From -

Rt. Rev. Msgr. Stapleton

August 26th. 1957.

( Community )

# THE THEOLOGY
## OF ST PAUL

# THE THEOLOGY
# OF SAINT PAUL

## BY FERNAND PRAT, S.J.

*Translated from the Tenth French Edition*

### BY JOHN L. STODDARD

## VOLUME II

THE NEWMAN BOOKSHOP
Westminster, Md.

1956

NIHIL OBSTAT:

T. McLaughlin, S.T.D.,
*Censor Deputatus.*

IMPRIMATUR:

Edm. Can. Surmont,
*Vicarius Generalis.*

Westmonasterii,
*die 17ª Martii, 1927.*

*Reprinted, 1946*
*Reprinted, 1950*
*Reprinted, 1952*
*Reprinted, 1956*

PRINTED IN THE UNITED STATES OF AMERICA

# NOTE

1. The bibliography and index will be found at the end of this volume.

2. Except when otherwise stated, the patristic references are to Migne's *Patrology,* the roman numeral indicating the volume and the arabic the column. The author's name indicates sufficiently whether the Latin or Greek Patrology is referred to. For example, Hilary, *De Trin.,* viii, 47, X, 22, means: the *De Trinitate* of St Hilary, book viii, No. 47, Migne's *Latin* Patrology, vol. X, column 22. The Greek or Latin fathers who have already appeared in the Leipzig or Vienna editions are quoted according to these editions. The quotations from Philo are usually from Mangey's edition, that of Cohn and Wendland being still incomplete.

3. The key-number printed after and above a title denotes the edition. Thus, Cornely, *Introd.*², means: second edition of the *Introductio historica et critica in S. Scripturam* of P. Cornely. When there is no possibility of confusion, the title is often given in an abridged form.

4. In the case of ancient or modern commentators, it has not seemed necessary always to mention the volume and page. If Estius or Theodoret is quoted on Rom. viii, 28, it will easily be understood that recourse must be had to the commentary on the text in question.

5. For the Greek text of St Paul, we usually follow Nestle's edition, which everyone has at hand (*Novum Testamentum Graece et Latine*⁵, Stuttgart, 1914); but we depart from it in regard to certain orthographical peculiarities, and sometimes also as regards punctuation. The Latin text is that of the Clementine Vulgate.

# CONTENTS

## BOOK I

## PAULINISM

## BOOK II

## PREPARATION FOR THE REDEMPTION

vii

# BOOK III

## THE PERSON OF THE REDEEMER

### CHAPTER I—THE PRE-EXISTENT CHRIST

### CHAPTER II—RELATIONS OF THE PRE-EXISTENT CHRIST

# CONTENTS

# BOOK IV

## THE WORK OF REDEMPTION

### CHAPTER I—THE REDEEMING MISSION

### CHAPTER II—THE REDEEMING DEATH

### CHAPTER III—THE IMMEDIATE EFFECTS OF REDEMPTION

# BOOK V

## THE CHANNELS OF REDEMPTION

### CHAPTER I—FAITH, THE PRINCIPLE OF JUSTIFICATION

### CHAPTER II—THE SACRAMENTS

### CHAPTER III—THE CHURCH

# CONTENTS

## BOOK VI

## THE FRUITS OF REDEMPTION

### CHAPTER I—THE CHRISTIAN LIFE

### CHAPTER II—THE LAST THINGS

## DETACHED NOTES

### L—PAUL'S MYSTERY AND PAGAN MYSTERIES

# CONTENTS

# BOOK I
## PAULINISM

# CHAPTER I

## DEFINITION OF PAULINISM

### I—THE GOSPEL OF PAUL

1. General Notion.  2. The Gospel of Paul and the Mystery of Christ.
3. Elements of Paulinism.

1.  **B**Y *Paulinism* is meant the teaching inculcated by
the Doctor of the Gentiles, considered in its
particular characteristics and in the organic
sequence of its ideas.  As the word corresponds
to an accurate conception, and as it has in its
favour the fact that it is really needed, we think it very
advantageous to retain it, after having first purged it of its
rationalistic dross.

The differences in tone, ideas, and style which give to the
sacred writers their distinctive physiognomy and individuality,
impressed historians and exegetes from the first.  To be convinced of this, we have only to read the prefaces in which St
Jerome characterizes the prophets, as well as the pages of St
Irenæus, Eusebius, and other Fathers on the symbolism of
the four animals of Ezechiel applied to the evangelists.  A
glance makes evident the fact that the Book of Wisdom does
not resemble Ecclesiastes, and that the Fourth Gospel has a
very different style to that of the three Synoptists, and that
St James has not the same point of view as St Paul.  The
preaching of the latter did not fail at first to excite some
astonishment in a section of the Christian community.  If
these did not dispute his right to preach to the Gentiles, they
were at least surprised that he exempted them from the
observance of the Mosaic Law.  The matter was deemed
sufficiently serious to be referred to the apostles and the
mother-church at Jerusalem.  There Paul won his case; but
this victory did not protect him from the calumnies and hostile
manœuvres to which he was exposed all his life.  Long
after, the Elders of Jerusalem occupied themselves with these
imputations, and Paul, on their advice, thought it well openly
to acknowledge the respect which he still felt for the religious
institutions of his people.  This does not prove at all that
Paul taught a doctrine of his own, or that there was in the
early Church a conflict between one pulpit or altar and
another ; but it is at least a sign that all the preachers of
the Gospel did not give the same prominence and importance
to the abolition of the Law, to the liberty of the Gentiles, and
to their perfect equality with the Jews ; otherwise the dis-

3

cussions, dissensions, and misunderstandings, instead of continuing, would have been cut short at once.

There are not two Gospels, two messages of salvation. The true, the only Gospel is that which Paul teaches in accord with all the other apostles.[1] Anathema to anyone who preaches another ! But, continues the Apostle, it is not another Gospel : " it is only the attempt of a few persons to spread discord among you and to pervert the Gospel of Christ."[2] He ironically concedes to the Corinthians that they would be justified in listening to his enemies, if these were preaching another Christ, or conferring another Spirit, or proclaiming another Gospel ;[3] but that is an absurd hypothesis, which is destroyed by merely stating it ; for there is only one Gospel, just as there is only one Christ and only one Holy Spirit. Yet, if there are not two Gospels, there are different ways of preaching the same Gospel, according to times, places, and persons. Paul declared that he had received, as his share of the work, the Gospel of the uncircumcision,[4] as Peter had received that of the circumcision.

Let us admit that the explanation given by Tertullian is correct : *Non ut aliud aliter, sed ut alter aliis praedicet:* that " the Gospel of the uncircumcision " means the preaching to the uncircumcised, and that the two apostles agree to limit not the exclusive field of their apostolate—neither of them ever understood it in this way—but the special field in which their action should be carried on. It always happens that a different audience necessitates, if not a different theme, at least a different mode of presenting the same Gospel subject. This is what the best authorities understand by the Gospel of Paul.[5]

2. He explains this himself in the final doxology of the Epistle to the Romans :

> Glory be to him, that is powerful to establish you according to my *gospel* and the preaching of Jesus Christ and the revelation of the mystery which was *kept secret* from eternity, but which now is *made manifest* to all nations by the scriptures of the prophets, according to the precept of the eternal God, for the obedience of faith.[6]

---

[1] 1 Cor. xv, 11.    [2] Gal. i, 7.    [3] 2 Cor. xi, 4.    [4] Gal. ii, 8.
[5] On the meaning of the word " Gospel " see Note N, p. 396.
[6] Rom. xvi, 25-26 :

| | |
|---|---|
| Τῷ δὲ δυναμένῳ ὑμᾶς στηρίξαι | 25. *Ei qui potens est vos confirmare* |
| A. (a) κατὰ τὸ εὐαγγέλιόν μου καὶ τὸ κήρυγμα 'I. X., | *secundum Evangelium meum et praeconium J. C.,* |
| (b) κατὰ ἀποκάλυψιν μυστηρίου χρόνοις αἰωνίοις σεσιγημένου, | *secundum revelationem mysterii temporibus aeternis taciti,* |
| B. φανερωθέντος δὲ νῦν | 26. *manifestati autem nunc* |
| C. (a) διά τε γραφῶν προφητικῶν | [*et*] *per Scripturam prophetarum,* |
| (b) κατ' ἐπιταγὴν τοῦ αἰωνίου Θεοῦ | *secundum praeceptum aeterni Dei,* |
| (c) εἰς ὑπακοὴν πίστεως | *in obeditionem fidei* |
| (d) εἰς πάντα τὰ ἔθνη γνωρισθέντος . . . | *in omnes gentes cogniti . . .* |

The principal idea of the passage is evidently the description of the three phases of the *Mystery:* formerly *hidden* in the depths of the divine counsels, but to-day *disclosed* providentially, and even *made known* to the whole world. This revelation of it is addressed, above all, to the Gentiles, whom it especially concerns; it has for its object to bring them to the faith by presenting to them the brilliant prospect of the blessings of the Gospel, which are destined for them as well as for others; it is done by means of the ancient prophecies now better understood; and this by the express command of the God the King of ages, to whom is to be ascribed all the glory of it, since he initiated it. Here St Paul identifies his Gospel with the message of Jesus Christ—that is to say, with the preaching which has Jesus Christ for its object, and he places it in connection with the mystery of the plans of redemption. The mystery itself, without being expressly defined in this place, is described by its manifold characteristics which the Epistles of the captivity relate minutely. Hinted at by the prophets, but having remained uncomprehended, it is now illumined by a new light and proclaimed to the Gentiles, whom it is to bring to the faith. All these traits combined show us that the mystery is the plan of salvation conceived by God from all eternity, hidden previously in the penumbra of the old revelation, but proclaimed to-day solemnly throughout the whole world—a plan by virtue of which all men are to be saved by the mediation of Christ and

---

As the present Vulgate is almost unintelligible, especially on account of the parenthesis which breaks the connection of the parts, we give beside the text the ancient and much more exact Latin version, adding, however, an *et* which the sense, in harmony with the original, demands.

Note the gradation : *A. Mystery formerly hidden* (χρόνοις αἰωνίοις σεσιγη-μένου), *B. now made manifest* (φανερωθέντος δὲ νῦν), *C. and even made known* (γνωρισθέντος).

Note also the four circumstances of its publication : (*a*) It is done by means of the ancient prophecies illumined by the Gospel (διά τε γραφῶν προφητικῶν—the particle τε, very important, is critically certain); (*b*) by order of God, whose secret it was (κατ᾽ ἐπιταγὴν τοῦ αἰωνίου Θεοῦ); (*c*) to the Gentiles specially interested (εἰς πάντα τὰ ἔθνη); (*d*) with the object of converting them (εἰς ὑπακοὴν πίστεως).

According to some, κατά in both cases, although not connected, should be co-ordinated and depend equally on στηρίξαι (God establishes you *according to* my Gospel, *according to* the mystery) ; the Gospel would thus be practically identified with the mystery, and the mystery would define the Gospel. According to others, in both cases κατά is subordinate : the first limits στηρίξαι, as above; the second explains κήρυγμα (God confirms you *according to* [that is, in] my Gospel and the message of Jesus Christ, which is *according to* the mystery). In reality, the meaning is scarcely changed, for the best interpreters understand by τὸ κήρυγμα Ἰησοῦ Χριστοῦ, not the message announced by Jesus Christ, but the message having Jesus Christ for its object. After this, the only question is to know whether the mystery is a second definition of the Gospel of Paul, or (which amounts to about the same thing) whether the message of Jesus Christ (that is to say, in fact, the Gospel of Paul) is *in conformity with* the mystery of the plan of redemption.

by their mystical union with him. Now the purport of this mystery is the essential theme of the Pauline Gospel.

The Epistles of the captivity will tell us how :

> I now rejoice in my sufferings for you and in my flesh fill up [gladly] those things that are wanting of the sufferings of Christ, for his [mystical] body which is the Church. Whereof I am made a minister according to the dispensation of God, which is given me that I may proclaim to you fully the word of God: the *mystery* which hath been hidden from ages and [past] generations, but now is manifested to his saints, to whom God would make known how rich unto the Gentiles is the glory of this *mystery*, which is *Christ in you, the hope of glory*.[1]

The word Gospel is not used here; but, in reality, Paul means nothing else when he speaks of his preaching, of the charge which has been confided to him, of the mission which he is fulfilling, and of the sufferings which he is enduring and is ready still to face, in order worthily to accomplish his task. Now all this tends to the promulgation of the *Mystery* among the heathen. This mystery, formerly hidden in the *arcana* of divine knowledge, but now brought to light and loudly proclaimed, is Christ, accessible not only to the Jews, but to the Gentiles themselves, the universal Saviour of men and their common hope. No more exceptions, favours, privileges : henceforth Christ belongs to all, and in the same measure. This is what Paul feels himself called upon to preach incessantly, this is what makes him brave persecu-

---

[1] Col. i, 24–27. For verse 24, see p. 295.—The phases of the mystery are here presented almost as in the preceding text; formerly kept *secret*, it is now made *manifest* (τὸ μυστήριον τὸ ἀποκεκρυμμένον ἀπὸ τῶν αἰώνων καὶ ἀπὸ τῶν γενεῶν, νῦν δὲ ἐφανερώθη, cf. Rom. xvi, 25-26 : μυστηρίου χρόνοις αἰωνίοις σεσιγημένου, φανερωθέντος δὲ νῦν) and is to be *made known* everywhere (γνωρίσαι, cf. Rom. xvi, 26 : γνωρισθέντος). This is the special duty of Paul. The Apostle has received in view of the Gentiles (Col. i, 25 : εἰς ὑμᾶς, cf. i, 27 : ἐν τοῖς ἔθνεσιν) a *ministry* or an *administration* (οἰκονομία) which constitutes him διάκονος τῆς ἐκκλησίας (i, 25) or οἰκονόμος Θεοῦ (Tit. i, 7; I Cor. iv, 1), because the Church is the house (οἶκος) of God.—This ministry consists in *preaching in its integrity, in its fulness* (πληρῶσαι) the word of God. The *word of God* is in general the Gospel (I Cor. xiv, 36 ; 2 Cor. ii, 17 ; iv, 2 ; I Thess. ii, 13), but two circumstances determine it here in a more special sense : the mission to the Gentiles and the identification of the word of God with the mystery. It is, therefore, practically the Gospel of Paul.—We have in this place a new and very concise definition of the mystery, i, 27 : ὅ ἐστιν Χριστὸς ἐν ὑμῖν ἡ ἐλπὶς τῆς δόξης. Whether the antecedent of ὅ ἐστιν (var. ὅς ἐστιν, by attraction) is πλοῦτος or μυστήριον matters little, for the *mystery* does not essentially differ from the *riches of the mystery ;* but it is grammatically and logically more probable that the antecedent is μυστήριον. It is this word, therefore, which is directly defined. —In the definition itself a comma can be put after ἐν ὑμῖν and two distinct thoughts are obtained: the mystery is (1) Christ in the midst of you, Gentiles ; (2) Christ your hope. Or one can read the words without a comma and gain one single thought : the mystery is Christ, the hope of glory in you (or for you). Formerly Christ, the Messiah, seemed to belong to the Jews alone, and the Gentiles were without hope (Eph. ii, 12 : χωρὶς Χριστοῦ . . . ἐλπίδα μὴ ἔχοντες). Now *Christ* is in the midst of them (ἐν ὑμῖν), he is theirs ; he is their *hope* ; he promises and guarantees them celestial *glory*.

tions, this is what consoles him for his sufferings : it is the proclamation of the great mystery, the Gospel of the un-circumcision.

These same ideas are more fully developed in the great digression in the Epistle to the Ephesians :

> I Paul, the prisoner of Jesus Christ for you Gentiles, if yet you have heard of the dispensation of the grace of God which is given me towards you, how that, according to revelation, the *mystery* has been made known to me, as I have written above in a few words ; as you, reading, may understand my knowledge in the *mystery* of Christ, which in other generations was not known to the sons of men, as it is now revealed to his holy apostles and prophets in the Spirit ; that *the Gentiles should be fellow-heirs and of the same body, and co-partners of his promise in Christ Jesus,* by the Gospel, of which I am made a minister. . . . To me the least of all the saints is given this grace to preach among the Gentiles the unsearchable riches of Christ, and to enlighten all men that they may see what is the dispensation of the *mystery* which hath been hidden from eternity in God who created all things. . . . Wherefore I pray you not to faint at my tribulations for you, which are your glory.[1]

Four thoughts stand out in this passage. The Apostle, as is customary with him, calls himself the prisoner of Christ, the captive of the Gospel, for the sake of the Gentiles. It is for having pleaded their cause that he has drawn down upon himself the hate of his compatriots ; it is for having defended their rights that he suffers persecution ; therefore his suffer-ings are for him a source of joy, and ought to be a subject of pride for them.[2] He claims for himself, not an exclusive, but a very special knowledge of the *Mystery,* of which his Epistle contains the clearest and most complete exposition ; above all, he claims to have the mandate to preach this article of faith everywhere ; and the remembrance of such an un-deserved favour calls forth in him an outburst of humble gratitude.[3] He identifies the mystery with the Gospel which

---

[1] Eph. iii, 1-13. The verses 2-13 form an immense parenthesis, and the thought of the phrase beginning at verse 1 (τούτου χάριν ἐγὼ Παῦλος) is carried on until verse 14 (τούτου χάριν κάμπτω τὰ γόνατά μου).

[2] Δέσμιος Χριστοῦ Ἰησοῦ (Philem. 1 and 9), ὁ δέσμιος τοῦ κυρίου (2 Tim. i, 8), ὁ δέσμιος τοῦ Χριστοῦ Ἰησοῦ (Eph. iii, 1), ὁ δέσμιος ἐν Κυρίῳ (Eph. iv, 1).— Frequent allusions to his chains (Phil. i, 7, 13, 14, 17 ; Col. iv, 18 ; 2 Tim. ii, 9 ; Philem. 10), which are the chains of the Gospel (Philem. 13 : ἐν τοῖς δεσμοῖς τοῦ εὐαγγελίου) because he has been imprisoned for having preached the rights of the Gentiles (Acts xxi, 28 ; xxii, 22) ; glorious chains for them (Eph. iii, 13 : ἥτις ἐστὶν δόξα ὑμῶν) and honourable for him (Col. i, 24). He likes to call himself an *ambassador* of Christ *in chains* (Eph. vi, 20 : ὑπὲρ οὗ πρεσβεύω ἐν ἁλύσει), and his sole ambition is to preach always with the same courage the *mystery of the Gospel* (*ibid.* : τὸ μυστήριον τοῦ εὐαγγελίου) or *the mystery of Christ for which* he is bound (Col. iv, 3 : τὸ μυστήριον τοῦ Χριστοῦ δι' ὃ καὶ δέδεμαι)—that is to say, the mystery which is the fundamental point of his Gospel and the mystery which has for its object Christ, the universal Redeemer.

[3] Eph. iii, 3-4 : ὅτι κατὰ ἀποκάλυψιν ἐγνωρίσθη μοι τὸ μυστήριον, καθὼς προέγραψα ἐν ὀλίγῳ, πρὸς ὃ δύνασθε ἀναγινώσκοντες νοῆσαι τὴν σύνεσίν μου ἐν τῷ μυστηρίῳ τοῦ Χριστοῦ. Paul explains what he has just said : εἴγε ἠκούσατε τὴν οἰκονομίαν τῆς χάριτος τοῦ Θεοῦ τῆς δοθείσης μοι εἰς ὑμᾶς. The word οἰκονομία is not to be taken in the active sense (administration)

he is commissioned to preach, not alone, but more than the others; a sublime ministry, having for its object to reveal to men the ineffable riches of the plans of redemption and to disclose to the angels themselves the depths of divine wisdom.[1]   Finally, the mystery—and consequently the Gospel of Paul—is once more defined with more precision than ever : " The Gentiles are co-heirs "—that is to say, heirs of grace and glory with the same right and in the same measure as the Jews, to whom the patrimony of heavenly favours had until then seemed to be reserved; they are " members of the same body," the mystical body of Christ, and consequently between them and the Jews there are neither privileges, differences, nor inequalities; they are " co-partners in the promise," the wonderfully liberal promise made to the patriarchs down the centuries, and they are all this " in Christ," who is the meritorious cause of it and " by the Gospel," which is its essential condition.[2]

---

but in the passive sense (establishment, divine institution) ; χάρις is not the grace of conversion but that of the apostolate, and in particular of the apostolate to the Gentiles, as is shown by the addition : τῆς δοθείσης μοι εἰς ὑμᾶς.   The genitive χάριτος is therefore an objective genitive (the dispensation in relation to grace) or, if it be preferred, an *epexegetical* genitive (the dispensation which consists of grace).   In verse 3, ὅτι does not mean *because*, but *that is to say :* the revelation of the mystery (κατὰ ἀποκάλυψιν ἐγνωρίσθη μοι τὸ μυστήριον) is precisely the *dispensation of grace* of which he has just been speaking.   When he adds, " as I wrote above in a few words " (καθὼς προέγραψα ἐν ὀλίγῳ), the Apostle refers to chap. ii, where he has indeed described the mystery of the incorporation of the Gentiles into the Church, with the assurance that his readers will recognize there how profound is his knowledge of this mystery.

[1] Eph. iii, 8-9 : ἐμοὶ τῷ ἐλαχιστοτέρῳ πάντων ἁγίων ἐδόθη ἡ χάρις αὕτη, τοῖς ἔθνεσιν εὐαγγελίσασθαι τὸ ἀνεξιχνίαστον πλοῦτος τοῦ Χριστοῦ, καὶ φωτίσαι τίς ἡ οἰκονομία τοῦ μυστηρίου.   The word ἐλαχιστότερος is curious : " lesser than the least of the saints."   It is a comparative of a superlative.   These formations are not rare, especially in low Greek, with irregular superlatives and comparatives.   We find in Aristotle ἐσχατώτερος and in St John μειζότερος (3 John 4).—The grace, the signal honour accorded to Paul, in spite of his unworthiness, is : (1) to preach to the Gentiles the unsearchable riches of Christ ; (2) to explain the dispensation of the great mystery.   The first message especially concerns the Gentiles because it is important for them to know that the riches of Christ are poured out upon them abundantly, and that they by this fact are as rich as their elders the Jews.   These riches of Christ are called unsearchable, incomprehensible or immeasurable, because they surpass human standards of value and because they can be extended to all men without being exhausted.   The second message is addressed to all, Jews as well as Gentiles, for all need to know the dispensation of the mystery, a dispensation comprising, as its name indicates, a mass of institutions, relations and points of view which until then had remained the secret of the Creator (sacramenti absconditi a saeculis *in Deo qui omnia creavit*), of which the angels themselves had no knowledge (*ut innotescat principatibus et potestatibus in caelestibus*) and in which the manifold wisdom of God bursts forth (ἡ πολυποίκιλος σοφία).

[2] Eph. iii, 6 : εἶναι τὰ ἔθνη συγκληρονόμα καὶ σύσσωμα καὶ συμμέτοχα τῆς ἐπαγγελίας ἐν Χριστῷ Ἰησοῦ διὰ τοῦ εὐαγγελίου.   Here are the contents and the definition of the mystery.   The principal idea is in the component

Our investigations bring us always to the same result. The *Gospel* of Paul, or, in other words, the mystery of God, the mystery of Christ, the mystery of the Gospel, or simply the mystery, is, in its broadest and most precise expression, the mystery of the redemption of all men by Christ and in Christ. Here and there the Epistles furnish us with a few more data on this subject, but we must be on our guard against the danger of supposing that the Apostle intends to call our attention to a characteristic point of his teaching every time he appeals to his Gospel. When, provoked by the disorderly conduct of the Corinthians in the celebration of the *agape,* he reminds them of the teaching of the Saviour on the subject of the Eucharist, he does not suggest that the other churches are less favoured in this respect ;[1] and when, in reply to their new-born doubts, he repeats a portion of his first instruction about the death, burial, and resurrection of Christ, he claims so little distinction for himself in this from the other apostles, that he immediately adds : " Whether I or they, so we preach, and so you have believed."[2] No doubt he must have insisted more than the others did on the soteriological importance of the burial and resurrection of Christ, but the proof that this point of view is not exclusively his, is that he supposes the symbolism of the mystical burial of the Christian in baptism to be already known to the Romans and Colossians,[3] who were not his disciples.

However, the mention of his Gospel, even when it does not necessarily imply a characteristic point of his preaching, at

---

proposition σύν found in the three adjectives: συγκληρονόμα, *co-heirs*—that is, heirs *with* (the Jews, etc.).—The word συλκληρονόμος is not employed by classic writers ; it has been found in Philo, *Legat. ad Caium*, 10 ; the verb συγκληρονομεῖν is in Eccli. xxii, 29. In the New Testament *heritage* (κληρονομία), being in general eternal life (Eph. i, 14, 18 ; v, 5 ; Col. iii, 24 ; 1 Pet. i, 4), συγκληρονόμος signifies co-heir of the kingdom of heaven. *Cf.* Rom. viii, 17 ; Heb. xi, 9 ; 1 Pet. iii, 7.—The meaning of σύσσωμα, *members of the same body*, is clear to anyone familiar with the theory of the mystical body. Did Paul himself invent this expressive term ? What would lead us to think that it is older is that in the *De Mundo* (iv, 30), attributed to Aristotle, we find συσσωματοποιεῖν.—The word συμμέτοχος is not found elsewhere than in Josephus ; but συμμετέχειν is employed in the classics, and the addition of τῆς ἐπαγγελίας makes the meaning entirely clear. Paul frequently explains what he means by the *promise* or the *promises* (Rom. iv, 13-20 ; ix, 4, 8, 9 ; xv, 8 ; Gal. iii, 14-29 ; iv, 23-28 ; Eph. i, 13 ; ii, 12, etc.) ; they are the engagements which God, on various solemn occasions, contracted with his people, and they include the sending of the Messiah.— The two conditions for receiving these blessings are to embrace the Gospel, which is for every believer the means of salvation (Rom. i, 16), and to be united to Christ the only Mediator (1 Tim. ii, 5), the depositary of all these gifts (Gal. iii, 16), and above all the crucible in which the intimate union of believers is effected (Gal. iii, 26-29).

[1] 1 Cor. xi, 28.
[2] 1 Cor. xv, 11.
[3] Rom. vi, 4 ; Col. ii, 12.

least gives the reader a hint. Before the text : " In the day when God shall judge the secrets of men by Jesus Christ, according to my Gospel,"[1] the best exegetes ask themselves what is the point aimed at by those words, " according to my Gospel " ; and they rightly conclude that it is neither the day of the Lord, nor the secret actions of men as matter for the divine judgement, nor the fact of judgement itself, but the way in which the judgement is to be delivered through the mediation of Christ. This is, in fact, one of Paul's favourite ideas. To the impudent detractors who accuse him of adulterating the word of God, of concealing it under miserable disguises, and of overloading it with arbitrary enigmas, he protests that he does not preach himself, but " Christ Jesus our Lord."[2] He puts the emphasis on the word Lord. We know, indeed, that he considered the confession of the *lordship* of Christ as a condensed profession of faith and as a résumé of the Gospel.[3] So, also, when he mentions his Gospel in reference to the Mosaic Law and sets it over against that of the Judaizers,[4] he makes us think of his principle doctrine concerning the nature of the Law, which is powerless in itself, independent of grace, and is good only for keeping rebels and criminals in the right path by means of terror and threatenings. In his second Epistle to Timothy he reminds him of still another point of his Gospel : " Be mindful that the Lord Jesus Christ of the seed of David, is risen again from the dead, according to my Gospel, wherein I labour even unto bonds, as an evil-doer."[5] The point aimed at is evidently not the descent from David ; it is, therefore, the resurrection of Jesus Christ, the remembrance of which is a comfort and encouragement to the Christian in the midst of disappointments and persecutions.

All these details scattered here and there warn us not to confine the Gospel of Paul in a too narrow formula, such as the liberty of the Gentiles in regard to the observances of the Law would be, or justification by faith without the works of the Law, or even the universality of God's plans of redemption. Paul's Gospel is not so much a particular thesis, as it is the whole body of Gospel teaching, regarded from a certain

---

[1] Rom. ii, 16 : *Indicari hac locutione aliquid videtur, quod ab ipso magis, quam a reliquis, doceatur ipsiusque praedicationi quasi sit proprium et essentiale* (Cornely). " The point to which St Paul's Gospel or habitual teaching bears witness is, not that God will judge the world (which was an old doctrine), but that he will judge it *through Jesus Christ*, as his Deputy " (Sanday).

[2] 2 Cor. iv, 5.      [3] Rom. x, 9-10.      [4] 1 Tim. i, 8-11.

[5] 2 Tim. ii, 8. " The emphasis of the thought is in the words ' risen again from the dead.' That is what Timothy must above all remember " (Lemonnyer). The Apostle exhorts his disciple to suffer with him (ii, 3 : συγκακοπάθησον) for the sake of the Gospel (i, 8), thinking of Jesus risen from the dead, who, being a man like ourselves, passed through the same trials before entering into glory.

angle and presented in a special light. It is a frame in which all the truths can find a place. Therefore, after having considered the indications given us by the Apostle, it is well to proceed to summarize his doctrine by way of counter-proof.

3. Let us then close his Epistles, as if he had said nothing of his Gospel, and let us ask the theologians best versed in his doctrine, without distinction in regard to schools or tendencies, what its essential points and constituent elements are. We have not again to group and classify them, but merely to draw up a list of them. Later on we shall examine whether they are really fundamental and cannot be ignored without altering the whole order of things, whether they are characteristic, at least when viewed from the Apostle's angle ; and whether they are susceptible of forming a coherent whole. Here, then, first, is the verdict of this referendum, in which the enumeration of the points follows without logical order :

*God's plan of redemption,* comprising the divine initiative of grace, eternal election and predestination in Christ, providential preparations and the completion of the redemptive work.

*The contrast of the two Adams,* the type and the antitype, summing up the history of humanity : the first Adam the cause of sin, death, and the fall ; the second Adam the author of justice, life, and restoration.

*The antithesis of flesh and spirit,* placed erroneously by some at the very foundation of Paulinism, but certainly of capital importance for the doctrines of salvation and of morals.

*The part played by the Law and its scope,* which, at first sight, would seem to be less closely allied to the Apostle's teaching, but the import of which cannot be called secondary in the Gospel of the teacher of the Gentiles.

*The redeeming death of Christ,* regarded by some with evident exaggeration as an exclusive creation of the mind of Paul, but which is certainly a central point of his doctrine.

*Justification by faith,* the counterpart of redemption and the subjective application of the redeeming death.

*The resurrection of Jesus Christ,* as the intrinsic complement of the redemptive work, and as the exemplary cause of our own glorious resurrection.

*The Church the mystical body of Christ,* fruit of his death and of his resurrection.

*Baptism,* the seal of faith and rite of incorporation into the mystical Christ, with the *Eucharist,* which gives to this body its nourishment and growth.

*Eschatology,* as the normal issue of the Christian life.

This list could no doubt be extended to include a few more

points; but in most cases they might be included in one of
the subjects already mentioned, or else they possess nothing
really characteristic or seem to be at the periphery of Pauline
thought.   Thus the apocalyptic element, in so far as it is
distinct from the eschatology, is wanting in originality, and
follows the traditional data; the demonology and angelology
are superficial ideas borrowed from popular language, and
without serious influence on the very foundation of the teaching; the theory of the origin, extent and dominion of sin is,
on the contrary, of capital importance, but in the antithesis
of the two Adams it holds the position of a part to the
whole; finally, the theodicy, in so far as it is specifically
Pauline, is entirely contained in the theory of the plans of
redemption.

This doctrinal summary, which constitutes the particular
teaching of the Doctor of the Gentiles, is what is called
Paulinism, and can be also called by a name which is perhaps
open to discussion, but is accepted now and sanctioned by
use, the *Theology of St Paul*.   Before going further, however, let us dispel a misunderstanding or ambiguity.   We
do not treat the sacred authors " as theologians," nor do
we consider their writings " as so many theological schemes,
or even sketches "; we do not look upon them " now
as revelation and now as theology," and we do not distinguish in them " on the one hand revealed data, and on
the other, the elaboration " of divine data.   The theology
of St Paul is one thing, the theology of St Thomas, for
example, is quite another.   The theology of St Paul is the
sum total of the divine revelations transmitted to us through
the agency of the Doctor of the Gentiles.   The theology
of St Thomas is his—however felicitous, nevertheless human
and fallible—interpretation of the data revealed by Paul
and by the other inspired writers.   Paul gives us the
elements of a theology, but he does not construct his theology
himself in the usual sense of that word.   He thinks
systematically—that is to say, in a consistent and coherent
manner, but the system itself is not his, and in order to reduce his thought to a system, it will be sometimes needful to
fill up the gaps, establish connections, and draw some conclusions.   This is the task of the theologian.   As a faithful and
loyal interpreter, he must aim at rendering with as little imperfection as possible the entire thought, and nothing but the
thought, of his inspired guide, without perverting it, without
influencing it, and without misrepresenting it either by excess
or by default.   We are not of those who wish to read in St
Paul " more than he says and more than he can say "; who
regard him as a simple " collaborator of grace and of the
master within "; and who, on the pretext that " the letter
killeth," refuse to be bound to his words and expressions.

These precise statements are necessary; for, although they do not seem to exceed the limits of an average intelligence, they often actually escape the notice of many cultivated minds.

## II—PAULINE THEOLOGY IN EMBRYO

1. Christ the Centre.  2. Not as Dying.  3. But as the Saviour.
4. Synoptical View.

1. If, in order to understand St Augustine's *City of God* or Bossuet's *Discourse on Universal History,* it is necessary to be thoroughly imbued with the thesis which these two great geniuses develop therein with such magnificence of style, it is no less needful, in order to read St Paul profitably, to examine attentively the governing principles of his thought. In works of the intellect, as in the creations of art or the spectacles of nature, there is always a point beyond which the proportions are disturbed and the perspective is perverted. This central point which gives unity, cohesion, and harmony to the whole and cannot be displaced without disturbing the entire arrangement of the work, is what is called the dominant idea. A thinker of the first rank, a powerful dialectician, and a philosophic mind capable of co-ordinating dissimilar facts, grasping their hidden relations and unifying them by vigorous synthesis, Paul had to put into his writings a small number of dominant ideas, or perhaps only one; and it is beyond all doubt that this idea, once known, is the leading thread of his doctrine.

The first bird's-eye view of this immense field is enough to convince us that its centre is Christ. Everything converges on this point; thence everything proceeds, and thither everything returns. Christ is the beginning, middle, and end of everything. In the natural order, as in the supernatural, everything is in him, everything is by him, everything is for him. A simple calculation confirms this impression. With the exception of the Epistle to the Hebrews, the name " Lord " occurs about 280 times in the writings of Paul; the name " Jesus," 220; the name " Christ," nearly 400 times. If he writes one of the Saviour's names in nearly every line of his Epistles, it is because he makes this the mark of all his thoughts and prayers. If we open his Epistles at random, we come infallibly on an allusion to the nature, the work, or the mediaton of the man-God.[1] Every attempt to under-

---

[1] The name *Christ* (Χριστός, with or without the article) appears alone 203 times; *Christ Jesus* 92 times; *Jesus Christ* 84 times ; *the Lord* (Κύριος, with or without the article) appears alone 157 times ; *the Lord Jesus* 24 times ; the *Lord Jesus Christ* 64 times ; *Jesus* alone is found only 16 times. Attention should be also paid to the other names, such as Saviour, Son of God, Well-beloved, etc., as well as to numerous phrases in which Jesus Christ, without being named, is the subject of the proposition. The figures given above are

stand any passage whatever, if we should eliminate the person of Jesus Christ, would end in certain failure.

This is forgotten by those theologians who make the foundation of the doctrine of Paul either the metaphysical notion of God, or the abstract thesis of justification by faith, or the psychological contrast between flesh and spirit.

The first are victims of an optical illusion. Jewish thought being profoundly religious, the idea of God fills the entire Bible. For St Paul, as for all his compatriots, God is the primary source of all, the universal providence, the supreme end of all beings; nothing is done without his initiative, nothing occurs except through him. From this point of view the theodicy of St Paul differs little from that of Isaias or St John; it is a heritage of the ancient revelation and the common patrimony of the Israelites. Now, it is not in points of agreement, but in divergences, that we must seek the inmost thought of an author and the root-idea of a work.[1]

Justification by faith must be set aside for another reason. It is a theme of controversy which owes its prominence to judaizing polemics. Once the controversy is ended, Paul seems to forget it or to lose his interest in it; a sure proof that it does not form part of the very foundation of his theology, at least in the acute form which the struggle against irreconcilable adversaries gives it. Luther never saw this when he made this doctrine the quintessence of the Gospel and the palladium of Protestantism.

Will the psychological dualism put forward by some rationalistic writers of our day give us any better key to the theology of St Paul? Impotence of man before the good which he loves, domination of sin which the Law incites rather than restrains, instinctive desire for a justice which proceeds from faith alone, and which individual failures cannot impede, and an inward feeling that Christ is sufficient to fulfil all the aspirations of our soul: such are the fundamental principles of this Gospel. In this manner, they say, the theology of St Paul is the mature fruit of his religious experience; he is indebted to no one for it; he owes it only to himself or, to use his own words, to the spirit of Christ;

---

only approximate, because certain passages offer different readings (*Jesus Christ* and *Christ Jesus*, for example, often being interchanged); but the sum total remains about the same.

[1] Findlay (in Hastings' *Dictionary of the Bible*, Vol. iii, p. 718) takes the theodicy as a point of departure: "The Apostle's doctrine is *theocentric*, not in reality anthropocentric. . . . St Paul's *Soteriology and Christology* are rooted in his *Theology*." He attributes the same line to Stevens. In fact, the latter (*The Pauline Theology*[2], New York, 1906, p. 96), after the preliminaries, begins with the Pauline conception of God, which is, he says, of capital importance for understanding the theology of the great Apostle. This exceptional importance of the idea of God does not appear in Stevens, *The Theology of the New Testament*, Edinburgh, 1899.

in his way of thinking, after as well as before his conversion, unity and continuity are always present; everything can be explained without the annoying intervention of the supernatural. But we have seen, on the contrary, that this explains nothing, neither his conversion nor the rest of his life. Is it likely that Paul, who regarded human wisdom with pity and disdain, would reduce his Gospel to a philosophical hypothesis? Could he have expressed his dominant idea in one single passage, the meaning of which is disputed?[1] No, neither man nor God forms the centre of Paul's theology, but Christ. Paul's doctrine is not a corollary of his anthropology or of his theodicy; it has its focus in the one and only mediator between God and men.

2. As the mediation of Christ consists only in his work as Redeemer, and as he is the Redeemer only by the cross, many theologians, even those who occasionally favour another system, see in the *verbum crucis* the corner-stone of Paul's Gospel: "The fact of the death of Jesus becomes thus the centre of the whole Pauline system. The Christianity of the Apostle is summed up in the person of Christ; but this person himself acquires all his redemptive importance only at the moment of his death on the cross."[2] The idea is all the more alluring because the formal declaration of Paul puts us on the track of it: "O foolish Galatians," he writes to some wavering converts, "who hath fascinated you . . . before whose eyes Christ hath been set forth crucified among you?"[3] He had *exposed to view, placarded,* before the eyes of the Galatians the image of the Crucified; he had made of Jesus

---

[1] Chap. vii of the Epistle to the Romans. See Vol. I, pp. 225-236.

[2] Sabatier, *L'Apôtre Paul*[3], p. 322. See also Beyschlag.

[3] Gal. iii, 1: *Ὦ ἀνόητοι Γαλάται,*    *O insensati Galatae, quis vos fasci-*
*τίς ὑμᾶς ἐβάσκανεν, οἷς κατ᾽ ὀφθαλμοὺς*    *navit non obedire veritati ante*
*Ἰ. Χ. προεγράφη ἐσταυρωμένος;*    *quorum oculos J. C. praescriptus*
   *est, in vobis crucifixus?*

The addition (*non obedire veritati*) in the Vulgate is merely an unimportant gloss, but the words *in vobis,* before *crucifixus* and after the comma, render the meaning difficult. If, with a certain number of manuscripts, we read in Greek ἐν ὑμῖν, it is clearly necessary to make these words refer to προεγράφη.—In place of *praescriptus,* it should be *proscriptus,* as the *Fuldensis* has it. *Proscribere,* προγράφειν, means to expose to view, to placard publicly, for example, a capital sentence; hence the edicts of *proscription* and the *proscribed.* St Paul had, in a way, exposed and placarded before the Galatians the image of Jesus crucified, in order that this image, always present to their view, might preserve them from seduction. —*Fascinare,* βασκαίνειν, means *to fascinate by the look,* as the serpent fascinates the little bird, or the cat the mouse. In order for the charm to be effective, the gaze of the fascinator must remain fixed upon the creature fascinated. If one or the other turns away his eyes, the charm is broken and the fascination ceases. The Galatians have only been bewitched by the seducers, because they have not, as they should have done, kept their gaze fixed on the Crucified.

on the cross a picture so vivid and so poignant, that he
cannot conceive how they have been able to divert their gaze
from it : if they would keep their eyes fixed upon his blood-
stained image, the charm of the seducer would have no hold
upon them.   It is certain that the preaching of the cross
always assumed in his first instructions great prominence :
" I determined to know among you only Jesus Christ and
him crucified."[1]   Jesus Christ is the general theme of his
preaching ; Jesus Christ crucified his special subject.   If he
always puts at the foundation of his preaching the mystery
of the cross, does he not give us a right to seek there the
substance of his Gospel and the root idea of his theology?

These reasons are more specious than solid.   In order that
Jesus Christ should save us by the cross, it was necessary
that the drama of redemption should be enacted at a certain
place and time, at the moment when the Jews had lost their
autonomy and the right of the sword, under the Roman
domination, which reserved this infamous punishment of
crucifixion for conquered peoples.   Now, although nothing
takes place by chance in the designs of God, is it likely that
St Paul should attach his principal theory of the salvation of
men to an accidental circumstance of place and time?   The
Apostle, it is said, determined not to know anything except
Jesus Christ crucified.   That is indeed what he affirms, but he
joins to it two limitations.   One is contained in the words
" among you," and refers to the special conditions of his
apostolate at Corinth.   After the rebuff he had met with at
Athens, he had understood that to the cavilling, frivolous
Greeks it was necessary to present the mystery of the cross
in all its disconcerting realism ; perhaps, under different
surroundings, he would have tried another method.   The
second limitation springs from his controversial purpose : he
is reproached with being ignorant of, or at least neglecting,
wisdom ; he replies that *his* wisdom, the only profitable
wisdom which they are capable of apprehending, is the
cross, a stumbling-block to the Jews and foolishness to the
Gentiles.   The paradox consists in opposing the foolishness
of the cross to the wisdom of the world, and in showing that
God triumphs over wisdom by foolishness ; but the Apostle

---

[1] 1 Cor. ii, 2 : Οὐ γὰρ ἔκρινά τι εἰδέναι ἐν ὑμῖν εἰ μὴ Ἰησοῦν Χριστὸν
καὶ τοῦτον ἐσταυρωμένον.   Here the word κρίνειν, *judicare*, means " to
judge good, to find proper," a meaning frequent in St Paul (1 Cor. vii, 37 ;
2 Cor. ii, 1) and elsewhere, as in the Ciceronian expression : *Mihi judicatum
est*.   It is a question of a practical, not of a speculative, judgement.   We must
not translate, therefore, " I judged that I did not know anything except Jesus
Christ crucified," for this judgement would be contrary to the truth, but :
" I did not judge it proper to know anything whatsoever, save Jesus Christ
crucified."   The negation is naturally related to the nearest word ἔκρινα.
To make the οὐ refer either to τι or εἰδέναι would be arbitrary, without,
moreover, especially modifying the sense.

does not give us the right to conclude in addition that the *verbum crucis* contains in embryo all his teaching.

To tell the truth, the death of Christ, considered in itself, independently of what gives it signification and value, would be without any effect on our salvation. By itself, far from being the instrument of redemption, it would be the supreme crime of humanity, which would seem to require a new redemption. It is meritorious for Christ and salutary for us only so far as it is on the part of the Son an act of reparation and the crowning act of a life of obedience. In order to confer upon Jesus' death a redeeming value, it is necessary to include in it an element which puts it in relation with God, with men, and with the Saviour himself : with the Saviour who offers it, with God who accepts it, and with men who benefit from it. On this condition only is it agreeable to God, whom it renders propitious to us.

A more serious reason for not limiting our attention to the death of Christ in order to find in it the primitive idea of Pauline theology, is that in the eyes of Paul Christ's death is inseparable from his resurrection, without which, from a soteriological point of view, it is incomplete. When the Apostle epitomized his Gospel for the converts of Corinth, he said to them : " I delivered unto you first of all which I also received, how that Christ died for our sins, according to the Scriptures, and that he was buried, and that he rose again the third day, according to the Scriptures."[1] This is what he taught at Antioch in Pisidia, at Athens, everywhere.[2] The death of Christ was never preached without the resurrection, for the one is the complement and corollary of the other. Not only was the glorious resurrection due to the Saviour as a recompense, but God owed it to himself to raise his Son from the dead, in order to seal his mission and to sanction his work. Since the death of Jesus was not the settlement of a personal debt, it has not its finality in itself; " Whom God hath raised up, as it was impossible that he should be holden by it " (death).[3] So, not content with affirming that Christ " died and has risen again for us," St Paul is not afraid to write the following words, whose natural meaning gives so much trouble to certain exegetes : " He was delivered up for our sins and rose again for our justification."[4] Whence it appears that the resurrection of Christ forms an integral part of the redemptive work.

3. However, the complex idea " Jesus dead and risen for us " is not yet the expression for which we are seeking. In addition to the fact that it is not sufficiently peculiar to Paul, it expresses only the objective side of our salvation. Now,

---

[1] 1 Cor. xv, 3-4.

[2] Acts xiii, 29-30 ; xvii, 31 ; xxvi, 23, etc.

[3] Acts ii, 24.

[4] Rom. iv, 25.

the Apostle never separates the two aspects of redemption.
It is useless to ransack all his Epistles; it is sufficient to
observe that if Jesus Christ dies for us, it is to make us die
mystically with him, and that, if he rises again for us, it is
to make us rise morally with him. *Si unus pro omnibus
mortuus est, ergo omnes mortui sunt.*[1] It matters not
whether this idea is presented under the form of a conditional proposition, with the Greek received text and the
Vulgate, or under the form of an enthymeme, in accordance
with the critical editions; for in both ways our mystical
death appears equally as the necessary consequence of
Christ's death. Much more: "If we be dead with Christ,
we believe that we live also together with him."[2] Our resurrection is involved in the Saviour's, as is our death in his
death.

In the writings of St Paul there is a long series of unusual
words, most of which can be translated into another language
only by an uncouth expression, or by a circumlocution. The
Apostle has invented them or revived them, in order to give
a graphic expression to the ineffable union of Christians with
Christ and in Christ. Such are: *to suffer with* Jesus Christ,
*to be crucified with* him, *to die with* him, *to be buried with*
him, *to rise from the dead with* him, *to live with* him, *to be
made alive with* him, *to share his form, to share his glory, to
sit with* him, *to reign with* him, *to be conformed with* him,
*united with* his *life, co-heir*. To these can be added *co-
partner, concorporate, built together with* and still others,
which do not directly express the union of Christians *with*
Christ, but designate the intimate union of Christians with
one another in Christ.[3] An examination of these curious

---

[1] 2 Cor. v, 15.                    [2] Rom. vi, 8.

[3] Here are the above-mentioned words with the Vulgate translation and
an indication of all the places where they occur:

(a) συμπάσχειν (*compati*, Rom. viii, 17 ; I Cor. xii, 26).

(b) συσταυροῦσθαι (*simul crucifigi*, Rom. vi, 6 ; *configi cruci*, Gal. ii, 20).

(c) συναποθνήσκειν (*commori*, 2 Tim. ii, 11 ; *cf.* 2 Cor. vii, 3).

(d) συνθάπτεσθαι (*consepeliri*, Rom. vi, 4 ; Col. ii, 12).

(e) συνεγείρειν (*conresuscitare*, Eph. ii, 6 ; passive, Col. ii, 12 and iii, 1).

(f) συζῆν or συνζῆν (*simul vivere cum*, Rom vi, 8 ; *convivere*, 2 Tim. ii, 11).

(g) συζωοποιεῖν (*convivificare*, Eph. ii, 5 ; Col. ii, 13).

(h) συμμορφίζεσθαι (*configurari*, Phil. iii, 10).

(i) συνδοξάζεσθαι (*conglorificari*, Rom. viii, 17).

(j) συγκαθίζειν (*consedere facere*, Eph. ii, 6).

(k) συμβασιλεύειν (*conregnare*, 2 Tim. ii, 12 ; *cf.* I Cor. iv, 8).

(l) σύμμορφος (*conformis*, Rom. viii, 29 ; Phil. iii, 21).

(m) σύμφυτος (*complantatus*, Rom. vi, 5).

(n) συγκληρονόμος (*coheres*, Rom. viii, 17 ; Eph. iii, 6).

(o) συμμέτοχος (*comparticeps*, Eph. iii, 6 ; v, 7).

(p) σύσσωμος (*concorporalis*, Eph. iii, 6).

(q) συνοικοδομεῖσθαι (*coaedificari*, Eph. ii, 22).

(r) συναρμολογούμενος (*constructus*, Eph. ii, 21 ; *compactus*, Eph. iv, 16).

(s) συμβιβαζόμενος (*connexus*, Eph. iv, 16 ; *constructus*, Col. ii, 19 ;
*cf.* ii, 2).

words suggests to us three interesting observations: our
mystical union with Christ does not extend to the mortal life
of Jesus; it originates only at the time of the Passion, when
Jesus Christ inaugurates his redemptive work; but, from
that moment on, it is continuous, and the *communicatio
idiomatum* between Christians and Christ is henceforth
complete.—That if we go back to the source of this union of
identity, we see that it exists by right and potentially at the
moment when the Saviour, acting in the name and for the
profit of guilty humanity, dies for us, and causes us to die
with him, but that it is realized, in fact and indeed, in every
one of us, when faith and baptism graft us upon the dying
Christ and make us participate in his death.—The author of
it is none other than God himself, who, clothing us with
the form and attributes of his well-beloved Son, recognizes
us as his children by adoption, and treats us thereafter as co-
heirs with Jesus.

We come back thus to what is perhaps most personal
and characteristic in St Paul's theology: I mean the expression *In Christo Jesu,* which comprises the whole of redemption from its first conception in the divine mind and its
potential execution on Calvary, to its successive realization
in each one of us, and its final consummation in eternity.
God has elected and predestined us in Christ; in Christ he
reconciled the world unto himself; in Christ we are born to
grace; in Christ we grow and persevere in grace; in Christ
we shall be made alive, raised from the dead, and glorified.
But is not this precisely the object of the *mystery,* which is,
as we have seen, the corner-stone of Paul's Gospel? Between the *communicatio idiomatum* pointed out above, the

---

All the words above enumerated are Pauline but (*b*), (*c*), (*j*) and (*n*); yet
they are all without exception Pauline in sense. Indeed, συσταυροῦσθαι is
employed by the evangelists only in the literal meaning, speaking of the
thieves *crucified with* Jesus (Matt. xxvii, 44; Mark xv, 32; John xix, 32);
συναποθνήσκειν, also in the literal meaning, referring to Peter who wishes
to *die with* Jesus (Mark xiv, 31); συγκαθίζειν also, in reference to the
people *seated with* Peter (Luke xxii, 55). Only συγκληρονόμος comes a
little nearer to the usage of Paul in Heb. xi, 9 (Abraham, Isaac and Jacob
*co-heirs* of the promise), and in 1 Pet. iii, 7 (husbands and wives *co-heirs*
of grace).

Quite a large number of other words, also Pauline for the most part, do
not figure in this list because, although they well express the union of the
faithful with one another through the communion of saints, they do not
explicitly declare their union with Christ or in Christ. These are:
συναγωνίζεσθαι (Rom. xv, 30); συναθλεῖν (*collaborare*, Phil. i, 27; iv, 3);
συνυπουργεῖν (2 Cor. i, 11); συγκακοπαθεῖν (2 Tim. i, 8; ii, 3); συγκοινωνεῖν
(Eph. v, 11; Phil. iv, 14; Apoc. xviii, 4); συγκοινωνός (Rom. xi, 17; 1 Cor.
ix, 23; Phil. i, 7; Apoc. i, 9); συμπολίτης (Eph. ii, 19); συμμιμητής
(Phil. iii, 17), etc.

One should bear in mind that the idea expressed by these composite verbs
is often translated by the simple verb with the component preposition separated from it (for example, Rom. vi, 8: εἰ ἀπεθάνομεν σὺν Χριστῷ).

phrase *In Christo Jesu* and the contents of the mystery, exist the closest and most enduring relations.  They are not so much three distinct truths as three particular aspects of the same truth, redemption by Christ and in Christ : only the mystery looks upon it from the standpoint of God, who takes the initiative in it and keeps its secret ; the *communicatio idiomatum* considers it from the standpoint of man who appropriates to himself its benefits and gathers its fruits ; the phrase *In Christo Jesu* apprehends it in the very person of the mediator.  In any case, the theology of St Paul is soteriological.

But how can we give it an expression comprehensive enough to keep us from omitting anything essential and short enough to avoid every useless additional burden? Perhaps the following statement, despite its imperfection, would be sufficiently explicit, provided the value of the words be precisely noted : " Christ as Saviour associating every believer with his death and life."  *Christ as Saviour* defines the person of the redeemer ; he is the Messiah, the messenger, the agent and the representative of God, the high priest of guilty humanity, the new Adam charged by God with the task of repairing the work of the first Adam.—*Every believer* specifies the subject of redemption, potentially universal, without distinctions, exclusions, or privileges ; and indicates at the same time the essential condition of salvation, faith. *Union with the death and life of Christ* comprises the redemptive plan, conceived by the Father from eternity, fulfilled in the course of the ages by the Son, who, making himself one with us, and uniting us to him by a bond of mystical identity, makes what is ours pass to him, and what is his own pass to us.

4. If we have succeeded in indicating the true central point of the Pauline doctrine, it seems necessary to place ourselves on Calvary, as on a lofty observatory, and there to contemplate, first, the mystery of our salvation under all its aspects : the mission of the Saviour, the efficacy of the redeeming death, and the immediate effects of redemption ; then, to fix our gaze upon the events which serve as a prelude to the great drama and also on the series of facts which prepare its denouement.  But this mode of procedure, however rational it may appear, is impracticable.  The work of redemption, conditioned by the history of the fall, is explained only by the light of the divine counsels, and is understood only in the work of the person of the Redeemer.  It is, therefore, necessary to examine, first of all, what led up to it— that is to say, the state of fallen humanity and the designs of God concerning it; then, the origin, relations and nature of him who assumes the task of saving the world.  Similarly,

the consequences of redemption comprise two distinct orders of benefits which we ought not to blend in one : I mean the channels established by God to convey to men's souls the efficacy of the redeeming blood, and the fruits of salvation which this divine nourishment causes to germinate. Thus, if we eliminate the subdivisions which the nature of the subject imposes or suggests, the theology of St Paul assumes the following schematic form :

I.—*Preparation for the Redemption.*

    1. Humanity without Christ.
    2. The Initiative of the Father.

II.—*The Person of the Redeemer.*

    1. The Pre-existent Christ.
    2. Relations of the Pre-existent Christ.
    3. Jesus Christ.

III.—*The Work of Redemption.*

    1. The redeeming Mission.
    2. The redeeming Death.
    3. The immediate effects of the Redemption.

IV.—*The Channels of Redemption.*

    1. Faith and Justification.
    2. The Sacraments.
    3. The Church.

V.—*The fruits of the Redemption.*

    1. The Christian Life.
    2. The Last Ends.

Instead of appearing at the head of this list, as one might have expected, the central idea occupies really its centre. By degrees we rise to the summit of the doctrinal teaching of the Apostle, and then descend from it. The scheme of redemption thus unrolls both behind and before us in a chronological picture of harmoniously receding vistas.

# CHAPTER II

## THE ORIGINS OF PAULINISM

### I—PAUL AND JESUS

1. Paul against Jesus. 2. Apparent Indifference of Paul to the Mortal Life of Jesus. 3. Clear Statement and Explanation of the Phenomenon.

1. THE pretended antagonism between Jesus and Paul is still an article of belief in certain rationalistic schools. For many critics Paul remains the founder of the Church, the creator of its theology, the propagator of asceticism, the promoter of the sacraments, and the determined enemy of everything free, spontaneous, vital, and vivifying in that individual religion which is the true religion of Jesus. On this account Nietzsche the superman, the mystical critic Paul de Lagarde, and Abbé Loisy devote a kind of personal hatred to St Paul. The German Bötticher, who calls himself Paul de Lagarde, treats the Apostle as a hallucinated fanatic with a disordered mind, who would have ruined the Gospel, if the Gospel could have perished. Nietzsche calls him ambitious, tricky, intriguing, and superstitious, and his writings a dishonour to Christianity. M. Loisy sees in him nothing but word-play and fantastic fancy, and warns us that "the mentality of Paul is not that of an educated man, but rather that of a primitive man dominated by his impressions and taking for realities the images which crowd one another in his brain."

Hostility towards the Doctor of the Gentiles has aroused in England and Germany a religious movement which expresses itself in the rallying cries: "Back to Christ! Los von Paulus!" In 1869 Renan predicted that the disastrous hegemony of Paul would soon reach its conclusion: "After three hundred years of being the Christian teacher par excellence, Paul, in our time, sees his reign ending; Jesus, on the contrary, is more vital than ever. It is no longer the Epistle to the Romans which is the résumé of Christianity, it is the Sermon on the Mount. True Christianity will endure for ever, and it comes from the Gospels, not from the Epistles. The writings of Paul have been a dangerous reef, the cause of the principal defects in Christian theology. Paul is the father of the subtle Augustine, the arid Thomas

Aquinas, the gloomy Calvinist, the crabbed Jansenist, and author of the ferocious theology which damns and predestines to damnation. Jesus is the father of all who seek the repose of their souls in dreams of the ideal."[1]

2. Some still bolder critics radically do away with the problem of the relations between Jesus and Paul, either by withdrawing from Paul the authorship of all his Epistles without exception or by disputing the very existence of Jesus; but in spite of the noisy successes which were won by the former in Holland and by the others in Germany, their paradoxes have met with so much indifference and disdain among the immense majority of critics in all lands and of all schools that we do not wish to make ourselves ridiculous by taking them seriously.[2]

One objection, however, is so specious that it must not be lightly pushed aside. How does it happen that the mortal life of Jesus occupies such a small place in the teaching of the Apostle, and that the Paul's Christ seems so different from the Christ of the Synoptists?

However this phenomenon may be explained, it cannot be attributed to ignorance. For is it possible that Paul, converted almost on the morrow of the resurrection, wished to know nothing of the life and teaching of him who had just appeared to him : and that he learned nothing from Ananias and the Christians of Damascus, with whom he lived on two occasions, before and after his journey to Arabia? Always in touch with the immediate disciples of Jesus, he had Barnabas for a collaborator at Antioch, in Cyprus and in Asia Minor; Silas accompanied him in his second mission, the duration of which was not less than three years; the two future historians of Jesus, St Mark and St Luke, lived intimately with him, one at the beginning and at the end of his apostolic career, the other during the last half. And I have not spoken of his relations with Peter and James and the deacon Philip and the faithful in Antioch and Jerusalem. Was ever a man better placed to become, fundamentally and in detail, acquainted with the words and deeds of the Saviour?

But, it will be said, he takes no interest in them. His Christ is not the Christ of history; he is the dead and risen Christ, the Christ seated in glory at the right hand of the Father, ready to return in the clouds of heaven to take his followers into his kingdom. Does he not confess this when he writes : " Henceforth we know no man according to the

[1] Renan, *Saint Paul*, pp. 569-570.
[2] We have spoken of the former in Vol. I, pp. 4-6. Whoever would learn more of the others should consult Fillion, *Jésus ou Paul ?* (five articles which appeared in the *Revue du clergé français* in 1912).

flesh; and if we have known Christ according to the flesh, yet now we know him [so] no longer "?[1]

To argue from a text so obscure that everyone interprets it to suit himself, is not a good method.  According to the best exegetes, Paul means that, on becoming a Christian, he adopted different thoughts and feelings in regard to everything.  He no longer ought to know anyone according to the flesh, and *even* if he had known Christ according to the flesh, he ought not so to know him any longer now.  This text proves clearly that Paul, when converted, has on every subject loftier, more spiritual, and more supernatural ideas, but it does not at all prove that he takes no interest in the earthly life of Jesus.

St Paul's portrait of Jesus, as we shall soon see, is not a mere sketch, it is a faithful picture which the evangelists

---

[1] 2 Cor. v, 16: "Ὥστε ἡμεῖς ἀπὸ τοῦ νῦν οὐδένα οἴδαμεν κατὰ σάρκα· εἰ καὶ ἐγνώκαμεν κατὰ σάρκα Χριστόν, ἀλλὰ νῦν οὐκέτι γινώσκομεν.

*Itaque nos ex hoc neminem novimus secundum carnem ; et si cognovimus secundum carnem Christum, sed nunc jam non novimus.*

The general idea of this difficult verse is furnished by the immediate context.  Whoever thoroughly understands the meaning of the death of Christ, comprehends that he is to live for him alone and to have henceforth no more terrestrial and carnal thoughts on any subject whatever (verse 15) ; hence (ὥστε) he, Paul—and those who resemble him—no longer appreciates and esteems anyone *according to the flesh*, not even Christ (verse 16) ; it is thus (ὥστε) that he becomes a new creature, a soul renewed in thoughts and affections (verse 17).

It follows: (1) That the *henceforth* (ἀπὸ τοῦ νῦν) has for its point of departure the moment when Paul realized the significance of the death of Christ for us (κρίναντας τοῦτο)—that is to say, the time of his conversion.—2. That the words *according to the flesh* (κατὰ σάρκα) have a subjective, not an objective, sense—that is to say, they qualify the Christian's manner of thinking and feeling, and not the object of his thoughts and feelings.  The place of the words *according to the flesh* shows that they refer to the verb (*novimus, cognovimus*, οἴδαμεν, ἐγνώκαμεν) and not to the objective case (*neminem, Christum*).  Moreover, whether the expression *according to the flesh* qualifies the subject knowing or the object known, really matters little ; since, any way, their mutual relation having changed through the effect of the mystical death of the Christian in Christ, the knowledge of this relation ought therefore to change also.—3. That Christ (Χριστός, without the article) signifies the person itself of Jesus Christ and not the Messiah.  This is the evident meaning of Χριστός in the whole context, and this appears very clearly in verse 16 from the contrast between *no one* (οὐδένα) and *Christ* (Χριστόν —Christ, meaning the Messiah, requires the definite article.

This being admitted, the whole question reduces itself to this : Is the hypothesis real or unreal ?  In other words, does Paul make a *concession* to his opponents, or does he start out from a *supposition*, possible but not proven, in order to emphasize his thought ?  If the hypothesis is the real meaning will be : " Formerly, it is true, I knew Christ according to the flesh, but now I do not wish to know him thus any more."  Many exegetes adopt this interpretation, but they are hard put to it to explain the *concession* of the Apostle reasonably.  They propose one of the three following paraphrases :

A. " Before my conversion I regarded Jesus Christ as a malefactor and justly put to death : now I have more correct notions concerning him " (Cornely, B. Weiss, Plummer [1915], Bachmann [1918], etc.).  But how can we suppose that Paul assumes so solemn a tone to end in such a truism ?

complete, without modifying its expression. But what is the
use of our lingering over a difficulty which exists only in the
imagination of the critics? The charge which is brought
against the Apostle of making so little use of the acts and
words of Jesus is inconclusive. If it had any foundation, it
would apply equally well—and even more so—to all the other
writers of the New Testament except the evangelists, whose
special aim it is to relate the Saviour's life. Regard being
had to relative proportions, allusions to the earthly life of
Jesus are not more numerous in these authors; it can even be
maintained with assurance that they are fewer in number.
The question, therefore, assumes a completely different
aspect. If any difficulty remains, it is not St Paul that it
specially concerns; it needs a general explanation.

Here, to begin with, are two evangelists: St John and St
Luke. Whether the author of the fourth Gospel is the beloved disciple or not, matters little for the moment; he
certainly composed the Epistle which serves as a preface to
the Gospel and in which he declares himself expressly to
have been an eye and ear witness. Now what does he teach
us there of Jesus? He mentions casually his incarnation, his
holiness, his love for us; he perhaps alludes discreetly to the
institution of baptism; and that is all. Will anyone accuse
him of ignorance? And will anyone say that the author of
the Acts, who is also certainly the author of the third Gospel,
was unacquainted with the life of Jesus? Yet in the Acts,
except in the first chapter, which is a continuation of the
Gospel history, he makes very few allusions to Jesus. He
reports only one saying of his, which he has not recorded in
the Gospel, and—a remarkable circumstance—he puts it in
the mouth of Paul. As Harnack has admirably said: " If we

---

B. " There was a time, I confess, *even after my conversion*, when I knew
Christ, his person and his work imperfectly; but my knowledge of him has
progressed and it is now spiritual and just" (Baur, Holsten, Jowett, etc.).
This exegesis, defended only by heterodox writers, is contrary to what we
have said above and contradicts the express and reiterated assertions of the
Apostle, who admits in his Gospel neither vacillation nor change.

C. " Before my conversion I knew Jesus living on the earth, mortal and
susceptible of suffering; but that was a carnal knowledge, of which I have now
divested myself" (Schlatter, J. Weiss, Moe, etc.).—But, supposing that Paul
had known Jesus personally—which is improbable—why should he wish to
forget it? And what would fit in with such forgetfulness?

Since the concession gives us no satisfactory meaning, we must fall back
on the unreal hypothesis. Heinrici, in his great commentary, and Reitzenstein (*Die hellenist. Mysterienrel.*, p. 195) show that from the philological
point of view there is no objection to it. The meaning then is: " Even if I
had known Christ according to the flesh—which is not the case and which
has nothing to do with the present question—I no longer wish to know him
thus." To know Christ *according to the flesh* is to know him after the manner
of the enemies of Paul; to know him *according to the spirit* is to know him
as his resurrection and glorification have taught us to know him in the light
of the Holy Spirit.

knew of this author only the Acts and not the Gospel, we should doubtless pass the following judgement on him : this man knows nothing of the Gospel history ; above all, he is absolutely ignorant of the synoptic tradition, since the only saying of Jesus that he has preserved is not found in this source." An absurd conclusion ; but a style of reasoning identical with that which we are reflecting.

Suppose that the first Epistle to the Corinthians had not been written, or that it had been lost : would the critics fail to assert that Paul is *ignorant* of the institution of the Eucharist and the circumstances of the resurrection? This hypothesis plainly shows the fallacy of the argument. The most natural explanation, both of St Paul and the others as well, is that they are addressing themselves to Christians already instructed in the life of Jesus, and that their writings take for granted catechetical teaching in the Church, but are not themselves imparting it.

3. The principal difference between Paul and the Synoptists lies in the manner of presenting the person and the work of Jesus. Whence comes this difference?

When Jesus wished to make himself recognized as the Messiah and the King of Israel, the delivery of this message encountered many and varied difficulties—the jealous susceptibility of the Romans, the fanatical and revolutionary infatuation of the patriotic Jews, and, above all, the lack of intelligence and the crude conceptions of the people. The ideas held in regard to the Messiah were far from being uniform ; but in general the people dreamed of a national hero, invested with power and glory, who would shake off foreign domination, annihilate or subdue the enemies of Israel, reassemble the *Diaspora,* and inaugurate at Jerusalem an era of justice, prosperity, happiness, and peace. All this was to burst forth suddenly, without human assistance, by a lightning-like intervention on the part of Jehovah. No idea of a poor, suffering Messiah was prevalent, or of a spiritual reign of God, demanding the inward co-operation of souls and establishing itself by degrees in intensity as well as in extent.

The very name Messiah conjured up in almost all the Jews of that time incomplete, incorrect, and actually false notions. It could be used only with circumspection. At the beginning of his preaching Jesus seems to avoid it purposely, as if he feared to be misunderstood. It is true, he does not reject it when it is applied to him ; he approves it solemnly six months before his death, when uttered by St Peter ; he lays claims to it before Pilate and the Sanhedrim, together with the title of the Son of God ; but, after all, he does not employ it habitually. The expression which he ordinarily uses to designate himself is that of *Son of Man*. This name had the advantage of being understood in a Messianic sense, without awakening the revolutionary passions of the zealots. Jesus, therefore, takes it as his usual appellation. When he is asked to prove his mission, if he sometimes invokes the testimony of the Baptist, of the Scriptures, and of his heavenly Father, he appeals most frequently to his miracles and, above all, to his resurrection, which remains the principal reason for credibility.

But, after the resurrection, three great changes occur in the way in which the apostles speak of Jesus. First, the name Son of Man has no further *raison d'être*. The evangelists preserve it in order to remain faithful to historical truth; but all the others replace it by more significant terms : *Christ* (that is to say, Messiah), *Lord* (translation of the name Jehovah in the LXX), and, above all, *Son of God*. This last title, the most comprehensive and just, was also that which the resurrection had best demonstrated.—Not only does the miracle of the resurrection eclipse all the others, but there is no more need of another miracle. St Peter is content to appeal to it. St Paul does the same. Henceforth, if we except the transfiguration, which was a kind of prelude to the glorious resurrection, no particular miracle will be mentioned in the New Testament, outside the Gospels. Finally, although the earthly life of Jesus always formed the subject of catechetical instruction, the chief effort was rather to show Christ to converts as he is now in glory, the invisible Head of the Church and the all-powerful intercessor with the Father.

What we have said of Christology applies in a still higher degree to the doctrine of salvation. Let us confine ourselves to one point only : the preaching of the *kingdom of God*.

It was in order to avoid giving offence to the Roman authorities and to correct the vague, erroneous or extravagant notions which the Jews entertained about the Messianic kingdom, that Jesus in the midst of his Galilean ministry had inaugurated his system of teaching by parables. In these he showed that the kingdom is not only God's claim upon the individual soul, but his social reign in a society in which the good and the bad are mingled. He made prominent the spiritual and universal character of this kingdom, in which the Gentiles have their appointed place, and from which the unbelieving Jews are excluded.

But, once the true notion of the *kingdom* was understood, and when the concrete realization of it was seen in the Church, the pedagogic rôle of the parables came to an end. We no longer find any trace of them outside the Synoptists, neither in St John, nor in the rest of the New Testament, nor in the apostolic Fathers. No doubt the parables always formed part of the elementary catechetical teaching, as a piece of history, together with an epitome of the life of Jesus; but they no longer served to illustrate the nature of the *kingdom of God,* the very name of which tended to disappear, to give place to that of the *Church.* On this particular point St Paul is still the one who comes nearest to the teaching of Jesus, as it is recorded in the Synoptists.

These brief remarks are enough to show why and how the Gospel preaching concerning the person and the work of the Saviour necessarily underwent a transformation in passing from Jesus to the apostles. The cause of this change was the very fact of the resurrection of Jesus and of the foundation of the Church on the day of Pentecost. And it has been proved that in this Paul does not differ at all from his colleagues in the apostolate.

## II—THE APOSTOLIC CATECHESIS

1. Its Existence.   2. Its Historical, Dogmatic, Liturgical and Moral Contents.

1. It is to-day generally conceded that St Paul derives his ideas from Jesus, and does not substitute his own notions for the teaching of the Master. It becomes even more and more evident that it is impossible to understand him clearly without a basis of religious instruction common to all the Christian communities. This statement is not a new one. Reuss wrote in 1852 : " The Epistles [of Paul] are addressed without exception to persons already familiar with the ideas of the Gospel ; they are by no means intended to give either elementary or complete instruction to their readers. Dogma is mentioned fragmentarily and as occasion calls for it ; often it is simply alluded to, as to something already known. The real Christian instruction had been given orally, and no doubt in sequence and entirety."[1]

Nothing is more certain. St John, at the end of his career, bequeaths his episodical and complementary Gospel to his faithful companions who had long been familiar with the life and works of Jesus. St Luke addresses his to a catechumen, not so much to initiate him into a knowledge of Christianity, as to make known to him " the truth of those words in which he had been instructed " orally.

As for St Paul, all his letters are enigmas, if we suppose that the persons to whom they are addressed are unacquainted with the elements of the Christian faith. These elements did not vary according to the fancy of the preachers ; they corresponded to a uniform type, to which all the teachers of the Gospel had to conform. Paul, on returning from his first

---

[1] *Theol. chrét. au siècle apost.*[3], Strasbourg, 1864, vol. ii, p. 9.

apostolic mission, expounded his Gospel in detail before the
whole assembly of Jerusalem; then, separately, to the
principal heads of this church, especially to James the
brother of the Lord, to Peter, prince of the apostles, and to
John, the beloved disciple.    The aim of this communication
was to show them that the Doctor of the Gentiles had not
gone astray, and was not departing from the teaching
common to them all.    The result was what was to be
expected.    "The pillars of the Church," said St Paul,
"added nothing to me."[1]    They found nothing to find fault
with, nothing to rectify, and nothing to add to in his doctrine.
They conferred upon him nothing but what he already
possessed, and they taught him nothing that he did not
know before.    But, on his part, he does not boast of having
taught them anything; for if, to a certain extent, there are
two ways of proclaiming the Gospel, according to whether
the hearers are Jews or Gentiles, there is, after all, really
only one Gospel, that of Jesus Christ.    Paul never pretends
to have instructed the other apostles, and he never finds in
them any error or doctrinal difference to criticize.    They and
he are subject to one and the same higher rule : the teaching
of Jesus Christ.

Such is the rule which both catechists and catechumens
have to obey.    "Let him that is instructed in the word,"
says St Paul to the Galatians, "communicate to him that
instructeth him, in all good things."[2]    The exact meaning of
this recommendation is a matter of dispute.    According to
some, the catechumen should try to participate in the spiritual
and intellectual possessions of the catechist by paying attention to the word of the Gospel, and especially by imitation.
According to others, whose interpretation is more widely
known and seems to us better, the catechumen should share
with his catechist the temporal goods which he possesses, in
exchange for the spiritual blessings which he receives from
him, because the preacher of the Gospel has a right to re-

---

[1] Gal. ii, 6 : ἐμοὶ οἱ δοκοῦντες οὐδὲν προσανέθεντο.    See Vol. I, p. 48.
Οὐδὲν προσανέθεντο does not mean, as certain exegetes wish to prove
(Sieffert, Lagrange, Loisy), "they did not impose any new burden upon me,"
but rather "they did not give me anything new *from what they possessed*"
(this explains the middle voice).    The beginning of the phrase *ab iis autem
qui videbantur aliquid esse* anticipates the complementary words *nihil
accepi vel didici*.    This is the thought which Paul expresses by changing
the construction, a thought which agrees well with the idea that precedes
and with the one that follows.

[2] Gal. vi, 6 : Κοινωνείτω δὲ ὁ κατηχούμενος τὸν λόγον τῷ κατηχοῦντι ἐν
πᾶσιν ἀγαθοῖς.    See, for details, Cornely, Lagrange or Lightfoot.    In
translating κατηχούμενος by *catechumen* and κατηχῶν by *catechist*, we do not
mean to give these words the technical sense which they received after the
institution of the catechumenate.    Here the *catechist* is one who teaches the
Christian doctrine (τὸν λόγον), and the *catechumen* is one who is taught,
whether he is baptized or not.

muneration. But this divergence of views is unimportant for our present investigation. It results clearly from our text that there were then catechists, who were charged by a competent authority with the task of instructing the new converts, or who assumed that duty voluntarily; also that there were catechumens to whom the Word was taught —namely, the Gospel of Christ; and that therefore there was a system of catechetical teaching, without which there could be neither catechists nor catechumens. The latter were probably not only the candidates for baptism, but rather all the converts whose religious instruction was still incomplete.

This system of instruction was not left to individual inspiration, but was identical in its import and uniform in its presentation. St Paul writes to the Romans: "You have obeyed from the heart unto that form (τύπος) of doctrine, into which you have been delivered."[1] But this form, this *type* of doctrine, is imposed no less imperiously on the preachers than on the faithful themselves. When the Apostle wishes to utter a warning against the awakening doubts of the Corinthians on the subject of the resurrection of the dead, he refers them to his oral teaching :

> I make known unto you, brethren, the Gospel which I preached to you, which also you have received and wherein you stand, by which also you are saved, if you hold fast what I preached unto you, otherwise you have believed in vain.
>
> For I delivered unto you first of all, which I also received, how that Christ died for our sins, according to the Scriptures; and that he was buried, and that he rose again the third day, according to the Scriptures ; and that he was seen by Cephas, and after that by the Twelve. Then was he seen by more than five hundred brethren at once, of whom the majority remain until this present, and some are fallen asleep. After that, he was seen by James, then by all the Apostles. And, last of all, he was seen also by me, as by an abortive. For I am the least of the Apostles and am not worthy to be called an Apostle, because I persecuted the Church of God. But by the grace of God I am what I am ; and his grace in me hath not been void ; but I have laboured more abundantly than they all. Yet not I, but the grace of God with me.
>
> Thus, whether I or they, so we preach, and so you believed.[2]

---

[1] Rom. vi, 17 : ὑπηκούσατε ἐκ καρδίας εἰς ὃν παρεδόθητε τύπον διδαχῆς. The grammatical attraction is, it seems, to be explained thus : τύπῳ διδαχῆς εἰς ὃν παρεδόθητε (*the type of doctrine to which you have been delivered*). Seeberg prefers to explain : εἰς τύπον διδαχῆς ὃν παρεδόθητε, but the construction appears forced and the meaning of it difficult.

Three conclusions result from this text : (*a*) The τύπος διδαχῆς means a fixed and uniform teaching, for τύπος signifies " a pattern," " an exemplar." Euthymius, following Chrysostom, thinks that it is a question especially of moral teaching.—(*b*) The converts have been *delivered to this rule of conduct*, because, expressing the will of God, it has for them an imperative character.—(*c*) But, when once it has become a rule valid for all the churches, the preachers also are obliged to conform to it.

[2] I Cor. xv, 1-11. The conclusion (εἴτε οὖν ἐγὼ εἴτε ἐκεῖνοι οὕτως κηρύσσομεν καὶ οὕτως ἐπιστεύσατε) proves clearly the fact of a catechetica system common to all the preachers and to all the believers in all the churches

Jesus Christ dead, buried, risen the third day, according to the Scriptures, and his appearance to Peter, to the Twelve, to more than five hundred disciples at once, to James, and to Paul himself; this is what all the faithful must have heard from the mouth of the Apostle and his colleagues. This text is extremely important as a specimen of the apostolic form of teaching, for it allows us to conclude that the facts concerning the Saviour's life occupied a far greater place in the preaching of the Apostle than in his writings, and that his first teaching was precise and, so to speak, stereotyped like a catechism. Paul does not pretend to reproduce all his oral Gospel; he transcribes only a fragment of it, that which is applicable to his present design, without adding, as elsewhere, that he has it from the Lord himself, for he can very well owe the knowledge of these facts to eye-witnesses. What he expressly affirms is that, on these fundamental points, the teaching of all the preachers and the faith of all the faithful are identical: *Sive enim ego, sive illi, sic praedicamus et sic credidistis.*

What are the principal articles of this primitive catechism? The Epistle to the Hebrews gives us a concise idea of it:

> Wherefore, leaving the word of the beginning of Christ, let us go on to things more perfect;
> Not laying again the foundation of penance from dead works and of faith in God,
> Of the doctrine of baptisms and imposition of hands,
> Of the resurrection of the dead and of eternal judgement.[1]

The author has just told the Hebrews that, having been Christians for a long time, the first elements of the faith are no longer suited to them, and that they need a stronger and

---

(*a*) Paul says that he has preached the resurrection ἐν πρώτοις, not necessarily *in the first place*, but as *a fundamental article*.

(*b*) He cites, as witnesses of the resurrection, only persons still living and of unquestionable authority; and curiously, no women.

(*c*) He makes no difference between the appearance of Christ to the first Apostles and the appearance with which Christ favoured him. As regards certainty and reality, these are facts of the same order.

[1] Heb. vi, 1-2: Διὸ ἀφέντες τὸν τῆς ἀρχῆς τοῦ Χριστοῦ λόγον ἐπὶ τὴν τελειότητα φερώμεθα, μὴ πάλιν θεμέλιον καταβαλλόμενοι μετανοίας ἀπὸ νεκρῶν ἔργων καὶ πίστεως ἐπὶ Θεόν,

βαπτισμῶν διδαχὴν ἐπιθεσεώς τε χειρῶν,
ἀναστάσεως νεκρῶν καὶ κρίματος αἰωνίου.

(*a*) The verb φερώμεθα could include the readers (let us go, *you and I*), but it is better to understand it of the author himself who is going to add example to words (ἀφέντες), and to whom alone it belongs to lay the foundations of faith (καταβαλλόμενοι). Moreover, the general sense remains the same.

(*b*) *The word of the beginning* concerning Christ (τὸν τῆς ἀρχῆς τοῦ Χριστοῦ λόγον) is defined by its contrast with a more perfect teaching (ἐπὶ τὴν τελειότητα) and by a similar phrase in the preceding chapter, verse 12. It is, therefore, the A B C of Christianity.

more virile nourishment. He exhorts them, therefore, not to
be content with the milk of children, but to assimilate solid
food corresponding to their age; or rather, he declares that
he is himself going to rise to loftier considerations, more
worthy of their maturity in the faith. He will, then, put
aside the *first teaching* concerning Christ, the *first elements*
of revelation. A variation from the original reading throws
some uncertainty on the text here. According to one version,
the rudiments of Christianity would comprise six items
grouped in pairs : penance and faith, baptism and confirmation, the resurrection and judgement. But the other reading,
which appears to us the better one, identifies penance and faith
with the foundation laid at the beginning by the preachers of
the Gospel, and then the composition of the *credo* consists
of four items, grouped thus : the *doctrine of baptisms* (no
doubt the distinction between the baptism of John and that
of Jesus, or between the ritual purifications of the Jews and
Christian baptism), and *the laying on of hands* (that is, confirmation conferred after the baptism) ; the dogmas of the
resurrection of the dead and of the last judgement. This
was, in fact, by the very nature of things, and according to
historical data, the most abbreviated early catechism used. It
will appear less concise if it be remembered that the understanding of baptism and of confirmation necessarily presupposes a knowledge of the Trinity and of grace, and that
the glorious resurrection substantially includes the work of
redemption.

2. History, dogma, liturgy, and morals : such were the
four primordial elements of the apostolic catechesis.

The *historical teaching* was concerned with the acts,
miracles, and teachings of Jesus. It is inconceivable that
the preaching of the apostles passed over in silence the life
and words of the founder of Christianity. Before believing
in him, the catechumens had to know what he had been,
done, and said. Assuredly certain features were made more
prominent than others : his descent from the lineage of
David, predicted by the prophets, his birth from a woman
(without any mention of a mortal father), his baptism and
the testimony of the Baptist, his life of obedience, humility,
and renunciation, the principal manifestations of his superhuman power, the institution of the Eucharist; the most remarkable circumstances of his passion, his resurrection on

---

(*c*) We adopt the reading διδαχήν in place of διδαχῆς. The accusative
διδαχήν is then in apposition with θεμέλιον, which he explains : " Let us
not lay again the *foundation*, which consists of penance for dead works and
of faith in God ; I wish to speak of the *doctrine* of baptisms," etc. If we should
read διδαχῆς, all these genitives would depend on θεμέλιον, and the foundation of the faith would comprise six elements, grouped in pairs.

the third day, his appearances to the disciples, and his triumphal ascension. But everything leads us to believe that the instruction was not confined to this brief résumé. Apollos had received a very incomplete training in this respect, since he still knew only the baptism of John; nevertheless, he was able *to teach accurately the things concerning Jesus*—that is to say, evidently—if these expressions are compared with similar utterances—the life, deeds, and discourses of the Master.[1] St Luke takes it for granted that Theophilus, the catechumen or neophyte, to whom he addresses his Gospel, is already acquainted with the Gospel history. And when we read that St Paul, while a captive at Rome, taught without hindrance and in full liberty *the things concerning the Lord Jesus*,[2] we must assume that he made explanations of importance, and admit that mere allusions by the way, or a few hurried details about the earthly life of Jesus would not at all justify the assertion of the author of the Acts.

More concise, no doubt, was the *dogmatic teaching*. It does not appear to us proved that the apostles had an almost stereotyped compendium, which they gave the neophytes to commit to memory in a nearly invariable form.[3] At least, perhaps excepting certain cases in which the teaching was completed after baptism, they set before them a rudimentary *Credo*, of which the dogma of the Trinity always formed a part. Indeed, all the *Symbols* said to be those of the apostles, in spite of their remarkable variations, are uniformly cast in a trinitarian mould. The baptismal formula, employed from earliest times, as well as the doxology *Glory be to the Father and to the Son and to the Holy Ghost,* in use at a very early date, proves that the three divine Persons were always

---

[1] Acts xviii, 25. For the expression τὰ περὶ Ἰησοῦ *cf.* Col. iv, 8; Eph. vi, 22.

[2] Acts xxviii, 31 : *Praedicans regnum Dei et docens quae sunt de Domino Jesu Christo* (τὰ περὶ τοῦ Κυρίου Ἰ. Χ.).

[3] *Cf.* Seeberg in *Der Katechismus der Urchristenheit*, Leipzig, 1903, and *Das Evangelium Christi*, Leipzig, 1905. But his apostolic *symbol* is much too limited. It may be reduced to this (*Katechismus*, p. 85) : " The living God, Creator of all things, sent his Son, born of the race of David, Jesus Christ, who died for us according to the Scriptures, was buried and rose again on the third day according to the Scriptures, sitteth at the right hand of God in heaven, having subjected to himself principalities, powers and dominions, and will return in the clouds of heaven invested with power and glory."

We grant Seeberg that his embryonic *Credo* did really form part of the apostolic system of instruction, but we do not think that this *Credo* was presented everywhere under an almost invariable form, and especially that it was limited to that form. The article of the last judgement by Christ could not have been wanting in the first preaching of St Paul (Rom. ii, 16 ; xiv, 10 ; 2 Tim. iv, 1 ; Acts xvii, 21, etc.), nor in that of the other Apostles ; for it was a fundamental and elementary dogma (Heb. vi, 2 ; *cf.* Acts x, 12 ; 1 Pet. iv, 5). But without stopping to deal with criticisms in detail, the primitive formulary of faith was certainly founded upon the dogma of the Trinity.

closely associated in the thought and adoration of the faithful. St Paul presupposes in all his converts, whatever may have been their origin, acquaintance with the person and activity of the Holy Spirit.[1] All the more must they have known what Christ was before the incarnation and what were the bonds uniting him, the Spirit, and the Father. Nor is it doubtful either that the subject of the incarnation and the value of the redemptive death of the Messiah, Son of God, entered into the framework of this primitive *Credo*. Let us note also that the teaching of the second coming of Christ, of the resurrection of the dead, and of the last judgement forms the foundation of all the sermons of Paul recorded in the Acts,[2] just as it is one of the fundamental points of the Church's elementary teaching, according to the Epistle to the Hebrews.

When a catechumen became a member of the Church, it was necessary to explain to him the meaning and the import of the sacred rites which united him to Christ. This is what may be called the *liturgical teaching*. All the Christians whom Paul addresses are supposed to know and understand perfectly the value and mystical signification of baptism, confirmation, and the Eucharist.[3] That this initiation was the end of the catechetical teaching can be concluded from the recital in Acts,[4] that it was common to all the faithful appears from the Epistle to the Hebrews, in which " the doctrine of baptisms and of the imposition of hands " is ranked among " the first elements of the oracles of God " and " the initial institution of Christ."[5] To liturgical teaching is united the Lord's Prayer, which it was the custom to recite three times a day, perhaps at the usual hours of Jewish prayer, and its general use is not in any case later than the appearance of the first and third Gospel.[6]

The *teaching of morals* was a matter of course, and the Talmud shows us that it was given regularly to proselytes from Judaism.[7] It would be easy but unnecessary to prove that this practice was in use throughout the whole Church from the end of the second century onwards ; and it can even be proved that it goes back much further, and probably to the very beginning. In the year 112, Pliny the Younger learned that Christians *took an oath* not to commit either

---

[1] Acts xix, 2 ; Gal. iii, 2-5, etc.

[2] Rom. ii, 16 ; xiv, 10 ; 2 Tim. iv, 1 ; Acts xvii, 31, etc. *Cf.* Heb. vi, 2 ; Acts x, 12.

[3] Rom. vi, 3 (baptism) ; 1 Cor. xi, 23 (Eucharist) ; Gal. iii, 2-3 ; Acts xix, 2-6 (confirmation).

[4] Acts xviii, 25.　　　　　　[5] Heb. vi, 2 and v, 12.

[6] The *Didache*, ix, 3, prescribes the recital of the Lord's Prayer three times a day. *Cf.* Bindemann, *Das Gebet um tägliche Vergebung der Sünden*, etc. Gütersloh, 1902.

[7] Mishna, *Gerim*, i, 1-4 ; Baraitha, *Yebamoth*, 47a-b.

theft, larceny, adultery, or cheating;[1] an oath which must have coincided with the reception of baptism. Indeed, St Justin defines converts as " those who are persuaded of the truth of our doctrines, and believe what we believe, and *pledge themselves to live accordingly.*"[2] The *Didache* also prescribes that the contents of the *Two Ways*[3] should be read to the catechumen before baptizing him. The apostles always concluded their first sermon with the words : " Therefore be converted and do penance."[4] It was, of course, necessary for them to explain what conversion meant and what the " dead works "[5] were, for which the proselyte was bound to do penance. The new converts had to " persevere in the doctrine of the apostles,"[6] to " obey from the heart unto that form of doctrine into which they had been delivered,"[7] and to avoid things contrary to the doctrine which they had learned.[8] All this presupposes a fixed and precise oral teaching, and this teaching was called the way of the Lord, the way of God, the way of salvation, or simply the *Way.*[9] St Paul calls it " his way "[10] because he was accustomed to impart it in all the churches which he founded. Did this brief moral code thenceforth become crystallized? Was it perhaps substantially identical with the little treatise known by the name of the *Two Ways,* which forms the first part of the *Doctrine of the Apostles,* was incorporated in the *Epistle of Barnabas,* and has been discovered in a very ancient Latin version? Was it in the main borrowed from the Synagogue, at first without any remarkable change, but later receiving an interpolation of a specifically Christian hue? These are interesting questions, but they lie beyond the scope of this volume.

[1] *Epist.*, x, 96.    [2] *Apol.*, i, 61.
[3] *Doctr. apost.*, vii, 1.
[4] Acts ii, 38 ; iii, 19 ; xvii, 30 ; xx, 21 ; xxvi, 20 ; *cf.* 1 Thess. i, 9, etc
[5] Heb. vi, 1.    [6] Acts ii, 42.
[7] Rom. vi, 17.    [8] *ib.* xvi, 17.
[9] Acts xiii, 10 ; xviii, 25 ; xvi, 17 ; xxii, 4 ; xxiv, 22.
[10] 1 Cor. iv, 17. *Timotheus vos commonefaciet* (ὑμᾶς ἀναμνήσει=will remind you of) *vias meas . . . sicut ubique in omni ecclesia doceo.* This rule of conduct (τὰς ὁδούς μου) is the moral teaching given formerly to the Corinthians by St Paul, *conformably* (καθώς) to what he *is accustomed to teach* (διδάσκω), *in every country* that he travels through (πανταχοῦ), *in all the churches* which he founds (ἐν πάσῃ ἐκκλησίᾳ). It is only a matter of refreshing the memory.

### III—FOREIGN INFLUENCES

1. Judaism.   2. Hellenism.   3. Hellenized Oriental Religions.   4. The
True Sources of Paulinism.

1. It would be a miracle if the many localities visited by
the Apostle had not more or less reacted on his way of thinking; for he did not live apart in a tower of ivory, sheltered
from contact from without.   Born in an active and learned
city, where perhaps more than elsewhere the blending of
Hellenism with Oriental ideas took place, brought up in the
very centre of Judaism and affiliated by his own choice as
well as by family tradition with the sect of the Pharisees, and
obliged to live in the centre of Greek cities and Roman
colonies, he must have yielded in some degree to the
pressure of these different currents.

The traces of rabbinism visible in him are, however, rare
and even questionable.   Moreover, the five or six examples
usually alleged[1] relate only to accessory matters, lying on the
extreme periphery of his thought; for we do not call the use
of the typical meaning of the Scriptures rabbinism, nor the
oratorical use of the accommodative sense, nor yet the
progress of doctrines contained in embryo in the ancient
revelation, such as the spirituality of the soul, the reversibility
of merits, and the habit of attributing to the Messiah titles
belonging to Jehovah.

The rabbinism of St Paul's time is unknown to us.   What
we call such is the artificial product of a school, formed after
the ruin of the Temple and successively transplanted to
Jamnia, Lydda, Sepphoris, and Tiberias.   As the most ancient
collection of rabbinical decisions, the Mishna, hardly goes
back as far as the end of the second century, its relations
with St Paul are always very doubtful.

Hence contemporary critics do not lay much stress on
them.   Some pretend that the Apostle is inspired rather by
those numerous speculations at the beginning of the Christian
era which are generally called apocalypses.   Does he not
quote as Scripture a passage from the Apocalypse of Elias?[2]

[1] They are found in J. Weiss, *Das Urchristentum*, Göttingen, 1917,
pp. 332-334.   We have discussed them in Vol. I, p. 19-21 ; for 1 Cor. x, 4,
see later, p. 147.

[2] 1 Cor. ii, 9 : Καθὼς γέγραπται· ἃ ὀφθαλμὸς οὐκ εἶδεν καὶ οὖς οὐκ ἤκουσεν,
καὶ ἐπὶ καρδίαν ἀνθρώπου οὐκ ἀνέβη, ὅσα ἡτοίμασεν ὁ Θεὸς τοῖς ἀγαπῶσιν αὐτόν.
Ambrosiaster and Origen (*Comment. in Matt.*, xxvii, 9) affirm that Paul
here quotes the *Apocalypse of Elias*.   But the date of this apocryphal work
is entirely unknown, and it is possible that it was interpolated by Christian
hands.   This is what happened to the *Ascension of Isaias*, which quotes the
same text as it is found in St Paul.   According to a passage preserved in the
*Catenae* (Cramer, *Catenae in Paulum*, Oxford, 1841, p. 42), Origen asked
himself whether the Apostle was quoting Isaias freely or whether he borrowed
his quotation from an apocryphal writer.   St Jerome defends the first

He must have read others, for this kind of literature was then very popular. What, it has been asked, is his theology if not an apocalypse? The expectation of the imminent return of Christ explains the temporary character of his moral teaching. All his thoughts are turned towards the future. He longs for one thing only—to enter into the kingdom which Christ is about to inaugurate.[1] Faith and justification are for him only the assurance of taking part in it; the sacraments (baptism and the Eucharist), which unite us mystically with Christ, are the conditions of being admitted to it. All Paul's theology lies in these few dogmas.

If, however, we reflect that his eschatology is precisely the least original aspect of his doctrine, that in this respect he does not pass beyond the horizon of the Gospels, that his eschatological ideas, far from progressing with time, decline little by little and tend to disappear, and that the prominence which they have in the first Epistles is due to local circumstances and accidental causes, we are forced to concede that apocalyptical Judaism accounts for Pauline thought no better than rabbinical Judaism does. Will the partisans of Hellenism be more fortunate?

2. By *Hellenism* is understood either classic Greek culture, or the whole collection of the religious and moral ideas of the Greek world after Alexander, or the mode of thinking of those Jews who were called *Hellenists* and adopted the Greek language and customs in the Diaspora.

If St Paul became impregnated with Hellenism, it certainly did not take place in his own family. His father was an ardent Pharisee, and he himself professed the purest Pharisaism. We have seen how small a part profane writers[2] occupied in his early education. Did his sentiments change afterwards? Every orthodox Jew, when confronted with paganism, experienced a feeling of disgust, indignation, and pity. What distinguishes Paul from his compatriots is that he joins to this instinctive repulsion for pagan doctrines and institutions a lively sympathy for individuals. Moreover, he does not limit himself to condemning heathen delusions and depravity, he stigmatizes with the same energy what

---

alternative vigorously (*Comment. in Is.*, lxiv, 4). In fact, Isaias writes: ἀπὸ τοῦ αἰῶνος οὐκ ἠκούσαμεν οὐδὲ οἱ ὀφθαλμοὶ ἡμῶν εἶδον Θεὸν πλὴν σοῦ, καὶ τὰ ἔργα σου ἃ ποιήσεις τοῖς ὑπομένουσιν ἔλεον. But Paul may have been influenced by the remembrance of Isa. lxv, 16: οὐκ ἀναβήσεται αὐτῶν ἐπὶ τὴν καρδίαν. See Cornely or Zahn (*Geschichte des Kanons*, vol. ii, p. 808).

[1] Schweitzer, *Geschichte der paulin. Forschung*, Tübingen, 1911, pp. 187-194. Schweitzer, who had had Kabisch for a predecessor, proposed to treat the question thoroughly in a new work; but he went as a missionary to the Congo, March 24, 1913; it is to be feared, therefore, that we may never have this fine judgement concerning apocalyptic Paulinism.

[2] See Vol. I, pp. 15-16.

appeared to be the best thing in paganism : its philosophy, its love of wisdom. This worldly and carnal wisdom he repudiates, and commands his converts to keep clear of it : " Beware, lest any man cheat you by philosophy and vain deceit, according to the tradition of men and the elements of the world, and not according to Christ."[1] All the Epistles are filled with similar passages. What the Apostle finds most favourable in paganism (not in order to admire it or to excuse it, but in order to condemn it with less severity) is the fact that it belongs to the ages of ignorance which preceded the coming of the light of the Gospel, when the world, still in its infancy, had received but an elementary education.[2] Who can believe that a man animated by such sentiments ever went to the schools of the pagans and knowingly borrowed their religious practices or doctrines? But perhaps he was influenced by them un-awares.

Tarsus was then the rendezvous of philosophers and the boulevard of the Stoics. St Paul has very possibly con-versed with them, if only to combat their theories, and derived from such intercourse more than one unconscious loan. If this hypothesis is false, it is nevertheless not with-out some likelihood ; yet if we examine it closely, nothing corroborates it. The Stoics used a peculiar phraseology, especially in treating the subject of morals. Their habit of defining and dissecting notions distinguishes them at first glance from other philosophers. In order to prove that the phraseology of Paul has no connection with theirs, it is sufficient to compare their respective lists of moral virtues. Of the four cardinal virtues : fortitude (ἀνδρεία) is not even named by the Apostle ; temperance (σωφροσύνη) is mentioned only once, in the Pastorals ; prudence (φρόνησις) also once only, and then applied to God ; as to justice (δικαιοσύνη) everyone knows that he gives this word a very different meaning. Nor does he show a trace of the secondary virtues which divide and subdivide the cardinal virtues ad infinitum. Only one word, benignity (χρηστότης), recalls vaguely the Stoics' vocabulary.

The doctrines differ even more than the phraseology. The Stoics often speak of God, the soul, providence, prayer, and benevolence ; but these terms have almost nothing in common with the corresponding Christian ideas. The God of the Stoics is not the personal, good, just, holy, all-powerful God whom the Christians adore ; he is the totality of beings, the great All, nature, or the law of the world, the intelli-gence of the universe, force opposed to matter. The soul

---

[1] Col. ii, 8 ; cf. Rom. i, 18-32 ; 1 Cor. i, 26-ii, 8, etc.
[2] Gal. iv, 8-9 ; Eph. ii, 11-13 ; v, 6-8 ; Col. iii, 7-10, etc.

is no more immortal than God is personal; it is dissolved
with the body, returns to the elements, and is lost in the great
All, of which it is only a tiny part.   Some, indeed, conceded to it a more or less lengthy survival of the body, but
not immortality.   With these ideas of God and the soul, we
can imagine what providence and prayer would be.   Their
providence is fatal destiny, the immutable law of the universe,
the inflexible decree of the blind intelligence which rules the
world, and is confounded with it.   Can there still be any
question of prayer?   What would any Stoic ask of the gods?
A deviation from the laws of the world?   But that is impossible and impious.   Happiness and virtue?   But these
depend on ourselves alone.   The typical prayer of the Stoic
is the formula of Cleanthes, an act of pure and simple resignation to inevitable Destiny—prayer as far from Christianity as possible.

Stoicism was the philosophy of despair; Christianity is the
religion of hope.   Against the evils of life, the Stoic had only
one antidote — pride; and only one sovereign remedy —
suicide.   Not that there is not something noble and touching in this effort to preserve human dignity, in this philan-
thropy, conformable to reason, but foreign to the feeling
of pity which was regarded as a weakness, and even in its
sad resignation to fatality; but there is nothing that resembles the Christian ideal.   Of all the forms of ancient
philosophy, there is not one more opposed to our religion
than Stoicism and Pyrrhonism, because the one denies reason
and the other deifies it.[1]

What St Paul owes to Stoicism is not his groundwork of
ideas, but his style of preaching.   The Cynics, the forlorn
hope of Stoicism, were accustomed to stop passers-by in the
streets in order to propound to them their system and their
philosophy of morals.   They proceeded by apostrophes, by
written dialogues, and by brusque and insistent questions.
They fenced verbally with imaginary adversaries and, to the
objections which struck them, they replied with irony or disdain rather than by lengthy reasonings.   They loved to repeat
certain words and sayings, which they finally forced into the
minds of their hearers.   There are traces of this in the
manner of Paul;[2] and, as St Augustine remarks, he has more

[1] Regarding the pretended relations between Seneca and St Paul, *cf.*
Aubertin, *Sénèque et St Paul*[3], Paris, 1872; G. Boissier, *La Religion romaine
d'Auguste aux Antonins*, Paris, 1878, vol. ii.   On Epictetus and St Paul
A. Bonhöffer, *Epiktet und das Neue Testament*, Giessen, 1911; Lagrange,
*La philosophie religieuse d'Epictète et le christianisme*, in the *Revue biblique*,
1912, pp. 5-21 and 192-212.
[2] R. Bultmann, *Der Stil der paulin. Predigt und die kynisch-stoisch.*,
*Diatribe*, Göttingen, 1910.   See also Martha, *Les moralistes sous l'empire
romain*[3], Paris, 1872, and Norden, *Antike Kunstprosa*, Leipzig, 1898.

oratorical artifices borrowed from the rhetoric of his day than we might anticipate.[1]

3. If, at the present time, there is little tendency to exaggerate Paul's Hellenism, his indebtedness to oriental syncretism is readily asserted. This modern view, though not likely to endure, is making at this moment considerable noise in the world, disturbing the timorous and disquieting those who have been hypnotized by German science. It has been trumpeted aloud by a small minority of philologists, who may be very clever in their own line, but are notoriously unfamiliar with scriptural studies.[2]

We must here emphasize what we have said above about the attitude of the Apostle in regard to the pagan world. If he was averse to paganism in general, the heathen mysteries must have filled him with horror. This is seen clearly in his reply to the Colossians, who were led astray by theories and practices somewhat analogous to the mysteries. But previously he had made once for all a solemn profession of his faith, when writing to the Corinthians. The Apostle showed them, by five antitheses, the absolute incompatibility between the Christian life and pagan customs. Christianity and paganism are as much opposed to each other as are yes and no, day and night, Christ and Belial, the temple of God and a den of uncleanness.

> Bear not the yoke with unbelievers,
> For what participation hath justice with injustice ?
> Or what fellowship hath light with darkness ?
> And what concord hath Christ with Belial ?
> Or what part hath the faithful with the unbeliever ?
> And what agreement hath the temple of God with idols ?[3]

---

[1] Examples in St Augustine, *De doctrina christiana*, book iv, and in J. Weiss, *Das Urchristentum*, Göttingen, 1917, pp. 303-330.

[2] See Note L, pp. 383 ff.

[3] 2 Cor. vi, 14-16:

> Μὴ γίνεσθε ἑτεροζυγοῦντες ἀπίστοις·
> Τίς γὰρ μετοχὴ δικαιοσύνῃ καὶ ἀνομίᾳ,
> ἢ τίς κοινωνία φωτὶ πρὸς σκότος;
> Τίς δὲ συμφώνησις Χριστοῦ πρὸς Βελίαρ,
> ἢ τίς μερὶς πιστῷ μετὰ ἀπίστου;
> Τίς δὲ συγκατάθεσις ναῷ Θεοῦ μετὰ εἰδώλων;

The prohibition is formulated in the first phrase ; the reasons for it are given in the five succeeding ones. In what does the prohibition consist ? Ἑτερο- ζυγεῖν signifies literally " to be coupled under the same yoke with an animal of a different race " (for example, an ox with an ass ; *cf.* Lev. xi, 19 ; Deut. xxii, 10 : ἑτερόζυγος). The pagans bear a yoke which Christians are not to share, and to which they should not be harnessed. Paul speaks of the yoke, of which every pagan is the slave, and which to that extent marks him as a pagan. The prohibition is, therefore, general and is not directed against any special relation between Christians and pagans. It is the *spirit* of paganism that it is necessary to avoid in everything.

In the eyes of every Christian and Israelite the mysteries of paganism branded on the foreheads of their adherents the stigma of idolatry. Yet it does not at all follow that Christians and Jews could not draw from these mysteries comparisons and metaphors. Philo, who speaks with supreme disdain of these shameful initiations, as the allies of secrecy and darkness and a refuge for thieves and prostitutes,[1] occasionally borrows without scruple the language of the mysteries and uses it to explain the symbolic meaning of the Scriptures.[2] The same phenomenon—and a still more striking one—is found in Clement of Alexandria. We know how drastically he pours out his sarcasm and ridicule upon the orgiastic worship and sacred rites of Eleusis.[3] Nevertheless, he does not hesitate to declare frequently that the perfect Christian is the true Eleusinian initiate, who has reached the end of his initiation.[4] St Paul could therefore employ the language of the mysteries, as he employs that of the stadium and theatre, especially if it were certain that such terminology was current in every day speech. However that may be, the Catholic exegete must always watch these comparative studies closely. There is nothing in them to alarm orthodoxy or disturb the faith of the believer.

We only ask the partisans of the *religionsgeschichtliche Methode* not to take an analogy for an imitation or a similarity of expression as a proof of a dependency of ideas; to proceed in the comparison of texts in some other way than by discovering concordances; and to avoid startling anachronisms, such as seeing in the late institution of the *taurobolium* the prototype of baptism, or classing St Paul's Epistles among the Hermetic Books. The novelty of these studies was formerly some excuse for mistakes and exaggerations; but we should now get rid of such early blunders.

It is difficult to understand how the champions of religious syncretism can see without demur a reminder of the pagan mysteries in the following text :

> We speak wisdom among the perfect; yet not the wisdom of this world, neither of the princes of this world, that come to naught. But we speak the wisdom of God in a mystery, the hidden wisdom, which God ordained before the ages to our glory.[5]

---

[1] *De sacrificantibus*, Mangey, vol. ii, p. 260 ; *Liber quisq. virt. studet*, vol. ii, p. 447.

[2] *De Cherubim*, vol. ii, p. 147 ; *De Sacrif. Abel et Cain*, vol. i, p. 173.

[3] *Protrepticus*, ii, 21-23 ; ed. Stählin, Berlin, 1905, pp. 10-17.

[4] *Stromata*, i, 28 ; ii, 10 ; iv, 23 ; v, 10-11 ; vii, 4, etc.

[5] 1 Cor. ii, 6, 7 : Σοφίαν λαλοῦμεν ἐν τοῖς τελείοις . . . ἀλλὰ λαλοῦμεν Θεοῦ σοφίαν ἐν μυστηρίῳ, τὴν ἀποκεκρυμμένην, ἣν προώρισεν ὁ Θεὸς πρὸ τῶν αἰώνων εἰς δόξαν ἡμῶν.

(a) Meaning of the word τέλειος.—Those who were initiated into the mysteries were not called τέλειοι but τετελεσμένοι, " having been the sub-

Two things here, they say, plainly suggest pagan initiations : the *mystery* and the mention of *perfect* men, who are none other than the initiated. But that is, to use a common expression, taking chalk for cheese. The *mystery* of Paul (μυστήριον in the singular) is just the contrary of the pagan mysteries (μυστήρια in the plural). The mysteries are sacred rites administered by the hierophants of Eleusis in the obscurity of the sanctuary ; the mystery of Paul is the secret of God regarding the plan of redemption. The mysteries are confided to the initiated under a pledge of such absolute secrecy that they cannot be divulged without incurring the vengeance of the gods ; the secret of Paul is no longer a secret, since God has revealed it, and the Apostle has received the commission to proclaim it everywhere. The mysteries are the property of a little band of privileged persons ; the mystery of Paul concerns all men, and all are to benefit by it. The mysteries are magical ceremonies which pretend to assure happiness in this life and the next, independently of moral virtues and spiritual character ; the mystery of Paul is a truth preached to all Christians to sustain their faith and revive their hope.

If the mystery of Paul is the very opposite of the pagan mysteries, so his *perfect man* has nothing in common with the Eleusinian initiate. Paul's perfect man is the adult, as contrasted with the child ; he is one who, having reached the age of maturity, must be nourished with stronger food, more solid doctrines. All Christians have not reached that maturity, but it is the duty of all to endeavour to attain to it. Between them is no water-tight partition, no impassable barrier ; there are no privileged hearers, as in the school of Pythagoras. The preacher of the Gospel has, of course, to

---

ject of a ceremony of initiation " (τελετή). What has made some people think of a connection here with the mysteries is Plato's word-play (*Phaedr.*, 249c, τελέους ἀεὶ τελετὰς τελούμενος τέλεος ὄντως μόνος γίγνεται), which proves nothing for this technical sense of τέλεος. The word τέλειος has in St Paul its ordinary meaning of " accomplished, perfect " (Rom. xii, 2 ; 1 Cor. xiii, 10 ; Phil. iii, 5 ; Col. iv, 12) ; it has the special and classic meaning of a *grown man* in antithesis to a *child* (Eph. iv, 13 ; 1 Cor. xiv, 20), and this is the case here, on account of iii, 1-2 : *tanquam parvulis in Christo, lac vobis potum dedi* (νηπίοις opposed to τελείοις).

(*b*) Meaning of the word μυστήριον.—Although ἐν μυστηρίῳ might refer to λαλοῦμεν, most and the best exegetes make it refer to σοφίαν. The absence of the article is no obstacle to this (Rom. v, 15 : δωρεὰ ἐν χάριτι). Then the expression ἐν μυστηρίῳ has almost the force of an adjective, " mysterious, which concerns the mystery or secret of God," the definition of which is often given by St Paul (Rom. xvi, 25 ; Eph. i, 9 ; iii, 3, 4, 9 ; Col. i, 26, 27 ; ii, 2 ; iv, 3). Nothing, either near or remote, makes us think here of the mysteries of Paganism.

See for details Robertson and Plummer, *The First Epistle of Paul to the Corinthians*[2], Edinburgh, 1914 (*Crit. exeg. Comment.*), or Bachmann, *Der erste Brief des Paulus an die Korinther*[2], Leipzig, 1910 (Zahn Collection).

come down to the mental capacity of his audience; but neither St Paul nor the early Church ever knew the system of esoteric teaching.

4. The true origins of Paulinism are now clear : they are the Bible and the teaching of Jesus. Having to preach and write in Greek, Paul prefers to read and to quote the Greek Bible. For him, as for all his compatriots, the Bible is the supreme and unquestionable authority, the word of God. It is the Book *par excellence,* the only one which contains all truth, the only one which deserves to be studied. It has not yet been proved that Paul knew or used any other. His language is modelled on that of the Septuagint; as we shall have occasion to show in regard to his psychology. It would also be easy, if it had not been already done, to extend the demonstration to other subjects as well; his religious conceptions, too, have their roots in the Old Testament. But neither his conceptions nor his language are stereotyped. Just as his field of vision far exceeds that of the prophets, so the words which he employs undergo an extension and an accumulation of meanings proportionate to the progress of his doctrines.

St Paul interprets the Old Testament in the light of the Gospel, which came to complete and to perfect it. We do not claim that he derived the teaching of the Master from written documents,[1] for the numerous and remarkable co-incidences of ideas and expressions between the evangelists and himself are very easily explained by oral tradition and apostolic teaching. This almost uniform catechetical instruction is an undeniable and informative fact. Outside the question of legal observances, there is not a trace of dissension between the Doctor of the Gentiles and his colleagues in the apostolate, and even this point, less theoretical than practical, was quickly and amicably settled. As for the rest, there are the same ideas about God, the person of Christ, salvation, the sacraments, and the final destinies of man. Peter, James, and John, in the assembly at Jerusalem, solemnly approved Paul's Gospel, and the latter has so little intention of separating from the others that, in order to cut short all doubts and abuses, he appeals to the practice and common teaching of the churches.

For all that, we do not overlook his own personal contribution. If he always attributes a divine origin to his preaching, if he affirms that he has received the Spirit of the Lord, if he lays claim to a special knowledge of the mystery

---

[1] This is the idea of Resch, *Der Paulinismus und die Logia Jesu,* Leipzig, 1904. St Paul, according to him, borrowed from an early Aramaic Gospel, which also served as a source to our three Synoptists. His book is full of interesting remarks, but his theory has had little success.

of man's salvation, it is because he is conscious of being illumined by a supernatural light. This inward inspiration, which reveals to him sooner and more distinctly than to his colleagues the secret of the redeeming plans, is called by rationalistic writers, religious experience, or a conclusion reached by reasoning, but we call it by the name which he himself gives to it—a revelation.

# BOOK II
## PREPARATION FOR THE REDEMPTION

# CHAPTER I

## HUMANITY WITHOUT CHRIST

### I—Pauline Psychology

1. Biblical Foundation.  2. Hellenic Contributions.  3. The Human
Composite.  4. Eclectic Language.

1.    CONTEMPORARY exegetes cannot be accused of
having left St Paul's psychology in the shade.
Several of them have devoted to it valuable
monographs.  All assign to it a chosen place in
the system of Pauline doctrine.  But is there, in
the strict sense of the word, any such thing as a psychology
of St Paul?  If no sacred book is a book of science, if the
inspired writers have not received a commission to teach us
the secrets of natural history or the elements of metaphysics,
Paul would have been the last to endure being lowered to
the level of those loquacious philosophers and pedlars of
human wisdom, whom he was wont to pursue with his
sarcasms.  He never intended to construct a system of
rational psychology.  He employs the usual vocabulary—for
he had to make himself understood, and he would not
have hazarded his teaching by inventing new words—but
he does not pride himself on the exclusiveness of his choice
nor on the constancy of his selections.  Any word is good
enough for him, provided it perfectly translates his thought
at the moment.  His language becomes richer and is
modified with age, with the countries through which he
travels, and with the localities which he frequents.  Individual
in his ideas, he is eclectic in his expression, and this medley
forms one of the most lifelike, picturesque, and agreeable
styles imaginable; but every attempt to extract from it a
coherent philosophic system is doomed in advance to certain
failure.

To convince oneself that the psychological language of the
Apostle is in substance that of the Septuagint, and that his
conception of man is, above all, biblical, it is sufficient to
consider the part he assigns to the heart in the drama of life.
The heart is, in his opinion, as in that of the Old Testament
writers, the centre of the whole emotional, intellectual, and
moral life, the seat of all the affections and passions, remembrance and remorse, joy and sorrow, holy resolutions
and wicked desires, the channel of all the inspirations of the

Holy Spirit, and the sanctuary of the conscience, on which are engraved in indelible characters the tables of the natural law, and into which no eye can penetrate, save that of God.[1] The truth enlightens it, infidelity blinds it, impenitence hardens it, hypocrisy perverts it, happiness dilates it, anguish contracts it, gratitude makes it exult.[2] The heart is the measure of the man ; in fact, the heart is the man himself, and that is why God, in order to appraise man at his just value, looks at his heart.[3]

Since the heart comprises almost all the phases of human activity, the role of the other organs is correspondingly reduced. The liver, seat of anger and envy ; the kidneys, the centre of the conscience ; and the spleen, the dwelling-place of sadness, are not even mentioned by St Paul.[4] The eyes denote intelligence, and the ears attention rather by metaphor than by metonymy. The figure by virtue of which the bowels express tenderness or mercy, becomes almost softened down.[5] Nevertheless, the Apostle does revive an old word beloved by Homer and the ancient writers of tragedies— namely, the diaphragm ($\phi\rho\acute{\eta}\nu$)—the organ of sentiment and judgement—and he makes it appear in a dozen derivatives or compounds which are peculiar to him.[6]

All the more remarkable, therefore, is the role which he assigns to the head. For the Hebrews, the head was only the emblem of superiority and pre-eminence. If the Greeks

---

[1] Functions of the heart : affection (2 Cor. vii, 3 ; Phil. i, 7), consolation (Eph. vi, 22 ; Col. ii, 2 ; iv, 18 ; 2 Thess. ii, 17), peace (Col. iii, 15 , cf. Phil. iv, 7), pain (Rom. ix, 2 ; 2 Cor. ii, 4), good desire (Rom. x, 1 ; 1 Thess. ii, 17), bad desire (Rom. i, 24), charity (1 Tim. i, 5), faith (Rom. vi, 17 ; x, 9-10), natural conscience (Rom. ii, 15 : τὸ ἔργον τοῦ νόμου γραπτὸν ἐν ταῖς καρδίαις αὐτῶν) and supernatural (2 Cor. iii, 2-3 : ἐγγεγραμμένη ἐν ταῖς καρδίαις ἡμῶν, ἐν πλαξὶν καρδίας σαρκίναις, cf. Rom. x, 8), habitation of the Holy Spirit (Rom. v, 5 ; 2 Cor. i, 22 ; Gal. iv, 6), and of Christ (Eph. iii, 17).

[2] Illumination (2 Cor. iv, 6 : ὃς ἔλαμψεν ἐν ταῖς καρδίαις ἡμῶν, Eph. i, 18 : πεφωτισμένους τοὺς ὀφθαλμοὺς τῆς καρδίας ὑμῶν), blindness (Rom. i, 21 : ἐσκοτίσθη, 2 Cor. iii, 15 : κάλυμμα ἐπὶ τὴν καρδίαν), dilatation (2 Cor. vi, 11 : ἡ καρδία ἡμῶν πεπλάτυνται), exultation (Eph. v, 19 : ψάλλοντες, Col. iii, 16 : ᾄδοντες), hardness (Eph. iv, 18 : πώρωσις, Rom. ii, 5 : σκληρότης, and Rom. ix, 18 : σκληρύνειν). Pure heart (1 Tim. i, 5 ; 2 Tim. ii, 22), simple (Eph. vi, 5 ; Col. iii, 22), upright (cf. 2 Thess. iii, 5), innocent (cf. Rom. xvi, 18), circumcised (cf. Rom. ii, 29), mad (Rom. i, 21), hard and impenitent (Rom. ii, 5), cf. Heb. x, 22 (sincere) ; iii, 12 (bad).

[3] God searcheth the hearts (Rom. viii, 27 : ἐραυνῶν), proveth our hearts (1 Thess. ii, 4 : δοκιμάζων), closed to every other eye (1 Cor. xiv, 25 : τὰ κρυπτὰ τῆς καρδίας).

[4] Ἧπαρ and σπλήν are not found in the New Testament. Ὀσφύς is employed once (Eph. vi, 11), but not as the seat of consciousness.

[5] Σπλαγχνίζεσθαι, "to be moved by compassion," and τὰ σπλάγχνα, "compassion, pity," are employed without allusion to their concrete origin. St Paul says : σπλάγχνα καὶ οἰκτιρμοί (Phil. ii, 1), as he says : σπλάγχνα οἰκτιρμοῦ (Col. iii, 12).

[6] Exclusively Pauline are : φρὴν (1 Cor. xiv, 20), φρεναπάτης (Tit. i, 10), φρεναπατᾶν (Gal. vi, 3), φρόνημα, ὑπερφρονεῖν, σώφρων, σωφρόνως, σωφρονίζειν, σωφρονισμός, σωφροσύνη.

made it the seat of thought, it is because they also made it the abode of the soul, an immaterial atom lying in wait at the portals of the senses to scrutinize the horizon and to direct the course, like the lookout on the topmast, or the pilot at the helm. But Paul, imbued with biblical ideas about the unity of the human composite, could not liken the soul to the motor of Descartes or the guide of Plato. Hence he speaks of the functions of the head in the economy of life in terms which suggest an echo of modern biological doctrines.

Let us not make him say, however, as a certain contemporaneous exegete does, that the brain monopolizes all the sensorial impressions, in order to telegraph the commands of the soul in all directions; yet one is inevitably led to think that in his theory of the mystical body the relation of Christ to the Church must have given him an intuition of what the head is in its relation to the human composite, so much more decisive is his language than that of the other sacred writers. We have elsewhere pointed out this interesting and remarkable phenomenon.

2. The influence exerted on Paul by Hellenic culture is not to be denied. It shows itself at first sight by the introduction of two words—conscience (συνείδησις) and reason (νοῦς)—which are now so generally used that it is hardly conceivable that we could ever have got along without them.

The word "conscience" is of quite recent creation. No writer of the age of Pericles was yet acquainted with it. The first to employ it was the comedian Menander in the famous maxim: "For every mortal conscience is a god."[1] Later, historians and philosophers vie with one another in its use, after having divested it of its old meaning of witness and accomplice, to make of it, according to the fine personification of Philo, that incorruptible judge which sits in the depths of the soul, endeavouring by its counsels and threats to bring back those who have imprudently strayed away, and to subdue the proud and the rebellious.[2] Not that the idea

---

[1] Fragment 654 (Didot, p. 103): Βροτοῖς ἅπασιν ἡ συνείδησις θεός. Variant (*ibid.* 597, p. 101): *Ἅπασιν ἡμῖν ἡ συνείδησις θεός.—Συνείδησις comes from σύνοιδα, "I know *together with* another" (as an eye- or ear-witness, or as an accomplice) something concerning this other, or common to both. Thence, by a kind of reduplication of the "me"—σύνοιδα ἐμαυτῷ—"I can testify to myself, I am conscious of." But this meaning, frequent among the classics, still had nothing to do with the *moral* conscience. The first time that συνείδησις appears in the writings of a philosopher, the word does not signify the moral conscience, but the instinct of self-preservation, or rather the feeling of this instinct: Πρῶτον οἰκεῖον εἶναι πάντι ζώῳ τὴν αὑτοῦ σύστασιν καὶ τὴν ταύτης συνείδησιν (Chrysippus, according to Diogenes Laertius, vii, 85).

[2] *De mundi opif.* (Mangey, vol. i, p. 30), *cf. De posterit. Caini* (vol. i, p. 136); *Quod Deus sit immut.* (vol. i, p. 291). Philo—as also Josephus and Plutarch—instead of συνείδησις employs τὸ συνειδός, "that which is conscious

of conscience is absent from the Bible, but the word itself
was wanting there.[1]  What may surprise us is the fact that,
when it was once found, the authors of the New Testament
abandon the use of it almost exclusively to Paul.  St Luke,
who twice puts it in the mouth of the Apostle, makes no use
of it himself, and it is found again only in the Epistle to the
Hebrews and the First Epistle of Peter, so closely related to
the style of Paul in ideas and vocabulary.  According to
Paul, conscience is an incorruptible law-giver, which formulates and promulgates the divine law, a truthful witness
whose testimony cannot be challenged, an impartial judge
whose verdict is beyond appeal.  Sure of the value of this
testimony and of this verdict, Paul appeals to his own conscience and to that of others.[2]  But conscience is for him
not only a tribunal where the past is inquired into and
judged; it is an inner light which warns man of his duties,
and a faithful guide which imperiously points out his way.[3]
Thus man ascends or descends the scale of moral perfection
in proportion as his conscience is good, pure, and without
reproach, or, on the contrary, bad, soiled, and seared; the
middle course is that of weakness.  Then it deserves in-
dulgence and careful treatment.[4]

The other word which Paul borrows from profane
language is no less fortunate; for the biblical λόγος signifying the word and not reason (νοῦς), used so frequently in
classical literature from Homer's time, had no exact equivalent in the Bible.  The νοῦς is not only the intellect and the

---

in us and testifies to ourselves."  Diodorus of Sicily, Dionysius of Halicar
nassus, Lucian and Epictetus have συνείδησις, the latter in a sense which
resembles the modern usage closely.

[1] For the idea, compare Job ix, 21 ; 2 Sam. xviii, 13, etc.  The word מַדָּע
(Eccl. x, 20), translated by συνείδησις, is rather thought than conscience
(Vulgate, in cogitatione tua).

[2] 2 Cor. i, 12 (τὸ μαρτύριον τῆς συνειδήσεως ἡμῶν) ; iv, 2 (συνιστάνοντες
ἑαυτοὺς πρὸς πᾶσαν συνείδησιν ἀνθρώπων); cf. v, 11.—In Rom. ix, 1
(ἀλήθειαν λέγω ἐν Χριστῷ, οὐ ψεύδομαι, συμμαρτυρούσης μοι τῆς συνειδήσεώς μου),
the testimony of Paul's conscience is added (σύν) to his express affirmation
(οὐ ψεύδομαι).—In Rom. ii, 15 (συμμαρτυρούσης αὐτῶν τῆς συνειδήσεως)
the testimony of the conscience of the pagans observing the natural law
confirms (σύν) the moral goodness of their act.

[3] It is a mistake to claim that in St Paul conscience is merely consequent ;
it is antecedent in all the cases where the Apostle orders a thing to be done or
not to be done, διὰ τὴν συνείδησιν, Rom. xiii, 5 : obligation to obey the
constituted authorities in conscience ; 1 Cor. x, 25, 27, 28, 29.—Moreover,
the conscience that judges the actions of others (2 Cor. iv, 2 ; v, 11 ; cf.
1 Cor. x, 29) supposes a criterion capable of discerning the objective goodness
and malice of acts, and this criterion belongs to the antecedent conscience,
since everyone can apply it to future actions.

[4] 1 Tim. i, 5, 19 (ἀγαθή) ; 1 Tim. iii, 9 ; 2 Tim. i, 3 (καθαρά) ; 1 Tim. iv, 2
(κεκαυτηριασμένη).  It is curious that St Luke, relating the discourses of
Paul, uses the word συνείδησις, unknown to his own vocabulary, and follows
it with the same epithets as Paul, Acts xxiii, 1 (ἀγαθή) ; xxiv, 16 (ἀπρόσκοπος

reason, but also the mode of thinking, opinion, sentiment.[1]
A born auxiliary of the conscience, with which it sometimes
seems to be confounded, the natural law is within its province,
but the supernatural is outside of its sphere, and the mysteries
of faith are beyond it. Unless it is assisted and renewed by
the πνεῦμα, it will be vain, corrupt, and reprobate. Powerless against the flesh, it can itself become carnal; and Paul,
always original, even in his selections from others, offers us
some strange combinations of words, such as " the spirit of
reason " and " the reason of the flesh," which make us comprehend the impossibility of applying to him the standard of
the classical vocabulary.

St Paul also seized upon that fine expression of Plato, *the
inward man,*[2] probably without knowing the origin of it, and
giving it the *outward man* as a pendant; but this contrast is
used too sporadically, and is too elementary a philosophy
to be the pivot of the whole Pauline psychology, as some
modern exegetes maintain. In the passage in the Epistle to
the Romans, where he affirms that he is delighted with the
Law of God according to the inward man,[3] the Apostle
clearly identifies this inward man with the reason, for he
adds : " With the mind I serve the Law of God, but with the
flesh the law of sin." The νοῦς is not to be confounded with
the πνεῦμλ; the latter, entering the lists against the flesh,
would come out of the struggle victorious, while the νοῦς is
invariably conquered. The antithesis *flesh* and *inward man*—
or, what amounts to the same thing, *flesh* and *reason*—is
therefore formed here of incongruous elements, the inward
man designating the intellectual nature, which is the very
essence of the man, and the flesh being his sinful nature,
whose present fall presupposes necessarily a primitive state
of elevation. But when the Apostle enjoins the Ephesians to
be " strengthened by his (God's) Spirit with might unto the
inward man," and when he writes to the Corinthians:

---

—The weak or the sickly conscience, 1 Cor. viii, 7-10 (ἀσθενής); 1 Cor. viii, 12
(ἀσθενοῦσα) can mean easily soiled (μολύνεται, 1 Cor. viii, 7). Compare
the μεμίανται (Tit. i, 15) of the Pastorals.

[1] Outside of Luke xxiv, 45 ; Apoc. xiii, 18 ; xvii, 9, the word νοῦς is found
only in St Paul, who employs it twenty-one times. Among the derivatives
or compounds of νοῦς, the following seven belong to him exclusively :
νόημα, εὔνοια, νουθετέω, νουθεσία, προνοέω, πρόνοια, ὑπόνοια, including the
discourses of the Acts.

[2] Plato says (*Republ.*, ix, 589A) : Τοῦ ἀνθρώπου ὁ ἐντὸς ἄνθρωπος ἔσται
ἐγκρατέστατος.—Plotinus, who expressly attributes the expression to Plato
(*Ennead.*, v, 1, 10 : Οἷον λέγει Πλάτων τὸν εἴσω ἄνθρωπον), calls the *inward
man* the true man (*Ennead.*, i, 1, 10) and opposes it to the body. So Philo,
*De Plantat.* (Mangey, vol. i, p. 336).

[3] Rom. vii, 22 : συνήδομαι τῷ νόμῳ τοῦ Θεοῦ κατὰ τὸν ἔσω ἄνθρωπον.
Three verses later (vii, 25), the *inward man* is identified with the νοῦς :
Ἄρα οὖν αὐτὸς ἐγὼ τῷ νοῒ δουλεύω νόμῳ Θεοῦ. It is evident that it is a
question of a νοῦς which the flesh dominates.

" Though our outward man is corrupted, yet the inward
man is renewed day by day,"[1] the inward man is no longer
merely the soul or the reason, it is the intellectual nature
enriched by the gifts of grace, the soul inhabited by the Holy
Spirit, and in possession of the πνεῦμα.

To sum up : The outward man is dependent on the physical
order ; the inward man belongs either to the physical order
or to the moral and religious order.—The inward man and
the outward man would exist in the state of nature, as they
exist in the state of supernatural elevation ; but, while the
notion of the outward man remains invariable in both cases ;
the comprehension of the inward man differs.—Thus the inward man is not simply the invisible and immaterial part of
the human composite, it is also what grace effects within us.
Under the influence of the Holy Spirit, the inward man is
strengthened and renewed ; left to himself, he is powerless
against the flesh and becomes carnal.

3. The flesh or body constitutes the outward man ; the
soul, the mind, the heart, the reason, and conscience are
different aspects or appellations of the inward man.   Strictly
speaking, the body and the flesh are not synonyms.   The body
is the organized matter, living or dead, of men and animals.
The flesh is the body minus the idea of organism, with, in
addition, the idea of life.[2]   The flesh, therefore, abstracts from
the homogeneity of the parts which the notion of the body
excludes, and it presupposes the vital principle abstracted by
the body.   With a few exceptions, Paul always attaches to
the body the idea of an organism and of a human organism ;[3]
we know with what felicity of expression he thus designates
the Church, the organic complement of the Saviour and an
integral part of the mystical Christ.   Nevertheless, a
synonymy between the body and the flesh exists for him
to a considerable degree.   When he says of himself that
he is " absent in the body but present in spirit " (1 Cor. v, 3)
or " absent in the flesh but present in the spirit " ; when he
wishes that the virgin should be holy " both in body and in
spirit," and that all the faithful should avoid the contamina-
tions " of the flesh and the spirit " ; when he desires that

---

[1] Eph. iii, 16 : κραταιωθῆναι διὰ τοῦ Πνεύματος αὐτοῦ εἰς τὸν ἔσω ἄνθρωπον.
Since the Holy Spirit intervenes, the *inward man*, submissive to its
influence, is the *spiritual* man and not the natural man.—2 Cor iv, 16 : εἰ καὶ
ὁ ἔξω ἡμῶν ἄνθρωπος διαφθείρεται, ἀλλ' ὁ ἔσω ἡμῶν ἀνακαινοῦνται ἡμέρᾳ καὶ
ἡμέρᾳ.   The contrast here is not between σάρξ and πνεῦμα, but between σῶμα
and πνεῦμα, or rather between the σῶμα considered independently, and the
νοῦς renewed by the πνεῦμα.   *Cf*. Eph. iv, 23.

[2] Flesh, destined to serve as nourishment, food, is called κρέας (Rom.
xiv, 21 ; 1 Cor. viii, 13).

[3] 1 Cor. xv, 37-40 (the body of plants and stars) ; Col. ii, 17 (ἅ ἐστιν σκιὰ
τῶν μελλόντων, τὸ δὲ σῶμα τοῦ Χριστοῦ ; this is the *shadow* [the figure or
type] of things to come, but the body [the truth or the realization] is of Christ
[belongs to him, concerns him]).

"the life of Jesus may appear in our bodies" or "in our mortal flesh"; and when he urges the Christian husband to "love his wife as his own body, for no man ever hated his own flesh," it is difficult to discover any difference in meaning between these two terms, for they can be almost always interchanged,[1] except in the case of some restrictions imposed by biblical usage, as, for example, the mention of the flesh instead of the body whenever reference is made to circumcision.[2] But when the flesh is put into relation with the soul or spirit, it acquires, by reason of this connection, several new meanings of considerable complexity.

The words *soul* and *spirit* had in Hebrew, as in Greek and Latin, similar careers, and followed an analogous course in their semantic evolution. From the etymological meaning of "breath, air in motion," they came to signify by turns "breathing," the sign and condition of life, then "life" itself, then "the vital principle," and, finally, "a living substance" distinct from matter and superior to it.[3] But while by usage the spirit freed itself more and more from matter, the soul, by a reverse process, tended to identify itself with the vital principle of animate beings. Nevertheless, among biblical writers, their general synonymy results from this triple law: first, that they correspond to each other very frequently in parallel phrases; secondly, that they are interchanged freely in the same phrase; and thirdly, that they receive almost without distinction the same attributes. If some have thought they had discovered that neither joy, nor fear, nor hope were ever attributed to the spirit, while sensuous desires and appetites were always referred to the soul,[4] these are perhaps accidental facts, the significance of which must not be exaggerated.

Paul, being accustomed to concentrate all the manifestations of life in the heart and to borrow from the classical

---

[1] Compare together the following four pairs of expressions : 1 Cor. v, 3 with Col. ii, 5 (ἀπὼν τῷ σώματι, παρὼν δὲ τῷ πνεύματι and τῇ σαρκὶ ἄπειμι, ἀλλὰ τῷ πνεύματι σὺν ὑμῖν εἰμι); 1 Cor. vii, 34 with 2 Cor. vii, 1 : (ἁγία καὶ τῷ σώματι καὶ τῷ πνεύματι and καθαρίσωμεν ἑαυτοὺς ἀπὸ παντὸς μολυσμοῦ σαρκὸς καὶ πνεύματος); 2 Cor. iv, 10 with iv, 11 (ἵνα καὶ ἡ ζωὴ τοῦ Ἰησοῦ ἐν τῷ σώματι ἡμῶν φανερωθῇ and ἵνα καὶ ἡ ζωὴ τοῦ Ἰησοῦ φανερωθῇ ἐν τῇ θνητῇ σαρκὶ ἡμῶν); Eph. v, 28 with v, 29 (ὡς τὰ ἑαυτῶν σώματα and οὐδεὶς γάρ ποτε τὴν ἑαυτοῦ σάρκα ἐμίσησεν).

[2] In the primitive institution of circumcision (Gen. xvii 9-14) the word *flesh* is constantly employed. The association of ideas recalls this word in reference to the circumcision, Rom. ii, 28 ; Gal. vi, 13 ; Eph. ii, 11, etc.

[3] In classic Latin *spiritus* and *anima* retained to the end the whole series of the meanings indicated, while *animus* was specially restricted to the intelligent soul.—Πνεῦμα and רוּחַ likewise kept all their successive meanings, and in Ecclesiastes are applied even to the souls of beasts. On the contrary, ψυχή lost its etymological sense of "breath" and its derivative meaning of "breathing," a meaning which נֶפֶשׁ yielded to נְשָׁמָה.

See Hatch, *Essays in Biblical Greek*, Oxford, 1889, pp. 94-130.

vocabulary new terms for the operations of the intellect, very
rarely calls the *soul* or the *spirit* the thinking principle.
According to Genesis, God, breathing into man's nostrils the
breath of life, made of him a " living soul "—that is to say,
a soul exercising vital functions in and by the flesh. Thenceforth, the flesh is not conceived without the soul, and the
soul is not defined without some relation to the flesh. The
flesh is the substratum of the soul, and the soul is the life of
the flesh. When Paul thanks Epaphroditus for having
" delivered " his *soul* for love of him, when he praises
Prisca and Aquila for having risked their heads to save
his *soul*, and when he assures the Thessalonians that he
would have liked to give them not only the Gospel, but his
*soul*, as a mother lavishes it upon her babes, it is clear that
he is speaking of life.[1]  Also a great number of psychic
phenomena are assigned without distinction to the flesh or
to the soul, because the soul, considered as the vital principle,
is not adequately distinguished from the flesh. " Every
soul " and " all flesh " are two equivalent expressions.[2]

Unless led to it by a wish for symmetry or by the desire
to accentuate a contrast, Paul seems also to avoid naming
*spirit,* the intelligent part of man.  But when, by exception, the spirit designates the thinking substance,[3] there is
between the soul and it a modal difference, which allows him
to say without tautology : " May the God of peace sanctify
you in all things, that your whole spirit and soul and body
may be preserved blameless."[4]  The body or the material
substratum, the soul or the sentient life, the spirit or the intellectual life, are three aspects of man which comprise his
entire being and all his activities ; they are not three distinct
parts of the human composite.  To look for Plato's tri-

---

[1] Phil. ii, 30 ; Rom. xvi, 4 ; 1 Thess. ii, 8.  So too ζητοῦσιν τὴν ψυχήν μου
Rom. xi, 3), but it is a quotation from 1 Kings xix, 10.

[2] 1 Cor. i, 29 ; Rom. iii, 20 ; Gal. ii, 16 (πᾶσα σάρξ, but the last two examples
are quotations).  Rom. ii, 9 ; xiii, 1 (πᾶσα ψυχή).

[3] 1 Cor. ii, 11, etc.  See note, p. 144.

[4] 1 Thess. v, 23 : ὁλόκληρον ὑμῶν τὸ πνεῦμα καὶ ἡ ψυχὴ καὶ τὸ σῶμα
ἀμέμπτως ἐν τῇ παρουσίᾳ τοῦ Κυρίου ἡμῶν Ἰ. Χ. τηρηθείη.  See E. von Dob-
schütz, Meyer's *Kommentar*[7], Göttingen, 1909 : *Exkurs zur Trichotomie*,
pp. 230-232.  The author shows that trichotomy is not biblical, that it is foreign
to Josephus and to Philo and even to the Greek philosophers, Plato and
Aristotle, and that it is derived from the Neo-Platonists, from whom it passed
to the Gnostics (St Irenaeus, *Adv. haeres.*, I, vii, 5), to the Montanists (Origen,
*Peri Archon*, IV, viii, 11), and to Apollinaris of Laodicea (*fragm.* 88 in
Lietzmann, i, 226).  He, like Chrysostom, Theodoret, Ambrosiaster, an
anonymous writer (in Cramer, *Catena*, p. 374), Pelagius and St Ambrose
(*In Luc.*, vii, 190) believes that St Paul means here by πνεῦμα " the new
element of life which comes into the Christians "; but the enumeration (τὸ
πνεῦμα καὶ ἡ ψυχὴ καὶ τὸ σῶμα) seems to prove that it is a question here of
grandeurs of the same order, and the adverb ἀμέμπτως could be with difficulty
applied to the supernatural work of the Holy Spirit within us.  Moreover,
it is certain that St Paul sometimes employs πνεῦμα as a synonym of νοῦς.

chotomy in these words is to lose sight of the fact that the Apostle's anthropology rests, as is well known, upon the scriptural conception, and that it cannot be admitted, without the most extreme unlikelihood, that he departs from that conception only once, in a casual phrase, in favour of a system incompatible with Jewish theology.

By his soul man has an affinity with the higher powers; by his flesh he stands in contrast to pure spirits : " My spirit, saith the Lord, shall not remain in man for ever, because he is flesh."[1] The Old Testament furnishes us with numerous examples of this antithesis :

> The Egyptian is *man* and not *God:*
> His horses are *flesh* and not *spirit.*[2]

Whether the antithesis is pronounced or hidden, it usually ascribes to the flesh an additional idea of weakness, impotence, wretchedness, and decline. Whatever is transitory, perishable, and terrestrial takes the name of flesh, and whatever is eternal, incorruptible, and celestial enters into the category of spirit.[3] In this sense the term flesh is often replaced by flesh and blood. We have to contend not " against flesh and blood, but against the spirits of wickedness in the high places."[4]

To this order of ideas is allied an expression, the analysis of which is somewhat difficult. The Jews usually said of their relatives : " He is my flesh " or " my flesh and bones." Paul designates[5] in the same way a community of origin and relations of kinship. In this we might see a simple physical contrast between the flesh transmitted by generation and common to the members of one family and the soul which comes from God. It is thus, in fact, that the Epistle to the Hebrews[6] regards it. But Paul unites the flesh and the soul too closely to distinguish the father of the soul from the father of the flesh. Between the children of the flesh and the children of God, between Israel according to the flesh and the Israel of God, between Ishmael born according to the flesh and Isaac born according to the spirit, and between Christ, the son of David, according to the flesh, and Son of God according to the spirit of sanctity,[7] the opposition is always ontological; it occurs between complete substances, and not between the component parts of one and the same substance.

4. We see what a disparity of elements, what a variety of influences, and what a complexity of combinations the

---

[1] Gen. vi, 3.  [2] Isa. xxxi, 3.
[3] 1 Cor. ix, 11 (τὰ σαρκικά, temporal goods); Rom. xv, 27.
[4] Eph. vi, 12 ; *cf.* Gal. i, 16 ; 1 Cor. xv, 50 ; Heb. ii, 14.
[5] Rom. ix, 3 ; xi, 14.  [6] Heb. xii, 9.
[7] Rom. ix, 8 ; 1 Cor. x, 18 and Gal. vi, 16 , Gal. iv, 29 ; Rom. i, 3-4.

anthropology of St Paul presents.  We are tempted to apply
to it what has been said of Philo : " He uses different terms
to express the same phenomena and the same terms to
designate different phenomena.  He borrows his vocabulary
sometimes from one philosophy, sometimes from another,
and most frequently from the Bible itself."   But the
eclecticism of the two writers has very different motives :
Philo, desirous of proving that nothing beautiful and true is
absent from the Bible, allows himself to be carried away by
his naturally fluctuating mind in the wake of all systems ;
Paul puts himself above all systems and blends their dissimilar products into a very personal form of teaching, which
touches by its ramifications almost all the essential points of
his theology.   His heterogeneous vocabulary causes verbal
collisions and shocks of ideas, which produce effects as
singular as they are unforeseen ; and what brings the difficulty of his style to a climax is his playful use of antitheses
and the employment of terms opposed to and reacting upon
one another ; as well as his habit of gliding imperceptibly
over the shades of meaning in the same word to the point of
running through the whole gamut of them in the same context.   But, in the main, his conception of the human composite is constantly inspired by biblical language.   From this
there results a very intimate union between the soul and the
body, by virtue of which all the activity of man can be referred to the heart, the focus of life.   The celebrated definition : " An intelligence served by organs," would not have
suited Paul's taste.   In order to grasp his thought, we must
put aside the dualism of Plato, Descartes, and Kant.   If he
casually compares our body to a garment or a tent, this
isolated figure of speech is of no importance.[1]   No more than
Philo, who paints the unity of the human composite in the
most realistic colours, and also represents the body occasionally as the dwelling, the sanctuary, or even the prison
and the tomb of the soul,[2] does Paul divide man's single
self into two parts ; if he subordinates the body to the soul,
as is just, he does not take it away from the personality.

The appearance of sin, also described conformably to
biblical data, causes a moral disturbance which destroys the

---

[1] 2 Cor. v, 1-4.  See pp. 367-9.

[2] Philo usually defines man as " a composite, a mixture, a tissue of soul
and body."  (De ebriet., 26, Mangey, vol. i, p. 372 : τὸ ψυχῆς καὶ σώματος
ὕφασμα ἢ πλέγμα ἢ κρᾶμα ἢ ὅ τι ποτὲ χρὴ καλεῖν ταυτὶ τὸ σύνθετον ζῷον).
Nevertheless, outside of the comparisons indicated, he sometimes divides the
soul into two parts (Quis rerum divin. heres, 11, vol. i, p. 480 (διχῶς) ; De
migrat. Abrah., i, vol. i, p. 436 ; De agric., 7, vol. i, p. 304); into three parts
(Leg. alleg., i, 22 ; iii, 38, vol. i, pp. 57 and 110 ; De confus. linguar., 7, vol. i,
p. 408 : τριμερής), or even into six parts (Quis rerum divin. heres, 45, vol. i,
p. 504).   These variations, which do not prevent his psychology from resting
on the Bible, show us how easily a Jew could accommodate himself to the
erminology of different schools of philosophy.

equilibrium of our faculties. Man, who was flesh both because he is animated matter and because he is not pure spirit,
becomes flesh by a new right because sin dwells within him.
Henceforth there is a conflict and a discord in his whole
being. To re-establish the interrupted harmony, the active
intervention of the Holy Spirit is necessary, whose presence
brings him qualities, functions, and relations—in a word,
a new nature which itself takes the name of spirit. Before
entering into this special sphere, we must study the origin,
invasion, and domination of sin.

## II—THE REIGN OF SIN

1. Origin of Sin. 2. Extension of Sin. 3. The Empire of Satan.
4. Elemental Spirits.

1. The corruption of the human race, a commonplace of
Jewish theology, had not failed to impress the pagans themselves.[1] We know how the first three chapters of the Epistle
to the Romans develop this thesis : " All have sinned and
do need the glory of God. . . . Both Jews and Greeks are
all under [the yoke of] sin."[2] The Apostle states the fact,
without proving it otherwise than by an appeal to experience,
which is confirmed, especially for the Jews, by the testimony
of Scripture. The twofold purpose which he pursues is to
show that there is no salvation outside the Gospel,[3] and that
the Jews, in spite of their disputable prerogatives, do not
possess, in the face of sin and supernatural justice, any
advantage over the Gentiles, who are the object of their
disdain.[4]
A general phenomenon must be traceable to the same
cause, and it might be supposed that the Apostle, after
having described the overflow of evil, would indicate its
common source. But two subsidiary ideas draw him elsewhere : he is eager to conclude that the Gospel promises and
gives what the Law made men hope for in vain ;[5] and he does
not wish to leave the reader under the impression that the
salvation brought by the Gospel is in contradiction to the
Law.[6] So, when he comes to the origin of sin, he does not
put it into direct relation with the moral corruption, the
gloomy picture of which he has just drawn ; he is satisfied
with drawing a parallel between it and the origin of justice,
which it makes clearer by analogy.[7] This is to go from the

[1] For the Jews, see Weber, *Jüdische Theol.*[2], pp. 233-239 ; for the pagans,
compare not the satirists, suspected of exaggeration, but the moralists and
philosophers, like Seneca, *Epist.*, xcv (general picture of pagan morals) ;
*De beneficiis*, i, 10 ; *De ira*, ii, 7 and 8, etc.

[2] Rom. iii, 23 and iii, 9.

[3] Rom. iii, 20.

[4] Rom. ii, 1, 25 ; iii, 9, 27.

[5] Rom. iii, 21-26.

[6] Rom. iii, 13 and the whole of chap. v.

[7] Rom. v, 12-21.

more known to the less known, and to proceed according to the rules of logic. No Jew, and indeed no proselyte, could be ignorant of the history of the creation and of man's fall, and it cannot be doubted that this history formed part of the elementary doctrines taught to every catechumen who came from the ranks of the Gentiles.

Now from the narrative in Genesis it is clear that Adam's disobedience brought upon the human race death, the enmity of God, and a share of misfortunes, of which the most humiliating is the rebellion of the senses. Composed of perishable elements, man found in the tree of life an antidote to his inborn corruptibility; it is sin which banished him from his earthly paradise and caused the fatal sentence of death to be passed upon him and his race. Then instead of the divine intimacy and gracious favours with which he had been blessed, he sees fall upon him one calamity after another: the infertility of the soil, the hard necessity of work and remote banishment from the face of God. Created in rectitude and innocence, Adam and Eve did not carry within them the germs of moral perversity; the incitement to evil had to reach them from without; but sin destroyed at once the harmony of their faculties, took away from them their domination over inferior powers, and with the sentiment of shame was born within them concupiscence. Without speculating much about these three scriptural statements, every sensible reader will conclude that a common penalty implies a common offence, that the loss of the divine friendship presupposes a previous state of favour and grace, that in order to bring down on all his descendants a sentence of condemnation, Adam must have represented them by virtue of a right which the mere quality of being the first man did not confer upon him, and that there was, therefore, in God's designs, between Adam and his race a union of solidarity, very unlike our modern ideas of extreme individuality, but very congenial to the ancient mode of thinking. Hence the dogma of the original fall of man could not cause any embarrassment to the contemporaries of Paul, since they unhesitatingly admitted, on the testimony of the Scriptures, that the result of the disobedience of Adam has been for us death, a tendency to evil, and the sad conditions of humanity to-day. The childish fables, subsequently added to the biblical foundation by the editors of the Talmud, did not alter the essence of the dogma.

Paul does not, therefore, intend to demonstrate the fact of the original fall; he takes it for granted as being known, just as he does the relation of solidarity, without which the original fall would be unintelligible: but he makes use of both ideas to explain the work of restoration. In fact, the reversibility of demerits in the person of Adam makes clear

the reversibility of merits in the person of Christ, provided
that the first truth is above all dispute, and that there exists
between Adam and Christ a relation easily admissible. This
being established, the teaching of the Apostle may be summed
up thus : Sin originates from Adam; death originates from
sin.

*Sin originates from Adam.* " By one man sin entered into
the world."[1] This man is evidently our first father; sin is
the power of evil which Jesus Christ will come to destroy;
" the world " indicates the human race, and the entry of sin
is not an isolated and transitory apparition, but a triumphant
invasion. Sin is not propagated merely by imitation and by
the contagion of example; it is transmitted by heredity.
" By the disobedience of one man many (οἱ πολλοί, whatever
their number) were made sinners." There is only one
fault committed, and, nevertheless, there are many condemned, many guilty, many sinners; the fault of one, therefore, was common to all.

*Death originates from sin.* " Death passed upon all men,
because all had sinned."[2] It is not a question here of
personal sins, but of one single sin common to all. Indeed,
if the Apostle were speaking of actual sins, he would assign
to death a *different* origin from that which he assigned at the
beginning of the phrase. He would assign to it an origin
notoriously *false,* since it is certain that all men die, yet that
all men are not guilty of actual sins. He would assign to it
a cause *refuted by himself,* for he adds immediately that " sin
was not imputed " as worthy of death, " for want of a law "
pronouncing against it the penalty of death, and that, nevertheless, " death had reigned even over those who had not
sinned after the similitude of Adam's transgression "; in
other words, " who were not guilty of actual sins." Hence
the best commentators, both Protestants and rationalists,
when they are working. as exegetes, not as theologians,
adopt our explanation, however contrary it may be to their
prejudices and their systems, because it seems to be the only
rational one and the sole explanation in harmony with the
evident intention of the Apostle.

The transmission of the original sin has its pendant in the
diffusion of the justice of Christ. It is necessary to hold fast
to this analogy. As the deprivation of original grace is
accomplished in law and principle by the disobedience of
Adam, acting in the name and to the detriment of all his
posterity, and as it awaits for its diffusion only our actual
entrance into the human family through natural generation,
so the merit gained by Jesus Christ, acting in the name and
for the benefit of humanity of which he is the representative,

---

[1] Rom. v, 12. See Vol I, pp. 213-4.
[2] On this text see Vol. I, pp. 215-6.

is acquired for us in law and principle once for all and awaits for its communication only our actual union with Christ our Redeemer by faith and baptism. If there still always remains something mysterious in this solidarity of merit and demerit, the mystery is the same on both sides; but the explanation of it is not the province of biblical theology.

2. Once having entered into the world and being firmly established in the centre of things, sin reigns there like a despot. The empire of evil increases and spreads more and more. The corruption of the heart gains possession of the mind and the perversion of the mind accelerates that of morals. In this way, in the opinion of St Paul, is explained the progress of idolatry and the inundation of vice. The divine being, perceived through the veil of creation and in the depths of the conscience, imposed on man three duties : to seek God who was apprehended imperfectly by reason, to honour him after having found him, and to thank him for his benefits in order to render him propitious. Far from that, the pagans, led astray by their depraved instincts, despised the happiness of knowing God, fettered the truth in order not to hear its urgent voice, basely offered divine honours to the most abject creatures, and carried their depravity to the point of taking delight in lies and malice. Consequently, the penalty of retaliation fell upon them, terrible and inexorable. First, their reason became darkened and their thoughts vain ; they were the sport of illusions and sophisms, and their madness became the more incurable, the more they plumed themselves on their wisdom. The blindness of their intellect, added to the hardness of their heart, soon gave them over to impure passions ; they abandoned themselves to vileness, and unintentionally made themselves the executors of divine vengeance.[1] Finally, as they had abandoned God, God abandoned them to their reprobate sense ; they were " full of inquity, wickedness, fornication, avarice, malice, envy, murder, contention, deceit, malignity ; whisperers, detractors, contumelious, proud, haughty, inventors of evil things, disobedient to parents ; foolish, dissolute, without affection, without mercy."[2]

This picture has often been compared with that which the author of the Book of Wisdom draws.[3] If there is here no literary dependence of Paul's description on the latter in the true sense of the word, and even no intentional imitation, it is difficult not to see in it at least a reminiscence. The absurdity of polytheism and the laxity of the pagans universally offended the moral sense of the Jews. What

[1] Rom. i, 18-28.  [2] Rom. i, 29-31.
[3] Wisd. xiii, 1-17 and xiv, 11-27. See this parallel in Sanday, *Romans*, pp. 51-52, or in the dissertation of Grafe (*cf.* Vol. I, p. 16, note).

distinguishes Paul from his compatriots is that, while condemning with great energy the vices of the Gentiles, he sympathizes with them as individuals, that he founds their guilt on the violation of natural morality, instead of attributing it to their ignorance of the Law, and that he explains the progress of idolatry and profligacy by a sort of psychological process, serving at the same time as punishment and remedy, and causing good to come out of the very excess of evil.

It has been asserted that, unfaithful to his own maxims, he does not connect the general corruption of humanity with the original fall. But what, then, does this statement mean? " We also walked in time past in the desires of our flesh, fulfilling the will of the flesh and of our [bad] thoughts, and were by nature children of wrath, even as the rest."[1] In whatever way we understand them, the words : " We were

---

[1] Eph. ii, 3 : ἤμεθα τέκνα φύσει ὀργῆς ὡς καὶ οἱ λοιποί. Haupt (*Meyer's Kommentar*[8]) thinks that the verb ἤμεθα has ἡμεῖς πάντες (verse 2) for subject and includes all Christians ; but then οἱ λοιποί designates the non-Christians, and the state of sin is affirmed definitely of all men, as in the other explanation. The exegesis adopted by St Augustine in numerous passages (*Retract.*, I, x, 3 ; xv, 6, etc.) has been followed by several commentators ancient and modern, St Thomas, Estius (*ex ipsa nativitatis origine, qua naturam a parentibus accipimus*), Bisping (*durch unsere natürliche Geburt*), etc. But the majority of the commentators since St Chrysostom (πάντες πράττομεν ἄξια ὀργῆς), have seen that it could not be a question here, *at least directly*, of original sin ; for (*a*) *Eramus natura filii irae* is explained by what immediately precedes : *et nos omnes aliquando conversati sumus in desideriis carnis nostrae*, and nothing indicates that there is a priority of time in ἤμεθα in relation to ἀνεστράφημεν, besides the fact that it is not clear what a mention of original sin has to do here.—(*b*) The Apostle contrasts the past with the present, the unhappy condition of the Jews *in time past* and the blessed state of those same Jews *now ;* indeed, *from the point of view of original sin*, the condition of the converted Jews is the same in both cases : in time past they were born with original sin which circumcision (or any other *remedium naturae*) effaced, and now they are born with the same original sin, which baptism effaces.—(*c*) The evident aim of Paul is to show that the Jews *were in time past* (ἤμεθα) on the same footing as the Gentiles (ὡς καὶ οἱ λοιποί) in regard to sin and to the divine wrath, and that they, as well as the Gentiles, are now in an entirely different state through the simple effect of God's mercy (ii, 4 : *Deus* autem, *qui dives est in misericordia, propter nimiam charitatem suam, qua dilexit nos*, etc.). The word which forms the antithesis to *naturae* is not therefore, as elsewhere, the Law (*cf.* Rom. ii, 14), nor theocratic adoption (Gal. ii, 15 ; Rom. xi, 24), nor teaching (1 Cor. xi, 14), in fine, nothing that distinguished the Jews from other nations and raised them above those nations, but only the mercy and grace of the present system. The Jews, like the Gentiles, *were by nature* (φύσει), through the evil inclinations inherited from their first father, sinners and addicted to vice ; but now, like the converted pagans, they *are by grace* (ἐλέει : ii, 4 ; χάριτι, ii, 5 ; *cf.* ii, 8) made alive, raised from the dead (ii, 5-6), and created in Christ Jesus for good works (ii, 10).—The existence of original sin is not, therefore, directly stated here, but it is presupposed ; and the word φύσει cannot be explained without this supposition. In fact, it cannot signify *wholly* (*omnino, πάντως*), as some commentators have thought, and everyone agrees that the exegesis of Ambrosiaster is inadmissible (*Natura cum mala voluntas supponitur fit natura irae*).

by nature children of wrath, like the rest," include necessarily all men without exception. Indeed, if "we" denotes
the Jews, according to the common explanation, "the rest"
are the non-Jews—that is, all the Gentiles; and if "we"
denotes the Christians, as certain commentators desire to
prove, "the rest" would be the non-Christians—that is, all
unbelievers, whether Jews or Gentiles. In both cases the
affirmation is universal. On the other hand, following
biblical analogy, the "children of wrath" are men worthy
of divine wrath and exposed to the punishments inflicted by
this retributive anger. The only question, therefore, is to
determine the meaning of the word "naturally" or "by
nature" (φύσει). As those dispositions which we bring with
us at birth are called *natural,* whether we derive them from
heredity or from any other cause, St Augustine thought we
were "children of wrath by nature," as men are blind from
birth, or racially negroes, because sin, without belonging to
the essential constitution of our being, is hereditary in us.
Calvin, while adopting this exegesis, as usual exaggerates
the thought of Augustine; he wishes to prove that we are
born with sin, as the serpent with its poison. Many Protestant theologians go so far as to pretend that original sin
is inherent in our nature. The Apostle does not say that.
He points out very clearly what it is that makes us "children
of wrath"; it is to obey "the desires and will of the flesh";
it is, in other words, to commit actual sin. When he adds
that we are so "by nature," the meaning of this word must
be determined by the latent contrast which it implies. Now
the only contrast suggested here by the context is that of
grace: *by grace* we are just, holy, and sons of God; *by
nature* we are sinners and sons of wrath—that is to say,
evidently by nature left to itself and without the intervention
of grace. If, then, original sin is not named here, it is
sufficiently indicated as the universal source of the evil
inclinations with which our nature is now tainted.

3. We come thus to trace the genealogy of evil. The reign
of sin is explained by the abuse of human liberty, and the
abuse of liberty is closely related to the corruption of man's
nature and to the dominion of the flesh; and natural corruption is derived from Adam's disobedience; but it is necessary
to go back still further. According to St Paul and St John,
both of them inspired by the story of Genesis and the Book
of Wisdom, the first instigator of sin was the devil, who, in
the form of a serpent, seduced Eve and, through Eve, our
first father, and, a murderer from the beginning, still
pursues continually his deadly work.[1]  He it is that creates

---

[1] Gen. iii, 1-4 (ὁ ὄφις); Wisd. ii, 24 (φθόνῳ δὲ διαβόλου θάνατος εἰσῆλθεν
εἰς τὸν κόσμον); 2 Cor. xi. 3 (ὁ ὄφις ἐξηπάτησεν Εὕαν ἐν τῇ πανουργίᾳ αὐτοῦ)

obstacles for the preachers of the Gospel and persecutions for
the faithful; he it is that foments idolatry, spreads doubt in
men's minds, and incites rebellion in their hearts. His usual
name is Satan, but Paul calls him also Belial and the serpent
in the Epistles to the Corinthians, and the devil in the Epistle
to the Ephesians, the Pastorals, and the Acts.[1] Sometimes
he describes him as a single person or as a collective
being representing the power of evil; at other times he dis-
seminates him among a multitude of evil spirits who inhabit
the higher spheres, the supramundane regions, or the darkness.[2] It is difficult to decide how far the Apostle uses the
commonly received vocabulary of that time on this subject,
without appreciating its full significance, for his formulas
are not generally the object of an express assertion, and
almost all of them are found in Jewish and rabbinical
theology.[3] What he affirms clearly is that the great enemy
has thus created for himself a kingdom, intended to oppose
the kingdom of God.

Every kingdom spreads through time and space, occupies territory and has a certain period of duration; the
territory in which the empire of Satan is powerful is *this
world;* the time which is assigned to it is *the present age.*

For the Jews of apostolic times the *present world* and the
*present age* were two similar expressions, which formed a
pendant to the world to come and the age to come—that is
to say, to the terrestrial reign of the Messiah and to the
heavenly reign of God in his saints. They drew from this
contrast a more or less pronounced unfavourable meaning
according to the view of the authors. It is not necessary to
be very familiar with the language of St Paul to have
observed that in his writings the world rarely denotes the
whole material creation. The world is often the abode, the
theatre, the actual condition of man; still oftener it is present
humanity, weak, blind, delivered over to its passions, far
removed from its original purpose.[4] Since the advent of sin,

---

1 Tim. ii, 14 (ἡ δὲ γυνὴ ἐξαπατηθεῖσα ἐν παραβάσει γέγονεν); John viii, 44
(ἐκεῖνος ἀνθρωποκτόνος ἦν ἀπ᾽ ἀρχῆς); 1 John iii, 8; Apoc. xii, 9, etc.
[1] *Satan:* Rom. xvi, 20 (God will crush him); 1 Cor. v, 5 and 1 Tim. i, 20
(to deliver over to Satan); 1 Cor. vii, 5 (Satan tempts); 2 Cor. ii, 11 (seeks
to destroy); xi, 14 (transforms himself into an angel of light); xii, 7 (buffets
the Apostle); 1 Thess. ii, 18 (obstacle to his projects); 2 Thess. ii, 9 (paves the
way for Antichrist); 1 Tim. v, 15 (attracts bad Christians to himself);
Acts xxvi, 18.—*The Devil:* Eph. vi, 11 (machinations); 1 Tim. iii, 6 (judgement); 1 Tim. iii, 7 and 2 Tim. ii, 26 (snares); Acts xiii, 10 (son of the devil);
Eph. iv, 27 (μηδὲ δίδοτε τόπον τῷ διαβόλῳ).—*Belial:* 2 Cor. vi, 15.—*The
Serpent:* 2 Cor. xi, 3. *Cf.* Apoc. xii, 9: ὁ δράκων ὁ μέγας, ὁ ὄφις ὁ ἀρχαῖος,
ὁ καλούμενος Διάβολος καὶ ὁ Σατανᾶς, ὁ πλανῶν τὴν οἰκουμένην ὅλην.
[2] Eph. ii, 2; vi, 12.     [3] See Note P, pp. 408 ff.
[4] In the sense of universe, κόσμος is rarely found except in Rom. i, 20;
Eph. i, 4 (*cf.* Acts xvii, 24). In 1 Cor. xiv, 10; Col. i, 6; 1 Tim. vi, 7, it is
already the world, as the abode of man. Elsewhere it is almost always
corrupted humanity. See Note Q, II, pp. 417 ff.

the world is the enemy of God; the wisdom of the world is opposed to the wisdom of God, the spirit of the world to the spirit of God, the sorrow of the world to the sorrow according to God, the things of the world to the things of God.[1] Paul expresses with remarkable energy this irreconcilable hostility by saying that he is crucified to the world and that the world is crucified to him. The same unfavourable meaning sometimes attaches to the present age by virtue of a manifest or unspoken antithesis to the age to come. The coming age is the era of unalloyed and endless happiness; the present age, exposed to miseries, death, and sin, is depraved in its principles and tendencies.[2] Thus the world and the age come to be almost synonymous; yet the etymological distinction remains and the synonomy is not absolute.[3]

The world thus understood is the kingdom of Satan; the age is the length of time assigned to his reign. The Epistle to the Hebrews, St John and St Paul express this domination by somewhat different formulas: St John calls Satan " the prince of this world ";[4] the Epistle to the Hebrews attributes to him " the power of death ";[5] St Paul, going still further, calls him " the god of this age."[6] After the final triumph, God will be all in all; but, during the period of conflict which will last till the *parousia*, the empire of the world is divided and the devil claims his share of sovereignty. He gathers round him the outlaws, the rebels, and the deserters, and blinds them by his sophisms; he draws them away from the

---

[1] Wisdom (I Cor. i, 20, 21, 24), spirit (I Cor. ii, 12), sorrow (2 Cor. vii, 10). *Cf.* I Cor. i, 27-28; vii, 33, 34 (τὰ τοῦ κόσμου . . . τά τοῦ κυρίου).

[2] Gal. i, 4: ἐκ τοῦ αἰῶνος τοῦ ἐνεστῶτος πονηροῦ.

[3] (Eph. ii, 2): κατὰ τὸν αἰῶνα τοῦ κόσμου τούτου, without tautology. The Hebrew עֹלָם (translated αἰών in the Septuagint and *saeculum* in the Vulgate) is derived from a root whose primordial meaning is to *hide*, and by means properly *the distant past*, which is lost in the night of ages; then, by extension, a *long, indefinite, limitless, eternal duration* either in the past or in the future. As there is a relation between the duration of the world and the world which endures, this word in rabbinical Hebrew and in Aramaic came finally to signify also *the world ;* and it is this last sense which alone has been preserved in Arabic.—In its most ancient and classic meaning the Greek word αἰών signifies *the whole duration of human life.* It is thus defined by the author of *De caelo*, i, 9, and by the lexicographers Eustathius (τὸ μέτρον τῆς ἀνθρωπίνης ζωῆς) and Hesychius (ὁ τῆς ζωῆς χρόνος). More often it is the normal *duration* of a man's life (seventy years), finally *any sort of duration*, provided it is considered as indefinite or very long. From this come the expressions ἀπ᾽ αἰῶνος, δι᾽ αἰῶνα, εἰς αἰῶνα, ἐξ αἰῶνος, *ab aeterno, in aeternum.* Having reached this stage of its evolution, αἰών became adapted to translate the Hebrew עוֹלָם, which evolved in a contrary manner: first indefinite duration, then long but limited duration.

[4] John xii, 31; xiv, 30; vi, 11 (ὁ ἄρχων τοῦ κόσμου τούτου).

[5] Heb. ii, 14 (τὸν τὸ κράτος ἔχοντα τοῦ θανάτου).

[6] 2 Cor. iv, 4: ὁ θεὸς τοῦ αἰῶνος τούτου. The metaphor is to be compared with *quorum deus venter est* (Phil. iii, 19; ὧν ὁ θεὸς ἡ κοιλία). It is curious to note that it is found also among the Rabbis: *Deus primus est Deus verus, ed Deus secundus est Samael.* (Jalkut Rubeni).

influence of the Gospel; he reigns over them completely; he is their god. As his domination can establish itself and endure only through error and lies, "the god of this age" is a god of darkness:

> Put you on the armour of God, that you may be able to stand against the deceits of the devil. For our wrestling is not against flesh and blood, but against principalities and powers, against the rulers of the world of this darkness, against the spirits of wickedness in the heavenly regions.[1]

The occult power which makes war upon us is sometimes concentrated in the person of its head, sometimes divided up among a multitude of hostile beings, "principalities and powers, princes of this world, spirits of wickedness." Their sphere of action is the world, darkness, the sublunar regions. If these terms are taken in their literal sense, the *celestial regions* can be only places adjoining our globe, and commonly known under the name of heaven. That the evil spirits should dwell there is a necessity of the war waged by them against humanity. St Paul recalls to the Ephesians the time when they walked "according to the course of this world, according to the prince of the power of the air, of the spirit that now worketh on the children of rebellion.[2] The precise meaning of almost all these words is

[1] Eph. vi, 11:

'Ενδύσασθε τὴν πανοπλίαν τοῦ Θεοῦ
πρὸς τὸ δύνασθαι ὑμᾶς στῆναι πρὸς τὰς μεθοδίας τοῦ διαβόλου.

12. ὅτι οὐκ ἔστιν ἡμῖν ἡ πάλη πρὸς αἷμα καὶ σάρκα.
ἀλλὰ πρὸς τὰς ἀρχάς, πρὸς τὰς ἐξουσίας.
πρὸς τοὺς κοσμοκράτορας τοῦ σκότους τούτου.
πρὸς τὰ πνευματικὰ τῆς πονηρίας ἐν τοῖς πο ἐπουρανίοις.

The hostile forces receive three qualifications: (*a*) They are the *principalities and powers* as contrasted to *flesh and blood ;* that is to say, to what is feeble and perishable, like man himself.—(*b*) They are the *rulers of this dark world :* κοσμοκράτωρ is used of a powerful monarch, such as the king of Egypt or Babylon; but here it is probably necessary to think of the etymological meaning (*mundi rectores*), giving to *mundus* the unfavourable sense of which we have spoken; then the *darkness* forms a sort of apposition to the world, and we can translate "of this world of darkness" or "of this dark world."—(*c*) They are *spirits of wickedness* (τὰ πνευματικά = spiritual beings) *in the celestial regions* (ἐν τοῖς ἐπουρανίοις). The special meaning of this last word will be noted. Elsewhere τὰ ἐπουράνια designates literally heaven, the abode of God and the angels (Eph. i, 3, 20; ii, 6; iii, 10); here it can signify only the lower heavens, the air, which is called in common parlance heaven (Matt. vi, 26: τὰ πετεινὰ τοῦ οὐρανοῦ).

[2] Eph. ii, 2:

περιεπατήσατε κατὰ τὸν αἰῶνα τοῦ κόσμου τούτου,
κατὰ τὸν ἄρχοντα τῆς ἐξουσίας τοῦ ἀέρος.
τοῦ πνεύματος τοῦ νῦν ἐνεργοῦντος ἐν τοῖς υἱοῖς τῆς ἀπειθείας.

Before their conversion, the Christians who came from the Gentiles had been living in sin, walking according to the course of this world and according to the prince of the power of the air, as the rule of their conduct. What is the meaning of this double rule (introduced by κατά) which is really only one ?

(*a*) *According to the course of this world.* It is a question of the present world (ὁ κόσμος οὗτος), of the corrupt world, hostile to Christ and to his work, subjected to the influence of the powers antagonistic to man, and opposed

disputed; nevertheless, one cannot escape the impression that the *air,* which is mentioned, is indeed the material atmosphere in which the demons are, so to speak, ambushed, ready to fall upon man unexpectedly, and where the " adversary the devil, as a roaring lion, goeth about seeking whom he may devour."[1] This conception was then common, and there is no anachronism in attributing it to St Paul.

Cannot the sin which dominates the human race and which has its seat in the flesh, instead of being a personification of evil, be a veritable person, the devil himself? Some Fathers have thought so and several heterodox theologians still maintain it.[2] But this opinion is not only unsupported by any solid reason, but meets with serious difficulties of exegesis. All that can and ought to be conceded is that the presence of a personal being behind the principle of evil facilitates greatly the constant personification of sin.

---

to the future world, where all will be justice and holiness. These two worlds exist at the same time; each has its own duration (αἰών), its distinct course. We can belong to one or the other, according as we place ourselves under its respective influence. The meaning is very intelligible and there is no reason why we should understand αἰών as a personal being, as the Gnostics did subsequently. This meaning is foreign to the language of the New Testament, where αἰών signifies duration and where ὁ αἰὼν τοῦ κόσμου τούτου therefore will mean the course of this corrupt world, the duration which measures it.

(*b*) *According to the prince of the power of the air.* Here the word prince (ἄρχων) designates a personal being, and this phrase is the explanation of the preceding one. There it was a question of an influence, here it is a question of a person who directs and controls this influence.—The precise meaning of ἐξουσία is a matter of dispute. Some see in it a collective noun (the power or the powers—that is to say, the demons), and this agrees well with the word *prince* or *chief,* but much less with the word *air,* which qualifies and specifies this power. It is better to regard ἐξουσία as an abstract noun : the prince of the domination of the air, or the prince of the power which is dominant in the air, the genitive ἀέρος being an objective genitive.—As to the word *air,* it is impossible to take it otherwise than its proper sense, for although ἀήρ signifies the dense air as contrasted to the imponderable ether, it does not mean obscurity or darkness ; on the other hand, it never has the meaning of an intellectual or moral atmosphere. On the air inhabited by demons, see Note P.

(*c*) *Of the spirit that now worketh on the children of rebellion.* Some exegetes think that τοῦ πνεύματος is put into the genitive by the attraction of the two preceding genitives, and that in reality it refers to τὸν ἄρχοντα (according to the prince . . . the spirit). The meaning would be good, but the construction is very hard, if not inadmissible. The simplest explanation is to put τοῦ πνεύματος in apposition with τῆς ἐξουσίας. If ἐξουσία were collective (domination for dominators), πνεῦμα would also be collective (the spirit for the spirits), which appears a little strange. If, on the contrary, ἐξουσία is abstract, πνεῦμα too will be so and will signify the manner of thinking, as one speaks of mentality, the spirit of the world, the spirit of the age. In this case Satan is represented as directing a power (τῆς ἐξουσίας), a perverse influence (τοῦ πνεύματος), rather than an army of personal beings, or demons.

[1] I Pet. v, 8. *Cf.* James iv, 7.

[2] Simon, *Die Psychologie des Ap. Paulus,* Göttingen, 1897, pp. 51-54, and also Pfleiderer, *Das Urchristentum,* vol. i, p. 197.

4. Does Paul know of a class of intermediate spirits, who are neither demons nor angels, although destined perhaps to become such some day, indeterminate beings, more malicious than wicked, usually hostile to man through love of mischief or by caprice, recalling the fauns, elfs, dryads, and nymphs of Greek and Latin mythology, the sprites, goblins, sylphs, and imps of medieval legends, the fairies and jinns of Arabian stories, the genii of the winds and waters of animist religions and of popular superstition? This is an exceedingly modern question which the ancient commentators have neither propounded nor suspected. Let us say at once that there is not in St Paul the slightest trace of this new conception. When he writes to the Galatians : " If we or an angel from heaven preach to you another Gospel, let him be anathema,"[1] he is speaking of good angels, of those who look upon the face of God ; but he does not seriously consider a case in which either an angel or himself should come to overturn what he has built. The hypothesis is impossible of realization ; only it is less repugnant to the reason than the truth of another Gospel would be.

Neither does the counsel given to the Corinthians presuppose the existence of disloyal angels. " The woman must have on her head " the veil, symbol of the marital " power," " because of the angels." The term " the angels," without any other explanation, never means any but good angels. We must not, therefore, think of those celestial spirits, neither definitely good nor bad, who, according to the Book of Enoch, fell in love with the daughters of men and sinned with them. This interpretation has the inconvenience of introducing a strange theme into the context, without having the advantage of corresponding to the Jewish ideas of the time; for the fall of the angels was for the Jews a fact of ancient history, the repetition of which was seen no more. A simpler and more natural exegesis is suggested by the attentive reading of the passage : " Knowing the bond of subordination which unites the woman to the man, either in the very act of creation or in the design of the Creator, the woman is to wear upon her head the sign of her dependency, because of the angels associated by God with the creative act and charged by him to promulgate the Law and to watch over its observation." It is less through respect for the angels who are witnesses of the eucharistic sacrifice than through fear of the angels appointed to the government of the world and the Church.

In favour of intermediate spirits, who are neither angels

---

[1] I Cor. xi, 10 : Διὰ τοῦτο ὀφείλει ἡ γυνὴ ἐξουσίαν ἔχειν ἐπὶ τῆς κεφαλῆς διὰ τοὺς ἀγγέλους. On this difficult text see Robertson and Plummer or Bachmann in the works cited above, p. 42, note. These authors regard our explanation as certain.

nor demons, the following text is also invoked : " We speak
wisdom among the perfect : yet not the wisdom of this world,
neither of the princes of this world that come to naught (τῶν
καταργουμένων) ; but we speak the wisdom of God in a
mystery, a wisdom which is hidden, which God ordained
before the world unto our glory.  Which none of the princes
of this world knew ; for if they had known it, they would
never have crucified the Lord of glory."[1]   Some Fathers
thought that " the princes of this world " were the demons ;
and certain modern commentators see in them the elemental
spirits who call into operation the physical forces of nature.
But, without speaking of the strange idea that demons or
elemental spirits crucified Christ and that they would not
have crucified him if they had had the true wisdom, the
context clearly indicates that the " princes of this world "
denote human beings, those who then governed the world
and who had the power to put Jesus to death.   Indeed, in
these first two chapters, Paul establishes a contrast between
human wisdom on the one side, wisdom according to
the flesh, the wisdom of this world, which is the property
of the philosophers, the noble, and the powerful, and on the
other divine wisdom, revealed by the Holy Spirit to the
humble, the weak, and the lowly, who form the bulk of
the Church.  The latter wisdom was unknown to the Herods,
the Caiaphases, and the Pilates of that time, for if they had
known it they would not have crucified the author of wisdom
himself.   Let not the faithful, therefore, blush for their low
social condition, their ignorance, and their insignificance
according to worldly standards, for they possess a wisdom
to which the geniuses and potentates of this world could not
attain.   Who does not see how much the introduction of
demons or elemental spirits would disturb the course of such
clear reasoning?

The theory of elemental spirits shelters itself sometimes
under the protecting shadow of an obscure text.   God,
" despoiling the principalities and powers, hath made of
them an open show, triumphing over them by the cross."[2]
It is unquestionable that " the principalities and powers "
include sometimes the infernal spirits.   But it is otherwise
here.   In fact, one cannot resist the impression that the
Apostle here refers to the " principalities and powers " which
he has just mentioned a few verses previously.   The Colossians had the habit of honouring them with a superstitious
worship (θρησκεία τῶν ἀγγέλων) on account of their intrinsic
dignity and because they knew them to be associated in the

---

[1]  1 Cor. ii, 6-8. See above, p. 42.
[2]  Col ii, 15.   We have given the explanation of this text in an article
entitled : " The Triumph of Christ over the Principalities and Powers "
(Recherches de science religieuse, vol. iii, 1912, pp. 201-229).

promulgation and guardianship of the Mosaic Law. Paul reminds them that God has nailed this superannuated Law to the cross of Jesus and divested the mediators of the ancient covenant of their power. There is now only one Mediator; the role of the angels has passed away and they now serve to promote the exaltation of the Crucified One, of whose triumphal chariot, so to speak, they are the escort. That they have been unfaithful to their mission the Apostle does not imply; but their mission is none the less ended, and the Colossians are wrong to make use of them to introduce a worship injurious to Christ.

### III—Slavery of the Flesh and Liberty of the Spirit

1. False Theories. 2. The Flesh and the Spirit. 3. The Flesh and Sin. 4. Résumé.

1. Since man possesses the three essential elements of moral life—knowledge of God, the natural law, and free will—what does he still lack in order to attain his highest end? The end of a being is not to be found outside of the sphere of its activity, and if man is destined for blessedness, he must be able to attain it. Yet the contrary seems to result from the doctrine of Paul, particularly in the Epistle to the Romans, where he teaches that the moral impotence of man comes from the flesh, and has no other remedy but the Spirit of God.

Between the spirit and the flesh we have already pointed out two oppositions: one physical, between the constituent parts of the same being; the other ontological, between complete substances, the respective character of which is spirituality and corporality. We must now join to these the moral and religious opposition, which is the principal, the most important, and really the only opposition characteristic of Paul's Gospel. The mistake of a great number of heterodox theologians has been practically to confound the moral antithesis " flesh and spirit," either with the physical or the ontological opposition. They hoped in this way to unify concepts and simplify theories, but instead of clearing up the problem they have only made it more obscure.

The first, who are all followers of the school of Baur, claim that Paul, here abandoning the ground familiar to Judaism, makes a rather unfortunate incursion into the domain of Greek philosophy. The monotheism of the Bible stops him, however, halfway; he does not go as far as metaphysical dualism, but still adheres to moral dualism.[1]

[1] Holsten, *Die Bedeutung des Wortes* σάρξ *im Lehrbegriff des Paulus*, Rostock, 1855 (pamphlet incorporated in *Zum Evang. des Paulus und Petrus*, Rostock, 1868). Holsten has been followed by Lüdemann, *Die Anthropologie des Ap. Paulus und ihre Stellung innerhalb seiner Heilslehre*,

Paul, it is said, has carried into the moral order the physical antithesis that the Old Testament is accustomed to establish between God and the world and between man and the Spirit of God, without perceiving his fallacious reasoning and without reflecting that this is to ascribe to the Creator of nature the origin of sin.

In order to maintain this paradox, it is necessary to impute to the Apostle many contradictions. If the flesh is inherently bad in so far as it is opposed to the spirit, how, then, can the flesh of Christ be holy? Now it is certain that St Paul gives to Christ a flesh similar to our own, and that he nevertheless denies that he has anything to do with sin.[1] This proves clearly that sin is not inherent in the flesh, from which it is separable. If our body is irremediably impure, how can it be the temple of the Holy Ghost?[2] How can it serve as an instrument for the works of justice?[3] How can it be offered up to God, as a living sacrifice pleasing unto him?[4] The Apostle invites us to avoid " all defilement of the flesh and of the spirit "[5]; but, if the relation of the flesh to sin were necessary and essential, it would be no more possible for us to defile it than it would be possible for us to preserve it from defilement. Could Paul, from a dualistic point of view, speak of a *redemption of the body* and present it as the perfect achievement of salvation? " Our salvation, on the contrary, should be perfect, as soon as our soul is freed from the fetters of matter."[6]

According to the dualistic theory, Adam has no significance; he is only the first sinner because he was the first man. Now there is more and more agreement among theologians that the anthropology of St Paul has its foundation in the Old Testament. The account in Genesis, with its two immediate corollaries—a personal God, superior to the world, and matter created and therefore good—is always present in his thought. To seek in his writings for the Gnostic dualism,

---

Kiel, 1872, pp. 50-71 ; by Pfleiderer, *Der Paulinismus*, Leipzig, 1873, p. 48 (with important restrictions and modifications in the second edition, 1890 ; and in *Das Urchristentum*, Berlin, 1887) ; and by Holtzmann, *Neutest. Theologie*, 1897, vol. ii, pp. 19-22. Holsten maintains that according to Paul sin is essential to man, for it is nothing but the sensuous appetite or ἐπιθυμία (*Paulinische Theologie*, Berlin, 1898, p. 81). Paul has not reflected on the consequences and has not succeeded in explaining how the pagans are capable of any good action (Rom. ii, 14-16). Refutation of the dualism of Holsten by Weiss, Beyschlag, Gloël, Sabatier, Juncker, Stevens, and above all by H. Sladeczek, *Paulinische Lehre über das Moralsubjekt*, Ratisbon, 1899.

[1] 2 Cor. v, 21. On this text, see p. 204.        [2] 1 Cor. vi, 19.
[3] Rom. vi, 13.        [4] Rom. xii, 1.        [5] 2 Cor. vii, 1.
[6] Sabatier, *L'apôtre Paul*[3], 1896, p. 309. But the author, in the appendix on the origin of sin added to this third edition, falls back into the dualistic explanation which he disputes in the main portion of the work ; according to him the flesh is no longer the *effect* of Adam's sin, but the *cause*.

which makes of matter an evil principle, is an audacious paradox, contradicted by all the texts, and irreconcilable with the biblical education of Paul and his repeated allusions to the first chapters of Genesis. The share of Hellenic influence upon him remains to be debated; but, however great it may be supposed to be, its importance is much diminished by the consideration that the psychology of the Apostle is only secondary in his teaching; it is not psychology that dominates and directs his theological doctrine; it is his theological doctrine that commands and determines his psychology.

From the fact that in Paul's writings the flesh is always the animate matter, that it includes the soul in its concept, that sins of the intellectual order are attributed to the flesh, and that in one passage the expressions " You are men " and " You are carnal " are exchanged as synonyms, other Protestant theologians conclude that the flesh, in the moral sense in which it is employed here, designates human nature. If sin dwells in the flesh, this means, according to them, that man, by virtue of his inborn imperfection, has the opportunity and the power of placing himself in opposition to God.[1] In order to be logical, they ought also to conclude— and some of them do not hesitate to do so—that man is carnal, not because he is man, but because he is a creature: from which there would result this triple paradox that Adam was as carnal as his descendants, that an angel is as carnal as a man, and that neither man nor angel can ever cease to be carnal, since they are essentially created beings. This is groundlessly to make Paul guilty of not knowing the difference between moral evil and metaphysical evil, between the deprivation of a quality which, according to the intentions of God, the rational nature was to possess and the absence of a perfection resulting from the limitation essential to every finite being. But independently of these absurd consequences, the system in question cannot maintain itself, for it is to the material organism of man that Paul attaches sin.

2. The flesh, especially from the moral point of view, which is the one that here concerns us, can hardly be defined except as a function of the spirit. In the Old Testament, the Spirit of God is the creator and preserver of things, the agent of miracles and of prophetic inspiration. In the New Testament its sphere of action is still more enlarged: it is the life-giving, regenerating, and sanctifying Spirit; all that relates to grace and to the *charismata* belongs to its sphere. Since

---

[1] Tholuck (*Ueber σάρξ als Quelle der Sünde* in *Stud. u. Krit.*, 1855, fasc. 3), Müller (*Lehre von der Sünde*³), B. Weiss (*Lehrbuch der bibl. Theol. des N.T.*⁷, Stuttgart, 1903, § 68*b*), and H. Wendt (*Fleisch und Geist im bibl. Sprachgebrauch*, Gotha, 1878), have maintained this system.

it is the soul of the mystical body, of which Christ is the head, there is established between it and the just man a close relation, a very intimate bond; its proper name, derived from its personal character, is the Holy Spirit; its presence in us is more than an inward renewal, it is a metamorphosis, a veritable creation, the production of a divine nature endowed with new qualities and activities.[1]

To this new nature Paul gives also the name of *spirit*. From having misconceived this, certain exegetes become involved in the most improbable explanations. They wish to make a distinction only between the spirit of man, or the rational soul, on the one hand, and the Spirit of God, or the third Person of the Trinity, on the other; but there is an intermediate term—namely, the spirit which the Holy Spirit forms within us and which is related to him as the effect is to its cause. When " the Spirit beareth witness to our spirit "[2] no ambiguity is possible, and since the spirit which beareth witness is assuredly the Spirit of God, the spirit in whose favour it beareth witness can be only this new sense produced in us by the Spirit and capable of perceiving divine things; for the understanding, if left to itself, knows nothing of our adoptive sonship. There are other examples of this division of our faculties. The possessor of the gift of tongues is not understood by those about him, nor by himself, but only by God, unless he has received, in addition, the gift of interpretation : " His $\pi\nu\epsilon\hat{\upsilon}\mu\alpha$ prayeth, but his $\nu o\hat{\upsilon}s$ is without fruit."[3] The ideal thing for him to do would be to pray both with the $\nu o\hat{\upsilon}s$ and also with the $\pi\nu\epsilon\hat{\upsilon}\mu\alpha$. A prayer made in an unknown tongue, under the impulse of grace, may be an excellent prayer, capable of edifying the speaker by the pious sentiments which it suggests, and, if inspired by the Spirit of God, it nourishes the spirit of man; but when it is not understood, it has no effect upon the intelligence. The spirit and the intellect are here distinct principles; one represents in us the natural, the other the supernatural element. From this point of view, the spirit includes the body as well as the soul; since our body, destined to become spiritual, has received in advance the germ of the Spirit and is the temple of the Holy Ghost.[4]

---

[1] 2 Cor. v, 17 ($\epsilon\check{\iota}$ $\tau\iota s$ $\dot{\epsilon}\nu$ $X\rho\iota\sigma\tau\hat{\omega}$ $\kappa\alpha\iota\nu\dot{\eta}$ $\kappa\tau\acute{\iota}\sigma\iota s$); Gal. vi, 15 ($\kappa\alpha\iota\nu\dot{\eta}$ $\kappa\tau\acute{\iota}\sigma\iota s$); Eph. ii, 15 ; iv, 24 ($\kappa\alpha\iota\nu\grave{o}s$ $\check{\alpha}\nu\theta\rho\omega\pi os$).

[2] Rom. viii, 16: $A\dot{\upsilon}\tau\grave{o}$ $\tau\grave{o}$ $\pi\nu\epsilon\hat{\upsilon}\mu\alpha$ $\sigma\upsilon\mu\mu\alpha\rho\tau\upsilon\rho\epsilon\hat{\iota}$ $\tau\hat{\omega}$ $\pi\nu\epsilon\acute{\upsilon}\mu\alpha\tau\iota$ $\dot{\eta}\mu\hat{\omega}\nu$ $\check{o}\tau\iota$ $\dot{\epsilon}\sigma\mu\grave{\epsilon}\nu$ $\tau\acute{\epsilon}\kappa\nu\alpha$ $\Theta\epsilon o\hat{\upsilon}$. There are two distinct testimonies ($\sigma\upsilon\mu\mu\alpha\rho\tau\upsilon\rho\epsilon\hat{\iota}$) : that of the Holy Spirit which expresses itself by *charismata*, and that of our spirit of sonship which manifests itself in confidence, desire, etc.

[3] 1 Cor. xiv, 14, 15 : $T\grave{o}$ $\pi\nu\epsilon\hat{\upsilon}\mu\acute{\alpha}$ $\mu o\upsilon$ $\pi\rho o\sigma\epsilon\acute{\upsilon}\chi\epsilon\tau\alpha\iota$, $\dot{o}$ $\delta\grave{\epsilon}$ $\nu o\hat{\upsilon}s$ $\mu o\upsilon$ $\check{\alpha}\kappa\alpha\rho\pi\acute{o}s$ $\dot{\epsilon}\sigma\tau\iota\nu$. $T\acute{\iota}$ $o\mathring{\upsilon}\nu$ $\dot{\epsilon}\sigma\tau\iota\nu$; $\pi\rho o\sigma\epsilon\acute{\upsilon}\xi o\mu\alpha\iota$ $\tau\hat{\omega}$ $\pi\nu\epsilon\acute{\upsilon}\mu\alpha\tau\iota$, $\pi\rho o\sigma\epsilon\acute{\upsilon}\xi o\mu\alpha\iota$ $\delta\grave{\epsilon}$ $\kappa\alpha\grave{\iota}$ $\tau\hat{\omega}$ $\nu o\hat{\iota}$. It is evident that " my spirit " ($\tau\grave{o}$ $\pi\nu\epsilon\hat{\upsilon}\mu\acute{\alpha}$ $\mu o\upsilon$) is neither the Holy Spirit nor the $\nu o\hat{\upsilon}s$.

[4] 2 Cor. i, 22 ; v, 5 ($\dot{\alpha}\rho\rho\alpha\beta\grave{\omega}\nu$ $\tau o\hat{\upsilon}$ $\pi\nu\epsilon\acute{\upsilon}\mu\alpha\tau os$) ; 1 Cor. vi, 19 ($\nu\alpha\grave{o}s$ $\tau o\hat{\upsilon}$ $\dot{\alpha}\gamma\acute{\iota}o\upsilon$ $\pi\nu\epsilon\acute{\upsilon}\mu\alpha\tau os$) ; Rom. viii, 23 ($\dot{\alpha}\pi\alpha\rho\chi\grave{\eta}\nu$ $\tau o\hat{\upsilon}$ $\pi\nu\epsilon\acute{\upsilon}\mu\alpha\tau os$ $\check{\epsilon}\chi o\nu\tau\epsilon s$).

If the *spirit* designates the entire man, as grace remakes him, the *flesh* also designates the entire man, as sin made him; the understanding becomes carnal when it is disordered; there exists, then, a carnal wisdom; the Corinthians are called carnal for keeping up intrigues and dissensions; the flesh has its thoughts and acts of volition, its affections and hatreds; finally, the sins which are due to the intelligence, such as idolatry, envy, enmity, and quarrels are ranked among the works of the flesh.[1] Nay, more, man is carnal from the one fact that he remains unresponsive to the influences of the Spirit of God. Wisdom according to the flesh, which of itself would be a thing of no importance, becomes evil from the moment that it comes into conflict with the spirit: "Whereas there is among you," he says to the Corinthians, "envying and contention, are you not carnal and walk you not according to man? While one saith: I indeed am of Paul, and another: I am of Apollos, are you not men?" If Paul can reproach the neophytes with being men and with walking according to man, it is because there is disorder in our nature; it is because man is no more what he ought to be according to the plans of God; it is because from the moral point of view there are within us two men, the old man and the new.

The old man is not Adam, nor is the new man Jesus Christ, as certain ill-informed exegetes have for very weak reasons maintained. The *old man,* who dies in principle at baptism, whom St Paul exhorts us to put off more and more, is the inheritance of our first father, that fallen and corrupt nature which he has bequeathed to us, that carnal self spoken of in the Epistle to the Romans. The *new man,* who succeeds him, is the regenerated man, in whom supernatural grace completes the divine image, outlined by the creative *Fiat.*

> Lie not one to another; since you have stripped yourselves of the old man with his deeds, and put on the new man, who is renewed unto [supernatural] knowledge according to the image of him that created him.
> Put off the old man, who is corrupted according to the desire of error, and be renewed in the spirit of your mind, and put on the new man, who according to God is created in justice and holiness of truth.[2]

---

[1] Col. ii, 18 (ὁ νοῦς τῆς σαρκός); 1 Cor. i, 20; iii, 19 (ἡ σοφία τοῦ κόσμου); ii, 5, 6, 13 (ἀνθρώπων, ἀνθρωπίνη, τοῦ αἰῶνος τούτου); 2 Cor. i, 12 (σαρκική); Rom. viii, 6, 7 (τὸ φρόνημα τῆς σαρκός); xiii, 14 (πρόνοια); Gal. v, 16 (ἐπιθυμία); Eph. ii. 3 (τὰ θελήματα τῆς σαρκός); Gal. v, 19, 20 (τὰ ἔργα τῆς σαρκός).

[2] Col. iii, 9. Μὴ ψεύδεσθε εἰς ἀλλήλους, ἀπεκδυσάμενοι τὸν παλαιὸν ἄνθρωπον σὺν ταῖς πράξεσιν αὐτοῦ,

10. καὶ ἐνδυσάμενοι τὸν νέον τὸν ἀνακαινούμενον εἰς ἐπίγνωσιν κατ' εἰκόνα τοῦ κτίσαντος αὐτόν.

Eph. iv, 22. ἀποθέσθαι ὑμᾶς τὸν παλαιὸν ἄνθρωπον τὸν φθειρόμενον κατὰ τὰς ἐπιθυμίας τῆς ἀπάτης·

9. *Nolite mentiri invicem, expoliantes vos veterem hominem cum actibus suis,*

10. *et induentes novum eum qui renovatur in agnitionem secundum imaginem etc.*

Eph. iv, 22. *Deponere vos veterem hominem qui corrumpitur secundum desideria erroris.*

While the inward man and the outward man, spoken of above, form the two parts of which man is composed, in whatever order of providence he is considered, the old man and the new are two consecutive states of the same man, delivered over at first to the influences of sin, of which Adam is the origin, and then to those of grace, of which Jesus Christ is the dispenser. According to the sense, therefore, the new man coincides with the spirit and the old man with the flesh.

3. But although the word "flesh" designates the entire man, as fallen from original justice, the Apostle frequently puts the flesh into special relation with the material part of the human composite : " I know that there dwelleth not in me, that is to say, in my flesh, that which is good."[1] Here the flesh is distinguished from the " me," as part from whole; the flesh belongs to the " me," but it is only the less noble part of it—namely, that which is opposed to reason, to the inward man, and St Paul also calls it " the law of sin which is in my members."[2] Undoubtedly, therefore, the seat of evil, the focus of sin, is the body itself. Thus the material part of man, without being in itself bad, is nevertheless the source of moral evil. How is this enigma to be solved?

---

23. ἀνανεοῦσθαι δὲ τῷ πνεύματι τοῦ νοὸς ὑμῶν

24. καὶ ἐνδύσασθαι τὸν καινὸν ἄνθρωπον τὸν κατὰ Θεὸν κτισθέντα ἐν δικαιοσύνῃ καὶ ὁσιότητι τῆς ἀληθείας.

23. *Renovamini autem spiritu mentis vestrae*

24. *Et induite novum hominem, qui secundum Deum creatus est in justitia et sanctitate veritatis.*

A. The first text is the easier. The only difficulty is to know whether the past participles ἀπεκδυσάμενοι and ἐνδυσάμενοι give a reason for the imperative, as we have supposed (Lie not, having stripped yourselves, that is to say, *since* you have stripped yourselves), and then allusion is made to baptism (Gal. iii, 27) ; or whether they agree for the time with the imperative which precedes and virtually have the sense of an imperative (Lie not, stripping yourselves, meaning " *but on the contrary*, strip yourselves ") ; in this case it would be a question of the progress of the Christian life, consisting of putting off more and more the old man and of more and more putting on the new. The parallel passage in the Epistle to the Ephesians, where all the infinitives are equivalent to imperatives, favours this second hypothesis.

B. The newness of the new man is expressed by two terms καινός and νεός. Properly speaking, καινός refers to the *quality* of what is new, without allusion to time ; νεός indicates rather a *recent* date. But the two adjectives can be considered in St Paul as synonyms, for they are interchanged, as well as their corresponding verbs. (Col. iii, 10: τὸν νεὸν τὸν ἀνακαινούμενον, and Eph. iv, 27 : ἀνανεοῦσθαι . . . τὸν καινόν.)

C. As in the two texts creation is mentioned (Col. iii, 10: κατ᾽ εἰκόνα τοῦ κτίσαντος αὐτόν, and Eph. iv, 24: τὸν κατὰ Θεὸν κτισθέντα), it is possible that the particle ἀνά in the compound verbs keeps all its force and signifies " anew," taking us back thus to a time anterior to the first sin, when the old man did not yet exist, and when the new man still retained the supernatural image of the Creator.

[1] Rom. vii, 18.　　　　　[2] Rom. vii, 22, 23.

First of all it results from the fact that sin, having entered into the world through the fault of Adam, invades all his posterity, because we are only one flesh with our first father. Thenceforth all flesh becomes sinful, with the exception of him who took upon himself " the likeness of sinful flesh," without, however, knowing sin, seeing that he did not issue from the sinful mass of humanity according to the laws of natural generation, and, moreover, because sin is absolutely incompatible with his person.

Nevertheless, it is necessary to recur to another consideration in order to justify the Apostle's language. It is a fact of experience, commonplace because so true, that the body hinders the upward flight of the soul. Paul understood this better than anyone, when he exclaimed : " Who shall deliver me from the body of this death?" By virtue of the intimate unity of all parts of the human composite, there is not perhaps a single action of the soul which does not react upon the body, nor an impression made upon the body which is not felt in the soul. Now the sensual appetites very often come into conflict with the end and aim of our higher nature, which is the true nature of man, and to complete this misfortune, they are essentially blind and selfish. Thus, while man finds in his reason a sure though insufficient source of aid against the attraction of evil, everything, so far as the senses are concerned, is only an obstacle. In order to re-establish equilibrium and to neutralize the temptation of the flesh, he needs the spirit—namely, an assistance superior to that which his own nature can render, a supernatural principle. Hence in St Paul *the carnal man, the psychic man, the natural man,* or simply *man,* are synonymous expressions which designate man left to himself and to his inborn corruption, without the antidote of the spirit.

Thus, the flesh, in its moral significance, which alone concerns us here, is at once the cause and the effect of sin ; and, of the two modes of action, it is the material part of our being which establishes this relation, because it is in some sort the vehicle of original sin and incites to actual sin. By this it is seen how different was the condition of the first man, and how different also would be the condition of humanity in a state of pure nature. By the free and kindly gift of the Creator the reason of the first man, possessing the mastery over the sensual appetite, caused harmony to reign in his entire being. This harmony, it is true, would not exist in a state of pure nature ; but, independently of sin, this would be merely a physical imperfection and not a moral disorder. It is with concupiscence—and with greater reason —as it is with death. In a state of pure nature both would be the simple resultant of our organic constitution ; in the present order of things, however, they mean a forfeiture, because they deprive us of a good which, according to the plans of God, we were intended to have ; they assume, therefore, a moral character as being the fruit of sin and, in the case of concupiscence, as being the living root from which sin germinates.

4. To sum up the argument : However varied may be the interpretations of the terms *flesh* and *spirit,* they are all connected with the fundamental meaning of *animate matter* and *immaterial being.*

The spirit and the flesh, in the moral sense characteristic of Pauline theology, include the entire man, considered from different points of view : the spirit is man under the influence of the Holy Spirit ; the flesh is man without the Holy Spirit.

The flesh, the material part of man, is in itself neither bad nor essentially sinful, since it is capable of being purified, sanctified, and glorified.

Nevertheless, the flesh, as it exists within us at present, implies a double connection with sin : an historical connection with the guilty head of our race, and a psychological connection with the guilty act to which it inclines.

The psychological connection is allied to the low, selfish, and blind instincts of our sensuous nature, which put it into continual antagonism with the essential good of our rational nature. In this conflict the understanding, if left to itself, is infallibly vanquished and becomes carnal ; but, with the additional support of the Holy Spirit, it comes out of the struggle victorious and the entire man becomes spiritual.

# CHAPTER II

## THE INITIATIVE OF THE FATHER

### I—DESIGNS OF MERCY

#### 1. The Will to Save.  2. Different Aspects of the Divine Will.

1. SINCE man cannot lift himself again by his own efforts or free himself by his own strength, it is necessary for God to extend his hand to him. This act of divine kindness, doubly undeserved both because man has no right to it and because he is positively unworthy of it, is called mercy. Paul extends to all men the merciful goodness of the heavenly Father, so long as they are still being tested.

> I desire therefore, first of all, that supplications, prayers, intercessions and thanksgivings be made for all men, [in particular] for kings and for all that are in high stations, that we may lead a quiet and a peaceable life in all piety and honour.
> For this is good and acceptable in the sight of God our Saviour, who will have all men be saved and to come to the knowledge of the truth. For there is one God, and one mediator of God and men, the man Christ Jesus, who gave himself a ransom for all.[1]

The thought of the Apostle is so clear that no sophism can obscure it. It amounts to this : It is necessary to pray for all men without exception, because God, who is the God

[1] 1 Tim. ii, 1-5.  *Cf.* Belser, *Die Briefe an Tim. und Titus*, 1907.

A. (1) Παρακαλῶ . . . ποιεῖσθαι δεήσεις, προσευχάς, ἐντεύξεις, εὐχαριστίας,
B. ὑπὲρ πάντων ἀνθρώπων, (2) ὑπὲρ βασιλέων καὶ πάντων ἐν ὑπεροχῇ ὄντων,
C. ἵνα ἤρεμον καὶ ἡσύχιον βίον διάγωμεν ἐν πάσῃ εὐσεβείᾳ καὶ σεμνότητι.
D. (3) Τοῦτο καλὸν καὶ ἀπόδεκτον ἐνώπιον τοῦ σωτῆρος ἡμῶν Θεοῦ,
E. (4) ὃς πάντας ἀνθρώπους θέλει σωθῆναι καὶ εἰς ἐπίγνωσιν ἀληθείας ἐλθεῖν.
(5) εἷς γὰρ Θεός, εἷς καὶ μεσίτης Θεοῦ, κτλ.

It is necessary to distinguish in this text the form, the object, the end, the motive and the reason for the prayer recommended by the Apostle.

A. *The precise form* and the distinction between the four kinds of prayers (δεήσεις, προσευχάς, ἐντεύξεις, εὐχαριστιάς) is of little importance for the general meaning ; but it cannot be reasonably doubted that here it is a question especially of public and solemn prayer.

B. *The object of the prayer* is twofold : (*a*) all men in general (ὑπὲρ πάντων ἀνθρώπων), (*b*) rulers in particular (ὑπὲρ βασιλέων καὶ πάντων ἐν ὑπεροχῇ ὄντων). The word βασιλεῖς comprises all who have supreme authority, kings or emperors (the Roman emperor was called in the East βασιλεύς) ; the expression οἱ ἐν ὑπεροχῇ ὄντες denotes all those who have a delegated authority, pro-consuls, proprætors, procurators and governors.

C. *The aim of the prayer* (ii, 2*b*) : to procure for the Church a period of peace and tranquillity (ἵνα ἤρεμον καὶ ἡσύχιον βίον διάγωμεν), favourable for its external development and not less so for the exercise of Christian

of all and whose Son has died for all, also desires the salvation of all.

*It is necessary to pray for all men without exception:* not only for Christians, but for the pagans themselves, particularly for princes, whatever may be the infamy of their conduct, because they can do more for good than for evil. This injunction is strikingly applicable, when it is remembered that the then reigning emperor was Nero, and that he had just unloosed upon the infant Church the most horrible persecution. An immediate corollary of the apostolic command is that prayer is profitable to all men; for who ever enjoins the impossible and absurd?

*God wills the salvation of all men:* which must be understood of all without exception, since no exception is indicated but is on the contrary excluded by the emphatic character of the discourse and by the repetition of the word "all" four times. It is in vain to object that the divine wish to save is necessarily limited by the addition "that all may come to the knowledge of the truth": for, we are assured, since this second proposition cannot be absolutely and universally true, the first one cannot be true either. The reply is easy: all human beings have not the use of their reason, but all, without a single exception, are capable of eternal salvation; thus, while the phrase referring to the knowledge of the truth limits itself naturally to men who are capable of knowing it, the other phrase is limited by nothing and should, according to the rules of sound exegesis, retain its full significance.

*God wills the salvation of all, because he is the God of all and because Jesus Christ, the universal Mediator, has submitted to death for all.* As God is one, he is of necessity the beginning and supreme end of all men. Is it not natural that he should desire to bring them all to the goal of their destinies? That is the consideration which the Apostle has already emphasized in the Epistle to the Romans.[1] Let no one here bring up as a counter argument the original fall, which, by breaking off the harmony between God and man,

---

virtues (ἐν πάσῃ εὐσεβείᾳ καὶ σεμνότητι. The last word, which the Vulgate translates *sanctitas*, signifies rather "gravity, dignity, respectability"). These lines were written in the midst of active persecution; now, although the hostility of the State cannot stop the expansion of the Church, the good-will of public officials is always to be desired.

D. *The motive of the prayer* for all men is to please God, because this act is morally good (καλόν) and acceptable to God.

E. *The reason for this prayer is twofold:* first, because God, being the only God, is necessarily the Creator, the supreme end and the Father of all men; secondly, because his Son, Jesus Christ, has suffered death for all. In regard to these last two verses see p. 167. For the practice of the early Church in regard to public prayers for sovereigns, see pp. 325-6.

[1] Rom. iii, 29, 30. *Cf.* x. 12.

has rendered the latter unworthy of divine benevolence. Beside the one and only God stands the universal Mediator, whose mission is precisely to re-establish good relations between earth and heaven, and who, by dying for all men, acquires for them all the same claim to mercy.

The different explanations imagined by prejudiced theologians to limit the divine will to save, are sufficiently refuted by a simple presentation of them : (a) God wishes *all those who will really be saved* to be saved. A self-evident truth. (b) God wishes *some men* of *every* country and of *every* condition to be saved. By means of what exegesis can " all " be made synonymous with " some " ? (c) *All* is hyperbolical and signifies *many*. But the Apostle, by repeating to satiety the word " all," has undertaken to refute this singular hypothesis. (d) God wishes *only* the salvation of the elect, but he wishes us to desire the salvation of *all* men. He wishes, therefore, to make us desire what is impossible and to make us wish what he himself does not wish ! Moreover, it is a question in this text of what God wishes and not of what he wishes us to wish. (e) God wishes the salvation of *all* in the sense that he does something for *all,* although this something is insufficient to save them. This really means that he does and yet does not wish ; in other words, that he does not wish seriously, or, more simply, that he does not wish at all. (f) Jesus Christ, *as man,* wills the salvation of all, with an inefficacious will, knowing that the object of his will cannot be realized. But it is not the will of Jesus Christ that is in question here, but the divine will. Moreover, why should Jesus Christ, even as man, will what his Father does not will?

It is indisputable that the Apostle takes his stand on the hypothesis of original sin ; for, by urging Christians to pray for all men, he affirms that God at present wills salvation for all, and that Jesus Christ has died for all. Will anyone dare to ascribe to Paul this lame sort of reasoning : Pray for *all* men because God wills the salvation of *some men,* inasmuch as Jesus Christ has died for *all?* To be logical it would be necessary at the same time to limit these three propositions, which are so closely connected, and to say, for example : " Pray for the elect only, because God wills the salvation of the elect only, and because Jesus Christ died for the elect only." But then we should remain logical only to be thrown into arbitrariness and to fall into heresy.

This is not the place in which to develop the corollaries of this teaching. A glance reveals the fact that the *positive reprobation* of Calvin is diametrically opposed to it, the antecedent will to save all men excluding *ipso facto* the antecedent will to damn some of them, even on the hypo-

thesis of original sin; for, as we have proved, this is the
hypothesis which the Apostle adopts. We could never understand how the defenders of *negative reprobation* succeed in
eluding our text. This reprobation is called negative either
because it expresses itself by a negation or because it is the
negation of a benefit; but it consists in a *positive* act of
God: the partisans of the system recognize it and, if they
denied it, it would be easy to demonstrate it. Now the
antecedent will to refuse eternal salvation to some men is
absolutely incompatible with the antecedent will to save them
all, for the first will destroys the second, of which it is the
contradiction. And it would be of no use to try to put these
two wills on a different footing by an appeal to original
sin; since, according to St Paul, the will to save remains
universal even on the hypothesis of original sin. No subtlety
of exegesis will ever escape this argument of elementary logic
and common sense. The will to save is not absolute, for otherwise it would not fail of accomplishment; it is conditional,
but with regard to a condition which does not depend upon
itself alone; if not, it would be illusory and could be stated
thus: " I would will, if I willed," which plainly amounts to
saying: " I do not will."

2. Just as it is unreasonable to seek in St Paul the present
scholastic terminology, so it would be equally rash and un-
scientific not to distinguish in him the different expressions of
the divine will. We must not confound the purpose (πρόθεσις),
the good pleasure (εὐδοκία), the counsel (βουλή), the will of
God (βούλημα, θέλημα). The *purpose* of God[1] is an eternal
and absolute act of consequent will, relating to a particular
benefit, like the efficacious call to faith: it is free, since it is
done according to his good pleasure; it is gracious, since it
does not depend upon the merits of man; it is absolute,
since it has for its effect the efficacious call; it is eternal,
since it is anterior to the ages. In reality, the divine purpose
is what best corresponds to predestination, a word which St
Paul does not use; only predestination implies, as regards
the order of execution, a precedence in time, which the
purpose does not by itself express.—The *good pleasure*,[2] as

---

[1] Rom. viii, 28; ix, 11; Eph. i, 11; iii, 11; 2 Tim. i, 9 (πρόθεσις).—
Rom. iii, 25; Eph. i, 9 (προτίθεσθαι).—See Vol. I, p. 434, and compare, for
the local meaning of πρό in the compound, Ps. liii (liv), 5: οὐ προέθεντο τὸν
Θεὸν ἐνώπιον αὐτῶν; Ps. c (ci), 3: οὐ προεθέμην πρὸ ὀφθαλμῶν μου πρᾶγμα
παράνομον.

[2] Eph. i, 5 (κατὰ τὴν εὐδοκίαν τοῦ θελήματος αὐτοῦ); i, 9 (γνωρίσας ἡμῖν
τὸ μυστήριον τοῦ θελήματος αὐτοῦ κατὰ τὴν εὐδοκίαν αὐτοῦ); Phil. ii, 13 (ὁ
ἐνεργῶν ἐν ὑμῖν καὶ τὸ θέλειν καὶ τὸ ἐνεργεῖν ὑπὲρ τῆς εὐδοκίας); 2 Thess. i, 11
(ἵνα ὁ Θεὸς πληρώσῃ πᾶσαν εὐδοκίαν ἀγαθωσύνης).—For εὐδοκεῖν, 1 Cor. i,
21; x, 5; Gal. i, 15; Col. i, 19.—On Eph. i, 5, 9 see pp. 88, 91; on Phil. ii, 13,
p. 83.—We repeat again, since some pretend to misunderstand, that the *good
pleasure* of God does not denote an arbitrary will. If we do not translate

the word indicates, denotes the spontaneity as well as the liberty of the divine will; it is used, therefore, only in reference to a benevolent and gracious act of will and is never applied to the permission of evil or to the punishment of crime.—*Counsel*[1] illumines and directs volition. St Paul could say without pleonasm that God "worketh all things according to the counsel of his will," because the divine will is neither blind nor arbitrary, obeys profound although often incomprehensible reasons for its decisions, and unfolds itself harmoniously in time and space in accordance with a plan conceived from all eternity.—Four *wills* of God can be distinguished :[2] the will of precept, the will of desire, the will of decree, and the will of permission. The first is evidently absolute, for it is one with the moral law; but the necessity which results from it refers to the obligation of the act, not to the existence of the act itself. The will of desire is a serious and active will, but its realization is conditioned by the exercise of a foreign will. The will of decree is absolute and inevitable; but when it has for its object the free acts of man, it is not anterior to all prevision of those acts, as we shall presently see. Finally, the will of permission is a sort of negative will which allows the human faculties their free operation, even for evil.

The will of God respects the liberty of his creatures and does not always attain its effect. That is why we pray every day that the will of God may be done more and more, on earth as in heaven. Nothing happens without some intervention of his will. Evil itself would not exist without tolerance on his part (ἀνοχή).[3] The prophets, in saying that God creates evil, mean physical evil, punishment of moral evil; but St Paul does not fear to affirm that God delivers the pagans over to their passions, their evil desires, and their reprobate senses.[4] When God turns evil into good by repairing or punishing it, it can be said that he wishes it by a will that is virtually twofold; on the one hand it permits evil, and on the other it directs it to good.[5]

---

εὐδοκία by "benevolence," it is because benevolence is a disposition, while εὐδοκία is the act of a benevolent will. Those who object that Paul "did not at all intend to signify 'good pleasure' in the sense, which the word has gained, of purely arbitrary choice," are merely forcing an open door.

[1] Eph. i, 11 (τὰ πάντα ἐνεργοῦντος κατὰ τὴν βουλὴν τοῦ θελήματος αὐτοῦ); Heb. vi, 17 (ἐπιδεῖξαι . . . τὸ ἀμετάθετον τῆς βουλῆς αὐτοῦ); Acts xiii, 36; xx, 27 (Paul's speech).—The word is again used in Luke vii, 30 and in Acts ii, 23; iv, 28.

[2] Some examples of these four wills of God in St Paul : (a) *Will of precept :* Rom. ii, 18; xii, 2; Eph. v, 17; vi, 6; Col. i, 9; iv, 12.—(b) *Will of desire :* 1 Thess. iv, 3; 1 Tim. ii, 4; Rom. ix, 22 (desire of showing his justice neutralized by the will to show his patience).—(c) *Will of decree :* Rom. ix, 18; Eph. i, 9, 11; and the formula "apostle by the will of God" (1 Cor. i, 1, etc.).—(d) *Will of permission :* Rom. i, 10; xv, 32; 1 Cor. iv, 19.

[3] Rom. ii, 1; iii, 26.    [4] Rom. i, 24-28.    [5] See Vol. I, pp. 256-8, 266-7.

## II—THE REDEEMING PLAN

1. Grace and Free Will.   2. Order of Intention and Order of Execution.
3. Extension of the Divine Plan.

1. Josephus somewhere attributes to the Pharisees of his
time a doctrine analogous to the Stoics' profession of faith,
expecting everything from God, except virtue.   According
to him, the Essenes referred everything to destiny; the
Sadducees nothing; the Pharisees, a part to destiny, part
to free will.   Does *destiny*—an idea totally foreign to Jewish
theology—here, perhaps, represent providence or the divine
decree?   Elsewhere Josephus modifies his description of the
theory of the Pharisees thus : " Although everything depends
on destiny, man remains none the less free, since God has
arranged a sort of equilibrium between the decree of destiny
and man's liberty."[1]   Nevertheless, the Pharisees had, in
practice, to diminish or attenuate the divine initiative.
Justice being for them only the carrying out of a contract
signed with God, they thought they were free from any
obligation of gratitude when they had faithfully observed it,
and regarded themselves even then as Jehovah's creditors.

That Saul shared this error before his conversion, nothing
leads us to suppose : so keen and profound in him is the twofold sentiment, first, that man can never boast in regard to
his salvation, and, secondly, that everything comes from God
in the supernatural, as well as in the natural, order.[2]   But if
he does not sacrifice to man's free will the sovereign domain
of God, no more does he build the sovereign domain of God
upon the ruins of that free will.   His repeated exhortations
would have no sense, if man were not free to do good and to
avoid evil.   Let us recall merely, in order not to come back
to a question which is so clear, the three following Pauline
assertions : Man is responsible for his actions, both good and
bad ; he must render an account of them to the Supreme
Judge,[3] he is without excuse if he does wrong, because he
knows that, by so doing, he merits death,[4] and because God,

---

[1] *Antiq. Jud.*, XIII, v, 9 : Οἱ μὲν Φαρισαῖοι τινὰ καὶ οὐ πάντα τῆς εἱμαρμένης
εἶναι λέγουσιν ἔργον, τινὰ δ'ἐφ' ἑαυτοῖς ὑπάρχειν, συμβαίνειν τε καὶ μὴ γίνεσθαι.
Here the things which depend on us are contrasted with those which
depend on· destiny.—On the contrary (*Antiq. Jud.*, XVIII, i, 3), *destiny*
extends to everything, without, however, discrediting free will : Πράσσεσθαί τε
εἱμαρμένῃ τὰ πάντα ἀξιοῦντες, οὐδὲ τοῦ ἀνθρωπείου τὸ βουλόμενον τῆς ἐπ' αὐτοῖς
ὁρμῆς ἀφαιροῦνται.   Here is a mixture (κρᾶσις) of the two.—Elsewhere
(*Bell. Jud.*, II, vii, 14) destiny and free will unite and co-operate : Εἱμαρμένη
τε καὶ Θεῷ προσάπτουσι πάντα, καὶ τὸ μὲν πράττειν τὰ δίκαια καὶ μὴ κατὰ τὸ
πλεῖστον ἐπὶ τοῖς ἀνθρώποις κεῖσθαι, βοηθεῖν δὲ εἰς ἕκαστον καὶ τὴν εἱμαρμένην.
But what can destiny here, being distinct from God, really be ?

[2] Rom. xi, 36.   See on this subject Vol. I, p. 177.

[3] Rom. ii, 12-16 ; xiv, 10 ; 2 Cor. v, 10, etc.

[4] Rom. i, 32.

not content with giving him the notion of good, does on his part all that is necessary to lead him to it.[1] The believer's act of faith is an act of obedience agreeable to God; unbelief is an act of insubordination, contempt, obstinacy, and wilful hardness of heart, which calls down upon him the divine wrath;[2] now whoever talks of obedience or disobedience, talks of freedom of the will.—But neither is the unbeliever lost beyond the possibility of repentance, nor the believer saved except by hope.[3] The latter must always fear and the former can always hope. The salvation of the believer is assured only on God's part, on man's it is conditional " if he perseveres in the faith,"[4] likewise the loss of the unbeliever is certain only if he persists in his unbelief. If he is converted, he will be saved in his turn.[5]

It is a remarkable thing that Paul unites in the same phrase these two ideas, which to so many heterodox theologians appear contradictory, and that he does not seem to see in this an antimony : " Work out your salvation with fear and trembling, for it is God who worketh in you both to will it and to do it."[6]

We must work for our salvation as if everything depended on us and abandon ourselves to God as if everything depended

---

[1] Phil. ii, 12, 13.          [2] Rom. ii, 8.          [3] Rom. viii, 24.
[4] Rom. xi, 22 ; Col. i, 23.          [5] Rom. xi, 23.
[6] Phil. ii, 12, 13 : μετὰ φόβου καὶ τρόμου τὴν ἑαυτῶν σωτηρίαν κατεργάζεσθε. Θεὸς γάρ ἐστιν ὁ ἐνεργῶν ἐν ὑμῖν καὶ τὸ θέλειν καὶ τὸ ἐνεργεῖν ὑπὲρ τῆς εὐδοκίας.—(a) The words φόβος and τρόμος are often put in proximity (Gen. ix, 2 ; Ex. xv, 16 ; Isa. xix, 16 ; 1 Cor. ii, 3 ; 2 Cor. vii, 15 ; Eph. vi, 5), and their union does not seem much to strengthen the idea. The Apostle appears to allude here to Ps. ii, 11 : Δουλεύσατε τῷ κυρίῳ ἐν φόβῳ καὶ ἀγαλλιᾶσθε αὐτῷ ἐν τρόμῳ.—(b) The compound verb κατεργάζεσθαι signifies "to accomplish, to finish, to bring to a good ending": usque ad metam (Bengel, Gnomon), for the salvation of the faithful is already begun.—(c) The connection between verse 12 and verse 13 (γάρ) is rather difficult. There is on this point a monograph by Schäder (Der Gedankeninhalt von Phil. ii, 12-13, in Greifswalder Studien, 1895). " Verse 13," says P. Lemonnyer (Épîtres de Saint Paul, Paris, 1905, vol. ii, pp. 21-22), " presents itself as the justification of the counsel formulated in verse 12. Its meaning remains doubtful. Are the Philippians to fear and tremble because God wishes their salvation and works in them to this end, and because they will incur his wrath if they do not respond to the action and desire of God ? Or are they to fear and tremble because, in the accomplishment of their salvation, they depend upon the action of God ? . . . It is impossible to reply with any degree of certainty." The meaning would indeed be very doubtful if the emphasis of the discourse rested upon the words " with fear and trembling "; but it is much less so if the emphasis is laid upon κατεργάζεσθε, as the best exegetes admit. It is necessary to work diligently for our salvation, for God is working for it too.—(d) The last words, ὑπὲρ τῆς εὐδοκίας, must not be interpreted as if they were κατὰ τὴν εὐδοκίαν, " according to his good pleasure." Certainly εὐδοκία is the " good pleasure " of God and not the " good will " of man ; but ὑπέρ means " for," " in view of." The sense is : God worketh in you the willing and the doing, in order to accomplish his benevolent designs towards you (cf. Rom. viii, 31). Let us not forget that here is a question of Christians already in possession of sanctifying grace.

on him. Nothing is more just than that we should enter on this work with fear and trembling, for our eternal happiness or our eternal misery is here at stake, and no one is guaranteed against the weakness of his will. Paul himself experiences this fear; he knows that, even if not conscious of doing any evil, he is not sure of being justified;[1] he mortifies his body and treats it as a slave for fear that, after having preached to others, he himself may be a castaway.[2] But here is a maxim which resembles a paradox. We must work out our salvation, *because* God worketh in us to will it and to do it.

Several Protestant theologians of our time see in these two parts of the phrase an irreducible opposition and severely blame St Paul for not having perceived it. Some excuse him by saying that here is an incomprehensible mystery. One of them, more disrespectful than the others, sends him unceremoniously from the school of Gamaliel to that of Aristotle, which taught better reasoning.[3] The argument of these great thinkers is simplicity itself: If God, they say, does everything in the work of salvation, man has nothing to do; and if man does everything, there remains nothing for divinity to do. Their error arises from the fact that they conceive the combined action of God and man, as if it were a joint work. If God and man were partial causes and of the same order of being, the objection would be conclusive; but this is not the case: God and man together produce the entire effect, but each in his own order;[4] and yet the effect could not be produced without their simultaneous co-operation. It is, therefore, the assurance of the divine co-operation, added to the feeling of his own weakness, that inspires in man both confidence and fear; and still more confidence than fear, for, the implied quotation from the Psalmist being

---

[1] I Cor. iv, 4 : οὐδὲν ἐμαυτῷ σύνοιδα, ἀλλ' οὐκ ἐν τούτῳ δεδικαίωμαι.

[2] I Cor. ix, 27 : ὑπωπιάζω μου τὸ σῶμα καὶ δουλαγωγῶ, μήπως ἄλλοις κηρύξας αὐτὸς ἀδόκιμος γένωμαι. The verb ὑπωπιάζειν signifies to " bruise with blows," from the noun ὑπώπιον, " blue, livid traces left by blows." The adjective ἀδόκιμος means properly " one who does not bear the test or examination," and then " rejected, discarded."

[3] The author of this clumsy jest is Fritzsche. Von Soden and Pfleiderer merely say that Paul does not perceive the contradiction, or that he acts as if he were not conscious of it. Holtzmann declares that Paul defends free will when he is speaking as a preacher or a moralist, but upholds the theory of determinism when he is speaking as a theologian (*Neutest. Theol.*, vol. ii, pp. 169-171). There is in Holtzmann (*ibid.*, pp. 171-174) a long, very condensed note on the attitude of the principal Protestant theologians of our day in regard to this teaching of St Paul.

[4] *Non sic idem effectus causae naturali et divinae virtuti attribuitur, quasi partim a Deo partim a naturali agenti fiat, sed totus ab utroque secundum alium modum* (St Thomas, *Contra Gentes*, III, lxx).—*Deus est qui operatur in nobis velle et operari ; certum est nos facere cum facimus, sed ille facit ut faciamus, praebendo vires efficacissimas voluntati* (St Augustine, *De gratia et lib. arbit.*, 16).

granted, the counsel to fear is here only secondary, and the emphasis of the discourse falls on the words : " Work out your salvation." Such is the profound but perfectly consistent thought of St Paul.

2. What God works in time he resolved to do from all eternity. The history of redemption is not unrolled before him like a panorama, which he contemplates while taking part in it, but like a vast drama the machinery of which he sets in motion, the events of which he combines, and the ending of which he prepares. St Paul frequently refers to this divine plan which he calls the " eternal purpose, before the formation of the world " ; and he sums it up magnificently in a passage whose lyrical tone and rhythmical charm remind us of a canticle or a hymn :

(Verse 3) Blessed be the God and Father of our Lord Jesus Christ ;

A. Who hath blessed us with spiritual blessings in heavenly places in Christ ;
(4) as he chose us in him before the foundation of the world, that we should be holy and unspotted in his sight in charity ;

B. (5) who hath predestinated us unto the adoption of children through Jesus Christ unto himself, according to the good pleasure of his will,
(6) unto the praise of the glory of his grace, in which he hath graced us in the Beloved,
(7) in whom we have redemption through his blood, the remission of sins, according to the riches of his grace. which he hath shed abundantly on us, in all wisdom and understanding.

C. (9) that he might make known unto us the mystery of his will, according to his good purpose formed in him,
(10) in the dispensation of the fulness of times, to re-establish all things in Christ, that are in heaven and on earth,

(a) (11) in him in whom we, the first to hope in Christ, were made heirs, predestined according to the purpose of him who worketh all things, according to the counsel of his will,
(12) to be unto the praise of his glory ;

(b) (13) in him in whom you also, after you had heard the word of truth, the gospel of your salvation, and also believed in it, were signed with the Holy Spirit of promise,
(14) the pledge of our inheritance, unto the [full] redemption of those whom he has acquired, unto the praise of his glory.[1]

---

[1] Eph. i, 3-14. The different parts of this text are explained later in detail. For the moment it is a question only of taking a general view of them. It is usually divided into two sections, enumerating the blessings mentioned in verse 3, first in the *order of intention* (4-6), then in the *order of execution* (7-14). But a mere reading is sufficient for us to see that this division is faulty, for the order of intention and the order of execution are everywhere

The theological notions accumulated in this passage would require a long commentary. For the moment it is sufficient to bring out the three principal ideas : to God alone are due the glory and the initiative of our salvation : predestination, election, remission of sins, the bestowal of grace, heavenly blessings in the widest sense, all are derived from him.—All this, both in the order of execution and in that of intention, is done in view of Christ, " the well-beloved Son."—Finally, the order of execution is unrolled through the centuries, according to the order of intention conceived by God from eternity.

Before investigating closely the mystery of the divine plan, it is well to define the concepts of predestination, election, and foreknowledge. The word *predestination* is not biblical, but the word *to predestinate* appears five times in St Paul in the following passages :

---

closely mingled. In examining the long phrase, we see that it turns on three participles : ὁ εὐλογήσας (3), προορίσας (5), and γνωρίσας (9), directly or indirectly dependent on the doxology, εὐλογητός (εἴη or ἔστω being understood). This gives us an excellent division : *Blessed* be God (A) because he hath *blessed* us conformably to his eternal election, (B) because he hath *predestined* us to grace and hath realized in us the effect of this predestination, (C) because he hath *made known* to us the mystery of his redeeming plan and hath executed it (a) first in the Jews, (b) then in the Gentiles. The two subdivisions which are connected with the third part are clearly indicated by the construction : (a) verse 11 (ἐν ᾧ), (b) verse 13 (ἐν ᾧ).

An important question from an exegetical point of view, but especially from a grammatical one, is to know whether the three participles εὐλογήσας, προορίσας and γνωρίσας are co-ordinated or subordinated—that is, whether they are all directly dependent on εὐλογητὸς ὁ Θεός, or whether the first one alone depends on it, and the other two on the sentence which precedes them. M. Coppieters (*La doxologie de la lettre aux Ephésiens*, in *Revue bibl.*, 1909, pp. 74-88) defends the former opinion, and he maintains also, at least as being more probable, the view that ἐν ἀγάπῃ is to be connected with προορίσας, and ἐν πάσῃ σοφίᾳ καὶ φρονήσει with γνωρίσας. The great majority of both ancient and modern commentators are of the contrary opinion, and it seems with good reason. It is less a matter of peremptory demonstration than of exegetical tact. It seems clear that προορίσας depends on ἐξελέξατο, and that therefore it is necessary to translate " after having predestined us " or " in predestining us." Similarly, everyone will agree that the words ἐν πάσῃ σοφίᾳ καὶ φρονήσει are *better* suited (to say nothing more) to the knowledge of man than to the knowledge of God, and that it is then necessary to refer them to ἐπερίσσευσεν εἰς ἡμᾶς and not to γνωρίσας. Consequently γνωρίσας explains the manner, the object and the origin of the knowledge which God gives us so liberally.

But grammatical construction is one thing, the march and progress of thought is another : grammatically, the two participles προορίσας and γνωρίσας are subordinated to what precedes them ; logically, they introduce a new development and the description of a new blessing. This gives to the style more freedom of movement and life, but makes the translation much harder.

Th. Innitzer (*Der Hymnus im Epheserbriefe*, i, 3-14, in the *Zeitschrift für kath. Theol.*, 1904, pp. 612-621) has proposed a strophic division, based upon the repetition of a sort of refrain, εἰς ἔπαινον δόξης, in verses 6, 12 and 14. Although it is possible to think of strophes in prose, few exegetes will adopt the practice. Form is thus too often sacrificed to substance and thought to expression.

We speak the wisdom of God in a mystery, a wisdom which is hidden, which God *predestinated* before the world unto our glory.

For whom he foreknew, he also *predestined* to be made conformable to the image of his Son, that he might be the firstborn among many brethren.

And whom he *predestined*, them he also called, and whom he called, them he also justified, and whom he justified, them he also glorified.

He chose us in him before the foundation of the world, that we should be holy and unspotted in his sight, by *predestinating* us unto the adoption of children through Jesus Christ.

In whom also we have received our share [of heritage], being *predestinated* according to the purpose of him who worketh all things according to the counsel of his will, that we may be unto the praise of his glory, we who before hoped in Christ.[1]

From all these passages it appears that the act by which God predestinates is very comprehensive. It is an eternal act, since it exists before all ages and is synchronous with or logically anterior to election, which is itself anterior to the foundation of the world. It is also an absolute act, and likewise an efficacious one in proportion as it is absolute, for it is the result of the " counsel " or " purpose " of God. Moreover, it is a sovereignly free act, for it takes place according to the purpose of him who worketh all things by the counsel of his will; it does not therefore, strictly speaking, find its origin in anything done by man, although it can have, as its *raison d'être,* a condition dependent on God. The divine acts succeed one another in the following order : foreknowledge, predestination, vocation, justification, glorification, the first two belonging to the order of intention, the last three to the order of execution. Predestination is, therefore, logically preceded by prescience : " those whom he foreknew he also predestinated " ; for it is in the nature of things that the act of will follows the act of intelligence and does not precede it. Finally, God predestines man to a favour, or a favour to man, but this favour is never directly eternal glory.

While predestination belongs only to the order of intention, election comprises also the order of execution. It adds to predestination or to the efficacious call an idea of *favour* with respect to those who are predestinated or efficaciously called, and an idea of *predilection* with respect to God who predestines or calls. A sort of pleonasm sometimes occurs to accentuate this twofold idea : " The Lord thy God hath chosen thee out of all the nations to be his special people." If all men were predestinated, they would not be *elected* in the peculiar sense employed in Scripture. Consequently, predestination does not necessarily presuppose election, but election necessarily presupposes predestination : " God hath blessed us with every kind of spiritual blessings, in heavenly places in Christ, as he chose us in him before the foundation

[1] I Cor. ii, 7 ; Rom. viii, 29, 30 ; Eph. v, 5, 14. To *predestinate* is used also in Acts iv, 28, in the sense of to " decree."

of the world, that we should be holy and unspotted in his
sight by predestinating us (*or* having predestinated us) to be
his children by adoption through Jesus Christ, according to
the good pleasure of his will.''[1] Like predestination, election
is eternal, since it exists in the divine decree before the
creation of the world. It takes place " in Christ," in view
of his merits and not independently of him, as Cajetan interprets it for all the saints and, as Catharin thinks, for a class
of elect souls. It has for its object a " holy and unspotted
life before God "; it has not, therefore, for a direct and
immediate aim eternal glory. Finally, it is the source of
spiritual blessings, for the order of execution is conformable
to (καθώς) the order of intention. In the passage which has
just been cited, election is indeed connected with the order of

[1] A. Eph. i, 3. Εὐλογητὸς ὁ Θεὸς καὶ πατὴρ τοῦ Κυρίου ἡμῶν Ἰησοῦ Χριστοῦ,
ὁ εὐλογήσας ἡμᾶς ἐν πάσῃ εὐλογίᾳ πνευματικῇ ἐν τοῖς ἐπουρανίοις ἐν Χριστῷ,

B. (4) καθὼς ἐξελέξατο ἡμᾶς ἐν αὐτῷ πρὸ καταβολῆς κόσμου, εἶναι ἡμᾶς
ἁγίους καὶ ἀμώμους κατενώπιον αὐτοῦ ἐν ἀγάπῃ,

C. (5) προορίσας ἡμᾶς εἰς υἱοθεσίαν διὰ Ἰησοῦ Χριστοῦ εἰς αὐτόν, κατὰ τὴν
εὐδοκίαν τοῦ θελήματος αὐτοῦ,

D. (6) εἰς ἔπαινον δόξης τῆς χάριτος αὐτοῦ ἧς ἐχαρίτωσεν ἡμᾶς ἐν τῷ
ἠγαπημένῳ.

Without troubling ourselves with difficulties of detail, we must first try to
follow the line of thought. The principal idea is expressed in verse 3:
" Blessed be God who hath blessed us." The Apostle then remembers that
these blessings, conferred in time, correspond to the eternal plan of election
(verse 4, καθὼς ἐξελέξατο). He explains this plan by the kindred idea of
eternal predestination (verse 5: προορίσας ἡμᾶς). He concludes by stating
clearly the finality of the divine plan which is the glory of God (verse 6). It will
be noticed that each of these acts is related to Christ: the blessings *in Christ*
(ἐν Χριστῷ), election *in him* (ἐν αὐτῷ), predestination to the adoption of
children *through Jesus Christ* (διὰ Ἰησοῦ Χριστοῦ), the grace conferred
upon us in his beloved Son (ἐν τῷ ἠγαπημένῳ); the reason of which is that
the dominating thought of the Epistle is Christ considered as the centre of
unity of all the faithful.

A. *The blessings* which God pours out upon us are: (*a*) very varied in
their manifestations (ἐν πάσῃ);—(*b*) but they are all of the spiritual order
(πνευματικῇ) because they come from the Holy Spirit and belong to the
domain of the spirit;—(*c*) they are given us in Christ (ἐν Χριστῷ), in so far
as we are united to him and are only one with him;—(*d*) they are in heavenly
places (ἐν τοῖς ἐπουρανίοις) by their origin and destination.—Notice the
connection: εὐλογητός . . . ὁ εὐλογήσας. The blessings of man are to
ascend towards God in proportion as the blessings of God descend towards
man; but while man blesses only in words, God blesses in acts.

B. *Election*, whence the blessings proceed, is: (*a*) before the foundation
of the world (πρὸ καταβολῆς κόσμου), an expression which designates eternity
(John xvii, 24; 1 Pet. i, 20);—(*b*) it takes place in Christ (ἐν αὐτῷ), and
consequently it is neither logically anterior to the decree of the incarnation,
nor independent of this decree;—(*c*) it has for its *direct* object our sanctification (εἶναι ἡμᾶς ἁγίους, κτλ.), and by this sanctification the acquisition of
heavenly glory.

C. *Predestination* is: (*a*) not an *immediate* destination to eternal glory,
but to filial adoption (εἰς υἱοθεσίαν) and, through the state of sonship, to
the celestial heritage;—(*b*) the sonship, the direct object of the predestination, is through Jesus Christ (διὰ Ἰησοῦ Χριστοῦ) as a meritorious cause,
and in him (εἰς αὐτόν) because we become children by adoption only by

intention; but everywhere else in St Paul it is the order of execution which it concerns. Then election is confounded with the efficacious call and all the faithful are named *elect:* "Labour," says St Peter, "to make your calling and *election* sure."[1] "I endure all things for the sake of the *elect* that they also may be saved," says St Paul.[2]

If predestination is logically subsequent to prescience and is made plain by it, it is all the more necessary to say this of election, which is logically subsequent to or at least synchronous with predestination. God first knows, and then predestines and elects according to his wisdom. Nevertheless, although prescience precedes and predestination follows, there is not a relation of causality between these two acts. In other words, God does not predestinate man to faith *because* God foresees that he will believe: neither faith nor the prevision of faith can be the cause of the predestination, since, on any hypothesis, the prevision of faith presupposes the prevision of grace freely offered. On the other hand, it cannot be strictly said that we believe *because* we are predestinated to believe, for the prevision of faith is logically previous to predestination. Predestination is only one particular aspect of supernatural providence, just as God's prescience is only one particular aspect of his omniscience. Now it is easy to understand that the prevision of a free act—that is to say, its vision in the future, is just as little contrary to liberty as its vision in the present; that the act thus foreseen comes to pass infallibly, yet not by necessity; and that prescience, therefore, effects no change in the course of events and proves only the infinite perfection of an intelligence destined by its very nature to perceive all truth.[3]

3. In general, the redeeming plan has our earth for its horizon, and comprises only the human race. Sometimes,

---

being united to and associated with the Son. Observe the force of the compound verb in the middle voice (ἐξελέξατο): he has chosen us for himself (ἐλέξατο, middle voice) from amongst several others (ἐξ).

D. One of God's aims (εἰς) in predestinating us to the adoptive sonship in Jesus Christ was the brilliant and glorious manifestation of his grace. The expression is very energetic. God wills his grace to be recognized, admired and praised (εἰς ἔπαινον) by men: and not his grace only, but "the glory of his grace" (δόξης τῆς χάριτος αὐτοῦ), his triumphant grace. This grace is "given us in the beloved Son" (ἐν τῷ ἠγαπημένῳ), and the only point is to know whether this is a question of objective grace, that which is in God and is the principle of his blessings, or of subjective grace, that which is in us and is the form of justification and sanctification. Catholics (St Thomas, Estius, Corn. a Lapide, Bisping, etc.) advocate in general the second, which the Fathers also assume (Chrysostom and the Greek commentators: ἐχαρίτωσεν = ἐπεραστοὺς ἐποίησεν) and the Council of Trent (*Sess.*, vi, cap. 7). Several Protestant exegetes are of the same opinion.

[1] 2 Pet. i, 10.  [2] 2 Tim. ii, 10.
[3] On prescience, election, and predestination, see Vol. I, pp. 433-7.

however, the prospect widens out and the divine plan comprehends the universality of beings, making the whole of creation converge towards Christ :

> That in all things he may hold the primacy : because in him it hath pleased (the Father) that all fulness should dwell ; and through him to reconcile all things unto himself, making peace through the blood of his cross, both as to the things that are on earth and the things that are in heaven.[1]

The dominant idea of the passage, as well as that of the entire Epistle, is the primacy of Christ. He is to be *first in all* because *all fulness* dwells in him. Let us give to this expression its broadest meaning, since St Paul does not think it expedient to limit it. It will then be the fulness of being as well as the fulness of graces. In order to have the primacy in everything, Christ must be without a peer in the two orders of grace and nature. And this primacy shines forth prominently in the fact that, through his mediation, God reconciles and pacifies all things. God does not reconcile them to himself, but reconciles them between themselves *through* Christ, by directing them *towards* him, as to their final end, and by making them converge *towards* him, as to their common centre. We have no right to refuse its proper value to the particle compounded with the verb to *re*concile, which is that of a *return* to a previous state of concord before the

---

[1] Col. i, 19-20.  *Cf.* Lightfoot, *Colossians.*

| | |
|---|---|
| 19. ὅτι ἐν αὐτῷ εὐδόκησεν<br> πᾶν τὸ πλήρωμα κατοικῆσαι | (A) 19. *quia in ipso complacuit,*<br> *omnem plenitudinem inhabitare,* |
| 20. καὶ δι' αὐτοῦ ἀποκαταλλάξαι<br> τὰ πάντα εἰς αὐτόν, | (B) 20. *et per eum reconciliare*<br> *omnia in ipsum,* |
| εἰρηνοποιήσας διὰ τοῦ αἵματος<br> τοῦ σταυροῦ αὐτοῦ, δι' αὐτοῦ, | (C) *pacificans per sanguinem*<br> *crucis ejus,* |
| εἴτε τὰ ἐπὶ τῆς γῆς<br> εἴτε τὰ ἐν τοῖς οὐρανοῖς. | (D) *sive quae in terris*<br> *sive quae in coelis sunt.* |

(*a*) *The subject of the phrase* can be only God, named in verse 15, and, moreover, easy to understand with a verb like εὐδόκησεν. To make Christ the subject is to create inextricable confusion without any motive for so doing.  The adoption of πᾶν τὸ πλήρωμα as the subject is still more arbitrary. For how can we then explain the participle εἰρηνοποιήσας in the masculine ?

(*b*) *The signification* of πᾶν τὸ πλήρωμα is not exactly that of πᾶν τὸ πλήρωμα τῆς θεότητος (Col. ii, 9), and is not to be restricted to the special sense of a plenitude of graces (*cf.* John i, 14) ; it is at the same time the plenitude of being and of spiritual gifts.

(*c*) *All the personal pronouns refer to Christ*, δι' αὐτοῦ marking his mediatory action, ἐν αὐτῷ the moral cause, εἰς αὐτόν the final cause. If, in this last case, Paul had had God in view, as certain exegetes think, he would have employed the reflective form, εἰς ἑαυτόν, much more necessary here to avoid a misunderstanding than in 2 Cor. v, 18, 19. Moreover, when he wishes to express reconciliation with God he always uses the dative (Rom. v, 10; 2 Cor. v, 18, 19, 20), never the accusative with εἰς.

(*d*) *The verb* εἰρηνοποιεῖν, extremely rare, is found only in Prov. x, 10, where it is intransitive, and in Stobaeus (*Ecl. phys.*, i, 52) where it is transitive.  The transitive meaning of *to pacify* is perfectly admissible, since there is given us the analogy of the similar compounds ὁδοποιεῖν and λογοποιεῖν con-

appearance of sin.    Henceforth all things recover their primitive unity, since they all come back under the hegemony of Christ.

The condition or resultant of the reconciliation of beings is their pacification. Paul does not speak of a *mutual* pacification of the things of heaven *with* those of earth—the expression which he uses is opposed to it—but speaks of a *general* pacification of all beings among themselves, *whether* on earth *or* in heaven.    All beings are pacified as well as reconciled *in* Christ, who is their centre of gravity and their point of convergence.

In the parallel passage the field of vision remains as wide, but the union of all beings under the sceptre of the incarnate Word is marked in it by a still more definite characteristic.

> Blessed be the God and Father of our Lord Jesus Christ . . . who hath made known unto us the mystery of his will (according to his good pleasure, which he hath purposed in him, in the dispensation of the fulness of times) to re-establish all things in Christ, that are in heaven and on earth.[1]

The object of the mystery or divine secret is expressed in Greek by a compound word which has given rise to different but not incongruous interpretations. The Latin commenta-

structed with an accusative, the first by Aristotle (*Rhetor.*, I, i, 2), the second by Thucydides (vi, 38). It is, therefore, natural to regard the clause D as dependent on C, and to translate it *pacifying . . . what is on the earth and what is in heaven*, instead of making C a parenthesis, beyond which the sentence B would continue. This construction is very simple, was adopted by Chrysostom, and eliminates every difficulty.

(*e*) Those who understand by ἀποκαταλλάξαι a reconciliation *with* God ought to understand by τὰ πάντα *only* rational creatures. Then the *things on earth* (τὰ ἐπὶ τῆς γῆς) would denote men, and the *things in heaven* (τὰ ἐν τοῖς οὐρανοῖς) the angels. There would remain to be explained how Christ reconciles the angels with God.

[1] Eph. i, 9, 10. *Cf.* Haupt, *Meyers Kommentar.*

| | |
|---|---|
| 9. γνωρίσας ἡμῖν τὸ μυστήριον τοῦ θελήματος αὐτοῦ, | (A) 9. *Ut notum faceret nobis sacramentum voluntatis suae,* |
| κατὰ τὴν εὐδοκίαν αὐτοῦ, ἣν προέθετο ἐν αὐτῷ | (B) *secundum beneplacitum ejus, quod proposuit in eo,* |
| 10. εἰς οἰκονομίαν τοῦ πληρώματος τῶν καιρῶν, | (C) 10. *in dispensatione plenitudinis temporum,* |
| ἀνακεφαλαιώσασθαι τὰ πάντα ἐν τῷ Χριστῷ, | (D) *instaurare omnia in Christo,* |
| τὰ ἐπὶ τοῖς οὐρανοῖς καὶ τὰ ἐπὶ τῆς γῆς. | (E) *quae in coelis et quae in terra sunt.* |

(*a*) *Construction of the phrase.*—Grammatically, the clause C could depend either on γνωρίσας or on μυστήριον or on ἀνακεφαλαιώσασθαι or on προέθετο ἐν αὐτῷ. The last construction is indisputably the most natural and satisfying and also the one most commonly accepted. The meaning will be therefore : " God formed in himself this plan with a view to the dispensation which the fulness of times brings." In its turn, the clause D can depend on τὸ μυστήριον τοῦ θελήματος αὐτοῦ or on εὐδοκίαν or on προέθετο, or may be only an explanation of the clause C. The first hypothesis is the

tors following the Vulgate and the ancient version, readily adopt the meaning suggested by the verb *instaurare* or *restaurare*. Thus Ambrosiaster writes : " Every creature in heaven and on earth is restored by the knowledge of Christ to the state in which it was created." And St Augustine sees this twofold restoration effected : *in heaven,* when the void made by the fall of the angels is filled by the elect ; *on earth,* when those who are predestinated, freed from the corruption of sin, are invested with eternal glory.[1] This exegesis is of an irreproachable theology, but of a doubtful philology ; for St Paul does not seem to have in view rational beings only, and a return to the primitive state by the reparation of sin does not express his whole thought.

Tertullian, expressly approved by St Jerome, translated the Greek word by *recapitulare.*[2] That is, indeed, the sense of the Greek, and St Irenæus explains it by saying that all things are summed up or epitomized in Christ.[3] This can be understood in three ways : in the *ontological* sense Jesus Christ, God and man, epitomizes in some way the whole

---

best one : ἀνακεφαλαιώσασθαι is then the content of the *mystery* or the divine secret which has been revealed to us, and the sentences B and C, qualifying A (not γνωρίσας, but μυστήριον), form a sort of explanatory parenthesis. The meaning is : *"God has revealed to us the mystery of his will* (conformably to the benevolent design which he conceived in order to execute it in the fulness of times) *to re-establish all things in Christ."*

(*b*) *Meaning of* ἀνακεφαλαιώσασθαι.—This word comes from κεφάλαιον (a neuter adjective, taken substantively, from κεφαλαῖος, "relating to the head "), which signifies ʼwhat is principal or capital "—for example, *the principal person* in a group, or the *capital point* of an affair ; then by extension the *capital,* contrasted with the interest, or the *summary* contrasted with its fuller details. The simple verb κεφαλαιοῦν meant " to sum up, to negotiate *for capital sums,"* sometimes to " depict in general features," oftener " to sum up (the parts)," and, in the passive, " to amount to (so much)"; the compound ἀνακεφαλαιοῦν was frequently used to denote the rhetorical procedure (ἀνακεφαλαίωσις, *recapitulatio*) of summing up a discourse by a final recapitulation. From this came the meaning to " repeat " (*Protevang. Jacobi,* xiii, 1). But these different meanings do not harmonize very well with our text, and Chrysostom's explanation is clearly preferable, if it can be justified. Now we believe it to be irreproachable from the philological point of view. It is true that κεφάλαιον, which sometimes signifies the *head* of fishes, vegetables, etc., is never used to designate the head of the human body, but it signifies in popular speech the *top* or *summit,* and is employed in this sense both for persons and things. Thus the principal philosophers are τὰ κεφάλαια τῶν μαθημάτων (Lucian, *Piscat.,* 14), and the commander-in-chief is τὸ κεφάλαιον τοῦ πολέμου (Appian, *Civ.,* v, 10). Why should not ἀνακεφαλαιοῦν τὰ πάντα ἐν τῷ Χριστῷ signify " to give a crowning touch, a head (not κεφαλή but κεφάλαιον) to all things in the person of Christ," in other words, " to place Christ on the summit of all things," as a principle of unity ? The middle voice is easily explained by the divine intention and by the interest which God takes in exalting his Son above all things.

[1] Augustine, *Enchirid.,* vi ; Ambrosiaster, *Commentary.*
[2] *Contra Marcion.,* v, 17 ; but *De Monogamia* 5 (*reciprocare*).
[3] *Haereses,* III, xvi, 6 ; xviii, 1 ; xxi, 9-10 ; IV, xl, 3 ; V, xx, 2, etc

creation, the world of spirits and the world of bodies; in the *soteriological* sense Christ epitomizes the whole scheme of redemption, since the prophecies all have in him their fulfilment, and all the work of God tends towards him as to its ultimate goal; from the *representative* point of view, Christ can epitomize all beings endowed with reason, as Adam comprised in himself the whole of humanity, of which he was the father.

If these considerations please the grammarians, they do not wholly satisfy the exegete. It is true that Christ realizes in his person the prophecies and metaphors of the old Covenant, and that his double nature contains admirably the highest qualities of all beings; but the general affirmation of our text is not the less limited by it in a very arbitrary manner, and this does not agree well with the recognized object of the Epistle to the Ephesians, which is to present Christ as a principle of universal union. Hence the best interpreters restrict Paul's thought still more, saying, for example, with St John Chrysostom: " God has given Christ to be the Head of all beings, both angels and men. In this way the union, the perfect connection, is formed when all things are grouped under only one head and receive from on high an indissoluble bond. . . ." The sin of the first man, we are told by St Paul, had produced throughout the whole of nature disorder, a division and a conflict of hostile tendencies. Jesus Christ re-establishes concord there—or at least brings harmony into it—because he is the natural chief of all rational beings and the dominating centre of the material creation.

We perceive now the close relations between our two texts, the first reading of which seemed to reveal some divergences. In both the plan of redemption, extending beyond our sphere, embraces both earth and heaven : in both Christ is a mediator of peace and an instrument of union, and he is so as man, in the fulness of the times; in both there is indicated—or insinuated—the return to a primitive state of harmony and concord; finally, in both the cosmic role of Christ serves as a prelude to the reconciliation of the pagans with God and to the reunion of the Jews and Gentiles in one and the same mystical body.

Even as man, Jesus Christ has, therefore, a kind of cosmic role; he is the head of the angels and has dominion over all creation. If we think of the disorder produced by sin in the entire work of God and of the harmony which the presence of Christ restores to it, we see that this cosmic role is in some way closely related to soteriology.[1] It is a sort of cosmical

---

[1] All creatures participate *to a certain degree* in the blessings of redemption. The glorification of man sheds its influence morally over the whole universe. For this idea see Rom. viii, 20, 21.

reaction of the incarnation and a sudden enlargement of the horizon contemplated by the Apostle, whose gaze does not usually go beyond the salvation of men.

### III—Providential Preparations

1. The First Stage of Humanity. 2. The Era of Promise. 3. The Régime of the Law. 4. The Elements of the World. 5. The Fulness of the Times.

1. The plan of salvation having been once decided, was it necessary to defer its execution? Since man cannot rise again alone, of what use is it to let him make a trial of his impotence? What glory can a delay, fatal to so many victims, bring to God? It is said in reply that the mission of Christ, having a retroactive effect, the value of his redeeming death is therefore imparted to previous generations. As there were righteous men before Jesus Christ, and as they could have been righteous only by the universal Mediator of grace, the saints of the ancient Covenant are the anticipatory results of Calvary. But, if the Apostle authorizes us to draw these conclusions, he does not draw them himself. He is content to appeal to the "purpose" of God which unrolls itself in "the course of ages";[1] at most, he invokes the providential necessity of letting the times come to their fulness and of allowing the human race to reach its majority.[2] It is a law of nature to advance by degrees to the stage of perfection, and man comes to maturity only by passing through childhood and youth. God has not disdained to adapt himself to these harmonious conditions, because they make his mercy and wisdom still more evident. He will, therefore, lead man to his ultimate goal by four successive stages : the law of nature, the time of the promises, the period of the Covenant, and the era of grace. Thus providence leads humanity onward by progressive degrees. This truly biblical idea, with which two of the most beautiful books that ever issued from the hands of men were inspired, is what it is agreed to call, in St Paul, the philosophy of history, and which could be more justly named his theology of providence.

The creation of the first human pair opens the religious history of humanity. St Paul does not tell us what would have been man's condition on the earth if he had not sinned. He does not like, any more than do his colleagues, to explore the nebulous regions of possibilities and hypotheses, and he rarely directs his gaze beyond the actual horizon. It is

---

[1] Eph. iii, 11 : κατὰ πρόθεσιν τῶν αἰώνων.

[2] Compare the expressions τὸ πλήρωμα τοῦ χρόνου (Gal. iv, 4), τὸ πλήρωμα τῶν καιρῶν (Eph. i, 10), and reread the famous passage about the role of the schoolmaster, tutors and stewards (Gal. iii, 23–iv, 7).

sufficient for him to refer us to the recital of Genesis, attributing man's loss of the divine friendship, death, and the inclination to evil to Adam's disobedience. He makes no allusion to a primitive revelation; for the *revelation* by which the pagans perceived the attributes of God in the mirror of the sensible world is a natural revelation, inherent in man's intelligence,[1] and the knowledge which they had of the eternal law was only the verdict of their conscience and their reason.[2] The solicitude, of which the pagans were constantly the object, even in their worst errors, that solicitude which had for its immediate aim to incite them to seek God, and for its final motive to lead them to him,[3] could be called supernatural providence only if it had been first proved that there is none other in the present order. It is by virtue of the same providence that God keeps them, as well as the Jews, under the dominion of sin. He intends to show mercy to them all.[4]

If it is said elsewhere that God "in past ages let all the Gentiles walk in their own ways,"[5] that he delivered them over to their perverse instincts and their depraved senses,[6] this cannot be understood as a total and absolute abandonment, since it is affirmed in the same passages that God has not ceased to bear witness of himself by his benefits,[7] that he remains the God of the Gentiles as well as of the Jews,[8] and that he intends to profit by their misery and even by their wickedness to draw them from the abyss.[9] The allegory of the good olive and the wild olive[10] shows clearly that the Jews had received from the heavenly Gardener special care, but does not allow us to conclude that the wild olive had been deprived of all care. On the contrary, the natural education of the Gentiles sometimes approached the supernatural education with which the chosen race was favoured. In both cases the moral and religious institutions which formed a prelude to the Gospel, however different they were, are ranged under the same concept of elementary doctrines, similar to an alphabet which the world, still in its infancy, was trying to decipher.[11]

The preparation of the Gentiles for faith may appear chiefly negative; but the spread of Christianity in pagan countries proves that it was none the less efficacious on that account. The contempt inspired by the absurd and indecent crowd of gods in the Greco-Roman pantheon, the disgust produced in the long run by unbridled corruption, the satiety of vice which little by little took possession of virtuous souls,

---

[1] Rom. i, 20. See Vol. I, pp. 194-202.
[2] Rom. ii, 14, 15.
[3] Acts xvii, 26, 27.
[4] Rom. xi, 32 ; Gal. iii, 22.
[5] Acts xiv, 16.
[6] Rom. i, 28.
[7] Acts xiv, 17.
[8] Rom. iii, 29.
[9] Rom. v, 20, 21.
[10] Rom. xi, 24.
[11] Gal. iv, 9 ; Col. ii, 8.

the intellectual confusion brought about by the utter failure of the philosophies, the aspiration towards a nobler religious ideal, the awakening of conscience, the vague suspicion of the unknown God, were all so many silent preachers, which cleared the way for the heralds of the Gospel.

2. Between the state of nature and the régime of the Law is inserted the age of promise. Its beginning can be sought in the first announcement of a redeemer, which was made the day after the fall, or in the hope given to Noe after the flood; but we know that the Apostle dates it from Abraham, who personifies it. The promise is almost always defined as a function of the Law.

> Why then was the Law? It was added because of transgressions, until the seed should come to whom he made the promise, being ordained by angels in the hand of a mediator. Now a mediator is not of one but God is one.[1]

---

[1] Gal. iii, 19, 20: Τί οὖν ὁ νόμος; τῶν παραβάσεων χάριν προσετέθη, ἄχρις ἂν ἔλθῃ τὸ σπέρμα ᾧ ἐπήγγελται, διαταγεὶς δι᾽ ἀγγέλων ἐν χειρὶ μεσίτου. ὁ δὲ μεσίτης ἑνὸς οὐκ ἔστιν, ὁ δὲ Θεὸς εἷς ἐστιν.—There will arise later on the question of the aim and end of the Law, but here we are concerned only with its promulgation and with the office of mediator.—Διατάσσειν νόμον is not properly to compose or draw up a law, but to give notice of it, to promulgate it. Two kinds of agents had concurred in the solemn promulgation of the Law: the angels and Moses. For the angels, cf. Deut. xxxiii, 2 (in the version of the Septuagint: ἐκ δεξιῶν αὐτοῦ ἄγγελοι μετ᾽ αὐτοῦ); Acts vii, 38 and vii, 53 (ἐλάβετε τὸν νόμον εἰς διαταγὰς ἀγγέλων); Heb. ii, 2 (ὁ δι᾽ ἀγγέλων λαληθεὶς λόγος is evidently the Law); Josephus, Antiq., XV, v, 3; Eisenmenger, Entdecktes Judentum, vol. i, pp. 309-310 (ridiculous stories of the Rabbis).—The name of mediator was the recognized title of Moses, Deut. v, 5 (κἀγὼ εἱστήκειν ἀνὰ μέσον κυρίου καὶ ἀνὰ μέσον ὑμῶν); Lev. xxvi, 46; Ex. xxxi, 18; Philo, Vita Mos., iii, 19 (Mangey, i, 160); Josephus, Antiq., XV, v. 3; Assumptio Mosis (in Fabricius, Cod. Pseudep. V.T., vol. i, p. 845: ἐθεάσατό με ὁ Θεὸς πρὸ καταβολῆς κόσμου εἶναί με τῆς διαθήκης αὐτοῦ μεσίτην); Aboth, by R. Nathan, i, 1 (Legem, quam Deus Israelitis dedit, nonnisi per manus Mosis dedit) and the texts quoted by Schoettgen (Horae, 738). The name of Mediator of the new Covenant, given to Jesus by Heb. viii, 6; ix, 15; xii, 24 (cf. Acts vii, 38) presupposes that Moses is the mediator of the ancient one. The mediator of whom St Paul speaks in reference to the Law is, therefore, certainly Moses. If the word μεσίτης has not the definite article, it is because Paul does not emphasize the person of the mediator, but his quality of mediator. It is necessary to translate "by means of a mediator," who is, indeed, Moses, but could be any other person without changing the reasoning of the Apostle, for all his argument aims at the meaning of the word mediator. The δέ (ὁ δὲ μεσίτης, verse 20) is not a mere particle of transition; nor is it adversative or limiting, but argumentative and should be translated by now (atqui). The definite article in ὁ μεσίτης indicates the kind, the generic notion, the content of the idea of mediator (cf. John x, 11; 2 Cor. xii, 12); it is no longer the mediator Moses, it is the mediator in general, any mediator whomsoever. This being settled, the meaning of the mysterious verse 20 can be only this: "Now the mediator is not [mediator] of only one [contracting party]; but God is one only." In the promise, God is only one and the promise depends only on him; in the Law, God is not one only, since there is a mediator. Hence, from this point of view, the promise has conditions of stability which

This last phrase must be very obscure to have suggested hundreds of explanations to the exegetes. However, as most of the commentators suppose, contrary to all the evidence, that the mediator here is Jesus Christ, and as almost all the others pay more attention to the words themselves than to the context, the number of really permissible interpretations is reduced remarkably. The mediator of the Law is not Jesus Christ, but Moses, and the aim of St Paul is not to show the advantage of the Law, but its imperfection and its instability. The inferiority of the Law, when compared with the promise, appears from merely contrasting them: the promise is a testament, the Law is a contract; the promise is absolute, the Law is conditional; the promise comes from God without an intermediary, the Law is promulgated by the mediator; the promise is confirmed by God with an oath, the Law is prepared and transmitted by the angels. Consequently, the promise is immutable, the Law is susceptible of abrogation; the promise, made with no temporal limit, is eternal, the Law, given under the reservation of the promise, is transient; the promise pledges the fidelity of God absolutely, the Law pledges the fidelity of God only in proportion to the fidelity of the people. All this may be summed up in the following formula: " The mediator," by his nature, " is not a mediator of one " contracting party. Wherever he comes in, there is a bilateral contract which, subordinated to two different wills, can be cancelled;

---

the Law has not. This quite simple meaning is adopted by the majority of modern commentators, Catholic (Bisping, Cornely, etc.) and Protestant (Lightfoot, Perowne, Sieffert, Reuss, etc.). The following is Reuss's commentary: " Whoever speaks of a *mediator* speaks of two contracting parties and consequently of two wills, which, even while uniting momentarily, can at other times be opposed to each other. A law promulgated by mediation is therefore always something uncertain and imperfect; while the promise, emanating from God *only*, having his will as its unique source and guarantee, is incomparably more certain and therefore more exalted. The Law could not therefore in any case be superior to the promises." The other exegetes mentioned above say the same thing more or less clearly. Several among them (Cornely, Sieffert, etc.) try to reconstruct the Apostle's argument by regarding the first as a major, and the second as a minor, proposition, with the conclusion understood. Cornely states it thus: *Legislatio per mediatorem Moysen data contractum constituit bilateralem, qui benedictiones conditioni legis impletae alligat; atqui promissiones Abrahae seminique ejus dictae utpote contractus unilateralis, benedictiones nulli conditioni alligant; ergo Lex in promissionum locum succedere easque abrogare non potuit.* Whatever one may think of the soundness of this syllogism, it is better to see in our text not an incomplete syllogism, but an antithesis: the Law, given by a mediator, is a *covenant* (διαθήκη in sense of בְּרִית); the promise, made without a mediator, is a *testament* (διαθήκη in the usual sense). In the consequences to be drawn from this contrast, it is essential to observe that St Paul does not propose here to exalt the Law above the promise, but on the contrary to make prominent the advantages of the promise in respect to the Law.

"but," in the promise, made by God with no restrictions or conditions, "God is the only one" responsible; no one can invalidate his irrevocable decision, and he owes it to himself not to withdraw it to the detriment of those interested. It follows that the Law, coming later than the promises, can neither abolish nor modify them; while the promise of God carries in itself its own guarantee.

St Luke, St Paul, and the author of the Epistle to the Hebrews are the only ones to speak of the promise in its technical sense. They understand by it the whole of the gracious prospects of the future revealed to the father of the faithful for him and for his race: the possession of a permanent abode, a progeny more numerous than the stars in the sky and the grains of sand in the desert, and, finally, above all, a blessing which was to flow out upon all the nations of the earth.[1] In the widest sense, the promise includes all the messianic blessings until their complete realization in heaven. As the object of it is at the same time single and multiple, the sacred authors speak sometimes of several promises and at other times of only one;[2] but it is certain that all the promises have their fulfilment in Jesus Christ: "It is by virtue of the promise that God has raised up to Israel a saviour Jesus . . . for all the promises of God are in him. Yea, therefore also [we say] by him *Amen* to the glory of God" in praise and thanksgiving.[3]

Who are the true heirs of the promise? At first sight the answer seems an easy one. Is not the possession of the promises one of the privileges of Israel?[4] Were not the Gentiles strangers to the promise, and therefore without hope?[5] Is not Christ the "minister of the circumcision to [prove] the truth of God, to confirm the promises made unto the Fathers?"[6] But, on the other hand, the Gentiles, when they have become Christians, are fully entitled to be co-partners of the promise,[7] and the Apostle affirms on several occasions that the promise was originally destined for them.[8] In order to solve the contradiction, it is necessary

[1] The three principal promises made to Abraham are : that of the promised land (Gen. xii, 7 ; xiii, 15 ; xv, 18 ; xxvi, 4), that of an innumerable posterity (Gen. xii, 2 ; xiii, 16 ; xv, 5 ; xxii, 17), that of the blessings (Gen. xii, 3 ; xviii, 18 ; xxii, 18 ; xxvi, 4).—In the New Testament the *promise* is often referred to Abraham (Rom. iv, 13-16 ; Gal. iii, 8-9, 16-18 ; Heb. vi, 15 ; xi, 9 ; Luke i, 54, 55, 73). The idea nearest to it in the Old Testament is Ps. cxiv, 8-9 : "He hath remembered his *covenant* for ever . . . which he made to Abraham and his oath to Isaac." Again the promise is regarded under the form of a covenant (בְּרִית). It is true that between the promise and the covenant there are many relations, which the Greek word διαθήκη comprises at the same time. *Cf.* Gal. iii, 15-17 ; Heb. ix, 16, 17.

[2] The promise (Rom. iv, 13, 20 ; ix, 8, 9 ; Gal. iii, 17, 29 ; iv, 23-28, etc.); the promises (Rom. ix, 4 ; xv, 8 ; 2 Cor. i, 20 ; Gal. iii, 16, 21, etc.).

[3] 2 Cor. i, 20.  
[4] Rom. ix, 4.  
[5] Eph. ii, 12.  
[6] Rom. xv, 8.  
[7] Eph. iii, 6.  
[8] 2 Cor. vii, 1 ; Gal. iv, 28, etc.

to discover the principle, according to which the blessings bequeathed to Abraham may be distributed and imparted. This is the triumph of the dialectician, trained in the subtleties of the schools. Paul calls attention to three remarkable peculiarities in the history of the promise. The promise does not extend to all the children of Abraham : it passes first to Isaac, with the exclusion of Ishmael, and then to Jacob, with the exclusion of Esau.[1] The principle of this difference is that of election, of the free choice of God : the carnal posterity will not inherit the blessings, but the spiritual posterity. In the second place, the promise made to Abraham is universal, since all nations are to be blest in him.[2] The principle of this extension is faith : those who shall share the faith of the father of the faithful will be the true sons of Abraham. Finally, the promise is collective, for it concerns not each one of the patriarch's descendants, but his race, his seed.[3] The principle of this collective relation is union with Christ, the unique source of the blessings ; the true heirs of Abraham are, therefore, not the Jews but Christians, in so far as they form with Christ one and the same mystical person, the spiritual lineage of Abraham. Thus the promise possesses three characteristics which liken it to the Gospel. Like that, it is universal ; like that, it is based upon faith ; like that, it is dependent on grace. The promise is the Gospel seen in perspective, and the Gospel is the promise realized.

3. If such are the prerogatives of the promise, does not the régime of the Law, instead of being a step forward, mark a retrogression in the progress of humanity? This objection has occurred to the mind of the Apostle, and he replies to it as follows : " What then? Do we (Jews) excel them (the Gentiles)? No, not entirely."[4] There are two points in which the equality exists and in which the Jews cannot boast of any privilege : the domination of sin and the mode of justification by faith ;[5] but that does not do away with all difference. " What advantage, then, hath the Jew? Or what is the profit of circumcision? Much in every way. First, indeed, because the words of God were committed to them."[6] Is it nothing to be the depositaries of the revelation? Divine revelation is a light for the intelligence and a guide for the will. The misuse of a blessing does not diminish its value. But the revelation is not all ; it is for the Jews the origin or the accompaniment of other honorary privileges.

---

[1] Rom. ix, 8.                [2] Gal. iii, 8.                [3] Gal. iii, 16.
[4] Rom. iii, 9 : οὐ πάντως means *non omnino* (not wholly) and not *nequaquam*. It is not a total negation, but a restriction.
[5] Gal. ii, 16 ; Rom. i, 21-24, 30 ; Rom. iii, 9, 23.
[6] Rom. iii, 1, 2. See Vol. I, pp. 203-4.

They are Israelites; to whom belongeth the adoption as of children and the glory and the covenants and the giving of the Law and the [legal] service of God and the promises: whose are the fathers and of whom, according to the flesh, is born Christ, God over all, blessed for ever.[1]

These nine prerogatives epitomize their pre-eminence. They are *Israelites*—that is, they bear the name of one of the greatest servants of Jehovah; this name, chosen by God himself, is not a mere national appellation; it is a glorious title, of which the Jews were always proud, which St Paul himself lays claim to with pride and does not fear to apply to Christians.—As a people specially chosen by God, they are *children by adoption;* God was able to say of them through the mouths of the prophets: "Israel is my first-born son;" this adoption, while collective, is none the less a precious source of divine blessings.—Jehovah dwells in the

[1] Rom. ix, 4:

| | |
|---|---|
| οἵτινές εἰσιν Ἰσραηλῖται | (A) *Qui sunt Israelitae,* |
| ὧν ἡ υἱοθεσία | (B) *quorum adoptio est filiorum,* |
| καὶ ἡ δόξα | (C) *et gloria,* |
| καὶ αἱ διαθῆκαι | (D) *et testamentum,* |
| καὶ ἡ νομοθεσία | (E) *et legislatio,* |
| καὶ ἡ λατρεία | (F) *et obsequium,* |
| καὶ αἱ ἐπαγγελίαι, | (G) *et promissa:* |
| ὧν οἱ πατέρες | (H) *quorum patres,* |
| καὶ ἐξ ὧν ὁ Χριστός. | (I) *et ex quibus est Christus.* |

(A) *Israelites.* St Paul is proud of this name (2 Cor. xi, 22 ; *cf.* Gal. ii, 15 ; Phil. iii, 3-5), the origin of which is glorious (Gen. xxxii, 28 ; Eccli. xvii, 15 : μερὶς κυρίου Ἰσραήλ ἐστιν. *Cf.* Psalm. *Sal.*, x, 7 ; xiv, 3 ; xvii, 50-51 ; *Jub.*, xxxiii, 18, etc.). This name will pass to the Christians (Gal. vi, 16).

(B) Ex. iv, 22 : *filius meus primogenitus Israel. Cf.* Deut. xiv, 1 ; xxxii, 6 ; Jer. xxxi, 9 ; Os. xi, 1.

(C) The supernatural splendour which at times surrounded the ark of the covenant in the desert (Ex. xvi, 10 ; xxiv, 16 ; xl, 34) and in the Temple (1 Kings viii, 14 ; x, 18 ; Ezech. i, 28 ; Heb. ix, 5), and which was the visible sign of the presence of God in the midst of his people, is called in Hebrew כְּבוֹד יְהֹוָה and is translated by δόξα (*gloria*). It is the שְׁכִינָה of the Rabbis. See Weber, *Jüdische Theol.*[2], pp. 185-190.

(D) Instead of the singular *testamentum*, it should be the plural, for the covenants (διαθῆκαι) were manifold : with Noe (Gen. vi, 18 ; ix, 9), with Abraham (Gen. xv, 18 ; xvii, 2, 7, 9), with Moses (Ex. ii, 24).

(E) *Legislatio* (νομοθεσία) denotes the whole of the Law of Moses. It forms part of the revelation (Rom. ii, 2 : *eloquia Dei*), of which the Jews have a right to be proud.

(F) The word *obsequium* translates λατρεία, which signifies the *divine worship* instituted by Moses by God's command. Simeon the Just (*Pirgê Aboth*, i, 2) said that the three supports of the world are the Law, *divine worship* and charity.

(G) On the promises, see above, pp. 96-9.

(H) Their great ancestors, Abraham, Isaac and Jacob (Acts iii, 13 ; vii, 32), were for the Jews a subject of pride, which was fundamentally legitimate, but excessive in its manifestations. The *Apocalypse of Baruch* (xxi, 24) affirms that the world was created for them. Already Ezechiel had reduced these pretensions (xiv, 14) which Jesus Christ never ceased to combat (Matt. iii, 8, 9 ; John viii, 33).

midst of his people and visibly manifests his presence by the *glory,* that supernatural splendour which at times enveloped the mercy-seat of the ark and recalled the luminous cloud that guided the Israelites across the desert.—Heirs of the patriarchs and, like them, an object of special divine favour, the Hebrews inherit also the *convenants* concluded between God and the holy men of the past, Noah, Abraham, and Moses; and these covenants, which guarantee the faithfulness of God, are for them a pledge of protection and assistance.—They alone, among all the nations of the earth, possess a *Law* come down from heaven and transmitted through the ministry of angels; if the Torah was a burden for them, it was also a supreme distinction: "God has not acted in the same way towards the other nations and has never revealed to them his judgements."—Together with the Law is revealed also the lawful *worship* of God, the only one agreeable to him, since it is the only one inspired and sanctioned by him, the only one which adds to its intrinsic worth a figurative signification which elevates and ennobles it.—The Hebrews are still in a special sense the retainers of the *promises* made by God to humanity; as these promises concern the Messiah, and as the Messiah is to be born among them, they have in some way the patrimony of them.—It is also for them a title of glory to have descended from these *patriarchs* whom God honoured most with his friendship; the glory of the Father is poured out upon the children, and the family shares in the celebrity of each of its members; although St Paul combats the exaggerated sentiment of the Jews in this respect, he does not dispute its principle: "If the root is sound, the branches will be equally so."—Finally, the climax of honour is that of being, according to the flesh, kinsmen of Christ, the Messiah, the God-man.

What distinguishes the Hebrews especially from other peoples is that they are the guardians of the revelation and have received the Law as their guide. When St Paul speaks of the Law, he always means the Mosaic Law; he knows no other, although he sometimes gives by analogy the name of law to other moral forces. Now—and on this point the Apostle never changed his opinion—the Law is good, just, noble, holy, spiritual, and given by God. It is not absolutely perfect, in the sense that nothing better could be imagined, but it is excellent, since it is summed up in what is the most excellent thing in the world—love; and one cannot impute to it the abuses of which it has been the occasion. Its imperfection appears only if it is compared with something still more perfect, or if one thinks of the troubles which arise from it.[1] This consideration can be formed from four points

[1] On the role, the sanctity and the imperfection of the Law, see Vol. I, pp. 182-4, 224-33.

of view: the historical, the psychological, the metaphysical, and the theological.

Historically, the promise made to the patriarchs is absolute and antecedent to the Law: the Law can, therefore, neither annul nor limit it; nor can justification, which is dependent on the promise, be dependent on the Law. The latter has not cured the Jews of their passions, and has opposed to the flood of evil in the world only a feeble dyke.—More could not be expected from it. For, after all, what is a law? It is at once a light and a barrier; a light that shows us the way and a barrier that forbids us to depart from it; a light inopportune for an irresolute will, a barrier provocative to a perverse will.[1] The law brings a new obligation, but without new assistance; it can, therefore, only manifest, aggravate, and increase sin.[2]—This is a matter of common experience. Man, in presence of a law, experiences instincts of rebellion, and feels at the same time that the aid offered to the law by his reason is not a sufficient counterpoise. He does not do the good which he loves, and he does commit the evil that he abhors. If he does not at all understand this contradictory phenomenon, he at least has no trouble in verifying it. He perceives also that the law is not the cause of evil, but only the occasion of it; but even so, conscious of the insufficiency of the law, he seeks assistance outside of it, and turns towards mercy.[3]—Here comes in the theological principle. One could conceive another order of providence in which the Law would justify and, on this hypothesis, " justice would truly be by the Law."[4] But in the system now prevailing man's salvation depends on grace, and man has no right to boast on that account.[5] Now, if the Law *alone* justified, man could boast of having performed by his own strength a magnificent deed of valour; but in that case we should have no more need of Christ, and " Christ would have died in vain."[6]

While declaring that the Law is " incapable of justifying," Paul, nevertheless, says that " those who have observed the Law shall be justified."[7] He assures us that the Law was given " unto life," and he asserts that it was superadded " to increase transgressions."[8] Is there not a flagrant contradiction in these statements? Not at all. The Law by itself is incapable of justifying, but the Jews were never left with the Law *only*. In giving the Law to the Hebrews, who were already the depositaries of the promises made to Abraham, God wished to confer upon them supernatural life, not by the Law alone (which was incapable of doing that), but by

[1] Rom. vii, 7-9.
[2] Gal. iii, 19; Rom. v, 20.
[3] Rom. vii, 5-25.
[4] Gal. iii, 21.
[5] Gal. vi, 14; Rom. iii, 27; iv, 2; Eph. ii, 9.
[6] Gal. ii, 21.
[7] Gal. iii, 21 (*cf.* Rom. viii, 3).
[8] Rom. vii, 10 and Gal. iii, 19.

grace superadded to the Law, as an external and independent principle. When God saw that his first intention was frustrated by the fault of the Jews, he sanctioned the accomplished fact and wished that sin might abound through the Law in order to make grace more abound.[1] The two finalities are not contradictory because they move along different planes.

It is evident from what precedes that the doctrine of St Paul in relation to the Mosaic Law is one of great complexity. Let us try to indicate its principal features :

As an expression of the divine will, the Law is good, holy, and spiritual ;[2] but, considered in itself, it is only a light illuminating the intelligence without strengthening the will, only a barrier provoking a spirit of revolt without efficaciously repressing it ; it is, therefore, for a corrupt being an accidental cause of transgressions, and it is in this sense that it increases sin and engenders wrath.[3]

From the historical point of view, the Law came after the gratuitous, absolute, universal, and eternal promise, which it could neither annul, supplant, limit, complete, nor restrain.[4] It was, therefore, by its nature temporary and local, destined for a single people and a fixed period of time.

It must not be concluded from this that it was injurious or useless. It was a blessing of God and a prerogative of Israel, not only as a revelation, but as an intimation of the divine will.[5] If it had been faithfully observed, it would have been a source of merits and a cause of justification.[6] This is indeed what God had in view at first in granting it : it was given to lead men to eternal life.[7] For, if by itself it does not confer the privileges of faith and grace, neither does it take them away. It was proposed to a people already in possession of the promise, from which the help necessary for the salutary observation of the Law could be obtained.

This first aim and end of the Law was, however, frustrated by the hard-heartedness of the Jews. The Law indeed opposed only a powerless barrier to the invasion of sin and the flood of evil.[8] Nevertheless, God maintained it for reasons worthy of his wisdom. He made of it a watchful guardian to preserve the Jews from dangerous contacts and a teacher charged with the task of bringing them to Christ. And if the pedagogic role of the Law was chiefly negative, it had none the less the honour of being the depositary of monotheism and of revealed truth.[9]

But it carried in itself many germs of decay, and when the

---

[1] Rom. v, 20.    [2] Rom. vii, 12 (ἅγιος) ; 14 (πνευματικός) ; 16 (καλός).
[3] Rom. v, 15-20 ; Gal. iii, 14.
[4] Gal. iii, 21.    [5] Rom. ix, 4 (νομοθεσία).
[6] Rom. ii, 13.    [7] Rom. vii, 10.    [8] Rom. viii, 3.
[9] Gal. iii, 24 (παιδαγωγὸς ἡμῶν εἰς Χριστόν) ; iii, 23 (ὑπὸ νόμον ἐφρουρούμεθα).

human race should reach maturity,[1] when the moment fixed by God for the emancipation of the world should come,[2] when the hour assigned for the fulfilment of the promise made to the father of the faithful should strike,[3] when Christ, who is its aim and limit, should appear, and when the system of grace, with which it is incompatible, should be inaugurated, the régime of the Law had to die a natural death.

4. Thus humanity in its march onward learns and progresses like a man who is to live for ever. This collective entity, seeking its destiny obscurely and finding it only in Christ, is for St Paul *the world*: the world, which in time past sin invaded,[4] which prides itself in vain upon its wisdom,[5] which God labours with that it may become reconciled to Christ,[6] which he compels to declare itself indebted to divine justice,[7] and which he will one day judge in company with the elect.[8] The learning which it acquires in the course of the centuries and of which it is so proud is, compared to the knowledge of Christ, merely a rudimentary education, like the alphabet which is taught to little children, and St Paul gives to this the significant name of *elements of the world*. Four times, in two distinct texts, the Apostle employs this expression which the context illumines. He writes to the Galatians :

> So we also, when we were children, were in bondage to the *elements of the world*. . . . But then indeed, not knowing God, you served them who by nature are no gods ; but now, after that you have known God, or rather are known by God, how turn you again to the weak and needy *elements*, which you desire to serve again ? You observe days and months and times and years.[9]

---

[1] Gal. iii, 25 : *ubi venit fides jam non sumus sub paedagogo.*
[2] Gal. iv, 4, 5.     [3] Gal. iii, 22.
[4] Rom. v, 12.     [5] 1 Cor. i, 20.
[6] 2 Cor. v, 19.     [7] Rom. iii, 19.     [8] 1 Cor. vi, 2.
[9] Gal. iv, 3 : Οὕτως καὶ ἡμεῖς, ὅτε ἦμεν νήπιοι, ὑπὸ τὰ στοιχεῖα τοῦ κόσμου ἤμεθα δεδουλωμένοι. . . .
8. Ἀλλὰ τότε μὲν οὐκ εἰδότες Θεὸν ἐδουλεύσατε τοῖς φύσει μὴ οὖσι θεοῖς·
9. νῦν δὲ γνόντες Θεόν, μᾶλλον δὲ γνωσθέντες ὑπὸ Θεοῦ, πῶς ἐπιστρέφετε πάλιν ἐπὶ τὰ ἀσθενῆ καὶ πτωχὰ στοιχεῖα, οἷς πάλιν ἄνωθεν δουλεῦσαι θέλετε;
10. ἡμέρας παρατηρεῖσθε κτλ.
A. In verse 3 the first person in the plural (ἡμεῖς, ἦμεν, ἤμεθα) denotes the Jews *only* and not the Jews and Gentiles at the same time. Indeed : (a) ὅτε ἦμεν νήπιοι clearly corresponds to ὁ νόμος παιδαγωγὸς ἡμῶν γέγονεν (iii, 24).—(b) ὑπὸ τὰ στοιχεῖα τοῦ κόσμου ἤμεθα δεδουλωμένοι corresponds no less clearly to ὑπὸ νόμον ἐφρουρούμεθα συγκλειόμενοι (iii, 23) ;—(c) before the fulness of the times the Gentiles were not heirs, even in hope (Eph. ii, 12) ; the Jews alone held the promises (Rom. ix, 4).—It results from this text that the *elements of the world* to which the Jews were subjected represent the *Mosaic institutions*.
B. Verses 8-10 concern Gentile converts, who formerly had served false gods (iv, 8). They wish to *go back* (ἐπιστρέφετε) *again* (πάλιν), to serve

The Apostle's thought is simple : *Formerly, not knowing God, you served beings who had nothing divine in them*; but *now, knowing the true God,* why do you wish to serve such vain things as the elements of the world? The contrast is between the past ignorance and the present knowledge, which renders the judaizing Galatians wholly inexcusable; and the emphasis is on the word " serve," which designates a voluntary subjection. Three details will help us to determine the meaning of the " elements of the world." Before their conversion, the Jews were like young children ( νήπιοι), which always denotes in St Paul a state of imperfect knowledge; but now, enlightened by faith, they have ceased to be pupils and are no more under a pedagogue. Formerly, they were under the yoke and guardianship of the Law; and so were subjected to the elements of the world. To be liberated from the Mosaic Law and to be delivered from the elements of the world is for the Apostle one and the same thing. As to the Gentiles, they also were under the domination of the elements of the world, and St Paul reproaches them, with a persistence not free from pleonasm, with wishing to fall back again into that servitude, because they observe the days, months, seasons, and years. The Galatians did not wish to return to idolatry, nor to a superstitious worship of angels or demons. Nothing in the Epistle suggests this hypothesis; it is everywhere only a question of legal observances or of prescriptions grafted on to the Law. St Paul must, therefore, include under one general notion the Mosaic ritual and the religious customs of the Gentiles, to qualify them all together as " weak and beggarly rudiments." It is the Christian religion which, by comparison, belittles and crushes them.

Those who wish to see in the elements of the world personal beings remind us that they are compared to tutors and superintendents, that they are called poor and feeble, and that the Galatians serve them as they formerly served idols. But these reasons are very weak, and it would be very difficult to take them seriously if they were not advanced with such

---

*once more* (πάλιν) as *formerly* (ἄνωθεν) the *weak and needy elements* (iv, 9). At first sight, one might be tempted to identify these *elements* with idols; but one sees quickly that this identification is absolutely impossible for : (*a*) nothing in the Epistle shows the least propensity on the part of the Galatians to fall back into idolatry ;—(*b*) if it were so, the Apostle would not fail to reprove them for it indignantly, as he so severely blames their inclination for Jewish practices ;—(*c*) moreover, he explains to them clearly what he means by this return : " You observe the days and months and times and years."

To put themselves voluntarily under the yoke of the Law and its rabbinical extension is to fall back into the servitude of former times, although in a different way ; it is to return to the *elements of the world*, to those human and ephemeral institutions from which the Gospel has delivered them.

assurance. For the Law also is compared to tutors and superintendents and even called a pedagogue, and yet is not a person; the Epistle to the Hebrews can mention the infirmity of the Law without for that reason conferring on it personality, and we know that the adjective *poor* (πτωχός) is often applied to things; finally, if the elements of the world assume a personal character from the fact that the Galatians serve them, what shall we say of the text of St Paul : " They serve their belly and not Christ?"

The passage in the Epistle to the Colossians says still more clearly what the elements of the world are :

> Beware lest any man cheat you by philosophy and vain deceit; according to the tradition of men, according to the *elements of the world* and not according to Christ. . . . If then you be dead with Christ to the *elements of this world*, why let laws be imposed on you as though living in the world ? Touch not [you are told], taste not, handle not : which all are unto destruction by the very use, according to the precepts and doctrines of men.[1]

The elements of the world could not be better defined, on the one hand, by their real identity with the tradition of men, and on the other by their opposition to the true doctrine of Christ. The synonymy between *elements of the world* and the *tradition of men* is all the clearer, because for St Paul the world means humanity left to itself or withdrawn from the life-giving influence of Christ, and because the whole context converges towards the idea of a philosophical, traditional, and elementary doctrine, to be corrected by the teaching of the Gospel. Let it not be urged that the Law of Moses,

---

[1] Col. ii, 8: Βλέπετε μή τις ἔσται ὁ συλαγωγῶν διὰ τῆς φιλοσοφίας καὶ κενῆς ἀπάτης, κατὰ τὴν παράδοσιν τῶν ἀνθρώπων, κατὰ τὰ στοιχεῖα τοῦ κόσμου καὶ οὐ κατὰ Χριστόν.

20. Εἰ ἀπεθάνετε σὺν Χριστῷ ἀπὸ τῶν στοιχείων τοῦ κόσμου, τί ὡς ζῶντες ἐν κόσμῳ δογματίζεσθε;

21. Μὴ ἅψῃ, μηδὲ γεύσῃ, μηδὲ θίγῃς· ἅ ἐστι πάντα εἰς φθόραν τῇ ἀποχρήσει, κατὰ τὰ ἐντάλματα καὶ διδασκαλίας τῶν ἀνθρώπων.

In the first part of this text the Apostle affirms the identity of the elements of the world with human traditions and their opposition to Christian teaching ; in the second part he reminds us that the Christian is dead to the elementary institutions of the world, in whatever manner they are expressed, whether as Judaizing practices (verse 9 : feasts, celebrations of the new moon, sabbath days, distinction between pure and impure foods), or as observances inspired by dualistic doctrines (verse 21 : touch not, taste not, handle not).

All the words of verse 20 should be carefully weighed :—(a) *Death with Christ* is, without any doubt, the mystical death of baptism, which puts an end to all our past servitudes, especially to dependence on the Mosaic Law. Cf. Rom. vi, 4 ; vii, 4-6 ; Gal. ii, 19, 20.—(b) *The world* must have the same meaning in both cases, in order that the reasoning may not be defective. It cannot be the physical world, for it is not the business of the Colossians to die to the world thus understood ; hence it is the *moral world*, humanity without Christ, subjected to influences other than those of Christ.—(c) *The word* δογματίζεσθε can only signify " to submit to laws " (in the passive), or better, " to allow laws to be imposed upon you " (in the middle voice, reflexive).

being a divine institution, could not be represented as a
human tradition; for, in fact, the false teachers of Colosse
mingled with the Mosaic observances practices of an extreme
asceticism; and, moreover, the Mosaic prescriptions have
now only the value of purely human traditions, since the
dying Christ has nailed them to his cross.   It is an imperfect
Law which the Gospel abrogates, a shadow which disappears
before the new light; the ancient legislation has had its day.

Even though the Mosaic Law should retain a certain value
for others, it would have no value for the Christian who is
dead in Christ to all past servitudes.   For " by the Law the
Christian is dead to the Law," he lives no longer " in the
world,"[1] which is foreign to the influences of Christ and still
subject to the rudimentary institutions of former times.
Henceforth these outworn restrictions have lost for him their
imperative force.   They are nothing but " human teachings
which are able to have an [unjustified] renown for wisdom,
spontaneous piety, humility, and austerity, but which, in
reality, even while mortifying the body, only feed the flesh,[2]"
the principle opposed to the action of the Holy Spirit upon us.

Mosaic prescriptions, traditions superimposed by the
Rabbis on the code of Sinai, practices suggested by religious
sentiment whether normal or misleading, these are what St
Paul always designates as the elements of the world, and
these are what the coming of Christ, in whom are centred all
the treasures of knowledge and wisdom, dispels like a shadow.

5. This sudden reversal, this startling transformation, is
brought about in the *fulness of the times* or in the *fulness of
time*.[3]   The two expressions are not perfectly synonymous;
the latter denotes the moment when humanity, having
emerged from childhood, and thenceforth fit for stronger and

---

[1] Gal. ii, 19; vi, 14; Col. ii, 20 (τί ὡς ζῶντες ἐν κόσμῳ δογματίζεσθε).

[2] Col. ii, 22, 23.   For the meaning see Vol. I, p. 284, note.

[3] Eph. i, 10: εἰς οἰκονομίαν τοῦ πληρώματος τῶν καιρῶν.   Gal. iv, 4:
ὅτε δὲ ἦλθεν τὸ πλήρωμα τοῦ χρόνου.   The expression πληροῦν χρόνον or
καιρόν signified, even among the classics (Plato, *Leg*., ix, 866A), " to complete
a definite period of time," the measure of time being considered as a kind of
receiver, which is continually filled by the addition of successive moments.—
The meanings of the words χρόνος and καιρός are not identical: χρόνος
refers only to duration, while καιρός means properly " the season, the
occasion"; χρόνος is uniform duration, καιρός is duration distinguished by
variations, such as the seasons of the year, the revolutions of the stars, the
periods of history or of human life.   St Paul says (Gal. iv, 4): ὅτε ἦλθεν τὸ
πλήρωμα τοῦ χρόνου, because he is alluding to the decree of the Father (iv, 2:
ἄρχι τῆς προθεσμίας τοῦ πατρός), fixing a certain period of delay for the
sending of his Son, during which time (iv, 1: ἐφ' ὅσον χρόνον) the human race
is regarded as young, like a child under age.   He says, on the contrary,
(Eph. i, 10): εἰς οἰκονομίαν τοῦ πληρώματος τῶν καιρῶν, because this long
duration is divided into periods, in which the providential action of God is
exercised in different ways.   These καιροί have some correspondence with the
αἰῶνες, Eph. iii, 11; 1 Cor. x, 11; 1 Tim. i, 17; Heb. i, 2.

more virile institutions, enters into possession of its rights, its privileges, and its heritage; the former implies a series of historical periods succeeding one another according to a plan determined in advance, just as the regular cycle of the seasons brings in turn the buds, the flowers, and the fruits. *The fulness of time* is the date freely appointed by divine wisdom; *the fulness of the times* is the coronation of the preparations made by Providence.

# BOOK III
## THE PERSON OF THE REDEEMER

# CHAPTER I

## THE PRE-EXISTENT CHRIST

### I—CHRIST BEFORE THE AGES

1. Paul and Christ.  2. Eternal Pre-existence of Christ.

1. MODERN historians of dogma are sometimes surprised, "after the simpler Christology of the first apostles, to hear St Paul attribute to the Saviour a celestial pre-existence before his terrestrial birth and even a participation in the creation of the world." Their astonishment may be due to an imperfect knowledge or to an inaccurate appreciation of the theology of the first apostles, but the fact remains none the less disconcerting for one who wishes to reduce the grandeur of Christ to human dimensions. And it is still more so if we take account of the two following facts : that St Paul was the first to state the Christian belief positively in writing ; and, secondly, that his Christology was never the subject of controversy. For this fact is undeniable, and is recognized in good faith by the critics who are least inclined to defend the traditional positions. This is what gives so much interest to St Paul's teaching about the person of Christ.

The way in which the converted Pharisee speaks of the lately crucified religious reformer Jesus of Nazareth, whose work and name he but yesterday thought it a glory and a duty to annihilate and abolish, is a strange phenomenon which seems to contradict all the laws of psychology and all the analogies of history. Paul, that proud genius, so conscious of his dignity, so disdainful of the idols of flesh and blood, is in ecstasy and adoration before his Master. He wishes to be his liege-man, his slave ; and also the slave of his brethren for love of him.[1] He allows no one to put him on a level with any created thing. Higher than the heavens, vaster than the universe, more powerful than death, sole victor over sin, the only mediator of grace and the one redeemer of the human race, Christ effaces all else by his splendour, fills everything with his plenitude, and is

[1] Rom. i, 1 ; Gal. i, 10 ; Phil. i, 1 (δοῦλος 'I. X.) ; 2 Cor. iv, 5 (nos servos vestros per Jesum—i.e., propter Jesum, διὰ 'Ιησοῦν).—The title of servant of Christ which applies to all Christians (Eph. vi, 6 ; Col. iv, 12 ; 2 Tim. ii, 24), should be compared with the injunction : Pretio empti estis, nolite fieri servi hominum (1 Cor. vii, 23).

antecedent to the ages.[1] Therefore every knee is to bend before him, in heaven, on earth, and in hell, for the most perfect of the celestial spirits recognize in him their Chief, their Creator, and their God.[2] Such is the picture of Jesus which the Apostle, soon after the passion, sets before the witnesses of his life and death and even before his persecutors and executioners.

What colossal proportions the image of the Crucified suddenly assumes in the mind of Saul? The transcendent character of this image is such that it can grow no more; to the infinite nothing can be added. All our efforts to trace its gradual development remain fruitless. From the first moment of his conversion, Christ is for him the incomparable, the unique; nothing stands above him or beside him. And this is not at the expense of his human nature. Jesus Christ is not a creation of the fancy. He is a very real being, still living in the memory of his disciples, who repeat his words and model their conduct on his own. When Saul became a Christian, *at most* only six or seven years had elapsed since the passion; when he began his public preaching, he was separated from it by scarcely ten years, and he wrote his first Epistles only twenty-two years subsequent to that memorable event. Jesus Christ, only a few years older than himself, was for him, in all the force of the term, a contemporary, whom he might easily have passed in the streets of Jerusalem or under the porticoes of the Temple; he was also a compatriot, if it be true, as St Jerome believes, that Saul's family was of Galilean origin. How is it that he has become his God? Neither the time which had elapsed, nor his Palestinian associates, nor the circumstances of the death of Jesus were favourable to an apotheosis; and the seriousness of Jewish monotheism did not lend itself to the ridiculous deifications which placed a Claudius or a Tiberius in the ranks of the immortals, assigning to them temples, priests, and sacrifices, and making them the peers of the gods of Olympus, who were indeed neither better nor worse.

When the flattery of the degenerate Romans, rivalling oriental adulation, decreed divine honours to the emperors, who accepted them with a certain reserve at first, but later quite shamelessly, the Jews were inflexibly opposed to this impious worship. The adoration of a man, were he king or emperor, was for them the abomination of desolation. It was actually necessary for Rome to yield to their invincible repulsion and to dispense them officially from an act more horrible in their eyes than death. The Christians also showed no less obstinacy in this respect, and often sealed with their

---

[1] Col. i, 18-20 ; Eph. i, 21-23 ; Rom. iii, 23-25 ; 1 Tim. ii, 5.
[2] Phil. ii, 9-11 ; Col. i, 16, 17 ; Rom. ix, 5 ; Tit. ii, 5. The Epistle to the Hebrews and St John have nothing stronger.

blood their refusal to concede to a man the titles and honours reserved for God. In vain did the pagans refuse any comprehension of their scruples, they could never triumph over them. For the Christians, still more than for the Jews, the cult of Cæsar was always the adoration of the Beast; and the temple of the Augusti was the throne of Satan. When St Paul protests that there is for us " only one God, the Father, and only one Lord, Jesus Christ," his profession of faith sounds like the indignant cry of the Christian conscience against the supreme aberration of expiring polytheism. Since that time, all the divine titles, " God, Son of God, God of God, Lord, or Lord God, Saviour, or God the Saviour," had been profaned by the adulation of the people and by the apathy of paganism; but Paul, by applying these terms to the pre-existent Christ, gives them the Jehovistic sense which they have in the Bible.

2. The pre-existence of the Son of God is clearly shown by what we shall have to say concerning his divine nature, his eternal relations to the heart of God, and his active part in the creation of the world; but it is also proved directly by three series of testimonies.

At a certain moment of time Christ " came into the world,[1] he appeared in the flesh;[2] being rich, he became poor, that through his poverty we might be rich."[3] Now it is clear that the exchange of the riches of heaven for the poverty of earth necessarily presupposes a mode of existence previous to the incarnation. Texts like the following : " God, sending his own Son in the likeness of sinful flesh and for sin, condemned sin in the flesh,"[4] or " God sent his Son, born of a woman, made under the Law . . . that we might receive the adoption of sons,"[5] have nothing in common with the biblical phrase : " God sent them a judge or a saviour " ; for, if the mission of the Son coincides with his earthly origin, his existence of necessity precedes it, since it is the likeness of sinful flesh, in other words, human nature, which is the goal of the mission.

Christ is the " firstborn of every creature."[6] It is absolutely impossible that this expression means the " firstborn among creatures " ; it signifies, therefore, " born before every creature " ; which implies first that Christ is not to be ranked in the category of created beings; and, secondly, that he possesses a mode of existence superior to and antecedent to every created being. In order that there

---

[1] I Tim. i, 15 : *X. 'I. ἦλθεν εἰς τὸν κόσμον ἀμαρτωλοὺς σῶσαι.* Not only does he come, but he comes with a *purpose*, which does not allow us to compare his coming with " every man coming into the world."

[2] I Tim. iii, 16.     [3] 2 Cor. viii, 9.     [4] Rom. viii, 3.
[5] Gal. iv, 4.     [6] Col. i, 15. See Vol. I, pp. 288-9.

may be no misunderstanding about this, Paul himself comments on it by saying that Christ "is before all things"; and he gives as a reason for this that "All things were created by him and for him."[1]   As it is necessary to exist before creating, the consequence is clear.

Not only did Christ exist, but he "subsisted in the form of God."[2]   The form of God cannot be acquired any more than it can be lost; it could not be supplanted by the form of a slave added thereto in time: where it is, it is from all eternity.   Therefore, "Jesus Christ was yesterday, is to-day, and will be for ever."[3]   Like the author of the Epistle to the Hebrews, St Paul is accustomed to distinguish in the life of Christ three states or phases: the eternal pre-existence of the Son with the Father, and what might be called his pre-history; his historical appearance on earth in the fulness of time; and the glorious exaltation of the risen Christ.   And it is evident that these three states, succeeding one another with no change of the subject, belong to the same person.

The recent hypothesis which attributes pre-existence to the soul of Christ needs no refutation: the pre-existence of souls was always antipathetic to Jewish thought, and not the slightest trace of it is found in the New Testament; moreover, why should St Paul honour Christ, in contradistinction to all the others, with a pre-existence which, according to this hypothesis, would be common to him and all men?

Some contend that the Apostle was inspired by Philo, and that his Christ is, after all, only the typical man of the Alexandrian philosopher;[4] but as Paul is ignorant of the Hellenist Plato, or in any case borrows nothing from him, and as his realistic

---

[1] Col. i, 16 : τὰ πάντα δι' αὐτοῦ καὶ εἰς αὐτὸν ἔκτισται.
[2] Phil. ii, 6.    [3] Heb. xiii, 8.
[4] A. Hilgenfeld (*Bemerkungen über den paulinischen Christus*, in *Zeitschrift für wiss. Theol.*, xiv, 1871, pp. 188-192) refers at the same time to the ideal man of Philo and to Plato's theory of pre-existent souls; but it is necessary to choose between these two dissimilar conceptions.  If the pre-existent Christ is only the pre-existent soul of Christ, according to the heresy of Apollinarius, he is no longer the ideal man of Philo.  We know that, according to Philo, the creation of the typal man is indicated in Gen. i, 27 (ἐποίησεν ὁ Θεὸς τὸν ἄνθρωπον κατ' εἰκόνα Θεοῦ), and the formation of the real man in Gen. ii, 7 (ἔπλασεν ὁ Θεὸς τὸν ἄνθρωπον χοῦν ἀπὸ τῆς γῆς). This ideal man is not the Logos, the idea of ideas and the archetype of reason, he is the *idea* of man (*cf.* J. Drummond, *Philo Judaeus*, London, 1888, vol. ii, p. 275), and therefore he has no connection with the really pre-existent Christ of St Paul.  Philo is very explicit: the celestial man (ὁ οὐράνιος ἄνθρωπος) is *incorporeal*, the terrestrial man (γήϊνος) has a body (*Leg. allegor.*, i, 12; Mangey, vol. i, p. 49); the latter is composed of a soul and a body; he is man or woman, and mortal; the former is an idea or seal (*i.e.*, the intellectual exemplar, which the artist stamps upon matter), intelligible, incorporeal, neither man nor woman, and immortal by nature (ὁ δὲ κατὰ τὴν εἰκόνα ἰδέα τις ἢ σφραγίς, νοητός, ἀσώματος, οὔτ' ἄρρην οὔτε θῆλυς, ἄφθαρτος φύσει, *De mundi opif.*, 46; Mangey, vol. i, p. 32).  Between this Platonic idea and the pre-existent Christ of St Paul there is nothing in common.  Philo's typal man is not the *second* Adam, but the *first*.

theology stands at the antipodes of the theosophic idealism of Philo, this new opinion completely lacks foundation and does not bear examination.

Other critics concede to us the fact that St Paul actually taught the real pre-existence of Christ, and that it is impossible to deny it without prejudice and dogmatic bias; but of his pre-existent Christ they entertain the strangest idea. According to them, Christ pre-existed, not as God, but as man: a real man, possessing already a luminous, ethereal, immaterial body; a human prototype, a divine image, a divine exemplar, on the model of which all other men will be formed; a celestial man, descended from heaven and destined to return thither after a period of earthly existence; a spiritual man, who is animated by the spirit of God and is himself spirit.[1]  We are also told that Paul borrowed his theory of the pre-existent Christ from the idle fancies of Palestinian Judaism concerning the existence of the Messiah; but this rabbinical conception is a very late one, and, moreover, is understood only as referring to an ideal pre-existence.[2]  Now the principal supporters of the theory which we thus set forth are obliged to recognize that the pre-existent Christ of St Paul is a reality. How could he be anything else than a real being, who creates and preserves the world, who is sent hither by God and exchanges the splendours of heaven for the humiliations of earth? But if Jesus Christ was a man before being born, he must, of course, be relegated to the

---

[1] Holtzmann, *Neutest. Theol.*, vol. ii, p. 82: *Im Geist des Paulus kommt die Vorstellung nur in der Form einer realen Präexistenz vor.*—Holtzmann builds up his strange theory of the *Urmensch* on the fact that Christ—whether pre-existent, historical or glorified—remains identical with himself; but he was man while on the earth, therefore he was man previously. But the mere presentation of this sophism reveals its error. The argument proves only that Christ is one and the same person, under his three phases of existence, but not that he has always been united to one body; for texts like Rom. viii, 3; Gal. iv, 5; Phil. ii, 7; 1 Tim. iii, 16, show most clearly that he assumed a body in time. One cannot without extreme difficulty succeed—if indeed one can do so at all—in forming any idea of the pre-existent Christ of Holtzmann, which is a fleeting image, floating between reality and fancy, and which can be for us, he assures us, only an idea, but which for St Paul is a person.—This hypothesis is excellently stated and refuted by Father Lagrange (*Revue bibl.*, vol. vi, 1897, pp. 468-474): in so far as "the lack of precision in its pretended depth" lends itself to a precise refutation.—Weizsäcker, *Das apost. Zeitalter*[3], p. 121, expresses ideas analogous to those of Holtzmann.

[2] The rabbis admitted indeed that the Messiah *existed* in the mind of God before the creation of the world, but this was by virtue of an *ideal* pre existence in the divine decree of predestination (*cf.* Weber, *Jüdische Theologie*[2] pp. 198, 348, 354). Wholly different is the later conception of the rabbis who, in order to explain the delay in the appearance of the Messiah, said that he *existed* already somewhere, but that God for various reasons kept him in reserve. It is no longer a question here of pre-existence, but of an actual existence in an unknown place (*cf.* Weber, *op. cit.*, p. 355). As to the vision of the Son of Man by Daniel (vii, 13), it is *prophetic*, and moreover implies no eternal pre-existence.

rank of creatures, since God alone is uncreated; and how, then, can St Paul affirm that every created being without exception in heaven and on earth has been created by him and for him? If Jesus Christ was man before being born, how can we explain the fact that he becomes man at his birth? And if Jesus, in rising from the dead, returns to his original state, which he had before his incarnation, what significance has the resurrection? That is what the authors of this curious invention have never tried to tell us, and this stamps their whole hypothesis, in whatever obscurity they envelop it, as absurd.

## II—JESUS CHRIST LORD

1. Our Lord Jesus Christ.  2. The Lord, God's Proper Name.  3. Prayers and Doxologies in Honour of the Lord Jesus.

1. The most concise résumé of Christology is contained in the formula: "Our Lord Jesus Christ, Son of God."[1] Although all the elements of it are anterior to him and go back to the apostolic preaching, it is stereotyped only in St Paul, who gives it an import and fulness of meaning which are of the utmost interest to the student of the history of theology.

In the synoptists the question is to know whether Jesus is or is not the Christ—that is to say, the Messiah, the descendant and antitype of David, the expectation and the hope of Israel. Herod ascertains the place where he is to be born, John the Baptist points him out, the demoniacs proclaim him, Peter confesses him, Jesus himself openly claims this title which epitomizes his mission, and the zealots of the Jews bestow it on him ironically.[2] But while the synoptists make us eyewitnesses, so to speak, of this work of gradual recognition, and while they always maintain a very clear notion of the bond which unites the character of the Messiah

---

[1] The entire formula is found in 1 Cor. i, 9: Πιστὸς ὁ Θεὸς δι᾽ οὗ ἐκλήθητε εἰς κοινωνίαν τοῦ υἱοῦ αὐτοῦ Ἰησοῦ Χριστοῦ τοῦ κυρίου ἡμῶν, and in Rom. i, 4, where υἱοῦ Θεοῦ is in apposition with Ἰησοῦ Χριστοῦ τοῦ κυρίου ἡμῶν.—The usual formula of St Paul is ὁ κύριος ἡμῶν Ἰησοῦς Χριστός (forty-four times as against eleven times in the Catholic Epistles, once in the Acts and one doubtful case, Acts xx, 21), less often ὁ κύριος Ἰ. Χ. (eighteen times as against once in the Epistle of James, twice in the Acts and a doubtful case, Acts iv, 33), or simply ὁ κύριος Ἰησοῦς, with or without ἡμῶν after κύριος (twenty-four times and two doubtful cases [1 Cor. v, 4; 2 Cor. iv, 14] as against ten times in the Acts, twice in Hebrews, twice in 2 Peter, once in Apoc., and finally Mark xvi, 19). We see that, apart from the end of Mark, these formulas do not appear in the Gospels. The expression "Son of God" is, on the contrary, frequent in all the books of the New Testament.

[2] Matt. ii, 4 (Herod), Luke iii, 15, 16; John i, 20-27 (John the Baptist), Luke iv, 41 (demoniacs), Matt. xvi, 16; Mark viii, 29; Luke ix, 20 (Peter), Matt. xxvi, 68 (executioners), Matt. xxvi, 63, 64 (Jesus).—In all these examples and in general in the Gospels ὁ Χριστός can be translated by the "Messiah."

with the fulfilment of the promises, for St Paul the identification of Jesus with the Christ is a definite and undisputed fact.
The Christ has visibly broken all the Jewish ties, and the
memory of them is almost effaced.    Christ becomes the
proper name of the Saviour, and as such can do without
the article.[1]   Christ dies to make us triumph over death,
rises from the dead to incorporate us with his life, reigns
glorious to associate us in his glory.    His work is super-
mundane, and the place where it is consummated is super-
terrestrial.    From the union of Christians with Christ there
results a new being, the mystical Christ, in whom there is
no longer any distinction between Jew and Gentile, Greek
and barbarian, slave and free man, because all are " one in
Christ Jesus."[2]    When we consider that Paul certainly
reflects the Christian thought of his time and that his
Epistles preceded the compilation of the Gospels, we can
but admire the effort at historical reconstruction which the
evangelists must have made, in order not to project into the
life and words of Jesus the ideas and sentiments of their own
surroundings.

2. It is well known that the word " Lord " is, in the
Septuagint, the usual translation of the ineffable name, the
sacred tetragram.    It could be given to the Messiah either
as a theocratic king, the representative of Jehovah, or as
designated by the Psalmist's prophecy : " The Lord said unto
my Lord."[3]   Yet the evangelists apply it to Jesus only rarely.
In St Mark and St Matthew the " Lord " is usually God himself, as in the Old Testament, and the appellation " Lord "
is most frequently merely a polite form, like " Master " or
" Rabbi."    As the Passion approaches, they depart a little
from their reserve.[4]   St Luke, and especially St John, begin

---

[1] The word Χριστός is employed without the article, as a proper name and
without allusion to the etymological meaning of Messiah, about ninety-four
times, not including the expressions ἐν Χριστῷ, σὺν Χ., Ἰησοῦς Χριστός, and Χ. Ἰ.
In the Gospels, on the contrary—except the expression Ἰησοῦς Χριστός, which
is very rare (title of Matt. and of Mark ; John i, 17 ; xvii, 3 and two doubtful
cases, Matt, i, 18 ; xvi, 21)—the word Χριστός is regularly accompanied by the
article.  When the article is wanting, the omission is required by the grammar,
Χριστός being in the vocative (Matt. xxvi, 68) or in apposition with an accusative (Luke xxiii, 2 ; John ix, 22 ; moreover, Mark i, 34 if Χριστὸν εἶναι is
authentic), or finally employed simply to explain the meaning of the word
" Messiah ": τὸν Μεσσίαν ὅ ἐστι μεθερμηνευόμενον Χριστός (John i, 42),
Μεσσίας ἔρχεται ὁ λεγόμενος Χριστός (John iv, 25).   The only exception is
Mark ix, 41 : ὅτι Χριστοῦ ἐστε.
[2] Gal. iii, 28.                                       [3] Ps. cix, 1.
[4] Mark xi, 3 ; Matt. xxi, 3 ; Luke xix, 31 (the Master [ὁ κύριος] has need
of him).—Mark xiii, 35 ; Matt. xxiv, 42 (the Lord will come).—Mark xii, 36,
37 ; Matt. xxii, 43-45 ; Luke xx, 42-44 (Jesus claims the title of " Lord,"
which belongs to him according to the prophecy of David).—Add the end of
Mark (xvi, 19, 20, and perhaps also xiii, 20).  Before Passion-week the first two
evangelists never call the Saviour thus, for " the Son of Man, master (κύριος)
of the Sabbath " (Mark ii, 28 ; Matt. xii, 8 ; Luke vi, 5), has another meaning.

to do this sooner;[1] nevertheless, both are far behind St Paul, and this slowness, in our opinion, can only be explained by a scruple about historic truth.    St Paul, apart from quotations from the Old Testament, regularly calls Jesus Christ " the Lord."    Probably the language of the Apostle does not afford a single exception.[2]    In every case " Lord " has become the proper name of Christ, and can, as such, dispense with the article.[3]    Furthermore, in taking the name of Jehovah, the Christ receives also all his attributes; Paul calls himself a servant of Christ, as the prophets liked to call themselves servants of Jehovah; in phrases expressing divine actions, such as creation, the dispensation of grace, sanctification, judgement, and final retribution, the names of God and of Lord are exchanged, as synonyms are interchanged according to the flow of utterance; finally, whatever Scripture relates of Jehovah, Paul understands unhesitatingly as applying to his Master.[4]

Jehovah was the " Rock of Israel " or simply " the Rock "; such was the familiar Old Testament usage.    Paul knows that better than anyone, yet it does not prevent him from affirming that the " Rock was Christ " pre-existent— *Petra autem erat Christus*.[5]    And he adds a little later : " Let us not tempt (the Lord, or) Christ, as some of them tempted (him) and perished by the serpents."[6]    One may read : " the Lord " or " Christ," the variation of the reading has little importance, because for St Paul the two terms are synonymous. Joel said, speaking of Jehovah : " Everyone that shall call upon the name of the Lord shall be saved."[7]    But the Lord is Christ, and the Apostle is able to comment on this text as follows : " There is no difference between the Jew and the Greek, since they all have the same Lord, merciful towards all those who call upon him, for [it is written] : Everyone that shall call upon the name of the Lord shall be saved."[8] Salvation, formerly connected with the invocation of Jehovah,

---

[1] John iv, 1 ; vi, 23 ; xi, 2 ; Luke vii, 13, 19 ; x, 1, 39, 41 ; xi, 39 ; xii, 37, 42 ; xiii, 15 ; xvii, 5, 6 ; xviii, 6 ; xix, 8.—In the Acts, St Luke applies to Jesus Christ the title of " Lord " (ὁ κύριος, always with the article) still more freely.    When he makes St Paul speak, he usually simply says ὁ κύριος (however, in xxi, 23 : τοῦ κυρίου Ἰησοῦ) ; when he speaks in his own name, he prefers to say ὁ κύριος Ἰησοῦς (except xviii, 8, 9, and in the expression ἡ ὁδὸς τοῦ κυρίου).

[2] Cremer, *Wörterbuch der neutest. Gräcität*[9], p. 619, says that *excepting in quotations from the Old Testament* St Paul employs κύριος in the sense of " God " at least in 1 Cor. x, 25 (τοῦ κυρίου γὰρ ἡ γῆ καὶ τὸ πλήρωμα αὐτῆς). How is it that this scholar has not remarked that there is here a *textual quotation* from Ps. xxiii, 1 ?—In reality not one plausible exception to the rule which we give has been pointed out.    There is no reason for admitting one in xvi, 7 : " I hope to remain with you if *the Lord* permits."

[3] Rom. xiv, 6 ; 1 Cor. vii, 22 ; Eph. vi, 8 ; Phil. ii, 11, etc.
[4] Am. iii, 7 ; Jer. vii, 35 ; Dan. ix, 6, etc.
[5] 1 Cor. x, 4.                   [6] 1 Cor. x, 9.    Allusion to Num. xxi, 5, 6.
[7] Joel iii, 5 (ii, 32)           [8] Rom. x, 13.

is now connected with the invocation of Christ, and, to prove it, Paul quotes the word of the prophet. It follows logically that in his eyes Christ is one with Jehovah. How could we otherwise explain his discourse to the Elders at Ephesus : " Take heed to yourselves and to the whole flock, wherein the Holy Ghost hath made you bishops to rule the Church of God, which he hath purchased with his own blood."[1] This phrase early scandalized some timorous theologians, who caused it to undergo various corrections, one of which, consisting in the substitution of the name " Lord " for the name " God," ended by invading most of the Greek manuscripts. Modern critics, however, have had recourse to the most extravagant hypotheses in order to explain away Paul's saying that " God has purchased the Church by his own blood." But the Apostle has no need of their assistance. His language in this passage is no more extraordinary than in many another. He limits himself, as is his custom, to identifying Jesus Christ with God, and applies to him an attribute which suits him only in his human nature. But the communication of idioms, of which he avails himself very extensively, authorizes his doing so.

Must we, then, still be astonished at the value which St Paul attaches to the text " Christ is Lord " ? He makes of it the pivot of orthodoxy and the criterion of the *charismata:* " No man, speaking by the Spirit of God, saith anathema to Jesus. And no man can say Jesus [is] Lord, but by the Holy Ghost."[2] He regards it as the most concise epitome of his Gospel : " We preach not ourselves, but Jesus Christ as Lord."[3] Much more ; he presents it as a profession of Christian faith, containing, in substance, the conditions of salvation : " If thou confess with thy mouth that Jesus is Lord and believe in thy heart that God that raised him up from the dead, thou shalt be saved ; for the Scripture saith : Whosoever believeth in him shall not be confounded."[4] Isaias had indeed said that of God and not of Christ ; but for Paul it is the same thing, and we must not be weary of repeating it, since his Christ is Lord and God.

3. If this be so, we should expect to see the Apostle place Christ above all that is not God, in a sphere inaccessible to created beings, to address hymns and prayers to him as to God himself, and to apply to him the doxologies which Scripture reserves for God. Nor are our expectations disappointed.

The Epistle to the Galatians opens with the words : " Paul, an apostle, not of men, neither by man, but by Jesus Christ

[1] Acts xx, 28. See pp. 427-9.
[2] 1 Cor. xii, 3.
[3] 2 Cor. iv, 5.
[4] Rom. x, 9. *Cf.* Isa. xxviii, 16, whence the quotation is drawn.

and God the Father."[1]   Paul denies absolutely to men any
causality, remote (ἀπό) or immediate (διά), as to his apostolate ;
he is neither the delegate nor the mandatory of men.   When,
therefore, he calls himself an apostle by the exclusive act of
Jesus Christ and God the Father, he clearly considers Christ
as a being superior to man, or, rather, as a person who is
more than a man.   Doubtless there are between God and
man an infinitude of degrees ; but if we reflect that Paul
certainly would not claim that grace—and especially a grace
like that of the apostolate—could come from a being inferior
to God, and that he includes Jesus Christ and God under one
and the same causative particle (διά), thus leaving to no one
the possibility of alleging that he establishes between the two
a subordination of authority or rank, since Jesus Christ is
here named even first, there can be no reasonable objection
offered to interpreters who see in these words a proof of the
divinity of the Son.   In order to defeat their reasoning, it
would be necessary to be sure beforehand that Jesus Christ
is not God, and that Paul did not believe him to be God ; but
such a prejudiced position renders all sound exegesis impossible.

Christians do not consciously separate Christ from God.
From the first they prayed to him, invoked him, sang to him,
and glorified him as God.   St Stephen, dying, exclaimed :
" Lord Jesus, receive my spirit. .    . Lord, lay not this sin
to their charge."[2]   The ardent supplication which Jesus on
the cross addressed to his Father, the first martyrs address
to Jesus himself.   Thenceforth " whosoever shall call upon
the name of the Lord shall be saved,"[3] and the Lord is none
other than Christ.   The faithful are " those who call upon
the name of the Lord " ; such is their distinctive and
characteristic title.   Paul writes " to the Church which is
at Corinth, to them that are sanctified in Christ Jesus, called
to be saints, with all that invoke the name of our Lord Jesus
Christ, in every place."[4]   Practice follows theory.   The

---

[1] Gal. i, 1 : Παῦλος ἀπόστολος, οὐκ ἀπ' ἀνθρώπων οὐδὲ δι' ἀνθρώπου, ἀλλὰ
διὰ 'Ιησοῦ Χριστοῦ καὶ Θεοῦ πατρός.

The preposition ἀπό designates the source, the preposition διά indicates
the channel of the call to the apostolate.   Paul has received the apostolate
*from God* in opposition to the false apostles ; and he has received it *directly
from him*, equally with the Twelve.   In the second part of the phrase, the
particle διά is used alone, in order to show that here the source and the channel
are identical.—The proof of the divinity of Christ, based upon this passage,
was developed by Origen at considerable length in his commentary (*cf.*
St Pamphilus, *Apologia pro Origene*, XIV, 1297–8).   It is repeated in substance by the Latin (Victorinus, Ambrosiaster, St Jerome, etc.) and by the
Greek commentators (St Chrysostom, Theodoret, etc.).

[2] Acts vii, 59 : Κύριε 'Ιησοῦ, δέξαι τὸ πνεῦμά μου. vii, 60 : Κύριε, μὴ στήσῃς
αὐτοῖς ταύτην τὴν ἁμαρτίαν.   In the acts of the martyrs many similar prayers
are to be found.

[3] Rom. x, 13.                              [4] I Cor. i, 3.

Apostle, feeling " a sting in his flesh, an angel of Satan,"
which buffets him and seems about to paralyze his ministry,
prays to the Lord three times to be free from it; and the
Lord says to him : " My grace is sufficient for thee."[1]   He
prays not to God the Father but to the Lord, because he
knows very well that to pray to the Lord is to pray to God
himself; and the Lord, the Author and Dispenser of grace,
promises him his all-powerful aid.

In the year 112 A.D. some who had formerly been Christians
told Pliny that before their apostasy they had been accustomed
to assemble to sing hymns to Christ as God : *Christo quasi
Deo*.[2]  This was not a novelty.   Evidence is given by
Eusebius to prove that the custom of composing psalms and
odes, in which the Word was celebrated as God, goes back
to the very beginning.[3]  This assertion can be verified by the
express testimony of St Paul : " Speaking to yourselves in
psalms and hymns and spiritual canticles, singing and
making melody in your hearts to the Lord."[4]  In the parallel
passage " the Lord " is replaced by " God,"[5] which proves
that the faithful addressed the same praises to God and to
Christ.   Short fragments of these primitive compositions,
more remarkable for their religious tone than for their poetic
inspiration, have very probably come down to us; such as the
following rythmical description of the " mystery of piety " :

> He manifested himself in the flesh,
> He was justified in the spirit,
> He appeared to the angels ;
> He was preached among the nations,
> He was believed in the world,
> He was taken up into glory.[6]

The doxology is a sort of abbreviated hymn.   The Hebrews
connected it only with the name of God, and this is what the
Apostle himself generally does : " To God alone be honour
and glory for ever and ever.   Amen."[7]  But already St Paul,

[1] 2 Cor. xii, 8, 9.   [2] *Epist. ad Trajan.*, 96.
[3] *Hist. Eccl.*, V, xxviii, 5 : . . . Ψαλμοὶ δὲ ὅσοι καὶ ᾠδαὶ ἀδελφῶν ἀπ'
ἀρχῆς ὑπὸ πιστῶν γραφεῖσαι τὸν Λόγον τοῦ Θεοῦ τὸν Χριστὸν ὑμνοῦσιν
θεολογοῦντες ;
[4] Eph. v, 19 : ᾄδοντες καὶ ψάλλοντες τῇ καρδίᾳ ὑμῶν τῷ κυρίῳ.
[5] Col. iii, 16 : ᾄδοντες ἐν ταῖς καρδίαις ὑμῶν τῷ Θεῷ.
[6] 1 Tim. iii, 16.  Another probable fragment is Eph. v, 14, and perhaps
1 Cor. ii, 9 ; but in the latter text there is no question of Christ.
[7] There are two kinds of doxology : one consists of a formula of benediction,
beginning in Hebrew with בָּרוּךְ, in Greek with εὐλογητός (*benedictus*) ; the
other takes the form indicated in the text, or a more complicated form.
The first, very frequent in the Old Testament and connected also with the
name of God in the New Testament (Luke i, 68 ; Rom. i, 25 ; 2 Cor. i, 3 ;
xi, 31 ; Eph. i, 3 ; 1 Pet. i, 3, and, for Christ God, Rom. ix, 5), is less special
and may be addressed exceptionally to a man, Luke i, 42 (Mary : εὐλογημένη σὺ
ἐν γυναιξίν) ; Judges v, 24 (Jahel : תְּבֹרַךְ מִנָּשִׁים, εὐλογηθείη ἐν γυναιξὶν Ἰαήλ) ;
Deut. xxviii, 3 (faithful Israelite : בָּרוּךְ אַתָּה, εὐλογημένος σύ); it is not

St John, St Peter, and the Epistle to the Hebrews, as if they had agreed among themselves to do so, imperceptibly substitute the name of the Son for that of the Father : " The Lord hath delivered me from every evil work and will preserve me [by making me enter] unto his heavenly kingdom. To whom be glory for ever and ever. Amen."[1] For, since it is from him that we expect grace, it is just that we should pay him honour and thank him for it : " I give thanks to Christ Jesus our Lord who hath strengthened me, that he hath judged me faithful by establishing me in the ministry."

The attribution of doxologies to Christ is, however, exceptional. When the Apostle's thought is fixed exclusively on the person of Jesus Christ, he can pray to him, invoke him, thank him, and exalt him, as if he were the only author of supernatural blessings ; but when he names him jointly with his Father, he establishes between them an order which he never changes. Then he thanks, implores, and glorifies God *through* Jesus Christ or *in* Jesus Christ. Nothing more natural. " The head of every man is Christ ; (as) the head of the woman is the man ; (but) the head of Christ is God."[2]

---

necessary, therefore, to see an express confession of faith in the divinity of Jesus Christ in the acclamation which greeted his triumphal entry into Jerusalem : *Benedictus qui venit in nomine Domini* (Matt. xxi, 9; Mark xi, 9 ; Luke xix, 38 [*cf.* Matt. xxiii, 39 ; Luke xiii, 35] : quotation from Ps. cxvii, 26).—The doxology, properly so called, is on the contrary exclusively reserved for God, and it never accompanies the name of any created being whatever, angel or man. In the New Testament this is also the usual rule : Rom. xi, 36 (αὐτῷ ἡ δόξα εἰς τοὺς αἰῶνας· ἀμήν) ; Gal. i, 5 (ᾧ ἡ δόξα κτλ) ; Phil. iv, 20 (Τῷ δὲ Θεῷ καὶ πατρὶ ἡμῶν ἡ δόξα κτλ) ; Eph. iii, 21 ; 1 Tim. i, 17 ; vi, 16 ; 1 Pet. v, 11 ; Jud. 25 ; Apoc. vii, 12, and two or three doubtful cases, subsequently discussed.

[1] 2 Tim. iv, 18 ; 'Ρύσεταί με ὁ Κύριος ἀπὸ παντὸς ἔργου πονηροῦ καὶ σώσει εἰς τὴν βασιλείαν αὐτοῦ τὴν ἐπουράνιον· ᾧ ἡ δόξα εἰς τοὺς αἰῶνας τῶν αἰώνων· ἀμήν. It is very important to note that the other apostles have similar doxologies whose application to Christ is beyond doubt. Thus 2 Pet. iii, 18 (αὐξάνετε δὲ ἐν χάριτι καὶ γνώσει τοῦ Κυρίου ἡμῶν καὶ σωτῆρος 'Ι. Χ. Αὐτῷ ἡ δόξα καὶ νῦν καὶ εἰς ἡμέραν αἰῶνος) ; Apoc. i, 6 (Τῷ ἀγαπῶντι ἡμᾶς καὶ λύσαντι ἡμᾶς ἐν τῷ αἵματι αὐτοῦ . . . αὐτῷ ἡ δόξα κτλ). The Apocalypse is remarkable in this, that it unites the Son and the Father in the same doxology, Apoc. v, 13 (Τῷ καθημένῳ ἐπὶ τῷ θρόνῳ καὶ τῷ ἀρνίῳ ἡ εὐλογία κτλ) ; vii, 10 (ἡ σωτηρία τῷ Θεῷ ἡμῶν . . . καὶ τῷ ἀρνίῳ). In view of these facts, we can only understand the doxology of Heb. xiii, 20, 21 as referring to Christ (ὁ δὲ Θεὸς τῆς εἰρήνης, ὁ ἀναγαγὼν ἐκ νεκρῶν τὸν ποιμένα τῶν προβάτων τὸν μέγαν ἐν αἵματι διαθήκης αἰωνίου, τὸν Κύριον ἡμῶν 'Ιησοῦν . . . ποιῶν ἐν ἡμῖν τὸ εὐάρεστον ἐνώπιον αὐτοῦ διὰ 'Ι. Χ., ᾧ ἡ δόξα εἰς τοὺς αἰῶνας τῶν αἰώνων· ἀμήν), for the relative ᾧ refers naturally to the nearest word, and moreover all the emphasis of the discourse rests upon the mediation of Christ. Less clear is the case of 1 Pet. iv, 11 (ἵνα ἐν πᾶσιν δοξάζηται ὁ Θεὸς διὰ 'Ιησοῦ Χριστοῦ, ᾧ ἐστιν ἡ δόξα καὶ τὸ κράτος εἰς τοὺς αἰῶνας τῶν αἰώνων· ἀμήν), because the idea of mediation appears accessory. As much can be said of Rom. xvi, 27.

[2] 1 Cor. xi, 3 : παντὸς ἀνδρὸς ἡ κεφαλὴ ὁ Χριστός ἐστιν, κεφαλὴ δὲ γυναικὸς ὁ ἀνήρ, κεφαλὴ δὲ τοῦ Χριστοῦ ὁ Θεός.—It is not a question here of the *conjugal* subordination of the woman, for the precepts of Paul refer to all women, even the unmarried ; nor of her *natural* subordination, for the

There is here a well-defined hierarchy: God, Christ, man,
woman. If we read the context attentively, we shall remark
first that it is a question here of Christ as the Head of the
Church in the system of redemption; secondly, that it concerns the relations of man and woman, viewed from the
Christian and social standpoint. In fact, the question treated
here concerns the conduct of women in church, a conduct
determined by the position of women in the Church. From
the individual point of view, the Christian woman is directly
united to Christ the Redeemer, just as the man is, but it
is not the same from the social point of view. Here there
is a hierarchy to be observed in theory and to be maintained in practice. As Head of the Church, Christ is directly
dependent upon God, of whom he is the envoy and mandatory. The man is directly dependent upon Christ, whom
he represents in the sacred functions of the ecclesiastical
hierarchy; and the woman—married or unmarried—is
directly dependent on the man, who alone has a part in
the government of the Church. And this subordination is
to be shown outwardly, in religious gatherings, by the veil,
a symbol of dependence, with which the woman is to cover
her head, and also by the fact that she is forbidden to
prophesy, or to teach or speak in public in the presence of
the faithful and their pastors.

God is, therefore, the Head of Christ the Mediator, and it
is in this relation that they are usually considered when they
are named together in the doxologies and solemn prayers.
Paul looks for grace, mercy, and other spiritual blessings
simultaneously from the Son and from the Father, and he
can ask the Father or the Son for them with equal readiness.[1]
But he seems to have established a regular rule for our prayers
when he says to the Colossians: "All whatsoever you
do in word or in work, do all *in the name* of the Lord Jesus
Christ, giving thanks to God and the Father *by him*. . . ."[2]
Since "all the promises of God have become *Yea in him*"
it is eminently just that we should address "*by him* the
*Amen*" of our benedictions.[3] Perhaps, an anxiety not to do

---

Apostle is thinking only of the Christian woman; nor of *individual* subordination, for all Christians are equal in Christ and depend directly on him
(Gal. iii, 28); it is a question, therefore, of her *social* and *religious* subordination (1 Cor. xiv, 34; 1 Tim. ii, 12). Further on, it is true, Paul confirms this subordination by the story of the creation (1 Cor. xi, 8, 9: the man
is the image and glory of God and the woman is the glory of man; *cf.* 1 Tim.
ii, 13, 14): but this is in an entirely different order of ideas.

[1] In the opening formula of many of the Epistles: χάρις ὑμῖν καὶ εἰρήνη
ἀπὸ Θεοῦ πατρὸς ἡμῶν καὶ Κυρίου Ἰησοῦ Χριστοῦ (Rom. i, 7; 1 Cor. i, 3;
2 Cor. i, 2; Gal. i, 3; Eph. i, 2; Phil. i, 2; 1 Thess. i, 1; 2 Thess. i, 2;
1 Tim. i, 2; 2 Tim. i, 2; Tit. i, 4; Philem. 3), and sometimes elsewhere
(Eph. vi, 23; 1 Thess. iii, 11; 2 Thess. ii, 16).

[2] Col. iii, 17.                    [3] 2 Cor. i, 20.

an injury, even in appearance only, to the strict maintenance
of Hebrew monotheism has something to do with this usage
introduced by the apostles and subsequently adopted by the
Church, a usage which moreover, as we have seen, does not
prevent Paul from occasionally praying separately to the Son
and from sometimes addressing to him the doxologies
reserved for God alone.[1]

### III—JESUS CHRIST GOD

1. The Divinity of Christ and Pagan Apotheoses.   2. Four Illuminating
Texts.   3. Synthetic View.

1. All the ancient civilizations—of Chaldæa, Egypt, China,
Persia, and India—deified their kings.  Alexander the Great,
in seizing the territory of those ancient monarchies, appro-
priated to himself the honorary titles of their sovereigns.
Naturally the generals who divided up his states among
themselves also inherited his titles.  After them the Cæsars,
although at first avoiding openly offending Roman ideas,
soon lent themselves to an apotheosis which served their
political policy without shocking oriental customs.  A beginning was made by deifying the emperors after death; subsequently divine honours were paid to them even while alive.
If they do not seem to have cared much for the name of
" Lord," so dear to the Ptolemies and Herods, they had no
scruples about letting themselves be called " God-Saviour,
Saviour, and God," or simply " God "; and also, if the
father already enjoyed apotheosis, " God, Son of God."[2]

---

[1] These conclusions concerning prayer to Christ are admitted in substance
by many Protestant authors : Chase (*The Lord's Prayer in the Early Church*
in *Texts and Studies*, vol. i, fasc. 3, Cambridge, 1891) ; Seeberg (*Die
Anbetung des Herrn bei Paulus*, Riga, 1891.  Zahn (*Die Anbetung Jesu
im Zeitalter der Apostel*, in *Skizzen aus dem Leben der alten Kirche*[3],
Leipzig, 1908, pp. 271-398).  E. von der Goltz (*Das Gebet in der ältesten
Christenheit*, Leipzig, 1901) admits in general the theses of Zahn and
Seeberg ; but he insists on the exceptional character of these invocations
and seeks for the explanation in the hypothesis that the name " Lord "
was applied to both the Father and the Son without a clear distinction of
persons.  Is it not simpler and more natural to believe that it is on account
of the identity of their nature ?

[2] See Beurlier, *Le culte impérial*, etc., Paris, 1891 (with the Latin thesis
of the same author), and Deissmann, *Licht vom Osten*, etc., Tübingen, 1908,
pp. 243-276.
  We will cite only one curious example, taken from the *Excavations in
Cyprus* in the *Journal of Hellen. Stud.*, vol. ix, 1888, p. 243.  King
Ptolemy VI, surnamed Philometor and claiming to be called *God*, had
dedicated to Venus of Paphos this votive inscription :

> ΒΑΣΙΛΕΑ ΠΤΟΛΕΜΑΙΟΝ
> ΘΕΟΝ ΦΙΛΟΜΗΤΟΡΑ
> ΠΑΦΙΑΙ

Subsequently, the original inscription was beaten out with a hammer, and
this pedestal was usurped for the *goddess* Julia, daughter of Augustus, *God,
Son of God:*

Domitian, however, appears to have been the first, after the madman Caligula, to have himself called *Dominus et deus noster*[1] even in his capital.

The Christians always repudiated with indignation these impious pretensions. The profanation of divine names and attributes inspired them with invincible horror. When the author of the Apocalypse says to the angel of Pergamus that he " dwells where the seat of Satan is,"[2] one cannot help thinking of the first temple erected to the god Augustus and the goddess Roma, a temple of dazzling marble which rose upon the summit of the acropolis of Pergamus; dominating the plain of the Caïcus and visible for a great distance in all directions. The protest of St Paul against the deification of men is not less energetic :

> There is no God but one. For though there be that are called gods [by an abuse of language] either in heaven or on earth ; so that men speak of gods many and lords many ; yet to us there is but one God, the Father, of whom are all things and we unto him : and one Lord Jesus Christ by whom are all things and we [are Christians] by him.[3]

So, when we see the Apostle giving to Christ the name and the attributes of God, we are far from thinking of pagan apotheoses, repudiated by him with so much force, and we give to these expressions the only meaning which Hebrew monotheism authorizes, added to the personal distinctions established in the depths of the divine life by the Christian revelation.

2. Four texts, taken purposely from all the epistolary groups, may teach us Paul's constant notion of the pre-existent Christ. Jesus Christ is " exalted above all, God blessed for ever " ; he is " our great God and Saviour " ; in him " dwelleth all the fulness of the Godhead " ; finally, he is " subsisting in the form of God." Let us briefly examine the import of these testimonies.

From the heart of Israel has come " according to the flesh, Christ who is exalted above all, God blessed for ever."[4] This phrase refers so clearly to Christ, whose transcendent and divine nature it explains, that it has never been understood differently by Christian tradition. In the

---

*(ΙΟΥ) ΛΙΑΝ ΘΕΑΝ ΣΕΒΑΣΤΗ(Ν)*
*ΘΥΤΑΤΕΡΑ ΑΥΤΟΚΡΑΤΟΡΟ(Σ)*
*ΚΑΙΣΑΡΟΣ ΘΕΟΥ ΥΙΟΥ ΘΕΟΥ κτλ.*

[1] Suetonius, *Domit.*, xiii : *Dominus ac deus noster sic fieri jubet.*
[2] Apoc. ii, 13 : *Scio ubi habitas ubi sedes* (θρόνος) *est Satanae.*
[3] 1 Cor. viii, 5, 6. *Cf.* Deissmann, *Licht vom Osten*, p. 255-258.
[4] Rom. ix, 5 : ἐξ ὧν ὁ Χριστὸς τὸ κατὰ σάρκα, ὁ ὢν ἐπὶ πάντων, θεὸς εὐλογητὸς εἰς τοὺς αἰῶνας· ἀμήν. For the textual criticism see Sanday, *Epistle to the Romans ;* for the exegesis and Patristic tradition, A. Durand, *La divinité de J.-C. dans S. Paul*, Rom. ix, 5 (*Revue biblique*, vol. xii, 1903, pp. 550-570).

East, St Dionysius of Alexandria and the bishops who signed
the synodal letter against Paul of Samosata, St Athanasius,
St Basil, St Gregory of Nyssa, St Epiphanius, St Cyril of
Alexandria; in the West, St Irenæus, St Hippolytus,
Tertullian, Novatian, St Cyprian, St Hilary, St Ambrose,
St Jerome : the Greek and Latin commentators, Origen,
Ambrosiaster, Pelagius, St Chrysostom, Theodore of
Mopsuestia, Theodoret, and the rest do not even suspect
that any other meaning could be given to it. One must come
down to Photius to find a dissenting voice ; for all that can be
concluded from the silence of Arius, Diodorus of Tarsus, and
the Arianizing writers of the fourth century is that our text
embarrassed them and that they avoided quoting it, as an
objection fatal to their thesis. Certain modern exegetes are
less scrupulous. They arbitrarily put a period either after
" Christ according to the flesh," or before " God blessed
for ever " ; and they obtain a fragment of a phrase which
they translate thus :

> A. He who is above all [is] God blessed for ever.
> B. God who is above all [is (or) may he be] blessed for ever.
> C. God [is (or) may he be] blessed for ever.

Everyone will agree that this kind of trimming gives to
the phrase an awkward appearance and a strange turn.
Assuredly it would never have occurred to anyone who was
not already fully persuaded that Paul cannot call Christ God,
and that he never addresses a doxology to him. If this
double hypothesis were justified, the conclusion drawn from
it would none the less be a fallacy, and would make it necessary for the same reason to expunge from the teaching of St
Paul all the assertions which appear only once in his
writings ; but the whole hypothesis is as false as it is
gratuitous : the Apostle does sometimes give to Christ the
name of God and does address him doxologies. Moreover,
our text is not, strictly speaking, a doxology; it is an affirmation pure and simple of the supereminent dignity of Christ,
ending in an *Amen* of benediction and praise. The *Amen*
alone, if you like, forms the whole doxology. It is easy to
show that the construction imagined by the rationalists is
contrary to logic and grammar. It is not the excellence of
the Father, but that of the Son, which the passage is to make
prominent. The words " according to the flesh " prepare us
for an antithesis : we expect a second aspect of the portrait
of Christ; the phrase " who is above all, God blessed for
ever " fulfils our expectation ; it completes the image of the
Saviour and finishes by an admirable stroke the picture of the
prerogatives of the Jews : the descent from Israel, the adoption of sons, the sensible presence of God, the Law transmitted by angels, the legitimate manner of worship, messianic

promises, the blood of the patriarchs, and human kinship with Jesus Christ, whose superior nature is poured out in glory upon them. For the detached phrase to be a doxology referring to the Father, it would be necessary either that the word " blessed " be given a prominent position instead of being submerged in the sentence, or else that the phrase should commence with a verb in the optative mood; a doxology, like the one proposed to us, in order to alter the natural meaning of St Paul, would be unexampled in the Greek language. The unusual construction, with which the third explanation comes into conflict, becomes entangled with the other two by a solecism.[1] It is, therefore, not surprising that the Greek Fathers, who know their language a little better than our modern exegetes, do not mention it, even to refute it.

Jesus Christ is not God in an unwarranted, participated, or analogous way; he is exalted above everything that is not God. As this quality of sovereign God can belong to one being only, the Son must necessarily be consubstantial with the Father and identical with him in nature. Paul will find nothing nobler to say of Christ when, at the very end of his career, he writes to Titus: " Looking for the blessed hope and coming of the glory of the great God and our Saviour Jesus Christ (τοῦ μεγάλου Θεοῦ καὶ σωτῆρος ἡμῶν Χριστου Ἰησοῦ).[2] It is consoling to see the exegetes of our day coming back more and more to the traditional interpretation. If it were a question of the Father, the Apostle would not add to God the epithet of " great," which naturally is the principle of divinity. Moreover, the *parousia* is always the glorious manifestation of the Son coming to judge the world, never

---

[1] The participle of the verb " to be," preceded by the definite article and followed by a preposition with its objective case, never qualifies a noun. One can say ὁ ἐπὶ πάντων, or ὁ ἐπὶ πάντων Θεός, or again ὁ ὢν ἐπὶ πάντων but not ὁ ὢν ἐπὶ πάντων Θεός, taking ὁ for the article of Θεός. In this expression the word Θεός is necessarily in apposition with ὁ ὢν ἐπὶ πάντων, and then the article with the present participle is equivalent to a relative referring to the noun which precedes, here therefore to Jesus Christ.

[2] Titus ii, 13: προσδεχόμενοι τὴν μακαρίαν ἐλπίδα καὶ ἐπιφάνειαν τῆς δόξης τοῦ μεγάλου Θεοῦ καὶ σωτῆρος ἡμῶν Χριστοῦ Ἰησοῦ.—Supposing that τοῦ Θεοῦ designates God the Father, the absence of the article before σωτῆρος ἡμῶν would be an intolerable mistake. For the same reason, 2 Pet. i, 1 (ἐν δικαιοσύνῃ τοῦ Θεοῦ ἡμῶν καὶ σωτῆρος Ἰ. Χ.) must be understood of Christ only. It must be added that at this time the expression Θεὸς καὶ σωτήρ was very much used as an honorary title. Moreover, ἡ ἐπιφάνεια τῆς δόξης clearly designates the glorious second coming of Christ. This fact is being more and more recognized. The Anglican revised version has corrected the old translation thus: *our great God and Saviour* (instead of " the great God and our Saviour"). Weizsäcker also translates: *Die Erscheinung der Herrlichkeit unseres grossen Gottes und Heilandes Jesus Christus.* Most modern commentators, even Protestants, support this exegesis. *Cf.* B. Weiss, *Meyers Kommentar*

that of the Father. Finally—and this argument is decisive —the two titles "great God" and "Saviour," being included in Greek under the same definite article, must refer to the same person; to be able to isolate them and to connect the second only to Jesus Christ, this latter name would have to be placed between the two. To object to this testimony under the pretext that Jesus Christ is not God and that St Paul should not have called him so, is to give up working as an exegete and to entrench oneself behind a prejudiced position of obstinate negation.

However illuminating these texts are, they are still only rapid flashes of accidental light. It is in the Epistles of the captivity that the portrait of the pre-existent Christ is set forth in the most admirable relief. Nothing more resembles the prologue of St John than the christological passages of the Epistle to the Colossians. The parallelism goes further than the order of ideas, and extends even to their expression : in both Christ is presented as a fountain of graces, the fulness of which overflows upon the entire race, and the union of divinity and humanity in his person is affirmed by a formula of equal boldness. But, while St John is pleased to consider the Logos in the bosom of the divine light, of which he is the eternal radiance, St Paul prefers to contemplate Christ at the head of humanity which he ransoms, and of the creation to which he restores its primitive harmony. For his principal aim, determined by the controversy with the false teachers of Colosse, is to show that Christ is first in all things, as man and as God, in time and in eternity; therefore he heaps upon his person, without troubling himself too much about their logical or chronological order, the honourable titles, exceptional qualifications, dignities, and prerogatives which put him absolutely beyond comparison and confer upon him a supereminent primacy.

Thus Christ is " *the* well-beloved Son " necessarily unique, and by virtue of this quality disposing of the kingdom of his Father as *his* kingdom.—He is the " image of the invisible God," the living portrait of the heavenly Father, alone perfectly resembling his archetype and capable of revealing him to men, because he alone knows the Father as he is known by him.—He " is the firstborn of every creature," because he existed before every creature.—He is the Creator and preserver of all things; and no created being, however exalted he may be in the heavenly hierarchies, escapes his creative activity or his providence.—He is the " sovereign head of the Church," the author of redemption and the remission of sins, the firstborn among the dead and the firstfruits of the resurrection, because, having to possess the primacy in all things, no pre-eminence can be wanting in him.—He possesses the plenitude of the graces requisite for

filling his role of universal reconciler and pacificator.[1]—
Finally, as a last characteristic, " all the fulness of the Godhead dwelleth in him bodily."[2] We must not confound this
text with the preceding one; they differ entirely; in one it
was the plenitude of graces, in the other it is the plenitude
of divinity; in the former it was a plenitude resting on the
person of Christ, in the latter it is a plenitude which dwells
in the body of Christ. The word employed by St Paul is not
ambiguous : " all the fulness of the Godhead " can be only
the divine nature itself.

It is, however, the great christological text in the Epistle
to the Philippians which gives the most complete expression
of Paul's thought. The Apostle, wishing to give his disciples
an example of self-abnegation and to show them that voluntary humiliation is a seed of glory, sets before them the
three stages—the divine life, the life of trial, and the glorified
life—through which Christ Jesus passed : " Who, being in
the form of God, thought it not robbery to be [treated as]
equal with God :—but emptied himself, taking the form
of a servant, being made in the likeness of men, and in
habit found as a man, he humbled himself, becoming obedient
unto death, even to the death of the cross ; for which cause
God also hath exalted him and hath given him a name which
is above every name : that in the name of Jesus every knee
should bow, of those that are in heaven, on earth, and under
the earth : and that every tongue should confess that the
Lord Jesus Christ is in the glory of God the Father."[3]

In each of these three stages of majesty, humility, and
glory there are, as it were, two distinct phases. Before all
ages Christ was in the form of God and was very God by
that fact, for the form of God belongs to his essence ; and,
as God, he had a right to divine honours as well as his
Father (τὸ εἶναι ἴσα Θεῷ). This majesty did not prevent him
from stooping down to us; he emptied himself (ἐκένωσεν
ἑαυτόν), not by rejecting the divine form, which was inseparable from his being, but by concealing his divine form
under his human form and by renouncing thus for a time the
divine honours which were due him; he humbled himself
(ἐταπείνωσεν ἑαυτόν) still more than his condition as man required, by submitting to death and the most ignominious
of deaths. In order to give to his voluntary renunciation a
proportionate recompense, God now compels every created
being to render homage to him and to confess his triumph.

3. At the risk of anticipating somewhat the contents of the
following chapter, let us try to outline the principal features
of this image.

[1] Col. i, 13, 20. See Vol. I, pp. 287-92.
[2] Col. ii, 9. See below pp. 151-2.
[3] Phil. ii, 6-11. See Vol. I, pp. 311-6, and note I, pp. 456-65.

Christ belongs to an order superior to every created being,[1] he is himself the creator[2] and preserver of the world;[3] all is by him, in him, and for him.[4] He is the efficient, exemplary, and final cause of all that exists, and is therefore God.

Christ is the image of the invisible Father;[5] he is the Son of God, but not like the other sons; he is so in an incommunicable way; he is *the* Son, God's own Son, the Beloved, and he has always been so.[6] He proceeds, therefore, from the divine essence, and is consubstantial with the Father.

Christ is the object of doxologies reserved for God;[7] Christians pray to him as well as to the Father;[8] they expect from him blessings which it is in the power of God alone to confer—grace, mercy, and salvation;[9] before him every knee must bow in heaven, on earth, and in hell,[10] as every knee bends in adoration before the majesty of the Most High.

Christ possesses all the divine attributes: he is eternal, since he is the firstborn of every creature and existed before all the ages;[11] he is immutable, since he is in the form of God;[12] he is all-powerful, since he has the power to make fruitful even nothingness;[13] he is immeasurable, since he fills the universe;[14] he is infinite, since the fulness of the Godhead dwelleth in him, or rather, he is the fulness of the Godhead;[15] all that is the special property of God belongs to him as the rightful owner; the tribunal of God is the tribunal of Christ,[16] the Gospel of God is the Gospel of Christ,[17] the Church of God is the Church of Christ,[18] the kingdom of God is the kingdom of Christ,[19] and the Spirit of God is the Spirit of Christ.[20]

Christ is the only Lord;[21] he identifies himself with the Jehovah of the old Covenant;[22] he is the God who has redeemed the Church with his own blood;[23] he is "our great God and Saviour Jesus Christ";[24] he is even "God exalted

---

[1] Eph. i, 21.    [2] Col. i, 16.    [3] Col. i, 17.

[4] Col. i, 16, 17.    [5] 2 Cor. iv, 4; Col. i, 15.

[6] 2 Cor. i, 19; Rom. viii, 3-32; Col. i, 13; Eph. i, 6, etc.

[7] Rom. ix, 5; xvi, 27; 2 Tim. iv, 18. Hymns: 1 Tim. iii, 16; Eph. v, 14.

[8] 2 Cor. xii, 8, 9; Rom. x, 12-14; 1 Cor. i, 2.

[9] Rom. i, 7; 1 Cor. i, 3; 2 Cor. i, 2; Eph. i, 2; Phil. i, 2; Col. i, 3; Philem. 3; 2 Thess. i, 2; 1 Tim. i, 2; Titus i, 4.—Rom. xvi, 20; 1 Cor. xvi, 23; 2 Cor. xiii, 13; Gal. vi, 18; Eph. vi, 23; Phil. iv, 23; 1 Thess. v, 28; 2 Thess. iii, 18; Philem. 25, etc.

[10] Phil. ii, 10.    [11] Col. i, 15-17.

[12] Phil. ii, 6.    [13] Col. i, 16.

[14] Eph. iv, 10; Col. ii, 10.    [15] Col. ii, 9.

[16] Rom. xiv, 10 (of God); 2 Cor. v, 10 (of Christ).

[17] Rom. i, 1; xv, 16 (of God); Rom. i, 9; 1 Cor. ix, 12 (of Christ).

[18] 1 Cor. i, 2; x, 32, etc. (of God); Rom. xvi, 16 (of Christ).

[19] Eph. v, 5.    [20] Rom. viii, 9.

[21] 1 Cor. viii, 6.

[22] 1 Cor. x, 4-9.    *Cf.* 1 Cor. ii, 16; ix, 21; Rom. x, 13.

[23] Acts xx, 28.    [24] Titus ii, 13.

above all things,"[1] dominating all created things by his infinite transcendence.   If he is not called God without an epithet, it is because God, in the language of Paul, denotes the person of the Father, and because a personal identity between the Father and the Son is contradictory.

[1] Rom. ix, 5.

# CHAPTER II

## RELATIONS OF THE PRE-EXISTENT CHRIST

### I—The Trinity in Unity

1. The Persons placed in Juxtaposition by Co-ordination. 2. Intervening in the Working of their Eternal Relations.

"THE theology of St Paul," writes Sabatier, " does not end like traditional theology; the dogma of the Trinity lies outside its sphere." A very decisive affirmation, somewhat modified, it is true, by the following concession : " Paul succeeds, however, in formulating some distinctions in the divine activity, which can be regarded as the point of departure of subsequent speculations and ecclesiastical metaphysics."[1] On the other hand, other liberal and rationalistic critics are struck by what they call the Apostle's trinitarian conception. Let us see if they are right.

1. The number of cases in which the three divine Persons are united in the same text is a surprising and unexpected phenomenon. Thirty such can be counted.[2] Not only are the Father, the Son, and the Holy Spirit constantly named together, without there being in this enumeration any fixed order, but they are distinguished from any and every creature and are placed in the category of the divine being. If we do not look in St Paul for the technical terms of present theology : " nature, substance, person " and still less " subsistence, consubstantiality, circumincession," we find in him a fund of ideas and mutual relations, destined, one day, to render the uniform adoption of all those terms necessary. Let us examine closely some of the texts in question, regretting, however, not to be able to gather them close together, for they lose much of their convincing force by the very fact of their isolation :

> The grace of our *Lord Jesus Christ*
> and the love of *God* [*the Father*]
> and the communion of the *Holy Ghost* be with you all.[3]

---

[1] A. Sabatier, *L'Apôtre Paul*[3], Paris, 1896, p. 366.
[2] In Note S, at the end of this work, we shall rapidly run over all those which are not studied here.
[3] 2 Cor. xiii, 13 :

> Ἡ χάρις τοῦ Κυρίου Ἰησοῦ Χριστοῦ
> καὶ ἡ ἀγάπη τοῦ Θεοῦ
> καὶ ἡ κοινωνία τοῦ ἁγίου Πνεύματος μετὰ πάντων ὑμῶν.

It is probable that it is a question here of the *communion* of which the Holy Spirit is the agent, and not of the communion of which he is the object; but this shade of meaning matters little. Paul attributes to the Son alone the grace which elsewhere he loves to refer to the Son and the Father conjointly; then goes back to the original source of grace—namely, to the active love of the Father which comprises and represents the whole divine nature; finally, he descends to the effective distribution of the graces which belongs to the Guest of the just soul, to the Spirit of sanctity. The three Persons, therefore, each in his appropriate sphere, together contribute to the common work of salvation, and their habitual order is changed, either to show that it does not imply essential inequality, or rather by virtue of the association of ideas. No less remarkable is the following text:

> There are diversities of *charismata*, but the same *Spirit*;
> and there are diversities of *ministries*, but the same *Lord*;
> and there are diversities of *operations*, but the same *God*,
> who worketh all in all.[1]

The only exegetical difficulties of this text are the exact value of the genitives and the precise meaning of κοινωνία. As the first two genitives are certainly subjective (the love which God has for us and the grace of which Jesus Christ is the dispenser), it is *a priori* very probable that the third genitive is subjective also: κοινωνία will, therefore, have to be understood in the active sense (that which is the work of the Holy Spirit) and not in the passive sense (the Holy Spirit communicated). Oecumenius, copied by Theophylact, explains the terms thus: " He wishes for them the *grace* of the Son, by which he has saved us freely, having been sacrificed for us: and the *love* with which the Father loved us, when he delivered up his only Son for us: and the *communion* of the Holy Ghost, namely his participation and reception (οἷον τὴν μετοχὴν αὐτοῦ καὶ μετάληψιν), by which we are all sanctified" (CXVIII, 1088).

If the sense of the genitive Πνεύματος were objective, as Oecumenius seems to suppose, the meaning of κοινωνία would be " common possession of the Holy Ghost "; if it is subjective, as we think, the meaning of κοινωνία will be " mutual communication, union of minds and hearts," produced in the faithful by the unction of the Spirit (*cf.* Gal. ii, 9: δεξιὰ κοινωνίας, Acts ii, 42: προσκαρτεροῦντες . . . τῇ κοινωνίᾳ, Rom. xv, 26; 2 Cor. viii, 4, and Heb. xiii, 16, where κοινωνία is joined to εὐποιία as a synonym).

These shades of meaning do not weaken the proof in favour of the Trinity which the Fathers—among others St John Chrysostom and Theodoret—derive from this passage. Harnack writes of this text (*Entstehung und Entwickelung der Kirchenverfassung*, etc., Leipzig, 1910, p. 187): *Zwar bietet sie [die trinitarische Formel] Paulus noch nicht als solemne oder gar exklusive Formel, aber er bietet sie doch.* Very good: but why not *solemn* and *exclusive*?

[1] 1 Cor. xii, 4-6: Διαιρέσεις δὲ χαρισμάτων εἰσίν, τὸ δὲ αὐτὸ Πνεῦμα· καὶ διαιρέσεις διακονιῶν εἰσιν, καὶ ὁ αὐτὸς Κύριος· καὶ διαιρέσεις ἐνεργημάτων εἰσίν, ὁ δὲ αὐτὸς Θεὸς ὁ ἐνεργῶν τὰ πάντα ἐν πᾶσιν.
The word διαίρεσις signifies " division " rather than " difference," but the difference results from the division. The difference refers to the various *charismata*, the divers ministries and the different operations, but does not imply the diversity of operations, ministries and *charismata* compared with one another. Thus the Greek commentators regard these three words as synonyms or, more exactly, as applying to the same objects. It is better to

We should not think here of an ascending scale and a sphere of unequal activity, in which the Holy Spirit, here named first and put into relation with the *charismata* only, is inferior to the other two.    There are three reasons against this.    The ministries and the operations can be, and sometimes are, included under the general name of *charismata*. Furthermore, the Holy Spirit distributes to each, according to his good pleasure, all the spiritual gifts, in the number of which operations are particularly mentioned.    Finally, although the operations, works of power, are naturally referred to the Father as belonging to him, and although the ministries are specially attributed to the Son, the ever-living Head of the Church, all these graces, being the common property of the three divine Persons, are awarded now to one, now to another, according to the subject and the occasion.    We do not even perceive here that sort of hierarchy of the Persons observable in some other passages.

2. Instead of being in juxtaposition by co-ordination, as in the texts quoted above, the Persons often appear in the discharge of their eternal relations or missions, which they receive from one another :

> When the fulness of the time was come, God sent his Son, made of a woman, made under the Law, that he might redeem them who were under the Law, that we might receive the adoption of sons.    And because you are sons, God hath sent the Spirit of his Son into our hearts crying : Abba, Father !    Therefore thou art not a servant, but a son, and if a son, an heir also through God.[1]

---

distinguish them separately ; the *operations* will then be the graces of healing, the gift of miracles and similar favours ; the *ministries* will denote the spiritual gifts which have to do with the active service of the Church or of its members ; the *charismata* will include, besides the two preceding categories, all the *gratiae gratis datae*, the enumeration of which follows : the gift of tongues, the discernment of spirits, the gift of interpretation, etc.    In fact, the Apostle three times (1 Cor. xii, 9, 28, 33) calls χαρίσματα ἰαμάτων the gifts of healing, which it would be necessary rather to name ἐνεργήματα (*cf.* 1 Cor. xii, 10), if the *charismata* did not embrace all the other graces.    He closes his list of *charismata*, operations and ministries by saying : " But seek zealously for the greater *charismata*," which proves again that the name *charismata* is the most comprehensive term.

[1] Gal. iv, 6 ; ὅτι δέ ἐστε υἱοί,

ἐξαπέστειλεν ὁ Θεὸς τὸ Πνεῦμα τοῦ Υἱοῦ αὐτοῦ εἰς τὰς καρδίας ἡμῶν, κρᾶζον· Ἀββᾶ, ὁ πατήρ· ὥστε οὐκέτι εἶ δοῦλος ἀλλὰ υἱός· εἰ δὲ υἱὸς καὶ κληρονόμος τοῦ Θεοῦ.

The two most striking features of this passage are the two sendings of the Son and the Holy Spirit by the Father, with the effects of these sendings.    The Apostle has just said that God, in the fulness of times, sent his Son (verse 4) : ἐξαπέστειλεν τὸν Υἱὸν αὐτοῦ.    This sending of the Son coincides with the incarnation : in the verb ἐξαπέστειλεν each of the two component particles can retain its own value, ἀπό marking the going away, the passage from heaven to earth, and ἐκ the emission or origin, although perhaps we ought not to insist too much on these shades of expression.    Paul now says that God sent (ἐξαπέστειλεν) his Spirit, called also the Spirit of the Son : it is a question here of a temporary and incidental sending of the Spirit into the just soul ;

Whosoever are led by the Spirit of God, they are the sons of God. For you have not received the spirit of bondage [to fill you] again with fear ; but you have received the spirit of adoption of sons, whereby we cry, Abba, Father ! For the Spirit himself unites with our spirit to bear witness that we are the sons of God ; and if sons, heirs also : heirs of God and joint-heirs with Christ.[1]

These two texts ought not to be separated, for they mutually throw light upon each other ; in both it is God the Father who sends the Spirit, who is the Spirit of the Son, and, therefore, is sent also by the Son ; in both the adoption of sons is attributed to the Holy Spirit, to the Son and to the Father ; finally, in both the presence of the Spirit presupposes filial adoption with all the rights which it brings with it, and the filial adoption presupposes the presence of the Spirit of God, without our being able to say with certainty which has the logical priority.

Sometimes the relations seem still closer ; what has just been affirmed of one person is, a moment later, affirmed of the other, or the simultaneous co-operation of the three is expressed as a function of their personal relations in the heart of the divine life. This is especially true when it is a question of the sanctification of souls :

> God . . . saved us by the laver of regeneration and renovation of the *Holy Ghost*, whom he hath poured forth upon us abundantly through *Jesus Christ* our Saviour.[2]

---

this is not the first time that the Holy Spirit has taken possession of the soul, but is the testimony of the divine indwelling manifesting itself by the charismatical gifts. Instead of " *because* you are sons," many translate : " [for a proof] *that* (ὅτι) you are sons."

[1] Rom. viii, 14 : ὅσοι γὰρ Πνεύματι Θεοῦ ἄγονται, οὗτοι υἱοί εἰσι Θεοῦ·

15. οὐ γὰρ ἐλάβετε πνεῦμα δουλείας πάλιν εἰς φόβον, ἀλλὰ ἐλάβετε πνεῦμα υἱοθεσίας ἐν ᾧ κράζομεν· Ἀββᾶ, ὁ πατήρ.

16. Αὐτὸ τὸ Πνεῦμα συμμαρτυρεῖ τῷ πνεύματι ἡμῶν ὅτι ἐσμὲν τέκνα Θεοῦ·

17. εἰ δὲ τέκνα, καὶ κληρονόμοι· κληρονόμοι μὲν Θεοῦ, συγκληρονόμοι δὲ Χριστοῦ.

The Father, the Son and the Holy Spirit are mentioned together with the personal attributes that distinguish them. The Holy Spirit, represented as a supernatural moving power (verse 14), renders testimony to our sonship in relation to the Father, and to joint-heirship with relation to the Son. *Father, son, heir, joint-heir* being essentially personal notions, the Son who is the heir of the Father, since we are his co-heirs, cannot be one and the same Person with the Father ; and the Holy Spirit, who attests our relations with the Father and the Son, must be distinct from the Father and the Son. Our *spirit*—that is to say, the supernatural instinct produced in us by the Holy Spirit—testifies that we are sons by our uttering the filial cry : *Abba, Father.* But to this subjective testimony is joined that of the Holy Spirit himself (συμμαρτυρεῖ = testifies *with*). The Greek Fathers saw this clearly : the Latin Fathers, following the Vulgate (*testimonium reddit spiritui nostro*) thought it meant a testimony rendered by the Holy Spirit *to* our spirit. But this divergence does not affect the present question.

[2] Titus iii, 4-6 : Ὅτε δὲ ἡ χρηστότης καὶ ἡ φιλανθρωπία ἐπεφάνη τοῦ σωτῆρος ἡμῶν Θεοῦ . . . ἔσωσεν ἡμᾶς διὰ λουτροῦ παλιγγενεσίας καὶ ἀνακαινώσεως Πνεύματος ἁγίου, οὗ ἐξέχεεν ἐφ' ἡμᾶς πλουσίως διὰ Ἰησοῦ Χριστοῦ τοῦ σωτῆρος ἡμῶν.—The whole effect of baptismal regeneration, instead of being attributed to the three Persons by co-ordination, as in Matt. xxviii, 19, is here

It is clearly a question here of the fruits of baptism : initial salvation, regeneration, and renovation. God the Father initiates them purely by an act of his mercy without any regard to the merits which we did not have and of which we were incapable, and he produces these effects by the bestowal of the Holy Spirit. On the other hand, regeneration and renovation belong to the sanctifying Spirit (παλιγγενεσίας καὶ ἀνακαινώσεως Πνεύματος ἁγίου) which is poured out upon us by God the Father, and at the same time by Jesus Christ, called by virtue of this our Saviour. Thus the baptismal re-birth is due to the Father of mercies, as the first source of divine being (it is he who is the subject of the whole phrase : ἔσωσεν, ἐξέχεεν) ; it is due also to Jesus Christ as mediator (διὰ Ἰησοῦ Χριστοῦ) ; and it is due in the last analysis to the Holy Spirit as the common envoy of the Father and the Son (οὗ ἐξέχεεν διά). All that had been indicated—but less clearly —in a declaration which recalls the trinitarian formula of baptism : " You are washed, you are sanctified, you are justified in the name of our Lord Jesus Christ and the Spirit of our God."[1] St Paul never has baptismal grace in mind without the co-operation of the Father, the Son, and the Holy Ghost.

The three Persons similarly intervene in the conferring and exercise of the apostolate :

> He that confirmeth us with you in *Christ* . . is *God*, who also hath sealed us, and given the pledge of the *Spirit*.[2]

---

attributed by subordination : the Father sanctifies, *in* the Spirit, *by* the Son.— The, so to speak, immediate sanctifier is the Holy Spirit : διὰ λουτροῦ παλιγγενεσίας καὶ ἀνακαινώσεως Πνεύμ. ἁγίου. Baptism is a "bath of re-generation," because it produces instrumentally a second birth of the spiritual order : and this regeneration is explained by a synonym, "the renovation of the Holy Ghost "; he it is who gives to the water of baptism its power to regenerate.—The intermediary sanctifier is Jesus Christ our Saviour ; for on the one hand he sends the Spirit and on the other he is Himself sent by the Father.—The primordial sanctifier is the Father, to whom is attributable the initiative of salvation ; he is moved only by his pity (κατὰ τὸ αὐτοῦ ἔλεος), by his goodness (φιλανθρωπία), and by his gentleness (χρηστότης) ; he saves us by sending his Son and by giving us through him his Spirit, without regard to works accomplished in a state of justice, impossible works, since the state of justice did not yet exist. For details *cf.* Meyer-Weiss (*Die Briefe Pauli an Timotheus und Titus*[1], Göttingen, 1902), or Belser (*Die Briefe an Timotheus und Titus*, Fribourg i. B., 1907).

[1] 1 Cor. vi, 11. See Vol. I, p. 171.

[2] 2 Cor. i, 21-22 :

> ὁ δὲ βεβαιῶν ἡμᾶς σὺν ὑμῖν εἰς Χριστὸν
> καὶ χρίσας ἡμᾶς Θεός, ὁ καὶ σφραγισάμενος ἡμᾶς
> καὶ δοὺς τὸν ἀρραβῶνα τοῦ Πνεύματος.

It is necessary to observe that *us* (ἡμᾶς, ἡμῶν) denotes only Paul and his colleagues. This appears from the whole context and in particular from the phrase " *with you* " (σὺν ὑμῖν). It is not, therefore, a question of confirma-tion, common to all the faithful, but of the apostolate, peculiar only to the preachers of the Gospel.—Moreover, the subject of the entire phrase is, without any possible dispute, *God the Father*, since he is placed in personal

God confirms Paul and his colleagues constantly ($\beta\epsilon\beta\alpha\iota\hat{\omega}\nu$) ; he anointed them one day with the spirit of courage ($\chi\rho\iota\sigma\alpha s$) and marked them as with a seal ($\sigma\phi\rho\alpha\gamma\iota\sigma\alpha\mu\epsilon\nu\sigma s$), conferring upon them the *charismata* which legitimate their apostolate in the eyes of the faithful. This seal, this pledge, is none other than the Holy Spirit, the dispenser of the *charismata*. And God works this miracle by constantly directing the apostles towards Christ ($\epsilon\iota s$ $\chi\rho\iota\sigma\tau\acute{o}\nu$) and binding them to him by his grace. We see how the divine Persons contribute to the endowment of the preachers of the faith: the Father as the original author of the spiritual gifts, the Son as the source of their supernatural life, and the Holy Spirit as the seal of their mission and the pledge of their success.

We find this co-operation of the three Persons in another text of singular force. Paul excuses himself for writing to the Romans with so much apostolic freedom; but by reason of the task which has been given him, he is:

> The minister of *Christ Jesus* among the Gentiles, devoted to the service of the Gospel of *God*, that the oblation of the Gentiles, sanctified by the *Holy Ghost*, may be made an acceptable [sacrifice].[1]

Here the phraseology of sacrifice is plain. The Apostle exercises in regard to the Gentiles a kind of priesthood; he

---

contrast to Christ and to the Spirit. The action of the Father is expressed by four participles : one in the present tense ($\beta\epsilon\beta\alpha\iota\hat{\omega}\nu$), denoting a permanent source of help which the apostles share in some measure with all Christians ; the other three, in the past tense, indicating a transitory act, accomplished once for all in the apostles only, the effects of which, however, can still endure.

[1] Rom. xv, 15, 16 :

$$\delta\iota\grave{\alpha} \ \tau\grave{\eta}\nu \ \chi\acute{\alpha}\rho\iota\nu \ \tau\grave{\eta}\nu \ \delta\sigma\theta\epsilon\hat{\iota}\sigma\acute{\alpha}\nu \ \mu\sigma\iota \ \grave{\alpha}\pi\grave{\sigma} \ \tau\sigma\hat{\upsilon} \ \Theta\epsilon\sigma\hat{\upsilon}$$
$$\epsilon\grave{\iota}s \ \tau\grave{\sigma} \ \epsilon\grave{\iota}\nu\alpha\acute{\iota} \ \mu\epsilon \ \lambda\epsilon\iota\tau\sigma\upsilon\rho\gamma\grave{\sigma}\nu \ X\rho\iota\sigma\tau\sigma\hat{\upsilon} \ {}^{,}I\eta\sigma\sigma\hat{\upsilon} \ \epsilon\grave{\iota}s \ \tau\grave{\alpha} \ \check{\epsilon}\theta\nu\eta,$$
$$\iota\epsilon\rho\sigma\upsilon\rho\gamma\sigma\hat{\upsilon}\nu\tau\alpha \ \tau\grave{\sigma} \ \epsilon\grave{\upsilon}\alpha\gamma\gamma\acute{\epsilon}\lambda\iota\sigma\nu \ \tau\sigma\hat{\upsilon} \ \Theta\epsilon\sigma\hat{\upsilon},$$
$$\iota\nu\alpha \ \gamma\acute{\epsilon}\nu\eta\tau\alpha\iota \ \dot{\eta} \ \pi\rho\sigma\sigma\phi\sigma\rho\grave{\alpha} \ \tau\hat{\omega}\nu \ \check{\epsilon}\theta\nu\omega\nu \ \epsilon\grave{\upsilon}\pi\rho\acute{\sigma}\sigma\delta\epsilon\kappa\tau\sigma s, \ \dot{\eta}\gamma\iota\alpha\sigma\mu\acute{\epsilon}\nu\eta$$
$$\grave{\epsilon}\nu \ \Pi\nu\epsilon\acute{\upsilon}\mu\alpha\tau\iota \ \dot{\alpha}\gamma\acute{\iota}\omega.$$

The conjunction of the five words, $\lambda\epsilon\iota\tau\sigma\upsilon\rho\gamma\acute{\sigma}s$, $\iota\epsilon\rho\sigma\upsilon\rho\gamma\sigma\hat{\upsilon}\nu\tau\alpha$, $\pi\rho\sigma\sigma\phi\sigma\rho\acute{\alpha}$, $\epsilon\grave{\upsilon}\pi\rho\acute{\sigma}\sigma\delta\epsilon\kappa\tau\sigma s$, $\dot{\eta}\gamma\iota\alpha\sigma\mu\acute{\epsilon}\nu\eta$, shows that this passage is a prolonged allegory or metaphor, having for its point of departure the consecration of the Gentiles to God in baptism, a consecration regarded under the figure of a sacrifice offered to God by the ministers of Christ, with the co-operation of the Spirit as sanctifier.—Paul takes part in this only as *a delegate of Christ to the Gentiles :* $\lambda\epsilon\iota\tau\sigma\upsilon\rho\gamma\acute{\sigma}s$ signifies generally " a sacred minister " (Heb. viii, 1, 2 : Jesus Christ is $\dot{\alpha}\rho\chi\iota\epsilon\rho\epsilon\acute{\upsilon}s$ and $\tau\hat{\omega}\nu \ \dot{\alpha}\gamma\acute{\iota}\omega\nu \ \lambda\epsilon\iota\tau\sigma\upsilon\rho\gamma\acute{\sigma}s$) ; but in the Septuagint this word often denotes a minister of inferior rank ($\sigma\iota \ \iota\epsilon\rho\epsilon\hat{\iota}s \ \kappa\alpha\grave{\iota} \ \sigma\iota \ \lambda\epsilon\iota\tau\sigma\upsilon\rho\gamma\sigma\acute{\iota}$ =priests and levites).—The role of Paul is only preparatory and indirect ; $\iota\epsilon\rho\sigma\upsilon\rho\gamma\epsilon\hat{\iota}\nu$ means " to perform a sacred rite," or else " to exercise a sacred ministry in regard to something," and is construed with the accusative ($\iota\epsilon\rho\sigma\upsilon\rho\gamma\hat{\omega}\nu \ \tau\grave{\sigma} \ \epsilon\grave{\upsilon}\alpha\gamma\gamma\acute{\epsilon}\lambda\iota\sigma\nu$ =" being a sacred minister of the Gospel," who prepares the Gentiles to be offered to God).—The words $\dot{\eta} \ \pi\rho\sigma\sigma\phi\sigma\rho\grave{\alpha} \ \tau\hat{\omega}\nu \ \check{\epsilon}\theta\nu\omega\nu$ are a genitive of apposition : " the offering, the sacrifice, of which the Gentiles are the subject and the material."—Under the old Law every victim offered up according to the prescribed rules was pleasing to God ($\epsilon\grave{\upsilon}\pi\rho\acute{\sigma}\sigma\delta\epsilon\kappa\tau\sigma s$, *acceptabilis*), and consecrated to God ($\dot{\eta}\gamma\iota\alpha\sigma\mu\acute{\epsilon}\nu\eta$). The offering of the Gentiles will become so by the presence and operation of the Holy Spirit ($\grave{\epsilon}\nu \ \Pi\nu\epsilon\acute{\upsilon}\mu\alpha\tau\iota \ \dot{\alpha}\gamma\acute{\iota}\omega$).—The text as a whole presents no difficulty, if the exact value of each term is established.

himself indeed does not offer up the sacrifice, but he is the aid and assistant (λειτουργός) of the one and only High Priest of the New Covenant, Jesus Christ. The victim to be offered (προσφορά) is the Gentiles; and, dying with Jesus Christ in baptism, in union with the Victim of Calvary, they, too, become victims pleasing to God. Paul prepares them for it by making himself the consecrated minister (ἱερουργοῦντα) of the Gospel, who, so to speak, leads catechumens to the foot of the altar. There remains only to render the victim acceptable to God and worthy of being offered to him; and this is the role of the Holy Spirit. In brief, it is the Father who receives the sacrifice; it is Jesus Christ who, by the ministry of Paul, presents it; and it is the Holy Spirit who sanctifies and consecrates it.

A detailed examination of all the trinitarian texts would carry us too far. In order to express this constant phenomenon of relative opposition and mutual interpenetration, and to make it consistent with the strict monotheism, which, as all concede, predominates in the writings of St Paul, only one exact formula is possible: Trinity in Unity.


## II—THE FATHER, THE SON, AND THE HOLY GHOST

1. God the Father. 2. The Son of God. 3. The Spirit of the Father and the Son.

1. The part of the divine paternity in the New Testament has been much exaggerated. Jehovah had for his people the care and solicitude of a tender father;[1] the Israelites, collectively and as a nation, were the sons of God or the son of God;[2] even the theocratic king, a type of the Messiah, was exceptionally entitled a son.[3] Nevertheless, the divine paternity assumes in the New Testament a greater amplitude and prominence. Father is henceforth the proper name for God. The Christian's cry of hope, the aspiration which the Holy Spirit continually brings to his lips, in proof of his filial adoption, is that appeal of the heart: *Abba, Father!*[4] As Father, love is the characteristic note of God. If Paul did not have the honour of inventing the formula *Deus*

---

[1] Deut. i, 31; viii, 5; xxxii, 6; Isa. lxiii, 16; lxiv, 8; Jer. iii, 4, 19; xxxi, 9; Mal. ii, 10; Ps. cii, 13; Wisd. ii, 18; Eccl. xxiii, 1, 4 (Κύριε πάτερ καὶ Θεὲ ζωῆς μου).

[2] Ex. iv, 22, 23 (*Filius meus primogenitus Israel. Dimitte filium meum*); Deut. xiv, 1, 2 (*Filii estote Domini Dei vestri*); Os. xi, 1 (*Quia puer Israel et dilexi eum: et ex Aegypto vocavi filium meum*); Isa. i, 2; Jer. xxxi, 20.

[3] Ps. ii, 7; 2 Sam. vii, 14; Ps. lxxxviii, 27. *Cf.* Heb. i, 4. The angels are sons of God, but none of them is *the* Son of God.—Nevertheless, the individual meaning of the expression "son of God" begins to appear in Wisdom and Ecclesiastes. *Cf.* Lagrange, *La paternité de Dieu dans l'A.T.* (*Rev. biblique*, 1908, pp. 481-499).

[4] Rom. viii, 15; Gal. iv, 6.

*caritas est,* he celebrates at every opportunity the love of God and the God of love, the Father of mercies, of whom goodness is the dominant trait.[1]

God displays his paternity in the three distinct spheres: of creation, of grace, and of his inner life. God is a Father, and is so by essence; his paternal providence extends to all rational beings, whom he loads with blessings; all that which in heaven or on earth forms a family is only a reflection, an image, a shadow of his paternity. In the sphere of grace God has as many sons as Jesus Christ himself adopts as brothers; their number is limitless, and includes potentially the whole human race. On the contrary, in the circle of his inner life, God has, and can have, only one Son; the production of a consubstantial Son exhausts his fecundity.

The paternity of God, as Creator, appears only once, and in a rather enigmatic text: " I bow my knees to the Father of whom all paternity (*toute famille,* πατριά) in heaven and earth is named."[2] It is almost always considered as a function of the sanctifying grace which renders us sons of God, and it is then expressed in various terms: *Father* or *Abba, Father* or *God the Father,* or *God and Father,* or *God our Father,* or *our God and Father.*[3]

All these formulas may also, in a different sense, be applied to the Father of the Word incarnate. When Paul offers his thanksgiving to the " God and Father of Jesus Christ,"[4] it is in vain that some timid interpreters propose to divide the sentence thus: " God, who is also the Father of the Lord Jesus." The Greek article, common to both nouns, is opposed to it. Moreover, the expression " God of our Lord

---

[1] 1 John iv, 8 (ὁ Θεὸς ἀγάπη ἐστίν);—Rom. v, 5; viii, 39 (ἡ ἀγάπη τοῦ Θεοῦ); 1 Cor xiii, 11 (ὁ Θεὸς τῆς ἀγάπης); 2 Cor. i, 3 (ὁ πατὴρ τῶν οἰκτιρμῶν).

[2] Eph. iii, 14: κάμπτω τὰ γόνατά μου πρὸς τὸν πατέρα, ἐξ οὗ πᾶσα πατριὰ ἐν οὐρανοῖς καὶ ἐπὶ γῆς ὀνομάζεται. The words *Domini nostri J. C.* have no equivalent in the Greek. Paul is addressing God as the author of grace and not as the author of nature; but he uses the occasion to announce the divine paternity in all its amplitude.—If it were possible to understand πατριά in the sense of πατρότης (as Theodoret and the author of the Vulgate do) the passage would be quite clear: " all paternity is a derivation from the paternity of God." But then we must ask what "the paternity in the heavens" may be Moreover, πατριά does not mean " paternity," but a " race, or tribe born of one father," and by extension "family or nation." The meaning, therefore, is: " All that can be called πατριά (*family* in the widest sense) derives its name (ὀνομάζεται) from the word πατήρ, which is the real name of God." The classes of celestial spirits are compared to families.

[3] *Father* simply (Eph. ii, 18; iii, 14): 'Αββᾶ, ὁ πατήρ (Rom. viii, 15; Gal. iv, 6).—*God the Father* (1 Cor. viii, 6; Gal. i, 1; Eph. vi, 23; Phil. ii, 11; 1 Thess. i, 3; 2 Thess, i, 2; 1 Tim. i, 2; 2 Tim. i, 2; Titus i, 4).—*God and Father* (Eph. iv, 6; v, 20).—*God Father* (Col. iii, 17).—*God our Father* (Rom. i, 7; 1 Cor. i, 3; 2 Cor. i, 2; Eph. i, 2; Phil. i, 2; Col. i, 2; 2 Thess. i, 1).—*Our God and Father* (Gal. i, 4; Phil. iv, 20; 1 Thess. i, 3; iii, 11, 13; 2 Thess. ii, 16).

[4] Rom. xv, 6; 2 Cor. i, 3; xi, 31.

Jesus Christ,"[1] which is found textually in St Paul and virtually in St John, has nothing unusual in it. It is only necessary to note that Christ's sonship and our own are related merely by analogy.

2. In the Synoptists it is sometimes difficult to determine the precise value of the name " Son of God." The testimony of Satan is hardly of a nature to enlighten us.[2] That of the centurion is no clearer.[3] Peter's confession, as it appears from its three different readings, may be only an explicit recognition of the messianic dignity.[4] The voice from heaven, heard at the baptism and at the transfiguration, by its two-fold allusion to a word from Isaias and the Psalms, seems equally to be based upon the Old Testament.[5] It is evident that, even in the Synoptists, Jesus is not *a* son like the others, but that he is *the* Son *par excellence,* and that there is, there-fore, a special relation between him and the Father, and we have a right to conclude that this relation, unique in its kind, is of a superhuman order. Thus Jesus never confounds his position in regard to the heavenly Father with that of his disciples ; he teaches them to say " our Father," but for his part he says : " My Father and your Father," never " our Father " when speaking of himself and of them together.[6] He is careful to put himself into a category apart by saying, for example, that of the day and hour of the *parousia* " no man knows, neither the angels in heaven, nor the Son, but the

---

[1] Eph. i, 17 ; ὁ Θεὸς τοῦ Κυρίου ἡμῶν ᾽I. X. *Cf.* John xx, 17 : *Ascendo ad Patrem meum et Patrem vestrum,* Deum meum *et Deum vestrum.* In I Cor. xv, 24, when Christ the victor restores his kingdom " to God and the Father," it is necessary likewise to understand it as " to his God and Father."

Another example is Col. i, 3 : τῷ Θεῷ πατρὶ τοῦ Κυρίου, provided that it ought not to read : τῷ Θεῷ καὶ πατρί.

[2] Satan's words to Jesus (Matt. iv, 3 ; Luke iv, 3) ; demoniacs of Gadara (Matt. viii, 29 ; Mark v, 7 ; Luke viii, 28).

[3] According to Matt. xxvii, 54 and Mark xv, 39, the centurion says : " Truly this man was *son of God*" (υἱός without an article) ; according to Luke xxiii, 47 : " Indeed this was a just man." Compare the challenge of his tormentors (Matt. xxvii 40) and the question of Pilate (Matt. xxvi, 63 ; Luke xxii, 70). *Cf.* Matt. xi, 3 ; Luke vii, 19 ; Matt. xiv, 33.

[4] Matt. xvi, 16 : " Thou art the Christ, the Son of the living God." These last words, " the Son of the living God," are omitted by Mark viii, 29 and by Luke ix, 20, as if they were virtually included in the name of " Christ " or " Messiah." They are indeed so included, since the Messiah announced by the prophets was to be the Son of God and God. See Knabenbauer's Commentary on these texts.

[5] Baptism (Matt. iii, 17 ; Mark i, 11 ; Luke iii, 22); transfiguration (Matt. xvii, 5 ; Mark ix, 7 ; Luke ix, 35). Compare these texts with Ps. ii, 7 and Isa. xlii, 1.

[6] Compare on the one hand Luke xxii, 29 ; xxiv, 49 ; Matt. x, 33 ; Mark viii, 38, and on the other Matt. vi, 32 ; vii, 11 ; Luke xi, 13 ; xii, 32.—Take into account the parable of the husbandmen, which shows that there is only *one* Son (Mark xii, 6 ; Matt. xxi, 37 ; Luke xx, 13), and the words of the archangel to Mary, Luke i, 35 : " He shall be called the Son of God."

Father."[1] By his acts and his words he shows that his sonship is transcendent; and the Jews understand him thus clearly, since they accuse him of blasphemy in having proclaimed himself the Son of God.[2] Nevertheless, if we considered the Synoptists alone, we might perhaps ask ourselves whether the title of Son, given to Christ, refers directly to his pre-existent being or to his messianic character, and it is a fact that he is not called Son of God by the Synoptists themselves, if, as many think, the words υἱοῦ Θεοῦ in the title of the second Gospel are an interpolation.[3]

With St Paul—as with St John and the writer of the Epistle to the Hebrews—no doubt is possible. The quality of Son refers plainly to his pre-existence : " When the fulness of the time was come, God sent his Son[4] . . . God, sending his own Son in the likeness of sinful flesh and for sin, condemned sin in the flesh."[5] He does not constitute him his Son by sending him—that is absurd—he sends him because he is his Son. He is *the* Son by antonomasia, or, again, *the* Son of God, his *own* Son, the Son of his love :[6] he must therefore be the Son in a way entirely different to our adoptive sonship, which is imperfect and shared with others ; he must be so by a special and incommunicable title; and he must be so by nature and by an inalienable right, although he can, in an inferior sense and by analogy, give himself adopted brethren and join to himself co-heirs, and merit thus the name of the " First-born among many brethren."[7]

If Christ was the Son of God previous to his earthly birth, this title is not a purely messianic appellation. It is often stated that in the days of the New Testament the appellation Son of God was synonymous with Messiah; but no one has ever furnished the proof of this assertion. For one who gave to the second Psalm a messianic sense the name Son of God must truly have been a title of the Messiah; but the question here is quite different : it is to know whether the Jewish contemporaries of St Paul, on hearing the Son of God named, could and must have understood, without further explanation, that the promised Messiah was spoken of. In reality, all the indications are opposed to this. Origen, who understood the subject well, laughs at Celsus for having made his Jew say that the *Son of God* would come to Jerusalem : " Never," · replies Origen, " would a genuine Jew have

---

[1] Mark xiii, 32.
[2] Matt. xxvii, 43.
[3] Mark i, 1.
[4] Gal. iv, 4.
[5] Rom. viii, 3. This text is explained later on, pp. 163-5.
[6] Rom. i, 3, 9 ; v, 10 ; viii, 29 ; 1 Cor. i, 9 ; 2 Cor. i, 19 ; Gal. i, 16 ; ii, 20 ; iv, 4, 6 ; Eph. iv, 13 ; 1 Thess. i, 10 (ὁ υἱὸς τοῦ Θεοῦ). Cf. Heb. iv, 14 ; vi, 6 ; vii, 3 ; x, 29.—1 Cor. xv, 28 (ὁ Υἱὸς by antonomasia). Cf. Heb. i, 2, 8. —Rom. viii, 3 (τὸν ἑαυτοῦ υἱόν, his own Son) ; Rom. viii, 32 (τοῦ ἰδίου υἱοῦ, his own Son).—Col. i, 13 (τοῦ υἱοῦ τῆς ἀγάπης αὐτοῦ).
[7] Rom. viii, 29.

spoken so. The real Jews ask us, on the contrary, what we mean when they hear us mention the Son of God."[1] If it be supposed that this title was one of the usual names of the Messiah, it ought to be found frequently in Jewish literature ; but there is not a trace of it outside of the Fourth Book of Esdras, which is subsequent to our era and has been several times interpolated by Christian hands, we do not know exactly to what extent.[2] The silence of the apocryphal writings is confirmed by the language of the sacred authors. For them the Messiah is indeed the Son of God, but the name " Son of God " is not the same thing as the rank of Messiah. And this is still more true of St Paul, the one who of all of them emphasised least the Messiahship of Jesus. Paul treats the appellation " Christ " as a proper name, without ever stopping to think of its etymological meaning, which was of little importance to his readers. The password of his orthodoxy, the epitome of his creed, is not : " Jesus is the Christ "—that is to say, the Messiah ; but " Jesus is the Lord." So, far from establishing an identity between the name of Christ and that of Son of God, he does not even indicate a connection between these two terms. And still more certainly does he not teach what certain exegetes too carelessly impute to him, that Jesus acquires all at once, at the moment of his resurrection, his universal lordship, his messianic dignity, and his divine sonship.

3. The personal character of the Holy Spirit appears only gradually in the Bible. It has been asked whether, in the beginning of Genesis, the " Spirit of God " denotes the blowing of the wind or a divine activity, and the same question

---

[1] *Contra Celsum*, i, 49 (XI, 753).

[2] That, in the *Life of Adam and Eve*, 42 (Kautzsch, *Die Pseudepigraphen des A. T.*, Tübingen, 1900, p. 520) the passage referring to Christ, the Son of God, has been interpolated by a Christian hand, it is impossible to doubt. As to the one solitary text of the Book of Enoch, cv, 2 (*ibid.*, p. 308), where there is question of the Son of God, that has likewise been doctored and retouched. Dalman and many others regard the fragment as a Christian addition. The only authority, therefore, is 4 Esdras, xiii, 32 (*et tunc revelabitur filius meus*), 37 (*Ipse autem filius meus arguet*, etc.), 52 (*Sic non poterit quisquam super terram videre filium meum*). For 4 Esdras, xiv, 9, see Kautzsch (*ibid.*, p. 398) ; the Latin version is quite different. There is still 4 Esdras, vii, 28 (*Revelabitur filius meus Jesus*), 29 (*Et erit post annos hos et morietur filius meus Christus*) ; but verse 28 is interpolated, as is to be seen from the different readings of the other versions : my son the Messiah (Syriac), my Messiah (Ethiopian), the Messiah of God (Armenian), the Messiah (Arabic). In *Psalm. Salom.*, xvii, 23 : ἴδε, κύριε, καὶ ἀνάστησον αὐτοῖς τὸν βασιλέα αὐτῶν υἱὸν Δαυίδ . . . τοῦ βασιλεῦσαι ἐπὶ Ἰσραὴλ παῖδά σου, it is Israel that is the *son of God*. Note that in the Pseudo-Esdras God speaks of the Messiah *his* Son (Ps. ii, 7), without the Messiah being called Son of God, which is very different.

In these conditions one can only subscribe to the conclusion of Stanton (*The Jewish and the Christian Messiah*, Edinburgh, 1886, p. 288) : " It [the name Son of God] could not with them be a mere title of Messiahship."

has been asked in regard to the spirit that reanimates and renews the face of the earth.[1]    But the concepts become finer in proportion as revelation progresses, and as the Spirit of God becomes more and more free from all material alloy. No confusion is possible in regard to the inspirer of the prophets and the sanctifier of the just.[2]    In the New Testament the Spirit scarcely assumes any form perceptible by the senses except by an allusion to the ancient prophecies.    Even on the day of Pentecost, when he appears in fire and tempest, St Luke speaks only of tongues *as of* fire and of a noise *as of* a hurricane.[3]    Its special emblem will thenceforth be *gushing water*.[4]

St Paul likes to associate him with the immaterial part of man and to put it in relative antithesis to the Son and to the Father.    The Spirit is sent by the Father and by the Son ; he is given by the Father and by the Son ; he is the Spirit of the Father and the Spirit of the Son.[5]    We rightly infer from this the distinct personality of the Holy Spirit and his simultaneous procession from the Son and the Father.    Although he never receives the name of God, he has the attributes of God.    Grace, the divine work *par excellence,* is derived from the Holy Spirit, as well as from the Father and the Son.    The operation of the Spirit is also that of Christ and of the Father.[6]    The faithful are called, equally, temples of the Holy Ghost and temples of God.[7]    The Father, the Son, and the Holy Spirit are inseparably united in the bestowal of baptism, and they dwell conjointly in the souls of the just.[8] No one is acceptable to God unless he is influenced by the Spirit of God,[9] and the greatest misfortune that could befall a Christian would be to grieve the Spirit,[10] without whom he is incapable of receiving any spiritual good.    Do these texts, taken by themselves alone, prove incontrovertibly that the Holy Spirit is God, and that he is a personal being, not a divine attribute personified?[11]    In any case, they should not

---

[1] Gen. i, 2 ; Ps. ciii, 30.

[2] 1 Sam. x, 10 ; xi, 6 ; xix, 20, 23, etc.—Os. ix, 7 (אִישׁ חָרוּחַ, πνευματοφόρος, *vir spiritus*).—Isa. xi, 1-3 : רוֹחַ יְחֹוָה is again here in the feminine, like its material symbol, which proves that the personification is not complete.

[3] Acts ii, 2, 3.

[4] John vii, 38, 39 ; Acts ii, 17, 18 (quoted from Joel ii, 28).

[5] Spirit of God (Rom. viii, 9, 11 ; 1 Cor. ii, 11, etc.), Spirit of Christ (Rom. viii, 9 ; 2 Cor. iii, 17, etc.). Given or sent by God (1 Thess. iv, 8 ; 1 Cor. ii, 12 ; 2 Cor. i, 22 ; v, 5).

[6] 1 Cor. xii, 11 ; Eph. iv, 11 ; *cf.* 1 Cor. xii, 6, 28.

[7] Temples of God (1 Cor. iii, 16) ; of the Holy Ghost (1 Cor. vi, 19).

[8] Titus iii, 4, 6 ; 1 Cor. vi, 11.

[9] Rom. viii, 9.          [10] Eph. iv, 30.

[11] Lebreton, *Les origines de la Trinité*[4], Paris, 1919, p. 405 : " In consequence of the point of view chosen by the Apostle, the action of the Spirit appears much more clearly than his person ; the distinct personality of the Son is manifested very plainly in his mortal and glorious life, and, even in his pre-

be taken by themselves or separated from the other trinitarian passages; for, when taken together, they acquire a
convincing force vastly superior to that which they possess
when considered apart; and their value increases still more
when they are connected with the uniform teaching of the
apostles and find a place again in the great current of
Catholic tradition.

Not that it is necessary to undervalue isolated texts. No
mind, St Paul tells us, can conceive the happiness which God
prepares for those who love him:

> But to us God hath revealed it by the Spirit, for the Spirit searcheth
> all things, even the deep things of God. For what man knoweth the
> things of a man, but the spirit of a man that is in him? So the things
> also that are of God, no man knoweth, but the Spirit of God. Now we
> have received not the spirit of this world, but the Spirit that is of God,
> that we may know the things that are given us from God.[1]

Three truths issue from this text. The Spirit of God *only*
is capable of revealing the mysteries of God, because he *only*
searches the depths of God: he does not belong, therefore, to
the category of created things; possessing omniscience, an
essentially divine attribute, he must himself be God. The
Spirit of God is to God what the spirit of man is to man; the
Spirit of God is, therefore, in God and is something divine.

---

existence, it has been more than once described by St Paul, especially when
he was incited to it by nascent heresies. On the contrary, the personality
of the Holy Spirit remains in shadow; he has not appeared to us in an incarnation, and the mysteries of his procession and eternal life are as yet only
indirectly illumined by the reflections of his action here below."

[1] 1 Cor. ii, 10: Ἡμῖν γὰρ (or δὲ) ἀπεκάλυψεν ὁ Θεὸς διὰ τοῦ
Πνεύματος· τὸ γὰρ Πνεῦμα πάντα ἐραυνᾷ, καὶ τὰ βάθη τοῦ Θεοῦ.

11. Τίς γὰρ οἶδεν ἀνθρώπων τὰ τοῦ ἀνθρώπου εἰ μὴ τὸ πνεῦμα τοῦ ἀνθρώπου
τὸ ἐν αὐτῷ; οὕτως καὶ τὰ τοῦ Θεοῦ οὐδεὶς ἔγνωκεν εἰ μὴ τὸ Πνεῦμα τοῦ
Θεοῦ.

12. Ἡμεῖς δὲ οὐ τὸ πνεῦμα τοῦ κόσμου ἐλάβομεν ἀλλὰ τὸ Πνεῦμα τὸ ἐκ
τοῦ Θεοῦ.

A. *Meaning of* ἡμεῖς.—Here *us* (ἡμεῖς) does not designate all Christians,
but only the preachers of the Gospel, those who can say with Paul: *Sapientiam
loquimur inter perfectos* (verse 6). It is to them that the Spirit has revealed
the mysteries of God, that they might transmit them to the faithful: *Quae et
loquimur non in doctis humanae sapientiae verbis sed in doctrina Spiritus*
(verse 13).

B. *Meaning of the word* πνεῦμα.—The Spirit of God (verse 11) and also
*Spirit* (verse 10) is certainly the Holy Spirit. The *spirit of man* which is in
man (verse 11) can be only the intellect; it is, therefore, a mere synonym
of νοῦς. The *spirit of the world* which we have not received is, according
to some exegetes, the devil; but, apart from the fact that this thought,
"We have not received the devil," is a very strange expression, the whole
beginning of the Epistle shows that it is a question here of the wisdom,
the mentality of the world; and this is also the opinion of most of the
commentators. The *spirit that comes from God* could be, strictly interpreted,
by virtue of the parallelism, supernatural mentality, wisdom inspired by
God. But, if we reflect how easily the Apostle passes from the effects of
the Holy Spirit to the Holy Spirit himself, and if we compare what he says
a little further on (verses 13 and 14): *in doctrina Spiritus, quae sunt Spiritus
Dei*, we shall not hesitate to believe that he is speaking here again of the
person of the Holy Spirit.

Finally, the Spirit of God is also the Spirit which comes from God (τὸ ἐκ Θεοῦ), proceeds from God, and is sent by him.

Another no less suggestive passage is the following:

> You are not in the flesh, but in the spirit, if so be that the Spirit of God dwell in you. Now if any man have not the Spirit of Christ, he is none of his. And if Christ be in you, the body indeed is dead, because of sin, but the spirit liveth, because of justice. And if the Spirit of him that raised up Jesus from the dead dwell in you, he that raised up Jesus Christ from the dead shall quicken also your mortal bodies by his Spirit, [or *because of his Spirit* that dwelleth] in you.[1]

The Holy Spirit is here presented as a personal being who dwells in us, influences us by his action, and bears witness to our spirit. He is in us as a principle of supernatural life, of sanctification, and of filial adoption, effects which are produced in us only by a divine influence. Moreover, the Spirit of the Father is the Spirit of the Son : he cannot dwell within us without the Son dwelling there also, and his absence involves that of the Son ; which presupposes an indissoluble union between them.

These relations between the Spirit and the Son have, however, a limit, since all the attributes of the Son are not adapted to the Holy Spirit. The latter is never called the

---

[1] Rom. viii, 9: Ὑμεῖς δὲ οὐκ ἐστὲ ἐν σαρκὶ ἀλλὰ ἐν πνεύματι, εἴπερ Πνεῦμα Θεοῦ οἰκεῖ ἐν ὑμῖν· εἰ δέ τις Πνεῦμα Χριστοῦ οὐκ ἔχει, οὗτος οὐκ ἔστιν αὐτοῦ.

10. Εἰ δὲ Χριστὸς ἐν ὑμῖν, τὸ μὲν σῶμα νεκρὸν διὰ ἁμαρτίαν, τὸ δὲ πνεῦμα ζωὴ διὰ δικαιοσύνην.

11. Εἰ δὲ τὸ Πνεῦμα τοῦ ἐγείραντος τὸν Ἰησοῦν ἐκ νεκρῶν οἰκεῖ ἐν ὑμῖν, ὁ ἐγείρας ἐκ νεκρῶν Χριστὸν Ἰησοῦν ζωοποιήσει καὶ τὰ θνητὰ σώματα ὑμῶν διὰ τοῦ ἐνοικοῦντος αὐτοῦ Πνεύματος (or διὰ τὸ ἐνοικοῦν αὐτοῦ Πνεῦμα) ἐν ὑμῖν.

A. *Meaning of* πνεῦμα.—(a) It is agreed that the Spirit of God and the Spirit of Christ (verse 9) as well as the Spirit of him who raised up Jesus from the dead (verse 11) denote the Holy Spirit.—(b) In the phrase : *vos autem in carne non estis sed in spiritu*, it is better to understand by " the spirit " the super-natural principle which animates a man in a state of grace ; first on account of the antithesis *in carne* (nature dominated by sin), then on account of the explanation *si tamen Spiritus Dei habitat in vobis*, the Holy Spirit being the living source of our *spirit*.—(c) In *spiritus vero vivit propter justificationem*, the sense will be the same by virtue of the contrast between the body and the spirit, and because it is not the Holy Spirit but our spirit (our supernaturalized being) that justification quickens.

B. *Two effects of the indwelling of Christ or the Spirit within us.*— (a) Henceforth, if the body is dead (by anticipation) on account of the original sin which caused death to come upon all the posterity of Adam, the spirit is life (full of vitality) on account of the justice which comes to us from Christ. Some give the explanation : " The body is dead (mystically and morally), namely in regard to sin (διὰ τὴν ἁμαρτίαν), to which it is no more subjected." But this exegesis is not a very natural one and does not take into account the adversative particle ἀλλά.—(b) One day the body, the tabernacle of the Holy Spirit, will be raised from the dead *on account* of the presence of the Spirit (διὰ τὸ ἐνοικοῦν) or *by the action* of the Spirit present in us (διὰ τοῦ ἐνοικοῦντος). The two readings are almost equally well attested and each gives an excellent interpretation.

Son of God and never takes the predicates of the historical Christ; on the other hand, he is the Spirit of the Son, and is sent by the Son; in a word, he seems still more distinct from the Son than he is from the Father. The heterodox exegetes who confound the Spirit of God with the Son of God rely on the supposed identity of the two expressions " in Christ " and " in the Spirit," and on two texts of St Paul skilfully handled. We shall examine these expressions later on, and shall prove that their identity has to do only with the work relating to the sanctification of souls.[1] As for the two texts: " The second Adam became a quickening spirit,"[2] and " the Lord is the spirit,"[3] we shall see that they have nothing to do with the Holy Spirit.

### III—External Relations

#### 1. Christ is First in All Things.    2. The Rock of Israel.

1. We have seen that Christ possesses the primacy in everything, both in the natural and the supernatural order: *in omnibus ipse primatum tenens*. This absolute primacy, which implies a pre-eminence of rank and a priority of existence, is the term which best expresses his relations with the exterior world. He is " the firstborn of every creature," not by virtue of a moral superiority, which would make of him the first and most eminent of creatures, for all created beings without exception, in heaven and on earth, owe their existence to him; but by virtue of a relation of temporal priority, and because he was born before the creation of the world, a fact which the Apostle explains by substituting for this title an equivalent which is free from any ambiguity:: " He is *before* all things."

The absolute primacy of the Son is expressed by this other formula: " All things are in him, all things are by him, all things are for him." All things are *in* him because, being the perfect image of God, he comprises the ideal and the model of all things possible, and is thus the exemplary cause of all contingent beings. All things are *by* him, as the efficient cause, God, in his outward operations, acting by the Son in the Holy Spirit in accordance with the order and harmony of his inmost life. All things are *for* him by a double right, both because the creation is his work and because God, embracing at a glance the whole multitude of his counsels, connected with his Son, in advance and by a special bond of finality, the world of nature and the world of grace. For these two relations of Christ as God and as man, as the author of nature and as the author of grace, are hardly

---

[1] See, later on, " The Life of the Church."
[2] 1 Cor. xv, 45. See pp. 172-3.    [3] 2 Cor. iii, 17. See Note T.

ever separated. But, whether he be considered as God or as man, his transcendent dignity comes originally from his primacy.[1]

2. It is, however, in the work of redemption that the Apostle is principally interested. Christ began that work before his human birth; for "the Rock from which the Israelites drank and which followed them in the desert, was Christ" himself: *Petra autem erat Christus*.[2] For one who bears in mind that Jehovah was the Rock of Israel, that he accompanied his people across the desert, that the pre-existent Christ is even here identified with Jehovah, the text which we have just quoted has in it nothing obscure. "Christ was the Rock," not the Rock of Horeb, struck by the staff of Moses, for that rock did not follow the Hebrews

---

[1] Col. i, 18 : ἵνα γένηται ἐν πᾶσιν αὐτὸς πρωτεύων. It is a *primacy* in every form, according to his divine and human nature, in the natural as well as in the supernatural order. We perceive in the description of Christ, under these two aspects, an exact and sustained parallelism which is no doubt intentional.

| In regard to creation. | In regard to the Church |
|---|---|
| A. πρωτότοκος πάσης κτίσεως | πρωτότοκος ἐκ τῶν νεκρῶν |
| B. ἐν αὐτῷ ἐκτίσθη τὰ πάντα | ἐν ᾧ ἔχομεν τὴν ἀπολύτρωσιν |
| τὰ πάντα ἐν αὐτῷ συνέστηκεν | |
| C. τὰ πάντα δι' αὐτοῦ ἔκτισται, | δι' αὐτοῦ ἀποκαταλλάξαι |
| δι' οὗ τὰ πάντα (1 Cor. viii, 6) | |
| D. τὰ πάντα . . . εἰς αὐτὸν ἔκτισται | τὰ πάντα εἰς αὐτόν. |

The formula A concerns Christ the *firstborn*, Col. i, 15 (creation); Col. i, 18 (the Church).—The formula B, Christ *the exemplary or formal cause*, Col. i, 16, 17 (creation); Eph. i, 7 (Church).—The formula C, Christ the *efficient cause*, Col. i, 16 ; 1 Cor. viii, 6 (creation); Col. i, 20 (Church). —The formula D, Christ *the final cause*, Col. i, 16 (creation); Col. i, 20 (redemption).

We must not, moreover, imagine that these expressions are peculiar to Paul, except perhaps in what concerns the final cause. The other three have their exact parallel in the Gospel of St John and in the Epistle to the Hebrews.

[2] 1 Cor. x, 4 : ἔπινον γὰρ ἐκ πνευματικῆς ἀκολουθούσης πέτρας· ἡ πέτρα δὲ ἦν ὁ Χριστός.—This phrase is connected with the preceding one, for which it gives the reason. It explains (the Vulgate translates *autem*, but the text reads γάρ) why the Hebrews in the desert had *spiritual* food and drink—that is to say, miraculous and, as the context clearly implies, typical—*for* they did not quench their thirst at a material rock, like the rock of Horeb, but at the *spiritual* Rock which accompanied them everywhere. And "the Rock" which I mean, adds Paul, was Christ.—This language would be incomprehensible if we did not remember that the Rock (צוּר) designated Jehovah. No Jew could be ignorant of this, the use of the term was so common. They said not only "the Rock of Israel" (2 Sam. xxiii, 3 ; Isa. xxx, 29), or "my Rock, our Rock," or "the Rock of my hope, the Rock of our salvation," etc., but also simply "Rock" (2 Sam. xxii, 32 ; Ps. xvii, 32 ; Isa. xliv, 8), and with the article "the Rock" (Deut. xxxii, 4).—The meaning is, therefore, clear ; "It was not a material rock which satisfied their thirst, it was the spiritual Rock, Jehovah, always present in the midst of them. Now Jehovah was the pre-existent Christ." For anyone familiar with the teaching of St John, St Paul and the Epistle to the Hebrews, this assertion contains nothing new

in their march, but the veritable Rock which served them as a refuge and a citadel, the spiritual Rock of which Moses had spoken to them.

The pre-existent Christ is the Rock, because he is one with Jehovah. If this identification between Christ and Jehovah awakened some doubt, the Apostle would remove it by adding : " Neither let us tempt Christ, as some of them tempted and perished by the serpents." The Israelites had tempted Jehovah ; but Jehovah, the Rock of Israel, was Christ. Thus the Son of God anticipating, so to speak, the incarnation and anticipating the role of Saviour, was in the midst of the Hebrews, served them as a guide and provided for their wants. It was he who rained down upon them the manna, a nourishment doubly spiritual, both because it was the result of a miracle and because it prefigured the eucharistic bread ; he it was, the angel of Jehovah and Jehovah himself, the mystical Rock, who quenched their thirst by a *spiritual* drink, so called by a twofold significance, as proceeding from a miracle, and as the type of the chalice of benediction. We are happy to say that the best interpreters of all schools return to this explanation, at once so simple and so natural, and recognize that the former incorrect and protestant translation : " The rock *signified* Christ," was inspired by biassed motives. Still less must we think here of the childish and ridiculous fables of the rabbis of the later period, whose imagination deliriously dreamed of a magical stone rolling on through mountains and valleys in the wake of the Hebrews, to furnish them with drinking water. Christ is the true Rock, as he is the true Vine ; but while the latter title belongs to the incarnate Word, the former applies to the pre-existent Christ.

# CHAPTER III

## JESUS CHRIST AS MAN

### I—THE HUMAN NATURE OF CHRIST

**1. Christ truly Man, but God-Man. 2. Mystery of this Union.**

I.

NOTHING equals the emphasis with which St Paul affirms that Christ, whose pre-existence he has just taught, is also truly man, like unto all other men, except as regards sin. This is because Jesus Christ can be a perfect mediator only on condition that he shares our nature : " There is one God and one mediator of God and men, the man Christ Jesus."[1] He is the conqueror of sin and death only by virtue of the solidarity, which makes his cause ours : "For by a man came death, and by a man [must also come] the resurrection of the dead."[2] These explicit statements leave no doubt as to the real meaning of certain expressions which, by themselves, might seem ambiguous. When St Paul says that " the second man is from heaven,"[3] he alludes to his eternal origin ; he contrasts him, from this point of view, with the first Adam formed out of dust and incapable of transmitting to his descendants any life other than the physical one. When he affirms that he who was " in the form of God " took " the form of a servant "[4] and appeared " in the likeness of men," far from denying the truth of his human nature, he adds immediately that Christ was " found as a man " through the experience of his entire life, since he was capable of obedience and was subject to death. Finally, when he speaks of the sending of the Son of God " in the likeness of sinful flesh," he evidently means to exclude the *sinful flesh* and not the flesh itself, for the sending was expressly meant " to condemn sin in the flesh."[5] And what perverse exegesis has ever been able to discover the slightest trace of Docetism in the following passage : " If we have known Christ according to the flesh, now we know him so no longer "?[6] It is one thing not to recognize the reality of the flesh of Christ, and quite another no longer to know Christ according to the flesh— that is, according to the low, earthly, carnal ideas of Paul's adversaries.

In order to fulfil his mission Christ must be truly man ;

[1] I Tim. ii, 5.  See pp. 167-8.          [2] I Cor. xv, 21 ; *cf*. Rom. v, 17.
[3] I Cor. xv, 47.  See pp. 173-4.        [4] Phil. ii, 6.  See Vol. I, pp. 312-6.
[5] Rom. viii, 3.  See pp. 163-5.          [6] 2 Cor. v, 16.  See pp. 24-25.

for, in the present order of things, he must be "the second Adam, the firstborn of the dead, the firstborn among many brethren," and the ideal "High Priest;"[1] now, if he were not truly man, he would be neither the new Adam, nor raised from the dead, nor high priest, and he would not have the saints for brethren. In the present order of providence, in which man falls and is raised again by the principle of solidarity, it was necessary that the Son of God should assume our nature and not a higher nature, and that he should be man and Son of man in order to be wholly devoted to our interests and capable of serving them. He had to borrow his flesh from the sinful mass in order to put into it a leaven of sanctification, and to assume the semblance of sinful flesh in order to condemn sin in the flesh.

Also he was "manifested in the flesh";[2] and the flesh means for the Apostle the soul united to the body, the human composite. He showed that he was man by his whole earthly life and his long intercourse with men, and notably by his weakness, his sufferings, his death, and his resurrection : *Habitu inventus ut homo.*[3]

He is descended from the patriarchs;[4] he is a child of Abraham ;[5] he is the son of David according to the flesh ;[6] he was born, or more exactly " made," of a woman[7]—that is to say, formed of the substance and blood of a woman, without the agency of man and contrary to the laws of natural genera-tion ; but this privilege, due to his transcendental dignity and to the necessity of breaking all connection with sin, which he came to destroy, does not prevent him from being also as really man as the first Adam, who came directly from the hands of his Creator.[8]

Being God and man at the same time, Jesus Christ must receive all the attributes which belong to God and man. This *communicatio idiomatum* is nowhere more remarkable than in St Paul. Christ's pre-existence, his historical exist-ence, and his glorified existence are quite often united in the same phrase, and referred to the same subject without any care for what we should call the chronological order :

---

[1] Rom. v, 14 ; 1 Cor. xv, 22-45 (New Adam) ; Col. i, 18 ; Rom. viii, 29 (firstborn) ; Heb. ii, 17 ; iv, 14 ; v, 1-10 (high priest), etc.

[2] 1 Tim. iii, 16.  [3] Phil. ii, 8.  [4] Rom. ix, 5.

[5] Gal. iii, 16.  [6] Rom. i, 3.  [7] Gal. iv, 4.

[8] (*a*) *Jesus Christ man :* Rom. v, 15 (ἐν χάριτι τῇ τοῦ ἑνὸς ἀνθρώπου Ἰ. Χ.) ; 1 Cor. xv, 21 (δι᾿ ἀνθρώπου ἀνάστασις νεκρῶν) ; xv, 47 (ὁ δεύτερος ἄνθρωπος ἐξ οὐρονοῦ) ; Phil. ii, 8 (σχήματι εὑρεθεὶς ὡς ἄνθρωπος) ; 1 Tim. ii, 5.

(*b*) *Son of a woman, of David, of Abraham, of the Patriarchs :* Gal. iv, 4 (γενόμενον ἐκ γυναικός) ; Rom. i, 3 (τοῦ γενομένου ἐκ σπέρματος Δαυεὶδ κατὰ σάρκα) ; Gal. iii, 16 (τῷ σπέρματι αὐτοῦ [᾿Αβραάμ] ; Rom. ix, 5 (ἐξ ὧν [πατέρων] ὁ Χριστὸς τὸ κατὰ σάρκα) ; 2 Tim. ii, 8 (᾿Ι. Χ. . . . ἐκ σπέρματος Δαυεὶδ).

(*c*) *The flesh or physical body of Christ,* Col. i, 22 (ἐν τῷ σώματι τῆς σαρκὸς αὐτοῦ) ; Eph. ii, 14 ; Rom. viii, 3.

(a) Subsisting in the form of God . . . (pre-existence)
(b) He took the form of a servant . . . (earthly existence)
(c) Therefore God has exalted him[1] (glorious existence).

(a) By him all things were made . . .
(b) He is the head of the body, the Church,
(c) He who is before all, the firstborn from the dead.[2]

(b) He made himself poor for us.
(a) He who was rich,
(c) that he might by his poverty make us rich.[3]

(a) On the subject of his Son,
(b) descended from the race of David according to the flesh,
(c) established Son of God by the resurrection from the dead.[4]

(b) In him dwells bodily
(a) All the fulness of the Godhead
(c) And you are filled in him.[5]

Since certain attributes do not belong to the human nature and others are incompatible with the divine nature, two natures must necessarily have existed in Jesus Christ; and it is equally necessary that there should have been in him but one person, since the possessor of the attributes remains the same.

2. How is the mystery of this union accomplished? Paul does not explain it. He lays the foundations of the doctrine; it is for theologians to draw the consequences. His two formulas of the incarnation are, on that account, none the less worthy of interest. " In him dwelleth all the fulness of the Godhead bodily."[6] The exegetes recognize that the

---

[1] Phil. ii, 6, 7, 9.     [2] Col. i, 16, 18.     [3] 2 Cor. viii, 9.
[4] Rom. i, 3, 4.     [5] Col. ii, 9, 10.
[6] Col. ii, 9 : 'Εν αὐτῷ κατοικεῖ πᾶν τὸ πλήρωμα τῆς θεότητος σωματικῶς. In ipso inhabitat omnis plenitudo divinitatis corporaliter.

(a) All the fulness of the Godhead.—The word θεότης is found only here, and its kindred term θειότης only in Rom. i, 20 and Wisd. xviii, 9. Trench, Synonyms of the N. T., § ii, states the difference clearly : θειότης is the character of that which is divine, θεότης is the character of that which is God. Among profane writers only three examples of θεότης are known (Lucian, Icarom., 9 ; Plutarch, De def. orac., 10 and De Isid. et Osir., 22), while θειότης is common ; but it can be said that they observe the distinction marked by etymology and thoroughly appreciated by the Greek Fathers. Augustine himself (De civit. Dei, vii, 1) noticed the difference of meaning : " Hanc divinitatem, vel ut dixerim deitatem, nam et hoc verbo uti jam nostros non piget, ut de Graeco expressius transferant id quod illi θεότητα appellant . . ." German translators also, who pride themselves on their exactitude, employ different words : Gottheit for θεότης, and Göttlichkeit (de Wette) or Gottesgüte (Weizsäcker) for θειότης.—This being granted, the meaning of " all the fulness of divinity " cannot be doubtful. The best exegetes are agreed on this point : Non modo divinae virtutes, sed ipsa divina natura (Gottheit und

fulness of the Godhead can be only the entirety of the divine essence, and consequently divinity itself. In fact θεότης (*deitas*) abstracted from θεός is not identical with θειότης (*divinitas*) abstracted from θεῖος. The latter word might be understood as referring to quality, the former must refer to nature. This meaning would apply still more forcibly in the case where Paul combats the error of the Colossians, which consisted in locating in the superior powers particles and emanations of divinity; but, in the main, it is independent of this hypothesis. What does " bodily " mean? Many of the

---

Göttlichkeit *ist zweierlei. Jenes deutet die göttliche Natur an : dieses den Glanz, Ehre, Würde, Aufzug, welche aus der göttlichen Natur hervorstrahlt und derselben von rechtswegen gebührt*), Bengel, *Gnomon N.T.*[8], Stuttgart, 1892, p. 800.—Haupt (in *Meyers Kommentar*[8], 1902) paraphrases very well : *die Fülle, d.h. der Gesamtinhalt, die Summe, alles dessen, was Gott zu Gott macht.*—Abbott (*Eph. and Col.*, Edinburgh, 1897) is more concise : " of the Godhead, that is, of the divine nature." The paraphrase of Lightfoot (*Col.*, p. 179 : " the totality of the divine powers and attributes ;") and of Stevens (*The Paul. Theol.*[2], p. 202 : " the plenitude of divine attributes ") is much less happy, but the latter author corrects himself a little further on (p. 214) by translating " the plenitude of Deity," and the former completes his definition immediately by adding : " of the Godhead."

(*b*) *Dwelleth in him bodily.* The word κατοικεῖν designates a permanent and fixed abode (Hebrew יָשַׁב) ; it is distinguished thus from παροικεῖν (גּוּר, *peregrinari*), with which it is often contrasted ; Philo says that whoever lingers in the *encyclical* sciences (preliminary sciences, such as geometry, astronomy, etc.) *passes through* philosophy but does not *reside* in it (*Sacrif. Abel et Cain*, 10, Mangey, vol. i, p. 170: παροικεῖ σοφίᾳ οὐ κατοικεῖ). Since the fulness of the Godhead dwells in Christ, the expression is very just.— The words ἐν αὐτῷ refer to Christ who has just been mentioned by name (ii, 8: οὐ κατὰ Χριστόν), and consequently refer to the incarnate Word, not to the Word before the incarnation, as certain exegetes carelessly suppose.— The precise meaning of σωματικῶς is not without difficulty. Since the *body* is once (Col. ii, 17) contrasted with *shadow*, like reality with the figure, some, following St Augustine (*Epist.*, cxlix), explain it by the word " really " ; but the body has this meaning only by virtue of an explicit antithesis with the type or figure. Several Fathers think that σωματικῶς is equivalent to οὐσιωδῶς, " substantially " (Isid. of Pelusium, *Epist.*, iv, 166). The Godhead dwells in the humanity of Christ not *accidentally* (οὐ σχετικῶς, St Cyril of Alex.), nor *partially* as in the saints (*nequaquam per partes*, St Jerome, *In Isaiam*, xi, 1 ; *cf.* St Hilarius, *De Trinit.*, viii, 54), but wholly and by a substantial union. All this is irreproachable theology and can be deduced from κατοικεῖν, but " body " does not signify " substance." Others have recourse to a metaphorical sense of the word " body." The fulness of the Godhead dwells in him, " in the body of the Church," or " as in a body "—that is, forming a kind of organism (Haupt).—It is useless to seek so far for explanations, when the obvious meaning is satisfactory at every point. " The fulness of the Godhead dwelleth in him bodily "—that is, incarnate. St John Chrysostom observes that the Apostle does not say : " The fulness of the Godhead dwelleth in a body " (ἐν σώματι), because a body cannot contain it ; but " in him " (ἐν αὐτῷ), in his person, and this " united to a body." We have here a formula of the incarnation comparable to John i, 14 : σωματικῶς expresses by one word the *Verbum caro factum est* of St John. The best exegetes understand it thus : " σωματικῶς—namely, assuming a bodily form, becoming incarnate " (Lightfoot).—" Not ἀσωμάτως, as in the λόγος before the Incarnation " (Abbott).

Fathers translate it by "really" or "substantially"; but the word "body" has this meaning only when it is contrasted with shadow. *Corporeally* signifies "in a body, in the form of a body"; this meaning is in every way suitable, and there is no occasion for seeking any other. Your pretended philosophy, said Paul, is only a vain deceit; you still linger in elementary, childish doctrines; you ask for the protectors and mediators of a chimerical world of the imagination, and you neglect him in whom, in a visible and tangible form, free from error and illusion, "dwelleth all the fulness of the Godhead bodily." As he possesses this absolute plenitude ($\pi\hat{a}\nu$ $\tau\grave{o}$ $\pi\lambda\acute{\eta}\rho\omega\mu\alpha$) permanently ($\kappa\alpha\tau o\iota\kappa\epsilon\hat{\iota}$), he will cause it to flow out upon you in spiritual graces, and you can therefore dispense with all other intercessors.

This text teaches, indeed, the fact of the union of divinity and humanity in the one person of Christ, but does not inform us how the union is made. Another passage lifts a little the veil of this mystery: "Being in the form of God, he thought it not robbery to be equal with God, but emptied himself, taking the form of a servant, being made in the likeness of men."[1] Without reverting to the previous detailed exegesis of this text, we consider the following points to have been established: the form of God is the divine nature, the form of the servant is human nature. The "emptying of himself" takes place by reason of the fact that Christ superadds to the divine nature, which he had from all eternity, the human nature which he assumes in time. There are, therefore, in one and the same subject, in one and the same person—namely, in Christ, two natures, the divine and the human.—Since the divine nature is immutable, and since it is elsewhere asserted that Christ retains it ($\acute{v}\pi\acute{a}\rho\chi\omega\nu$), the self-renouncement cannot consist in the abandonment or the diminution of that nature. If this self-renouncement signifies anything else than abasement and complete humiliation, resulting from the assumption by the Word of an inferior nature, it can be only the voluntary abandonment of the divine honours to which Christ had a right as man ($\tau\grave{o}$ $\epsilon\hat{\iota}\nu\alpha\iota$ $\emph{\iota}\sigma\alpha$ $\Theta\epsilon\hat{\omega}$), and might have claimed by virtue of the hypostatic union. His human nature is not absorbed in this union, for Christ remains truly man and is recognized as man by his outward appearance ($\sigma\chi\acute{\eta}\mu\alpha\tau\iota$), which is not deceptive, and by the entire course of a life of obedience, humiliations and sufferings.

[1] Phil. ii, 6-7. See Vol. I, pp. 312-16, and Note I, pp. 456-65.

## II—The Historical Figure of Jesus

1. What Paul tells us of Jesus. 2. What he could tell us of him.

1. When Renan was accompanying with his little bells the deafening orchestra of German criticism at that time so much in vogue, he wrote : " Paul can say what he will ; he is inferior to the other apostles.  He has not seen Jesus ; he has not heard him speak.  The divine *logia,* the parables, are scarcely known to him.  The Christ, who gives him personal revelations, is his own phantom ; it is himself that he hears, while thinking that he is hearing Jesus."[1]  Thirty years later Renan, with his plastic, versatile genius, would have doubtless agreed with the then more progressive criticism, and would perhaps have subscribed to the following judicious reflections of Sabatier : " According  to  the  school  of Tübingen, Paul either knew the life and historical teaching of Jesus very imperfectly, or disdained that tradition as being a knowledge of Jesus according to the flesh, which made his Gospel dependent on that of the first apostles. But neither of these theories is better founded than the other. . . .  We cannot see how the traditional knowledge of the acts, sufferings, and teachings of Jesus could have harmed the independence of his apostolate and the originality of his Gospel."[2]

The fact is that the positions have greatly changed since that time.  To-day it is generally admitted that Paul was acquainted with the life and teaching of the Master, that he was inspired by his spirit, and that he faithfully reflected his mind.  The allusions to the earthly life of Jesus are as numerous in Paul's Epistles as in the other apostolic writings, outside of the Gospels, whose object was precisely to narrate it.  Proportionally there are even fewer allusions to the facts of the Gospels in the Apocalypse, in the Catholic Epistles, in the Epistle to the Hebrews, and in the Acts of the Apostles than in the letters of the Doctor of the Gentiles. Let us judge of this by the following brief sketch.

Before coming to this earth, Christ pre-existed in the form of God ;[3] he was rich with all the riches of heaven.[4]  At the end of the providential preparations for the event and at the time indicated by the divine decrees, he, the Son of God, is sent by his Father to accomplish the work of salvation.[5] Jesus is the descendant of Abraham,[6] the son of David,[7] the glory of the Hebrew people.[8]  He is born of a woman under

---

[1] Renan, *Saint Paul*, Paris, 1869, p. 563.
[2] A. Sabatier, *L'Apôtre Paul*[3], 1896, p. 61.
[3] Phil. ii, 6.
[5] Gal. iv, 4 ; Rom. viii, 3 ; iii, 25, 26 ; v, 7.
[7] Rom. i, 3 ; xv, 12 ; 2 Tim. ii, 8.
[4] 2 Cor. viii, 9.
[6] Gal. iii, 16.
[8] Rom. ix, 5.

the régime of the Law;[1] he lives in the midst of Jews,[2] and Jerusalem is the centre of his Church.[3]  He is truly man, in all respects like ourselves,[4] yet without sin.[5]  He has brethren according to the flesh,[6] one of whom, James, is designated by name.[7]  In order that they should collaborate with him and continue his work, he surrounds himself with apostles,[8] to the number of twelve;[9] three among them, Peter, James, and John, are expressly mentioned;[10] but Cephas-Peter occupies the highest rank among them.[11]  In confiding to the apostles the care of preaching his doctrine, he gives them the right to live by the Gospel[12] and the power to work miracles.[13]  After having led on earth a life of poverty,[14] subjection,[15] obedience,[16] and holiness,[17] he voluntarily gives himself up to his enemies,[18] the Jews, who put him to death.[19]

The institution of the Eucharist is related by Paul with more precision of detail than in the Gospel.  Paul mentions especially the *treason* of that tragic *night,* which recalls the sinister *nox erat* of St John.  If the passion is described on broad lines, we know that, in speaking to catechumens, the Apostle made a striking picture of it.[20]  He tells us often of the cross,[21] the blood,[22] and even of the nails.[23]  The executioners of Jesus are the Jews[24] and the princes of this world.[25]  The passion took place towards Easter, at the time of the azymoi,[26] under Pontius Pilate.[27]  The burial is not forgotten,[28] because it gives to baptism its figurative value.[29] But Paul lays more stress on the resurrection on the third day and on the different manifestations of the risen Christ.[30] Jesus Christ has ascended into heaven,[31] is seated on the right hand of the Father,[32] and will return to judge the living and the dead.[33]  These are articles of the *Credo,* the form of which is largely borrowed from the Apostle to the Gentiles.

Such is an epitome of Paul's picture of Jesus.  It is more than a sketch; it is a lifelike portrait drawn with firm lines, which the evangelists complete without altering its expression.

This is not all.  After deeds, words; after the Master's physiognomy, the substance of his teaching.

[1] Gal. iv, 4.

[2] Gal. i, 17 ; Rom. xv, 19-27.

[3] Gal. i, 19 ; ii, 29.

[4] Rom. v, 15 ; 1 Cor. xv, 21, 22 ; 1 Tim. ii, 5.

[5] 2 Cor. v, 21.

[6] 1 Cor. ix, 5.

[7] Gal. i, 19 ; ii, 29.

[8] 1 Cor. ix, 5, 14.

[9] 1 Cor. xv, 5.

[10] Gal. i, 18, 19 ; ii, 9.

[11] 1 Cor. ix, 5.

[12] 1 Cor. ix, 15.

[13] 2 Cor. xii, 19.  *Cf.* Rom. xv, 19.

[14] 2 Cor. viii, 9.

[15] Phil. ii, 8.

[16] Rom. v, 19.

[17] Rom. i, 4.

[18] Gal. i, 4 ; ii, 20.

[19] 1 Thess. ii, 15.

[20] Gal. iii, 1.

[21] 1 Cor. ii, 2, etc.

[22] Rom. iii, 25, etc.

[23] Col. ii, 12.

[24] 1 Thess. ii, 15.

[25] Eph. i, 7 ; ii, 13.

[26] 1 Cor. v, 6-8.

[27] 1 Tim. vi, 2.

[28] 1 Cor. xv, 4.

[29] Rom. vi, 4 : Col. ii, 12.

[30] 1 Cor. xv, 4-7.

[31] Eph. iv, 8-10.

[32] Eph. i, 20 ; ii, 6.

[33] 1 Thess. i, 10 ; Phil. iii, 20.

Paul has saved from oblivion the saying of Jesus: "It is more blessed to give than to receive."[1] He reproduces the words of the Last Supper more completely than the evangelists themselves, except, perhaps, Luke.[2] In speaking of marriage, he refers to the teaching of Christ, as it is found in St Matthew and St Mark, and distinguishes it expressly from his own precepts.[3] When he proclaims the right which the preacher of the Gospel has to live by the Gospel, we are irresistibly reminded of the measures taken by Jesus on behalf of the heralds of the faith,[4] and this impression is changed into certainty on reading St Paul's verbal quotation from St Luke: *Dignus est operarius mercede sua.*[5] When he relies on a word of the Lord in order to instruct the faithful on the subject of the *parousia,* the most natural sense is certainly to take the "*word of the Lord,* not for an inward voice, but for a word really pronounced by Jesus in the course of his earthly life."[6]

The Apostle only thinks of making laws in his own name when he cannot invoke a command of the Lord.[7] Everywhere else he appeals to the law of Christ, which, he takes it for granted, is known by his neophytes,[8] a law which is binding upon him, as well as on simple believers.[9] The moral law, which he teaches to the catechumens, is not derived from him, but from Jesus;[10] to fail to conform to it would be to disobey Jesus;[11] and the duty of the faithful is to *learn* Christ, as that of the apostles is to *teach* Christ to them.[12]

Finally, in order to verify the results of this rapid review, we ought to take some terms of comparison; for example, the Sermon on the Mount or the great eschatological Discourse.[13] Here the numerous similitudes, both in substance and in form, are instantly obvious, and can be traced back evidently to the same source—namely, the teaching of Jesus. The fact is so clear that no sensible critic will dispute it.

2. Thus, whether we collect the allusions to the earthly life of Jesus scattered through the writings of Paul or compare his moral teaching with that of Jesus or examine the similarities of expression too numerous to be accidental, we cannot say either that the Apostle is ignorant of the contents of the Gospel history, or that he disdains them. This study

---

[1] Acts xx, 35.
[2] I Cor. xi, 24-26.
[3] I Cor. vii, 10-12.
[4] I Cor. ix, 14.
[5] I Tim. v, 18 ; Luke x, 7. *Cf.* Matt. x, 10 (*cibo suo*).
[6] I Thess. iv, 15.
[7] I Cor. vii, 25.
[8] Gal. vi, 2.
[9] I Cor. ix, 21.
[10] I Thess. iv, 1-2.
[11] I Tim. vi, 3, etc.
[12] Eph. iv, 20, 21 ; Col. ii, 6, 7.
[13] For the eschatology, see Vol. I, pp. 73-4, 79.

has been made by others, and we have not to remake it here.[1] We shall limit ourselves to formulating the following conclusions.

The allusions to the life and teachings of Jesus, whether open or concealed, are much more numerous in St Paul than a superficial examination would lead us to suppose; in proportion, there are more of them than in the rest of the New Testament, apart from the Gospel.

These allusions sometimes touch upon minute details and imply consequently a larger and more general acquaintance with the facts which are merely incidentally mentioned.

The manner in which they are made testifies to the existence, in both the author and in his readers, of a common stock of instructions and memories, which it is sufficient to call up to be understood by all.

Finally, the picture that results from them is a faithful portrait, and he who drew it can be justly proud of having " the spirit of the Lord."

But we must not be weary of repeating that Paul's task is not to write the biography of Jesus, which he includes among the elements of faith of which no neophyte can be ignorant; that he returns only by accident to this elementary teaching; that instead of laying emphasis upon it he contents himself most frequently with merely alluding to it; and that he knows infinitely more than he can write about it. If it had not been for the disorders of the *agapae* and the doubts of the Corinthians on the subject of the resurrection, should we ever suspect that, in regard to the circumstances of the institution of the Eucharist and the appearance of the risen Jesus, he possessed so many accurate and precise details, which the evangelists have omitted to tell us?

[1] It is sufficient to refer to P. Feine, *Jesus Christus und Paulus*, Leipzig, 1902; Knowling, *The Testimony of St Paul to Christ*, London, 1905; Dausch, *Jesus und Paulus*, Münster, 1911 (collection *Biblische Fragen*); Olaf Moe, *Paulus und die evangelische Geschichte*, Leipzig, 1912; Dausch is Catholic, the others are conservative Protestants. For objections, Goguel, *L'Apôtre Paul et Jésus-Christ*, Paris, 1904.

# BOOK IV
## THE WORK OF REDEMPTION

# CHAPTER I

## THE REDEEMING MISSION

### I—THE AMBASSADOR OF GOD

1. Object of the Redeeming Mission.  2. The Mediator of the New Covenant.
3. No other Mediator but He.

1. WE have already said that the initiative of our salvation originates always with the heavenly Father. It is to him that St Paul loves to ascribe all the redeeming plans, the execution of which is confided to the Son, the natural mediator between God and men :

> When the fulness of the time was come,
> God sent his Son,
> made of a woman, made under the Law,
> that he might redeem them who were under the Law,
> that we might receive the adoption of sons.[1]

This short phrase expresses the fact, the time, the manner, and the object of the redeeming mission.—*The fact.* God the Father sends his only Son, sufficiently distinguished from all those who are to share in the name of sons by his very

---

[1] Gal. iv, 4, 5.  Other details in Sieffert and Cornely.

A. (4) ὅτε δὲ ἦλθεν τὸ πλήρωμα τοῦ χρόνου,      *At ubi venit plenitudo temporis,*

B. ἐξαπέστειλεν ὁ Θεὸς τὸν Υἱὸν αὐτοῦ,      *misit Deus Filium suum*

C. γενόμενον ἐκ γυναικός, γεν. ὑπὸ νόμον,      *factum ex muliere, factum sub lege,*

D. (5) ἵνα τοὺς ὑπὸ νόμον ἐξαγοράσῃ ἵνα τὴν υἱοθεσίαν ἀπολάβωμεν.      *ut eos, qui sub lege erant, redimeret, ut adoptionem filiorum reciperemus.*

The four principal circumstances of the sending are found stated in the four sections of this phrase.

A. *The time.*—The adversative particle δέ refers to what has just been said : *quanto tempore heres parvulus est* (iv, 1) . . . *cum essemus parvuli* (iv, 3). Consequently, *the fulness of the time* corresponds to the *time appointed by the Father* (ἄχρι τῆς προθεσμίας τοῦ πατρός, iv, 2) ; this is what St Paul expresses elsewhere by *dispensatio plenitudinis temporum* (Eph. i, 10) or by *fines saeculorum* (1 Cor. x, 11 ; cf. Heb. ix, 26) ; but it is also, independently of the divine decree, the termination of that period of childhood which made humanity incapable of seconding God's redeeming plan.

B. *The fact.*—In the compound verb ἐξαπέστειλεν, the two component prepositions can retain their proper value : ἐξ " from the bosom of God " (John viii, 44 : ἐγὼ ἐκ τοῦ Θεοῦ ἐξῆλθον), ἀπό " from heaven " (John vi, 38 : καταβέβηκα ἀπὸ τοῦ οὐρανοῦ), a meaning which agrees perfectly with the only other case where St Paul employs this compound verb (Gal. iv, 6.) The paraphrase of Bengel : *ex caelo a sese*, would therefore gain, if reversed.

isolation and by the incommunicable relation which unites
him to the Father; he sends him from himself and from the
highest place in heaven, as indicated by the forceful compound word (ἐξαπέστειλεν) employed by the Apostle, he
sends him at a precise moment of time, but he does not constitute him his Son by the act of sending him, for this
mission clearly presupposes the real pre-existence of the
Son.—*The time*. It is the fulness of the times, an expression
which refers at the same time to the expiration of the delays
freely appointed by the Father, and to the end of the
providential preparations which were to make the world

---

*ex sese a caelo*. Let us remember, however, that in late Greek, especially
in St Luke (four times in the Gospel and seven times in the Acts), the
compound ἐξαποστέλλειν often has the meaning of the simple στέλλειν.

C. *The manner*.—The Son of God is the subject of a twofold becoming:
he becomes the son of a woman and a subject of the Law.—(*a*) The expression
γενόμενον ἐκ γυναικός recalls γενόμενος ἐκ σπέρματος Δαυεὶδ κατὰ σάρκα
(Rom. i, 3). The reading γεννώμενον, which is that of the present Vulgate
(*natum ex muliere*), and which Bede defends so vigorously (*In Luc.*, xi, 27,
XCII, 480 : *quia Christus conceptus ex utero virginali carnem non de nihilo,
non aliunde, sed materna traxit* ex carne), is not defensible from a critical
point of view.  Moreover, it would not give a satisfactory sense, for Christ
was born formerly, but is no longer *born* now ; it would therefore need the
perfect or the aorist, as Photius remarks (*Amphil. qu.*, 228, CI, 1024).—The
expression γενόμενον ἐκ γυναικός is not opposed to the virginal conception
of Jesus, but does not prove it either, as Tertullian and others think (*De carne
Christi*, 20 : Factum *potius dicit quam* natum ; *simplicius enim enuntiasset*
natum ; factum *autem dicendo et* Verbum caro factum est *consignavit et
carnis veritatem ex Virgine factae asseveravit*) and Pelagius (*In eo quod
dicit* ex muliere, *monstrat non more solito ex conventu viri et feminae, sed
per Spiritum S. ex matre tantum Christum incarnationem hominis suscepisse*).
—(*b*) The expression γενόμενον ὑπὸ νόμον signifies that Christ was born subject
to the Law, in so far as he was born a member of the Hebrew people, also
subject to the Law ; and this Law he observes from his birth, in regard to the
cirumcision, the presentation in the Temple, the yearly pilgrimage, etc.  But
he does not observe it as regards the arbitrary interpretations of it by the
Pharisees, or in opposition to the moral law ; and he shows that he is superior
to the Law.

D. *The object*.—It is twofold : to redeem those who were under the Law
(that is, to deliver them from the yoke of the Law) and to confer on all the
adoption of sons.  These two partial ends correspond inversely to the two
aspects of the manner of the sending.

(*a*) Made of a woman.              (*b*) To redeem those subject to the
                                                    Law,
(*b*) Made under the law.          (*a*) To confer on all filial adoption.

The two ends are subordinated to one another, for it was necessary first to
deliver the Jews and to free them from their burdensome privileges, in order
to be able to extend to all, equally, the prerogative of sonship.

The Latin Fathers sometimes notice the iterative sense of *redimere* and
*recipere*.  Thus St Jerome in his commentary says : Redempti *dicuntur
qui primum de Dei parte fuerint et postea esse cessaverint ;* and St Augustine :
*Non dixit* accipiamus *sed* recipiamus, *ut significaret hoc nos amisisse in
Adamo*.  But the Greek ἐξαγοράζειν does not indicate this idea of return ;
and in ἀπολαμβάνειν, the component preposition ἀπό marks rather the fulfilment of the promise by which the filial adoption is given, as several Greek
Fathers observe.

ready for this great event.  Subsequently, it would have been too late ; previously it would have been too soon ; the termination of the messianic prophecies was to coincide with the maturity of the human race.—The *manner* is synthetized in that brief formula " made of a woman, made under the Law." It was indeed fitting that the Son should partake of the nature of those whom he came to redeem, by being born of a woman, like all other men, in order that he might have the right to call them his brethren and make them share in his quality of Son; it was fitting also that he should be subject to the Law, that he might deliver his compatriots from its yoke ; a seemliness which becomes a necessity in the actual plan of redemption, in which God had resolved to save men through the principle of solidarity.—The twofold *object* of the mission corresponds to the twofold condition of the divine envoy : it was to deliver the Jews from the tyranny of the Law in order to bring them under the Gospel ; and to confer upon all men, Jews and Gentiles without exception, the adoption of sons.

Another text as famous for its intrinsic difficulty as for the confused interpretations of it by the exegetes is quite similar to the preceding one, yet differs from it in one point : the principal idea, expressed by the personal verb, is no longer the Son's mission, but the condemnation of sin in the flesh resulting from this mission :

> For what the Law could not do, in that it was weak through the flesh,
> God sending his own Son in the likeness of sinful flesh, and for sin,
> Condemned sin in the flesh, that the justification of the Law might
> be fulfilled in us.[1]

---

[1] Rom. viii, 3-4.  *Cf.* Cornely and Lagrange ; Sanday, B. Weiss, and Zahn.

| | |
|---|---|
| A. (3) τὸ γὰρ ἀδύνατον τοῦ νόμου ἐν ᾧ ἠσθένει διὰ τῆς σαρκός, | *Nam quod impossibile erat legi, in quo infirmabatur per carnem,* |
| B. ὁ Θεὸς τὸν ἑαυτοῦ Υἱὸν πέμψας | *Deus Filium suum mittens* |
| C. ἐν ὁμοιώματι σαρκὸς ἁμαρτίας καὶ περὶ ἁμαρτίας | *in similitudinem carnis peccati et de peccato,* |
| D. κατέκρινε τὴν ἁμαρτίαν ἐν τῇ σαρκί, | *damnavit peccatum in carne,* |
| E. (4) ἵνα τὸ δικαίωμα τοῦ νόμου πληρωθῇ ἐν ἡμῖν τοῖς μὴ κατὰ σάρκα περιπατοῦσιν ἀλλὰ κατὰ πνεῦμα. | *ut justificatio legis impleretur in nobis, qui non secundum carnem ambulamus, sed secundum spiritum.* |

This text, like the preceding one, may be regarded as bearing on the redeeming mission, and we may consider : A the motive ; B the fact; C the manner and immediate object ; D the result ; E the remote object of this mission.

A.  *The motive.*—It is the recognized powerlessness of the Law to struggle against sin, and still more to conquer it.—Τὸ ἀδύνατον τοῦ νόμου can be active and signify " the impotence of the Law," or rather, " that in which the Law was impotent "; or it can be passive and signify " that which was impossible to the Law."—The second meaning is simpler and more comformable to usage ; above all, it fits in better with the addition ἐν ᾧ ἠσθένει διὰ τῆς σαρκός.  This last part of the phrase is also susceptible of a double meaning : " inasmuch as, in that," or " because."  In the first case the writer explains

All doubtful points aside, it appears evident from this complex phrase that one of God's motives in sending his Son was to remedy the thenceforth recognized impotence of the Mosaic Law. The Law revealed to man the path of justice, and was intended to lead him thither ; but it had been fettered and paralysed by the flesh—that is to say, by the inclination to evil which at present vitiates human nature. In order to vanquish and destroy sin in its own domain, God sends his Son "in the likeness of sinful flesh." Paul does not say " in the likeness of the flesh " ; for he would thus let us

---

*in what* the impotence or impossibility of the Law consisted ; in the second, the *reason* for it is given : but the general signification remains about the same.—As to the construction, the most competent philologists agree to-day in regarding the clause τὸ ἀδύνατον τοῦ νόμου ἐν ᾧ ἠσθένει διὰ τῆς σαρκός as a nominative, or better as an accusative absolute put in apposition with the following phrase : " God condemned sin in the flesh, that the justification of the Law might be fulfilled in us, *which was impossible to the Law*, because it was weak (and rendered powerless) by the flesh." There are some examples of this accusative in the best classics : Plato, *Theaet.* 153C ; Sophocles, *Oedipus Tyrannus*, 603 ; compare 2 Cor. vi, 13 : τὴν δὲ αὐτὴν ἀντιμισθίαν, πλατύνθητε καὶ ὑμεῖς. *Cf.* Sanday, *Romans*[5], p. 191.

B. *The fact.*—The mission is indicated here by the verb πέμπειν, a less expressive synonym of ἐξαποστέλλειν. The emphasis is on τὸν ἑαυτοῦ Υἱόν, *his own Son*, the only being fitted to fill well the mission which God wished to entrust to him.—" The relation of the aorist participle πέμψας with the verb κατέκρινε is neither that of priority nor that of simultaneousness ; it is here not a relation of time, but of manner : *en faisant l'acte d'envoyer* (Godet)." We see by this that the mission presupposes the pre-existence of the Son, as the best commentators agree.

C. *The manner and the immediate object.*—In the Vulgate this clause presents two noteworthy differences : (*a*) The accusative *in similitudinem carnis* designates the incarnation itself as the object of the mission, while ἐν ὁμοιώματι lets us extend the mission to the entire life.—(*b*) The punctuation *et de peccato damnavit peccatum* appears to have been suggested by John xvi, 8 (*arguet mundum de peccato*) ; but not to mention the difficulty of explaining the expression *damnare peccatum de peccato*, the conjunction (καί, *et*) cannot begin the principal phrase, for there is no other personal verb ; it announces, therefore, a circumstantial complement, co-ordinated with *in similitudine carnis peccati.*—In the Septuagint, Ps. xxxix, 7 ; *cf.* Heb. x, 6-18, περὶ ἁμαρτίας (θυσία being understood) takes sometimes the meaning of " sacrifice for sin." But, as nothing here suggests the idea of sacrifice, and as the elliptical expression would be hard to understand, it is better to adhere to the natural sense, which is perfectly suitable : *for sin, i.e.* to break the dominion of sin, as will be seen.

D. *The result.*—What does " to condemn sin in the flesh " mean ? *Sin* can here be only the power of evil, the consequence of the first fault, which invaded all Adam's posterity and has its special seat in the flesh. It is *the* sin described in chapter v, while in the preceding clause it was a question of sin in general (περὶ ἁμαρτίας). *To condemn* sin is not only to declare it bad ; all the commentators are agreed on that, as is shown by their paraphrases : ἐνίκησεν (Chrysostom), κατέλυσεν (Theodoret), *interfecit* (Grotius), *virtute privavit* (Bengel), *destruxit* or *debilitavit* (S Thomas), *devote to ruin* (Godet). Reflection shows that the condemnation of sin is determined by the context in two ways :—(*a*) " To condemn sin in the flesh " was precisely what the Law could not do : it could indeed declare sin bad¦and unjust, but it could neither curb it nor dislodge it.—(*b*) The effect of this condemnation is to permit us to fulfil the precepts of the Law (τὸ δικαίωμα=what the Law

understand either that Christ did not have real flesh, or that his flesh was of a nature different from ours. Nor does he say " in a flesh of sin," which could let us suppose that Christ had assumed sinful flesh. He says, with rare felicity of expression, " in the *likeness* of sinful flesh " ; for the flesh of Christ is indeed real flesh, which nothing distinguishes from our own physically, but it is only in appearance a flesh of sin, since it is neither the heritage, nor the seat, nor the focus, nor the instrument of sin.

As he had for his mission the condemnation of sin in the

---

declared just). It is not, therefore, a simple sentence of condemnation, and Weiss (*Meyers Kommentar*[9]) gives the meaning well : " He condemned it to lose its power and to be vanquished by Christ."

But where, when, and how is this condemnation of sin effected ?

(*a*) Most interpreters suppose that ἐν τῇ σαρκί means in the flesh of Jesus, and moreover that the condemnation took place at the death of Christ. This being affirmed, Baur and his usual disciples (Holsten,[1] Pfleiderer, Schmidt, etc.) think that God, by killing the flesh of Christ on the cross, has killed sin itself. This explanation encounters two impossibilities ; it implies the existence of sin in the flesh of Jesus, which is absolutely contrary to 2 Cor. v, 21 ; and it imputes to St Paul the absurdity of saying that the death of the sinner kills sin in him and in others.

(*b*) Several refer to 2 Cor. v, 21 and Rom. vi, 6-11 : " By the death on the cross, a death endured in his human nature, he breaks for ever all contact with sin, which could touch him only by that nature. Thenceforth sin has no more claim upon him, and no more claim on the believer, since the believer is dead with Christ " (Sanday).—Rückert, Olshausen, Philippi, Hofmann and others have much the same opinion. According to this theory, Christ condemned sin to impotence, while according to St Paul it is God who condemns it. Moreover, Christ by his death escaped from sin ; but sin could not touch him (2 Cor. v, 21), and it is not plain, therefore, how death has withdrawn him from it.

(*c*) Others, dissatisfied with this exegesis, connect the condemnation of sin with the whole mission of Christ. In carne *quam Christus puram assumpsit, puram per totam vitam servavit, puram in cruce Patri obtulit, Deus peccatum damnavit, atque illa ipsa in re, in qua et per quam peccatum regnum tenuerat virtutemque suam exseruerat, illud devicit prostravitque* (Cornely). Bisping has a similar explanation. This interpretation shows clearly how Jesus Christ vanquished sin in his own flesh, but does not explain how he vanquished it in the flesh in general. Now this is precisely what the Apostle means to express, as the following sentence proves : *ut iustificatio legis impleretur in nobis.* This last phrase is the key to the mystery.

E. *The remote end.*—The Law required justice from man without being able to give it ; the Son of God gives the justice demanded by the Law (τὸ δικαίωμα τοῦ νόμου=what the Law declares just and imposes as such ; *justificatio legis* renders the idea imperfectly). This justice will be fulfilled *in us*, thanks to the means of salvation brought by the Son of God (ἐν ἡμῖν, not ὑφ' ἡμῶν, " by us ") ; on condition, however, that we do not " walk according to the flesh," and do not obey the instincts of concupiscence, but that we " walk according to the spirit " and obey the impulses of grace : a condition which the Apostle supposes realized in all Christians (τοῖς μὴ κατὰ σάρκα περιπατοῦσιν, equivalent to *quippe qui non ambulamus secundum carnem*).—We see that, if the thought of the Apostle turns upon the word flesh, it converges towards this central idea, of giving the Christian what the Law had not been able to give him.

flesh, Jesus Christ could, of necessity, have nothing in common with sin. God sends him expressly " on account of sin " (περὶ ἁμαρτίας)—namely, to expiate and atone for sin; not only original sin (it is not περὶ τῆς ἁμαρτίας), but sin in general, whatever may be its nature and source. The best exegetes of all schools have seen very clearly that here is no question of a simple condemnation by comparison, like that which might occur to a sinful man from the sight of the sinless flesh of Christ, nor of a platonic sentence which would leave things as they were before. They give to the word " condemn," the strongest equivalents : " to conquer, to strike down, to destroy, to abolish, to annul, to expel, to kill, to exterminate," and they are no doubt right, for God's condemnation being efficacious, cannot fail to produce its effect; but the idea of effective condemnation, with which St Paul contents himself, is sufficiently clear, and it is better to stop there. God condemns to impotence the sin which was reigning in the flesh; and he condemns it in the flesh itself, since the flesh of Christ is ours. By having tried to find in this text what Paul never put there, the majority of commentators have closed their minds to its truth. They have completed it arbitrarily, each to suit himself, either by understanding the words " for sin " as meaning " sacrifice for sin," or by supposing that the condemnation of sin takes place in the flesh of Christ *only,* as if there were any sin " in *his* flesh "; or by forgetting that the condemnation of sin is here the work of the Father who commands the ·Son to execute it.

2. This mission constitutes Jesus Christ the ambassador of God and representative of men; in other words, a Mediator. In the Jewish religion there were three kinds of mediators : kings, priests, and prophets. The prophet brings to men the messages of God; the priest administers the things of God in the name of men; the theocratic king was the lieutenant of God. Priests and prophets are equally mediators between God and man; only, on the mysterious ladder which unites heaven with earth, the priest ascends and the prophet descends; the prophet, a messenger from God, descends towards men; the priest, a delegate of men, ascends towards God. No doubt, when their mission is completed, their movements are reversed; the prophet then returns towards God to render an account of his message; the priest descends again towards his constituents to distribute among them the blessings of heaven; but it is their first direction which characterizes them. As for the theocratic king, his throne is " the throne of Jehovah " itself.[1] David, clad with the ephod, blesses the people in the name of God;[2] and in the

---

[1] Ps. xliv, 7; *cf*. Heb. i, 8.  [2] 2 Sam. vi, 18.

messianic psalms the king, a descendant of David, presents himself as the accredited intermediary between God and the people.

Did the Jewish contemporaries of Jesus Christ suspect the triple mediation of the Messiah as king, prophet, and high priest? Had they any idea of any other priest than the levitical hierophant, and did they generally recognize the Messiah in the " priest for ever according to the order of Melchisedech?" Was the prophet whom they expected the Messiah himself, or a forerunner of the Messiah? These are thorny questions, confused by controversies, and obscured by vagueness or by the uncertainty arising from contradictory data. The writers of the New Testament certainly show us in Jesus Christ spiritual royalty, the fulness of the prophetic spirit, and the eternal priesthood, but without ever grouping these three attributes together; they seem rather to divide them up among themselves, the Synoptists giving more prominence to the office of the messianic king, St John to the authority of the prophet *par excellence,* and the Epistle to the Hebrews to the dignity of the high priest, who is the first to open the way to heaven. Paul, indeed, calls Christ neither priest, nor king, nor prophet; and although he assigns to him royal, sacerdotal, and prophetic functions, this threefold division of the offices of Christ was foreign to the messianic speculations of the Jews,[1] almost unknown by the Fathers, introduced or put into use, after very curious, wavering attempts, by the reformers of the sixteenth century, and is not at all in harmony with Pauline theology.

The Apostle gives the name of mediator only once to Jesus Christ. "For there is one God; and one mediator of God and men, the man Christ Jesus, who gave himself a redemption for all."[2] To extend to all the blessing of the divine

---

[1] The *Testaments of the Patriarchs* indeed group together the attributes of high priest and king (*Simeon,* 7: ἀναστήσει γὰρ Κύριος ἐκ τοῦ Λευεὶ ὡς ἀρχιερέα καὶ ἐκ τοῦ Ἰούδα ὡς βασιλέα, Θεὸν καὶ ἄνθρωπον); but is not this clearly a Christian interpolation?

[2] 1 Tim. ii, 5: Εἷς γὰρ Θεός, εἷς καὶ μεσίτης Θεοῦ καὶ ἀνθρώπων, ἄνθρωπος Χριστὸς Ἰησοῦς.—The particle γάρ gives the reason for what has just been said, namely that God desires the salvation of all men. The reason is in part twofold : the *one* God, necessarily the same for *all* men, the beginning and supreme end of all, the *one* mediator who has offered himself as a sacrifice for *all* men.—The word εἷς is put first, for it is the pivot of the whole argument. So it must not be translated : " One God exists," or " There is one God," or " God is one," but " Unique is God," or if one prefers, " One only (being) is God," regarding εἷς as the subject, Θεός and μεσίτης as the predicate; hence the absence of the definite article before μεσίτης.— The addition ἄνθρωπος Χριστὸς Ἰησοῦς explains the title of mediator, a natural intermediary between the two extremes : as man, he proceeds from men ; as Christ, he proceeds from God. Jesus Christ is mediator *ratione personae* and *ratione muneris,* as the following verse indicates. He is mediator equally *ratione status* (in so far as he is at once *comprehensor* and *viator ;* cf. Augustine, *De civit. Dei,* ix, 15), but this is not what the Apostle says here.

will for man's salvation by rendering God propitious through the voluntary sacrifice of life, which he offers as the representative of the human race : such is the end, the means, and the condition of his all-powerful mediation. The special office of mediator being to serve as a bond of union between two parties, in order to reconcile them if they are in conflict, and to strengthen the bonds between them, if they are at peace, the God-Man was eminently fitted to fill this role ; since, by his two natures, he identifies himself with the two extremes, and since, by his theandric nature, he associates them in an indissoluble union. Jesus Christ was, therefore, a mediator, not only by reason of his intermediary position between the way and the end, between the trial and the crown, nor by reason of his person, the harmonious union of humanity and divinity, but, above all, as a dispenser of the divine blessings of which he is the unique depositary.

For the Christ of St Paul is not simply a natural mediator, like the Logos of Philo ; he is a mediator of supernatural life. By him, in fact, we have grace[1] and salvation, begun here below, consummated in heaven ;[2] by him, justice and the fruit of justice ;[3] by him, justification,[4] redemption,[5] and reconciliation ;[6] by him, peace[7] and general pacification ;[8] by him, free access to God[9] and a sure refuge against the divine wrath ;[10] by him, spiritual consolation[11] and a confidence which nothing can disturb ;[12] by him, the gift of the Holy Spirit[13] and the adoption of sons ;[14] by him, the victory over

---

—On the argument itself, Cornelius à Lapide remarks : *Apostolus hic probat id quod dixit, Deum scilicet velle omnes homines fieri hoc argumento : Unus est omnium hominum, tam fidelium quam infidelium Deus, id est creator, provisor et pater, qui summe bonus omnes homines quasi filios suos amat ac salvos esse cupit : ideoque dedit Christum mediatorem ut scilicet unus et idem Christus omnium omnino hominum esset redemptor, utque per Christum omnes homines jungeret ac salvaret.* The first part of the text is well expounded, the second less well. There are indeed *two* proofs of the will universal to salvation : the oneness of God and the oneness of the redeemer. It is perfectly true that the mission of the redeemer comes from the divine initiative, but this is not St Paul's point of view here, who makes both arguments converge to the same end, without subordinating one of them to the other. The emphasis of the discourse is, therefore, laid upon the words *qui dedit semetipsum redemptionem pro omnibus,* from which comes the oneness of the mediator. Consequently St Paul has in view *chiefly* redeeming mediation and not *ontological* mediation—that is to say, the union of the two natures, divine and human, in the one person of Christ. On 1 Tim. ii, 2-4, see pp. 77-9.

[1] Rom. i, 5 ; v, 21.
[2] 1 Thess. v, 9 ; 2 Tim. iii, 15.
[3] Rom. iii, 27 ; Phil. i, 11.
[4] Rom. v, 18 ; Gal. ii, 16.
[5] Rom. iii, 24 ; Eph. i, 7.
[6] Rom. v, 10-11 ; 2 Cor. v 18 Eph. ii, 16 ; Col. i, 20-22.
[7] Rom. v, 1.
[8] Col. i, 20.
[9] Rom. v, 2 ; Eph. ii, 18.
[10] Rom. v, 9.
[11] 2 Cor. i, 5.
[12] 2 Cor. iii, 4.
[13] Titus iii, 6.
[14] Eph. i, 5.

all our enemies;[1] by him, the endless reign in heaven.[2] It is by him alone that we are able to glory in God,[3] and that we must address our thanksgivings to him;[4] for, as all the divine promises have had in him their *Yea*—that is to say, their fulfilment, by him also the faithful pronounce their *Amen*, in an act of sincere and grateful faith, in order to ascribe all honour and glory to God.[5] In a word, in the order of grace still more than in the order of nature " all things are by (or for) him and we by him,"[6] since he is the principle of our life and of our whole being.

3. Thenceforth there is no other mediator above or beside him. By a badly understood cult of angels, connected in their thought with the observance of the Mosaic Law, the Colossians detracted from the universal mediation of Christ. " They had been told that the Law had been given by angels, because they had lent their ministry to its promulgation, and because they would not look with indifference upon any contempt of the Torah,"[7] of which they were the guardians. Anyone who violated it, therefore, was exposed to the wrath and vengeance of the heavenly spirits. The Apostle assures them that there is nothing in this :

> *Despoiling* [of their past functions] *the principalities and powers, God hath made an open show of them in the eyes* [of all, thus despoiled and deprived of their honours], *leading them in triumph* [in the train of Christ the conqueror, enthroned] *on* [or *by*] *the Cross.*[8]

St Paul knows only two kinds of supernatural beings, the good and the bad, the spirits of light and the spirits of dark-

---

[1] Rom. viii, 37 ; 1 Cor. xv, 57.    [2] Rom. v, 17.
[3] Rom. v, 11.    [4] Rom. i, 8 ; vii, 25 ; xvi, 27.
[5] 2 Cor. i, 20.
[6] 1 Cor. viii, 6 ; δι' οὗ (variant : δι' ὅν) τὰ πάντα καὶ ἡμεῖς δι' αὐτοῦ.
[7] Theodore of Mopsuestia (edit. Swete), vol. i, p. 294. Theodoret on Col. ii, 15 has a similar explanation.
[8] Col. ii, 15 : 'Απεκδυσάμενος τὰς ἀρχὰς καὶ τὰς ἐξουσίας ἐδειγμάτισεν ἐν παρρησίᾳ θριαμβεύσας αὐτοὺς ἐν αὐτῷ. *Expolians principatus et potestates traduxit confidenter, palam triumphans illos in semetipso.*
There are few texts of Scripture about which the Greek and Latin commentators, ancient and modern, are in more thorough disagreement. Not only is the meaning of all the words without exception disputed, but there does not exist any foundation of agreement either as a whole, or in detail. See *Le triomphe du Christ sur les principautés et les puissances* in *Recherches de science relig.*, vol. iii, 1912, pp. 201-229, where we attempt to prove : (*a*) that God and not Christ is really the subject of the phrase, a point generally admitted to-day ; (*b*) that ἀπεκδυσάμενος is transitive and has for its object τὰς ἀρχάς; (*c*) that τὰς ἀρχὰς καὶ τὰς ἐξουσίας denotes the angels and not demons or earthly powers; (*d*) that ἐδειγμάτισεν ἐν παρρησίᾳ means : " He exposed publicly to the gaze of all " the angels thus deprived of their past prerogatives, so that no one could be deceived in them ; (*e*) that θριαμβεύσας means " leading them in triumph " in the suite of Christ the conqueror—a meaning which θριαμβεύειν has in Greek and *triumphare* in Latin ; (*f*) that ἐν αὐτῷ refers to the cross (σταυρός) which has just been named : *on* the cross, or *by* the cross.

ness, the angels of God and the angels of Satan. Nowhere is there discoverable in him the conception of intermediate beings, destined, perhaps, to become angels or demons, but who are at present neither demons nor angels. For the Jewish contemporaries of St Paul and for St Paul himself, the angels connected with the promulgation of the Law were good angels, and he never had any idea that they had overstepped the mandate given them, or had turned against God the authority with which they were invested. Nor did the Colossians, who paid them honour, have a different idea of them, and the Apostle would not have been understood if he had advocated another hypothesis. Nothing, therefore, suggests to us that the angels have transgressed; nevertheless, when the Law had been abolished, their role was ended and their mediation was useless. Jesus Christ, exalted infinitely above the super-terrestrial powers, alone capable of revealing to us the Father, of whom he is the perfect image, and the only appointed intermediary between God and men, is thenceforth a substitute for the heavenly spirits, promulgators and guardians of a law which, instead of favouring the redeeming plan, has rather been an obstacle to it. So, when the Law is put aside, they share in a certain way its disgrace, and their ministry has no more reason for existing.

God makes them serve as an escort to the triumphant Christ. In itself this would be an honour; but it is also a loss, for it marks the end of their autonomy, and is a proof that they are only the subordinates and satellites of the great mediator.

Why, then, is St Paul, in speaking of Christ, so chary of the name of mediator? Is it perhaps because, in the opinion and common parlance of the Jews of that time, Moses was the mediator *par excellence?*[1] But the author of the Epistle to the Hebrews, who is not ignorant of this, nevertheless calls Jesus Christ the mediator of the new covenant.[2] The reason is to be sought elsewhere. A mediator, in the usual sense of the word, is a stranger to both the parties whom he brings into harmony. It is otherwise with Christ, in whom dwells the fulness of the Godhead bodily, yet who has really entered into the human family. He is a mediator, but not an ordinary mediator; he is the new Adam. This is a title which St Paul creates expressly for him and which, while containing pre-eminently the role of mediator, renders it henceforth unnecessary.

---

[1] Gal. iii, 19 (ἐν χειρὶ μεσίτου). See pp. 96-7.
[2] Heb. viii, 6 (κρείττονός ἐστι διαθήκης μεσίτης); cf. ix, 15 ; xii, 24.

## II—The New Adam

1. Parallel between the Two Adams.   2. Role and Quality of the
Second Adam.

1. The most complete, fruitful, and original figure of the
redeeming mission of Christ which the Apostle draws for us
is that of the new Adam.   It is exceedingly doubtful whether
is was suggested to him by contemporary Jewish theology, for
the appellation " second " or " last Adam " appears only in
some writings of doubtful authority and a very late date, and
there is every reason to believe that the expression *Adam-ha-
Rishon,* so frequently met with, does not signify the first
Adam, but simply the first man.[1]   In any case, it was
reserved for Paul to express its doctrinal value and to show
what harmonious relations it establishes in the whole system
of Christian soteriology.   Adam and Christ summarize the
two periods of humanity ; they do not merely symbolize them,
they realize them in their person by a mysterious identification.   The first time the parallel presents itself under Paul's
pen it takes this antithetical form :

[1] In his *Horae hebraicae et talmudicae,* referring to 1 Cor. xv, 45, Schöttgen
says : *Nomina illa duo* (primus et secundus Adam) *Judaeis sunt familiaria.*
This inopportune remark has deceived the commentators who rival one
another in affirming that the typology employed by St Paul was familiar
to his contemporaries.   In reality, even if the expression אדם הראשׁין
(in Aramaic אדם קדמאה) is very common among the Rabbis—see Buxtorf,
*Lexicon chaldaic., talmud. et rabbin.,* under the word אדם—the corresponding expression אדם האחרון appears only very late in the Middle Ages, at
the time of the Zohar and the Cabbala.   The text usually quoted is from
the *Neve Shalom,* ix, 9 : *Adam postremus est Messias* (האחרין הוא המשׁיה
האדם), but the author lived in the fifteenth century ; and is there not an
unconscious Christian infiltration here ?   Adam being in Hebrew both a
proper name and appellative noun, אדם הראשׁון can be translated either
*first Adam* or *first man,* and it is the second translation that the absence of
the second Adam suggests.   There is, however, a difficulty : in this expression the word אדם is without the article in Hebrew and without an
emphatic position in Aramaic, which would lead us to suppose that it was
regarded as a proper name, and it is thus indeed that Josephus takes it,
*Antiq.,* I, iii, 3 (ἀπὸ ᾿Αδάμου τοῦ πρώτου γεγονότος) ; VIII, iii, 1 (ἀπὸ τοῦ
πρώτου γενηθέντος ᾿Αδάμου).   Perhaps the expression is, therefore, elliptical :
*Adam the first* (man), the omission being made easier by the double
meaning of אדם.   However this may be, the idea of opposing a second Adam
to the first came only very late ; and this was on the occasion of the twofold
account of the creation of man in Genesis.   According to some interpreters,
the first Adam was an hermaphrodite ; but they were so far from seeing
the Messiah in the second Adam, that some of them, playing on the words
(אַהֲרוֹן, אַהֲרוֹן), found in them Aaron.   See Schiele, *Die rabbinischen
Parallelen zu* 1 Cor. xv, 45-50 (in *Zeitschr. f. wiss. Theol.,* 1899, pp. 20-31).
The author rightly concludes (p. 31) that this text has no parallel in the
writings of the Rabbis ; but he is wrong when he adds that Paul is indebted
to the Greeks for its ideas and terminology.

If there be a psychical body, there is also a spiritual body.

Thus is it written : the first man Adam became a living soul ; the last Adam a quickening spirit.

Yet that was not first which is spiritual, but that which is psychic ; afterwards that which is spiritual.

The first man was of the earth, earthly ; the second man [is] from heaven.

Such as is the earthly, such also are the earthly ; and such as is the heavenly, such also are they that are heavenly ;

And as we have borne the image of the earthly, we shall also bear the image of the heavenly.[1]

Without allowing ourselves to be diverted by the accessory ideas and explanatory parentheses—such as the existence and origin of the spiritual body and the origin, nature, and priority of the psychical body—let us adhere to the central idea. The Apostle has just said : " It is sown a psychic

---

[1] 1 Cor. xv, 44-49. See, below, the exegesis in detail.

A. (44) Εἰ ἔστι σῶμα ψυχικόν, ἔστι καὶ πνευματικόν· οὕτως καὶ γέγραπται
B. (45) Ἐγένετο ὁ πρῶτος ἄνθρωπος Ἀδὰμ εἰς ψυχὴν ζῶσαν
C. ὁ ἔσχατος Ἀδὰμ εἰς πνεῦμα ζωοποιοῦν.
D. (46) Ἀλλ' οὐ πρῶτον τὸ πνευματικὸν ἀλλὰ τὸ ψυχικόν, ἔπειτα τὸ πνευματικόν.

A. *Rightfulness of the conclusion : Si est corpus animale, est et spiritale.*—This conclusion is asserted by St Paul rather than proved. After all, it can do without proof, for if a body is called *psychical*, when considered as being animated by the soul, it can be called *spiritual*, when considered as being animated by the spirit. The scriptural citation does not apply to the whole of the conditional proposition, but to the condition only : " There is a psychical body, *thus* it is written : Adam became a living soul (ψυχή)." The present Vulgate (*sicut scriptum est*) awakens the idea of a real argument here, but formerly the reading was *sic et scriptum est*, which is conformable to the Greek text, and indicates merely a biblical comparison. There is here then no argument.

B. *The living soul.*—When God, having formed man from the slime of the earth, breathed into him a breath of life, man (Gen. ii, 7) became a living soul : וַיְהִי הָאָדָם לְנֶפֶשׁ חַיָּה. There is here a double Hebraism : *fieri in*, γίγνεσθαι εἰς, signifies simply *to become* this or that, and a *living soul* means " to be animated by a principle of life, to be living, animal." St Paul adds two words to the text quoted : *Adam*, because he wishes to prepare the idea of the new Adam ; and *first*, because he wishes to make prominent the typical signification of Adam.—By virtue of this infusion of the soul into matter, man has a *psychical body* (σῶμα ψυχικόν)—that is to say, a body which the soul (ψυχή) causes to live, or rather a body in which the soul exercises the functions of life. The soul is not for the body the *adequate principle* of life, since the body needs food in order to live and because the soul cannot preserve life in it indefinitely ; hence it is living, but not quickening, vivifying.—St Paul, following the story in Genesis, speaks here only of what the first man retained from the fact of his creation. And rightly : for Adam did not preserve and therefore did not transmit to his posterity the preter-natural gifts with which God had endowed him. Moreover, these gifts did not essentially change his nature (as St Augustine well remarks, *De civit. Dei*, xiii, 23-24), and did not prevent his body from being *psychical* and from needing a periodical antidote against death.

C. *The quickening spirit.*—This expression is suggested by the biblical phrase *a living soul*, and is modelled after it. Just as the living soul is, by synecdoche, a being living from the life of the soul, so the *quickening spirit* will be a being living from the life of the spirit. As the commentators remark with reason, St Paul does not say a *living spirit*, but a *vivifying* or

body; it shall rise a spiritual body," and he concludes, after his long explanation, as follows: "As we have borne the image of the earthly, we shall also bear the image of the heavenly." The natural (*psychical*) body is the perishable body, such as we consign to the earth, and such as the first man received from the hands of the Creator. The body of Adam was moulded out of earth (ἐκ τῆς γῆς) or, more exactly, out of slime (χοῦς, whence comes χοϊκός); but when God had breathed into him the breath of life he became *a living soul*: it is thus that Scripture designates an animated being, endowed with a vital principle. Adam can transmit to his descendants only what he possesses by nature, a natural and mortal body. It need not be objected to this that he was endowed with sanctifying grace and destined to immortality. These supernatural gifts, which were not inherent in him, and which he was unable to keep, do not form part of his heritage. Earthly himself, he gives birth only to an earthly progeny.

Entirely different is the condition of the second Adam. He is from heaven, not only because heaven is his centre of gravitation and the actual place of his sojourn, whence he will return in glory at the moment of the *parousia,* but he is from heaven, above all, by reason of his divine pre-existence and the celestial gifts which it confers upon him for himself and for those who are his own.[1] He is *heavenly* by every

*quickening spirit* (Theophylact: Οὐκ εἶπεν· εἰς πνεῦμα ζῶν, ἀλλὰ ζωοποιοῦν, τὸ μεῖζον εἰπών). There are, in fact, two extreme differences: first, the quickening spirit causes its possessor to live—that is to say, it is an adequate cause of life, and the body which it animates is for ever *a spiritual* body (σῶμα πνευματικόν); secondly, it makes others live, on condition that they are united to it, and it is precisely on that account that it is called vivifying. That Paul has in view this kind of vivification appears from 1 Cor. xv, 22 (οὕτως καὶ ἐν τῷ Χριστῷ πάντες ζωοποιηθήσονται) and from xv, 49 (φορέσωμεν τὴν εἰκόνα τοῦ ἐπουρανίου). The commentary of St Thomas is, therefore, excellent: *Sicut Adam consecutus est perfectionem sui esse per animam, ita et Christus perfectionem sui esse, in quantum homo, per Spiritum sanctum. Et ideo cum anima non possit nisi proprium corpus vivificare, ideo Adam factus est in animam non vivificantem sed viventem tantum; sed Christus factus est in spiritum viventem et vivificantem.*

D. *Priority of the spiritual over the psychical.*—Nature and grace proceed from the less perfect to the more perfect. "Not that which is spiritual comes first, but that which is psychical." The principle is a general one, and there is no occasion to understand σῶμα after τὸ πνευματικόν and τὸ ψυχικόν. Paul applies this general rule to the particular case in question and thus shows by a plausible reason that the second Adam was bound to come after the first. This is not an accidental succession, but an order conformable to divine wisdom. By his insistence on justifying this order, the Apostle refutes in advance the rationalistic systems, which make of the second Adam the ideal or heavenly man, whose existence had preceded the creation of the first man.

[1] 1 Cor. xv, 47:

ὁ πρῶτος ἄνθρωπος ἐκ γῆς χοϊκός,    *Primus homo de terra, terrenus:*
ὁ δεύτερος ἄνθρωπος ἐξ οὐρανοῦ.      *secundus homo de caelo, caelestis.*

In the two parts of the phrase, the verb *to be* must be understood: "The

right, and his resurrected body is spiritual, in order to be freed from the limitations of matter and entirely dominated by the Spirit. If the psychical body is that which serves as an organ to the sensitive soul and is adapted to it, so the spiritual body will be that which serves as an instrument to a principle of activities of a superior order—called by St Paul *spirit*—and which shares in its perfections. It is at the moment of the resurrection that Jesus Christ actually assumes this spiritual body, to which he is entitled by the fulness of the Holy Spirit possessed from the moment of his miraculous conception, and by the merit acquired in the work of redemption; and it is also at the instant of the resurrection that he *becomes a quickening spirit,* capable of bestowing and transferring the supernatural life with which he is endowed. Thus, while the first Adam bequeaths death to all who are one with him by the fact of natural generation, the second Adam bequeaths life to all who are one with him by the fact of supernatural regeneration. Adam is " of the earth," he is " earthly," he becomes a " living soul " at the instant of his creation, when he begins to be the head of the human race; the parallelism invites us, therefore, to refer the three contrasted terms to the moment when Jesus Christ becomes the glorious Head of humanity restored. The Apostle, after a long détour, returns to his point of departure : " By a man came death, and by a man the resurrection of the dead; for as in Adam all die, so also in Christ

---

first man (made) from earth *is* earthly : the second man *is* from heaven." The Vulgate adds the word *caelestis*, employed in the following verse and contained as to its meaning in *de caelo*. It is very easy to understand why the first man is earthly or, more exactly, made out of slime, mud (χοϊκός) ; it is because, according to Genesis, he was formed out of the slime of the earth (ii, 7 : χοῦν λαβὼν ἀπὸ τῆς γῆς. *Cf.* Eccl. iii, 20 ; xii, 7 ; I Mac. ii, 63). The question shows that it is necessary to take *earthly* in a physical sense and not in a moral sense (having earthly inclinations—that is to say, low and bad ones) as certain commentators think, after the example of Chrysostom. The same remark applies to the word *heavenly* in the succeeding verse.

In what way is the second man from heaven ? This phrase, in order to correspond to the first, must describe the *origin* and the *nature* of the new Adam—that is, Jesus Christ, as the *principle of the supernatural life.* Now, from this point of view, the new Adam is not from heaven because he will come from heaven on the day of the *parousia*, nor because he was conceived miraculously by the action of the Holy Spirit (that does not constitute a new Adam), nor because, before appearing on earth, he possessed a heavenly body (for, independent of the other absurdities of this strange theory, he would not thus be the second Adam, but the first). He is from heaven by reason of his divine nature, by his personality and by the right which it gives him to possess the fulness of the Holy Spirit for himself and for those who are united to him. And he becomes, in the full force of the term, a heavenly man, a quickening spirit, at the moment when he receives actually in his soul and in his body the glory which is due him, and when, the work of redemption being accomplished, he can make us partakers of this glory.

all shall be made alive.''[1] The character of both the first and second Adam is essentially a representative one. Adam bears in himself the whole human race; hence what applies to the father applies also to the children. Being, according to the flesh, the descendants of an earthly man, we shall be earthly like him; being, according to the spirit, the descendants of a heavenly man, we shall, like him, be heavenly. We receive in turn the image of each.[2]

[1] I Cor. xv, 21-22 : *Quoniam quidem* (=enim, γάρ) *per hominem mors, et per hominem resurrectio mortuorum. Et* (=etenim, γάρ) *sicut in Adam omnes moriuntur, ita et in Christo omnes vivificabuntur.*—This text plays a great rôle in Pauline soteriology which constantly finds its support in the principle of solidarity. The meaning is a little obscured in Latin by the suppression of the two words γάρ, which should be translated by *enim* and *etenim ;* but in the original it is very clear: verse 21 gives a reason for the appellation *primitiae dormientium*, which has just been given to Christ; and verse 22 justifies and confirms this reason. It can be paraphrased thus : Christ is called *the first fruits of them who sleep*, not only because he is the first of those raised to die no more, but also because he is for the others the pledge and promise of the glorious resurrection. *For* (verse 21) as all die *by the deed* (διά) of one man, it is proper and even *necessary* (in our present providential order) that all should be made alive by the deed of one man. *Indeed* (verse 22) it is so ; since if all *die in* Adam (ἐν), being united to him by a bond of carnal solidarity, so all shall be likewise *made alive in* Christ, being united to him by a bond of spiritual solidarity. A parallel, doubled by a contrast, between the two Adams.

Several Fathers and ancient commentators thought that to *make alive* meant to *recall to life*, and must be understood as referring to the resurrection of both the good and the wicked, according to John v, 29 and Acts xxiv, 15. But many others (St. Augustine, St Leo the Great, St Cyril of Alexandria), with the majority of the moderns, have clearly understood that this exegesis is impossible. Indeed : (*a*) in the whole of this chapter St Paul is speaking exclusively of the resurrection of the just ; (*b*) he speaks here of Christ as the *first fruits of them who sleep ;* (*c*) he speaks of those who shall be made alive *in* Christ (verse 22) because they belong to Christ (*qui sunt Christi*, verse 23). It is a question here, therefore, of the glorious resurrection only.

[2] I Cor. xv, 48, 49:

| | |
|---|---|
| Οἷος ὁ χοϊκός, τοιοῦτοι καὶ οἱ χοϊκοί, καὶ οἷος ὁ ἐπουράνιος, τοιοῦτοι καὶ οἱ ἐπουράνιοι· | 48. *Qualis terrenus, tales et terreni, et qualis caelestis, tales et caelestes.* |
| Καὶ καθὼς ἐφορέσαμεν τὴν εἰκόνα τοῦ χοϊκοῦ, φορέσωμεν καὶ τὴν εἰκόνα τοῦ ἐπουρανίου. | 49. *Igitur, sicut portavimus imaginem terreni, portemus et imaginem caelestis.* |

The reasoning is clear. Sons resemble their father ; consequently, the descendants of the first Adam, who is earthly, will be earthly, like him, while the descendants of the second Adam will partake of his heavenly nature. —In the following verse, the meaning differs a little, according as one reads the future indicative φορέσομεν or the aorist subjunctive φορέσωμεν. At first sight, the indicative seems preferable, for this clause is the end of a series of deductions, and nothing in Greek announces an exhortation (the present Latin *igitur*, which could suggest this meaning, corresponds in Greek to the simple copula καί). But the subjunctive, which is better attested, allows also an excellent explanation. St Paul very often passes naturally from teaching to moral exhortation ; and here the transition was all the easier since the Apostle, as usual, includes under only one concept grace and glory, which he calls by the same name : *the image of the heavenly man* (ἡ εἰκὼν τοῦ

The text which we have just studied is made up entirely of antitheses : differences, between the two Adams, in their origin, nature, action, and destiny; the text which is now to engage our attention (Rom. v, 12-21) unites the parallel with the contrast, although the contrast dominates :

" Wherefore, as by one man sin entered into this world, and by sin death," so by one man has justice entered into this world, and, by justice the life which was lost in " Adam, who is the figure of the Adam that is to come."—*First similitude.*

" But not as the offence, so also is the gift. For, if by the offence of one, many (οἱ πολλοί = all, whatever their number) died, much more the grace of God and the gift by the grace of one man, Jesus Christ, hath abounded unto many "—that is, unto all.—*First contrast.*

" And not as it was by one sin [by the act of one sinner] so also is the gift; for judgement [proceeds] from one [bad act to end] in condemnation, but the free gift [proceeds] from many offences unto justification."—*Second contrast.*

" For if by one man's offence death reigned by the [deed of] one [Adam], much more they who receive abundance of grace and of the gift of justice shall reign in life through one, Jesus Christ."—*Third contrast.*

" Therefore, as by one sole fault [judgement falls upon] all men unto condemnation, so also by one sole meritorious act [grace comes] upon all men unto justification of life."—*Second similitude.*

" For as by the disobedience of one man many (οἱ πολλοί = all, whatever their number) were made sinners, so also by the obedience of one many (that is to say, all whatever be their number) shall be made just."—*Third similitude.*

" Now the Law entered in, that sin might abound; but where sin abounded, grace did superabound; that as sin hath reigned by death, so also grace might reign by justice unto life everlasting through Jesus Christ our Lord."[1]—*Résumé of the parallel and the contrast.*

All in all, without counting the final conclusion, there are three analogies and three contrasts. The first analogy refers to *a fact:* the introduction into the world and universal diffusion of sin and death on the part of Adam, and of justice and life on the part of Christ. Quite a long

---

ἐπουρανίου). It depends on us to preserve on earth this still imperfect image, and this is the condition of our some day being clothed upon with the glorified image. If we adopt the future reading, it would follow that, at present, we should have neither the image of the first Adam, which we formerly wore, but which we wear no longer (ἐφορέσαμεν), nor the image of the second Adam, which, according to this hypothesis, we do not yet wear (φορέσομεν). This is a serious objection to the reading φορέσομεν.

[1] Rom. v. 12·21. See, for the meaning of the words and the construction of the phrase, Vol. I, pp. 215-19.

parenthesis, explaining that all men die in Adam since all have sinned in Adam, disturbs the parallelism a little; but the typological connection, recalled by a word (τύπος), is none the less clear. The second analogy concerns the *manner:* the union of solidarity, which exists between the entire race and its respective heads, without regard to the number of individuals represented. The third analogy relates to the meritorious *cause;* here the obedience of Christ, there the disobedience of Adam; one has made all men sinners, as the other will constitute them just. Side by side with the analogies stand the contrasts. The first opposes the *instruments* to each other: sin and grace, but good proves superior to evil, and grace is more powerful to save than sin is to destroy. The second compares the *effects:* here only one sin which is transmitted, there one single act of grace which effaces and atones for innumerable sins; there is an evident excess in favour of grace. The third contrasts the *persons:* on the one hand, only a man; on the other, Jesus Christ, whose name is above every name.

2. To atone for sin and to conquer death was the role of the second Adam. He will atone for sin by the gift of justice; he will conquer death by associating us with his life. " Christ Jesus came into this world to save sinners."[1] This motive was necessary to draw him down to earth. On this point the teaching of the Apostle to the Gentiles has in it nothing peculiar to himself; St John, St Peter, as well as the author of the Epistle to the Hebrews and the Synoptists speak in absolutely the same way. All portray the mission of Christ as having a relation with sin; all of them present his death as the expiation of our transgressions; not one of them gives us to understand that he would have come to this earth if there had not been sinners here to save.[2] As nothing makes up for the silence of revelation, when we search into the mystery of the divine counsel, the hypothesis of the incarnation for another providential order can have only a precarious foundation,[3] unless we impose upon God, in his

[1] 1 Tim. i, 9. It is necessary to compare the texts relating to the mission of Christ (Rom. viii, 3-4; Gal. iv, 4) with those which say that Jesus Christ's end is the salvation of the world (Gal. i, 4; 1 Cor. xv, 3; 2 Cor. v, 21, etc.).

[2] Heb. x, 4-7 (the Word becomes incarnate in order to supplement the inadequacy of the ancient sacrifices); Luke xix, 10 (the Son of Man comes to save that which was lost); 1 John iv, 10 (God sends his Son as a propitiation for our sins); John iii, 17 (God sends his Son to save the world).— Compare also Heb. i, 3; ii, 17; v, 1-3; ix, 26-28; 1 Pet. iii, 18; 1 John i, 7; ii, 2; iii, 5; Apoc. i, 5, etc.

[3] This is the reason given by St Thomas, *Summa Theol.*, IIIa, qu. 1, art 3.— The Fathers, whose texts will be found in Petavius, do not assign to the incarnation any other motive than that of saving the human race. The contrary thesis can evidently end only in a *perhaps*, not in a definite conclusion. It would be otherwise if it were proved that the grace of the angels is derived

activities *ad extra,* the obligation of the most perfect, which is the very negation of liberty.

Besides the special mission which accredits him, the second Adam must possess two essential qualities: human nature and exemption from sin.

That Jesus Christ is exempt from sin is the teaching of St John, St Peter, the author of the Epistle to the Hebrews, and of St Paul himself. In St John, Jesus challenges his enemies to find him guilty of sin: *Quis ex vobis arguet me de peccato?* For him, as for the other evangelists, the sinlessness of Jesus is a fact of experience; it results from a wholly pure and saintly life. The writer of the Epistle to the Hebrews deduces it from the priesthood of Christ: since the ideal priest must be " holy, undefiled, and separated from sinners " by an impassable barrier, " tempted in all things like as we are, without sin." St Peter deduces it from the character of the victim: " Christ also died once for our sins, the just for the unjust," and we have been redeemed " by the precious blood of Christ as of a lamb unspotted and undefiled." As for St Paul, it is on the mission of the second Adam that he founds the sinlessness of the Saviour. Jesus Christ receives a mission " to conquer sin in the flesh," and he can conquer it in others only after having conquered it in himself; also, although he has a flesh entirely like our own, he has a sinful flesh only in appearance. Not only has he no experience of sin, but he could not have anything in common with sin; therefore " God made him sin for us, that we might be made the justice of God in him," sure that, far from being defiled by contact with sinners, Christ would communicate to them his own justice.[1]

But sin is one thing and human nature another. " If Christ was not truly man," said Tertullian, " all his life is nothing but a lie ": his virgin-birth was a lie, his agony and passion, his death on the cross and his glorious resurrection; and, concludes St Irenæus, " the whole scheme of redemption is a lie." In fact, if Jesus Christ was not truly man, he would not be our brother; if he were not our brother, he would not be our Head in the strict sense of the word; if

---

from Christ, *and* that the predestination of the angels is anterior (*signo rationis*) to the prevision of the sin of Adam. But neither of these two theses is absolutely established, and it would be necessary for them to be proved *together;* for it might be that God, foreseeing the fall of man and the sending of his Son as the Saviour of the human race, had resolved to grant his grace to the angels also through the mediation of his beloved Son.

[1] A comparison of the four authors is instructive. For St Paul, Rom. viii, 3, see pp. 163-5; 2 Cor. v, 21, see p. 204.—For St Peter, 1 Pet. i, 19 (ἀμνοῦ ἀμώμου καὶ ἀσπίλου Χριστοῦ); iii, 18 (δίκαιος ὑπὲρ ἀδίκων).—For the Epistle to the Hebrews, vii, 26 (ὅσιος, ἄκακος, ἀμίαντος, κεχωρισμένος ἀπὸ τῶν ἁμαρτωλῶν); ix, 14 (ἄμωμος); iv, 15; ix. 28 (χωρὶς ἁμαρτίας). *Cf.* ii, 14-18.—For St John, viii, 46 (τίς ἐξ ὑμῶν ἐλέγχει με περὶ ἁμαρτίας).

he were not our Head, he would not be our representative; his grace would be peculiar and personal to himself and his justice would not be ours by any right. Thus is explained the insistence with which Paul incessantly teaches the reality of the human nature of Christ.

# CHAPTER II

## THE REDEEMING DEATH

### I—SACRIFICE OF THE CROSS

1 Real Sacrifice.   2. Realizing the Ancient Types.   3. Voluntary
Sacrifice.

1.     A SACRIFICE, a religious rite in which a
sentient object is destroyed in honour of the
divinity, differs from immaterial offerings —
prayers, vows, voluntary fasts—and from simple
offerings of a material order—presents of money,
natural gifts, votive monuments, the erection of temples and
oratories, consecration of persons—in a word, from all obla-
tions designed to perpetuate liturgical ceremonies and to
maintain the permanent service of the divinity. It is not
expedient to specify further, by including in the definition
of sacrifice either the manner of offering it, or the immediate purpose intended by the worshippers, or the mode
of operation, real or supposed, of the sacred rite, for a too
explicit definition has the twofold inconvenience of not being
applicable to every sacrifice, and of being founded on
debatable theories. Sacrifice is prayer in action. Man has
always the intention of pleasing the divinity and rendering him
propitious to himself; but the means employed vary infinitely
according to the gross, naïve, lofty, or sublime conceptions
which the worshipper entertains of his deity, and according
to the feelings of gratitude, homage, respect, impetration,
repentance, or obedience, which he wishes to express. When
the object to be sacrificed is a living being, the death of the
latter is the usual condition of it : from this are evolved two
kinds of sacrifices, bloody and unbloody. In both cases,
the partial destruction of the victim suffices for the symbolism, and a total destruction is required only for certain
special sacrifices. After a part of the object sacrificed has
been consumed by fire, or poured out in libation, or destroyed
in any way, the remainder generally is utilized for a sacred
banquet, a natural complement of the sacrifice, or else is
reserved for the exclusive use of the priests, the accredited
representatives of the divinity.

It is not easy to see how anyone, who cherishes no pre-
conceived theory or dogmatic prejudice, can deny that
Christ's death means for St Paul a sacrifice. Before
approaching the formal proofs of this, it is well to pass in
review the less explicit texts which stand by themselves, but

the impression of which as a whole tends to evoke irresistibly the idea of sacrifice and indeed of a bloody sacrifice.

*All the effects of redemption are ascribed to the blood of
Christ:* We have redemption through his blood[1] . . . God
hath pacified through the blood of his cross the things that
are on earth and the things that are in heaven.[2] You
(Gentiles) who some time were afar off are made nigh in
the blood of Christ. . . .[3] Justified now by his blood, much
more shall we be saved from wrath through him.[4] To drink
of the consecrated chalice is the communion of the blood of
Christ,[5] and the unworthy communicant profanes the blood
of Christ because the consecrated chalice contains the blood
which seals the new covenant.[6]

*When it is not directly to the blood, it is to the violent
death of Christ that the effects of redemption are attributed:*
Christ died for our sins according to the Scriptures. . . .[7]
He died for us in order that those who live may live no more
for themselves but for him who died for them and rose
again. . . .[8] When we were still sinners, Christ died for us.
If, when we were enemies, we were reconciled to God by the
death of his Son, how much more, being reconciled, shall we
be saved by his life? . . .[9] Now he hath reconciled us in
the body of his flesh through death to make us holy and unspotted and blameless. . . .[10] Jesus Christ died for us that,
whether we watch or sleep, we may live together with him.[11]
Jesus Christ " gave himself to be a ransom for all;"[12] we
have been " bought with the great price " of his blood;[13]
" he hath redeemed us from the curse of the Law, being
made a curse for us "[14] on the cross; if justice, the fruit of
redemption, came to us from elsewhere, " Christ would have
died in vain."[15] All this points to one and the same idea of a
bloody sacrifice.

2. The apostolic doctrine of Christ as victim was, for the
contemporaries of St Paul, a strange novelty. The Jews
knew well the value of trials accepted with resignation, the
efficacy of the prayers of the just, the reversibility of merits
and demerits, but, except with extreme repugnance, they
never honoured the idea of a suffering Messiah nor accorded
any expiatory value to such sufferings. The *sufferings of
the Messiah*[16] are not his personal sufferings, but the
terrestrial calamities and cosmical commotions which are to

---

[1] Eph. i, 7.                    [2] Col. i, 20.                  [3] Eph ii, 13.
[4] Rom. v, 9.                   [5] 1 Cor. x, 16.               [6] 1 Cor. xi, 27.
[7] 1 Cor. xv, 3.                [8] 2 Cor. v, 15.               [9] Rom. v, 8-10.
[10] Col. i, 22.                 [11] 1 Thess. v, 10.            [12] 1 Tim. ii, 6.
[13] 1 Cor. vi, 20 ; vii, 23.
[14] Gal. iii, 13.                                                [15] Gal. ii, 21.

[16] חֶבְלֵי הַמָּשִׁיחַ; *cf.* Mark xiii, 8 ; Matt. xxiv, 8 : ἀρχὴ ὠδίνων.

precede his coming; they are in some way like the world's *pangs of childbearing* in bringing forth the Messiah. To the question : Did the Jews of that time believe that the Messiah was destined to suffer, and that his sufferings would result in expiating the crimes of men, a decidedly negative answer must be given.

Neither the Targum nor the Talmud of Jerusalem make the slightest allusion to a suffering Messiah. There is nothing more curious than the Targum of Jonathan on chapter liii of Isaias, recognized as messianic. "All that is said of the sufferings of the servant is violently distorted from its natural meaning and applied to the people."[1] If the Talmud of Babylon, a compilation of the fifth century, mentions three times the sufferings of the Messiah, they are the sufferings endured by the Messiah before entering upon his role of Saviour. Raymond Martin believed indeed that he had discovered a text which treats of a suffering Messiah ;[2] only it is very probable that the learned Dominican made use of a copy interpolated by a Christian hand, for his famous passage is not found in any other manuscript. Nor have we any more authority for maintaining that the Jews divided into two their originally unique Messiah, in order to attribute to the Messiah, son of Joseph, the expiatory sufferings, while they had reserved for the Messiah, son of Judah, the glory and the triumphs. "The Messiah, son of Joseph, is not a suffering Messiah, he is a slain Messiah."[3]

In St Paul, on the contrary, the immolation of Jesus Christ is expressly likened to the sacrifice of the paschal lamb, to the sacrifice which seals the new covenant, to the sacrifice of the great day of expiation, and to another sacrifice which is perhaps the burnt sacrifice, but which it is not possible surely to determine.

*Paschal Lamb.*—St Paul writes to the Corinthians : "Know you not that a little leaven corrupteth the whole lump? Purge out the old leaven, that you may be a new paste, as you are unleavened ; for Christ our pasch is sacrificed."[4] Two circumstances gave to these recommendations greater actuality and appropriateness. Easter was

---

[1] Condamin, *Le livre d'Isaie*, 1905, p. 326.

[2] *Pugio fidei*, fol. 675, quoting the *Sifrâ* (midrash of Leviticus).

[3] Lagrange, *Le Messianisme chez les Juifs*, 1909, p. 236.

[4] 1 Cor. v, 7 : Ἐκκαθάρατε τὴν παλαιὰν ζύμην, ἵνα ἦτε νέον φύραμα καθώς ἐστε ἄζυμοι· καὶ γὰρ τὸ πάσχα ἡμῶν ἐτύθη Χριστός. There is here an evident allusion to Ex. xii, 21 (θύσατε τὸ πάσχα, xiii, 6-9. Compare 1 Pet. i, 19 ([ἐλυτρώθητε] τιμίῳ αἵματι ὡς ἀμνοῦ ἀμώμου καὶ ἀσπίλου Χριστοῦ) and Apoc. v, 6, 12 (τὸ ἀρνίον τὸ ἐσφαγμένον) ; vii, 14 (ἐν τῷ αἵματι τοῦ ἀρνίου), etc. Jesus is called "the Lamb" twenty-nine times in the Apocalypse. We may admit that there and also in John i, 29, 30 (ἴδε ὁ ἀμνὸς τοῦ Θεοῦ) the name of the Lamb is derived from the prophecy of Isa. liii, 7 (*cf.* Acts viii, 32) ; but 1 Cor. v, 7 and 1 Pet. i, 19 certainly refer to the paschal lamb, the symbolism of which St John also points out (John xix, 36 ; Ex. xii,

approaching, and at that period the Gentile Christians celebrated the solemnity commemorative of their salvation, not in the Jewish manner by abstaining from fermented bread, but in a spiritual way, by being themselves *azymoi*— that is, pure from all moral corruption. Now, the presence among the Christians of Corinth of a man who was guilty of incest was a blot upon the entire church. The Apostle orders the expulsion of the author of this scandal: " Put away the evil one from among yourselves ;" for he may end by corrupting you, as a little leaven corrupteth the whole lump of fresh dough. If, in itself, this exhortation is not applicable to all times, how much more impressive is it on the anniversary of the sacrifice of the cross : " Our paschal Lamb, Christ, is sacrificed ; therefore let us feast, not with the old leaven, nor with the leaven of malice and wickedness, but with the unleavened bread of sincerity and truth." What the Pasch is for the Jews, Christ sacrificed is for us ; he is the sacrifice of our deliverance, the sacred feast which puts an end to our servitude ; thus the types have had their fulfilment, the shadows have disappeared, and we are henceforth in the region of spiritual realities.

*Sacrifice of the New Covenant.*—Christ, the true paschal Lamb, is also the victim who seals the new covenant. At the moment of concluding the old covenant, Moses offered burnt sacrifices and peace-victims, poured out part of the blood at the foot of the altar and sprinkled the people with the remainder, saying : " Behold the blood of the covenant which Jehovah hath concluded with you." Familiar with the story of the Exodus, the witnesses of the Last Supper could not mistake his meaning when they heard Jesus say in offering them the eucharistic cup : " This chalice is the blood of the new covenant," or " This chalice is the new covenant [made] in my blood."[1] Whether he referred directly to the

---

46).—The leaven was the symbol of corruption (Matt. xvi, 6 ; Gal v, 9). and its rapid action was proverbial (Matt. xiii, 33 ; Luke xii, 1 ; Gal. v, 9). Christians are to be *azymoi*, that is to say, as St Paul explains, free from all leaven of wickedness and malice. The figure in 1 Cor. v, 7 (ἵνα ἦτε φύραμα καθώς ἐστε ἄζυμοι) is therefore clear, and it is superfluous to attribute to ἄζυμος the unusual meaning of " abstaining from leaven " (by analogy with ἄσιτος, ἄοινος). The Apostle says: " By your pure conduct and your sincere faith be like *fresh dough*, νέον φύραμα (νέος means recent in regard to time ; καινός, new, in regard to quality), because you are—or ought to be, as Christians—*azymoi*, free from the fermentation of corruption." We see that the metaphor is suitable to all periods, although it is more appropriate to the time of the passover, which suggested it. Similarly the typology of the paschal lamb does not seem to require that Jesus should die on the day and at the hour when the paschal lamb was sacrificed. But this controversy is foreign to the present topic.

[1] 1 Cor. xi, 25.—It is necessary to compare it with the story in Ex. xxiv, 8 ; with the typical application of Heb. ix, 15-22 ; with the allusion in 1 Pet. i, 2 (εἰς ὑπακοὴν καὶ ῥαντισμὸν αἵματος Ἰ. Χ.) ; also Mark xiv 24 ; Matt. xxvi, 28.

sacrifice of the altar or to that of Calvary matters little to the
present inquiry; for, after all, it is the same sacrifice, and
the Saviour's words would have no meaning if the blood of
the Eucharist were other than the blood of the cross. Now,
this divine blood has for its special efficacy to seal the
covenant predicted by Jeremias, just as the blood of the
victims offered by Moses sealed the covenant of Sinai; with
this twofold difference, however, that it purifies souls by
reaching their bodies and that it produces holy dispositions
instead of merely confirming them.

*Sacrifice of expiation or propitiation.*—The sacrifice for
sin is the most characteristic and most common part of the
Mosaic ritual. The Epistle to the Hebrews develops its
typology. With this category of sacrifices are often compared two passages of St Paul which really are connected
with quite a different order of ideas.[1] On the other hand, the
Epistle to the Romans compares the death of Jesus to the
sacrifice of expiation which was *par excellence* the sacrifice
for sin : " God hath proposed Christ Jesus to be a propitiation through faith in his blood."[2] Whatever may be the
precise meaning of ἱλαστήριον — victim of propitiation,
instrument of propitiation, or even mercy-seat—it follows
inevitably from this text that the sacrifice of the cross is
for Christians and carried out in a more excellent manner
what the solemn day of *Kippurim,* the annual sacrifice of
expiation or propitiation, was for the Jews. " It is impossible," says Sanday in his commentary, " to eliminate
from this passage the twofold idea of a sacrifice and a
sacrifice of propitiation." Godet, too, writes : " The idea of
sacrifice, if it is not in the word itself, appears from the
expression *by my blood.* For what is a *means of propitiation
into which blood enters as an agency* if it be not a sacrifice?"
The discordant voices of some heterodox theologians, desirous
of avoiding an embarrassing text, are now scarcely heeded.

*Sacrifice in general.*—" Christ hath loved us and hath
delivered himself for us, an oblation and a sacrifice to God
for an odour of sweetness."[3] We recognize here a clear

---

[1] For 2 Cor. v, 21 see p. 204; and for Rom. viii, 3 see pp. 163-5.

[2] Rom. iii, 25. The generic sense of ἱλαστήριον is determined by the
twofold fact that ἱλάσκεσθαι or ἐξιλάσκεσθαι correspond to the Hebrew
*kippēr* " to expiate, to render propitious," and that the day of Kippurim or
Expiation is called ἡ ἡμέρα τοῦ ἱλασμοῦ (Lev. xxv, 9). *Cf.* Lev. xxiii, 27, 28
(ἔστιν γὰρ ἡμέρα ἐξιλασμοῦ αὕτη ὑμῖν ἐξιλάσασθαι περὶ ὑμῶν ἔναντι Κυρίου) ;
Num. v. 8, etc. In the New Testament this word and its derivatives are
rare : Heb. ii, 17 (ἱλάσκεσθαι) ; 1 John ii, 2 ; iv. 10 (ἱλασμός) ; Rom. iii, 25
(ἱλαστήριον) ; Heb. ix, 5 (ἱλαστήριον, in the sense of the mercy-seat) ; but
the fundamental meaning " to expiate, to render propitious," appears always
clearly. *Cf.* Vol. I, pp. 429-32.

[3] Eph. v, 2 : ὁ Χριστὸς ἠγάπησεν ὑμᾶς καὶ παρέδωκεν ἑαυτὸν ὑπὲρ ἡμῶν
προσφορὰν καὶ θυσίαν τῷ Θεῷ εἰς ὀσμὴν εὐωδίας. There is a manifest allusion
to Ps. xxxix, 7 : θυσίαν καὶ προσφορὰν (זֶבַח וּמִנְחָה) οὐκ ἠθέλησας, σῶμα δὲ

allusion to the words of the Psalmist : " Sacrifice and oblation thou wouldest not ; burnt offering and sin offering thou
didst not require." But if it is certain that Paul is speaking
of Christ offering himself in sacrifice, the nature of the
sacrifice is not indicated.

Of the four words of the passage appealed to—the (peace)
victim, the oblation, the burnt offering, and the sacrifice for
sin—which correspond to the four principal kinds of Mosaic
sacrifice, the Apostle retains only the first two, which, in
reality, include the other two. It is, therefore, probable that,
having in view the general idea of sacrifice, of which Jesus
Christ is the perfect antitype, he denotes by " victim " (θυσία)
the bloody sacrifice of Calvary, and by "oblation" (προσφορά)
the voluntary and loving offering which Christ makes of himself to his Father. The two notions of priest and victim
would, therefore, be associated here ; and, as in the Epistle to
the Hebrews, be reunited in the person of Jesus.[1]


3. Certain theologians think they are doing enough if they
show that the death of Christ is a true sacrifice, realizing the
typical meaning of the sacrifices of the old Law ; and they
hasten to conclude that the sacrifice of the cross operates in
the same way as that of the victims of the Jewish ritual,
although, it is true, in a more excellent manner, since the
antitype eclipses the type and the reality effaces the symbols.
That is a defect of logic and of method. On Calvary Jesus
Christ is not merely a victim ; he is the sacrificing priest ; and
he is so by his Father's will. These three things—the
passive immolation of Christ, the oblation which he makes
of himself, and the command of God—form one act, the
elements of which we can clearly distinguish without, however, having the right to dissociate them. Let us see how
St Paul presents these two new aspects of the drama of
redemption.

Jesus Christ delivered himself up to death ; he delivered
himself up in order to save us ; and he delivered himself up
through love : this is the epitome of his active part in the
tragedy of Calvary. St Paul is never tired of repeating :

---

κατηρτίσω μοι· ὁλοκαύτωμα καὶ περὶ ἁμαρτίας (עוֹלָה וַחֲטָאָה) οὐκ ᾔτησας.
What makes one think that the Apostle has this text in view is the analogy
of the ideas, the quotation repeated from the Epistle to the Hebrews (x. 5-8),
and the fact that προσφορά is not found elsewhere in the Septuagint.
[1] The Epistle to the Hebrews (ix, 22-26 and elsewhere) generalizes the
theory of sacrifice and shows the necessity of it for the two Testaments ;
formerly, there was no remission of sins without the shedding of blood ;
now, it is the same, only the victim is perfect and consequently unique ;
formerly, there was a succession of high priests who repeated unceasingly
their offerings for themselves and the people ; now, there is only one high
priest, eternal and immaculate, who gives an infinite value to the sacrifice
offered once for all.

" Christ hath loved us and hath delivered himself for us, an oblation and a sacrifice [agreeable] to God for an odour of sweetness.[1] Christ has loved the Church and has delivered himself up for it, in order to sanctify it.[2] I live in the faith of the Son of God, who loved me and gave himself for me.[3] Jesus Christ gave himself for our sins that he might deliver us from this present wicked world, according to the will of God and our Father.[4] The mediator of God and men, the man Christ Jesus, who gave himself a redemption for all."[5] These texts need no commentary. Paul crowns the work by reminding us of the glorious manifestation " of our great God and Saviour, Christ Jesus, who gave himself for us, that he might redeem us from all iniquity."[6] In this teaching, taken purposely from all the groups of the Epistles, two points are to be noticed : first, if Jesus Christ offers himself for us, as a sacrifice to save us, it is because he alone has the power to do so, since he is the *only* mediator between God and men ; and secondly, he does so only according to the intention and with the sanction of his Father, who has given him a formal mandate for that purpose. This last consideration brings us naturally to the second series of texts, in which the divine initiative is manifest.

By the very fact of sending his Son to save the world, God made him his plenipotentiary. Jesus Christ had thenceforth only to consult his Father's will and conform to it. Therefore the offering which he makes of himself, at the command of God, has the value of an act of obedience, a meritorious act which, on the one hand, annuls and atones for the disobedience of Adam,[7] and, on the other, earns a reward for its author. Christ Jesus " humbled himself, becoming obedient unto death, even to the death of the cross, wherefore God also hath exalted him."[8] By virtue of the divine command, received and executed by the Son, the Apostle can say indifferently either that Christ offers himself as a victim for our salvation, or that his Father delivers him up to death for us. " He spared not even his own Son, but delivered him up for us all. God commendeth his charity towards us because, when as yet we were sinners, Christ died for us."[9] The dominant idea of these passages is that the command intimated by the Father and the voluntary obedience of the Son are, on the part of both the Son and the Father, an equal and sovereign manifestation of love. There is hardly need to recall the fact that St John follows this teaching of the Apostle to the Gentiles very closely.[10]

The writer of the Epistle to the Hebrews comes still nearer

[1] Eph. v, 2.
[2] Eph. v, 25.
[3] Gal. ii. 20.
[4] Gal. i, 4.
[5] 1 Tim. ii, 6.
[6] Titus ii, 13.
[7] Rom. v, 19.
[8] Phil. ii, 8, 9.
[9] Rom. viii, 32 ; v, 8.
[10] John iii, 16.

to it in thought, if not in expression. The picture of the priestly victim, consecrated by the Father, corresponds exactly, feature for feature, with the portrait which we have drawn above, according to the teacher of the Gentiles. The name of priest, it is true, is here wanting, but the sacerdotal act is not the less clearly described. In both cases there is a victim, who is none other than Jesus Christ; it is the victim who offers himself, delivers himself up and gives himself; and the Father intervenes, not only to accept the offering, but to command it. In both cases, the oblation constitutes an act of obedience and an obedience prompted by love. In both cases the sacrifice has for its object and result to expiate, efface, and destroy sin, to render God propitious and to open to mankind the gates of heaven. This being so, the mention of the priest in the Epistle to the Hebrews is of only secondary importance, more interesting from the point of view of special terminology than as the basis of the teaching itself.

On the part of Christ his redeeming death is an act of obedience; and this act is meritorious in regard to the humanity which it saves, in regard to the Father whom it renders propitious, and in regard to the Son who owes his exaltation to it. We conclude from this, both directly and by analysis, that this act was free, since without freedom its merit is not conceivable; and that it was a response to a divine command, since there is no obedience where there is no command. St John expressly affirms these two conclusions, but does not teach us, any more than does St Paul, the means of reconciling them with the sinlessness of Jesus Christ. That is a purely scholastic question, the solution of which must not be asked of the inspired authors. I say *purely scholastic,* for it depends on five or six problems discussed in the school, which revelation alone does not solve. Whence comes the sinlessness of Christ? Is it derived from the beatific vision, or from the hypostatic union? And, in the latter case, is it derived from the fact itself of the union, or from a special providence due to the Man-God? Does this freedom presuppose—not indeed the power of admitting a bad act as possible, for that is evidently an imperfection—but the power of delaying the doing of a good or indifferent act *in sensu composito,* as it is put, of all the conditions requisite for acting? Would the freedom, possessed by the blessed in heaven, to make a selection among several possible boons—besides the essential one of blessedness—suffice to render their actions meritorious, if God had not, by a definite arrangement, fixed the time-limit of merit at death? To what degree was Jesus at the same time *viator* and *comprehensor?* And within what limits were the natural effects of the beatific vision neutralized in him in order to allow him

to fulfil his role as redeemer? Was the divine command,
which he obeyed by dying, a precept in the strict sense of the
word, or the manifestation of a simple desire? And if it was
a precept, was it absolute or conditional, subordinated to the
acceptance of the incarnate Word, or anterior to any acceptance? Finally, did it refer to the mere fact of death, or to the
circumstances of the passion?

We believe, for our part, that Christ was not only without
sin, but that he was absolutely exempt from the possibility
of sin, and this by virtue of the hypostatic union; also that
the command to die was a genuine precept from the time that
the incarnate Word had accepted death for our salvation;
that this acceptance by Christ was really free, and consequently meritorious; and that it sufficed to render Christ
obedient unto death, even if it was no longer possible to
retract it; but we are far from imputing all these theological
deductions to St Paul.

## II—The Value of the Redeeming Death

1. Subjective or Moral Value. 2. Three Explanations of the Objective
   Value : Redemption, Substitution, Satisfaction. 3. Doctrine of the
   Fathers.

1. The passion of Christ is a manifestation of justice
which, in the divine purpose, must be recognized and
appreciated by men. When the conscience of the sinner is
blinded, he must have a new revelation of divine sanctity;
and this revelation God gives him in the spectacle of the
Just One bearing the punishment of others' sins. But if the
Just One, suffering for the guilty, remained purely passive
and did not accept with filial submission the role of
mediator, his suffering would not be a real homage to
infinite holiness. " The satisfaction offered to divine justice
by the sacrifice of Christ does not, therefore, consist in his
death alone, but in his death united with two moral facts
which accompany it, one of which takes place in the consciousness of the mediator, the other in the consciousness of
the believer."[1] Such is the explanation, not so new perhaps
as they imagine, which certain modern theologians propose to
us. The danger and error would be in believing that it
explains all the mystery, or that it exhausts the subject. It
so little exhausts it that the passion of Christ—always in the
order of subjective efficacy—can just as properly be regarded as an example of heroic self-abnegation and as an
incentive to love.

[1] Godet, *Comment. sur l'ép. aux Romains*[2], vol. i, p. 370. In a long note
(*L'Expiation d'après Saint Paul*, pp. 369-377) Godet refers to Gess (*Zur
Lehre der Versöhnung und der Notwendigkeit des Sühnens Christi* in *Jahrbücher für deutsche Theol.*, 1857, 1858, and 1859), whose ideas he professes
to adopt.

The drama of Calvary speaks an eloquent language to every noble heart : if Christ died for us, who were nothing to him, how much more ought we to live for him, who is everything to us ; and if Christ gave his life for strangers, how much more ought we to give ours for our brethren ? Jesus, in giving himself up for us, wished his example of self-abnegation not to be lost ; thereby he counted on triumphing over our selfishness, and this is one of the considerations which the Apostle emphasizes by saying that the love of Christ constrains him and leaves him no rest.[1]  Jesus Christ redeems us only by identifying himself with our race, and we participate in his redemption only by identifying ourselves with him by faith : whence there results the imperative duty of imitating his conduct and modelling our own lives after his.  When St Peter lays down the great principle of the imitation of Christ, founded on the example of his passion,[2] he is in perfect accord with St Paul, who loves to present the crucified Saviour to neophytes[3] as a model, whose condition of death he himself tries to reproduce,[4] and whose bleeding image he is proud to bear in his body.[5]

That the redeeming death of Christ is valuable for us as an example, a lesson, and an encouragement is, therefore, perfectly clear.  The great mistake of Abelard was to believe that it was only that : a manifestation of love, designed to produce in us a responsive love.  If Abelard's theory is sometimes obscure, the confession of faith which was imposed upon him, the retractation of his former disciple, Geoffroy de Clairvaux, and the refutations of St Bernard and of William of St Thierry, clarify and give it precision.  Little liked by its contemporaries and almost forgotten, it was revived by Socinus and his pupils ; but his compromising patronage was not calculated to recommend it to Protestants, and still less to Catholics.  It is Ritschl who gave it a certain vogue in heterodox circles.  The redeeming work of Christ, according to this theory, consisted merely in revealing, by his life and, above all, his death, the love of the heavenly Father, who is so essentially a Father that he is always disposed to pardon the sinner.  This revelation, by restoring our confidence, destroys sin in us, which is only a want of confidence in respect to God ; so that it justifies and reconciles us ; it delivers us also from the punishment of sin, for this punishment is, according to Ritschl, only the perception of our fault and the conviction that the evils of life are the just punishment for it.  The majority of Protestant theologians, it must be said, reject a theory which is too openly opposed to the teaching of St Paul.  They confess that Christ's death has for the Apostle an objective value, which results from the

[1] 2 Cor. v, 14, 15.  See below, pp. 201-3.          [2] I Pet. ii, 21.
[3] Phil. ii, 8.                    [4] 2 Cor. iv, 10.          [5] Gal. vi, 17.

redeeming act itself, and which exists apart from any consideration for us and independently of our knowledge.

2. Redemption is essentially the destruction of sin. There are as many aspects of redemption as there are of sin; if sin is a fall, redemption will be an uplifting; if sin is an infirmity, redemption will be a remedy; if sin is a debt, redemption will be its payment; if sin is a fault, redemption will be an expiation; if sin is a bondage, redemption will be a deliverance; if sin is an offence, redemption will be a satisfaction as regards man, a propitiation as regards God, and a mutual reconciliation between God and man. It is the restoration of humanity by the Word made flesh which Alexandrian speculation, guided by apologetical considerations, preferred to consider. The incarnation was put in the foreground, and redemption, in the strict sense of the word, by the death of Christ, was relegated to a second place. It was reiterated that the Word became incarnate in order to deify—they even said "wordify"—human nature, in order to honour it by his presence and to heal it by his contact, and to restore the immortality and incorruptibility lost at the time of the original sin, as well as to give light to its darkness and to dissipate its errors. All this made the benefit of the incarnation perceptible, but did not tell the reason for the redeeming death nor the manner of its operation.

The theories invented to explain the objective value of this death may be reduced to three: that of redemption or ransom, that of expiation and penal substitution, and that of satisfaction. We must briefly present the proofs which corroborate them and show, if necessary, their weak points and incompetency.

*Theory of redemption or ransom.*—The value of Christ's death is quite often expressed in Scripture by a commercial metaphor. Paul says that Jesus Christ has *acquired* us, *bought* us, *ransomed* us; the *price* is expressly mentioned: it is the blood of the Son of God. Once even, in a passage which has its exact parallel in the first two Synoptists, the word *ransom* is mentioned. Moreover, the idea of ransom is contained in the etymological meaning of the words *to buy back* and *redemption* ($\lambda \nu \tau \rho o \tilde{\nu} \sigma \theta a \iota$ and $\dot{a} \pi o \lambda \dot{\nu} \tau \rho \omega \sigma \iota \varsigma$ from $\lambda \dot{\nu} \tau \rho o \nu$).

In order to appreciate the purport of this concept, we must go back to its origin. Israel was the property, the private possession of Jehovah; this was a consequence of the Mosaic theocracy: "Thou shalt be a holy people to the Lord thy God; the Lord thy God hath chosen thee to be his peculiar people out of all peoples that are upon the earth."[1]        God

---

[1] Deut. vii, 6; xiv, 2; xxvi, 18 (עַם סְגֻלָּה, λαὸς περιούσιος).

imposed, however, one condition : " If you will hear my voice and keep my covenant, you shall be my peculiar possession above all people ; for all the earth is mine."[1] This possession God established by his sovereign right and by his voluntary choice :

> " The Lord hath chosen Jacob,
> Israel for his own possession."[2]

But he had taken pains to assure it to himself ; he could say by the mouth of Isaias : " This people have I formed for myself ; they shall show forth my praise,"[3] and he could protest by the voice of Moses and of the Psalmist that he possessed it by right of conquest.[4] Thenceforth it was permissible for him to dispose of it at his pleasure ; therefore he frequently threatens to give it away and to abandon it to its enemies :[5]

> Otherwise the Rock will sell them ;
> And the Lord will deliver them up.[6]

God applied to his faithless people the *lex talionis ;* he abandoned them in proportion as he was himself abandoned. It was not a complete, absolute, final abandonment with no hope of return, but a partial and temporary one, revocable on the day of their repentance. God never renounced the right of redeeming his repentant people, made wise through misfortune. He even bound himself to do this on two grounds : one by virtue of the covenant made with the posterity of Abraham and with the children of Israel, a covenant which obliged him to bring his people out of Egypt—and subsequently from Babylon—to deliver them from their oppressors and to preserve them from ruin ; the other in his character of redeemer, which imposed upon him the task of liberating his people which had fallen into servitude, and of avenging them on their enemies.[7] In all these metaphors there is no cause for anxiety about the price to be paid, for God is the master ; and as the act of abandonment did not confer upon the

---

[1] Ex. xix, 5.                    [2] Ps. cxxxiv, 4.

[3] Is. xliii, 21 : λαόν μου ὃν περιεποιησάμην (יָצַרְתִּי).

[4] Ex. xv, 16 ; Ps. lxxiii, 2.   Here it is the verb קָנָה, to acquire.

[5] Judges ii, 14 ; iii, 8 ; iv, 2, 9 ; x, 7 ; 1 Sam. xii, 9 ; Is. l, 1 ; lii, 3 ; Ezech xxx. 12.

[6] Deut. xxxii, 30.   We know that צוּר (rock, refuge) is a name for God.

[7] The word *to redeem* (λυτροῦν) appears very often (90 times) in the Septuagint and usually has God for subject. It corresponds : (*a*) to the word גאל (44 times), " to set at liberty " in the character of *gō'ēl* (*redemptor*, near relative) ; we know that God was the *gō'ēl* of his people ;— (*b*) to the word פדה (41 times), " to redeem, to deliver, to save ";—(*c*) to the word פרק (5 times), " to snatch away," for example, from a danger.— In all these cases, when it is a question of God, the etymological meaning of " to deliver in return for the payment of a ransom (λύτρον) " is wholly absent.

adversaries of Israel a veritable right of ownership, neither does the new act of liberation, which annuls the first contract, give them a claim for compensation.

> You were sold *for nothing;*
> And you shall be redeemed *without money.*[1]

Once only the idea of compensation appears : " I am the Lord thy God, the Holy One of Israel, thy Saviour ; I have given Egypt, Ethiopia, and Saba for thy ransom."[2]   But this solitary allusion, which the historical fact of the conquests of the liberator of the Jews explains, makes only the more noticeable the number of cases in which the ransom and redemption are accomplished without the least mention of a compensating payment, and with the evident impossibility of determining the individual to whom the debt or ransom ought to be paid.

Let us now see what part the ideas of acquisition, purchase, redemption, price, and ransom play in the writings of St Paul.   The texts can be divided into two series : those in which price and purchase are spoken of, and those in which redemption and ransom are named.   In the discourse addressed to the Elders of Ephesus, the Apostle says to them : Feed " the Church of God, which he hath purchased with his own blood."[3]   This is a clear allusion to the passages in the Old Testament which bestowed on Israel the name of an " acquired people "[4]—that is to say, purchased by the Lord as his particular possession ; only since it is here a question of the Church, the price of purchase can only be the blood of Christ.   The Epistles hardly offer us a wholly similar example ; yet the assertion, twice repeated, " You were bought with a [great] price "[5] should be regarded as parallel, for there is no doubt that the *price* in question is the Saviour's blood.   By virtue of this purchase we become the inalienable property of God, and it is no longer permissible for us to subject ourselves to anyone whomsoever. Speaking particularly of the Jews, St Paul says again : " Christ hath redeemed us from the curse of the Law, being

---

[1] Is. lii, 3 : Δωρεὰν ἐπράθητε καὶ οὐ μετὰ ἀργυρίου λυτρωθήσεσθε.   The text is interesting on account of the use of λυτροῦν.

[2] Is. xliii, 3 : Ἐποίησα ἄλλαγμά σου (בָּפְרְךָ).

[3] Acts xx, 28 : ἣν περιεποιήσατο διὰ τοῦ αἵματος τοῦ ἰδίου.   Elsewhere (Luke xvii, 33 ; 1 Tim. iii, 13) God is not the subject of περιποιεῖσθαι.

[4] Titus ii, 14 : ἵνα καθαρίσῃ ἑαυτῷ λαὸν περιούσιον (*cf.* Deut. xiv, 2 ; Ex. xix, 5) ; 1 Pet. ii, 9 : λαὸς εἰς περιποίησιν (Is. xliv, 20, 21).   Compare Eph. i, 14 : εἰς ἀπολύτρωσιν τῆς περιποιήσεως.

[5] 1 Cor. vi, 20 ; vii, 23 (τιμῆς ἠγοράσθητε).   The verb ἀγοράζειν is used in the same metaphorical sense (2 Pet. ii, 1 ; Apoc. v, 9 ; xiv, 3, 4).   It appears elsewhere only in the expression " to redeem the time or the occasion " (Eph. v, 16 ; Col. iv, 4).   St Paul, in the two examples below, uses the compound ἐξαγοράζειν.

made a curse for us;"[1] and elsewhere: "God sent his Son, made of a woman, made under the Law, that he might redeem them who were under the Law."[2] Thus Jesus Christ, as the Jehovah of the old covenant, acquires, purchases, and ransoms his people. He gives for them an inestimable price, his blood; or, indeed, he assumes a burdensome and ignominious mode of life, the observance and curse of the Law. But the metaphor is not carried too far, and no one intervenes to demand or receive the price.

St Paul twice gives to the word "redemption" an eschatological meaning: we wait for the "redemption of our body"[3]—namely, deliverance from the miseries of mortality; and the Holy Spirit has sealed us "unto the day of redemption,"[4] which is that of final liberation and of the complete triumph of life over death. Everywhere else redemption is connected with the actual work of salvation; it is "redemption in Christ Jesus," or, what amounts to the same thing, "redemption by his blood."[5] The Apostle, no doubt alluding to an utterance of the Master, says also that "Jesus Christ hath given himself [as] a redemption for all,"[6] giving himself up to death. What is the exact purport of these statements? In the Old Testament the *redemption* effected by God contains only the idea of deliverance, and never suggests the notion of a price to be paid or received. With all the more reason must it be so in the New, where the word redemption acquires a technical meaning, complete in itself and including the entire work of our salvation, the remission of sins, sanctification, and glorification,[7] without the idea of deliverance being specially indicated in it.

In any case, the *price,* mention of which is sometimes made, can only be a burdensome condition to be fulfilled by the Redeemer. In fact, if it were a question of satisfying or indemnifying someone, it would evidently be the one who had held us in bondage, and from whom Christ Jesus snatches us away. Now, according to St Paul, we were slaves of sin, vices, and passions,[8] and we are delivered from

---

[1] Gal. iii, 13.                                    [2] Gal. iv, 5.
[3] Rom. viii, 23.                                   [4] Eph. iv, 30.
[5] Rom. iii, 24: 1 Cor. i, 30; Eph. i, 7, 14; Col. i, 14. Outside of St Paul, Luke xxi, 28; Heb. ix, 15; xi, 35; and for the synonym λύτρωσις, Luke i, 68; ii, 38; Heb. ix, 12.—The title of redeemer (λυτρωτής) is given once to Moses (Acts vii, 35), never to Jesus Christ. But the verb λυτροῦν, *redimere,* is applied three times to the work of redemption: Tit. ii, 14 (ἵνα λυτρώσηται ἡμᾶς ἀπὸ πάσης ἀνομίας); Luke xxiv, 21; 1 Pet. i, 18.
[6] 1 Tim. ii, 6: ὁ δοὺς ἑαυτὸν ἀντίλυτρον ὑπὲρ πάντων. See p. 197.
[7] Col. i, 14 (ἐν ᾧ ἔχομεν τὴν ἀπολύτρωσιν, τὴν ἄφεσιν τῶν ἁμαρτιῶν); 1 Cor. i, 30 (δικαιοσύνη τε καὶ ἁγιασμὸς καὶ ἀπολύτρωσις); Rom. viii, 23 (ἀπεκδεχόμενοι τὴν ἀπολύτρωσιν τοῦ σώματος ἡμῶν); Eph. iv, 30 (εἰς ἡμέραν ἀπολυτρώσεως). Elsewhere (Rom. iii, 24; 1, 14) the word is employed absolutely in the general sense of redemption, with no special allusion to a deliverance.
[8] Rom. vi, 6, 17, 19, 20; vii, 14, 23; Tit. ii, 3; iii, 3.

all iniquity;[1] the Jews are redeemed from the curse of the
Law;[2] the pagans were enslaved to the elements of the
world, God had delivered them over to their impure desires.[3]
Will it be said that the price of redemption is paid to sin, to
iniquity, and to carnal passions? The devil never appears in
this business; and with all the more reason is the grotesque
conception of a bargain struck with the devil, whom a fair
compensation would succeed in buying off, totally absent
from the writings of St Paul. If we wish to push the
metaphor to the extreme limit, it is to God himself that the
price of our ransom would be paid; for it is God whom
the work of redemption appeases and renders propitious, and
it is in relation to God alone that Christ " propitiates." The
Saviour is our ransom ($\lambda \acute{v} \tau \rho o \nu$), and it is well known that, in
the Mosaic code, this word denotes the tax or the sacrifice
required by God for the ransom of the firstborn.[4] But once
again, nothing allows us to assert that the metaphor should
be pushed so far.

In the times when ideas of purchase, price, and ransom
were operative, the temptation was great to change the
metaphor into an allegory and to complete the similitude by
making up for the silence of the sacred authors. Several
Fathers did not resist it, and there escaped from them some
unfortunate expressions which have drawn down upon them
the anathemas of our modern historians of dogma. The facts
hardly justify these virulent diatribes. The burlesque theory
of the devil's right to us was never common in the Church;
and they ought not to be called theories, but rather fugitive
allusions or oratorical amplifications, quickly corrected by
explanations of flawless accuracy. If we put aside St Justin
and St Irenæus, wrongly accused, since they confine themselves to paraphrasing the utterances of the Apostles, and if
we eliminate from Origen, St Basil, and St Jerome some
offensive lines, there remain only the well-known and too
much expounded passages of St Ambrose and St Gregory of
Nyssa. It is in two letters only that St Ambrose carries the
allegory to the extreme by affirming that the price of ransom
was paid by Jesus Christ to the devil himself and that man,
having sold himself to Satan, was an insolvent debtor; a
prisoner for debts for whom it was necessary for Christ to
pay, and thus to destroy the authentic document upon which
man's indebtedness was inscribed. To whom, therefore, did
Christ pay the price of his blood? To the infernal creditor:
the Bishop of Milan does not recoil from this horrible con-

---

[1] Titus ii, 14.　　　[2] Gal. iii, 13 ; iv, 5.　　　[3] Rom. i, 24, 26, 28.

[4] The word $\lambda \acute{v} \tau \rho o \nu$ in the Septuagint corresponds seven times to פִּדְיוֹן,
six times to כֹּפֶר, five times to גְּאֻלָה or words of the same root, and once to
מְחָר. Now the first of these words signifies the compensation given to G
for the firstborn, Num. xviii, 15 ($\lambda \acute{v} \tau \rho o \iota \varsigma \ \lambda v \tau \rho \omega \theta \acute{\eta} \sigma \epsilon \tau \alpha \iota \ \tau \grave{\alpha} \ \pi \rho \omega \tau \acute{o} \tau o \kappa \alpha$).

clusion, and St Gregory of Nyssa reaches the same point by another road. The redemption of the human race must safeguard all the attributes of God : justice, as well as wisdom and goodness. Now since we had been delivered over to the devil by a document well and correctly drawn, we were his property, and he would not consent to abandon his claim to us without fair compensation. He thought he had found this compensation in the death of the Saviour, but perceived too late that he had made a bad bargain ; for man remained none the less beyond his attacks and demands. In order not to judge these juridical negotiations and this strange haggling too severely, we must remember that the saintly teacher is addressing his remarks to unbelieving readers, and that he is not expounding nor even speaking of theology in the strict sense of the word, but arguing apologetically, and let us add, if we must, badly. However, his example teaches us how dangerous it is, in these delicate matters, to venture " beyond what is written."

*Theory of penal substitution.*—There are many theologians who discover at the foundation of every sacrifice the idea of substitution. Sacrifice, it is said, has essentially for its aim to recognize the sovereign right of God to what is his, and also the unworthiness of man in his present fallen state. Under these conditions, the religious instinct suggests to the guilty man, conscious of his faults and of the punishment which they deserve, the thought of substituting for himself an innocent victim among the animals most necessary to his subsistence. If such a sentiment is difficult to discover among primitive peoples, where the sacrifice often assumes a joyous character, it is thought possible at least to establish its existence among the Israelites, who received it by revelation. The ritual common to sacrifices for sin seems to indicate this substitution quite clearly ; the victim must be immaculate ; the priest who sacrifices it lays his hands upon it to signify the transfer of the fault ; it is killed instead of the criminal ; its blood, shed before God, and its body consumed by the flames, complete the symbolism of the expiation. In support of this the following text from Leviticus is quoted : " The life of living beings is in the blood ; and I have given it you for the altar to make propitiation for you ; for it is the blood that maketh propitiation because it is the life."[1] Blood must be abstained from because life is in the blood ;

---

[1] xvii, 11, trans by Reuss, *L'histoire sainte et la loi*, vol. i, Paris, 1879, p. 150. Reuss avoids the literal translation (the soul of the flesh) because it gives a false meaning in French, the *soul* hardly signifying life, nor *flesh* living beings. He adds the three following reflections : " Literally, of the *flesh*, an expression which includes men and animals It will be remarked that the principle of animal life is located in the blood, as elsewhere in the breath (Gen. ii, 7) ; it is not at all a question of what we call the *soul* in a

life ceases with the blood and passes away when the blood
flows from the body; this fact of experience is sufficient to
cause the blood to be considered as the vehicle of life, as the
very life. Now the life of animals belongs to God only; he
reserves it for himself and grants the use of it to man only in
view of sacrifice. To offer the blood is to offer the life, and
God accepts it on the altar, but only as a means of expiation
or propitiation : the Hebrew word *kipper* signifies both.

This ingenious theory raises many objections. How is it,
for example, to be applied to peace-offerings, to votive
sacrifices and to sacrifices of thanksgiving? Even if restricted to the sacrifice for sin, it encounters serious difficulties. The Mosaic Law did not admit sacrifices for
transgressions which merited death. The sacrifice consisted
less in the immolation itself, which a layman sometimes performed, than in the manipulation of the blood, which was
reserved for the priest only. Has it ever been proved that
the laying on of hands, which is susceptible of such varied
symbolism, signified precisely the transfer of the guilt? And
if it did signify that, why did the victim, instead of being
defiled, become so holy that only the priests partook of it? A
bloody death is absent precisely in the ceremony of the scape-
goat, in which the idea of substitution is most obvious and in
which, as might be expected, the animal which is sym-
bolically laden with the sins of the peoples becomes impure
and accursed.

Moreover, the theory of penal substitution, when isolated
and exaggerated, presents grave dangers. It tends to establish a repugnant conflict between the justice and the love of
God on one side and between his anger and mercy on the
other. God persecutes a God; he proceeds against him with
all the apparatus of justice; he regards him as an enemy and
as one who deserves all his vengeance; he declares open war
upon him; he delivers him over, as a victim, to the fury of
his irritated justice and inflicts upon him in a certain way the
punishment of the damned. How much better than these
oratorical figures and exaggerated metaphors, the hyperbole
of which must be reduced, is the simple doctrine of St
Thomas that God gave up his Son by decreeing his death for
the salvation of the world, by inspiring him with the willingness to die for us, and by not protecting him against his
enemies.

It is said that the innocent is punished for the guilty; but
this is not exact nor even intelligible. Punishment cannot be
transferred from one person to another without changing its

---

philosophical or psychological sense.—There is a use for the blood, but it is
intended not for nourishment but for sacrifice.—The author has in mind
the expiatory sacrifice ; the life of the animal is given to God in compensation
for the life of sinful man."

nature. A debt can indeed be paid by an intermediary, but a punishment cannot be undergone by proxy. Punishment is essentially a personal thing, inseparable from the sin; if it falls upon a stranger, it is no longer a punishment. If the law of nations has sometimes allowed the fault of one of their members to be imputed to a family, a city, or a nation, it is because the family, city, or nation were considered as moral entities; it is not by virtue of the principle of penal substitution, but by virtue of the wholly different principle of solidarity.

If we suppose that St Paul really had in mind the theory of substitution, how comes it that he never formulated it? Why does he *always* say that Christ was crucified *for* us (ὑπέρ, and exceptionally περί), *for* all men, *for* sinners,[1] that he went to death *for* us,[2] that he was made a curse *for* us,[3] that he was made sin *for* us,[4] and that he gave himself up *for* our sins;[5] and why does he *never* say that Christ died *in our place* (ἀντί),[6] which logically would dispense us from dying? No doubt what one person does *for* another is often done *in his stead;* it is what he ought to have done, and makes up for his lack of ability, and therefore is somehow done by way of substitution; but it does not follow that the two expressions have the same meaning. In the New Testament not a single example of this equivalence is quoted, and even if to die *for* men can be understood, in the last analysis, as being a substitution of the innocent for the guilty, can " to die *for* their sins " be interpreted in the same way? Is this not a clear proof that the idea of substitution does not convey the whole thought of the Apostle, and that it must be corrected or completed by a notion of another kind?

Ever since the principle of penal substitution has been

---

[1] Rom. v, 6, 7, 8; xiv, 15; 1 Cor. i, 13; 2 Cor. v, 15; 1 Thess. v, 10 (περί).

[2] Rom. viii, 32; 1 Cor. xi, 24; ii, 20; 1 Tim. ii, 6; Tit. ii, 14.

[3] Gal. iii, 13.                              [4] 2 Cor. v, 21.

[5] Gal. i, 4; 1 Cor. xv, 3; *cf.* Rom. viii, 3.

[6] St Paul changes the *logion* (Matt. xx, 28; Mark. x, 45: δοῦναι τὴν ψυχὴν αὐτοῦ λύτρον ἀντὶ πολλῶν) in a way which seems intentional (1 Tim. ii, 6: ὁ δοὺς ἑαυτὸν ἀντίλυτρον ὑπὲρ πάντων). In the new version the idea of substitution is so attenuated that it almost disappears; for ἀντίλυτρον (like ἀντιμισθία, Rom. i, 27; 2 Cor. vi, 13 for μισθός, and ἀντάλλαγμα, Mark viii, 37; Matt. xvi, 26 for ἄλλαγμα) does hardly more than strengthen the meaning of λύτρον and does not indicate the exchange of this ransom *for* the persons liberated. The relation with the interested parties is expressed as usual by ὑπέρ. After this, it is superfluous to inquire whether ὑπέρ is not sometimes equivalent to ἀντί. Let us note, however, that the two examples cited in Thayer's dictionary (4th edit. *sub voce*) are not very reliable. In fact, we know that baptism *for* (ὑπέρ, 1 Cor. xv, 29) the dead was conferred by the Corinthians *in favour* of the dead, but we do not in the least know whether in was *in their place*. As to Philem. 13, it may be granted that ὑπὲρ σοῦ is almost equivalent to ἀντὶ σοῦ, but many authors (Vincent, Haupt, St John Parry, etc.) dispute it, precisely because this is contrary to Paul's usage. See, however, Lightfoot on this last passage and on Col. i, 7: πιστὸς ὑπὲρ ὑμῶν (or ὑπὲρ ἡμῶν) διάκονος.

applied, there has been a temptation to exaggerate it. This is what a great number of Protestant theologians did, especially in Lutheranism. They maintained that Christ had suffered identically the punishment due for sin : death, the divine curse, and damnation itself. Thus Jesus suffered the anguish of hell in Gethsemani, when his soul was oppressed with a deadly sadness ; he suffered the tortures of the damned on Calvary, when he uttered that cry of agony : " My God, why hast thou forsaken me?" He suffered all this also, not *extensively*, according to duration of time, but *intensively, essentially*. This line of thought has been generally abandoned ; but these absurd consequences have thrown upon the theory of penal substitution an amount of discredit which it is far from overcoming.

*Theory of satisfaction.*—In his famous *Cur Deus homo,* St Anselm reasons thus : Sin is an offence against God ; but the wisdom and the holiness of the Most High cannot let an offence against his honour go unpunished. The sinner remains, therefore, a debtor to divine justice, until the offence has been atoned for. Now, no created being, whether man or angel, can restore to God the outward glory which sin takes from him ; for the act of every finite being is by its nature finite, while sin, by attacking God, acquires on account of this fact an infinite wickedness. Therefore, one of two things is true : either sinful man was irremediably lost, or it was necessary that a God-Man should come to his aid. But it is repugnant to divine goodness to abandon its plans of love and mercy. Hence we see the moral necessity for the incarnation of the Word, in order to offer to God, in the name of guilty humanity, a satisfaction equal to the offence. By virtue of the hypostatic union, the divine person confers upon the acts of his human nature an infinite value, and the redeeming death, voluntarily accepted by Jesus, as a supreme proof of filial obedience, for the purpose of restoring the honour of God, restores it with interest.

This dialectical arrangement, the power and harmony of which no one will fail to recognize, may be criticized as pertaining too much to the spheres of pure speculation. Pushed to its ultimate consequences, it would end in philosophic optimism and the absolute necessity of the incarnation. Yet the author of *Cur Deus homo* was able to steer clear of the difficulties and his interpretation of the redeeming death marks a real progress. Let us add that it finds a solid foundation in Paul. It is indisputable that God, in the actual plan of salvation, had in view the display of his wisdom and justice. It will be said that it is a question here of justifying justice ; but justifying justice is only one particular aspect of the divine attribute of justice ; it is justice which, having inflicted upon sin the treatment which it deserves, spares the sinner who is united to Jesus by faith. The blood of Christ is a "means of propitiation" (ἱλαστήριον). Whether the propitiation is a direct effect of the redeeming death or whether it springs directly from the expiation produced by the sacrifice of the cross, the result is the same; in either way, the blood of Christ atones for the offence against God and renders him propitious to us. It effects also a reconciliation and puts an end to the mutual hatred which formerly existed between sinful man and an outraged God; and this reconciliation presupposes that the wrongs against God no longer exist; in other words, that God has received satisfaction for the offences committed against him.

The theory of satisfaction completes and corrects to a great degree that of penal substitution. Considering sin no longer as a debt to be paid or a punishment to be undergone, but rather as an injury to be repaired, it renders superfluous the material proportionality between sin and its expiation; a moral proportion is sufficient, which results superabundantly from the value conferred upon the acts of Christ's human nature through his divine personality. It explains, moreover, the necessity of uniting the active obedience of the Redeemer with his passive obedience; for the reparation of an offence can be made only by a free and conscious act. Nevertheless, as it is generally presented, it is open to serious objections. It presupposes in the first place that every sin must necessarily be punished or atoned for: *Necesse est ut omne peccatum satisfactio aut poena sequatur* is the maxim repeated several times by St Anselm. Now sin can be forgiven and also remitted even after an inadequate reparation. This is not the case in the present order of things, for the satisfaction of Christ is more than sufficient, but it might be the case; and then the theory, which is based upon philosophic speculation and not upon the positive facts of revelation, would be defective. In the second place merit cannot be transferred any more than punishment can. If a family is honoured or recompensed out of consideration for one of its members, it is because it forms a moral unity, and because its members are not strangers to one another. Similarly the atonement for an offence can be effected only by the offender in person or by someone who forms with him morally one and the same person. On any hypothesis, we emerge from the principle of substitution to enter that of solidarity, the only one that gives us the key to the Pauline doctrine. There is, therefore, room for further improvements in this matter, and the final word is not spoken.

3. It is not, however, in the writings of the Fathers that we must seek it. They have been often wrongly accused of giving too little prominence to this fundamental dogma, for

in their writings are found as many allusions to the work of redemption as to any other article of faith, perhaps even more. But various circumstances explain their reticence. In the first centuries no heresy ever directly attacked the dogma of redemption; hence the Fathers were not obliged to defend it, and they limited themselves in general to repeating the traditional formulas without troubling themselves about harmonizing them or investigating their profound meaning.

Given the public which they addressed and the plan which they proposed to follow, the apostolic Fathers and the apologists had hardly any need to speak of the redeeming death. Later, when confronted by sceptical pagans, the chief problem was : Why had a God become man? Several, following the example of Origen in his refutation of Celsus, thought they could make the mystery of an incarnate God. more intelligible by proving the necessity of redemption. Such is also the dominant idea of the first works in which redemption is treated in a learned manner. St Athanasius entitles his work *De incarnatione Verbi;* if he insists far too much, to suit us, on physical redemption—that is to say, on the restoration of human nature by the union of the Word with our flesh—his aim, and his readers as well, forced this plan upon him. The apologetical aims of St Gregory of Nyssa, in his *Great Catechesis,* are not less marked. We do not hesitate to confess that in this he makes a bad use of medical comparisons, and takes an excessive amount of pleasure in describing medicinal methods employed to heal mankind; but the Catholic doctrine of salvation by the cross of Jesus is neither forgotten nor concealed; it is made secondary in prominence, that is all. " Our nature was ill," says St Gregory, " and had need of a physician; fallen man waited for a helping hand to lift him up; fatally stricken, it was necessary for someone to restore him to life; having gone astray in the paths of evil, he called for a guide to lead him to the good; imprisoned in darkness, he yearned for the light. The captive needed a redeemer; the prisoner a helper; the slave a liberator." All this tends to prove the expediency of the incarnation, but throws only a faint light on the nature of the work of redemption itself.

### III—DOCTRINAL SYNTHESIS

1. The Great Principle of Solidarity.  2. Soteriological Value of the Resurrection of Christ.  3. Unity and Harmony of Paul's Doctrine.

1. The preceding pages have shown how many and varied are the aspects of redemption. All these viewpoints are to a certain degree just, and all should be presented, yet they can be presented only one after another; moreover, all of them are incomplete, and it is because they have been

isolated, one being exaggerated to the detriment of the other, that contradictory systems have been imagined, all insufficient in their narrowness and, above all, false by their exclusiveness. Each of them represents a part of the truth, but not the whole truth.

The theory of ransom is right, for sin really made us debtors to God, and we were unable to pay our debt; but it is not a stranger who pays it for us; it is the human race itself which discharges it through its representative, Jesus Christ. The theory of substitution is right, for Christ has endured for us a punishment which he did not deserve; but the substitution is incomplete, since he who expiates our faults is the Head of our family, and thus we expiate them in him and by him. The theory of satisfaction is right, but only if it is not based exclusively upon a substitution of persons, for an offence is really washed away only if the offender takes part in the reparation as he took part in the offence. Thus, whichever road is taken, unless indeed we halt on the way, we always end by coming to the principle of solidarity.

This illuminating principle was not only perceived but clearly formulated by the Fathers of the Church. All of them say in about the same words that Jesus Christ had to become what we are, in order to make us become what he is; that he became incarnate in order that the deliverance should be accomplished by a man, as the fall had been accomplished by a man; that Christ, as redeemer, comprises and summarizes all humanity; and that God wished to restore our nature by itself and by its own resources, by means of the Incarnate Word. Several of them, far from failing to recognize the principle of solidarity, exaggerated its application. Modern theologians also will enter more and more into this category of ideas; Catholics, in order to find in it a necessary complement to the doctrine of satisfaction; Protestants, in order to obtain a no less necessary corrective for the theory of substitution, the terminology of which they religiously retain. It is a happy sign; we are advancing by degrees towards a conception of the redemptive death, which puts a stop to many difficulties and will end by rallying into one group all those who concede an objective value to the redemption. We shall see that it interprets the Apostle's thought correctly.

> The charity of Christ presseth us : judging this, that if One died for all, then all died ; and that One died for all, that they also who live may not now live to themselves, but unto him who died for them and rose again.[1]

----

[1] 2 Cor. v, 14, 15 : Ἡ γὰρ ἀγάπη τοῦ Χριστοῦ συνέχει ἡμᾶς κρίναντας τοῦτο ὅτι (A) εἰς ὑπὲρ πάντων ἀπέθανεν· ἄρα οἱ πάντες ἀπέθανον·

14. *Charitas enim Christi urge nos : aestimantes hoc, quoniam* (A) *si unus pro omnibus mortuus est, ergo omnes mortui sunt ;*

The theory of penal substitution would force us to conclude : If one died for all, then all have no more to die. St Paul reaches the very opposite conclusion : " If one died for all, then all died" ideally and mystically in him and with him. This is because he starts from the principle of solidarity which makes the death of Christ our death and the life of Christ our life. Instead of writing " One died *in the place* (ἀντί) of all," he writes, perhaps intentionally : " One died in favour and to the profit (ὑπέρ) of all."

The commentators who, carried away by St Augustine's authority, understand by this death original sin, fall into inextricable difficulties. Their explanation is refuted by grammar, for Paul does not say, " If one died for all, then all *were dead*" before him, but " If one died for all, then all *died*" simultaneously and by that very fact. Moreover, what would the mention of original sin have to do here, even supposing that the original sin, with no other qualification, can be called death? How would the recollection of original sin

---

(B) καὶ ὑπὲρ πάντων ἀπέθανεν ἵνα οἱ ζῶντες μηκέτι ἑαυτοῖς ζῶσιν ἀλλὰ τῷ ὑπὲρ αὐτῶν ἀποθανόντι καὶ ἐγερθέντι.

15. (B) *et pro omnibus mortuus est Christus : ut, et qui vivunt, jam non sibi vivant, sed ei, qui pro ipsis mortuus est et resurrexit.*

*Differences between the Vulgate and the original text.*—(a) The *quoniam* which seems causative (*because*) must be understood as ὅτι (considering this, *that*).—(b) The Latin conditional *si* is found also in many Greek manuscripts. But whether εἰ has been omitted by the copyists before εἷς or added in order to render the phrase more flexible does not affect the meaning at all ; in the one case, we have a conditional proposition (*if one died for all, then all died*) ; in the other case, we have an argument with only one proposition (*One died for all, therefore all died*) ; the result is the same.—(c) The words *mortuus est, mortui sunt*, which appear to be a past indefinite or even a present, if we take *mortuus* and *mortui* as adjectives, do not render very well the aorist ἀπέθανεν, ἀπέθανον (died, singular and plural).—(d) The word *Christus*, added to verse 15, does not change the sense at all, but suggests the idea of an argument, which does not exist here.—(e) The present participle, *aestimantes*, in place of the aorist κρίναντας, has no influence on the thought.—(f) On the contrary, the addition of *et* (in *et qui vivunt*) makes the phrase obscure.

*Signification of some terms.*—(a) Nearly everyone is agreed that the love of Christ designates here the love which Christ has for us. The context requires it, although one thinks of the rule that a personal genitive after ἀγάπη is *always* a subjective genitive, and never an objective genitive.—(b) The word συνέχει signifies *urget* and *cohibet*. It can keep this double meaning quite consistently. Chrysostom translates : *leaves me no rest* (οὐκ ἀφίησι ἡσυχάζειν με) ; Theodoret : *inflames us* (πυρπολούμεθα) ; the exact meaning seems to be : *possesses us unreservedly, dominates us and urges us, animates us and keeps us from thinking of ourselves.*—(c) The words κρίναντας τοῦτο ὅτι mean : *having considered this* (namely) *that.* For this meaning of κρίνειν *cf.* 1 Cor. x, 15 ; xi, 13. For the expression τοῦτο ὅτι, *cf.* Rom. ii, 3 ; vi, 6 ; 2 Cor. x, 7, 11 ; Eph. v, 5.—In this way, τοῦτο ὅτι includes the two following considerations united by the copulative conjunction (καί) after which ὅτι must be understood.

*Doctrinal import of the text.*—The love which Christ feels for us inflames the devotion and self-abnegation of the Apostle, because it suggests two reflections : (A) *First consideration :* " One died for all, hence all died."

stimulate the self-abnegation of the apostles? On the contrary, it is easy to understand that the mystical death with Jesus Christ makes it obligatory for us to live in him and to model our sentiments on his. Finally, the exegesis of Augustine has for its point of departure an error of fact suggested by the Latin version. In the words *et pro omnibus mortuus est Christus* the conjunction *et,* owing to the interpolation of the word *Christus,* has the appearance of resuming the unfinished argument. Now this is not the case : the reasoning is complete in the first phrase, and the copulative merely introduces a second consideration well fitted to support the Apostle in the way of abnegation. Thus the whole text awakens, not the idea of substitution, but that of solidarity. For, in order that Jesus may associate us with his death, it is essential that we should be wholly one with him at the moment when he dies for us. No doubt we are associated

---

The explanation of some old theologians (Theodoret, Ambrosiaster, etc.), " therefore all had to die a physical death," is as contrary to logic as to grammar here. That of St Augustine (*Contra Julian.,* vi, 4 ; *De peccat. merit. et remiss.,* i, 27 ; *De civit. Dei,* xx, 6, etc.) followed by many scholastic commentators, " therefore all were spiritually dead through sin," is no more admissible than the other, for there would be needed, not the aorist (ἀπέθανον) but the pluperfect ; moreover, this consideration does not agree at all with the context or with the evident object of St Paul, as Estius has very well remarked : *Hic commentarius . . . etsi veram sententiam contineat, non admodum quadrat Apostoli instituto, nec connecti facile potest cum iis quæ sequuntur.* If the death of all is neither a physical nor a spiritual death (the death of sin), it is then either a moral death or a mystical death. Almost all the modern exegetes declare their adherence to one or the other of these two deaths. St Thomas proposes three meanings : (*a*) spiritual death, as St Augustine, (*b*) mystical death (*ut omnes mortui dicantur veteri vitae, nec significetur quid sit sed quid esse debeat*), (*c*) moral death (*ita quisque debet reputare ac si mortuus esset sibi ipsi*). He regards the last sense, which is that of the gloss, as more literal. Nevertheless, the commentators, and with reason, generally prefer the second. In fact, this is not an exhortation, but the presentation of a fact ; or at least the exhortation is indirect and originates, as a consequence, from the fact itself. It is a question, therefore, of the mystical death of all men, which ideally took place on Calvary in the physical death of Jesus Christ, their common representative, and which really took place for each of them at baptism, in the act of their incorporation with Christ. Bengel expresses this with his usual conciseness : *Mors facta in morte Christi.* Bisping explains it well : *Wirklich und wahrhaft sind wir in Christi Tode mitgestorben und miterstanden. . . . Deutlich wird hier, wie in so vielen paulinischen Stellen, der Tod Christi als ein stellvertretender bezeichnet.* So also Plummer (in *Cambridge Bible for Schools and Colleges*) : " The principle assumed is that of representation. In one sense all died in Adam (1 Cor. xv, 22), in quite another, all died in Christ."—(B) The *second consideration* draws its consequence from the first, a consequence formally wished for by the dying Christ : " He died for all, *in order that* all who live may not live for themselves but for him who died and rose again for them."

To sum it all up, the Apostle considers that he no longer belongs to himself, but that he owes himself entirely to the service of Jesus Christ and his brethren, because, *firstly,* he has died a *mystical death* with the dying Christ, and *secondly,* this mystical death implies and demands a *moral death* to himself and to his selfishness.

with the dying Christ only in an ideal way, as our representative, but his death is realized in us mystically through faith and baptism, and St Paul has accustomed us to this language : " As in Adam all die "—ideally in Eden by the very act of disobedience, and subsequently really, by the fact of natural generation—" so shall all be made alive in Christ "—ideally and potentially on Calvary, and really and actually by the fact of supernatural regeneration.

It is still the principle of solidarity which is set forth in another passage of astonishing boldness : " Him, who knew no sin, he (God) hath made sin for us : that we might be made the justice of God in him."[1]

The Apostle has just said : " For Christ we beseech you, be reconciled to God." He hastens to add that this reconciliation is possible and easy, because God has taken the initiative and prepared the ways. The thought assumes, therefore, this paradoxical turn : By a sublime condescension on the part of God, the Just One becomes sin, in order that sinners may become justice. Here again there is, properly speaking, no substitution of persons, but solidarity of action. Sin is not transferred from men to Christ, but it proceeds from men to embrace Christ as the representative of human nature, just as the justice of God is not transferred from Christ to men, but proceeds from Christ to embrace men, when the latter, by filial adoption, are clothed with the divine nature. This idea is more clearly expressed in the second sentence, for we become the justice of God only *in* Christ; that is to say, only in so far as we are united with him; but the two parts of the phrase are parallel and are intended mutually to explain each other. The Apostle, in using the general terms " sin " and " justice," does not employ exactly the abstract for the concrete, which would not be suitable here; he means to express a collective idea. Jesus Christ, as the Head of the human race, whose cause he represents and whose

[1] 2 Cor. v, 21 : *Τὸν μὴ γνόντα ἁμαρ-*     *Eum, qui non noverat peccatum,*
*τίαν ὑπὲρ ἡμῶν ἁμαρτίαν ἐποίησεν,*     *pro nobis peccatum fecit, ut nos*
*ἵνα ἡμεῖς γενώμεθα δικαιοσύνη Θεοῦ*     *efficeremur justitia Dei in ipso.*
*ἐν αὐτῷ.*

It is certain that the negative *μή* (instead of *οὐ*) expresses a subjective sentiment either on the part of the writer, or (much more probably) on the part of God himself who treated Jesus thus, *although* he knew him to be without sin, or *on account of* that.

It is likewise certain that *ἁμαρτία* cannot here signifiy " sacrifice for sin." This rendering, unknown to the authors of the New Testament and foreign to the language of the Septuagint (except perhaps Lev. vi, 18), would not have been understood by the Corinthians. Moreover, it does not harmonize with the context. Jesus Christ must become " sin " for us, as we become " justice " in him. This is what almost all the modern exegetes have clearly seen ; hence they generally abandon the explanation of Ambrosiaster, Pelagius, and St Augustine (*Enchirid.*, 41 ; *contra Maximin.*, i, 2, etc.), who has as usual drawn after him a large number of Latin commentators and even some Protestant exegetes (Ewald, Ritschl, etc.).

interests he includes, personifies sin; he is made "sin for us," not in our place, but for our advantage; for, by making himself a joint partaker of our fate, he associates us with his destiny; thus, being made sin for us, he causes us to be made the justice of God in him. Jesus is neither a sinner nor sin, personally, but as a member of a sinful family, with which he identifies himself. It is in the same sense that he is made a "curse," like a branch of an accursed tree. Similarly, on account of our union with him who is justice itself, we participate in his "justice." Jesus, being by his nature impeccable, cannot be made a sinner by his contact with sinners, while our moral union with the Just One *par excellence* renders us really just ourselves. And this justice, because it comes from grace and not from us, is rightly called the "justice of God."

The same order of ideas, or nearly so, prevails in the following passage from the Epistle to the Galatians :

> Christ hath redeemed us from the curse of the law, being made a curse for us (for it is written : Cursed is everyone that hangeth on a tree), that the blessing of Abraham might come on the Gentiles through Christ Jesus ; that we may receive the promise of the Spirit by faith.[1]

St Paul has just said that all those who are dependent on the works of the Law, and who put their hope exclusively in it, are under its curse. In fact, the Law curses all its trans-

---

[1] Gal. iii, 13, 14 :

13. Χριστὸς ἡμᾶς ἐξηγόρασεν ἐκ τῆς κατάρας τοῦ νόμου γενόμενος ὑπὲρ ἡμῶν κατάρα, ὅτι γέγραπται· ἐπικατάρατος πᾶς ὁ κρεμάμενος ἐπὶ ξύλου,

14. ἵνα εἰς τὰ ἔθνη ἡ εὐλογία τοῦ Ἀβραὰμ γένηται ἐν Ἰησοῦ Χριστῷ, ἵνα τὴν ἐπαγγελίαν τοῦ Πνεύματος λάβωμεν διὰ πίστεως.

13. *Christus nos redemit de maledicto legis, factus pro nobis maledictum : quia scriptum est : Maledictus omnis qui pendet in ligno :*

14. *ut in Gentibus benedictio Abrahae fieret in Christo Jesu, ut pollicitationem Spiritus accipiamus per fidem.*

(A) *The sequence of ideas.*—All those who put their hope in the works of the Mosaic Law (ὅσοι ἐξ ἔργων νόμου εἰσίν) are under a curse, for the Law pronounces the curse upon whoever violates one of its precepts (verse 10) ; on the other hand, it cannot remove this curse by justifying man, since it is faith that justifies (verse 11), and the law is not based on the principle of faith, but on the principle of works (verse 12). There is here a complete syllogism, in which the conclusion is put first, and St Thomas rearranges it thus : *Justitita est ex fide ; sed Lex ex fide non est ; ergo Lex justificare non potest.* —Verses 11 and 12 form, therefore, a parenthesis designed to prove that the Law is powerless to revoke the curse which it has pronounced. Verse 13 is thus connected with verse 10 without any grammatical link : " The Law has cursed us ; Christ delivers us from this curse."—It is to be noted that ἡμᾶς refers to *the Jews only*. In fact, the Law curses only those who violate it, and only those can violate it who are legally subjected to it. Moreover, in the following verse, the *us* is formally put in contrast to *the Gentiles ;* hence it cannot include them. It is the Jews only, then, who are cursed by the Law and who are delivered by Christ from this curse ; but their deliverance has for its result to open to the Gentiles the source of blessings.

(B) *The twofold curse.*—The curse pronounced by the Law against its transgressors is one thing, the curse whose object is the executed criminal is quite

gressors and gives them no means of escape from the male-
diction which it pronounces. It was necessary, therefore,
that Christ should come to remove this curse, for it is incompatible with the blessing, of which their father Abraham
constituted them presumptive heirs, and by which the Gentiles
will profit only after the Jews are fit to receive it. How will
the Saviour proceed to do this?

In order to save men, he took their sin on himself, or,
rather, entered into communion with their sinful nature;
similarly, to save the Jews—and the Gentiles after the Jews—
he takes their curse upon himself, or, rather, makes himself
a participant of their curse. The curse which weighs upon
him is, however, very different from that which weighs upon
the Jews. Both are pronounced by the Law, but the latter is

---

another. Against its transgressors the Law (Deut. xxvii, 26) pronounces a curse
which falls upon *all* those who are subject to the Law and who have no other
source of help than the Law ; for according to the doctrine enunciated elsewhere
by the Apostle (Rom. iii, 20 ; iv, 15), the Law by itself is a light, but not a
force ; it enlightens but does not sustain : *Maledictus* omnis *qui, non perman-
serit in* omnibus. The words *omnes, omnibus,* added in the Septuagint, are
not found in the Hebrew text, but are implicitly contained in the universal
proposition and are required by the Apostle's argument.—Very different is
the other curse. The death of the cross was not customary among the Jews,
but the corpse of one condemned to death was suspended from a gibbet.
It was an aggravation of the penalty, and above all a spectacle tending to
inspire terror. The corpse had to be taken down and buried the same
day for the following reason (Deut. xxi, 21) : הַלּוּי כִּי־קִלְלַת אֱלֹהִים, ὅτι
κεκατηραμένος ὑπὸ Θεοῦ πᾶς κρεμάμενος ἐπὶ ξύλου. St Paul quotes the
text freely, according to the Septuagint : ἐπικατάρατος πᾶς ὁ κρεμάμενος
ἐπὶ ξύλου. He keeps the addition ἐπὶ ξύλου, which is a just commentary
and which applies perfectly to Jesus crucified. He keeps also the πᾶς,
implicitly contained in the general proposition of the Hebrew text. He
changes κεκατηραμένος to ἐπικατάρατος, in order to make the parallelism
between the two curses closer. He leaves out ὑπὸ Θεοῦ, which would not
be applicable to Christ, or would be so only if explained. In this way there
is one curse (κατάρα) which rests upon the Jews, and another curse (κατάρα)
which rests upon Jesus ; but the curse of the Jews consists in the fact that,
having violated the Law, they find themselves cursed by the Law (Deut. xxvii,
26 : ἐπικατάρατος ; in Hebrew, אָרוּר) and consequently under the penalty
of the curse (ὑπὸ κατάραν εἰσίν, Gal. iii, 10) ; the curse of Jesus consists in the
fact that, although innocent, he finds himself in a condition which the Law
declares accursed.

(C) *Inadequate explanations.*—(*a*) That of Hilgenfeld has had little
success : The Law has lost its right to curse the Jews by pronouncing an
undeserved curse upon Jesus Christ, and the Jews have by that very fact been
freed from the tyranny of the Law.—(*b*) Nor has the theory of Everett (*The
Gospel of Paul*) met with any great favour : Christ crucified, being cursed
by the Law, was legally impure and unable to observe the Law ; his disciples,
in their turn, being crucified with him, were likewise impure from the legal
point of view, and, therefore, exempt from the Law. But as where there is
no Law there is no sin (Rom. v, 13), their deliverance from the Law would
bring with it their deliverance from sin. See the refutation of this theory
in Stevens, *The Theol. of the N. T.*, Edinburgh, 1899, pp. 405-406 (note).
It is in vain for Everett to protest that his method is the right one and that his
opponents (Bruce, Briggs, Holtzmann, Mead etc.) are blinded by dogmatic

real and the former apparent; one is valid in the eyes of God, the other has validity only in the erroneous estimation of men; one proceeds from a transgression of the Law, the other results from an external fact which has no connection with the Law; one has for its cause the just death of the guilty, the other has for its cause the unjust death of the innocent. We must not arbitrarily complete the thought of Paul, at the risk of falsifying it or making a travesty of it. Paul does not insinuate that the Law, by erroneously cursing the innocent, loses thenceforth the right to curse the guilty; nor that the Law, by obtaining the death of Christ, receives all its due and has no longer anything to claim. These are the mere fancies of exegetes at bay. Simpler and less enig-

---

prejudice; he will found no school.—(c) A third system of interpretation is presented as follows by M. Tobac, who also adopts it (*Le problème de la iustification*, p. 190): " The Law pronounced a curse against its transgressors; that is to say, this curse. in the mind of Paul and probably also in the thought of the New Testament Jews and the adversaries of the Apostle, was death and thus exclusion from the kingdom. To this curse Christ submitted for our sake; bearing the weight of our transgressions he was condemned by the sentence of death which the Law had passed, and was crucified by the Law. But how is this death at the same time a death to the Law? By being made accursed for our sake, Christ redeemed us from the curse of the Law: we are no longer cursed by it, and we are no longer its debtors; its claim is wiped out; thenceforth also we have in a certain way shaken off its yoke. Just as Christ, by undergoing the punishment of death, delivered us at least legally from its power, so in an analogous way, by taking on himself the Law's curse, he put an end, legally, to its domination." All this is very complicated and very distorted; it takes for granted as implicitly expressed a mass of ideas which Paul never does express and which agree very little with his thought. The explanation rests upon two false principles: the total substitution of Jesus Christ for sinners (ἀντί instead of ὑπέρ), and the hypothesis that Jesus Christ delivers us from sin and the Law by suffering the punishment due to sin and pronounced by the Law, in our place.

(D) *Meaning of the passage.*—The participle γενόμενος, from a grammatical point of view, can be merely descriptive and circumstantial (*being made a curse for us*), or causative (*being made, or because he is made, a curse for us*). The above-named exegetes adopt this last meaning, and they have then to explain why and how Christ has delivered the Jews from the curse of the Law by putting himself into the condition of being *materially* cursed by the Law. They succeed in doing this only by means of subtle reasonings and by reading between the lines a quantity of things which Paul does not say and against which he would protest. It is best to add nothing to what he states; for his thought is quite clear and appears plainly in all the analogous passages (Gal. iv, 4; Rom. viii, 3; 2 Cor. v, 21, etc.). The parallelism with Gal. iv, 4 is especially striking, since the circumstance is expressed by the same participle (γενόμενος) and the conclusion by the same conjunction (ἵνα).

| Gal. iii, 13, 14: | Gal. iv, 4: |
|---|---|
| *Christus nos redemit de male-dicto legis,* | *Misit Deus Filium suum* |
| factus *pro nobis maledictum:* | |
| ut *in gentibus benedictio Abrahae fieret,* | factum *sub muliere,* factum *sub lege,* ut *eos, qui sub lege erant, redimeret,* |
| ut *pollicitationem Spiritus accipiamus.* | ut *adoptionem filiorum reciperemus.* |

matic is the real thought of the Apostle. The curse
materially pronounced by the Law and accepted by the
Saviour is not the means, but the condition, of our salvation.
In other terms, Jesus Christ does not liberate the Jews from
the yoke of the Law by the fact of taking upon himself the
curse of the Law; but he takes upon himself the curse of the
Law in order to be capable of freeing the Jews from the yoke
of the Law. Why? Because, according to St Paul and the
writer of the Epistle to the Hebrews, in our providential
order, where redemption is effected according to the principle
of solidarity, Jesus Christ has to be man in order to redeem
men, subject to the Law in order to deliver those who are
also subject to the Law, and a member of a sinful family in
order to save sinners, clothed also with flesh in order to
subdue the flesh in its own sphere, closely associated with the
guilty in order to pour out upon them his justice; in a word,
he must be subject to all our infirmities and miseries in order
to be the ideal high priest, capable of opening for us the
gates of heaven.

2. This leads us to a statement of the highest importance—
the soteriological value of the Resurrection : *Christ was
delivered up for our sins and rose again for our justification.*[1]

The first clause is a tacit quotation from Isaias, and the
context shows that it is a question of the Messiah delivered
up to death as a remedy for the sins of the people. This is
an idea common to the whole New Testament. Jesus Christ
delivered himself up to death, and if he was delivered up by
Judas and the Jews, he was delivered up also by his Father.[2]

---

In both cases it is not the *manner* of the redemption which is indicated, but
the *condition*. Jesus Christ does not deliver the Jews from the yoke of the
Law, and does not confer on all of us the adoption of sons *by the fact itself*
that he is subject to the Law and that he is born *of* a woman like all others ;
but it is here an *essential condition* of the redemptive work, it being supposed
that God wishes to save men by the principle of solidarity. Thus Christ,
*in order to* remove the Law's curse from the Jews, wishes to share in this curse.
How, as a matter of fact, he will deliver them, Paul teaches us elsewhere ;
but we must not seek in each text the whole body of his doctrine.

[1] Rom. iv, 25 :

ὃς παρεδόθη διὰ τὰ παραπτώματα ἡμῶν
καὶ ἠγέρθη διὰ τὴν δικαίωσιν ἡμῶν.

The first part is an almost textual quotation of Isa. liii, 12 : διὰ τὰς ἀνομίας
αὐτῶν παρεδόθη, where the immediate context shows that it is necessary
to translate it *delivered up to death* (παρεδόθη εἰς θάνατον).

The διὰ with the accusative is final ; but the finality can refer to the past
or the future *pro subjecta materia*. When it is a question of sins committed
which are to be expiated, it refers to the past ; when it is a question of a
justification still absent and to be secured, it naturally refers to the future.
Therefore, in the first part of the phrase we translate : *on account of* our sins,
and in the second : *in view of* our justification.

[2] Delivering himself up (Gal. ii, 20 ; Eph. v, 2), delivered up by the Jews
(Matt. xx, 19 ; John xx, 11), delivered up by God (Rom. viii, 32 ; John iii, 16).

This last meaning is made necessary here by the parallelism. Christ was delivered up *by God on account of our sins,* which his death alone, in the present providential order, could expiate. The difficulty is not there.

But why did he *rise again for our justification;* or, what amounts to the same thing, why did God raise him again for our justification? It is not because Christ earned justification for us by rising from the dead, since after death he was no more capable of earning merit. Nor is it because the remission of sins and justification are separable; if it is permissible to distinguish them as the negative and positive sides of our salvation, it would not be possible to separate them so much that one could ever go without the other. Certain heterodox authors propose this exegesis: "Jesus Christ is justified in his resurrection, and on account of our intimate union with him we are justified at the same time"[1] What a confusion of ideas and what nonsense! How is Jesus justified in his resurrection? Is it because God then proclaims him just? But had he not proclaimed him so during his mortal life, especially at his baptism? Is it because he then appears just in the eyes of men? But what relation can that have with our own justification? The following exposition is no better, even though it did lead a certain Catholic author to adopt it: "As our sins have, morally, ended in the death of Christ, so has our justification, morally, ended in his resurrection. Our condemnation had killed him, our justification has raised him from the dead."[2] What does this enigma signify? Does it mean that, after having justified us by dying for us, Christ had no more reason for remaining dead, and that it is, therefore, we who, being justified, are in some way the involuntary cause of his resurrection? But how is this rather overstrained commentary deducible from the words of St Paul?

Some Catholic interpreters, following the example of St Augustine, seek the key to the mystery in the fact that, since the Saviour's resurrection is the foundation of our faith and the principal reason for its credibility, if Jesus Christ had not risen from the dead, we should not believe in him, and, through failing to believe in him, should not be justified; or else in this other fact that it was God's plan that the Gospel was not to be preached until after Christ's resurrection and that thus our faith—and consequently our resurrection—depend on it. But the connection established between Christ's resurrection and our justification—the latter especially—is very frail, very external, very superficial, and how can we suppose that the Apostle leaves so much to be read between the lines?

[1] Candlish in *Expositor,* 1893, 4th ser., vol. viii, pp. 466-470; Everett, *Gospel of Paul,* pp. 199-200, Otto, Ménégoz, etc.

[2] Godet, in his *Commentary,* and some others.

St John Chrysostom grasps the question more closely. For him Christ's death and resurrection are only the two faces of one and the same redemptive act, so that the results of redemption can be impartially ascribed to one or the other. If our justification is related to the resurrection rather than to the death of Christ, it is, according to St Thomas, because Jesus Christ is in his death the meritorious cause, while in his resurrection he is the exemplary cause of our justification; he rose from the dead, therefore, to serve for us as a model in the acquisition of a new life. All this appears very conformable to the mind of Paul; perhaps, however, one last touch is wanting.

Jesus Christ did not come to this earth simply to die; he came to unite us with him and to associate us with his triumph. It was not therefore sufficient for him to die for us; he had also to rise again for us.[1] His death was only half of the redemptive work, which requires his resurrection as its necessary complement. In fact, the justification of each one of us is produced by faith and baptism; and it is easy to see how the resurrection of Jesus influences these two causes; for our faith in Christ is not a faith in Christ dead, but in Christ living and risen from the grave; and baptism is not only the efficacious symbol of the death of Christ, but also of his glorious life.

So the act and the rite which incorporate us with Christ are put in constant relation with his resurrection. In this very text the Apostle has just said that faith will be imputed to us for justice, as it was to Abraham, "if we believe in him that raised up Jesus Christ our Lord from the dead."[2] A little further on he says: "If thou confess with thy mouth tne Lord Jesus, and believe in thy heart that God hath raised him up from the dead, thou shalt be saved."[3] Without the resurrection faith has not its real object, nor has baptism its complete symbolism. In baptism, indeed, we die and rise again with Jesus Christ; we die mystically with him inasmuch as we are associated with his death, and we rise again ir smuch as we are sacramentally associated with his resurrecticn. Eliminate the resurrection, and baptism and faith itself, which does not justify without some connection with baptism, lose their significance and hence their efficacy. This is one of the reasons for which Jesus Christ "rises again" in view of our justification.

There is another and still deeper reason—that Christ's resurrection is for us the most solid ground for our faith, the providential condition of the sending out of the apostles, and the sure pledge of our own resurrection; that it is for him the just recompense for his merits, the natural result of his

[1] 2 Cor. v, 15 : *qui* pro ipsis *mortuus est et resurrexit.*
[2] Rom. iv, 24.    [3] Rom. x, 9. *Cf.* ii, 24 ; 1 Thess. iv, 14.

fulness of graces, the worthy coronation of his redemptive
work; and that it is for God the seal placed upon redemption,
a declaration of peace given to men and the expression of his
favour finally regained. All these are common-sense truths.
But it is something more and better than that; it is closely
connected with the result of the redemptive death and with
the gift of the Holy Spirit. It is at the moment of the
resurrection that Jesus Christ becomes a "quickening
Spirit."[1] Previously he had indeed the Spirit in its fulness,
but the Spirit which dwelt within him, fettered by the limitations inherent in the scheme of redemption, could not there
exercise all its living power. Above all, Christ himself was
not yet able to communicate to others the fulness of life.
This privilege had, for a preliminary condition, the death and
the resurrection. " It is expedient that I go away," Jesus
had said; " for, if I do not go away, the Paraclete will not
come to you; but if I go away, I will send him to you."[2]
And as he was himself to come with the Paraclete, he added :
" I will not leave you orphans, I will come to you."[3]   St Paul
expresses the same thing under this concise and enigmatical
form. Christ glorified becomes a "quickening Spirit"; he
becomes for his disciples a permanent source of graces and
life. " The work of Christ includes two things—what he has
done for all men and what he still does for each of them;
what he did once for all and what he now does incessantly;
what he has done for us and what he does within us; what he
has done on earth and what he is doing in heaven; what
he has done in person and what he is doing by his Spirit; he
reconciles by offering himself upon the cross, he justifies by
sending us his Spirit "[4] and by himself working within us in
spirit.

3. This twofold complementary role naturally explains the
curious duality pointed out with pleasure by many heterodox
theologians.[5] According to them, St Paul had two theories
of redemption, different, if not incongruous, sometimes running parallel to one another without any tendency to meet,
sometimes approaching each other to the point of touching
and blending ; one, which may be called juridical, because it
is based on the principle of compensation, penal substitution,
and vicarious satisfaction, attributes to the death of Christ an
objective value, independent of the individual application;
the other, which shall be called moral, because it is based
upon the fact of inward restoration, recognizes in redemption

[1] I Cor. xv, 45 ; see pp. 172, 173.                    [2] John xvi, 7.
[3] John xiv, 18.
[4] Newman, *Lectures on Justification*[6], London, 1892, ix, Note 1.
[5] Particularly by Holtzmann (*Neutest. Theol.*, vol. ii, pp. 114-121), whom
the above statement follows.

only a subjective value, in so far as man makes it his own by faith and union with Christ. In the first theory reconciliation takes place outside of the soul, and is accomplished by virtue of a sort of contract concluded between God and humanity, with Christ as mediator; in the second it is a product of the conscience itself. The juridical theory deals with the ideas of expiation, propitiation, sacrifice, substitution; in a word, with the categories of popular Judaism; it is a remnant of the pharisaical education of Saul; the moral theory is derived rather from Hellenic thought and reflects the religious experience of Paul after the transformation which took place in him on the road to Damascus. The same duality of theories is found in the explanation of the origin of sin, which he sometimes connects with the historical fact of the first fall, and at other times refers to the psychological determinism of the flesh; it is found also again in the concepts of justification, salvation, and judgement; in a word, it dominates all the Apostle's teaching. Some declare that a reconciliation between them is impossible and maintain that in Paul's mind the synthesis was not made; others try to solve the contradiction, but do so by eliminating one of the two points of view; some, again, are of the opinion that it is necessary to leave both systems independent, without attempting to combine them or to subordinate one to the other, through fear of changing their nature by seeking to unite them.

These are but vain scruples. St Paul took care to bring the two aspects of the redemptive work face to face and to set forth their close relations : " Being justified freely by the grace of God, through the redemption that is in Christ Jesus, God hath sent him forth as a propitiation, through faith in his blood, to show his justice now, that he may be just and the justifier of him who believeth in Jesus Christ."[1]

According to this passage, three initiatives on the part of God, three operations on the part of Christ, and three sentiments on the part of man concur in the redemptive work. God, seeing us incapable of getting free from sin by our own efforts, decides to justify us freely; this is the initiative of grace. He also decides to make Christ an instrument of propitiation and to exhibit him as such to the gaze of the world; this is the triumph of wisdom. He wishes thus to demonstrate that he is and was always just, in spite of his former apparent indifference in regard to sin; this is the amends made by justice. Christ, on his side, accomplishes the work of redemption—that is, the deliverance of sinners— and this redemption, far from being opposed to grace, acts in harmony with it. He accomplishes the propitiation when, *expiating* sin, which had raised a barrier between God and ourselves, he makes God *propitious* to us. He effects redemp-

---

[1] Rom. iii, 24-26. For exegetical details, see Vol. I, pp. 204-6.

tion and propitiation *as a victim;* the efficacy of salvation is in his blood. Man, however, does not remain passive; his salvation is not concluded without his co-operation; his contribution is faith, faith in Christ the Saviour; he meditates upon the lesson of Calvary and understands that he must respond to so much love with gratitude; finally, in view of this demonstration of divine justice, he learns to dread the wrath of God and to trust in his mercy.

In this way the doctrine of redemption forms a coherent whole, in which the most diverse points of view harmonize.

The fact of man's restoration corresponds exactly to the history of his fall. Calvary is the reply to Eden. Humanity falls and rises again in its respective representatives. An act of disobedience ruins it, an act of obedience saves it. What light is thus thrown upon the unity of the redemptive plans, human brotherhood, and the communion of saints !

God is no more the creditor eager for the payment of his debt, nor the sovereign jealous of avenging his rights at any price; he is the eminently good, holy, just and wise Father, who, in his persistent love for guilty man, takes the initiative in order to save him, and brings into action his omnipotence to carry out a plan which best conciliates all his attributes— goodness, holiness, justice and wisdom.

Jesus Christ is always the victim, whose blood expiates sin, effects propitiation, seals the covenant, and opens heaven; but he is no longer an inert victim endowed with a kind of magic virtue; his blood, however precious it may be, is valid only through the free and loving offering which he makes of it to his Father in the name of the humanity contained in him as its head. It is no longer a question of a substitution, by which the innocent should undergo the punishment of the guilty, but of a sublime condescension which leads the Son of God to identify his cause with that of sinners; nor is it a question of an external satisfaction given to God in order to extort from him the pardon of criminals, but of a filial homage which, thanks to Jesus Christ, the human race pays of itself and which God accepts because he initiated it and has the principal part in it.

The resurrection of Jesus is no more a supernatural luxury offered to the admiration of the elect, nor a simple recompense accorded to his merits, nor merely the support of our faith and the pledge of our hope; it is an essential complement and an integral part of redemption itself.

Finally, man is no more the passive witness of a drama which is being played outside of him, and in which he has no part; he dies ideally on Calvary with the dying Christ and lives again mystically in him in the act of faith and the sacred rite which apply to him the fruit of the redemptive death.

# CHAPTER III

## THE IMMEDIATE EFFECTS OF REDEMPTION

**M**AN'S redemption takes three steps—at Calvary, the Baptism, and the *Parousia*. On Calvary it is accomplished by right, in principle, and in power; at baptism it is realized in fact and in deed, although still imperfectly; on the day of the *parousia* it will be finished and consummated. Intrinsically connected with the death of Christ, potential redemption is independent of its more or less extended applications, and, so to speak, of its historical success. The immediate effects of it are the reconciliation of the human race with God and the victory of Christ over the enemies of humanity.

### I—THE RECONCILIATION EFFECTED

1. The Wrath of God.   2. Aspects of the Reconciliation.

1. God hates sin in the same proportion as he loves moral order—namely, infinitely. Hatred of evil is as essential to him as the love of good, for both proceed from his sanctity. If contempt is added to the offence committed, the wrath of God is kindled. We know in what lurid imagery the Bible depicts the divine anger. God rises in fury to avenge his ignored rights; he rushes to the combat like a warrior; like a devouring fire he scatters and consumes his enemies. When his people, forgetful of the covenant, prefer strange gods to him, he calls himself a jealous God; and his jealousy bursts forth in terrible reprisals against the unfaithful and their seducers. Fundamentally his wrath is no more anthropomorphic than his love, for it is only the necessary reaction of outraged love. We may, therefore, refine as much as we like the concept of the divine wrath, but let us take care not to eliminate it entirely under the pretext that it is incompatible with infinite perfection. Precisely because it is transcendental, infinite perfection can include contrasts which in a finite being would be contradictions. Far from excluding mercy, the wrath of God presupposes and completes it; it will be all the more dreadful the slower it was to move, and all the more efficacious in destroying sin, because it leaves the door open for repentance. This is why the sacred writers so frequently couple the wrath of God with his mercy and his forgiveness with his vengeance, as if there were nothing more easily reconcilable than this contrast.

The same order of ideas reigns throughout the New Testament. No doubt the wrath of God usually assumes an eschatological turn and has for its goal the last judgement, called by antonomasia the day of wrath; it tends to become rather individual, instead of being, above all, collective; it is provoked by every infraction of the divine will, instead of being provoked in general, as formerly, by the violation of the covenant. But apart from these reservations, which belong to the difference between the two systems, God's attitude towards the sinner remains identical. Before their conversion Jews and Gentiles were "by nature children of wrath";[1] that is to say, retaining the strength of the biblical language, deserving of the divine wrath, the dreadful consequence of which weighed upon them. Hardened sinners, "fitted for destruction," are called "vessels of wrath,"[2] because they are actually the object of God's wrath, which would be let loose upon them at once were it not for the counterweight of his long-suffering. The Mosaic Law, by augmenting sin, "worketh wrath";[3] every transgression invites it, and the guilty one accumulates upon his "head treasures of wrath against the day of wrath."[4] But it is not always neutralized, even here below, by mercy; from this time forward it bursts forth against the unbelieving Jews[5] and applies the law of retaliation[6] to the pagans, blinded by their criminal passions. It is not, therefore, permissible to say that in the New Testament, and particularly in the Epistles of St Paul, the wrath of God is a purely eschatological concept. If, however, it does begin to manifest itself on earth, it is there almost always counterbalanced by mercy, and it will reach its complete, universal, and final manifestation only on the day of judgement.[7]

Wrath, kindled by an offence, necessarily implies a certain

---

[1] Eph. ii, 3: ἤμεθα τέκνα φύσει ὀργῆς. See pp. 61, 62.

[2] Rom. ix, 22. They are *now* "vessels of wrath" (σκεύη ὀργῆς) since God has need of all his patience to endure them (ἤνεγκεν ἐν πολλῇ μακροθυμίᾳ) despite his desire to manifest at once the wrath which he feels towards them (θέλων ἐνδείξασθαι τὴν ὀργήν). See Vol. I, pp. 256, 257.

[3] Rom. iv, 15: ὁ νόμος ὀργὴν κατεργάζεται.

[4] Rom. ii, 5.

[5] I Thess. ii, 16: ἔφθασεν ἐπ᾽ αὐτοὺς ἡ ὀργὴ εἰς τέλος. The wrath of God, which will pursue the impenitent Jews *to the end* (εἰς τέλος) has already fallen upon them (ἔφθασεν).

[6] Rom. i, 18: ἀποκαλύπτεται (present) ὀργὴ Θεοῦ.

[7] Rom. ii, 5: θησαυρίζεις σεαυτῷ ὀργὴν ἐν ἡμέρᾳ ὀργῆς; *cf.* ii, 8: wrath and indignation (ὀργὴ καὶ θυμός) await the rebels.—The wrath is again eschatological in I Thess. i, 10 (᾽Ιησοῦν τὸν ῥυόμενον ἡμᾶς ἐκ τῆς ὀργῆς τῆς ἐρχομένης) and also no doubt in Col. iii, 6 (δι᾽ ἃ ἔρχεται ἡ ὀργὴ τοῦ Θεοῦ) and in Eph. v, 6 (διὰ ταῦτα ἔρχεται ἡ ὀργὴ τοῦ Θεοῦ ἐπὶ τοὺς υἱοὺς τῆς ἀπειθείας) on account of the similarity of expression; likewise in Rom. v, 9 (σωθησόμεθα δι᾽ αὐτοῦ ἀπὸ τῆς ὀργῆς), in I Thess. v, 9 (οὐκ ἔθετο ἡμᾶς ὁ Θεὸς εἰς ὀργήν) and in Rom. iii, 5 (μὴ ἄδικος ὁ Θεὸς ὁ ἐπιφέρων τὴν ὀργήν;). However, the last two cases are debatable; above all, the last, which may be understood of a wrath manifested by God against unbelievers already in this life.

hostility, on the part of the person wounded in his honour
and his rights, against the person of the offender. So the
not very scriptural formula that " God hates sin while loving
the sinner " would not have the approval of Paul. Without
speaking of the quotation from Malachias—" I have hated
Esau "[1]—which could not be understood as referring to a
relative love, the Apostle represents God as pursuing the
guilty man with his enmity. God, it is true, becomes the
enemy of man after man has declared himself the enemy
of God; but from that moment the hatreds are mutual,
although in an infinite being the hatred does not exclude love.
" If, when we were enemies, we were reconciled to God by
the death of his Son, much more, being reconciled, shall we
be saved by his life."[2] The word " enemies " is here put into
opposition to the word " reconciled," which is itself explained
by the expression " saved from wrath." It designates, therefore, not the enmity of sinners to God, but the enmity of
which sinners were the object on the part of God. The
necessity of the reasoning here, as well as the movement of
the thought, requires this exegesis, for it is the change of
God's attitude towards us which guarantees to us in future
his kindly sentiments and bases our hope on an immovable
foundation. When Paul, speaking of the unbelieving Jews,
says to the pagan converts, " They are enemies for your sake
as concerning the Gospel, but as touching the election they
are most dear for the sake of the fathers,"[3] the same idea is
presented with complete proof. Collectively, as a nation, the
Jews are at the same time detested and loved by God;

---

[1] Rom. ix, 13, quoting Mal. i, 3-4. See Vol. I, pp. 252-4.

[2] Rom. v, 10. See subsequently pp. 218-9.

[3] Rom. xi, 28 : κατὰ μὲν τὸ εὐαγγέλιον ἐχθροὶ δι' ὑμᾶς, κατὰ δὲ τὴν ἐκλογὴν
ἀγαπητοὶ διὰ τοὺς πατέρας. The subject of the phrase is clearly Israel (πᾶς
'Ισραήλ, verse 26 ; αὐτῶν, verse 27) ; the Israelites are therefore, at the same
time, from two different points of view, enemies and friends, not of Paul, but
of God, as the following verses (29-30) prove beyond the shadow of a doubt.
The phrase, skilfully constructed, is wholly composed of antitheses : ἐχθροί
corresponds to ἀγαπητοί; κατὰ τὸ εὐαγγέλιον corresponds to κατὰ τὴν εκλογήν ;
δι' ὑμᾶς to διὰ τοὺς πατέρας, and the contrast is accentuated by the particles
μέν and δέ.—The opposition with ἀγαπητοί (beloved of God) shows that ἐχθροί
is passive and signifies " hated by God." The motive and end which inspire
God show it no less : it is " on account of the Gospel " not in itself, for the
Gospel excludes no one, but inasmuch as it has been rejected by the Jews;
and it is " with a view to the Gentiles " (δι' ὑμᾶς) because the unbelief of the
Jews, foreseen by God, has had for its effect to hasten the evangelization of the
pagans (verses 11, 15, 19).—However, from another point of view, Israel
remains the favourite of Jehovah : it is " on account of the election " of which
Israel was formerly the object (Deut. iv, 37) and which is not revoked (verses
2 and 29) ; and it is " on account of the patriarchs," the sacred root (verse 16)
which communicates to the branches something of its goodness.—The text
in its entirety and in its details could not be clearer, and we see how it would
be so obscured as to be unintelligible if theological notions foreign to the
subject were mixed up with it ; for example, by taking " election " in the
concrete sense, as referring to those " elected to celestial glory " (St Augustine).

detested on account of the Gospel which they have refused to accept, yet nevertheless loved on account of the gracious election of which they were formerly the object and because they are of the lineage of the patriarchs. If it be objected that the theocratic election is annulled in all its results by the present unbelief of Israel, Paul replies that " the gifts of God are without repentance."[1] Israel, therefore, is at the same time worthy of love and of hate from two different points of view; it feels now the effects of the hate which excludes it from the messianic kingdom, and it will experience subsequently the effects of love, when it shall be assembled *en masse* within the bosom of the Church.

2. These preliminaries bring us naturally to the biblical concept of reconciliation. Reconciliation is bilateral or unilateral according as the injuries are reciprocal or all on one side; in both cases it re-establishes good relations between the contending parties by suppressing the cause of their disagreement. Sin being an act of hostility directed against God, it is man who assumes the offensive, and God merely defends his injured honour; but the hatreds are reciprocal, although the real injuries are not. It follows that the reconciliation also must be reciprocal, and that it is not enough that God lays aside his anger if man on his part does not adopt new feelings towards God. It is on this account that it appears sometimes to be a direct consequence of man's conversion, and at other times a simple change of attitude on the part of God. And according as one fixes his gaze on the one or the other of these aspects, one is disposed to see, with official Protestantism, only an arbitrary act of God, forgetting the sin without regard to man's dispositions, or else, with the school of Ritschl, only the gradual transformation of the sinner in presence of a God always equally well disposed to man, in spite of sin.

The words " to reconcile " and " reconciliation " are united in four or five texts which are very different in appearance.[2] Once the reconciliation effected by the blood of Christ expands to the point of embracing the totality of created beings.

---

[1] Rom. xi, 29 : ἀμεταμέλητα γὰρ. τὰ χαρίσματα καὶ ἡ κλῆσις τοῦ Θεοῦ. The free gifts (χαρίσματα) are, for example, the honorary titles of Israel (Rom. ix, 4-5). The vocation (κλῆσις) is the theocratic vocation which, according to the plans of God, leads to the Gospel.

[2] If we omit 1 Cor. vii, 11 (μενέτω ἄγαμος ἢ τῷ ἀνδρὶ καταλλαγήτω), where it is a question of the reconciliation of separated husbands and wives, the words which express reconciliation with God, or effected by God, are gathered into five passages : Rom. v, 10, 11 ; Rom. xi, 15 ; 2 Cor. v, 18-20 ; Col. i, 20, 21 ; Eph. ii, 16. But as in Rom. xi, 15 the reconciliation is mentioned only casually, the doctrine is to be derived from the other texts, where the substantive καταλλαγή recurs three times, the verb καταλλάσσειν four times, and the doubly compounded verb ἀποκαταλλάσσειν twice.

It hath well pleased the Father to make all fulness dwell in him,
and by him to reconcile all things unto himself,
making peace through the blood of his cross,
by him [I say] whether the things that are on earth or the things that
are in heaven.[1]

The meaning is not obscure provided we avoid any useless complication. God, to whom always belongs the initiative of the salvation of men and of the redemptive plans, has been pleased to make all fulness dwell in Christ—fulness of being and fulness of graces—in order to pacify and reconcile all things in Christ, who is the centre of creation and the bond of union between all beings.

Everywhere else the Apostle's vision does not go beyond the salvation of men, and the reconciliation of which he speaks is made with God.

If, when we were enemies, we were reconciled to God by the death of his Son; much more, being reconciled, shall we be saved by his life.
And not only so : but also we glory in God through our Lord Jesus Christ, by whom we have now received reconciliation.[2]

---

[1] Col. i, 19, 20. This text has been previously explained, pp. 90-92.

[2] Rom. v, 10 : εἰ γὰρ ἐχθροὶ ὄντες κατηλλάγημεν τῷ Θεῷ διὰ τοῦ θανάτου τοῦ υἱοῦ αὐτοῦ, πολλῷ μᾶλλον καταλλαγέντες σωθησόμεθα ἐν τῇ ζωῇ αὐτοῦ.

11. οὐ μόνον δέ, ἀλλὰ καὶ καυχώμενοι ἐν τῷ Θεῷ διὰ τοῦ κυρίου ἡμῶν Ἰ. Χ., δι' οὗ νῦν καταλλαγὴν ἐλάβομεν.

A. 10. Si enim cum inimici essemus, reconciliati sumus Deo per mortem filii ejus, multo magis reconciliati, salvi erimus in vita ipsius.

B. 11. Non solum autem : sed et gloriamur in Deo per Dominum nostrum J. C. per quem nunc reconciliationem accepimus.

A. Verse 10 is a confirmation (γάρ) of the preceding verse, to which he adds a new conclusion. The Apostle has just said, verse 9 : " If, when we were sinners, Christ died for us, much more, being now justified by his blood, shall we be saved from wrath through him." He adds : " For if, when we were enemies, we were reconciled to God by the death of his Son, much more, being reconciled, shall we be saved by his life." This new *a fortiori* is more general ; it contains the preceding one with something more ; instead of *sinners*, we read now *enemies ;* instead of *justified, reconciled ;* instead of a *refuge against wrath, salvation ;* instead of the *death of Christ as a guarantee of pardon*, there is *his life as a pledge of life eternal.* The *a fortiori* is, on the one hand, based upon the fact that the glorious life of the Saviour has a symbolical value superior to his death, for his death expresses the negative side and his life the positive side of redemption (*cf.* Rom. iv, 25) ; on the other hand, it is based upon the difference of the subjects to which redemption applies : here, reconciled (or justified) ; there, enemies (or sinners).—The whole context makes prominent God's dispositions in regard to us and the divine action which responds to these dispositions. It results from this that ἐχθροί must be taken in the passive sense (object of the divine hostility) and that κατηλλάγημεν τῳ Θεῷ must signifiy " we were reconciled to God," who abandoned his causes of complaint ; the reason for this change of attitude is indicated : " by the death of his Son."

B. It is not enough to be reconciled and saved ; we are to glory in God, the author of our reconciliation and salvation. Verses 9, 10 and 11 take up point by point the proposition announced at the beginning of the chapter : we are justified, we have peace with God, we glory in him (verses 1-2) ; we are justified by the blood of Christ (verse 9) ; we are reconciled to God by his death (verse 10) ; and we glory in God through our Saviour Jesus Christ the instru-

God is the author of the reconciliation; Jesus Christ is the instrument and the meritorious cause of it; man is its subject, and, as it were, its recipient. It is always God who reconciles and man who is reconciled. It does not follow at all that the reconciliation is one-sided; but this manner of speaking, certainly intentional, shows that the initiative proceeds from God, that man has no valid complaints, and that it is therefore for him to receive the peace, not to offer it. The reconciliation, in fact, comes down from God to man and does not ascend from man to God; it begins by the abandonment of the Creator's complaints against his creature. Enemies of God and objects of his wrath, which our sins had provoked and which we were powerless to mitigate, it was absolutely necessary for God, the offended party, to reconcile us *to* him. There is here a very fine shade of expression which, without eliminating the co-operation of man, leaves to God all the honour of the result. Hence, if man has no right to glory in himself, he can glory in God who works great things in him, yet does not do them without him.

To the Corinthians still more than to the Romans the Apostle presents the reconciliation under its many aspects:

> But all things are of God, who hath reconciled us to himself by Christ and hath given to us the ministry of reconciliation. For God indeed was in Christ, reconciling the world to himself, not imputing to them their sins; and he hath placed in us the word of reconciliation.
>
> For Christ therefore we are ambassadors, God as it were were exhorting by us. For Christ's sake we beseech you, be reconciled to God.[1]

---

ment of reconciliation (verse 11: δι' οὗ νῦν τὴν καταλλαγὴν ἐλάβομεν). The construction of verse 11 is a little difficult, if we read with the critical editions καυχώμενοι instead of καυχώμεθα. The simplest is to understand ἐσμέν after καυχώμενοι, as in 2 Cor. vii, 5; viii, 19; *cf.* Rom. iii, 24. We can also mentally supply σωθησόμεθα from the preceding phrase: not only (shall we be saved) but (we shall be saved) in glorying in God. Another difficulty is that the reconciliation appears sometimes potential and objective (verse 10), sometimes actual and subjective (verse 11); but we know that the Apostle likes to unite the two ideas of redemption closely.

[1] 2 Cor. v, 18, 19, 20:

A. 18. τὰ δὲ πάντα ἐκ τοῦ Θεοῦ τοῦ καταλλάξαντος ἡμᾶς ἑαυτῷ διὰ Χριστοῦ καὶ δόντος ἡμῖν τὴν διακονίαν τῆς καταλλαγῆς,

B. 19. ὡς ὅτι Θεὸς ἦν ἐν Χριστῷ κόσμον καταλλάσσων ἑαυτῷ, μὴ λογιζόμενος αὐτοῖς τὰ παραπτώματα αὐτῶν, καὶ θέμενος ἐν ἡμῖν τὸν λόγον τῆς καταλλαγῆς.

C. 20. Ὑπὲρ Χριστοῦ οὖν πρεσβεύομεν ὡς τοῦ Θεοῦ παρακαλοῦντος δι' ἡμῶν· δεόμεθα ὑπὲρ Χριστοῦ· καταλλάγητε τῷ Θεῷ.

A. 18. *Omnia autem ex Deo, qui nos reconciliavit sibi per Christum: et dedit nobis ministerium reconciliationis.*

B. 19. *Quoniam quidem Deus erat in Christo mundum reconcilians sibi, non reputans illis delicta ipsorum, et posuit in nobis verbum reconciliationis.*

C. 20. *Pro Christo ergo legatione fungimur, tanquam Deo exhortante per nos. Obsecramus pro Christo, reconciliamini Deo.*

A. Paul has just said: "If then any be in Christ, he is a new creature. The old things are passed away; behold all things are made new." (The Vulgate is susceptible of taking this meaning by dividing the phrase thus:

Here, as always, the initiative comes from the Father. It is not, therefore, man who reconciles himself to God, but the Father who reconciles us *to* himself by Christ or in Christ. The reconciliation is made in several stages. First, God, having constituted his Son a victim of expiation, forgets the crimes of men out of regard for this Son. It is still only a potential reconciliation; for it to become actual there must be in man a movement to return to him, a movement which is effected with the co-operation of man at the call and instigation of God. The apostles are the first to be invited to this reconciliation, of which they are made the heralds and the agents, because they receive the official command to promulgate and transmit it. Their message, briefly stated, is this: " Let yourselves be reconciled to God," or, " Be reconciled to

---

*Si qua [creatura] in Christo, nova creatura. Vetera transierunt : ecce facta sunt omnia nova.*) He continues in these words : " All things are of God " —that is to say, God takes the initiative in all this transformation which he works through Christ. And this transformation begins by the Apostles, more especially concerned, because they are accused of having human thoughts. No, these thoughts are foreign to them (verses 14, 15); they no longer know anyone according to the flesh (verse 16) ; their entire being is renewed (verse 17). God is the author of this change, he who reconciles them to himself in Christ, and who has confided to them the ministry of reconciliation (verse 18 ; the pronoun ἡμᾶς, ἡμῖν, designates the Apostles only, since it is a question of them alone and since they only have received the mission to reconcile men to God.)

B. From this particular case of the Apostles, Paul rises to the general principle. The transition, which moreover is a natural one, was suggested by the statement : *Vetera transierunt, ecce facta sunt (omnia) nova.* We must not translate : "God was in Christ reconciling the world to himself," but rather : " God was reconciling the world to himself in Christ "; for the circumlocution ἦν καταλλάσσων is equivalent to an imperfect, with this one difference, that instead of expressing simply the action of God, it shows God *in the process* of acting. The world is evidently " the human race," a meaning which the word κόσμος with or without an article often has in St Paul. The two participles which follow do not express the *mode* of the reconciliation, but the *circumstances* which accompany it, for it is evident that God does not reconcile the world to himself *by* confiding the message of reconciliation to the Apostles. The reconciliation here referred to is objective, *ideal,* and concerns all humanity ; it designates the new attitude of God towards the human race. *In view of Christ* (ἐν Χριστῷ), God takes no account of the sins of the human race ; he acts in regard to men, as if those sins did not exist (μὴ λογιζόμενος αὐτοῖς τὰ παραπτώματα αὐτῶν) ; even more, he commands the apostles to announce to all his benevolent dispositions (καὶ θέμενος ἐν ἡμῖν τὸν λόγον τῆς καταλλαγῆς).

C. All is ready now for the *subjective* reconciliation on the part of man. The apostles are the ambassadors of God, they exhort in his name (πρεσβεύομεν ὡς τοῦ Θεοῦ παρακαλοῦντος δι' ἡμῶν), since they have the message (λόγος) and the ministry (διακονία) of reconciliation, and are the heralds and, what is more, the agents of it. Their message is short : " We beseech you *for* Christ (ὑπέρ, in his interest and for his service) be reconciled with God." To καταλλάγητε a reflexive sense is rightly given (let yourselves be reconciled to God, do on your part what is necessary for this); indeed, the exhortation proves that there is on the part of man a condition to be fulfilled in order that the reconciliation, both subjective and effective, may be accomplished.

God." Finally, in order that the reconciliation may be effective, men must prepare, by their free assent to faith, a soil propitious for the divine action. The initiative of the heavenly Father, the apostolic message, the response of man to this message—such are the three phases or stages of the reconciliation. Wherever the reconciliation is mentioned, it is God who accomplishes it through the mediation of Christ; but if it begins by a change of attitude on the part of God towards man, it must be completed always by a change of attitude of man towards God.

The epistles written in captivity offer us a somewhat different conception. In the Epistle to the Ephesians one and the same word seems to express at once the mutual reconciliation of the Jews and Gentiles to one another and their common reconciliation to God, without our being able to say certainly whether these two reconciliations are simultaneous or whether one is presented as the logical antecedent of the other.[1] Nevertheless, the fact is that this double reconciliation is always accomplished by the cross of Christ and by a union in his mystical body. The passage in the Epistle to the Colossians is still more remarkable;[2] it is a question there of a double reconciliation which includes at the same time the conversion of men to God and the mutual reconciliation of his creatures, who up to that time have been at war with one another. The horizon of reconciliation becomes enlarged, and we see that all things again find concord and harmony in Christ, the universal peacemaker.

## II—THE VANQUISHED ENEMIES

### 1. Sin, the Flesh and Death. 2. The Mosaic Law.

1. The death of Christ has borne its fruits, and his sacrifice has not been in vain. Why did he come to earth? In order to destroy sin and to abolish its deadly consequences. This aim was realized.

> There is now therefore no condemnation to them that are in Christ Jesus. For the Law of the Spirit of life hath delivered thee, in Christ Jesus, from the law of sin and of death. For what the Law could not do, in that it was weak through the flesh, God sending his Son, in the likeness of sinful flesh, hath condemned sin in the flesh.[3]

This condemnation is a sentence of death. Thenceforth sin has no strength; it reigns no longer over humanity, and we are delivered from its tyranny. We have seen in the Epistle to the Romans what the sad condition of our slavery to sin was and what has been the mode of our liberation from it.

If Jesus Christ, in dying for us, had merely proposed to

[1] Eph. ii, 16. See pp. 225-7.    [2] Col. i, 19, 20. See pp. 90-92.
[3] Rom. viii, 1-3. See above, pp. 163-165.

restore to us what Adam had caused us to lose, the redemptive death would have had to put us again in possession of our original integrity and immortality ; but the plan of salvation adopted by God, instead of giving us back exactly the privileges that we had lost, substitutes for them something more excellent. Our present lot is different but better ; instead of abolishing the decree of death, God grants us a glorious immortality ; instead of extinguishing the fires of concupiscence, he gives us, with the certainty of conquering, all the reward of victory. While awaiting the final triumph, " our body is mortal on account of sin," but death is powerless to keep its prey ; we have to contend against the flesh, but we are not its slaves ; the inclination to evil continues its attacks, but we are freed from its domination. " The law of the Spirit of life hath delivered us in Christ Jesus from the law of sin and death." The force by which sin and death once maintained their empire is broken by a superior force— grace ; sin can no more subjugate us in spite of ourselves, nor can death retain us in its grasp.

This is why St Paul does not hesitate to say that " our Saviour, Christ Jesus, has destroyed death and brought life and immortality to light." Death has been destroyed, or, rather, rendered powerless ; this is an acquired result, a first-fruit of Calvary, a blessing granted at the very moment when the springs of life gushed forth. The effect is not immediate, for it is only too evident that men continue to die. No doubt hereafter "neither death nor life can separate us from the love of God in Christ," and " whether we live or die we are the Lord's," but death none the less retains a remnant of its empire ; though conquered by Christ, it is not annihilated ; it will be the last of the hostile powers to be exterminated, when at the hour of the resurrection it will be swallowed up in the supreme triumph of the Redeemer. *Novissima autem inimica destruetur mors.*

Death is natural to man, for it results from his organic constitution ; but, raised to the supernatural level, it is also a punishment for sin. Those who consider the death of Christ as a debt paid for us, or as a penalty endured in our place, find themselves here in an embarrassment, from which no subtlety can extricate them ; for a debt, once paid, is no more subject to demand, and a penalty, once undergone, is not inflicted a second time. The Christian ought not, therefore, to die ; nor the unbeliever either, since Jesus Christ died for all men. But we know already that the death of Christ has for us another significance and another kind of efficacy. We see, therefore, nothing contradictory in these two assertions of St Paul : " No more condemnation now unto those who are in Christ Jesus," and " The body is doomed to death on account of sin." In our present providential order death is indeed a *consequence,* a *result* of sin, since without sin it would not exist. Must it still be called a *punishment,* even in the just man, who is the object of no "condemnation," inasmuch as he is "in Christ Jesus"? That is a question of words, with no great theological importance.

Nevertheless, it is a fact that the liberation of the Christian is not instantaneous but progressive. It is ideal on Calvary, where Christ undoes the work of Adam in order to remake the lot of humanity better; it is real, although imperfect, at baptism, when the Christian begins to participate practically in the destinies of Christ; it is complete at the resurrection, when the divine plan is consummated.

2. With the Mosaic Law the conditions are very different. Since its maintenance or abrogation is independent of man's co-operation, it is not necessary to seek for successive moments in its annulment. It disappears naturally with the coming of Christ, who is its end, when it has no more reason for existence, and when the promises which are irreconcilable with it are realized. But even though it should retain its validity in principle, the Christian, by the fact of baptism, is released from its empire.

> My brethren, you also died to the Law by the body of Christ, that you may belong to him, who is risen again from the dead, and to bring forth fruit to God. For when we were in the flesh, the passions of sins, stirred by the Law, did work in our members to bring forth fruit unto death. But now we are loosed from the Law and dead to the Law wherein we were held [captive], we serve [God] in newness of spirit and not in the oldness of the letter.[1]

If the details of this text give room for discussions, the general meaning is not open to doubt. At baptism the Christian "dies to the Law," which is no more anything to

---

[1] Rom. vii, 4-6. See Vol. I, pp. 226-7, for the general sense of the passage.

(*a*) Verse 4 (*Itaque et vos mortificati estis legi per corpus Christi*) is directly connected with verse I (*lex in homine dominatur quanto tempore vivit*), from which it draws the conclusion (*itaque*) : " You no longer live, for ycu are dead mystically in Christ; therefore you are dead to the Law." Paul alludes to baptism, which grafts us into the death of Christ, or into the dying Christ (Rom. vi, 3-5). The *body of Christ* is, therefore, the mystical body into which baptism incorporates us. The physical death of Christ also kills the Law objectively (Col. ii, 14; Eph. ii, 14, 15), but, if we except baptism, it does not cause us to die personally to the Law.

(*b*) There is a notable difference in verse 6 between the Vulgate (*nunc autem soluti sumus a lege mortis, in qua detinebamur*) and the best attested original text (νυνὶ δὲ κατηργήθημεν ἀπὸ τοῦ νόμου, ἀποθανόντες ἐν ᾧ κατειχόμεθα). Instead of ἀποθανόντες the translator reads τοῦ θανάτου. However, both readings affirm the capital point—namely, the Christian's liberty in relation to the Law. In the Greek phrase ἀποθανόντες ἐν ᾧ κατειχόμεθα the antecedent of the relative is understood : " being dead (*to that*) in or *by which* you were held (captive)," and the commentators ask whether this antecedent which is understood denotes the Law itself (as we have supposed in our translation) or the old man subject to the Law. The meaning of the phrase is not seriously affected by this controversy.

him; if he was formerly a Jew, the Law loses all its power over him; if he was a pagan, the Law can no more make any claim upon him. Baptism, in fact, is a mystical death in which we are united to the dying Christ. Now, death, which is the end of past obligations, extinguishes, therefore, our debt; and thus the Law of Moses will have no more claim to urge against us. This is also the thought hidden in the enigmatical passage : " I, through the Law, am dead·to the Law. . . . I am crucified with Christ."[1] We can easily understand that the fact of being crucified with Jesus Christ is a death to the Law. St Paul has familiarized us with this idea; but how " through the Law am I dead to the Law"? Is there a connection between these words and the following sentence, and in that case is it a question of the ideal union with Christ crucified on Calvary, or of the mystical union with him in baptism? Whatever explanation is given of this obscure text, it remains certain that if, as is impossible, the

---

(c) The great majority of exegetes think that the allegory of marriage is continued in verses 4-6; that in *ut sitis alterius* (verse 4) it is necessary to understand *viri* and not *domini ;* and that *fructificare* (verses 4 and 5) indicates the fecundity of the husband and wife. However, some good modern commentators, reverting to the explanation of Origen and Chrysostom, are of the opinion that the allegory is ended, that the idea of marriage with the risen Jesus is not suitable here, that in *mortificati estis legi per corpus Christi, ut sitis alterius* it is necessary to understand *domini* (*cf.* Rom. vi, 6), and that the fruits are those spoken of above (Rom. vi, 21, 22: liberati *a peccato,* servi autem facti Deo, habetis fructum). Verse 6 (soluti *sumus a lege . . . ita ut* serviamus), where the idea of service is clearly substituted for that of marriage, is strongly in favour of their exegesis.

[1] Gal. ii, 18: εἰ γὰρ ἃ κατέλυσα    18. *Si enim quae destruxi, iterum*
ταῦτα πάλιν οἰκοδομῶ, παραβάτην    *aedifico: praevaricatorem me con-*
ἐμαυτὸν συνιστάνω·    *stituo.*
19. ἐγὼ γὰρ διὰ νόμου νόμῳ ἀπέθανον    19. *Ego enim per legem, legi mor-*
ἵνα Θεῷ ζήσω· Χριστῷ συνεσταύρωμαι.    *tuus sum, ut Deo vivam . . . Christo*
*confixus sum cruci.*

The ideas of this passage are closely connected with one another (notice γάρ twice), and the difficulty is to present a coherent exposition of them. Verse 18 is connected with the preceding one, of which it gives the proof (γάρ). Paul has just said : " If, while we seek to be justified in Christ, we ourselves also are found sinners, is Christ then the minister of sin ? God forbid !" Verse 18 furnishes the reason of this *absit :* " Far be it ! for (on the contrary) if I rebuild what I have destroyed (in proclaiming necessary to salvation a Law which I have recognized as useless) I make myself a prevaricator "— that is to say, a violator (παραβατήν) of the Law. Why ? Verse 19 informs us : " For I through the Law am dead to the Law." To live again to the Law is, therefore, to go against the intentions of the Law ; it is to violate it. No doubt it can be asked how, through the Law, Paul is dead to the Law. As it is impossible to translate : " Through the Law of the Gospel I am dead to the Law of Moses," seeing that one cannot give to the Law in this expression διὰ νόμου νόμῳ two such different meanings, the most reasonable reply will be that of St Augustine and St Chrysostom : " Through the Law which led me to Christ, and showed him to me (Gal. iii, 24 : ὁ νόμος παιδαγωγὸς εἰς Χριστόν), I am dead to the Law which had no more reason for existing after it had fulfilled this office."

Mosaic Law were not abrogated for everyone, it would be so for the Christian.

Besides the death of the Christian to the Law and what may be called the natural death of the Law, which had become decrepit through age, there is a violent death of the Law which St Paul describes in two passages of remarkable force. The two texts offer great analogies of thought and expression, though with profound divergences, which are explained by the different purpose the author has in each. The fundamental thought is the same : the pagans, formerly buried in their sins, owe to the abolition of the Law the fact that they have been made alive in Christ. But the abolition of the Law is presented to the Colossians as the deliverance from an odious and crushing yoke, while to the Ephesians it is portrayed as the cessation of past discords and a pledge of union between the two sections of the new humanity ; for the Epistle to the Colossians wishes to establish Christian liberty under the sole mediation of Christ, and the Epistle to the Ephesians has for its object to show the perfect equality of the elements which compose his mystical body. The picture drawn in this latter Epistle is one of solemn and tragic grandeur. Here is the slightly paraphrased translation of it.

> Remember that formerly you pagans in the flesh, treated as uncircumcised by those who are called circumcised [and who are so] in the flesh by the hand of man, [remember] that at that time you were without Christ, excluded from the theocracy of Israel, strangers to the covenants of the promise, without hope and without God in the world.
>
> But now, in Christ Jesus, you who were formerly afar off have been made nigh by the blood of Christ.
>
> For he is our Peace, who hath made of the two [peoples] one, having broken down the wall of partition, [the cause of] the enmity, and destroyed in his [sacrificed] flesh the law of commandments [consisting of many] ordinances, in order to form in himself one new man with the two [peoples] which he has pacified, and to reconcile them both in one body, by the cross, destroying the enmity by it.
>
> And he came to announce peace to you who were afar off, and peace [also] to those who were near ; for by him we both have access to the Father in one and the same Spirit.[1]

---

[1] Eph. ii, 13, 14, 15, 16:

13. Νυνὶ δὲ ἐν Χριστῷ Ἰησοῦ ὑμεῖς οἱ ποτε ὄντες μακρὰν ἐγενήθητε ἐγγὺς ἐν τῷ αἵματι τοῦ Χριστοῦ.

14. Αὐτὸς γάρ ἐστιν ἡ εἰρήνη ἡμῶν, ὁ ποιήσας τὰ ἀμφότερα ἓν καὶ τὸ μεσότοιχον τοῦ φραγμοῦ λύσας, τὴν ἔχθραν, ἐν τῇ σαρκὶ αὐτοῦ,

15. τὸν νόμον τῶν ἐντολῶν ἐν δόγμασι καταργήσας ἵνα τοὺς δύο κτίσῃ ἐν αὐτῷ εἰς ἕνα καινὸν ἄνθρωπον ποιῶν εἰρήνην,

13. Nunc autem in Christo Jesu vos, qui aliquando eratis longe, facti estis prope in sanguine Christi.

14. Ipse enim est pax nostra, qui fecit utraque unum, et medium parietem maceriae solvens, inimicitias in carne sua :

15. legem mandatorum decretis evacuans, ut duos condat in semetipso in unum novum hominem, faciens pacem.

The thought presented by this sentence, so full of sub-clauses, is, on the whole, quite simple. The Apostle conceives of the two peoples, whose reunion will form the Church, the Jews and the Gentiles, as separated from each other by an insurmountable barrier and animated by an irreconcilable hostility against each other. The barrier is the Law; the cause of the hostile sentiments is again the Law. In fact, the Law gave to the Jews all the privileges, consisting of Messianic hopes, theocracy, divine covenants, and the knowledge of the true God. Being strangers to all this, the Gentiles were treated with contempt by the children of the circumcision; and what was still more serious, they were without Christ, without God, and without hope. They were

---

16. καὶ ἀποκαταλλάξῃ τοὺς ἀμφοτέρους ἐν ἑνὶ σώματι τῷ Θεῷ διὰ τοῦ σταυροῦ, ἀποκτείνας τὴν ἔχθραν ἐν αὐτῷ.

16. *et reconciliet ambos in uno corpore, Deo per crucem, interficiens inimicitias in semetipso.*

A. *Contrast between the two states of the converted Pagans.*—*Formerly* (ii, 12 : τῷ καιρῷ ἐκείνῳ) deprived as they were of Christ (χωρὶς Χριστοῦ), they were : (*a*) banished from the theocracy of Israel and its religious privileges (ἀπηλλοτριωμένοι τῆς πολιτείας τοῦ Ἰσραήλ) ; (*b*) strangers to the covenants of the promise and to the blessings that came from them (ξένοι τῶν διαθηκῶν τῆς ἐπαγγελίας) ; (*c*) without hope, since the divine promises did not concern them directly (ἐλπίδα μὴ ἔχοντες) ; (*d*) without God in the world, since the gods whom they worshipped were nothing (ἄθεοι ἐν τῷ κόσμῳ). Nor is this all : (*e*) they were formerly (ii, 11 : ποτέ) the uncircumcised, treated with disdain by the children of the carnal circumcision (οἱ λεγόμενοι ἀκροβυστία ὑπὸ τῆς λεγομένης περιτομῆς ἐν σαρκὶ χειροποιήτου). —*Now*, on the contrary (νυνὶ δέ), being united to Christ Jesus (ἐν Χριστῷ Ἰησοῦ) : (*a*) they have been brought near to the true Israel in such a way as to make only one body with it (ii, 13 : ἐγενήθητε ἐγγύς) ; (*b*) they are the fellow-citizens of the saints and of the family of God (ii, 17 : ἐστὲ συμπολῖται τῶν ἁγίων καὶ οἰκεῖοι τοῦ Θεοῦ) ; (*c*) they have obtained peace with God and with the Jews. Thus the words of Isaias (lvii, 19) and of Micheas (v, 4) are verified.

B. *Peace brought to the Gentiles by the Messiah.*—What peace is here in question ? Peace with God, or peace between the parties constituting the Church ? Haupt (*Meyer's Kommentar*[7],) energetically defends the first meaning for two main reasons. Nothing in the context, he says, makes one think of a conflict between the Jews and Greeks ; in what precedes it is said that the Gentiles were *afar off* from Israel, but that does not imply hostility ; in what follows it is a question of *union*, and this proves that they were indeed *separated*, but not that they were at war. Moreover, Jesus Christ came " to preach peace to you who were afar off and peace to them who were nigh " (ii, 17) ; the repetition of the word " peace " denotes a distributive significance ; it is not a relative and reciprocal peace, but an absolute peace which is preached on the one hand to the Jews and on the other to the Greeks. —These reasons have some force, but they are not decisive. Haupt is compelled to regard the word " enmity " (τὴν ἔχθραν), mentioned in verse 16 and which completely spoils his thesis, as interpolated. Moreover καὶ ἀποκαταλλάξῃ τοὺς ἀμφοτέρους can be understood only as referring to a mutual reconciliation between the two peoples ; now reconciliation presupposes a previous state of hostility, to which Christ " our peace " puts an end.— We have, however, to ask ourselves whether we are obliged to choose between two interpretations. When the Apostle, following the prophet, says that Christ is our peace, can we not give the word " peace " its most extensive meaning, which will subsequently be limited, according to the needs of the

far removed from the Jews in every way, and the reciprocal hostility which reigned between them increased the distance.

The idea which pervades the mind of Paul, as he writes these lines, is God's plan to form with these heterogeneous elements one family, one house, which shall be the Church, and one moral person, one body, which shall be the mystical Christ. At the same time, he is haunted by two scriptural texts, which are strikingly related to his subject : one from Micheas, predicting that the Messiah will be *peace*—that is to say, the supreme peace-maker ; the other from Isaias, announcing that the Messiah will bring peace to those who

---

context, to a peace with God or to a peace between the hostile sections of humanity ? The peace with God is indeed the condition of the other. Ewald in his *Commentary* (Zahn's collection) proposes this explanation, which seems to us satisfactory in every particular.

C. *Destruction of the Law, the condition of unity.*—In order to bring together what was afar off and to unite what was separated, it was necessary to break down the wall of separation, to form a whole out of the incongruous elements, and to pacify men with one another and with God.—(*a*) *God breaks down the wall of separation—that is to say, the Law and the privileges possessed by Israel.* The phrase καὶ τὸ μεσότοιχον τοῦ φραγμοῦ λύσας, τὴν ἔχθραν, ἐν τῇ σαρκὶ αὐτοῦ τον νόμον τῶν ἐντολῶν ἐν δόγμασι καταργήσας has been taken in at least four ways, but the best exegetes rightly agree that only one interpretation is acceptable, although it is not without some difficulty. It is that which makes of τὴν ἔχθραν an apposition with τὸ μεσότοιχον and sees in ἐν τῇ σαρκὶ αὐτοῦ a circumstantial complement of λύσας. The meaning then is : "Having in his flesh destroyed the intermediary wall which served as a barrier—that is to say, the enmity—having abolished the law of commandments [consisting] of decrees." The word μεσότοιχον is extremely rare, but presents no difficulty as regards the sense. The genitive τοῦ φραγμοῦ is a genitive of apposition : "the intermediary wall consisting in a barrier": φραγμός signifies properly "an enclosure, a palisade," and the idea of separation belongs rather to μεσότοιχον. This barrier was all that isolated the Hebrew people and kept them from contact with foreigners ; the Law, religious privileges, the national, chauvinistic spirit, all provoked and fomented the hatred of other peoples and could be called figuratively "enmity" (ἔχθρα) for the same reason as the Saviour is called "peace." The Greek verb λύειν, "to destroy," is taken equally well with τεῖχος (or μεσότοιχον) or with ἔχθρα. We have just seen that the wall of separation (μεσότοιχον) is more general than the Law ; but the abrogation of the Law itself deserved special mention : it is reduced to nothing (καταργεῖν means exactly "to render vain, nothing, without effect, to enervate, to deprive of its force"). The expression τὸν νόμον τῶν ἐντολῶν ἐν δόγμασιν offers a certain difficulty. It is certain that the Law is the Mosaic Law ; the genitive τῶν ἐντολῶν is a genitive of apposition : "the Law consisting in precepts, in commandments." As for δόγμα, it signifies "decree, peremptory order" (Luke i, 2 ; Acts xvi, 4 ; xvii, 7). But it is impossible to join ἐν δόγμασιν with καταργήσας and to understand it in an instrumental sense, as Chrysostom and his school with Theodore of Mopsuestia do : "having abolished by *his* decrees [by the Law of the Gospel] the Law of commandments [the Mosaic Law]."—(*b*) *Unification of the incongruous elements.* (a) They are both made nigh to Christ and consequently nigh to each other (verse 13) ; (β) both form henceforth only one being in the moral order (verse 14 : ὁ ποιήσας τὰ ἀμφότερα ἕν ; (γ) the moral person thus constituted is "a new man" (verse 15) ; (δ) the union is effected in the mystical body of Christ (verse 16), of which the faithful, both Jews and Gentiles, are the living members.

are *near* and to those who are *afar off*. How will this double
prophecy be accomplished? By eliminating all the causes of
hatred and discord, by annihilating the distance separating
the two peoples, and by breaking down the barrier which
divided them and which was none other than the Mosaic
Law with its burdensome and hateful privileges. Jesus
Christ accomplished all this by blending the two peoples into
one in the identity of his mystical body.

The old legislation had crushed the Jews under its intolerable weight, and for the Gentile Christians it is a conspicuous
favour that they are freed from it. They owe it to Christ :

> And you, when you were dead in your sins and the uncircumcision of
> your flesh, God hath quickened together with him [Christ], forgiving us
> all our offences ; blotting out the handwriting of the decree that was
> [drawn up] against us ; and he hath taken the same away, fastening it to
> the Cross.[1]

It is perfectly certain that " the authentic deed, consisting
of commandments," denotes the Law of Moses. This
document was " against " the Jews because it imposed upon
them numerous and rigorous duties and exposed them, in

---

[1] Col. ii. 13, 14 ; *Vos cum mortui essetis in delictis et praeputio carnis,*

13. συνεζωοποίησεν ὑμᾶς σὺν αὐτῷ,    13. *convivificavit cum illo, donans*
χαρισάμενος ἡμῖν πάντα τὰ παραπτώ-    *vobis omnia delicta ;*
ματα,

14. ἐξαλείψας τὸ καθ' ἡμῶν χειρό-    14. *delens quod adversus nos erat*
γραφον τοῖς δόγμασιν ὃ ἦν ὑπεναντίον    *chirographum decreti, quod erat con-*
ἡμῖν, καὶ αὐτὸ ἦρκεν ἐκ τοῦ μέσου,    *trarium nobis, et ipsum tulit de medio,*
προσηλώσας αὐτὸ τῷ σταυρῷ.    *offigens illud cruci.*

A. *Subject of the phrase.*—It is God, not Christ : (*a*) This appears from
the parallel passage, Eph. ii, 5.—(*b*) God is always the subject of such verbs
as συνεγείρειν, συζωοποιεῖν, which denote a mystical identification of the
Christian with (σύν) Christ.—(*c*) It is grammatically much simpler to derive
the understood subject from τοῦ Θεοῦ than from the pronoun αὐτόν of the
preceding phrase.—(*d*) The last words of verse 12 : *qui suscitavit illum a
mortuis* have evidently God as subject, but the καὶ ὑμᾶς which follows shows
that the same subject persists, since the object is placed first : " God hath
raised his Son from the dead and you also hath he quickened."—(*e*) The only
reason for regarding Christ as the subject of the phrase is that verse 15 would
not be appropriate to God ; but we shall show elsewhere the worthlessness
of this reason.

B. *Meaning of the personal pronouns.*—The pronouns ὑμᾶς, ὑμῶν, denote
clearly the converted pagans ; we might think that the pronouns ἡμῖν, ἡμῶν,
which follow them designate by contrast the converted Jews. But it is
preferable to understand thereby all Christians, for the blessings enumerated
(the pardon of sins and even the abolition of the Law) concern them all,
although in a rather different way. Perhaps the Apostle changes the person
because the Jews are *more directly* interested in the Law's abrogation.

C. *Meaning of* χειρόγραφον.—This word signifies any kind of " autograph," particularly a " note signed by a debtor who acknowledges that he
owes a sum of money and promises to pay it back " (Tob. v, 3 ; ix, 5). Some
commentators regard the solemn acceptation of the Hebrew people (Ex. xxiv,
3 ; xxvii, 14-26) as the *signature* set to the Law and giving it its validity ;
but it is not necessary to push the metaphor so far ; the meaning *authentic
deed* is sufficient. All are now of the opinion that τὸ καθ' ἡμῶν χειρόγραφον

case of violation of the Law, to severe penalties; it was "contrary" to them for the same reasons, and also because it retarded the accomplishment of the Messianic promises. It was also no less contrary to the Gentiles whom it excluded from the theocracy. Thus, "the code of the commandments" is annulled; God causes it to disappear in order that no one can claim its authority to proceed against the disciples of Christ; he nails it to the Saviour's cross, as if to punish it for its misdeeds and to give more brilliancy to its abrogation. The Law, which carried within itself so many germs of decay, here expires by a violent death, and its tyranny comes to an end: "Let no man judge you in regard to meat or drink, or in respect of a festival day, or of the new moon, or of the sabbaths, which are a shadow of things to come."[1] The Mosaic Law concludes its dramatic career on the cross; it has killed Christ, and Christ kills it in his turn.

---

can designate only the Mosaic Law; this appears clearly from the parallel passage (Eph. ii, 15: τὸν νόμον τῶν ἐντολῶν ἐν δόγμασιν). The dative τοῖς δόγμασιν, after χειρόγραφον, is rather difficult; some make it depend on καθ' ἡμῶν (which was against us *by* its decrees); others on ὃ ἦν ὑπεναντίον ἡμῖν (which was contrary to us *by* its decrees); the simplest construction and the one most conformable to Eph. ii, 15 is to make it depend on the participle γεγραμμένον, virtually contained in χειρόγραφον (the deed written *in* decrees). It is known that the Greeks (Theodore of Mopsuestia, Severianus, Chrysostom and his school) as well as St Jerome, Estius and others, make it depend on ἐξαλείψας (having suppressed the act of the Law *by the Gospel's decrees*), which grammatically is without difficulty, but meets with objections of another kind: (*a*) The parallel passage Eph. ii, 15; (*b*) the impossibility of understanding τὰ δόγματα, without more explanations, as the Gospel teaching; (*c*) the conclusion of the Apostle (ii, 30: τί δογματίζεσθε;) which supposes the abolition of the δόγματα.

D. *Treatment inflicted on the Law.*—The Law is effaced, put aside, nailed to the Cross: (*a*) *Effaced*. The word ἐξαλείφειν signifies "to wipe away" (tears), "to efface" (for example, an autograph, in smoothing down the wax of the tablet with the other end of the stylus); if it is a question of a law, "to abrogate, to abolish." The aorist participle ἐξαλείψας grammatically might be simultaneous with χαρισάμενος. The meaning would then be: "having pardoned us all our sins by abrogating the Law"; but that is scarcely intelligible. It is, therefore, better to give the second aorist its relation of priority: "having pardoned us all our sins *after having* abolished the Law." There are in this case two distinct benefits, and the second is the condition and the preparation of the first.—(*b*) *Put aside*. The expression αἴρειν ἐκ τοῦ μέσου simply means "to make disappear" that which is annoying, that which is an obstacle, that which interferes. The idea that this obstacle exists *between two* persons is not expressed. The perfect tense ἦρκεν indicates that the result still persists.—(*c*) *Nailed to the Cross*. The Cross is that of Jesus Christ; hence the article. God by a sort of vindictive revenge nails to the Cross of his Son the Law which has contributed to crucify him. We must not weaken this sublime idea by supposing that it was customary to abolish laws by piercing them by a nail, a hypothesis which has, moreover, no historical foundation.

[1] Col. ii, 16. See Vol. I, p. 282.

# BOOK V
## THE CHANNELS OF REDEMPTION

# CHAPTER I

## FAITH, THE PRINCIPLE OF JUSTIFICATION

### I—JUSTIFYING FAITH

1. Protestant Faith and Catholic Faith.  2. Nature of Faith.  3. Object of Faith.  4. Value of Faith.

1. IT is very difficult to know what the reformers of the sixteenth century understood by *the faith that justifies,* for we find among them no precise definitions, and especially no uniform notions of it. Their texts, when compared, leave a strong impression of obscurity and incoherence. The leaders of Protestantism were indeed agreed in denying that a formless faith is a true faith; but as they wished to eliminate the intellectual element from the act of faith, while nevertheless leaving it certitude, their embarrassment in trying to define their special faith was extreme. If they said with Calvin that faith is " an unshaken and certain knowledge of divine good will towards us," they had to make long commentaries in order to explain that such an act proceeds from the heart and not from the mind, and they did not know where to locate the reality of this faith, the object of which, at the moment when it was perceived as existing, did not yet exist. If they preferred Luther's definition : " a certain and profound confidence in the divine goodness and in the grace manifested and known by the Word of God," it was impossible to say how this confidence can be certain, unless it be admitted that it is itself preceded by an act of intellectual faith.

We have no right to expect any greater clearness and precision from modern Protestants. The majority, even of those who might be thought disposed to emancipate themselves from Lutheran orthodoxy, always consider confidence as the unique or principal element of faith. We note, however, among many of them, an anxiety to avoid what in the Protestant conception is too shocking or openly contrary to Scripture. Thus B. Weiss unites confidence with intellectual adhesion and understands by *confidence,* especially the kind of confidence shown to God by believing in his word; it is the *pius credulitatis affectus* of Catholic theologians. On the other hand, certain rationalists maintain without hesitation the radical ideas of the first reformers, and thereby expose the fundamental absurdity of them. In the opinion of Baur, for example, " faith, as a principle of justification, is the persuasion, founded on Jesus Christ, that what is not, nevertheless is "; and he asks with amazement what influence such an act can have upon our salvation. This, indeed, sets us thinking, for it is the pure and simple denial of the principle of contradiction. But the strain of absurdity continues : " Faith," according to Fricke, " is a receptive seizing of something which is, however, first rendered possible by the reception of grace prepared in God before any reception !" What sphinx could solve this enigma? It is not to be wondered at that the Protestant notion of faith is wanting in clearness; for, according to the author of the definition which has just been read, the thought of Paul is so profound that very few men have comprehended it, and before Luther it had been wholly misunderstood for more than a thousand years. According to Harnack, the first to understand it was the heretic Marcion, and even he did so very imperfectly.

In contrast to these fluctuations of interpretation, let us state the unchanging doctrine of the Catholic Church, thus formulated in the council of the Vatican : " Faith is a supernatural virtue, by which, through the influx and with the aid of grace, we believe those things which have been revealed, to be true, not because of their intrinsic truth, accessible to the natural powers of reason, but because of the authority of God himself who reveals them and who can neither be deceived nor deceive us." The Council of Trent declares that "we are justified by faith, because faith is the origin, foundation and the root of all justification," and that "we are justified freely because nothing that precedes justification, neither faith nor works, can merit the grace of justification."[1] Faith is the *origin* of our salvation because it marks the first disposition towards it, and because without it the sinner can really neither hope, nor repent, nor love God sincerely. Faith is the *foundation* of our salvation, because all the rest is based upon it; if it falls, the entire structure crumbles with it, while it is able to maintain itself amid the ruin of the other virtues. Faith is also the *root* of our salvation; not because it is the spontaneous and infallible germ of the other supernatural dispositions, but because it concurs, with divine assistance, in producing and sustaining them.

Before examining how faith justifies, let us study St Paul on the nature, object, and value of justifying faith.

2. In this analysis three errors of method are to be avoided. The first is to explain biblical usage by profane usage; Christian faith and pagan faith are entirely different; they have not a common standard of measurement; the classics indeed furnished the sacred writers with the word " faith," but

[1] *Concil. Vatican.*, Sess. iii, cap. 3 ; *Concil. Trident.*, Sess, vi, cap. 8.

nothing more.[1] A second danger is to take as a point of departure the etymology of the Greek word. When the apostles—and before them the Septuagint—adopted this word, the idea of faith had behind it a long history; being the product of a different race and civilization, its Greek etymology throws but little light upon it.[2] Finally, the last danger to be avoided is to proceed from the notion of " faith " to the notion of " believing." The reverse procedure is necessary; for in Hebrew, where the concept of Christian faith is elaborated, the grammatical derivation, in conformity with the logical evolution of the idea, passes from the verb " to believe " to the substantive " faith "; which hardly ever assumes the religious meaning which the verb " to believe " usually possesses.[3]

Every attentive reader is struck by the fact that St Paul, as the editor of the Epistle to the Hebrews, likes to connect the Christian faith with the faith of the Old Testament, and seems to make no difference between them; a fact all the more curious from the circumstance that in the Old Testament the role of faith seems at first quite obliterated; one hopes in God, obeys him, fears him, loves him, but never thinks of esteeming it meritorious to believe in him, for to refuse to do that is the error of a " fool " only. Faith is scarcely mentioned save in exceptional cases where it has obstacles to overcome, doubts to surmount or serious duties to fulfil; then, it is true, it is the principal virtue, just as its opposite, unbelief, is the most odious crime. The salvation or the ruin of the people depended on its faith : " If you will

---

[1] (a) Among the classics, the active meaning is rare and of comparatively recent date (later than Thucydides); the passive sense is much more common; one says πίστιν or πίστεις διδόναι, ποιεῖσθαι, δέχεσθαι, to give or receive guarantees, pledges (oaths, hostages, etc.). In biblical Greek the contrary is true ; the passive meaning is quite exceptional.—(b) In profane Greek, πίστις and πιστεύειν very rarely express a religious act, and even this is only a purely intellectual act : πίστις θεῶν is not faith in the gods, but either the gods called upon to witness, or the belief in the existence of the gods, founded on general opinion. In the Greek of the New Testament, the meaning is almost always religious : πίστις Θεοῦ, Χριστοῦ is faith in God or Christ founded on their testimony.—(c) In profane Greek πίστις and πιστεύειν, taken absolutely, signify nothing ; in biblical Greek they express a complete notion, which need not be determined by an object or govern anything.

[2] Πίστις comes from πείθειν, " to persuade or seek to persuade " (2 Cor. v, 11 ; Gal. i, 10) ; in the middle voice πείθεσθαι, " to let oneself be persuaded or convinced," in the second perfect πεποιθέναι, " to be convinced, to have confidence "; πεποιθώς and πεποίθησις coming from πεποιθέναι, follow its meaning.

[3] Πιστεύειν (from πιστός) is of relatively recent date ; πίστις and πιστός are derived in a parallel manner from πείθειν, of which they are the noun and the verbal adjective. In Hebrew, on the contrary, the noun and the adjective are derived from the verb ; the latter is much more employed, אֱמוּנָה being very rare in the sense of faith (the only certain example is Habac ii, 4).

not believe, you shall not continue."[1]  " Believe in the Lord
your God and you shall be secure."[2]  Such was the faith of
Abraham, and of the Ninivites, the faith of which Habacuc
speaks, and the faith of Israel at the time of the flight
from Egypt : " They believed the Lord and in Moses, his
servant."[3]  Everywhere faith is stated as an assent to the
Word of God or of his prophet, but the intellectual element
is rarely isolated ; there is almost always added to it a sentiment of security, confidence, abandonment, obedience, and
filial love ; the adhesion of the mind produces a thrill of the
heart.

In passing from the Old Testament to the New, we
measure at a glance the road we have traversed.  Faith is
no more pointed out as an exceptional fact, it is henceforth
the normal attitude of the Christian ; the two words " faith "
and " to believe " are found on every page in almost equal
proportions ; the profane sense, completely eliminated from
the substantive, tends to disappear also from the verb ;
finally, the two terms have acquired a technical sense which
allows us to employ them absolutely ; *faith* is the acceptance
of the Gospel, and *to believe* is to profess Christianity.[4]
The fulness of meaning renders the analysis of the Christian
faith difficult ; however, a careful comparison of the texts
suggests to us the following remarks.  Faith is not a pure
intuition, a mystical tendency towards an object more
suspected than known ; it presupposes preaching : *Fides ex
auditu ;* it is the yielding of the mind to divine testimony.[5]—
Faith is opposed to sight, both as regards the object known
and the manner of knowing ; one is immediate and intuitive,
the other takes place through an intermediate agent.[6]—
Nevertheless, faith is not blind ; it is ready to give a reason
for itself, and aspires always to more clearness.[7]—It is closely
united, on the one hand, to charity and hope, with which it
forms an inseparable trio, and, on the other hand, to
obedience and to the conversion of the heart.[8]—Faith, however firm and unshakable it is in its adhesion, has neverthe-

---

[1] Is. vii, 9.  *Cf.* xliii, 10.

[2] 2 Paral. xx, 20.     [3] Ex. xiv, 31.

[4] See Note V.

[5] Rom. x, 17 (ἡ πίστις ἐξ ἀκοῆς) ; Gal. iii, 2-5 (ἀκοὴ πίστεως) ; 1 Thess
ii, 13 (λόγος ἀκοῆς).

[6] 2 Cor. v, 7 : διὰ πίστεως γὰρ περιπατοῦμεν, οὐ διὰ εἴδους.

[7] 2 Cor. iv, 4-6.  (The Gospel is a light [φωτισμός], and on the contrary
it is unbelief that is *blind*) ; 1 Cor. viii, 1 (faith is perfectly compatible with
knowledge) ; Phil. iii, 8-10 (faith and knowledge go together).   St Paul asks
God for knowledge (γνῶσις or ἐπίγνωσις) for his neophytes : Eph. i, 17, 18 ;
iv, 13, 14 ; Col. i, 9 ; ii, 2, etc.   The true Christian must be ready to give a
reason for his faith, 1 Pet. iii, 15 ; and 2 Pet. i, 16-21 present some of the
motives which make faith reasonable.

[8] For the trio, faith, hope and charity, see p. 332.—For obedience (Rom.
i, 5), *cf.* Vol. I, p. 174.

less degrees, and can increase in intensity and perfection.[1]—
Finally, being derived from grace, it possesses an intrinsic
value which renders it agreeable to God.[2]  Before examining
whence its value comes, let us state its object.

3. It is necessary to distinguish in the act of faith the
formal object—the motive for believing—and the material
object, to which faith is directed.  That which incites the
mind to adhesion is always the testimony of God, whether it
is produced directly or comes through the intervention of the
authorized preachers of revelation.  God himself spoke to
Abraham and Moses; he speaks to us by the prophets and
apostles; but this difference in the manner of transmission
changes nothing in the divine testimony itself: " When you
had received of us the word of God, you received it not as
the word of men, but (as it is indeed) the word of God."[3]
The Gospel is not an invention of the apostles, for they
" have not received it of man, but by the revelation of Jesus
Christ."[4] who is Wisdom incarnate.  Thenceforward the
word of the Gospel is the word of God, or simply the Word,
and to believe God's messengers is to believe God himself.

While the formal object does not change, the material

---

[1] 1 Cor. iii, 1, 2 (childhood in the faith); 2 Cor. x, 15 (crescentis *fidei
vestrae*); Col. ii, 7; 2 Thess. i, 3 (supercrescit *fides vestra*), etc

[2] Eph. ii, 8.  See Vol. I, p. 177, and Vol. II, p. 240.

[3] 1 Thess. ii, 13 : παραλαβόντες λόγον ἀκοῆς παρ' ἡμῶν τοῦ Θεοῦ ἐδέξασθε
οὐ λόγον ἀνθρώπων ἀλλὰ καθώς ἐστιν ἀληθῶς λόγον Θεοῦ, ὃς καὶ ἐνεργεῖται ἐν
ὑμῖν τοῖς πιστεύουσιν.  It is difficult to render well all the shades of meaning
in this phrase : (a) παραλαμβάνειν does not signify merely " to receive,"
but " to receive a thing transmitted by someone " (παρά); δέχεσθαι is also
not simply " to receive " but " to welcome, to accept."—(b) ὁ λόγος ἀκοῆς
παρ' ἡμῶν τοῦ Θεοῦ forms one single complex expression : ἀκοῆς is a modal
genitive, " the word of hearing "—that is, the word which is heard, which
reaches the mind only by passing through the ear ; τοῦ Θεοῦ is a genitive
of author or origin, " the word which comes from God, which is spoken by
him "; παρ' ἡμῶν is not an object of παραλαβόντες—which would be a pleonasm
—but a word qualifying ὁ λόγος τῆς ἀκοῆς, " the divine word given by hearing,
which we have transmitted to you."—(c) ἐδέξασθε οὐ λόγον ἀνθρώπων ἀλλὰ . . .
λογον Θεοῦ, " You have welcomed, accepted, not a word of men (that is, *a
human word*—remark the absence of the definite article), but a word of
God " (*divine* in its origin and nature, since men are only the bearers of it) ;
ἐδέξασθε expressing not only the *fact* of the reception but the *persuasion* of
the Thessalonians, the Vulgate rightly translates *non ut verbum hominum ;*
yet the Greek is more energetic.—(d) ὃς καὶ ἐνεργεῖται refers to λόγον and
not to Θεοῦ, for with the name of a person the active voice of the verb
ἐνεργεῖν is employed (1 Cor. xii, 6; Gal. ii, 8; iii, 5; Phil. ii, 13), while
with the name of a thing the middle voice is used (Gal. v, 6; Eph. iii, 20;
Col. i, 29).

Three corollaries follow from this text : (a) The preaching of the Apostles
is not a human word, in spite of the human medium, it is a divine word, the
testimony of God.—(b) Faith is not an intuition of the mind, but the acceptance of a testimony, called λόγος ἀκοῆς because it must be offered to man's
external senses.  *Cf.* Rom. x, 17; Gal. iii, 2-5.—(c) Faith is not inactive :
it works (ἐνεργεῖται) in the hearts of believers.

[4] Gal. i, 12.

object varies infinitely. It can be concerned with revelation as a whole, or with a group of truths, or with a particular dogma : " If we be dead with Christ, we believe that we shall live also together with Christ.—If thou confess with thy mouth the Lord Jesus and believe in thy heart that God hath raised him up from the dead, thou shalt be saved."[1]—" If we believe that Jesus died and rose again ; even so them who have slept through Jesus, will God bring with him."[2] Here faith is an intellectual adhesion to an historical truth, without any accessory idea of confidence or self-abandonment ; nevertheless, it is genuine Christian faith, since salvation is connected with it. In fact, however limited the material object may be, the formal object remains always the same, and this it is which specifies the kind of faith.

It is when it is not expressed that the material object is most comprehensive. St Paul likes to call the faithful " believers " because faith is the vast and universal sentiment which epitomizes best the Christian character. " Faith " is the profession of the whole Gospel, and is also, objectively, the Gospel in its broadest sense. In a word, " to believe " is to be a disciple of Christ; for, besides the intellectual adhesion, sincere faith implies a tacit and essential submission to the duties which Christianity imposes.

When the object of faith is indicated—aside from certain exceptional expressions like " faith in the Gospel, faith in truth "—it is always God or Christ. And then, since the material object coincides with the formal object, the notion of faith is quite complex. If to believe God ($\Theta\epsilon\tilde{\omega}$) (à Dieu) can be only to have faith in his testimony, to believe in God adds to this concept some delicate shades of thought, the meaning of which is rendered well by the Greek particles. To believe in God is not only to believe in his existence, but to rest upon him ($\epsilon\pi\lambda\ \Theta\epsilon\tilde{\omega}$) as on an immovable support, to take refuge in him ($\epsilon\pi\lambda\ \Theta\epsilon\delta\nu$) as in a sure place of shelter, to tend towards him ($\epsilon\iota\varsigma\ \Theta\epsilon\delta\nu$) as to one's supreme end.

In recent years it has been denied that " the faith of Christ is faith towards Christ "; it is claimed that it is the faith which Jesus himself had had during his mortal life. Happily, the whole body of theologians and exegetes, Protestant as well as Catholic, resisting the enthusiasm which a new opinion always excites, however arbitrary it may be, continue to see in " the faith of Christ " the faith of which Christ is the object on the part of the faithful.[3]

There is no more adequate expression of the justifying faith of Paul.[4] Jesus Christ is not only the plenipotentiary of God and the one and only mediator of the new covenant; he is, moreover, the epitome of the Gospel, since he is the

---

[1] Rom. vi, 8 ; x, 9.
[2] 1 Thess. iv, 14.
[3] See Note V.
[4] Gal. ii, 16.

centre of the scheme of salvation, and all God's promises are fulfilled in him. Hence to preach Christ is to preach the Gospel, to confess Christ is to profess the religion which he came to found, to believe Christ is to accept him as a Saviour, to trust in his meditation and to submit to his law. We are justified by the faith of Jesus Christ, and we live in the faith of the Son of God,[1] because this faith, far from being confined to the domain of the intellect, is a practical, active, obedient faith, which receives its form and merit from charity.

4. Even when stripped of its accidental modes, such as confidence and submission to the divine will, the act of faith possesses an intrinsic moral value. In fact, it could not exist in the simplest form without the *pius credulitatis affectus* by which man voluntarily bows to the authority of God and confesses implicitly the truth of his testimony. "Without faith it is impossible to please [God]; for whosoever cometh to God must believe that he is, and that he is a rewarder of them that diligently seek him."[2] We have here the most intellectual form of faith, the form most liberated from moral conditions, the one with which the will has least to do; yet the inspired author affirms that without this faith it is impossible to please God, and that with it it is possible to do so. A proof of this is Henoch: Scripture says nothing of his faith, but renders this testimony in regard to him that he pleased God; and our author concludes from it that it is by faith that he did so, since without faith we cannot please him.[3] Hence it follows necessarily that faith possesses in itself a moral value capable of winning man the divine favour.

Nor is it otherwise with the faith of which Habacuc speaks. God said to the prophet: "Though the vision tarry, wait for it; because it will surely come, it will not fail"; and he adds: "Behold how he faileth whose soul is not upright, but the just shall live by his faith."[4] The meaning of the first clause cannot be determined with certainty; but three

---

[1] Gal. ii, 20.    [2] Heb. xi, 6.    [3] Heb. xi, 5.
[4] Habac. ii, 4: צַדִּיק בֶּאֱמוּנָתוֹ יִחְיֶה (ὁ δὲ δίκαιος ἐκ πίστεώς μου ζήσεται, *justus autem in fide sua vivet*). The Vulgate translation agrees exactly with the Massoretic Hebrew text. The Septuagint reads בֶּאֱמוּנָתִי and expresses the instrumental בְּ by ἐκ. St Paul quotes from the Septuagint, omitting however the possessive μου (Rom. i, 17; Gal. iii, 11, without δέ); the Epistle to the Hebrews (x, 38) follows another Greek version: ὁ δὲ δίκαιός μου ἐκ πίστεως ζήσεται. It appears clearly from the text and the translations that ἐκ πίστεως must be connected with ζήσεται and not with δίκαιος. It is, therefore, entirely arbitrary to claim, as some modern exegetes do, that it is different in the quotation of St Paul and that it must be translated: "The just by faith (that is, he who is justified by faith) shall live." Why impute to the Apostle a false reading and a sophism when he is merely quoting the Septuagint?

things are beyond doubt : there is a contrast between the lot of the unbeliever, that of the haughty man who refuses to believe in the prophetic vision, and that of the just and pious man who has faith in it. Faith consists precisely in believing that the prophecy made in God's name will be fulfilled; this, therefore, is indeed the faith which we have described, a steadfast adhesion to the divine word. The fruit of faith is the fact that by it the just shall live—that is to say, shall be the object of providential preservation.

For the contemporaries of St Paul, as well as for St Paul himself, the faith of Abraham is the typical faith. It avoids three defects which would deprive it of its merit and value; these are incredulity, doubt, and hesitation. The matter of it was difficult, incredible, and, humanly speaking, impossible; yet the patriarch did not give way to incredulity, but, on the contrary, believed against all likelihood, and, if it is permissible to say so, against all reason : *qui contra spem in spem credidit*.[1] He was not checked by inducements to doubt—his age, his feeble body, the advanced age of Sarah—but he believed with a steadfast, immovable faith : *confortatus est fide*. Much more, directing his thoughts immediately towards him whose truth equals his power, he was not troubled for a moment : *non haesitavit diffidentia*. His faith was prompt, steadfast, complete, and perfect : hence it was rewarded; "God," says the Scripture, "imputed it to him for justice." Although there is neither equality nor equivalence between faith and justice, it is nevertheless absolutely necessary that there should exist a certain proportion between justice and faith; for that which is nothing is not imputed to anything. Moreover, St Paul takes care to tell us how agreeable to God the faith of Abraham was, and why it received its reward. It is because the patriarch, by the steadfastness of his belief, by his implicit acknowledgement of divine truth, by his confident attitude in regard to promises which seemed impossible, and by the promptitude of his obedience, had rendered glory to the author of all good : *dans gloriam Deo*. Such is the intrinsic, moral value of faith.

Not that faith derives this value from itself, nor that man can boast of its possession. Even if it is in us and even if it is not without our co-operation—since it is a human act—the Apostle teaches that in the last analysis it is not of us, but of God : " By grace you are saved through faith; and that not of yourselves, for it is a gift of God—not of works, that no man may glory."[2] To be saved at the

---

[1] Rom. iv, 16-22. See Vol. I, pp. 177*ff*, and 208-9.

[2] Eph. ii, 8: τῇ γὰρ χάριτί ἐστε σεσωσμένοι διὰ πίστεως·

καὶ τοῦτο οὐκ ἐξ ὑμῶν, Θεοῦ τὸ δῶρον·

(A) 8. *Gratia enim estis salvati per fidem,*

(B) *et hoc non ex vobis ; Dei enim donum est,*

same time by faith and by grace appears contradictory, and would really be so if faith originated in ourselves; but no, replies the Apostle, all that is a gift of God; you cannot attribute it either to yourselves or to your works. Moreover, faith is an operation, a product of the Holy Spirit, or, as the Apostle again says, a fruit of the Spirit.[1] And it is to its supernatural origin that it is indebted for its value.

We are now in possession of the three elements of Christian faith, as St Paul describes it: the *intellectual element* is never absent. In cases where the twofold object, material and formal, is clearly evident, we might possibly conceive

---

9. οὐκ ἐξ ἔργων, ἵνα μή τις καυχήση-     (C) 9. *non ex operibus, ut nequis*
ται.                                         *glorietur.*

(A) The words ἐστὲ σεσωσμένοι, in the perfect, signify " you have been saved *and you are now* in the way of salvation." Salvation is sometimes represented as present, sometimes as past (Tit. iii, 5), sometimes as future (Rom. v, 10), sometimes as past and future at the same time (Rom. viii, 24). The words τῇ χάριτι repeat with greater emphasis verse 5 (χάριτί ἐστε σεσωσμένοι, where χάριτι was inserted only incidentally and had scarcely more than the value of the adverb χάριν or δωρεάν, " gratuitously "); here τῇ χάριτι refers to the " riches of the grace" of God (verse 7: τὸ ὑπερβάλλον πλοῦτος τῆς χάριτος αὐτοῦ), who has just been mentioned. The words διὰ πίστεως determine with more precision the τῇ χάριτι which precedes: " You are saved by grace, and that by faith, as an instrument of divine grace."

(B) The method employed by God to " save us gratuitously by faith " has for corollaries the impotence of man left to himself (*hoc non ex vobis*) and the insufficiency of works (*non ex operibus*). The *hoc* (τοῦτο) does not refer to faith alone, for it is not clear why St Paul should make use of the neuter pronoun; above all, this would make it necessary to put *et hoc non ex vobis, Dei donum est* in parentheses and to disunite *non ex vobis* and *non ex operibus*, which seem closely co-ordinated; it refers, therefore, to the whole idea " salvation by faith." Salvation by faith is not of us, it is a gift from God; but if so, then it is absolutely necessary that faith also should be a gift from God. The consequence is evident: (*a*) from the fact that *per fidem* is only an explanation and a definition of *gratia*; (*b*) from the manifest intention of the Apostle to refute in advance the possible objection that, if salvation is through faith, therefore it comes from us and from our works. The refutation is valid only if faith is not from us but from God. It was, therefore, right for the second Council of Orange (A.D. 529) to cite this text as a proof that the *initium fidei* is a gift of grace (can. 5). The question is merely to know whether St Paul affirms *explicitly* that faith is a gift of God, or whether he allows himself only to conclude it, by the fact that he establishes an equivalence between the formulas " *to be saved by faith* " and " *to be saved by grace.*" Most commentators do not express a clear opinion on this point, although they are agreed on the main thesis. Thus Corn. à Lapide: *Pronomen* hoc *demonstrat ṅon* τὸ salvati estis, *sed* τὸ per fidem. *Quod per fidem salvati estis hoc non ex vobis est quia fides non est ex vobis, sed Dei donum est.* Are these words—*quia fides non est ex vobis*—a conclusion of the interpreter or a direct assertion of Paul?

(C) The question arises whether *ut nequis glorietur* expresses the end which God purposed, or only the result which he has obtained. As we know that God, in establishing justification by faith, wished that man should not be able to glory in regard to his salvation (Rom. iii, 27; iv, 2; 1 Cor. i, 28-31), there is no difficulty in giving the preposition *ut* (ἵνα) its final signification, which is certainly the most common one.

[1] Gal. v, 22; *cf.* Rom. xii, 3; 1 Cor. xii, 9.

faith without the co-operation of the will, but never without
the co-operation of the intelligence.  A faith, in which the
will had no part, would not be a free, meritorious, theological
faith; yet by an extension of meaning the name of faith
could be given to it, as is done by St James; a faith in which
the intelligence has no part is not even conceivable, for all
faith is a conviction, and every conviction supposes an assent
of the mind.—A second element of faith is *confidence,* which
can be understood in two ways : confidence in the one who is
speaking, and confidence in the one who is promising.  The
first is inherent in the act of faith; it is very nearly the *pius
credulitatis affectus* of the theologians.  The other, being
accidental, is only a modality of the material object, when
this consists of a present aid or of a promised benefit : *Contra
spem in spem credidit.*—The third element of living faith is
a *twofold obedience:* obedience of the mind to the word of
God evinced by the prompt and steadfast acceptation of the
divine testimony, and obedience of the heart ready to conform in everything to the divine will so far as it is manifested.

## II—Justification by Faith

### 1. The Justice of God.   2. How Justice is born of Faith.

1. The Council of Trent recognizes two meanings in the
expression " justice of God " : the justice by which he is just
and the justice by which he renders us just.[1]  Since Ritschl's
time, several heterodox writers and one or two Catholics,
contrary to the general opinion, find this distinction illusory;
they maintain that the justice of God is always in Scripture,
and even in St Paul, his intrinsic and inherent justice.  What
must we think of their utterances?

As a divine attribute, " the justice of God is, properly
speaking, the activity of his holiness in relation to the moral
part of creation."[2]  While his holiness is an absolute
attribute, God's justice appears in the Bible as a relative
attribute.  The just God rises to punish guilty Israel or to
destroy sin ; he seats himself on his throne in order to cast
down the oppressor and to do justice to the oppressed :

(Jahve) put on justice as a breast-plate, and a helmet of salvation
upon his head ;

---

[1] Sess. vi, cap. 7 : *Unica formalis causa* [*justificationis*] *est justitia Dei,
non qua ipse justus est, sed qua nos justos facit.*  We do not claim that this
incidental phrase settles the question of exegesis.

[2] J. Monod, in *Encycl. des sciences relig.*, vol. vii, p. 562.  This other
definition (p. 561) is a less happy one : " The justice of God is that perfection,
by virtue of which he wishes in an absolute and unchangeable manner all
that is conformable to the good, that is to say, to the sovereign law of his
being."

he put on the garments of vengeance and was clad with zeal, as with
a cloak.
As were man's deeds, so was his revenge:
wrath to his adversaries and reprisals to his enemies; . . .
I will set judgement in weight and justice in measure.[1]

But the justice of God is not only the vindictive justice
which punishes crime, nor the distributive justice which
rewards every man according to his merits; it is sometimes—
especially in the Psalms of the captivity and in the second
part of Isaias—tutelary and saving. It is then placed on an
equal footing with salvation, grace, goodness, and mercy.
The prophet prays God to guide him, protect him, save him,
and hear him with favour in his justice.[2]

In thy justice thou wilt bring my soul out of trouble
And in thy mercy thou wilt destroy my enemies.[3]

This association of ideas is still more striking in the second
part of Isaias:

My justice is at hand, my salvation cometh;
and my arms shall bring the people justice.
Keep ye judgement and do justice;
for my salvation is near to come and my justice to be revealed.
It is I that speak justice
and am a defender to save.[4]

It is not difficult to explain this phenomenon. The second
part of Isaias is a message of consolation. The prophet is
commanded to cry aloud to Jerusalem:

that her evil is come to an end,
her iniquity is forgiven;
she hath received of the hand of the Lord
double (punishment) for all her sins.[5]

Thenceforth the justice of God will be exercised only in
mercy for Israel and in vengeance against her enemies. We
are thus prepared for the justice of the New Testament,
which, far from excluding mercy, includes it as an essential
element, and for that saving and redeeming justice which
will manifest itself only in regard to Christian believers,
when Jesus Christ, to whom they are united by faith, shall
have made propitiation for their sins. But this particular
aspect of it must not make us forget the others.

The expression " justice of God" is not very common in
the New Testament, it appears once in St Matthew, once in

[1] Is. lix, 17-18; xxviii, 17.
[2] Ps. v, 8; xxx, 1; cxviii, 40; cxlii, 1, etc.
[3] Ps. cxlii, 1.
[4] Is. li, 5; lvi, 1; lxiii, 1. This association of ideas is not wholly peculiar
to the second part. *Cf.* Is. xxx, 18.
[5] Is. xl. 2. This is the programme of the message of consolation.

the Epistle of St James, and eight or nine times in St Paul.[1] In the first two cases the meaning remains doubtful, although the justice of God seems to indicate something which is in man or which man can acquire; but it is the language of Paul which principally interests us. Here we find ourselves confronted by two very different accepted meanings. When it is said that " our injustice commends (or makes prominent) the justice of God,"[2] it clearly means an attribute of God— his fidelity or truth. On the other hand, in the text : " Him who knew no sin [God] hath made sin for us that we might be made the justice of God in him,"[3] the justice of God cannot be a divine attribute : firstly, the contrast with sin is opposed to it; and secondly, it is impossible to conceive how we could be made a mode of divinity; it is, therefore, a justice that is in us, although derived from God. Similarly in this other text : " For they, not knowing the justice of God and seeking to establish their own, have not submitted themselves to the justice of God,"[4] the antithesis exactly distinguishes the meaning of the terms. Indeed, man's own justice is elsewhere contrasted with the justice of God, where no misunderstanding is possible. " I desire," the Apostle says to the Philippians, " that I may be found in him, not having my justice, which is of the Law, but that which is of the faith of Christ Jesus, which is of God : justice [grounded] on faith."[5] Here " the justice of God," which replaces man's own justice, being made the property of man, is therefore inherent in man.

There remain two passages about which the present controversy chiefly rages : " For the justice of God is revealed therein [in the Gospel] from faith unto faith, as it is written : The just man shall live by faith."[6] At first glance the meaning of uncreated justice appears satisfactory; for this saving justice is, in truth, revealed in the Gospel by the salvation of believers, just as the wrath of God is revealed outside of the Gospel by the destruction of the wicked; not to mention the

---

[1] Rom. i, 17 ; iii, 5, 21, 22, 25, 26 ; x, 3 ; 2 Cor. v, 21 ; Phil. iii, 9 (τὴν ἐκ Θεοῦ δικαιοσύνην). Outside of St Paul, Matt. vi, 32 (ζητεῖτε δὲ πρῶτον τὴν βασιλείαν καὶ τὴν δικαιοσύνην αὐτοῦ) ; James i, 20 (ὀργὴ ἀνδρὸς δικαιοσύνην Θεοῦ οὐκ ἐργάζεται). See what is said in Vol. I, pp. 192-4.

[2] Rom. iii, 5.　　　　　　　　　　[3] 2 Cor. v, 21.

[4] Rom. x, 3.　　　　　　　　　　[5] Phil. iii, 9.

[6] Rom. i, 17 : Δικαιοσύνη γὰρ Θεοῦ ἐν αὐτῷ ἀποκαλύπτεται ἐκ πίστεως εἰς πίστιν, καθὼς γέγραπται· ὁ δὲ δίκαιος ἐκ πίστεως ζήσεται. Cf. Vol. I, pp. 192-4. The sequence of thought is as follows : " The Gospel is an agent of salvation for every believer (16 : δύναμις Θεοῦ εἰς σωτηρίαν παντὶ τῷ πιστεύοντι) because (γὰρ) the justice of God which is of faith is revealed in it, as it is written (καθὼς γέγραπται) : " The just man shall live by faith." The sense of the passage is, therefore, conditioned by the meaning of the scriptural quotation which serves as a proof or confirmation of the apostolic assertion. The faith of Habacuc corresponds to the faith of the Apostle ; just (δίκαιος) corresponds to justice (δικαιοσύνη) ; and shall live (ζήσεται) corresponds to salvation (σωτηρία).

fact that the revelation of God's justice is an expression quite usual in the prophetic writings, where it undoubtedly denotes the manifestation of some divine activity. But on examining the text more closely, doubts arise. How can the intrinsic justice of God be "from faith unto faith" in any possible interpretation of the words? What has the quotation from Habacuc to do here, and what connection is there between the manifestation of eternal justice and that assertion of the prophet : " The just man shall live by faith "? On the contrary, it is easy to see how the justice produced by God in man is "from faith" (ἐκ πίστεως), since faith is necessary condition for its development ; and how it progresses thence " unto faith " (ἐις πίστιν), since faith remains its source, its measure, and its ideal ; also how it is revealed in the Gospel which announces and realizes it ; and, finally, how it exists and is revealed in conformity to ancient prophecies (καθὼς γέγραπται), for the prophet Habacuc certainly speaks of a justice inherent in man.

The other text is not more obscure : " But now, without the Law, the justice of God is made manifest, being witnessed by the Law and the prophets, even the justice of God, by the faith of Jesus Christ, [a justice which is extended] unto all them that believe."[1]

The justice of God through faith in Jesus Christ is a justice which dwells in man, and this St Paul affirms in the clearest manner, adding, moreover, that it is intended for all believers. And it is not difficult to see how this justice of God through faith is supported by the testimony of the Law and the prophets, for Abraham, according to Genesis, owed his justification to faith, and the just man, according to the prophet Habacuc, lives by faith. It is objected that, a little further on, God shows or demonstrates his justice—evidently his intrinsic justice—by proposing and exposing the crucified One as a means of propitiation, and it is urged that one and the same expression ought always to keep the same meaning in the same context. Much could be said in regard to this principle. As far as St Paul is concerned, it is certainly false ; and if it were strictly applied, we should often end in an exegesis that is forced, childish, and absurd. Can we ignore the fact that the Apostle likes mentally to revolve about the various meanings of a word, frequently running through the whole gamut of definitions of a term, and that even here the notions of faith and law certainly change in the course of the phrase? Moreover, the divine attribute of justice and the justice which comes from God are two kindred concepts which are called by the same name and attract each other mutually, since God shows himself just, in justifying the sinner who is united to Jesus Christ.

[1] Rom. iii, 21, 22. Commented on in Vol. I, pp. 204-6.

On the whole : The " justice of God " is presented by St Paul under two distinct but not incongruous aspects : the justice which is in God and the justice which comes from God.

The intrinsic justice of God is not merely a vindictive or distributive justice, it is also—and sometimes chiefly—redemptive justice ; instead of excluding or ignoring goodness, grace, and mercy, it includes them.

The justice inherent in man is not, therefore, unrelated to the intrinsic justice of God. God is just and manifests his justice by justifying man. Created justice is the effect and the reflection of uncreated justice.

2. In looking through the Epistles of St Paul before making any detailed analysis of them, one is struck by the fact that he constantly associates justice and man's justification with the act of faith. Thus " the justice of God [is] *by* the faith of Jesus Christ,[1] justice [comes or results] *from* faith,[2] justice [rests] *on* faith,"[3] in a word it is " the justice of faith."[4] Similarly man " is justified by faith ;"[5] all, Jews and Gentiles, are " justified by reason of faith ;"[6] God " justifies whosoever is of the faith of Abraham ;"[7] finally, to every believer " faith is imputed unto justice."[8] If we examine these texts closely, we shall see that faith is not a simple, essential condition, the presence of which is required for some reason which we hardly understand, but that it exercises a real causality in the moral order. To speak accurately, it is not faith that justifies, it is God who justifies by faith ; for faith is neither the principal efficient cause, nor the formal cause, but only the instrumental cause of our justification. God justifies *by* faith (πίστει or διὰ πίστεως) as a channel of grace ; he justifies *in view of faith* or *in regard to faith* (ἐκ πίστεως) as a beginning of man's inward restoration ; and he justifies *on* faith (ἐπὶ πίστει) as a foundation of salvation. The instrumentality of faith appears especially in the justification of the father of the faithful : " Abraham believed God and it was imputed unto him for justice."[9] St Paul does not say that justice was imputed to Abraham ; he says—what is quite different—that faith was imputed to him for justice.

[1] Rom. iii, 22 : δικαιοσύνη Θεοῦ διὰ πίστεως 'I. X.

[2] Rom. ix, 30 : δικαιοσύνην τὴν ἐκ πίστεως.

[3] Phil. iii, 9 : τὴν [δικαιοσύνην] διὰ πίστεως Χριστοῦ.

[4] Rom. iv, 11, 13 : τῆς δικαιοσύνης τῆς πίστεως . . . διὰ δικαιοσύνης πίστεως.

[5] Rom. iii, 28 : λογιζόμεθα δικαιοῦσθαι πίστει ἄνθρωπον.

[6] Rom. iii, 30 (δικαιώσει περιτομὴν ἐκ πίστεως καὶ ἀκροβυστίαν διὰ τῆς πίστεως) ; Gal. ii, 16 (ἵνα δικαιωθῶμεν ἐκ πίστεως Χριστοῦ) ; iii, 8 (ἐκ πίστεως δικαιοῖ τὰ ἔθνη) ; iii, 24 (ἵνα ἐκ πίστεως δικαιωθῶμεν).

[7] Rom. iii, 26 : δικαιοῦντα τὸν ἐκ πίστεως Ἰησοῦ.

[8] Rom. iv, 5 : λογίζεται ἡ πίστις αὐτοῦ εἰς δικαιοσύνην.

[9] Gen. xv, 6 ; Rom. iv, 3, 22, 23 ; Gal. iii, 6 ; Jas. ii, 23.

Nor does he say that faith is the equivalent of justice; for then this imputation would belong to man by right, whereas it is, according to Paul, an act of grace.[1] He says that faith was imputed for justice because faith is inferior to justice and justice is nevertheless conferred on account of faith. God does not recognize the equivalency of faith and justice, but he accepts it by grace; it is his mercy that makes up what is wanting. However, as his gifts are not illusory, justice, when credited to man's account, becomes really the belonging and the property of man.

In the eyes of official Protestantism justifying faith has no moral value; it is a sort of passive instrument, a purely receptive power of justification, which exercises no causality and is only a condition *sine qua non;* it is only by an abuse of language that one can say that it justifies. The justification of the ungodly man takes place wholly in God; it changes nothing and effects nothing within man; it is a synthetic judgement, by virtue of which the wicked man, who remains wicked, is declared just. God, seeing his faith, but not on account of his faith, imputes to him the justice of Christ, without, however, giving it to him. Thus the ungodly man, though justified, is always in himself ungodly, but before God who has decreed to him the attribute of justice, he is just.

This statement is hard to understand. How can the false be true, or how can God declare true what he knows to be false? Why is faith required, if it is inactive, and why has God any consideration for it, if it is valueless? By what right is it affirmed that the justice of Christ is imputed to us, when St Paul declares, on the contrary, that our faith is imputed to us for justice? Can we be surprised that many *liberal Protestants* reject this system as arbitrary, immoral, and incoherent? For them faith is not without value; it is a germ of virtue, an aspiration towards what is good, the starting-point of a new life. They tell us that on God's part justification consists in being satisfied with this germ, in judging man by his ideal, in taking the tendency for the accomplished fact, in seeing in the humble acorn the noble oak which will evolve from it. God declares that the ungodly man is just because, by believing, he has already begun to be just, and because he will some day become wholly so.

We admit without hesitation that the justification of man suggests usually in the Old and even in the New Testament the idea of a divine judgement, that it is possible to discover it there without doing violence to the texts, and that in a small number of cases the justification is purely affirmative. It is so, for example, every time when it is a question of the

---

[1] Rom. iv, 16 : διὰ τοῦτο ἐκ πίστεως ἵνα κατὰ χάριν.

last judgement, which does not produce justice in man, but presupposes it : " For not the hearers of the Law are just before God : but the doers of the Law shall be justified."[1] Here the justification is only the verdict of the sovereign Judge; nevertheless, by virtue of the equation between " being justified " and " being just before God," the divine judgement is not arbitrary ; it is founded on truth, not on a legal fiction.  But that is not the ordinary sense ; and what proves this is the impossibility of replacing, in most cases, the verb " to justify " by its so-called equivalents " to declare just " or " to treat as just."

Even when the justification presents itself under the form of a declaratory sentence, it supposes or produces justice. For how is it possible to conceive of a divine declaration not being true and a judgement of God being based upon error? When " God justifies the ungodly," say the leaders of Protestantism, the justification is not an analytical judgement, but a synthetic one, the attribute of which is not included in the notion of the subject.  An analytical judgement would be : " The ungodly man is not just."  But the judgement which God pronounces, when he justifies us, is wholly different : it is " The ungodly man is just."  So that the wicked man, though justified, finds himself at the same time (in sensu composito) in possession of two contradictory qualities, one of which belongs to him as an ungodly man, while the other is attributed to him by a divine declaration. It would be like saying that a circle is round and square at the same time, if God pronounced it to be square : round essentially, but square by virtue of the *synthetic judgement* formulated by God.  " In justifying the sinner, God does not recognize in him any attribute (of justice) ; on the contrary, he gives him an attribute while he is still a sinner—namely, that of justice."[2]  Is it surprising that such a doctrine has called forth protests from the day of its birth?  Moreover, those who still defend it give up trying to understand it, and while claiming for it the authority of Paul, gladly take refuge in mystery.

For a man to be just before God and for God to pronounce him just, one of two things is necessary : either that God has made him just previously, or that he makes him just by this pronouncement itself.  In the latter hypothesis, the justification of the wicked would be declaratory in form but effective in reality.  The divine sentence of justification would then produce its effect after the manner of sacramental formulas, like the words of consecration or like the words of Christ when working miracles.  In this way, there would be kept for the word " justification " that judicial meaning which

---

[1] Rom. ii, 13 : *factores legis justificabuntur.*
[2] Franks, *Justification* (*Dict. of Christ and the Gospels*, vol. i, p. 919).

many modern exegetes regard as essential, while excluding that fictitious justification due to a divine judgement contrary to truth.

Most of the heterodox theologians of our day complain of finding a most singular duality in St Paul. They find that he has a juridical, objective, and imputed justification, and also a real, moral, subjective, and inherent one. In the first, the Holy Spirit intervenes only as a witness; in the second, he is an active agent, a pledge, and an instalment of the justification. In the one case faith is presented as a mystical bond that unites us with Christ; in the other, on the contrary, faith is only a simple intellectual recognition of the scheme of salvation. The forensic justification is connected with the concept of redemption by ransom and penal substitution, while the subjective justification has for its counterpart the deliverance from sin and the flesh. According to Pfleiderer, these two conceptions " are like two rivers which flow in the same bed without mingling their waters." Some declare them irreconcilable, or at least maintain that the reconciliation was not effected in the mind of Paul; others endeavour to reconcile them, but are led astray by their prejudices and end in illogical solutions.

They are persuaded that " it is impossible to harmonize the Apostle's doctrine, save by regarding the justice of God as a quality in no way present in the believer, but surely promised him in the future." This would be a kind of prophetic judgement by anticipation, which God will confirm and at the same time realize at the last day. Such is the famous *forensic* and *eschatological* justification meant to clear up all the mystery, but which, in reality, only accentuates the darkness.

How much more simple, rational, and conformable to the letter and spirit of the Apostle is the Catholic solution, every detail of which can be justified by a word from St Paul:

*God takes the first steps;* he alone is the author of the inward appeal as well as of the external call; it is the initiative of grace, and it is thus that faith is of God.

*Man then responds to the appeal,* but not without divine help; he glorifies God by accepting his testimony, bending under his hand, and yielding himself entirely to him; this is a merit, certainly, but a merit the honour of which he cannot ascribe to himself.

*God intervenes again;* he imputes faith for justice; he gives justice freely in return for faith, but not as the equivalent of or compensation for faith. Up to this time grace has always had the preponderating part.

The justice granted to man *binds him to do, and gives him the power to do good works.* Man, equipped with habitual grace, can go from virtue to virtue; but the fruits which he obtains, although belonging to him, are not exclusively his, for he is working with the capital furnished by God, and with the advances from it which God allows him.

Finally, *God crowns his work;* he justifies man for ever; this time by declaring him just, because, in fact, man is so. A wonderful combination, in which God is always active without either suppressing or fettering man's activity, and in which man works out his own salvation without in any respect infringing on the sovereign domain of God.

## III—Sanctification

### 1. The Idea of Sanctity.  2. Justice and Sanctity.

1. The abyss which separates Christianity from classic paganism appears nowhere broader and deeper than in the concept of sanctity. The ancient religion of the Greeks and Romans did not even suspect such a thing as the sanctity of their gods; in any case, the epithet saintly was not applied to the gods of Olympus. Biblical phrases such as " Be ye holy, because I am holy," or " I who sanctify you am holy," would have sounded strangely to pagan ears.

However obscure may be the original and etymological meaning of the word *holy* in Hebrew, the phases of its philological evolution and the degrees of spiritualization through which it passed in the course of ages, as revelation progressed, it is certain that the biblical notion of sanctity is essentially religious and moral, pertaining to God *par excellence* and to finite beings by reason of their relation to God.[1] In the Old Testament the saint was a man who was united to God by a bond of consecration and special dependence; in the New Testament he is one who shares in the holiness of God itself.

[1] The Hebrew root קָדַשׁ in all its present forms has no longer any save religious meanings and it is difficult to go back to its original physical signification. It seems, however, that the primordial idea was that of *separation.* God was holy, first by reason of his majesty, transcendence and inaccessibility; then because of his aversion to everything impure, profane and morally evil. Holy persons and things were those which a special appointment or consecration separated from common usage and reserved for the service of God.

In order to translate the words derived from the root קָדַשׁ the Septuagint employed the adjective ἅγιος and its derivations ἁγιάζειν, ἁγιασμός, ἁγιότης, ἁγιωσύνη. All these derivations were hardly ever used in profane literature; in passing to the New Testament, they kept their biblical signification, with a tendency to become always more spiritualized. The Greek word ἅγιος had not much in common with the corresponding Hebrew word. It was not used in speaking of the gods and rarely in reference to men. Applied to things, it signified " august, sacred," if it were a question of an object consecrated to the gods of heaven; but if it referred to an object dedicated to the duties of the nether world, it meant " cursed, execrable." Moreover, its use in any case was extremely rare.

If, in order to distinguish them, justification and sanctification are compared, the latter appears like a positive perfection, susceptible of indefinite progress, while the former presents itself under its negative aspect—the remission of sins—which does not seem to permit such progress at all. Sanctification includes indeed the notion of justification, but the contrary is not true; so that it is possible to conceive a providential order of things in which sinful man would be simply declared just, whereas it is impossible to imagine a saint whose sins should not have been forgiven. From this point of view, justification logically precedes sanctification, for which it serves as a foundation.

2. Let us hasten to say that in the present order of things, with which alone we are interested, justification and sanctification are inseparable. We prove this by two series of texts.

St Paul writes to the Corinthians:

> Know you not that the unjust shall not inherit the kingdom of God ? Do not err : neither fornicators, nor idolaters, nor adulterers, nor the effeminate, nor liers with mankind, nor thieves, nor covetous, nor drunkards, nor railers, nor extortioners shall possess the kingdom of God. And such some of you were. But you washed yourselves, but you were sanctified, but you were justified in the name of our Lord Jesus Christ and the Spirit of our God.[1]

The Apostle enumerates, apparently at random, half a score of the commonest vices among the pagans, especially at Corinth. He reminds his readers that a certain number of them—he does not generalize too much in order not to offend them—have formerly been guilty of those vices; but, no matter ! baptism has washed all that away. Baptism effects at one single stroke the purification, sanctification, and justification of the sinner. It is in vain that excessively subtle exegetes labour to find a gradation in these three effects of the sacramental grace. It does not exist; but by placing sanctification between the other two fruits of baptism, St Paul shows that it is not posterior to them. To the Ephesians he addresses the same language; only here he

---

[1] I Cor. vi, 9-11; on the last verse, see Vol. I, p. 171. Ἀλλὰ ἀπελούσασθε, ἀλλὰ ἡγιάσθητε, ἀλλὰ ἐδικαιώθητε. (a) The three verbs are aorists, not perfects, because they do not express a final result which cannot be lost, but a grace accorded at a precise moment of time, at baptism.—(b) While the last two verbs are passive, the first is in the middle voice : a shade of thought worthy of note. It must not be rendered *vous avez été* lavés ou purifiés (Crampon, Lemonnyer, Second. etc.), but *vous vous êtes* purifiés (*ihr liesset euch abwaschen*, Weizsäcker, Bachmann) ; because allusion is made to the co-operation of the catechumen, who has not been merely passive.—(c) The attempt of Estius to establish a certain gradation between purification, sanctification and justification is not successful..

applies to the whole Church what is applied in the other passage to every Christian :

> Christ loved the Church and delivered himself for it, that he might sanctify it, cleansing it by the laver of water in the word of life, that he might present it to himself, a glorious Church, not having spot, or wrinkle, or any such thing, but holy and without blemish.[1]

Sanctity is not the privilege of a few chosen ones; it is the appanage of all Christians worthy of the name. When the Apostle writes to the *saints* of Rome, Corinth, Philippi, or any other city, he does not establish various categories of the faithful : he addresses them all indiscriminately.[2] Every Christian is for him a *saint;* and he gives to this word its full value. In a few rare texts he may indeed speak only of an external and legal sanctity, which does not rise above the level of the Old Testament; as when he says, for example, in regard to mixed marriages : " For the unbelieving husband is sanctified by the believing wife; and the unbelieving wife is sanctified by the believing [husband]; otherwise your children should be unclean; but now they are holy."[3]

The conjugal union being so intimate that the two parties to it form only one flesh and one moral person, the sanctity of the one is imparted to the other; the unbelieving partner and his children are, as it were, immersed in an atmosphere of sanctity, which envelops and will finally penetrate them, as water, when mingled with wine, assumes the taste and the colour of the latter. But this way of speaking is exceptional. The Christian, from the fact of his baptism, is sanctified by the Holy Spirit whose temple he is,[4] he becomes the friend of God[5] and he is called to sanctity;[6] and we know that for St Paul the call is always an efficacious call, that produces its effect. The sanctity of the Christian is,

---

[1] Eph. v, 25-27. See the explanation of this text later, p. 256.

[2] *Saints* is put for Christians at least thirty times.

[3] 1 Cor. vii, 14. Paul speaks of the case where one of the married pair has become a Christian *after* marriage ; for he forbids the marriage of a Christian with an unbeliever (vii, 32 ; 2 Cor. vi, 14). Another example of external and legal sanctity is mentioned in Rom. xi, 16 : *Quod si delibatio sancta est, et massa ; et si radix sancta, et rami.* The *root* is the chosen people, which communicates a sort of external sanctity to the *branches*—that is to say, to the members of that people. In the same way a blessing, pronounced over food, *sanctifies* it, and causes it to be no more unclean and profane (1 Tim. iv, 5).

[4] 1 Cor. iii, 16 ; 2 Cor. vi, 16.          [5] Col. iii, 12 ; Rom. i, 7.

[6] 1 Cor. i, 2 : ἡγιασμένοις ἐν Χ. Ἰ., κλητοῖς ἁγίοις. Rom. i, 7 : *omnibus qui sunt Romae, dilectis Dei, vocatis sanctis.* Note here that Paul (*a*) addresses all the faithful ; (*b*) he calls them all friends of God (ἀγαπητοὶ Θεοῦ) ; (*c*) he supposes that all are called to sanctity (κλητοὶ ἁγιοι). Now κλητοὶ ἁγιοι must be understood as is κλητὸς ἀπόστολος (Rom. i, 1 ; 1 Cor. i, 1) " called to sanctity " with an effective and efficacious call which puts them in possession of sanctity.

therefore, not merely a potential sanctity, but a sanctity which is at least initial, the germ of which needs only to fructify.

Thus in the present order of things justification is not merely a remission of sins; it is a reconciliation with God,[1] who restores to us the divine friendship, and with it the privileges lost in Adam. Hence it is represented as a transformation of our entire being, a metamorphosis, which makes of every Christian " a new creature."[2]

[1] Rom v, 10-11 ; 2 Cor. v, 18, 19.
[2] 2 Cor. v, 17 : εἴ τις ἐν Χριστῷ καινὴ κτίσις. *Cf.* Eph. ii, 10 ; Col. iii, 10.

# CHAPTER II

## THE SACRAMENTS

THERE exists in the New Testament no general term designating the symbolic rites instituted by Jesus Christ to confer grace. As μυστήριον, frequently translated by *sacramentum* in the Latin Bible, has sometimes the meaning of symbol or sacred sign, it seemed the most fitting word to express the visible vehicles of grace, when a single appellation was desired to include them.[1] At an early date, baptism, with the laying on of hands which seals it and the Holy Communion which accompanies it, were thus named; but the special nature of these three rites which make the neophyte a member of the Christian fold and remind us of the religious initiations of paganism, made the extension of the name *mysteries* to the other sacraments difficult. The corresponding Latin word *sacramentum* was, from its very vagueness, better adapted to denote the different Christian institutions, the common feature of which was indeed their sacred character, but whose analogies were, at first sight, less striking than their specific differences : hence this word was applied to all, or nearly all, the sacraments by St Augustine, who, in doing so, only made general the usage of Tertullian and St Cyprian.

Of the seven sacraments of the Church St Paul does not mention extreme unction nor, probably, penance.[2] But, on the other hand, his allusions to baptism are quite frequent ; his teaching regarding the Eucharist is more complete than that of the evangelists ; and his statements about Holy Order and Matrimony allow us to conclude that he regards them as sacred signs conferring grace, although we cannot infer *directly* from them that he believes them to have been instituted by Jesus Christ.

### I—BAPTISM

1. Manifold Symbolism of Baptism.  2. Mystical Death and Resurrection.
3. Faith and Baptism.

1. The rite of baptism by immersion, which was the usual practice of the primitive Church, can be considered under at

[1] See later, Note L.
[2] We speak of penance as a *sacrament*. The " ministry of reconciliation " (2 Cor. v, 18) which was confided to the Apostles is not the power of the keys. The Epistles mention indeed a sort of public penance consisting of putting

least four symbolical aspects : as a *sacred bath*, symbol of internal purification ; as a *return to the light*, symbol of spiritual illumination ; as a *mystical burial*, symbol of death to the old man and of union with the death of Christ ; and as a *mystical resurrection*, symbol of regeneration and of a new life.

Later, this symbolism was enriched by two new elements : anointing, emblem of the grafting of the neophyte into the true olive-tree, and the change of dress, emblem of moral transformation ; but this twofold symbolism, whether suggested or not by St Paul's language, must not occupy our attention here, for nothing proves that it goes back to the apostolic age.[1] Of the four aspects pointed out above, the first—the one which the etymology of the word first evokes, and which most naturally suggests itself to the mind—was also the most common at the beginning. The second was specially honoured from the second century onwards ; after the time of St Justin, *to illumine* and *illumination* became synonymous with " to baptize " and with " baptism."[2] These forms of speech and of thought are common to St Paul. Christians have " the eyes of their heart enlightened " ;[3] they are " children of the light and children of the day " ;[4] much more, the light which penetrates them at baptism changes them into luminous centres, which reflect it and disperse it, as a crystal, illumined by the sun's rays, becomes glittering and radiant ; they shine like "lights in the world,"[5] and are themselves " light in the Lord."[6] Nor is Paul unaware of the fact that baptism is a " bath of regeneration and renovation " ;[7] that all the faithful are " puri-

---

the offender in quarantine and excluding him from the Christian community until he amended his conduct (2 Thess. iii, 6, 14, 15 ; 1 Cor. v, 3-5 ; 2 Cor. ii, 6-10) ; but this is still not sacramental penance.

[1] This manifold symbolism is well presented by St Cyril of Jerusalem (*Catech. Mystag.*, ii.) : (*a*) Divestment, or rejection of the old man (ii, 2 ; XXXIV, 1077).—(*b*) Anointing with consecrated oil (ἐλαίῳ ἐπορκιστῷ) or grafting into the true olive tree (1080). This unction differs from the unction of the chrism (μύρον χρίσμα) which forms part of the sacrament of confirmation, and of which more is said later (*Catech. Mystag.*, iii).—(*c*) Triple immersion, or death and burial (1080-81).—(*d*) Triple emersion, or spiritual resurrection and illumination (*ibid.*).—(*e*) White garments, or sanctifying grace (*Catech. Mystag.*, iv, 8 ; XXXIV, 1104).—The same symbolism, but less methodical, in the *De Mysteriis* and the *De Sacramentis*, attributed to St Ambrose.—The *De Baptismo* of Tertullian, which is polemical rather than dogmatic, scarcely stops at symbolism. *Cf. De corona*, 3.

[2] St Justin is the first to use the word φωτισμός in the sense of baptism (*Apol.*, i, 61 ; καλεῖται δὲ τοῦτο τὸ λουτρὸν φωτισμός) ; but his manner of speaking seems to show clearly that this term was in general use in his time.

[3] Eph. i, 18 : πεφωτισμένους τοὺς ὀφθαλμοὺς τῆς καρδίας ὑμῶν.

[4] 1 Thess. v, 5 : πάντες γὰρ ὑμεῖς υἱοὶ φωτός ἐστε καὶ υἱοὶ ἡμέρας.

[5] Phil. ii, 15 : φαίνεσθε ὡς φωστῆρες ἐν κόσμῳ.

[6] Eph. v, 8 : νῦν δὲ φῶς ἐν Κυρίῳ· ὡς τέκνα φωτὸς περιπατεῖτε.

[7] Titus iii, 5 : ἔσωσεν ἡμᾶς διὰ λουτροῦ παλιγγενεσίας. See below, p. 259.

fied, sanctified, justified ";[1] and that Jesus Christ, wishing
to prepare for himself a spouse perfect and worthy of him,
sanctifies it (the Church), "cleansing it by the laver of water
in the word."[2]  Certainly it is not a question here of a
material purification : the baptismal application owes its
efficacy to the all-powerful word which elevates it to the
dignity of a sacramental rite.  It is not, however, the purification of the soul through the remission of sins, or the
illumination of the intellect by faith, that St Paul wishes to
make prominent when he speaks of baptism; it is the
mystical death and resurrection, represented and produced
by the sacrament.

2. The rebirth of man has a previous death as its essential
condition.  Jesus Christ is a Saviour only by the cross, and
he saves us only by associating us with his death.  But to
become capable of saving us, this ideal death must be
realized in each one of us, and this is what takes place at
baptism :

> Know you not that all we who are baptised in Christ Jesus are baptised
> in his death ?  For we are buried together with him by baptism into
> death ; that, as Christ is risen from the dead by the glory of the Father,
> so we also may walk in newness of life.  For if we have been planted

---

[1] I Cor. vi, 11 : ἀπελούσασθε . . . ἡγιάσθητε . . . ἐδικαιώθητε.

[2] Eph. v, 26 : ἵνα αὐτὴν ἁγιάσῃ καθαρίσας τῷ λουτρῷ τοῦ ὕδατος ἐν ῥήματι.
The sequence of thought is this : Jesus Christ delivered himself up to death
for his Church, *in order to* sanctify it by purifying each one of its members
in baptism (ἵνα denotes immediate purpose, because baptism has efficacy
only by virtue of the redemptive death), *in order to* prepare for himself a
spouse wholly pure and wholly beautiful (ἵνα παραστήσῃ, remote purpose,
because it is obtained only by means of baptism, application of the redemptive
death to individuals).—It is quite probable that the Apostle here alludes to
the *bath* which was for a bride the prelude to the nuptial toilette, but it is
beyond doubt that τὸ λουτρόν τοῦ ὕδατος denotes baptism.  The Saviour
wishes to sanctify his Church in order that it may be worthy of him, and he
sanctifies it *by purifying it* " by the bath of water " (καθαρίσας, in relation
to the aorist ἁγιάσῃ, marks not priority but simultaneousness.—What does
the expression ἐν ῥήματι refer to and what does it mean ?  It cannot be
made to refer to ἁγιάσῃ, which is much too remote, nor to τῷ λουτρῷ τοῦ
ὕδατος, because it cannot form one expression either with λουτρόν or with
ὕδωρ, and because the repetition of the article (τῷ ἐν ῥήματι or του ἐν ῥήματι)
would consequently be indispensable; it refers, therefore, to καθαρίσας.
Some Protestant writers think that ἐν ῥήματι signifies " by the word of the
Gospel " ; but ῥῆμα, especially without an article, never signifies and never
can signify the Gospel; it would require a determining complement, such as
ῥῆμα τῆς πίστεως (Rom. x, 8), Χριστοῦ (Rom. x, 17), Θεοῦ (Eph. vi, 17 ;
Heb. vi, 5).  Others (St Chrysostom, etc.) think that it refers to the formula
of baptism; but, if this formula were *directly* and *distinctly* indicated, the
article (ἐν τῷ ῥήματι) would be necessary.  The only admissible meaning,
therefore, is : " by purifying it by the baptism of water (instrumental dative)
*by means of* a word " (ἐν instrumental).—The baptismal water *alone* has not
the power to purify the soul ; there must be added to it " a word," which is
indeed the formula of baptism, although it is designated here only generically :
*Accedit verbum ad elementum et fit sacramentum* (Augustine).

together in the likeness of his death, we shall be also in the likeness of his resurrection. Knowing this, that our old man is crucified with him, that the body of sin may be destroyed, to the end that we may serve sin no longer ; for he that is dead is freed from sin.[1]

This text condenses into a few words of admirable fulness of meaning the direct effects of baptism, the benefits which it assures us in the future and the duties which it imposes on us now. Through failing to distinguish these different points of view, exegetes and theologians amalgamate incongruous ideas and thus make of one of the most beautiful pages of St Paul a piece of insipid nonsense. We have to consider here only the immediate fruits of baptism. To be baptized into the death of Christ is to be baptized into the dying Christ—that is, to be incorporated with Christ in the very act by which he saves us, to die mystically with him who suffered death in the name and for the benefit of all. This mystical death is a reality, for the effects of it are very real : death to sin, death to the old man, death to the Law.

If we are to believe certain Protestant commentators, death to sin is only the result of a legal fiction : God, they say, regards us as dead, in the same way as he treats us as just, although no change has taken place in us. At most, they make the change consist in a decisive breaking-off from sin on the part of the will, with its instincts and desires, and this under the continually renewed power of faith in the death of Christ *for* sin. This explanation explains nothing. That the Christian from the very fact of his baptism is in duty bound to persevere in a state of death in relation to sin, no one disputes ; but this duty, if it is analysed, implies an internal change of the moral order. St Paul is not satisfied with saying : " Die to sin," but he says : " You are dead to sin." To die to sin, therefore, is to lay aside the taint of sin ; but it is at the same time to be delivered from its tyranny and to be enabled to resist its further attacks. There is no restriction, no exception ; original sin, present sins, all that is called sin in the true sense of the word, has disappeared at baptism ; for " there is now no more condemnation for them that are in Christ Jesus."[2] Yesterday they may have been idolaters, fornicators, thieves, calumniators, and blasphemers ; now they have been " purified, sanctified, and justified in the name of our Lord Jesus Christ."[3]

Death to the old man is a consequence of death to sin. When we were baptized into the death of Christ, " our old man was crucified with him."[4] The old man denotes all that we have in common with the first Adam, and all that we inherit directly or indirectly from him, as the religious Head

---

[1] Rom. vi, 3-7. *Cf.* Vol. I, p. 222.
[3] 1 Cor. vi, 11.
[2] Rom. viii, 1.
[4] Rom. vi, 6.

of humanity. All this perishes through the fact of our union with the second Adam. It is very evident that death to the old man is progressive, for the inclination to evil persists even in regenerate man; but the old man has received a mortal blow; with the antidote of grace, concupiscence, called here "the body of sin," is rendered inert and harmless.

It seems clear also that Christian baptism is a death to the Mosaic Law: "For I, through the Law, am dead to the Law, that I may live to God; with Christ I am nailed to the cross. And I live, now not I, but Christ liveth in me.—My brethren, you also are become dead to the Law by the body of Christ. . . . Now we are loosed from the Law of death, wherein we were detained."[1] In this latter passage the allusion to baptism appears evident: it is, in fact, baptism which puts an end to all our servitudes: "He who is dead is freed from sin" and from all its consequences. It is probable that as much must be said also of the preceding text; for at what moment has the Apostle been crucified with Jesus Christ, if not in the baptismal rite, which united him to the dying Christ?

It is not without a reason that the Apostle always establishes a connection between the spiritual death and the spiritual resurrection. Indeed, it is impossible to die to sin without beginning to live to grace: "If we be dead with Christ, we believe that we shall live also together with Christ. . . . If we have been planted together in the likeness of his death we shall also be in the likeness of his resurrection."[2] Our new life may not be apparent, but it exists of necessity, because it is a corollary of our death: "You are dead and your life is hid with Christ in God."[3] How could it be otherwise, since baptism, which is the grave of the old man, is also the cradle of the new?[4]

In order to appreciate this language, it is necessary to compare the following expressions: "to be baptized into (εἰς) Christ" and "to put on Christ."[5] We cannot agree with those who claim that the etymological meaning of "to baptize" and the figurative meaning of "to put on" have wholly disappeared from these modes of speech. To be baptized into Christ is to be plunged into the mystical Christ, as into the natural element of our new life; it is, therefore, substantially the same thing as to be baptized into the body of Christ—that is to say, incorporated into his mystical body. Similarly, to put on Christ, is to be enveloped with that divine atmosphere, made a living member of Christ and

---

[1] Gal. ii, 19; Rom. vii, 6.
[2] Rom. vi, 8 (cf. 2 Tim. ii, 11); vi, 5.
[3] Col. iii, 3.
[4] Col. ii, 12: *consepulti ei in baptismo, in quo et resurrexistis.*
[5] For the phrase "to be baptised into Christ," see Note X.

subjected to that supernatural force, known as the soul of the Church, which is nothing else than the Holy Spirit. The Apostle likes to speak of putting on Christ, or the Lord Jesus Christ, of putting on the new man, of putting on immortality, weapons of light, the armour of God, the helmet of salvation, the breastplate of faith and of charity; in all these instances the figurative meaning is clear. We put on Christ not so much as a mantle that covers our poverty, as a vital form which makes us participate in his life.

Almost all the fruits of baptism considered as the beginning of a new life are admirably grouped together in the following texts : " He (God) saved us by the laver of regeneration and renovation of the Holy Ghost, whom he hath poured forth upon us abundantly through Jesus Christ our Saviour; that being justified by his grace, we may be heirs, in hope, of life everlasting."[1] According to this, passing over the collateral points, baptism is a bath of regeneration and renovation : a *bath* which purifies the soul of all its past stains ; *of regeneration,* because it is a second birth by water and by the Holy Ghost, which renders us children of God, as the first birth rendered us slaves of sin ; *of renovation,* because under the influence of the creative Spirit, the neophyte puts off the old man, puts on the new, is transformed in his entire being, and becomes a new creature.— Baptism is, moreover, the gift of the Holy Spirit poured into our hearts by the Father, with the mediation of the Son.— Finally, baptism renders us heirs of eternal life by conferring upon us the adoption of sons : true heirs, although the effec-

---

[1] Titus iii, 5-7 : ἔσωσεν ἡμᾶς διὰ λουτροῦ παλιγγενεσίας καὶ ἀνακαινώσεως Πνεύματος ἁγίου, οὗ ἐξέχεεν ἐφ᾽ ἡμᾶς πλουσίως διὰ Ἰησοῦ τοῦ σωτῆρος ἡμῶν, ἵνα δικαιωθέντες τῇ ἐκείνου χάριτι κληρονόμοι γενηθῶμεν κατ᾽ ἐλπίδα ζωῆς αἰωνίου. (*a*) The subject of the phrase is certainly God, who has just been named (τοῦ σωτῆρος ἡμῶν Θεοῦ) and to whom mercy rightly belongs (κατὰ τὸ αὐτοῦ ἔλεος).—(*b*) The genitive ἀνακαινώσεως might strictly depend on διά, which would give us *two* instruments of salvation : baptism and renovation ; but it is much more natural to make it depend (as the Vulgate does) on λουτροῦ. Baptism is then described as a regeneration and a renovation.—(*c*) The laver (λουτρόν) is certainly baptism. The figurative meaning *purification,* imagined by some exegetes to account for the absence of the article before λουτρόν, is to-day universally rejected.—(*d*) This laver is a bath of *regeneration,* because it *produces* regeneration, as almost all exegetes, even heterodox ones, concede (see B. Weiss, *Meyer's Kommentar*[7], 1902, p. 369). The word παλιγγενεσία is not explained by Matt. xix, 28 (the only other example in the N.T.), where it signifies the renovation of the world after the *parousia.* It is necessary rather to compare John iii, 3 (*nisi quis renatus fuerit denuo*) ; iii, 4-7.—(*e*) *Renovation* (ἀνακαίνωσις) is another aspect of *regeneration.* Regeneration expresses the *fact* of a *second* birth (πάλιν) because the first birth makes us heirs of sin (John iii, 7 : δεῖ ὑμᾶς γεννηθῆναι ἄνωθεν, whether ἄνωθεν signifies *again,* as Nicodemus understands it, or *from on high,* the necessity of a second birth is not thus less) ; renovation expresses the *quality* of this second birth, presented everywhere as a *creation,* as the production of a *new* being, as a *metamorphosis* (2 Cor. v, 17 ; Gal. vi, 15 ; Rom. xii, 2 ; 2 Cor. iii, 18 ; Eph. ii, 15 ; iv, 24 ; Col. iii, 10, etc.)

tive enjoyment of our patrimony is deferred, and although by this title we are only heirs in hope (κληρονόμοι κατ' ἐλπίδα), prospective heirs; but we know also that, so far as God is concerned, our hope is certain of fulfilment.

3. All the effects which we have just assigned to baptism— justice, life, salvation, adoption of sons, and the possession of the Holy Spirit—are attributed by St Paul also to faith. Whence comes this close union, this mutual interpenetration of faith and baptism? In the first place, there is synchronism. Almost all those to whom Paul addressed his Epistles had received baptism at the same time as the gift of faith : both these recollections were blended in their memory. The instruction of the catechumens was then concise : the Saviour had said, as he ascended to heaven : " Whoever believeth and is baptized shall be saved," as if the two actions were simultaneous. In fact, the three thousand men converted by Peter, at the first Pentecost, were baptized that same day ;[1] the eunuch of Queen Candace descended from his chariot to receive baptism at the hand of the deacon Philip who had just instructed him ;[2] St Paul's gaoler was baptized with all his family the very night on which he had embraced the faith ;[3] the twelve disciples at Ephesus, who had as yet received only the baptism of John, " believed on Jesus and were baptized."[4] A similar formula epitomizes the labours of the Apostle at Corinth.[5] There was no interval between faith and baptism.

To this first external bond—the resultant of the simultaneousness of the two acts and the identity of the two memories —is added another, still more intimate and pertaining to the nature of things. For St Paul concrete, normal faith, the faith that justifies, is not a simple assent of the intellect to a speculative truth ; it is the consent of the reason, the will, and the whole man to the Gospel—that is to say, to the plan of salvation of which God is the author and Jesus Christ the proclaimer. This initial faith, with which Paul especially concerns himself, for it was for him, as well as for his first readers, the decisive point of his life and the critical moment of his destiny, necessarily includes therefore, together with the offering of himself to God, the implicit desire for baptism. Not only is the baptism of an adult inconceivable without faith, since it is inconceivable without repentance (μετάνοια) and conversion to God—but sincere and justifying faith is also inconceivable without a desire for baptism. Hence our spiritual regeneration is attributed sometimes to faith, sometimes to baptism, because the act and the rite are mutually dependent on each other and exercise a common causality.

[1] Acts ii, 41.  [2] Acts viii, 38.  [3] Acts xvi, 33.
[4] Acts xix, 5.  [5] Acts xviii.

The case of a catechumen overtaken by death before receiving the sacrament is not chimerical; but it is accidental and exceptional, and a theory does not take into consideration exceptions and accidents : " You are all the children of God by faith in Christ Jesus. For as many of you as have been baptized in Christ have put on Christ."[1] Thus the adoption of sons is attributed at the same time to faith and to baptism. You are no longer, says the Apostle, *little children* (νήπιοι, παῖδες), as the Jews had previously been, still in tutelage and under a pedagogue; you are children of God (υἱοὶ Θεοῦ) who have reached a mature age, are emancipated from the Law, and in full possession of your patrimony and all your rights; and you are all this by the living faith which unites you to Christ Jesus and makes you participate in his prerogatives. How should you not be children of God? Baptized in Christ, you have put on Christ, you have the form of Christ, and consequently also the adoption of sons inherent in that form. It is indeed union with Christ which makes us children of God, and this union is effected by faith and by baptism; but neither can the effective union of baptism be produced without the effective union of faith, nor the effective union of faith be produced without some intrinsic relation with the effective union of baptism; it is because the effective union of faith tends essentially to the effective union of baptism that it becomes itself effective; and the two conceptions, far from being opposed, are reunited.

## II—CONFIRMATION

The bestowal of the Holy Spirit through the laying on of hands, being so closely united with baptism, the two acts seemed to be only integral parts of one and the same rite. No doubt St Paul's question to the disciples of

---

[1] Gal. iii, 26, 27 : *Πάντες γὰρ υἱοὶ Θεοῦ ἐστε διὰ τῆς πίστεως ἐν Χριστῷ Ἰησοῦ. ὅσοι γὰρ εἰς Χριστὸν ἐβαπτίσθητε Χριστὸν ἐνεδύσασθε.*—(a) The first γάρ gives the reason of the preceding affirmation (*At ubi venit fides, jam non sumus sub paedagogo*). The reason is that we are now *children of God* (υἱοὶ Θεοῦ) who have come to maturity, and that we are no longer, as formerly, before the coming of Christ, νήπιοι (iv, 13) or παῖδες (the idea contained in παιδαγωγός), *young children.*—(b) The emphasis is on the word πάντες, placed prominently at the beginning of the phrase and still more accentuated by ὅσοι of the following phrase. The Apostle was obliged to prove only that the Jews are no more under the Law (*non* sumus *sub paedagogo*), but he proves more; he proves that no Christian can be under the Law, *for* all are children of God, all are baptised in Christ.—(c) The words ἐν Χριστῷ Ἰησοῦ might depend on πίστις, for in biblical Greek we sometimes find πιστεύειν ἐν and also πίστις ἐν (Eph. i, 15 ; Col. i, 4), which allows the suppression of the definite article before ἐν Χ. Ἰ. We should therefore be children of God *by faith in Christ Jesus*. Nevertheless it is better to make ἐν Χριστῷ Ἰησοῦ, as well as διὰ πίστεως, refer to υἱοὶ Θεοῦ ἐστε (You are children of God by faith in Christ Jesus, or, You are children of God in Christ Jesus by faith).

Ephesus, who he thought had been baptized with Christian baptism, shows plainly that these acts were not only distinct, but separable;[1] and indeed, the Samaritans, baptized by the deacon Philip, received the Holy Spirit only later, on the arrival of the apostles;[2] nevertheless, as there was no other reason for separating confirmation from baptism than the absence of a legitimate minister, they were usually conferred together and formed two connected articles of the elementary Christian instruction.

St Paul, supposing that Christians had received the Holy Ghost at baptism, does not mention the laying on of hands except in connection with the sacrament of Holy Order. Many theologians think they see an allusion to confirmation in the following passage : " He that confirmeth us with you in Christ and that hath anointed us is God, who also hath sealed us and given the pledge of the Spirit in our hearts."[3]

The argument founded on this text is very uncertain. It can hardly be supported by the verbs to fortify or confirm (βεβαιῶν, qui confirmat), to seal (σφραγισάμενος, qui signavit), to anoint (χρίσας, qui unxit); for these terms were applied to confirmation only at a later date, and they have God for their subject, not the sacred minister. Moreover, it is not a question here of all the faithful, but of Paul and his companions, especially Sylvanus and Timothy ; and it is not clear how these last could attribute to a gift, which was common not only to them, but to all Christians, the courage necessary to the apostles for the worthy exercise of their ministry. The unction from which this divine strength is derived is their vocation to the apostolate itself ; and the seal which marks them with its imprint is seen in the operations of the Holy Spirit, by which their mission is authorized.

There is, however, a clear allusion to confirmation in a text in which the majority of theologians do not perceive it : " For as the body is one and hath many members, and all the members of the body, whereas they are many, yet are one body, so also is Christ; for in one Spirit were we all baptized into one body, whether Jews or Gentiles, whether

---

[1] Acts xix, 2.                    [2] Acts viii, 17, 18.

[3] 2 Cor. i, 21, 22 : Ὁ δὲ βεβαιῶν ἡμᾶς σὺν ὑμῖν καὶ χρίσας ἡμᾶς Θεός, ὁ καὶ σφραγισάμενος ἡμᾶς καὶ δοὺς τὸν ἀρραβῶνα τοῦ Πνεύματος ἐν ταῖς καρδίαις ἡμῶν.—The word βεβαιοῦν has in itself nothing relating to a sacramental rite (cf. Rom. xv, 8 ; 1 Cor. i, 6, 8 ; Col. ii, 7). The strength which God confers on the Apostles has for its effect to increase their adhesion, or perhaps their devotion and their fidelity to Christ (εἰς Χριστόν), and consequently aids them better to fulfil their ministry.—The verb χρίειν denotes everywhere else the anointing of the Messiah (Luke iv, 18, quotation from Is. lxi, 1 ; Heb. i, 9, alluding to Ps. xliv, 8; Acts iv, 27 and x, 38, alluding probably to one of these two texts). Here it is the anointing preparatory to the apostolic mission : Spiritus Domini unxit me, evangelizare pauperibus misit me.—As for σφραγίζειν, it does not necessarily denote the seal imprinted by the Holy Spirit in the sacrament of confirmation.

bond or free; and in one Spirit we have all been made to drink."[1] Four reasons make us think that this infusion of the Spirit denotes the sacrament of confirmation: the aorist (ἐποτίσθημεν) indicates neither a permanent state nor an action often repeated, but a transitory rite analogous and parallel to that of baptism.—Further, we cannot think of baptism itself, which has just been mentioned, nor of drinking the Eucharist, which cannot be recognized under this figure.—Paul's words describe the formation of the mystical body: by baptism the neophyte is grafted on to Christ, immersed in Christ, incorporated into Christ; then intervenes the Holy Spirit, the soul of the Church, in order to infuse a new life into it; the gift of the Holy Spirit completes the incorporation of baptism.—In the Old Testament as well as in the New, the mission of the Spirit of God is usually presented under the symbol of an outpouring, a rain, or an exhalation,[2] and can there be a more appropriate figure than this by which to designate the sacred rite which renews and perpetuates in the bosom of the Church the miracle of Pentecost?

### III—THE EUCHARIST

1. Paul's Formulas.  2. Allusions to Sacrifice.

1. If baptism gives birth to the mystical body, the Eucharist feeds it and makes it grow. St Paul presents the type of the two sacraments together. The Hebrews, he says, "were baptized in Moses, in the cloud and in the sea; and did all eat the same spiritual food, and all drank the same spiritual drink."[3] The manna and the water from the

---

[1] I Cor. xii, 13: καὶ γὰρ ἐν ἑνὶ Πνεύματι ἡμεῖς πάντες εἰς ἓν σῶμα ἐβαπτίσθημεν . . . καὶ πάντες ἓν Πνεῦμα ἐποτίσθημεν. The received Greek text has εἰς ἓν πνεῦμα (in unum Spiritum), a reading which the present Vulgate favours (in uno Spiritu). But the critics who possess most authority prefer the reading adopted by us, which is that of the principal Greek manuscripts, of a great number of the Fathers (Athanasius, Chrysostom, Ambrose, Augustine, etc.), of the Syriac, Coptic, Armenian, Ethiopian, Gothic, Italic, and even of the original Vulgate, to judge from the most ancient codices, such as Amiatinus (Omnes unum Spiritum potati sumus).—It could be more forcibly translated: "We were drenched with the same Spirit," or "We drank, we inhaled the same Spirit."

[2] Is. xii, 3; xxxii, 15; xliv, 3; Jer. ii, 13; Ezech. xlvii, 1; Zach. xii, 10; xiv, 8; Joel ii, 28, etc.—John vii, 39, 40; Acts ii, 17, 18, 33; Titus iii, 6, etc.

[3] I Cor. x, 1-2. The Israelites received a figurative baptism and participated in a figurative Eucharist (πνευματικὸν βρῶμα, πνευματικὸν πόμα). St Paul employs the general terms for food and drink, the better to indicate their relation to the Eucharistic elements. This food and this drink were spiritual, because they had a typical or spiritual meaning (x, 6: Ταῦτα δὲ τύποι ἡμῶν ἐγενήθησαν. Compare, for this interpretation of the word "spiritual," Apoc. xi, 8). They were also spiritual in another way, because they were not purely material, but miraculous, and because they came from the spiritual Rock (x, 4: πνευματικὸν ἔπιον πόμα· ἔπινον γὰρ ἐκ πνευματικῆς πέτρας. Note the γάρ, which gives the reason for the epithet πνευματικόν, and compare for this meaning I Pet. ii, 5).

rock are called *spiritual,* both because they were the result of a miracle and because they prefigured the two elements of the Eucharist, the food and drink of the man regenerated by baptism.

It is to a fortuitous combination of circumstances that we owe the teaching of Paul concerning the Eucharist. He had delivered it orally to the Corinthians, as to all his other catechumens, and would not have repeated it in writing but for the doubts of the new Christians in regard to meats offered to idols, and but for their irreverent conduct during the celebration of the *agape.* We can readily believe that his oral teaching was more developed, but it could hardly have been more precise. The Apostle first indicates to us the source of his information, Jesus Christ himself : " I have received from the Lord that which I delivered unto you."[1] In describing the institution of the Eucharist, he lays stress upon the circumstances of time—" the same night in which he was betrayed to his enemies," " after he had supped," " at the end of the [farewell] meal "—in order to fix the scene more perfectly in the minds of the neophytes, or rather in order to put it in direct connection with the death of the Lord Jesus.

The formula of the consecration of the bread could not be more clear. It would be not only obscure, but unintelligible and contradictory if the Saviour had said : " This bread is my body " ; for it is absolutely impossible that a thing should be and not be at the same time, and the difficulty would not be removed by including the body of Christ in ordinary bread, for it would still be untrue that the real bread *is* the real body of Christ. But Jesus speaks unequivocally : " This is my body, which [is] for you."[2] The subject of the phrase is the demonstrative pronoun " this "—that is to say, what you see before you, that which I indicate to you by a gesture, that which is designated still neither as ordinary bread nor as the body of Christ, but the meaning of which will be

---

[1] 1 Cor. xi, 23.

[2] 1 Cor. xi, 24 :

| | Luke xxii, 19: | Mark xxiv, 22: | Matt. xxvi, 26: |
|---|---|---|---|
| τοῦτο μού ἐστιν | τοῦτό ἐστιν | τοῦτό ἐστιν | τοῦτό ἐστιν |
| τὸ σῶμα | τὸ σῶμά μου | τὸ σῶμά μου. | τὸ σῶμά μου. |
| τὸ ὑπὲρ ὑμῶν. | τὸ ὑπὲρ ὑμῶν | | |
| | διδόμενον. | | |

The essential part of the formula is identical in the four texts. For the text of St Luke, from a critical point of view, *cf.* W. B. Frankland, *The Early Eucharist* (A.D. 30-180), London, 1902, pp. 115-119 (according to him the *long account* is indeed by St Luke, but does not belong to the first edition of the Gospel).—For the addition of κλώμενον in the passage of St Paul, an addition attested by numerous witnesses, but with many different readings (θρυπτόμενον, *frangitur, frangetur, traditur, tradetur, datur*), see Scrivener-Miller, *Introduction*[4], 1894, vol. ii, pp. 381-382. The various readings are a strong argument against the authenticity of κλώμενον. If it is retained, it will be necessary to understand it of the *eucharistic body,* comparing 1 Cor. x, 16.

determined at the end of the proposition, when something shall have been affirmed concerning it. The substantive verb, which serves as a copula, expresses as always the identity pure and simple between subject and predicate. It is a consolation to see to-day the Protestant and rationalistic exegetes agreeing with the Catholics to recognize such an elementary truth and to reject the biassed exegesis which translated "to be" by "to signify," contrary both to biblical and profane usage. Should the ambiguity be in the predicate? Ought the word "body" to be taken figuratively as a symbol of the body? The hypothesis is already unacceptable for the reason that it distorts without reason the natural meaning of the terms, but still more is its absurdity perceived, on substituting for the word "body" its pretended equivalent: "This is the symbol of my body, which symbol is for you. Whoever shall eat the bread and drink the chalice unworthily is guilty of the symbol of the body and of the symbol of the blood of the Lord." As to the identification of the eucharistic body with the Church, it is best to say nothing about it. Certain systems need no refutation, and they are pointed out only to show to what desperate solutions the abandonment of the only natural and legitimate meaning drives us.[1]

Taken by itself, independently of the allusions and circumstances which determine it, the other formula of consecration: "This chalice is the new covenant in my blood,"[2]

[1] Axel Andersen (*Das Abendmahl in den zwei ersten Jahrhunderten nach Christus*, Giessen, 1904) advances the theory (p. 4) that the *body* of Christ, here as elsewhere, signifies the Church, and (p. 6) that the death of Christ not being, in the eyes of Paul, a sacrifice, the blood of Christ (in Rom. iii, 25; Eph. i, 7, etc.) is not therefore true blood, but denotes simply his violent death.—After his work was finished, the author learned that the identification of Christ's body with the Church had been already proposed by Baur and adopted by Pfleiderer, Schmiedel, and especially by Hoffmann. The erudition of the professor of Christiania is not profound; he does not suspect that his "discovery" is as old as Erasmus and Zwingli.

[2]

| 1 Cor. xi, 25: | Luke xxii, 20: | Mark iv, 24: | Matt. xxvi, 27: |
|---|---|---|---|
| τοῦτο τὸ ποτήριον | τοῦτο τὸ ποτήριον | τοῦτό ἐστιν | τοῦτο γάρ ἐστιν |
| ἡ καινὴ διαθήκη ἐστὶν | ἡ καινὴ διαθήκη | τὸ αἷμά μου | τὸ αἷμά μου |
| ἐν τῷ ἐμῷ αἵματι. | ἐν τῷ αἵματί μου τὸ ὑπὲρ ὑμῶν ἐκχυννόμενον. | τῆς διαθήκης τὸ ἐκχυννόμενον ὑπὲρ πολλῶν. | τῆς διαθήκης τὸ περὶ πολλῶν ἐκχυννόμενον εἰς ἄφεσιν ἁμαρτιῶν. |

For the import of these texts from the point of view of the Eucharistic sacrifice, *cf.* Franzelin, *De eucharistiae sacramento et sacrificio*, Rome, 1868, th. xi, pp. 335-341. On the traditional meaning of the Church in relation to the sacrifice of the altar, *cf.* Rauschen, *Eucharistie und Busssakrament in den ersten sechs Jahrhunderten der Kirche*, Freiburg i. B., 1908, pp. 46-69 (criticism of Wieland, *Mensa und Confessio*, Munich, 1906). Convenient review of the patristic testimony of the first two centuries in Frankland (*op. cit.*,

would offer obscurities. There are in it two metonymies, one of which takes the container for the contained, while the other takes the effect for the cause, the new covenant concluded in the blood of Christ for the blood of Christ itself which seals the new covenant. The first, however, is so commonly employed that " this chalice " awakens in the mind immediately the idea of a drink. Moreover, unless the vague demonstrative " this " were retained, the metonymical language would be obligatory. Jesus could not indeed say : " This wine is my blood " without uttering an error and imposing on the faith of his disciples an unintelligible equation. The second metonymy is a little less usual ; but it is explained when replaced in its context : the contents of a material cup not being able to be the covenant sealed in the blood, this must be the blood of the covenant.—Jesus Christ acts in the same way (ὡσαύτως) in both consecrations ; between the two acts there reigns a complete parallelism ; hence if, by virtue of the sacramental words, there is on the one hand the body of Christ, on the other hand, there will be his blood.—The manifest allusion to the account in Exodus leaves no more room for doubt. Moses sprinkling the people with the blood of the sacrifice, says : " Behold the blood of the covenant." The blood of the covenant and the covenant in the blood are, therefore, the same thing.

Assuredly in both formulas the word of the Son of God is creative. The truth announced is not anterior to the enunciation itself, as in ordinary affirmations ; it is the product of it. But Jesus Christ had accustomed his disciples to these miracles of his speech, and he who healed by a word, by saying " Your son is healed," or " You are freed from your infirmity," deserved the same credence, when, by an analogous formula, he conferred the promised gift of his body and his blood.

St Paul adds to the double consecration the command given by Christ to the apostles to perpetuate the Eucharist till the end of time.[1] St Luke does not mention it until after

pp. 3-29) ; but the author, an Anglican, does not admit the reality of the Eucharistic sacrifice : " In the Eucharist is an oblation of God's natural gifts, with offerings of thanks and praise upon an heavenly altar ; but the divine Gifts are received, not offered " (p. 111).

[1] The rationalistic critics who deny that the Eucharist was instituted by Jesus Christ do not dispute the fact that the primitive Church and the Apostles themselves believed in this institution. But they say that the Apostles misunderstood the meaning of the words of Jesus. What, then, did Jesus mean ? According to Spitta (Zur Geschichte und Litteratur des Urchristentums, Leipzig, 1893, vol. i, pp. 207-337 : Die urchristl. Traditionen über Ursprung und Sinn des Abendmahls), Jesus was so obsessed by his eschatological ideas that he thought he was present at a messianic feast, and invited his disciples to eat and drink at this feast (p. 333).—A. Jülicher (Zur Geschichte der Abendmahlsfeier in der ältesten Kirche in the Theolog. Abhandlungen in honour of Weizsäcker, Freiburg i. B., 1892, pp. 215-250)

the consecration of the bread, and the other two Synoptists pass it over in silence, considering it perhaps superfluous on account of the living tradition of the Church.

2. By reason of the divine command and the explanation furnished by the Apostle, the Eucharist became a commemorative rite : " Do this in remembrance of me. For as often as you shall eat this bread and drink this chalice, you shall show the death of the Lord until he come." But the eucharistic rite is not a simple commemoration of the sacrifice of the cross; it is itself a commemorative sacrifice. St Paul does not say : " This chalice is commemorative of the new covenant concluded on Calvary in my blood "; he says : " This chalice is itself the covenant "; in other words : " The blood contained in this cup seals the covenant." It is, therefore, the blood of a victim; and the rite which sheds it mystically will have the character of a sacrifice. This appears still more clearly from the parallel passage of St Luke : " This chalice is the new covenant in my blood, which is shed for you." St Luke does not say that the blood *will be* shed at the moment of the Passion : he says that the blood *is* shed now, at the hour of the accomplishment of the eucharistic rite; he even says still more forcibly that the chalice—that is to say, the blood contained in it—is shed for men. Taken separately, the formula of the consecration of the bread would not suggest the idea of sacrifice : " This is my body, which is for you." One could understand here the words : " which is given you in nourishment," instead of " which is immolated for you." And the more explicit text of St Luke would not wholly remove the doubt : " This is my body which is given (or delivered) for you." It is true, we might ask whether a body given in nourishment is not, by that very fact, an immolated body, and especially

---

believes that Jesus simply intended to make a parable or a concise comparison, as when he said : " I am the Vine." Filled with the thought of his approaching death, Jesus *compared* the bread to his body about to be tortured and the wine to his blood about to be shed. His words had no deeper significance and the Eucharist is due only to a misunderstanding.—J. Hoffmann (*Das Abendmahl im Urchristentum*, Berlin, 1903) affirms that the Eucharist originated in the repasts taken in common by the first disciples, awaiting together the *parousia* of the Lord, which was regarded as imminent. As the *parousia* became more and more delayed, they remembered the tragic ending of Jesus, and finally came to associate the daily meal with the recollection of the Last Supper. On that day the Eucharist was instituted. Subsequently the idea of the redemptive death became connected with it.—Andersen takes a step further in the path of paradox (*Das Abendmahl*, etc.). The dogmatic evolution of the Eucharist, he thinks, has followed this ascending route : (A) *A religious repast*, the centre of which was, at first, God, and then, insensibly (in the apostolic era), Christ.—(B) *Eating the flesh of Christ* (from the time of St Justin).—(C) *Sacrifice of the flesh of Christ* (from the time of St Cyprian). Where will the fancy of the historians of dogma end ?

whether the words "given for you" really signify "given in nourishment," and whether they do not signify, as everywhere else, the act by which Christ offers himself as a victim. But a certain obscurity would always remain, even apart from the parallelism.

Another passage of St Paul furnishes us with additional light. Wishing to show to the Corinthians that participating in idolatrous banquets is forbidden, whatever intention one may bring to them, because it is a scandal, a danger, and a formal act of idolatry, the Apostle appeals to their consciences: "I speak as to wise men: judge ye yourselves what I say. The chalice of benediction which we bless, is it not the communion of the blood of Christ? And the bread which we break, is it not the communion of the body of Christ? Because there is one bread, we, being many, are one body, for we partake of that one bread. Behold Israel according to the flesh. Are not they that eat of the sacrifices partakers of the altar?" And St Paul, deducing a code of morality from this doctrine, concludes in these words: "The things which the heathens sacrifice, they sacrifice to devils and not to God. I would not that you should be made partakers with devils. You cannot drink the cup of the Lord and the cup of devils; you cannot be partakers of the table of the Lord and of the table of devils."[1] If the arguments of the Apostle are not fallacious, the eucharistic communion is for Christians what the eating of food sacrificed to idols was for the Gentiles and what the sacred repast was for the Jews. Now the sacred banquet has a religious significance: it constitutes an act of worship in that it is a complement of the sacrifice and unites the faithful with the sacrificing priest, with the altar where the victim was immolated and with the victim itself.

## IV—HOLY ORDER

The rite of the inauguration of the sacred ministers of the Church was always and everywhere the laying on of hands. Indeterminate in itself, this rite receives its precise signification from the circumstances which surround it or from the words which accompany it. We see in Scripture that hands are laid on, by the superior to bless, by the worker of miracles to heal, by the apostles to confer the Holy Ghost, and by those endowed with ecclesiastical authority to communicate the power with which they are invested.[2] The idea

---

[1] 1 Cor. x, 15-21. *Cf.* Vol. I, pp. 117, 118.

[2] In the New Testament the only example of a benediction through the laying on of hands is Matt. xix, 13. Everywhere else hands are laid on either to restore health or life (Matt. ix, 18 ; Mark v, 23 ; xvi,18 ; Luke iv, 40 ; Acts ix, 12, 17 ; xxviii, 8), or to confer the Holy Ghost or the power of Order ( Acts vi, 6 ; viii, 17 ; xix, 6 ; 1 Tim. iv, 14 ; 2 Tim. i, 6 ; Heb. vi, 2).

common to these four modes is the transmission of a spiritual gift, a supernatural favour, or a sacred power.

All the faithful had concurred in the election of the seven Hellenist deacons, but it was the apostles only who laid their hands upon them. It was a question of rendering them fit for a sacred function of a similar nature, for the celebration of the *agape* was still closely associated with the Eucharist. Hence care had been taken that the candidates should be filled with the Holy Spirit, and the laying on of hands had been performed amid public prayers; the ceremony being finished, the Seven, besides the care of the tables, had assumed the ministry of preaching and the administration of baptism, but without claiming to confer the Holy Spirit, which was an act exclusively reserved for the apostles. Their institution had had a religious character, and their power was of the spiritual order, although remaining subordinate.[1]

The laying on of hands was used also for the intermediate degree of the priesthood. When Paul writes to Timothy: "Lay not hands lightly upon any man,"[2] he speaks particularly of *elders*, in the ecclesiastical sense, and not of men advanced in age.

Finally, the same rite—if we exclude the words or prayers which accompanied it—served equally for the higher grade of the hierarchy; and here the texts are a little more explicit. We can hardly resist the impression that the laying on of hands, described in Acts xiii, had for its object to transmit to Barnabas and Saul the supreme power of Orders. A simple farewell benediction would not have been surrounded with so much solemnity, preceded by fasts and accomplished during the liturgy, by the command of the Holy Spirit. The missionaries are specially designated for the conversion of the Gentiles — that is to say, for the foundation of new churches in which the power of Orders is indispensable to them. In fact, immediately after, we see them appointing *elders* ($\pi\rho\epsilon\sigma\beta\upsilon\tau\acute{\epsilon}\rho\upsilon\varsigma$) in the cities where they have established Christian communities. Probably no one would have understood the passage in the Acts otherwise had it not been for the difficulty of finding a suitable minister in Antioch. If Barnabas, who was, according to all appearances, the principal person in that church, was not a bishop, how can we suppose that the other prophets and teachers named after him were so rather than he? On the other hand, St Luke does not mention the presence of the apostles in Antioch in this episode. It is true, it can be said that he had no need to mention it, if it was recognized, as everything leads us to believe, that a power is never conferred except by the one who possesses it. Even if it were a question here of a simple benediction, the difficulty would

---

[1] Acts ii, 1-6    [2] I Tim. v, 22.

still remain, since a benediction descends from a superior and does not proceed from inferiors or from equals.

With the consecration of Timothy by St Paul we are on firmer ground. The Apostle writes to his disciple : " Neglect not the grace (χάρισμα) that is in thee, which was given thee by prophecy (or on account of prophecies), with the imposition of the hands of the college of presbyters.—I admonish thee that thou stir up the grace of God (χάρισμα), which is in thee by the imposition of my hands."[1]  We have here an

[1] 1 Tim. iv, 16 :

Μὴ ἀμέλει τοῦ χαρίσματος

ὃ ἐδόθη σοι διὰ προφητείας
μετὰ ἐπιθέσεως τῶν χειρῶν τοῦ πρεσβυτερίου.

2 Tim. i, 6, 7:

Ἀναμιμνήσκω σε ἀναζωπυρεῖν τὸ χάρισμα τοῦ Θεοῦ,
ὅ ἐστιν ἐν σοὶ
διὰ τῆς ἐπιθέσεως τῶν χειρῶν μου.
Οὐ γὰρ ἔδωκεν ἡμῖν ὁ Θεός, κτλ.

According to these two texts, compared together : (A) Timothy *actually possesses* a charisma ( ὅ ἐστιν ἐν σοί) *which has been given him previously* once for all (ὃ ἐδόθη σοι) ; (B) in view of or *on account of the prophecies* which designated him for this office (διὰ προφητείας); (C) *by the laying on of the hands* of the Apostle (διὰ τῆς ἐπιθέσεως τῶν χειρῶν μου) ; (D) *with the co-operation of* the presbyters who had also imposed hands (μετὰ ἐπιθέσεως τῶν χειρῶν τοῦ πρεσβυτερίου).

(A) The meaning of *charisma* is explained by 2 Tim. i, 7 : *Non enim dedit nobis Deus spiritum timoris ; sed virtutis et dilectionis et sobrietatis.*  The spirit of power, of love and of moderation—such is the *charisma* which the disciple is to *stir up* in the dangerous combination of circumstances in which he and his master find themselves.  This *charisma* is dormant but not dead, for it is the principle of the grace of a calling ; it is, therefore, indestructible, like that grace itself.

(B) The clause διὰ προφητείας is ambiguous. If προφητείας is regarded as the accusative plural—which appears more satisfactory from every point of view—the meaning will be " on account of the prophecies "—that is to say, the utterances concerning him made by the faithful endowed with the *charisma of prophecy.  Cf.* 1 Tim. i, 18 : *Commendo tibi, secundum praecedentes in te* prophetias, *ut milites in illis militiam bonam.*  If it be taken in the genitive singular, as the Vulgate has it, prophecy (that is to say, the prophetic utterance, as above, or the prophetic *charisma* possessed by Timothy) would be the determining, and so to speak the moral, cause (διά) of the promotion of Timothy.

(C) The clause διὰ τῆς ἐπιθέσεως τῶν χειρῶν μου indicates without any ambiguity the instrumental cause (physical or moral according to the classification) of the production of the special *charisma ;* this is the sacramental rite of the laying on of hands.

(D) Finally, the use of the preposition μετά instead of διά leads us not to attribute to the imposition of hands on the part of the presbyterate the same value as to the laying on of Paul's hands ; the latter is active and produces the effect (διά), while the former is only concomitant (μετά) ; one is essential to the rite, the other enhances its brilliancy.

The Council of Trent (*Sess.* xxiii, cap. 3) quotes 2 Tim. i, 6 as an indubitable proof that Holy Order is a sacrament.  Timothy had received this Order in all its fulness, since he had the power of laying on hands in his turn (1 Tim. v, 22).  But one ought not to deduce from our texts that the episcopal consecration, *as distinct from sacerdotal ordination*, is a sacrament.  It is, indeed, very probable that all the powers of Order were conferred on Timothy by *one single* imposition of hands.  Nothing is opposed to this in theory, as Bellarmine recognizes, and Petavius thinks that such was the practice of the early Church.

external rite—the laying on of hands—and an internal grace produced by the rite. What is this grace, this *charisma?* Evidently it is not the purely gratuitous gift which the Holy Spirit bestows or withdraws at will, which is not permanent, and which no one has the right to call into being or revive. Nor is it, as some think, the episcopal character, the power of Order, for this has no need of being revived, since it is incapable of diminution or decline. This *charisma* is rather the supernatural fitness received for the worthy exercise of a sacred ministry; something like what we call the grace of a calling—that is to say, the totality of spiritual gifts and the right to the actual graces which the duties of the episcopate require. Although associated with the character and power of Holy Order, it is nevertheless distinct from them. While the character is indelible and the power inalienable, this *charisma* may become enfeebled through a want of effort or of vigilance; if it does not reach the point of extinction, it needs at least to be rekindled. St Paul indicates very plainly the nature of this *charisma,* when he adds : " For God hath not given us the spirit of fear, but [a spirit] of power, and of love, and of sobriety." This *charisma* brings with it, therefore, an increase of internal grace, together with the actual graces made necessary by the episcopal office. Now all this is conferred " by (διὰ) the laying on of the hands " of the Apostle, yet not without the co-operation and assistance (μετὰ) of the presbyteral college of Ephesus if, as is probable, it is at Ephesus that the consecration took place.

We have, therefore, in the ordination of Timothy, the three principal elements of what the Church to-day calls a sacrament : first, an external rite—the laying on of hands ; then a permanent grace(χάρισμα)—the source (produced by this rite) of various graces of condition (διά) ; and lastly, an internal grace corresponding to the symbol of the external rite, which symbol is determined in its signification by a number of circumstances, such as the prophetic designation and the mission to which Timothy was destined. Divine institution, with its direct or indirect promulgation by Jesus Christ, acts, of course, when it is a question of imparting grace to a rite.

## V—MARRIAGE

To the quotation from Genesis : " The man shall leave his father and mother, and shall cleave to his wife, and they two shall be one flesh," St Paul adds the following reflection : " This is a great mystery (μυστήριον) ; but I speak of Christ and the Church."[1] According to the Council of Trent, the

---

[1] Eph. v, 32 : Τὸ μυστήριον τοῦτο μέγα ἐστίν, ἐγὼ δὲ λέγω εἰς Χριστὸν καὶ εἰς τὴν ἐκκλησίαν. What is the mystery—that is, the *hidden sense*—indicated by the Apostle ? One of three things : either the mystery is the

Sacrament of marriage is *suggested* in this text.[1]  That is the most appropriate word.  In the absence of an express affirmation, there is here an indication which the theologian must take into account.

Not that nothing can be deduced from the Latin translation : *Sacramentum hoc magnum est.*  The biblical meaning of *sacramentum* (μυστήριον) is not sacrament.  It is either a secret design of God regarding the salvation of men or a word or deed containing a symbolical signification.  The reasoning, based upon the text of the Apostle, to prove that marriage is a real sacrament, is much more complex, and, whatever pains may be taken to support it, there will always remain in it some weak points.  That the conjugal union has a sacred character—that it is a sacrament in the widest signification of the word—no one disputes.  In the opinion of St Paul the primitive institution of marriage or, what amounts to nearly the same thing, the story of Genesis relating to this institution, is a great mystery which symbolizes the union of Christ and his Church, and is consequently the sign of something eminently holy : *Sacramentum hoc magnum est, id est sacrae rei signum, scilicet conjunctionis Christi et Ecclesiae,* says St Thomas.  If here we have a real type, marriage would be on this ground a sacrament as rightfully as circumcision and the sacrifices of the ancient Law.  We are still very far from the visible sign instituted by Jesus Christ to produce the grace which it signifies.  The efficacious production of the grace once proved, the divine institution would certainly be naturally deduced from the fact that it is the prerogative of God alone to add grace to an external rite ; and the promulgation by Christ would follow as a corollary, since Jesus Christ is the only and universal mediator of the new covenant.  Thenceforth the principal question is to know if our text allows us to conclude that a Christian marriage, as soon as contracted, confers sanctifying grace.  No Catholic theologian has maintained the affirmative of this question with more scholastic subtlety and scriptural erudition than Father Palmieri.  His reasoning can be summed up as follows.  The figurative rites of the new law are by their nature practical and not speculative—that is to say, they produce the grace which they signify ; now Christian marriage, according to St Paul

---

text of Genesis itself, as typical ; or it is marriage, as figurative according to its primitive institution ; or it is the union of Christ and the Church.  The last hypothesis cannot stand, for it implies a tiresome tautology.  This mystery—namely, the union of Christ and the Church—is great: I mean relatively to Christ and the Church.  In reality the other two hypotheses form only one ; for whether it be the biblical text or the thing expressed by the text, which constitutes the mystery, matters little.

[1] *Sess.* xxiv, *Paulus innuit.*

typifies the union of Christ and his Church; hence it produces the grace signified by this union. If the Christian marriage *in facto esse* imposes supernatural obligations on the parties to it, it necessarily confers *in fieri* an internal grace proportionate to these obligations.

It will be objected that the symbol of the mysterious hymen of Christ and his Church is marriage in itself, not Christian marriage; and therefore that, if the preceding argument proved anything, it would be that every marriage is a sacrament. But this objection can be met. In the first place, Christian marriage—St Paul here speaks only of this because he is addressing the faithful exclusively—imposes on the husband and wife special duties, requiring the assistance of special graces. Christian consorts, in their mutual relations, must model themselves after Christ and his Church; on the one side respectful submission to the point of sacrifice, on the other, devoted love till death. This source of supernatural obligations presupposes a corresponding source of supernatural graces; and St Paul argues well, in presenting this hypothesis, when he adjures them to realize in their own lives the marriage of the Church and Christ, of which their own union is the emblem. In the second place, every marriage can indeed be a sign, yet for all that may not be an efficacious sign, as Christian marriage is. The rites of the new Law are commemorative, not prophetic; they do not look towards a potential future, but towards the past, which they revive; they are practical, not speculative; they do not merely represent grace, but produce it. If circumcision had been maintained by Jesus Christ as a sign of his Covenant with humanity, there is every reason to believe that it would have become a sacrament in the strict sense of the word. If its aim and significance had been changed, and if it had been turned towards the past and not towards the future, it would have been capable of producing effectively the grace of the Covenant; but, having been left to itself, as an inferior and uncouth rite, it lost all its value after the death of Christ. Similarly marriage, which was formerly the type of the union of Christ and his Church, changes its signification when this union is consummated on Golgotha; from being prophetic, it becomes commemorative; from being speculative, it becomes practical; from being inert, it becomes efficacious.

Nevertheless, for the argument drawn from our text to be decisive, it would be necessary to prove: that the symbolism indicated by St Paul is not a creation of his mind or a mystical relation imagined by him—*ego autem dico*—but that it really exists *a parte rei* from the fact of a positive act of will on the part of God; that this symbol is not a simple prophetic type, but a practical and commemorative sign; that the grace attached to marriage does not come merely

from the new obligations inherent in the conjugal state—
as happens, for example, in the religious state—but that it is
conferred *instrumentally* by the very rite of the matrimonial
contract *in fieri*. Now all this is *suggested* rather than
affirmed in the Apostle's words. When we know beforehand that marriage is a sacrament, we can find in this text a
more or less clear allusion to the sacramental rite; otherwise
we should perhaps be wiser not to look for it there.

# CHAPTER III

## THE CHURCH

### I—THE PAULINE CONCEPTION OF THE CHURCH

1. The Names of the Church.  2. The Church of God.
3. Notes of the Church.

1. THE chosen race was sometimes represented as the *vineyard* guarded and cultivated by God with jealous care, as in the famous allegory of Isaias, to which the Synoptists refer,[1] some-times as the vine transplanted into Canaan and susceptible of unlimited growth:

> The shadow of it covered the hills,
> And the branches thereof were as the cedars of God;
> It stretched forth its branches unto the sea
> And its boughs unto the river.[2]

St John gives a different turn to this symbol so dear to the prophets;[3] St Paul substitutes for it the olive-tree.[4] Paul indeed conceives of baptism as a graft which, grafting us on Christ, makes us draw up the divine sap; it was natural, therefore, for him to conceive of the Church under the figure of an olive-tree plunging its roots into the depths of the ancient system and growing infinitely by the addition of new branches. The allegory is clear: the " sacred root and blessed trunk" are the patriarchs; the olive-tree is the Church, growing out of the Synagogue by a kind of vital

---

[1] Is. v, 2-7.  *Cf.* Matt. xxi, 28-41 ; Mark xii, 1-9 ; Luke xx, 9-16.  The idea most similar to this in St Paul is I Cor. iii, 9 : *Dei agricultura.*

[2] Ps. lxxix, 11, 12.  The vine was the queen of plants (Judges ix, 12). Pliny said of the vine : *Nullo fine crescit.*

[3] Os. x, 1 ; Jer. ii, 21 ; Is. xxvii, 3-6 ; Cant. i, 6 ; viii, 12, etc.  In St John (xv, 1-5) it is no longer Israel that is the vine, but the epithet " true " shows the allusion to the old allegory.

[4] Rom. xi, 16-24.  The new symbol adopted by St Paul can be justified by Jer. xi, 16 ; Os. xiv, 7-9.  While the vine is propagated by suckers and shoots, the wild olive is grafted with branches from the cultivated olive. St Paul describes the reverse procedure, as Origen has remarked in his commentary (Rufinus trans.) : *Sed nec hoc quidem lateat nos in hoc loco, quod non eo ordine Apostolus olivae et oleastri similitudinem posuit quo apud agricolas habetur.  Illi enim magis olivam oleastro inserere et non olivae oleastrum solent ; Paulus vero apostolica anctoritate ordine commutato res magis causis quam causas rebus aptavit.*  It is therefore useless to collect in antiquity examples of the proceeding described by St Paul.  However, see Ramsay, *The olive-tree and the wild-olive,* in the *Expositor,* 6th series vol. xi, 1905, pp. 16-34, 152-160.

process; the boughs are the members of the Church, some (the Christians of Jewish extraction) having come naturally upon the true olive, the others (the Gentile Christians) grafted from the wild stock.   It is unbelief that breaks off the former; it is faith that engrafts the latter; but the broken branches always retain the hope of being again restored, and the grafted boughs must always fear being rejected in their turn.

Israel was also represented as the *house,* the *kingdom,* and the *people* of Jehovah; Jehovah was their father, king, and God.   The Church, the heir of the Synagogue, will also be all this pre-eminently.   The starting-point of the metaphor " House of Jehovah " seems to be the idea of a family rather than a house, although the thought of a building appears clearly in some passages.[1]   The Apostle rarely applies to the Church militant the notion of the Jewish theocracy, for he generally gives the " kingdom of God " an eschatological meaning.[2]   Nor does he call it " the people of God," unless it be in reminiscences of the Old Testament.[3]

It was the great honour of the holy nation to be the *daughter* and *spouse* of Jehovah.   But, in passing over into the new order of things, the title of child changes its character; from being collective, as it had been, it becomes individual; thenceforth it is no more the Church which is the daughter of God; it is the children of the Church who possess the adoptive sonship, personally.[4]   The name of spouse ought naturally to have followed a similar evolution.   But this symbol of marriage which plays so great a role in the prophets[5] finds little room in the New Testament.   St John and St Paul remember it, the former when describing the marriage of the Lamb,[6] the latter when he calls marriage a great mystery " in respect to Christ and his Church,"[7] and

---

[1] Num. xii, 7; Os. viii, 1; Jer. xii, 7.   *Cf.* Heb. iii, 6: *Christus tanquam filius in domo sua, quae domus sumus nos.*   The *domestici* (οἰκεῖοι) *fidei* (Gal. vi, 10) and the *domestici Dei* (Eph. ii, 19) belong to the same order of ideas.   This last text offers a curious example of the gradual passage from the idea of a family (verse 19) to that of a building (with foundations and corner-stone, verses 20-21) and of a temple (verse 22) of which the faithful are the living stones (συνοικοδομεῖσθε).   The Christians are the temple of God because God dwells within them (2 Cor. vi, 16), but this habitation of God suggests the idea of a material construction which is built and can be destroyed (1 Cor. iii, 9-17).

[2] On the kingdom of God, see pp. 376-81.

[3] 2 Cor. vi, 16, quoting Lev. xxi, 11, 12, with a possible allusion to Ezech. xxxvii, 27.   *Cf.* Rom. ix, 25, 26, quoting Os. ii, 25 and i, 10; Titus ii, 14, alluding to Ex. xix, 5.

[4] Rom. viii, 14: *Quicumque spiritu Dei aguntur ii sunt filii Dei.*   The adoptive sonship is the individual prerogative of Christians.   Rom. viii, 15-23; Gal. iv, 5; Eph. i, 5.   Instead of υἱὸς Θεοῦ, St Paul says also τέκνον, preferred by St John.

[5] Especially Osee.

[6] Apoc. xxi, 6-9; xxii, 17.

[7] Eph. v, 32.   *Cf.* pp. 271-2.

when he attributes to himself the functions and the feelings
of the bridesman entrusted with the duty of leading his
affianced bride to Christ.[1] But the prophets' idea of a
jealous God did not pass on to the evangelists; hence the
allegory of marriage did not follow its normal development,
which would have made of the individual soul the bride of
Christ. There are, however, in St Paul and the Gospel
allusions enough to justify the language of the mystical
writers.[2] The mystery of the incarnation was needed—a
God made man and a man made God, two natures infinitely
distinct yet joined without confusion in the unity of one and
the same Person—to give a faint idea of a union still more
intimate than that of husband and wife. The minds of men
were already prepared for it by the turn which the allegory
of the vine had taken in the mouth of the Saviour. In
promising the Eucharist, and after having instituted it, Jesus
had spoken of his union with communicants in terms which
implied an identity of operations, functions, and life. His
words laid the foundation of the doctrine of the mystical
body which St Paul took up, elaborated and studied under all
its aspects, finally making it the culminating point of his
moral system and the centre of his teaching.

The *body of Christ* and *the Church* are thenceforth the
most characteristic names of the spouse of Jesus Christ : the
former title belongs to her rightfully, the latter she inherits
partly from the Synagogue.

2. In the Old Testament two almost synonymous words
(*qāhāl* and *'edāh*) designated the religious assembly of the
chosen people under the invisible presidency of Jehovah represented by his mandatories. The Septuagint and the later translators—Aquila, Symmachus, and Theodotion—usually render
the first of these terms by ἐκκλησία, the second by συναγωγη.
But, at the time of the Gospel, συναγωγή signified the edifice
in which the Jews assembled on Sabbath days, and it appears
also to have been generally used for the meetings themselves. For the Christian community this was an imperative
reason for adopting the other term, and in order to distinguish itself from the Synagogue, it called itself Church. To
believe that this word was borrowed from the turbulent

---

[1] 2 Cor. xi, 2 : *Aemulor enim vos Dei aemulatione ; despondi enim vos
uni viro, virginem castam, exhibere Christo.* The Church of Corinth
collectively, is the spouse. Paul has betrothed it to Christ, in the quality
of bridesman, an intermediary entrusted in the East with matrimonial
negotiations. As such, he is jealous *with the jealousy* even of God, whom he
represents and whose sentiments he shares.

[2] Parable of the ten virgins awaiting the bridegroom (Matt. xxv, 1-10) ;
Jesus Christ compared to the bridegroom (νύμφιος, Matt. ix, 15 ; Mark ii, 19,
20 ; Luke v, 34, 35 ; John iii, 29) ; moreover, the texts of the Apocalypse cited
above.

assemblies of the Greek democracies is to sacrifice uselessly all the probabilities and all the positive data of history to the spirit of system.

By reason of its historical origin, this word had first to designate the Church universal, before being applied to individual churches; and this is indeed exactly what we maintain. Jesus Christ proposes to found upon Peter *his Church*, which is necessarily unique; St Luke also knows only one Church, in spite of the diversity of places and nations, which he sees on his travels; St Paul himself remembers how he had persecuted the *Church of God*, and when he identifies this Church with the body of Christ, or makes Christ its Head, he plainly excludes all plurality. To specify local churches, he will say, for example, " the church which is at Corinth," or, by derivation, " the church of the Thessalonians "; unless the Church, in the singular, is indicated by the context.[1] The Church is neither the aggregate of the believers, nor the sum total of the individual

---

[1] The word ἐκκλησία occurs in the New Testament 125 times (of these 63 times in St Paul and 23 times in the Acts). The Gospels do not contain it, except in Matt. xvi, 18 and xviii, 17 (*bis*). In St John, where it appears 23 times (20 times in the Apoc. in regard to the letters to the churches of Asia and three times in 3 John), its use has nothing remarkable in it. It is found once in the Epistle of James (v, 14 : *Infirmatur quis in vobis ? Inducat presbyteros Ecclesiae*) ; twice in Hebrews, but only in a quotation from the Old Testament (ii, 12), and in an allusion to the ancient order of things (xii, 23). It is, therefore, hardly anywhere except in the Acts and St Paul that its significance can be studied.

The word " church " enjoys, in the Acts, a great variety of meanings. It is (*a*) the profane assembly of the Greek cities (classic sense, Acts xix, 39, 41); (*b*) the people of Israel (in Stephen's speech, vii, 38) ; (*c*) the Christian assembly (xiv, 27 ; xv, 3, 4, 22) ; (*d*) a particular church (xi, 22, 26 ; xiii, 1 ; xiv, 23 ; xviii, 22 ; xx, 17), the churches (xv, 41 ; xvi, 5); (*e*) the Church (v, 11 ; viii, 1, 3 ; ix, 31 ; xii, 1, 5 ; xix, 32) or the Church of God (xx, 28) ; but this last text, which recalls Paul's language, is in fact taken from a speech of St Paul.

In St Paul the word " church " has become technical and is used only of the Christian Church. It can signify the universal Church or a particular church ; sometimes, exceptionally, the assembled church. (*a*) The universal Church is called simply the *Church*, especially in the Epistles of the captivity (Phil. iii, 6 ; Col. i, 18, 24 ; Eph. i, 22 ; iii, 10, 21 ; v, 23, 24, 25, 26, 27, 29, 32 ; 1 Cor. xii, 28 ; 1 Tim. v, 16) or the Church of God (Gal. i, 13 ; 1 Cor. x, 32 ; xv, 9 ; 1 Tim. iii, 5, 15).—(*b*) The local church is designated by the context or by the mention of the place : the *church which is at* (Rom. xvi, 1 ; 1 Cor. i, 2 ; 2 Cor. i, 1), the *church which is in* (a private house, Rom. xvi, 5 ; 1 Cor. xvi, 19 ; Col. iv, 15 ; Philem. 2), more rarely the *church of* (Col. iv, 16 ; 1 Thess. i, 1 ; 2 Thess. i, 1).—(*c*) The plural is used to signify the totality of the churches, either absolutely (Rom. xvi, 16 ; 1 Cor. vii, 17 ; xi, 16, 22 ; xiv, 33 ; 2 Thess. i, 4), or with a restriction expressed or implied (Rom. xvi, 4 ; 1 Cor. xvi, 1 ; 2 Cor. viii, 1, etc.) ; also *every church* (1 Cor. iv, 17), *no church* (Phil. iv, 15).—(*d*) In certain cases ἐκκλησία, again approaching its original sense, denotes the *church actually assembled*, the religious meeting of the faithful, 1 Cor. xiv, 31-35 : *Mulieres in Ecclesia taceant. . . . Turpe est enim mulieri loqui in Ecclesia. Cf.* 1 Cor. xi, 18 : συνερχομένων ὑμῶν ἐν ἐκκλησίᾳ. This is no question of the sacred building.

communities, but a moral being to which unity is essential. " Not only is the part in the whole, but the whole is in the part." [1] This is why St Paul addresses " the Church of God which is at Corinth " ; in fact, whether it is at Corinth, at Ephesus, or elsewhere, it is always the Church; and it is always the Church of God, since the Church is essentially one. This is also why the Apostle calls a particular church the temple of the Holy Ghost and the bride of Christ, because that particular church is only an extension of the universal church, and would keep the name of church only by an abuse of language if it were separated from the one and only Church.

3. The metaphors which serve to designate the Church well indicate its characteristics and what we should call to-day its notes. As the mystical body of Christ, the Church is *one;* as being his bride, it is *holy;* as the temple of God, it has for its foundation the *apostles;* as the kingdom of heaven, it is *Catholic* or universal. But Paul does not make it a point to be constant in the use of his metaphors; he passes continually from one to the other; and this mixture of different figures would engender some confusion, if we interpreted them with the strictness of a purist. Let us rapidly survey these four characteristics of unity, catholicity, apostolicity, and holiness, without going outside of the Epistle to the Ephesians where these traits are especially marked. [2]

Our common incorporation into Christ is the great principle of unity. To one single head belongs one body; otherwise we have a monstrosity. As there is only one natural Christ, it is impossible that there should be more than one mystical Christ.

> Be careful to keep the unity of the Spirit in the bond of peace. One body and one spirit ; as you are called in one hope of your calling ; one Lord, one faith, one baptism ; one God and Father of all, who is above all, and through all, and in us all. [3]

---

[1] The formula is Harnack's (*Entstehung und Entwickelung der Kirchenverfassung*, etc., Leipzig, 1910, p. 36). A little later (p. 37): *Sie* (*die Kirche*) *ist also eine himmlische Grösse, d.h. im Grunde nicht Einzelgemeinde, sondern Erscheinung des Ganzen in dem Teil.* Cremer (*Biblischtheol. Wörterbuch*[9], 1902, pp. 548-550) shows that the notion of the universal Church preceded that of the local church.

[2] *Cf.* Méritan, *L'ecclésiologie de l'ép. aux Ephésiens* (*Rev. bibl.*, 1898, pp. 343-369). In this article, written in regard to two Anglican works (Ch. Gore, *The Epistle to the Ephesians*, London, 1898, and Hort, *The Christian Ecclesia*, London, 1897), the author studies only the two notes of unity and catholicity.

[3] Eph. iv, 3-6: Σπουδάζοντες τηρεῖν τὴν ἑνότητα τοῦ πνεύματος ἐν τῷ συνδέσμῳ τῆς εἰρήνης·

ἓν σῶμα,

καὶ ἓν Πνεῦμα,

Seven elements—three intrinsic, three external, and one transcendental—enter into the constitution of the Church and bind its unity closely. The Church in its material principle is one, since it is one single body; it is one in its formal principle, since it is animated by one Spirit; it is one in its tendency and final cause, which is the glory of God and of his Christ through the happiness of the elect. It is one also by the authority which governs it; one by the common faith which serves it as a rule and an external standard; one by its efficient cause, the baptismal rite, which gives it existence and growth. St Paul sums up these six principles of union in one phrase: " You are all one in Christ Jesus."[1] There remains the seventh principle: " The God and Father of all men." It is not clear at first what relation can exist between the unity of God and the unity of the Church. But the Apostle elsewhere defines his thought. He informs us that all mankind is destined hereafter to form one family in the house of a common Father, one theocracy under the sceptre of one king.[2] From this point of view the unity of the Church is identified with both oneness and catholicity.

The word *Catholic,* quite common to profane writers from the time of Aristotle, is not in the Bible; but, after St Ignatius of Antioch, it serves to express a very biblical idea —the universality of the Church. This universality was announced by the prophets, and the apostles are charged to make it real by preaching the Gospel to the very limits of the world. Jewish exclusiveness has come to an end; the ancient theocracy has had its day; the régime of privilege has ceased: " Is God the God of the Jews only? Is he not also of the Gentiles?"[3] These despised Gentiles, strangers to the covenants, strangers to the promises, without Christ, without God, without hope, are now blended into one single national body together with the chosen people. No more strangers

---

καθὼς καὶ ἐκλήθητε ἐν μιᾷ ἐλπίδι τῆς κλήσεως ὑμῶν·
εἷς Κύριος,
μιά πίστις,
ἓν βάπτισμα·
εἷς Θεὸς καὶ πατὴρ πάντων, ὁ ἐπὶ πάντων καὶ διὰ πάντων καὶ ἐν πᾶσιν.

As usual Paul bases his moral teaching on dogma : he recommends his readers to maintain " the unity of the Spirit in the bond of peace," in consideration of the multiple unity which is of the essence of the Church. Our Epistle is the only one where this abstract word " unity " (ἑνότης) is employed.

[1] Gal. iii, 28 : πάντες γὰρ ὑμεῖς εἷς ἐστε ἐν Χ. ᾿Ι. The Apostle does not say ἕν (one thing) but εἷς (" one moral person ").

[2] The idea of a kingdom is not rare in the Epistles, and the same is true of the idea of a house; but the most explicit text, from the point of view which here concerns us, is the following passage in which the Christians are represented as one family whose members nothing can or ought to separate (Eph. ii, 14-22). All are συμπολῖται and οἰκεῖοι τοῦ Θεοῦ.

[3] Rom. iii, 29. *Cf.* x, 12, etc.

and foreigners; all are members of the Church, without distinction of origin; all are henceforth " fellow-citizens with the saints and the household of God."[1] The whole world is hereafter to form only one kingdom, one city, one house, of which God, with Christ his representative, will be the sole King, the sole Chief, the sole Father.

From the moment that it is certain that God extends his plans of redemption to all men and that he wishes to save them only by incorporating them into Christ, it follows of necessity that the Church is one in essence and universal in its destination. It is one and universal because it is the bride of Christ, including potentially the whole human race : because it is the body of Christ, in whom all those, who died in the first Adam, are to be born again ; and because it is the kingdom of God, the true Israel, succeeding to the ancient theocracy the particularism of which it destroys.

If St Paul stopped there, his teaching would have in it nothing very peculiar. Its originality consists in the fact that he derives these two attributes precisely from his notion of the Church. The Church, as he conceives it, is essentially one and universal, in other words, Catholic, because it eliminates everything that is opposed to unity and universality, by suppressing, from a religious point of view, all national, social, and individual differences, together with all inequalities of rights and privileges, by infusing into all its members a common current of life and action possessing inexhaustible energy. " You are all the children of God by faith in Christ Jesus. For as many of you as have been baptized in Christ have put on Christ. There is neither Jew nor Greek, there is neither bond nor free, there is neither male or female; for you are all one in Christ Jesus. [2]—There is neither Greek nor Jew, circumcision nor uncircumcision, Barbarian nor Scythian, bond nor free; but Christ is all and in all."[3] The differences of race, education, social rank, even sex, have disappeared. The quality of a child of God has effaced all those distinctions. No one, therefore, is now excluded from the new system, since Scythians, the most barbarous of barbarians, are admitted to it.

It was not enough to carry the message of salvation to the confines of the world[4] and to preach the Gospel to every creature under heaven ;[5] it was also necessary to remove the obstacles which would prevent the perfect blending of those heterogeneous elements. The most formidable of these obstacles was Jewish particularism. The Jewish theocracy, national by nature and expressly closed to certain foreign nations, did not aspire to be the religion of the whole world ; for, in ceasing to be national, it would lose its character of a

[1] Eph. ii, 19.     [2] Gal. iii, 26-28.     [3] Col. iii, 11.
[4] Rom. x, 18.     [5] Col. i, 23.

privileged institution. It could indeed increase by the addition of new adepts, but the humiliating inferiority in which it kept them and the degrees of difference which it left between them, not to mention the prohibitions which it pronounced, showed clearly that it did not at all aim at making the whole race one religious family. The barrier of the Law, which had formerly protected the monotheistic faith of the chosen people, kept it thereafter in a fatal isolation. Jesus Christ, in order to assure the unity and universality of his Church, had first of all to break down the wall of separation. He nailed, therefore, to the cross the ancient handwriting which resisted the fusion of the peoples of the earth;[1] he also opened wide the doors of the new order to the nations which until then had been afar off; and thus all men become by the same right fellow-citizens of one kingdom and members of one family; in a word, all, reconciled with one another and with God, are united in Christ in one mystical body.[2]

One and Catholic in essence, the Church must be also *apostolic*. Paul writes to the Ephesians: " You have been built upon the foundation of the apostles and prophets, Jesus Christ himself being the chief corner-stone."[3] The grammarian may interpret this foundation in four ways: the foundation upon which the apostles are built; the foundation on which the apostles build; the foundation which the apostles have built; and the foundation which is identified with the apostles. It is the apostles and prophets themselves who are the foundation of the Church. In this building, of which Christ is the corner-stone and the faithful the living stones, the foundation must be of the same nature and symbolize persons. Are the prophets named here those of the New Testament or those of the Old? Perhaps those of the New, because, since in Greek the same definite article includes the two words, it seems to place them in the same category, and because the prophets and apostles of the New Testament are generally grouped together without any possible misunderstanding. Nevertheless, the other hypothesis seems better. That the prophets of the New Testament are the foundations of the Church is not a very natural thought, and we find no trace of it elsewhere. The prophetic *charisma* of the New Testament *edifies,* but does not *lay a*

---

[1] Col. ii, 14.    [2] Eph. ii, 14-19. *Cf.* Col. i, 20-22.
[3] Eph. ii, 20: *Superaedificati super fundamentum Apostolorum et Prophetarum.* Were these the prophets of the Old Testament or of the New? In favour of the latter are urged: (*a*) the analogy more apparent than real (Eph. iii, 3; iv, 11); (*b*) the position of the words, the Apostles being named first; but nothing proves that St Paul intends to follow the order of time rather than the order of dignity; (*c*) the one article ($\tau\hat{\omega}\nu$), which seems to show that Apostles and prophets are placed in one category; but this reason is not decisive, for the Apostles of Christ and the prophets of the ancient Law can very well be considered under the same aspect of pillars of the Church.

*foundation.* On the contrary, we know how eager Paul is to establish the new system on the foundations of the old, and to represent the apostles to us as the heirs of the prophets.

The *sanctity* of the Church is so often proclaimed that it is superfluous to give a list of testimonies thereto. It is enough to recollect that Christians, by the fact of their baptism and as members of the mystical body, are *saints* by antonomasia ; that the Church is the bride of Christ, whose sanctity is bestowed upon it; and that Jesus gave his blood to purify and sanctify it that it might be " without blemish, holy, and spotless."

## II—THE LIFE OF THE CHURCH

1. The Mystical Christ. 2. The Mystical Body of Christ. 3. The Holy Spirit, Soul of the Church. 4. The Spirit and Christ. 5. The Communion of Saints. 6. *In Christ Jesus.*

1. In connection with the Epistle to the Ephesians we have studied the collective entity formed by the union of Christ and the Church, its analogy with the human body, its principal properties, and its relations with the mystery of redemption.[1] We must now follow this doctrine still further, deduce its consequences, and examine their import.

The Church is " the complement of Christ "[2] as the trunk is the complement of the head and as the limbs are the complement of the organism. The head is helpless without the body; the organism can function normally only if it possesses every one of its organs. So Christ without the Church would be an incomplete being; incomplete as a Redeemer, since the grace which he possesses for the purpose of bestowing it would remain inactive ; incomplete also as

---

[1] Vol. I, pp. 300-307. Especially on the *mystery*, Vol. II, pp. 4-11.

[2] Eph. i, 23 : ἥτις ἐστὶ τὸ σῶμα αὐτοῦ, τὸ πλήρωμα τοῦ τὰ πάντα ἐν πᾶσι πληρουμένου. We translate: " [The Church] which is his body, the complement of him who is completed in all in every way." The other possible translation, " him who perfects everything, who brings everything to its perfection," would also be in the spirit of Paul ; but the former commends itself for many reasons. First, the ancient versions in general authorize it. Moreover, the participle πληρούμενος appears never to have a transitive meaning, but always a passive or reflexive one. Finally, since the last part of the phrase explains in what way the Church is the complement of Christ, this gives more sequence and connection to the discourse. This clearer and more beautiful meaning is, moreover, favoured by the Fathers. St Jerome writes : *Sicut adimpletur imperator, si quotidie ejus augeatur exercitus et fiant novae provinciae et populorum multitudo succrescat ; ita et Dominus noster J. C. in eo quod sibi credunt omnia.* The thought and expression are taken from Origen : ἐννόει βασιλέα μὲν πληρούμενον τῆς βασιλείας καθ' ἕκαστον τῶν αὐξόντων τὴν βασιλείαν, κενούμενον δὲ ταύτης ἐν τοῖς ἀφισταμένοις, κτλ. St Chrysostom says more briefly, referring to the allegory of Paul : καὶ γὰρ πλήρωμα κεφαλῆς σῶμα, καὶ πλήρωμα σώματος κεφαλή. " The body completes the head and the head completes the body ; for the body is composed of all its parts and has need of each of them." St Thomas and others say the same with more or less clearness.

second Adam, because he is so only by his representative character; incomplete even as Christ, for Christ is also, in St Paul, a collective personality. Thus Christ " is completed in all in every way " : in the members of the sacred hierarchy as Head of the Church, and in the humble faithful as Saviour and Sanctifier.

On our text Origen makes a very penetrating reflection : " The Church is the body of Christ; but must we consider it as the trunk, distinct from the head and governed by it, or is not the entire Church of Christ rather the body of Christ animated by his divinity and filled with his Spirit, after the analogy of the human body, of which the head is itself a part? In the second case, what there is human in him will be an element of the body and what there is divine and vivifying will form, as it were, the divine presence, which animates the whole Church."[1] Apart from some expressions which require explanation, the question is thus very well stated. St Paul indeed looks upon Christ and the Church in two very different ways. Sometimes the Church is compared to the trunk in contrast to the head, and then the Church and Christ are the two integral parts of the mystical body. This is the case with all passages in which the person of Christ is likened to the head.[2]

But it is not always so. Often the Church and Christ are synonymous or are distinguished only by a scarcely perceptible shade of meaning; Christ and the Church are one complete whole; the Church is in Christ and Christ is in the Church; and for either of them may be substituted " the body of Christ " without any appreciable change of signification. This phenomenon takes place in three series of texts : first, when Christ is presented as a *collective personality,* as the true lineage of Abraham and " his [spiritual] seed, which is Christ,"[3] as the total sum of the members, the whole of whom constitute the body *" of Christ."*[4] Here we may apply the comment of St Augustine, who of all the Fathers has most frequently and most fittingly spoken of the mystical body : *Totus Christus caput et corpus est.*—Then in the expressions : *to put on Christ, to be baptized into Christ, to be grafted on to Christ:* " For all of you who have been baptized in Christ (εἰς Χριστόν) have put on Christ. . . ."[5] " If thou wert, contrary to Nature, grafted into the wild olive-tree, how much more shall they [that are the natural branches] be grafted into their own olive-tree?"[6]—Finally, in the characteristic formula *In Christo, in Christo Jesu.*[7]

---

[1] In Gregg, *Journal of Theol. Studies,* iii, 1902, p. 399.
[2] Eph. i, 22 ; iv, 15 ; v, 23 ; Col. ii, 19 (*cf.* Col. ii, 10 ; i, 18). See Vol. I, p. 302.
[3] Gal. iii, 16.        [4] 1 Cor. xii, 12.        [5] Gal. iii, 27.
[6] Rom. xi, 24.        [7] See Vol. I, p. 300, and below, pp. 297 *ff.*

2. The comparison of political societies with the organism of the human body is as old as the world, as is proved by the apologue, " signal among fables," related by Titus Livius, and put into verse by La Fontaine. To the plebeians who complained that the Senate decreed to itself all honours and arrogated to itself all privileges, Menenius Agrippa pointed out that the stomach, that voracious and idle organ, for which all the other members laboured arduously, is not the least necessary for the public good. St Paul employs the same comparison to make his readers understand that the diversity of spiritual gifts, far from being injurious to the union of the faithful, tends, on the contrary, to bind it closer.

> For as in one body we have many members, but all the members have not the same office ; so we, being many, are one body in Christ, and each one members one of another.[1]

Other societies can indeed assume metaphorically the name of body, because the tendency to the same end, the bonds of authority and dependence, and mutual rights and duties give them a moral unity which assimilates them to a living organism. But the union of the mystical body of Christ is of a higher nature. If it is called *mystical,* it is not in order to deny its real properties, but rather to distinguish it from the *physical* body, assumed by the Word in the body of Mary, in order to mark its relation to what Paul calls the *Mystery,* and, above·all, in order to express certain *mysterious* properties of the supernatural order which, because they cannot be verified by the experience of the senses, are none the less realities. There are in this marvellous composite first a real action of the head on each and all the members, then a reaction of the members upon one another through the communion of the saints, and lastly, a real interpenetration of the Holy Spirit, who vivifies the entire body and forms in it the most perfect of bonds—charity. What distinguishes the mystical body essentially from the moral entities, incorrectly named " bodies," is that it is endowed with life and that its life comes from within.

The text which has just been read merely outlines the doctrine. In it Paul proposes only to admonish each of the faithful to be content with his allowance of graces through the consideration that the spiritual blessings of the Church, to whichever member they individually belong, are, so to speak, common to all. He gives, however, to his union of

---

[1] Rom. xii, 4, 5. It is to justify the lesson of modesty which St Paul has just given : *sapere ad sobrietatem, et unicuique sicut Deus divisit mensuram fidei.* The *and* (*et*) is superfluous and is wanting in the Greek. In verse 5, οἱ πολλοί = *all, as many as we are;* τὸ καθ' εἷς (a late Greek expression) = *each one separately.*

solidarity a fuller and more complete expression in his first
Epistle to the Corinthians :

> For as the body is one and hath many members, and all the members
> of the body, whereas they are many, yet are one body ; so also is Christ.
> For in one Spirit were we all baptised into one body, whether Jews or
> Gentiles, whether bond or free ; and in one Spirit we have all been made
> to drink.
>
> For the body also is not one member, but many. If the foot should
> say : Because I am not the hand, I am not of the body, is it therefore not
> of the body ? And if the ear should say : Because I am not the eye,
> I am not of the body, is it therefore not of the body ? If the whole body
> were the eye, where would be the hearing ? If the whole were hearing,
> where would be the smelling ? But now God hath set the members,
> every one of them in the body, as it hath pleased him. If they were
> all one member, where would be the body ? But now there are many
> members indeed, yet one body.
>
> The eye cannot say to the hand : I need not thy help ; nor again
> the head to the feet : I have no need of you. Yea, much more
> those that seem to be the more feeble members of the body are more
> necessary ; and such as we think to be the less honourable members
> of the body, about these we put more abundant honour ; and those that
> are our uncomely parts have more abundant comeliness ; for our comely
> parts have no need.
>
> Thus God hath tempered the body together, giving to that which wanted
> the more abundant honour ; that there might be no schism in the body,
> but that the members might be mutually careful one for another. And
> if one member suffer, all the members suffer with it ; or if one member
> be honoured, all the members rejoice with it.
>
> Now you are [all together] the body of Christ and each one of you
> individually its members.[1]

The diversity of organs in a human body is not only an element of beauty, but an essential condition of life. Among the
members of the mystical body it does not arise from the fact
that they are Christians, since in this respect there is no
difference between them ; nor from their being men, for the
differences which nature establishes do not count from the
Christian point of view ; Paul ascribes it to those gratuitous
gifts which the Holy Spirit grants to the faithful for the
common good of the Church : the apostolate, prophecy, dis-

---

[1] I Cor. xii, 12-27. This passage offers no remarkable difficulties of
exegesis. For verse 12, see above, p. 263.

(a) The comparison to the human body must be explained as a parable
rather than as an allegory. It is therefore not necessary to ask what the
different organs signify : the ears, the eyes, the feet, the hands, the head, etc.
The scholastics, following St. Gregory, see in the members used for locomo-
tion the figure of active life, and in the organs of sense the image of the
contemplative life. The less noble members are imperfect Christians ; the
dishonourable parts denote figuratively sinners, etc. But that is an accommodative interpretation which easily excites ridicule.

(b) In verse 27 the Vulgate *Vos estis corpus Christi et membra* DE MEMBRO
requires the reading καὶ μέλη ἐκ μέλους. But the critics rightly prefer καὶ
μέλη ἐκ μέρους, which means : " and its members *in particular*" (*i.e.*, each
one in particular). If we read ἐκ μέλους, it will mean : " members depending
on other members and intended to help them." A very just idea in itself
and clearly expressed in Rom. xii, 5, as we have just seen.

courses marked by wisdom or learning, discernment of spirits, power to heal the sick and to work miracles, aptitude for governing, teaching, helping the poor, consoling the afflicted, and performing other works of mercy. These examples are well chosen, since the *charismata* are definitely social peculiarities and have for their author the Holy Spirit himself, who fashions as he likes the mystical body, of which he is the soul; but all that the Apostle says could also be applied to the ordinary hierarchy, and perhaps even to the inequality, which the difference in their co-operation in the various calls of grace produces among the saints.

Man is essentially a social being. A pagan philosopher says : " We were made for common action. . . . To oppose one another is contrary to nature."[1] If each of the organs could instinctively attract everything to itself, the entire body would soon perish. It would be the same with the social body ; but nature warns us against selfishness. It makes us understand that we are not sufficient for ourselves, that each member has its sphere of usefulness, that the weakest are often the most necessary, that the least honourable are those who are usually treated with the most honour, that the general health depends upon the proper working of the whole, and that the welfare of all is dependent on the good condition of each one. This truth is proved especially by its very obviousness, and we should not insist upon it, if St Paul did not furnish us with the true formula of Christian altruism : " We are members of one another."[2] The other members are not strangers to us ; they are a part of us ; they work for us as we work for them ; we need their aid and we owe them ours.

The social function, which sums up the activity of the organic body, is community of life. The member does not live from its own life, but from the life of the body. For this it must be united not only to the head, from which the living influx proceeds, but also to the other members, each of which, in its own sphere, transmits that life to it. Separated from the head, the member no longer lives ; isolated from the other members, it would lead only an imperfect and precarious life. St Paul teaches us this when he describes that visionary of Colosse, " who holds not the head, from which the whole body, being supplied with nourishment and com-

---

[1] Marcus Aurelius, *Thoughts*, ii, 1 (Γεγόναμεν πρὸς συνεργίαν) ; vii, 13. *Cf.* Cicero, *De offic.*, iii, 5 ; Xenophon, *Memorab.*, ii, 13.

[2] Rom. xii, 5 : *singuli autem alter alterius membra.* Read the fine commentary of St Augustine (*In Psalm.* cxxx, No. 6, Migne, XXXVII, 1707): *Auris videt in oculo, oculus audit in aure. . . . Ita cum auris dicit : Oculus mihi videt, oculus dicit : Auris mihi audit, oculi et aures dicunt : Manus nobis operantur,* etc. If a thorn enters the foot, the eyes and the hands are used to extract it ; and all the body bends over and exerts itself to share in the operation.

pacted by its joints and bands, groweth with the increase of God " ; for it is through Christ " the Head that the whole body, being compacted and fitly joined together by the mutual help of the members each working in its own measure, maketh increase and is edified in charity."[1]

The mystical body of St Paul has often been compared to the allegorical vine of St John.[2] The similarities of thought are evident. In both cases the supernatural life is likened to the growth of a living being, a growth due to an internal principle and having union with the centre of life as its essential condition. But the differences are not less striking. In St John the branches, joined directly to the stock, get the sap directly from it; while in St Paul the members, united to the head by the other members, receive the flow of life through their means. The first considers rather the individual life of the believers, while St Paul has especially in view the social life of the Church, which regulates and measures the growth of each Christian. But for both the agent of the supernatural life is the Holy Spirit.

3. The Holy Spirit is the soul of the mystical body. As the soul by its presence ennobles the human body, vivifies it by its contact and moves it by its activity, so does the Holy Spirit animate the mystical body of Christ. He is the divine guest of the Church and of each one of its members; he is the only agent and motive power in the supernatural order; he is the joint gift of the Father and the Son, and gives himself also as the most precious of his gifts.

The Holy Spirit dwells in us as in his temple. This temple is sometimes the entire Church, sometimes a Christian community, and sometimes the individual soul : " The Spirit of God dwelleth in you."[3]—" Your body is the temple of the Holy Ghost which is in you."[4]—" If the Spirit of him that raised up Jesus from the dead dwell in you, he that raised up Jesus from the dead shall quicken also your mortal bodies because of his Spirit that dwelleth in you."[5] The Holy Spirit being the Spirit of the Father and the Spirit of the Son, where he dwells the Father and Son dwell also : " Know you not that you are the temple of God?"[6]—" The temple of God is holy, which you are."[7]—" We are the temple of the living

---

[1] Col. ii, 18 ; Eph. iv, 12-16.   Texts explained in Vol. I, pp. 304-8.

[2] John xv, 1-6.   The allegory of the olive tree (Rom. xi, 16-24) can also be compared.   See above, p. 273.

[3] 1 Cor. iii, 16 (τὸ Πνεῦμα τοῦ Θεοῦ ἐν ὑμῖν οἰκεῖ); Rom. viii, 9 (εἴπερ Πνεῦμα Θεοῦ οἰκεῖ ἐν ὑμῖν); 2 Tim. i, 14 (διὰ Πνεύματος ἁγίου τοῦ ἐνοικοῦντος ἐν ὑμῖν).

[4] 1 Cor. vi, 19 : τὸ σῶμα ὑμῶν ναὸς τοῦ ἐν ὑμῖν ἁγίου Πνεύματός ἐστιν.

[5] Rom. viii, 11.   See p. 145.

[6] 1 Cor. iii, 16 : οὐκ οἴδατε ὅτι ναὸς Θεοῦ ἐστε ;

[7] 1 Cor. iii, 17 : ὁ ναὸς τοῦ Θεοῦ ἅγιός ἐστιν· οἵτινές ἐστε ὑμεῖς.

God."[1]—" You are built into a temple of God in the Spirit."[2]
—" That Christ may dwell by faith in your hearts."[3]

As the guest of our soul, the Spirit of holiness is not in-active there. All the florescence of our spiritual life expands at a breath from him. Therefore he is called by St Paul the " Spirit of Life,"[4] and by St John a " quickening Spirit."[5] All the *charismata,* of whatever nature, are conferred by him.[6] It is to him that the Apostle owes the revelation of the great mystery, which is the fundamental article of his Gospel; for the Spirit who searcheth the deep things of God, reveals them to whom he will.[7] His action extends to all Christians and to all manifestations of the supernatural life, from baptismal regeneration to everlasting blessedness. To obey the motions of grace is commonly called " walking in the Spirit, being moved by the Spirit " ;[8] the aggregate of all virtues is " the fruit of the Spirit " ;[9] all that lifts us above our carnal and psychical nature, all that forces us into a divine atmosphere, and all that transforms us into *spiritual* beings, according to Paul's favourite expression, receives the general name of *spirit,*[10] alluding to the source from which it emanates.

The Holy Spirit is love, and the characteristic of love is to give, giving oneself with one's gifts. The love with which God loves us is manifested by the gift of the Spirit, and at the same time by an outpouring of sanctifying grace, which is an effect of the Spirit present in us. This outpouring of grace is not transitory; it is inherent, and it continues in-separably united with the Holy Spirit, who is its source: " The love of God is poured forth in our hearts by the Holy Ghost who is given to us."[11] There is, therefore, in us some-thing else besides the Spirit, there is the product of his activity. As this outpouring is necessarily finite, since it is received in a finite being, it is susceptible of indefinite increase. Hence Paul says sometimes that we have received " the firstfruits,"[12] or " the earnest of the Spirit."[13] We have indeed received the Spirit wholly, for the Spirit is indivisible; but we have received only a portion of the bless-ings which he intends for us, and that the smallest, or rather, the least apparent portion of them.

The question has been raised whether, in order to do justice to all these affirmations of the Apostle and to the interpreta-tions of the Fathers, it would not be necessary to accord to

---

[1] 2 Cor. vi, 16 : ἡμεῖς γὰρ ναὸς Θεοῦ ἐσμεν ζῶντος.
[2] Eph. ii, 22. συνοικοδομεῖσθε εἰς κατοικητήριον τοῦ Θεοῦ ἐν Πνεύματι.
[3] Eph. iii, 17 : κατοικῆσαι τὸν Χριστὸν διὰ τῆς πίστεως ἐν ταῖς καρδίαις ὑμῶν.
[4] Rom. viii, 2.        [5] John vi, 63.        [6] 1 Cor. xii, 4.
[7] 1 Cor. ii, 10.        [8] Rom. viii, 4, 14, etc.        [9] Gal. v, 22.
[10] See pp. 406-7.        [11] Rom. v, 5.  See Note S, p. 432.
[12] viii, 23 : αὐτοὶ τὴν ἀπαρχὴν τοῦ πνεύματος ἔχοντες.
[13] 2 Cor. i, 22 ; v, 5 (ὁ δοὺς ἡμῖν τὸν ἀρραβῶνα τοῦ πνεύματος).  *Cf*. Eph. i, 14.

the Holy Spirit a special kind of presence. Is the union of
the just soul with God made directly with the divine nature,
or by the mediation of the Holy Spirit? In the first case, it
would pertain to all the three Persons by the same right, and
could be referred to one of them only by appropriation; in
the second case, it would be peculiar to the Holy Spirit, and
the other two Persons would participate in it only by con-
comitance, by virtue of that mutual interpenetration which
does not permit them to exist separately. We know that the
theologian Petavius imagined for the indwelling of the Holy
Spirit in us something analogous to the union of the Word
incarnate with human nature. He makes here, however, a
difference; in the hypostatic union of the Word, a substantial and indissoluble bond unites the two extremes; while
in the indwelling of the Holy Spirit, the bond is only
accidental—because it takes place with a faculty of the soul,
not with its substance, and because it can be broken—but it
would nevertheless be personal to the Spirit of holiness. This
attractive theory is very difficult to conceive. Its inventor
does not himself succeed in explaining it. "It is not yet,"
he says, "sufficiently elucidated."[1] In fact, on what would
be founded the special relation of consecration or possession
which would unite the just soul to the Holy Spirit? What

[1] The opinion of Petavius is not to be confounded with the theory of Peter
Lombard. The latter taught not only that the Holy Spirit is present in a
special way in the just soul, but that he takes there the place of the virtue of
charity, the act of which he produces in us. Some of his disciples said even
that the Holy Spirit, inasmuch as he dwells in us, is called grace, and that
since he unites himself to our will, he is the charity by which we love God.
Petavius admitted a grace and love which are created and consequently distinct from the Holy Spirit; he only said, with some reservations: *Certa
quaedam ratio est, qua se Spiritus sancti persona sanctorum justorumque
mentibus applicat, quae ceteris personis eodem modo non competit* (*De Trinit.*,
VIII, vi, 6). The Holy Spirit is veluti forma *qua sancti Deoque grati et
adoptivi filii sunt* (*ibid.*, No. 3) . . . quasi forma *sanctificans et adoptivum
reddens sui communicatione filium* (*ibid.*, No. 8). This presence is peculiar to
the Holy Spirit, although it is difficult to say how (*ibid.*, No. 6). It is secundum
hypostasim, *non secundum essentiam* (*ibid.*, No. 6), otherwise it would be
common to the three Persons; however, it is not *hypostatic* (*ibid.*, No. 2)—
that is to say, it takes place with the person itself of the Holy Spirit, but there
does not result from it a *person*, a hypostasis, as in the union of the Word with
humanity.—The great difficulty is that tradition does not know and the two
cannot conceive of any other union *peculiar to a divine person* than the hypa-
static union; it is not clear indeed what a divine Person can give of his own
(*en propre*) to a finite nature, if it is not his personality, since he has nothing
else of his own. Petavius knew no more than we do about this, or, if he did
know more, he kept it to himself: *Nostra quae privatim sit opinio, vel non
dico, quia rem nondum compertam satis habeo; vel hoc loco non dico* (*ibid.*,
No. 6). Consequently, Petavius thinks that the Holy Spirit was present in
the just souls of the Old Testament only by his operation (κατ' ἐνέργειαν),
while he does dwell substantially (οὐσιωδῶς) in those of the New (*De Trinit.*,
VIII, vii, 1 and 5). But this is another serious disadvantage of his system.—
*Cf.* B. Froget, O.P., *De l'habitation du Saint Esprit dans les âmes justes
d'après la doctrine de St Thomas*[2], Paris, 1900, pp. 447-475.

hypostatic (or partly hypostatic) function can the Holy
Spirit exercise in the soul? And if he unites himself to it by
an operation like the production of sanctifying grace, why
should his union be direct, when the other two Persons, who
have shared in his activity, are united only through an
intermediary?

On the other hand, the common explanation, which sees in
the indwelling of the divine Persons only different degrees of
appropriation, does not seem to harmonize sufficiently with
the language of the Fathers and the Scriptures. We are
told that it is by sanctifying grace that God dwells in us, as
in his temple; but ordinary grace, a product of the entire
Trinity, unites us directly to God without distinction of
Persons. There is not, therefore, in regard to the way in
which the three divine Persons are present, any other distinction possible than that of appropriation, by virtue of which
we are accustomed to ascribe to the Father being and power,
to the Son knowledge and wisdom, and to the Holy Ghost
love and sanctity, because we perceive in these different
attributes a certain relation to their personal characteristics.
This theory is worthy of respect, but it is nevertheless only
a theory.

In any case, the Fathers and the sacred writers do not
seem to look at things in this way. In their opinion the God-
assimilating union is accomplished, first, with the Persons
and then by the Persons with human nature; and sanctifying
grace is not the condition, but the result of the presence of
the divine guests. When God wishes to sanctify souls, he
sends his beloved Son, the universal mediator of grace; and
the Son in his turn, conjointly with his Father, sends the
Spirit of sanctity. The sanctifying action, therefore, takes
place in accordance with the order of the eternal processions
(of the Trinity), and it is the same with the presence of the
three Persons in the sanctified soul. Only in this last case
the order is reversed; the Holy Spirit, having been given and
giving himself to the soul, first of all enters into contact with
it. It is, of course, a priority of thought, not of time, but a
priority founded upon something real, for the sending of the
Persons is not equivalent to the appropriation of their
attributes. Some texts, like the following, do not appear
susceptible of any other exegesis: *Caritas Dei diffusa est in
cordibus nostris per Spiritum sanctum qui datus est nobis.*
Here a vast field opens before us, but we cannot enter it
without passing beyond the limits of biblical theology.

4. All that we have just said shows how intimate is the
union of the Son and the Holy Spirit in the work of sanctification. The observation is certainly not a new one; St
Epiphanius says: " Christ is sent by the Father and the

Holy Spirit is also sent; Christ speaks in the saints, the Holy Spirit speaks also; Christ heals and the Holy Spirit likewise heals; Christ sanctifies and so does the Holy Spirit."[1]   Then follows a very long series of texts, in which this common action is affirmed.    In fact, grace, the *charismata,* filial adoption, good works, salvation, eternal glory; in a word, all the manifestations of the divine life are referred sometimes to Christ, sometimes to the Spirit.    Thus " we live by the Spirit " and nevertheless " Christ is our life."[2]   The Holy Spirit is the dispenser of all the *charismata,* and yet these are conferred " according to the measure of the gift of Christ."[3]   It is by Jesus Christ that we received the adoption of sons; nevertheless, the Holy Spirit is the Spirit of adoption and " all those who are moved by the Spirit of God are sons of God."[4]   The dead will rise from the dead " by a man," Jesus Christ; and yet God will raise us " because of the Spirit " or " by the Spirit that dwelleth " in us.[5]   Let us add still another fact often pointed out : the equivalence of the two formulas *in Christ* and *in the Spirit.*    This equivalence does not go so far as is usually supposed, far from it; but it is nevertheless suggestive.    Some examples will show this :

| | |
|---|---|
| Justified in the Spirit | = justified in the Lord.[6] |
| Sanctified in the Holy Spirit | = sanctified in Christ Jesus.[7] |
| Holy temple in the Spirit | = holy temple in the Lord.[8] |
| To be sealed in the Spirit | = to be sealed in Christ.[9] |
| Joy in the Holy Spirit | = joy in the Lord.[10] |
| Peace in the Holy Spirit | = peace in the Lord.[11] |

To explain this phenomenon, must we say that Christ and the Spirit are identical in Paul's thought, or that the Spirit is only the mode of Christ's operation, or that Christ, after his resurrection, totally transformed himself into the Spirit? There is a simpler and more natural explanation, which has, moreover, the advantage of avoiding absurdity.    Let us remark first that the equivalence in question is a very limited one.    The pre-existent Christ is never identified with the Spirit; the historical Christ is never identified with the Spirit; and Christ as Saviour is never identified with the Spirit in the work of redemption.    The points of contact between Christ and the Spirit concern only the glorified Christ, and even this is not in his physical, personal life at the right hand of the Father, but in his mystical life in the bosom of the Church. In other terms, the Holy Spirit and the glorified Christ, who

---

[1] *Ancoratus,* 68 (XLIII, 140).     [2] Gal. v, 25 and Col iii, 4 ; Phil. i, 21.
[3] 1 Cor. xii, 11 and Eph. iv, 9.
[4] Eph. i, 5 (*cf.* Gal. iv, 5-6) and Rom. viii, 15.
[5] 1 Cor. xv, 21 and Rom. viii, 11.
[6] 1 Cor. vi, 11 and Gal. ii, 17.                    [7] 1 Cor. vi, 11 and i, 2.
[8] Eph. ii, 22 and ii, 21.                             [9] Eph. i, 13 and iv, 39.
[10] Rom. xiv, 17 and Phil. iv, 4.                  [11] Rom. xiv, 17 and v, 1.

appear everywhere else as two distinct Persons, seem to become identical in their role of sanctifiers of souls.[1] There, indeed, their sphere of influence is the same and their fields of action blend; for Christ is the head or, under a somewhat different figure, the organism of the mystical body, the soul of which is the Holy Ghost; now in ordinary language, chiefly in that of St Paul, almost all vital phenomena can be referred equally to the soul or to the head.

But for the identity of operation on the part of Christ and the Spirit in the lives of the just there exists a much deeper cause. Christ, as man, possessed the fulness of the Spirit[2] and was to cause it to be poured out upon us as soon as he had accomplished his redemptive work. Then, at the moment of the resurrection, he becomes actually for himself and for us a " quickening spirit " ;[3] for himself, since the grace with which he abounds fills his body and renders it spiritual, and for us, because he communicates to us lavishly all the gifts of the Holy Spirit and the Holy Spirit himself. Henceforth, from the supernatural point of view, we live by the Son and also by the Spirit; or, more exactly, we live by the Spirit sent by the Son. It is an identity of operations without confusion of Persons. Let us take, for example, filial adoption. It comes to us from the Son who has adopted us and causes us to be accepted as brothers; God " predestines us for it by Jesus Christ " and confers it upon us by faith and baptism— that is to say, by the act and rite which put us " into fellow-ship with the Son of God."[4] The Holy Spirit is none the less called the " Spirit of adoption " and all those whom he leads are truly " sons of God."[5] This is because God adopts us as sons by giving us his Spirit, and Christ adopts us as brothers by sending us his Spirit; " for if any man hath not the Spirit of Christ, he is none of his."[6] The proof that " you are sons, is that God hath sent the Spirit of his Son into your hearts, where he cries : Abba, Father ! Therefore now he is not a slave but a son; and if a son, an heir also through God."[7] The Holy Spirit is the witness, the messenger, the agent, and the pledge of our sonship.

Thus, far from being a source of obscurity, the active interpenetration of the Son and Holy Spirit is for us a source of intense light. Thanks to it, we better understand why Christ had to rise from the dead in order to send us his Spirit and to become himself a quickening Spirit. It also throws light upon the nature of the mystical body, which is not a fiction, a simple metaphor or a pure moral entity, but a

[1] Col. i, 19.  [2] 1 Cor. xv, 45.  Cf. pp. 172-3.
[3] Gal. iv, 5 (the Son becomes incarnate in order to confer upon us the adoption of sons) ; Eph. i, 5 (προορίσας ἡμᾶς εἰς υἱοθεσίαν διὰ ʾI. X.); Gal. iii, 26 (πάντες υἱοὶ Θεοῦ ἐστε διὰ τῆς πίστεως, ἐν Χριστῷ ᾽Ιησοῦ).
[4] 1 Cor. i, 9.  [5] Rom. viii, 14-15.
[6] Rom. viii, 9.  [7] Gal. iv, 6-7.

composite of the supernatural order, receiving at the same time the vital influx from the head, the centre of the organism and from the soul, the principle of life. Thenceforth the consoling doctrine of the communion of saints is no longer a theory artificially connected with the theology of the Apostle, but a corollary of his teaching, clear and easy to understand.

5. The communion of saints is the bond of corporate life which unites the members of Christ with their Head and with one another under the common action of one and the same Spirit. This definition has the double advantage of agreeing with Pauline terminology and of being sufficiently elastic to adapt itself to all later precise interpretations, without prejudice to the meaning of the article subsequently inserted in the Creed.[1]

The Apostle calls " saints " all those who are in communion with Jesus Christ, or, preferably, all those " who are in Christ." Whether they are still contending in the arena or whether they have already received their crown, makes no difference in his eyes ; for the charity that " never faileth " unites them all alike to Christ Jesus ; living or dead, they are always " with him, in him " ; and they form part of his kingdom and of his mystical body. It is remarkable that Paul constantly uses this word " saints " as a simple synonym for Christians and applies it without distinction to all the faithful, even in cases where grave abuses have to be reformed. Is it because he supposes them all to be individually worthy of this title, leaving to him who searcheth the reins and the hearts of men the task of classifying them? Or does he take this name in the theocratic and social sense which it had under the Old Covenant, and does it constitute a sufficient right to it to belong to the Church, the sançtity of which is imparted to each of the members? What favours the second hypothesis is that Paul recognizes only two ways of leaving the mystical body : one on account of unbelief, the other by excommunication. By unbelief the baptized member separates himself from the Head whence all the flow of life is derived ; by excommunication he is cut off officially. Who-

---

[1] For the origin and meaning of and motive for the insertion in the Creed of the words *sanctorum communionem, cf. Revue d'histoire et de littér. réligieuses*, vol. ix, 1904, pp. 222-252 (Dom Morin) and *Diction. de théol. cathol.*, vol. iii, 1906, col. 350-354 (P. Bernard). The addition was made about the beginning of the fifth century or the end of the preceding one and very probably in Gaul. The word *sanctorum* is not neuter (of sacred things), as Zahn has claimed, but masculine. The saints denote certainly, besides the faithful, or the saints on earth, the elect of heaven. We may merely ask if the introducer of the formula did not intend to designate especially the blessed souls in heaven ; the communion of terrestrial saints with one another was a matter of course and could not be doubted by anyone, while the communion between the saints of earth and the saints of heaven had just been vigorously disputed in southern Gaul.

ever, having once entered into the unity of the mystical body, either has not wholly detached himself from it, or has not been formally expelled from it, belongs, therefore, to the sphere in which the communion of saints is in operation.

A certain community of joys and sorrows is essential to all society. All the members of a moral body lend one another mutual aid. The humblest have need of the noblest, and the noblest have need of the humblest. The welfare or unhappiness of some is shared to some degree by all. The honour or dishonour of some is reflected morally upon all. And this is even truer of the Christian society, whose more intimate union is symbolized by the human body. Each Christian works for the development of the body of Christ. The very person of Jesus Christ possesses a fulness to which nothing can possibly be added; but the mystical Christ is susceptible of indefinite growth which he receives from the individual growth of his members. Thus the Church rises by degrees " into a holy temple in the Lord," and the body of Christ acquires little by little its full stature and becomes " a complete man," thanks to the continual progress of its organism. No part gains anything which is not profitable to the whole; but, inversely, the whole gains nothing which is not of profit to the parts. In this way there is produced a kind of vital circulation, bringing to the centre all the product of the life-giving energy to distribute it in all directions, as the ocean absorbs into itself the rivers whose origin it feeds. But there is this difference to the advantage of the mystical body, that it retains all that it has received and gives it back without losing anything.

The communion of saints has for its aim to enrich the treasure of the Church and to distribute this subsequently to this or that member. The first result is obtained by every meritorious act; the second chiefly by prayer. " Now," says the Apostle, " I rejoice in my sufferings for you and fill up those things that are wanting of the sufferings of Christ in my flesh for his body, which is the Church.[1] According to his dogmatic prejudices, every reader is tempted to see in this text too much or too little; but there are at least three

---

[1] Col. i, 24 : Νῦν χαίρω ἐν τοῖς παθήμασιν ὑπὲρ ὑμῶν, καὶ ἀνταναπληρῶ τὰ ὑστερήματα τῶν θλίψεων τοῦ Χριστοῦ ἐν τῇ σαρκί μου ὑπὲρ τοῦ σώματος αὐτοῦ ὅ ἐστιν ἡ ἐκκλησία.—The substantive ὑστέρημα, " that which is wanting," opposed to περίσσευμα, " that which abounds " (2 Cor. viii, 13-14), expresses the need of being completed (ἀναπληροῦν, 1 Cor. xvi, 17 ; Phil. ii, 30 ; or προσαναπληροῦν, 2 Cor. ix, 12 ; xi, 9 ; or καταρτίζειν, 1 Thess. iii, 10). The word is found in St Paul only in these eight texts, and the meaning of it cannot be doubtful.—The meaning of the verb ἀνταναπληροῦν, which is met nowhere else in the Bible and is very rare in profane writers, is also perfectly certain; it is " to complete what is incomplete." As St Paul usually puts with ὑστέρημα the verbs ἀναπληροῦν or προσαναπληροῦν, it may be asked what is the exact meaning of the component particle ἀνά. Does it merely strengthen the idea ?

facts certain : First, the tribulations of Christ are not sufferings comparable to those of *Jesus,* but rather the pains and
torments endured by *Christ* during his mortal life. These
tribulations, in spite of their infinite value, present from one
point of view a sort of deficit ; the word employed by the
Apostle (ὑστέρημα) can have no other meaning.—It is man's
duty to fill up this deficit and thus to complete the work of
Christ, and this is what Paul is proud and happy to do by
completing (ἀνταναπληρῶ) what is wanting in the tribulations
of his Master.

Here the exegete can advance only with hesitation. What
are the tribulations of Christ which are to be made up for the
good of the Church? Are they the sufferings of Gethsemani
and Calvary, in themselves more than sufficient for the salvation of mankind, but the application of which to individual
souls remains to be assured? Or are they the persecutions
endured in order to found the kingdom of God, persecutions
of which all the apostles and, after them, all the preachers
of the Gospel are to have their share? In the first hypothesis
the dogma of the communion of saints is directly taught. In
the second we learn at least that Jesus Christ established the
salvation of the human race upon the principle of solidarity,
and that those who carry on his work are to share in it in
order to realize his merciful designs.

When we speak of solidarity, we mean a reversibility of
merits and demerits. This idea was current among Paul's
contemporaries. Without stopping to justify it, the Apostle
takes it for granted when he affirms that the Church of
Corinth expiates by sicknesses and bereavements the
irreverence shown by some in the celebration of the Lord's
Supper ; that the Christian husband sanctifies the unbelieving
wife and that the believing wife sanctifies the pagan husband,
and that charity makes up in some way for inequality among
the disciples, the rich giving to the poor the superfluity of
their temporal goods and the poor recompensing them in
higher goods.[1] He has such confidence in this exchange of
spiritual graces that he does not cease to implore the prayers
of those to whom he writes, offering them in return the aid of
his own prayers and exhorting them to pray for one another :
" By all prayer and supplication, praying at all times in the
Spirit . . . and with supplication for all the saints and for
me that speech may be given me that I may open my mouth
with confidence, to make known the mystery of the Gospel."[2]
He attributes to these prayers his deliverance, the protection
with which God surrounds him and the success of his preaching ; for, when supplication reaches such a degree of intensity

---

[1] 1 Cor. xi, 30-32 ; vii, 14 ; 2 Cor. viii, 13-15.
[2] Eph. vi, 18-19.

that it can be called a struggle, a combat, it is all-powerful with God.[1]

The prayer of the just is useful not only to the living; it is also profitable for the dead. A Christian of Ephesus, Onesiphorus, had just died, having lavishly bestowed upon Paul the most touching proofs of affection and devotion. In order to repay his debt of gratitude, the Apostle is not content to recommend to Timothy the family of Onesiphorus, but he himself recommends the soul of the deceased to God : " The Lord grant unto him to find mercy of the Lord in that day."[2] Several Protestant commentators record the fact rather ungraciously and not without astonishment. But what can be more natural, if the Church is one and if it includes the dead as well as the living?

6. Under whatever aspect we consider the life of the Church, we inevitably come to the formula *In Christo Jesu,* which is certainly " one of the pillars of St Paul's theology " (Sanday). Without being strictly his, since St John makes a restricted use of it, it has in Paul a plenitude of meanings and a variety of applications which are thoroughly characteristic.

In his first Epistle St John several times declares that charity establishes between God and us a relation of mutual interpenetration. " God is charity, and he that abideth in charity abideth in God and God in him."[3] Our act of charity, finite as it is, not only has God for its immediate object, but is really a taking possession of God who is infinite love. Charity, so far as it is in us, unites us, therefore, to him by an indissoluble bond. And what is true of the Father is true also of the Son, since they are of the same substance : *Ego et Pater unum sumus.* So that, in the Epistle, it can be sometimes asked whether St John means to speak of the Son or of the Father. But, in the Gospel, his language is wholly different. Jesus said to his disciples : " He that eateth my flesh and drinketh my blood abideth in me and I in him."[4] It is not by virtue of the real union of the flesh of Christ with ours that Jesus Christ *abideth* in us, it is as the spiritual nourishment of our soul that he dwells in us, even after the corruption of the sacramental elements ; and we abide in him because this heavenly food has the admirable property of transforming us into him, contrary to what occurs with every other food. The case is a little different in the allegory of the vine : " Abide in me and I in you. . . . He that abideth in me and I in him, the same beareth much fruit."[5] We abide in him by a living faith, as the branch is attached to the

[1] Rom. xv, 30.          [2] 2 Tim. i, 18.          [3] 1 John iv, 16.
[4] John vi, 56.          [5] John xv, 4-5.

trunk by the fibres and the bark; and he dwells in us by charity, which puts us into vital contact with him and by which he communicates the divine sap to us.

On passing from St John to St Paul, we have the impression that the horizon is no more the same. At the very first we remark two capital differences in the use of the formula. Unlike St John, St Paul never says *in Jesus* or *in Jesus Christ;* he always says *in Christ* or *in Christ Jesus:* a clear proof that he is not considering the individual person of Jesus, but rather his office as the Messiah, his quality as the second Adam; in a word, his representative character. Moreover, while St John establishes the reciprocity between Jesus and ourselves, St Paul refrains from doing so or at least speaks of Jesus Christ in us only in very rare cases, the precise meaning of which remains to be discussed.[1]

The formula *In Christo Jesu* is clearly connected with the doctrine of the mystical body. This point is, in fact, not contested. Let us see, therefore, how St Paul describes the incorporation of the Christian in Christ:

> You are all the children of God by faith in Christ Jesus; for as many of you as have been baptised in Christ have put on Christ. There is neither Jew nor Greek, there is neither bond nor free . . . for you are all one in Christ Jesus.
>
> Know you not that all we who are baptised in Christ Jesus are baptised in his death? For we are buried together with him by baptism into his death; that, as Christ is risen from the dead by the glory of the Father, so we also may walk in newness of life. For if we have been planted together in the likeness of his death, we shall be also in the likeness of his resurrection.[2]

As the etymological meaning of to *baptize* is to *plunge into the water,* it is hardly doubtful that in describing the effects of baptism St Paul is thinking of the external rite of immersion and emersion, the efficacious symbol of death and a new life. The effect of baptism is to plunge us into Christ, to graft us upon Christ, to incorporate us in Christ, to identify us in part with Christ. When it is said that the Christian is *in* Christ, as the bird is *in* the air or the fish *in* the water, this realistic expression is below the truth; for we are not in Christ as in a foreign element, but as in an entirety, of which we ourselves form a part. To tell the truth, the best commentary on the formula *In Christo Jesu* is the following

---

[1] Rom. viii, 10 (εἰ δὲ Χριστὸς ἐν ὑμῖν) seems to be the exact counterpart of 2 Cor. v, 17 (εἴ τις ἐν Χριστῷ). By the fact that we are in Christ, Christ dwells in us.—Gal. ii, 20 (ζῇ ἐν ἐμοὶ Χριστός, *cf.* Phil. i, 21) recalls the Christ-Life of St John.—2 Cor. xiii, 5 (*An non cognoscitis vosmetipsos quia Christus Jesus in vobis est?*) is very remarkable. It is not a question of the presence of Jesus Christ in the church of Corinth, but of his dwelling in the hearts of the faithful. Von Soden adopts the reading Χριστὸς Ἰησοῦς, which the Vulgate presupposes; but good authorities have Ἰησοῦς Χριστός. If the latter reading is the true one, it justifies the expression *Jesus in us.*

[2] Gal. iii, 26-28; Rom. vi, 3-5.

text of St Paul : " By a man came death, and by a man shall come the resurrection of the dead ; for as *in Adam* all die, so also *in Christ* all shall be made alive."[1]  Adam and Christ represent here all mankind, and one can say with St Augustine, provided that we understand him rightly : *In Adam Christus et Christus in Adam.*[2]  All men are in Adam and all are in Christ, although in a very different way : " All die in Adam," said St Cyril of Alexandria, " because, on account of his transgression, human nature was condemned in him ; thus all shall be justified in Christ because, thanks to his redemptive act, human nature is once more blessed in him."[3]

It is not quite correct to say that " The Christ of the formula *In Christo Jesu* is always Christ glorified as πνεῦμα, and not the historical Christ " (Sanday).  It is not precisely the glorified Christ, but Christ the Saviour, the new Adam, that is indicated by the formula ; and he is so from the moment when he inaugurates his redemptive mission—that is to say, from the moment of his Passion.  Thenceforth we suffer and die with him and we rise from the dead and reign with him ; we share his form, his life, and his glory.  Thenceforth also we are called, justified, elected, and predestined in him, and in him also we obtain all the heavenly blessings, grace, filial adoption, sanctification, and eternal life.

Such is the normal value of the formula *In Christo Jesu,* but it is susceptible of receiving a remarkable increase or diminution of meaning.  When the Apostle wishes to express the ineffable union of Christians with one another and with Christ in the identity of the mystical body, the formula attains its maximum value ; but when he confines himself to indicating the principle of Christian solidarity, the signification becomes weak and faded ; then to be in Christ is to move in the sphere of the Gospel or to live according to the spirit of Christianity.

### III—THE GOVERNMENT OF THE CHURCH

1. Ecclesiastical Dignitaries.  2. Coercive Power of the Church.
3. Résumé and Conclusions.

1.  All the churches founded by St Paul were directly dependent upon him.  Upon him in truth rested " the care of all the churches."  It may perhaps be asked whether this centralization, by prolonging the period of tentative Church methods, did not retard the evolution of the monarchical episcopate, but it was necessary at the beginning, in order to

---

[1] 1 Cor. xv, 21-22.  See Vol. I, pp. 135, 136.
[2] *In Psalm.* ci, *Sermo* i, No. 4 (XXXVII, 1296).  *Cf. Sermon.* ccxciii, No. 9. (XXXVIII, 1333).
[3] *Fragm. in* 1 Cor. xv, 22 (LXXI, 901).

weld together the bonds of unity and to obviate the danger
of schism.[1]

We should not, however, conclude from this that Paul's
churches were without any hierarchical organization. As
soon as a church had passed the embryonic stage, it always
received leaders and directors. St Luke tells us that Paul
and Barnabas, on returning from their common missionary
journey in Asia Minor, chose *elders* (πρεσβυτέρους) where-
ever they went. This selection, attended with prayers and
fastings, was not a simple appointment of the candidates, but
a liturgical ceremony inaugurating their new functions; for,
however far back we go, we find that the consecration of the
sacred ministers is always performed in the midst of fasts and
solemn supplications. As the chronicle of the Acts is representative in character, and as St Luke is not accustomed to
repeat what is a matter of course or what he has already said
once for all, there is nothing surprising in the fact that this
allusion is an isolated one, but, on the contrary, it should be
taken for granted that this was everywhere the practice of
the missionaries. In this case it happens to be a statement
concerning the *Elders* of Ephesus,[2] whose nomination is
nowhere recounted. At Thessalonica, a few months after the
foundation of that church, we remark the presence of
labourers, presiding officers, and exhorters, to whom the
faithful owe love, respect, and gratitude. We do not know
whether they had voluntarily assumed these tasks with the
consent of the converts, or whether they had been conferred
upon them by the Apostle; at all events the fact is recognized
and sanctioned by him. Paul reminds them of their duties:
" Rebuke the unquiet, comfort the feeble-minded, support
the weak, be patient towards all men, see that none render
evil for evil."[3] These men, whose function it was to labour
on God's work, to preside over religious gatherings, to warn
the brethren, and, if need be, to admonish them, and who, in
return had a right to esteem, affection, and gratitude, occupy
an official or quasi-official position. Have they the rank of
deacons and of elders? Analogy would lead us to think so,
although they do not bear those titles. A tradition, already
old in the time of Origen, regarded Caius, St Paul's host at
Corinth, as the first bishop of Thessalonica.

The church of Corinth is often cited as the type of a democratic assembly. It is true, the Apostle leaves it to the free
choice of the Corinthians to appoint the arbiters charged
with the settlement of litigation and the delegates who were
to bring to Jerusalem the sum of money that had been collected;[4] but he none the less keeps that turbulent community

---

[1] Cf. *Ecclesiastical Dignitaries*, vol. i, pp. 341 *ff*.
[2] Acts xx, 17.                          [3] I Thess. v, 12-14.
[4] I Cor. vi, 4, 5 ; xvi, 3.

under his immediate supervision, and has himself represented there almost constantly by his coadjutors;[1] and it is always he who regulates, judges, and, in the last appeal, decides.[2] Side by side with the transitory and charismatic ministry, which was so flourishing at Corinth, did there exist a hierarchical and permanent ministry? Who presided over the *agape*, and who celebrated the Lord's Supper? We cannot say, for our information is very fragmentary and relates to the very first beginnings of church polity, and to the three or four years following its foundation. But, though precise details are lacking, we think that the church of Corinth was organized on the model of the other churches.

The community at Philippi was hardly ten years old when the Apostle sent thither a special greeting to the priests (ἐπίσκοποι) and deacons.[3] Perhaps these persons had taken a prominent part in the collection made for Paul when a prisoner; perhaps also Paul wished to recognize their services and reinforce their authority. The collective reference to the ἐπίσκοποι does not prove absolutely that they formed a company of equals; it might have included the president himself, if it be supposed that Epaphroditus, "the brother, fellow-labourer, and fellow-soldier" of Paul[4] held the first place there. However, it is more probable that here, as elsewhere, the supreme jurisdiction devolved on the representative of the Apostle.

At Ephesus and in Crete the situation is clear. Paul's delegates, invested with his authority, are instructed to establish priests and deacons, to repress heretics and quarrelsome persons, and to punish offenders, not excepting the clergy, provided that legal procedure be observed.[5] When they have to be replaced, they will be so by one person only, so that the government of these churches is almost monarchical in form.[6] At the head is the representative of Paul, who exercises a sovereign jurisdiction; below him is the college of priests, whose prerogatives are not yet clearly defined. In the lowest rank of the clergy are the deacons. No allusion is made to a charismatic ministry. The hierarchical organization is developing; it is advancing gradually towards a definite constitution.

The Apostle had taken good care not to grant complete autonomy to the recently founded churches. His lieutenants were constantly at work, visiting and reforming the communities which depended upon him. He was the only pastor of the immense diocese which he had conquered for the faith

[1] I Cor. iv, 27; ii, 13; vii, 6-14; viii, 6; xii, 18.
[2] I Cor. v, 1-13; xi, 2-34; xiv, 27-40; 2 Cor. xiii, 1-10, etc.
[3] Phil. i, 1.
[4] Phil. ii, 25. *Cf.* iv, 3 (Clement and the other helpers).
[5] I Tim. i, 3; iii, 1-15; iv, 11; vi, 2; Titus i, 5; ii, 10; I Tim. v, 19-22.
[6] Titus iii, 12 (Artemas or Tychicus); 2 Tim. iv, 12 (Tychicus).

of Christ.   Neither in Greece, nor in Macedonia, nor in Galatia, nor in Crete, nor at Ephesus was there, during his life, any other bishop besides himself and his delegates. The old tradition which regarded Caius of Corinth as the first bishop of Thessalonica may, indeed, be true, for nothing specially suggested Caius for that distant post ; but it is not said, and it is not at all probable, that Caius was bishop during Paul's lifetime.   Nor were Titus and Timothy so, either.   Titus, left in Crete to organize that church, was to rejoin his chief on the arrival of a substitute.   The position of Timothy at Ephesus was also hardly more stable, and the Apostle soon recalled him.   In a word, the churches of Paul were served by deacons and governed by a council of dignitaries, called indifferently πρεσβύτεροι or ἐπίσκοποι, under the always alert surveillance and the ever active direction of their founder or his substitutes.

In the very earliest years, when a church consisted merely of a little nucleus of believers, the *charismata* might for a time make up for the absence or the imperfection of the ordinary hierarchy, for several of these graces were gifts of instruction or government.   Perhaps this state of things lasted for a short time at Corinth, which was distinguished for the abundance of its charismatic gifts.   Let us not forget that, with the exception of Southern Galatia, no ecclesiastical foundation of Paul preceded his martyrdom by more than fifteen or sixteen years.   Almost all the churches were much younger at the time when the Apostle was busy with their affairs. Even at the epoch of the Pastorals, the church of Ephesus was not more than twelve years old, and those of Crete had just come into existence.

The way in which the appointment of the sacred ministers was made had to vary according to the necessities of place and time.   The first seven Hellenist deacons of Jerusalem were nominated by the faithful and ordained by the apostles. This was perhaps an act of condescension suggested to the Twelve by the desire to take from the discontented every pretext for insubordination and every motive for complaint. But Paul and Barnabas, without going clearly counter to the converts' wishes, and without overlooking the capabilities of candidates, seem to have consulted only themselves when they gave *Elders* to each recently founded church.[1]   In the

[1] Acts xiv, 23 : Χειροτονήσαντες αὐτοῖς κατ' ἐκκλησίαν πρεσβυτέρους. Note the word αὐτοῖς, which accentuates the initiative of the Apostles and seems to exclude the active participation of the faithful.   The verb χειροτονεῖν, taken here in the sense of to *establish*, signifies to *elect* in the only other text in which it appears, 2 Cor. viii, 19 : χειροτονηθεὶς ὑπὸ τῶν ἐκκλησιῶν συνέκδημος ἡμῶν.   At Athens it retained its etymological meaning of " to vote with lifted hands," in particular " to choose someone with lifted hands " in the assembly of the people.   But outside of the Greek republics, the etymological meaning was early lost and, at the New Testament epoch,

domain of Paul we do not find that the rank and file of the faithful ever took part in the election of ecclesiastical dignitaries properly so called, for the arbiters and those who were commissioned to bring the alms of Corinth to Jerusalem, do not belong to the sacred hierarchy, since they were elected by the votes of the people. It is certain that neither Titus nor Timothy had among his instructions the command to submit the choice or the approbation of the deacons and priests to the faithful in general, although they are ordered to take into account the good reputation of the candidates, both in the church and outside of it.[1] Thus even if the government of the Apostle was neither despotic nor arbitrary, a democratic régime was little to his taste.

2. Like every perfect society, the Church possesses the inalienable right to govern itself, to defend itself, and to perpetuate itself, which is derived directly from its right to exist.

The power to govern itself comes to it from God. " Take heed to yourselves and to the whole flock, wherein the Holy Ghost hath set you as guardians, to rule the Church of God, which he hath purchased with his own blood,"[2] says St Paul to the Elders of Ephesus, who had hastened to receive his last instructions. This text is to be carefully considered. The persons in question have only a subordinate authority and yet they watch over, inspect, and govern the faithful of Jesus Christ. Although they have been appointed and constituted officials, through the medium of man, they hold their authority from the Holy Spirit, from whom in the last analysis it is derived. Their charge is a local one and their jurisdiction restricted, yet they govern the Church of God, because the Church is one and indivisible. The power of legislating Paul reserves to himself. He knows only one authority higher than his own—namely, that of Christ, and he knows very well how to distinguish the precepts of his Master from his own,[3] but he is conscious also of commanding in the name of him whose ambassador he is : " If any seem to be a prophet or spiritual, let him know the things that I write to you, they are the commandments of the Lord,"[4] writes Paul to the Corinthians, to whom he has just given various in-

---

χειροτονεῖν meant usually " to elect in any way whatever," or even " to designate, institute (or) establish," without any accessory idea of a vote or an election. Cf. Josephus, Antiq., VII, xi, 1 ; XIII, ii, 2 (nomination of the high priest) ; VI, xiii, 9 ; VII, ix, 3 (of the king) ; Philo, ed. Mangey, vol. ii, pp. 58 and 76 (Joseph established governor), etc.

[1] 1 Tim. iii, 1-14 ; Tit. i, 5-7. Impose not hands lightly upon any man (1 Tim. v, 22), nor ordain a neophyte (1 Tim. iii, 6), and let the deacon be proved before being raised to a higher rank (1 Tim. iii, 10-13).

[2] Acts xx, 28.   [3] 1 Cor. vii, 8, 10, 25.

[4] 1 Cor. xiv, 37.

junctions. Terrible are his threats to the rebels and the disobedient.[1] Let no one take his humble exterior and mean appearance for weakness: "For the weapons of our warfare are not carnal, but mighty [with all the might] of God, unto the pulling down of fortifications, destroying counsels, and every height that exalteth itself against the knowledge of God, and bringing into captivity every thought unto the obedience of Christ; and having in readiness to punish all disobedience when your obedience shall be fulfilled."[2] He arrogates to himself, therefore, an entire sphere of sovereignty, not only over the will of the faithful, but even over their intelligence—a power truly superhuman, and, as he himself says, divine.

But although the Apostle, neither at Corinth nor elsewhere, admits any authority capable of restraining his own, he recognizes in all the churches an authority on a level with his and below it. He invests Titus and Timothy with his power;[3] he calls upon the Thessalonians and Corinthians to make use of theirs; he congratulates the latter on having used it with moderation;[4] and he reminds the elders of Ephesus of their right and duty to govern the Church of God.[5]

If the primitive Church offered to their enemies from without only a passive resistance, the *non possumus* of which the apostles had given both the formula and the example,[6] it needed other weapons against internal enemies, subjected to its jurisdiction by the fact of their baptism.[7] In menacing the seditious of Corinth with his severity, Paul does not dream that his right to punish the guilty can be questioned: "Behold, this is the third time I am coming to you; in the mouth of two or three witnesses shall every word stand. I have told before and foretell, as present and now absent, to them that sinned before and to all others, that if I come again, I will not spare. . . . I write these things, being absent, that, being present, I may not deal more severely according to the power which the Lord hath given unto me unto edification and not to destruction."[8] Everywhere the Apostle claims with the same energy his right to punish. His repression will not be despotic and he will keep within legal forms, but he will chastise the offenders according to their fault and will pardon only if they repent.[9] He prescribes to Timothy the same course: "Against an *elder* receive not an accusation but under two or three witnesses. Them that sin reprove before all, that the rest also may have fear."[10]

[1] 2 Cor. xiii, 10.  
[2] 2 Cor. x, 4-6.  
[3] 1 Tim. i, 3; Titus i, 5.  
[4] 1 Thess. v, 14; 1 Cor. v, 2, 13; 2 Cor. ii, 10, 11.  
[5] Acts xx, 28.  
[6] Acts iv, 20; v, 29.  
[7] 1 Cor. v, 12, 13.  
[8] 2 Cor. xiii, 1, 2, 10.  
[9] 2 Cor. xii, 21.  
[10] 1 Tim. v, 19, 20.

The punishments inflicted by St Paul were a reprimand, temporary exclusion, and the anathema. One of the first duties of the heads of the Church is to reprove those who do evil. There were evidently two kinds of admonitions : one, paternal or fraternal, which could be private ; the other more official and severe, which had to be public. St Paul seems to indicate, as does the Gospel, that these two reprimands followed each other and served as a prelude to a more serious punishment. "A man that is a heretic ($αἱρετικὸν ἄνθρωπον$, a promoter of schism and divisions), after the first and second admonition, avoid, knowing that he that is such an one is subverted and sinneth, being condemned by his own judgement."[1] Moreover, excommunication itself had two entirely different forms : one was the simple putting into quarantine of turbulent, quarrelsome, or scandal-causing Christians, the temporary cessation of all relations with them until they had amended their conduct; such were the idlers of Thessalonica, the public sinners of Corinth,[2] and the innovators of the Pastoral Epistles, unless these last belong to the category of those obstinate and incorrigible criminals whom Paul delivers over to Satan to teach them not to blaspheme. He had pronounced that anathema upon Hymenæus and Alexander.[3] For a moment he had thought of fulminating it against the man guilty of incest in Corinth, but he soon contented himself with a milder penalty,[4] and even congratulated the Church on having pardoned him, for the right to be severe towards rebels implies that of forgiving the penitent.

The care with which certain Greek clubs of revellers and social circles sought to prevent the interference of the State in their internal affairs, and the penalties which they inflicted on offending members, such as fines in money or in kind, exclusion from festivals and banquets, and even expulsion from membership, cast very little light upon the primitive constitution of the Christian communities, which were not formed on this model. The organization of Jewish societies in the Diaspora would give a more correct idea of them. But these Jewish societies, being legal associations, had in case of need the support or at least the tolerance of the public officials. The council of the elders enjoyed in them a discretionary power in both civil and religious matters; and it dispensed floggings with astonishing liberality, as well as a simple excommunication and a solemn exclusion accompanied with an anathema which was doubtless only a mild equivalent of stoning, in cases where the latter was not practicable. On the contrary, we do not find among the early Christians any example of corporal punishment; the penalties were reduced to reprimands, to temporary exclusion, and to excom-

---

[1] Titus iii, 10.    [2] 2 Thess. iii, 14 and 1 Cor. v, 2-7.
[3] 1 Tim. i, 20.    [4] 1 Cor. v, 5 ; 2 Cor. ii, 5-9.

munication, coupled with a delivering up of the guilty party into the hands of Satan. Not one of these punishments, not even the last mentioned, was purely vindictive. This is because the Church does not forget the injunctions of its divine Founder; its aim is not domination; its ideal is not to inspire fear and to make a show of its force; the measure and limit of its power is the protection of the truth, of which it is " the pillar and ground."[1]

3. Let us sum up in a few words the conception of the Church as it appears from the writings and practice of the Apostle.

All the churches under Paul, from their foundation or very soon after, are provided with clergy appointed by him or by his delegates. This clergy, besides the deacons, comprises other persons called indifferently πρεσβύτεροι or ἐπίσκοποι. The names may have been synonymous without their functions being so; but the synonymy of the names might also extend to the functions. Hence we have three distinct hypotheses; either the superior dignitaries were all bishops; or some of them were priests and others bishops, although their names were the same; or finally they were all merely priests. Of these three hypotheses the last is the only satisfactory one. The first, which once satisfied Petavius, is absolutely devoid of proof and encounters serious objections. The second is no less precarious, for what essentially distinguishes the bishop from the priest is the power of holy order; and we do not find the slightest trace of this power in the *resident clergy* of Paul's churches.

---

[1] 1 Tim. iii, 15 : [Ταῦτά σοι γράφω] ἵνα εἰδῇς πῶς δεῖ ἐν οἴκῳ Θεοῦ ἀναστρέφεσθαι, ἥτις ἐστὶν ἐκκλησία Θεοῦ ζῶντος, στῦλος καὶ ἑδραίωμα τῆς ἀληθείας. The instruction is addressed to Timothy, but it is a general one and applies to all the ecclesiastical dignitaries mentioned in chapter iii, and perhaps to the classes of Christians whose duties are indicated in chapter ii. It is necessary therefore to translate πῶς δεῖ ἀναστρέφεσθαι by " how it is necessary to behave," and not by " how it is necessary to behave *thyself*."—The expression οἶκος Θεοῦ, introduced by iii, 5 (*si quis domui suae praeesse nescit quomodo Ecclesiae Dei diligentiam habebit ?*), signifies *family* of God (*domus Domini*, Os. viii, 1 ; ix, 8, 15) ; and thus we avoid the inconvenience of comparing the Church (which in the N.T. never denotes a material edifice) first to a *house* and then to a *column*. The meaning, therefore, is " how it is necessary to behave in the family of God, *seeing that it is* (ἥτις is argumentative) the assembly of the living God."

A *column* serves either to support a roof or an architrave, or to lift into the air, to expose to view, a commemorative monument. The latter sense is preferable both on account of the use of the singular (one column alone cannot support a roof), and because the first meaning is expressed more forcibly by the other term. In fact *firmamentum* (ἑδραίωμα from ἑδραῖος) denotes all that gives solidity to an edifice and assures its duration, like its footings, basements, buttresses and pillars. If, therefore, it is the Church's mission to show forth the truth to men, it is because she is visible ; and it is her duty to defend this truth against external assaults and the wear and tear of centuries, because she is infallible.

Whenever a new community was founded or *priests* and *deacons* were to be ordained in it, Paul intervened personally or sent some one of his delegates : Timothy, on whom he had himself laid his hands ; Titus, his most active fellow-labourer ; probably Luke, who seems to have organized the church of Philippi ; perhaps Tychicus or Artemas, who were to replace Titus in Crete, when the latter was called elsewhere ; and no doubt others also. But it would be a fallacy to suppose that things went on everywhere in the same way, for the situation of the churches at Jerusalem, Antioch, Rome, and Alexandria may have been very different. The hierarchy with three degrees of rank must have existed ever since the apostolic age.

While not forming part of the clergy, the *widows* aided them and sometimes took their place in dealing with women. They did not enter into the order of widows simply because they were widows, but by their express profession of widowhood with the formal ratification of the Church, which took them under its charge under certain conditions. As to the so-called *deaconesses,* by these Paul probably means only the wives of the deacons or persons who had received from the Holy Spirit the special *charisma* of διακονία.[1]

If, in spite of all this, the organization of the Pauline churches seems rather rudimentary, and the role of the resident authorities a very subordinate one, we must take into consideration four circumstances which we are too apt to lose sight of.

All the churches, into whose interior life St Paul's Epistles allow us to cast a furtive glance, are extremely young. The oldest have had at most only eight or ten years of existence ; the others have just been born. Ought we to be surprised at finding them still in tutelage, and can we expect them to have already attained their complete growth?

The cities, which the Apostle had made it his special prerogative to present to Christ, were considered to be among the most turbulent and undisciplined of the Roman world. If he had left these foundations to themselves, instead of keeping them directly under his hand and governing them by his delegates, he would have run the risk of seeing them ruined by intrigues and intestine quarrels, after the fashion of the democratic assemblies of that time, and, indeed, of all times.

There was also the danger of isolation to be guarded against. The union of the Jewish Christian communities was cemented by national sentiment as much as, if not more than, by religious sentiment. The first of those bonds was wanting in the Gentile churches, for love of country did not

[1] Concerning priests, deacons, widows and *deaconesses,* see Vol. I, pp. 341 *ff*.

exist in the Hellenic world, or was confounded with pride in the city itself. Under these conditions, a too complete or a too hasty autonomy offered a constant danger of schism and heresy.

Perhaps the charismatic gifts, more abundant at the beginning, made up in some measure for the lack of hierarchical organization. This state of things was transitory, but it was able to serve as a period of transition between the infancy of the churches and the epoch of their maturity.

# BOOK VI
## THE FRUITS OF REDEMPTION

# CHAPTER I

## THE CHRISTIAN LIFE

### I—THE PRINCIPLES OF MORALITY

1. Foundations of Christian Morality. 2. The Will of God. 3. Baptismal Regeneration. 4. New Relations.

1. **I**NSTEAD of rolling on in endless sentences, complicated with sub-clauses and causative particles, crammed with digressions and parentheses which leave no respite to the eye and mind, like the dogmatic parts of Paul's Epistles, the *moral* parts, cut, chopped, and slashed into minute clauses, are shelled out usually like peas from a pod in a monotonous litany without apparent sequence, grammatical connection, or any real relation to the dominant idea. Nothing is more disconcerting than this contrast, and the reader is at times repelled by such an inopportune and disconnected ethical discourse, which seems to be suited to all situations and all recipients. Even if the moral teaching of the two Epistles to the Ephesians and Colossians does form a consistent and summary rule for home-life, and even if that of the Epistle to the Romans outlines the principal duties of the citizen towards the governmental authority and towards his fellow-men, it is not clear why the Apostle connects them just with those letters rather than any others. Only in the Epistle to the Galatians does the moral teaching spring from dogma, and even there nothing reminds us of the consummate art of the Epistle to the Hebrews, where dogma and morality unite in one harmonious whole. They are almost always lists of counsels and precepts like the following :

> Rebuke the unruly ;
> Comfort the feeble-minded ;
> Support the weak ;
> Be patient towards all men. .
> Quench not the Spirit ;
> Despise not prophecies ;
> Prove all things ;
> Hold fast that which is good ;
> Avoid all appearance of evil.[1]

This phenomenon is not peculiar to the short Epistles ; the long ones furnish us with numerous examples of it :

---

[1] 1 Thess. v, 14, 19-22.

> Give alms with simplicity;
> Rule with carefulness;
> Show mercy with cheerfulness.
> Let love be without dissimulation;
> Hate that which is evil, cleave to the good.
>   Be joyful in hope,
> Patient in tribulation;
> Persevering in prayer;
> Provident for the necessities of the saints;
> Pursuing hospitality.
> Bless them that persecute you;
> Bless and curse not.
>   Rejoice with them that rejoice;
> Weep with them that weep.[1]

In this long series of phrases with no grammatical connection or logical unity, it is difficult to see a governing principle of moral teaching. For that is precisely the delicate—
I was about to say the weak—point of Paul's moral teaching:
after having completely done away with the Mosaic Law,
he never says clearly with what he replaces it. The Law of
Moses is abolished past return; Christ is its end and the goal
towards which it tends, no doubt, but he is also the limit
where it dies.[2] The code of Sinai has been destroyed, nailed
to the cross.[3] Christians are dead to the Law and the Law
is dead for them.[4] Children of the free woman, not of the
bondwoman, it is their right and duty to persevere in the
liberty which Christ has won for them.[5] In seeing Paul
intent on destroying the whole edifice of the ancient Law,
without appearing to think of reconstructing it, we ask
with anxiety where this work of demolition is going to stop,
and on what foundation the obligation of the new dispensation is to rest. For the distinction imagined by certain
exegetes between the ceremonial and the moral law, one of
which survives and continues to serve as a standard, while
the other is stricken to death by Christ whom it has killed
first, this fine distinction is unknown to the Apostle. For
him the Sinaitic code is indivisible; it is an edifice that stands
or falls in one block. Nor is there any reason to inquire
whether his attitude in regard to the Law was modified with
time, either in the sense of extreme inflexibility or in that
of conciliation. His ideas, fully fixed after the apostolic
gathering of A.D. 50, before he had written a single line of
his Epistles,[6] thereafter never varied. At all times he was
able to use condescension and to tolerate practices which were
unimportant and consecrated by usage and by religious
memories, yielding, if necessary, to the occasion,[7] but from

---

[1] Rom. xii, 8-15.       [2] Rom. x, 4.       [3] Eph. ii, 15; Col. ii, 14.
[4] Rom. vii, 4, 6; Gal. ii, 19; Col. ii, 20, etc.
[5] Gal. iv, 21, 31; v, 1.
[6] Gal. ii, 3-7, 14-21, and the incident of Antioch.
[7] Acts xvi, 3 (circumcision of Timothy); xviii, 18 (vow of St Paul);
xxi, 26 (sacrifices in the temple and ritual purification); Rom. xiv, 1-6

one end of his career to the other he maintained, as a matter of principle, the total abolition of the Torah, for the Jews as well as for the Gentiles.

As the ever increasing light thrown upon the natural law by revelation is an irrevocable fact, an attempt might be made to reconstruct on the ruins of the Torah a new code which would be only the natural law illumined in its darkest corners by divine revelation. But this system, however ingenious it may be, has not the approval of Paul. The Apostle certainly recognizes the existence of the natural law ; he declares that the heathen are inexcusable for having violated it ;[1] he describes conscience as summoning men to the bar and pronouncing, according to circumstance, verdicts of acquittal or sentence of condemnation ;[2] but he does not give to this internal standard the name of law,[3] because law is for him the expression of a positive will. Moreover, he would not allow the Christian, freed from the Law, to retrograde to the state of nature. The Mosaic Law necessarily marks a stage in the ascent of humanity, and, if it has to disappear, it must be replaced by something better. So, at the very moment when he contrasts the régime of the Law with the régime of grace, implying that the two states are incompatible, he vigorously desires his exemption from all law, and declares that he is subject to the Law of Christ. Such is the paradox : the Christian is so essentially free that he cannot be under the yoke of the Law, yet, nevertheless, he is subject to a law. This is because the new system is a true law, if one considers its obligatory character, and it is not a law, if one thinks of the imperfections of the Mosaic Law. In calling it a law of grace, we are in accordance with the mind of the Apostle ; in calling it a law of Christ, we are in harmony with his language.[4]

2. The liberty of the children of God is not licence, and the deliverance from the Mosaic yoke is not exemption from all restraint.[5] Paul had to protest many times against the false

---

(tolerance of the weak who distinguish between meats and days). In Gal. ii, 3-4, Paul makes it clearly understood that he might have consented to the circumcision of Titus, as he subsequently decided that of Timothy, if the Judaizing Christians had not tried to force it on him. 1 Cor. ix, 20, 21 formulates the general principle of this tolerance : *Factus sum Judaeis tanquam Judaeus ut Judaeos lucrarer.*

[1] Rom. i, 32.  [2] Rom. ii, 14, 15.

[3] Paul's *law* is always the positive law. In Rom. ii, 14 (οὗτοι νόμον μὴ ἔχοντες ἑαυτοῖς εἰσι νόμος), the natural law is not called *law*, but the pagans are *their own law* by analogy, because they find in themselves a light which replaces the Law. The Gentiles have no Law, they are ἄνομοι, 1 Cor. ix, 21 ; Rom. ii, 12.

[4] Gal. vi, 2 (ὁ νόμος τοῦ Χριστοῦ) ; 1 Cor. ix, 21 (ἔννομος Χριστοῦ) ; Rom. vi, 15 (οὐκ ἐσμὲν ὑπὸ νόμον ἀλλὰ ὑπὸ χάριν).

[5] Gal. v, 13.

interpretation of his thought.[1]  He was misunderstood.  He never said that God has abrogated the ancient system without substituting for it a more perfect one.  At the moment when Jesus abolished the régime of the Law, he laid the foundation of the régime of grace.[2]  There is here no solution of continuity ; the New Testament takes over the moral law of the Old, which it supplants.  Not content with sanctioning it, it perfects and completes it : " Whatsoever things are true," writes Paul to the Philippians, " whatsoever honourable, whatsoever just, whatsoever holy, whatsoever pure, whatsoever lovely, whatsoever of good fame, virtuous, and praiseworthy, think on these things."  There we have all the natural law under its various aspects, proposed to the faithful; but it is no more merely as a natural law that it compels them : " All that you have both learned and received [from me]," adds Paul, " this do ye."[3]  Thanks to the revelation of the Gospel, the natural law—as also the code of Sinai in its moral part— becomes again a positive law.  Only the relation of man to the law is no longer the same.  The principal defect in the ancient Law was that of being external to man and little adapted to our present fallen state.[4]  In order to restore equilibrium, it was necessary either to lower the Law to the level of fallen man, or to raise man to the level of the divine Law.  It had been imposed upon the Israelites through the double mediation of Moses and the angels amid the terrors of Sinai.[5]  Born subject to the Law as well as a member of the chosen race, the Jew, from the first dawn of reason, had to endure its burden whether he liked it or not, which was rendered more crushing through the feeling of his own impotence.[6]  Here was nothing spontaneous, free, generous, and filial.  The slave of the Law could only have the thoughts of a slave : thoughts of fear, distrust, and melancholy.

Entirely different is the condition of the Christian.  By the act of faith and by baptism, which is its seal, he has given himself freely to the service of God and has become a soldier of Christ.  He escapes from the yoke of the Law only by abdicating his independence.  The will of God, accepted with his whole heart and embraced in advance in the measure in which it is manifested, becomes his rule of conduct : " Know you not that by yielding yourselves as slaves to obey anyone,

---

[1] Rom. iii, 8 ; vi, 1-15.

[2] Matt. v, 17 (οὐκ ἦλθον καταλῦσαι ἀλλὰ πληρῶσαι).  The word πληρῶσαι, employed absolutely, must be understood in the most comprehensive sense : to *verify* the prophecies and to *perfect* the Law.  In fact, in the Sermon on the Mount the ancient Law is abrogated only in order to be at once re-established more perfectly (Matt. v, 21, 22, 27, 28, 31, 33, 34, 43, 44).  Each opposition to the Law of Moses gives place to a *crescendo* (*Dictum est antiquis . . . ego* autem *dico vobis*).

[3] Phil. iv, 8, 9.

[4] Rom. vii, 14.

[5] Gal. iii, 19.

[6] Rom. vii, 5-11,

his slaves you are whom you obey? . . . Now, being made free from sin and being subject to God, you have your fruit unto sanctification and the end life everlasting. For the wages of sin is death; but the gift of God is life eternal in Christ Jesus our Lord."[1] It is hardly to be doubted that Paul, when writing these lines, had in view the Jewish slave and the Roman soldier. Among the Hebrews slavery differed little from ordinary home-life; for compatriots it could not in any case be prolonged more than six years without the express consent of the interested party. If this consent was given, the slave entered with full right and for ever into the house of his master, but his position had nothing humiliating or degrading in it; he was part of the family; he enjoyed the religious privileges of the nation; he was a man and a citizen, not, as among the Gentiles, a beast of burden. So Paul, who so forcibly repudiates any suspicion of cringing and servility, loves to call himself the slave of Christ, and even the slave of his brethren for the love of Christ. Though a slave of Christ, he is also the soldier of Christ. It is well-known that the Roman legions enrolled only free men. The enrolment of *servi,* even after a previous enfranchisement and in case of compulsion, had always been considered as a bad example, incompatible with the dignity of the eagles. The recruits, on taking oath, consecrated their life to the *imperator* and bound themselves to an absolute obedience, often harder than slavery, but elevated and ennobled by their quality as citizens and by the sentiment of a duty freely assumed. This is why the Apostle is so fond of using military language, which recalls to him the engagement contracted at baptism and the state of dependence in which he has voluntarily placed himself by the act of faith which made him a Christian. He preferably gives to his disciple the title of a soldier of Christ,[2] the most honourable that he knows; he adjures the Thessalonians to put on the armour of theological virtues, the breastplate of faith and of charity, and the helmet of hope;[3] in a famous panoply he distributes to the Ephesians the whole equipment of the legionary, the breastplate, the helmet, the short two-edged sword, and the long hide-covered shield, without forgetting the sandals and the sword-belt of leather,

---

[1] Rom. vi, 13-23.—Δοῦλος (with its derivatives δουλεύειν, δουλοῦν) is the pivotal word of the chapter. The whole moral discourse revolves around this contrast: *formerly* you were *slaves* of sin, *now* you are *slaves* of justice and of God.—The military metaphor, sufficiently indicated by the context, where sin personified appears like an *emperor* having weapons and soldiers (vi, 12-14), is emphasized still more by the word *wages* (ὀψώνια). It would have more prominence if we translated χάρισμα by *donativum* (the imperial gift granted to the soldiers in addition to their regular pay), as Tertullian does, *De resurr. carnis,* 47.

[2] 2 Tim. ii, 3. He also calls Epaphroditus (Phil. ii, 25) and Archippus (Philem. 2) his comrades in arms.

[3] 1 Thess. v, 8. Reminder of Isa. lix, 17 and of Wisd. v, 17-20.

and he sees in these the symbol of as many Christian virtues. [1]
If the metaphors of weapons, of combat, of wages, of
soldiery and the like recur constantly in his writings, [2] it is
because he has continually in mind the oath by which he constituted himself the liegeman of Christ, an oath which obliges
him " not to embarrass himself with the cares of this life,
but to think only of pleasing his master." [3]  As a soldier and
voluntary slave of Christ, the Christian belongs, therefore,
no longer to himself.  The rule which he must follow, having
freely accepted it, is the will of God, the will of the Lord. [4]
Such is also the external standard which no Christian can
ignore.

One of the most certain facts of the apostolic age, although
the critics have taken some time to ascertain it, is the existence of a catechetical teaching of morals, quite uniform in

---

[1] Eph. vi, 13-17.  The Christian's six pieces of armour are (a) the *sword-
belt*, which symbolizes *the truth*, alluding to Is. xi, 5 : *Et erit justitia cingulum
lumborum ejus et fides cinctorium renum ejus* (Fides = אֱמוּנָה, ἀλήθεια
[LXX], fidelity, veracity).  The Christian has need of it in order to foil the
artifices of the father of lies.—(b) The breastplate (θώραξ), symbol of *justice*
according to Isa. lix, 17 : *Indutus est justitia ut lorica.*  Justice means here
the totality of the virtues, all necessary for the protection of the heart, the
centre of the moral life.—(c) *Sandals*, narrow and light, emblem of *promptitude* in God's service.  The Roman legionaries of the time of Polybius wore
greaves above the left foot; but the Apostle does not allude to them.—(d) The
*buckler*, which, like lively *faith*, preserves us from the sharp arrows of the
enemy.  Paul does not speak here of the little round buckler (ἀσπίς), but of
the large, rectangular buckler (θυρεός), measuring about 4 by 2½ feet, formed
of a frame of bronze covered with fresh skins, which protected the entire
person except the lower part of the leg.—(e) The *helmet* (περικεφαλάια)
is *salvation* (Is. lix, 17) or the hope of salvation (1 Thess. v, 8).  In fact, it
protects the head, which is the point at which the adversary aims.—(f) *The
sword of the Spirit* (μάχαιρα), the sword furnished by the Spirit, or the
spiritual sword, is the *word of God,* which assists us to repel the attacks of
error and falsehood.  It is not a question of the long sword (ξίφος), but of the
short sword with a stout blade and two edges (μάχαιρα).—On the complete
equipment of the Roman legionary see Polybius, *Histor.,* vi, 23 and Josephus,
*Bell. Jud.,* III, v, 5.  It will be remarked that St Paul says nothing of offensive
weapons, such as the lance (λόγχη, δόρυ, κόντος), the javelin (ἄκων), etc.
[2] Here are some of these texts : 1 Thess. v, 8 ; 1 Cor. ix, 7 ; 2 Cor. vi, 7 ;
x, 3-6 ; xi, 8 ; Rom. vi, 13, 14, 23 ; xiii, 12 ; Phil. i, 30 ; ii, 25 ; Col. i, 29 ;
ii, 1 ; iv, 10 ; Eph. vi, 10-18 (cf. iv, 8) ; Philem. 2 and 23 ; 1 Tim. i, 18 ; iv, 10 ;
vi, 12 ; 2 Tim. ii, 3, 4 ; iii, 6 ; iv, 7.—*Cf.* Howson, *The Metaphors of St Paul,*
London, 1883, and, for the Fathers, Harnack, *Militia Christi, die christl.
Religion und der Soldatenstand in den ersten drei Jahrhunderten,* Tübingen,
1905.  The military language of Tertullian, St Cyprian and Origen is remarkable.  The following phrase of St Ignatius (*Ad. Polyc.,* vi, 2) is to be
compared with the panoply of St Paul : Ἀρέσκετε ᾧ στρατεύεσθε (cf.
2 Tim. ii, 1) ἀφ' οὗ καὶ τὰ ὀψώνια κομίζεσθε (cf. Rom. vi, 23 ; 1 Cor. ix, 7) ;
μή τις ὑμῶν δεσέρτωρ (*desertor*) εὑρεθῇ.  Τὸ βάπτισμα ὑμῶν μενέτω ὡς ὅπλα
(cf. Rom. vi, 13), ἡ πίστις ὡς περικεφαλαία (cf. Eph. vi, 17 ; 1 Thess. v, 8),
ἡ ἀγάπη ὡς δόρυ, ἡ ὑπομονὴ ὡς πανοπλία (cf. Eph. vi, 11-13).  Τὰ δεπόσιτα
ὑμῶν τὰ ἔργα ὑμῶν (*deposita ;* for the idea cf. 2 Tim. i, 12), ἵνα τὰ ἄκκεπτα
ὑμῶν ἄξια κομίσησθε (*accepta* = what is put to your credit, what is due to you).
[3] 2 Tim. ii, 3, 4.
[4] Rom. xii, 2 ; Eph. vi, 6 ; 1 Thess. v, 18 ; Eph. v, 17.

its content. St Paul clearly makes allusion to it, when he writes to the Corinthians : " Timothy will put you in mind of my *ways,* which are in Christ Jesus, as I teach everywhere in every church.''[1] The *ways* of Paul are not his conduct, but as the word plainly indicates, and as the incidental explanatory clause makes indubitable, his supernatural moral teaching. Some may find it astonishing, if they will, that so free and impulsive a genius should bind himself to a regular and, so to speak, stereotyped method of instruction ; but his positive testimony is there; he taught " everywhere, in every church " the same things in the same way, to such a degree that it was sufficient for him subsequently to send one of his disciples to refresh their memories concerning it. Still more, this catechetical teaching existed also elsewhere, and St Paul writes to the Romans, to whom he had not preached the Gospel: " You have obeyed from the heart unto that form of doctrine which has been delivered unto you," or perhaps with greater force " into which you have been delivered."[2] All the context shows that this *type of doctrine* is a moral teaching, and the very name of *type* shows that the transmission of it was not left to caprice or to individual inspiration. Paul forbids the Thessalonians to have any intercourse with the brethren who may depart from the *tradition* received from him, and he lays the same injunction on the Romans relative to the faithful who may go counter to the *doctrine* that has been taught them.[3] Way, tradition, doctrine, type of doctrine, *didascalia*—and even the word *catechesis*[4]—all these terms come astonishingly from the Apostle's pen in a sense so akin to that of succeeding generations. Thus the will of God, proclaimed by Christ, [5] and promulgated by the apostles, [6] awakened in the neophytes a very concrete idea. When Paul said laconically : " Do not act as do the Gentiles who have not the Law, or like the Jews who have only the Law ; let your conduct be worthy of saints, worthy of your vocation,

---

[1] I Cor. iv, 17.   See p. 35.          [2] Rom. vi, 17.

[3] 2 Thess. iii, 6 and Rom. xvi, 17.

[4] Gal. vi, 6.

[5] Feine, *Jesus Christus und Paulus,* 1902, pp. 68-69, claims that the precepts of Jesus have not the force of law in Paul's eyes, and he gives for this the curious reason that Paul does not consider himself bound to observe them. But, in the example which he cites (1 Cor. ix, 14 : *Dominus ordinavit iis qui Evangelium annuntiant de Evangelio vivere*)—the obligation regarding the faithful—the Apostles can evidently give up their right.—When Jesus has spoken, Paul has only to transmit his orders, 1 Cor. vii, 10, 12, 25 ; ix, 14 ; Acts xx, 35.—The number of direct appeals to the authority of the Lord is not very great, but they must have been much more so in his oral preaching.   Moreover, there are more allusions to Christ's words in Paul's Epistles than one would at first suppose.   *Cf.* Resch, *Der Paulinismus und die Logia Jesu,* Leipzig, 1904, and Juncker, *Die Ethik des Ap. Paulus,* Halle, 1904.

[6] 2 Cor. v, 20 ; x, 5.

worthy of the Gospel, worthy of Christ, worthy of God,"[1]
these short phrases said a great deal. They reminded the
neophyte of the moment when, embracing the faith, he had
broken with the past, had given himself to God and submitted to the law of Christ; they summed up in a word the
apostolic teaching, of which doubtless nothing can give us
a more correct idea than the *Ways,* that little compendium
of morals inserted in two of the most ancient specimens of
Christian literature, the *Teaching of the Apostles* and the
*Epistle of Barnabas.*

3. If it be objected that we put the Christian back again,
by a subterfuge, under the yoke of the Law from which
Christ had freed him, and that the situation of the baptized
infant, inheriting the obligation before knowing what it is,
is identical with that of the Jewish infant born subject to the
Law, we reply that such is not the case. No doubt the
Apostle, addressing himself to converts of recent date, is
thinking of the actual faith of adults; but his doctrine can
be applied also to the habitual faith of the Christian child.
Faith, whether actual or habitual, has always the same tendency; it is by nature a spontaneous impulse of the mind
and heart, by which man gives over into the hands of God
his intelligence and will. If there is a difference, it is wholly
in favour of habitual faith, for here the Holy Spirit works
alone and nothing impedes his action. Now the intimate
impulse of the Holy Spirit cannot be compared to an external
compulsion; it elevates man instead of oppressing him; it
takes from obedience its servile character. The Christian is
made by baptism subject to the law of grace, as he is born
subject to the law of nature; but, properly speaking, he
is not *under* the law, because he is not, like Israel, under the
yoke of the Law. For no one will maintain that the natural
law, inherent as it is in our being, is for man a foreign yoke.
Now the law of Christ is to the Christian what the natural
law is to man. Our incorporation into the mystical Christ
is not only a transformation and a metamorphosis, it is
a real creation, the production of a new being,[2] subject to
new rights and consequently to new duties: " Know you not
that all we who are baptized in Christ Jesus are baptized in
his death? We are buried together with him by baptism
into death; that, as Christ is risen from the dead by the glory
of the Father, so we also may walk in newness of life. For
if we have been planted together in the likeness of his death,

---

[1] Rom. xvi, 2 (ἀξίως τῶν ἀγίων); Eph. iv, 1 (ἀξίως τῆς κλήσεως ἧς ἐκλήθητε);
Phil. i, 27 (ἀξίως τοῦ εὐαγγελίου); Col. i, 10 (ἀξίως τοῦ Κυρίου); 1 Thess.
ii, 12 (ἀξίως τοῦ Θεοῦ).—Negative rule: do not act like pagans, 1 Cor. vi, 11;
Eph. iv, 17-21; Titus iii, 3-7, etc.
[2] 2 Cor. v, 17 (εἴ τις ἐν Χριστῷ, καινὴ κτίσις); Eph. ii, 10 (κτισθέντες ἐν
Χ. 'I.); Gal. vi, 15; Eph. ii, 15; ii, 22, etc.

we shall be also in the likeness of his resurrection.  Knowing
this, that our old man is crucified with him, that the body of
sin may be destroyed, to the end that we may serve sin no
longer.''[1]  For everyone who has become familiar with Paul's
thought this untranslatable phrase has nothing obscure.  The
rite of baptism, doing what it signifies, causes us to be born
into divine life.  It causes us to die to ourselves by burying
us in the death of Christ; it infuses into us the divine nourishment by grafting us on him; he envelops us with his grace
and spirit by immersing us into his mystical body.  Thenceforth '' it is no more I that live, but Jesus Christ that liveth
in me.''

It is evident that this new being required new operations :
*Operatio sequitur esse*.  In order to know the nature and
extent of our obligations, it is enough to become acquainted
with ourselves, and in order to do that it is sufficient to reflect upon the mystery of our supernatural birth.  What do
we see at baptism?  A death, a resurrection, a burial, a
return to the light, and these four things produced by the
sacramental rite which symbolizes them are destined to
endure for ever; and not only to endure, but to grow and
develop.  The death of sin is in itself finished and final, for
Jesus Christ, in dying, breaks the sceptre of sin, and in
causing us to die with him makes us participants in his
victory; but, unlike physical death, death to sin is susceptible
of more and of less; it is not enough to affirm it; it is necessary to carry it out to completion.  '' You are dead and your
life is hid with Christ in God . . . mortify, therefore, your
members which are on the earth : fornication, uncleanness,
lust, evil concupiscence.''[2]  The ideal is always to carry the state
of the death of Jesus still further.  The life of grace, eternal
by its nature, desires also to be constantly strengthened and
renewed : '' Therefore, if you be risen with Christ, seek the
things that are above . ... mind the things that are above,
not the things that are upon the earth.''[3]  Our burial in
Christ must follow an analogous process; hence the Apostle,
after having said : '' For as many of you as have been baptized
in Christ have put on Christ,'' does not fail to add : '' Put
on the Lord Jesus Christ,''[4] for this act permits of unlimited
degrees.  Finally, Paul begs more and more clarifying light
for the neophytes, illumined by baptism, and urges them to
proceed from glory to glory.[5]

[1] Rom. vi, 3-6.  The principal verb is in the aorist (ἐβαπτίσθημεν, συνετάφημεν, συνεσταυρώθη) because it expresses the sacramental rite which passes ;
but the results produced are in the present, and the consequences for the
moral or glorified life are in the present or future (σύμφυτοι γεγόναμεν, τῆς
ἀναστάσεως ἐσόμεθα).  *Cf.* Gal. ii, 20.

[2] Col. iii, 5.                                   [3] Col. iii, 1-2.

[4] Gal. iii, 27 ; Rom. xiii, 14.

[5] Eph. i, 18 ; 2 Cor. iii, 18, etc.

4. Paul's moral teaching plainly has a solid foundation;
it is supported on the one side by the positive will of God,
proclaimed by Jesus Christ, promulgated by the apostles, and
accepted freely by the neophytes in their first act of faith;
and, on the other side, by baptismal regeneration and by the
new relations which it engenders; for, from the supernatural being received at baptism, special relations with each
of the three divine Persons are derived:

A relation of sonship with the Father;
A relation of consecration to the Holy Spirit;
A relation of mystical identity with Jesus Christ.

To analyze these three relations and to deduce the corollaries from them would be to expose in detail the whole of
the Apostle's moral system. Such is not our aim here; we
wish only to outline our route with a few landmarks; but this
rapid glance will reveal to what heights Paul rises and lifts
us.

Between the *adoptive sonship* of the New Testament and
the theocratic sonship of the Old there yawns a gulf. The
latter was collective and came to the individual only through
the medium of the chosen people. It was, properly speaking, Israel, and not the Israelites, who was the son of God.
If anyone in the Old Testament receives this title exceptionally, it is because he bears upon his brow a prophetic reflection of the Son *par excellence*. The Christian, on the
contrary, is a son individually and by full right; the Holy
Spirit puts upon his lips the name of Father, which marks
his new relation to God; but with the prerogatives of a son
he assumes also the duties of gratitude, confidence, and love.[1]

*The presence of the Holy Spirit,* which consecrates us, as
a temple, creates between him and us a new bond, difficult
to define, but impossible to deny. Now, every new relation
is a source of new obligations: hence, for the Christian the
duty not to grieve the Spirit,[2] nor to quench it,[3] and, above
all, not to destroy or profane his temple.[4] But it is also the
source of glorious privileges. As a guest in the just soul, the
Spirit is not inactive there; he produces in it *charismata,*
gifts, and permanent graces; he pours out upon it unction
and light; he engraves upon it the law of God in indelible
characters. Thus is explained that enigmatical phrase: "If
you are led by the Spirit, you are not under the Law."[5] The

---

[1] Rom. viii, 15-17.—Here we are only dealing with the *progress of revelation* and with the *different way* in which the two Testaments describe the life
of the just. *In reality*, the saints of the Old Testament possessed, like those
of the New, sanctifying grace, participation in the divine nature, adoptive
sonship and the presence of the Holy Spirit.

[2] Eph. iv, 30.                                    [3] 1 Thess. v, 19.
[4] 1 Cor. iii, 16-17; vi, 19; 2 Cor. vi, 16; Eph. ii, 21.
[5] Gal. v, 18.

Christian can obey the law, without being under it, because the law is no more for him an external, oppressive yoke, but an inward principle which guides him and urges him forward. Far from enslaving and crushing him, " the law of the Spirit of life delivers him from the law of sin and death."[1]

*The doctrine of the mystical body,* Paul's masterpiece, is no less fruitful in morals than in dogma. The first time he presents it, he himself makes the application of it with a clearness that leaves nothing to be desired. Showing that the diversity of the members and the unity of life are essential to this body of which Christ is the head and the Holy Spirit the soul, he deduces from it the reciprocal duties of love, justice, and solidarity, with the obligation for each of the members to collaborate for the general good.[2] It is all a concise programme of social morality, the originality of which consists in reconciling the demands of the common welfare, certainly not with selfishness, but with the instinctive quest of personal interest. One can hardly ascribe to chance the fact that the other three descriptions of the mystical body serve precisely as a preface to the second part of the Epistles, in which morals are clearly separated from dogma.[3] The intention appears manifest in the Epistle to the Romans, and hence the miscellaneous recommendations recently quoted are not to be wondered at. Precepts and counsels, unlike in appearance, find their unity in this principle : " We are one body in Christ and individually members one of another." Is it not evident that the corollary of this principle is our duty " to love one another with the charity of brotherhood " and " with honour to prefer one another?"[4] The doctrine of the mystical body is presented under a somewhat different aspect in the Epistles to the Ephesians and the Colossians. The obligation, which comes from it for each of the members, is to aspire to the perfection of the Head ;[5] for, in order that there may be harmony and proportion, each Christian must strive to grow to the measure of Christ.

## II—PRECEPTS OF SOCIAL MORALITY

1. The Christian and the Civil Authority. 2. The Christian Family.
3. Christian Marriage.

1. Baptismal regeneration is a second birth which renders Christians equal and free. " For as many of you as have been baptized in Christ have put on Christ. There is neither Jew nor Greek ; there is neither bond nor free ; for you are

[1] Rom. viii, 2.　　　　[2] I Cor. xii, 12-27. See above, pp. 286-7.
[3] Rom. xii, 4, 5 ; Eph. iv, 12-16 ; Col. ii, 19.
[4] Rom. xii, 10.
[5] Col. ii, 19. It is the mystical Christ who effects his own growth (τὴν αὔξησιν τοῦ σώματος ποιεῖται) ; the members have only to oppose no obstacle to it. *Cf.* Eph. iv, 15, 16.

all one in Christ Jesus."[1]  Differences of nationality, condition and sex no longer count for anything and disappear before that higher unity which reconciles them; they are in some way absorbed by the new specific form which the neophyte puts on, and which is nothing else than Christ. So much for equality.  Christian liberty is born from the same principles.  Set free by Christ, the Christian belongs thereafter only to Christ; the liberty received by him at baptism is inalienable : " Christ has given you liberty; stand fast, and fall not back again under the yoke of bondage."[2]  The reference here is to the yoke of the Law; but the application of the principle is general : " Ye are bought with a price; become not the slaves of men."[3]  One can imagine how evilminded people could abuse these maxims.  Both St Paul and St Peter had therefore to protest against the false interpreters of their thought : " You are free," says one, " but you are also servants of God; use not your freedom as a mask to disguise your wickedness."[4]  " You have been called unto liberty," says the other, " only make not liberty an excuse for the flesh."[5]  Do not imagine that you are exempt from the bonds of subordination and dependence and of engagement and contracts, of relations established by nature or created by casual circumstance.  Christian equality consists in the fact that from a religious point of view all have the same rights and the same duties, are dependent on the same sovereign judge and treat directly with the same God.  If Christian liberty delivers us from the slavery of sin and from the old Law, it does not at all suppress the hierarchical relations of society and the family.  Fraternity itself, the most characteristic mark of Christians, which would seem naturally to bring with it only privileges, also imposes duties : mutual support, tolerance, and the obligation to avoid scandal.  Thus the social duties of the Christian are in direct ratio to his rights.

The word of Jesus, " Render unto Cæsar the things that are Cæsar's, and unto God the things that are God's," is a remark so incisive that it must have graven itself deeply into the memories of all who heard it.  It was no less appropriate to inculcate this duty and to show the reason for it ; and this is what St Paul does in chapter xiii of the Epistle to the Romans :

> Let every soul be subject to higher powers.  For there is no power but from God ; and those that are are ordained of God.  Therefore he that resisteth the power resisteth the ordinance of God ; and they that resist purchase to themselves damnation.  For princes are not a terror to good deeds, but to the evil.
> Wilt thou then not be afraid of the power ?  Do that which is good

---

[1] Gal. iii, 27, 28.      [2] Gal. v, 1.      [3] 1 Cor. vii, 23.
[4] 1 Pet. ii, 16.      [5] Gal. v, 13

and thou shalt have praise from the same. For he is God's minister to thee for good. But if thou do what is evil, fear; for he beareth not the sword in vain. For he is God's minister, an avenger to execute wrath upon him that doth evil. Wherefore be subject of necessity, not only for wrath, but also for conscience' sake.

For therefore also you pay tribute; for they are the ministers of God, serving diligently unto this purpose.

Render therefore to all men their dues; tribute to whom tribute is due; custom to whom custom is due; fear to whom fear; honour to whom honour.

There has been much discussion about the seasonableness of these recommendations. As the Jews at Rome were notorious for their turbulence, and as the lawfulness of the tax paid to foreigners was a burning question in Israelite circles, it has been supposed that the neophytes were won over by the revolutionary ideas of the Palestine patriots. But neither Suetonius nor Arrian hint that the turbulence of the Roman Jews was directed against the established power; and the Jews of the Diaspora, far from claiming independence on theocratic grounds, like the zealots of Palestine, were, on the contrary, proud of their fidelity and loyalty; the empire had no more submissive subjects. Moreover, the Jewish element formed only a small part of the Church of Rome. There is, therefore, no use in seeking any special seasonableness in this teaching of the Apostle, who seems here purposely to use the most general terms, "every soul, the power, higher authorities, ministers," avoiding thus every allusion to local conditions. We find ourselves, consequently, confronting a theoretical rule regarding the attitude of Christians in respect to the civil power.

Paul formulates these three propositions: By right and in principle all power comes from God.—In fact and in practice the established power is from God.—Furthermore, the power is exercised in the name of God.

The first two propositions were almost an axiom among Paul's Jewish contemporaries. The Apostle confines himself to proclaiming them, distinguishing them, as is proper, and adding to them the evident consequence that to resist the power established by God is to resist the command of God himself.[1] He insists even more upon the third proposition.

[1] Rom. xiii, 1-2: Πᾶσα ψυχὴ ἐξουσίαις ὑπερεχούσαις ὑποτασσέσθω· οὐ γὰρ ἔστιν ἐξουσία εἰ μὴ ὑπὸ Θεοῦ, αἱ δὲ οὖσαι ὑπὸ Θεοῦ τεταγμέναι εἰσίν· ὥστε ὁ ἀντιτασσόμενος τῇ ἐξουσίᾳ τῇ τοῦ Θεοῦ διαταγῇ ἀνθέστηκεν.—(a) The precept is a general one: it is addressed to *every soul* (a biblical expression for every person, every individual) and concerns *all higher authority*, all the possessors of public authority by whatever name they may be called. The Latin word *sublimioribus* gives us to understand that the reference is only to the supreme authority, and ὑπερεχούσαις, if it adds anything to ἐξουσίαις, must have this meaning. Cf. 1 Pet. ii, 13 (εἴτε βασιλεῖ ὡς ὑπερέχοντι); Wisd. vi, 5 (where the kings are also ὑπερέχοντες). In fact, St Paul subsequently speaks of princes who bear the sword, levy tribute and execute vengeance; all of which can apply only to the supreme

The prince is the "minister of God" (διάκονος), "the lieutenant of God" (λειτουργός), whose duty it is to promote the welfare of society; especially to praise and reward good citizens and to terrify and punish the bad. If he bears the sword, it is in the name of God that he does so; if he avenges crime, it is also in the name of God. "It is necessary, therefore, to obey him, not only through fear of the punishment to be avoided, but also on account of the dictates of conscience," for the wrath with which the prince menaces the rebellious is just and sanctioned by God. It is also a matter of conscience to pay one's taxes. In demanding them, the sovereign is no less the minister of God, appointed to this office for the defence and good organization of the society of which he has the custody.[1] The phrase which sums it all up : " Render, therefore, to every man his due," shows that this it not of simple counsel, but of real obligation.

---

authority.—(b) Authority, considered in itself and in the abstract, is established by God (ὑπὸ Θεοῦ) ; God, the founder of society, is also the institutor of authority, without which no society can exist. Moreover, we cannot conceive of an authority which is not derived from God, the principle of all physical and moral being.—(c) The concrete authorities (αἱ δὲ οὖσαι—ἐξουσίαι being understood—means the authorities which actually exist : that is to say, the actual possessors of authority) are constituted, sanctioned and willed by God. It is, then, a universally received truth that princes receive their power from God : Wisd. vi, 3 (ἐδόθη παρὰ τοῦ κυρίου ἡ κράτησις ὑμῖν καὶ ἡ δυναστεία παρὰ ὑψίστου) ; John xix, 11 (Non haberes potestatem adversum me ullam, nisi tibi datum esset desuper) ; Josephus, Bell. Jud., II, viii, 7 (οὐ γὰρ δίχα Θεοῦ περιγίνεσθαί τινι τὸ ἄρχειν) ; Enoch, xlvi, etc. Of course, St Paul teaches us nothing about the origin of power, whether direct or indirect, mediate or immediate. Nor does he say what is to be done in case the authority is doubtful, contested, clearly usurped and illegitimate. He takes his standpoint in the normal conditions of life.—(d) In whatever way the actual authority may proceed from God, it governs in the name of God, and to resist it is to resist the will and the command of God (τῇ διαταγῇ). The consequence is evident.

[1] Rom. xiii, 3-6. The exercise of power is also derived from God : (a) Princes (ἄρχοντες are equivalent to chiefs of State, whatever their particular name may be) have to promote the public welfare : Θεοῦ γὰρ διάκονός ἐστιν σοὶ εἰς τὸ ἀγαθόν. Only the wicked are to fear them ; the good have nothing to fear, for princes are the "ministers of God for the good" of society, as well as for the good of individuals (σοί).—(b) But they are also the ministers of his vengeance : Θεοῦ γὰρ διάκονός ἐστιν, ἔκδικος εἰς ὀργὴν τῷ τὸ κακὸν πράσσοντι. They do not bear the sword, the symbol of the right of life and death, in vain—a formidable right which can come only from the Master of life. Their acts of vengeance are those of God himself ; it follows that it is necessary to obey them not only on account of the prospect of punishment (διὰ τὴν ὀργήν, cf. verse 2 : κρίμα λήψονται), but on account of conscience (διὰ τὴν συνείδησιν) because the principle of punishment inflicted by them is a just one.—(c) They are also commissioned by God to levy the taxes necessary for the good administration of a State : λειτουργοὶ γὰρ Θεοῦ εἰσιν εἰς αὐτὸ τοῦτο προσκαρτεροῦντες. The word λειτουργός is still stronger than διάκονος, for it often expresses a sacred function. Princes are diligently occupied (προσκαρτεροῦντες) in this work (εἰς αὐτὸ τοῦτο), and that as λειτουργοὶ Θεοῦ.

At the moment when the teacher of the Gentiles wrote these lines, the imperial authority appeared everywhere under its most favourable aspect; the famous *quinquennium* of Nero was still in existence; the world was governed by sages and philosophers; in spite of the abuses, vexations, and exactions of some of its delegates in the provinces, Rome symbolized order, justice, and liberty; Paul had had scarcely any occasion to do otherwise than be well pleased with the Roman magistrates whom he met with in his journeyings. But even when the feeling of the authorities changed towards the Church, the teaching of the Church did not change. It was then that Paul enjoined upon Timothy to cause prayers to be made " for kings and for all in authority,"[1] and that he ordered Titus to preach submission and obedience to established powers.[2] It was then that Peter wrote : " Be ye subject, therefore, to every human institution for God's sake; whether it be to the king as supreme, or to governors as sent by him for the punishment of evildoers and for the praise of the good. For so is the will of God."[3] A modern commentator claims to have discovered a curious contrast in these two apostles. Peter is thought to have been a republican, and Paul a monarchist; the Roman citizen being an imperialist in politics as well as in theology, while the Galilæan Jew shares the revolutionary tendencies of his compatriots.[4] That shows too much imagination for a critical commentator. The contrary paradox could also be maintained; for St Peter speaks of the " king " (the name of the Roman emperor in the East) and of his delegates, proprætors or proconsuls; while St Paul, to render his teaching independent of times and places, abstains from every special designation. A less illusory difference is the fact that the teacher of the Gentiles, by what is perhaps a unique exception, keeps himself constantly on the ground of natural right and indicates to the faithful their duty as citizens and as men, while his colleague, placing himself on the ground of Christian right, appeals to the will of God and to the command of the Lord.

Obedience to the civil law has for its limit the divine law; but it was not well to bring up the hypothesis of a conflict between the law of God and the law of man. If the case occurred, the faithful had the Gospel precept for their guide;[5] their reason would tell them that the higher authority ought to prevail, and the conduct of the apostles before the Sanhedrin would dictate to them the answer to make. With this exception, which does not detract from the general principle to obey established authority, the Christians of the first centuries were always distinguished for their submission. Their

---

[1] I Tim. ii, 1-2.      [2] Titus iii, 1.      [3] I Pet. ii, 13-17.
[4] Bigg, *The Epistles of St Peter*, etc.  Edinburgh, 1901, p. 139.
[5] Matt. xxii, 21 ; Mark xii, 17 ; Luke xx, 25.

deference to the public authorities was the triumphant defence of their apologists and the immediate refutation of popular calumnies about a pretended hostility of the Christians to imperial institutions. St Clement of Rome, St Polycarp, St Justin, Tertullian, and Origen, not to mention others, teach us with what zeal the infant Church conformed to the instructions of St Paul.[1] If, so long as the empire remained pagan, the Church did not favour the participation of its members in public functions, and regarded with special disfavour the military profession,[2] it was because these duties, which were moreover optional, almost always exposed the neophyte to acts of idolatry, and put him often to the alternative of choosing between apostasy and martyrdom. And let us not forget that the Church, from the beginning, was conscious of being a distinct society, invested by its divine founder with the power of governing and perpetuating itself. It is acting on this principle that Paul judges and punishes Christians guilty of creating scandals, and condemns so strongly a recourse to pagan tribunals.[3]

2. God is the author of the family, as he is the author of society; but in the Christian family, he is the prototype of the master, the father and the husband, while the servant, the son, and the wife find their symbol and model in the Church. Christianity does not break marriages, it consolidates them by sanctifying them; it does not loosen the natural ties between fathers and children, it sanctions and strengthens them; it respects the legitimate relations between masters and slaves, but it supernaturalizes them. The great principle inculcated in his converts by St Paul is to change nothing in the external conditions of their life, provided that these agree with the precepts of the Gospel. To put off vice and to put on Christ, but to remain in the post assigned to them by Providence, such is his word of command and countersign.[4]

This recommendation referred above all to slaves, who pressed forward in crowds to the Church's open arms. You need not be troubled any more about your condition, the Apostle said to them; in Christ you are all brethren and the equals of free men; serve them for the love of Jesus Christ, but without enslaving yourselves to them morally. With a firm hand he points out to both masters and slaves their

---

[1] Fine prayer for the rulers in St Clement, *Ad Corinth.*, lxi. *Cf.* St Polycarp, *Ad Philipp.*, xii, 3; St Justin, *Apol.*, i, 14, 71; St Athenagoras, *Legat.*, 37; Theophilus, *Ad Autol.*, i, 11; Tertullian, *Apol.*, 30-36; *Ad Scapul.*, 2; Origen, *Contra Cels.*, viii, 73.

[2] *Cf.* Harnack, *Militia Christi, die christl. Religion und der Soldatenstand in den ersten drei Jahrhunderten*, Tübingen, 1905.

[3] 1 Cor. vi, 1-6. *Cf.* Vol. I, pp. 103-104.

[4] 1 Cor. vii, 20: ἕκαστος ἐν τῇ κλήσει ᾗ ἐκλήθη ἐν ταύτῃ μενέτω.

reciprocal duties.[1] Slaves are to "obey their masters according to the flesh, in all" that is not contrary to the law of God. They are to do so with a sentiment of apprehension inspired by the fear of the Lord, and not by the fear of punishment; "in simplicity of heart," without hypocrisy or dissimulation; "from the depths of their souls," with a spirit of faith and from a supernatural motive; with a view to pleasing God and not to flattering their master by a redoubled zeal shown in his presence. They are also to stimulate their obedience by the prospect of their future reward and think that it is an affair of justice, that their conscience is concerned in it and that they will have to render an account of their conduct at the tribunal of the supreme Judge. In their turn Christian masters must "observe in regard to their slaves the written and natural law"; go beyond the strict law and apply to them rules of "equity"; abstain from those horrible and degrading "threats" of which the pagans were so lavish; and finally, remember their common Master and Judge who is no respecter of persons.[2] Such is the rule that will henceforth govern the relations between

---

[1] Col. iii, 22-25; Eph. vi, 5-8. (A) *Extent of obedience*: it is universal (κατὰ πάντα), but this universality is limited by two things: by the fact that the Apostle is addressing himself here to Christian slaves and masters, which permits him to suppose that the latter will order nothing contrary to the divine law, and by the addition "according to the flesh," which defined the earthly and temporal sphere to which the authority of the masters and the subjection of the slaves is confined.—(B) *Qualities of obedience*: (a) *sincere*, "in simplicity of heart," exempt from all pretence and duplicity;—(b) *mingled with fear* (μετὰ φόβου καὶ τρόμου, Eph. vi, 5), a fear inspired not by men, but by the Lord (φοβούμενοι τὸν Κύριον, Col. iii, 22);—(c) *internal*, "from the heart" (ἐκ ψυχῆς), and consequently the same, whether out of the master's sight or under his inspection (μὴ ἐν ὀφθαλμοδουλίαις, Col. iii, 22; μὴ κατὰ ὀφθαλμοδουλίαν, Eph. vi, 6), for it is not its purpose to flatter the man or to please him (ὡς ἀνθρωπάρεσκοι);—(d) *supernatural*, dictated by the thought of doing the will of God (ποιοῦντες τὸ θέλημα τοῦ Θεοῦ, Eph. vi, 6) and of serving Christ (τῷ Κυρίῳ Χριστῷ δουλεύετε, Col. iii, 24).—(C) *Motives of obedience*: prospect of heavenly rewards (Eph. vi, 8; Col. iii, 24) and the punishments with which injustice is threatened (Col. iii, 25).

[2] Col. iv, 1: Οἱ κύριοι τὸ δίκαιον καὶ τὴν ἰσότητα τοῖς δούλοις παρέχεσθε, εἰδότες ὅτι καὶ ὑμεῖς ἔχετε κύριον ἐν οὐρανῷ.

Eph. vi. 9: Καὶ οἱ κύριοι τὰ αὐτὰ ποιεῖτε πρὸς αὐτούς, ἀνιέντες τὴν ἀπειλήν, εἰδότες ὅτι καὶ αὐτῶν καὶ ὑμῶν ὁ κύριός ἐστιν ἐν οὐρανοῖς, καὶ προσωπολημψία οὐκ ἔστιν παρ' αὐτῷ.

According to Colossians, masters are to observe *justice* towards their slaves (τὸ δίκαιον), which proves that if the slaves are not protected by human law, they are protected by divine law. The masters are moreover to maintain *equity* (ἰσότης), which sometimes goes beyond strict legal right, for it is inspired not only by justice, but by charity. The word ἰσότης does not denote *equality of treatment* in regard to all the slaves, nor the *Christian equality* which is to be maintained between slaves and masters, as several commentators think.—The expression τὰ αὐτὰ ποιεῖτε πρὸς αὐτούς signifies: "Act in the same way towards them; maintain towards them a line of conduct analogous to that which I recommend to them; be inspired by the same principles."

master and slave. But when the Apostle lays aside his role of legislator and speaks as counsellor and father, his heart makes him speak for the slave Onesimus in sublimely pathetic and tender accents. Never had been heard such a lesson in fraternity.

The position of Christian slaves under a pagan master might become almost intolerable. St Paul does not, like St Peter,[1] limit himself to reminding them that they will on that account have more merit in God's eyes. Titus is commanded to enjoin on such converts " to be obedient to their masters, to please them in all things, not gainsaying and not defrauding, but showing them a good fidelity, that they may adorn the doctrine of God our Saviour in all things."[2] The poor slaves are transformed into apostles; they become by their patience and submission to every trial mute preachers of the faith. Who can say how many recruits to the infant Church were gained by the heroism of the Christian *slaves?* Yet certain of them, less impregnated with the Christian spirit, were more anxious to secure their rights than to perform their duties. Some served pagans unwillingly, thinking they did them too much honour, and thus gave them occasion to blaspheme the name of the true God and to calumniate the Gospel. Others behaved with negligence in the service of Christian masters precisely because they were Christians; but this, the Apostle told them, is to repay the gentleness and kindness of your benefactors with ingratitude.[3]

There was no need of insisting much on the mutual duties of parents and children. If the Jews by a perverse casuistry sometimes eluded the fourth commandment of the Decalogue,[4] they could not be ignorant of it; and the Gentiles, when they were wanting in the respect and obedience due to their parents, did not escape the sting of conscience.[5] Paul therefore deals very briefly with this subject : " Children, obey your parents in all things, for this is well pleasing to the Lord. Fathers, provoke not your children, lest they be discouraged."[6] In addressing children, he does not mention the exceptional and almost chimerical case of Christian parents ordering their offspring to do something contrary to the divine law. In the parallel passage the commandment of the Decalogue is quoted, less as a proof of additional

---

[1] 1 Pet. ii, 18.     [2] Titus ii, 9, 10.     [3] 1 Tim. vi, 1.
[4] Matt. xv, 3-6.     [5] Rom. i, 30.
[6] Col. iii, 20 : Τὰ τέκνα ὑπακούετε    Eph. vi, 1-3 : Τὰ τέκνα, ὑπακούετε τοῖς γονεῦσι κατὰ πάντα, τοῦτο γὰρ   τοῖς γονεῦσιν ὑμῶν ἐν κυρίῳ· τοῦτο γάρ εὐαρεστόν ἐστιν ἐν κυρίῳ.       ἐστι δίκαιον. Τίμα κτλ. (Ex. xx, 12).

According to Colossians the obedience of children must be universal (κατὰ πάντα); for this, from the Christian point of view (ἐν κυρίῳ), is "pleasing" to God and men. According to Ephesians the obedience must proceed from a supernatural motive (ἐν κυρίῳ refers to ὑπακούετε and not to γονεῦσιν).

authority than by reason of the promise with which the Hebrew lawgiver accompanies it. It was unnecessary to command parents to love their children; that is a sentiment which nature imprints upon the heart; it was sufficient to remind them of their duty to rear them as becomes Christians.[1] Nevertheless, force must not degenerate into harshness, nor firmness into tyranny. A Spartan mode of education is not to Paul's taste. He does not want parents to make their children timid by reason of their unreasonable demands. By stifling all spontaneity, confidence, and freedom in them, or by an uncalled-for severity, they will produce in them dissimulation, slavish fear, and the habit of lying.

It is impossible to offer husbands and wives a loftier ideal than that which Paul proposes to them : " Wives, be subject to your husbands, as it behoveth in Christ. Husbands, love your wives and be not bitter towards them."[2] If he had limited himself to this laconic precept, we should never have suspected the profound reason for it. Fortunately he comments on it himself in the Epistle to the Ephesians : " Let women be subject to their husbands, as to the Lord ; because the husband is the head of the wife, as Christ is the head of the Church, which is his body, whereof he is the Saviour. Therefore, as the Church is subject to Christ, so also let the wives be to their husbands in all things. Husbands, love your wives, as Christ also loved the Church and delivered himself up for it, that he might sanctify it, cleansing it by the laver of water in the word of life, that he might present it to himself, a glorious Church, not having spot or wrinkle or any such thing."[3] The duties of the wife are comprised in submission inspired by a supernatural motive ($\dot{\omega}_S \tau \hat{\omega} K \upsilon \rho i \omega$). The obligation of the husband includes love, devotion, and a constant care to assure the happiness of his wife, in imitation of Christ sacrificing himself for the Church. Sublime model for both of the Christian consorts ! The Old Testament was fond of employing the allegory of marriage, in order to make comprehensible the intimate union—unique in its way—which existed between Jehovah and the chosen race ; St Paul, for his part, wishes that the still closer union of Christ with his Church should serve as a rule and standard for the intimacy of the conjugal tie.

---

[1] Col. iii, 21 : Οἱ πατέρες, μὴ ἐρεθίζετε τὰ τέκνα ὑμῶν, ἵνα μὴ ἀθυμῶσιν.

Eph. vi, 4 : Καὶ οἱ πατέρες, μὴ παροργίζετε τὰ τέκνα ὑμῶν, ἀλλὰ ἐκτρέφετε αὐτὰ ἐν παιδείᾳ καὶ νουθεσίᾳ κυρίου.

Parents have the duty of not irritating their children unreasonably and on every occasion (ἐρεθίζειν in a good sense means to " stimulate," but in a bad sense to " irritate "—for example, to tease animals in a cage ; παροργίζειν, used more frequently, has only the second meaning).

[2] Col. iii, 18, 19.          [3] Eph. v, 22-28.

3. The revelation of justice and perfection that Christianity brought to the world, and which was destined to revolutionize it, appears nowhere with more clearness than in the new conception of marriage. Progress, which cannot fail to react upon the mutual relations of husbands and wives, characterizes it from the beginning in four ways : unity, indissolubility, equal rights, and sanctity.

Under the influence of Roman legislation, which forbade it, polygamy was tending to disappear. Nevertheless, it is too much to say that " at that epoch there was no more question of bigamy or polygamy among real Jews." Neither the Talmud nor the Gospel shows any trace of those real Jews who would have had scruples about making use of the legal permission. Josephus cites the Mosaic provisions at length without speaking of their having become obsolete or feeling obliged to apologize for them. It does not appear that Herod was blamed for having nine wives at the same time. In reality, for the Jews of that time, as for the Mohammedans of to-day, a plurality of wives, although still lawful, was a luxury which only the rich could allow themselves. On the contrary, it was opposed to the principles of Christianity. Jesus abolished it by reminding men of the fact that in the designs of the Creator the man and the woman were intended to become one flesh.[1] Such an intimate union excluded all promiscuity, and the symbolical signification of the Christian marriage, representing the marriage of the Church and Christ, excluded it still more. Moreover, ecclesiastical history does not offer a single example of bigamy officially tolerated; it was necessary to wait until the Reformation of the sixteenth century before seeing this monstrous abuse sanctioned.

The doctrine of the indissolubility of marriage is no more peculiar to Paul than is that of its unity. He merely proclaims it in the name of the Lord;[2] but perhaps he does teach it more clearly than the Evangelists; for to the party separated from the other for any cause whatever, he leaves only two alternatives: either to become reconciled or to abstain from a new marriage,[3] which presupposes in any hypothesis that the previous marriage still exists. The exception which he appears to make in the case called " Paul's privilege " is not a real exception, since it does not refer to a Christian marriage.[4]

More characteristic is the teaching concerning the equality of rights between husbands and wives. This does not mean an absolute equality which would destroy the subordination essential to the conjugal union. The relation of the head to

[1] Mark x, 8 ; Matt. xix, 5 (quoting Gen. ii, 24).
[2] I Cor. vii, 10 : τοῖς δὲ γεγαμηκόσιν παραγγέλλω, οὐκ ἐγὼ ἀλλ' ὁ κύριος.
[3] I Cor. vii, 11 ; ἐὰν δὲ χωρισθῇ, μενέτω ἄγαμος ἢ τῷ ἀνδρὶ καταλλαγήτω.
[4] I Cor. vii, 12-16 ; cf Vol. I, pp. 114-115.

the body is a relation of inequality.[1]  The natural subjection
of the woman to the man, a subjection symbolized by the
veil, appears in several ways in the story of creation.[2]  The
man was not taken from the woman, but the woman from
the man;[3] the man was not created for the woman, but the
woman for the man;[4] the woman is the reflection of the
man, as the man is the reflection of God.[5]  The following
ascending gradation can be established : the woman, the man,
Christ, God.[6]  And to follow Paul to the end, let us add that
the man was created first and was seduced only after the
woman.[7]  However, there are compensations.  If the woman
has need of the man, man also has need of the woman, and
if the first woman was taken from man, man is now born of
the woman.[8]  But the conjugal rights and duties are the
same ; the privilege of Paul has to do with every married
convert, with the wife as well as the husband;[9] and both are
equally bound to maintain the stability of the Christian home,
although the declaration of this duty insinuates, by a delicate
shade of meaning, the wife's subordination.[10]

The moral masterpiece of Christianity is the sanctification
of marriage.  The conjugal duty is plainly lawful—this is
the express teaching of Paul—and the name of duty alone
would prove its lawfulness.[11]  If marriage in general is good,
as a divine institution, Christian marriage is holy, as a
visible sign of a sacred thing.  Certainly virginity is better;[12]
but that is a grace which Paul is happy to have received and
desires for other Christians,[13] but imposes upon no one.  Not
only is virginity better, but widowhood even is preferable.[14]
A second marriage bars the candidate on the threshold of
admission to the clergy.[15]  However, there are cases where
marriage and even a second marriage are to be advised; all
depends upon the circumstances and the persons ; provided,
of course, that there is no previous engagement, for it is a
sin to violate pledged faith.[16]  Such is the sanctity of the conjugal tie that, in mixed marriages, it is imparted to the pagan
consort and to the children of the union.[17]  Christian marriage
prepares recruits for baptism and candidates for heaven.  The
Apostle puts the crown upon his teaching by these consoling
words : " The woman shall be saved through child-bearing

---

[1] 1 Cor. xi, 3 : κεφαλὴ δὲ γυναικὸς ὁ ἀνήρ.

[2] 1 Cor. xi, 5-10.  [3] 1 Cor. xi, 8.  [4] 1 Cor. xi, 9.
[5] 1 Cor. xi, 7.  [6] 1 Cor. xi, 3.  [7] 1 Tim. ii, 13-14;
[8] 1 Cor. xi, 11-12.  [9] 1 Cor. vii, 12, 13.
[10] 1 Cor. vii, 11 : γυναῖκα μὴ χωρισθῆναι . . . καὶ ἄνδρα γυναῖκα μὴ ἀφιέναι.
[11] 1 Cor. vii, 3.  [12] 1 Cor. vii, 1.  [13] 1 Cor. vii, 7.
[14] 1 Cor. vii, 40.
[15] The πρεσβύτερος or ἐπίσκοπος must be μιᾶς γυναικὸς ἀνήρ (having been
married only once, 1 Tim. iii, 2 ; Titus i, 6), and the deacon also (1 Tim. iii. 12),
Similarly a widow, officially recognized by the Church, must be ἑνὸς ἀνδρὸς
γυνή (1 Tim. v, 9).
[16] 1 Tim. v, 11, 12.  [17] 1 Cor. vii, 14.

(διὰ τεκνογονίας), provided she continue in faith and charity and sanctification with modesty."[1]

## III—PRECEPTS OF PERSONAL MORALITY

1. The Three Theological Virtues.   2. Pre-eminence of Charity.
3. Virtues and Vices.   4. Prayer.   5. Little Virtues.

1. Faith, hope, and charity are the foundation, the centre, and the summit of the Christian life. Faith begins, charity completes, and hope is the bond of union between them. Paul loves to classify these by themselves and to indicate the distance which separates them from the other virtues. He exhorts the Thessalonians to put on " the breastplate of faith and charity and the helmet of hope,"[2] because faith increased with charity renders the Christian invulnerable, and because hope teaches him to fear nothing and to dare everything. He praises in them " the work of faith and labour and charity and the enduring of hope,"[3] because sincere faith is active, true charity indefatigable, and supernatural hope capable of suffering everything. In contrast to the *charismata* which pass away and whose role is transitory, " faith, hope, and charity abide."[4] The number of cases in which the three virtues follow one another is significant, and it will appear still more surprising if one of its synonyms is substituted for hope, or if we remember that it is virtually comprised in faith and charity, the pair which occur so often in the Apostle's writings.[5]

---

[1] 1 Tim. ii, 15 : σωθήσεται διὰ τῆς τεκνογονίας.

[2] 1 Thess. v, 8 : ἐνδυσάμενοι θώρακα πίστεως καὶ ἀγάπης καὶ περικεφαλαίαν ἐλπίδα σωτηρίας. St Paul's metaphor is inspired by Is. lix, 17 (ἐνεδύσατε δικαιοσύνην ὡς θώρακα καὶ περιέθετο περικεφαλαίαν σωτηρίου ἐπὶ τῆς κεφαλῆς), but he changes the name of the virtues in order to bring in his trio : faith, hope, and charity. In Eph. vi, 14-17 his aim is different ; it is necessary there to have a *complete defensive* armour from the helmet to the feet. These two texts should be compared with Wisdom v, 19 and Baruch v, 2.

[3] 1 Thess. i, 3 : μνημονεύοντες ὑμῶν τοῦ ἔργου τῆς πίστεως καὶ τοῦ κόπου τῆς ἀγάπης καὶ τῆς ὑπομονῆς τῆς ἐλπίδος τοῦ Κυρίου ἡμῶν Ἰ. Χ. It is very probable that the last words qualify only hope (Bisping, Schäfer, Bornemann, etc.), which has for its object and stimulant the triumphal return of Christ.

[4] 1 Cor. xiii, 13 : νυνὶ δέ μένει πίστις, ἐλπίς, ἀγάπη, τὰ τρία ταῦτα.

[5] Outside of the texts already cited, the three virtues are enumerated together in the following passages: Gal. v, 5-6 (ἐκ πίστεως ἐλπίδα ἀπεκδεχόμεθα . . . πίστις δι' ἀγάπης ἐνεργουμένη) ; Rom. v, 1, 2, 5 (δικαιωθέντες ἐκ πίστεως . . . καυχώμεθα ἐπ' ἐλπίδι . . . ἡ δὲ ἐλπὶς οὐ καταισχύνει ὅτι ἡ ἀγάπη τοῦ Θεοῦ κτλ.) ; Col. i, 4-5 (ἀκούσαντες τὴν πίστιν ὑμῶν . . . καὶ τὴν ἀγάπην . . . διὰ τὴν ἐλπίδα) ; Eph. i, 15, 18 ; iii, 17 (compared with Col. i, 23) ; *cf.* 1 Cor. xiii, 7 ; Heb. vi, 10-12 ; x, 22·24.—With ὑπομονή instead of ἐλπίς : 2 Thess. i, 3, 4 ; 1 Tim. vi, 11 ; 2 Tim. ii, 2 (ὑγιαίνοντες τῇ πίστει, τῇ ἀγάπῃ, τῇ ὑπομονῇ).—The pair " faith and charity " : 1 Thess. iii, 6 ; Philem. 5 ; 1 Tim. i, 14 ; ii, 15 ; iv, 12 ; 2 Tim. i, 13 ; ii, 22.—Observe, however, that in Gal. v, 5 it is a question of the *object* of hope (which further presupposes subjective hope), and that in Rom. v, 5 it is a question directly of the *love* of God (who pours forth in our hearts the virtue of charity).

When associated with charity and hope, faith is no longer the first movement of the soul's approach to God and the acquisition of justice; it is then a supernatural habit which gives to the different manifestations of the Christian life their impulse, their direction, and their tone. This character of stable faith is much more emphasized in the Pastoral Epistles, where the formula " in the faith " appears stereotyped; but it is by no means absent from the other Epistles. The Apostle admonishes the Corinthians to be firm in the faith, and to test themselves to see if they are in the faith; the Colossians, to persevere in the faith and to strengthen themselves in the faith; he rejoices to see the Thessalonians anchored in the faith; he himself lives in the faith of the Son of God. Evidently in all these examples faith is not a passing act but a virtue that abides.[1]

In the Greek classics hope was an expectation, more or less vain or well founded, of an event, fortunate or unfortunate. This meaning is foreign to the Bible; here, hope is always the certain expectation of a coming good. We fear evil, we do not hope for it. Hope has always in view the divine promises: salvation, eternal life, the resurrection of the dead; it includes the whole matter of faith in so far as it concerns us and is to come.[2] As it must be founded on reason, it is the attribute of Christians only. The Gentiles have no hope;[3] the hope of the godless, being only a deceitful illusion, will perish; on the contrary, that of the Christians is certain; " it confoundeth not,"[4] because it relies upon faith; it is, therefore, for them a never-failing source of courage, joy, and inward happiness. Hope and faith mutually help each other; for if faith acts upon hope, hope reacts also upon faith; each draws from charity its value and its worth, but each of them in turn kindles charity and stimulates it to action.[5] Hope especially, symbolized by the helmet and distinguished by ardour, intrepidity, and audacity, is checked by no obstacle, terrified by no danger, discouraged by no delay: " Tribulation worketh constancy, and constancy proved virtue, and proved virtue hope."[6] Hope is at the same time the beginning and the end of this evolution towards the better; for the Christian virtues partially interpenetrate and mutually stimulate one another.

2. Faith, hope, and charity readily keep step together, but charity always takes precedence of her two sisters. One should read without interruption St Paul's wonderful chapter in its praise which has been justly called the hymn of charity:

---

[1] See Note V.
[2] Heb. xi, 1.
[3] Eph. ii, 12; 1 Thess. iv, 13.
[4] Rom. v, 5.
[5] 1 Cor. i, 4-5.
[6] Rom. v, 4. Compare for the idea Jas. i, 3-4.

Be zealous for the best *charismata* ; but I will show you a far more excellent way.

If I speak with the tongues of men and of angels, and have not charity, I am become as sounding brass or a tinkling cymbal. And had I the gift of prophecy and such faith as to remove mountains, if I have not charity, I am nothing. And if I should distribute all my goods to feed [the poor], and if I should deliver my body to be burned, if I have not charity, it profiteth me nothing.

Charity is patient, is kind ; charity envieth not, vaunteth not itself, is not puffed up, doth nothing unseemly, seeketh not her own, is not provoked to anger, thinketh no evil ; rejoiceth not in iniquity, but rejoiceth with the truth ; excuseth all things, believeth all things, hopeth all things, endureth all things.

Charity never faileth. If [there be] prophecies, they shall vanish away ; if tongues, they shall cease ; if knowledge, it shall vanish. For we know in part and we prophesy in part ; but when that which is perfect shall come, that which is in part shall vanish away. When I was a child, I spoke as a child, I thought as a child, I reasoned as a child. But when I became a man, I put away the things of a child. We see now through a mirror, in reflected images, but then [we shall see] face to face. Now I know in part, but then I shall know even as I am known.

And now there remain faith, hope and charity, these three ; but the greatest of these is charity.[1]

This lyrical passage is clearness itself, and any commentary would only obscure it. Let us try merely to disengage its dominant ideas by grouping them under three headings.

*Charity is the queen of virtues.* *Charismata* are indeed precious gifts and must be estimated at their full value, preference being given to the most useful rather than to the most brilliant. But there is a way incomparably loftier and surer, the royal road of love. Without charity the most excellent of *charismata* are nothing and do no good. The gift of tongues is then a useless babble of words ; prophecy is a passing gleam, which will be eclipsed at the day of the beatific vision. Charity alone will never fail. Faith and hope, which share with her the privilege of having God for a direct object, will disappear in heaven, where the elect see instead of believing and can no longer hope for what they already possess without the possibility of loss ; but charity is

[1] 1 Cor. xii, 31-xiii, 13.—The verse xii, 31 serves as a means of transition : *Aemulamini autem charismata meliora, et adhuc excellentiorem viam vobis demonstro.* St Paul has reproached the Corinthians with striving to obtain the most unusual and *conspicuous* charismata. Now he urges them to desire the greatest or the best charismata ($\mu\epsilon i\zeta o\nu a$ or $\kappa\rho\epsilon i\tau\tau o\nu a$)—that is to say, the most useful, as he has explained. It is better to take the verb $\zeta\eta\lambda o\hat{v}\tau\epsilon$ in the imperative ; the indicative, with an interrogation point after the first part of the phrase, would give a rather distorted meaning : " Are you zealous for the best *charismata ?* Well, I will show you a more excellent way." But this presupposes that charity is a *charisma*, which is contrary to the Apostle's language and thought. On the contrary, with the imperative the meaning is perfectly natural ; the first part of the phrase is the conclusion of what has been said on the subject of *charismata ;* then Paul shows something more excellent and desirable.—The expression $\kappa a\theta'$ $\dot{v}\pi\epsilon\rho\beta o\lambda\dot{\eta}\nu$ has the value of an adjective qualifying $\delta\delta\delta s$.

immortal and does not change essentially in nature when transformed into glory.

*Charity is the summary of the commandments,* for it includes an implicit submission to the divine will in all its extent. The Master said: " On these two commandments (love of God and of one's neighbour) depend the whole Law and the prophets." The disciple said in his turn: " All the other commandments are comprised in one word: Thou shalt love thy neighbour as thyself. . . . Love, therefore, is the fulfilling of the Law."[1] And again: " For all the Law is fulfilled in this word: Love thy neighbour as thyself."[2] Or, with enigmatical conciseness: " The end of the commandment is charity."[3]

*Charity is the bond of perfection.*[4] This it is which holds tightly together, like a sheaf of fragrant flowers, the virtues whose entirety constitutes Christian perfection. Or, to vary the metaphor, it is keystone of the vault designed to hold together all the stones and mouldings of our spiritual structure, which without it would crumble.

St Francis de Sales tells us in his usual graceful style that " charity never enters a heart without also quartering therein all her escort of the other virtues." The pious Bishop of Geneva appears to have drawn his inspiration from St Paul, who thus describes the train of the minor virtues which attend their sovereign: " Charity is patient "; she possesses that tolerant forbearance which the Scriptures describe as the peculiar characteristic of the divine Fatherhood.—" She is full of benignity," and practises in all fraternal relations that

---

[1] Matt. xxii, 40 and Rom. xiii, 9, 10.     [2] Gal. v, 14.

[3] 1 Tim. i, 5.

[4] Col. iii, 14. *Super omnia autem haec, charitatem habete, quod est vinculum perfectionis.* Ἐπὶ πᾶσι δὲ τούτοις τὴν ἀγάπην, ὅ ἐστι σύνδεσμος τῆς τελειότητος. As the reference has just been to the virtues which were to be put on (verse 12) one might be tempted to translate: " Over all these (virtues, put on) charity." Charity would then be like a large mantle covering the other virtues with its folds, or like a broad girdle binding them round the Christian. But it is probable that the proper meaning of ἐνδύσασθε is no longer obvious here; the Vulgate has replaced it by the colourless *habete*. In this case, ἐπὶ πᾶσι τούτοις will mean " more than all this," or " in preference to all the rest."

The principal point is to know to what charity serves as a *bond*. Is it to the other virtues, or to the Christians themselves? The first explanation is the most common. Thus Chrysostom says: πάντα ἐκεῖνα αὕτη συσφίγγει. So also Lightfoot, Abbott, etc. Some compare it to the word of the Pythagoreans, who make friendship the *bond* of all the virtues: σύνδεσμος πασῶν τῶν ἀρετῶν. The genitive τῆς τελειότητος would then be objective: charity is *that which binds*, ties together and unites the virtues, the whole of which constitutes perfection. The idea is beautiful, but the expression has something a little peculiar in it; one binds, it is true, the parts of a whole, but what is the bond of a whole?—Hence the second explanation keeps its probability. Charity is thus the powerful bond that unites Christians to one another. The genitive τῆς τελειότητος would then be a genitive of quality (a perfect bond); or a genitive of apposition (a bond consisting in perfection); or, perhaps, even a possessive genitive (a bond for the use of perfection, of the perfect).

amiable gentleness the charm of which the Apostle tells us.—
" Charity is not envious," because she is unpretentious, and
because the happiness and success of others cannot offend
her.—" Charity does not blow her own trumpet " ; she does
not imitate the Pharisees who proclaim their services or their
charities with the sound of a trumpet.—" She is not puffed
up with pride," because she pays less attention to the good
that she does than to that which she is powerless to do.—
" She doth nothing unseemly " in her language or her attitude, carefully avoiding everything that is of a nature to
wound or scandalize her neighbour.—" She seeketh not her
own advantage," for she needs to forget herself in order to
live, and selfishness would kill her.—" She is not irritated,"
whether she is misunderstood or calumniated, so far is she
above terrestrial cares.—" She thinketh no evil " of incon-
siderate behaviour in others.—" She rejoiceth not in
iniquity," even when it is successful and profitable.—" On
the contrary, she rejoiceth with the truth," and applauds its
triumph.—" She excuseth all things," leaving to God, the
searcher of hearts, the care of judging man's secret intentions.—" She believeth all things " that are told her, in good
faith and simplicity.—" She hopeth all things " that are
promised her, without suspicion or distrust.—" She endureth
all things," even indifference and ingratitude.[1]

---

[1] 1 Cor. xiii, 4-7 :

| | |
|---|---|
| Ἡ ἀγάπη μακροθυμεῖ, | (a) charitas patiens est, |
| χρηστεύεται ἡ ἀγάπη, | (b) benigna est, |
| οὐ ζηλοῖ, | (c) charitas non aemulatur, |
| ἡ ἀγ. οὐ περπερεύεται, | (d) non agit perperam, |
| οὐ φυσιοῦται, | (e) non inflatur, |
| οὐκ ἀσχημονεῖ, | (f) non est ambitiosa, |
| οὐ ζητεῖ τὰ ἑαυτῆς, | (g) non quaerit quae sua sunt, |
| οὐ παροξύνεται, | (h) non irritatur, |
| οὐ λογίζεται τὸ κακόν, | (i) non cogitat malum, |
| οὐ χαίρει ἐπὶ τῇ ἀδικίᾳ, | (j) non gaudet super iniquitate, |
| συγχαίρει δὲ τῇ ἀληθείᾳ, | (k) congaudet autem veritati, |
| πάντα στέγει, | (l) omnia suffert, |
| πάντα πιστεύει, | (m) omnia credit, |
| πάντα ἐλπίζει, | (n) omnia sperat, |
| πάντα ὑπομένει. | (o) omnia sustinet. |

Some terms require a word of explanation : (b) χρηστεύεσθαι is to practise
the Pauline virtue of χρηστότης (benignitas).—(d) Περπερεύεσθαι is to be
πέρπερος, " a boaster " or " a sycophant "; but the second meaning is less
appropriate here on account of the nearness of οὐ φυσιοῦται.—(f) Ἀσχημονεῖν
is to have something shocking and offensive for others in one's external
appearance ;—(i) Λογίζεσθαι τὸ κακόν could signify " to attribute bad conduct to others in order to avenge oneself when a chance occurs "; but it is
better to translate it, " to think ill of something "—that is, to assume its
intention was evil.—(j and k) The word ἀδικία does not denote an injustice
done to a neighbour, and the word χαίρει does not express the sentiment
of pleasure which this sight awakens in the jealous. The idea is a more
general one : " Charity detests all injustice, but on the contrary rejoices at
the triumph of the truth " (συγχαίρει, she rejoices with the truth which
triumphs).—(l) Στέγειν may mean " to support "; but as this idea is ex-

We will not try to classify these fifteen virtues, the companions of charity. By seeking to find in them a strict order, our exegesis would be sacrificed to a system. Paul was able to prolong or shorten his list as he liked, and the enumeration is made rather as an example than as an effort to exhaust the subject.

3. The unequalled rank assigned to charity has the natural effect of throwing the other moral virtues rather into the shade. Their lack of prominence is due, however, to another cause. As they were included in the apostolic catechetical teaching and belonged consequently to the rudiments of the faith, the sacred writers had scarcely any reason for referring to them again. When Paul sees fit to allude to them, his lists of virtues and vices are neither complete nor methodical, and they teach us but little. Let us mention merely the characteristic traits of the Pauline vocabulary; they are humility and goodness among the virtues, and covetousness and dissension among the vices.

*Humility* is a specifically Christian virtue, of which the pagans do not seem to have had any idea. For them " humble " (ταπεινός) was synonymous with " low, vile, abject, servile, and ignoble."[1] Among the Hebrews it was entirely different. The man who was oppressed and conscious of his nothingness and misery, accepted the trial with patience as a means of expiation, put his hope in God and had for his persecutors neither hatred nor ill will, was the ideal of the just man. He was designated by a word which is translated either by " poor," " meek," or " humble." When Jesus Christ said of himself : " I am meek and lowly of heart," the Jews who heard him had no difficulty in comprehending him.[2] Humility and gentleness are the face and the reverse of the same virtue : humility before God, gentleness towards men. St Paul is fond of uniting them : he wishes that " each with all humility should esteem others better than himself," and he urgently recommends his converts to be " full of gentleness towards all men,"[3] Thus do these twin

---

pressed later (*o*), it is better to adhere to the classical idea of " passing over in silence, or excusing."—(*m* and *n*) These two phrases are best understood by referring them to our neighbour rather than to God. Paul does not mean that charity nourishes faith and hope in a theological sense, but that she is without mistrust and suspicion.

[1] *Cf*. Trench, *Synonyms of the N.T.*, xliii.

[2] Matt. xi, 29 : ὅτι πραΰς εἰμι καὶ ταπεινὸς τῇ καρδίᾳ. Originally distinct in meaning and etymology, the two adjectives עָנָו and עָנִי became subsequently synonyms, and are translated indifferently by πραΰς or ταπεινός. *Cf*. Cremer, *Wörterbuch, sub voce.*

[3] The word ταπεινοφροσύνη (Eph. iv, 2 ; Phil. ii, 3 ; Col. ii, 18, 23 ; iii, 12 ; Acts xx, 19, Paul's speech) is elsewhere met with only in 1 Pet. v, 5. The word πραΰτης (1 Cor. iv, 21 ; 2 Cor. x, 1 ; Gal. v, 23 ; vi, 1 ; Eph. iv, 2 ;

virtues, one of which was profoundly despised and the other scarcely known by the ancient world, become the test of the true Christian.

*Goodness* is no less characteristic of Paul's code of morality. It is expressed by two words, peculiar to him alone, one of which (ἀγαθωσύνη) is really "goodness," the other (χρηστότης) "kindness" or "mildness."[1] St Jerome has well caught the shade of difference in meaning : "Kindness is a sweet, amiable, tranquil virtue, of gentle speech, affable manners, and a happy mixture of all good qualities. Goodness is very like it, for it also seeks to give pleasure; but it is distinguished from it by the fact that it is less prepossessing and of a severer aspect, and also, although prompt to do good and render a service, lacks that urbanity and suavity which win all hearts."[2] Goodness characterizes more the foundation, benignity more the form of devotion. Kindness includes goodness, but it adds to it something which doubles its value. One can say without pleonasm "the kindness of goodness," but not "the goodness of kindness." Kindness is the special prerogative of God ; and it is also the most easily recognizable imprint of the Creator on his creatures. However, neither Christian goodness nor Christian kindness degenerate into easy-going complaisance and weakness, as is often the case in the works of secular writers.

Of all the vices the most hateful to Paul is the spirit of *discord*. He met with it almost at the commencement of his career, threatening to fetter his ministry and to destroy his work. He found it again at the end of his course, always disturbing, disquieting, and jealous. He condemns it under many names, some of which really belong to it, such as disputes, dissensions, factions, animosity, envy, and a love of

---

Col. iii, 12 ; 2 Tim. ii, 25 ; Titus iii, 2) is also found in James i, 21 ; iii, 13 ; 1 Pet. iii, 15. St Paul unites the two nouns in Eph. iv, 2 ; Col. iii, 12. He also uses πραϋπαθία (1 Tim. vi, 11).—St Bernard defines humility thus : *Virtus qua quis ex verissima sui cognitione sibi ipsi vilescit.* St Chrysostom says less aptly that to be humble is ὅταν τις μέγας ὢν ἑαυτὸν ταπεινοῖ. He was no doubt thinking of the humility of Christ. St Basil calls humility (*Constit. mon.*, 16) γαζοφυλάκιον ἀρετῶν. Trench, *loc. cit.*, establishes the synonymy thus : "Πραΰτης, or meekness, is more than mere gentleness of manner, if indeed the Christian grace of meekness of spirit must rest on deeper foundations than its own : on those namely which ταπεινοφροσύνη has laid for it, and can only subsist while it continues to rest on these. It is a grace in advance of ταπεινοφροσύνη, not as more precious than it, but as presupposing it, and as being unable to exist without it."

[1] The word ἀγαθωσύνη (goodness) is exclusively Pauline (Rom. xv, 14 ; Gal. v, 22 ; Eph. v, 9 ; 2 Thess. i, 11) ; χρηστότης (kindness) also (Rom. ii, 4 ; iii, 12 ; xi, 22 ; 2 Cor. vi, 6 ; Gal. v, 22 ; Eph. ii, 7 ; Col. iii, 12 ; Titus iii, 4), as well as χρηστεύεσθαι (1 Cor. xiii, 4) and χρηστολογία (Rom. xvi, 18).

[2] *Comment. in Galat.*, v, 22. *Cf.* St Basil (*Regul. brev. tract.*, 214): Πλατυτέραν οἶμαι εἶναι τὴν χρηστότητα εἰς εὐεργεσίαν τῶν ὅπως δηποτοῦν ἐπιδεομένων ταύτης, συνηγμένην δὲ μᾶλλον τὴν ἀγαθωσύνην καὶ τοῖς τῆς δικαιοσύνης λόγοις ἐν ταῖς εὐεργεσίαις συγχρωμένην.

schisms and of sects.[1] He expressly commands Titus to shun
the heretic—that is, the fomenter of troubles and divisions.
It might be sometimes thought that his moral code consists
in causing unity, good understanding, harmony and peace to
prevail among his converts.

Another vice, which is quite prominent in Paul's writings
(πλεονεξία, πλεονέκτης) and characteristic of his vocabulary,
is hard to define.[2] The Vulgate always translates it by
*avaritia*; but it is rather *carnal desire* than cupidity. In
fact, this vice is almost always associated with sins of impurity, and it is not any too clear what avarice has to do in
this company. Moreover, it is presented as the dominant
mark of paganism and is even identified once with idolatry;
now avarice does not seem to have been the particular vice
of the pagans, while idolatry and fornication or impurity
were synonyms. Finally, the command given to the
Ephesians not to speak of it: *Fornicatio et omnis immun-*

---

[1] The following words are Pauline: ἔρις (dispute), Rom. i, 29; xiii, 13;
1 Cor. i, 11; iii, 3; 2 Cor. xii, 20; Gal. v, 20; Phil. i, 15; 1 Tim. vi, 4;
Titus iii, 9;—διχοστασία (dissension), Rom. xvi, 17; Gal. v, 20;—ἐριθία
(discord), Rom. ii, 8; 2 Cor. xii, 20; Gal. v, 20; Phil. i, 17; ii, 3 (except
James iii, 14, 16).

[2] The verb πλεονεκτεῖν, peculiar to Paul (2 Cor. ii, 11; vii, 2; xii, 17-18;
1 Thess. iv, 6), is rendered in the Vulgate by *circumvenire; πλεονέκτης*, also
peculiar to Paul (1 Cor. v, 10, 11; vi, 10; Eph. v, 5), is rendered by *avarus*;
πλεονεξία in St Paul (Rom. i, 29; 2 Cor. ix, 5; Eph. iv, 19; v, 3; Col. iii, 5; 1
Thess. ii, 5), and elsewhere (Mark vii, 22; Luke xii, 15; 2 Pet. ii, 3, 14) is
rendered by *avaritia*. Now, in many of these texts, the idea of avarice is
difficult to justify: (*a*) Eph. v, 3 (*Fornicatio et omnis immunditia aut* avaritia
*nec nominetur in vobis*) is much better translated by *carnal concupiscence*
than by avarice, first because of the adjoining words, and then because of
the singular verb and the word *aut* (καὶ ἀκαθαρσία πᾶσα ἢ πλεονεξία), which
seems to mean that it is a question here of the same vice under different
names, and finally because it is not clear why it would be objectionable to
*mention* avarice by name.—(*b*) Nor is it easy to see what connection there can
be between *avarice* and idolatry: Col. iii, 5 (καὶ τὴν πλεονεξίαν, ἥτις ἐστὶν
εἰδωλολατρεία); Eph. v, 5 (πλεονέκτης, ὅς ἐστιν εἰδωλολάτρης); while the Bible
and history agree in showing us the close connections between idolatry and
the carnal passions.—(*c*) The word πλεονεξία is usually associated with sins of
impurity: Col. iii, 5; Eph. v, 3; v, 5; Rom. i, 29; 1 Cor. v, 10-11; 2 Pet.
ii, 14; Mark, vii, 21 (the true order is κλοπαί, φόνοι, μοιχεῖαι, πλεονεξίαι).

In the Decalogue the prohibition to *covet thy neighbour's wealth* and to
*desire his wife* is expressed by the same verb: Ex. xx, 11 (*Non concupisces
domum proximi tui, nec desiderabis uxorem ejus, non ancillam, non bovem,
non asinum, nec omnia quae illius sunt;* in Greek it is the same verb ἐπιθυμεῖν,
in Hebrew also *ḥāmad*). Although cupidity and covetousness were differentiated at an early age (in Deut. v, 8 the verbs differ), they were able to continue being expressed by the same word. Perhaps this remark explains
1 Thess. iv, 6 (τὸ μὴ ὑπερβαίνειν καὶ πλεονεκτεῖν ἐν τῷ πράγματι τὸν ἀδελφὸν
αὐτοῦ). πλεονεκτεῖν τινα means usually "to prejudice, to wrong someone by cupidity or avarice by depriving him of his due"; can it not
signify "to wrong someone by unlawful desire" in deceiving him in the
matter (ἐν τῷ πράγματι) of marriage? This meaning agrees very well with
the preceding verse, where the reference is to the chaste use of marriage, and
it also agrees well with the reason given in the following verse (*non enim
vocavit nos Deus in immunditiam*). It is not surprising, therefore, that
St Jerome, Estius, and others adopted it.

*ditia aut avaritia nec nominetur in vobis,* is much better translated by *carnal desire.* We must remember that in the primitive moral code, before the varieties of evil desires had been differentiated, the same word signified at once an impure desire and cupidity or avarice. The special usage of St Paul brings us back to those distant beginnings : such is the most natural solution of a linguistic problem which engrosses the attention of exegetes.

4. What has gone before is sufficient to show what an abyss separates the moral code of Paul from that of the Stoics. As has been well said : " Stoicism is the result of despair " : despair in religion in view of the decadent and absurd mythologies ; despair in politics, when the Macedonian conquest had dispelled all men's dreams of independence ; despair in philosophy, at the sight of all its impotent and contradictory systems.[1] But Christianity is the religion of hope, and Paul's moral code is the code of love. There is no common standard of measurement between these heights. As almost all the Stoics were of Eastern origin, and as many of them had established themselves in Tarsus or in Cilicia, some have suspected the teacher of the Gentiles of having come under their influence ; and, indeed, by dint of laboriously examining the writings of Epictetus and Seneca, we may discover therein a certain number of maxims which are quite similar in tone and expression to those of Paul. But these resemblances must not deceive us ; they are external and superficial. We recognize at first the complete absence of the Stoic vocabulary ; but what especially differentiates the teachings is their spirit. The Stoics considered it supremely ridiculous to ask God for virtue and to honour him for it ; now nothing is more characteristic of Paul's moral teaching than prayer and thanksgiving.

His injunctions in this respect border on hyperbole : " Pray without ceasing; give thanks in all things.—In everything by prayer and supplication, with thanksgiving, let your petitions be made known to God.—Whatsoever you say or do, do all in the name of the Lord Jesus, giving thanks through him to God the Father.—Make at all times in the spirit all prayers and supplications."[2] He himself sets the example. He writes to the new Christians : " We pray always for you with thanksgiving. . . . We cease not to pray for you."[3] The Acts

[1] Lightfoot, *Epistle to the Philippians,* pp. 271, 272 ; Appendix, *St Paul and Seneca,* pp. 270-333. See *ibid.,* p. 299, an erudite note on the country of all the Stoics of renown. R. Bultmann (*Der Stil der Paulinischen Predigt und die Kynisch-Stoische Diatribe,* Göttingen, 1910) has tried to prove how much St Paul owes to the school of Stoics and Cynics in all that pertains to methods of argumentation. The proof has, in our opinion, nothing convincing, but the idea should be taken into consideration.

[2] 1 Thess. v, 17 ; Phil. iv, 6 ; Eph. vi, 18.
[3] 1 Thess. i, 2 ; Col. i, 9, etc

reveal him to us as praying in all the serious circumstances of his life; at the moment when he goes to Ananias to be baptized by him,[1] in the Temple after his conversion,[2] before receiving the laying on of hands,[3] when he appoints *elders* for the new churches,[4] in the prison at Philippi,[5] at Miletus before the assembled elders,[6] when saying farewell to the Christians of Tyre,[7] after his miracle at Mitylene,[8] and at the Three Taverns on the road to Rome.[9] He prays for his disciples[10] and for the Jews;[11] he prays also for himself;[12] he exhorts the faithful to pray frequently[13] especially for him,[14] and relies upon their prayers.[15] We know that, like the pious Jews of his time, he was accustomed to pray before meals.[16]

His Epistles also, interlarded with doxologies, generally begin with an act of thanksgiving which sometimes continues through the whole Epistle of which it forms the frame. His final wish again almost always finds its expression in a form of prayer.

If we do not insist further on this point, it is because there is in it nothing peculiar; for the practice of frequent prayer is a habit formed by St Paul when a devotee of Pharisaism. All devout Pharisees loved to adorn their writings and discourses with prayers and doxologies. St Paul scarcely distinguishes himself from them except by the earnestness of his supplications and by the fact, already pointed out elsewhere, that in his invocations he associates the Son with the Father and makes the Holy Spirit the principal master and agent of Christian prayer.

5. Let us mention, in closing, three modest virtues very dear to the Apostle: work, order, and decorum. He no sooner arrived in a new mission than he installed himself in one of those narrow shops which lined the market-place; there he took up his trade of weaver, in order to provide for his needs, to give a good example to all and to preserve his independence. To the elders of Ephesus, who had come to Miletus to receive his farewells, he showed with pride his wrinkled hands, used to hard work day and night.[17] To the Thessalonians, obsessed with the vision of the approaching end of the world, he recalled emphatically the law of labour:

---

[1] Acts ix, 11.
[2] Acts xxii, 17.
[3] Acts xiii, 3.
[4] Acts xiv, 23.
[5] Acts xvi, 25.
[6] Acts xx, 36.
[7] Acts xxi, 5.
[8] Acts xxviii, 8.
[9] Acts xxviii, 15.
[10] Rom. i, 9, 10 ; 2 Cor. xiii, 7 ; Eph. iii, 14 ; Phil. i, 3, 9 ; Col. i, 3.
[11] Rom. x, 1.
[12] 2 Cor. xii, 8 ; 1 Thess. iii, 10.
[13] Rom. xii, 13 ; 1 Cor. vii, 5 ; xi, 5-13 ; xiv, 13 ; Phil. iv, 6 ; Col. iv, 2 ; 1 Tim. ii, 1-4.
[14] Rom. xv, 30-32 ; 2 Cor. i, 11 ; Eph. vi, 18 ; Col. iv, 3, 18. 2 Thess. iii, 1-2.
[15] Phil. i, 19 ; Philem. 22.
[16] Acts xxvii, 35.
[17] Acts xx, 34.

" We were not idle among you, and we have not eaten any man's bread for nothing."[1] His maxim was that whoever would not work should not eat.[2] Wealth which protects one from want, is not an excuse for idleness. Paul wishes that everyone should work in order to escape a want of occupation and—if a more Christian motive is needed—in order to dispense charity more generously.[3] Labour in itself is a good work, but charity increases its value ten-fold.

Order was no less dear to the heart of the Apostle and he was a living example of it. He prescribed that in the religious assemblies all should be done in order.[4] Nothing pleased him so much as the charm of fair order in a young church.[5] He required that the idle members who troubled and scandalized the others should be fraternally reproved and, in case of backsliding, punished with a sort of kindly excommunication, capable of bringing them back to duty.[6]

Decorum was in his eyes the result of order and work : " Let everything be done decently," he often said. " Behave with decorum, as in the full day of Gospel light. Act properly in your relations with strangers " to our faith.[7] The convert must not be an exile from the world ; he may accept the invitations of unbelievers, but everywhere he must leave an influence unto edification.[8] Merely not to be a stumbling-block to Jews and Greeks[9] is too little; the Christian in his deportment and his entire conduct must convey to others a high idea of his faith and do honour to the Gospel.[10] Thus exalted, little virtues become great, and they are called devotion and apostolate.

St Paul's code of morals is full of contrasts. With incomparable ease he associates the most sublime mysticism with the most practical asceticism. While his eyes explore the depths of space, his feet never lose contact with the earth. Nothing is above, and nothing is beneath him. At the moment when he declares himself crucified to the world and living from the very life of Christ, he is able to address to his children delightful words of kindliness and grace and to descend to the most minute instructions about the veiling of women, good order in the assemblies, the duty of manual labour and the care of a weak stomach. Thus his spirituality offers to the humblest hearts a nourishment which is always savoury and to noble souls an inexhaustible mine of profound meditations.

---

[1] 2 Thess. iii, 5.   [2] 2 Thess. iii, 10.   [3] Eph. iv, 28, 29.
[4] 1 Cor. xiv, 40.   [5] Col. ii, 5.
[6] 1 Thess. v, 14 ; 2 Thess. iii, 6-11.
[7] 1 Cor. xiv, 40 ; Rom. xiii, 13 ; 1 Thess. iv, 12 ; Col. iv, 5.
[8] 1 Cor. x, 27, 28.   [9] 1 Cor. x, 32.   [10] Titus ii, 10.

## IV—CHRISTIAN PERFECTION

1. The Way of the Counsels. 2. The Imitation of Jesus Christ.
3. Christian Asceticism. 4. The Eucharist, the Seal of Perfection.

1. The reader must have perceived that Paul's exhortation goes far beyond strict obligation and is often an ideal rather than an imperative rule. How could it be otherwise? When he says to the faithful: "Have the same mind that was in Christ Jesus," he opens wide the door of the evangelical counsels. Ever since the *Si vis perfectus esse* of the divine Master was heard, a multitude of generous souls have voluntarily undertaken to tread this path and the apostles urge them thither, without, however, imposing it on them as a rigorous duty. At the moment when St Paul highly praises virginity and recommends the continence which he himself professes, he is very careful to say that it is a gift of God and that it demands a special call of grace; but this grace is generously offered and it is man's part to respond to it. Since our soul is a canvas upon which the living image of Jesus should be depicted, there will necessarily be some traits offered for our imitation which are not imposed upon our consciences; to pay one's debts is justice, to render more than one's due is generosity or gratitude; to give all without counting, is love.

Protestants must take their stand in regard to these things, and some do it with a fairly good grace. One of them writes, concerning the advice about virginity, which had just been discussed: " Christian celibacy does not deserve to be despised; it is, or can be, worthy of admiration; under its best aspect, it is clearly preferable to marriage. . . . Protestants do not like to hear this assertion, but it is necessary to bow to facts, and it is a fact that St Paul encourages continence; and the Protestant himself can, if he wishes, discover reasons for sympathizing with Paul's teaching."[1] The Catholic, on the other hand, finds Paul's doctrine quite natural, for to him it is a direct echo of the teaching of Jesus.[2]

Perfection is a career that has no limits. To whatever degree the Christian has attained, he can always aspire to rise higher, and it is the task of the preacher to stimulate him to this noble effort: " We preach Christ, admonishing and teaching every man in all wisdom, that we may present (to God) every man perfect in Christ."[3] But life will be ended

---

[1] R. Mackintosh, "Marriage Problems at Corinth," in the *Expositor*, 7th series, vol. iv (1907), p. 350.

[2] Matt. xix, 12 ; xix, 21. But *non omnes capiunt verbum istud*.

[3] Col. i, 28 : *ut exhibeamus omnem hominem perfectum* (τέλειον) *in Christo*. Τέλειος in St Paul has its ordinary meaning: " finished, accomplished, lacking nothing suitable to its nature " (Rom. xii, 2). Τὸ τέλειον (1 Cor. xiii, 10) denotes the perfection of the future life, in contrast to the imperfection of the present life. But often, as in the classics, τέλειος in-

before the aim is fully realized, for the standard proposed
to the Christian as a member of the mystical body is the perfection of the Head, Jesus Christ, and it is evident that he
will never come near that.

2. Some have wrongly claimed that St Paul, unlike the
Evangelists, does not present the historical Christ for our
imitation—that is to say, the person of Jesus Christ considered during his mortal life. No doubt there are in the
earthly life of Jesus many traits, such as his miracles and his
manifestations of divinity, which cannot be imitated. Where
he can be followed, and even urges us expressly to imitate
him, is when he lowers and effaces himself, when he kneels
before his disciples to wash their feet, when he accepts in-
sults and outrages, and when he takes upon himself the
cross through love of us.[1] This is also the model that St
Paul presents to us. In order to induce us to please others
" unto good, to edification," he quotes the example of Christ,
" who pleased not himself."[2] To teach us the merit and the
value of giving alms, of self-abnegation and of obedience, he
reminds us that Christ voluntarily exchanged the riches of
heaven for the poverty of earth, that he made himself of no
value by assuming a body like our own, and pushed the
heroism of obedience even to the death of the cross.[3]

If, however, the mortal life of Jesus plays a rather limited
role in Paul's moral as well as his theological teaching, it is
because the Apostle loves to consider Jesus Christ as he is
at present in his glorified life ; and he not only exhorts us to
imitate him and to model ourselves after him, but to transform ourselves into him. He invites us to put on Christ, to
fill ourselves with the thoughts of Christ and to live from the
life of Christ : " I live, yet now not I, but Jesus Christ liveth
in me."[4] Why speak of imitation, when the Apostle aims at
mystical identity?

It is true also that in giving us Jesus Christ as a model,

---

dicates the maturity of age as contrasted with infancy (Eph. iv, 13) ; it
then forms an antithesis to νήπιος (1 Cor. ii, 6). Let us observe that here
on earth perfection is only relative, since it is always susceptible of growth
(1 Cor. xiv, 20 ; Phil. iii, 15).

[1] John xiii, 15 ; Matt. xvi, 24 ; 1 Pet. ii, 21 ; cf. Matt. x, 24 : xi, 29, etc.

[2] Rom. xv, 3 : καὶ γὰρ (etenim) ὁ Χριστὸς οὐχ ἑαυτῷ ἤρεσεν.

[3] 2 Cor. viii, 9 ; Phil. ii, 5-11 ; cf. Heb. xii, 2.

[4] Gal. ii, 20. To put on Christ (Rom. xiii, 14 ; Gal. iii, 27), to be transformed into his image (2 Cor. iii, 18), to grow in him (Eph. iv, 5), to live in
him (Rom. vi, 11), etc., are only different expressions of the same thing. It is
less the direct imitation of Jesus than the effort to assimilate to ourselves
always more and more the divine nourishment of grace which makes the
Christian another Christ. St Paul is not afraid to propose to us Jesus Christ
as a model in his divine pre-existence (2 Cor. viii, 9 ; Phil. ii, 5-7). Why
should he not do so, since he exhorts us to imitate God (Eph. v, 1 : γίνεσθε οὖν
μιμηταὶ τοῦ Θεοῦ)?

Paul likes to interpose himself between Christ and us, as a living image of the Master. Eight or nine times in his Epistles this text recurs in similar forms : " Imitate me, as I imitate Christ."[1] This is the shortest and most efficacious example of his teachings. But the whole life of St Paul was a perpetual system of morals in action. What is curious in this silent preaching is that it was a carefully thought out procedure and an intentional complement of his oral teaching. There was in it neither ostentation nor vainglory, but that paternal condescension which can accommodate itself to weakness and, in order better to instruct, address the eyes, the intelligence and the heart in turn. He said to the Thessalonians : " Yourselves know how you ought to imitate us. For we were not disorderly among you. Neither did we eat any man's bread for nothing, but in labour and in toil we worked night and day, lest we should be chargeable to any of you. Not as if we had not power, but that we might give ourselves a pattern unto you, to imitate us."[2] The language of the preachers of the Faith is indeed eloquent when their conduct lends such support to their teaching.

The imitation of Christ opens limitless horizons to perfection. It is the death of selfishness and self-seeking. Here are some of the maxims which it suggests to St Paul : " Let none consider his own advantage, but that of others.— Rejoice with them that rejoice and weep with them that weep.—Bear the infirmities of others and let everyone of you try to please his neighbour unto good, to edification.—Remember . . . that it is more blessed to give than to receive."[3] It is in the Epistle to the Romans that Paul advances the theory of this voluntary renunciation for the sake of charity. In Rome there were over-scrupulous persons who abstained from certain foods and drinks and made distinctions between the different days of the year, the month or the week. These timorous souls did not form a definite group and had no established system, but, like all scrupulous people, were slaves to their own vain apprehensions and unreasonable aversions. They did not try to impose their ideas upon

---

[1] I Cor. xi, I ($\mu\iota\mu\eta\tau\alpha\ell$ $\mu o\nu$ $\gamma\ell\nu\epsilon\sigma\theta\epsilon$ $\kappa\alpha\theta\dot{\omega}s$ $\kappa\dot{\alpha}\gamma\dot{\omega}$ $X\rho\iota\sigma\tauo\hat{\nu}$). This counsel is a continuation of I Cor. x, 32, 33, and the division of the chapters is not a happy one. The other passages in which the Apostle exhorts the faithful to imitate him or praises them for having done so, are : I Cor. iv, 16 ($\mu\iota\mu\eta\tau\alpha\ell$ $\mu o\nu$ $\gamma\ell\nu\epsilon\sigma\theta\epsilon$—the addition *sicut et ego Christi* of the Vulgate is not in the text) ; vii' 7 (*volo omnes vos esse sicut meipsum*) ; vii, 8 (*bonum est illis si sic permaneant sicut et ego*) ; Phil. iii, 17 (Be *ye all* followers of me [$\sigma\nu\mu\mu\iota\mu\eta\tau\alpha\ell$ $\mu o\nu$ $\gamma\ell\nu\epsilon\sigma\theta\epsilon$], and observe them who walk so as you have our *model* [$\tau\acute{\nu}\pi o\nu$]) ; iv, 9 (*quae et didicistis, et accepistis, et audistis et vidistis in me, haec agite*) ; 2 Thess. iii, 7-10 (see below) ; I Tim. i, 16 ; 2 Tim. i, 13 (these last two are less striking). Compare, too, the remark of St Paul to the Elders of Ephesus (Acts xx, 35).

[2] 2 Thess. iii, 7-10 : *Ipsi scitis quemadmodum oportet imitari nos*, etc;

[3] Phil. ii, 1 ; I Cor. x, 24 ; Rom. xii, 15 ; xv, 2 ; Acts xx, 35.

others in the form of a doctrine, but "weak in the faith," they were above all weak in character, and were consequently exposed to the influence of example, even in actions which had wounded their badly instructed consciences. Were they, unconsciously, under the influence of Judaism? It is possible after all, although they seem to have been rather led astray by an ascetic and unwise ideal, although in itself worthy of respect.[1] In any case they were not aggressive Judaizers, like those in Antioch, Jerusalem, and Galatia, nor Manichean dogmatizers like those of Colosse. Otherwise the Apostle, so prompt to anathematize all the advocates of false doctrines, would not treat them with so much mildness and circumspection. He wishes the *strong*—that is to say, the enlightened Christians—to support the *weak,* who were subject to scruples, without even troubling them with sterile discussions; to abstain from condemning and judging them; much more, to avoid shocking and saddening them by a mode of conduct contrary to their own. The maintenance of peace and unity is well worth these sacrifices: "It is good [for thee] not to eat flesh and not to drink wine nor anything whereby thy brother is offended, or scandalized, or made weak. . . .[2] Wherefore if meat scandalize my brother, I will never eat flesh, lest I should scandalize my brother."[3]

3. Whoever wishes to walk in the footsteps of Jesus must be prepared for all sacrifices. See Paul, his faithful imitator. As a herald of the Gospel, he could live of the Gospel, but, as an Apostle to the Corinthians, he ought to be maintained by them. The soldier is fed by his commander and the workman by his employer; and it is to make us understand this truth of common sense that Moses forbids men to muzzle the ox that treadeth out the corn.[4] Yet Paul never made use of this right. He takes pains, as a handworker, not to be a burden on any one. He makes it his glory and his duty to preach the word of God without pay "in order to put no obstacle in the way of the [spread of the] Gospel."[5] Inspired by this aim, he accepts in advance all renunciations: "Free as to all, I made myself the servant of all that I might gain the more. . . . I became all things to all men, that I might save at least some."[6] It is not zeal alone that impels him; he obeys a still nobler motive.

Know you not that they that run in the race, all run indeed, but one receiveth the prize? So run that you may obtain.

And everyone that striveth for the mastery refraineth himself from all things. And they indeed that they may receive a corruptible crown, but we an incorruptible one.

---

[1] Rom. xiv, 1-xv, 4.
[2] Rom. xiv, 21.
[3] I Cor. viii, 13
[4] I Cor. ix, 1-15.
[5] I Cor. ix, 12.
[6] I Cor. ix, 19-22.

> I therefore, so run, not as at an uncertainty ; I so fight, not as one beating the air. But I chastise my body and bring it into subjection, lest perhaps, when I have preached to others, I myself should become a castaway.[1]

We know how long and severe the preparation for the athletic contests was among the ancients. For ten months or more a minute and tyrannical rule determined for the candidate the hours and duration of his exercises, his meals, and his sleep, which he took on a couch too hard for his body to leave an impression on it. He had to harden himself against hunger, cold and heat, the sun and dust, fatigue and the inclemencies of the weather. Not only were the pleasures of the table and of love severely prohibited, but he was forbidden to drink wine, because it heats the blood, while cool drinks were excluded under the pretext that they are debilitating. And all that for the chance of receiving a leafy crown which was to ornament the head of the fortunate victor.

St Paul, comparing the present life to an arena, likens himself to a competitor who is contending for the prizes offered for running and pugilism. Like the runner in the stadium, he keeps his gaze fixed on the goal which he does not lose sight of for a moment ; like the pugilist, he strikes terrible blows at his adversary, who is none other than himself. In order to comprehend the frightful realism of his words, one must have stood before those antique statues which represent the pugilist standing, with bruised ear, swollen eye, hanging lip, broken teeth, and his entire face dotted with bloody protuberances. When one of the fighters, panting and half dead, lay on the ground, his rival planted his knee

---

[1] 1 Cor. ix, 24-27. All the terms of this passage are metaphorical and are borrowed from the games of the arena. Verses 24-25 contain the presentation of the allegory, and verses 26-27 its application. In the presentation we note the place of the contest, the *stadium* (στάδιον) ; the *rival competitors* (ὁ ἀγωνιζόμενος), and in particular the *runners* (τρέχοντες) ; the *training*, which consists above all in a severe abstinence (πάντα ἐγκρατεύεται) ; the victory, which is awarded the one who first *touches* the goal and *secures* the palm (καταλαμβάνειν) ; the *crown* (στέφανος) of parsley or pine, destined to adorn the brow of the victor ; and the *prize* (βραβεῖον), in cash or in kind, which often supplements the crown.—In the application, Paul compares himself by turns to a runner and to a pugilist : as a runner, he looks steadfastly at the goal, never losing sight of it for a moment ; as a pugilist, he is careful not to beat the air but to hit his adversary, who in this case is none other than himself. The blows which he delivers are described by a word of singular force : the verb ὑπωπιάζειν denotes literally " to bruise the face," to give it *livid contusions* (ὑπώπιον). I think that δουλαγωγεῖν must be explained in harmony with the preceding metaphors : " to throw upon the ground, to keep down, to hold at one's feet like a slave." For the same reason κηρύσσειν, which could be translated " to preach," ought here to retain its etymological sense of " to serve as a herald, to proclaim the order of the contests or the name of the victor," etc.—It is known that the word ἀδόκιμος (in the Vulgate *reprobus*) means " rejected, refused," like a coin of base mixture and like a competitor unworthy of the prize.

upon his breast in order to demonstrate his defeat. This is the treatment which the Apostle inflicts upon his body; he beats it unmercifully like a mortal enemy and keeps it under foot like a vanquished slave.

What the accomplishment of his ministry must have cost him in fatigues, dangers, privations, and sufferings we could easily guess, even if we did not have his discreet disclosures on that point.[1] He endured all with resignation and even with joy; for he knows that the Apostle, after the example of his Master, saves others only by the cross: "I rejoice in my sufferings for you and fill up those things that are wanting of the sufferings of Christ, in my flesh, for his body, which is the Church."[2] To the trials occasioned by men or sent by God, he adds voluntary renunciations. All his ambition is "to carry about in his body everywhere the crucifixion of Jesus,"[3] and "to bear in his flesh the marks" of the Crucified.[4]

This attitude in regard to his fellow-creatures and to himself, however generous it may be, nevertheless presents only the negative, and as it were the reverse, side of perfection. It has for its effect to break all the ties which attach the soul to earth and to remove the obstacles which hinder its flight towards heaven. Such was the disposition of St Paul from the first moment of his conversion: "The things that were gain to me, the same I have counted loss for Christ. Furthermore, I count all things to be but loss for the excellent knowledge of Jesus Christ, my Lord, for whom I have suffered the loss of all things, and count them but as dung, that I may gain Christ and may be found in him, not having my justice which is of the Law, but that which is through faith in Christ, which is of God, [grounded] on faith."[5] Not content with purifying his soul from earthly

---

[1] 2 Cor. xi, 23-30.      [2] Col. i, 24. *Cf.* p. 295.

[3] 2 Cor. iv, 10. *Cf.* p. 189.

[4] Gal. vi, 17.

[5] Phil. iii, 7-9. Verse 7 has nothing obscure in it: *quae mihi fuerunt* (better *erant*) *lucra*=all the just enumerated human gains—descent from the purest Hebrew blood, a spotless reputation in regard to legal justice, etc. —these I have counted loss for Christ, from whom they alienated me.—The difficulty is in verse 8. Many interpreters see in it a simple repetition of verse 7. Formerly I despised these things; now I despise all that ($\pi\acute{a}\nu\tau a = \check{a}\tau\iota\nu a$). The contrast is then between the past ($\mathring{\eta}\gamma\eta\mu a\iota$) and the present ($\mathring{\eta}\gamma o\hat{u}\mu a\iota$). But this interpretation is a weak one and the application unsatisfactory, for: (*a*) The present ($\mathring{\eta}\gamma o\hat{u}\mu a\iota$) is not in opposition to the perfect ($\mathring{\eta}\gamma\eta\mu a\iota$), which expresses an action or a state *which still endures.*— (*b*) It is assumed gratuitously that $\pi\acute{a}\nu\tau a$ is equivalent to $\check{a}\tau\iota\nu a$, for it would be necessary to have at least $\tau\grave{a}$ $\pi\acute{a}\nu\tau a$=all that I have just spoken of.—(*c*) The structure of the phrase indicates a progress in the thought ($\grave{a}\lambda\lambda\acute{a}$ . . . $\kappa a\acute{\iota}$), which can be translated by *much more.*—The meaning therefore is: not only have I regarded and still regard the temporal gains, which I sacrificed for Christ, as loss, *but even* ($\grave{a}\lambda\lambda\grave{a}$ $\kappa a\acute{\iota}$) I consider *all* earthly goods ($\pi\acute{a}\nu\tau a$) as refuse ($\sigma\kappa\acute{u}\beta a\lambda a$).

affections, he turns towards the inimitable model and endeavours to reproduce him.

> Not as though I had already attained, or were already perfect; but I follow after, if I may by any means apprehend, wherein I am also apprehended by Christ Jesus.
> Brethren, I do not count myself to have apprehended. But one thing I do: Forgetting the things that are behind and stretching myself forth to those that are before, I press towards the mark, to the prize of the heavenly calling of God in Christ Jesus.[1]

The allegory of the race is here perfectly plain. To look behind is for the runner in the stadium as useless an act as it is dangerous. He must keep his gaze fixed constantly before him, in order not to swerve from the straight line and also to prevent the surprises, accidents, and obstacles which would retard his progress and cause his fall. The desire to win gives him wings, and he strains all his nerves and thoughts towards that goal, knowing well that a moment's relaxation might cost him the victory. See, for example, the old statues of nimble runners whose feet scarcely touch the earth, whose breasts are thrown forward and their arms stretched out towards the goal which they devour with their eyes.

On the road to perfection there is no halting or resting. Therefore St Paul *forgets* gladly what he has already accomplished; he effaces it from his memory and dispels the thought of it. To go forward constantly, to get nearer and nearer to the goal, and little by little to diminish the distance that separates him from his sublime Model, that is his only anxiety. That ceaseless striving for what is better, that constant tension of soul, Paul expresses with an untranslatable force when he says: *ad ea quae priora sunt extendens meipsum*.

Nevertheless, St Paul foresees that all the faithful are not yet prepared for this teaching. Many will not hear it or will understand it amiss. But with these minds, more sluggish than disobedient, he knows how to temporize, and stoops to their level of weakness, saying to them: "Let all of us therefore who are perfect be thus minded; and if

---

[1] Phil. iii, 12-14. One phrase of this text is ambiguous both in Latin and Greek. *Sequor autem, si quomodo comprehendam in quo et comprehensus sum a Christo Jesu:* διώκω δὲ εἰ καὶ καταλάβω ἐφ' ᾧ καὶ κατελήφθην ὑπὸ X. 'I. We have adopted in the text the simplest translation, which understands before ἐφ' ᾧ the antecedent ἐκεῖνο [*illud*] *in quo*, " that for which," and makes it governed by the two verbs *sequi* and *comprehendere*. However, the Greeks (Chrysostom, Theodore of Mopsuestia, Theodoret) take ἐφ' ᾧ in the sense of *because*, a meaning which *in quo* also possesses; I pursue [the ideal of perfection] in order to try to seize (*or* attain it), *because* I have myself been seized by Christ: κατεδίωξέν με ὁ Χριστός, καὶ φεύγοντα ἀπ' αὐτοῦ κατέλαβεν, καὶ ἐπέστρεψεν (Theophylact). The idea is just and beautiful and the interpretation attractive, but in the other explanation the phrase is clearer and smoother.

in anything you be otherwise minded, this also God will reveal to you."[1]

4. Is it possible, without the Eucharist, to reach this ideal state of perfection? "Except you eat the flesh of the Son of man," said Jesus, "and drink his blood, you shall not have life in you. . . . For my flesh is meat indeed and my blood is drink indeed." Understood in their natural sense, these words teach us that the eucharistic bread and wine are as necessary for the maintenance and progress of the life of the soul as material food is for the life of the body. We can be born to the life of grace without the Eucharist, and that is why baptism, actual or desired, is necessarily the only means; but we cannot long retain, strengthen, and increase this life without the eucharistic food, unless by a miracle comparable to that of a human body growing in strength and stature, although deprived of all nourishment. The Eucharist is therefore necessary, not only as an act of obedience to the commands of God or the Church in order to avoid the death of sin, but as the condition normally requisite to perfect in ourselves the life of Christ.

St Paul reaches the same point by an entirely different road. While St John considers the part played by the Eucharist in the life of the individual soul, Paul regards it in its relations to the mystical body : "The chalice of benediction which we bless, is it not the communion of the blood of Christ? And the bread which we break, is it not the communion of the body of Christ? For there is only one bread, and we all make one body, since we all partake of that one bread."[2] Chrysostom's commentary is very acute :

---

[1] Phil. iii, 15, 16: *et siquid aliter sapitis, et hoc vobis Deus revelabit* (ἀποκαλύψει).

[2] 1 Cor. x, 16-17. In verse 16 the Vulgate translation *communicatio sanguinis* and *participatio corporis* is not a happy one; it is *communio* (κοινωνία) that is needed in both cases.

In many of the Latin manuscripts verse 17 reads thus : *Quoniam unus panis* ET *unum corpus multi sumus omnes qui de uno pane participamus.* The ordinary gloss commented thereon as follows : Unus panis, *unione fidei, spei et charitatis.* Corpus *est per subministrationem charitatis ; quia unum sumus et unum sentire debemus* (Migne, CXIV, 536). An obscure commentary copied by the Scholastics.—P. Cornely, without reading *et* between *panis* and *corpus,* thinks that the two words are co-ordinated and that it is necessary to render it " We are one bread, one body, because we partake of the same bread." He invokes the authority of Ambrosiaster, Chrysostom and other Greek Fathers ; but I do not see any such thing in Ambrosiaster, whose whole commentary is as follows : *Quoniam unum sumus, alter alterius membra, unum nos sentire debere dicit, ut fides una unum habeat opus.* And there is nothing in the Greek Fathers with the exception of Cyril of Alexandria who, without commenting on it, quotes our text in a very singular manner (*In Joan.* x, Migne, LXXIV, 341): Οἱ γὰρ πάντες ἐν σῶμά ἐσμεν ἐν Χριστῷ, ὅτι εἷς ἄρτος οἱ πολλοί ἐσμεν· οἱ γὰρ πάντες ἐκ τοῦ ἑνὸς ἄρτο υ

" Paul does not say *participation,* but *communion,* because
he wishes to express a closer union. For, in receiving Holy
Communion, we not only participate in Christ, we unite with
him. In fact, as this body is united with Christ, so by this
bread we are united with Christ. . . . But why do I speak
of communion? Paul says that we are identically this body.
For what is this bread? The body of Christ. And what do
we become by receiving this bread? The body of Christ :
not many bodies, but one only."

It seems, therefore, that without the Eucharist, which is
" the sacrament of piety, the [efficacious] sign of unity and
the bond of charity," according to the famous expression of St
Augustine, the mystical body would not have all the perfection which is its due. Christians would neither be united
with Christ nor with one another by that ineffable union
which Holy Communion produces and which the Lord meant
for his Church when he instituted the Eucharist. If our incorporation into Christ by faith and baptism is sufficient for
salvation, communion with Christ is indispensable for the social
perfection of the mystical body and even, normally, for the individual perfection of the Christian. The consequence is
evident to everyone who remembers that the eucharistic food,
unlike ordinary nourishment, has the power of transforming
us into it.

---

$\mu\epsilon\tau\acute{\epsilon}\chi o\mu\epsilon\nu$.—The majority of modern exegetes and translators (Segond,
Crampon, Lemonnyer, Weizsäcker) explain the verse as we have done,
understanding $\acute{\epsilon}\sigma\tau\acute{\iota}\nu$ after $\acute{o}\tau\iota$ $\epsilon\acute{\iota}s$ $\acute{a}\rho\tau os$, which serves as the protasis, while
$\acute{\epsilon}\nu$ $\sigma\hat{\omega}\mu a$ $o\acute{\iota}$ $\pi o\lambda\lambda o\acute{\iota}$ $\acute{\epsilon}\sigma\mu\epsilon\nu$ is the apodosis, and the words $o\acute{\iota}$ $\gamma\grave{a}\rho$ $\pi\acute{a}\nu\tau\epsilon s$ $\acute{\epsilon}\kappa$
$\tauo\hat{\upsilon}$ $\acute{\epsilon}\nu\grave{o}s$ $\acute{a}\rho\tauo\upsilon$ $\mu\epsilon\tau\acute{\epsilon}\chi o\mu\epsilon\nu$ give the reason for the complete assertion:
" Because there is one [eucharistic] bread only, we are all one [mystical]
body ; since we all partake of this same [eucharistic] bread." The exegesis
is very simple and the grammar unobjectionable.

# CHAPTER II

## ¡THE LAST THINGS

### I—Points of Contact with Jewish Eschatology

1. Difficulty of the Subject.    2. The Present Age and the Age to Come.
3. The True Sources of New Testament Eschatology.

1.     UNDER the comprehensive name of *eschatology*
are often designated death and the intermediate
state, the *parousia* with its precedent signs, the
resurrection, the judgement, the retribution of
the good and the wicked, and the consummation
of all things.   The special word *apocalypse* is reserved for the
moral and religious crisis which is to precede the last day,
with its preliminary phases and the dramatic conflict waged
between the powers of heaven and hell in regard to the human
race.   These terms have passed into common use and we shall
employ them, for the sake of brevity, conjointly with that
of the " last things," which includes, besides individual
destinies, the final lot of humanity and the ultimate transformation of the universe.

We know that the eschatological teaching of St Paul clearly
tends to diminish.   After having played such a great role in
the Epistles to the Thessalonians and still holding a notable
place in the great Epistles, it appears only incidentally and at
long intervals in the writings of the captivity and in the
Pastoral Epistles.[1]   From the day when the theory of the
mystical body of Christ was set by him in high relief, his whole
attention was concentrated on that subject : eschatology is
thenceforth only the normal ending, the regular coronation of
the moral life.   Far from being the most original feature of
Paul's theology, eschatology would be only an appendix to
it of little interest, if it were not so closely connected on the
one hand with the primitive teaching of the apostles and by
that very fact with the first transfiguration of Jewish hopes,
and on the other hand with the doctrine of the mystical body,
which St Paul has made specially his own.   We shall outline its principal characteristics by grouping them under four
heads : 1. Points of contact with Jewish eschatology.   2.
Death and the resurrection.   3. *Parousia* and the judgement.
4. The consummation of all things.

If an accurate knowledge of New Testament times is
nowhere more desirable for the historian of the origins of

---

[1] The principal eschatological texts, in the order of dates, are 1 Thess.
iv, 13-v, 5 ; 2 Thess. i, 4-12 ; ii, 2-12 ; 1 Cor. xv ; 2 Cor. v, 1-10 ; Rom. viii,
17-23 ; xi, 25-29 ; Phil. iii, 21 ; 2 Tim. iv, 1-8.

Christianity than precisely in questions of eschatology, nowhere also is that knowledge more difficult to obtain. The Hellenist writers of the epoch, Philo and Josephus, anxious to adapt Jewish thought, one to the taste of his pagan readers, the other to the postulates of Greek philosophy, were able only to alter, veil or attenuate it. Rabbinical works, of a date so uncertain and in general so late, ought to be utilized only with extreme circumspection. The Targums of Onkelos and of Jonathan, even if they are of the first century, as is commonly believed, and not of the third century, as some recent critics vigorously maintain, throw but little light upon the subject of contemporary eschatology, for one of them, even in paraphrasing, does not wish to abandon his role of interpreter, and the other is only a scrupulously exact translator. The clearest sources of Jewish traditions—the *Mishna,* written apparently towards the end of the second century, and the *Tosephta,* composed perhaps at the dawn of the third—regarded as pandects, touch upon eschatology but very incidentally. It is through the *Gemara* of the two Talmuds and through the *Midrashim* that eschatological ideas run most abundantly; but if we read Weber's *Jewish Theology* or any other similar book, we see what can be extracted from that confused, incoherent, and contradictory mass of trash.

There remain the Jewish apocalypses, which were so numerous about the beginning of the Christian era. Here again we are assailed by difficulties of every kind. It has been justly said : " It is a delicate task, to put a little order into this chaos, at the risk of sacrificing many a fine shade of thought to the necessity of finally reaching some general ideas ; a necessary task nevertheless on account of the extreme —and let us say at once disproportionate—importance which is to-day ascribed to these productions of a feverishly agitated and exhausted age." It would not be too severe to describe them as a " gigantic effort in the void, or a tedious dream enlivened by a few flashes of common sense in the nightmare of a sick man, yet containing at times real beauties of style, with a religious and still more nationalistic tone, at once sincere and passionate."[1] But the trouble of disentangling this chaos is not the only one. The Jewish apocalypses, as they have come down to us, swarm with Christian interpolations. How can we recognize with certainty the hand of the forger and the extent of his forgeries? It is an arduous problem, always complicated and often insoluble.

As apostolic times approached, Jewish eschatology became at once more universal, more individual, and more spiritual : more universal, because it now looked beyond the national

[1] Lagrange, *Le messianisme chez les Juifs,* Paris, 1909, p. 39.

horizon and busied itself with the destinies of all peoples; more individual, because, having ceased to blend in one mass the lot of individuals in the history of Israel, it evolved with ever-increasing intensity the sense of personal responsibility; and finally more spiritual, because it rose at times above the dreams of an exaggerated patriotism and a vulgar realism: if the idea of an earthly kingdom still haunted the imagination, it no longer formed the sum total of the messianic hopes. This can be truly said in general; yet this systematic view might involve us in the risk of going astray. In every advance there are halts, deviations from the route, and even retrograde movements to be taken into account. Each document requires a separate treatment. But this study, fortunately, does not belong to our subject and we shall confine ourselves here to pointing out an idea of considerable importance in the evolution of eschatology.

2. The prophets regarded the appearance of the Messiah as the beginning of a new era: it was the starting-point of *the end of days*,[1] the beginning of the reign of holiness and justice which the day of the Lord was to precede or to conclude. The fulfilment of the messianic promises and the final destinies of all the nations were grouped together in a picture without perspective, in which all the events seem to blend. Sometimes it might be said that all this future is contained in only one indivisible moment. The exegesis of the Rabbis was based upon these data. In proportion as it separated the earthly reign of the Messiah from his eternal reign and by fantastic calculations assigned to the first reign a duration of forty, seventy, a hundred, six hundred, a thousand years or more, it obtained for the end of days a double point of departure, the origin of which it fixed either at the commencement or the end of the terrestrial kingdom. In principle, the history of humanity was divided into two periods, the present age and the age to come, and there were two worlds measured by these two periods, the present world and the future world. To what age and to what world did the temporal kingdom belong? Naturally, the apocalypses without a Messiah had not to face this question; but the others could solve the problem in two ways: either the whole eschatology was referred to the future world, or it was divided, so to speak, into two judgements, two resur-

---

[1] The expression בְּאַחֲרִית חַיָּמִים (*in fine dierum*) is found in Gen. xlix, 1; Num. xxiv, 14; Deut. iv, 30; xxxi, 29; Is. ii, 2; Jer. xxiii, 20. xxx, 24; xlviii, 47; xlix, 39; Ezech. xxviii, 16; Os. iii, 5; Mich. iv, 1; Ezech. xxxviii, 8 employs the synonym בְּאַחֲרִית חַשָּׁנִים (*in fine annorum*). Kimchi rightly remarks in regard to Is. ii, 2: *Ubicumque leguntur haec verba, ibi sermo est de diebus Messiae.* Indeed, all the texts in which this expression is met are to some extent messianic.

rections, two messianic reigns, and two restorations. As each writer represented only his own personal authority, we do not know to which system it is proper to award the preference; and if we think of the retouchings, manipulations and interpolations which these documents have undergone, and of the heaps of heterogeneous writings which are presented to us under one and the same title, the confusion knows no limits.

That which essentially distinguishes Christian from Jewish eschatology is its faith in the double advent of Christ. The messianic hopes are indeed already realized, yet only in part; the ancient prophecies are explained and precisely indicated in the light of history; the vistas recede and become harmonious; all the points of view are changed by the fact itself: the resurrection, the judgement, the final retribution are carried on into the future and are all connected with the second advent. The horizon may appear more or less distant, the supreme crisis more or less near; but that is a secondary point, and Christian eschatology acquires a clearness of contours and a relative firmness in its lines which Jewish eschatology never had.

Nevertheless, the terminology which it inherited did not adapt itself easily to the new conceptions. From this fact come uncertainties of expression and differences in the use of words. Thus the end of the age coincides, in St Matthew, with the end of the world; in the Epistle to the Hebrews, conformably to the language of the prophets, with the dawn of the messianic age. St Paul gives the same meaning to the fulness of the times and also to the end of the ages.[1] The limit of the last days is scarcely more definite. According to the different points of view, we have either already reached them or are still awaiting them.

We have seen what an exceptional role the conception of the *world* or of *the present age* plays in the New Testament, and especially in St Paul. But the corresponding notion of *the world* or *the age to come* has not by any means the same

---

[1] The expression ἡ συντέλεια τοῦ αἰῶνος (*consummatio saeculi*) in St Matt. denotes five times (xiii, 39, 40, 49; xxiv, 3; xxviii, 20) the epoch of the *parousia*. In the Epistle to the Hebrews (ix, 26 : νυνὶ δὲ ἅπαξ ἐπὶ συντελείᾳ τῶν αἰώνων) it coincides with the messianic era. This is also the meaning of τὸ πλήρωμα τοῦ χρόνου (Gal. iv, 4) or τῶν καιρῶν (Eph. i, 10).—The end of all things in the *Prima Petri* (iv, 7 : πάντων τὸ τέλος) is eschatological; the end of the ages in St Paul (1 Cor. x, 11 : τὰ τέλη τῶν αἰώνων) is messianic and recalls the prophecies referring to the end of the times.—The last day and the last hour are always associated, in the fourth Gospel, with the resurrection and the judgement. Elsewhere the meaning varies: it is eschatological in James v, 3; 1 Pet. i, 5; it includes the messianic age in 2 Tim. iii, 1 (ἐν ἐσχάταις ἡμέραις); 1 Tim. iv, 1 (ἐν ὑστέροις καιροῖς); 1 Pet. i, 20 (ἐπ' ἐσχάτου τῶν χρόνων); 2 Pet. iii, 3 (ἐπ' ἐσχάτων τῶν ἡμερῶν); Jud. 18 (ἐπ' ἐσχάτου χρόνου). In some of these cases this may be the *last phase* of messianic times, as also in 1 John ii, 18 : ἐσχάτη ὥρα ἐστίν.

importance. St Paul mentions only once " the age to come,"[1]
and once " the ages to come ";[2] on the other hand, the
Epistle to the Hebrews mentions once " the powers of the
world to come,"[3] and twice " the world or the city to come."[4]
And that is all. How are we to explain the rarity of this
expression, when the phrase which forms a pendant to it is
so frequent? This phenomenon, attributed by Bousset to
mere accident, seems, however, to be attributable to other
causes than chance. It is because the writers of the New
Testament give the present age or present world only a
moral value; the present age has lost its notion of duration
and the present world its idea of space; thenceforth, the
present age and the age to come can interpenetrate each
other; there is no chronological interval between them; there
are only opposing influences. On the one hand, the idea of a
sudden catastrophe inaugurating the reign of the Messiah
and of an instantaneous cataclysm caused by God alone,
without the co-operation of man, who will be only a passive
spectator, gradually gives place to that of a messianic
kingdom developing by degrees until the consummation of all
things. In these conditions the Jewish concept of the age
or the world to come was almost inapplicable and it was
necessary to replace it by eternal life.[5]

3. On the whole, the Apocrypha and the Talmud offer very
little help to an understanding of New Testament eschatology.
All those who use this method in the hope of finding some
light therein return from the effort disappointed, and those
who send us thither with so much confidence make us suspect
that they have not pursued the path very far themselves.
A text from Daniel casts perhaps more light on the eschatology of the New Testament than all the rabbinical writings
put together :

> At that time shall Michael rise up, the great prince, the defender of
> the children of thy people. And a time of tribulation shall come such
> as never was from the time that nations began. And at that time shall

---

[1] Eph. i, 21.     [2] Eph. ii, 7.     [3] Heb. vi, 5.
[4] Heb. ii, 5 ; xiii, 14.
[5] To what epoch can we trace back the distinction between *the present age*
and *the age to come?* The Hebrew text of the O.T. gives us no indication
of it; nor do the deutero-canonical books (except perhaps Tob. xiv, 5 :
ἕως πληρωθῶσιν καιροὶ τοῦ αἰῶνος); the words πατὴρ τοῦ μέλλοντος αἰῶνος
of the Codex Alexandrinus (Is. ix, 7) are a Christian correction for the
true translation of the Septuagint μεγάλης βουλῆς ἄγγελος. Nor is it in
Philo. But on the contrary, it is found quite frequently in the fourth book
of Esdras viii, 1 : *Hoc saeculum fecit Altissimus propter multos, futurum
autem propter paucos.* So also vi, 7, 9, 20 ; vii, 12-13, 42-43, etc. In the
*Apocalypse of Baruch* the " age " is replaced by its synonym the " world,"
xlviii, 50 : *Sicut in hoc mundo qui praeterit laborem multum pertulistis, ita
in mundo illo cui finis non est accipietis lucem magnam.* Cf. xiv, 13;
xv, 7-8 ; xliv, 15.

thy people be saved, every one that shall be found written in the book of life. And many of those that sleep in the dust of the earth shall awake, some unto life eternal and others unto eternal shame and reproach. But they that are wise shall shine as the brightness of the firmament, and they that have instructed many to justice, as stars for all eternity.[1]

This passage, which has been the object of numberless allusions and reminders, informs us of the unequalled role of the archangel Michael in the Jewish-Christian eschatology, the times of extreme tribulation which are to precede the great day, the Book of Life in which the names of the just are inscribed and in which are recorded their claims to a glorious immortality, the resurrection common to both the good and the wicked, the eternal life of the just and the incomparable glory of the elect, the endless opprobrium and ignominy which are the lot of the rejected, and the final division of the good and the bad, separated " for ever and ever " by an impassable barrier. These are the seven principal truths which sum up the doctrine of the last things.

Daniel, the second part of Isaias, the portions of the prophets referring to the judgement and the end of days, and the Books of the Machabees constitute the true sources of the New Testament eschatology. In the slough of the Apocrypha and the rabbinical writings a few particles of gold can be sometimes met with, but with how much dross are they combined !

## II—DEATH AND THE RESURRECTION

1. Death and the Hereafter.   2. The Resurrection of the Just.
3. The Fate of the Living.

1. *Death* has meanings as varied as those of its antithesis, *life*.[2]   Besides natural death or the physical destruction of the human composite, St Paul mentions a spiritual death, the death of sin, which is opposed to the life of grace and, at the end of the era of probation, becomes eternal death. The wicked deserve death and sin works death ; " death is the wages of sin."[3]   Physical death, spiritual

---

[1] Dan. xii, 1-4.

[2] Kabisch (*Eschatol. des Paulus*, pp. 109-110) and Tobac (*Problème de la justific.*, p. 79 and *passim*) claim that death in St Paul's writings must always be understood as *physical* death. This thesis seems wholly untenable. " Death " and " to die " are used figuratively in many texts, for example : Rom. i, 32 ; vi, 2, 7, 8, 11, 16, 21 ; vii, 4, 6, 10 ; viii, 6, 13 ; 2 Cor. v, 14 ; vii, 10 ; Gal. ii, 19 ; Eph. ii, 1, 5 ; Col. ii, 13, 20 ; iii, 3 ; 1 Tim. v, 6 ; 2 Tim. ii, 11. It is impossible to escape the force of these texts by subtle arguments or by doing violence to the natural meaning of the words. On the other hand, others (Schmidt, *Die Lehre des Ap. Paulus*, pp. 35-49) maintain that death, as the consequence of sin, always means spiritual death. The truth lies between the two.

[3] Rom. vi, 23. The meaning appears here from the opposition : τὸ δὲ χάρισμα τοῦ Θεοῦ ζωὴ αἰώνιος. So also Rom. vi, 24 (*finis illorum mors est*).

death, eternal death, all these directly or indirectly go back to a common source, the transgression of Eden. But there is a fourth death, a remedy for the three others, mystical death in Christ, which is for the soul and for the body the prelude and the pledge of a glorious immortality: " You are dead, and your life is hid with Christ in God."—" One died for all, therefore all have died "[1] mystically with him.

It is as a punishment for sin that death is terrible. To the instinctive horror of dissolution is added the fear of the Judge and the uncertainty of what lies beyond. In the metaphorical language of St Paul, " sin is the sting of death."[2] Death uses sin as a poisoned dart to widen his empire, or perhaps rather as a piercing arrow to terrorize men and lead them at his will. Jesus Christ, the conqueror of sin, takes from death its malevolent and painful sting and will one day render it powerless and harmless. If it retains to the last a remnant of its ancient power and yielded only last of all to the triumph of the cross, it has already lost its terrors. In spite of natural repugnances, the feeling of Christian resignation, preached to the faithful of Thessalonica and of Corinth, makes its appearance, and also the more heroic feeling of fond desire for death, which Paul, without giving up conformity to the divine will, frequently reveals. Thenceforth, life is a duty to accept and death a gain to which to aspire.

What becomes of the soul when separated from the body? What are its relations with God, with the living, and with the dead? On all these problems St Paul gives but little information and still less in the way of teaching. Quite a large number of heterodox theologians claim that the Apostle imagines the soul to be inactive, torpid, or asleep, while awaiting the hour of the resurrection.[3] Like the shadowy forms which hovered on the shores of the mythological Erebus, it had no longer any feeling, memory, consciousness, or personality; and there it needed nothing less than the blast of the last trumpet to draw it from its lethargy. The advocates of this theory rely upon the word " sleeping "

---

[1] Col. iii, 1 ; 2 Cor. v, 14.—So also Rom. vi, 2 (*mortui sumus* peccato, dative and not instrumental ablative).

[2] 1 Cor. xv, 56 : τὸ δὲ κέντρον τοῦ θανάτου ἡ ἁμαρτία.

[3] The partisans of this theory can be divided into three classes : (*a*) those who admit it and seek proofs of it everywhere in the N.T.; (*b*) those who attribute it specially to Paul without distinction of time (Dähne, Köstlin, etc.); (*c*) those who claim that Paul maintained it until after the first Epistle to the Corinthians (Usteri, Pfleiderer, etc.). Later, he is believed to have altered his mind when the prospect of a speedy *parousia* commenced to recede and he perceived that he might die before the return of Christ. His acquaintance with Apollos, who was imbued with Hellenist ideas about immortality, may have had something to do with this change of opinion.

It must be said that many Protestants do not share these views. Messner finds the theory arbitrary (*Lehre der Apostel*, p. 283) ; Beyschlag thinks it rather unnatural (*Neutest. Theol.*[3], vol. ii, p. 272) ; Weiss combats it (*Bibl. Theol. des N.T.*[6], pp. 395-396), as do Schmidt and Wendt.

sometimes given to the dead;[1] but this support is very weak.
In all literatures death and sleep are brothers; sleep is the
living image of death, and to die is to sleep. This metaphor
suits Christian death still better, since this is a bond of union
between two lives, a short interlude between two acts of one
and the same existence. If death involved the loss of thought,
death would have nothing desirable in it. Paul teaches expressly that it does not separate the just from Christ.[2] To
depart from the body is for the soul to leave this world to
go to the Saviour and to live with him.[3] The crown awaits
the victor at the end of the struggle, which is a figure of the
present life.[4] That which sleeps in us is, therefore, not the
soul, it is the body resting in the dust of the tomb, for which
the resurrection will be an awakening.

If the just enter at once into the possession of the state of
blessedness without waiting for the last day, it is natural
that sinners should undergo their punishment at once after
the end of their earthly trial. Nevertheless, the Apostle says
nothing on this subject. Nor does he speak to us of the
individual judgement which decides the destiny of each man
immediately after his decease. But this immediate discrimination is in the nature of things, and from this fact it appears
that neither the happiness of the elect nor, by analogy, the
punishment of the rejected is deferred until the *parousia*.
Perhaps the way in which the Epistle to the Hebrews brings
the judgement close to death without, apparently, any interval
between the two events, authorizes the same conclusion.[5]

---

[1] The dead are those who are asleep (οἱ κεκοιμημένοι, 1 Cor. xv, 20;
Matt. xxvii, 52); who have fallen asleep (οἱ κοιμηθέντες, 1 Cor. xv, 18;
1 Thess. iv, 15); who sleep (οἱ κοιμώμενοι, 1 Thess. iv, 13).—To sleep
(κοιμᾶσθαι) is again taken metaphorically in the sense of dying, John xi, 11;
Acts vii, 60; xiii, 36; 1 Cor. vii, 39; xv, 51; 2 Pet. iii, 4.—By means of a
similar metaphor, death is a *rest* (Heb. iv, 3, 11; Apoc. xiv, 13).—It is
noteworthy that Jesus Christ himself is called " the firstfruits of them that
sleep " (1 Cor. xv, 20: ἀπαρχὴ τῶν κεκοιμημένων), and consequently forms
part of those who slept (note the perfect participle of the verb and the force
of the word ἀπαρχή); whence it follows that death does not involve any
more for us than for Christ the loss of intellectual activity and consciousness.

[2] Phil. i, 21, 23: ἐπιθυμίαν ἔχων εἰς τὸ ἀναλῦσαι καὶ σὺν Χριστῷ εἶναι,
πολλῷ γὰρ μᾶλλον κρεῖσσον. It is evident that the dissolution of the body
and life with Christ are simultaneous; if there were to be an interval, life
would be preferable to death.

[3] 2 Cor. v, 6-8. The simultaneousness of *being absent from the body* and
*being present with the Lord* is evident, because of the antithesis (*dum sumus
in corpore peregrinamur a Domino*). But *praesentes esse ad Dominum* is
*ambulare per speciem :* to enjoy the beatific vision.

[4] 2 Tim. ii, 5.—In 2 Tim. iv, 8, the (solemn) coronation of the victor is
referred to the last day (ἐν ἐκείνῃ τῇ ἡμέρᾳ), but ii, 5-6 does not imply such
a long interval between the victory and the reward, or between the labour and
the harvest; the reward is decreed immediately after the contest and the
harvest follows the work at once.

[5] Heb. ix, 27: ἀπόκειται τοῖς ἀνθρώποις ἅπαξ ἀποθανεῖν, μετὰ δὲ τοῦτο
κρίσις. Scholastic theologians in general understand by this text the
particular judgement; but the exegetes are much divided, and the reasons

We do not find either any positive teaching about the fate of the just who end life with venial or not entirely expiated faults. Nothing impure enters heaven, and no one is received in the bosom of God without having paid his debt to the uttermost farthing : the doctrine of purgatory is based upon these biblical data and upon tradition ; but the text of St Paul, invoked by many, furnishes rather an indication than an incontrovertible proof.[1] This want of details about conditions beyond the grave ought not to surprise us, since all the interest of the Apostle centres in the fact of the resurrection and in the dominant truth that the just are intimately united to Christ in death as in life.

2. We know from the Epistle to the Hebrews that the resurrection of the dead was, together with the last judgement, one of the cardinal points of the apostolic catechetical teaching.[2] Paul never failed to place at the foundation of his teaching the resurrection of Jesus, to which he united our own resurrection as a corollary.[3] Neither the railleries of the Athenians[4] nor the sarcasm of the procurator Festus[5] nor the scepticism of the king Agrippa[6] nor the incredulity of the Sadducees[7] could induce him to conceal so essential a truth. He would have blushed to purchase his liberty at the price of a dishonourable silence, and he gloried in having been persecuted for this article of faith. We know what were his surprise and indignation on learning that doubts had arisen about such a fundamental dogma in a church founded by him.[8]

He had preached at Cæsarea the general resurrection of the just and the unjust,[9] and it was undoubtedly thus that the doctrine of the resurrection had usually to be presented, the well-known text of Daniel and the positive teaching of Jesus being cited, which were in this respect in accord with the most authorized opinion of the Jews of that time.[10] Nevertheless,

---

alleged by both sides leave a doubt. See Atzberger, *Eschatologie*, pp. 204-209. —As to 2 Cor. v, 10, almost all the exegetes see in it only the last judgement.

[1] 1 Cor. iii, 11-15. *Cf.* Vol. I, pp. 94-96.—For the texts of the N.T. in favour of purgatory see Atzberger, *Die christl. Eschat.*, Freiburg i. B., 1890, pp. 269-282.

[2] Heb. vi, 2 : ἀναστάσεως νεκρῶν καὶ κρίματος αἰωνίου. These two articles belong to the foundation (θεμέλιον) of the Christian doctrine.

[3] 1 Cor. xv, 1-13. Note the final protestation : *Sive enim ego, sive illi : sic praedicamus et sic credidistis*. From this point of view Paul's preaching had nothing special about it.

[4] Acts xvii, 32. *Cf.* Vol. I, p. 62.　　　　[5] Acts xxvi, 24.

[6] Acts xxvi, 27, 28.　　　　[7] Acts xxiii, 6-8.

[8] 1 Cor. xv, 12 : πῶς λέγουσιν ἐν ὑμῖν τινες ὅτι ἀνάστασις νεκρῶν οὐκ ἔστιν; only *a few* do so; but even this fractional doubt appears to him unlikely.

[9] Acts xxiv, 15 : ἀνάστασιν μέλλειν ἔσεσθαι δικαίων τε καὶ ἀδίκων.

[10] Dan. xii, 2 : *Et multi de his qui dormiunt in terrae pulvere evigilabunt : lii in vitam aeternam et alii in opprobrium ut videant semper*. In place of *ut videant semper*, it should read *in ignominiam sempiternam ;* but this

in his Epistles, Paul seems to pay attention merely to the resurrection of the just; his arguments are valid only for that resurrection, and his context most frequently imposes a limitation which it is proper to extend by analogy to two or three doubtful expressions. It is true that in the First Epistle to the Corinthians he mentions without any distinction the resurrection of the dead,[1] but all the rest of the argument shows that he is speaking of the glorious resurrection; and when, in the Epistle to the Philippians, he expresses the wish to " attain to the resurrection from the dead,"[2] his thought is not ambiguous; it is to the glorious resurrection that he aspires. Good exegetes are of the opinion that the signal victory won by Christ over death presupposes or requires for its meaning the universal resurrection; for they say, if all the dead did not rise, the defeat of death would be only partial, and St Paul would not have the right to say: *Novissima autem inimica destruetur mors.*[3] This argument does not appear to us very decisive. The victory of Christ over sin will be complete also, like his victory over death; and that does not involve the conversion of all sinners. The fact is that the fruits of redemption, though universal in principle, are in reality conditioned by the co-operation of man. The victory of Christ over death will be absolute in those who unite with him to share in his victory; in the others it could be only potential, like the victory over sin. Weaker still appears the argument drawn from the text: " Everyone [shall rise] in his own order: the firstfruits, Christ; then they that are Christ's, at his coming; afterwards the end."[4]

---

error does not obscure the text as regards the *two categories of the resurrected.* The Hebrew word *rabbim (multi),* which signifies properly " the multitude," is used for the totality and the whole as well as of the part. *Cf.* John v, 28, 29 : *Omnes qui in monumentis sunt, audient vocem Filii Dei ; et procedent qui bona fecerunt, in resurrectionem vitae ; qui vero mala egerunt, in resurrectionem judicii.* For the doctrine of Judaism, see pp. 475-6.

[1] 1 Cor. xv, 42 (ἡ ἀνάστασις τῶν νεκρῶν); *cf.* xv, 12, 13, 21 (ἀνάστασις νεκρῶν).

[2] Phil. iii, 11 : εἰ πως καταντήσω εἰς τὴν ἐξανάστασιν τὴν ἐκ νεκρῶν.

[3] 1 Cor. xv, 26. Cornely and Godet among others are of this opinion.

[4] 1 Cor. xv, 23-24: Ἕκαστος δὲ ἐν τῷ ἰδίῳ τάγματι· ἀπαρχὴ Χριστός, ἔπειτα οἱ τοῦ Χριστοῦ ἐν τῇ παρουσίᾳ αὐτοῦ, εἶτα τὸ τέλος, κτλ.

In the preceding verses St Paul has just said that Christ has risen from the dead as the firstfruits of them that sleep, that the resurrection is the deed of one man (Jesus Christ), as death was the deed of one man (Adam) ; and that all shall be made alive in Christ, as all die in Adam. This quickening—the resurrection of the dead—is accomplished in a certain order which forms the subject of the present verse. Let us remark at first that the text of the Vulgate is paraphrased in a rather unhappy way : *Unusquisque autem in suo ordine : primitiae Christus ; deinde ii qui sunt Christi qui in adventu ejus crediderunt.* The words in roman type are added. By omitting them the meaning becomes simple : " Every one [shall rise] in his own order : Christ, the firstfruits ; then those who [belong to] Christ, at the time of his appearance." The question is to know : (A) what the word *order* (τάγμα) signifies. (B) How many orders are enumerated.

Some would like to make this the *end* of the resurrection and the third order of the resurrected, of those who do not belong to Christ; but this is to read too much between the lines. It is a fact, however, that the resurrection of sinners has no great interest for the Apostle, because it is not connected with his doctrine and usually remains beyond his field of vision.

As for the resurrection of the just, it is proved by half a score of arguments: the argument by *reductio ad absurdum,* founded on the pernicious consequences of the contrary thesis;[1] the argument of *tradition* which rests upon the doctrine and the constant teaching of the apostles;[2] the argument *ad hominem,* drawn from the inward, spontaneous, irresistible conviction of the faithful themselves;[3] the argument of the *meritorious cause,* based on the truth that Jesus Christ

---

(A) *Meaning of the word* τάγμα.—We know that τάγμα was often used to signify " a body of troops," especially " the Roman legion " (references in Thayer, *A Greek-English Lexicon of the N.T.*[4]). But it was also frequently employed in the sense of " order, rank, class, series," etc. Sextus Empiricus speaks of the class of atheists (*Adv. Math.*, ix, 54: ἐκ τοῦ τάγματος τῶν ἀθέων), Josephus places the Sadducees in the second rank of the Jewish sects (*Bell.*, II, viii, 2, 14: Σαδδουκαῖοι δὲ τὸ δεύτερον τάγμα), and Theophylact inserts τάγμα between two words which signify conduct and kind of life (*In* 1 *Cor.*, vii, 20: ἐν οἵῳ βίῳ καὶ ἐν οἵῳ τάγματι καὶ πολιτεύματι). The two meanings can apply here, and perhaps the military interpretation harmonizes better with the habitual language of St Paul, especially if, as St Clement would like to prove (*Ad Corinth.*, i, 37, 41), the Chief alone can constitute a τάγμα. However this may be, we can consider in a τάγμα both the order of time and the order of dignity. It is the latter that the Apostle seems to have chiefly in view. Although all the just rise from the dead in Christ, and by Christ, there are among the resurrected different categories corresponding to the various grades of merit and of glory. *Cf.* 1 Cor. xv, 41-42: *Alia claritas solis, alia claritas lunae, et alia claritas stellarum. Stella a stella differt in claritate ; sic et resurrectio mortuorum.* But besides the order of dignity, the order of time seems also indicated in the context, in such a manner, however, that the attention of the Apostle refers *exclusively* to the *priority* of Jesus Christ as the *firstfruits : Unusquisque in suo ordine, primitiae Christus ; deinde,* etc.

(B) *How many orders in the resurrection ?*—A special and unique category is formed by Jesus Christ, who shares with no one as *firstfruits* (ἀπαρχή), and thus unites the priority of time with the priority of dignity. The risen just (οἱ τοῦ Χριστοῦ), emerging *together* from the tomb, yet *after* Christ (ἔπειτα), constitute the second class, divided into distinct groups. Some commentators see a third group indicated in the words εἶτα τὸ τέλος. They understand by τέλος " the end of the resurrection "—namely, the resurrection of sinners ; thus Theodoret (ἡ κοινὴ πάντων ἀνάστασις), Cajetan, Bengel, Meyer, Grimm, *Zeitschr. für wiss. Theol.*, 1873, p. 385, etc. Cornelius à Lapide gives the interpretation of Cajetan the second place without expressing his own view. St. Cyril of Alexandria identifies the third class of the resurrected with the *just* already dead before the coming of Christ. All this is quite arbitrary, for the expression *deinde finis* does not by any means denote a new order of the resurrected, any more than it indicates an interval between the resurrection of the just and the moment when Christ offers his Father the homage of his royalty.

[1] 1 Cor. xv, 12-19. *Cf.* Vol. I, pp. 133, 134.
[2] 1 Cor. xv, 30-32.
[3] 1 Cor. xv, 29.

came to rebuild the ruins wrought by sin and to restore to us the blessings lost through the first Adam;[1] the argument of the *exemplary cause,* connected with the theory of the mystical body and with the solidarity of Christ and the saints;[2] the argument of the *seal* imprinted within us by the Holy Spirit, who, making us his own, binds himself to keep us, body and soul, eternally;[3] the argument of the *earnest-money* given by this same Spirit, the first instalment of a coming glorious immortality;[4] the argument of the temple, the sacred and imperishable dwelling of this Spirit;[5] the argument of the *first-fruits,* in other words of grace, the seed of glory;[6] the argument of the *supernatural desire* which the Holy Spirit kindles within us and which makes us sigh for the glorification of this body, associated with the conflicts of the soul and the instrument of its victories.[7]

Many of these arguments are so akin to one another that they touch and combine together: they are not so much distinct proofs as different aspects of the same proof. What is rhetorical in them, we have not to examine; but we must be careful not to consider them as philosophical conclusions. They are theological inductions in the full force of the term, finding their support in the teaching of the Apostle. Taken apart from the assertions of Paul, who affirms their premises as verities of faith, some of them would seem to rest on a begging of the question or to move in a vicious circle.

The five arguments placed at the head of the list have been studied in connection with the First Epistle to the Corinthians.[8] The other five, the elements of which are scattered through various Epistles, are all based upon the supernatural activity of the Holy Spirit. One can say that they all come back to this: " If the Spirit of him that raised up Jesus from the dead dwell in you, he that raised up Jesus Christ from the dead shall quicken also your mortal bodies, because of his Spirit that dwelleth in you."[9] Is it because the body of the just is his temple? Perhaps. Nevertheless, apart from the two texts where the Holy Spirit figures as the soul of the mystical body, rather than the guest of an individual temple,[10] the reasoning of the Apostle takes another turn. He says: " You are sealed by the Holy Spirit unto the day of redemption."[11] You are his property, one day he will reclaim you for his own; on that day the body, after the soul, will be avenged for the outrages of death. The seal of which St Paul speaks is imprinted upon us at baptism. This

---

[1] I Cor. xv, 21. *Cf.* Rom. xii, 18.
[2] I Cor. xv, 20-23. *Cf.* vi, 13, 14 and 2 Cor. iv, 14; Rom. viii, 11.
[3] Eph. iv, 30.
[4] 2 Cor. v, 5; Eph. i, 14.
[5] I Cor. vi, 19.
[6] Rom. viii, 23.
[7] Rom. viii, 15, 17, 23-26.
[8] See Vol. I, pp. 133-138.
[9] Rom. viii, 11.
[10] I Cor. vi, 19; 2 Cor. vi, 16.
[11] Eph. iv, 30.

sacramental rite, which incorporates us into the mystical
body, confers upon us also the "earnest of the Spirit,"[1]
another guarantee of eternal blessedness. The earnest is a
sum advanced "on account," as a pledge for the entire payment. It is not distinct from the Holy Spirit; it is the Holy
Spirit, as it were a gift possessed by souls, a gift identical
in its essence, but susceptible of progress in intimacy and
perfection. The just, quickened by grace, have received,
already in this world, the firstfruits of the immortality of
glory; they are "saved in hope," and the promised salvation
concerns the body as well as the soul. Paul never establishes
a rigid line of demarcation between grace and the glory
which is its tardy but assured florescence. Whoever is grafted
upon Christ is by that very fact associated with his immortal
and glorified life.

The proof derived from desire appears at first a sophism,
and would be so in fact, if it were a question here of a purely
natural desire, for there would then be a disproportion
between the tendency and the end in view. But the Apostle
assumes and affirms that this desire is a supernatural one,
created and maintained within us by the Holy Spirit himself. In bringing to our lips that cry of the heart : *Abba,
Father!* the Spirit testifies to our adoptive sonship, and
attests the fact that we are heirs of God and coheirs of Christ.
But the glory of the resurrected body forms an integral part of
this heritage. Thenceforth creation's anxious aspirations are
no longer wanted to foretell our return to original immortality :
"We ourselves, who have the firstfruits of the Spirit, even we
ourselves groan within ourselves, waiting for the [consum-
mated] adoption of sons, and for the [glorious] redemption
of our body."[2] The desire given us by grace will not be
illusory; for why should the Holy Spirit put within our hearts
an aspiration which he cannot or will not satisfy?

3. St Paul affirms, on several occasions, that the just, who
shall be witnesses of the *parousia,* will not die. Hence he
never says, "All the just shall rise from the dead," but
"The dead who are in Christ shall rise."[3] Sometimes he
presents his thought under this dilemma : "Either we shall
rise or we shall be changed."[4] He starts from the principle
that "flesh and blood cannot inherit the kingdom of God."[5]
Flesh and blood mean always to him human nature, in so far
as it is weak, changeable, and perishable, especially as opposed to the divine nature, which is eternal, unchangeable, and
incorruptible. His point here, therefore, is not, as certain

[1] 2 Cor. i, 22; v, 5 (ὁ δοὺς ἡμῖν τὸν ἀρραβῶνα τοῦ Πνεύματος); Eph. i, 14
(ὅ ἐστιν ἀρραβὼν τῆς κληρονομίας ἡμῶν).

[2] Rom. viii, 24.                                              [3] I Thess. iv, 16.

[4] I Cor. xv, 52.                                              [5] I Cor. xv, 50

Fathers thought, that nothing impure will enter into the kingdom of heaven, nor that the flesh will have no part in the glorious resurrection, as many modern interpreters think, thus adding a doctrinal error to a fault of exegesis. Paul teaches that the body of the just, in order to enter into glory, needs transformation. And this transformation, which he has described minutely for the dead who are restored to life, is equally necessary—and still more mysterious perhaps—for the living whom death has spared. Here is his message from the Lord himself to the Thessalonians:

> We who are alive, we who remain unto the *parousia* of the Lord, shall not rise before those who sleep [the sleep of death]. For the Lord himself with a word of command, with the voice of an archangel and at the sound of the trumpet of God, shall descend from heaven, and the dead [who are] in Christ shall rise first ; then we who are alive, who are left, shall be rapt together with them into the clouds of the air to meet Christ ; and so shall we be always with the Lord.[1]

From this revelation, which is not at all obscure provided it be read without dogmatic prejudices, three truths follow: Those who died in a state of grace (οἱ νεκροὶ ἐν Χριστῷ) will rise *before* the catching up into the air of the just who are then alive.—The resurrected dead and the living will be caught up *together* into the air to meet Christ.—All the just, the resurrected dead and the living, will be *for ever* with the Lord.

The Apostle says nothing of sinners, either living or dead, but concerns himself only with the just and especially with the living at the time of the *parousia*. The latter will have no advantage over their brethren who have died, but they must themselves be the object of a glorious transformation in order to enjoy eternally, unchangeably, and persistently the society of the glorified. If it were otherwise, would not their lot be a deplorable one? Paul had no need to insist upon a doctrine which the converts of Thessalonica did not doubt.

He returns to it subsequently in order to reply to the doubts of the Corinthians: " Behold, I tell you a mystery. We shall not all die, but we shall all be changed. In a moment, in the twinkling of an eye, at the last trumpet; for the trumpet shall sound and the dead shall rise again incorruptible, and we shall be changed. For this corruptible [body] must put on incorruption, and this mortal [body] must put on immortality."[2] St Paul announces that he is going to unveil a mystery, something hidden and mysterious (μυστήριον). The mystery consists in the fact that even *the just*, who have been spared by death, must *be transformed,* as truly as the just who died in Christ.—This transformation, common both to the living and the dead, will take

---

[1] 1 Thess. iv, 15-17.    [2] 1 Cor. xv, 51-53.

place *instantaneously* and *simultaneously*, at the first blast of the trumpet announcing the *parousia*.—The reason for this necessary transformation is that " flesh and blood cannot inherit the kingdom of God, neither corruption incorruption." Corruption and incorruptibility are two contradictory and consequently incompatible things. Therefore this corruptible body must cease to be corruptible and this mortal body must cease to be mortal. It is in this that the transformation consists.

To put on immortality without experiencing the terrors of death is an enviable privilege. The Corinthians, knowing by the teaching of Paul in his first Epistle that this will really be the lot of the just who shall be found on the earth at the moment of the *parousia,* began to desire it. The Apostle does not blame them for it, for this desire springs from the very depths of our nature :

> For which cause we faint not ; but though our outward man perish, yet the inward man is renewed day by day . . .
> For we know if the tent in which we dwell on earth be dissolved, that we have a building of God, a house not made with hands, eternal in heaven.
> For this also we groan, desiring to be clothed upon [over our earthly tent] with our house that is from heaven ; yet so that we be found clothed, not naked.
> For we also, who are in this tent, do groan, being burdened ; because we would not be unclothed, but clothed upon [with immortality] over [our perishable body], that that which is mortal in us may be swallowed up of life.
> Now he that maketh us for this very thing is God, who hath given us the earnest of the Spirit.[1]

It is almost impossible to translate this passage without commenting upon it more or less, so full is it of ideas. The difficulty rises first from a want of harmony in the metaphors, since Paul pictures our body now under the figure of a garment and now under that of a house, and sometimes blends the two metaphors together; but the difficulty is due also to other causes. This is a case in which we must have recourse to the principle of exegesis, which says that what is obscure is to be explained by that which is clear. Now the two following points seem to be indubitable : " The tent of our earthly house " denotes the corruptible body, which is here the abode of the soul.—We would not be unclothed or stripped of this body, abject though it be; we fear for our soul a *nakedness* contrary to its nature and aspirations ; we desire consequently to put on our celestial garment without quitting our terrestrial one. Such is the exact value of the Greek word, untranslatable in French.

To what does this heavenly garment correspond? What means the dwelling which is eternal in heaven? Here the

[1] 2 Cor. iv, 16 ; v, 1-5.

controversies begin. Let us at the start reject unhesitatingly an hypothesis advanced by a small number of heterodox exegetes and even by one or two Catholic commentators. According to this, the just receive at baptism the germ of a glorious body which develops here on earth through the use of the sacraments, especially through that of the Eucharist; this temporary body follows the soul after death and will be subsequently exchanged, at the moment of the universal resurrection, for the definite final body. There is not a trace in St Paul of this strange conception. The just, at death, depart from the body and, on rising from the dead, take again their body, which is then transfigured; there is nowhere a suggestion of an intermediate body between the perishable body and the glorified body.

This hypothesis being discarded, two opinions confront us. According to one, the spiritual habitation denotes metaphorically the glorified body; according to the other, it designates celestial glory. The first interpretation is the more common. Since " the earthly tent " represents the mortal body, is it not natural that " the heavenly house " should stand for the glorified body? Doubtless we do not actually possess it immediately after death, as the conditional proposition of the Apostle would seem to indicate; but we do possess it thenceforth ideally, and it can even be said that we have a right to it; we possess it, not with the relative certainty of hope, but with the full and absolute certainty of a claim that has to be paid. Now the Scriptures very often express the certainty of a coming good by a verb in the present tense. The only serious difficulty is that in reality we do not put on the glorified body over the mortal body: these are not two entirely distinct things; the material elements are common to both; only, the mode of being differs. This difficulty does not exist in the second theory. Here the holy soul really puts on the celestial glory *as soon as* the mortal body is separated from it; and the just who witness the *parousia* will put on this same glory over their real body, of which they will never have been divested. The allegory is therefore harmonized and Paul's language is strictly exact. If we die before the *parousia,* we shall have our vestment of glory immediately; if, on the contrary, we live to the last day, the glory will envelop us like a royal cloak according to the desire which the Holy Spirit kindles in our hearts, and so what is mortal in us will be absorbed by the fulness of life.

There remains a sub-clause, the precise meaning of which is much debated. According to the Vulgate, the sense would be: We desire to put on the glory over the actual body, *si tamen vestiti non nudi inveniamur;* " if nevertheless [at the moment of the *parousia*] we are found clothed [with the body], not naked "—that is to say, deprived by death of our earthly garment. This is such a natural explanation that it is not surprising to see it adopted by so many Fathers and ancient and modern commentators. Survival " until the day of the *parousia* " is then presented as an indispensable condition for the realization of our desire. But a number of contemporary scholars, in the name of philology, protest against so simple an interpretation. In order to safeguard the propriety of the terms, they propose to translate it as follows : We desire to put on the glory over the mortal body, " seeing that, having been once clothed [with heavenly glory] we shall not be found naked, since death will no more have any hold on us."[1] The sub-clause no longer expresses the *condition* to be fulfilled in order to realize the wish stated in the preceding verse, but rather the very *object* of the wish or the *circumstance* which makes it desirable. However great may be the divergence in this point of detail, the whole idea of the passage remains about the same.

At all events, the Apostle is certain that a glorified and immortal body awaits him in heaven, and this prospect enables him to confront the tribulations of this life with joy and consoles him for seeing the dissolution of his perishable body.

If he experiences the natural desire to live till the *parousia,* it is not just from fear of death, for he knows well that nothing can separate him from Christ, the sole object of his love ; it is on accouunt of the instinctive repugnance which we all feel to the thought of undergoing, even for a time, the dissolution of man's composite being.

Like the faithful in Thessalonica and Corinth, whose wishes

---

[1] 2 Cor. v, 3 : εἴ γε καὶ ἐνδυσάμενοι οὐ γυμνοὶ εὑρεθησόμεθα. The Western reading has too little support to have any chance of being authentic. And unless the double metaphor " clothed " (ἐνδυσάμενοι) and " naked " (γυμνοί) is to escape absurdity, it must be taken in the physical, not in the moral, sense (*clothed with* or *stripped of* virtues or good works).

The usual exegesis regards οὐ γυμνοί as a synonym explanatory of ἐνδυσάμενοι and makes the whole depend on εὑρεθησόμεθα. But this construction has not its exact counterpart in the examples with which it is compared to justify it, 1 Cor. iii, 2 (γάλα οὐ βρῶμα) ; Rom. ii, 29 (ἐν πνεύματι οὐ γράμματι) ; 1 Thess. ii, 17 (προσώπῳ οὐ καρδίᾳ). Moreover, it obliges us to take ἐνδυσάμενοι adjectivally, which would be possible with the perfect participle ἐνδεδυμένοι, but not with the aorist participle, which always keeps its value as a participle and, when joined with a verb in the future, acquires the sense of the past future ; it becomes then the subject instead of being the attribute. This is a difficulty, but is it invincible ?

In the other explanation : εἴγε has not a dubitative meaning but an affirmative under the dubitative form of the indirect style (not *si tamen,* but *siquidem,* a meaning which εἴγε or εἴγε καί really possesses); ἐνδυσάμενοι=ἐπενδυσάμενοι and the aorist participle agreeing with the future=a past future, "when we shall have been clothed"; finally, the negative οὐ qualifies the verb, not the adjective, and οὐχ εὑρεθησόμεθα=οὐκέτι : " Once *clothed* with glory, we no longer risk being found *naked* [*i.e.,* bereft of the body], since death is no more to be feared, and that is just what we desire." This is clear ; but is it not a truism ?

he approves and shares, he would like to go, still living, to meet the triumphant Christ and enter into a glorious immortality without passing through the experience of death.

He does not put forward survival till the *parousia* as something either certain or probable; but he speaks of it as possible; otherwise his desire would be aimless. Moreover, he affirms that the author of this desire is the Holy Spirit; which again indicates its possibility. The condition laid down for the realization of this desire is expressly stated, if we interpret the sub-clause as the Vulgate and ordinary exegesis do; it is at least assumed, if we interpret it as do the majority of modern philologists.

Nevertheless, the wish in question is not so imperative that it deprives us of peace and resignation. We know that our earthly pilgrimage is an exile far from the Lord, and that to depart from this mortal body is to go to the Lord. In order to be resigned to this change, in spite of the instinctive desires of nature and grace, we need nevertheless courage and intrepidity, feelings with which faith inspires us. In any case, we aim at pleasing the Lord, whether present with him or absent from him. That is the essential thing; the rest does not depend on us.[1]

---

[1] Concerning the fate of the last generation of the just, see Vol. I, pp. 76-78. The opinion of universal death is more common to-day among theologians, perhaps on account of these words from the *Catechism of the Council of Trent* (I, ii, 6) : *Huic sententiae quae asserit omnes morituros esse nemine excepto Ecclesiam acquiescere ipsamque sententiam magis veritati convenire, scriptum reliquit S Hieronymus : idem sentit et S Augustinus. Neque vero huic sententiae repugnant Apostoli verba ad Thessalonicenses* (1 Thess. iv, 6). . . . *Nam S Ambrosius cum ea explanaret ita inquit : In ipso raptu mors praeveniet,* etc.—Unhappily, there are in these lines three serious inaccuracies which reduce the proof of authority to nothing : (*a*) The author of the commentary cited is not St Ambrose, but Ambrosiaster, a learned layman, probably orthodox, but not a doctor of the Church.—(*b*) St Augustine is entirely neutral on the subject (*Retract.*, ii, 33 : *Aut non morientur aut . . . mortem non sentient*); he is rather favourable to the contrary opinion. See Vol. I, p. 77.—(*c*) The words attributed to St Jerome are not his, but from Acacius of Cæsarea, quoted by St Jerome (*Epist.* 119 *ad Minerv.*, XXII, 970-971). Here St Jerome is only a reporter : *Haec celeri sermone dictavi, quid eruditi viri de utroque sentirent loco et quibus argumentis suas vellent probare sententias vestrae prudentiae exponens* (*ibid.*, 978). But elsewhere he lets us know his personal opinion (*Epist.* 59 *ad Marcell.*, XXII, 587) : *Hoc ex ipsius loci continentia sciri potest, quod sancti qui in adventu Salvatoris fuerint deprehensi in corpore, in iisdem corporibus occurrent ei ; ita tamen ut inglorium et corruptivum et mortale gloria et incorruptione et immortalitate mutetur, ut qualia corpora mortuorum surrectura sint in talem substantiam etiam vivorum corpora transformentur.* It would be impossible to be more explicit.

## III—THE DAY OF THE LORD

1. The *Parousia*.   2. The Last Judgement.   3. Separation of the Good
from the Wicked.

1. *Parousia,* literally " presence," further meaning " the
coming," is a technical term used in the New Testament to
denote the second advent of Jesus Christ, which is called
also " the revelation " or " apparition " or " the Day of the
Lord." [1]

At the time when St Paul wrote his Epistles, *parousia* was
the name given to the solemn visit of a sovereign or of some
great personage, particularly of the emperor himself. Polybius mentions in this sense the *parousia* of king Antiochus,
and an inscription of the third century before Christ informs
us that the *parousia* of Saïtapharnes to Olbia cost the inhabitants nine hundred gold pieces. [2]

Such an extraordinary circumstance, celebrated by festivals,
games, and sacrifices, and perpetuated by statues, foundations, commemorative medals, and sometimes by the establishment of a new era, was of a nature to strike the imagination of nations and left a lasting impression on the memories
of men.   No expression, therefore, was more appropriate for
the triumphal return of Christ, who comes to inaugurate
his reign.

The *parousia* borrows its dramatic setting and colouring of
the Day of Jehovah, of which it is the typical realization,
largely from the prophets.   In both instances the Day of the
Lord closes the history of humanity and marks the end of the
ages.   In both cases, it appears near without it being possible
to say whether it is so in reality or whether the illusion is
due to the prophetic style employed, which eliminates all perspective and projects remote events upon the same plane.
In both occurrences it arrives escorted by a formidable display, announces its coming by cosmical convulsions, and
leaves all nature purified and renovated.   Finally, in both the

---

[1] *Parousia* and synonyms. — (*a*) Παρουσία (Christ's or the Lord's),
1 Thess. ii, 19; iii, 13; iv, 15; **v**, 23; 2 Thess. ii, 1, 8; 1 Cor. xv, 23; Jas. v,
7, 8; 2 Pet. i, 16; iii, 4, 12; 1 John ii, 28; Matt. xxiv, 3, 27, 37, 39.   The
word is also used for the *coming* or the *presence* of other persons; Stephanas
(1 Cor. xvi, 17), Titus (2 Cor. vii, 6, 7), Paul (2 Cor. x, 10; Phil. i, 26; ii, 12),
Antichrist (2 Thess. ii, 9).—(*b*) Ἡμέρα (the Lord's), 1 Cor. i, 8; v, 5;
2 Cor. i, 14; 1 Thess. **v**, 2; 2 Thess. ii, 2; (Christ's), Phil. i, 6, 10; ii, 16; (the
Day by antonomasia), 2 Thess. i, 10; 2 Tim. i, 12, 18; iv, 8 (ἡ ἡμέρα ἐκείνη);
1 Cor. iii, 13 (ἡ γὰρ ἡμέρα δηλώσει).   *Cf.* Rom. ii, 16 and xiii, 12; 1 Thess.
v, 4.   Elsewhere, Acts ii, 20; Heb. x, 25 (βλέπετε ἐγγίζουσαν τὴν ἡμέραν);
1 Pet. iii, 10, 12; Apoc. xvi, 14 (τοῦ Θεοῦ).—(*c*) Ἐπιφάνεια, 1 Tim. vi, 14;
2 Tim. i, 10; iv, 1, 8; Titus ii, 13.   Note 2 Thess. ii, 8 (τῇ ἐπιφανείᾳ τῆς
παρουσίας αὐτοῦ). — (*d*) Ἀποκάλυψις, 1 Cor. i, 7; 2 Thess. i, 7; *cf.* 1 Pet. i,
7, 13; iv, 3.

[2] Polybius, *Hist.*, xviii, 31; Dittenberger, *Syllog.*[2], No. 226, l. 85, 86.
*Cf.* Deissmann, *Licht vom Osten*, Tübingen, 1908, p. 270.

Saviour presents himself as Judge, Saviour, and Avenger; a universal Judge, Saviour of his own, Avenger of the oppressed. But unlike the Day of Jehovah, the *parousia* is always closely connected with the resurrection of the dead; its character is more spiritual; it is Christ, rather than God, who pronounces the judgement.

In every prophecy and apocalypse the part of the type, the symbol and allusion to former prophecies is difficult to make out. The prophecy is not to be explained like an historical narrative, nor the apocalypse like an ordinary prophecy. This literary form allows the use of traditional symbols which it would be dangerous to take literally, and the meaning of which, conditioned by a series of predictions still more ancient, remains always mysterious and fluctuating. Like all similar compositions, Paul's apocalypse is an echo of other apocalypses. There is found in it a multitude of reminiscences of Daniel, Isaias, Ezechiel, and the Psalms, with various features borrowed from the eschatological discourse of Jesus. Moreover, it has a special difficulty, since it refers to an oral teaching the purport of which we do not know.

The exterior setting of the *parousia* in St Paul is almost the same as in the Synoptists. The blast of the trumpet summons the dead and the living to the great tribunal of the human race, the Son of Man approaches with the angels for his escort and the clouds for his chariot; a single dramatic stroke changes in the twinkling of an eye the face of the whole world and fills the spectators with surprise, alarm, and consternation. The physical transformation of the universe, so emphasized in the eschatology of the prophets, is scarcely alluded to by St Paul, and we find in him no certain trace of the conflagration, so dramatically described in the First Epistle of St Peter.[1]

---

[1] The following are the features relating to *the final call* and to *the triumphal cortège*.

(A) *The final call.*—(*a*) *The command* (1 Thess. iv, 16: αὐτὸς ὁ Κύριος ἐν κελεύσματι καταβήσεται ἀπ' οὐρανοῦ). Κέλευσμα is the *cry* used to rouse up animals (horses, dogs, etc.) or men (sailors, soldiers, etc.). Who utters this cry? Is it God giving Christ the signal for the *parousia* (Tillmann, *Die Wiederkunft Christi*, p. 152)? Is it Christ assembling the angels of his escort (Wohlenberg, *Thessalonicherbriefe*, p. 100)?—(*b*) *The voice of the archangel* (1 Thess. iv, 16: ἐν φωνῇ ἀρχαγγέλου). It is commonly believed that this is Michael; cf. Dan. x, 21; xii, 1.—(*c*) *The sound of the trumpet* (1 Cor. xv, 52: ἐν τῇ ἐσχάτῃ σάλπιγγι.—1 Thess. iv, 16: ἐν σάλπιγγι Θεοῦ). The trumpet usually announced theophanies, Ex. xix, 13, 16; Ps. xlvi, 6; Isa. xxvii, 13; Joel ii, 1; Soph. i, 16; Zach. ix, 14. But here it sounds the summons of the dead. *Cf.* Matt. xxiv, 31. It is called *last*, not that it is *the last* of a series, but because it will sound at the *last* day. It is called the trumpet *of God* because it proclaims the command of God. Estius sagely remarks: *Significatur metaphorice signum aliquod universale, evidentissimum et praeclarissimum, quo velut instrumento divinae virtutis omnes mortui suscitandi sunt ad vitam et convocandi ad tribunal judicis Christi, quomodo tubae sonitu solebat olim populus convocari.* Cf. St Augustine, *Epist. ad Honorat.*, p. 34.

Of the three preliminary signs of the *parousia*—besides the
physical phenomena—the final conversion of the Jews is
peculiar to Paul; the general apostasy is common to all, and
it is probably so with the appearance of Antichrist, although
the Synoptists speak of a great number of false Christs, and
although St John seems to divide up among several persons
the role assigned by St Paul to the Man of sin, the Son of
perdition. As St John informs us that the coming of one
Antichrist only formed part of the teachings of the apostles,
it may be admitted that the many antichrists were regarded
as the lesser agents or precursors of the great adversary.[1]

2. Having already spoken of the two points peculiar to St
Paul's apocalypse—the mysterious obstacle which is opposed
to the immediate manifestation of Antichrist and the privilege enjoyed by the just who shall witness the *parousia*—we

---

(B) *The cortège.*—(a) *Angels* (2 Thess. i, 7 : μετ' ἀγγέλων δυνάμεως αὐτοῦ).
It is the usual escort of God and of Christ the Judge, Matt. xxv, 31 ; Mark
viii, 38 ; Luke ix, 26, etc.—(b) *Saints* (1 Thess. iii, 13 : μετὰ πάντων τῶν ἁγίων
αὐτοῦ). The allusion to Zach. xiv, 5 (καὶ ἥξει κύριος ὁ Θεὸς καὶ πάντες οἱ
ἅγιοι μετ' αὐτοῦ) seems evident. But from the fact that in the text of
Zacharias and elsewhere the saints denote angels, we cannot conclude (with
Lüdemann, Bornemann and other exegetes) that it is the same in St Paul.
The word *saints*, used to designate the *angels*, is unexampled in the N.T.
The reference is, therefore, to the souls of *all* the elect (πάντων), who accompany the Saviour and reassume their bodies at the given signal.—(c) *Clouds*
(1 Thess. iv, 17) form part of the setting of the *parousia* (Matt. xxiv, 30 ;
xxvi, 64 ; Mark xiii, 26 ; xiv, 62 ; Luke xxi, 27) as of theophanies in general.
—(d) *Fire* also (1 Cor. iii, 13 : ἐν πυρὶ ἀποκαλύπτεται.—2 Thess. i, 8:
ἐν πυρὶ φλογὸς διδόντος ἐκδίκησιν). *Cf.* Acts vii, 30 (the burning bush);
Ex. xix, 12, 13, 16, 17, 18 (apparition on Sinai, with the principal characteristics of theophanies : *trumpet, voice, cloud, fire*).
[1] The preliminary signs of the last day are :
(a) *The general apostasy* (2 Thess. ii, 3 : ἐὰν μὴ ἔλθῃ ἡ ἀποστασία πρῶτον).
This is not a *political defection*, as several Fathers believed, for here St Paul
keeps constantly to the religious ground ; nor is it *a heresy in the heart of
Judaism*, as several modern commentators think, refuted by Tillmann (*Die
Wiederkunft Christi*, 1909, pp. 131-133), but *an apostasy from the Christian
faith*, foretold by Jesus Christ in his great eschatological discourse (Matt.
xxiv, 12 ; Luke xviii, 8) and announced also by St Paul (2 Tim. iii, 1-10).—
(b) *Antichrist* (2 Thess. ii, 3, 8 : " the son of perdition, the man of sin ").
This is not Satan in person, for he is expressly distinguished from Satan
(2 Thess. ii, 9), nor Belial (2 Cor. vi, 15), whatever Bousset says of him (*Der
Antichrist in der Ueberlieferung des Judentums, des N.T. und der alten
Kirche*, Göttingen, 1895, p. 99). He is a personal being as his titles indicate,
in particular his character as an adversary of Christ. The apostasy which is
spoken of above will prepare the way for Antichrist (2 Thess. ii, 7), who in
his turn will spread abroad the spirit of seduction and error (2 Thess. ii,
10-12). H. Kellner (*Jesus von Nazareth und seine Apostel im Rahmen der
Zeitgeschichte*, Ratisbon, 1908, p. 320) has brought up again the hypothesis
of Grotius, which identifies Antichrist with Caligula and the " obstacle "
with Petronius, governor of Syria. But Caligula had been dead about ten
years when St Paul wrote. As for the *obstacle* which is opposed to the appearance of Antichrist, see Vol. I, pp. 81-83.—(e) *The conversion of the Jews.*
See Vol. I, pp. 265-267.

shall add only a few words concerning the last judgement, as to which Pauline theology presents nothing very original. The judgement is so closely connected with the *parousia* that it is impossible to separate those two scenes of the same drama, which the Church has united in one article of the Creed. Jesus Christ comes and he comes to judge the quick and the dead. The apostles did not fail to insert this dogma in their first discourse to pagans, and St Paul does so with more insistence than the others because, at least at the beginning, he gave the *parousia* very great prominence.

The judgement will be universal and based upon works : " We must all appear before the judgement-seat of Christ, that everyone may receive retribution for what he hath done in the body, whether good or evil."[1] This refers solely to adults, who alone are capable of moral actions ; and in spite of the authority of St Augustine, who has carried with him as usual many interpreters, it is impossible to include little children in their number ; but the absolute universality of the judgement was expressed by a formula which is free from ambiguity : " He will come to judge the living and the dead,"[2] both the risen dead and the living witnesses of the *parousia*. In whatever way we interpret the words living and dead, there is no middle point between these two terms, which necessarily include all mankind without exception. It follows from this that the saints, who are assessors of the sovereign Judge, will also be judged. Moreover, " we shall judge angels " ;[3] and not only the fallen angels, but the angels who remained faithful ; the wicked angels do not receive this name without some qualification. To conclude, the judgement will have the same extent as the merit and the demerit. Whether angels or men, all those who have been put to the test, whether they have come out of it victors or not, will have to appear before the judgement seat of God.

The catechumens were taught that the judgement will be " eternal "[4] in its effects and consequences—that is to say, it will be final and irrevocable. In regard to the just, St Paul could not be more explicit ; they will be " *for ever* with the Lord " ;[5] the *eternal* life which they have secured makes them safe from a second death. The sentence pronounced against the wicked is no less unchangeable ; they are doomed to " *eternal* perdition."[6] Those who pretend that St Paul, after the Epistles to the Thessalonians, changed his mind, have given no proof of this supposed retractation. In all the apostolic writings, death is represented as the limit of fears

---

[1] 2 Cor. v, 10. *Cf.* Rom. ii, 16 ; xiv, 10 ; Acts xvii, 31.
[2] 2 Tim. iv, 1 (κρίνειν ζῶντας καὶ νεκρούς) ; 1 Pet. iv, 5 ; Acts x, 42.
[3] 1 Cor. vi, 3 (οὐκ οἴδατε ὅτι ἀγγέλους κρινοῦμεν ;).
[4] Heb. vi, 2. See p. 31-32.
[5] 1 Thess. iv, 17 : καὶ οὕτως πάντοτε σὺν κυρίῳ ἐσόμεθα.
[6] 2 Thess. i, 9: οἵτινες δίκην τίσουσιν ὄλεθρον αἰώνιον.

and hopes. The fate of both the elect and the rejected is, therefore, no more subject to fluctuations and vicissitudes.

3. A passage from St Paul recalls the pathetic separation of the good from the wicked described by St Matthew and outlined by St John in the Apocalypse. It is a rhythmical and lyrical passage, a sort of hymn or Psalm, which binds the principal features of Christian eschatology together, as it were, into a sheaf. The Apostle tells the converts to console them for the persecutions which they are enduring.

> It is a proof of the just judgement of God, who would make you worthy of the kingdom of God for which you suffer ;
> For it is a just thing with God to repay tribulation to them that trouble you, and to you, who are troubled, rest with us ;
> When the Lord Jesus shall be revealed from heaven with the angels of his power, in a flame of fire ;
> To punish them who know not God and who obey not the Gospel of our Lord Jesus Christ :
> They shall suffer punishment in eternal destruction, far from the face of the Lord and from the glory of his power ;
> When he shall come to be glorified in his saints and to be made wonderful in all them who have believed.[1]

Paul proves the necessity of the judgement by the spectacle of the actual world, in which the innocent are so often victims. This momentary derangement of the moral order must sooner or later cease. The world to come will be the reverse of the present one ; then sorrow and shame will be the portion of the persecutors, while rest and glory will be given to the

---

[1] 2 Thess. i, 5-10. As we read this passage we see that it is filled with biblical allusions and reminders. As this fact closely concerns the interpretation, it is well to point out some similarities : (A) *The just judgement of God* (i, 5: ἔνδειγμα τῆς δικαίας κρίσεως τοῦ Θεοῦ). Cf. Ecclus. xxxii, 22 (κρινεῖ δικαίως καὶ ποιήσει κρίσιν).—(B) *The judgement of retribution for good and evil* (i, 6, 7 : ἀνταποδοῦναι τοῖς θλίβουσιν ὑμᾶς θλῖψιν καὶ ὑμῖν τοῖς θλιβομένοις ἄνεσιν). Cf. Is. xxxiv, 8 (ἡμέρα κρίσεως κυρίου καὶ ἐνιαυτὸς ἀνταποδόσεως) ; xxxv, 4 (κρίσιν ἀνταποδίδωσι καὶ ἀνταποδώσει) ; lxi, 2 ; lxiii, 4, 7 ; lxvi, 4 ; Jer. xxviii, 6, 21, 56 ; Lam. iii, 64 (ἀποδώσεις αὐτοῖς ἀνταπόδομα) ; Abdias 15, etc.—(C) *Theophany amidst angels and avenging fire* (i. 7, 8 : μετ᾽ ἀγγέλων δυνάμεως αὐτοῦ ἐν πυρὶ φλογός). Cf. Ex. iii, 2 (ὤφθη ἄγγελος κυρίου ἐν πυρὶ φλογός) ; xix, 18 ; Deut. iv, 11 ; Is. iv, 5 ; xxix, 16 (φλὸξ πυρὸς κατεσθίουσα) ; lxvi, 15, 16 (Κύριος ὡς πῦρ ἥξει . . . ἀποδοῦναι ἐν θυμῷ ἐκδίκησιν αὐτοῦ καὶ ἀποσκορακισμὸν αὐτοῦ ἐν φλογὶ πυρός· ἐν γὰρ τῷ πυρὶ κυρίου κριθήσεται πᾶσα ἡ γῆ) ; Dan. vii, 9 (ὁ θρόνος αὐτοῦ φλὸξ πυρός), etc.— (D) *Punishment of the wicked and those who know not God* (i, 8 : διδόντος ἐκδίκησιν τοῖς μὴ εἰδόσι Θεὸν καὶ τοῖς μὴ ὑπακούουσιν τῷ εὐαγγελίῳ). Cf. Is. lix, 1, 8 (ἀνταποδώσων ἀνταπόδοσιν ὄνειδος τοῖς ὑπεναντίοις) ; lxvi, 6 (φωνὴ κυρίου ἀνταποδιδόντος ἀνταπόδοσιν τοῖς ἀντικειμένοις) ; Jer. x, 25 (ἔκχεον τὸν θυμόν σου ἐπὶ ἔθνη τὰ μὴ εἰδότα σε) ; Ps. lxxviii, 6.—(E) *Eternal perdition of the wicked far from the face of God* (i, 9: δίκην τίσουσιν ὄλεθρον αἰώνιον ἀπὸ προσώπου τοῦ κυρίου καὶ ἀπὸ τῆς δόξης τῆς ἰσχύος αὐτοῦ). Cf. Jer. xxv, 12 (ἐκδικήσω τὸ ἔθνος ἐκεῖνο καὶ θήσομαι αὐτοὺς εἰς ἀφανισμὸν αἰώνιον) ; Is. ii, 10 (κρύπτεσθε εἰς τὴν γῆν ἀπὸ προσώπου τοῦ φόβου κυρίου καὶ ἀπὸ τῆς δόξης τῆς ἰσχύος αὐτοῦ) ; ii, 19, 21.—(F) *God glorified in his saints* (i, 10: ὅταν ἔλθη ἐνδοξασθῆναι ἐν τοῖς ἁγίοις αὐτοῦ). Cf. Is. xlix, 3 ἐν σοὶ ἐνδοξασθήσομαι) ; Ezech. xxviii, 22 ; xxxviii, 23 ; xxxix, 21.

persecuted. God subjects us to trial in order to render us worthy of the crown; in awarding us that, he performs an act of justice, and pronounces a judgement equally just in refusing to give the crown to the wicked; in both cases there is retribution.[1] It would be impossible to state more clearly that the kingdom of God is won by conquest, gained, and merited. Certainly, on the other hand, Paul's thought would be travestied, if we supposed that this merit, real and personal as it is, can be the fruit of our efforts only. It is God who, after having given us the power to deserve it, incites and helps us to make use of it, who makes his grace triumph in us and who renders us worthy of the kingdom. It is none the less true, however, that the merit is ours and creates for us a genuine claim upon God. Thus the Apostle writes to Timothy: "There is laid up for me a crown of justice, which the Lord, the just Judge, will render to me in that day; and not only to me but to them also that love his coming."[2] The crown of "justice" is a reward lawfully gained; and the "Judge," if he is "just," is bound to award it without either arbitrariness or injustice. "There is no respect of persons with God; for whosoever have sinned without the Law shall perish without the Law; and whosoever have sinned in the Law shall be judged by the Law; for not the hearers of the Law are just before God, but the doers of the Law shall be justified."[3] The judgement will be carried out with due consideration to the amount of light which men have had and according to their works. Hence the day of retribution is called, in reference to the wicked, "the day of wrath," and, in regard to all, "the manifestation of the just judgement of God." It is unnecessary to add that the "works," which are to be the standard of the judgement, are not merely outward actions; for the eye of the sovereign Judge penetrates into the most secret recesses of the human conscience.

The punishment of the wicked consists of two things: they are banished far from the Lord and deprived of his glory—this is what is called to-day the punishment of the lost—and they experience in their souls tribulation and anguish; for their lot is ruin—eternal death.[5] The recompense of the elect is just the opposite: it is tranquillity, repose, and mental serenity, caused by the satisfaction of all legitimate desires, and it is above all the kingdom of God, union with Jesus their Head, in peace and happiness that know no end.[6] Moreover, human language is inadequate to express these

[1] 2 Thess. i, 6, 7 : εἴπερ δίκαιον παρὰ Θεῷ ἀνταποδοῦναι τοῖς θλίβουσιν ὑμᾶς θλίψιν καὶ ὑμῖν τοῖς θλιβομένοις ἄνεσιν μεθ' ἡμῶν.

[2] 2 Tim. iv, 8.          [3] Rom. ii, 11-13.

[4] 1 Cor. iv, 5 : φωτίσει τὰ κρυπτὰ τοῦ σκότους καὶ φανερώσει τὰς βουλὰς τῶν καρδιῶν. Cf. Rom. viii, 27 ; 1 Thess. ii, 4.

[5] 2 Thess. i, 9 : δίκην τίσουσιν ὄλεθρον αἰώνιον ἀπὸ προσώπου τοῦ κυρίου.

[6] 2 Thess. i, 7.

marvels, because " the eye of man hath not seen, nor ear
heard, neither hath it entered into the heart of man, what
things God hath prepared for them that love him."[1]    All
that can be said is that the vision of God without a veil or
intermediary will replace for us the present dim light of faith;
we shall see God face to face and we shall know him, even
as we are known by him.[2]

### IV—THE CONSUMMATION OF ALL THINGS

1. The Kingdom of God and of Christ.    2. The End.

1. The kingdom of God, that striking feature of Christian
preaching in the Synoptists, assumes another character in the
rest of the New Testament, and particularly in St Paul.    This
is due to a difference of view which is easily explained.    At
the beginning of our era, men believed themselves to be on
the eve of that day when the prophecies announcing the
coming of the king born of the lineage of David were to be
fulfilled, that king who was to make the theocracy of Israel
flourish again in augmented splendour and to establish on
earth the reign of peace, justice, and holiness.    It was necessary, therefore, that Jesus, if he wished to be recognized as
the Messiah, should claim this royalty, explaining, however, the
spiritual nature of the kingdom which he was coming to found.
I know, of course, that, with few exceptions, the writings of
the Rabbis, all of them subsequent to the Gospel, do not
represent the " kingdom of God " in direct connection with

---

[1] 1 Cor. ii, 9.

[2] 1 Cor. xiii, 12 ; 2 Cor. v, 7.    These two texts have some resemblance,
but with differences which should be noted.    In 2 Cor. v, 7 ($\delta\iota\grave{\alpha}$ $\pi\acute{\iota}\sigma\tau\epsilon\omega\varsigma$
$\pi\epsilon\rho\iota\pi\alpha\tau\sigma\hat{\upsilon}\mu\epsilon\nu$, $\sigma\grave{\upsilon}$ $\delta\iota\grave{\alpha}$ $\epsilon\check{\iota}\delta\sigma\upsilon\varsigma$), $\delta\iota\grave{\alpha}$ indicates not the instrument but the time
or method ; now we are *under the régime* (in the state or condition) *of* faith.
This classic sense is frequent in the N.T.    The word $\epsilon\check{\iota}\delta\sigma\varsigma$ designates not
the vision ($\check{\sigma}\psi\iota\varsigma$) but the appearance, the *immediate* presence of the object
contemplated.    The Apostle means : " Here below, exiled *far* from the Lord
Christ, we see him only by faith *indirectly ;* in heaven, *near* to the Lord,
we shall see him *face to face*."    Note that the reference here is to Christ.—
In 1 Cor. xiii, 8-11 Paul affirms that the *charisma* of " knowledge " ($\gamma\nu\hat{\omega}\sigma\iota\varsigma$),
being partial and imperfect, because it is based upon faith, must disappear
when the state of perfection comes.    In xiii, 12 he adds : " for we see now
through a glass ($\delta\iota'$ $\epsilon\sigma\acute{\sigma}\pi\tau\rho\sigma\upsilon$) confusedly ($\epsilon\nu$ $\alpha\grave{\iota}\nu\acute{\iota}\gamma\mu\alpha\tau\iota$), but then face to
face."    The word $\epsilon\sigma\sigma\pi\tau\rho\sigma\nu$ does not designate those half transparent scales
of gypsum which were called " specular stones " ($\delta\acute{\iota}\sigma\pi\tau\rho\sigma\nu$), with which the
rich adorned their windows ; but, like $\kappa\acute{\alpha}\tau\sigma\pi\tau\rho\sigma\nu$, the metallic mirrors which
the ancients used and which reflected only a more or less confused image.
The Apostle contrasts the *direct* and *distinct* vision of the future life with
the *indirect* and *confused* perception characteristic of the present life.    In
order to accentuate this contrast, he concludes : " Now I know ($\gamma\iota\nu\acute{\omega}\sigma\kappa\omega$) in
part, but then I shall know clearly ($\epsilon\pi\iota\gamma\nu\acute{\omega}\sigma\sigma\mu\alpha\iota$)—notice the force of this compound word—even as I am known " by God, from all eternity.    My know-
ledge will not be *comprehensive ;* but it will be *intuitive*, like that of God,
and consequently incompatible with faith.    Faith and vision differ not only
in *degree*, but in *kind*.    That is why one cannot apply to charity — in the
state of trial and in the state of glory—what St Paul says of faith.

messianic hopes ; they indicate by that term the divine government in the world, and not so much the work of God in men's
souls as the free acceptance of the " yoke of the Law " by
the profession of Jewish faith.[1]  But one of two things must
have been true : either the separation of the kngdom of God
from the kingdom of the Messiah was general among the
Pharisees of that time, and it was supremely important that
Jesus Christ should correct this false idea, so prejudicial to
the success of his mission ; or else it was suggested later to
the Rabbis by their spirit of hostility to Christianity ; in that
case it is easier to understand why the evangelical doctrine
of the kingdom of God raised, from the first, no objection on
the ground of principle.  On any hypothesis, the announcement of the kingdom was necessarily a fundamental article of
the preaching of Jesus during that phase of his public
ministry which was characterized by the teaching by parables
and which the Synoptists prefer to present to us.

But this doctrine passes to a subordinate place when the
Christian idea of the kingdom once becomes realized in the
Church.  If by force of habit they still speak of " preaching
the kingdom,"[2] as they might speak of " preaching the
Gospel," they were careful to avoid misunderstandings and to
consider the susceptibilities of the Roman authorities, by
transporting the kingdom outside of the sphere in which the
interests of this world are active.  This is why St Paul,
although often using that expression, generally gives it an
eschatological meaning :[3] " The unjust and thieves do not

---

[1] Cf. Lagrange, Le messianisme chez les Juifs, 1909, pp. 148-157.

[2] Thus in the Acts: i, 3 ; viii, 13 ; xix, 8 ; xxviii, 23, 31.

[3] St Paul uses " the kingdom of God " in three distinct senses :

(A) The eschatological kingdom, eternal glory.

(a) 1 Cor. vi, 9 : ἄδικοι Θεοῦ βασιλείαν οὐ κληρονομήσουσιν.

(b) 1 Cor. vi, 10 : οὐχ ἅρπαγες βασιλείαν Θεοῦ κληρονομήσουσιν.

(c) 1 Cor. xv, 50 : σάρξ καὶ αἷμα βασιλείαν Θεοῦ κληρονομῆσαι οὐ δύναται.

(d) Gal. v, 21 : οἱ τὰ τοιαῦτα πράσσοντες βασιλείαν Θεοῦ οὐ κληρονομήσουσιν.

(e) Eph. v, 5 : οὐκ ἔχει κληρονομίαν ἐν τῇ βασιλείᾳ τοῦ Χριστοῦ καὶ Θεοῦ.

(f) 2 Thess. i, 5 : εἰς τὸ καταξιωθῆναι ὑμᾶς τῆς βασιλείας τοῦ Θεοῦ.

(g) 2 Tim. iv, 1 : τὴν ἐπιφανείαν αὐτοῦ καὶ τὴν βασιλείαν αὐτοῦ.

(h) 2 Tim. iv, 18 : σώσει εἰς τὴν βασιλείαν αὐτοῦ τὴν ἐπουράνιον.

(B) The Church militant, alone or with the Church triumphant.

(i) 1 Cor. xv, 24 : ὅταν παραδιδῷ τὴν βασιλείαν τῷ Θεῷ καὶ πατρί.

(j) Col. i, 13 : μετέστησεν εἰς τὴν βασιλείαν τοῦ υἱοῦ τῆς ἀγάπης αὐτοῦ.

(k) Col. iv, 11 : οὗτοι μόνοι συνεργοὶ εἰς τὴν βασιλείαν τοῦ Θεοῦ.

(l) 1 Thess. ii, 12 : καλοῦντος ὑμᾶς εἰς τὴν ἑαυτοῦ βασιλείαν καὶ δόξαν.

(m) Acts xx, 25 : ἐν οἷς διῆλθον κηρύσσων τὴν βασιλείαν.

(C) The spirit of Christianity, the essence of the Gospel.

(n) Rom. xiv, 17 : οὐ γάρ ἐστιν ἡ βασιλεία τοῦ Θεοῦ βρῶσις καὶ πόσις

(o) 1 Cor. iv, 20 : οὐ γὰρ ἐν λόγῳ ἡ βασιλεία τοῦ Θεοῦ.

The last two texts will be studied later.  Perhaps there could be added
to this list Acts xiv, 22 (καὶ ὅτι διὰ πολλῶν θλίψεων δεῖ ἡμᾶς εἰσελθεῖν εἰς τὴν
βασιλείαν τοῦ Θεοῦ), if it were certain that the speeches of Paul and Barnabas
were reported in their actual words.  This would be a new example of the
eschatological meaning, the only one in the Acts.

inherit the kingdom of God "; the impure and idolaters
" have no share in the kingdom of Christ and God "; persecution " renders us worthy of the kingdom of God," which
" flesh and blood cannot inherit." From this point of view,
the kingdom of God begins at the triumphal return of Christ
and is identified with eternal life. However, it is not always
so. The kingdom of God also exists already for us; we
possess it by anticipation, as we possess life, redemption,
salvation, and glory, in a state of imperfection which does not
exclude the reality. The vocation by which God calls us
" to his kingdom and glory " can be taken in the eschatological sense, but not the act by which he has " translated
us to the kingdom of the Son of his love." Sometimes the
meaning is more doubtful. " The kingdom of God," says
the Apostle, " is not eating and drinking, but justice and
peace and joy in the Holy Ghost."[1] Here it is evidently not
the society of the faithful, and still less the society of the
saints in heaven, that the word kingdom designates; it is
rather the *kingdom of God* as it is presented in the writings
of the Rabbis. The meaning would hardly be changed, if
we substituted for the word kingdom the Gospel or Christianity. Similarly " the kingdom of God is not in speech
but in [works of] power ";[2] it does not consist in much
speaking, after the fashion of the agitators of Corinth, but
in acting with energy, as Paul proposes to do on his return.
On the whole, the kingdom of God denotes usually the life
eternal, where the just will reign with Jesus Christ; more
rarely the Church militant, where they are fighting for him;
sometimes the essence and leading principles of the Gospel.

For St Paul, as well as for the Evangelists, the kingdom of

---

[1] Rom. xiv, 17. The main question is to know if the reference here is to
the *kingdom of God in the individual soul*, or to the *social kingdom of God
in the Church*. Those (like Meyer and Weiss) who defend the first interpretation, understand by justice, peace and joy the possession and enjoyment
of these three virtues. The kingdom of God in the soul does not consist
of eating and drinking (the reading is not βρῶμα καὶ πόμα, namely " food and
drink," but βρῶσις καὶ πόσις, " the act of eating and drinking "): it
consists of possessing supernatural justice, of enjoying the peace which is a
result of this justice, and of tasting the joy which is born of peace. Those
who hold the second interpretation (Sanday, Cornely, etc.), which appears
to us the better, explain it thus : The kingdom of God consists, on its positive
side, in practising *justice* towards others, justice which would be violated if
one were to scandalize them and were a stumbling-block to them (*cf*. verses
13, 15, 20); in causing brotherly *peace* to prevail (*cf*. verse 19 : *itaque quae
pacis sunt sectemur*); and in promoting mutual *joy*, instead of saddening the
brethren (*cf*. verse 15) for the sake of things which are not worth the trouble,
such as eating and drinking. One sees how much better this second explanation is adapted to the context. In any case there may be an allusion to the
coarser ideas of the contemporary Jews concerning the kingdom of God,
which they conceived after the fashion of a Mohammedan paradise.

[2] 1 Cor. iv, 20. Here again we have the *social kingdom of God ;* not the
society of the faithful on earth or in heaven, but the principles and laws which
govern this society. It is, therefore, the Gospel rather than the Church.

God is also the kingdom of Christ. The establishment of the kingdom is the aim of the redemptive mission; when this aim is once attained, the mandate of the Saviour expires : " Afterwards the end, when he shall have delivered up the kingdom to God and the Father, when he shall have brought to naught all principality and power and virtue. For he must reign until he hath put all his enemies under his feet. And the last enemy to be destroyed shall be death. . . . And when all things shall be subdued unto him, then the Son also himself shall be subject unto his Father, that God may be all in all."[1]

---

[1] 1 Cor. xv :

24. εἶτα τὸ τέλος, ὅταν παραδιδοῖ τὴν βασιλείαν τῷ Θεῷ καὶ πατρί, ὅταν καταργήσῃ πᾶσαν ἀρχην, καὶ πᾶσαν ἐξουσίαν καὶ δύναμιν.

*Deinde finis, cum tradiderit regnum Deo et patri, cum evacuaverit omnem principatum, et potestatem et virtutem.*

25. Δεῖ γὰρ αὐτὸν βασιλεύειν ἄχρι οὗ θῇ πάντας τοὺς ἐχθροὺς ὑπὸ τοὺς πόδας αὐτοῦ.

*Oportet autem illum regnare donec ponat omnes inimicos sub pedibus ejus.*

26. Ἔσχατος ἐχθρος καταργεῖται ὁ θάνατος.

*Novissima autem inimica destruetur mors.*

(A) *The end of the present world.*—It results from verse 23 that the end, of which the Apostle speaks, is neither directly nor indirectly the end of the resurrection. It is necessary, therefore, to take it in its ordinary sense, the only one which could occur to the minds of his readers (the end of the present world and the beginning of a new order of things). *Cf.* Matt. xxiv, 14 (τότε ἥξει τὸ τέλος) ; Mark xiii, 7 ; Luke xxi, 9 ; 1 Pet. iv, 7. Twice in the Epistles to the Corinthians the end is put in connection with the *parousia* (1 Cor. i, 8 ; 2 Cor. i, 13, 14). Moreover, to prevent all doubt, Paul defines the end by means of two circumstances which can apply only to the consummation of all things : (*a*) " when he shall have delivered up the kingdom to his Father " (a relation of simultaneousness), consequently when his work shall be ended ; (*b*) " when he shall have brought to naught all his enemies " (relation of priority), consequently when the cycle of conflicts and victories shall be closed.—We, in common with the best authorities, adopt the reading παραδιδοῖ or παραδιδῷ. The reading ὅταν παραδῷ, which is that of the received text and of the Vulgate (*cum tradiderit*), comes to the same thing, provided that only a logical succession is established between the giving up of the kingdom to the Father and the end of the world. With the reading which we adopt, the end coincides with the giving up, and the two words ὅταν are no longer co-ordinated but subordinated. We must not translate " when he *shall have* delivered up the kingdom to his Father and brought all his enemies to naught," but " when he *shall deliver up* the kingdom and *when he shall have* brought to naught," etc. The two events are successive, at least logically, the last one to be announced preceding the other.

(B) *Destruction of his enemies.*—The word καταργεῖν, employed twice in this passage, signifies " to render vain, without force, without effect, without value ; to reduce to impotence, to nothingness," etc. As it is here a question of enemies, the reference is to a complete, final victory over them. One naturally asks if these " enemies " are terrestrial or infernal powers. We prefer to see in them all the powers hostile to God, all those which hinder the work of Christ, of whatever nature they may be. Observe that death is counted in the number of these enemies. In any hypothesis, " the principalities, powers and virtues " are not the angels, whose office and ministry would then cease (St Augustine, *De Trinit.*, i, 8 ; St Thomas and other Latin commentators). The case of Col. ii, 15 is entirely different.

(C) *The giving up of the kingdom to the Father.*—The kingdom of the Word, as Creator, is independent, inalienable and universal ; it includes

The end referred to here is not the *aim* of the resurrection, a meaning which the Greek word no more allows than does the context; nor the end of the resurrection, as numerous exegetes would have it; it is the completion of the work of Christ and the consummation of all things. This point can be considered as established, even without appealing to the parallel passages, since St Paul indicates clearly and in two ways the precise moment which marks that end; on the one hand, the delivery of the kingdom to the Father; on the other, the complete triumph over all enemies. So long as the conflict was being waged, so long as his adversaries were still standing, the mission of the Son of God was incomplete. Now that all his enemies are prostrate at his feet, not excepting even death, which remained the last on the field of battle, his dictatorship comes to an end and he gives back to his Father the mandate received from him, together with the fruit of his victories, as a vassal pays homage to his suzerain for the kingdoms he has conquered.

Such is Paul's thought, which a simple exposition justifies. But the fear of appearing to limit the kingdom of Christ suggested to exegetes the most cunningly devised solutions. To deliver up the kingdom to the Father would be to make the elect who form this kingdom contemplate God; or to lead them to submit to God; or to organize the kingdom, extirpate its abuses and banish the rebels from it. These subtleties are useless. Christ, as God, as Creator, reigns for ever with his Father. As man, he keeps the primacy of honour and the universal domination which the hypostatic union confers upon him. If the Church is a body, he is always its head; if it is a religious society, he is always its high priest; if it is a kingdom, he is always its king. From this point of view, his kingdom will never end; he will reign for ever and " we shall reign with him." But he is also head of the Church militant, charged to vindicate God's honour, to lead to victory those who march under his banner, and to punish rebels and subdue them. This temporary viceroyalty ceases with the functions which constitute it; the mandate of a dictator or commander-in-chief expires at the moment when

---

all rational beings, angels and men, good and bad. The kingdom of Christ, as Redeemer, includes only the elect; even as man, everything is subject to him and he exercises his domination over all things; yet he reigns, properly speaking, only in the saints. It is this kingdom, conquered by him, which he delivers up to him from whom he holds his mandate. He pays homage for it " to the God and Father " (τῷ Θεῷ καὶ πατρί), to him who is at the same time his God and his Father (*cf.* Eph. i, 17; John xx, 27). Moreover, the delivery of the kingdom to the Father does not at all imply the loss or abandonment of the kingdom; otherwise it would be necessary to say that God loses or abandons the domain of the universe when he delivers it to his Son (Luke x, 22). For the patristic exegesis of these verses, see in particular Cornely.

there are no more combats or hostile forces. God, in committing this extraordinary power to his Son, took care to assign its end : " He must reign until he shall have put all his enemies under his feet."

As head of the Church militant, Christ enjoyed a sort of autonomy and had an actual authority of his own. His mission ended, he has only to take his place far above his subjects, but far below God. The cession of his mandate is voluntary, as was also the act by which he took it up ; both are governed by the divine will. St Paul here so evidently speaks of Christ as *man,* that one can hardly conceive why so many Fathers—even the most illustrious—have here thought either of Christ subsisting in the divine nature or of the mystical body of Christ. The mystical body of Christ is not called " the Son of God," nor *a fortiori* " the Son himself," and it is to do violence to the text to pass abruptly from the work of redemption, which is the subject of this whole passage, to the relations of the inner life of the Word.

2. The theological sentimentalism of our days, reviving the fancies of Origen, prolongs the redemptive action of Christ far beyond his triumphal return. According to such thinkers, the *parousia* brings with it only the resurrection and glorification of the just ; in regard to the others, nothing is yet final. The end will come later, when Christ shall have completed his victory by subjecting all his enemies through persuasion, and when God, realizing his plans of love, shall have shown mercy to all men. But St Paul cannot be made responsible for a system which contradicts a great many of his clearest assertions. According to him, the saving will of God, universal as it is, still respects the liberty of man ; the redemption which is offered to all, is not forced upon anyone, and Christ, the only mediator, associates with his victory only those who accept his mediation and are united to him by love. And so the partisans of universal restoration see themselves constrained to abandon the ground of theology and exegesis, to take their stand upon the foundation of rational philosophy, which looks to them more solid. Thither we cannot follow them.

When man has once arrived at the term of his destinies, what will become of his former dwelling-place? Only one text of the Apostle authorizes us to make some rather uncertain inferences on this subject.[1] It represents the material creation as awaiting with anxiety and impatience the glorification of the elect, in which God has promised to make it participate.

Without laying undue stress upon this poetical word-

[1] Rom. viii, 19-22. *Cf.* Vol. I, pp. 238-239.

picture, it is evident that the material creation—for it is of this that the Apostle speaks, in contrast to rational things— was associated in some measure with the fall of man and that it will to some degree participate in his glorification. Indeed it now groans over its present condition as over a state of violence contrary to its legitimate aspirations, and it accepted its subjection to vanity only in obedience to the commands of the Creator and on the assurance that this odious yoke would be removed from it at the moment of the perfect deliverance of man. The whole point is to ascertain whether it is a question here of a physical or a moral fall, and of a physical or a moral rehabilitation. This isolated text does not allow us to reply to this question with certainty. The curse pronounced by God upon the earth punished man directly, but affected the earth only by reaction. Did the soil lose its natural fertility, or did man lose the providential aid which protected him from the hard law of toil? And will the earth one day find again that wonderful fertility which the Sibylline Oracles and other apocryphal writings, not to mention the compilers of the Talmud, promise it? Of this we know absolutely nothing: " God alone can say what the new heavens and the new earth will be. They will certainly be what is best adapted to manifest the divine goodness and the glory of the blessed. It is, therefore, useless to lose ourselves in vain conjectures in a sphere where reason is impotent and revelation mute." These wise words of Scotus might have spared theologians many idle fancies and exegetes many digressions. We should ask Paul, less than anyone, to describe to us the destinies of the material creation. All his interest is concentrated on the history of humanity. Even this history, in proportion as it progresses, becomes bounded within an ever-narrowing horizon; first the human race, then the Church militant, then the elect associated with the triumph of Christ, and finally, God all in all.

# DETACHED NOTES

## NOTE L—PAUL'S MYSTERY AND PAGAN MYSTERIES

### I—BIBLICAL AND CLASSICAL MEANING OF ΜΥΣΤΗΡΙΟΝ

1. IN classical writers μυστήριον means a *secret*; thus in Menander (Fragm. 695): Μυστήριόν σου μὴ κατείπῃς τῷ φίλῳ. Everything leads us to believe that this was the usual meaning in the spoken language; for Cicero, whose letters are embellished with current Greek words, writes to Atticus (iv, 18) that their letters are so full of *mysteria* that one does not dare to intrust them to secretaries. Sometimes, by extension, μυστήριον means *the secret of a thing*, *e.g.*, of nature, as in Herodian (VIII, vii, 8): ὁ στρατιωτικὸς ὅρκος, ὅς ἐστι τῆς ῾Ρωμαίων ἀρχῆς μυστήριον, and Marcus Aurelius (iv, 5): ὁ θάνατος τοιοῦτον οἷον γένεσις φύσεως μυστήριον. Especially was the plural μυστήρια used in speaking of the religious initiations, *e.g.*, of Samothrace and Eleusis, which imposed upon the initiated the most absolute *secrecy*: for μυστήριον comes from μυεῖν, and μυεῖν τὸ στόμα is a synonym for κλείν τὸ στόμα (to shut the mouth). The fundamental idea is, therefore, *secrecy* and the definition of Theodoret (on Rom. xi, 25) is correct: Μυστήριόν ἐστι τὸ μὴ πᾶσι γνώριμον ἀλλὰ μόνον τοῖς θεωρουμένοις.

In the Bible we discover three new meanings which are very closely connected with the generic notion. Mystery is used especially in speaking of the *secret of God in reference to the salvation of men by Christ*, a secret which has ceased to be one since now made known. (Rom. xvi, 23: μυστηρίου χρόνοις αἰωνίοις σεσιγημένου, φανερωθέντος δὲ νῦν.)—Mystery signifies also the *hidden, symbolical*, or *typical meaning* of an institution, of story or picture: Dan. ii, 18, 27, 30 (the meaning of Nabuchodonosor's dream); Eph. v, 32 (typical meaning of marriage); Apoc. i, 20; xvii, 5, 7 (symbolical meaning of a thing or name). A mystery is also *a thing the working of which is hidden* (2 Thess. ii, 7: the mystery of iniquity) or not really known (1 Cor. xv, 51: μυστήριον ὑμῖν λέγω).

The language of philosophy used the word mystery for the secret or inner nature of a thing; in ecclesiastical language it subsequently meant a symbolic rite effecting the grace which it signified—especially the three rites (baptism, confirmation, and the Eucharist), which are, as it were, the Christian's initiation—and finally something incomprehensible, too high for the light of reason.

Thus the following scale of meaning may be laid down :

(a) The *secret* of a person or a secret thing.

(b) The *hidden meaning* of a type, a symbol, or an allegory.

(c) The *secret of God* as to the salvation of mankind.

(d) *Religious initiations* imposing secrecy on the initiated.

(e) *Baptism and the Eucharist,* as rites of initiation.

(f) *Sacraments* in the sense of a sacred sign, then of an efficacious sign.

(g) *Inner nature* of a thing, for example of generation.

(h) A *truth incomprehensible* to reason.

2. The word μυστήριον is frequently met with in the translation of Daniel in the Septuagint and in the deutero-canonical books of the Old Testament; it is also found occasionally in the fragments of Symmachus and Theodotion. It is found twenty-eight times in the New Testament, twenty-one of these being in St Paul. Outside St Paul it is encountered only in the Apocalypse (four times), and in a parallel passage of the three Synoptists (Matt. xiii, 11 ; Mark iv, 11 ; Luke viii, 10).

The Vulgate renders it generally by *mysterium,* but sixteen times by *sacramentum,* though the difference in translation cannot be justified by the difference of meaning. The eight cases where μυστήριον is rendered by *sacramentum* in the New Testament are the following :

Eph. i, 9 : Sacramentum *voluntatis* (redeeming plan).

Eph. iii, 3 : *Notum mihi fecit hoc* sacramentum (*idem*).

Eph. iii, 9 : *Quae sit dispensatio* sacramenti *absconditi* (*idem*).

Eph. v, 22 : Sacramentum *hoc magnum est* (type or symbol).

Col. i, 27 : *Notas facere divitias* sacramenti (scheme of redemption).

1 Tim. iii, 16 : *Magnum est pietatis* sacramentum (secret?).

Apoc. i, 20 : Sacramentum *septem stellarum* (symbolical meaning).

Apoc. xvii, 7 : *Dicam tibi* sacramentum *mulieris* (*idem*).

The ancient Latin version had *mysterium* throughout. This is seen from the six examples from St Paul in the commentary of Ambrosiaster and from the four examples from the Epistle to the Ephesians in the commentary of Victorinus. The most curious thing about this is the fact that St Jerome, in the explanation of this Epistle, always retains *mysterium* except in Eph. v, 32 : *Sacramentum hoc magnum est.* It is true that the commentary was written in A.D. 386 or 387, and that the revision of the ancient version of the Pauline Epistles must have been later.

3. The significant and most interesting evolution of the word *sacramentum* is of considerable importance to the theologian. The study of it cannot find a place here ; besides, the elements for it are still wanting, except in Tertullian. See A. Réville, *Du sens du mot sacramentum dans Tertullien* (Bibl. de l'école des Hautes-Études, sciences relig., vol. i, 1889, pp. 195-204) ; A. d'Alès, *La Théologie de Tertullien,* Paris, 1905, pp. 321-23, and the monograph of the Abbé De Backer (Sacramentum, *le mot et l'idée représentée par lui dans les œuvres de Tertullien,* Louvain, 1911) which exhausts the subject.—The article by H. von Soden, ΜΥΣΤΗΡΙΟΝ *und* Sacramentum *in den ersten zwei Jahrhunderten der Kirche* (in *Zeitschrift f. d. neutest. Wissenschaft,* vol. xii, 1911, pp. 188-227), is instructive but too systematic. A work signed by several collaborating authors is announced to appear soon in the *Spicilegium sacrum Lovaniense* under the title *Pour l'histoire du mot* Sacramentum.

## II—Alleged Borrowings of St Paul from the Pagan Mysteries

1. For a long time attempts have been made to explain the origin of Christianity by the hidden action of its religious environment. This is what is called in Germany *die religionsgeschichtliche Methode.* But the application of the system to the theology of St Paul dates back only a few years, at least as regards the Hellenized Oriental religions.

The most prominent representative of the new *method* is at present Reitzenstein. After having prepared the ground in his *Poimandres, Studien zur griechisch-ägyptischen und frühchristlichen Literatur,* Leipzig, 1904, Reitzenstein seeks to prove his thesis in his work *Die hellenistischen Mysterienreligionen,* Leipzig, 1910. It is one of the most erudite of books, but also one of the most nebulous and undigested that I know. It is made up of a dissertation in which the most incongruous ideas assume an obscurity which one could almost believe intentional (pp. 1-62) ; all the rest consists of notes and Excursuses (pp. 63-212). The author apologizes for meddling, as a philologist, with theological questions about which he is notoriously incompetent, and he must be praised for having scented the danger, but blamed for having knowingly exposed himself to it. The following is the statement of his thesis (p. 59) : " However obscure the Apostle Paul's religious development may be, one fact appears always increasingly evident : he made a serious effort to become a Greek with the Greeks. He must have read their religious literature ; he speaks its language ; he is penetrated with it ; and the ideas which he draws from it necessarily ally themselves with the ideas which originate from his new experience and go very far beyond those of Judaism.''

As was to be expected, M. Loisy quickly followed in the steps of his German forerunner, and developed his ideas in a series of articles which appeared from 1911 to 1914 in the *Revue d'histoire et de littér. relig.* and were published separately under the title *Les mystères paiens et le mystère chrétien,* Paris, 1919. They can be summed up as follows. In order to spread through the world, Christianity had to be transformed into an Oriental mystery, which was all the easier because at heart the Gospel of Paul is only the mystery of a God who has died and risen again in order to save those who are united with him by a rite of initiation, as happens in the religions of Osiris, Attis, and Adonis. And it is Paul who is the author chiefly responsible for this transformation, since he makes Christ's death and resurrection a myth of salvation.

A few other critics maintain similar ideas, but as most of them are not specially concerned with St Paul, here we need only refer to Heitmüller, *Taufe und Abendmahl bei Paulus,* Tübingen, 1903, and Böhling, *Die Geisteskultur von Tarsos im augusteischen Zeitalter mit Berücksichtigung der paulin. Schriften,* Göttingen, 1913.

2. *Vices of the new system in regard to method*—(a) *Vicious circles.*—All practices suggested by the religious instinct have a certain analogy between them. Thus it is that ritual ablution is everywhere considered as a purification and that, in the sacred repast which concludes the sacrifice, those who partake of it always regard themselves as the guests and table-companions of the god whom they honour. There is nothing to be drawn from this common fund of religious ideas, and it would be an unpardonable fallacy to transform these similitudes into proofs of interdependence. The wise reflections of Cumont (*Les religions orientales,* 1906, preface, pp. xi-xiii) should be read on this subject. But, if the fact of imitation were proved, first we have to inquire which party was the imitator (*ibid.,* p. xi) : '' After Christianity became a moral power in the world, it imposed itself even on its enemies. The Phrygian priests of the Great Mother openly opposed their festivals of the spring equinox to the Christian Easter and attributed to the blood shed at the sacrifice of bulls the power of the blood of the Lamb of God.'' The Fathers accuse the devil, that ape of God, of having inspired these parodies of Christian worship. They may be mistaken ; yet the question of priority must be studied without prejudice. But that is what the partisans of the *religionsgeschichtliche Methode* constantly forget, and it is well to remind them of it.

(b) *Anachronisms.*—For one religious form to influence another, it is necessary that the first should be anterior to the second, or at least that they should be contemporaneous. Now a contact between infant Christianity and Mithraism, for example, is *a priori* so improbable that it can be rejected unhesitatingly. Mithras, that barbarous god, carried about the world by slaves and soldiers, acquired a place in the Roman pantheon under Commodus and attained his highest prominence in the third century. However, in A.D. 248, Origen (*Contra Celsum,* vi, 23) treats Mithraism as an obscure sect and a negligible quantity. Organized in little autonomous groups of at most a hundred adepts, from which women were excluded, it never aimed at universality. Left to itself, it soon disappeared in indifference and oblivion. It cannot be claimed with any degree of probability that Paul borrowed anything from it. Such is the opinion of Cumont (*Les religions orientales,* p. xv), of Harnack (*Mission und Ausbreitung des Christentums*[2], Leipzig, 1906, vol. ii, 273), and of Toutain (*Les cultes paiens dans l'empire romain,* vol. ii, Paris, 1911, pp. 150-59). *Cf.* A. d'Alès, *Mithra* in the *Dict. apol. de la foi cathol.,* fasc. xiv, 1918.

It would be a still more intolerable anachronism, or rather a purely imaginative one, to explain the meaning and the value of Christian baptism by the repugnant rite of the sacrifice of bulls (*taurobolium*), practised in honour of Cybele and Attis, of which Prudentius (*Peristephanon,* x, 1011-50) has left us a detailed description. In fact the *taurobolium* (i) is not a ceremony of initiation ; (ii) it is not considered as a new birth or as a pledge of eternal life ; (iii) it is of a relatively recent date and, far from having influenced Paul and the first Christian writers, may very well have itself been influenced by Christianity. *Cf.* Lagrange, *Attis et le christianisme,* in the *Rev. bibl.,* 1919, p. 419.

But the most shocking anachronism is the attempt to prove Paul's dependence on Oriental religions by the *Hermetical Books* and the *Magical Papyri* as Reitzenstein notably does. The Magical Papyri are not anterior to the third or fourth century of our era, although they no doubt contain more ancient documents. As for the Hermetical Books, they are also, in their present form, of the fourth century, or, at the earliest, of the third. *Cf.* Ménard (*Hermès Trismegiste*[2], Paris, 1867), and Kroll (*Die Lehren des Hermes Trismegistos,* Münster i. W., 1914).—Stock, *Hermes Trismegistus* (in *Encycl. of Religion and Ethics,* vol. vi, 1913), thinks that they were composed between 313 and 330, for Lactantius is the first to quote them. He gives this opinion of them (p. 626) : " Take Plato, the Stoics, Philo, Christianity, Gnosticism, Neo-platonism, Neo-pythagorism, and mix them all together, throwing in a strong dose of Egyptian ideas, and you will have something resembling Hermes Trismegistus, as we possess it." To seek for the source of Paul's thought in these hybrid compilations of uncertain date and origin is certainly not a good method. Is it not enough to doom a thesis to ridicule to support it by such arguments? For further details see our article *St Paul and Paulinism* in the *Diction. apol. de la foi cathol.,* fasc. xviii, 1922.

(c) *False reasonings.*—We shall point out only two of the most common, for to treat of them all would require too much space.

(i) People often reason as if they knew the Oriental religions as they might have been known by St Paul. Now, except for the religion of the Mother of the gods, which has very little similarity to the Apostle's doctrine, all the documents which we possess are later than the first century of our era. It is the *Golden Ass* of Apuleius, that satirical and licentious romance written in the second half of the second century, which is our principal and almost unique source of information, outside the Church Fathers, for the study of the mysteries of Isis. Curious and superstitious as he was, Apuleius may very well have had himself initiated into those mysteries; but in his grotesque recital it is not easy to distinguish between truth and fiction, between sincere piety and persiflage. In any case, we are already far from the early Church, and a relation of dependence of the latter on the former, if it really existed, might be indeed reversed.

(ii) Or else men build a coherent and well-arranged religious system on the meagre information at our disposal, by filling up the gaps in our knowledge, by interpreting obscure data, and by devising agreements between these diverse elements. Then they compare this artificial creation with Paul's theology, and are surprised to find in it resemblances which they themselves have put there. In a popular pamphlet, Brückner (*Der sterbende auferstehende Gottheiland in den orient. Relig. und ihr Verhältnis zum Christentum,* 1908) furnishes us a typical example of this. But Loisy (*Les Mystères paiens et le Mystère chrétien,* Paris, 1919) goes far beyond him. Père Lagrange critically discusses this work in the *Revue biblique,* xxix, 1920, pp. 420-446.

3. *St Paul and pagan mysteries.*—The question is not, whether the Apostle was or was not acquainted with the religious initiations called mysteries. It is impossible for him to have been ignorant of the famous mysteries of Eleusis, and it may indeed be conceded that he had a more or less perfect knowledge of the Oriental pairs whose cult was beginning to spread quietly through the Roman empire: Isis and Osiris, Cybele and Attis, the *Dea Syria* and Adonis, and even, perhaps, the cult of Mithras imported from Persia. The question is, whether and how far he was influenced by them.

In view of Paul's aversion to everything which savours of the adoration of idols, an intentional and deliberate imitation on his part of pagan mysteries is most improbable; but he may have been unconsciously influenced by them and have adopted their language to express his own ideas. It is a question of fact, to be studied without prejudice by a comparison of texts.

Now we notice at the outset that the vocabulary of the mysteries is completely foreign to St Paul, even in what relates to the mysteries of Eleusis, the terminology of which had passed into the language of the people. He never speaks either of *initiation* (τελετή, μύησις) nor of an *initiate* (μύστης, τετελεσμένος, τελεσθείς) nor of an *initiator* (ἱεροφάντης) nor of mystical contemplation (ἐποπτεία, τὰ ἐποπτικά), etc. On the other hand, we have shown that his *mystery* is the very opposite of the pagan mysteries, that his use of the word *perfect* (τέλειος, which, moreover, does not belong to the vocabulary of the mysteries) is not different from its classical use (*cf.* pp. 41, 42), and finally, that his psychological vocabulary (in particular πνεῦμα, πνεματικός, ψυχή, ψυχικός) is directly derived from the Old Testament (*cf.* pp. 43-55).

How, then, do the partisans of the *religionsgeschichtliche Methode* prove their statements? Here is a typical example of their reasoning. St Paul calls Timothy a *soldier of Christ,* and calls himself a *prisoner of Christ.* Now Reitzenstein affirms that these appellations are borrowed from the language of the religions of the mysteries (*Die hellenistischen Mysterienreligionen,* Leipzig, 1910, pp. 66-83). Harnack could have taught him that " the description of Christians as soldiers of Christ is in no way due to the influence of foreign religions " (*Militia Christi,* Leipzig, 1905, p. 122). But the testimony of this scholar was not needed to show that the life of man in all literatures, from Job to Stoicism, is often compared to a conflict. As for the title *prisoner of Christ,* the reasoning of Reitzenstein is quite astounding. In the Serapeion at Memphis there were persons known as κάτοχοι. Reitzenstein alleges that these κάτοχοι were " novices, serving in the temple, in the hope of an initiation, which often had to be waited for during many years, sometimes a whole lifetime " (p. 80); and this, he thinks, suggested to St Paul the idea of calling himself a *prisoner of Christ* (Philem. 1 and 9; and Eph. iii, 1). Were the κάτοχοι voluntary prisoners of Isis or of Serapis? Preuschen (*Mönchtum und Serapiskult*[2], Giessen, 1903), and Wilcken (*Papyruskunde,* vol. i, Part II, pp. 130-132) think they were *possessed.* But even if κάτοχος did signify *prisoner,* what would that have to do with the δέσμιος of the Apostle?

After this we cannot be astonished that the paradoxes of the new school have called forth many protests. Anrich, in his masterly study (*Das antike Mysterienwesen in seinem Einfluss auf das Christentum*, Göttingen 1894), denied any influence of pagan mysteries on primitive Christianity. Cumont (*Les religions orientales*, Paris, 1906, pp. xi-xv), and Toutain (*Les cultes paiens dans l'empire romain*, vol. ii, Paris, 1911, pp. 150-59) think the same. C. Clemen in his two works (*Religionsgesch. Erklärung des N.T.*, Giessen, 1909, and *Der Einfluss der Mysterienreligionen auf das älteste Christentum*, Giessen, 1913) reduces the influence of the mysteries almost to vanishing point. Such is also the opinion of Groton (*Dict. of the Apostolic Church*, Edinburgh, 1918, vol. ii, p. 62), who notes only certain resemblances in terminology covering totally different ideas. Such is almost the position of Kennedy (*St Paul and the Mystery Religions*, London, 1913), and of M. Jones (*The N.T. in the Twentieth Century*, London, 1914, pp. 120-161). It would be easy to prolong the list; but we cannot omit Schweitzer (*Geschichte der paulin. Forschung*, Tübingen, 1911, pp. 141-184), whose criticism, although severe, is often judicious and acute. Let us mention also J. Gresham Machen, *The Origin of Paul's Religion*, N.Y., 1921 (chapters vi and vii), a solid work which a Catholic could unreservedly approve, if the author (pp. 284-88) did not attack the efficaciousness of the sacraments *ex opere operato*.

On their side, Catholics have diligently and abundantly refuted these systems : Mangenot, *La doctrine de St Paul et les mystères paiens* (in *Revue du clergé*, vol. lxxiv, pp. 1 and 258); *La langue de St Paul et celle des mystères paiens* (*ibid.* vol. lxxv, 1913, p. 129), *St Paul et les mystères paiens* (in *Revue prat. d'apol.*, vol. xvi, 1918, pp. 176, 241, 339); Jacquier, *Les mystères paiens et St Paul* (in *Dict. apol. de la foi cathol.*, vol. iii, 1920, cols. 964-1014), where the reader will find an extensive bibliography ; Venard, *Le christianisme et les religions de mystères* (in *Rev. du clergé*, vol. ciii, pp. 182 and 283) ; see also the article by P. Lagrange, *Attis et le Christianisme* (in *Rev. biblique*, vol. xvi, 1919, pp. 419-80), and his review of the work of M. Loisy, *Les mystères païens et le Mystère chrétien* (*ibid.*, vol. xvii, 1920, pp. 420-446).

## NOTE M—IN CHRIST JESUS

### I—USE OF THE PHRASE

One of the most characteristic expressions in the theological language of St Paul is the phrase *In Christo Jesu*. It can be said to be peculiarly his own, for he employs it 164 times, while it is wholly absent from the Synoptists and other writings of the N.T. with the exception of St John, Paul's discourses in Acts (iv, 2 ; xiii, 39), and 1 Peter (iii, 16, 19 ; v, 10, 14), whose close resemblance of language and ideas to Paul's style is well known. St John uses an analogous phrase twenty-four times, especially in the allegory of the Vine (xv, 2, 4, 5, 6, 7) and in the recommendation made by Jesus to his disciples to abide *in* him (vi, 56 ; xiv, 20 ; xvi, 33 ; xvii, 21 ; 1 John iii, 5, 6, 8, 24, 27 ; iii, 6, 24 ; v, 11, 20) as he himself is *in* his Father. The Apocalypse has once ἐν Κυρίῳ (xiv, 13), like Paul, and another time ἐν Ἰησοῦ (i, 9), which Paul never uses, for Eph. iv, 21 is entirely different.

The formula is as common in St Paul as it is rare elsewhere. It recurs in all his Epistles except in the one to Titus ; and the exception is purely accidental, since the three Pastorals are evidently by the same author. However, it is not everywhere distributed equally. As one might have anticipated, it is much more frequent in the Epistles of the captivity, the principal subject of which is the mystical union of Christians with Christ. The following statistical table is furnished by Deissmann (*Die neutestam. Formel "in Christo Jesu,"* Marburg, 1892), who has made the study of this phrase a speciality :

| Epistle. | Number. | Proportion. | ἐν Χ. Ἰ. | ἐν Χριστῷ. | ἐν Κυρίῳ. | ἐν ᾧ ἐν αὐτῷ. |
|---|---|---|---|---|---|---|
| 1 Thess. | 7 | 0'87 | 2 | 1 | 4 | 0 |
| 2 Thess. | 3 | 0'75 | 0 | 0 | 3 | 0 |
| Gal. | 9 | 0'75 | 5 | 3 | 1 | 0 |
| 1 Cor. | 23 | 0'68 | 7 | 6 | 9 | 1 |
| 2 Cor. | 13 | 0'58 | 0 | 7 | 2 | 4 |
| Rom. | 21 | 0'59 | 8 | 5 | 8 | 0 |
| Phil. | 21 | 2'47 | 8 | 2 | 9 | 1 |
| Col. | 18 | 2'12 | 1 | 2 | 4 | 11 |
| Eph. | 35 | 2'69 | 7 | 6 | 8 | 12 |
| Philem. | 5 | 3'33 | 1 | 2 | 2 | 0 |
| 1 Tim. | 2 | 0'22 | 2 | 0 | 0 | 0 |
| 2 Tim. | 7 | 1'00 | 7 | 0 | 0 | 0 |
| Titus | 0 | 0 | 0 | 0 | 0 | 0 |
| | 164 | 0'98 | 48 | 34 | 50 | 29 |

Besides there are Phil. iv, 13 (ἐν τῷ ἐνδυναμοῦντί με), Eph. i, 6 (ἐν τῷ ἠγαπημένῳ), and Eph. iv, 21 (καθὼς ἔστιν ἀλήθεια ἐν τῷ Ἰησοῦ).

## II—Meaning of the Phrase

1. *In St John.*—The phrase which expresses the *circumin-cession* of the divine Persons : "I am in my Father and my Father in me" (John x, 38 ; xiv, 10, 11), is extended by the author of the fourth Gospel to the relations of Christ and his disciples : "In that day you shall know that I am in my Father, and you in me and I in you" (John xiv, 20). Else-where he affirms that by the possession of the Spirit of God (1 John iii, 24 ; iv, 13), or, what amounts to the same thing, of love, we are in God and God in us (1 John iv, 15-16) : Ὁ Θεὸς ἀγάπη ἐστίν, καὶ ὁ μένων ἐν τῇ ἀγάπῃ ἐν τῷ Θεῷ μένει καὶ ὁ Θεὸς ἐν αὐτῷ μένει. Through love indeed we partake of the nature of God (2 Pet. i, 4) and of his activity, since our super-natural act is at the same time one of God and of ourselves ; there takes place, therefore, in us something analogous to the relations of the divine Persons between themselves. St John immediately explains his thought by the allegory of the Vine (John xv, 1-10). The vine and the branches live the same life, are nourished by the same sap, and work together in the production of the same fruit. They form one being, they have one and the same action. There is here plainly a union similar to that of the mystical body of St Paul, and the language used in both cases is almost identical : The *body* corresponds to the *vine-stock* and the *members* correspond to the *branches.* Compare, for example, John xv, 5 with 1 Cor. xii, 12, 27. The only difference is that St John, representing Jesus Christ as the speaker, says ἐν ἐμοί (xv, 4 : μείνατε ἐν ἐμοί, κἀγὼ ἐν ὑμῖν) : while Paul, speaking of Christ, says ἐν Χριστῷ. For St John, to abide in the Son is to abide in the Father and reciprocally (1 John ii, 24) ; for St Paul, to be in Christ and to be in the Holy Spirit are also equivalent expressions.

2. *In St Paul.*—The monograph of Deissmann comes to this conclusion (*op. cit.*, p. 97) : "The phrase ἐν Χριστῷ Ἰησοῦ, created by St Paul under the influence of earlier profane use, characterizes the relation of the Christian to Jesus Christ as a kind of local presence in the spiritual (mystical) Christ. This idea, which has its counterpart in no other relation of man to man, we can conceive by the analogy of the expressions ἐν Πνεύματι and ἐν τῷ Θεῷ, which represent a mode of existence in a spiritual element comparable to the air. Is it necessary to conceive of this local presence in its literal meaning and not as a simple rhetorical figure ? It is impossible to say with certainty, but the local sense is very probable."

Karl (*Beiträge zum Verständnis . . . des Ap. Paulus*, 1896) accepts in general the conclusions of Deissmann, but he is wrong to compare the formula in question with the expression ἐν βεελζεβούλ (Matt. xii, 27-28), where ἐν is a pure Hebraism. Johannes Weiss, *Paulin. Probleme* (*in Stud. u. Krit.*, 1896, first number), also adopts the meaning of Deissmann, but he believes that the expression was in frequent use at the time of Paul ; that the influence of the Septuagint, in the case where ἐν is found connected with God (2 Sam. xx, 1 ; xxii, 30 ; Ps. xvii, 30 ; Zach. xii. 5), may have acted here; and finally that ἐν, including the idea of limit, often indicates the sphere in which the action takes place. Sanday (*The Epistle to the Romans*[5], Edinburgh, 1907, p. 161), although he also praises the pamphlet of the learned professor, finds that his method is rather too systematic and his conception somewhat too realistic. That is indeed the impression made by Deissmann, who writes as a grammarian rather than an exegete. Without violence the expression cannot be reduced to a perfectly identical concept. It is necessary to take into account the force of habit which blunts the meaning of ordinary expressions, of the reaction produced by analogous ideas, and of the influence exercised by certain associations of words and other phenomena of the same nature.

Here is the result of an attentive examination of the different elements of the problem : (*a*) In virtue of the theory of the mystical body, we form an integral part of Christ, we *put on* Christ, we are buried in Christ, Christ is in us and we in him. Such is the ordinary, and so to speak the technical, meaning of the phrase *In Christo Jesu* in St Paul, especially when it is a question of the supernatural life of the Christian or of the union of Christians with one another. In such a case the expression *In Christo Jesu* can be replaced by the words *In Spiritu*, without the necessity on that account of admitting the identity of Christ and the Holy Spirit, an identity which a mistaken exegesis wishes to draw from 2 Cor. iii, 17.—(*b*) But quite frequently the meaning becomes less clear, and the phrase *In Christo* signifies scarcely more than *in a Christian manner*, from the Christian point of view, or conformably to the principles of Christianity, and could be replaced by *In evangelio*, which is sometimes substituted for it : Gal. i, 22 (ἐκκλησίαι ἐν X.) ; 2 Cor. xii, 2 (Οἶδα ἄνθρωπον ἐν X.) ; 1 Cor. iii, 1 (νήπιοι ἐν X.). *Cf.* Rom. xvi, 17 ; 1 Cor. xv, 58 ; 2 Cor. ii, 12 ; Col. iii. 18-20. The antithesis to ἐν Χριστῷ would then be ἐν τῷ Ἰουδαϊσμῷ (compare Gal. i, 13, 14 with 1 Cor. iv, 17) or else ἐν τῷ νόμῳ (compare Rom. iii, 19 with 1 Thess. ii, 14), etc.—(*c*) We must also take into account the influence of the Septuagint, much greater than Deissmann admits, especially if we consider the deuterocanonical books. The Hebrew particle ב, translated by ἐν in the Septuagint,

designates the *instrument, support, society, limit*. The Apostle
construes with ἐν the verbs *to boast* (2 Thess. i, 4; 1 Cor. i, 31;
iii, 21; 2 Cor. v, 12; x, 15, etc.); *to have confidence* (1 Thess.
ii, 2; Phil. iii. 3-4); *to rejoice* (Col. i, 24; Phil. i, 18). The
Septuagint often does the same with the verb *to hope;* we
may therefore suppose that in these cases the formula *In
Christo Jesu* follows the analogy of the other complements,
and has not its own special value.


### III—*In Christ* AND *In the Spirit*

Gunkel (*Die Wirkungen des h. Geistes*, Göttingen, 1888) has
emphasized the close and constant relations which exist
between the form ἐν Χριστῷ and ἐν πνεύματι. He concludes
(p. 97): "All the operations of the πνεῦμα appear in other
places as operations of Christ." Indeed, the virtues and
supernatural gifts are accompanied by either form indifferently: πίστις (1 Cor. xii, 9; Gal. iii, 26), ἀγάπη (Col. i, 8;
Rom. viii, 39), εἰρήνη (Rom. xiv, 17; Phil. iv, 7); also the
verbs expressing action or state: εἶναι (Rom. viii, 9; 1 Cor.
i, 30), στήκειν (Phil. i, 27; 1 Thess. iii, 8), σφραγίζεσθαι (Eph.
iv, 30; i, 13), λαλεῖν (1 Cor. xii, 3; 2 Cor. ii, 17), ἡγιασμένος
(Rom. xv, 16; 1 Cor. i, 2), πληροῦσθαι (Eph. v, 18; Col. ii, 10).
In this list the first citation refers to the form ἐν πνεύματι, the
second to the form ἐν Χριστῷ or a similar one.

The best way to study this phenomenon of identity is to
run through a concordance, noting the form ἐν Χριστῷ, and
trying to replace it by ἐν πνεύματι, then to make the counter-
proof by replacing ἐν πνεύματι by ἐν Χριστῷ. It will be
observed (A) that the form can be very often changed
without appreciably altering the sense; and that in every
case where ἐν Πνεύματι denotes *with certainty* the Holy Spirit
it can be replaced by ἐν Χριστῷ, unless it is specially a
question of *charismata* (as in 1 Cor. xii, 3; xiv, 16).—
(B) That the exchange is, nevertheless, impossible in three
cases: (*a*) when the reference is to God loving us, choosing
us, or predestinating us "in Christ" (Rom. viii, 39; 2 Cor. v, 19;
Eph. i, 3, etc.); (*b*) when it is a question of Christ as the
second Adam—that is to say, in his redemptive mediation
(Rom. iii, 24; 1 Cor. xv, 22; Eph. ii, 13; iv, 32; 2 Tim. ii, 10,
etc.); (*c*) when the expression ἐν Χριστῷ is equivalent to
"from the Christian point of view," or "as a Christian," etc.
(Rom. xvi, 3, 9, 10; 1 Cor. iii, 1; iv, 15, 17; 2 Cor. xii, 2;
Gal. i, 22; Phil. i, 13, etc.).—(C) That even where the substitution is absolutely possible, it almost always causes the loss
of a very delicate shade of meaning, like that which would be
produced by putting soul instead of head, or *vice versa*, in the
description of the mystical body.

Deissmann (*op. cit.*, p. 84) asserts that the formula ἐν πνεύματι is taken by St Paul fifteen times out of nineteen in the specific sense of ἐν Χριστῷ. But if we examine each case strictly we shall make a very different reckoning. (*a*) Thus 1 Cor. xii, 9 (ἑτέρῳ πίστις ἐν τῷ αὐτῷ πνεύματι) and Gal. iii, 26 (υἱοὶ Θεοῦ ἐστε διὰ πίστεως ἐν Χριστῷ Ἰησοῦ) have only an apparent resemblance ; for, besides the fact that the first example concerns charismatical faith, and the second justifying faith, it is very probable that ἐν X. 'I. ought to be connected with υἱοὶ Θεοῦ ἐστε, and not with διὰ πίστεως (see p. 261).—(*b*) Rom. viii, 9 (οὐκ ἐστε ἐν σαρκὶ ἀλλὰ ἐν πνεύματι) and 1 Cor. i, 30 (ἐξ αὐτοῦ ὑμεῖς ἐστε ἐν X. 'I.) are not to be made equivalent without some reservations, for it is not sure that ἐν πνεύματι designates the Holy Spirit, and ἐν Χριστῷ depends not on ἐστε but on ἐξ αὐτοῦ ἐστε.— (*c*) Phil. i, 27 (στήκετε ἐν ἑνὶ πνεύματι, μιᾷ ψυχῇ) cannot be paralleled with Phil. iv, 1 (στήκετε ἐν κυρίῳ), because πνεῦμα is not the Holy Spirit, as the synonymy of ψυχή proves.— (*d*) 1 Cor. xii, 9 (χαρίσματα ἰαμάτων ἐν τῷ αὐτῷ πνεύματι) and Rom. vi, 23 (τὸ χάρισμα τοῦ Θεοῦ ζωὴ αἰώνιος ἐν X. 'I.) have nothing in common, because χάρισμα there designates very different things, and especially because ἐν X. 'I. is applied to ζωὴ αἰώνιος.—(*e*) Col. i, 8 (τὴν ὑμῶν ἀγάπην ἐν πνεύματι) must not be compared with Rom. viii, 39 (ἀπὸ τῆς ἀγάπης τοῦ Θεοῦ τῆς ἐν X. 'I.), for in the latter case it is a question of the love of God *for us*, and Jesus Christ fulfils his usual office of mediator.—(*f*) In Rom. ii, 29 (περιτομὴ καρδίας ἐν πνεύματι οὐ γράμματι) is it a question of the Holy Spirit, in order that we may be authorized to compare Col. ii, 11 (ἐν ᾧ [Χριστῷ] καὶ περιετμήθετε) ?—(*g*) Gal. v, 16 (πνεύματι περιπατεῖτε) does not offer the typical form, and one cannot compare Col. ii, 6 (ἐν αὐτῷ [Χριστῷ] περιπατεῖτε).—(*h*) 1 Cor. xii, 3 (ἐν πνεύματι Θεοῦ λαλῶν) and 2 Cor. ii, 17 (ἐν Χριστῷ λαλοῦμεν) have only a deceptive similitude : the proof is that the two expressions could not be exchanged one for the other.

On the whole, the equivalency of the formulas ἐν Χριστῷ and ἐν Πνεύματι is a very limited one, and even where it does exist there is a fine shade of meaning which is not negligible.

# NOTE N—THE GOSPEL

## I—THE "GOSPEL" APART FROM ST PAUL

1. *Use of the Word.*—The word "gospel" occurs sixty times in St Paul as against sixteen times elsewhere; and the verb "to evangelize" twenty times as against thirty-three times elsewhere.—It is found that both these words are wanting in the Epistle to the Hebrews, that St John uses them only in the Apocalypse (once the substantive, and twice the verb *in the active voice*), and that St Luke frequently makes use of the verb, but seems purposely to avoid the substantive, for he puts it only into the mouths of St Paul and St Peter (Acts xv, 7; xx. 24).—The absence of the word "gospel" in St Luke, St John, and the Epistle to the Hebrews is all the more extraordinary since this term formed part of the Christian vocabulary at a very early date. Can it be because the specific meaning of "good news" was not yet sufficiently known to the non-Christian public?

2. *Meaning of the Word in the Synoptists.*—Εὐαγγέλιον (in the singular in Homer, in the plural in the Attic dialect) signified *the present given to the bearer of good tidings,* or *the sacrifice offered on the occasion of good news.* Later it was also used of the *good news* itself; but this meaning, which has not been found previous to the age of Augustus, is foreign to the language of the Septuagint, for in 2 Sam. iv, 10 and xviii, 22 the meaning is a "present for good tidings"; and in 2 Sam. xviii, 25 it is almost certainly necessary to read εὐαγγελία in the feminine (as in 2 Sam. xviii, 20, 27) instead of εὐαγγέλια (Swete).

The comparison of the Synoptists is curious and instructive:

| Mark. | Matthew. | Luke. |
|---|---|---|
| (a) τὸ εὐαγγέλιον 'I. X., i, 1 | | |
| (b) τὸ εὐαγγέλιον τοῦ Θεοῦ, i, 14 | | |
| (c) τὸ εὐαγγέλιον, i, 15 | | |
| (d) | τὸ εὐαγ. τῆς βασιλείας, iv, 23 | (iv, 13) |
| | τὸ εὐαγ. τῆς βασιλείας, ix, 35 | |
| (e) ἕνεκεν ἐμοῦ καὶ τοῦ εὐαγ., viii, 35 | (xvi, 25) | (ix, 24) |
| (f) ἕνεκεν ἐμοῦ καὶ τοῦ εὐαγ., x, 29 | (xix, 29) | (xviii, 29) |
| (g) τὸ εὐαγγέλιον, xiii, 10 | τὸ εὐαγ. τῆς βασιλείας, xxiv, 14 | |
| (h) τὸ εὐαγγέλιον, xiv, 9 | τὸ εὐαγγέλιον τοῦτο, xxvi, 13 | |
| (i) τὸ εὐαγγέλιον, xvi, 5 | | |

St Mark, six times out of eight (*c*, *e*, *f*, *g*, *h*, *i*), has the
"Gospel" only, as if it were a question of a well-known idea.
Once only (*a*) it is "the Gospel of Jesus Christ," and once
(*b*) "the Gospel of God." St Matthew has three times out of
four—(*d*) forming a doublet and (*g*) the stereotyped form—
"the Gospel of the kingdom." St Luke avoids the word in
the three cases (*d*, *e*, *f*), where his text runs parallel to that of
the other Synoptists.

The first time that St Mark speaks of the Gospel (after his
preface) he defines its contents, i, 14, 15 : *Postquam traditus
est Joannes, venit Jesus in Galilaeum, praedicans* Evangelium
regni Dei *et dicens : Quoniam impletum est tempus, et appropin-
quavit regnum Dei : poenitemini et credite* Evangelio. Harnack
limits the content of the Gospel too much when he makes it
consist merely of the approach of the kingdom (*Entstehung
und Entwicklung der Kirchenverfassung*, etc., Leipzig, 1910,
p. 202). No, the Gospel is not merely the *approach* of the
kingdom, it is rather the *kingdom* that is approaching. In
fact, (*a*) in Mark viii, 35 and x, 29, Jesus says : "Whosoever
shall sacrifice everything *for my sake and for the Gospel* shall
receive an hundredfold." Is it possible to explain those
words as meaning for the *approach* of the kingdom of God ?—
(*b*) St Matthew in the parallel passages (xvi, 25 ; xix, 29)
omits the word "Gospel," no doubt because he considers it
implicitly contained in Christ, whose message the Gospel is.—
(*c*) St Luke does the same once (ix, 24), while the other time
(xviii, 29) he replaces ἕνεκεν τοῦ εὐαγγελίου by ἕνεκεν τῆς
βασιλείας τοῦ Θεοῦ, considering the contents of the Gospel
as equal in extent to the kingdom itself.—(*d*) Whatever may
be the precise meaning of the title of St Mark (Ἀρχὴ τοῦ
εὐαγγελίου Ἰ. Χ.), it does not favour Harnack's contention.

## II—THE "GOSPEL" IN ST PAUL

1. "*Preaching the Gospel" and the "Gospel*."—It is well to
begin with the verb εὐαγγελίζεσθαι, less technical than the noun
εὐαγγέλιον. This verb is once used by St Paul in the secular
sense (1 Thess. iii, 6), but everywhere else it is in the religious
sense popularized by the Septuagint (Is. xl, 9 ; lii, 7 ; lx, 6 ;
lxi, 1, etc.). It is often employed in an absolute way and
signifies by itself "to preach the Gospel" (nine times out of
nineteen) like our "to evangelize"; then it can be accompanied by an object in the dative (Rom. i, 15 ; 1 Cor. xv, 2 ;
Gal. i, 8, 11 ; iv, 13) or in the accusative with εἰς (2 Cor. x, 16).
—When the object of the predicate is expressed, it is the
Gospel itself (1 Cor. xv, 1 ; 2 Cor. xi, 7) or a synonym of the
Gospel (Gal. i, 8, 9) : messianic blessings (Rom. x, 15, quoting
Is. lii, 7), faith (Gal. i, 23), peace (Eph. ii, 17, alluding to
Is. lvii, 19), the unfathomable riches of Christ (Eph. iii, 8),

and finally Christ himself (Gal. i, 16). This last expression
" to preach Christ" is to be remembered.

St Paul also frequently employs the word "Gospel" in an
absolute way (twenty-eight times out of sixty). It is then, in
its full extent, the good news which Jesus Christ came to
announce to the world. It is hardly necessary to point out
that the Gospel never signifies the totality of the Saviour's
actions and discourses, and still less the book in which those
deeds and discourses are related ; nor does St Paul contrast
the Gospel with the Law; he knows only the antithesis of
faith and law; it was perhaps Marcion who created the antithesis of Gospel and Law (cf. Tertullian, Adv. Marcion. i, 19,
21 ; iv, 1, 4 ; St. Irenæus, Haereses, iv, 3). On the contrary,
the Gospel is often put into correlation with the promise : the
Gospel is the promise realized ; the promise is the Gospel in
prospect (cf. Rom. i, 1, 2 ; Eph. iii, 6 ; Acts xiii, 32).

The Gospel having already taken on a technical sense which
allows it to be employed absolutely, the etymological notion
of "good news" is no longer always discernible ; the more so
as in the Septuagint the words εὐαγγελίζεσθαι and εὐαγγέλιον
need to be investigated in order to know if they express good
news (2 Sam. xviii, 27 ; 1 Kings i, 42 ; Is. lii, 7 : εὐαγγελιζόμενος
ἀγαθά), and Josephus (Bell., II, xvii, 4) was able to say δεινὸν
εὐαγγέλιον. From this it appears also that the Gospel has
a tendency to mean no longer merely a collection of truths
but of salutary institutions : Virtus enim Dei est in salutem omni
credenti (Rom. i, 16). The same significant evolution begins
to appear in the case of a synonym of the Gospel, the Mystery
(1 Cor. iv, 1 : dispensatores mysteriorum Dei).

When the Gospel is not employed in an absolute sense it
is determined either by an adjective (2 Cor. xi, 4 ; Gal. i, 6 :
εὐαγγέλιον ἕτερον), or by a subclause (Gal. i, 11 ; ii, 2 ; 1 Cor.
xv, 1 : the Gospel which I preach), or by a genitive of the
thing (2 Cor. iv, 4 : the Gospel of the glory of Christ ;
Gal. ii, 7 : the Gospel of the circumcision and of the uncircumcision ; Eph. i, 13 : the Gospel of your salvation ; vi, 15 :
the Gospel of peace ; 1 Tim. i, 11 : the Gospel of the glory of
the blessed God), or more frequently by a genitive of the
person (God six times, Christ ten times, Paul six times). In
the case of the Gospel of God the meaning is not doubtful; it
is the Gospel of which God is the author (Rom. i, 1 ; xv, 16 ;
2 Cor. xi, 7 ; 1 Thess. ii, 2, 8, 9). As to the Gospel of Paul
and the Gospel of Christ, the meaning is less certain.

2. The Gospel of Paul.—When St Paul speaks of his Gospel,
whether he means "the Gospel preached by him" or his
"preaching of the Gospel," the difference is very little as
regards the sense, and the question has hardly any interest
except from the point of view of philology. Now it must be

confessed that the active signification (preaching) is not suggested by the form of the Greek word ; that, if it exists, it is at least exceptional and that it is not absolutely required in any example we possess. Indeed in the phrase : "They who preach the Gospel should live by the Gospel" (1 Cor. ix, 14), the Gospel is not the preaching but the Gospel preached; otherwise it would be necessary to take the word "Gospel" in two different senses in the same phrase. *Living by the Gospel* (by evangelical institutions), is used as we speak of living by the altar. In the same way "the Gospel of the circumcised and the uncircumcised" (Gal. ii, 7) may very well be the Gospel intended for the Jews or for the Gentiles, and not preaching to the one or the other. If the latter meaning finds support in the context (ii, 8), the former is favoured by the text itself (πεπίστευμαι τὸ εὐαγγέλιον τῆς περιτομῆς ; *cf.* 1 Tim. i, 11; 1 Thess. ii, 4). It is, therefore, better to understand by these expressions "my Gospel, our Gospel" (Rom. ii, 16 ; xvi, 25 ; 2 Cor. iv, 3 ; 2 Thess. ii, 14 ; 2 Tim. ii, 8), the Gospel committed to Paul, rather than the proclamation of the Gospel. This meaning is confirmed by the identification of the Gospel with the mystery (Eph. vi, 19 : τὸ μυστήριον τοῦ εὐαγγελίου) and by texts like Rom. xvi, 25 : κατὰ τὸ εὐαγγέλιόν μου καὶ τὸ κήρυγμα Ἰ. Χριστοῦ, where κήρυγμα is not the preaching of Christ but the message regarding Christ (passive sense) ; and that other text (1 Cor. xv, 1 : τὸ εὐ. ὃ εὐηγγελισάμην ὑμῖν). *Cf.* Gal. i, 11 : τὸ εὐ. τὸ εὐαγγελισθὲν ὑπ᾿ ἐμοῦ ; Gal. ii, 2 : τὸ εὐ. ὃ κηρύσσω.—However, the active sense seems preferable in 1 Thess. i, 5 : *Evangelium nostrum non fuit ad vos in sermone tantum, sed et in virtute, et in Spiritu sancto, et in plenitudine multa, sicut scitis quales fuerimus in vobis propter vos.* It would be appropriate also in Rom. i, 1-9 ; 2 Cor. ii, 12 ; viii, 18 ; x, 14, etc.

### III—THE GOSPEL OF CHRIST

Zahn (*Einleitung in das N.T.*[3], Leipzig, 1907, vol. ii, pp. 169-171), Harnack (*Entstehung der Kirchenverfassung*, etc., 216-217), and Seeberg (*Das Evangelium Christi*, Leipzig, 1905, pp. 45-47) wish to see in this genitive a genitive of the author (the Gospel brought or promulgated by Christ). They advance five arguments in favour of this opinion : (*a*) The analogy of the expression "Gospel of God."—(*b*) The analogy of the expression "my Gospel," where we have equally a subjective genitive.—(*c*) The expression "the Gospel of our Lord and Saviour Jesus" (2 Thess. i, 8), where there cannot be a question of a Gospel having Jesus as object, but certainly of a Gospel preached by Jesus.—(*d*) The analogy of the phrase "the testimony of Christ" (1 Cor. i, 6)—that is to say, the testimony furnished by Christ.—(*e*) The fact that, when he wishes to speak of the Gospel *concerning* Christ, Paul says explicitly: "the Gospel of God . . . *concerning* his Son" (Rom. i, 3).

However, the great majority of exegetes are in favour of the other meaning: the Gospel relating to Christ, having Christ as object.—(*a*) In fact, the Apostle always establishes a close relation between the Gospel of Christ and preaching on the subject of Christ. When he says that he has proclaimed the *Gospel of Christ* as far as Illyria, he adds by way of commentary: "I have desired to preach the Gospel where the name of Christ has never been uttered" (Rom. xv, 20).— (*b*) Instead of the *Gospel of Christ*, he uses also "the Gospel of the glory of Christ" (2 Cor. iv, 4)—that is to say, of Christ glorified; and it is clear that here the meaning is not subjective but objective, as in "the Gospel of our salvation (Eph. i, 13), the Gospel of peace" (Eph. vi, 15).—(*c*) The analogies invoked are precarious and several can be turned the other way: thus the *testimony of Christ* is not the testimony rendered by Christ, but that which is rendered *to* Christ. See Heinrici or Cornely on 1 Cor. i, 6.

It results from all this that there is no serious reason for abandoning the traditional exegesis on this point and that the *Gospel of Christ* in St Paul is not the Gospel brought to mankind by Christ, but the Gospel of which Christ is the object and principal theme.

# NOTE O—PSYCHOLOGICAL LANGUAGE OF ST PAUL

Seven terms are characteristic and frequently used: the *heart* (καρδία), the reason or rather the *mind* (νοῦς), the *conscience* (συνείδησις), the *body* (σῶμα), the *flesh* (σάρξ), the *soul* (ψυχή), and the *spirit* (πνεῦμα). We shall not revert to the first three terms, which are moreover sufficiently clear. The four others are divided into two groups—the body and the flesh, and the soul and the spirit—which constitute the outward and the inward man.

## I—NOTION OF THE WORD "BODY"

1. *Use of the Word.*—In Homer, σῶμα always means a *corpse*; the living body is called δέμας. But the usage of it changed subsequently and σῶμα designated the organism, living or dead, of men and animals. For St Paul the two essential conditions are the diversity of the organs and the unity of the vital principle. In eighty-nine cases the word "body" is used by St Paul as follows: sixty-six times in the sense of a *human body*, living or dead; five times, by extension, it means the *body* of plants and stars, the latter in speaking of the resurrected human body (1 Cor. xv, 37-40); fifteen times it designates figuratively the *mystical body* of Christ; once it means *reality* as contrasted with the shadow (Col. ii, 11). Three cases remain to be considered.

2. *Remarkable Cases.*—(*a*) Rom. vi, 6: "Our old man was crucified with him, that the body of sin might be destroyed." The *body of sin* (τὸ σῶμα τῆς ἁμαρτίας) can hardly be anything but the body in so far as it is under the influence of sin. The body is not itself destroyed by baptism; it is so, however, *as belonging to sin;* it is so in such a way "that we are no longer in the service of sin." Compare the expressions "sinful flesh" (Rom. viii, 3), "the body of death" (Rom. vii, 24), "the body of the flesh" (Col. ii, 11). The old explanation which sees in "the body of sin" the whole sum-total of sin seems to be rejected both by etymology and context.—(*b*) Col. ii, 11: "You are circumcised with a spiritual circumcision [which consists] in the despoiling of the body of the flesh." It is necessary to interpret *the body of the flesh* like the body of sin; it is the carnal body, given over to the instincts of the flesh. One can despoil this body by eliminating the relation which attaches it to the flesh. The same expression, Col. i, 22 (where it is a question of the body of Jesus), has an entirely different meaning; it signifies "the body of the flesh" in its literal meaning.—(*c*) Eph. ii, 16: Christ proposes to reconcile

Jews and Gentiles "in one body." The expression ἐν ἑνὶ σώματι is equivalent in its idea to εἰς ἕνα καινὸν ἄνθρωπον of the preceding verse. It designates, therefore, the *mystical body of Christ* and not his real crucified body, as St Chrysostom and his school, as well as several modern exegetes have thought, basing their opinion on the parallel passage (Col. i, 22 : ἐν τῷ σώματι τῆς σαρκὸς αὐτοῦ).

## II—NOTION OF THE WORD "FLESH"

1. *The Word "Flesh" in its Bad Sense.*—Certain phrases of the Old Testament tended to give to the word "flesh" a derogatory meaning : "All flesh had corrupted its way" (Gen. vi, 12). —"My spirit shall not remain in man for ever because he is flesh" (Gen. vi, 3). The philosophical language of the Stoics had a similar tendency. After Epicurus had made the flesh the seat of pleasure and pain and the source of bliss, the Stoics did their best to depreciate the flesh. The proof of this is found in Seneca, Plutarch, Marcus Aurelius, and especially in Epictetus, who takes pleasure in designating the flesh by a contemptuous diminutive (σαρκίδιον). See Heinrici, *Meyer's Kommentar*[8], on 1 Cor. ii, 16, pp. 112-114. It is very possible that this reaction of Stoicism against the doctrine of Epicurus may have influenced the language of St Paul. On the contrary, the dualism of Plato, even when softened by Philo, has nothing in common with the Pauline conception of the flesh. According to St Paul, the flesh is imperfect if compared to the spirit ; it is weak and impotent in contrast to supernatural blessings ; it is bad as soon as it opposes the action of the Holy Spirit. The bad sense of the word *flesh* originates always from one of these antitheses expressed or implied. An examination of the texts will show this.

2. *The "Flesh" in the Language of Paul.*—The word *flesh* (employed ninety-one times by St Paul) has three principal meanings.

(A) *Flesh is animated matter.*—More exactly it would be the fibrous and muscular part of the body in contrast to the bones (Luke xxiv, 39) and the blood ; but St Paul takes the part for the whole, and, practically, the flesh is for him the body minus the idea of an organism. This shade of meaning does not hinder the general synonymy of the terms, which can be often exchanged without any appreciable difference of meaning : "absent in body (Col. ii, 5), to live, abide, walk in the flesh (Gal. ii, 20; Phil. i, 24 ; 2 Cor. x, 3), our mortal flesh (2 Cor. iv, 11), the likeness of the flesh (Rom. viii, 3), infirmity of the flesh (Gal. iv, 13, 14), the sting of the flesh (2 Cor. xii, 7), tribulation in the flesh (1 Cor. vii, 28 ; *cf.* Col. i, 24 ; 2 Cor. vii, 5), my face in the flesh (Col. ii, 1), the flesh of

Christ (Eph. ii, 14 ; Col. i, 22 ; *cf.* 1 Tim. iii, 16)." Sometimes
biblical usage requires *flesh* instead of body : when it is a
question of circumcision (Rom. ii, 28 : circumcision in the
flesh ; Gal. vi, 12-13 ; Eph. ii, 11 ; Col. ii, 13), and when the
reference is to marriage (1 Cor. vi, 16 ; Eph. v, 31 : *erunt duo
in carne una* [or better *in carnem unam, εἰς σάρκα μίαν*] after
Gen. ii, 24).—The converse of the flesh is not the sensitive
soul (ψυχή)—for this forms part of the notion of flesh—but the
*intellectual soul* (πνεῦμα), 1 Cor. v, 5 : *tradere hujusmodi satanae
in interitum carnis, ut spiritus salvus sit in die Domini.* The
word *flesh* may assume a bad significance from the fact of this
physical opposition.

(B) *The flesh is human nature, with an accessory idea of weakness ; by extension, it means descent or natural kinship.*—Conformably to biblical usage, " all flesh " signifies " every man "
(Rom. iii, 20 ; 1. Cor. i, 29 ; Gal. ii, 16). The additional idea
of weakness is specially rendered by the expression " flesh and
blood " (1 Cor. xv, 50 ; Gal. i, 16 ; Eph. vi, 12). It can also
come from a tacit opposition to something superior to nature :
to glory according to the flesh (2 Cor. xi, 18), not to have
confidence in the flesh (Phil. iii, 3-4), to know no man
according to the flesh (2 Cor. v, 16), wise according to the
flesh (1 Cor. i, 26), lords according to the flesh (Eph. vi, 5 ;
Col. iii, 22), dear in the flesh (Philem. 16).—The same
opposition, expressed or understood, can affect the word *flesh*
in the sense of descent " or natural relationship." Jesus
Christ is descended from David according to the flesh
(Rom. i, 3 ; *cf.* ix, 5) ; Abraham is the ancestor of the Jews
according to the flesh (Rom. iv, 1) ; Paul is their brother
according to the flesh (Rom. ix, 3), and he calls them his
flesh (Rom. xi, 14). But " Israel according to the flesh "
(1 Cor. x, 18) makes a pendant to Israel according to the
spirit, to the " Israel of God " (Gal. vi, 16) ; the "children
of the flesh" are placed in opposition to the children
of God (Rom. ix, 8) ; Isaac and Ishmael are children of
Abraham, one according to the flesh, the other according to
the spirit, because the latter is the son of the miracle and
the son of the promise (Gal. iv, 23-29).

(C) *Finally, the flesh is human nature, as it is in the present
order, vitiated by sin and infected with concupiscence.*—The
bad sense, instead of being simply physical, as in the preceding paragraph, here becomes moral. The flesh is no
longer merely the weak, failing, material, terrestrial, human
part ; it has a relation—either of origin, or tendency, or
affinity—with sin. This meaning, frequent in chapters vii
and viii of the Epistle to the Romans and chapter v of the
Epistle to the Galatians, is also met elsewhere (2 Cor. x, 2 ;
Eph. ii, 3 ; Col. ii, 18, etc.). Then the flesh is often personified ; it has desires, projects, and a will ; it is the

antagonist of the Holy Spirit or of the new spirit which grace creates in us. However, the moral bad sense of the word is sometimes so attenuated that it is almost indistinguishable from the physical sense.

### III—Notion of the Word "Soul"

The soul (anima or animus, cf. ἄνεμος, "wind"; ψυχή from ψύχω, "to breathe"; Hebrew néfésh, "breath," cf. the Assyrian napâshu, "to blow") is properly the vital breath, the sign of life, and, by extension, life itself.—St Paul employs this word only thirteen times, including two quotations (Rom. xi, 3, quoting 1 Kings xix, 10, and 1 Cor. xv, 45, from Gen. ii. 7), and gives it four meanings :

(A) Individual life (distinct from ζωή = life in general).— Rom. xi, 3 (they seek my soul = my life); Rom. xvi, 4 (they have risked their heads for my soul = my life) ; 1 Thess. ii, 8 (we would gladly impart unto you not only the Gospel, but also our own souls) ; Phil. ii, 30 (having hazarded his soul = risking his life).

(B) The subject of life, the person.—Rom. ii, 9 ; xiii. 1 (every soul = every person) ; 1 Cor. xv, 45 (Adam was made into a living soul = an animated being, endowed with life).

(C) The soul itself as distinct from the body.—2 Cor. i, 23 (I call God to witness upon my soul) ; xii, 15 (I most gladly will spend myself for your souls). Here belongs the expression ἐκ ψυχῆς (Eph. vi, 6 ; Col. iii, 23), "from the soul," an expression equivalent to ἐκ καρδίας, ἐκ πνεύματος. And indeed in Phil. i, 27 (στήκετε ἐν ἑνὶ πνεύματι μιᾷ ψυχῇ συναθλοῦντες τῇ πίστει) the expression μιᾷ ψυχῇ is almost equivalent to ἑνὶ πνεύματι.

(D) The soul as the principle of the sentient life.—1 Thess. v, 23 (τὸ πνεῦμα καὶ ἡ ψυχὴ καὶ τὸ σῶμα). In this sense the soul is distinguished from the spirit, as the vital principle is distinguished from the reason, although both proceed from one substance.

The adjective ψυχικός possesses an ethical meaning which it is very important to observe. It is in implicit opposition to πνευματικός. Now the latter indicates a relation to the Spirit of God, source of the supernatural; and this is what ψυχικός excludes, or rather does not include. The man who is ψυχικός is one who has only the natural life, without being quickened by the Holy Spirit. He is very well defined by St Jude 19 : ψυχικοὶ πνεῦμα μὴ ἔχοντες. But the man deprived of the Spirit of God is in reality carnal, and therefore ψυχικός and σαρκικός come to be almost synonymous (1 Cor. ii, 14 : Animalis [ψυχικός] homo non percipit ea quae sunt Spiritus Dei ; James iii, 15 : sapientia . . . terrena, animalis [ψυχική], *diabolica*). Nevertheless, this bad sense is less pronounced in 1 Cor. xv, 44, 46, where ψυχικός and πνευματικός mark above all a gradation.

## IV—Notion of the Word "Spirit"

1. Perhaps no word causes so much perplexity to exegetes of the New Testament as this. Out of 145 cases where it is employed by St Paul, the *precise* sense of half of them remains more or less doubtful and disputable. Let us hasten to add, however, that these shades of meaning but rarely affect the general meaning of the phrase; nevertheless, they have a great interest for the commentator anxious to grasp as nearly as possible the thought of his text.—In the proper sense of the word πνεῦμα signifies "the wind, the air in motion," and by derivation "breath, the air expelled from the lungs." But we can pass over these two meanings, the first of which is not met with in St Paul, while the second appears in his writings only once (2 Thess. ii, 8: *ille iniquus, quem Dominus Jesus interficiet* spiritu *oris sui*), and that taken tacitly from Isaias (xi, 4).—Another very common meaning in the Bible and profane writers, that of an "intelligent and immaterial substance, angel or demon," is also probably wanting in St Paul, for the two alleged examples (Eph. ii, 2 and 1 Tim. iv, 1), understood by many interpreters to be personal beings, may very well bear an impersonal sense.

2. The different meanings of the word "spirit" can be reduced to three: the thinking principle in man, the activity of the Holy Spirit, the Person of the Holy Spirit.

(A) *The spirit as the thinking principle in man.*—The classical example of this meaning is 1 Cor. ii, 11, where the spirit denotes the psychological consciousness of man: *Quis enim hominum scit quae sunt hominis, nisi* spiritus *hominis qui in ipso est?* Similarly 1 Cor. vii, 34; 1 Thess. v, 23; *cf.* 2 Cor. ii, 13; vii. 13.—A kindred meaning is that of "thought" in the antithesis: absent in body, present in spirit (1 Cor. v, 3, etc.).—Finally, the spirit often denotes "the manner of thinking or conceiving, sentiment, mentality." Frequent in the Old Testament (Num. v, 14, 30: spirit of jealousy; Is. lxi, 3: spirit of dejection; Hosea iv, 12: spirit of fornication), it is also not rare in St Paul: spirit of stupefaction (Rom. xi, 8, from Is. xxix, 10), spirit of the world (1 Cor. ii, 12), spirit of fear (2 Tim. i, 7). This is not the place to examine whether the conception of a spiritual being, good or bad, exercising his influence in man, is not at the origin of this expression. In Eph. ii, 2 (spiritus *qui nunc operatur in filios diffidentiae*) we hesitate between the two meanings of an impersonal influence and of a personal being.

(B) *The activity of the Holy Spirit in man, or man under the influence of the Holy Spirit.* When St Paul says to the Corinthians : *Quoniam aemulatores estis* spirituum (1 Cor. xiv, 12 : ἐπεὶ ζηλωταί ἐστε πνευμάτων), he evidently means the *charismata*, which he also calls "spiritual gifts" (xiv, 1 : ζηλοῦτε τὰ πνευματικά). These *spirits*, he adds, are subject to the prophets (xiv, 32 : spiritus *prophetarum prophetis subjecti sunt*), because the possessors of the *charismata* have the free use of them. It is thus also that the following passage is explained (1 Cor. xiv, 14, 16) : *Nam si orem lingua*, spiritus (πνεῦμα) *meus orat, mens* (νοῦς) *autem mea sine fructu est. Quid ergo est? Orabo* spiritu, *orabo et mente; psallam* spiritu, *psallam et mente. Ceterum si benedixeris* spiritu, *qui supplet locum idiotae, quomodo dicet, Amen, super tuam benedictionem? quoniam quid dicas, nescit.* It is a question here of the *charisma* of the *gift of tongues*, permitting a neophyte to pray in a language not understood by himself or his hearers. His *spirit* (that is, he himself under the influence of the Holy Spirit) prayed and blessed God ; but his intellect was inactive, and the ordinary hearer (*idiota* = the simple Christian, un-endowed with the *charisma* of interpretation) could not join in his prayer and thanksgivings by saying *amen* as usual.— Besides the numerous cases where *spirit* signifies the charis-matical manifestation of the Holy Spirit (1 Thess. v, 19; 2 Thess. ii, 2), *spirit* has the same meanings as in the pre-ceding paragraph with the addition of the supernatural element. Thus in the final salutation of the Epistles the Apostle says indiscriminately : *Grace be with you* (Rom. xvi, 24; 1 Cor. xvi, 23 ; 2 Cor. xiii, 13; Eph. vi, 14; Col. iv, 18, etc.), or *with your spirit* (Gal. vi, 18; Phil. iv, 23 ; 2 Tim. iv, 22 ; Philem. 25). The expression "spirit of strength, charity, and temperance" is modelled on "spirit of fear" (2 Tim. i, 7); "the spirit of sonship" on "the spirit of servitude" (Rom. viii, 15) ; so, too, the "spirit of faith" (2 Cor. iv, 13), "the spirit of meekness" (Gal. vi, 1). The question is to know whether, in such usual expressions, the relation to the Holy Spirit is always distinctly perceptible.

(C) *The Person of the Holy Spirit.*—In a general way it can be stated as a principle that the *Spirit of God*, the *Spirit of Christ*, and the *Holy Spirit* all designate the actual Person of the Holy Spirit and not his action in us. Yet the rule requires caution in use (Acts vi, 5; x, 38; xi, 24; xiii, 52), even in the case of St Paul (2 Cor. vi, 6 : *in suavitate, in Spiritu sancto, in charitate non ficta* [a long list of works and virtues, amidst which appears the Holy Spirit]). In any case, the surest rule is to examine whether any personal functions are attributed to the Spirit, or whether he is placed in opposition to the other two Persons.

3. All exegetes are agreed in declaring that the distinction is a very delicate one. This will be appreciated if Rom. viii, 2-16 be examined. Out of seventeen cases where the word *spirit* appears, the present Vulgate writes *Spiritus* with a capital letter only four times (apart from the requirements of punctuation)—that is to say, when the Spirit is in opposition to the Son or to the Father, or forms an antithesis to our *spirit*, our supernaturalized intellect. It writes *spiritus Dei*, doubtless taking *Dei* in the sense of *God without distinction of Persons* and correcting the Sixtine MS., which had adopted the reading *Spiritus Dei*. Cornely finds the Holy Spirit in the majority of cases (eleven times out of seventeen).

Another very instructive example is Gal. v, 16-25. Here, out of seven cases, the Vulgate only once regards *Spiritus* as a proper name; for the initial capital letter is due to the punctuation, as the context proves. Cornely, who is not very consistent with himself, puts small letters everywhere. On the contrary, Lightfoot (*Galatians*, 1892, p. 210) thinks that "in this whole passage the πνεῦμα is clearly the divine Spirit; for the human spirit, left to itself, is not the enemy of the flesh." No doubt; but the essential point is to know whether it is a question here of the Person of the Holy Spirit or of his action in us, of the sanctifying and quickening Spirit or of the sanctified and quickened soul.

# NOTE P—ANGELS AND DEMONS

## I—Jewish Ideas of the World of Spirits

*The Sources.*—On seeing the immense rôle which supernatural beings play in the literature and religion of the
Semitic peoples, we are struck by the small amount of space
they occupy in the Old Testament, without even excepting
the deuterocanonical books. Oesterley has indeed tried to
prove that this contrast is only apparent, and that there is in
the Bible a multitude of latent allusions to spirits and demons
(*The Demonology of the O.T.* in the *Expositor*, seventh series,
vol. iii, 1907, pp. 316-332, 527-544), but he has not succeeded
in making his thesis probable. What a difference between
the Bible and the Apocrypha : the *Book of Enoch*, the *Testaments of the Twelve Patriarchs,* the *Book of the Jubilees,* and the
*Life of Adam !* Here, a mad phantasmagoria peoples heaven
and earth with supernatural beings, bearing fantastic names
and having strange forms, who seem by themselves alone to
fill the terrestrial stage. In the rabbinical theology it is still
worse, except in the Mishna, where these speculations have
little chance to display themselves. Whoever is interested in
these extravagant dreams of disordered brains can consult
one of the numerous authors who treat of the subject ; he
will be embarrassed to know what to choose out of the mass.
Let us cite only : Kohut, *Die jüdische Angelologie und Dämonologie*, Leipzig, 1866 ; Eisenmenger, *Das entdeckte Judentum,*
Königsberg, 1711 (very curious details of the origin, habitat,
functions, and daily occupations of the demons) ; Weber,
*Jüdische Theologie auf Grund des Talmud und verwandter
Schriften*[2], Leipzig, 1897 ; Schwab, *Vocabulaire de l'angélologie
d'après les manuscrits hébreux de la Biblioth. nat.*, Paris, 1897,
and *Supplément au Vocab. de l'angél.*, 1899 ; Edersheim, *Life
and Times of Jesus*, London, 1901 (Appendix xiii : *Jewish
Angelology and Demonology*, vol. ii, pp. 748-763) ; Bousset,
*Die Religion des Judentums im neutest. Zeitalter*[2], Berlin, 1906 ;
L. Hackspill, *L'angélologie juive à l'époque néo-testamentaire* in
*Rev. Bibl.*, xi, 1902, pp. 527-550 ; J. B. Frey, *L'angélologie
juive au temps de J.C.* in *Rev. des sciences phil. et théol.*, v, 1911,
pp. 75-110 ; articles on *Angelology* and *Demonology* in the
*Jewish Encyclopedia*, vols. i and iv ; articles on *Angel, Demon,
Devil* in the *Diction. of the Bible* and the *Diction. of the Apost.
Church*, by Hastings.

## II—Distinction between Angels and Demons

1. *Gradual distinction of good and bad Angels.*—In profane
literature the word ἄγγελος (masculine or feminine) signifies
always a messenger or envoy (it is the special title of Iris,

*messenger* of the gods) ; it never has the sense which we give to the word *angel*.—In Homer, δαίμων and θεός are almost synonymous. However, a notable difference appears in the adjective δαιμόνιος, which is no more the equivalent of θεῖος. Δαίμων signifies the divine influence rather than the divine person, and it is generally an ill-omened influence. For Hesiod the δαίμονες were demigods, descendants of the race created by the gods of Olympus in the golden age. Later, among the writers of tragedies, the δαίμων was destiny, but rather a fatal one. Nevertheless the bad meaning did not become general and, during the most brilliant period of Greek literature, δαίμων was used in a good as well as in a bad sense.—The accusation against Socrates was that of importing strange gods into Athens (Xenophon, *Memorab.*, i, 1, 1 : καινὰ δαιμόνια εἰσφέρειν; cf. Plato, *Apol.*, 26B). It is curious to see the Athenians imputing the same designs to Paul (Acts xvii, 18 : ξένων δαιμονίων καταγγελεύς).—On the contrary, although in the Septuagint, and even in the New Testament, the word ἄγγελος is sometimes taken in the common meaning of messenger, it denotes almost always a celestial spirit acting as an intermediary between God and men. On the other hand, the neuter adjective taken as a noun, δαιμόνιον has always an unfavourable sense, if Acts xvii, 18 be excepted, where St Luke makes the pagans speak their ordinary language. The word δαίμων is not used in the Bible, except in Mark viii, 31.

On this point we know that Philo abandons biblical and Jewish tradition, in order to accommodate himself as much as possible to the language and ideas of the Greek philosophers.

2. *According to the Talmud and the Bible, too, angels and demons are good creatures, as originally made by God; and demons are only fallen angels.*—The Jews never cast a doubt upon this truth, so thoroughly did the dogma of one only God, Creator of all things, profoundly rooted in their minds, make them immune from the assaults of Greek or Persian dualism. They merely discussed the date of the creation of the angels, fixed by some on the second day and by others on the fifth, but all agreed in saying (according to Job xxv, 3 ; Dan. vii, 10) that their number rose to millions and thousands of millions.

What was the origin of the bad angels ? In the *Life of Adam and Eve*, 12-16 (Kautsch, *Pseudepigr.*, pp. 513-514), Satan relates how, when God had formed man in his image and likeness, Michael invited all the angels to come and adore the image of God; but Satan and his companions refused under the pretext that man was inferior to them ; that is why they were banished from heaven and driven down to earth. The *Book* (in the Slavonic language) *of the Secrets of Enoch* (xxix, 4-5, rec. A; cf. xxxi, 36) gives a

picturesque description of this fall. Another version, reconcilable moreover with the first, although admittedly the story
of another fall of angels, was well accredited in the early
Church, thanks to the *Book of Enoch* (vi-xi) : Two hundred
angels, commanded by Semyaza, fell in love with the beauty
of the daughters of men and wedded them. For having
taught men magic, astrology, and other fatal sciences, they
were placed in chains by the four archangels and await the
day of judgement in a dark dungeon, which does not, however, prevent them from pursuing their evil deeds (xix).
Their descendants, as wicked as they are, complete their
work.—Fanciful speculations about the origin of the demons
are infinite. R. Bechai claimed that Satan had been created
at the same time as Eve, and he advanced for this the
singular proof that the letter *samech*, by which the name of
Satan was sometimes written in Hebrew, does not appear
before Gen. ii, 21, where the formation of woman is related.
Others think that the demons were created on the sixth day,
at the moment when the Sabbath was about to begin, so that
God had not the time to give them a body. Some say that,
for 130 years after his transgression, Adam abstained from all
conjugal connection with Eve in order not to condemn his
children to the curse. But, while he was asleep, the female
demon *Lilith* had connection with him, while a male demon
took advantage of Eve without her knowing it. From the
fact that Adam, at the age of 130 years, " begat a being in his
own likeness " (Gen. v, 3), it was concluded that he had, up
to that time, begotten beings of a different nature. In Weber
(*Jüdische Theol.*[2], pp. 253-254) and in Eisenmenger (*Entdecktes
Judentum*, vol. ii, chap. viii, pp. 406-415) many similar
stories are found.

3. *In the Bible, the Apocrypha, and the Talmud, the demons, by
whatever name they are called and whatever may be their origin,
are always represented as perverse and maleficent beings, as the
enemies of God, the adversaries of man, and the instigators of sin.
—Neither the Bible, nor the Apocrypha, nor the Talmud recognize
a class of spiritual beings, intermediary between the angels and
demons, and who are to be classed neither with the demons,
the subjects of Satan, nor with the angels, the servants of God.*—
These two propositions, of indisputable truth and extreme
importance, proceed from the fact that the demons, always at
war with man, God and the good angels, are designated by
names which put them in relation with evil or with sin. The
word " demons " always has an unfavourable meaning in the
Bible. Indeed, δαιμόνια, in the Septuagint, is the translation of
the various appellations of the false gods, שדים, שעירים, אלילים,
etc., and an idea of impiety and perversity is necessarily
connected with it. Each time that the demons are given a

favourable or neutral name, an epithet or definitive term fore-stalls misunderstanding. Jewish theology—and the New Testament—give the demons very characteristic names, which do not allow us to confound them with the good angels or to rank them in a special category, between good and evil. It calls them מַזִּיקִין (malefactors), רוּחִין בִּשִׁין (wicked spirits), רוּחִין טוּמְאַה (impure spirits).

### III—HIERARCHY OF ANGELS AND DEMONS

The angels of the Old Testament are hardly distinguishable from one another. Their whole reason for existing is to deliver messages or to execute a divine command. Thus the person disappears behind the function. Yet the fact that they are sometimes represented as an army proves that a certain hierarchy was established among them ; for there is no organized army without a recognized authority. Three of these chiefs are named in the most recent books : Michael, "the prince of Israel" (Dan. x, 21) or "the great prince" (Dan. xii, 1) ; Gabriel, who explains to Daniel the prophecy of Jeremias concerning the seventy weeks (Dan. viii, 15, 16) ; Raphael, "one of the seven angels who stand before the throne of God to offer to him the prayers of the saints" (Tob. xii, 12-15 ; Apoc. i, 4). *Cf.* Lebreton, *Origins du dogme de la Trinité*[4], 1919, *Note H, On the seven spirits who are before the throne of God.*

In the period of Judaism, the group of the archangels was the most celebrated. It included sometimes *seven* names, arranged thus in the *Book of Enoch*, xx: Uriel, Raphael, Raguel, Michael, Sariel, Gabriel, Remiel ; sometimes *six*—for example, in the targum of Jonathan on Deut. xxxiv, 6; at other times only *four* (*Enoch*, ix, 1 : Michael, Uriel, Gabriel, Raphael), enumerated without any fixed order (*cf. Enoch*, x, 1, 4, 9, 11 ; xl, 2, 9; liv, 8, 9, 12) ; sometimes *five* with different names (*Orac. Sibyll.*, ii, 214-215). Another group of celestial spirits, often referred to, were the *Seraphim*, the *Cherubim*, and the *Ophanim*, "who never sleep and who guard the throne of the divine majesty" (*Enoch*, lxxi, 7).

The military organization of the demons is much more complete than that of the good angels. The *Book of Enoch* mentions, besides the commander-in-chief of the two hundred fallen angels, their twenty decurions (vi, 7, 8) ; elsewhere centurions are spoken of, and chiefs of fifty and decurions (lxix, 3). But usually the organization is not carried so far ; only one supreme chief is named, to whom the crowd of subjects yields obedience. This chief is called by different appellations which can be changed with one another.— (a) *Satan, or the devil.* Satan is a Hebrew word, which signi-fies "adversary" or "accuser" (an adverse party in a court of justice) and has passed into Arabic (*shaytân*) and into Syriac (*satana*) with the Hebrew meaning. Akin to it is the Assyrian *mushtatinu* (hostile) and probably also the Ethiopian *Mastêma*, which designates the chief of the demons. In Hebrew Satan is an appellative noun and takes the definite article (*the* Adversary *par excellence*), except in 1 Chron. xxi, 1 where, becoming a proper noun, it omits the article. The Septuagint translated it by διάβολος, out of which the Arabs have made *Iblis:* the Greek equivalent κατήγορος, under the form of קטיגור, is found among the Rabbis and in the Apocalypse (xii, 10 : ὁ κατήγωρ). The authors of the N.T. use indifferently ὁ σατανᾶς and ὁ διάβολος, and the Apocalypse formally establishes the synonymy between the two terms (xx, 2 : ὁ ὄφις ὁ ἀρχαῖος, ὅς ἐστιν Διάβολος καὶ ὁ Σατανᾶς).— (b) *Belial.* This word in Hebrew is not a proper name ; it signifies etymologically—although the etymology is disputed —" profitless, useless," and by litotes "bad, pernicious." Belial appears more than thirty times in the *Testaments of the Patriarchs* under the form of Beliar, also found in St Paul (2 Cor. vi, 15). The identity between Satan and Belial appears, for example, in the *Ascension of Isaias* (ii, 1-4), where the expressions "to serve Satan" and "to serve Belial" are synonymous.—(c) Sammael, in the same place in the *Ascension of Isaias,* is another synonym of Satan. He is often mentioned in the Talmud, where he is called the "chief of the satans" (*Debarim rabba,* c. 11).—(d) *Asmodeus* is called "king of the demons" in the Hebrew and Aramaic versions of the Book of Tobias (iii. 8-17), he is presented as "chief of the demons" in the Talmud (*Sofa,* 48, a-b), and in the Targum of Ecclesiastes (i, 12). It was once generally admitted that Asmodeus is derived from the Persian *aêshma daeva,* but Moulton (*Expository Times,* vol. xi, 1900, pp. 257-260) contests this derivation.— (e) Belzebuth (*Ba' al-zebûb* = "the god of [*i.e.*, who keeps off] flies" of Accaron) is, under the form of Βεεζεβούλ or Βεελζεβούλ, named by the Synoptists "prince of demons" (Matt. xii, 24 ; Luke xi, 15 : ὁ ἄρχων τῶν δαιμονίων), and is consequently identified with Satan. It results clearly from the context that the word is borrowed from the terminology of the Jews.

The synonymy of all these words (the devil, Satan, Belial, Asmodeus, Sammael, Belzebuth) is certain : each of these persons is represented as the supreme chief of all the demons and as the leader of all the legions hostile to God. What is attributed to one of them, is in the same work or in different works attributed to the other.—They are never opposed to one another ; and, when they are named together, they fill the same rôle. Finally, the synonymy is positively stated in a certain number of texts.—But it is especially important to note that all these names are used in two very different meanings : as individual beings guiding the army of demons,

and as collective beings representing all the powers hostile to
God and personifying the evil principle.

## IV—The Demons in the Theology of St Paul

St Paul's doctrine of demons has nothing characteristic
about it. It can hardly be called a doctrine, as the Apostle
for the most part uses current speech without making it a
subject of formal affirmation. We shall limit ourselves to
three remarks which give rise to interesting comparisons.

1. *Demons and Sin.*—Satan was a "murderer from the
beginning" (John viii, 44) because of his active part in man's
first sin. All the sacred authors have in mind the story of
Genesis (iii, 1-13), according to which "the Serpent seduced
Eve by his subtlety" (2 Cor. xi, 3), and they know that in consequence of sin "death entered into the world through the
envy of the devil" (Wisd. ii, 24). But the great seducer
pursues his work of death. He is the Tempter *par excellence*
(1 Thess. iii, 5: ὁ πειράζων; *cf.* 1 Cor. vii, 5). There is no
snare that he does not set for the faithful (2 Cor. ii, 11;
1 Tim. iii, 7; 2 Tim. ii, 16), nor difficulty that he does not
raise for the preachers of the Gospel (2 Cor. ii, 11; 1 Thess.
ii, 18); but a sincere faith protects us from his darts
(Eph. vi, 16), and God will never permit a temptation beyond
our strength (1 Cor. x, 13: *cf.* Rom. xvi, 20).

These same ideas are met at every step in Jewish theology.
According to the Apocrypha and the Talmud, Satan made use
of the serpent to ruin the first human pair. Since then he
stirs up the tendency to evil (יצר הרע) with which he seems
sometimes to be confused. *Cf.* Weber, *Jüd. Theol.*[2], pp. 237
and 252. Before man had lost the image of God, he was a
sacred being (קדיש); but subsequently he became unholy (חל)
and subject to maleficent spirits (*Bereshith rabba*, c. 23). The
Ethiopian *Enoch* (lxix, 6) thinks that he knows the name of the
seducer of Eve; he is called, he says, Gadreel.

2. *Abode of the Demons.*—The demons like to dwell (*a*) in the
*atmosphere* (Eph. ii, 2: ἄρχων τῆς ἐξουσίας τοῦ ἀέρος), in the lower
heavens bordering on the earth (Eph. vi, 12: πρὸς τὰ πνευματικὰ
τῆς πονηρίας ἐν τοῖς ἐπουρανίοις);—(*b*) in *desert places* (Matt. xii, 43;
Luke xi, 24: δι' ἀνύδρων τόπων; *cf.* Is. xiii, 21; xxxiv, 14, and
the ceremony of the scape-goat sent to Azazel in the desert);
—(*c*) near *tombs* (Mark v, 2; Matt. viii, 28; Luke viii, 27);—
(*d*) in general in *dark and filthy places* (Mark v, 12; Matt. viii, 31;
Luke vii, 33 [the swine of Gadara]; Eph. vi, 12: πρὸς τοὺς
κοσμοκράτορας τοῦ σκότους τούτου, but this is perhaps a figurative
expression; *cf.* Col. i, 13: τῆς ἐξουσίας τοῦ σκότους).

That the demons inhabit the air is an opinion quite common
in Jewish literature. According to Philo, the air (that is to

say, the space included between the earth and the moon)
" is the abode of disembodied souls" (*De somniis*, i, 22,
Mangey, i, 641) ; it is thus that he calls the δαίμονες, who are
his angels and demons. For "those whom the philosophers
call δαίμονες, Moses was accustomed to call angels, and
these are the souls which fly in the air " (*De gigant.*, 2 ;
Mangey, i, 263 : ψυχαὶ δέ εἰσι κατὰ τὸν ἀέρα πετόμεναι). See
Lemonnyer, *L'air comme séjour d'anges d'après Philon*, in
*Revue des sciences phil. et théol.*, 1907, pp. 305-311.—According
to R. Bechai (*Explic. du Pentat.*, fol. 90, col. 1), the demons are
divided into three classes : some reside in the air, and it is they
who send us dreams ; others dwell in man to incite him to
sin ; and others are immersed in the depths of the sea, where
they create earthquakes.

3. *Demons and Idols.*—The Old Testament identifies the
gods of the pagans with demons, Ps. xcv, 5 : πάντες οἱ θεοὶ
τῶν ἐθνῶν δαιμόνια, and Deut. xxxii, 17 : ἔθυσαν δαιμονίοις καὶ οὐ
θεῷ (they offered sacrifices to demons and to a *non-god* = someone who was not God). St Paul tacitly refers to this last
text in his teaching concerning the meats offered to idols,
1 Cor. x, 20 : ἃ θύουσιν δαιμονίοις καὶ οὐ θεῷ θύουσιν. This brings
the application : *Nolo vos fieri socios daemoniorum*. The idea
was common in Judaism. *Cf. Enoch*, xcix, 7 (quoted by
Tertullian, *De idol.*, 4) ; *Jubil.*, i, 11 ; xxii, 17. It is certain that
the demons are the instigators of idolatry and that the worship
paid to idols is advantageous to them, whatever may be the
intention of the idolaters themselves.

V—The Choirs of Angels according to St Paul

The list of nine choirs of angels has been made, as everyone
knows, by taking as a central nucleus the five names furnished
by St Paul (Eph. i, 21 ; Col. i, 16: principalities, powers,
virtues, dominations and thrones), then by putting at the head
of these the seraphim and cherubim of the Old Testament, and
at the end the archangels and angels mentioned here and there
in the Bible. It is difficult to understand what principle could
have directed the classification of the intermediary choirs,
since St Paul has no fixed order. The Pseudo-Dionysius the
Areopagite divides them into three classes (διακοσμήσεις), and
describes them in this order, beginning with the most perfect
(*De cael. hierarchia*, vi-ix, Migne, III, 200-272). The enumeration of the beginning differs a little.

    (I) 1 Seraphim. 2 Cherubim. 3 Thrones.
    (II) 4 Dominations. 5 Virtues. 6 Powers.
    (III) 7 Principalities. 8 Archangels. 9 Angels.

*The order* is different in St Gregory the Great (*Moralia*,
xxxii, 23, No. 48, LXXVI, 665 : angels, archangels, thrones,

denominations, virtues, principalities, cherubim and seraphim, and *In Evang. homil.* xxxiv, *ibid.* 1249 : angels, archangels, virtues, powers, principalities, dominations, thrones,
cherubim and seraphim). St Gregory depends upon the
Pseudo-Dionysius ; but we cannot say, as has sometimes been
done, that the division of the angels in nine choirs is an
invention of the latter, for it is found already in St Ambrose
(*Apol. Proph. David* 5, XIV, 900) : *Dominus noster Jesus . . . cui
angeli et archangeli, virtutes et potestates et principatus, throni et
dominationes, cherubim et seraphim indefesso obsequio serviebaut.*
The tract is authentic and dates from about 385 ; the text is
that of the critical edition of Schenkl. As it is not probable
that Dionysius borrows from Ambrose, both have probably
borrowed from some previous Greek source, and in fact the
Pseudo-Dionysius refers to an anonymous authority (iii, 200) :
πάσας ἡ θεολογία τὰς οὐρανίους οὐσίας ἐννέα κέκληκεν ἐκφαντορικαῖς
ἐπωνυμίαις· ταύτας ὁ θεῖος ἡμῶν ἱεροτελεστὴς εἰς τρεῖς ἀφορίζει
τριαδικὰς διακοσμήσεις.

Apart from these two exceptions—three counting St
Gregory—the theory of the nine orders is entirely unknown to
the Greek and Latin Fathers. The interpolator of Ignatius,
*Ad Trallian.*, 5 (Funk, vol. ii, p. 64) counts *nine* classes of
angels, but he includes in them the *æons* and the *armies*.
St Irenaeus, *Contra haeres.*, ii, 54 (VII, 818), enumerates once
*seven* (omitting the cherubim and the seraphim), and once
*six* (omitting also the thrones). The *Apostolic Constitutions*
have once *ten*, viii, 12 (I, 1093 : here are also the æons and
the armies, but without the dominations), and once *eleven*
(I, 1101 : the dominations included). Origen has sometimes
*four* of them, *Contra Cels.*, iv, 29 (XI, 1069 : thrones, dominations, powers and principalities), sometimes *five*, adding either
angels, *Contra Cels.*, vi, 71 (XI, 1405), or the gods, *In Joan.*,
i, 34 (XIV, 79). St. Cyril of Jerusalem enumerates *eight*,
omitting only the seraphim, *Catech.*, xxiii, *Mystag.*, v, 6 (XXXIII,
1113) ; but see below. St Athanasius, *ad Serap.*, ii, 4 (XXVI,
614), enumerates *nine*, substituting for thrones παράδεισος, but
the text is very uncertain ; elsewhere, *ad Serap.*, i, 13 (XXVI,
561), he has only *seven*, omitting the virtues and the powers.
There are *seven* also in Titus of Bostra, *Contra Manich.*, iii, and
*eight* in Basil of Seleucia, *Orat.*, xxxix, 2 (LXXXV, 429 : the
archangels are wanting). St Basil the Great, *De spiritu sancto*,
38 (XXXII, 136), enumerates only *five* (principalities, powers,
virtues, thrones, dominations), but he adds: καὶ εἴ τινές εἰσιν
ἕτεραι λογικαὶ θύσεις ἀκατονόμαστοι. St Gregory Nazianzen, *Orat.*,
xxviii, 31 (XXXVI, 72), finds *eight*, replacing the cherubim
and seraphim by their Greek translation ἀναβάσεις, λαμπρότητες
and qualifying all the orders enumerated as νοερὰς δυνάμεις
ἢ νόας, which proves that he does not see a special order in
the virtues. St Gregory of Nyssa, *Contra Eunom.*, i (XLV, 345,

348), expressly identifies the cherubim with the thrones, the
seraphim with the virtues, and mentions neither the angels
nor the archangels; elsewhere, *In Cantic. hom.*, xv (XLIV,
1100) his enumeration is still more difficult. The author of
the *Dialogues* attributed to St Cesarius, *Dial.*, i, qu. xliv
(XXXVIII, 912-913), reduces the number of choirs to *seven*,
eliminating also the cherubim and seraphim. It is idle to
push our investigations further; we should not get much from
St Methodius, *De resurr.*, 10 (XVIII, 280), nor from Eusebius,
*De laud. Constant.*, i, 1 (XX. 1320); we should rather get only
difficulties from them. But St Ephrem (*Opera syriaca*, vol. i,
p. 270) furnishes us with *ten* choirs, the first of which is
formed of the *gods;* Theodoret *eight*, by regarding the
virtues as a generic term, or by identifying thrones and
cherubim.

The Fathers who carry with them most authority warn us
that our researches will be endless. We have heard what St
Basil says. St Hilary, *In Psalm*, cxxxv. 10 (IX, 773-774), is
no more encouraging: *De numero Apostolus nihil docuit; et
nescio an tacuerit an ignoraverit.* From Origen we get scarcely
any hope, *De Princip.*, I, v, 1 (XI, 157) on Eph. i, 21: *Ex quo
ostendit esse quaedam praeter haec quae commemoravit, quae
nominentur quidam in hoc saeculo, non tamen ab ipso enumerata
nunc fuerint, forte nec ab alio aliquo intellecta: esse vero alia
quae in hoc saeculo quidam non nominentur, in futuro tamen
nominabuntur.* St Jerome, commenting on the same text
(XXVI, 461), seizes on this idea; especially *Contra Jovin.*, ii, 28
(XXIII, 325): *Et cetera ministeriorum vocabula, quae nec nos
possumus nominare, nec ipsum Paulum puto, ut in gravi
corpusculo constitutum, enumerare valuisse.* The text of St
Augustine is well known, *Contra Priscill.*, ii (XLII, 678): *Certe
ait Apostolus:* Sive sedes (θρόνοι), sive dominationes, sive
principatus, sive potestates. *Et esse itaque sedes, dominationes,
principatus, potestates, in caelestibus apparatibus firmissime
credo, et differre aliquid indubitata fide teneo. Sed quo me con-
temnas, quem magnum putas esse doctorem, quaenam ista sint et
quid inter se differant nescio. Cf. Enchirid.*, 58 (XL, 259); *In
Psalm.*, lxxix, 2 (XXXVI, 1021); *In Psalm.*, xcviii, 3 (XXXVII,
1259); *Coll. cum Maxim.*, 9 (XLII, 727), etc.—St Chrysostom,
who once enumerates nine orders (*In Genes. hom.*, iv, 5), likewise believes that there are others, *De incomprehens. hom.*, iv
(XLIX, 729): Εἰσὶ γὰρ εἰσὶ καὶ ἕτεραι δυνάμεις ὧν οὐδὲ τὰ ὀνόματα
ἴσμεν. Finally, St Cyril of Jerusalem, *Catech.*, xv, 12 (XXXIII,
705), makes a virulent attack on the heretics who flatter
themselves that they know all the mysteries of Christ, yet are
powerless to say in what respect the angels differ.

In the face of these disagreements and uncertainties of
Catholic tradition, all speculation on the subject would be
in vain.

# NOTE Q—THE ELEMENTS OF THE WORLD

In this volume we have studied at sufficient length the two texts giving four times the remarkable expression τὰ στοιχεῖα τοῦ κόσμου, *elementa mundi* (Gal. iv, 3, 9 ; Col. ii, 8, 20). As there is less agreement than ever as to the precise meaning of this utterance, it is well to submit it to an exact analysis, examining : (1) The meaning of the word στοιχεῖον ; (2) the meaning of the word κόσμος in St Paul ; (3) the sense of the entire phrase.

## I—THE SIGNIFICANT EVOLUTION OF THE WORD στοιχεῖον

1. The word στοιχεῖον—from στοῖχος, *rank, file*, from στείχω, *to align, to march in order*—denotes things arranged, placed in ranks. Aristophanes calls the shaft of a gnomon or sundial by this word (*Ecclesiaz*, 65 : ὅταν ᾖ δεκάπουν τὸ στοιχεῖον, "when the gnomon [*i.e*, the shadow of it] is ten feet long "). The στοιχεῖον sometimes signifies a *column*, a *shaft*, a *statue*, but the original meaning seems to be a *base*. Thence, in a parallel manner two meanings were derived from a usage common in the classic age : the στοιχεῖα were the letters of the alphabet, not so much as signs as sounds, not so much as forms of writing as *elements* of speech (Dionysius of Halic., *De comp. verb.*, 14) ; and they designated also the *elements* of which the material world is composed (fire, air, water, and earth). Empedocles, who had fixed the number of these at four, called them ῥιζώματα, but Plato, as Eudemus assures us, designated them by the name of στοιχεῖα (*Sophist.*, 252B ; *Tim.*, 48B), because the word ῥιζώματα was unknown in Attic speech. This name of στοιχεῖα, to denote the *elements of matter*, was adopted by the philosophers of the Lyceum and the Portico ; only Aristotle added a fifth element—the ether. Later, the Epicureans called the atoms στοιχεῖα ; Lucretius translated this by *elementa*.

2. The alphabetical meaning gave rise to a metaphorical signification, by virtue of which the *elements* (στοιχεῖα) became the rudiments, the first principles and, so to speak, the alphabet, the *a b c* of a science or art. This signification, which goes back at least to Isocrates, and was made popular by the *Elements* of Euclid, was very common in New Testament times, when στοιχειοῦν was used to denote " teaching the rudiments," and στοιχείωσις for " instruction, education." See the examples in Passow. Everyone knows that *elementa* in Latin possessed the same figurative meaning (Horace, *Sat.* I, i, 20), which we shall also find in the Epistle to the Hebrews (v, 12 : πάλιν χρείαν ἔχετε τοῦ διδάσκειν ὑμᾶς τινα τὰ στοιχεῖα τῆς

ἀρχῆς τῶν λογίων τοῦ Θεοῦ). So far we are completely on classic ground.

3. Under the influence of astrology a new meaning was subsequently given a place of great honour in the schools of both the Stoics and the Pythagoreans. It became the custom to designate the seven planets by the seven vowels of the Greek alphabet and to call them "the celestial elements" (τὰ στοιχεῖα οὐράνια). See Diels, *Elementum, eine Vorarbeit*, etc., Leipzig, 1899, p. 44. This appellation was afterwards extended to all the constellations and to the twelve signs of the Zodiac, unless indeed these signs and constellations had been previously named thus as being the primordial elements of which the heavens are composed. It is not at all certain that this usage goes back to the beginning of the Christian era. The first known example is found in Diogenes Laertius (vi, 9), who relates, according to Hippobotos, that Menedemus, among other eccentricities, wore on his head an arcadian hat on which were woven the twelve signs of the Zodiac (τὰ δώδεκα στοιχεῖα) ; but it is not certain that the expression comes from Hippobotos, and, if it does, that would not take us back to St Paul. However, from the second century examples abound. St Justin speaks of the celestial elements (τα οὐράνια στοιχεῖα, *Apol.*, ii, 5 ; cf. *Tryph.*, 23) ; Polycrates of Ephesus, in his letter to Pope Victor, calls the Apostles John and Philip μεγάλα στοιχεῖα (in Eusebius, *Hist.*, III, xxxi, 3) ; see also Athenagoras, *Apol.*, 16 ; Theophilus, *ad Autol.*, i, 4 (ἥλιος καὶ σελήνη καὶ ἀστέρες στοιχεῖα εἰσίν). This meaning passed into Latin and is found in Lactantius (*Instit.*, ii, 6) and in St Jerome (*Epist.*, cxx, 4 : *Omnis hebdomada . . . quam ethnici idolorum et elementorum nominibus appellant*).

4. At a later period the derivation is more difficult to follow ; but we find it less interesting the further we go from the apostolic age. At that time it was universally believed that the stars were endowed with life. It was, therefore, quite natural to name στοιχεῖον not only the star itself, but the spirit which inhabits it, or rather the occult influence which it was thought to produce. Thanks to the progress of magic, every mysterious influence was called thus, whether good or bad, astral or otherwise. The στοιχεῖον becomes "a charm, a talisman," and forms the derivations στοιχειοῦν (to enchant) and στοιχείωσις, στοιχειωματικοί. Examples of this sort abound in Byzantine literature. See Sophocles, *Greek Lexicon*. Finally, the Greeks of our time give this name to everything the influence of which their superstition fears, to the nymphs of the groves and streams, to ghosts, and to the evil eye. An enchanted spring is for them στοιχειώμενο πηγάδι ; a haunted house is στοιχειώμενο σπίτι. Cf. G. F. Abbott, *Macedonian*

*Folklore*, Cambridge, 1903, pp. 249-250. The source of this meaning may be relatively ancient. *Cf. Apotelesmata Apollonii Tyanensis*, ed. Nau, in Graffin's *Patrol. syriaca*, vol. ii, 1376-7 (at a certain hour every στοιχεῖον of birds, serpents and quadrupeds is enchanted).

This scale of meanings therefore ensues :

   (*a*) *A column, support, shaft, the pointer of* a sun-dial (Aristophanes).

   (*b*) *Elements of matter and speech* (fifth and fourth centuries B.C.).

   (*c*) *Elements of arts and sciences* (classic age).

   (*d*) *Elements* of the heavens, planets, constellations, Zodiac (second century A.D.).

   (*e*) *Astral or magical influence of* celestial bodies (Byzantine age).

   (*f*) *Everything that casts a spell* (modern folklore).

## II—THE "WORLD" IN THE WRITINGS OF ST PAUL

The primordial meaning of κόσμος, which remained classic, is "beauty" and "order." This is also the usual meaning in the Septuagint, but the only example of it in the New Testament is in 1 Pet. iii, 3 (ἐνδύσεων ἱματίων κόσμος).

1. *The world is the universe, the whole of the material creation.* —Pythagoras is said to have been the first to call κόσμος either the universe (according to Plutarch, *De placit. philos.*, ii, 1 ; *Op. mor.*, p. 886B) or the heavens (according to Favorinus quoted by Diogenes Laertius, viii, 48) on account of their order and beauty. The first meaning is not known to the writers of the Septuagint ; but it often appears in the deuterocanonical books, as well as in the New Testament, and *always*, it seems, in relation to the creative act or sovereignty of God : ʿActs xvii, 24 (ὁ Θεὸς ὁ ποιήσας τὸν κόσμον) ; Rom. i, 20 (ἀπὸ κτίσεως κόσμου) ; Eph. i, 4 : (πρὸ καταβολῆς κόσμου). Κόσμος is never met with in the Bible in the special sense of "heaven" which it frequently has in the classics (Plato, *Tim.* 28B [οὐρανὸς ἤ κόσμος] ; Isocrates, iv, 179 [γῆς ἀπάσης τῆς ὑπὸ τῷ κόσμῳ κειμένης] ; Xenophon, *Memor.*, i, 1, 11).

2. *The world is also "the earth as the abode of man," or, more generally, "the milieu in which the human race moves."*—This meaning, unknown to classic Greek and rare in the profane literature of any epoch, is quite common in the New Testament. At birth, man brings nothing into the *world* (1 Tim. vi, 7) ; in order to avoid contact with sinners, it would be necessary to go out of the *world* (1. Cor. v, 10) ; Abraham

was the heir of the *world* (Rom. iv, 13) ; an idol is nothing in the *world* (1. Cor. viii, 4) ; the Gentiles, before their conversion, were without God in the *world* (Eph. ii, 12) ; the faith is preached in the whole *world* (Col. i, 6 ; *cf.* Rom. ¹, 8 ; 1. Tim. iii, 16). Yet several of these examples may be taken as referring not to the terrestrial globe, but to the human race which inhabits it, and we thus revert to the following meaning ; or else a secondary idea is mingled with it, and this we shall consider later.

3. *The world is also the human race, the earth's inhabitants.*—This meaning is clear in all the passages in which God is represented as the Judge of the *world* (Rom. iii, 6 [πῶς κρινεῖ ὁ Θεὸς τὸν κόσμον; *cf.* 1 Cor. vi, 2 ; xi, 32), and the *world* as a debtor to divine justice (Rom. iii, 19 : ὑπόδικος . . . πᾶς ὁ κόσμος τῷ Θεῷ) ; but it is indisputable in many other cases : " God in Christ was reconciling the *world* to himself " (2 Cor. v, 19) ; " by one man sin entered into the *world* " (Rom. v, 12 ; *cf.* v, 13), and has thus brought into all men the principle of death ; Paul declares that his conduct in the *world*—that is, among men—has not been inspired by carnal wisdom but by the grace of God (2 Cor. i, 12). The expression " refuse of the world " is explained by " the offscouring of all " (1 Cor. iv, 13) ; and if the other Apostles are called " lights in the world " (Phil. ii, 15), it is doubtless in order to enlighten the human race rather than the terrestrial globe.

4. *Finally, St Paul often uses the world, either as the present abode of man or as the totality of present humanity, in a derogatory sense, due to an expressed or implied contrast with a superior world or a regenerated humanity.*—The world thus understood is not always a corrupt and perverse world, but it is at least the world left to itself, destitute of divine grace, such as it is, and not such as it ought to be in order to correspond with God's designs ; in a word, it is the natural world, expressly or tacitly contrasted with the supernatural world. " God hath made foolish the wisdom of the world " (1 Cor. i, 20); "the world by wisdom knew not God " (i, 21) ; therefore God hath chosen to accomplish his work " the foolish things of the world, the weak things of the world, the base things of the world " (1 Cor. i, 27, 28 : τὰ μωρὰ τοῦ κόσμου, τὰ ἀσθενῆ τοῦ κόσμου, τὰ ἀγενῆ τοῦ κόσμου), for by choosing them he transforms them. The Christian has not the spirit of the world, because he has received the Spirit of God and because these two spirits exclude one another (1 Cor. ii, 12) ; indeed, " the wisdom of this world is foolishness with God " (1 Cor. i, 19). We see from these examples, especially the last, what sort of antithesis helps the derogatory meaning to slip in. The world is properly speaking *this*

*world* (ὁ κόσμος οὖτος), where everything is weakness, impotence, corruption, nothingness, the world as measured by the standard of the present age (Eph. ii, 2: κατὰ τὸν αἰῶνα τοῦ κόσμου τούτου) ; the world, the fashion of which passeth away, which it is necessary to use but not abuse (1 Cor. vii, 31, 32), the sorrow of which worketh death (2 Cor. vii, 10). The derogatory sense is more or less accentuated according to the implied contrast; it reaches its climax when the world forms an antithesis to God or to his Spirit : " The world is crucified to me and I to the world " (Gal. vi, 14) ; between us there is nothing in common. But the contrast is not always so violent: the married man and woman " think on the things of the world " (1 Cor. vii, 33, 34) ; it is an obstacle to holy meditations, but not an absolute bar to them. Moreover, the opposition is not radical and essential ; it is so only so far as the world remains apart from supernatural influences; but " God in Christ reconciles the world to himself " (2 Cor. v, 19), and the obstinacy of Israel, from the providential point of view, has been "the riches of the world" (Rom. xi, 12) and " the reconciliation of the world " (xi, 15), because it has contributed to the conversion of the Gentiles. Here the world does not mean all humanity, but that portion of it deprived of the Mosaic revelation. We have purposely omitted the disputed expression τὰ στοιχεῖα τοῦ κόσμου, but what we have just said may contribute to define its exact signification, or at least to exclude all the interpretations which would not harmonize with the Pauline notion of κόσμος.

III—MEANING OF THE EXPRESSION τὰ στοιχεῖα τοῦ κόσμου

In his *Entwicklung*, published in 1851, Usteri wrote in regard to Gal. iv, 3, 9 : "It is agreed to recognize that στοιχεῖα means *prima institutionis elementa*, and carries on the metaphor begun by νήπιοι." If he were living to-day Usteri would have to concede that the agreement is broken, although the common interpretation still remains that of the best exegetes and lexicographers (Lightfoot, Sieffert, Grimm, Cremer, etc.).

(A) Zahn (*Galaterbrief*², pp. 195-6) tries to revive an explanation already proposed by some old commentators. According to this, στοιχεῖα ="the matter and the material things of which the world is made—the world itself as far as it is material." From the point of view of classical philology this translation of τὰ στοιχεῖα τοῦ κόσμου might pass ; and, indeed, it has behind it the authority of a passage in Lucian (*Amor.*, 19) and of St Irenæus (*Haeres.*, I, iv, 2 ; v, 5 : τὰ σωματικὰ τοῦ κόσμου στοιχεῖα). But it is impossible to adapt it to the teaching of St Paul in the text quoted.

(B) Lagercrantz (*Elementum. Eine lexicologische Studie,*

Upsala, 1911), relying on a text from the *Shepherd* of Hermas (*Vis.*, III, xiii, 3), which he considers to have been mis-understood by his predecessors, seeks to establish in all the passages in the New Testament the meaning of *foundation*. His study will probably convince no one on this point, but should certainly be read, in spite of some fanciful hypotheses, in order to counteract the equally conjectural derivations of Diels, the principal advocate of the following explanation.

(C) The στοιχεῖα τοῦ κόσμου are, according to this, the *elemental spirits*, conceived of as personal or personified beings. All the partisans of this opinion are agreed on this word. But when they are asked what they mean by *ele-mental spirits* they give the most incongruous definitions, if, indeed, they deign to try to give one. Sometimes the *Elementargeister* are the angels who direct the courses of the stars, as imagined by rabbinical theology; sometimes they are the spirits concealed in the material objects of animistic religions; sometimes the deified forces of Stoic philosophy (λόγοι, δυνάμεις), or the planetary influences of mediæval astrology, or superterrestrial powers uniting in themselves, in fantastical confusion, irreconcilable characteristics. Ritschl, who was perhaps the first to introduce this exegesis, thought only of the angels who were the promulgators of the Law (*Rechtfertigung und Versöhnung*[3], vol. ii, 252); and Spitta likens them to the στοιχεῖα of 2 Pet. iii, 10, which, however, does not elucidate the question.

Taking these divergencies into account, among the de-fenders of the *Elementargeister* are : Everling, *Paulin. Ange-lologie und Dämonologie*, 1888, p. 55 ; Diels, *Elementum, eine Vorarbeit zum griech. und latein. Thesaurus*, Leipzig, 1899, pp. 44-47 ; Deissmann, in *Encycl. Biblica*, vol. ii, p. 1259 ; Reit-zenstein, *Poimandres, Studien zur griechischägypt. und früh-christlichen Literatur*, Leipzig, 1904 ; Bousset, *Die Religion des Judentums*[2], 1906, p. 372 ; Haupt, on Col. ii, 8, 20, in Meyer's *Kommentar;* Tobac, *Le problème de la justification dans St Paul*, 1908, pp. 54-62 ; Protin, *Les éléments du monde dans la pensée de St Paul*, in *Revue augustinienne*, vol. xiv, 1909, pp. 71-74 ; Pfister, *Die στοιχεῖα τοῦ κόσμου in den Briefen des Ap. Paulus*, in *Philologus*, vol. lxix, 1910, pp. 411-427.

We think that this interpretation of the στοιχεῖα τοῦ κόσμου has now reached and passed beyond the maximum of its popularity, and that it will decline little by little in proportion as its defects and difficulties are better estimated, and that its advocates will not let themselves be fascinated by its specious attractiveness at first sight. We do not hesitate to reject it for the following reasons : (*a*) It gives στοιχεῖον a meaning which was not in common use at the time of the New Testament and only appeared much later in the

Byzantine language. Now, is it not absurd, for the better understanding of St Paul, to refer us to a very late text the meaning of which is in dispute? (*Testam. Salomonis* in Fleck, *Anecdota sacra*, Leipzig, 1837, and Migne, CXXII, 1316-7 : " We are the στοιχεῖα, the dominators of the world, deception, discord, destiny [κλώθων], and tempest ").—(*b*) It does not safeguard the Pauline sense of the word κόσμος, and, to speak more correctly, it does not agree with any recognized meaning of this word.—(*c*) It imputes to St Paul a conception of " intermediary spirits" which is totally foreign to his Epistles, to the other writings of the New Testament, and even to contemporary Jewish thought. The Jews of that period admitted, indeed, that the stars and atmospheric agencies were directed by spirits, but they called those spirits πνεύματα and not στοιχεῖα, and it is not clear that they paid them a superstitious form of worship.—(*d*) It does not harmonize with the text and context of the two passages which are to be explained. The exegesis of these passages ought to have proved this.—(*e*) Finally, it is impossible to expound it with any clearness without discovering its weak points, untenable positions, and contradictory aspects. Only its vagueness makes it acceptable.

# NOTE R—CHRISTOLOGICAL TEXTS

## I—List of Texts

The entire work of Paul is fundamentally only a Christology, since it all centres in the Person or the mission of Christ; but it has been thought right to take from it a certain number of variously remarkable extracts which concern the nature or the functions of the Son of God. It will suffice to refer the reader to the explanation of these passages.

(a) Rom. iii, 21-26, Vol. I, pp. 204, 205.
(b) Rom. v, 12-21, Vol. I, pp. 212-221.
(c) Rom. viii, 3-4, Vol. II, pp. 163-165.
(d) 1 Cor. xv, 44-49, Vol. II, pp. 172-176.
(e) 2 Cor. v, 14-15, Vol. II, pp. 201-203.
(f) 2 Cor. v, 16, Vol. II, pp. 24-25.
(g) 2 Cor. v, 18-20, Vol. II, pp. 219-220.
(h) 2 Cor. v, 21, Vol. II, pp. 204-205.
(i) 2 Cor. viii, 9, Vol. I, p. 151.
(j) Gal. i, 1, Vol. II, pp. 120-121.
(k) Gal. iii, 13, Vol. II, pp. 205-208.
(l) Gal. iii, 19-20, Vol. I, p. 184; Vol. II, p. 96.
(m) Gal. iv, 4-5, Vol. II, pp. 161-163.
(n) Eph. i, 3-14, Vol. II, pp. 85-92.
(o) Eph. i, 23, Vol. II, p. 283.
(p) Eph. iv, 12-16, Vol. I, pp. 305-307.
(q) Phil. ii, 5-11, Vol. I, pp. 312-322; 456-465.
(r) Col. i, 14-20, Vol. I, pp. 287-292.
(s) Col. ii, 9, Vol. II, pp. 151-152.
(t) Col. ii, 13-14, Vol. II, pp. 228-229.
(u) Col. ii, 18-19, Vol. I, pp. 304-305.
(v) Col. ii, 20, Vol. I, p. 282; Vol. II, p. 106.
(w) 1 Tim. ii, 5, Vol. II, pp. 167-168.
(x) Titus iii, 4-6, Vol. I, pp. 331-332.
(y) Heb. i, 1-3, Vol. I, pp. 367-374.
(z) Heb. v, 1-4, Vol. I, pp. 374-380.

For the texts concerning the eternal relations of the Word to the heart of divinity, see the following note. We add below the exegesis of three other texts which have not found a place elsewhere.

## II—The Superscription of the Epistle to the Romans
### (Rom. i, 1-7)

1. *Theological Ideas.*—It has been possible to say without exaggeration that the beginning of this Epistle is an abbreviated Christology; indeed few passages of Scripture concentrate in less words more theological ideas.—(a) Definition of the apostolate of Paul, his election, vocation, and special mission to the Gentiles.—(b) Intimate and essential relation between the two Testaments, the first of which is the prophecy and type of the second, while the second is the antitype and realization of the first.—(c) Jesus Christ, Lord and Son of God, author of the divine call and of grace.—(d) Jesus, born of the blood of David according to the flesh. —(e) Jesus Christ established Son of God according to the spirit of sanctity. This last phrase requires an explanation which we give below.

2. *Construction of the Phrase.*—This is a series of parentheses enclosed in one another. As an example, we can bring out this peculiarity of Paul's style by using special type :

(*a*) Paulus, servus Jesu Christi, vocatus Apostolus, segregatus in Evangelium Dei,

    (*b*) QUOD ANTE PROMISERAT PER PROPHETAS SUOS IN SCRIPTURIS SANCTIS DE FILIO SUO,

        (*c*) **qui factus est ei ex semine David secundum carnem, qui praedestinatus est Filius Dei in virtute secundum spiritum sanctificationis ex resurrectione mortuorum,**

    (*b*) JESU CHRISTI DOMINI NOSTRI (better CHRISTO DOMINO NOSTRO)

        (*d*) per quem accepimus gratiam, et Apostolatum ad obediendum fidei in omnibus Gentibus pro nomine ejus,

            (*e*) *in quibus estis et vos vocati Jesu Christi :*

(*a*) omnibus qui sunt Romae, dilectis Dei, vocatis sanctis. Gratia vobis, et pax a Deo Patre nostro, et Domino Jesu Christo.

The principal proposition (*a*), printed in roman type (small pica), is cut in two by four incidental phrases superimposed, so to speak, one upon another. The first of these (*b*), in small capitals, which defines the Gospel, is itself cut in two by the second subclause (*c*), in heavy face, which defines the Son of God. The third clause (*d*), in brevier type, announces a new attribute of the Son, author of the apostolate of Paul to the Gentiles. Finally, the fourth (*e*), in italics, recalls the fact that the Romans belong to Paul's sphere of influence, and thus leads them back, by a long detour, to the principal idea which is now brought to an end without further difficulty. In the Vulgate two inaccuracies are to be noted : the words *Jesu Christi Domini nostri* ought to be in the ablative, as being in apposition with *de Filio suo;* moreover, nothing in the Greek corresponds to the word *ei* in the phrase *qui factus est ei.*

3. *The Son of God according to the Flesh and according to the Spirit.*

τοῦ υἱοῦ τοῦ γενομένου ἐκ σπέρματος Δαυεὶδ κατὰ σάρκα,
τοῦ ὁρισθέντος υἱοῦ Θεοῦ ἐν δυνάμει κατὰ πνεῦμα ἁγιωσύνης
ἐξ ἀναστάσεως νεκρῶν.

For an exegesis of this text, however incomplete, there is no room here. Let us confine ourselves to erecting a few guide-posts. The subject of attribution of the whole phrase is "the Son of God" (περὶ τοῦ υἱοῖ αὐτοῦ). This Son is defined

or described by two attributes expressed by the participles
(τοῦ γενομένου . . . τοῦ ὁρισθέντος). The first clause presents
no difficulties : " He who is the Son of God *becomes* of the
race of David according to the flesh." Paul does not say that
he becomes Son, for he is that already, but that he becomes
of the race of David—namely, a descendant of David—and that
from a special point of view, " according to the flesh," that is
to say, as man.

In the second clause, almost all the words offer room for
discussion. (A) *Meaning of* ὁρισθέντος. Let us observe in
passing that we have here not προορισθέντος (Vulg. *qui prae-
destinatus est*) but ὁρισθέντος, which signifies " declared " or
" established." The exegetes are divided between these two
explanations which really differ very little from each other.
Indeed the act indicated by the participle ὁρισθέντος does not
concern the nature of the Son or his essential being, but his
historical position ; thenceforth, "to declare " or " to establish " (that is to say, to cause to be recognized, to instal in
his dignity) amounts to almost the same thing : (*a*) It is impossible for Christ to be *constituted* Son of God by the
resurrection, since he is so at the moment of his human birth
(τοῦ υἱοῦ τοῦ γενομένου) and since he is sent to this earth in the
quality of Son (Gal. iv, 4 ; Rom. viii, 3).—(*b*) We must compare our texts with Acts x, 42 (οὑτός ἐστιν ὁ ὡρισμένος ὑπὸ τοῖ
Θεοῦ κριτὴς ζώντων καὶ νεκρῶν) and xvii, 31 (κρίνειν τὴν οἰκουμένην
. . . ἐν ἀνδρὶ ᾧ ὥρισεν). Christ was a Judge by right and by
power, but an authentic act of God declares and establishes
him as Judge ; in the same way he was Son really and by full
right, but he needed to be acknowledged as such.—(*c*) Every
difficulty is removed, if, as some good commentators (Cornely,
Weiss, etc.) think, ἐν δυνάμει ought to be joined to υἱοῦ Θεοῖ.
Then Christ is not declared or established mere Son of God,
but "*powerful* Son of God," the emphasis falling on the
epithet. The position of the words favours this interpretation.
—(B) *Meaning of* κατὰ πνεῖμα ἁγιωσύνης. Since these words
make an antithesis to κατὰ σάρκα " according to human
nature," we are inclined to understand by them the divine
nature, and it is thus that many exegetes, even Protestants,
explain them. The majority, however, refuse to see the
divine nature in so unusual a designation ; for from the fact
that the divine nature is spiritual and infinitely holy, it does
not follow that it can be recognized in the expression πνεῖμα
ἁγιωσύνης. So much the more as the flesh is not usually
contrasted with the divine nature, but either with the Person
or the effects of the Holy Spirit. It is, therefore, between
these two very kindred meanings that the choice must be
made. The Fathers, in general, prefer the former, and we
know indeed that the Holy Spirit is closely related with the
resurrection (Rom. viii, 11 ; 2 Cor. iv, 14). Nevertheless the

expressions "spirit of fear and adoption" (Rom. viii, 15), "spirit of faith" (2 Cor. iv, 13), "spirit of wisdom" (Eph. i, 17), invite us to take πνεῦμα ἁγιωσύνης also, in an analogous sense, as the fulness of sanctity—that is, of graces and of spiritual gifts, with which the humanity of Christ is adorned.—(C) *Meaning of ἐξ ἀναστάσεως νεκρῶν.* Many exegetes explain this as if it read ἐκ νεκρῶν, by which they understand the resurrection of Jesus himself. But "the resurrection of the dead" is more than the resurrection of Jesus, although it includes the resurrection of Jesus, the first-fruit of the resurrected and the first-born among the dead. The meaning is simple: Jesus Christ, in consummating the redemptive work *by the resurrection of the dead*, of which he is the meritorious and exemplary cause, is solemnly installed by his Father in the office of Judge and the dignity of Son of God, to whom men owe homage (*cf.* Phil. ii, 11).

*According to the flesh*—that is to say, according to carnal descent—Jesus Christ *becomes son of David;* but according to the *spirit of sanctification*—that is to say, according to the substantial sanctification which is poured out upon his humanity from the fact of the hypostatic union, and according to the accidental sanctification which the fulness of graces and gifts of the Holy Spirit confers upon him, a sanctity which wins for him the distinction of being the first of those who rise again and the first-fruit of the resurrection from the dead, Jesus Christ is declared, established and *enthroned as the Son of God.* He is so by the fact of the resurrection from the dead, which he inaugurates in his own person and which shows his true nature, and he is so in a striking manner by means of a sovereign act of divine power, *in virtute.*

We may compare, for the antithesis: *mortificatus quidem carne, vivificatus autem spiritu* (1 Pet. iii, 18) or *manifestatum est in carne, justificatum est autem in spiritu* (1 Tim. iii, 16); and for the expression: *crucifixus est ex infirmitate sed vivit* ex virtute *Dei* (2 Cor. xiii, 4).

### III—"GOD WHO HATH PURCHASED THE CHURCH WITH HIS OWN BLOOD"

(Acts xx, 28)

| | |
|---|---|
| Προσέχετε . . . παντὶ τῷ ποιμνίῳ, ἐν ᾧ ὑμᾶς τὸ Πνεῦμα τὸ ἅγιον ἔθετο ἐπισκόπους, | *Attendite . . . universo gregi, in quo vos Spiritus sanctus posuit episcopos,* |
| ποιμαίνειν τὴν ἐκκλησίαν τοῦ Θεοῦ, | *regere Ecclesiam Dei,* |
| ἣν περιεποιήσατο διὰ τοῦ αἵματος τοῦ ἰδίου. | *quam acquisivit sanguine suo.* |

1. *The True Reading.*—Besides some sporadic readings (τοῦ Κυρίου Θεου, τοῦ Κυρίου τοῦ Θεοῦ, τοῦ Θεοῦ καὶ Κυρίου) the versions soundly attested are:

(a) τοῦ Θεοῦ—B minusc., Vulg. Pat. multi.
(b) τοῦ Κυρίου—A C D E minusc., Copt. Arm. Pat. multi.
(c) τοῦ Χριστοῦ—Ethiop. Pesh.
(d) τοῦ Κυρίου καὶ Θεοῦ—C³ H L P minusc. plus 100.

Evidently the text has been intentionally manipulated, as everything leads us to believe, for dogmatic reasons.—Reading (d), which is that of the immense majority of recent manuscripts, is certainly false. In addition to the fact that it is not supported by any version or by a single one of the oldest manuscripts, or by any ecclesiastical author previous to the tenth century, it is clearly made up of a fusion of the readings (a) and (b).—The reading (c), insufficiently attested, has no chance of being an early one and is only a modification of (b). —The readings (a) and (b), if one counts up the testimonies in their favour, have about the same amount of support; but several considerations make the balance turn to the side of (a). Among the oldest Fathers we find the extraordinary expression αἷμα Θεοῦ, sanguis Dei ; St Ignatius of Antioch, Ad Ephes., i, 1 (ἐν αἷματι Θεοῦ, which the Latin version softens into Christi Dei, and in which the interpolator substitutes Χριστοῦ for Θεοῦ, cf. Ad Roman., vi, 3) ; Clement of Alexandria, Quis dives salvetur, 34 (αἷματι Θεοῦ Παιδός, cf. Ibid. 37) ; Tertullian, Ad uxor., ii, 3. Although these authors do not cite our text, their testimony is indirectly in favour of the primitive reading Θεοῦ, for it is difficult to believe that they both adopted such an expression without scriptural authority. We know that the reading αἷμα Θεοῦ always shocked many ecclesiastical writers, especially when the heretics had made a bad use of it. From this came the temptation to modify our text by substituting for τοῦ Θεοῦ either τοῦ Κυρίου or τοῦ Κυρίου καὶ Θεοῦ. And so the most recent critics, such as Westcott-Hort and Weiss, accept the reading τοῦ Θεοῦ as primitive and reject as arbitrary the supposition that the word υἱοῦ has disappeared after τοῦ ἰδίου, without leaving any traces of having been there. However, as the sense scandalizes them, Weiss proposes to translate διὰ τοῦ αἷματος τοῦ ἰδίου " by the blood of his own," (Son understood), and Hort suggests " by the blood which is his," as being that of his Son. These fantasies need no refutation.

2. *The Meaning.*—The only admissible translation is : Govern " the Church of God which he has purchased with his own blood." In order to explain what is a little shocking in this phrase, we must bear in mind that St Paul borrows at the start the language of the Old Testament where Israel is " the Church of God " and " the people that he has purchased." In writing these words, which he takes in a figurative sense, it may be that Paul does not yet have Christ

distinctly in mind; but, in the rest of the discourse, he identifies Christ with Jehovah, as he often does.

## IV—THE HYMN TO CHRIST TRIUMPHANT
### (1 Tim. iii, 16)

Ὅς [or Θεὸς] ἐφανερώθη ἐν σαρκί,     *Quod manifestatum est in carne.*
ἐδικαιώθη ἐν πνεύματι,     *Justificatum est in spiritu,*
ὤφθη ἀγγέλοις,     *apparuit angelis,*
ἐκηρύχθη ἐν ἔθνεσιν,     *praedicatum est Gentibus,*
ἐπιστεύθη ἐν κόσμῳ,     *creditum est in mundo,*
ἀνελήφθη ἐν δόξῃ.     *assumptum est in gloria.*

1. *The True Reading.*—Should we read ὅς or Θεός? The variant reading, so important for the meaning, depends on a very little thing; for in the uncial writing ΘΕΟC, abbreviated into ΘC, is scarcely distinguishable from ΟC.

(A) The reading Θεός is that of the immense majority of manuscripts, of more than 200 cursive, and of the three uncials KLP. The reading ὅς has in its favour only the cursives 17, 73, 181, and, among the uncials, the *Sinaiticus*, the twin texts F and G, and perhaps the first hand of C. The *Alexandrinus* is doubtful, and the *Vaticanus* has not this passage at all. Codex D reads, like the Vulgate, ὅ (quod).

(B) On the contrary, all the ancient versions presuppose the relative, either in the masculine or neuter; and the Latin Fathers naturally follow the reading of the Latin version; but the Greek Fathers are divided. St Chrysostom, St Gregory of Nyssa, Didymus, Theodoret and others later clearly support Θεός. St Epiphanius, Theodore of Mopsuestia, and St Cyril of Alexandria are for ὅς. To the first are sometimes added St Ignatius (*Ad Ephes.*, xix, 3: Θεοῦ ἀνθρωπίνως φανερουμένου) and St Hippolytus (*Ad. Noet.*: Θεὸς ἐν σώματι ἐφανερώθη); but, however precious these texts are for the theologian, to whom they show what was thought about the incarnate Word in the second century, it is not certain that these are quotations from St Paul—they lack the characteristic expression ἐν σαρκί—and we may ask whether they have not rather influenced the reading Θεὸς ἐφανερώθη of the more recent manuscripts and contributed thus to introduce a dogmatic alteration into the Epistle unconsciously.

(C) The critics are unanimous for the reading ὅς ἐφανερώθη. Thus Griesbach, Lachmann, Tregelles, Tischendorf, Westcott-Hort, Weiss, and von Soden. We must concede that they are right, not by virtue of the very untrustworthy principle: *Lectio magis ardua praestat,* but because the versions, some of which are much earlier than our oldest manuscripts, take it for granted, and because the testimony of the Fathers is undecided.

2. *The Meaning*.—The Apostle has just mentioned the *mystery of godliness*. He now passes without transition to the description of that mystery, identical in reality with Christ the redeemer, to whom the masculine relative (ὅς) refers for the meaning—unless we prefer to explain the lack of grammatical harmony by an abrupt quotation. In any case we must not look in this phrase for a complete and independent proposition the first part of which would be the protasis and the other five the apodosis, or the first three the protasis and the last three the apodosis (Seeberg). It matters little for the sense whether the six parts are parallel to one another or whether it is necessary to divide them, either into two triplets or into three pairs (Weiss).

(*a*) Christ *was made manifest in the flesh* at the moment of his earthly birth. This recalls the *Verbum caro factum est* of St John. St Peter also uses for Christ the word φανεροῦσθαι (1 Pet. i, 20), which St Paul applies elsewhere to the *Mystery* (Rom. xvi, 26; Col. i, 26; iv, 4).

(*b*) *He was justified in the spirit* (or *in the Spirit*). The glorious resurrection *justifies* the claim which Jesus made to be the Messiah and the Son of God (*cf.* Rom. i, 4). The *spirit*, as opposed to the flesh, is here not the divine nature, but either the Holy Spirit as agent of the resurrection (Rom. viii, 11), or the spirit of sanctification to which Jesus owes his resurrection and the fact that he became thus the first-fruits of the glorious resurrection.

(*c*) *He appeared to the angels*, not in any mere casual way, for the fact would thus have no significance, but as a conqueror having thenceforth a special right to the homage and adoration of the heavenly spirits (Phil. ii, 10, 11; *cf.* Col. ii, 15).

(*d*) *He was preached among the nations;* while he triumphed in heaven, his kingdom assumed ever-increasing proportions on earth.

(*e*) *He was believed on in the world ;* the world means here, as usual in St Paul, the human race.

(*f*) *He was taken up in glory*, at the moment of his glorious ascension. The verb ἀνελήφθη is employed in the same sense by St Luke (Acts i, 2, 22), and the addition of ἐν δόξῃ does not allow us to understand it differently. It is objected that this explanation disturbs the chronological order, but it has not been proved that the author wishes to confine himself to a strict order of events, and here he had a special reason for ending his enumeration with Christ's striking triumph.

# NOTE S—TRINITARIAN TEXTS

## I—List of Texts

The passages in which the three divine Persons are named together are numerous. Forty could be cited, including the Epistle to the Hebrews; but some belonging to the same context ought not to be counted separately; and in other cases the simultaneous mention of the three Persons either is only apparent or purely accidental. We give twenty-six of them, arranged in two categories.

### 1. TEXTS ALREADY STUDIED IN THIS WORK

(a) 1 Cor. ii, 10, 12, Vol. II, p. 143.
(b) 1 Cor. vi, 11, Vol. I, p. 171.
(c) 1 Cor. xii, 4, 6, Vol. II, p. 133.
(d) 2 Cor. i, 21, 22, Vol. II, p. 136.
(e) 2 Cor. xiii, 13, Vol. II, p. 132.

(f) Gal. iv, 5, 6, Vol. II, p. 134.
(g) Rom. viii, 9, 11, Vol. II, p. 145.
(h) Rom. viii, 14, 17, Vol. II, p. 135.
(i) Rom. xv, 15, 16, Vol. II, p. 137.
(j) Eph. i, 13, 14, Vol. II, pp. 85-86

(k) Titus iii, 4, 6, Vol. II, pp. 135-136.

### 2. TEXTS TO BE EXAMINED HEREAFTER

(l) 1 Thess. v, 18, 19.
(m) 2 Thess. ii, 13, 14.
(n) 1 Cor. vi, 15, 20.
(o) 1 Cor. xii, 3.
(p) 2 Cor. iii, 3.

(q) Rom. v, 1-5.
(r) Rom. xiv, 17, 18.
(s) Rom. xv, 30.
(t) Gal. iii, 11, 14.
(u) Col. i, 6, 8.

(v) Eph. ii, 18.
(w) Eph. ii, 22.
(x) Eph. iii, 14, 17.
(y) Eph. iv, 4, 6.
(z) Eph. v, 18, 20.

Many will perhaps find this list too short. They will search it in vain for texts to which they are accustomed to give a Trinitarian interpretation—for example, Rom. xi, 36 : *Quoniam ex ipso, et per ipsum et in ipso sunt omnia ; ipsi gloria in saecula :* but this speaks of God without distinction of Persons. St Augustine and the Latin commentators who understand by *ex ipso* the Father, by *per ipsum* the Son, and *in ipso* the Holy Spirit, have been led into error by the Latin version. In the Greek the third term εἰς αὐτόν hardly suits this application.— The passage in Acts xx, 28 (*Attendite vobis et universo gregi, in quo vos Spiritus sanctus posuit episcopos regere Ecclesiam Dei quam acquisivit sanguine suo*) contains in appearance only the mention of the three Persons ; for God, identified with Christ, cannot be God the Father. See Note R.

## II—Criticism of Several Texts

(l) 1 Thess. v, 18-19.—*In omnibus gratias agite; haec est enim voluntas* Dei *in* Christo Jesu *in omnibus vobis.* Spiritum *nolite extinguere.* The association of the three Persons appears fortuitous, since the two phrases are not connected. It is not even certain that *Spiritus* denotes the Holy Spirit, for it is paralleled with *prophecy*, nor is it very clear how anyone could *quench the Spirit*, unless in the *charismata* of which he is the author.

(*m*) 2 Thess. ii, 13, 14.—*Nos autem debemus gratias agere Deo semper pro vobis, fratres dilecti a* Deo, *quod elegerit vos* Deus *primitias in salutem in sanctificatione* Spiritus *et in fide veritatis : in qua et vocavit per Evangelium nostrum in acquisitionem gloriae* Domini nostri Jesu Christi. If we suppose that *Spiritus* signifies the Holy Spirit, the three divine Persons are distinguished according to their sphere of appropriation and represented as co-operating in our salvation : the Father, as author of the election and call ; the Holy Spirit, as the principle of sanctification ; Jesus Christ, as the meritorious or exemplary cause of eternal life (according as περιποίησις is taken in the active or the passive sense). The doubt in regard to the word *Spiritus* is difficult to remove, ἐν ἁγιασμῷ πνεύματος being able to signify the sanctification (active) which the Holy Spirit operates in us, or the sanctification (passive) of our spirit or our supernatural being. In the latter case, the reference to the Holy Spirit would be only indirect. The Vulgate writes *spiritus* without a capital.

(*n*) 1 Cor. vi, 15, 20.—Our bodies are the members of *Christ* (verse 15) and the temple of the *Holy Ghost* (verse 19) ; to respect one's body is to honour *God* (verse 20) ; to be joined to the *Lord* is to be one and the same *spirit* with him (verse 17). —Naturally we seem here to recognize three agents co-operating in our sanctification, whose action is so interwoven as to appear identical ; but the Greek δοξάσατε δὴ τὸν Θεὸν ἐν τῷ σώματι ὑμῶν does not express clearly the indwelling of the Father, and the Latin *et portate* is a gloss.

(*o*) 1 Cor. xii, 3.—*Nemo in* Spiritu Dei *loquens dicit anathema* Jesu. *Et nemo potest dicere* Dominus Jesus, *nisi in* Spiritu sancto. (No one speaking when moved by the Spirit of God says : Anathema be to Jesus ! and no one can say : Jesus is the Lord, unless by the Holy Spirit.)—From the point of view which concerns us here, there is hardly anything to be noted in this text except the simultaneous mention of the three Persons, the Spirit of God being the Spirit of the Father.

(*p*) 2 Cor. iii, 3.—*Epistola estis* Christi, *ministrata a nobis et scripta non atramento, sed* Spiritu Dei *vivi*. Is this the Holy Spirit ? The Vulgate writes *spiritu*.

(*q*) Rom. v, 1-5.—It is by Jesus Christ that we are reconciled with God the Father (v. 1), and it is by the Holy Spirit that the love of God is spread abroad in our hearts. (v. 5) There are here two personal contrasts of Christ and the Spirit with God the Father, but the three Persons are not placed simultaneously in connection with one another.

(*r*) Rom. xiv, 17, 18.—*Non est enim regnum* Dei *esca et potus, sed justitia et pax et gaudium in* Spiritu sancto : *qui enim in hoc servit* Christo *placet* Deo. We find here the names of the three Persons with an intimate relation between them, but no personal contrast.

(s) Rom. xv, 30.—*Obsecro vos per Dominum nostrum* Jesum Christum, *et per caritatem* sancti Spiritus, *ut adjuvetis me in orationibus vestris pro me ad* Deum. Among the texts of a secondary order, this is one of the best. The Greek, it is true, has only τοῦ πνεύματος, but it can hardly be doubted that it is the Holy Spirit (on account of the parallelism with the first clause), and the distinction of the three Persons is clearly marked.

(t) Gal. iii, 11, 14.—The allusion to the three Persons is too disconnected. Moreover, if *pollicitatio Spiritus* is the promised Holy Spirit, we ask whether in *nemo justificatur apud Deum* God signifies the Father or God without distinction of Persons.

(u) Col. i, 6-8.—The bond between *God*, from whom grace is derived (v. 6), *Christ Jesus*, of whom Paul is the minister (v. 7), and the *spirit*, which is perhaps not the Holy Spirit (v. 8 : *dilectionem vestram in spiritu*), is too weak to furnish a solid argument in favour of the Trinity.

(v) Eph. ii, 18.—*Per ipsum* [Christum] *habemus accessum ambo in uno* Spiritu ad Patrem. The mention of the three divine Persons is explicit, supposing that *spiritus* designates the Holy Spirit; it would be only indirect, if *spiritus* designated a gift or an effect of the Holy Spirit. Catholic exegesis in general understands by πνεῦμα the Holy Spirit (St Chrysostom, St Thomas, Estius, Bisping, etc.). Several Protestants are of the same opinion (Meyer, Westcott, Abbott, etc.). Yet Theodoret, St Jerome, and others think differently. Cornelius à Lapide leaves it to the choice of the reader.

(w) Eph. ii, 22.—*In quo* [Domino] *et vos coaedificamini in habitaculum* Dei *in* Spiritu. It is the same question here as above. The Latins who read in their text *in Spiritu sancto* (like St Thomas, Estius, etc.) understood by it the Holy Spirit. Chrysostom and his school regard ἐν πνεύματι as equivalent to an adjective (πνευματικός = a *spiritual* temple). Among the Protestant exegetes, several consider the mention of the Holy Spirit as evident : so Abbott, Moule, etc. German commentators are more inclined to treat ἐν πνεύματι as a common noun.

(x) Eph. iii, 14-17.—Although *Domini nostri J.C.* is wanting in the original, the personal contrast is very clear : Paul asks the *Father* to send *his Spirit*, that *Christ* may dwell in our hearts.

(y) Eph. iv, 4-6.—*Unum corpus et unus* Spiritus. . . . *Unus* Dominus, *una fides, unum baptisma. Unus* Deus et Pater *omnium, qui est super omnes, et per omnia et in omnibus nobis.* This text recalls I Cor. xii, 4-6, where the order of the divine

Persons is the same: the Spirit, the Lord, and God. It seems indeed that here again *Spiritus* denotes the Holy Spirit, soul of the mystical body; and we can understand also by the preceding verse (*solliciti servare unitatem Spiritus in vinculo pacis*) the union produced by the Holy Spirit. Yet Chrysostom thinks that πνεῦμα can signify here feeling or "good will" (προθυμία).

(z) Eph. v, 18-20.—*Implemini* Spiritu *sancto . . . gratias agentes semper pro omnibus, in nomine* Domini *nostri* Jesu Christi Deo *et* Patri. The question is always to know whether there is a *direct* reference to the Holy Spirit. In Latin, thanks to the addition of the adjective *sancto*, the thing is not doubtful; but the Greek has only πληροῦσθε ἐν πνεύματι, and these words form a counterpart to μὴ μεθύσκεσθε οἴνῳ. If the Holy Spirit himself is designated, we have here the formula of the Christian prayer which is addressed *to* the Father, *by* the Son (or *in the name* of the Son), *in* the Holy Spirit.

# NOTE T—*DOMINUS AUTEM SPIRITUS EST*

## (2 Cor. iii, 17)

### I—THE PRESENT POSITION

One of the most delicate and subtle problems of Pauline exegesis is, no doubt, to ascertain when the word "spirit" should be written with an initial capital. Let someone make a trial of this in chapter viii of the Epistle to the Romans, in which the word recurs seventeen times in the first sixteen verses, and where the orthographical variations of the Vulgate are not always easy to justify. But the most pertinent example is still our text: *Dominus autem spiritus* (or *Spiritus*) *est.* Exegetes here differ as widely as possible. A concise presentation of the position is found in L. Krummel (*Studien und Kritiken*, vol. xxxii, 1859, pp. 39-100), and a conscientious, systematic, and well reasoned out account of it in a learned monograph by P. Holzmeister (*Dominus autem Spiritus est*, Innsbruck, 1908). To the old interpretations many others have been added, and we feel, when running through them, that we are wandering haphazard in an inextricable labyrinth. More recently P. Nisius (*Zeitschrift f. kath. Theol.*, vol. xl, pp. 617-676) has proposed a new explanation, which perhaps will satisfy no one; because, as the *Biblische Zeitschrift* (vol. xiv, 1917, p. 376) remarks, the author "deals much with dogmatic and speculative considerations"; which, in exegesis, is not a good method. An evident result of this mixture is that no explanation makes an impression on the Catholic exegete, who remains thus free to choose as he likes. If the theologians of our day rarely appeal to this text to prove the divinity of the Holy Spirit, they must have good reasons for not doing so. When a text is generally abandoned by theologians, as are to-day 1 John v, 7 for the Trinity, and 2 Cor. iii, 17 for the divinity of the Holy Spirit, this abandonment is symptomatic. Its cause must be sought either in a serious doubt concerning its authenticity or in an insurmountable difficulty in its exegesis.

To proceed in an orderly manner, we will examine successively: (1) What is the subject of the phrase; (2) the meaning of ὁ Κύριος; (3) the meaning of τὸ πνεῦμα; (4) the sense of the entire clause.

### II—THE SUBJECT OF THE PHRASE IS ὁ Κύριος, not τὸ πνεῦμα

1. In the phrase ὁ Κύριος τὸ πνεῦμα ἐστιν, for the inversion to be admissible, Κύριος must not have the definite article if we are to regard it as a predicate, as in the passage in St John

(iv, 24) : πνεῦμα ὁ Θεός. *The text of St Paul is entirely different and nothing in it justifies the inversion.*

Contemporary interpreters are unanimous on this point, and perhaps now there is no dissentient voice ; but it was not always so. Walafrid Strabo, the author of the usual Gloss, says : *Ordo verborum est : Spiritus sanctus est Dominus* (or rather *dominus*.) He was followed by a great number of Latin commentators, such as Lanfranc, Haymo of Halberstadt, Hervé, Nicolas of Lyra, Dionysius the Carthusian. Peter Lombard and St Thomas gave his explanation the first place. For these authors and for those who share their views, *dominus* is not a proper but an appellative noun, as appears clearly in the paraphrase of Strabo (*dominus—i.e., potest operari quod vult*), or in that of St Thomas (*dominus—i.e., operatur ex proprio libertatis arbitrio*). The absence of an article in Latin made the confusion possible.

2. *This entirely differentiates their intrepretation from the exegesis of St John Chrysostom and the other Greek Fathers.* They also make τὸ Πνεῦμα the subject of the phrase, understanding thereby the Person of the Holy Spirit ; but no subtlety can obscure their thought, which is clearness itself. Their reasoning amounts to this: Moses formerly addressed the Lord (that is to say, God) ; the Christian addresses the Spirit. Now the Spirit also is himself *the Lord* (that is to say, God). Therefore to address the Spirit is to address God. They prove the minor proposition in two ways :

(a) In our text it is not Christ who is called the Spirit, it is the Spirit who is called Lord ; thus Chrysostom (LXI, 448 : καὶ τοῦτο [Πνεῦμα] Κύριος ἐστιν) ; Theodoret (LXXXII, 397 : Δῆλον ὡς τὸ πανάγιον Πνεῦμα Κύριον προσηγόρευσε) ; Theodore of Mopsuestia (LXVI, 896 : Δῆλον ὅτι μὴ τὸν Κύριον πνεῦμα λέγει, ἀλλὰ τὸ Πνεῦμα Κύριον). St Basil, enumerating the passages in which the Spirit is called Lord, adds our text to them (XXXII, 163-166). So too St Athanasius in *De Trin. et Spir. S.*, for a long time ascribed to Vigilius of Tapsus (XXVI, 545). Oecumenius well sums up the usual exegesis of the Greeks when he says (CXVIII, 955 : Μὴ φοβοῦ, καὶ πρὸς τὸ Πνεῦμα ἐπιστρέφων πρὸς Κύριον ἐπιστρέφεις. Κύριος γὰρ τὸ Πνεῦμα καὶ ὁμοπροσκύνητον καὶ ὁμοούσιον Πατρὶ καὶ Υἱῷ.

(b) The following verse says that, in beholding the glory of the Lord, we are transformed from glory to glory, καθάπερ ἀπὸ κυρίου πνεύματος. But the Greek is grammatically ambiguous and can be translated : as by the Lord the Spirit (ἀπὸ Πνεύματος Κυρίου). It is thus the Greek Fathers generally understand it. They conclude from it again that the Holy Spirit is called Lord (κυριολογεῖται), that is to say God ; for they suppose the synonymy between God and Lord to be established.

We cannot fail to notice that the Greek Fathers always

omit the article of ὁ Κύριος, so keenly do they feel that such a statement as τὸ Πνεῦμα ἐστιν ὁ Κύριος would be incorrect or at least very singular. What made them accept such an unnatural textual disturbance is the double conviction that τὸ Πνεῦμα is here a proper noun and that ὁ Κύριος denotes God and not Christ.

### III—ʹΟ Κύριος SIGNIFIES CHRIST

Here is another point on which modern exegetes are almost unanimously agreed. Indeed, an attentive study of the context and the Pauline vocabulary hardly allow any other view. Suffice it to indicate briefly the three principal reasons for it.

1. *St Paul, speaking for himself*—that is to say, apart from quotations from the Old Testament—*always understands by Κύριος* (with or without the article) *the Son of God and never God himself*. This fact is generally recognized, though a few admit some rare exceptions. Thus Cremer (*Biblisch-theol. Wörterbuch⁹*, p. 619) claims that κύριος *without* an article is used exceptionally as a divine name in 2 Cor. viii, 21 ; Eph. v, 8 ; 1 Thess. iv, 6, and *with* the article in 1 Cor. iv, 19 ; x, 9, 26 ; Eph. v, 17, 19 ; 2 Thess. iii, 5 ; but he hastens to add that in all these examples, except 1 Cor. x, 26, Κύριος or ὁ Κύριος may quite well mean Christ. The remark is a very wise one, for no reason is apparent in the cases cited for diverting the word Κύριος (or ὁ Κύριος) from its usual meaning. As for the one exception asserted by Cremer (1 Cor. x, 26: τcῦ Κυρίου γὰρ ἡ γῆ καὶ τὸ πλήρωμα αὐτῆς), that is a verbal quotation from the Septuagint, Ps. xxiii, 1, and it is singular that the learned lexicographer has not perceived it. Pauline usuage does not, therefore, allow a single exception (at least no certain one), and the exegetes have no right to suppose without good proof that the Apostle gives to Κύριος in 2 Cor. iii, 17 a meaning contrary to his whole customary usage. Here, as everywhere else, ὁ Κύριος must signify Christ. Whoever maintains the contrary must prove it.

2. *This meaning is further imposed by the preceding verse.* No one disputes the fact that the meaning of Κύριος in verse 16 ought to be the same as that of ὁ Κύριος in verse 17 ; otherwise, there would be a manifest lack of coherence in the discourse and a fallacy in the reasoning. Now the Lord in verse 16 can only be Christ : Ἡνίκα δὲ ἐὰν ἐπιστρέψῃ πρὸς Κύριον, περιαιρεῖται τὸ κάλυμμα. In order to remove the veil, symbol of blindness and servitude, it is sufficient to turn to the Lord and be converted to him—the figurative meaning of ἐπιστρέφεσθαι is not without an allusion to the proper sense of the word, applicable only to Moses—but it is in Christ alone that

the veil is taken away (verse 14: ὅτι ἐν Χριστῷ καταργεῖται) ; it is therefore to him that it is necessary to go to find light and liberty. Does anyone imagine that St Paul places the characteristic difference between the Jews and the Jewish Christians in the fact that the latter have become converted to God? As a Jew, Paul is conscious of having always served God (Acts xxiii, 1; 2 Tim. i, 3), but that which has made him a Christian is faith in Christ (Gal. i, 15 ; Phil. iii, 8).

3. *The following verse also enforces the equation:* " *The Lord = Christ.*" If the Lord means God, it can only be God without distinction of Persons, for that is the only intelligible meaning of the equation: The Lord (God) is the (Holy) Spirit; but then the "implied sense" of the word "Lord" will change in the following phrase, since, if the Spirit is the Person of the Holy Spirit, the Lord (God) can be only the Father or the Son. On the contrary, if we understand that the Lord means Christ, the same meaning is maintained to the end, and we can speak without ambiguity of the "spirit of the Lord" and of the "Lord [who is] spirit."

## IV—Τὸ πνεῦμα IS NOT THE PERSON OF THE HOLY SPIRIT

Even if ὁ Κύριος should signify God and not Christ, it is not clear how τὸ Πνεῦμα could denote the Person of the Holy Spirit. Indeed, in the proposition: "God is the Holy Spirit," either *God* is God the Father, and the proposition is manifestly false, or else *God* is the divine nature without distinction of Persons; and the proposition is so difficult to justify, that all the skill of the exegetes is insufficient to explain it. We can very well say : The Holy Spirit is God, because God, though he is one, subsists in three Persons ; but we cannot, on the contrary, say : God is the Holy Spirit, because the Holy Spirit does not exhaust all the fulness of the divine essence. Chrysostom and his school instinctively felt this, and that is why they made τὸ Πνεῦμα the subject of the phrase. Admitting that ὁ Κύριος is a divine name and, in fact, a synonym of God, they obtained in that way a proposition of irreproachable orthodoxy : The Holy Spirit is the Lord—that is to say, God. But if, with all the moderns, we reject as inadmissible the transposition of subject and attribute, we cannot intelligibly explain how the Lord can be the Holy Spirit.

If, on the contrary, as we have proved, ὁ Κύριος signifies Christ, τὸ πνεῦμα cannot be the Person of the Holy Spirit. Indeed, it is evident that one divine Person cannot be identified with another, and that such an equation as "the Father is the Son," or "the Son is the Holy Spirit," is absolutely refuted by the very notion of Person. In order to defend it, it would be necessary to maintain, with contemporary rationalists, either that the Holy Spirit is not a personal being, or that neither Christ nor the Spirit is a Person, but that they are merely influences, forces, spiritual *atmospheres*. For these systems of thought see Holzmeister, *op. cit.*, pp. 18-27. Having elsewhere proved that Christ and the Holy Spirit are distinct Persons, we shall not pause to consider this explanation.

## V—Tὸ πνεῦμα IS THE SPIRIT AS OPPOSED TO THE LETTER

If the spirit is not the Holy Spirit, can it be a "spiritual substance" as in the phrase "God is spirit" (John iv, 24), which has a false air of resemblance to ours? Several exegetes have thought so, such as Eusebius of Caesarea (*De eccles. theol.*, iii, 5; XXIV, 1012, etc.), Didymus the Blind (*De Spir. S.*, 54 and 58, XXXIX, 1079 and 1081), Walafrid Strabo in the common Gloss (CXIV, 555), and after him a goodly number of scholastics. But this explanation cannot be granted; for πνεῦμα could not then be in any way accompanied by the definite article. All modern exegetes, Protestant and Catholic, are agreed on this point.

The meaning is clearly suggested by the context which must be resumed from a rather remote previous point. Let us not forget that the first three chapters are an apology. Paul, accused of duplicity, disloyalty and shameful concealments, repudiates these reproaches indignantly and with an insistence for which he feels obliged to apologize. He needs no letters of recommendation, he declares; the Corinthians whom he has converted are themselves his letter of recommendation, written not with ink but with the spirit of the living God (iii, 3). Thenceforth the antithesis "letter" and "spirit" is the keynote of his defence. His words and acts are stamped with an apostolic liberty and frankness (πεποίθησις, παρρησία, ἐλευθερία) in consideration of the ministry which he fills:

It is not the ministry of the *old covenant*, but that of the *new* (iii, 6).
It is not the ministry of the *letter*, but that of the *spirit* (iii, 6 and iii, 8).
It is not a ministry of *death*, but one of *life* (iii, 7).
It is not a ministry of *condemnation*, but one of *justice* (iii, 9).

He contrasts the Gospel with the old covenant considered in itself, independently of the new and actually in conflict with the new. From this point of view, the Mosaic Law is a decrepit institution, a dead letter, which has actually produced death and condemnation; the Gospel is, however, a *spiritual* principle, quickening and justifying; for "the *letter* killeth," if it be left alone, isolated from the spirit; but the *spirit* quickeneth (iii, 6); the new dispensation, which bears a relation to the old, such as the spirit bears to the letter, gives life and supernatural justice. Here the purest Pauline doctrine is easily recognized.

Nevertheless, the ministration of the old covenant, in spite of its imperfection, was so glorious that its brilliancy was depicted on the face of Moses and obliged him to cover it with a veil. How much more glorious will be the ministration of the new covenant! (iii, 7-11). But the Apostles nevertheless show their faces unveiled; they do not borrow Moses' veil, which is a symbol of fear and blindness (iii, 12, 13); they leave it to the unbelieving Jews, who read the *letter* of the Law without grasping its *spirit* (iii, 14, 15). This veil Christ alone makes void (iii, 14), and when the Jews turn to the Lord and are converted to him, they will perceive this veil fall from their eyes (iii, 16). " Now the Lord is the spirit " (iii, 17)—that is to say, the spiritual and prophetic sense hidden under the letter. "Where the spirit of the Lord is, there is liberty," freedom exempt from cowardice and concealment. " But we all," concludes the Apostle, "beholding with open face the glory of the Lord, are transformed from glory to glory (and from brightness to brightness) into the same image, as by the Lord the spirit."

We have thus the advantage of keeping the antithesis "letter and spirit" in its natural and usual meaning (Rom. ii, 28, 29: *Non enim qui in manifesto Judaeus est; neque quae in manifesto, in carne, est circumcisio; sed qui in abscondito Judaeus est; et circumcisio cordis* in spiritu, non littera). The Christian is circumcised not literally but spiritually; not according to the letter of the Mosaic Law, but according to the spirit—that is to say, according to the typical and prophetic meaning of this law.—So also Rom. vii, 6: *Nunc autem soluti sumus a lege mortis (mortis* is gloss) *in qua detinebamur, ita ut serviamus* in novitate spiritus et non in vetustate litterae.—The Vulgate is right, in both cases, to write *spiritus* without an initial capital, for here there is no question of the Person of the Holy Spirit, although we can very easily pass from the activity of the Holy Spirit to his Person. Grammatically, the last words ἀπὸ Κυρίου πνεύματος can be translated in four ways:

    (*a*) By the Lord of the spirit (πν. depending on κυρ.).
    (*b*) By the Spirit of the Lord (κυρ. depending on πν. inversely).
    (*c*) By the Spirit (who is) Lord (apposition inversely).
    (*d*) By the Lord (who is) the spirit (natural apposition).

But (*a*) does not give a satisfying or even an intelligible sense. We can say the "Spirit of the Lord," but what is "the Lord of the Spirit"? (*b*) and (*c*) present an inversion which nothing allows us to assume or to accept, for this would be to go in search of ambiguity for its own sake. Therefore, the last of the above translations becomes imperative ; and it does so irresistibly, if we reach the equation : " The Lord is Christ," as almost all contemporary exegetes do.

Our interpretation is not new. Origen and St Thomas had already proposed it. In spite of some differences of detail, Origen maintains constantly : (*a*) That *the Lord* is Christ ; (*b*) that the *spirit* is not the third Person of the Trinity ; (*c*) that the *spirit* is the contrary of the letter. (*Contra Celsum*, vi, 70 ; *In. Matt.*, x, 14 ; *In Joan.*, xiii, 53 ; *In Exod. hom.*, xiii, 4.)—St Thomas has two explanations : the first is that of the usual Gloss, which it was not advisable to omit, however unsatisfactory it might be ; the second is the following : *Alio modo, ut per Dominum intelligatur Christus ; id est spiritus potestatis, et ideo, ubi est spiritus Domini, id est lex Christi spiritualiter intellecta, non scripta litteris, sed per fidem cordibus impressa, ibi est libertas ab omni impedimento velaminis.*—Many other commentators have remarked that the antithesis *letter* and *spirit* dominates this entire chapter. To cite only the most recent ones : Lebreton, *Origines du dogme de la trinité*[4], 1917, note F, p. 569, and Lemonnyer, *Epîtres de S Paul*, 1906, vol. i, p. 197 : " We ask whether this verse (iii, 17) does not refer to iii, 16 [*non littera sed Spiritu*], and whether the phrase : The Lord is the Spirit, is not implicitly parallel to this other : Moses is the Law." Very good ; but I should be much more affirmative.

If the free questions of exegesis, like this one, are not settled by an appeal to authority, it is always a consolation for an exegete to find himself in good company.

# NOTE U—PATRISTIC THEORIES OF REDEMPTION

Most of the texts are collected in the work of the Abbé J. Rivière (*Le dogme de la Rédemption, essai d'étude historique,* Paris, 1905), to which we refer the reader. Leaving aside the heterodox theory of subjective redemption, we shall confine ourselves to stating succinctly the three principal views of the Fathers : the theory of ransom, the theory of substitution, and the theory of solidarity.

## I—The Theory of Redemption and the Rights of the Devil

1. *Reprehensible Patristic Texts.*—When the Fathers are content to say that sin makes us slaves and even slaves of the devil, that Jesus Christ is our ransom, that he purchases us by his blood, there is nothing to object to, since their language is Scriptural. But some of them affirm or insinuate that the devil had claims to us, that compensation was due to him, that he would not have released us without it—in fact, that a ransom was paid him. Here are the incriminated passages :

(A) *Origen,* among other irreproachable explanations, insists a little too much on the ideas of ransom and redemption, which he seems to take in their literal sense. *Cf. In Roman.,* iii, 7 (XIV, 945) ; *In Joan.,* i, 39 and vi, 35 (XIV, 92 and 292). He likes to describe sin under the figure of a contract, by virtue of which we sell ourselves to the devil. *Cf. In Exod. hom.,* vi, 9 (XII, 338); *In Jerem. hom.,* xv, 5 (XIII, 433); *Iu Roman.,* v, 3 (XIV, 1026) ; *In Luke hom.,* xxii (XIII, 1862). Once he even asks whether the ransom has not been paid to Satan, *In Matt.,* xvi, 8 (XIII, 1397) : Τίνι δὲ ἔδωκε τὴν ψυχὴν αὐτοῦ λύτρον ἀντὶ πόλλων ; οὐ γὰρ δὴ τῷ θεῷ· μήτι οὖν τῷ πονηρῷ; οὗτος γὰρ ἐκρατεῖ ἡμῶν ἕως δοθῇ τὸ ὑπὲρ ἡμῶν αὐτῷ λύτρον ἡ τοῦ Ἰησοῦ ψυχὴ ἀπατηθέντι ὡς δυναμένῳ αὐτῆς κυριεῦσαι. *Cf. In Roman.,* ii, 13 (XIV, 145).

(B) If Origen hesitates, St Gregory of Nyssa is categorical : *Oratio catech. magna,* 22-24 (XLV, 60-66). The contract of sale concluded with the devil is valid ; we really belong to him ; God could doubtless liberate us forcibly from our master, but he prefers to observe equity and justice with him ; therefore a ransom is paid him : Ἔδει μὴ τὸν τυραννικὸν ἀλλὰ τὸν δίκαιον τρόπον ἐπινοηθῆναι τῆς ἀνακλήσεως · οὗτος δέ ἐστί τις τῷ ἐπικρατοῦντι ποιήσασθαι πᾶν ὅπερ ἂν ἔθελοι λύτρον (*ibid.* 23, XLV, 61).

(C) St Ambrose is also fond of describing the bargain which delivers us over to Satan. The devil buys us at auction. *Cf. De Jacob,* I, iii, 10 (XIV, 632) ; *In Psalm,* xxxvi, No. 46 (XV, 1036); *In Luke,* vii, Nos. 114-117 and x, No. 66

(XV, 1727-8 and 1913). From that to saying that the devil had to be indemnified was only a step. St Ambrose took this step once at least : *Pretium nostrae liberationis erat sanguis Domini Jesu, quod necessario solvendum erat ei cui peccatis venditi eramus* (*Epist.*, lxxii, 8-9 [XVI, 1299-1300]). Cf. *Epist.*, xli, 7-8 (XVI, 1162-3).

(D) St Jerome has something like it : *Nec ante veniam accipere possumus delictorum et servi esse cessamus, nisi pretium pro nobis cruentus quondam victor accepit* (*In Ephes.*, i, 7 [XXVI, 450-1]). The whole passage seems to betray the influence of Origen.

(E) I do not know whether it is necessary to add to this list St Basil by reason of a phrase rather rhetorical than dogmatic, *In Psalm.* xlviii, 3 (XXIX, 437) : ὑποχειρίους ὑμᾶς λαβὼν [ὁ διάβολος] οὐ πρότερον ἀφίησι πρὶν ἄν τινι λύτρῳ ἀξιολόγῳ πεισθεὶς ἀνταλλάξασθαι ὑμᾶς ἕληται.

But St Irenæus ought not to figure in this list in any way, for he protests quite frequently that the devil had no real claims upon us. *Cf.* P. Galtier, *La rédemption et les droits du démon dans Saint Irénée*, Paris, 1911 (extract from the *Recherches de science relig.*, vol. ii, part 1).

2. *An Entirely Different Conception.*—It is thus presented by M. J. Rivière, *Le dogme de la rédemption*, p. 396 : " The devil has received from God the power to put men to death on account of their sins ; but in attacking Jesus Christ, who is innocent, he seriously overstepped his constitutional rights ; it is, therefore, perfectly just that God, for this abuse of power, should deprive him of his captives. The devil no longer receives a ransom, but the just punishment of his crime." This conception is met with especially in the Latin Fathers : St Hilary, *In Psalm.* lxviii, 8 (IX, 475); St Pacian, *De baptismo*, 4 (XIII, 1092); Ambrosiaster, *Comment. in Col.*, ii, 15 (XVII, 431) and *passim ;* St Augustine, *De lib. arbitrio*, III, x, 29-31 (XXXII, 1285-7); *De trinitate*, XII, xii, 16-19 (XLII, 1026-9); St Leo, *Serm.*, xxii, 3-4 (LIV, 196-7) and *passim;* St Caesarius of Arles, *Hom. de Paschate*, iii (LXVII, 1049); St Gregory the Great, *Moral.*, XVII, xxx, 46-47 (LXXVI, 32-33). But it is found also in the Greek Fathers : St Chrysostom, *In Joan. hom.*, lxviii, 2-3 (LIX, 372-373); Theodoret, *De provid.*, x (LXXXIII, 748); St Cyril of Alexandria, *De incarn. Domini*, xi (LXXV, 1433-6); St John Damascene, *De fide orth.*, iii, 1 (XCIV, 984), whence it passed to St Thomas, *Summa theol.*, III$^a$, qu. 1, a. 1.

The idea is often presented in another form. The devil, thinking his triumph easy, attacks Jesus Christ, and himself rushes to his own defeat. He deceives himself, he is the dupe of his hatred, he is caught in the snare, on the hook, in the trap : St Gregory of Nyssa, *Oratio cat. magna*, 24 (XLV, 66);

St Augustine, *Serm.*, cxxx, 2 (XXXVIII, 726 : *Redemptor . . . tetendit* muscipulam *crucem suam ; posuit ibi quasi escam sanguinem suum*) and *passim ;* St Gregory the Great, *Moral.*, xxxiii, vi, 12-13 (LXXVI, 677-680 : In *hamo* captus est, quia inde interiit unde devoravit) and *passim ;* St Isidore of Seville, I, xiv, 12 (LXXXIII, 567 : *Illusus est diabolus morte Domini quasi avis. Nam ostensa Christus suae carnis mortalitate, quam interimendam ille appetebat, abscondit divinitatem, ut* laqueum *quo eum velut avem improvidam prudenti irretiret* decipula).

These metaphors are of more than doubtful taste, especially when it is Jesus Christ who, with the connivance of his Father, prepares the snare or the hook; but they do not affect the purity of the theological doctrine, since it is understood that the devil has no claims on us, or that he has only those which God allows him for our punishment.

3. *Criticism of the Rights Possessed by the Devil.*—This begins at an early date. We find it from the third century onwards, in the anonymous author of the *De recta in Deum fide*, attributed falsely to Origen (XI, 1756-7). The indignant protestation of St Gregory of Nazianzus, *Orat.*, xlv, 22 (XXXVI, 653) deserves to be cited. The saintly doctor asks himself to whom the ransom offered by Christ has been paid : Εἰ μὲν τῷ πονηρῷ, φεῦ τῆς ὕβρεως, εἰ μὴ παρὰ Θεοῦ μόνον, ἀλλὰ καὶ τὸν Θεὸν αὐτὸν λύτρον ὁ λῃστὴς λαμβάνει καὶ μισθὸν οὕτως ὑπερφυῆ τῆς ἑαυτοῦ τυραννίδος, δι' ὃν καὶ ἡμῶν φείδεσθαι δίκαιον ἦν. St John Damascene, *De fide orth.*, iii, 27 (XCIV, 1096), condemns this repugnant idea with no less force. But it is Abelard (*In Roman.*, ii, 3 and *Epit. theol.*, 23, CLXXVIII, 833-5 and 1730-1) and St Anselm (*Cur Deus homo*, i, 7 and *Medit.*, xi, CLVIII, 363-8 and 763-4) who gave the theory of the devil's rights the death-blow. After them there was merely a repetition of their arguments, which were decisive.

## II—SUBSTITUTION AND SATISFACTION

1. The Fathers rarely develop the theory of *substitution*, but they always take it for granted when they say that Jesus Christ has paid our debt or our ransom, or has undergone the punishment which was due to us in our place. They often express this idea by compound words formed with the particle ἀντί. Jesus Christ is πάντων ἀνθρώπων ἀντάξιος (St Basil, in *Psalm.* xlviii, XXIX, 440 ; St Cyril of Alexandria, *Glaphyr. in Levit.*, LXIX, 548 ; Clement of Alexandria, *Quis dives salvetur*, 37, IX, 641, etc.), ἀντίψυχος (Eusebius, *De theoph.*, 3, XXIV, 616; Procopius of Gaza, *In Isaiam*, liii, LXXXVII, 25, etc.), or ἀντάλλαγμα (St Gregory Nazianzen, *Orat.*, i, 5, XXV, 400, etc.). These forms of speech, of which there are numberless examples, are authorized by St Paul (1 Tim. ii, 6 : ἀντίλυτρον).

More than any other theory, that of substitution lent itself to exaggerations and erroneous deductions. The curious history of it will be found in Rivière (*op. cit.*, pp. 373-445), and, for Protestants, in Lichtenberger (art. *Rédemption* in *Encycl. des sciences relig.*, vol. xi, 143-4). M. Rivière (*Les conceptions catholiques du dogme de la rédemption*, in *Rev. prat. d'apologétique*, vol. xiii, 1911, pp. 5-32, 104-120, 161-176), affirms (p. 119) that "it is the Reformation which is responsible for putting into the foreground the notion of punishment and reducing Redemption to a mystery of bloody substitution." He is of opinion (p. 120) that "the idea of penal expiation is entirely accessory and that consequently, if given the front rank, it can only end in fallacies and disastrous errors."

2. The theory of *satisfaction*, at least as St Anselm presents it, is based upon the idea of substitution. It does not appear that the *present meaning* of the terms "to satisfy" and "satisfaction" existed before St Anselm. It is not found notably in the two frequently quoted texts of St Hilary (*In Psalm.* liii, 12 ; IX, 344) and of St Ambrose (*De fuga saec.*, vii, 44 ; XIV, 589). Tertullian, St Cyprian, and other Latin Fathers make use of the terms frequently in order to signify the works of penitence by which the sinner seeks to appease God, but not to denote the work of redemption. According to M. Rivière (*op. cit.*, p. 289), Raoul Ardent, towards the end of the eleventh century, was the first to give them this last meaning, without, however, applying them yet to the death of the Saviour. For the theory of the Archbishop of Canterbury, *cf.* Bainvel, *Anselme (Saint)* in *Dict. de théol. cathol.*; and, among more recent authors, B. Funke, *Satisfaktionstheorie des hl. Anselm von Canterbury*, Münster-i.-W., 1903 (*Kirchengesch. Studien*, vol. vi, part 3) ; L. Heinrichs, *Die Genugtuungstheorie des hl. Anselmus von Canterbury*, Paderborn, 1909 (*Forschungen zur christ. Liter. und Dogmengesch.*, vol. ix, part 1); Hugon, O.P., *Le mystère de la rédemption*, in the *Rev. thomiste*, vol. xviii (1909), pp. 406-421, 663-677 (and separately, Paris, 1910) ; G. C. Foley, *Anselm's Theory of the Atonement*, London, 1910.

The first scholastic doctors corrected little by little what was inaccurate or indefinite in St Anselm's system. Peter Lombard called attention to the fact that the death of Christ was not the only way which God made use of to save men. Alexander of Hales and St Bonaventure taught that neither the Incarnation nor the Passion was absolutely and strictly required for our salvation, but only by an obligation of propriety or in consequence of the divine decree. St Thomas insisted that the merit of Christ is ours, since Christ is our Head and we are his members. Duns Scotus went beyond all bounds in declaring that the satisfaction of Jesus Christ neither possessed an infinite value nor needed to possess it to be adequate.   But he had few followers.


### III—THE PRINCIPLE OF SOLIDARITY

This principle, as we have said, has been recognized from the beginning and is becoming ever more and more recognized.   We limit ourselves to a few salient features.

1. *St Irenæus* speaks very often of the summing up of all things in Christ : *Haeres.*, III, xviii, 1 ; xxi, 10 ; V, i, 2 ; v, 1-2 ; xxi, 1, etc.   The idea resulting from all these passages and other similar ones is that Christ begins the work of Adam again in the reverse way ; that he comprises all humanity in himself, as Adam, of whom he is the antitype, also comprised it ; and that therefore he must belong to the human family, in order to be its representative.   All this tends to the notion of solidarity both in the fall and in the rehabilitation of mankind.   But this idea is by no means peculiar to St Irenæus.

2. *Many Fathers* go further.   Not only do they say that Jesus Christ had to be a man in order to save men, but they make the union between Christ and humanity represented by him so close, that the flesh is sanctified by his presence and healed by his contact.   The result is always that in their eyes the human race is contained in Christ as in its chief and legal representative, so that the acts of Christ are morally the acts of the human family.   Here are some texts chosen from the most concise, but not always the most expressive, statements : "God refashions and restores Adam by himself" (St. Hippolytus, *De Christo et Antichristo*, 26 : 'Ἀναπλάσσων δι' ἑαυτοῖ τὸν 'Αδάμ).—*Deum in primo quidem Adam offendimus, non facientes ejus praeceptum; in secundo autem Adam reconciliati sumus, obedientes usque ad mortem facti* (St Irenæus, *Haeres.*, V, xvi, 3).—*Ergo ex nobis accepit quod proprium offerret pro nobis, ut nos redimeret ex nostro. . . . Nam quae erat causa incarnationis nisi ut caro quae peccaverat per se redimeretur* (St Ambrose, *De incarnationis sacram.*, vi, 54 and 56, XVI, 832).—*In eo* (*Christo*) *per naturam suscepti corporis quaedam universi generis humani congregatio continetur* (St Hilary, *In Matt.*, iv, 12 ; IX, 935).   These significant texts are not rare.

3. The majority of modern authors adopt the principle of solidarity, already clearly stated by St Thomas.   It is necessary to remark, however, that several of them do not understand it rightly.   For them solidarity consists in the fact that

the Son of God, by assuming our nature and associating himself with our destinies, accepts in advance his sufferings and death, which is, on his part, the greatest evidence of love. In this way the solidarity can be reconciled with the theory of a purely subjective redemption. Nevertheless, almost all these writers honestly warn their readers that their doctrine, which they claim is conformable to the teaching of Jesus, is not in harmony with that of Paul.

# NOTE V—"FAITH" IN ST PAUL

## I—Statistics and Evidence

1. *The Verb " to Believe."*—Out of *fifty-four* cases, πιστεύειν is employed *fourteen* times absolutely (especially in the participle ὁ πιστεύων = the believer, the faithful). Of the *forty* other cases we must eliminate *seven* where πιστεύεσθαι in the passive has the classical meaning of "to take in charge" (Rom. iii, 2; I Cor. ix, 17; Gal. ii, 7; I Thess. ii, 4; 2 Thess. i, 10; I Tim. i, 11; Titus i, 3).—In the *thirty-three* remaining cases, the indirect object is expressed *twenty-six* times and the direct object *seven* times. The indirect object is found: (*a*) With the dative (*eight* times) either of the thing (2 Thess. ii, 11, 12; Rom. x, 16), or of the person (Rom. iv, 3, 17; Gal. iii, 6; 2 Tim. i, 12; Titus iii, 8).—(*b*) With εἰς (Rom. x, 14), *twice* (Gal. ii, 16; Phil. i, 29).—(*c*) With ἐπί and the dative (Rom. ix, 33; x, 11; I Tim. i, 16).—(*d*) With ἐπί and the accusative (Rom. iv, 5, 24).—The direct object is found: (*a*) With the infinitive (Rom. xiv, 2: πιστεύει φαγεῖν, but the meaning is peculiar.—(*b*) With ὅτι (Rom. vi, 8; x, 9; I Thess. iv, 14).—(*c*) With the accusative (μέρος τι πιστεύω, I Cor. xi, 18; πάντα πιστεύει, I Cor. xiii, 7; but the sense of the first example is not religious nor perhaps that of the second). In I Tim. iii, 16 (ἐπιστεύθη ἐν κόσμῳ), the subject of the passive, and consequently the object of the corresponding active, is Christ.

2. *The Word " Faith."*—The word πίστις appears in all the Epistles without exception *a hundred and forty-two* times (not including the Epistle to the Hebrews). When we have discarded the very rare cases in which faith assumes a special meaning: *faithfulness* (Rom. iii, 3), *good faith* (Rom. xiv, 22, 23), *sworn faith* (I Tim. v, 12), or again *charismatical faith, faith working miracles* (Rom. xii, 3, 6; I Cor. xii, 9; xiii, 2), we observe that "faith" is almost always employed absolutely or, by exception, accompanied either by a qualifying word or by a genitive, which may be possessive or objective. We perceive also that faith, according to the context, designates an act, a habit, or an object, which is none other than the Gospel or the Christian dispensation. Sometimes we hesitate between these three meanings. We may, however, lay down the following rules: (*a*) Faith is *actual* when it is related to the justification which it produces (Rom. iii, 22, 28, 30; iv, 5, 9, 11, 13, 16; v, 1; Gal. ii, 16; iii, 8, 9, 11; Phil. iii, 9).— (*b*) Faith is usually *habitual* when it has a personal pronoun in the genitive (Rom. i, 8, 12; I Thess. i, 3, 8; iii, 2, 5, 6, 7, etc.),

when it is found in a list of virtues (Gal. v, 22 ; 2 Thess. i, 4 ;
1 Tim. i, 14, etc.), when it is a question of the faith that abides
(1 Cor. xiii, 13), increases (2 Cor. x, 15), or of the Christian
who lives (Gal. ii, 20), walks (2 Cor. v, 7) or perseveres in
faith (1 Cor. xvi, 13, etc.).—(c) The faith is *objective* whenever
it can be replaced by the word "Gospel," which happens, in
particular, when it is put in opposition to the Law (Rom.
iii, 31 ; iv, 14, etc.), and in a certain number of expressions,
such as to preach the faith (Gal. i, 23), the word of faith
(Rom. x, 8), obedience to the faith (Rom. i, 5 ; xvi, 26 ;
Gal. iii, 2, etc.), the faith that comes and will come (Gal. iii,
23, 25, etc.).

The genitive that follows the word "faith" is naturally
possessive when it is a personal pronoun : "our faith, your
faith"; it is objective when it is the name of a thing: 2 Thess.
ii, 13 (ἐν πίστει ἀληθείας), Col. ii, 12 (συνηγέρθητε διὰ τῆς πίστεως
τῆς ἐνεργείας τοῦ Θεοῦ), Phil. i, 27 (συναθλοῦντες τῇ πίστει τοῦ
εὐαγγελίου) : faith *in* the truth, *in* the power of God, *in* the
Gospel.

## II—Justifying Faith, the Form of which is Charity

In contrast to the Judaizers who expect justification or the
perfection of justice from the observance of the Law, the true
Christian expects justice from faith : Ἡμεῖς γὰρ πνεύματι ἐκ
πίστεως ἐλπίδα δικαιοσύνης ἀπεκδεχόμεθα (Gal. v, 5 : *Nos enim
spiritu ex fide, spem justitiae expectamus*. Read this without
any comma, which the sense excludes). The last words
ought not to be translated "we have the hope"—that is to
say, "we hope"—for ἐλπίς here is not subjective (hope) but
objective (the thing hoped for), as in a very similar passage
(Titus ii, 13: προσδεχόμενοι τὴν μακαρίαν ἐλπίδα). In its turn the
expression ἐλπίς δικαιοσύνης cannot be a genitive of apposition
(the justice hoped for), if we understand by justice *justification*,
since St Paul is speaking expressly of those who are already
Christians. Consequently either δικαιοσύνη expresses an increase of justice—and we thus obtain an idea which harmonizes well with the pretended perfection of justice which
the Judaizers expect from the observance of the Law—or
else, as is more generally admitted, it is a possessive genitive :
"the blessings which justice hopes for." In any case, it is
from faith (ἐκ πίστεως) that we expect either the progress or
the recompense of justice.

The Apostle gives the following reasons for this (Gal. v, 6):

Εν γὰρ Χ. Ἰ. οὔτε περιτομή τι    *Nam in Christo Jesu neque
ἰσχύει οὔτε ἀκροβυστία, ἀλλὰ    circumcisio aliquid valet, neque
πίστις δι' ἀγάπης ἐνεργουμένη.    praeputium, sed fides quae per
                                      charitatem operatur.*

Thus, in conformity with the true principles of Christianity and for the true Christian (ἐν Χριστῷ 'Ιησοῖ) circumcision avails no more than uncircumcision, but faith alone can avail anything (ἰσχύει τι, for it is a question of obtaining justice or an increase of justice), on condition that it is united to charity. There has been much and indeed too much discussion over the question whether ἐνεργουμένη is *passive* (faith made active or put into operation by charity), as profane usage, the Greek Fathers in general, and a great number of commentators would have it, or whether it is a *means* (faith which works by charity, which acts through charity), as the Latin Fathers and the majority of modern commentators think, in accordance with the ordinary usage of the New Testament. In both cases faith acts only by virtue of its union with charity and because it derives its efficacy therefrom. *Juxta Apostolum* (says Palmieri, *Comment. in Gal.*, 1886, p. 207) *fides quae valet in Christo Jesu, est fides operans per charitatem, conjuncta proinde charitati et ab ea formata; atqui fides, quae justificat, est certe fides quae plurimum valet in Christo, cum nos eidem conjungat: ergo fides justificans est fides formata charitate. Neque Protestantes unquam rationem reddent cur charitas non requisita ad justificandum, requiratur ad conservandam justitiam, aliis verbis, cur, si justus fio sola fide, nequeam perseverare justus, sola perseverante fide.* It is surprising to see the Protestants always repeating the objection that if charity is the *form* of faith, it is an essential part of faith. St Thomas refuted this quibble in advance : *Non dicitur esse forma fidei charitas per modum quo forma est pars essentiae, sic enim contra fidem dividi non posset; sed in quantum aliquam perfectionem fides a charitate consequitur, sicut in universo elementa superiora dicuntur esse ut forma inferiorum* (*De Verit.*, qu. xiv, a. 5 ad 1). All Catholic theologians express themselves in the same way.

There is an important monograph on this subject by J. Wieser (*Pauli apost. doctrina de justificatione ex fide sine operibus et ex fide operante*, Trent, 1874), but we dare not recommend it, because the author makes Paul think too much after the fashion of the scholastic categories and because he does not seem to us to have always apprehended the meaning of the Apostle. On the contrary, the study of B. Bartmann (*S. Paulus and S. Jacobus über die Rechtfertigung*, 1897, in *Biblische Studien*, vol. ii, part 1) deserves to be read.

### III—THE PROTESTANT THEORY OF JUSTIFYING FAITH

1. *The Dogma " Sola Fide."*—All the Protestant confessions of faith agree on this formula, although they understand it differently. The *Augsburg Confession* of 1530 understands by it *special* faith: *Fide hoc beneficium [justificationis] accipiendum*

*est, qua credere nos oportet, quod propter Christum nobis donen-
tur remissio peccatorum et justificatio.* It is true one reads
a little further on : *Fides hic* non tantum *historiae notitiam
significat, sed significat credere promissioni misericordiae quae
nobis per Mediatorem Christum contigit.* The *non tantum* contradicts the preceding assertion; but that merely proves the
usual indecision of the reformers. Moreover, most of the
confessions adhere to the general formula : *Credimus nos* sola
fide *fieri hujus justitiae participes.* The *Gallican Confession*
(formulated in 1559, presented to Charles IX in 1561 at the
Conference of Poissy), No. 20—Sola fide *nos justificari doctrina est saluberrima.* The *Anglican Confession of* 1562,
Art. 11—*Merito cum Paulo dicimus : Nos* sola fide *justificari
seu fide absque operibus. The Acts of the Synod of Dordrecht*
of 1561, No. 22. Similarly the *Confession of Bâle* of 1547,
the *Saxon Confession* of 1551, the *Swiss Confession* of
1566, etc.

There were two difficulties : that faith is never alone, and
that it is not any kind of faith that justifies, but living faith.
Why, then, has faith only the power to justify rather than
charity which accompanies it, and what is the *life* of faith ?

The leaders of Protestantism did not contest the fact that
living faith ought to be accompanied by other dispositions.
Luther admitted the need of hope (*In Gal.*, v, 5 : *Fides et spes
vix discerni possunt*). Calvin apparently included charity
also. But Luther vigorously denied that faith owed to
charity its power to justify (*In Gal.*, iii, 12 : *Haec fides* sine *et*
ante *charitatem justificat*). Melancthon's merit was to discover the convenience of this distinction. When it was
objected : Faith, according to you, is confidence; but in confidence there is charity ; therefore it is charity that justifies ;
he replied : *Concedo in fiducia inesse dilectionem et hanc virtutem
plerasque alias adesse oportere.* But it is not, he added, on
account of the other virtues that one is justified, but on
account of faith. The other virtues are concomitant, because
they are not adequately distinguished from faith or because
they are inseparable from it, but it is *faith only* that is active
or receptive, according to the system adopted.

2. *How and Why Faith Justifies.*—The founders of Protestantism taught at first that faith was the *formal cause* of our
justification—namely, that in which our justification consists.
Thus Luther on Gal. ii, 16 : *Ea [vera fiducia cordis] est* formalis
*justitia propter quam homo justificatur, non propter charitatem,
ut sophistae loquuntur.* Which Thomas Illyricus explained as
follows : *Fiduciam in Christum esse nostram formalem justitiam
seu imputari nobis in justitiam;* but here there is a contradiction in terms. Calvin also calls faith "the formal or instrumental cause of justification" (*Instit.*, III, xiv, 17); but the

formal and the instrumental cause mutually exclude each other. On the other hand, the *Augsburg Confession* seems to teach that faith justifies merely by its *presence*, without any influence or causality on its part: *Cum dicimus* Fide justificamur, *non hoc intelligimus quod justi simus propter ipsius virtutis dignitatem. Sed haec est sententia: Consequi nos remissionem peccatorum et imputationem justitiae per misericordiam propter Christum.*

The official doctrine of Protestantism is, however, that faith is the *instrument of* justification : ὄργανον ληπτικόν. Only some imagine this instrument to be a purely *receptive* power, while others concede it a certain *activity*. Moreover, the majority refuse to examine the question how faith justifies ; this, according to them, would be a superfluous and harmful curiosity. Luther, when urged to do so, burst out in invectives against sophists and their pernicious, pestilential, infernal, devilish, satanic, and blasphemous sophisms. It was sufficient, he said, to know the part which faith plays, without being necessary to scrutinize its nature. Protestants have always preferred the negative definition of justifying faith : " It is neither belief in mysteries, nor belief in historical facts, not even in the fact of redemption, nor miracle-working faith, nor the simulated faith of Simon the Magician." They can be divided into two great theological schools, one of which accords to faith no moral value, while the other recognizes in it a certain value.

(A) *Justifying Faith, a Purely Receptive Power.*—Luther constantly protested that faith was not indebted to charity for the power to justify, because it justified "without charity and *before* it" (*In Epist. ad Gal.*, iii, 12), because " it is not charity which ornaments and animates faith, but faith which ornaments and animates charity" (*In Gal.*, ii, 19). Yet Melancthon—and Calvin too, apparently—made no difficulty in conceding that faith was inseparable from at least an initial charity and from several other virtues (which Luther could not deny in the case of hope), but they maintained that we are justified on account of faith only, and not because of these concomitant virtues. Since then certain writers, more Lutheran than Luther, have endeavoured to prove that faith is not an *act*, but something purely *passive*, since St Paul opposes it to *works ;* and that it is without moral value, so jealous are they to maintain that it has no positive influence on salvation, and that it is only the condition of it pure and simple. But then they are obliged to give up explaining why it is pleasing to God and glorifies him, and why it is required for justification. Very early the idea occurred to them to say that faith justified because it took possession of (*apprehendebat*) Christ as Redeemer. Gerhard, in his *De justificatione*, is the one who has presented this point of view most clearly (section 153) : *Fides non justificat vel meritorie, vel per modum disposi-*

*tionis, sed* organice [*i.e.*, as an instrument, ὄργανον] et per
modum apprehensionis, *quatenus meritum Christi in verbo
Evangelii oblatum complectitur.* Consequently, justifying faith
is defined (*ibid.*, § 117): *Fiducialis apprehensio Christi Media-
toris ac beneficiorum ejus, quae in verbo Evangelii nobis offer-
untur.* Faith seizes upon Christ, takes possession of him,
renders him present in us, and makes us possess him; it is
the eye that perceives and the hand that receives. In this
there is, as a student of philosophy would see at once, a great
confusion between *real* possession and *intentional* possession,
between the effective and the ideal presence of the object in
the cognitive faculty. By this mode of reckoning the desire
for a treasure would make us rich and the contemplation of a
beautiful scene would make us beautiful.

(B) *Justifying Faith the Germ of Virtue.*—It can be said that
the preceding conception has been somewhat given up in our
time. "We are so accustomed," says Feine (*Theolog. des
N.T.*, Leipzig, 1910, p. 424), "to the Protestant formula
'justification by faith only,' that many Christians imagine that
this formula existed already in St Paul, and think that the
Apostle always conceives of faith as something passive, as
opposed to works. This is an erroneous idea." In fact, the
analysis of faith shows that there is in it an active principle
and a moral value. "Faith," says Beyschlag (*Neutest. Theol.*[2],
1896, vol. ii, p. 179), "is a convinced trust and a trustful
conviction" (*ein überzeugtes Vertrauen, ein vertrauensvolles
Ueberzeugtsein*). Indeed, to believe in *anyone* it is necessary
to *trust in him*, to *have confidence* that he will keep his word.
"Consequently faith is fit to constitute the moral foundation
of the whole life." Pfleiderer's conclusion is not very
different (*Der Paulinismus*[2], p. 169): Religious faith is the
act of holding a thing to be true (*Ein Fürwahrhalten*) without
logical grounds, but by virtue of the moral disposition of
having trust in God, of trusting in his veracity, power and
faithfulness; in this consists the respect due to God, the
honour which is given him, and hence the fundamental
disposition from a religious point of view (*worin eben die
schuldige Achtung gegen Gott, das* ihm die Ehre Geben, *also
die religiöse Grundstimmung besteht*). Holtzmann also says
(*N.T. Theol.*, vol, ii, 1, 122: "We believe anyone because
we trust him" (*Man glaubt einem, weil man ihm traut*).

These observations have brought about two changes in
Protestant exegesis and dogmatics. In the first place, no
more difficulty is found in admitting the moral value, the
ethical character of faith—that which is called its *vis activa ;*
we thus gain a better comprehension of the influence of faith
on justification, an influence so often affirmed by St Paul.
and also of the influence of living faith on the production
of good works, an influence wholly unintelligible in a system

of purely receptive faith. In the second place, little stress is now laid upon the total distinction between justification and sanctification, and it is conceded that these two things are inseparable, that they are two different aspects of the same thing, and that justification could not be conceived of without the principle or germ of sanctification. But then the whole Protestant theory of justification must be transformed, for nothing remains but traditional formulas, which Protestants still try to maintain by conviction or force of habit, but by depriving them of their original meaning.

## IV—THE FAITH OF JESUS CHRIST

J. Haussleiter (*Der Glaube Jesu Christi und der christl. Glaube, ein Beitrag zur Erklärung des Römerbriefs*, in *Neue kirchl. Zeitschrift*, vol. ii, 1891, pp. 109-145 and 205-230), while recognizing that he is going against common opinion, maintains that *the faith of Jesus Christ* must signify, *at least in the Epistle to the Romans*, the faith which Jesus had (subjective genitive): (*a*) The readers of Paul would not have otherwise understood him (Rom. iii, 26 : δικαιοῦντα τὸν ἐκ πίστεως Ἰησοῦ) ; for the first Christians believed that Jesus had become Christ and Lord only after his resurrection ; hence, there could not have been for them any question of faith *in* Jesus. —(*b*) The parallel expression (Rom. iv, 16 : τῷ ἐκ πίστεως Ἀβραάμ), which clearly signifies the subjective faith of Abraham, invites us to take τὸν ἐκ πίστεως Ἰησοῦ in the same sense.—(*c*) "The Apostle purposely chooses the expression πίστις Ἰησοῦ to show that he means the faith which Jesus himself had during his mortal life. The expression πίστις Χριστοῦ would be ambiguous." Rom. iii, 22, διὰ πίστεως Ἰησοῦ Χριστοῦ, must be understood in the same way, because the name of Jesus comes first.—Haussleiter, in *Neue Kirchl. Zeitschrift*, vol. ii (1891), pp. 507-520, resumes his subject under the title : *Eine theol. Disputation über den Glauben Jesu.* He has discovered a dissertation by a certain Ritter, read at the University of Greifswald, August 29, 1704 (*De fide Christi, sive utrum Christus habuerit fidem ?*), in which Ritter maintains the thesis of Christ's subjective faith, and cites in support of it four Protestant theologians.

In spite of this patronage, Haussleiter's thesis was not cordially received. Hilgenfeld (*Zeitschrift für wissensch. Theol.*, vol. xxxv, p. 391) criticized it very severely. Almost alone, G. Kittel (Πίστις Ἰησοῦ Χριστοῦ *bei Paulus*, in *Stud. und Krit.*, lxxix, 1906, pp. 419 436) gave him his support, without, however, bringing forward any new arguments. "In themselves," he says (p. 419), "both opinions are equally probable ; grammatically also they are equally possible ; in fact, if there is a faith *in* Christ, there must have been a faith *of*

Jesus." Why? Schläger, *Bemerkungen zu* Π ι σ τ ι ς ᾿Ιησοῦ Χ ρ ι σ τ ο ῖ in *Zeitschrift für N.T. Wissenschaft*, vol. vii (1906), pp. 356-8, referring to the article of Kittel, proposes a radical solution: in Rom. iii, 22 and iii, 26, the words ᾿Ιησοῦ and ᾿Ιησοῦ Χριστοῦ do not belong to the primitive text. For Gal. ii, 16 and iii, 22 he proposes the same remedy. It is true there is neither testimony nor any indication whatever in favour of this elimination, " but," says Schläger, "it is now or never the time to have recourse to the principles of high criticism to correct a difficult text." It is plain that criticism aided by the imagination is not the monopoly of the so-called Dutch school.

In spite of Haussleiter and his few followers, modern exegetes, Catholics, Protestants, and Rationalists, persist in seeing in "the faith *of* Christ" faith *in* Christ. Four decisive reasons for this can be given :

(*a*) Independently of the difficulty of conceiving of a *subjective* faith in Jesus Christ, the New Testament is completely unaware of such a faith. The verb "to believe" never has Christ for a subject. Even in Heb. xii, 2 (*auctor fidei et consummator*) it is not a question of an act of faith on the part of Jesus. This presumption is fatal to the opposite theory.

(*b*) On the contrary, Christ is constantly represented as the *object* of Christian faith (Gal. ii, 16 ; Col. ii, 5 ; Philem. 5, etc.). *Jesus* is as truly the object of faith as Christ himself (Rom. x, 9 ; 1 Cor. xii, 3 ; 2 Cor. iv, 5, 14)—a fact which annihilates the quibbles of Haussleiter.

(*c*) In the other Books of the New Testament the faith of Christ is incontestably faith in Christ (James ii, 1 ; Apoc. ii, 13 ; xiv, 12), as the faith *of* God is faith *in* God in St Mark xi, 22, as also in Philo and the Talmud. Even in St Paul himself one can invoke the analogy of the expressions "faith *of* the Gospel" (Phil. i, 27), "faith *of* the truth " (2 Thess. ii, 13), "faith *of* the power of God" (Col. 1i, 12).

(*d*) Finally the context shows that it is a question of the faith of the faithful in Christ, and not the personal faith of Christ.

# NOTE W—MAN'S JUSTICE AND GOD'S JUSTICE

## I—JUSTICE IN MAN

1. *Preliminary Notions.*—" Just " and " justice " are relative notions, while " good " and " goodness " are absolute notions. A thing is *good* (ἀγαθόν) by reason of its intrinsic excellence ; a thing is *just* (δίκαιον) when it conforms to a rule—for example, to the custom (δίκη) considered as the expression of what is right, right itself being regarded as the expression of the divine will ; for in all primitive societies the customary or positive idea of right is believed to go back ultimately to the gods.—The epithet δίκαιος is applied *metaphorically* to every object (a car, the earth, a horse, a writer, a doctor, etc.) which realizes *normal* conditions (compare the Latin *justum volumen*) ; but we cannot say, by catachresis, "a just thief" as we can say " a good thief " (excellent in his way), because he does not correspond to the standard of right. In the same way, although the prevailing laws were in general regarded as the expression of the right, the ancients had nevertheless the notion of " unjust " laws, when they were opposed to the higher law which nature writes in the conscience ; and the observance of these laws did not make a man just.—Whatever may be the fundamental meaning of the root צדק (" to be right," in opposition to what is tortuous or crooked, "to go to the goal," in opposition to that which turns aside), it is certain that the Hebrew צַדִּיק (just) and צֶדֶק (justice) designate the Greek δίκαιος and δικαιοσύνη, conformity to the right ; only the right is fully identified with the will of God, known by revelation. Among the Greeks justice was a social virtue ; it was piety (εὐσέβια) which comprised duties towards the gods, unless those duties were regulated by law, in which case they returned to the category and concept of justice. Among the Hebrews justice is a religious virtue ; a person is just when, in his whole conduct, he conforms to the divine will ; a thing is just when it corresponds to the will of God, manifested in the Torah. It is only metaphorically that they speak of a just weight, balance, or measure—that is, as corresponding to the normal standard.

2. *Forensic Justice or Real Justice ?*—But it is one thing to affirm that the justice of man is a *relative* concept in the sense that it implies an essential relation to an external rule, and it is another thing to claim that it is a purely *forensic* notion. This thesis, maintained among others by Cremer, fortified by a great supply of texts and quotations (*Wörterbuch*[9] and *Die paulin. Rechtfertigungslehre*), rests only on an ambiguity. Cremer relies

upon the fact that the words " just " and " justice " are very
often put into correlation with the words " judge, to judge" and
" judgement " ; but it is entirely natural that the ideas of right
and justice frequently call up the ideas of judgement and judge,
and this does not at all prove that the former are *forensic*—that
is to say, exist only through their relation to the latter.   The
judge must judge according to the law, must recognize justice
and do justice to the just (Lev. xix, 15, etc.) ; it follows that
justice exists before the verdict of the judge, and is not constituted by him.   The judge "who justifies the wicked and
taketh away the justice of the just from him " (Is. v, 23) does
not alter in the least the intrinsic nature of the just and
unjust ; which proves that his self-interested verdict does not
constitute justice, although it takes for granted its existence.
Similarly, God condemns the wicked and justifies the just
(1 Kings viii, 31), because his judgement is conformable to
truth—another proof that the just are just *before* the divine
verdict and not by virtue of it, as the wicked are wicked
before their condemnation.

3. *Justice Imputed or Justice Inherent ?*—According to the
Catholic doctrine, those whom God has justified are really
and truly just : St Augustine, *De spir. et lit.*, 26 : *Gratia Dei
justificamur, hoc est justi efficimur.   Opus imperf.*, ii, 65 :
*Justificat impium Deus non solum dimittendo quae mala fecit sed
etiam donando caritatem ut declinet a malo et faciat bonum per
Spir. S.*   The Greek Fathers speak as do the Latins.   St
Chrysostom (on Rom. iv, 5) thus explains the justification of
the wicked (LX, 456) : οὐχὶ κολάσεως ἐλευθερῶσαι μόνον, ἀλλὰ καὶ
δίκαιον ποιῆσαι.   The Council of Trent epitomizes its teaching
in these terms (*Sess.* vi, cap. 7) : *Justificatio non est sola
peccatorum remissio, sed et sanctificatio et renovatio interioris
hominis per voluntariam susceptionem gratiae et donorum.
Unde homo ex injusto fit justus.*   Moreover, the leaders of
Protestantism did not pretend to rely upon tradition ; and
they declared that the Fathers had not understood the
doctrine of the Apostle at all.   Luther and Calvin did not
make an exception even of St Augustine, and with greater
reason they abandoned the others with a light heart.   Bucer
and Chemnitz acknowledged that the majority of the Fathers
understand " to justify " in the sense of " to make just "; but
they cared nothing about them.   In our days these avowals
are still not rare.   Franks writes in *Hastings' Diction. of
Christ and the Gospels*, vol. i, p. 920 : "The doctrine of Paul
was a dead letter until the day when the Reformation revived
it."   Of which doctrine does he speak ?   The Protestants had
several of them at the beginning, and they have not succeeded
in coming to an understanding on so fundamental a subject.
It is true, after long hesitation, they almost agreed on the

formula of *imputed justice*, but they have always understood
it in two very different ways. They said either that *the
justice of Christ is imputed to us by God in consideration of faith*
(faith being only a condition whose presence is necessary for
some reason), or that *faith is imputed to us as justice* (that is to
say, that God regards faith as taking the place of the absent
justice). What is more extraordinary is that they thought
they were employing the very formulas of Paul. They perceived a little later that the imputation of the justice of Christ
lacks a Scriptural foundation, and that the Apostle speaks
of faith imputed *to* justice, and not of faith imputed *as* justice ;
but when people hastily construct new dogmas, they never
think of all the difficulties that may arise. However that may
be, here are their formulas : " Justification is an act by which
God . . . moved merely by pity and because of the redemption accomplished by his Son, *imputes the justice of Christ* to
every believing sinner " (*Formula of Concord*).—" Justification
consists in the remission of sins and in the fact that *the Justice
of Christ is imputed to us* " (Calvin, *Institut.*, III, xi, 2).—*Deus
propter solum Christum passum et resuscitatum propitius est
peccatis nostris nec illa nobis imputat,* imputat autem justitiam
Christi pro nostra (*Swiss Confession* of 1566, cap. xv).—
*In sola J. C. obedientia prorsus accquiescimus,* quae quidem
nobis imputatur (*Gallican Conf.* of 1559, No. 18).—*Meritum
J. C. " fit* nostrum *per fidem* " (*Würtemberg Conf.* of 1552).—
*J. C. nobis imputans omnia sua merita* (*Acts of the Synod of
Dordrecht* of 1561, No. 22).

By this system the justice of Christ is imputed to us without
being given to us. Protestations against this doctrine commenced early. From 1550 onwards, Osiander maintained
that justification is an act of the God of truth, and that God
would be unjust if he held someone to be just who is really
not just. That was precisely what all the Catholics said :
*Quando Deus justificat impium, declarando justum, facit etiam
justum, quoniam judicium Dei secundum veritatem est* (Bellarmine, *De justific.*, ii, 3).—*Verbum Domini ejusque voluntas
efficax est, et hoc ipso quod aliquem justum esse pronunciat, aut
supponit eum justum esse, aut reipsa justum facit, ne verbum
ejus mendax sit* (Vasquez, qu. cxii, disp. 202, c. 5).

4. *Eschatological Justice or Actual Justice ?*—Ever since
Kant's day, the Protestants have been emancipating themselves more and more from the confessions of faith. They
admit, as an axiom, that faith is a germ or a principle of the
virtuous life, and they say, with Kant, that God judges us
according to our ideal, and that he considers as already produced all the fruit that will develop from this germ; or, with
Neander, that in the eyes of God all that is to issue from the
principle is the same as if realized in the principle itself.

This is the point of departure of that *eschatological* justification of which so much is said to-day. It is thought that thus everything will be safeguarded: the moral value of faith and its active energy and the truth of the divine judgement and the act of grace, which imputes to us more than we really have. On the numerous Protestant theologians who subscribe to this new theory, *cf.* A. Matter, *Justification*, in *Encycl. des Sciences relig.*, vol. vii, pp. 570-571.

It is not without surprise that we see a Catholic advance theories which have at least verbal resemblances to the system of eschatological justification. For example: "In St Paul justification always consists in the decree of admission to the messianic kingdom. . . . Present justification is at the same time future justification; he knows only one, namely messianic justification. . . . He wishes to show the certainty of eternal life for those who are *now* reconciled with God by Jesus Christ. . . . The Christian possesses in himself the pledge of divine adoption and salvation, and is certain of the verdict of justification on the day of judgement. . . . Man is justified by his faith in Christ and possesses the certainty of his justification, as long as he believes." These and other similar phrases call for corrections or explanations. A Catholic cannot say that the Christian is, henceforth, *sure of his justification, sure of his salvation, and sure of his future admission to the messianic and eschatological kingdom.* The certainty of hope is one thing, the certainty of salvation is quite another. *The hope of salvation is certain*, because it is founded on the infallible promise of God (a formal object); *the fact of salvation itself* is not certain, because it is conditioned by the inconstancy of a will that is always fallible.

## II—Paul's Idea of the Justice of God

Until these later years it was universally admitted that St Paul gives to the expression "justice of God" two not incongruous but certainly different meanings (the justice which is in God and the justice which comes from God): the former is found in Rom. iii, 5, 25, 26, the latter in Rom. i, 17; iii, 21, 22; x, 3; 2 Cor. v, 21; *cf.* Phil. iii, 9. In 1890, in the explanation of the Epistle to the Romans which forms part of the *Pulpit Commentary*, p. xi, J. Barmby modified the usual opinion thus: "In the whole Epistle, δικαιοσύνη Θεοῦ signifies the eternal justice of God and, even in the passages where a justice that comes from faith is mentioned as communicated to man, the essential basic idea is the personal justice of God including believers in itself." The suggestion was accepted with some reservations by Robertson (*The Thinker*, November, 1893), taken up again by its author in an article in the *Expositor* (5th series, vol. iv, 1896, pp. 124-139), and applied to

Rom. i, 17 ; iii, 21, 22, but with no allusion to Rom. x, 3 and 2 Cor. v, 21, where the application would seem contrary to any sound exegesis. H. Beck (*Die* Δικαιοσύνη Θεοῦ *bei Paulus* in *Neue Jahrbücher f. deutsch. Theol.*, vol. iv, 1895, pp. 249-261) seized upon the thesis of Barmby, but without citing him, according to a custom quite extensively employed among the scholars beyond the Rhine. Much more substantial is the dissertation by Kölbing (*Studien zur paulin. Theol.* in *Theol. Studien und Kritik.*, vol. lxviii, 1895, pp. 1-51), which limits itself exclusively to the exegesis of Rom. i, 17 and iii, 25. According to Kölbing, in the two verses in question the justice of God must be understood as a "just conduct of God, which consists in the bestowal of justice on man or rather contains in itself that bestowal." In the following year appeared the monograph of Häring (Δικαιοσύνη Θεοῦ *bei Paulus*, Tübingen, 1896) approved by Holtzmann (*Theol. Literaturzeitung*, vol. xxi, 1896, pp. 645-646), who regrets not having been able to utilize it for his *Theologie des N.T.* A little later, C. Bruston (*La notion de la justice de Dieu chez St Paul* in *Revue de Théol. et des questions relig.*, vol. vii, 1898, pp. 86-95) espoused the explanation of Barmby, reproaching Sanday for not adhering to it. More recently, the Abbé Tobac (*Le problème de la justification dans St Paul*, Louvain, 1908, pp. 116-129) has defended the new exegesis fully and with conviction.

In reality, as M. Tobac justly remarks (*op. cit.*, pp. 117-118), this exegesis goes back to Ritschl, who "understood by the justice of God in the New Testament not a quality of man, but a divine attribute; not repressive or retributive justice, but a normal and consistent line of conduct, conformably to which the heavenly Father remains faithful to his promises and pursues in the world the ultimate salvation of his children. Since Ritschl, this conception of the justice of God as a divine attribute (subjective genitive) has been widely circulated, but with such complex shades of opinion that it would be impossible to go into the details of the different explanations." *Cf.* Frutsärt, *La justice de Dieu dans St Paul* (*Recherches de science relig.*, vol. ii, 1911, pp. 161-182).

We have already said what reasons prevent us from adopting the exegesis inaugurated by Ritschl : (*a*) In Rom. i, 17 ; iii, 21, 22, the context requires a justice which is within the Christian and not outside of him.—(*b*) In Rom. x, 3 and 1 Cor. v, 21 this explanation enforces itself with still greater clearness.—(*c*) Phil. iii, 9 defines without a possible doubt the subjective character of this justice.—(*d*) Finally, the conception of the justice of God as a divine attribute, in the system of Ritschl, is inadequate.

## NOTE X—ON BAPTISM

### I—To Baptize and Baptism

1. The word βαπτίζειν seems to be the frequentative of βάπ-τειν, " to immerse," which is found only four times in the New Testament, but is common in the Septuagint, where, on the contrary, βαπτίζειν is found only four times (2 Kings v, 14; Is. xxi, 4 [figuratively]; Eccli. xxxiv, 30 ; Judith xii, 7).

*To baptize* signifies, therefore, etymologically, " to dip into the water several times." But this etymological sense is modified by usage. Indeed, 2 Kings v, 14 and Judith xii, 7 prove that βαπτίζεσθαι was used of a legal purification or of a simple lotion without any idea of immersion, and still less of repeated immersion. This is also the meaning which we find in the New Testament whether for the verb or for the substantive : Mark vii, 4 (ἀπ' ἀγορᾶς ἐὰν μὴ βαπτίσωνται οὐκ ἐσθίουσιν ; another reading ῥαντίσωνται) ; Luke xi, 38 (οὐ πρῶτον ἐβαπτίσθη πρὸ τοῦ ἀρίστου) ; Heb. ix, 10 (ἐπὶ βρώμασι καὶ πόμασι καὶ διαφόροις βαπτισμοῖς). The word was used again figuratively to signify " to plunge into " affliction, calamities, etc., as in Is. xxi, 4 (ἀνομία με βαπτίζει). This meaning is found again in Mark x, 38, 39 ; Luke xii, 50. But in general, "baptism" and " to baptize " denote absolutely the baptism of John or Christian baptism.

The series of meanings of the word "to baptize " is, therefore, the following :

A. *To dip* (into the water) several times, or simply to dip, immerse.

B. *To purify* by plunging into the water, or simply to wash.

C. *To confer baptism* by immersion or otherwise.

2. In St Paul the word "baptism" appears only three times and always denotes Christian baptism : twice as a mystical burial, once as a principle of unity in the Church :

(a) Rom. vi, 4 : συνετάφημεν αὐτῷ διὰ τοῦ βαπτίσματος.
(b) Col. ii, 12 : συνταφέντες αὐτῷ ἐν τῷ βαπτίσματι.
(c) Eph. iv, 5 : εἷς Κίριος, μία πίστις, ἒν βάπτισμα.

It will be noticed that the Apostle does not use the active form βαπτισμός, but the passive form βάπτισμα, which denotes rather the result of baptism, although in practice the two forms are almost equivalent.

The word "to baptize " appears thirteen times ; but three times it is a question of a baptism by analogy : 1 Cor. xv, 29 (twice), it is a question of the obscure rite called baptism for the dead (οἱ βαπτιζόμενοι ὑπὲρ τῶν νεκρῶν) ; 1 Cor. x, 2 : " All were baptized *in* Moses (εἰς τὸν Μωϋσῆν) in the cloud and in the sea," as Christians are baptized in Christ. The ten other examples are included in four texts.

(*a*) Rom. vi, 3 (twice) : to be baptized in Christ Jesus (εἰς Χριστὸν Ἰησοῦν) or in his death (εἰς τὸν θάνατον αὐτοῦ).

(*b*) Gal. iii. 27 : to be baptized in Christ (εἰς Χριστόν).

(*c*) 1 Cor. xii, 13 : to be baptized into one body (εἰς ἓν σῶμα).

(*d*) 1 Cor. i, 13, 15 : to baptize in the name of someone (εἰς τὸ ὄνομα) ; i, 14, 16 : to baptize someone ; i, 17 : to baptize (absolutely).

We see that the Apostle uses both these remarkable expressions, which it is opportune to study closely : to baptize *in* (εἰς) someone or something, and to baptize *in the name* of someone (εἰς τὸ ὄνομα).

## II—To Baptize in Christ (εἰς Χριστόν)

1. How must we interpret the Pauline expressions " to be baptized in Christ " (Gal. iii, 27 : εἰς Χριστὸν ἐβαπτίσθητε) or " in Christ Jesus " (Rom. vi, 3) ? Does the preposition εἰς express a simple relation, or is it to be taken in an almost local sense, Christ representing the element, the medium, into which we are immersed by baptism ? Several exegetes see in it only a simple relation, for : (*a*) To baptize does not necessarily signify to dip, but can mean to wash, to purify.— (*b*) The analogous expressions, βαπτίζεσθαι εἰς μετάνοιαν, εἰς ἄφεσιν ἁμαρτιῶν, show that εἰς does not express the entry into a medium or element, but marks only the tendency or aim.— (*c*) A comparison with 1 Cor. x, 2 (πάντες εἰς τὸν Μωϋσῆν ἐβαπτίσαντο) seems to prove the same thing.

It is very true, as we have said above, that βαπτίζειν does not always signify to immerse into a medium. But if this meaning is not demanded by the word itself, neither is it excluded, and it can very well be expressed by εἰς (Mark i, 9 : ἐβαπτίσθη εἰς τὸν Ἰορδάνην). The essential thing is to know whether it is required by the context. Now when St Paul speaks of baptism in Christ, he seems clearly to be considering the mystical Christ as a sort of divine element, a supernatural atmosphere, into which we must be plunged. Indeed : (*a*) In Rom. vi, 3, the consequence of baptism in Christ is that we are *buried* with him by baptism [which is] in his death, and that we are σύμφυτοι with him. Sanday is therefore right to paraphrase thus : " The act of baptism was an act of *incorporation* into Christ." Meyer-Weiss says the same thing with less conciseness and more realism. Col. ii, 12 (*consepulti ei in baptismo*) is explained well only by this hypothesis ; for the rite of immersion accounts very well for being " buried in baptism," but why " buried *with* him," if we are not " immersed in him "?—(*b*) In Gal. iii, 27, 28, baptism in Christ (ὅσοι εἰς Χριστὸν ἐβαπτίσθητε) has two results: the first is to *clothe* us with Christ (Χριστὸν ἐνεδύσασθε); the second is to *unify us in* Christ (πάντες ὑμεῖς εἰς ἐστε ἐν Χριστῷ Ἰησοῖ). But all this is intelligible only if Christ is considered as an element in which we live, or as a common form which envelops us. —(c) In I Cor. xii, 13, the same order of ideas prevails, although the expression is a little different (ἡμεῖς πάντες εἰς ἓν σῶμα ἐβαπτίσθημεν): we have been baptized *into* one and the same mystical body because we are immersed in the same mystical Christ. The result is always the same—namely, to make of us all one and the same Christ (xii, 12: οὕτως καὶ ὁ Χριστός).

To avoid all ambiguity, let us repeat that the meaning indicated comes from the context and not from the verb βαπτίζειν (which had become a technical term signifying "to administer baptism"), nor from the preposition εἰς (which could indicate a simple relation, a tendency, an end, etc.). It is the context and the context only that invites us to retain for the word "to baptize" the etymological meaning of "to plunge" (to immerse). If the context changes, this meaning must be abandoned.

## III—To Baptize in the Name of Christ (εἰς τὸ ὄνομα)

1. This formula has been specially studied by J. Boehmer, *Das biblische* "IM NAMEN." *Eine sprachwissenschaftliche Untersuchung über das hebräische* בשם *und seine griechischen Æquivalente (im besonderen Hinblick auf den Taufbefehl,* Matt. xxviii, 19), Giessen, 1898. The author believes that the five following expressions are synonymous because they go back to the same origin and are the translation of the same בשם: (a) ἐν τῷ ὀνόματι, I Cor. v, 4; vi, 11; Eph. v, 20; Phil. ii, 10; Col. iii, 17; 2 Thess. iii, 6 (we only give the texts of St. Paul).— (b) εἰς τὸ ὄνομα, I Cor. i, 13, 15.—(c) διὰ τοῦ ὀνόματος, I Cor. i, 10.—(d) ἐπὶ τῷ ὀνόματι.—(e) τῷ ὀνόματι. The meaning of the formula would everywhere be "with the power or authority of someone," or "in the company or presence of someone." For example, Matt. xxviii, 19 would be: "Make for me disciples of all nations, baptizing them in the presence (*or* with the assistance *im Beisein*) of the Father, the Son, and the Holy Ghost" (p. 75). The author, as Deissmann reproaches him for doing (*Theol. Literaturzeitung,* vol. xxi, 1900, pp. 71-74), starts from a double postulate which is not proved and cannot be—namely, that the formula εἰς τὸ ὄνομα originated on the soil of Palestine, and that the five expressions enumerated above all correspond to the Hebrew בשם. Brandt ('Ονομα, *En de doops formule in het Nieuwe Testament* in *Theol. Tijdschrift,* Leyden, vol. xxv, 1891, pp. 565-610) had already shown that the equivalent of εἰς τὸ ὄνομα in late Judaism

is לְשֵׁם and not בְּשׁ. The expression is, in fact, found in the Talmud (*Yebamoth*, 48*b*): "The proselyte must be bathed in the name of Jehovah (לְשֵׁם הַשָּׁמִים). Moreover, although the difference between ἐν and εἰς tends to diminish towards the New Testament era, the identification is far from being proved, and in every case it is necessary to refer to the context. Now the assertion of Böhmer (*op. cit.*, p. 85) that the formula εἰς τὸ ὄνομα, as well as the formula ἐν τῷ ὀνόματι, always applies to the administrant of baptism and not to the candidate to be received into the Church, is untenable; for, except in Matt. xxviii, 19, this formula is found precisely with a verb in the passive, where the administrant of baptism is neither named nor indicated (Acts viii, 16; xix, 5; 1 Cor. i, 13, 15). At the most it could apply either to the priest who baptizes, as the author of the new relation of the baptized candidate to Christ, or to the candidate himself, the subject of this relation.

2. The question has been discussed in *The Journal of Theol. Studies* by Armitage Robinson (*In the Name*, vol. vii, 1906, pp. 186-202), and by Chase (*The Lord's Command to Baptize*, vol. vi, 1905, pp. 481-521, and vol. viii, 1907, pp. 161-184). The former maintains the equivalency of the two formulas ἐν τῷ ὀνόματι and εἰς τὸ ὄνομα. Here is his résumé (p. 197): "A confession of faith *in the Name* was the prelude to baptism, the invocation *of the Name* was an essential part of the ceremony. The baptized person accepted a new Master. Thanks to the commission (given to the Apostles, Matt. xxviii, 19) to make disciples by baptizing them *in the Name of the three* divine Persons, the administrant of baptism acted with authority *in this Name;* and he had the right to invoke *this Name:* a thought which does not exclude the preceding one." Chase, however, combats Robinson's thesis with much erudition and logic; but, in our opinion, he weakens his proof by the extravagance of his conclusions: that the word βαπτίζειν signifies everywhere "to immerse," and should be *translated* in our modern languages instead of being *transcribed;* in εἰς τὸ ὄνομα, ὄνομα is synonymous with "person," and βαπτίζειν εἰς τὸ ὄνομα Χριστοῦ means "to immerse in the person of Christ"—in other words, "in Christ himself"; the formula ἐν τῷ ὀνόματι has the same meaning.

W. Heitmüller, in a study remarkable for the number of texts and facts therein accumulated, but too systematized (*Im Namen Jesu. Eine sprach-und-religionsgesch. Untersuchung zum N.T. speziell zur altchristl. Taufe*, Göttingen, 1903), undertakes a new mode of explanation and comes to this conclusion (p. 127): "The expressions βαπτίζειν ἐν and ἐπὶ τῷ ὀνόματι describe the operation of the baptism; they signify

that the baptism is accomplished by uttering the name of
Jesus. On the contrary, the expression βαπτίζειν εἰς τὸ ονομα
expresses an (the) aim and a (the) result of the baptism; it indicates that the baptized person becomes an appurtenance or
property of Jesus. But the utterance of the name (of Jesus)
is also implied in the formula β. εἰς τὸ ονομα."—It is very true,
as we shall see, that the latter phrase expresses a property
relation; but neither formula necessarily implies the act of
invoking or of pronouncing the name of Jesus over the recipient of the baptism.

3. Three considerations put us on the right track:
(A) In the New Testament era the *name* was sometimes
almost synonymous with the *person;* there would therefore
be nothing extraordinary in the equivalence of the expressions
*to baptize in* (εἰς) *Christ* and *to baptize in the name* (εἰς τὸ ὄνομα)
*of Christ.* Cf. Acts i, 15; Apoc. iii, 4; xi, 13; Matt. x, 41-42.
There is the same manner of speaking in the Talmud;
cf. Lightfoot, *Horae hebraicae*, vol. ii, p. 118. The rabbinical
axiom is well known: "His Name is He, and He is his Name,"
in speaking of God (שמו הוא והוא שמו). For profane examples
see Deissmann, *Bibelstudien*, pp. 143-145, and *Neue Bibelst.*,
pp. 24-26. Noteworthy also is the equivalence of the two
formulas "to swear to the emperor" (ὀμόσαι εἰς, Plutarch,
*Otho*, 18) and "to swear in the name of the emperor (ὀμόσαι
εἰς ὄνομα, Herodian, ii, 13).
(B) The Fathers seem to make no difference between "to
baptize *in* Christ" and "to baptize *in the Name* of Christ."
St. Cyril of Jerusalem, *Catech.*, xvi, 19 (XXXIII, 945: εἰκότως
βαπτιζόμεθα εἰς πατέρα καὶ εἰς υἱὸν καὶ εἰς ἅγιον πνεῦμα). So also
St Athanasius, *Contra Arian.*, iv, 21 (XXVI, 500); *Épist.* iv *ad
Serap.*, xii (XXVI, 653); St Gregory Nazianzen, *Orat.*, xxxiv, 17
(XXXVI, 236); St Gregory of Nyssa, *Contra Eunom.*, xi (XLV,
881); *In baptisma Christi* (XLVI, 585); the Pseudo-Ignatius,
*Philipp.* ii (ed. Funk, 106), the *Apostolic Canons*, 49, etc.
Tertullian here speaks like the Greeks, *Adv. Prax.* 26:
*Novissime mandans ut tingerent in Patrem et Filium et Spiritum
sanctum, non in unum.* Thus "to baptize in the Father" and
"to baptize in the name of the Father" is all one.
(C) The examination of the passages in which appears the
formula εἰς τὸ ὄνομα confirms us in this opinion. Neither
Matt. xxviii, 19 nor Acts viii, 16 furnish any light; but, in
Acts xix, 5, the words ἐβαπτίσθησαν εἰς τὸ ὄνομα τοῦ Κυρίου
Ἰησοῦ seem to correspond clearly to εἰς τί οὖν ἐβαπτίσθητε;
(Acts xix, 3): which tends to establish the equivalence of
the two expressions. In 1 Cor. i, 13, 15 the matter is still
clearer. The converts' saying: "I am of Paul," made the
Apostle indignant. No, he said to them in substance, you
do not belong to me; you belong only to Jesus Christ.

"Was Paul crucified for you," and did he redeem you with his own blood? (*cf*. Acts xx. 28). "Were you baptized *in the name* of Paul," to become his property, his possession? If the reasoning is correct, the expression εἰς τὸ ὄνομα must indicate a relation of appurtenance.

To sum up: the expressions "to be baptized in (εἰς) someone or in the name (εἰς τὸ ὄνομα) of someone" are, *in themselves*, almost synonymous, and signify "to be, by the fact of baptism, consecrated, dedicated, subjected, to some-one, to become his subject, his slave, his property." Yet, *when it is a question of Christ*, there is reason to distinguish them, because the name Christ can be taken in two ways, either as that of the mystical Christ or that of the physical Christ. The expression βαπτίζεσθαι εἰς Χριστόν is applied to the mystical Christ, whose baptism clothes us as with an element or a new form; the expression βαπτίζεσθαι εἰς τὸ ὄνομα τοῦ υἱοῦ (Matt. xxviii, 19) or τοῦ Κυρίου Ἰησοῦ (Acts viii, 16; xix. 5—Χριστοῦ is not found anywhere—is applied to the physical person of the Son of God, the Lord Jesus, the Head of the Church: the first denotes a relation of union and mystical identity; the second marks a relation of appur-tenance, subjection, and consecration.

### IV—BATH OF THE PROSELYTES AND CHRISTIAN BAPTISM

1. *Statement of the Problem.*—If the controversy about the baptism of the proselytes still exists, it is perhaps because the problem is very badly stated. Two very different questions are usually confounded: "Had the proselytes to be bathed before being admitted to participate in the rites and religious privileges of Judaism?" and "Had this bath a significance which makes it resemble Christian baptism?" To the first question the reply of the historians should be unanimous. We may dispute about the precise meaning of the texts of Arrian (*Dissert. Epist.*, ii, 9) and of the *Sibylline Books* (iv, 165: ἐν ποταμοῖς λούσασθε ὅλον δέμας ἀενάοισιν), although it is difficult not to see in them a clear allusion to the bath of the proselytes; but the whole Jewish tradition, after the second century, takes this bath for granted, and it is not likely that the usage was introduced after the appearance of Christianity. In order to become a proselyte, in the strict sense of the word, there were necessary: (1) circumcision; (2) the bath of purification (מְבִילָה); (3) a sacrifice. After the destruction of the temple, the third was no longer possible for anyone, and for women everything was restricted to the bath. The Talmud is explicit: *Kerithoth*, 81*a*; *Yebamoth*, 46*a*. Already the *Mishna* leaves no doubt about the tradi-tional practice. See the treatises *Gerim*, i, 1-2; *Pesachim*, viii, 8 (=*'Eduyoth*, v, 2). This last text settles an interesting

case of conscience. It was a question whether a proselyte, circumcised on the 14th of Nisan, could eat the passover. The school of Shammai allowed it, provided that on the same day he had taken the required bath ; the school of Hillel, on the contrary, compared the converted pagan to a man defiled by contact with a corpse. Both schools therefore considered the proselyte as impure ; but for Shammai it was a minor impurity, lasting only till evening, provided that he had previously been purified ; for Hillel it was a major impurity, lasting seven days (cf. Num. xix, 11, 12) ; but for both the bath of the circumcised proselytes was a matter of course.

2. *The Baptism of Proselytes* was, therefore, a levitical purification, designed to put an end to the legal impurity inherent in the state of idolatry from which the proselyte was emerging. Schürer, *Geschichte*[4], vol. iii, p. 185, asks in what this baptism differed from the Christian baptism, since in both cases the name was identical (טבילה) and the rite also (a full bath). But he himself points out in a note an essential difference—namely, that the baptism of the proselytes tended to restore levitical purity, while Christian baptism symbolized moral purity [which it effected in symbolizing it]. Now, that the choice of the symbol was suggested by the Jewish practice is possible, but it is not proved. In reality, the symbol was suggested by the nature of things.

See S. Krauss, *Baptism* in *Jewish Encycl.*, vol. ii, 1902, pp. 499-500 ; C. Clemen, *Das Evang. Christi*, Leipzig, 1905, pp. 97-102 ; Isr. Levi in *Revue des études juives*, vol. liii, 1907, pp. 59-61 ; Schürer, *Geschichte des jüd. Volkes*[4], vol. iii, 1909, pp. 181-185 ; above all Edersheim, *The Life and Times of Jesus, App.* xii, vol. ii, 1901, pp. 745-747.

3. *Proselyte and Neophyte.*—We often find in the Babylon Talmud this kind of proverb : " The proselyte is like a new-born infant " (גר שנתגייר כקטן שנולד דמי), *Yebamoth, 22a, 48b, 62a, 97b.* This makes us think of St. John's *Nisi quis renatus fuerit denuo* etc. Read the entire passage (John iii, 3-10) and compare it with 1 Pet. i, 23 ; ii, 2 (*sicut modo geniti infantes*), with Titus iii, 5 (*lavacrum regenerationis*), and the expression *ex Deo natus*, frequently in 1 John.

On considering it closely it will be seen that the analogy is fallacious, and that there is no relation between the New Testament and the Talmud. In the latter it is not at all a question of a *supernatural rebirth*, of a *spiritual regeneration*, but only of a *new judicial state* which, by virtue of a legal fiction, changes the former relations of the proselyte. Therefore the situation of the proselyte is continually compared to the condition of an emancipated slave. Both enter into a

new sphere of social rights and duties.  The proselyte is
considered to have no longer parents and relations, and
Maimonides draws from this strange doctrine the following
consequences : " The pagan who has become a proselyte
and the emancipated slave are *like a newly born child*.  The
parents whom one or the other, once had when he was a
pagan or a slave are his parents no longer.  Legally, a pagan
may marry his own mother or his sister if they have become
proselytes.  But the wise men forbid those marriages, in
order that it may not be said that the proselyte descends
from a superior state of sanctity to an inferior one, and that
what was yesterday forbidden him is to-day allowed " (*Issure
Biah*, xiv, 13, quoted by Lightfoot; *Horae hebr.* on John iii, 3).

# NOTE Y—VIRTUES AND VICES

## I—St. Paul's Lists

### 1. *Lists of Christian Virtues*

(*a*) Fifteen virtues accompanying charity (1 Cor. xiii. 4-7).

(*b*) Five virtues typical of the Christian : mercy, kindness, humility, gentleness, long-suffering (Col. iii, 12 ; Eph. iv, 2).

(*c*) Nine *fruits* of the Spirit : charity, joy, peace, long-suffering, kindness, goodness, faith, gentleness, continence (Gal. v, 22-23).

(*d*) Three *fruits* of the light : goodness, justice, and truth (Eph. v, 9).

(*e*) Virtues required of a priest (1 Tim. iii, 2-6). *Cf.* Vol. I, pp. 346-348.

(*f*) Virtues required of a deacon (1 Tim. iii, 8-13). *Cf.* Vol. I, pp. 348-349.

(*g*) Special virtues recommended to Timothy : justice, piety, faith, charity, gentleness, peace (1 Tim. vi, 11 ; 2 Tim. ii, 22).

### 2. *Lists of Vices and Sinners*

(*a*) Fifteen *works* of the flesh : fornication, impurity, immodesty, idolatry, witchcraft, hatred, discords, jealousy, violent anger, disputes, dissensions, factions, envy, drunkenness, gluttony, and *other similar things* (Gal. v, 19-21).

(*b*) Six *works* of darkness : gluttony, drunkenness, lewdness, immodesty, discord, jealousy (Rom. xiii, 13).

(*c*) Twenty-one pagan vices : full of injustice, wickedness, avarice (or sensual covetousness), malice, envy, murder, contention, fraud, malignity, tale-bearers, calumniators, impious, proud, haughty, boasters, inventors of evil, disobedient to parents, without understanding, loyalty, pity, and mercy (Rom. i, 29-31).

(*d*) Eleven vices unworthy of Christians : discord, jealousy, resentments, disputes, detractions, calumnies, boastfulness, disorder, impurity, fornication, immodesty (2 Cor. xii, 20-21).

(*e*) Six kinds of sinners to be avoided : fornicators, avaricious (or voluptuaries), idolaters, insulters, drunkards, thieves (1 Cor. v, 11).

(*f*) Ten kinds of sinners excluded from heaven : fornicators, idolaters, adulterers, effeminate, sodomites, thieves, avaricious (or voluptuaries), drunkards, insulters, ravishers (1 Cor. vi, 9-10).

(*g*) Ten *members* of the old man : fornication, impurity, lustfulness, evil concupiscence, covetousness, anger, indignation, malice, blasphemy, and filthy speech (Col. iii, 5-8).

(h) Fourteen kinds of sinners who need to be restrained by the Law: the lawless and disobedient, ungodly and sinners, sacrilegious and profane, murderers of fathers and mothers, man-slayers, fornicators, sodomites, men-stealers, liars, perjurers, and *others like them* (1 Tim. i, 9-10).

(i) Nine sorts of unbelievers: the foolish, disobedient, led astray, slaves of passion and pleasure, subject to malice and envy, hateful and hating one another (Titus iii, 3).

(j) Nineteen vices of certain heretics who are lovers of themselves, of money, boasters, proud, blasphemers, disobedient to parents, ungrateful, ungodly, without feeling, dishonest, slanderers, detractors, incontinent, unmerciful, enemies of the good (or of good people), traitors, stubborn, puffed up with pride, lovers of pleasures more than lovers of God, hypocrites (2 Tim. iii, 2-5).

We have said that between the vocabulary of Paul and the terminology of the Stoics there is neither dependence, imitation, nor even a distant analogy. On the contrary, if we compare the pamphlet of the *Two Ways*, as it is found in the *Teaching of the Apostles* (chaps. i-v), in the *Epistle of Barnabas* (chaps. xviii-xx), and in the ancient Latin version discovered and published by J. Schlecht (*Die Apostellehre in der Liturgie der kath. Kirche*, Freiburg-im.-B., 1901), we feel immediately that we are on common ground. Christian moral teaching, being built upon the foundation of the Old Testament, has a very uniform terminology. The decalogue forms its framework with its positive commandments (love of God and of one's neighbour and obedience to parents), and its negative precepts (prohibition of idolatry, murder, sins of the flesh, theft, lying, and evil desires).

## II—THE WORDS DENOTING CHARITY

To express love and friendship the Greeks had four words, the different shades of whose meaning our language is powerless to convey. These are φιλεῖν, στέργειν, ἐρᾶν and ἀγαπᾶν.— (a) Φιλεῖν is the most general term, and includes every kind of love: that of persons and things which are dear (φιλά) to us, the love of God and of men, the love of others and of ourselves, pure love and guilty love. It is the contrary of to hate (μισεῖν, ἐχθραίνειν) ; it is a feeling of attraction or of habit (φιλεῖν with the infinitive = to like).—(b) Στέργειν denotes a tender but not a sensual love, a tranquil feeling, equable and constant, dictated by one's nature, or produced by family intimacy. It is the love of parents for their children and *vice versa*, the mutual love of husband and wife, the love of country. The word is not used in the New Testament.— (c) 'Ερᾶν means an ardent, passionate, and most frequently a sexual love—a love accompanied by a violent desire which presupposes its object absent or imperfectly possessed. Joined with φιλεῖν it forms a gradation : " A mild and beneficent prince," says Dion Chrysostom, "ought not to be simply loved by men, but passionately loved " (Orat., i : μὴ μόνον φιλεῖσθαι ὑπ᾽ ἀνθρώπων, ἀλλὰ καὶ ἐρᾶσθαι). We find the same gradation in Xenophon, Hieron, xi, 11. The verb ἐρᾶν is not employed in the New Testament any more than ἔρως and ἐραστής. It was a word tainted by the association of impure ideas. Plato had tried in vain to rehabilitate it in the Symposium and in the Phaedo ; it still remained none the less prostituted, in ordinary usage, to sensual and unnatural love. The authors of the New Testament replace it by ἐπιθυμεῖν and ἐπιθυμία with an unfavourable meaning. It remained under the ban of Christian language for the reason which Origen discloses in his Commentary on the Canticle of Canticles (Prolog., xiii, 68). The phrase of St Ignatius of Antioch : "My love has been crucified " (Roman., vii, 2 : ὁ ἐμὸς ἔρως ἐσταύρωται), is applied to Christ only by a singular misinterpretation, which the reading of the context makes plain.—(d) Ἀγαπᾶν is to love with esteem and choice. The Vulgate translates it very well by diligere (except in 2 Pet. ii, 15, amare), while amare serves to express φιλεῖν. There is, indeed, in ἀγαπᾶν an idea of choice and preference founded on esteem or duty, whereas φιλεῖν expresses rather a spontaneous feeling formed by natural sympathy or intimate relations. The distinction indicated by Aristotle is very just : ἀγαπᾶν, προαιρεῖσθαι, διώκειν (Eth. Nicom., i, 3) ; τὸ δὲ φιλεῖσθαι ἀγαπᾶσθαι ἐστὶν αὐτὸν δι᾽ αὐτόν (Rhetor., i, 11). According as it is desired to make one or the other idea prominent, ἀγαπᾶν (diligere) is stronger than φιλεῖν (amare) or vice versa. Cf. Xenophon, Comment., II, vii, 9 ; Cicero, Ad Famil., xiii, 47 ; Ad Brut., i. Dion Cassius, xliv, 48, makes Antony, speaking of Cæsar, say : "You have loved him as a father and cherished him as a benefactor" (ἐφιλήσατε αὐτόν ὡς πατέρα, καὶ ἠγαπήσατε ὡς εὐεργέτην). Study also the delicate shades of meaning in John xxi, 15-17.

If the verb ἀγαπᾶν is frequently employed by secular writers, the noun ἀγάπη is peculiar to the Bible. It is found eighteen times in the Old Testament (the deuterocanonical books included), ten of which occur in the Canticle of Canticles. It is always the translation of the Hebrew אַהֲבָה. Deissmann (Bibelstudien, p. 80) believed that he had read it in a papyrus antedating the Christian era ; but the reading is recognized as false (cf. Neue Bibelstudien, pp. 26-28), and it can no longer be cited except as an example of Philo (Quod Deus immut., 14, Mangey, vol. i, p. 283), who naturally borrows it from the Septuagint, and another of a commentator on Thucydides (ii, 51) of uncertain date.

The two words (ἀγαπᾶν and ἀγάπη) are very common in the New Testament, especially in St Paul and St John. There is no need to say how suitable they are to express the love of God for us, our love for God, love for our brethren, and in particular the Christian feeling of love for one's enemies. Jesus Christ says : ἀγαπᾶτε τοὺς ἐχθροὺς ὑμῶν (Matt. v, 44 ; Luke vi, 27), for charity is free and depends upon the will ; if he had said : φιλεῖτε τοὺς ἐχθροὺς ὑμῶν, he would have almost demanded the impossible. Yet God not only *cherishes* us, but *loves* with tenderness because he is our Father (φιλεῖ, John xvi, 27), and St Paul pronounces an anathema against whoever does not love him who has so loved us (1 Cor. xvi, 22 : εἴ τις οὐ φιλεῖ τὸν Κύριον ἤτω ἀνάθεμα).

### III—St Paul's Asceticism

The ascetical doctrine of St Paul would deserve a separate study. We have indicated some characteristics of it in an article entitled *Un aspect de l'ascèse dans St Paul* (*Revue d'ascétique et de mystique*, vol. ii, 1921, pp. 3-22), and more briefly in the course of this work, especially in Vol. II, pp. 344-350. The principal passages to be considered are 1 Cor. ix, Phil. iii, 2 Tim. ii-iv, etc. We will add here two interesting texts :

(A) 2 Cor. iv, 10. πάντοτε τὴν νέκρωσιν τοῦ Ἰ. ἐν τῷ σώματι περιφέροντες ἵνα καὶ ἡ ζωὴ τοῦ Ἰησοῦ ἐν τῷ σώματι ἡμῖν φανερωθῇ.

*Semper mortificationem Jesu in corpore nostro circumferentes ut et vita Jesu manifestetur in corporibus nostris.*

11. ἀεὶ γὰρ ἡμεῖς οἱ ζῶντες εἰς θάνατον παραδιδόμεθα διὰ Ἰ., ἵνα καὶ ἡ ζωὴ τοῦ Ἰ. φανερώθῃ ἐν τῇ θνητῇ σαρκὶ ὑμῶν.

*Semper enim nos qui vivimus in mortem tradimur propter J. ut et vita J. manifestetur in carne nostra mortali.*

These two verses are to be compared, for they mutually explain each other. The word νέκρωσις—the equivalent of the classic θανάτωσις—is sometimes passive, "the state of death" (Rom. iv, 19); but it seems to be active here, "the putting to death, the crucifixion." The Apostle means that the suffering of Jesus is always (πάντοτε), and everywhere (περιφέροντες) being renewed in his body. It is the *quotidie morior* of 1 Cor. xv, 32. He alludes to his persecutions and sufferings— beatings with rods, scourgings, stonings, etc. (2 Cor. xi, 23-30)—and also doubtless to his voluntary bodily mortifications (1 Cor. ix, 26-27). His life, saved miraculously so many times (2 Cor. i, 10 ; 2 Tim. iii, 11 ; iv, 17, etc.), is a kind of continual miracle and a proof that Jesus, his supporter and liberator, lives in glory in heaven. It is thanks to him that he can always say : *quasi morientes et ecce vivimus* (2 Cor. vi, 9).

(B) Gal. vi, 17. τοῦ λοιποῦ      *De cetero nemo*
    κόπους

μοι μηδεὶς παρεχέτω·      *mihi molestus sit ;*
ἐγὼ γὰρ τὰ στίγματα τοῦ Ἰησοῦ      *ego enim stigmata Domini Jesu*
ἐν τῷ σώματί μου βαστάζω.      *in corpore meo porto.*

In spite of the brevity of the text, the meaning is not
doubtful. " Henceforth (τοῦ λοιποῦ, imperfectly rendered by *de
cetero*) let no one molest me," nor cause me any more embarrass-
ments by his attacks, calumnies, and hostile manœuvres, like
those of which the Galatian Judaizers have been guilty towards
me ; " for I bear in my body the marks of Jesus," and those
glorious marks show that I belong to him, and that I am his
servant, his agent, and his apostle. The στίγματα were marks
that were inflicted with a red-hot iron : in the West on
fugitive slaves ; in the East on all slaves and sometimes on
soldiers, to indicate their master and their chief ; in all
countries on animals to make known their owners. St Paul
refers to the Eastern usage, and he clearly alludes to the scars
of the wounds so many times received for the name of Jesus.
These scars are the *marks of Jesus*, not only because they
liken him to his Master, but because they indicate him as the
slave and soldier of Jesus, and have been imprinted on his
body not indeed by Jesus himself, but for his sake.

# NOTE Z—JEWISH ESCHATOLOGY

The greatest difficulty which the study of Jewish eschatology presents is its almost inextricable amalgamation with messianic conceptions and apocalytic ideas, changeable and fleeting as dreams. We consider it useless to involve ourselves in this labyrinth, and we limit ourselves to two observations which can throw some light, by analogy or contrast, on the exegesis of the New Testament.

## I—THE DURATION OF THE MESSIANIC TIMES

The prophets assigned to the Messiah a never-ending reign (Jer. xxiv, 6 ; xxxiii, 17-22 ; Ezech. xxxvii, 25 ; Joel iv (iii), 20; Dan. vii, 27). That is also the teaching of the oldest extra-canonical authors (*Enoch*, lxii, 14 ; *Sibyll.*, iii, 49-50, 766; *Psalm. Salom.*, xvii, 4). *Cf.* John xii, 34 : *Nos audivimus ex lege, quia Christus manet in aeternum*. Nevertheless, together with the thesis of the eternal reign of the Messiah, the idea of a temporal reign, serving as a prelude to a never-ending heavenly kingdom, subsequently found credence. The *Apocalypse of Baruch*, while admitting the eternal duration of the messianic kingdom (lxxiii, 1), does not hesitate to say (xl, 3) : *Et erit principatus ejus stans in saeculum*, donec finiatur mundus corruptionis. *The Fourth Book of Esdras* even fixes a limit (xii, 34 : *quoadusque veniat* finis, dies judicii) and a date (vii, 28-29 : annis quadringentis. *Et erit post annos hos et morietur filius meus Christus*).—The rabbinical speculations are summed up in a passage of the Talmud of Babylon, *Sanhedrin*, 96b-99a. *The days of the Messiah* are *forty* years according to Ps. xciv (xcv) 10, and according to Deut. viii, 3 compared with Ps. lxxxix, 15 ; or *seventy* years according to Is. xxiii, 15 ; or *three generations* according to Ps. lxxi, 5 ; or *four hundred* years according to Ps. lxxxix, 15 compared with Gen. xv, 13.—To these hypotheses the *Pesiqta rabbathi* adds the following : *six hundred* years (with no Scriptural authority) or a *thousand* years according to Ps. lxxxix, 4 and Is. lxiii, 4 ; or *two thousand* years according to Ps. lxxxix, 15 ; or *seven thousand* years according to Is. lxii, 5, or *three hundred and sixty-five thousand* years (one year of the days of the Lord) according to Is. lxiii, 4.—All these calculations are based upon the principle that the messianic age of happiness must equal the length of the period of trial, or that a day of the Lord is as a thousand years.—Another tradition, which was to exert a great influence on the first Christian writers, is recorded in the Talmud of Babylon ('*Aboda Zara*, 9a and *Sanhedrin*, 97a-98a), and starts from a different notion. It makes the world last six thousand years, as the work of creation lasted six days : two thousand years of chaos (תוהו), two thousand years of the law (תורה), and two thousand years of the days of the Messiah (ימות תמשיח). *Cf.* Weber, *Jüd. Theol.*², 372-373, 349.

## II—THE RESURRECTION OF THE DEAD

About the time of the Christian era, did the Jews believe in a universal resurrection ? Let us divide this period into three sections.

1. *The Time Preceding the Appearance of Christianity.*— The Second Book of the Machabees occupies itself solely with the resurrection of the just (2 Mac. vii, 9, 14, 23 ; xii, 43-44 ; xiv, 46), and particularly of the martyrs, who seemed to have a special right to the resurrection (*cf.* Apoc. xx, 4). The famous passage in Daniel (xii, 2 : *Et multi de his qui dormiunt in terrae pulvere evigilabunt, alii in vitam aeternam et alii in opprobrium*), while mentioning the resurrection of the wicked, can by a strict interpretation be understood as referring to a partial resurrection, although the idea of totality is not excluded. But from the moment that the principle of the resurrection of the wicked was admitted, there was no more reason to limit its extent. The different parts of the Book of Enoch contain very different conceptions. According to xxii, 13, the sinners who have undergone their punishment here on earth will not rise from the dead ; xxv, 5 seems to suppose that the others will rise again to receive their punishment. As to the just, their resurrection is not doubtful.

2. *First Century of our Era.*—(A) *The rationalistic school*, represented especially by the Sadducees, denied absolutely the resurrection and even the immortality of the soul (Josephus, *Bell. jud.*, II, viii, 14 ; *Antiq.*, xviii, 1-4) ; but as their number was small, the Sadducees, in order not to shock the mass of the people, were obliged to conform to the language of the Pharisees (Josephus, *loc. cit.*), *cf.* Matt. xxii, 23 ; Mark xii, 18; Luke xx, 27 ; Acts iv, 1, 2 ; xxiii, 8.—(B) *The Hellenist school*, represented by Philo and the Fourth Book of the Machabees, admitted the immortality of the soul, but denied or feigned to ignore the resurrection of the body. According to Josephus (*Bell.*, II, viii, 11 ; *Antiq.*, XVIII, i, 5) the Essenes shared this opinion.—(C) *The orthodox school*, represented by the Pharisees, admitted the resurrection of the just, and even more generally the resurrection of all men, Jews and non-Jews, good and bad. Thus the Fourth Book of Esdras, vii, 32 : *Et terra reddet quae in ea dormiunt, et pulvis qui in eo silentio habitant, et promptuaria reddent quae eis commendatae sunt animae.* If the *Apocalypse of Baruch*, xxx, speaks only of the just, it

subsequently expressly mentions the wicked (i) : *Restituet
terra tunc mortuos quos recipit nunc ut custodiat eos, nihil
immutans in figura eorum, sed sicut recepit ita restituet eos.*
The alteration in the appearance of the resurrected good and
wicked will be visible only after the judgement (li) : *Et cum
praeterierit ille dies statutus, immutabitur aspectus eorum qui
damnati fuerint et gloria eorum qui justificati fuerint. Fiet
enim aspectus eorum qui nunc impie agunt pejor quam est, ut
sustineant supplicium,* etc. (trad. Ceriani, *Monumenta sacra et
prof.*, Milan, vol. i, 1866, p. 86). *The Testament of Benjamin*,
x, 8 (Charles, *The Testaments of the Twelve Patriarchs*, Oxford,
1908, p. 229), is still more explicit : καὶ οἱ πάντες ἀναστήσονται,
οἱ μὲν εἰς δόξαν, οἱ δὲ εἰς ἀτιμίαν (*Armenian* : Τότε πάντες ἀλλα-
γησόμεθα, οἱ μὲν εἰς δόξαν, οἱ δὲ εἰς ἀτιμίαν, *cf.* I Cor. xv, 51-52).
But it is necessary always to discount the chances of Christian
interpolation.

3. *Rabbinical Judaism.* — The primitive opinion, which
remained traditional, is that the dead will rise again at the
end of time for judgement. Towards the end of the second
century of our era, it seems, a dissenting school conceived of
a resurrection of the just to enjoy the messianic kingdom on
earth ; but this school did not succeed in becoming dominant.
More and more, the resurrection was made the counterpart of
the creation. This presupposes a universal resurrection in
conformity with Dan. xii, 2, although naturally the resurrection of the just formed the principal subject of thought.
*Cf.* Lagrange, *Le Messianisme*, pp. 122-131 and 176-185.
Consult also : F. Schwally, *Das Leben nach dem Tode nach den
Vorstell. des alten Israels und des Judentums*, 1892; A. Bertholet,
*Die israel. Vorstellungen vom Zustand nach dem Tode*, Freiburg-
im-B., 1899; R. H. Charles, *A Critical History of the Doctrine of
Future Life in Israel, in Judaism and in Christianity*, London,
1899; P. Volz, *Jüdische Eschatologie von Daniel bis Aqiba*,
Tübingen, 1903.

# APPENDIX

These alternatives in the translation have been recommended to us as a result of an examination of the latest amended French edition and have the support of very high authority. (The references are to page and line number.)

## VOLUME I

| | | |
|---|---|---|
| 1, l. 28. | adds to analysis synthesis | adds analysis to synthesis |
| 1, l. 31. | thought. Its | thought; but its |
| 2, l. 2. | theology. It | theology; it |
| 2, l. 5. | theology; and it | theology. It |
| 2, l. 34. | by a special command | by a special circumstance |
| 3, l. 33. | overflow into questions | overflow with questions |
| 5, l. 12. | falsely critical | pseudo-critical |
| 6, l. 33. | to delay acknowledging | to waste one's time at |
| 7, l. 24. | of which the Church of Ephesus was the mother | of which province Ephesus was the metropolis |
| 8, l. 44. | Adolf Harnack. But then we used to think that he placed the sacred rights of history above the petty prejudices of national infatuation. The only question. | the learned Professor Adolf von Harnack who, from 1908 until his death (June 1930), has strongly claimed for St. Luke the paternity of the Gospel and of the Acts. A question |
| 10, l. 37. | the events | the voyages |
| 14, l. 2-3. | But figures . . . and his technical | Figures . . . but his technical |
| 18, l. 24. | was constrained to render | would later on render |
| 18, l. 47. | ultimate designs | the last things |
| 20, l. 21. | accommodating | accommodated sense |
| 20, l. 22. | to a fact or to an analogous case | to an analogous fact or case |
| 21, l. 30. | its design is changed | it is purposely changed |
| 22, l. 1. | and that this | and this |
| 23, l. 8. | participle | particle |
| 24, l. 43. | sacrifices | concessions |
| 27, l. 4. | on the authority of documents | as documents |
| 30, l. 14. | neither possible nor | either impossible, or not |
| 31, l. 4. | quality | turn |
| 32, l. 8. | the fact of the Eucharist and the manner of its institution | the fact and the manner of institution of the Eucharist |
| 42, l. 10. | proofs | proofs from the Scriptures |
| 42, l. 38. | Nevertheless | Meanwhile |
| 44, l. 24. | two in Lycaonia | two in Phrygian Pisidia (Antioch and Iconium), two in Lycaonia |
| 46, l. 29. | admirably suited . . . offered himself | at all events admirably suited . . . yet offered himself |
| 47, n., l. 16. | si (si | whether (si |
| 48, n., l. 7. | Whatever their authority might be elsewhere | Whatever, moreover, their authority might be |
| 49, l. 6. | amplified greatly | fully supported |
| 49, l. 7. | proclaimed with equal power | implicitly proclaimed |
| 49, l. 15. | from marriage with blood-relatives, which were forbidden | from such marriages with blood-relatives as were forbidden |
| 51, n., l. 6. | before all | "to the face" |
| 53, l. 13. | had assumed at that time | in that case assumed |
| 54, l. 2. | the teaching of Christian doctrine in the true sense | the catechesis in the proper sense |
| 55, l. 10. | unorthodox | orthodox |
| 58, n. 2, l. 1. | have feelings | are passible |
| 65, l. 2. | such a letter | many a letter |
| 65, l. 48. | Moreover | Hence |
| 70, l. 31. | and the phrases | therefore the phrases |
| 72, l. 14. | reveal | set off |
| 74, n. 2, l. 5. | Sap. v, 19 | Sap. v, 19; Bar. v, 2 |
| 79, l. 6. | Ecce, veniam | Etiam venio |
| 82, l. 16. | command to preach the Gospel | decree to have the Gospel preached |
| 87, l. 19. | for a short time | later on |
| 88, l. 20. | incorrectness, full of | incorrectness, or his discourses full of |
| 89, l. 8. | grievious palliations of wrongdoing | regrettable attenuations |
| 93, l. 14. | the peculiar business | the gift proper to |
| 97, n. 2, l. 7. | contiguity of | comparison with |
| 102, n. 5, l. 3. | what are rightly called nature's laws | the precepts, properly so called, of the law of nature |
| ibid. | and it is certain that | and, of course, |
| 104, l. 37. | will be | were |
| 106, n. 1, l. 2. | Περὶ δὲ 'Απολλιὼ | Περὶ δὲ τῆς λογίας .xvi, 12: Περὶ δὲ 'Απολλὼ |

| | | |
|---|---|---|
| 107, l. 17. | comes straight to the point | restores just proportions |
| 108, l. 33. | counsel, however, when | counsel which, however, sounds like an order, when |
| 109, l. 24. | while unable | without our being able |
| 110, l. 12. | and, if not there, it is shown in | and, in the opposite case, in |
| 110, n., l. 5. | must not be | is not |
| 113, l. 27. | takes into account only | addresses himself only to |
| 113, l. 33. | either part | the latter |
| 114, l. 33. | Objection has been unjustly made to an application of the Pauline privilege | It is by error that an application of the Pauline privilege has been found |
| 114, n., l. 2. | does not make good | is not yet a case of |
| 115, l. 15. | allows it to continue | leaves it in force |
| 117, l. 31. | the imminent danger of scandal | the scandal and of the imminent danger |
| 120, l. 29. | the power of rule | the power of order |
| 122, l. 29. | which is usually followed | but which it more often followed |
| 127, l. 29. | the poison of serpents | venom and poison |
| 129, l. 17. | Moreover, the gifts | The gifts, therefore, |
| 133, l. 10. | sanctifying grace | the grace of one's state |
| 135, l. 12. | Paul's testimony | the witnesses accumulated by St. Paul |
| 139, l. 18. | profoundly mysterious | radical |
| 140, n. 2, l. 15. | changed in place | transferred |
| 144, l. 7. | difficulties, but it is of less moment than the | difficulties. It depends on the |
| 144, l. 26. | outbreak | leaven of discord and revolt |
| 144, l. 27. | among | with |
| 147, l. 27. | sufficient to think anything of ourselves, as of ourselves | of ourselves sufficient to think anything as [coming] from ourselves |
| 148, l. 40. | excellency | immeasurable value |
| 148, l. 41. | of the power of God | of God |
| 153, l. 6. | place | circumstances |
| 154, l. 32. | " You would bear " or " You bear | " You did bear " or even " You do bear |
| 155, n., l. 4. | I have done nothing less | in nothing I am less |
| 167, l. 13. | even cut off, who trouble you | mutilated, who agitate and trouble you |
| 168, l. 15. | is Christ then . . . of sin? | then Christ would be . . . of sin. |
| 171, l. 32. | Moreover | Elsewhere |
| 173, n. 2, l. 5. | arrangement | disposition |
| 174, l. 3. | involuntarily | spontaneously |
| 174, n. 3, l. 4. | Rom. iii, 25; xi, 20; 1 Cor. i, 24) | πίστει (Rom. iii, 28; xi, 20; 2 Cor. i, 24) |
| 175, l. 31. | even if | although |
| 176, l. 25. | essentially | virtually |
| 176, l. 27. | he is justified only by | (he is not justified) except by |
| 178, l. 9. | admitting that | supposing such a justification |
| 178, l. 13. | due to | belonging to the sphere of |
| 178, l. 14. | obtain it | obtain it, so to speak, |
| 180, l. 33. | which is | which are |
| 183, l. 36. | cannot himself love evil | cannot love evil itself |
| 184, l. 4. | occasions | stages |
| 184, l. 5. | overlooking | passing over |
| 184, l. 6. | being | over |
| 184, l. 11. | intermediary | intermezzo |
| 191, l. 13. | a fundamental thesis | a thesis, although a fundamental one |
| 191, l. 26. | God's salvation | of salvation in God's intention |
| 192, l. 34. | strictly speaking | in all strictness |
| 193, l. 28. | foretold by | foretold both by |
| ibid. | and by the signs | and by the indications |
| 193, l. 29. | and especially by | especially of |
| ibid. | was | remained |
| 193, n. 2, l. 2. | This . . . God: | It . . . God: |
| 195, n. 1, l. 8. | all probability | any hypothesis |
| 196, n. 2, l. 10. | the word qui twice | the last two qui |
| 198, l. 37. | bearing witness to them | also bearing witness |
| 199, n., l. 17. | bearing witness | also bearing witness |
| 201, l. 9. | elements | stages |
| 209, l. 27. | restored | transferred |
| 211, l. 19. | a queen but a suzerain | a queen also but subordinately |
| 212, l. 32. | every sin is not | not every sin is |
| 213, l. 25. | concludes . . . completes | conclude . . . complete |
| 214, l. 1. | heaping up | excess |
| 215, n. (C), l. 3. | nevertheless | , however, |
| 217, l. 1. | one sin of a nature | a sin of nature |
| 217, l. 11. | it is explained still less by the fact that | it can be explained still less since |
| 218, n., l. 12. | Finally | To sum up |
| 218, n., l. 14. | no more couples | and two couples |
| 220, l. 9. | Also | Hence |
| 221, n., l. 8. | grace | gratuity |

| | | |
|---|---|---|
| 222, l. 37. | a part of him as another self | a part of himself, another Christ |
| 223, n. 2, l. 2-3. | ἀδλὰ . . . μλοιώματι | 'αλλὰ . . . ὁμοιώματι |
| 224, l. 21-22. | he . . . he . . . he | it . . . it . . . it |
| 225, l. 12. | above all | still less |
| 225, l. 22. | it | he |
| 225, n. 2, l. 18. | is subject to | enslaves |
| 226, l. 42. | of a woman | of the woman |
| 228, l. 37. | no longer | neither |
| 230, l. 1. | because | that |
| 230, l. 22. | all the force it now possesses | all its force |
| 233, l. 15. | acting through | correlative to |
| 235, n. 1, l. 2. | etc., the | etc. The |
| 238, l. 11. | invoke | call for |
| 238, n. 2, l. 10. | submits | submitted |
| 240, l.14. | God that justifieth | It is God that justifieth |
| 242, l. 10. | arrangements for . . . arrangements | dispositions regarding . . . dispositions |
| 242, l. 23. | arrangements | dispositions |
| 242, l. 30. | modifying | attenuating |
| 243, l. 27. | in that | especially because |
| 243, l. 30. | construction | member |
| 244, n., l. 15. | explains this conformity exactly | precisely explains this conformity |
| 245, l. 29. | an aorist either gnomic or habitual | a gnomic or habitual aorist |
| 246, l. 17. | for us. | for us? |
| 246, l. 30. | lie | still continue |
| 246, l. 37. | proof | testimony |
| 247, l. 41. | whom God foresees destined to believe | who God foresees will believe |
| 247, l. 46. | erroneously extended | misunderstood |
| 248, l. 22. | misunderstood | overlooked |
| 249, l. 23. | cannot | may not |
| 250, l. 1. | It is asserted | It is now a certainty |
| 250, l. 12. | with | among |
| 251, l. 32. | contrasts | contracts |
| 252, n. 2, l. 17. | modify | attenuate |
| 255, l. 10. | and blinded him | and he blinded him |
| 255, l. 19. | Also the hardening | The hardening, therefore, |
| 256, l. 17. | drew its moral | drew the moral |
| 257, l. 4. | sin; | sin, |
| 257, l. 6. | Moreover | Hence |
| 257, n., l. 28. | his anger "; from now on he is | his anger" from now on, he is |
| 258, l. 3. | enemy | opponent |
| 261, l. 21. | it is best to postpone the question | it is therefore possible to restate the question |
| 262, l. 3. | the context and consultation | the context, the consultation |
| 263, l. 10. | persisted obstinately in their attitude to | run against |
| 263, l. 19. | individualism | particularism |
| 264, l. 20. | remove | transfer |
| 267, l. 2. | can we not here adore | can we here not adore |
| 267, n., l. 2. | some individuals excepted | leaving aside the question of individuals |
| 273, l. 14. | circumcision | mutilation |
| 279, l. 15. | without the | except in the case of |
| 279, l. 16. | foreseen the possibility | foreseen as a quite ordinary occurrence |
| 279, l. 17. | given as quite an ordinary occurrence. | given. |
| 280, l. 12. | determined | determinate |
| 280, l. 28. | and, finally, the description | and the final description |
| 280, l. 29. | There are also in the portions peculiar to each | Yet, even in the portions peculiar to each, there are |
| 280, l. 34. | restored if lost | reconstructed |
| 281, l. 13. | One after another these sectarians have been called | These sectarians have successively been called |
| 281, l. 35. | Christ | that of Christ |
| 282, l. 20. | very use according | very use. [Yes, but only] according |
| 283, l. 8. | based upon | blended into |
| 284, n., l. 3. | no account is taken of the fact | it does not make us realize |
| 285, l. 25. | in a word Docetism | and finally Docetism |
| 288, l. 13. | belongs especially to him | belongs to him |
| 289, n. 1, l. 26. | named | set up as |
| 293, l. 16. | very efficacious | hardly apparent |
| 294, l. 33. | Also | Hence |
| 294, l. 36. | nourishment | influx |
| 295, n., l. 23. | perfectly | frequently |
| 295, n., l. 37. | is fulfilled | completes himself |
| 297, l. 32. | Moreover | Elsewhere again |
| 298, n. 2, l. 19. | to | in |
| 299, l. 3. | It is in vain that . . . plenitude; | Although . . . plenitude, |

| | | |
|---|---|---|
| 299, l. 16. | union | total |
| 299, l. 30. | face to face with | quite naturally to |
| 300, l. 34. | incomprehensible | entirely misunderstood |
| 302, l. 36. | is fulfilled | completes himself |
| 303, l. 3. | Also | Hence |
| 303, l. 33. | is fulfilled | completes himself |
| 306, n., l. 17. | similarly | both equally |
| 306, n., l. 18. | similarly | both equally |
| ibid. | than on πρός | than πρός |
| 306, n., l. 39. | its | his |
| 307, n., l. 26. | supplying through every contact | by every contact with the supplying centre |
| 308, l. 35. | also | hence |
| 313, l. 26. | The other . . . language, almost to the point of enthusiasm. | Excepting the enthusiasm, the other . . . language. |
| 314, l. 1. | with the incarnation, logically occurs after it in point of time | with the incarnation in point of time, logically occurs after it |
| 314, l. 6. | It would not, therefore, be | It would not be |
| 315, l. 12. | voluntatis notionalis (purely personal) | of the notional will |
| 314, l. 14. | distinctively personal (hypostatic) function | hypostatic function |
| 314, l. 17. | a mind like that which was | an attitude of mind conformable to what took place |
| 314, l. 29. | calls his glorious exaltation a recompense | calls for his glorious exaltation as a recompense |
| 318, l. 11. | at least, those | at least those |
| 319, l. 34. | is its crown | which it crowns |
| 319, n., l. 3. | In this text again | In this text, however, |
| 320, l. 19. | strongly maintained | maintains, it is true, |
| 320, l. 37. | had not himself been able to empty himself | could not have emptied himself |
| 321, l. 27. | ego, and | ego; |
| 322, l. 22. | could | might |
| 325, l. 4. | Resemblances | Probabilities |
| 325, l. 15. | take for granted already | already suppose |
| 325, l. 32. | the paternity | the Pauline paternity |
| 326, l. 33. | used it to designate | thought of reserving it for designating |
| 327, l. 9. | strictly speaking | for all that |
| 328, l. 34. | and | but |
| 330, l. 1. | specious in a different way | much more specious |
| 330, l. 11. | choice | argument |
| 331, l. 14. | evidently hold an intermediate position | hold a position which is about intermediate |
| 332, l. 9. | belongs rightly to | is peculiar to |
| 332, l. 11. | by the Father and the Son without distinction | without distinction either by the Father or by the Son |
| 333, l. 5. | Paul does not commonly | Paul, as usual, does not |
| 333, l. 26. | It is expedient | We should |
| 334, l. 14. | doubtful | obscure |
| 336, n. 1. l. 7. | from | in |
| 337, l. 11. | he does | we do |
| 337, l. 29. | observe | compare |
| 337, n., l. 3. | by | upon |
| 339, l. 10. | animals | creatures |
| 340, l. 9. | or of | of |
| 342, n. 4, l. 5. | Gentile | Hellenist |
| 343, l. 6. | Gentile | Hellenist |
| 345, l. 14. | After having sent | Having summoned |
| 347, l. 13. | retires from the clergy | foregoes the clerical state |
| 348, n. 2, l. 2. | This | It |
| 350, l. 2. | were employed | had business |
| 350, n. 2, l. 23. | serious in another way | much more serious |
| 358, l. 48. | would | did |
| 359, l. 22. | doubtfully | unspecified |
| 361, l. 17. | As for the rest | Besides |
| 361, l. 28. | served him as an archetype | served as an archetype for the former |
| 361, n. 5, l. 2. | and definitely | and, in fine, |
| 362, l. 22. | shared again | still shared |
| 364, l. 19. | civilization | worship |
| 365, l. 23. | introduction | blending |
| 368, l. 6. | the lightning and the tempest also | hence the lightning and the tempest |
| 372, l. 17. | and the founder | or the founder |
| 373, l. 29. | to hold fellowship with his co-heirs | to associate co-heirs with himself |
| 375, l. 5. | on a large scale | roughly |
| 378, l. 33. | to him | in his case |

| | | |
|---|---|---|
| 379, l. 8. | make prominent either the oblation (the Eucharist) which | emphasize either the oblation which |
| 379, l. 9. | or the victim who | or the victim which |
| 379, l. 23. | Gospel | Epistle |
| 381, l. 5. | the infinite value | the infinite value, of that sacrifice |
| 381, l. 28. | above all | pre-eminently |
| 381, n., l. 10. | and to | and with |
| 382, l. 14. | It is not necessary to | It is necessary not to |
| 382, l. 28. | being a priest by their consent | according to them, being a priest |
| 382, l. 30. | being only | only |
| 385, l. 17. | in almost identical words | , though not in as many words |
| 386, l. 3. | revocable blemishes | irremediable defects |
| 386, l. 26. | its | their |
| 387, n. 4, l. 8. | which is found elsewhere | which, however, is found |
| 389, l. 35. | to be refuted | for refuting |
| 393, l. 32. | This rest of God is Jesus | This rest of God, it is Jesus |
| 395, l. 8. | author (or chief) | chief |
| 405, l. 36. | import | license |
| 406, l. 7. | this he expresses quite clearly elsewhere | this, moreover, he expresses clearly enough |
| 406, l. 12. | Philippi | Philip |
| 406, l. 15. | plundered wealth | inheritance |
| 408, l. 15. | some time | a fairly long time |
| 410, after l. 43. | The most recent and most complete work on the chronology of St. Paul is Plooij. De Chronologie van het leven van Paulus, Leiden, 1919. (A good summary by Jones in the Expositor, May, June, August, 1919.) The author puts the conversion of St. Paul in the year 30-31, his second visit to Jerusalem in 45-46, the assembly of the Apostles in 48, Paul's arrival at Corinth at the beginning of 50, the captivity in 57. He stops, as does the Acts, at the end of the captivity—Spring, 62. | |
| 415, l. 1. | it is true, with the variations | with, it is true, variations |
| 415, l. 50. | modification, cited from | modification of |
| 421, l. 18. | danger to one's neighbour | proximate danger |
| 424, l. 36. | eagerly sought for | readily assumed |
| 425, l. 37. | the prisoners, or the sick | whether in prison or sick |
| 427, l. 44. | dialect | slang |
| 430, l. 7. | one who | that which |
| 431, l. 21. | through | with reference to |
| 434, l. 6. | everything : ῞Ωστε | everything ; for he foresees the free acts, but does not predestine them : ῞Ωστε |
| 434, l. 8. | foreknowledge, which is something that | foreknowledge that which |
| 435, l. 13. | or of having it in mind | or of placing it before one's mind |
| 436, l. 28. | favour | initiative |
| 436, l. 40. | things to be done | the order of execution |
| 437, l. 20. | elsewhere | everywhere else |
| 440, l. 12. | whatever | notwithstanding |
| 440, l. 35. | admittedly the way in which | the way in which, in order to avoid misunderstanding, |
| 445, l. 1. | are precisely those | happen to be among those |
| 450, l. 3. | like the | as |
| 450, l. 35. | *predecessors* | as predecessors |
| 451, l. 30. | Also | Hence |
| 451, l. 37. | After | As early as |
| 451, l. 41. | returns | refers |
| 452, l. 10. | to Jacob | of Jacob |
| 455, l. 20. | to see | to show |
| 455, l. 29. | justice | truth |
| 455, l. 36. | so little is understood | there is so little agreement |
| 456, l. 36. | originates in | is proved already by |
| 458, l. 39. | was, even in his eyes, | was, in his eyes, even |
| 462, l. 46. | Finally | To sum up |
| 463, l. 39. | usual commentary | Glossa ordinaria |
| 463, l. 41. | commentary | Glossa |
| 464, l. 8. | Finally | To sum up |
| 454, l. 22. | mean | belong to |
| 464, l. 33. | it is surprising that the Fathers did not think of it. Also it is | it would be surprising if the Fathers had not thought of it. In fact, it is |
| 465, l. 33. | in exchange for | for |
| 467, l. 8. | depends | could depend |
| 467, l. 19. | union of | agreement in |
| 468, l. 12. | acquired by the Church after | existing already at |
| 468, l. 13. | These letters | At that date, these letters |
| 468, l. 22. | does not hesitate to write | writes nevertheless |
| 469, l. 40. | systematic | repeated |

| | | |
|---|---|---|
| 470, l. 26. | received readings | meanings |
| 471, l. 20. | etymology | vocabulary |
| 472, l. 15. | admirably | well |
| 475, l. 11. | he can be ranked indiscriminately | he cannot be ranked without reserve |
| 479, l. 15. | Gospel | Epistle |
| 492, l. 41. | injustice than to do that. | injustice. |
| 492, l. 42. | such a fault | it |
| 493, l. 38. | the party | one |
| 501, l. 25. | willingly find their preaching doubtful | find purposeful obscurity in their preaching |
| 506, l. 37. | schoolmaster | pedagogue |
| 508, l. 24. | by | to |
| 517, l. 6. | losing the faith | violating their sworn faith |
| 519, l. 11. | the husband of one wife | married only once |

Omissions:

| | | |
|---|---|---|
| 201, l. 33. | enough conscience among the heathen to | among the heathen a degree of ignorance sufficient to |
| 295, n., l. 15. | tackle | crew |
| 299, l. 10. | who is wholly completed | who completes himself wholly |
| xi, l. 12. | Resemblances | Probabilities |

## VOLUME II

| | | |
|---|---|---|
| 4, l. 26. | It always happens | It still remains |
| 4, l. 34. | and the revelation | , according to the revelation |
| 4, l. 36. | manifest to all nations | manifest, [and] is made known to all nations |
| 5, n., l. 14. | κατά in both cases | the two κατά |
| 5, n., l. 18. | in both cases κατά is subordinate | the second κατά is subordinate to the first one |
| 19, l. 7. | That if | If |
| 19, n., l. 21. | translated | rendered |
| 20, l. 44. | in the work of | in its relation to |
| 25, n., l. 11. | And what would fit in with such forgetfulness? | And what would be the meaning of that "divesting"? |
| 26, l. 7. | reflecting | refuting |
| 28, l. 38. | make known | confirm |
| 29, n., l. 6. | anticipates | would lead us to expect |
| 29, n., l. 7. | by changing | , although he changes |
| 31, l. 26-27. | Of the doctrine . . . and imposition Of the resurrection | The doctrine . . . and of imposition Of resurrection |
| 32, l. 7. | A variation of the original reading | A variant of the original text |
| 32, l. 8. | version | reading |
| 32, n., l. 2. | he | it |
| 34, l. 7. | subject | motive |
| 34, l. 35. | from | of |
| 37, n. 1, l. 5. | this fine judgment concerning | the final exposition of |
| 39, l. 34. | written dialogues | dialogues |
| 41, l. 38. | in a mystery | [which refers] to the mystery |
| 42, n., last l. | | *erste Brief des Paulus an die Korinther*,[a] Leipzig, 1910 (Collection Zahn). |
| 49, l. 17. | much more decisive is his language than | different is his language from |
| 50, l. 24. | for the biblical λόγος signifying the word and not reason (νοῦς), | for, since the biblical λόγος signifies the word and not reason, the νοῦς, |
| 52, l. 26. | abstracted by the body. | from which the body abstracts. |
| 52, n. 2. | food | meat |
| 56, l. 17. | his playful use | the interplay |
| 57, l. 24. | disputable | indisputable |
| 63, l. 11-13. | uses the commonly received vocabulary of that time on this subject, without appreciating its full significance, for . . . | uses without comment the commonly received vocabulary of that time on this subject, for . . . |
| 75, l. 35. | of the two modes of action | in both cases |
| 78, l. 6. | more for good than for evil. | more, for good as well as for evil. |
| 85, l. 7. | while taking part in it | passively |
| 92, n., l. 12. | to negotiate for capital sums | to treat per summa capita |
| 93, l. 18. | restrict Paul's thought still more | come nearer to Paul's thought |
| 95, l. 31. | sometimes approached | is sometimes compared with |
| 99, l. 25. | perspective | prospect |
| 106, l. 17. | use, according | use. [Yes, but only] according |

| | | |
|---|---|---|
| 107, l. 3. | extreme | arbitrary |
| 112, l. 30. | his Palestinian associates | the Palestinian milieu |
| 113, l. 19. | to the heart | in the bosom |
| 116, l. 28. | zealots | satellites |
| 120, l. 22. | Christians do not consciously | Christian sentiment does not |
| 127, l. 28. | naturally is | is superfluous when applied to |
| 132, l. 4. | Intervening in the Working of | Their Intervention according to |
| 133, l. 11. | appropriate sphere | sphere of appropriation |
| 134, l. 11. | as belonging to him | by appropriation |
| 134, l. 19. | in the discharge of their eternal relations or missions | in connection with their eternal relations or with the missions |
| 143, l. 14. | it | him |
| 149, l. 21. | physical | psychical |
| 153, l. 5. | occasion | need |
| 153, l. 31. | since it is elsewhere asserted | since, on the other hand, it is asserted |
| 156, l. 11. | St. Paul's verbal quotation from St. Luke | in St. Paul textually the same passage as in St. Luke |
| 168, l. 10. | by his theandric nature, he associates them in an indissoluble union. | by his theandric unity, he associates them in an indissoluble bond. |

N. B.  This last formula " *his theandric nature* " is directly *heretical.*

| | | |
|---|---|---|
| 169, l. 17. | because | that |
| 169, n. 8, l. 15. | deceived in them | mistaken |
| 173, n., l. 2. | two extreme differences | two differences in addition |
| 174, n., l. 7. | question | quotation |
| 180, l. 7. | sentient | material |
| 183, l. 11. | is not applicable | is applicable |
| 194, l. 19. | In the times when ideas of purchase, price, and ransom were operative | As soon as the ideas of purchase, price, and ransom were made use of |
| 195, l. 34. | the priest who sacrifices it | the one who offers it |
| 196, l. 29. | between the justice and the love of God on one side and between his anger and mercy on the other | between the justice and the love of God, between his anger and his mercy |
| 196, l. 36. | punishment of the damned | pain of loss |
| 198, l. 7. | tortures of the damned | pain of loss |
| 207, l. 5. | cause | effect |
| 211, l. 4. | regained.  All | regained—all |
| 228, n., l. 19. | we shall show elsewhere | we show elsewhere (See p. 169, Note 8) |
| 241, l. 10. | In cases where the twofold object | If the twofold object |
| 241, l. 11. | is clearly | were clearly |
| 245, l. 46. | are called by the same name | call·for |
| 254, l. 27. | to baptism are | to baptism and, by concomitance, to confirmation, are |
| 254, l. 33. | from them | from that fact |
| 255, l. 18. | after the time of St. Justin | from St. Justin on |
| 259, n., l. 5. | rightly belongs | belongs by appropriation |
| 261, l. 21. 23. | effective(ter) | affective |
| 266, l. 36. | does not mention it until | mentions it only |
| 269, l. 6. | a sacred function of a similar nature | a function of a sacred nature |
| 271, l. 5. | which no one had the right to call into being or revive. | to revive or to call which into being belongs to nobody. |
| 271, l. 10. | grace of a calling | grace of one's state |
| 271, l. 32. | graces of condition | graces of one's state |
| 271, l. 37. | acts, of course, | is, of course, assumed |
| 273, l. 19. | argues well, in presenting this hypothesis | really argues on this supposition |
| 273, l. 23. | can indeed be a sing, yet for all that may not be | could indeed be a sign, without, however being |
| 275, n. 4, l. 2. | suckers and shoots | cuttings and layers |
| 278, l. 7. | maintain | see |
| 280, l. 32. | into one single national body | into the body of one single nation |
| 282, l. 26. | with the apostles.  It is | with the apostles.  But the exegete does not hesitate.  It is |
| 290, n., l. 19. | the two | that we |
| 291, l. 1. | partly hypostatic | quasi-hypostatic |
| 291, l. 12. | ordinary grace | habitual grace |
| 291, l. 26. | with human nature | with the divine Nature |
| 296, l. 2. | *Jesus* | Jesus |
| 296, l. 3. | *Christ* | Christ |
| 298, l. 27. | planted together | grafted into him |
| 300, l. 20. | In this case it happens to be a statement concerning | In fact, there is an accidental mention of |
| 302, l. 38. | without going clearly | without, of course, going |
| 304, l. 16. | on a level with | besides |
| 305, l. 28. | clubs of revellers and social circles | corporations such as the Eranists and Thiasites |

| | | |
|---|---|---|
| 307, l. 12. | ever | in those churches |
| 313, l. 23. | desires | denies |
| 314, l. 26. | as well as | —because |
| 315, l. 32. | preferably gives to his disciple | gives to his disciple of predilection |
| 319, l. 22. | of sin | to sin |
| 326, l. 32. | but | and yet |
| 326, l. 33. | is his word of command and counter-sign. | are his watchword and his orders. |
| 338, l. 30. | really belong to it | are peculiar to him |
| 345, l. 4. | This is the shortest and most efficacious example of his teachings. | Example is the shortest and most efficacious teaching. |
| 346, l. 3. | had wounded | would wound |
| 346, l. 9. | Manichaean | dualistic |
| 346, l. 26. | Gospel, but, as | Gospel; as |
| 350, l. 12. | baptism, actual or desired, is necessarily the only means | baptism alone, actual or desired, is necessary with a necessity of means |
| 356, l. 15. | On the one hand | On the other hand |
| 357, l. 14. | incomparable glory | different degrees of glory |
| 359, l. 22. | from this fact it appears | is proved by this fact |
| 362, l. 5. | has | which has |
| 362, l. 6. | doctrine and usually | doctrine, usually |
| 366, l. 47. | Greek word, untranslatable in French. | untranslatable Greek word. |
| 368, n., l. 2. | reading has | reading 'εκδυσάμενοι has |
| 375, l. 36. | punishment of the lost | pain of loss |
| 385, l. 1. | The significant and most interesting evolution of the word sacramentum is | The evolution of the meaning of the word sacramentum is most interesting and is |
| 387, l. 21. | a purely imaginative one | pure imagination |
| 388, l. 23. | and a relation of dependence of the latter on the former, if | and the relation of dependence, if |
| 393, l. 22. | and of | of |
| 393, l. 23. | words and other | words, and of other |
| 397, l. 5. | and (g) the stereotyped form— | and (g)—the stereotyped form |
| 397, l. 43. | predicate | predication |
| 398, l. 21. | need to be investigated in order to know if they express | need some further qualification in order to express |
| 402, l. 42. | absent in body | absent in the flesh |
| 410, l. 1. | reconcilable moreover with the first, although admittedly | reconcilable, however, with the first, if it be taken as |
| 415, l. 1. | principalities, cherubim | principalities, powers, cherubim |
| 417, l. 10. | The Significant Evolution of the Word στοιχεῖον | The Evolution of the Meaning of στοιχεῖον |
| 417, l. 13. | shaft | pointer |
| 417, l. 15. | the gnomon | the pointer of a gnomon |
| 417, l. 18. | from a usage common | and commonly used |
| 417, l. 33. | The alphabetical meaning | The meaning " alphabet " |
| 418, l. 3. | Under the influence of astrology a new meaning was subsequently given a place of great honour | A new meaning was subsequently added under the influence of astrology, which was in great honour |
| 418, l. 16. | who relates, according to Hippobotos | who, on the authority of Hippobotos, relates |
| 424, l. 25. | to the heart of divinity | in the bosom of the divinity |
| 428, l. 25. | both | all |
| 433, l. 3. | contrast | opposition |
| 436, l. 5. | usual Gloss | Glossa ordinaria |
| 436, l. 43. | the Lord the Spirit | the Spirit Lord |
| 439, l. 18. | common Gloss | Glossa ordinaria |
| 441, l. 4. | reach | admit |
| 441, l. 13. | usual Gloss | Glossa ordinaria |
| 445, l. 42. | made use of | could have made use of |
| 452, l. 45. | to them | to some authors |
| 456, l. 10. | positive idea of right | positive right |
| 456, l. 25. | designate the Greek | designate, as do the Greek |
| 457, l. 14. | although it takes for granted | but presupposes |
| 457, l. 29. | its | their |
| 457, l. 37. | with greater reason | still more readily |
| 458, l. 9. | a little later | a little too late |
| 464, l. 6. | proved | an accomplished fact |
| 470, l. 12. | slanderers, detractors, incontinent | slanderers, incontinent |
| 470, l. 41. | tender | sensuous |
| 481, l. 24. | has the remarkable faculty of explaining | by a stroke of genius explains |
| 482, l. 17. | These form the vicissitudes | Beyschlag invites us to contemplate the vicissitudes |
| 482, l. 19. | of the parousia, which Beyschlag . . . | of the parousia. |
| 493, l. 3. | as the plan of redemption in action. | from the point of view of the redemptive act. |

# BIBLIOGRAPHY

FAR from seeking to lengthen this bibliography, we have made special efforts to abbreviate it. The mere enumeration of all that has been written on St Paul, from the third century to our own day, would fill a large volume. Such a list would, moreover, be of little interest and moderate utility, the greater part of these works being of no intrinsic value and having justly fallen into oblivion. We exclude from our lists six sorts of works.

1. *All authors previous to the nineteenth century*, because they are thought to be known to the reader, in case they are of any real value.

2. *All ancient and modern commentaries*, because they are enumerated, and generally with a short estimate of them, in all Introductions to the New Testament.

3. All the *great compilations* or anonymous collections, like dictionaries of the Bible, encyclopedias, etc.

4. Almost all *articles in reviews*, as well as most of the theses given for baccalaureate and licentiate degrees. M. U. Chevalier, in his *Bio-bibliographie*[2] (1907, vol. ii, cols. 3515-3535), gives a sufficiently long list of them.

5. *The Lives of St Paul and the Histories of the apostolic age*, although several of these works treat of history and theology at the same time.

6. Finally, with few exceptions, the *studies of topography and chronology* and researches into the composition, moral condition and vicissitudes of the Pauline churches.

The names of Catholic authors, unhappily still too rare, are marked by an asterisk.

## I—THEOLOGIES OF ST PAUL

### 1. PERIOD OF THE FIRST ATTEMPTS

We mention merely for remembrance those works which are already forgotten, and for the most part not without reason.

G. W. Meyer: *Entwicklung des paulin. Lehrbegriffes*, Altona, 1801.

*J. B. Gerhauser: *Character und Theologie des Ap. Paulus aus seinen Reden und Briefen*, Landshut, 1816.

L. Usteri: *Entwicklung des Paulinischen Lehrbegriffes, in seinem Verhältnisse zur bibl. Dogmatik*, Zürich, 1824 (6° ed., 1851).

485

K. Schrader: *Die Lehre des Ap. Paulus*, Leipzig, 1833.

Dähne: *Entwicklung des paulin. Lehrbegriffes*, Halle, 1835.

Lützelberger: *Grundzuge der paulin. Glaubenslehre*, Nuremberg, 1839.

Lutterbeck: *Die neutestam. Lehrbegriffe oder Untersuchungen über das Zeitalter der Religionswende*, Mainz, 1852.

E. Reuss: *Histoire de la théologie chrétienne au siècle apostolique*, Strasbourg, 1852, 3ᵉ édit., 1864.

Hahn: *Die Theologie des N.T.*, Leipzig, 1854.

H. Messner: *Die Lehre der Apostel*, Leipzig, 1856.

Schmid: *Bibl. Theologie des N.T.*[3] (ed. Weizäcker), Stuttgart, 1863.

F. C. Baur: *Vorlesungen über neutestam. Theologie*, Leipzig, 1864.

J. J. van Oosterzee: *De Theologie des Nieuwen Verbonds*, 1867 (2ᵉ ed., 1872).

Opitz: *Das System des Paulus nach seinen Briefen*, Gotha, 1874.

A. Immer: *Theologie des N.T.*, Berne, 1877.

*H. T. Simar: *Die Theologie des heil. Paulus*[2], Freiburg-im-B., 1883 (1st ed., 1864).

The first two essays are only humble and timid outlines; but the work of Usteri was epoch-making. Usteri was the first to reduce St Paul's theology to a system. He conceived it as a sort of philosophy of history, including the times of ignorance and the fulness of times, with the advent of Christ at the point of their intersection. The plan is thus unfolded:

*Part I—Paganism and Judaism.*—(1) Men gradually lose the knowledge of God and fall little by little into a general state of sin. (2) Relation between the sins of all men and the sin of the first man. (3) Relation of sin and death to the Mosaic Law. (4) Relation of the Law to justice. (5) Final aim of the Law, or relation of the Law to faith. (6) Desire of redemption inspired by the insufficiency of the Law.

*Part II—Christianity.*—(1) The redemption of the individual. (2) The birth and formation of the Christian community. (3) The consummation of the Christian community.

This contrast, suggested by the first chapters of the Epistle to the Romans, lends itself easily, through the vagueness of its outlines, to the most varied developments. But it has the fault of relegating to the background the Person of Christ, who makes his appearance only at the end of the work, immediately before the *parousia*.

The successors of Usteri tamely followed in his footsteps. They differ little from him in regard to the method of procedure and general point of view. Almost all of them hold to the Epistle to the Romans, as if that were the quintessence of Paul's doctrine, and, without denying the authenticity of the other Epistles, they make little use of them. It is always the antithesis between the past and the present, between the reign of sin and the reign of justice, between the impotence of man without Christ and his restoration by Christ. There is visible here the perhaps unconscious influence of official Protestantism, which regards justification by faith as the foundation of Christianity and the Epistle to the Romans as the résumé of Paul's doctrine. All equally neglect the moral part of the Apostle's teaching.

Simar himself, whose chief merit was to show the way to Catholic writers, is of the opinion that, without excluding the other Epistles, Romans—the freest from polemics and the least subordinated to external circumstances and to the special needs of those addressed—reveals the most complete and genuine expression of Paul's doctrine and of what might be called his scheme. He finds the fundamental idea of it (Grundgedanke) in "the universality of the salvation which is prepared by God for all men, without regard to persons, and which is equally necessary for all." The fullest yet most concise expression of this thesis is in the utterance of the Apostle— "The Gospel is the power of God unto salvation to every one that believeth, to the Jew first and also to the Greek; for the justice of God is revealed therein from faith unto faith"— provided that the texts which affirm the universality of sin and also those which explain the plan of redemption are compared with it. According to that, as Simar justly observes, the scheme of a theology of St Paul would admit of only two parts: (1) The need of redemption common to all men; (2) the fact of redemption considered in the person and work of the Redeemer. But reasons of symmetry make him divide up the second part into three subdivisions: (1) Universal redemption in Christ; (2) subjective redemption (the individual acceptance of redemption); (3) the consummation of all things. In this way the work includes four principal sections. It is, in short, the traditional route pursued ever since Usteri.

The presentation of the subject by Reuss, which is still read because it is written in a clear style, is also associated with the idea of Usteri, but while the latter made the theology of St Paul agree with the religious history of mankind, the Strasburg professor prefers to see in it the portrait of the life of the Apostle, divided into two periods " by the simple and sudden fact of his miraculous conversion on the road to Damascus." However, after this attempt at synthesis, Reuss seems to abandon any systematic plan, and his chapters succeed one another without any apparent order.

## 2. CONTEMPORARY WORKS

O. Pfleiderer: *Der Paulinismus, ein Beitrag zur Geschichte der urchristl. Theologie*[3], Leipzig, 1890 (1st ed., 1873).

J. Bovon: *Théologie du N.T.*, Lausanne, 1893-4 (2ᵉ éd., 1902-5).

W. F. Adeney: *The Theology of the N.T.*, New York, 1894.

A. Sabatier: *L'Apôtre Paul, esquisse d'une histoire de sa pensée*[3], Paris, 1896 (1 édit., 1871).

W. Beyschlag: *Neutestam. Theologie*[2], Halle, 1896.

H. J. Holtzmann: *Lehrbuch der neutest. Theologie*, Freiburg-im-B., 1897.

W. Schmidt: *Die Lehre des Ap. Paulus*, Gütersloh, 1898.

C. Holsten: *Das Evangelium des Paulus*, Berlin, 1898.

G. B. Stevens: *The Theology of the N.T.*, Edinburgh, 1899.

B. Weiss: *Lehrbuch der bibl. Theologie des N.T.*[7], Stuttgart, 1903.

G. B. Stevens: *The Pauline Theology*[2] (*a study on the origin and correlation of the doctrinal teachings of the Apostle Paul*), New York, 1906.

A. Schlatter: *Die Lehre der Apostel*, Tübingen, 1910.

P. Feine: *Theologie des neuen Testaments*, Leipzig, 1910 (2nd ed., 1912).

H. C. Sheldon: *New Testament Theology*, New York, 1911.

H. Weinel: *Biblische Theologie des Neuen Testaments*, Tübingen, 1911.

Holsten, Pfleiderer, and Holtzmann are more or less directly dependent on Baur and belong to the liberal (or, as it would be called in France, the radical) school; Beyschlag, B. Weiss, A. Sabatier, and Stevens represent different shades of so-called conservative Protestantism, but the last two have subsequently evolved in the liberal—that is, the rationalistic—direction; Feine and Schlatter, and above all Bovon, sound a more conservative note. We have read less of Adeney, Schmidt, and Weinel.

Side by side with profound divergencies, Pfleiderer and Holtzmann have numerous points of resemblance. Thanks to the progress of historical criticism, these two belated pupils of the Tübingen school admit the authenticity of the Epistles to the Thessalonians, at least that of the first, and of the Epistle to the Philippians and of the note to Philemon; they even consent to recognize in a large measure Pauline ideas in the Epistles to the Colossians and Ephesians. Both of them, although freed from belief in the supernatural and denominational opinions, nevertheless protest against what they call *rationalism*—that is to say, against the tendency to ascribe to the sacred writers the philosophic or religious ideas of our own age. Both believe that the theology of St Paul was derived from his conversion, or rather, from the psychological postulates which had rendered that conversion possible and necessary. But there their harmonious relations cease. While Pfleiderer is intent upon the most obscure texts and submits them to a keen analysis, unfortunately spoiled by an excess of ingenious subtlety, without troubling himself about what others have thought and said before him, Holtzmann displays with satisfaction a prodigious acquaintance with contemporary exegesis—I mean with German exegesis, for in his opinion real science begins in Tübingen and rarely crosses the German frontiers. The former exhibits in all his writings such an effort to be clear that his thought is almost never ambiguous, but he changes his opinion so easily that one is never sure of having reached his final conclusion. The latter wraps himself in a protective obscurity; he proceeds by allusions and insinuations·rather than by direct proofs; at every moment we must stop in order to verify his statements, and that is difficult; we ask ourselves anxiously whether we understand him, and whether he thoroughly understands himself. Whereas Pfleiderer uses every means to make the reader's course an easy one, Holtzmann seems to make it his business to impede it; but he regains his superiority in his presentation of the systems differing from his own and in his general views of the subject, wherein he excels.

Holsten has the remarkable faculty of explaining the conversion of Paul by his theology, and his theology by his conversion. He thinks that, through much meditating on Christian arguments in favour of the resurrection of Jesus, Paul finally convinced himself first, that Jesus could have been raised from the dead, and then that he really had been; and that this persuasion produced the hallucination on the road to Damascus. But this new fact—the apparition of Jesus—had little by little upset and transformed all his former ideas about the justice of God, salvation, morals, and eschatology. In his presentation of Paul's theology, Holsten reaches or surpasses the extremest limit of fantastic and arbitrary speculation.

Weiss and Beyschlag take different conceptions of Lutheranism, and are opposed to each other in mind, method, principles, and tendencies, as is seen by their incessant use of satirical notes. B. Weiss distributes Paul's writings, according to chronological order, into four groups, which are studied separately. Each chapter is divided into four paragraphs, and each paragraph into four sections. The latter are summed up at the head of the paragraph in the form of a thesis, and developed in the body of the article with the aid of many texts, notes, and references. Can all the Apostle's doctrines be so easily cast into one uniform mould of four divisions ? Clearly this system of water-tight compartments narrows all horizons, shortens all vistas, and renders all synthesis impossible. Order and clearness redeem in part this want of breadth, but the work resembles a concordance more than a theological presentation. Nevertheless, if to read it is painful, to consult it is useful. Unlike Weiss, Beyschlag does not aim at being complete. He devotes himself to the principal doctrines or to those which he deems such, and pursues them to the furthest limit. His exposition gains thereby in breadth, cohesion, and interest; but, unfortunately, he makes the whole theology of St Paul depend upon an antithesis, about which, as he himself confesses, exegetes indulge in a great confusion of ideas. This is the antithesis of " flesh and spirit." He thinks that the theology of the Apostle is the effort to solve this antithesis, which at once suggests another: " Adam and Christ." The two great historic figures of humanity explain the psychological enigma of the flesh and the spirit, and enable us to foresee the final victory of the latter. These form the vicissitudes of that struggle which has lasted since the decree of God in eternity, and will last till the final triumph at the time of the *parousia*, which Beyschlag invites us to contemplate.

The characteristics of the style and exposition of Sabatier are well known. His *Apôtre Paul*, in which history occupies a prominent place, has all the interest of an historical work. In the last part the author presents to us the *Organisme du système théologique de Paul*, or rather, the psychological evolution of Paul's thought under the influence of his "religious experience." What he has felt in himself Paul applies, by way of generalization, to every man, and from this comes his anthropology, his conceptions of sin and of the flesh, of faith and the Law, of justice and the new life. From the psychological sphere the Christian principle is then transported into the social and historical domain; from the individual it passes to the universal. There remains one last ascent to be made in order to reach the metaphysical sphere and find in God "the first and ever-active Cause of this great evolution of justice and life," which has been contemplated successively in the human conscience and the history of the world. These three different zones, he thinks, correspond to the three great periods in the life of Paul and to the three groups of his Epistles, from which Sabatier excludes, as doubtful, the Pastorals. But nothing justifies this concordance. What finally stamps upon the entire system the seal of arbitrariness is the fact that the notion of God is made its crown and climax. Now it is certain that the notion of God, an inheritance from Judaism, is one of the least characteristic points of Paul's doctrine.

Stevens does not, like Sabatier, pride himself on determining the progressive stages of Pauline theology. Commencing where Sabatier ends, he takes for the basis of his presentation the notion of God, with which he connects all the rest with no apparent bond. In the *Theology of the New Testament* by the same author, the notion of God loses its primacy, and the " point of departure is anthropological." Stevens redeems this inconsistency, however, by a clearness of exposition and a brilliancy of style which contrast favourably with the other theologies of St Paul, that of Sabatier excepted.

Only a word concerning more recent authors. Feine is a believer. He admits the divinity of Jesus Christ and the miraculous character of the conversion of St Paul; but, like a good Protestant, he maintains the *forensic* value of justification and the *symbolical* meaning of the words of consecration, and makes modern criticism a multitude of concessions which considerably weaken his conservative principles. His work has, nevertheless, very real merits, and can be studied with profit even by Catholics.

Schlatter, more conservative in tone than Feine, does not claim to make a critical theology, but merely a simple presentation of the teaching of the Apostles. His profound acquaintance with Rabbinism allows him to produce interesting comparisons with Jewish contemporary doctrines.

## II—PARTICULAR QUESTIONS

### 1. Paul's Conversion, his Gospel and Influence

Irons: *Christianity as Taught by St Paul*, 1876.

J. F. Clarke: *The Ideas of the Apostle Paul translated into their Modern Equivalents*, Boston, 1884.

O. Pfleiderer: *The Influence of the Apostle Paul on the Development of Christianity*, London, 1885 (*Hibbert Lectures*).

C. Everett: *The Gospel of Paul*, Boston, 1893.

A. B. Bruce: *St Paul's Conception of Christianity*[2], Edinburgh, 1894.

O. Cone: *Paul, the Man, the Missionary, and the Teacher*, New York, 1898.

Thackeray: *The Relation of St Paul to contemporary Jewish Thought*, London, 1900.

C. Anderson Scott: *The Gospel according to St Paul, its Character and Course* (in *Expositor*, 1900, vol. ii, pp. 202-10).

*V. Rose: *Comment Paul a connu le Christ* (in *Revue bibl.*, 1902, pp. 321-46).

*Bourgine, *Conversion de saint Paul. Saint Paul a-t-il été halluciné ?* Paris, 1902.

*E. Moske: *Die Bekehrung des heil. Paulus, Eine exegetisch-kritische Untersuchung* (complete Catholic bibliography), Münster, 1907.

Du Bose: *The Gospel according to St Paul*, London, 1907 (popular).

Th. Ohler: *Der Ap. Paulus und sein Evangelium als Autorität für den Glauben*, Bâle, 1907.

*S. Protin: *La théologie de S Paul. L'évangile de S Paul* (in *Revue Augustinienne*, Avril, 1908).

A. Seeligmüller: *War Paulus Epileptiker ? Erwägungen eines Nervenarztes*, Leipzig, 1910.

A. C. Headlam: *St Paul and Christianity*, London, 1913.

J. G. Machen: *The Origin of Paul's Religion*, New York, 1921.

## 2. PSYCHOLOGY. FLESH AND SPIRIT. SIN

Tholuck: *Ueber σάρξ als Quelle der Sünde*, in *Stud. und Krit.*, 1855, fasc. 3.

Holsten: *Die Bedeutung des Wortes σάρξ im Lehrbegriff des Paulus*, 1855, in his *Zum Evangelium des Paulus und Petrus*, Rostock, 1868.

Krumm: *De notionibus psychologicis Paulinis*, 1858.

L. Ernesti: *Vom Ursprung der Sünde nach paulin. Lehrgehalte*, Göttingen, 1862.

O. Pfleiderer: *Das paulinische Πνεῦμα*, in *Zeitschrift für wiss. Theol.* XIV. (1871), pp. 161-182.

Ecklund: *Σάρξ vocab. quid apud Paulum significet*, Lund, 1872.

H. Lüdemann: *Die Anthropologie des Ap. Paulus*, Kiel, 1872.

H. Wendt, *Die Begriffe Fleisch und Geist im bibl. Sprachgebrauch*, Gotha, 1878.

W. P. Dickson: *St Paul's Use of the Terms Flesh and Spirit*, Glasgow, 1883.

J. Gloël: *Der Stand im Fleische nach paulinischem Zeugniss*, Halle, 1886; *Der Heilige Geist in der Heilsverkündigung des Paulus*, Halle, 1888.

H. Gunkel: *Die Wirkungen des Heiligen Geistes, nach der populären Anschauung der apost. Zeit. und nach der Lehre des Ap. Paulus*, Göttingen, 1888 (3rd ed., 1909).

A. Westphal: *De Epist. Pauli ad Romanos septimo capite (7-25) commentatio critico-theologica*, Toulouse, 1888.

T. Simon: *Die Psychologie des Ap. Paulus*, Göttingen, 1897.

*H. Sladeczek, *Paulinische Lehre über das Moralsubjekt, als anthropologische Vorschule zur Moraltheologie des heil. Ap. Paulus*, Ratisbon, 1899.

R. Trümpert: *Die Lehre von der Sünde nach den Schriften des N.T.*, Darmstadt, 1901.

E. Sokolowski: *Die Begriffe Geist und Leben bei Paulus in ihren Beziehungen mit einander. Eine exegetisch-religionsgesch. Untersuchung*, Göttingen, 1903.

H. Windisch: *Die Entsündigung des Christen nach Paulus*, Leipzig, 1908.

J. Arnal: *La notion de l'Esprit. I. La doctrine paulinienne*, Paris, 1908.

R. Steinmetz: *Das Gewissen bei Paulus*, Berlin, 1911.

## 3. THEODICY AND PREDESTINATION

Poelman: *De Jesu Apostolorumque, Pauli praesertim, doctrina de praedestinatione divina et morali hominis libertate*, Groningen, 1851.

B. Weiss: *Die Prädestinationslehre des Ap. Paulus* (in *Jahrb. f. deutsche Theologie*, t. II, 1857, pp. 54-115).

*Lamping: *Pauli de praedestinatione decretorum enarratio*, Liége, 1858.

W. Beyschlag: *Die paulin. Theodicee*, Berlin, 1868 (2nd ed., 1896).

E. Ménégoz, *La prédestination dans la théologie paulinienne*, Paris, 1884.

Gœns: *Le rôle de la liberté humaine dans la prédestination paulinienne*, Lausanne, 1884.

*V. Weber: *Kritische Geschichte der Exegese des 9 Kapitels resp. der verse 14-23 des Römerbriefes bis auf Chrysostomus und Augustinus einschliesslich*, Wurzburg, 1889.

K. Müller: *Die göttliche Zuvorersehung und Erwählung nach dem Evang. des Paulus*, Halle, 1891.

J. Dalmer: *Die Erwählung Israels nach der Heilsverkündigung des Ap. Paulus*, Gütersloh, 1894; *Zur paulin. Erwählungslehre* in *Griefswälder Studien*, Gütersloh, 1895.

Kühl: *Zur paulin. Theodicee* (in *Theol. Studien*), Göttingen, 1897.

E. Weber: *Das Problem der Heilsgeschichte nach Röm. 9-11*, Leipzig, 1911.

## 4. CHRISTOLOGY AND SOTERIOLOGY

Full bibliography in H. Schumacher: *Christus in seiner Präexistenz und Kenose*, etc., Rome, 1914 (*Biblioth. de l'Institut Biblique*), pp. xiii-xxx. *Cf.* t. I, p. 533.

R. Schmidt: *Die paulin. Christologie in ihrem Zusammenhange mit der Heilslehre des Apostels*, Göttingen, 1870.

A. Dietzsch: *Adam und Christus, Rom. V*, 12-21, Bonn, 1871.

E. Ménégoz: *Le péché et la rédemption d'après saint Paul*, Paris, 1882.

W. Weiffenbach: *Zur Auslegung der Stelle Phil. II*, 5-11, *zugleich ein Beitrag zur paulin. Christologie*, Leipzig, 1884.

A. Seeberg: *Die Anbetung des Herrn bei Paulus*, Riga, 1891.

W. P. Du Bose: *The Soteriology of the N.T.*, New York, 1892.

A. Seeberg: *Der Tod Jesu in seiner Bedeutung für die Erlösung*, Leipzig, 1895.

Karl: *Beiträge zum Verständniss der soteriologischen Erfahrungen und Spekulationen des Ap. Paulus*, Strasburg, 1896.

E. H. Gifford: *The Incarnation, a Study of Phil. II*, 5-11, New York, 1897.

D. Somerville: *Saint Paul's Conception of Christ or the Doctrine of the Second Adam*, Edinburgh, 1897.

\*J. Labourt: *Notes d'exégèse sur Phil. II*, 5-11 (in *Revue bibl.* VII, 1898, pp. 402-415 et 553-563).

\*V. Rose: *Jésus-Christ, seigneur et fils de Dieu* (in *Revue bibl.*, 1903, pp. 337-361).

J. Denney: *The Death of Christ ; its place and interpretation in the N.T.*, London, 1903.

M. Brückner: *Die Entstehung der paulin. Christologie*, Strasburg, 1903.

A. Arnal: *La personne du Christ et le rationalisme allemand contemporain*, Paris, 1904.

J. F. S. Muth: *Die Heilstat Christi als stellvertretende Genugtuung*, Munich, 1904.

E. Ménégoz: *La mort de Jésus et le dogme de l'expiation*, Paris, 1905.

\*C. Van Crombrugghe: *De soteriologiae christianae primis fontibus*, Louvain, 1905.

Stevens: *The Christian Doctrine of Salvation*, Edinburgh, 1905.

\*H. Couget: *La divinité de Jésus-Christ. L'enseignement de saint Paul*, Paris, 1906.

Wetzel: *Grundlinien der Versöhnungslehre*[2], Leipzig, 1906.

Anonymous: *The Fifth Gospel, being the Pauline Interpretation of the Christ*, London, 1907.

\*A. Royet, *Étude sur la christologie des Épîtres de saint Paul*, Lyon, 1907.

J. Kögel: *Christus der Herr. Erläuterungen zu Phil. 2*, 5-11, Gütersloh, 1908.

W. Olschewski: *Die Wurzeln der paulin. Christologie*, Kœnigsberg, 1909.

## 5. FAITH AND JUSTIFICATION

Lipsius: *Die paulin. Rechtfertigungslehre*, Leipzig, 1853.

J. Winter: *Essai sur la prédestination d'après saint Paul*, 1862.

\*J. Wieser: *Pauli apostoli doctrina de justificatione ex fide sine operibus et ex fide operante*, Trent, 1874.

G. Schnedermann: *De fidei notione ethica paulina*, Leipzig, 1880.

Fricke: *Der paulin. Grundbegriff der* δικαιοσύνη Θεοῦ *erörtert auf Grund von Röm. 3*, 21-26, Leipzig, 1887.

G. Schwarz: *Justitia imputata ? Eine neue Erklärung der entscheidenden Ausprüche des Ap. Paulus über die Rechtfertigung*, Heidelberg, 1892.

E. Schäder: *Die Bedeutung des lebendigen Christus für die Rechtfertigung nach Paulus*, Gütersloh, 1893.

\*B. Bartmann: *St Paulus und St Jacobus über die Rechtfertigung*, Freiburg-im-B., 1897 (*Bibl. Studien*, fasc. II, t. I).

E. Riggenbach: *Die Rechtfertigungslehre des Ap. Paulus*, Stuttgardt, 1897.

H. Cremer: *Die paulin, Rechtfertigungslehre im Zusammenhange ihrer geschichtl. Voraussetzungen*, Gütersloh, 1900.

H. F. Nösgen : *Der Schriftbeweis für die evangelische Recht-fertigungslehre*, Halle, 1901.

Lütgert: *Die Lehre von der Rechtfertigung durch den Glauben*, Berlin, 1903.

E. Kühl: *Rechtfertigung auf Grund Glaubens und Gericht nach den Werken bei Paulus*, Kœnigsberg, 1904; *Die Stellung des Jacobusbriefes zum alttestam. Gesetz. und zur paulin. Rechtfertigungslehre*, Kœnigsberg, 1905.

K. Müller: *Beobachtungen zur paulin. Rechtfertigungslehre*, Leipzig, 1905.

J. H. Gerretsen: *Rechtvaardigmaking bij Paulus*, Nimègen, 1905.

E. Cremer: *Rechtfertigung und Wiedergeburt*, Gütersloh, 1907 (in *Beiträge zur Förderung christl. Theologie*, Year XI, fasc. 5).

*E. Tobac: *Le problème de la justification dans saint Paul*, Louvain, 1908.

### 6. MORALS AND MYSTICISM

L. Ernesti: *Die Ethik des Ap. Paulus in ihren Grundzügen dargestellt*[2], Göttingen, 1880 (1st ed., 1868).

Von Soden: *Die Ethik des Paulus* (in *Zeitschrift f. Theol. u. Kirche*, 1892, pp. 109-146).

*H. Sladeczek: *Paulinische Lehre über das Moralsubjekt*, Ratisbon, 1899.

H. Jacoby: *Die neutest. Ethik*, Kœnigsberg, 1899 (pp. 243-406).

Titius: *Der Paulinismus unter dem Gesichtspunkt der Seligkeit*, Tübingen, 1900.

*Ch. Calippe: *Saint Paul et la cité chrétienne*, Paris, 1902.

G. Bindemann: *Das Gebet um tägliche Vergebung der Sünden in der Heilsverkündigung Jesu und in den Briefen des Apostels Paulus*, Gütersloh, 1902.

*A. Rademacher: *Die übernatürliche Lebensordnung nach der paulin. und der johann. Theologie*, Freiburg-im-B., 1903.

A. Juncker: *Die Ethik des Apostels Paulus*, Halle, 1904; 2nd part: *Die konkrete Ethik*, Halle, 1920 (important work on the theology of St Paul from the moral point of view).

*V. Ermoni: *Saint Paul et la prière*, Paris, 1907.

W. E. Chadwick: *The Pastoral Teaching of St Paul*, Edinburgh, 1910.

A. B. D. Alexander: *The Ethics of Paul*, Glasgow, 1910.

*K. Benz: *Die Ethik des Apostels Paulus*, Friburg-im-B., 1912 (complete bibliography).

*H. Bertrams: *Das Wesen des Geistes nach der Anschauung des Apostels Paulus*, Munster-im-W., 1914.

*W. Reinhard: *Das Wirken des heiligen Geistes im Menschen nach den Briefen des Apostels Paulus*, Freiburg-im-B., 1919.

K. Deissner: *Paulus und die Mystik seiner Zeit²*, Leipzig, 1921.
*J. Duperray: *Le Christ dans la vie chrétienne d'après saint Paul²*, Gand, 1922.

## 7. ESCHATOLOGY

Stähelin : *Zur paulin. Eschatologie* (in *Jahrb. f. deutsche Theol.*, 1874, pp. 199-218).
Fr. Köstlin: *Die Lehre des Ap. Paulus von der Auferstehung* (in *Zeitschrift f. deutsche Theol.*, 1877, p. 259).
*L. Atzberger: *Die christliche Eschatologie in den Stadien ihrer Offenbarung im A. und N. Testament*, Freiburg-im-B., 1890.
R. Kabisch: *Die Eschatologie des Paulus*, Göttingen, 1893.
Slotemaker de Bruine: *De eschatologische Voorstellingen in I en II Corinthe*, Utrecht, 1894.
E. Teichmann: *Die paulin. Vorstellungen von Auferstehung und Gericht und ihre Beziehung zur jüdischen Apocalyptik*, Leipzig, 1896.
P. Volz: *Jüdische Eschatologie von Daniel bis Akiba*, Tübingen, 1903.
Kennedy: *St Paul's Conceptions of the Last Things*, London, 1904.
E. Kühl: *Ueber 2 Korinther 5, 1-10. Ein Beitrag zur Frage nach dem Hellenismus bei Paulus*, Kœnigsberg, 1904.
*Fr. Tillmann: *Die Wiederkunft Christi nach den paulinischen Briefen*, Freiburg-im-B., 1909.

## 8. THE CONTROVERSY—PAUL OR JESUS ?

P. Wernle: *Die Anfänge unserer Religion*, Tübingen, 1901.
P. Feine: *Das gesetzesfreie Evangelium des Paulus nach seinem Werdegang dargestellt*, Leipzig, 1899 et *Jesus Christus und Paulus*, Leipzig, 1902; cf. *Rev. bibl.*, 1904, pp. 117-120.
Goguel: *L'Apôtre Paul et Jésus-Christ*, Paris, 1904.
Weinel: *Paulus, der Mensch und sein Werk*, Tübingen, 1904.
W. Wrede: *Paulus*, Leipzig, 1905.
Kaftan: *Jesus und Paulus*, Tübingen, 1906 (deals with Bousset and Wrede).
Kölbing: *Die geistige Einwirkung der Person Jesu auf Paulus*, Göttingen, 1906.
A. Meyer: *Wer hat das Christentum begründet, Jesus oder Paulus ?* Tübingen, 1907.
A. Jülicher: *Paulus und Jesus*, Tübingen, 1907.
J. Weiss: *Christus. Die Anfänge des Dogmas*, Tübingen, 1909; *Paulus uud Jesus*, Berlin, 1909.
Wustmann: *Jesus und Paulus. Die Abhängigkeit des Apostels von seinem Herrn*, Gütersloh, 1909.
Scott: *Jesus and Paul*, London, 1909 (*Cambridge Bibl. Essays*).
*P. Dausch: *Jesus und Paulus*, Münster, 1910 (*Bibl. Zeitfragen*).

For a fuller bibliography see *Dictionnaire apologétique de la foi catholique*, our article *Paulinisme*.

## 9. Different Questions

Rogge: *Die Anschauungen des Ap. Paulus von dem relig.-sittl. Character des Heidenthums*, Fürstenwalde, 1887.

Beyschlag: *Hat der Ap. Paulus die Heidengötter für Dämonen gehalten?* Halle, 1894.

B. Duhm: *Pauli apost. de Judaeorum religione judicia*, Göttingen, 1873.

A. Zahn: *Das Gesetz Gottes nach der Lehre und Erfahrung des Ap. Paulus*[2], Halle, 1892.

E. Grafe: *Die paulin. Lehre vom Gesetz nach den vier Hauptbriefen*[2], Leipzig, 1893.

Schulz: Τί οὖν ὁ νόμος ; *Verhältniss von Gesetz, Sünde und Evangelium nach Gal.* 3 (in *Stud. und Krit.*, 1902, pp. 5-55).

Kähler : *Auslegung von Kap.*, 2, 14-16 *im Römerbrief* (in *Stud. und Krit.*, t. XLVII, 1874, pp. 261-306).

Giesecke: *Zur Exegese von Röm.* 2, 11-16 (*Ibid.*, t. LIX, 1886, pp. 173-182).

O. Everling: *Die paulinische Angelologie und Dämonologie*, Göttingen, 1888.

*J. Quirmbach: *Die Lehre des hl. Paulus von der natürlichen Gotteserkenntnis und dem natürlichen Sittengesetz*, Freiburg-im-B., 1906.

M. Dibelius: *Die Geisterwelt im Glauben des Paulus*, Göttingen, 1909.

*G. Kurze: *Der Engels-und Teufelsglaube des Apostels Paulus*, Freiburg-im-B., 1915.

*B. Bartmann: *Paulus. Die Grundzüge seiner Lehre und die moderne Religionsgeschichte*, Paderborn, 1914.

*P. Tischleder: *Wesen und Stellung der Frau nach der Lehre des heiligen Paulus*, Munster-im-W., 1923.

A great many other works have been mentioned in regard to special questions treated in the detached notes. It is sufficient for us to refer the reader to them.

# GENERAL TABLES

THE tables which follow are common to both volumes.

The first is an analytical summary of the principal points dealt with in the course of the work, necessarily very incomplete, and intended merely as a general guide to the reader.

The second is an alphabetical index of subjects; without duplicating the preceding, it will serve as an easier mode of reference in some cases.

The third is an index to the passages of St Paul and of the Acts which are commented on or discussed; texts which are merely quoted are not included.

The last is a list of Greek words studied from the symbolical, syntactical, or morphological standpoint.

In each table the roman numerals indicate the volume, the arabic the page. References may be either to text or notes.

# I—ANALYTICAL SUMMARY

SINCE the theology of Saint Paul is, above all, a doctrine of salvation, it has to be considered as the plan of redemption in action. The author has tried to effect a reconciliation between the usual divisions of dogmatic theology and the Apostle's point of view. His teaching has been grouped under four general headings, which are subdivided into sections as simple and comprehensive as possible.

## I—PAUL AND HIS WORK

## II—GOD AND CHRIST

## III—MAN AND CHRIST

## IV—CHRIST THE SAVIOUR

# II—ALPHABETICAL INDEX

# III—EXEGETICAL INDEX

In this list have been included only those passages from St Paul, Hebrews, and Acts which are the subject of *ex professo* comment or explanation at some length.  Other scriptural texts, and Pauline texts merely cited, are not included.

# IV—PHILOLOGICAL INDEX

CATHERINE NOVAISTRY

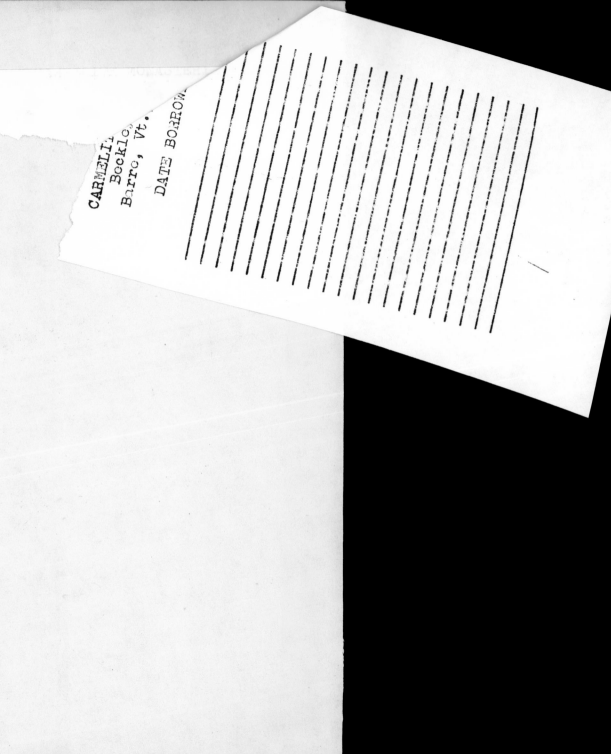

CARMELI
Beckl
Barre, Vt.

DATE BORROW

RANEAN SEA

uyotville
St-Eugéne
ALGIERS

Philippeville          Bône
Ménerville        Bougie          St-Charles     El-Hallia
        Tizi-Ouzou          El-Milia        Jemmapes
ufartk  Palestro  Ft.National    Catinat    El-Arrouch
                              Condé-Smendou    Guelma
        Tazmalt        Sétif    Constantine    Oued-Zenati
ISSER  SOUMMAM                              Souk-Ahras
                              Ain-Abid
                    T'lergma

                    Batna        Tébessa
        HODNA MTS.
        M'Sila    Lambèse              Khenchela
        CHOTT EL-HODNA    Arris    DJEBEL-HELIA
        Bou-Saâda              GHANIMNE

                    Biskra

                    CHOTT MELRHIR

                    Touggourt

                    ↓

                    TO TAMANRASSET

                    Miles
        0    25    50        100

                map by palacios

A        R        A

# THE STRUGGLE FOR ALGERIA

# THE STRUGGLE
## FOR *ALGERIA*

## BY *JOSEPH KRAFT*

DOUBLEDAY & COMPANY, INC., GARDEN CITY, NEW YORK

*FOR POLLY*

# CONTENTS

# 1.  NATIVE GROUNDS

A MELTING glacier issues in countless trickles, not a single river. So with the thaw in the Cold War. Before its onset, Moscow and Washington were twin poles of power around which the rest of the world clustered as satellites or client states. Now Paris, Bonn, Warsaw, Belgrade, Cairo, Baghdad, New Delhi, Djakarta, Rabat, Mexico City, Ottawa, and Rangoon are all independent centers of authority. London pushes an unwilling America toward the summit; Peiping restrains an eager Russia. Bandung and Accra are as much at the summit as Geneva. For better or worse, there has occurred a fragmentation of the diplomatic field. But is it for better or worse?

For better would surely have been the universal answer not many years ago. In their own eyes and in those of most of the rest of the world, Russia and America were grotesque monsters—"the elephant and the whale." Young, huge, and pulsing with energy, they were accused of being materialistic, hence crude and insensitive; and doctrinaire, hence inflexible and insensitive. Both were supposed to be in the hands of oversized

military machines; their politics in tow of Zhdanovs and Mc-
Carthys. Neither knew the restraining efforts of ancient cul-
tures or sentimental philosophies or careworn masses, wanting
only to die in peace. Spartans and Athenians, Greeks and Persians were cited to show that no two powers, armed to the
teeth and hostile, had ever confronted each other without a
war. That these two, waging their insensate quarrel over the
prostrate body of humanity, would ultimately plunge the
world into ruin was the conventional wisdom. The one way
out, it was thought, was the interposition of some humane,
civilized buffer.

As favorite candidates for that role, there stepped forward
the newly independent and largely underdeveloped countries
of the southern continents. Strangers to the central struggle,
they were supposedly peopled by gentle folk, poor, simple, and
freighted with good will. Democratic socialism, mixing features of both the American and Soviet systems, was billed as
their political ethos. Their leaders were represented as breathing the quality of saints. To their slogans—Third Force, Neu-
tralism, Five Principles—there was imparted the aura of man's
best hope.

A few years have shown the fear to be liars and seen the
hopes made vain. The seat of unmendable trouble has not been
Washington or Moscow, or even those few extensions of diminishing empire where the two systems meet. On the contrary,
the East-West rivalry has been engrossed in the struggle between North and South. War and revolution find their home
in the peripheral areas of the world, so remote from the axes
of power that the Big Two cannot bring to bear their full influence. Cuba, Laos, and Congo are cases in point. So is Algeria, the subject of this book.

It has been, for the past six years, the scene of the world's
only continuous shooting war. A guerrilla conflict, the Algerian struggle has been low on casualties and bare of major
military operations. But it has absorbed directly the energies

of a French force of over 400,000 men, and of a nationalist rebel army of some 30,000 soldiers. Inside Algeria a million persons have been displaced by the fighting; institutions have been crushed; opinion pulverized; the routine of life disrupted. Outside, the consequences are beyond measure.

For France, the war has made Algeria the touchstone of foreign and domestic policy. From it have emerged the forces which produced the largest upheaval in the postwar politics of western Europe: the third coming of General Charles de Gaulle, and the fourth defeat of a French republic. Midwife to the Fifth French Republic, the Algerian struggle still casts over that regime the baleful shadow of an executioner. It has been the decisive factor in two national elections, in the fall of four successive governments, in a conversion that renders uncertain the loyalties of the French army. It has, in short, stood upon its head the old colonial slogan *"Algérie c'est la France."* If anything, France has become Algeria.

Extensive if less dramatic effects have touched the rest of the world. The Algerian war has put a strain upon all of France's allies, not least the United States. Repeatedly the fighting has spilled over to the fledgling states bordering Algeria, Morocco, and Tunisia—states which have provided bases for the rebels and sanctuary for thousands of refugees. All the other African states, and most of the Asian ones, have aligned themselves with the nationalist cause. The Communist world, and especially the paladins of Peiping, have found in the struggle a means of embarrassing the West while shoring up ties in Africa and Asia. Since 1955, Algeria has been an unremitting headache for the United Nations.

If much of this turmoil expresses the universal unrest set up by the new countries, it also finds roots in special geographic and historic circumstance. Geographically Algeria is a meeting place of East and West. A seaboard state fronting on the south shore of the Mediterranean just opposite France, its coast line runs 600 miles from Tunisia in the east to Morocco in the

west. Its hinterland stretches back a thousand miles into
Africa and includes much of the Sahara Desert. Total area is
over 800,000 square miles, about four times the size of France.
But not 200 miles from the coast line, and parallel to it, there
rises a chain of rough, folded mountains, the Atlas ranges.
Lateral fingers of these penetrate the coastal plain at many
junctures. The range itself divides the littoral from the African
hinterland. Until the recent discovery of oil in the Sahara, virtually everything that happened in Algeria happened on the
coastal plain, or Tell.

Historically Algeria has played the role of cork on swelling
seas. A miserable country—poor in soil, short until very recently in energy resources, and tricky, where it is not impossibly
arid, in weather—Algeria has never been a matter of intrinsic
interest to the mighty. But the coast looks across the sea to the
heartland of the West, and down the coast to the centers of
Arabic civilization. It is one of destiny's relay points, a way
station on the road to Mediterranean hegemony.

About the original inhabitants, the Berbers, or Kabyles as
they are called in Algeria, almost nothing save their language
seems certain. The rest has been washed away by successive
waves of invasion. The Phoenicians and Carthaginians established trading posts on the Algerian coast centuries before the
birth of Christ. Roman cohorts made of Algeria the "granary of
empire," and midst the wheat (and figs and olives) there also
flourished a Christian civilization exemplified by such patristic
philosophers as Tertullian, St. Cyprian, and St. Augustine.
Genseric and the Vandals drove out the Romans, only to fall
themselves before the Byzantine forces of Belisarius. In the
seventh century, and again in the eleventh, Arab followers of
Mohammed swept over the land, leaving in their wake Islam
and the Arabic tongue. When Spain and the Ottoman Turks
battled to rule the Mediterranean waves, Algiers was a principal point of conflict; and it became, after the Spanish defeat,
the seat of a notorious Turkish pirate state, capital of the in-

famous Barbary Coast. Rich as it was in the sixteenth century, with some 30,000 Christian captives, including Cervantes, the corsair state declined under blows from the maritime powers. When France invaded in 1830, it sank without a trace.

Beneath these turbulent comings and goings, there subsisted in a life of changeless routine an underlying peasant population. Bound by tribal ties and an ecumenical religion, it never found the middle ground of nation-state. Numidia, Africa Minor, Ifriquiya, Mauretania, El Djezair—these were among the titles bestowed on what a Frenchman was to call "the country without a name." Sporadic bursts of revolt (the Donatist heresy of the fourth century, for example, or the seventh-century rebellion of the Berber Jewess, al-Kahina) were its principal witness to history. For the most part, it accepted foreign trespass as an incurable, and not very serious, disease. "I depended," Belisarius said of his conquest, "much less upon the numbers, or even the bravery, of my troops than upon the friendly disposition of the natives."

As others before them, the French conquerors found in the natives friendliness checkered by sporadic revolt. Like the others too, they won battles and then imposed settlers and foreign ways. But they alone brought effective administration and sharply defined frontiers. And they alone bore with them the gift of modern technology. With it, they quickened into historic life the submerged population of Algeria, the Moslem masses.

One of the end products of that process, an Arab doctor, once said:

> How could anyone imagine that I would not be a nationalist? Of course, I speak French, and I went to French schools. I also wear European dress, and in restaurants I eat European food. Many Frenchmen tell me I am French, and some of them even believe it.
>
> But in my home, everything was different. We spoke a different language. We practiced a different religion. Our women, my

mother and my sisters, were veiled. Our family relations were all
different. We lived in a different quarter. We had different
friends and different relatives.

All my experience, you see, taught me that I was different;
that I was not French. All the French taught me was that I was
Algerian.

Telescoped into those words is a mild version of historic developments reaching back a century and a quarter.

II

SOME three million people inhabited the country without a
name when the French troops arrived in 1830. A hundred thousand, perhaps, lived in the overgrown villages around the ports
of Bône, Algiers, and Oran. A Mediterranean mélange, with a
large dose of Christians and not a few Jews, the urban population included the Turkish administration (beylic) and its mer-
cenary soldiers (the Janissaries); the corporation of pirates
(Taïfa des Raïs); and a crowd of hanger-on merchants and
artificers. Commerce with southern Europe was a principal activity, and several of the European powers, France included,
had established missions at the beylical court. There also
thrived a catering business, supplying furnishings and clothes
and (most of all) loans to the ruling beylical and pirate families. Except for trade in olive oil and grain, conducted largely
in port markets, the city dwellers had almost no contact with
the surrounding countryside.

The beylical writ, to be sure, ran nominally within borders
much resembling those of present Algeria. But its chief, the
Dey of Algiers, was a distant official of a crumbling empire: the
Ottoman Porte, or sick man of Europe. Within the provincial
administration, there had been built up neither settled routine
nor legitimacy: over a stretch of nearly three hundred years,
half the beys died violent deaths. Soldiers of the Dey controlled
the principal market places, and through that control exercised

a monopoly on the grain trade, buying it at forced prices, and selling it relatively dear. In extreme cases the Janissaries could subject refractory tribes to punishing raids: one chronicler tells of a victory parade including 2,000 camels, 10,000 sheep, and three mules bearing baskets filled with the heads of rebellious tribesmen. But day-to-day administration was in the hands of local chiefs, religious leaders, and village elders. Dubbed emirs, or caids, or amins, or sheiks, these notables in effect presided over the native population.

Of these, about 2.5 million, the lion's share, by far, were seminomadic Arabs. Spread out evenly across the flat marsh land of the coastal plain, they were grouped in tribes running in number from several hundred to several thousand. Livestock made up their principal wealth, the source of milk, wool, meat, leather; and all summer long, living in tents, they grazed goats and sheep over broad, loosely marked tribal domains. Come winter, they settled in mud huts, and, with primitive plows, practiced grain farming in the adjoining terrain. Over all they farmed about 5.5 million acres.

In the few mountainous regions along the coast (the massifs) there dwelt some 300,000 Kabyles. Descendants of the original inhabitants, they had long since been converted to Islam but had fled the Arabs of the plain to mountainous retreats where they still spoke the Berber tongue. More sharply challenged than the Arabs, they had, in Toynbee's formula, responded by making further progress in the civilized arts. They were grouped in villages presided over by councils of elders (the djemma). Though like the Arabs they kept livestock and planted grain, their principal occupation was the cultivation of fig and olive trees. From the olives they pressed truly vast supplies of oil (over half a million gallons in 1834, for instance). The oil they sold in the coastal markets, and in connection with the oil trade they developed a transport business. Out of that there grew a small artisan industry, producing, among other things, chests, jewels, and tiles.

Not for any of these people was life a pastoral Arcady. Ignorant and superstitious, they were plunged in a perpetual battle for survival by disease, famine, and nearly constant tribal skirmishings. Extremes of heat and cold plagued them; while spring rains often threatened to flood them out, summer was an endless quest for water and shade. Because Moslem law proscribed pork, they relied heavily on goats, which, as everywhere else in the Arab world, swept clean most natural vegetation. "No where," a European resident of Algiers wrote toward the end of the eighteenth century, "is life so miserable as among the people who live in the hills and fields around Algiers."

Still custom assigned to each tribe or village enough land to scratch out a livelihood. Marabouts, or Moslem holy men, mitigated the ravages of war, as the Church did in twelfth-century Europe. Plague and famine kept the number of mouths in roughly even phase with available resources. If primitive farming methods meant backbreaking labor, at least there was work for all. Though hardly glorious, there did prevail a civilization with a delicate inner balance. This balance the French occupiers destroyed.

### III

Not, as so many Arab nationalists like to believe, by pillage, rapine, and seizure of land. To be sure, the French conquest was anything but easy. The Turkish administration surrendered without much of a fight, as did most of the tribes directly under the beylical thumb. Marshal Louis de Bourmont, who commanded the French expedition, predicted that all Algeria would be subdued in fifteen days. But as French troops pressed inland, they ran into pockets of resistance.

By far the strongest centered back of Oran in western Algeria around the figure of the Emir Abdel Kader. The breakdown of Turkish authority had emboldened Abdel Kader to expand his tribal domains. Between 1832 and 1839, in a series of raids against neighboring tribes, he acquired dominion over much of western Algeria. French forces formally opened hostilities against the Emir in 1840. In riposte Abdel Kader rallied tribes and villages all across Algeria, and notably in the mountainous country of the Kabyles, in something of a national campaign of resistance to the French. His forces were defeated in two pitched battles in 1843 and 1844, and in 1847 he surrendered. The defeat of Abdel Kader, except for two Kabyle risings in 1851 and 1871, in effect brought the military conquest to a close. Casualties had been low, probably no more than two thousand in any battle. But in the course of the raiding back and forth, thousands of livestock had been destroyed and hundreds of villages. Like all modern armies pitted against native forces, the French had found the most effective tactics to be the tactics of attrition. Figures are not available, but the whole military operation, from the landing in 1830 to the final suppression of the Kabyle revolt of 1871, can probably be summed up in one of the reports of the leading French commander in Algeria. "We have burned a great deal," Marshal Bugeaud wrote, "and destroyed a great deal."

Rude settlers followed the soldiers. By 1870 well over 200,000 Europeans had settled in Algeria. Almost evenly divided between small peasant holders and town dwellers serving the French army and administration, the early settlers kept close to coastal strong points around Algiers, Oran, and Bône. At their instigation, the French forces expropriated vast tracts of land from the native holders: 5 million acres, for example, after the Kabyle defeat of 1871. But much of the sequestered land had formerly comprised beylical domain, while in other cases tribes deprived of their lands found and cultivated new terrain. Most important of all, contact between the European and tribal civilizations remained severely limited.

In these circumstances, the traditional civilization survived with no great strain. There was a slight population drop (2.8 million in 1870 as against an estimated 3 million in 1830) chiefly because of a famine in 1868 and a cholera epidemic in 1849. But as before the Moslem population of the plains had about 5.5 million acres in grain. Livestock, the prime source of wealth, increased, if anything, in numbers. Thus forty years after the French landing, the Moslems of Algeria were still living as they had for centuries. Lust and greed may have inspired the coming of the French, and malevolence may have governed their behavior thereafter. But against the violent instincts, the traditional society was proof. What it could not resist, what destroyed it in the ensuing years, was the favorable atmosphere of peace, science, education, and the cash economy.

IV

THE *bel époque* in Algeria, as in France, began not long after 1870. From that point forward a French peace was upon the land; not until 1914, in Europe, was there to be much spilling of Moslem blood in military ventures. Disease persisted, and with it epidemic, but quinine and vaccines, dispensed through "tribal inoculation weeks" and native nurses, severely curtailed their toll. And modern transport put an end to famine.

In the absence of these traditional checks, the Moslem population began a steady climb. After holding nearly stable at a figure of around 3 million for centuries, it rose in the fifty years after 1870 to nearly 5 million: a growth of more than 60 per cent.

Accompanying the demographic burst was a striking decline in the traditional base of subsistence. At least 2.5 million acres of tribal and village domain passed into the hands of the Europeans, either by sale or expropriation. Slightly improved farming methods, and the opening of new lands to cultivation, made up some of the loss. Still, in 1920 the total acreage under cultivation by Moslems was slightly under that in 1830. Much of the new land was marginal, and more intensive cultivation wore out some of the old. Strict French enforcement of property rights put an end to the easy grazing of other days. Livestock herds dropped precipitously, sheep, for instance, falling from 11 million in 1886 to 6 million in 1911. Thus, if anything, the traditional economy was even less able in 1920 than in 1830 to support the traditional population of 3 million. And, in fact, there were nearly 5 million Moslems—2 million extra.

These did the one thing that was possible. Squeezed out of traditional society, they migrated into the European sector of the economy. From 1880 through 1920, there flowed a steadily rising stream of people from the tribes and villages of the countryside into the centers of European colonization. In general, the more advanced hill people, the Kabyles, moved directly into town, entering the French army in droves or setting up shop as petty artisans and small traders. "Between 1880 and 1920," one French writer has put it, "the Kabyle was our constant helper." The excess tribal population generally sought and, in the beginning anyway, often found, employment as agricultural laborers on the European farms. Between 1880 and 1920, the density of the Moslem population on the European-held land back of Oran, for instance, rose by more than one third.

These two internal migrations spelled a revolution. For one thing, the Moslem population, once spread out evenly across the country, began to congregate in cities like Algiers, or in zones of European agriculture such as the Chéliff back of Oran, and the Sahel and Mitidja plains near Algiers. As a result, for the first time large aggregates of Moslems and Europeans came to live side by side, in close daily contact. Lastly, an important segment of Moslem society came to depend entirely on the cash economy. In 1870 not many thousand Moslems were city dwellers or paid farm workers. By 1920 at least a million Moslems depended on wages or buying and selling for a livelihood. A foot was inside the door of the closed world of the traditional society.

Still, there looked to be a new balance in the making, and

the prospect of a gentle transition. For those who could no longer find room in the decaying ways of yore, there seemed to be a place in the rising sun of a modern economy.

v

ALAS, what shaped up as a gentle transition has shown itself in the years since 1920 to be a brutal dislocation. The twentieth-century scourges of war and depression have waged a losing struggle against the advances of twentieth-century medicine, sanitation, and transport. In consequence, the Moslem population of Algeria has continued to grow apace. Up by 25,000 every year in the 1920's, it mounted by over 100,000 annually in the early 1940's, and by nearly 200,000 yearly in the decade of the fifties. It now advances at a rate of 2.5 per cent annually: one of the steepest demographic curves in the world. In effect, the Moslems are doubling their ranks every twenty years. Three million in 1830, they now number 10 million and will reach 20 million in 1980, 40 million at the turn of the century.

Concentration in the cities and the saturated European rural zone has even outpaced the population growth. Between 1920 and 1950 the Moslem contingent living in the farming districts back of Oran and Algiers tripled itself. City Moslems doubled in number: from about 12 per cent of the total in 1920 to 23 per cent in 1950. Algiers, which was growing at a rate of about a thousand persons per year before 1920, picked up 2,000 annually in the late thirties; and about 4,000 annually in the late 1940's.

The population trends have strained to the breaking point all of Algeria's sparse resources. At one extreme, the dying agony of the traditional society has been prolonged. Far from withering away, the closed medieval economy has expanded. It now cultivates an area of 6 million acres (fully 10 per cent more than in 1870) while supporting a population of

2.5 million persons, about the same as in 1870. These are heavily dependent upon a single crop—wheat—and unable to break into cultivation of such relatively profitable items as cotton, vegetables, fruits, or wine grapes. They have been pushed from the best lands to stony and steep terrains in the hills and valley sides: in some cases land tilting at a 40-degree angle is farmed. Unable to move freely as in the past, they have worked the land to exhaustion: yields are less than one half of what they are in the better lands; and despite the growth in surface cultivation, production is below what it was fifty years ago. Livestock herds have increased barely, if at all. Subdivided over and over again, the plots average about fifteen acres, but the case of one man owning a tree and another the land under it is not unknown. Complicated tenure, indeed, forms a pattern refractory not only to tractor farming in the modern manner but also to the extension of credit—the *sine qua non* of all agricultural progress. Under these circumstances, the standard of living among the traditional farmers has barely altered in 130 years. Shoes and store-bought clothes, appliances, steel plows, books, cars are all unknown. Meat is eaten about once a month. Average income is estimated at $50 annually, barely enough to buy rudimentary tools and seed for the coming year. "We are like the chickens," a piece of wisdom proverbial among the traditional farmers says. "If we don't scratch the ground, we don't eat."

If the old society has not been allowed to die, the new one, so far as the Moslems are concerned, still struggles to be born. It is a measure of the situation that while there are more than 200,000 new births every year, the number of new jobs is about 20,000 annually. In all, perhaps 800,000 Moslems (with 4 million dependents) have found permanent places in the modern economy. That group includes a few hundred wealthy Moslem landowners and a comparable number of rich Moslems in trade and the professions. The overwhelming majority are agricultural laborers and industrial workers. These average earnings of about $300 a year, live in stone houses, send their children to school, and know the benefits of social security. Still, they generally spend something like 80 per cent of their earnings on food and shelter. They are, moreover, subject to a galling inequality. Next to them are the homes, not sumptuous but far more comfortable, of the Europeans. Just above them, as foremen, white-collar workers, straw bosses, are the same Europeans. While half the Moslems in industry are classed as unskilled laborers, only 8 per cent of the Europeans fall in that category. Nearly a third of the Europeans employed on the land are foremen, as against less than one fifth of one per cent of the Moslems. Twenty-three per cent of the Europeans employed outside agriculture are in the liberal professions or administration, compared to one per cent of the Moslems. Lastly, though comfortable by Algerian standards, the position of the Moslems with regular work is one of extreme insecurity. For behind them, eying their jobs and their homes with a hunger born of desperation, is an immense subproletariat.

Some 2.5 million Moslems—a quarter of the total—uprooted but not yet established anew, have slipped into the gulf between the society waiting to die and the one waiting to be born. Most of them remain upon the land as migratory workers helping on the European farms during peak times of sowing and harvest, or sharecroppers working parcels of Moslem-held land on the most onerous terms. Sharecropping alone (the so-called *khamessat*) occupies 150,000 families. Except for an occasional odd job, a typical tenant farmer is idle all winter long. The bare necessities—a mud hut and a little grain—he receives from his landlord, who also advances money for seed. In summer he tills an area generally under five acres, raising chickens, grain, occasionally tobacco. At harvest time comes the reckoning with the landlord. Generally the tenant is entitled to one fifth of the crop (*khame* is the Arabic word for fifth). In rare good years, receipts outrun the winter advances, and the tenant emerges with a pittance for buying clothes. In bad years, advances exceed the return from the crop. The tenant either gets out or sinks into the serfdom of debt.

As to the subproletariat of the cities, most live in the *bidon-villes* (or tin-can towns) that have sprung up around every population center in Algeria. Three shoulder-high boards, a swinging door, and a tin roof held down by stones make up each dwelling. Inside there is barely room for a family of four to lie down. Cooking is done outside over open fires; washing, in trenches of muddy water. For work there is the casual employment of the streets: peddling laces or brushes, running messages, opening and closing doors, watching parked cars, shining shoes, outright begging. Reliable figures on the number of people in such straits are not available—which is not to say that it is small. In Algiers alone, just before the rebellion burst, there were ten bidonvilles with nearly 150,000 inhabitants.

One escape hatch has in recent times opened up for the landless and homeless Moslems: temporary migration to France. Set in motion in the 1890's when Marseilles shippers imported Algerian labor to fight a dock strike, the Moslem migratory wave swelled during World War I and the early twenties, ebbed during the Great Depression and World War II, then swept back in the postwar years. With a labor shortage current in France, and a surplus in Algeria, it has become a major feature of both economies. During the present decade, the number of Algerian Moslems working in France has reached the 300,000 mark. They take mainly heavy-duty jobs in mines and factories. Minimum French wages are theirs, supplemented by family benefits. Almost all are able to send important sums of money back home. Still, the great bulk of the Algerian workers in France live without their families in crowded slum quarters. Many succumb to tuberculosis. Pimping, smuggling, and the currency black market pull others into the underworld. And when they return home, usually after two or three years, they face desolation.

For there must be no mincing of words. Malicious design

may not have motivated the French settlers, administrators, and soldiers in Algeria. If not always spurred by feelings of pure benevolence, they at least supposed themselves to be acting as agents of progress. Still, they left untouched much of what unfitted Algeria for modernity. The great majority of the people remain steeped in a medieval religion. While 70 per cent are Arab in tongue, large minorities, in the Kabyle district and the Aurès, speak a different language. And after a century of progress, the social condition of the Algerian Moslems was the condition of a ravaged people. A quarter were locked within the confines of a primitive economy. Another quarter were displaced persons, landless, homeless, jobless; hollow men of rural slums and the cruel cities: civilization's waste. The rest had entered the modern economy, but on the worst of terms, and at the lowest level. They had their daily bread, but upon it was the bitter spice of invidious grief. "I am a one-eyed man in the realm of the blind," a Moslem novelist put it. "But I am not king."

## VI

MOVEMENTS of protest inevitably sprang up at every level of Moslem society. Among the dispossessed there took root a revolutionary party: the North African Star, founded in 1923 among Algerian Moslems working in France by a World War I veteran and factory worker, Messali Hadj. A middle-class movement, Young Algeria, was established by a pharmacist, Ferhat Abbas, of Sétif, in 1921. Though most of the caids and marabouts served the French administration, traditional society put forth a reform religious movement: the Association of Ulemas (or Arabic teachers), founded in 1935 by the Sheik Abdelhamid ben Badis.

Tiny to begin with and hopelessly unequal to the problems they confronted, these groups pursued the most divergent aims. The North African Star sought an independent, urbanized, socialist Algeria and chose as means subversive action by the proletariat. Ferhat Abbas's Young Algeria disavowed nationalism, favoring "economic and political emancipation" within the context of a "durable French Algeria." The Ulemas, bearing a puritanical Moslem doctrine strongly influenced by religious leaders in the Middle East, sought regeneration and independence through a return to the pure practices of Islam.

On one point though, all agreed. Messali Hadj and the North African Star worked for "intimate collaboration between Algerians and Frenchmen," and they allied themselves first with the Communist party of France, then with the French Socialists. "*La France*," Ferhat Abbas proclaimed, "*c'est moi*." "The Algerian nation," Ben Badis wrote, "is not France, cannot be France, and does not want to be France." But to gain independence he trusted to "time and the will of France." To achieve their goals, different as they were, in short, all three groups looked to France.

The faith was touching, but a mark of weakness. Not that there was no sympathy. An inquiry into mistreatment of the Algerian Moslems was launched by the Chamber of Deputies in 1832, and thereafter the theme of reform in Algeria filled French books, reviews, newspapers, and the annals of parliamentary debate continually. But good will was never fortified by interest. About French policy in Algeria there was from the beginning something frivolous. Supposed to be a distant land peopled by exotic beings, Algeria was, for a full century, a mere plaything of the changing needs of French politics. "I'd rather have the meanest hold on the Rhine," a French deputy once put it, "than all of Algeria."

From 1815 to 1870, as Sir Lewis Namier has pointed out, France relived in slow motion the epopee of the Revolutionary and Napoleonic wars: history repeating itself as farce. The Bourbon Restoration of 1815–30 reproduced the uneasy compromise between King and Estates of 1789–91. From 1830 to 1848 the July Monarchy of Louis-Philippe recapitulated the bourgeois ascendancy of the Directory. Louis Napoleon worked at being "my uncle's nephew." In this historical dumb show, Algeria was to supply in little the élan Valmy and Austerlitz had given the earlier generation.

French schoolbooks say that in 1827, the Dey of Algiers, "an irritable character named Hussein . . . one day struck his fan several times against the arm of the French consul. An expedition against Algiers became necessary." Economic historians know that the big stake was a considerable sum of money owed to two Jewish merchants, Bacri and Busnach, who had financed grain shipments from Algeria to France beginning in 1793. No doubt both versions of the genesis of the French occupation have their truth. But what immediately touched it off was the need of the last of the Bourbons, Charles X, for a great success with which to overwhelm a refractory parliament. "For lack of a conquest on the Rhine," Emile Bourgeois put it, "he started with all speed a grand expedition against . . . Algiers."

Apart from the dispatch of the expedition, no plans had been drawn. It is a mark of the levity suffusing the whole project that in the initial proclamation, the French commander, Marshal Bourmont, addressed the Algerians as Moroccans. And during the first three weeks after the landing, only two messages passed between Paris and the Algerian expedition. One gave instructions for the collection of flora and fauna for a Paris museum. The other requested that sixty camels be shipped across the Mediterranean for acclimitization in France.

With the fall of Charles X, it was widely assumed that the whole Algiers venture would be abandoned. But even more than the Bourbons the House of Orléans had need for glories won on foreign fields, and if Louis-Philippe was cautious in Europe, he could be confident that in Algeria there were no Waterloos. "What difference does it make," he said, "if a hundred thousand rifles fire in Africa? Europe doesn't hear them." Napoleon III, before seizing power, had also hinted he had no use for the new territory. "Algeria," he said in 1851, "is a ball and chain." But what better place to push the Bonapartist myth of founding new nations. There might be no chance for re-establishing his uncle's kingdom of Poland. Napoleon III could, and did in 1852, declare Algeria to be "the kingdom of the Arabs." "We stayed in Algeria," E. F. Gautier wrote, reviewing the early years in the centenary history of 1930, "because we couldn't get out. It was a conquest *à contre-coeur*." "While the British Empire was built by businessmen wanting to make money," said another Frenchman, "the French Empire was built by bored officers looking for excitement."

For there was, at least, work for the army. Administrative powers were centered in a military Governor General, first Marshal Bugeaud himself, based in Algiers. Bureaux Arabes manned by career officers supervised tribal affairs. Beginning in 1840, the army began to lay out the magnificent road system of Algeria. In the tribal fighting dozens of military reputations were made, and some political ones. General Louis Eugène Cavaignac, liquidator of the 1848 revolt in Paris and thereafter briefly chief of the French state, was Governor General after Bugeaud. Marshal Patrice de Macmahon, second President of the Third Republic, held the office from 1864 to 1870. As Prévost-Paradis noted in 1868, Algeria was "an exercise field for the army."

Empire and army were both discredited in the debacle of Napoleon II in 1870. But no more than kings or emperors did republicans address themselves seriously to Algerian realities. They merely projected a different set of French institutions. From 1875 through 1940, the writ of the Assembly ran in Algeria as in France. A civilian, named by the French Premier, sat as Governor General in Algiers. The army's Bureaux Arabes were dismantled. As France was divided for administrative purposes into departments ruled by a prefect and elected general council, so Algeria was split into three departments. As private enterprise ran unchecked in France, so in Algeria huge speculative corporations, helped by franchise and other public grants, began the building of cities and railroads and all-out commercial exploitation of agriculture.

Two special exceptions—marks of unusual concern for Algerian peculiarities—were made. First, the Code d'Indigénat recognized the right of the Moslems to conduct their private affairs by Koranic law; only Moslems abandoning that privilege were permitted to vote in elections for the General Councils and Chamber of Deputies. Thus, while theoretically universal male suffrage prevailed in Algeria as in France, in practice all but a handful of Moslems were denied the vote. Secondly, in 1900, Algeria was endowed with fiscal autonomy. From that point through 1946, Algerian taxes and budgets were voted by the Financial Delegations—a group composed of picked representatives of the Moslem and settler communities. Behind this exception was a will to relieve European France of the heavy costs occasioned in Algeria by public improvements. Thus in both instances when France itself paid special attention to Algeria, the ruling principal was a shirking of responsibility. In each case Paris divorced itself from Algeria, and notably from its Moslem inhabitants.

By 1920, when the Moslem malcontents began taking their troubles back to Paris, there had elapsed ninety years of the "reluctant conquest"—ninety years of neglect. Changes meeting the needs of the Moslems were still theoretically possible— along one of two lines. There was assimilation, or integration as it came to be called: raising the Moslems to a footing of economic and political equality with Frenchmen. There was independence. Both involved enormous practical difficulties. Equality, in effect, meant making a poor, overpopulated country short of natural resources the equal of a rich one: a huge drain on French resources. Independence meant abandoning an attribute of sovereignty and prestige, and a reservoir of manpower. Apart from intrinsic difficulties, moreover, both ran athwart a determined, entrenched opposition. As test after test developed, it became plain that in the course of a century's neglect, Paris, nearly as much as the Moslems, had lost control over Algeria. A third force had taken charge—the European settlers.

## 2.   THE SETTLERS

"THE agricultural scum of the European countries," Marshal Bugeaud called them; and modern Frenchmen, not less contemptuously, speak of the settlers as *"pieds noirs"* —the black feet. But it is a native son that has best caught the national character. Mersault, the hero of Camus's novel *L'Etranger*, is the archetype of the Algerian settler. "A poor and naked man," he lives the life of an office worker, but is a child of nature at home in the sun and the sea and a stranger to the sophistication of abstract codes and ideas. What happens in his firm or even to the closest members of his family barely touches him. "Mother died today," he says, introducing himself with grotesque insouciance. "Or maybe yesterday." But it happened to him, without deeply willing it, to shoot an Arab. Dimly the sense of transgression is borne home: "I knew that I had shattered the equilibrium of the day, the spacious calm of this beach where I had been happy."

II

EVERY nation has its border peoples, cruder than the settled population of the interior and therefore an object of fun and contempt, but tougher and more energetic, better at working and at fighting. Absorbed as the pioneers in this country, the frontiersmen add dynamic leaven to a nation. Dominant, as the Prussians became in Germany, they impose harsh rule and set foot on the road to disaster. Midway between the two falls the case of the European settlers of Algeria. Not powerful enough to become dominant, they have proved too lumpy for good mixing. From ordinary Frenchmen they are set apart by reason of racial origin, occupation, a clawing struggle for survival, and the circumstance of being an outnumbered minority. In outlook a sea as unbridgeable as the Mediterranean divides them from European France. "You reason like a Frenchman of France," a group of settlers once complained to an official involved with Algerian matters. "You must reason like a Frenchman of Algeria."

Frenchmen of Algeria: it is one of many myths. Of the roughly 1,000,000 persons classed as Europeans in 1954, about 325,000 concentrated in the Oran district were of Spanish descent; another 100,000, living chiefly around Constantine and Bône, had Italian lineage; another 50,000, located in the same region, came originally from Malta. There were also 140,000 Jews, made French citizens by the Crémieux decree of 1870, but half of the indigenous to North Africa, most of the rest remnants of the Spanish persecutions of the sixteenth and seventeenth centuries. Even by French figures, in short, well over half the Europeans of Algeria issue from non-French stock.

Except for the Jews, what is most common to the settler pedigree is origin in the backward, rural districts of southern Europe. The great majority of the Spanish immigrants were day laborers, *braceros* from Andalusia. Calabrian and Sicilian sharecroppers made up the bulk of the Italians. Similarly with most of the *français de souche*, or Frenchmen by descent. Attention has been directed to the special cases: the case of the 400 Rhinelanders who left Le Havre for America in 1832, only to find themselves cast up by crooked sea captains as the first

Algerian settlers; the case of the 13,000 unemployed Parisians transported south in 1848 after the riots of the June days; the case of the 5,000 Alsaoian refugees from the German victory of 1870. But most of the French immigrants too came from the backward agricultural provinces. Not the south coast of France which is so close, still less the North or Parisian region where industry is concentrated, but Corsica and the poor farming sections of southeast and southwest France provided by far the lion's share of the French colonizers. These had more in common with the *braceros* of Spain and the farm workers of the Mezzogiorno than with their own countrymen. In Algeria they combined to form a homogeneous settlement.

Land drew them in the beginning. After 1840 plots expropriated from the beylical domain, and thereafter from native holders, were made available to soldiers serving in the French forces; then to groups of official colonists transported by the French government. After 1873, in keeping with the free-enterprise doctrines of the Third Republic, private-property law was applied to what had been joint Moslem holdings: purchasing Arab land became for a European about as easy, and not much more expensive, than taking candy from a baby. In one notorious transaction of 1885, a settler bought for twenty francs a small share of a 700-acre parcel of land belonging jointly to 513 Arabs; he divided the whole parcel into shares for each holder, charging for his troubles 11,000 francs; when that fee could not be met, he acquired in payment the whole 700 acres.

Getting the land, though, proved easier than working it. Uncertain weather and thin soil afflicted the European peasant as much as the Moslem fellah. More than two thirds of the 1870 immigrants had failed as farmers within five years. "Algeria," Marshal Bugeaud, one of the stanchest of the colonizers, said in a moment of desperation, "cannot be cultivated." Disease took an even heavier toll. A third of the workers transported in 1848 died of cholera within a year. "Only the cemeteries," one soldier wrote back home, "are prosperous." Moreover, for the "agricultural scum," movement off the land was a step up the social ladder. From the beginning, accordingly, scores of Europeans headed for the towns after the briefest fling on the land. By 1870, when the settlement numbered 245,000 Europeans, 60 per cent were in the towns. By 1920, when the immigration began to cease, 70 per cent of the 820,000 Europeans were urban. In 1954, only an eighth of the European population was on the land. Far more than Frenchmen of France, the Europeans had become a community of city dwellers. Similar in social origins, they found their unity further cemented by a common urbanism.

Even more are they bound together—and sociologically distinguished—by an absence of extremes in wealth. Sharp differences, to be sure, mark the fortunes of those—130,000 in all —who have stayed upon the land. At least 7,500 are unskilled agricultural laborers. Nearly that many, *gros colons* on the other end of the scale, live off huge tracts of land planted in wine or fruits and farmed by the most modern methods. Private holdings of 50,000 acres are not unknown. Henri Borgeaud, a former senator from Algeria known as the wine king, controls a domain of 2,500 acres of prime land from which have grown important interests in banking, tobacco, and transport, as well as wine. But in the urban sector of the settler population there is astonishing uniformity. Of the 200,000 active Europeans working in the cities, perhaps 10 per cent are workers in light industry. But administration and the liberal professions (32 per cent), services (9.2 per cent), trade (8 per cent), transport (10 per cent), highly skilled workers (14 per cent) make up nearly 75 per cent. Three quarters of the Europeans, in other words, are solid middle class. They work in offices, shops, or small factories; they live in modest homes or apartment houses; move about in cars, buses, and trolleys; communicate by telephone; send their children to local public schools; read local newspapers; amuse themselves in listening to the radio or watching television, at cafés, cinemas, team sports, and, above all, by the sea. Average income in 1950 was about $600 annually, almost the same as in France.

An immense social plant, or infrastructure, is required to meet these needs; and like settlers almost everywhere, the Europeans of Algeria have been builders on the grand scale. Forty thousand miles of straight road crisscross the territory. An excellent railroad fronts the coast and sends spurs into the hinterland back of Bône in the east, Algiers in the center, and Oran in the west. Algiers, Oran, Bône, Bougie, and Philippeville are all busy modern ports, the first two being the third and fourth most active in all French-ruled territory. The traveler approaching from the Mediterranean sees rising above the ports row upon row of immense apartment houses, office buildings, post offices, hotels. Hospitals and schools, some of them better appointed than in France, dot all the big cities. If there are European slums, for example Bab-el-Oued in Algiers, there are also magnificent structures, seaside villas, the palatial St. George Hotel, the ultra modern Government General building, overlooking the beautiful blue Bay of Algiers.

One thing the settlers could not build: inner economic balance. For labor, the farms, mines, docks, and light industry are dependent upon the Moslems. From their ranks come nearly 100,000 workers on European land: over 90 per cent of the total. They supply over 150,000 workers in the mines, docks, and light industry: about two thirds of the total employed. Not so crudely, but in as binding a way, the settler economy depends upon European France. French capital supplied, and supplies, most of the funds for development. The French market, protected and heavily subsidized, buys up nearly all the produce of the settler farms—which otherwise probably could not be sold competitively. Many shops and almost all industry in Algeria are projections of French firms. The external transport business is almost exclusively transport to and from France. The administration, which directly supports 18,-

ooo settler families, is the French administration. Only by backing from the French Treasury could Algeria pay the enormous social-service costs—in schools, roads, pensions, power plants—levied by settler needs.

Homogeneous as few other communities, in short, the settlers are doubly dependent upon the outside world. They need first the Moslems, next European France. Out of that condition there emerges the strange phenomenon of settler politics.

### III

"Art thou my master? or am I thine?"—George Meredith called that "the parent question of mankind." For its answer civilized men have traditionally turned to politics: a way of waging war, to reverse Clausewitz's famous dictum, by peaceful means. Wherever there are not universally accepted standards for singling out superiority, there politics will flourish. It enters, of course, into the designation of civic leaders, but as much if not more into the awarding of fellowships and contracts, the promotion of executives and army officers, the matter of who gets the corner office. It is, as Max Weber pointed out, the art of getting something for nothing: a phenomenon bred in the bone of virtually all communities.

Settler politics are strange precisely because at first glance they seem not to exist at all. System makers and pleaders of causes may single out "ultras" and "*enragés*," identifying them with the *gros colons* and petit bourgeoisie respectively. But in fact Mersault, the child of nature, is apolitical. His kind has produced no important leader. For heroes the settlers take French figures—Drumont in the 1890's, Pétain in the 1940's, Soustelle in the fifties. Still less have the settlers produced any original ideas. "The Algerian settler," Charles-André Julien, one of the great experts on the subject, has written, "never had *l'esprit politique*" (the political mind). Nor did he have the party habit. A handful of intellectuals in the liberal professions

and trade unions may have supported the Socialists and Communists. But of the traditional French parties only the Radicals struck root in Algeria, and they, even in France, were less
a party than a collection of notables and their clients. Most
settler parties were ad hoc affairs, put together for one electoral
test or another, then junked. Poll after poll was won by lists
bearing such general, nonparty names as Algerian Union. And
hardly anyone cared anyhow. "Only journalists and candidates," a settler once said, "care about elections."

On reflection, however, the absence of politics is a mirage;
what seems emptiness is a void filled to the brim. The settlers
had no need for political leadership, for programs or party organizations. Among themselves, there was virtually nothing in
conflict. "No cleavage," as E. F. Gautier wrote, "has appeared
in the bloc of the European settlers." "In Algeria," Marc
Lauriol, one of the most penetrating of the settlers, and himself a deputy, once noted, "the difference between right and
left is glossed over . . . The candidates have, on all the major
issues, practically the same opinion. The voters come from almost the same social background. Uniformity of interests and
of opinions is the striking fact of public life among the Europeans . . . It is only natural that the political debate is distinguished by indifference . . . Serenity is the characteristic
trait of the country's politics."

Except in the two areas of dependence. On all matters
touching the nerve of relations with the Moslems or with
France, the parent question came surging to the surface. On
the one hand, the settlers regarded themselves without equivo-
cation as the masters of the Moslems. On the other, their
supremacy depended upon backing from metropolitan France.
In both these areas the settlers threw themselves into the
political fray with the unchecked fury of men backed against
the wall in a struggle for survival. Apolitical among themselves, they were strangers to the sense of moderation and
compromise, the willingness to support ambiguity and live

with problems that is perhaps the most cherished bounty of active popular participation in public affairs. Mistrustful of party, and of the complicated workings of representative government, they looked instead to direct action—through chambers of commerce and agriculture; through professional, veterans', and school associations; through the local administration; by plot, if need be, or mob pressure. There thus evolved a unique brand of apolitical politics: colonial fascism. The settler community was not divided by party. It was itself a party. It was engrossed in an oppressive authoritarian movement aimed at asserting mastery over both the native population in Algeria and the parent government in France.

Upon the Moslems the settlers fastened a regime of barefaced inequality. "It is difficult," Jules Ferry wrote in 1892, "to make the European settler understand that there are other rights than his in an Arab country, and that the natives are not a race subject to taxes and forced labor at will." "Contempt for the Moslems" Jacques Soustelle found in 1955 to be "a constant theme." In a well-known trial the judge was told that there were five witnesses: "two men and three Arabs." In the settler lingo the Moslems were "*melons*" (simps), "*ratons*" (coons). "They weigh in the scales," a settler mayor, Raymond Laquièrre, once told me, "as feathers against gold." Another reporter recalls hearing on European lips the phrase: "He was an Arab, but dressed like a person." As to the settlers, one of them, Louis Bertrand, once wrote:

> We Frenchmen are in our own homes in Algeria. We have mastered the country by force, for a conquest can only be accomplished by force, which necessarily implies victors and vanquished. When they were mastered, we were able to organize the country, and the organization confirmed the superiority of the victor over the vanquished, of the civilized being over the inferior man.

On those master-race principles the settlers pitched the government of Algeria. Up to 1944 all European males, but only the merest handful of Moslems, voted in elections for Algerian delegates to the French Assembly. The Financial Delegations, which from 1900 through 1944, had the major voice in budgetary decisions, were composed of three sections: two with forty-eight representatives in all for the Europeans; one with twenty-four representatives for the Moslems. In local government, towns where the settlers predominated were endowed with full powers (hence the name Communes de Plein Exercise) and elected a municipal council which in turn named a mayor; but where Moslems predominated the towns, called Communes Mixtes, were administered from above. Except for tribal affairs where hand-picked caids held sway, the whole administrative apparatus—including the local police, the bureaucracy of the Government General, and the Algerian branches of the French ministries—were in settler hands. "Between the settlers and the government of Algeria," E. F. Gautier wrote, "there is a symbiosis . . . The result is that the Government General is imbued with the settler spirit."

The discriminatory nature of that spirit showed itself in all domains. Independent Moslem political movements were savagely persecuted by the army, the administration, and settler vigilantes; "the call for bloody repression" Jacques Soustelle found to be another constant settler theme. Direct taxation which would have borne heavily on the settlers was much less used as a revenue producer than indirect levies, paid mainly by the Moslems. As late as 1954 the income of the poorest 100,000 families in Algeria, all Moslem, was taxed at a rate of 12 per cent. The income, several hundred times larger, of the richest 10,000 families, almost entirely European, was taxed at a rate of 29 per cent. Schooling, in theory, was open to all. But as late as 1957, whereas all European children were receiving an education, over 80 per cent of the Moslems had no school. No doubt the population explosion counted for something in that figure; but so did settler prejudice. "Instruction of the natives," one settler group proclaimed, "is a veritable peril." "The

Arab," said another, "is an inferior race, ineducable." In theory, also, the Native Code was designed to protect Moslem *moeurs*. In settler hands it became an instrument for the denial of civil rights. As the settlers claimed to see it, only Moslems who renounced the Native Code for the Civil Code of France could fairly enjoy the full rights of French citizens. "If, compared to us," the settler deputy Etienne Morinaud once wrote, "they don't have full sovereignty, they have only themselves to blame. Let them accept the Civil Code, and they are our equals." Just let them try! In seventy years only 2,500 Moslems renounced the Moslem for the Civil Code—and little wonder. The full force of settler power was turned against those Moslems who tried to opt for the Civil Code. One settler, a deputy from Algiers, reported that when a tribal group came to Bougie seeking the status of the Civil Code "the military authorities put the most influential in prison in order to intimidate the others." An Arab schoolteacher who wanted the Civil Code reported this reception from the local administration: "What? You're a native, and that isn't good enough? Don't you think there are enough Frenchmen without you?" And one settler even pretended that such discrimination was in keeping with republican tradition. "Fraternity," he wrote, "is a part of the republican motto. It inspires and ennobles. Let us conserve its dignity and beauty. Let us not offer it as a gift, as bait, to indifferent or hostile races. France, at her purest, deserves to be sought after."

If less than keen to make Frenchmen out of Moslems, the settlers, in dealing with their other sore point, European France, played the super-Frenchmen. One settler leader described his fellow settlers as "valiant Frenchmen maintaining here [in Algeria] the French flag and sovereignty." "With the settlers," General Georges Catroux, one of them but no lover of the breed, once acknowledged, patriotism is a "primitive, instinctive reflex." But there was a proviso, noted by Léon Blum.

"What they call French sovereignty," he wrote in the *Populaire*, "is nothing but their own domination."

In keeping with authoritarian instincts, the settlers repeatedly aligned themselves with the extreme right wing in French politics. In the 1890's Algeria was a focal point of anti-Dreyfusard sentiment. The scene of vicious pogroms in 1897, next year it elected out of a total of six representatives, four blatantly anti-Semitic deputies, among them Edouard Drumont, the author of *Jew France*. During the regime of Léon Blum, Jacques Doriot launched his French Fascist party from Algiers. Marshal Pétain's National Revolution found enthusiastic support among the settlers. One of them, a student, for example, protested the application of the 3 per cent limit on Jewish students in the Algerian school system. "French students," he wrote, "have accepted the 3 per cent with sadness. What they really want is 0 per cent." Jacques Soustelle, later to become one of the settler heroes, wrote of their attitude toward Pétain, "If the National Revolution had not existed, it would have had to be invented. Whipped up by family, race, and caste hates, open to [Italian] Fascist influence from Tunis and [Spanish] Falangist influence from Oran . . . our North Africans offered a promised land for the Marshal's propaganda. Nowhere in France or in the Empire did one find it spread out so blatantly in enormous slogans defacing the walls, and in giant portraits of the 'good dictator'." M. Soustelle put the Pétainist support down to opportunism. A more convincing explanation comes from General Catroux: "Pétain gave the settlers just the kind of order they wanted, that is the submission of the natives . . ." And when that order began to crack, they turned in dizzying succession to the holders of might, backing first the Allies, next General Giraud, then the Free French, then the Communists, and, after 1947, the Gaullists. At one stage some of the settlers even threatened an appeal to the United Nations.

Authoritarian traditions also inspired settler treatment of

French representatives on Algerian soil. To men they mistrusted they opposed base rumor, spectacular gestures of contempt, and administrative sabotage. Maurice Viollette, Governor General from 1925 to 1927, they called Viollette l'Arbi; Yves Chataigneau, who held the position from 1945 through 1947, was Chataigneau ben Mohammed. Jacques Soustelle, when he arrived in 1955, was hailed as a Jew from Constantine: Ben Soussan. The settlers trampled upon a wreath he sent to a funeral. His orders, he admits long after being converted to the settler cause, "were not always obeyed." So fearful was he of being cut off from information that he found it necessary to tell his subordinates that letters marked personal were not to be intercepted. And to such gentle pressures there were added, in extreme cases, violent measures. Like all parties of the Right, the settler community nursed a corps of political racketeers. Useful as claques at demonstrations, or to cow individual Moslems, they also made themselves available for terror tactics against French officials. Well before the rebellion got under way, political assassination was an Algerian tradition. The bullet of a European assassin ended Admiral Darlan's life in Algiers in 1942. Next year an attempt was made on General Giraud. The strange bazooka plot against General Salan in 1956 was simply more of the same. Not altogether different were the settler uprisings of May 1958, and January 1960.

In striking contrast, but also in the authoritarian spirit, was the treatment meted out to French officials who expounded settler views. Feted in the villas of the rich, praised beyond measure in the press, saluted in endless parades by the military, they were accorded a dizzying popular acclaim. "To resist the Algerian sirens," Pierre Nora put it, "a man had to be lashed to the mast, like Ulysses." As the Fascists cheered Mussolini from the Forum, as the Nazis hailed Hitler from the Sportspalast, so the settlers found their political theater on a huge terrace just beneath a balcony of the Govern-

ment General building in Algiers. To the Forum, as the terrace came fittingly to be called, they thronged by the thousands at moments of political stress. Hatless and coatless, they
would stand by the hour, shouting in a frenzy of enthusiasm.
Amid such thunder claps of glory, the merest civil servant saw
himself a liberating Caesar. "From high on the balcony," Alfred Fabre-Luce wrote of that experience, "he feels himself
borne upon a shield. Above the vibrant crowd the air shim-
mers, as above a flame. Through this halo, beyond the noble
staircases running down to the sea, he imagines the France of
his dreams. The present seems less close than the antiquity of
the Latins, and most recent seems Algeria's role as a platform
for Liberation. Once again, Europe offers to a martial foot, a
soft underbelly. No more is it fascist Italy; it is republican
France."

## IV

FOR half a century the tactic of apolitical politics held both the
Moslems and the Paris government in thrall. From 1870
through World War I, every official act of France in the
Algerian domain served the settler interest. Even conflicting
principles were invoked to their advantage—a sure mark of un-
challenged supremacy. Thus in 1873 the French Chamber
passed the Loi Warnier, extending the private-property code to
some jointly held Moslem land. Behind the legislation was the
principle of "assimilation," summed up in the slogan "Algeria
is France." In theory the law conferred upon the benighted
Moslems the blessings of modern (French) land tenure. In
practice it only made it easy for settlers to buy Moslem-held
land on the cheap. Conversely in 1900 the Chamber endowed
Algeria with financial autonomy. Behind that law was the
principle of the "Algerian personality": a theoretical recognition that Algeria was not France. But in practice, the act of

1900 merely made possible settler domination through the Financial Delegations.

World politics forced the first break in the pattern. During World War I over 100,000 Algerian Moslems, drafted into the French army, served on the Western Front. For the nascent Moslem protest movements, conscription was a foot in the political door. "We are willing to pay the blood tax," a group of Young Algerians declared, "but in compensation for our help we ask the rights of French citizens." The Paris government, in the person of Premier Raymond Poincaré, accepted the gage. Throughout the war years a series of projects expanding Moslem political rights in Algeria were introduced to the Chamber. From the settlers came a chorus of nay-saying. The Financial Delegations declared itself "opposed with all its force." The Prefect of Constantine warned that reforms would lead to "bloody troubles and insurrection." His opposite number in Algiers foresaw "currents of discord, dangerous for the future of our colony." Still, in 1919, Georges Clemenceau, a foe of the settlers since the Dreyfus days, and now, as "le Père du Victoire," at the height of his powers, forced through a reform bill: the so-called Algerian Charter. A watered-down piece of legislation, it did not extend full voting rights to all Moslems, as Jean Jaurès had proposed; it did not even give full voting rights to Moslem veterans, as Clemenceau himself had vehemently demanded. It affected mainly the Financial Delegations and Municipal Councils where the Moslems representatives, making up a third of the total, had been picked by the administration. The reform did not even upset the European domination over both bodies. What it did was to make it possible for the Moslems to choose their representatives by vote. But even for that trivial change it took all of Clemenceau's immense prestige to override settler resistance. "The natives," one settler said in debate in the French Senate, "have done their duty toward us and deserve to be rewarded. But is it necessary to take imprudent steps?"

For twenty-five years, Clemenceau's charter was the high-water mark of reform in Algeria. For fifteen the settlers fought off any reopening of the question of Moslem rights. Then in 1936, a project to supplement the 1919 reform was put forward by the Popular Front Premier, Léon Blum, and his Minister of State, the former Governor General, Maurice Viollette. The Blum-Viollette proposal was based on Clemenceau's original idea. It accepted the refusal of Moslems to enter French political life at the cost of renouncing the Native Code. It opened the way for Moslems to achieve full citizenship rights while retaining their private statute. It provided that Moslems in certain categories—veterans, teachers, lawyers, members of the Legion of Honor—could, without abandoning their native status, vote in elections for the French Chamber and Senate and for settler representatives in the local assemblies. In all, it would have extended the franchise to about 21,-000 Moslems: 4 per cent of the total.

The settlers responded as though they were being forced to convert to Islam. This project, wrote Elisée Sabatier in the *Revue des Deux Mondes*, "would debase the name of citizen, and destroy the unity of the French nation in Algeria. It would be the end, not to say the death, of France's work of colonization and civilization in North Africa." To this patriotic *cri de coeur* were added the most vicious personal attacks. "All the anti-Frenchmen," wrote the fascist mayor of Oran, the Abbé Lambert, "are for the Viollette project." Blum, exulted one of the settler anti-Semites, "cares only about the protection of his own RACE, of his own NATION, the *jew Race*, the *jew Nation*." Viollette, said another broadside, was "a music-hall proconsul . . . a complete driveler." The climax of the protest was a meeting of the 308 settler mayors in Algiers in January 1937. All but two declared themselves against the project and resigned their offices in a general strike against the authority of Paris. Before this show of force, the government collapsed. The Blum-Viollette project was withdrawn without even coming to a vote. Its epitaph was written by one of the settlers, M. Abbo, who organized the revolt of the mayors: "I sabotaged the Blum-Viollette project, and the government capitulated."

That boast was made ten years after, in 1947. Appropriately enough, for the war years unsealed the settler victory of 1937 and put the whole question up for grabs once more. For the first time well-organized Moslem protest groups entered the arena. The liberating armies of the United States and Great Britain were pledged to the principles of the Atlantic Charter. Aversion to the settlers was a dominant mood among the Free French forces which followed in the Allied baggage train. The same sentiments were shared by the interior resistance, composed largely of Communists, Socialists, and liberal Catholics, which collaborated with General de Gaulle in setting up the first postwar governments. Before those combined forces, the settlers, occupied for a while and discredited by collaboration with Vichy, were powerless.

In these circumstances two breaches were opened in the wall of settler supremacy. In March 1944, General de Gaulle in effect decreed an expanded version of the Blum-Viollette project: some 60,000 Moslems were given European voting rights without renunciation of the Native Code; Moslem representation on local councils was raised from one third to two fifths; and in French representative bodies the Moslems were given equal representation with the settlers. On September 20, 1947, the French Assembly passed the Algerian Statute, in effect the first constitution ever given to the territory as a whole. The statute defined Algeria as "a group of departments," subject to the constitutional, civil, and criminal codes adopted by the French Assembly, and to an executive power vested in a Governor General appointed by the Paris government. But it recognized the Algerian personality. It established an Algerian Assembly, "charged with managing, in cooperation with the Governor General, special Algerian affairs," notably budgetary matters. The Assembly was to be made up of 120 members:

half elected by European voters plus the 60,000 Moslems given European voting rights; the other half elected by Moslem voters. Though obviously inequitable in according to the European minority parity with the Moslems in the Assembly, the Algerian Statute had real merits. It provided an institutional basis for the separate political expression of the two Algerian communities. As Leon Blum wrote at the time, "It breaks once and for all with . . . the politics of assimilation. It addresses itself to the reality of the Algerian problem. It tries to order . . . the relationship of two peoples, living on the same land, but different and distinct, unassimilable, and intending to remain independent of one another."

He reckoned without the settlers. Hostile to the statute at all times, they were by 1948 able to take action. The liberating armies, including the bulk of the Free French forces, had long since moved out. The Moslems had been cowed in the Sétif riots of 1945. In Paris, the wartime unity of the resistance forces was wearing thin; the stain of collaboration all but erased. In May 1947, the Communists left the government. In December there took office the first postwar Premier to have voted the induction of Marshal Pétain—Robert Schuman. With him there came to important office, for the first time in the postwar years, a settler representative: Finance Minister René Mayer, deputy from Constantine. Through his offices, the settlers were able to rid themselves of the moving spirit behind the 1944 and 1947 reforms, Governor General Yves Chataigneau. On February 11, 1948, he was replaced as Governor General by Marcel-Edmund Naegelen. A Socialist patriot from Alsace, Naegelen had spent most of his political life warring against the pro-German separatists of his native province, and it was through those glasses that he saw the Moslems of Algeria. "We shall," he said in one of his first speeches, "attempt to reason with those who might be tempted to pursue other goals, or who, carried away by pride and vanity, claim to be able to get along without France, and if they refuse to see the bright light of truth, it will be no fault of ours, and we shall not be responsible." "The threshold of a new era," proclaimed the chief settler organ, the *Echo d'Alger*. Within a matter of months, the settlers and M. Naegelen had contrived to empty the Algerian Statute of all content. Their weapon was systematic, unblushing electoral fraud.

Under M. Chataigneau there had been, in the immediate postwar years, relatively free elections. Among the Moslems, parties favoring a sharp whittling down of settler privileges, and in some cases independence itself, had demonstrated an impressive following. They swept the board in the first Constituent Assembly elections of October 21, 1945; and again in the second Constituent Assembly elections of June 2, 1946. In October 1947, they won 60 per cent of the vote in municipal elections, seating, for the first time, several mayors.

Six months later, in April 1948, there took place the first elections under the rule of M. Naegelen—elections to the Algerian Assembly. It was a seeming miracle. Of the sixty Moslem seats, only seventeen went to the protest parties. The other forty-three were won by the Administration's picked candidates, the so-called Beni Oui Oui. In the town of Blida, the vote for one protest party dropped from 10,000 to 2,000; of another from 2,000 to 16. At Guelma it fell off from 2,000 to 700; at Bône from 6,000 to 87. That these results were achieved by the most flagrant electoral rigging—proscription of some voters, forced attendance by others, stuffed ballot boxes, irregular counting—is by now abundantly plain. Thirty-two of the fifty-nine candidates of one Moslem group were put in prison before the vote. Well-attested reports indicate that at one polling place the local police commissioner presided over the urns; that at another the voting cards were not distributed; that at another tanks stood guard; that at still another military planes flew overhead. M. Naegelen himself, according to Alfred Fabre-Luce, used later to boast of "how he organized elections in Algeria." A French Catholic deputy, present during the poll, reported that "it is not the voters who choose the candidate, it is the administration . . . The fact is not only indisputable. It is even avowed." "The rigging of the second college elections," wrote a correspondent for *Le Monde*, "is the talk of Algeria." And one of the Moslems told him, "These elections are a comedy."

With those kinds of polls assuring the docility of the Moslem group in the Algerian Assembly, the settlers, as a sympathetic observer, Michael Clark, writes, "could breathe easy." Thereafter the junking of reform was child's play. Nothing came of proposals to expand educational opportunities for the Moslems. A constitutional provision that would have given Moslem women the vote was ignored. So were official declarations of intent by the Paris government to bring more Moslems into the administration. A section of the Algerian Statute calling for suppression of direct administration over Moslem towns in the Communes Mixtes was indefinitely postponed. Barely two years after the Algerian Statute had passed, the settlers were able to treat it openly as a dead letter. "Let us speak clearly," one of them told the Algerian Assembly in February 1950, "the statute was voted in a climate very different from the present climate."

v

IF THE climate had changed for the settlers, it had changed for the Moslems as well. The liberal wisdom is to suppose that the Blum-Viollette project and the Algerian Statute, if enforced, would have brought France and Algeria together on amicable terms. "Gentlemen," M. Viollette told the French Assembly, "these Moslems have no political country . . . They ask for admission into yours. If you refuse, you must beware lest they soon create one of their own." And M. Julien speaks of the failure to put the reform proposals into effect as "missed opportunities."

In fact, there is little evidence to suppose that concessions to the Moslems would have cut off the nationalist growth. Some Moslems opposed the Blum-Viollette reforms at the time as too little too late. On the same grounds almost all fought the Algerian Statute. Two years after one reform that went through—the 1919 charter—the Moslems were already screwing up their demands. Had the Algerian Statute been honestly administered, there can be no doubt the nationalists would have very quickly come to dominate the Moslem college, using it as a sounding board for independence.

Still, if honest application of the reforms would not have satisfied the Moslems, shameless violation of the rules did worse. It created a self-evident grievance, a talking point beyond dispute, that promoted the accession of Moslems to extreme nationalism. It bred among the Moslems a spirit of mistrust for France. It blocked off all hope for making progress in cooperation with France. As one of the most trenchant of the nationalists, Ahmed Boumendjel, put it at the time:

> The French Republic has cheated. It has duped us. And we will now have the right to make the choice dictated by despair . . . the choice against France.

In the rebellion of 1954, they made that choice.

Settler reaction to the rebellion followed predictable lines. A handful of individuals and organizations not dependent upon French control of Algeria worked beneath the tide of events to maintain rapport between the Moslem and European communities. Of these the least important and most invidiously interested was the Algerian Communist party, largely dominated by Europeans. It tried to penetrate the rebel organization, and despite ignominious failure continued to parade pro-rebel sentiments in a bid for Moslem support. By far the most important group working for harmony was the Catholic Church. Archbishop Duval of Algiers spoke repeatedly of "peaceful cohabitation of the spiritual communities" and called for what slanted very close to the line of negotiations: "a brotherly dialogue." Catholic social service missions continued to do charitable work for Moslems in trouble, whether nationalist or not. Three missions—in Algiers, Oran, and Souk Ahras—quite clearly gave aid and comfort to rebel fighters; one of the priests when apprehended said, "I was deeply anxious to bridge the gap between the communities through common social work." To these strange bedfellows there was added a commercial interest. Almost alone among the big business groups of Algeria, the esparto grass monopoly of M. Georges Blachette was independent of subsidy from France: the whole crop is sold, at a good profit, to Britain, where it is converted to vellum paper. Able to do business with or without France, M. Blachette, and even more his political ally, former Mayor Jacques Chevallier of Algiers, sought to work with the Moslems for a settlement by negotiation. M. Chevallier pursued in Algiers a vast public housing program, aimed chiefly at providing dwellings for Moslems. To stop the troubles, he told *Le Monde* in 1955, there were necessary "profound reforms . . . having as their object the improvement of the lot of the Moslem mass." Twice in the next year he came out openly for direct negotiations between France and the rebels. "Why persist," he asked a correspondent from *France-Soir* in September 1957, "in treating the Algerian affair as if it were a war? In reality it is a revolution . . . which to be cured must be treated politically . . . It is not by imposing solutions that success will be achieved. It is by restoring the broken contacts, by resuming a dialogue, by discussing solutions together. There is no point in discussing with those who agree with us. Discussion must be with those who disagree."

But after innumerable indignities at the hands of his fellow settlers, Chevallier was forced from office in 1958. The Communist party was banned in Algeria in September 1955. As to the Church, the Archbishop came to be widely known in settler circles as Mohammed Duval; one of its missions was expelled from Algeria; members of two others were brought to trial before military tribunals, found guilty of aiding the enemy, and sentenced to prison terms.

For faithful to its traditions, the overwhelming majority of settler opinion took toward the rebellion a posture of defiant intransigence wrapped in the cloak of French patriotism. From the top of the social scale to the bottom, the Europeans looked on the rebels as bandits pure and simple; called in impassioned tones for swift and harsh repression; disdained reforms as a mark of weakness; and looked on negotiations as a gage of treason. The tone was set at the top of the scale by the Grands Seigneurs of French Algeria: Henri Borgeaud, senator in Paris, and in Algeria proprietor of one of the largest wine domains; Laurent Schiaffino, owner of a shipping empire based on trans-Mediterranean traffic between Marseilles and Algeria; Count Alain de Serigny, publisher of the *Echo d'Alger*. Only a day after the hostilities had begun, Borgeaud had pronounced judgment: "The evil ringleaders must be hunted out. They are known. It will be enough to reinforce the security measures . . . A blow must be struck at this handful of agitators and struck at the top; the organization must be decapitated."

Local officialdom fell into line very quickly. The day after M. Borgeaud spoke, François Quillici, deputy from Oran, told *Le Monde*, "Years of weakness and especially ideological dreaming, have brought us to this pass . . . The admirable Algerian peace, French peace in Algeria, is ruined . . . Weakness always encourages new adventures." Spurred on by rebel attacks, there went up from all the Algerian mayors a chorus of demands for more troops, martial law, arming of the settlers. "The population of Philippeville," Mayor Benquet-Crevaux proclaimed after the attacks of August 1955, "requires the urgent establishment of an organization which will make it possible for the civilian population to cooperate legally in the maintenance of order . . . It demands once again the procla-

mation of martial law and the initiation of a policy of authority . . . It holds the authorities responsible once and for all
for all failures to come, for the disorders, and for the needless
loss of life that perseverance in the present policy cannot help
but engender. Determined to defend this portion of France
which is Algeria, it holds tantamount to the crime of treason,
any policy that by weakness, improvidence, or incompetence,
could lead it to ruin, or to separation from its home country."
By May of the next year the mayors were calling for execution
of all rebel terrorists. "There have been enough stupid and
criminal subterfuges," Henri Baretaud, mayor of Cherchell,
told a minister visiting from Paris. "You do not treat with hired
killers, still less when they style themselves soldiers of liberation . . . Any political concession can only strengthen the position of the nationalists and swell their ranks. We look to the
government for action . . ."

Further down the social scale, dozens of semiprivate organizations echoed the mayors, in even sharper terms. By 1956,
every party organization from the Poujadists on the extreme
Right to the Socialists had been captured by violent partisans
of French Algeria. Fifty-two veterans' organizations had come
together in a common front, the Comité d 'Entente des An-
ciens Combattants, pledged, in the words of Michael Clark, to
"maintain French sovereignty in Algeria"; to "re-establish order and security"; to "effect the execution of all sentences
imposed by the courts, notably the death sentence." The
European students' organization of Algiers closed ranks as a
paramilitary group and filled its offices with tracts and pictures
showing mutilated European children over the legend, "Do
you want this to happen to you?" A group of European doctors
issued a pamphlet showing many of the same pictures and arguing the theme that "mutilation is an inbred trait of the
Arabs."

In the underworld of politics, beneath these legitimate
groups, there sprang up a gaggle of ad hoc vigilante organiza-

tions. Using force to protect Europeans and terrorize Moslems, they maintained close relations with the regular army, and with militia units formed by the army among the settlers. Clandestine, they emerged to public view suddenly in moments of crisis, only to fade and then re-emerge under different names. Among the best known were UFNA (Union Française Nord-Africaine); ORAF (Organisation de Résistance de l'Algérie Française); FNF (Front National Français); MPIC (Mouvement pour l'Instauration d'un Ordre Corporatif); URA (Union Royaliste Algérienne). In and around these organizations there moved a shadowy group of political adventurers. Among many others, there was Joseph Ortiz, a handsome barrel-chested café owner, born in Algeria of Spanish extraction, and at home with the poor settlers of Bab-el-Oued who knew him as "Uncle Jo" or "Jo Jo Fat Arms." There was Bernard Lefèvre, a slim, bespectacled doctor from Algiers, nursed on the corporate-state theories of Maurras and Mussolini, who considered Salazar of Portugal as the beau ideal of the modern ruler, and who counted among his disciples a deaf-and-dumb pretender to the French throne. There was Pierre Lagaillarde, the moody ("a character in search of an author," he was called), bearded son of two liberal lawyers from Blida, who once counted many Moslems among his friends, until, after a spell in the paratroops, he became, at twenty-six, a student leader dedicated to the mission of converting the French Assembly into "an officers' mess." There was Robert Martel, a healthy bronzed vineyard owner from the Mitidja plain outside Algiers, who combined the tending of his vines by plane with the peasants' traditional hatred of all modernity.

A Runyonesque cast to be sure, but a fit projection of French Algeria. In origin all were simple men of the people, amateurs in politics which they entered under pressure of events. As with so many amateurs, a touch of the ideal invested their projects. Martel, for instance, took as his motto "God, Nature, Family, Country," and borrowed his emblem from the cross and heart of the Père Foucauld. "In this godless century," he once said, "I believe in the primacy of Spirit; I believe in the supernatural; I believe in miracles. France has had Joan of Arc; Algeria, the Père Foucauld. I pray to Père Foucauld not to abandon us." To the force of high-sounding principle, they joined direct objectives. "We will defend French Algeria with arms," Ortiz used to say. "We will cleanse France of traitors . . . We will do justice ourselves . . . From Algeria we will bring the revolution to Paris." Above all they were ready and willing to act. They and their kind organized countless terroristic acts against Moslems. They set up secret courts to try and execute supposed rebel sympathizers. They attacked in every way Frenchmen suspected of wishing to negotiate with the rebels. They were the authors of the tomato fusillade against Guy Mollet in February 1956, of the bazooka attack on General Raoul Salan in January 1957, of the May 13 demonstrations against Pierre Pflimlin and the Fourth Republic in 1958, of the October and January plots against Charles de Gaulle in 1959 and 1960. From 1956, forward indeed, they were the movers and shakers of every major settler action in Algeria. They had become the cutting edge, the true political expression, of Algerian settlerdom.

## 3. THE REBELS

For believers in the hero in history, the rise of the "underdeveloped" provides welcome text. Nehru in India, Sihanouk in Cambodia, Nyerere in Tanganyika, Nkrumah in Ghana, Bourguiba in Tunisia, Norman Manley in Jamaica—almost everywhere the struggle for independence has been identified with a single, dominant figure.

Not in Algeria. There, interpenetration of the two communities raised a genuine possibility of joint development under French auspices, while dependence of so many Moslems on the settlers for employment magnified the risk of revolt against French authority. The three Moslem protest groups which arose in the late 1920's reached unity only thirty years later, and in the heat of battle. By that time, feuding had bred in their bones an invincible aversion to one-man rule. Experience had taught them, as it taught no other Arab movement, one of the finest, if most disparaged, of the modern political arts: committee management. Throughout all the ups and downs of Algerian nationalism, overriding the rise and fall of different groups and men, eclipsing the comic vaporizing of some

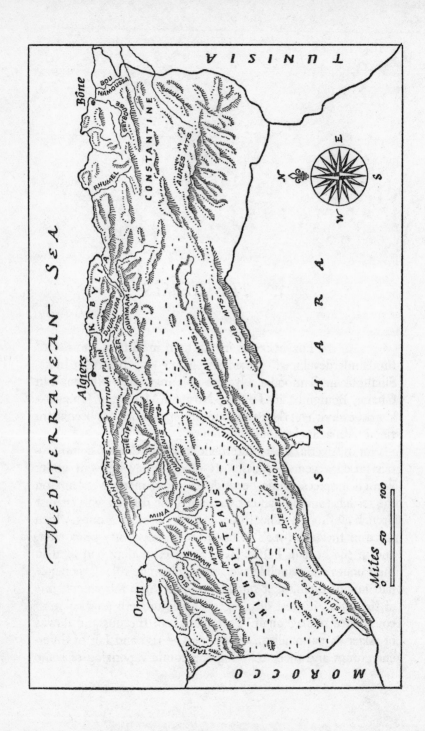

and the blind intransigence of others, there remained a basic, underlying organization. "Above everything else," a very young nationalist once told me, "it is organization that counts. With it you can do everything. Without it nothing. What is the difference between the little grills where we roast lamb, and your giant steel furnaces? Only organization."

## II

At THE heart of the organizational tradition was the protest movement that began life in 1925 as the North African Star. Founded as an adjunct of the French Communist party at a time when the Third International was cultivating the colonized, the Star was a catchall device aimed at "defending the material, moral, and social interests of North African Moslems." Within two years it had caught, and then been caught by, one of the more talented agitators of modern times—Messali Hadj. Born with the century in the Islamic center of Tlemcen, Messali served in the French army in World War I, married a girl from Lorraine, then settled down in Paris, entering working-class circles while following courses at the Sorbonne. From the Islamic background he retained the robes, beard, and whirling words of the prophets. A stranger to consistency, he was, over the years, to found four different parties, to make common cause with Moscow, to take the pilgrim's way to Mecca, to align himself with the French Fascists of Jacques Doriot. Egotistical beyond measure, he spoke of himself to strangers as "the father of Algerian nationalism," enjoined his followers to call him El Zaim—Leader—and warned those who thought of breaking away that "the day cannot begin without the sun." Still, from the Communists he had acquired the principle of solid organization from the ground up, and he applied it with the unflagging fervor of the born revolutionary. Named head of the North African Star in 1927, he found the organization dissolved by French authorities in

1929 and himself imprisoned in 1933. Released in 1935, he
fled, under the shadow of another jail term, to Geneva, returning when the Popular Front took office in 1936. As head of
a new organization, the National Union of North African Moslems, he toured Algeria, stirring wild crowds around Tlemcen
and attracting at one famous mass meeting in Algiers a throng
of 11,000 people. In January 1937, the Blum government dissolved the National Union. Within ninety days, Messali had
started a third organization, the Algerian People's Party (PPA).
Under that banner he went back to Algiers in the spring, organizing on July 14 a massive parade at which an Algerian
flag was displayed. A month later Messali was once more arrested. Except for very brief spells, he has not since then been
outside official custody. But by then the groundwork had already been laid.

Organizationally the PPA resembled the Communist party:
a central committee was at the top; from it depended regional
units (called *villaya* after the Turkish name for provinces);
each *villaya* was broken into smaller sections; which in turn
encompassed cells of about ten persons. Members were bound
to one another as brothers. A sharply defined program had been
worked out with national independence as the watchword. The
program also called for "confiscation of huge land holdings"
and their distribution among the peasantry; repeal of the
"odious" Native Code; the right to organize in trade unions.
The appeal of that program was manifest wherever anything
like free elections were possible. In the Algiers municipal elections of 1937, its first appearance at the polls and with Messali
already in jail, the PPA came second on the party list. Next
year Algiers elected one PPA candidate as a Moslem representative on the City Council, and another to the Departmental
Council. In particular, the party became a magnet for discontented youth; the workers in Paris and Algeria; students; soldiers in the French forces. By the time World War II broke,

it numbered 10,000 adherents in Algeria; another 4,000 in France. It had become Algeria's first mass party.

Of the two other protest groups, one very quickly came to work hand in glove with Messali's men. The Ulemas, or teachers, were essentially a religious revival movement, sprung from the Middle East late in the nineteenth century. Aiming at a return to the pure principles of Islam, they ran athwart France, as the standard-bearer of modernity. Their special enemies were the religious leaders, or marabouts, who had consented to enter into the French administration. "Islam," one of the Ulema leaders wrote in 1931, "is my religion, Arabic is my language, Algeria is my country." "The marabouts," he later set down, "are the domestic pets of colonialism." Too small in numbers for political action, the Ulemas established Arab schools, or *medersas*, in every major city, and not a few small villages. The *medersas*, drilling into thousands of students the separate qualities of Arabism, became a breeding ground of young nationalists. When Messali broke definitely with the Communists in 1937, the Ulemas were already a principal adjunct of his PPA.

The third of the Moslem protest groups stood apart for decades. Secular and essentially middle class, the Young Algeria movement lacked the Islamic inspiration of the Ulemas and the drive for social betterment of the PPA. Promotion for individual Moslems to the full rights of French citizenship was its original goal, and its leaders especially reflected that aspiration. Ferhat Abbas, the most important of these, was born in 1899 near Constantine, the son of a caid in the French administration. Educated in the classical tradition in French schools, he made his public debut as a pamphleteer—under the pseudonym Kemal (for the Turkish leader) Abençerage (after one of Chateaubriand's literary heroes). Politics he entered as the founder and first president of a group of Moslems studying in French schools: the Association of Moslem Students. After settling down in Sétif as a pharmacist (one of the few liberal professions, along with law, then attractive to Algerian Moslems), he was elected a Moslem representative, first on the Departmental Council, then on the Town Council, eventually on the Financial Delegations. Voluble by nature (he once granted a five-minute interview but talked for the better part of an hour before admitting a first question), he picked up in the various assemblies the back-slapping affability of the French politician. With his own career seeming to promise promotion for all Moslems within the frame of French rule, he turned his back on Algerian nationalism. In 1936, he stated his case in one of the most incautious statements ever made by any political leader:

> If I had discovered an "Algerian nation," I should have become a nationalist and would not have been ashamed of it . . . I did not find it. I consulted history, the living and the dead. I visited the cemeteries; and no answer came . . . You cannot build on air. We have driven away the clouds and the chimeras once and for all in order to bind our future to the French work of construction in this country. Six million Moslems live on this soil which has been French for a hundred years; they live in hovels; go barefoot, without clothing and often without bread. Out of this hungry mass, we shall make a modern society . . . elevate them to human dignity, so that they may be worthy of the name of Frenchmen . . .

"*La France c'est moi,*" Abbas called that statement; and even after the defeat of the Blum-Viollette reforms his sense of being French did not flag. When war broke out in 1939, he presented himself as a volunteer for French forces. But the defeat of 1940, the harsh rule imposed by Vichy, and then the deliverance by Allied troops shattered the faith. At the end of 1942, Abbas was writing:

> Like all the submerged peoples, the people of Algeria are becoming aware of their personality. To the problem of liberation they see a solution only in the framework of *la patrie algérienne.*

*Patrie,* the magic word, was out, and with Abbas's rallying to the nationalist cause there was prefigured an eventual alliance of all three protest groups. What remained to be found was a time to strike.

III

THE classic dilemma of reform versus direct action bedeviled the nationalist groups for fifteen years. At all times the obscure militants and field organizers of Messali's party favored violent strikes. But their leaders sought alliance with Ferhat Abbas and the Ulemas, and these counseled more moderate ways. Three times—in 1943, in 1947, and in 1951—alliances were struck. Twice—in 1945 and in 1950—they were broken by premature action from below which went awry. The third strike from below precipitated the Algerian war.

A first stab at cooperation came with the Algerian Manifesto of February 10, 1943. Written by Abbas, it owed its genesis to pressure from the Ulemas and Messali's PPA, notably Messali's number two man at the time, Mohammed Lamine-Debaghine. Both groups saw the document in composition and approved its contents. In form it was a serving of notice to the French government of Moslem expectations. Finis was formally written to Abbas's old hope of assimilation: "The European bloc and the Moslem bloc are distinct from one another, and without any common spirit . . . Henceforth an Algerian Moslem will ask only to be an Algerian Moslem." A claim was staked to both the social goals of the PPA ("a great agrarian reform"; "free compulsory education"; "absolute equality without distinction . . . . of race or religion") and the cultural aims of the Ulemas ("recognition of Arabic as an official language"; "freedom of religion for all"). Discretion veiled the political aims, but only slightly. The manifesto made reference to "*le Président Roosevelt*" and the Atlantic Charter. It spoke of the "application to all countries, large and small, of the right of popular self-determination" (*le droit des peuples à disposer d'eux-mêmes*). It demanded an Algerian constitution guaranteeing "the immediate and effective participation of Algerian Moslems in the government of their country."

The French response was General de Gaulle's edict enacting an expanded version of the Blum-Viollette project. A far cry from the demands of the manifesto, it was unacceptable to all three Moslem groups. These reacted by forming a joint organization—the Friends of the Algerian Manifesto, or AMA, formally established by Ferhat Abbas on March 14, 1944, a week after the Gaullist edict. Within a year, the AMA counted an estimated 500,000 Moslems as adherents, including many returning veterans. Belkacem Krim, a corporal who joined the movement, spoke of "the irresistible wave sweeping the Algerian people into the AMA." But while for Abbas the AMA was simply a gesture of nonviolent mass support for the principles of the manifesto, for Messali's men in the PPA, and notably for its principal leader at the time, Dr. Lamine-Debaghine, the AMA offered a front behind which there could be organization for action. All through 1944 Lamine brought into the PPA new groups, armed and alerted for a strike. By April 1945, their existence was an open secret. "Everywhere," a settler group wrote to the Prefect of Constantine, "insecurity is increasing. There have been reports of attacks on property, of willful damage to water mains, of undisguised threats on the lives of isolated French inhabitants. In the cities, despite the official ban on processions, the streets are full of demonstrators openly proclaiming that Algeria belongs to the Arabs. Local organizations—combat groups and groups formed to replace the French administration—have burgeoned in front of our eyes." The PPA, in a word, was preparing a mass uprising.

Occasion presented itself on May 8, 1945, when the war in Europe came to a close. All across Algeria there were to be victory parades. In Sétif, Ferhat Abbas's home and long-time residence of Lamine-Debaghine, the local Moslems, under PPA instructions, asked and received permission to stage a separate, nonpolitical victory parade. As they marched through the streets, they suddenly broke out a green Algerian flag and hoisted banners proclaiming the PPA slogans: Long Live Independent Algeria; Down with Colonialism; Free Messali. A police officer ordered them to put away the banners, and when they refused grappled with the demonstrators. There was a shot, apparently fired by the police. The demonstrators broke, and while the majority dispersed, one band of PPA militants opened fire on the police, then poured through the streets of Sétif, knifing and clubbing such settlers as they could find. Word of the encounter spread rapidly through the region, and by afternoon a Moslem reign of terror gripped the surrounding territory. In Guelma, there was a pitched battle with police. In Bône, official buildings were besieged. In smaller towns, European men were attacked and mutilated, their wives raped. In all, over a hundred Europeans were killed.

There followed a blind repression. Martial law was declared. Planes, tanks, and in one case a cruiser bombarded Moslem villages. After the bombing came infantry detachments burning villages, searching huts, shooting suspects. Thousands of Moslems were bundled into barbed-wire camps. "Summary executions," Edouard Sablier of *Le Monde*, an eyewitness, recounts, "struck more often than not at random." Estimates of the Moslems killed range from 40,000 to the official figure of 1,500.

Politically the settlers turned the trouble to immediate account. Moving about as armed militia, they cowed thousands of Moslems, seizing them in their homes, applying third-degree tactics, shooting some out of hand. Upon the Government General they loosed a flood of demands for harsh punishment. "When the house burns, and the ship is sinking," the *Echo d'Alger* wrote, "you don't call the insurance man or the dancing master. For the house, for the ship, it is the time of the fireman, the time of the savior. For North Africa it is the hour of the policeman." A settler tract demanded "summary execution of all the leaders, first of all Ferhat Abbas; recall of the Gover-

nor General; nomination of a civil governor born in Algeria and
armed with powers necessary to carry out a just and energetic
policy." Under the force of such pressure, the Paris government
caved in. Not only was the PPA officially dissolved and Messali exiled to Brazzaville, but something like 5,000 other Moslem political leaders wholly unconnected with the events of
May 8 were arrested. Ferhat Abbas was sentenced to a two-
year prison term; the sheik Brahimi, who had replaced Ben
Badis as head of the Ulemas, received the same treatment.
Still, in the long run the blind repression worked against the
settler interest. Rightly or wrongly, the events of May 8 became a part of the nationalist mythology. "It was in 1945 at
Sétif," the novelist Katib Yacine has written, "that for the first
time my humanity was confronted by the most atrocious of
sights. I was sixteen. I have never forgotten the shock of the
pitiless butchery which caused the death of thousands of Moslems. There my nationalism was cemented." "All those I have
met," the Swiss journalist C.-H. Favrod wrote a decade later
of the rebel leadership, "have told me the awful tale of the
nights and days of May."

Moreover, the jailed nationalist leaders were not long in
prison. Freed under a general amnesty in 1946, they were back
in business within the year. Sétif had underscored the danger
of direct action, and all three groups turned in their own ways
to nonviolent organization. Brahimi and the Ulemas continued
to teach—by 1950 they counted some 50,000 students. Abbas
divorced himself from Messali and founded a new party to campaign for the manifesto—UDMA, the Democratic Union for
the Algerian Manifesto. Messali, back from Brazzaville but
under surveillance in a villa outside Algiers, converted the PPA
into an above-ground party—MTLD, the Movement for the
Triumph of Democratic Liberties. Both Abbas's and Messali's
parties concentrated their efforts on elections to various assemblies, and both scored marked success. In the National Assembly elections of June 1946, Abbas's UDMA won three quarters

of the vote in the second, or Moslem, college, and elected eleven of thirteen deputies. Messali's MTLD, participating in a poll for the first time, won a third of the votes and elected five deputies in the general elections of November 1946. In municipal elections of October 1947, the MTLD won 31 per cent of the poll; the UDMA 28 per cent. But the passage of the disappointing Algerian Statute at the end of 1947, and the initiation of systematic election rigging under Naegelen in April 1948 precipitated within Messali's movement a new drive for direct action.

In May 1948, the MTLD set up an underground agency—the Organisation Spéciale, or O.S. A secret group spread across Algeria, the O.S. had the function of extending and deepening the Messalist organization while at the same time striking blows of terror and sabotage against French rule. Its members, obscure men at the time, included some of the most daring and tough of Messali's organizers, veterans, all, of the PPA and the MTLD and, in many cases, of the French army. The nominal coordinator of the operations was Mohammed Khider, a self-educated transport worker from Algiers who had been elected to the French Assembly in 1946 and thus enjoyed parliamentary immunity. Among the most important members were Ahmed ben Bella, a decorated sergeant from the French army, in the Oran district; Hocine Ait-Ahmed, Belkacem Krim, Amar Oumrane, and Rabah Bitat in the Kabylia; and, in the Constantine district, Mohammed Boudiaf, Mustafa ben Boulaid, Larbi ben M'hidi, Lakhdar ben Tobbal, Yussef Zirout, and Abdelhafid Boussouf. Working underground, they picked up where the PPA left off after the abortive rising of Sétif. Most of their work was organizational—building cells and sections in the back country and in Moslem quarters of the big city; storing caches of arms; settling scores with Moslems loyal to the French: a caid here, a forest guard there. Interspersed were some spectacular acts of violence. Early in 1949, an assassination attempt was made on Governor General Naegelen at Mostaganem. In April, Ben Bella staged a daring holdup of the main post office at Oran and made off with nearly $10,000. But in March 1950, two O.S. commandos were apprehended when a third Moslem whom they were trying to kidnap overcame chloroform and gave the alarm. Investigation led all the way up the ladder. Ben Bella, Ben Boulaid, and Zirout were arrested. Virtually every other O.S member went into hiding. Ait-Ahmed and Khider fled to Cairo. Boudiaf hid in Paris. Though Ben Bella was later to escape to Cairo, and Ben Boulaid and Zirout to the hill country in Algeria, the O.S. was shattered.

Its death opened in the ranks of the parent MTLD a crisis from which it never recovered. Drawing the lesson from the second failure in five years, the party's Central Committee, sitting in Algiers, decided to abandon direct action for cautious reform in tandem with Ferhat Abbas and the Ulemas. In August 1951, they struck a new alliance in the Algerian Front for the Defense and Respect of Liberty. Hocine Lahouel, secretary general of the party, became a municipal councilor in Algiers. So did the party comptroller, Abderrahmane Kiouane. "The MTLD considers," the Central Committee wrote in one of its publications, "that the struggle for immediate advances is not incompatible with the struggle for liberation."

To this reform doctrine Messali himself was bitterly opposed. A trip to Mecca in 1951 had exposed him anew to the hot breath of Middle Eastern nationalism. In Paris, in January 1952, he had been in touch with Tunisians and Moroccan nationalists embarking on the drive that was to win their countries' independence in the next four years. Back in Algeria in April, he began, over the protests of the Central Committee, a barnstorming tour across Algeria. Frenzied crowds turned out to meet him at Souk-Ahras and Philippeville and Blida and Orléansville, and almost everywhere there were demonstrations and clashes with police. Then on May 14, as the Central Committee had feared, Messali was arrested and deported to France.

From that point forward tension between Messali and the Central Committee waxed steadily. Messali accused the Centralists of "turning the party into the rut of reform," and gathered around him a group of faithful followers, including Moulay Merbah and most of the organization inside France. The Central Committee, forming ranks around Lahouel, rang the chimes on the theme of one-man rule, claiming that Messali, in custody for so much of his life, was out of touch with events. "El Zaim," one broadside said, "is outmoded." The fight came to a head in the summer of 1954. On July 15, at a congress of the MTLD in Hornu, Belgium, followers of Messali voted El Zaim full powers over the party and excluded the Centralists. In riposte at a congress in Algiers, held August 13–16, the Centralists voted to strip Messali of all authority and to vest full powers in the Central Committee. At the top, in other words, the party had split asunder.

There remained the basic organization. Stirred by Messali's speeches, open to winds of change blowing from Cairo, emboldened by French defeat in Indochina, and stimulated even more by the pace of nationalist progress across the borders in Morocco and Tunisia, the militants inside Algeria were as never before restless for action. "Everywhere," one of the nationalist leaders later recalled, "there was popular pressure to raise the standard of revolt." And if the top leadership was too preoccupied with internal bickering to raise the standard, there existed a resolute corps of intermediary leadership. Discovery had broken up the O.S. in 1950, but most of its former members had survived. Ahmed ben Bella had escaped from prison in 1952 and reached Cairo along with Hocine Ait-Ahmed and Mohammed Khider; by 1953 they were in touch with Colonel Nasser's Revolutionary Committee. Belkacem Krim and Amar Oumrane were at large, already undertaking guerrilla action in the Kabylia. Larbi ben M'hidi and his lieutenant, Abdelhafid

Boussouf, had transferred their activities from Constantine to western Algeria, where they were helping Moroccan nationalists. In eastern Algeria, Mustafa ben Boulaid had dug in in the wild Aurès Mountains, while Mourad Diddouche, Yussef Zirout, and Lakhdar ben Tobbal had gone underground in the fastness of the Collo Peninsula just west of Philippeville. One member of the O.S., perhaps the most remarkable of them all, had escaped to France. He was Mohammed Boudiaf, born in 1919 in M'Sila, south of Constantine. Though a chronic victim of tuberculosis, he received a good education at the College of Bou-Saâda, then absorbed administrative experience as an adjutant in the French army and a clerk in the French administration. A leading O.S. member in the Constantine district, he hid out in Algiers from 1950 to 1953, then moved to Paris where he became head of the MTLD's French Federation. In 1953, Boudiaf tried, and failed, in an effort to make peace between Messali and the Central Committee. Disgusted with both camps, he began, early in 1954, to weave together a plan for separate action by O.S. members.

In March he established contact with the delegation in Cairo: Ben Bella, Ait-Ahmed, Khider. On the tenth of the month, he inaugurated in Algiers a group of meetings with regional leaders from all parts of the territory. Initially his aim was to "preserve the unity of the party." But as the split between Messalists and Centralists deepened, Boudiaf set foot again on the road to direct action. In July, after further meetings in Berne and Algiers, there was formed a nine-man club, the Revolutionary Committee for Unity and Action (CRUA). It included Boudiaf, Ben Bella, Khider, and Ait-Ahmed from outside Algeria. On the inside were regional leaders: Mustafa ben Boulaid for the Aurès; Mourad Diddouche for Constantine; Rabah Bitat for Algiers; Larbi ben M'hidi for Oran; Belkacem Krim for the Kabylia. In August and September last-minute attempts to bring unity between Messali and the Centralists were tried and collapsed. On October 10, at a final meeting in Algiers, Boudiaf and the five regional commanders fixed their rendezvous with destiny. D-Day was to be November 1, 1954; H-Hour was 1 A.M.

That night armed bands struck in fifty different actions all across Algeria. Biskra was rocked by bomb explosions. In Batna the French army barracks was attacked and two sentries killed. Two bombs exploded in downtown Algiers. Arris was besieged. At Boufarik the European-owned agricultural cooperative was destroyed. In the Tighanimine Gorge armed bands stopped a bus, hauled out a caid and two Europeans, and shot them on the spot. In the Kabylia two policemen were killed and a storage depot was burned to the ground. Near Oran two settler farms were burned, a motorist killed, a power plant attacked. From Cairo, the *Voice of the Arabs* announced establishment of a Front of National Liberation (FLN): "Today . . . at one o'clock in the morning, a powerful elite of the free children of Algeria started the insurrection of Algerian freedom against French imperialism in North Africa."

The war was on.

IV

FEW enterprises can have seemed more hopeless at the outset. To be sure, on the political front the rebels, though divided at the top, could count on some popular support for their objectives, and a small, disciplined organization. But as a military force the Army of National Liberation (ALN) was contemptible. When operations began it numbered about 300 men, armed with rifles and a few bombs. It lacked arms and ammunition, trained personnel, safe bases, uniforms, and regular systems of command, communications, and logistics. To acquire these was a first order of business.

Tactics varied almost from village to village, but from the outset there was apparent an over-all strategy. French observers have likened it to the Communist guerrilla strategy laid down by Mao Tse-tung, and it is true that like the Communists the Algerian rebels were more interested in winning masses of men than masses of land. It is also true that occasionally rebel leaders cited Mao's words: notably, that an army should be to the people as a fish to water. But in fact the ALN strategy had a far more respectable pedigree. The rebels borrowed it not from the Communists, whom they barely knew, but from a revered French military hero known all too well. In essence what the rebels did was to apply what Marshal Lyautey, years before, called the *tache de l'huile*—the grease-spot strategy.

Only in reverse. Lyautey, battling anarchy, massed forces in a settled area and then spread in widening circles a French peace. The rebels, at odds with that peace, started with one or two zealots from remote points outside the French system. Here they dug in with the local population from which they drew recruits, food, hiding places, and sentries. Impregnated in depth, these first grease spots then became the center for widening circles of rebel penetration. Eventually the rebels reached settled areas where they came to grips with French security forces. By deliberately creating disorder—by assassinations, bombings, strikes, boycotts, economic sabotage, and direct assaults on security forces—the organized bands of rebels moved to disrupt the French peace. In many cases the bands were able to break French influence and themselves fill the void. In many others French repression cast moderate Moslems into the arms of the rebels. In any event, by the end of 1956 the rebels had achieved striking success. With only slight exaggeration one of the principal rebel leaders, Ramdane Abane, wrote at that time, "The small groups of the Army of National Liberation, badly armed and isolated from each other, have not only held in check the formidable forces of French colonialism, but have spread the grease spot to . . . the whole national territory."

The grease-spot strategy was inaugurated in the wild Aurès-

Nementcha mountain range, home of the Chouia Berbers in the southwest corner of the Algerian Tell. For years prior to the active fighting, Mustafa ben Boulaid, a PPA militant, O.S. and CRUA member who owned a mill in Lambèse and a coffeehouse in Batna, had been organizing the region. In August 1954, after direct talks with Ben Bella and Boudiaf, he began converting from a political to a military basis. By November 1, he had mustered 150 men, divided them into five commando units, equipped them with rifles, cartridges, and second-hand uniforms. They constituted the main ALN striking force on the Algerian D-Day. During the next month, Ben Boulaid pulled back his forces, bivouacking them in a group of tiny villages on the western slopes of the main peak in the Aurès, Chelia. In December he moved south, made contact with two nomadic bandit groups on the fringes of the Sahara, and organized a southern supply line: from Egypt through Libya south of Tunisia, then up through a string of Saharan oases to the Aurès. In February 1955, Ben Boulaid was captured by the French while on a mission in Tunisia. His place was immediately taken by his deputy, Bahir Chihani. By March, Chihani had established a rebel stronghold of some 2,000 square miles in the heart of the Aurès. A special headquarters staff had been set up, and there was a primitive liaison system and a special supply group. Five different units sat astride the approaches to the mountain stronghold. By April, these were making their presence known. On April 13, one of the bands ambushed a convoy of three military trucks, seizing seventeen rifles and a machine gun. Three days later another band intercepted a military jeep, and after burning the vehicle slaughtered its two occupants, a French army major and a chaplain. On April 24, still a third band stopped a convoy of two trucks and a jeep, killing four French soldiers and the local French administrator, and winning to their own ranks thirty Moslems in the French army. Next month the imposition of a boycott on cigarettes signalized rebel penetration of the two big towns in the Aurès: Khenchela and Batna. And with summer the rebel bands began fanning out to all sides: east to Tébessa on the Tunisian frontier, thence north to Souk-Ahras and the pass leading into Tunisia; northwest toward Sétif; south toward Biskra and Touggourt; due north to the fringes of Constantine; due west to the Hodna Mountains leading into the Kabylia range. Villaya I, the Villaya of the Aurès, was in place.

Villaya II, north of the Aurès and stretching from Constantine to the sea, followed a similar path at a slightly slower pace. Its base was a small strip anchored in the wild and trackless hill country of the Collo Peninsula, and running inland into the triangle formed by the cities of El Milia, Philippeville, and Constantine. Only slight disturbances marked the area in the first months of the rebellion. By January 1955, some 500 guerrilla soldiers had been raised, and they were pushing out toward the towns. A first engagement with French forces on January 18 cost the rebels dear; though they killed one policeman and wounded another, they lost to French counterattack six of their own men, including the villaya chief, Mourad Diddouche. Into his place there stepped Yussef Zirout, a blacksmith from the town of Condé-Smendou, formerly a member of the O.S., who had been hiding in the Collo region since 1951. By spring Zirout's bands were once again showing their teeth. On May 1, a band of sixty stole from a forestry station at Jemmapes a score of rifles and over 800 rounds of ammunition. Next day at El Milia two policemen were wounded by gunfire. Six days later at Collo a forest guard was murdered. On May 10, the town of El Milia was cut off when rebel bands chopped off all telephone poles and blocked road approaches by felling trees. Two policemen trying to reach the town were killed next day. Not long thereafter, a crowd of Moslem villagers, pushed on by one of Zirout's bands, assaulted with stones and rotten fruit a paratroop command post at El Arrouch. Then, in August, Zirout brought off the most spectacular armed coup achieved by the rebels in the whole course of the war. Timed to coincide with Moroccan strikes on the August 20 anniversary of the ouster of Sultan Mohammed ben Youssef, it took the form of an organized burst of violence at many different places across a wide area. Altogether over thirty different points were struck. At Constantine in the south, bombs were exploded in a police station, a barracks, and a movie house, while political personalities working with the French, one of them a nephew of Ferhat Abbas, were assassinated. At Oued-Zénati crowds of screaming Moslem women, pushed on by the rebels, stormed the city hall. At Ain-Abid, St. Charles, and El Arrouch European pedestrians were shot in the street. At the zinc mines of El-Hallia, outside Philippeville on the coast, the European community was massacred. In all 123 persons, including seventy-one Europeans, were killed. French troops, counterattacking immediately, chased the bands back into the fastness of the Collo Peninsula. But from there they continued intermittent sallies, and there was no bridging the harsh gulf opened between Moslems and Europeans. From that day forward, Villaya II was in business.

What Collo was to Villaya II, the plunging Kabylia range was to Villaya III. As early as 1950 two Kabyle veterans of the French army and Messali's PPA—Belkacem Krim, a former corporal, and Amar Oumrane, a former sergeant—had assembled a band of nationalist marauders. Tireless organizers, they had ever since been laying the groundwork for guerrilla activities. "There was no village, no hamlet, no cell," Krim was to write later of his early organizing, "that I did not visit." For months after the formal outbreak of war on November 1, 1954, Krim and Oumrane continued their work behind the scenes. At the beginning of 1955, they emerged in force. As usual there were political assassinations. Twenty-one different murders in the town of Tazmalt, for instance, wiped out all local Moslems holding office in the French administration. In another commune the rebels killed in one year four caids, five native policemen, and six municipal administrators. There followed assault by ambush on the main lines of communication. In one day in February 1956, three buses and a truck were intercepted and destroyed along a single stretch of road. Not long thereafter, the regular transportation companies suspended service in Kabylia. Added to that was an unusual complement of daring military operations. Oumrane launched direct attacks on French military groupings near Tizi-Ouzou, Palestro, and Bou Zegza. In Operation Bluebird, three rebels under orders from Krim volunteered in the fall of 1955 to organize a Kabyle opposition to the ALN. For a full year they maintained the deception, outfitting and equipping at French expense twenty-three different bands. In September 1956, the whole lot deserted back to Krim. With them they brought over 200 new weapons, including twenty-three machine guns. By that time *Le Monde*, while still considering the Aurès to be the principal theater of operations, had long since come to speak of Kabylia as "the second front."

Third front might have been more appropriate, for from Kabylia, Krim's operations reached out to hit Villaya IV, Algiers itself. Rebel operations there had been off to a slow start. While Ben Boulaid in the Aurès had been able to raise a following in the name of Messali Hadj, in the big city the divisions among Messalists, Centralists, and CRUA survived the outbreak of hostilities, making organization difficult where it did not lead to open factional fights. Moreover, the Algiers police, serviced by an army of Moslem informers, seized a goodly number of the leading nationalists in the opening months of the rebellion. One of their catches, in March 1955, was Rabah Bitat, first chief of Villaya IV. By June of that year, however, Krim's bands had penetrated to the outskirts of the city, and he himself established a *pied à ville* in a bakery in the Casbah. There he was joined by two remarkable political personalities, Ramdane Abane and Benyussuf Benkhedda, both newly released from prison. Abane, a Kabyle born in 1919, a graduate of the *lycée* at Sétif, and formerly an official in the French administration, became Krim's political adjutant. Benkhedda—an Arab born in 1920, a graduate of the college at Blida, and a talented editor and leading Centralist figure—was made head of the Zone of Algiers, in effect Villaya IV.

Using the Casbah as a redoubt—much as the Aurès, Collo, and Kabyle massifs had been used elsewhere—Abane and Benkhedda built an extraordinary political underground. Hierarchically organized, it reached from the top down to virtually every Moslem home and store in Algiers. Special groups were charged with fund raising, supply, intelligence, communications, and direct action. The net included clandestine presses, a laboratory for making bombs, a trade union, a corps of women volunteers. By far its most spectacular action was a campaign to spread terror by leaving time bombs in public places. No accurate count is possible, but between the fall of 1956 and the summer of 1957 several hundred bombs must have been detonated in Algiers alone. Among the most notorious incidents were the blasts of September 30, 1956, and June 9, 1957. The first hit the Milk Bar, a popular café in downtown Algiers, severely wounding thirty Europeans. The second destroyed a popular dancing spot outside Algiers, the Casino de la Corniche, killing eleven Europeans and wounding scores, many of them teen-agers. Much more important, however, was the political work of the Algiers underground. By mid-1955, Abane and Benkhedda had eliminated or enlisted in their own cause most of Messali's following in Algiers. They then brought pressure to bear on moderate Moslems in the various legislative bodies of Algeria and France—among them Ferhat Abbas. At their urging, the moderates in September 1955 formed themselves into a group—"the 61"—and condemned French policy for "blind repression" of the rebellion. In December, "the 61" voted a boycott of the Algerian Assembly, in effect wrecking that body. Thereafter the Algiers underground began piloting some of the more prominent—including Abbas—to the FLN delegation in Cairo. With the moderates in camp, Benkhedda took in tow the mainly European, Algerian Communist party. In April, two Algerian Communists serving in the French forces deserted to the ALN, one of them, officer candidate Henri Maillot, bringing with him a truckload of 135 machine guns. Thereafter both men were cut adrift and left to die at the hands of French troops. And in March 1956, Benkhedda formed, over the vigorous protests of the Communist-dominated union, the CGT, an Algerian trade union, the UGTA. In July, the UGTA was admitted to the anti-Communist International Confederation of Trade Unions, and though officially barred, it held the support of a large segment of the Moslem workers in Algiers. In January 1957, it was the backbone of a week-long general strike, timed to coincide with a United Nations debate on Algeria. On the first day of the strike, January 28, 1957, almost all Moslem shops were closed, there was a complete walkout of the rail and dock workers, and 71 per cent of the postal and telegraph workers failed to show up. "Algiers," a Tunisian correspondent reported, "was a dead city." Though the paratroopers of General Jacques Massu broke the strike, and in the course of 1957 dismantled much of the underground network, Algiers remained thereafter a center of flickering, but inextinguishable, resistance.

Among those captured when the paratroopers moved in to break the Algiers strike was Larbi ben M'hidi, chief of Villaya V, embracing most of western Algeria. A veteran organizer and O.S. member from eastern Algeria, Ben M'hidi and a young lieutenant, Abdelhafid Boussouf, had been in hiding around Oran from 1950 through 1954. That year, they established an organizational base in Nador, on the Mediterranean in what was then Spanish Morocco. For the first year after the opening of the fight in Algeria, Nador served as headquarters for the Moroccan Army of Liberation. When Morocco won independence in November 1955, Ben M'hidi and Boussouf transferred their base to Oujda, just inside the Moroccan frontier and athwart the main rail and road lines into Algeria. In December

1955, Ben M'hidi went on mission to Cairo, leaving the villaya in Boussouf's charge. On his way back through the Constantine area, Kabylia and Algiers, he was picked up by the paratroopers and eventually killed. But in Boussouf's hands, penetration moved on apace. In January 1956, there took place the first of many derailments on the line running along the frontier south from Oran to the mines at Sidi-bel-Abbès. On February 9, a mutinous Moslem corporal in the French army collaborated with one of Boussouf's bands in an attack on a railroad guard post west of Tlemcen in which six French soldiers were wounded. A week later a group of rebels dressed as French soldiers marched into the center of Tlemcen, opened fire on a noncom barracks, and escaped without harm. On February 20, fifty-five Moslem soldiers in a French company deserted in the thick of a running battle with one of Boussouf's bands. In the ensuing slaughter, eleven French soldiers including a lieutenant were killed; twenty wounded. The rebels made off with over a hundred rifles and eight machine guns. Villaya V, in the western extremity, had come alive. The isolated and ill-armed bands, as Abane boasted, had spread the grease spot all across Algeria.

V

THE symbol of that spread was a congress of the major rebel leaders held under the noses of French forces in Algeria. Originally called for July 31, 1956, the meeting was postponed when French forces got wind of it. It was convened eventually on August 20 in an abandoned forestry station in the Soummam Valley. By force of circumstance two important groups were not represented. A delegation from the exterior under Ben Bella was held up in Italy when the original congress was canceled and never did make Soummam. The Aurès villaya, then beginning to fall apart, sent only a secondary figure, Omar ben Boulaid, the brother of Mustafa. But at least 200 persons did make the meeting. Among the leaders were Yussef Zirout and his deputy, Lakhdar ben Tobbal, from Villaya II; Krim and his deputy Ramdane Abane, from Villaya III; Amar Oumrane and Benyussuf Benkhedda from Villaya IV; and Larbi ben M'hidi from Villaya V. The proceedings of the Soummam Congress, made public on November 1, 1956, the third anniversary of the war, announced sweeping decisions in the military and political fields.

In the military field, Soummam marked the formal designation of the Army of National Liberation (ALN) as a regular armed force, in the field for the long pull. The congress declared that the rebel army "extended over the whole national territory" and was "a living reality." As a primary military objective the congress fixed, not victory, but "the weakening of the French army, to make it impossible for it to achieve armed victory." "Our guide," Belkacem Krim, the most important of the rebel military men put it, "is survival. If the French mass, we disperse. If they guard the cities, we ambush the mountain roads. If they chase us in the mountains, we hole up in the city. We don't want to waste our forces."

To that end, the ragged guerrilla bands were engrossed in a system of regular command. The congress established a hierarchy of operational theaters (villayas, zones, regions, sectors); of units (group: 11 men; section: 35 men; company: 110 men; battalion: 350 men); and of grades (ranging from corporal to colonel, but no higher). Over this apparatus there was placed a five-man general staff: the Committee for Coordination and Execution (C.C.E.). The members named at Soummam were: Ramdane Abane, Belkacem Krim, Yussef Zirout, Benyussuf Benkhedda, Larbi ben M'hidi. With the new command structure went a new strategy. Having come alive, the rebel army was determined to stay alive. Its aim, pure and simple, was to keep the war going.

The political implications of Soummam overshadowed by far

its military consequences. Underlying the principle of the fight for survival was the expectation of eventual political settlement. "Our war aims," the Soummam declaration put it, "are simply to achieve the end of the war . . . a cease-fire or an armistice with a view to negotiation." But if France would obviously be party to the negotiation on one side, she required what came to be known as an *interlocuteur valable*—a valid spokesman—on the other. For that role the FLN at the outset had only the poorest claims. Apart from those concerned primarily with military operations on the inside, its leadership on the outside numbered only four people: Ben Bella, Khider, Ait-Ahmed, and Boudiaf. They were at odds with every reputable element in the nationalist tradition—with Messali, with the Centralists, with Ferhat Abbas's UDMA, with the Ulemas. Their status, in short, was zero.

Not for long. At the beginning the FLN adopted an open-house policy. Provided other organizational ties were severed, all Algerian nationalists could join the Front as individuals. Negotiations for Messali's support lasted from November 1954 through January 1955, breaking down when Messali instead of joining the Front established a rival group—the Algerian National Movement (MNA). Still, Messali's chief foe, the Centralist leader Hocine Lahouel, reached Cairo in November 1954 and joined the FLN within the month. Lahouel was ailing, and many of his followers, marked men in Algeria, were immediately picked up by the French police. But it was not long before the bulk of Centralist leadership had rallied to the FLN. M'hammed Yazid, a former student leader in France, came over with Lahouel. In March, Mohammed Lamine-Debaghine, former secretary general of the PPA, came to Cairo; in April, Abderrahmane Kiouane, former Algiers municipal councilor, and Ahmed Mehri, an organizer from Constantine with a wide knowledge of Arab affairs, showed up. In May, Benyussuf Benkhedda, released from prison, joined the Algiers underground headed by Belkacem Krim and Ramdane Abane.

Pressure from Benkhedda and Abane landed the big fish. On April 6, 1956, a leader of the Ulemas, Tewfik el Madani, arrived in Cairo. Next day Ferhat Abbas left Algeria en route for France. On April 20, he was in Cairo; and five days later, at a press conference held in the presence of Ben Bella and Khider, he announced his support for the Front. With Abbas in camp, the Front commanded the loyalties of every well-known Moslem politician save Messali Hadj. Abderrahmane Farès, a former president of the Algerian Assembly, was only underscoring the obvious when he asserted, in September 1956, that: "The only valid *interlocuteur* at the present time is the FLN, which has been able to muster behind it the Algerian people, almost to a man."

Having achieved status, there remained work. Procuring arms was by far the most pressing need, and Ben Bella, a former noncom in the French army who enjoyed good relations with the Nasser regime, inevitably took in charge that matter—thereby rapidly becoming the most prestigious of the rebel leaders. Boudiaf, the principal organizer of the November 1 strike, went to Spain to handle supplies going in through Morocco, as well as relations with FLN supporters in France. In addition there was the matter of relations with foreign states. In Cairo an ad hoc political committee was set up under Mohammed Khider and Lamine-Debaghine to coordinate missions to the outside world. Ahmed Mehri, the best, if not the only, Arabist in the lot, went to Damascus. Hocine Ait-Ahmed and M'hammed Yazid toured Asia, dropping in at the Bandung conference, then establishing a mission to the United Nations in New York. Still on probation, Ferhat Abbas, and his brother-in-law and fellow UDMA leader, Ahmed Francis, were assigned to drum up support in Latin America.

The existence of internal and external organizations inevitably bred tensions, and by the time of the Soummam Congress a major rift had opened. One practical matter at issue was the arms supply—always a chronic problem and aggravated especially through 1956 by the troubles in the main highway to the interior, Villaya I. A connected issue was Ben Bella himself. As the principal controller of the arms flow, he had acquired both power and prestige. Legends of his prowess and ubiquity circulated through Algeria. Apart from that of Abbas, his name was the only one widely known among the rebel troops. In Cairo, he allowed himself to be called "General ben Bella." The leaders of the interior, still bitterly mindful of Messali's domination and with grievances over arms shortages to boot, came to look on Ben Bella's rising star with deep misgivings. The more so as underlying both the arms and the Ben Bella problems was a third question—the question of legitimacy. A child of rebellion, living in a climate of revolution, and void of statutes, organs, and tradition, the FLN had no accepted means for reaching decisions and imposing authority.

Arms, the man, and legitimacy were the three problems comprising the agenda at the Soummam Congress. On the first, Soummam proclaimed that in the allocation of resources there should be "priority for the internal over the external" needs: it named the head of Villaya II, Yussef Zirout, to take in charge his troublesome neighbor, Villaya I. As to Ben Bella, the congress stipulated that "the rank of general will not come into use until after the liberation." It also endorsed "the elimination of personal power and the acceptance of the principle of collective leadership." And by its answer to the legitimacy question it put a further check on one-man authority. In its most important act, the congress created a National Council of the Algerian Revolution (CNRA) composed of seventeen full, or voting, members, and seventeen associates. The Council represented all strains of FLN membership. It included the nine members of the original CRUA (among them Ben Bella and Krim); three men who had subsequently risen inside Algeria (Zirout, Abane, and Oumrane); and lastly, the politicos, Abbas for the UDMA; and Benkhedda and Yazid for the Centralists. The CNRA was endowed with plenary powers as "the highest organ of the revolution." Ascendancy over the military —and specifically over the C.C.E., or war council created at Soummam—was assured by a provision that there should be "priority for the political over the military organization." Lastly, the Council was shaped as an agency for making decisions on the international front, especially as regards negotiations with France. In the report of the Soummam proceedings, it was described as "the sole body authorized in the last resort to take decisions relative to the country's future." "Only the CNRA," the report said, "is capable of ordering a cease-fire."

Whether Soummam could have settled the struggle between interior and exterior is doubtful. The Congress itself was obviously dominated by the interior—and notably by Krim's political adviser, Ramdane Abane. Ben Bella, absent from the meeting, harbored important reservations on its decisions. But before the issue was ever forced, events achieved what the conference could not. On October 22, 1956, the four CRUA members on the exterior (Ben Bella, Boudiaf, Khider, and Ait-Ahmed) were captured by the French as they flew from Morocco to Tunisia. Simultaneously a wave of troubles hit leaders on the inside. Yussef Zirout was killed on his way home from Soummam; though Zirout's deputy, Lakhdar ben Tobbal, took over in Villaya II, he was not able to take in hand the arms traffic through Villaya I. In January 1957, Larbi ben M'hidi was arrested in Algiers. His capture, amid circumstances suggesting betrayal, raised an immediate threat for all other members of the C.C.E. By February 1957, the military leaders were streaming into Tunis. The interior had fused with the exterior.

Urgent questions of military leadership were settled very quickly. Belkacem Krim, loaded with prestige from his successful leadership of Villaya III and the only member of the CRUA not dead or in prison, took Ben Bella's post as supreme military man. One of his deputies, Amar Oumrane, assumed responsibility for supply. In March 1957, he reached accord with President Bourguiba of Tunisia on a plan establishing Tunisia as main rebel staging ground for operations in Algeria. In exchange for FLN agreement to keep hands off Tunisian affairs, the rebels were granted a large reservation on the Algerian frontier which they eventually converted into a base for 20,000 troops. Before the summer was out, the affairs of Villaya I, across the border from the Tunisian base, were also straightened out. The feuding chiefs of rival bands were liquidated, and, with Krim's blessing, control over Villaya I passed into the hands of Mahmoud Cherif, a former regular officer in the French army and follower of Ferhat Abbas's UDMA, who had joined the rebels in 1955.

For political supremacy, however, there was a long period of jostling within the FLN. The surface issue was the so-called *préalable*, or guarantee: whether or not as a condition for truce negotiations with France there should be an advance guarantee of Algerian independence. Beneath the surface was a bitter personal struggle. Ferhat Abbas opposed the *préalable*, confident that once serious negotiations were joined, independence was bound to emerge. He had the backing of the FLN diplomats in the field, notably Yazid at the U.N. and Ahmed Mehri, responsible for dealings with the Arab countries. President Bourguiba, an old friend, and fearful besides that fighting might spread to Tunisia, was equally an Abbas supporter. So were Ben Bella and the other leaders captured by the French in October 1956. The main force against the *préalable*, was Belkacem Krim's chief political adviser, Ramdane Abane. Too little known to take political leadership himself, he put up in the struggle against Abbas, Mohammed Lamine-Debaghine, former secretary general of the PPA. Behind Lamine-Debaghine, he lined up Krim, Oumrane, and most of the military.

For most of 1957, Abane and Lamine held the whip hand. Lamine was named head of the external delegation, the chief political post. In March 1957, at a much publicized press conference in Tunis, he took the chair and did most of the talking, though Abbas was also present. Among other things, Lamine said:

> The Algerian nation cannot be satisfied with a solution which does not imply in advance [*au préalable*] the recognition of Algerian independence.

In July in a signed article on the front page of the FLN weekly paper, Abane insisted that "good sense and wisdom do not lie in searching for a . . . compromise with the oppressor; they demand resolute struggle up until the liberation of the country and its independence." In October, a formal FLN statement declared that "there can be no negotiation without advance recognition of Algerian independence." Still, Lamine, Abane, and the hard line at no time won complete victory. On the contrary, their failure to achieve domination marked the major FLN meeting of 1957—the first session of the CNRA, held in Cairo at the end of August.

The chief business of the meeting was to adjust FLN structure to the change in circumstance that had supervened since Soummam. Thus, in keeping with the merger of interior and exterior, the Council abolished previous distinctions between the two: "all those who participate in the liberating struggle, with or without uniform, are equal." For the same reason, the five-man general staff set up at Soummam was translated into a general fourteen-man (the Committee for Coordination and Execution, or C.C.E.) executive with the broadest responsibilities. The assumption of such broad responsibilities by the C.C.E. trenched inevitably on the original concept of the CNRA. As a mark of slight decline, the Council was expanded from thirty-four to fifty-four members, all of them with voting rights.

While practical considerations dictated most of these decisions, the effect on the struggle for power was clearly evident. That the meeting was held in Cairo was a leg up for Lamine, who was based there. He was confirmed during the meeting as head of the external delegation. His influence was further reflected in the composition of the new fourteen-man C.C.E. It included, besides himself, five supporters: Abane, Belkacem Krim, Amar Oumrane, Abdelhafid Boussouf, and Lakhdar ben Tobbal. On the other hand, Abbas was a member of the C.C.E., along with Ahmed Mehri and Mahmoud Cherif; the five leaders held prisoner by the French who were ranged with Abbas in the struggle were included in the C.C.E. as ex-officio members. Moreover, on one vote, Lamine's main supporter, Abane, was put in the minority. Thus, while Lamine still was top dog, the Cairo meeting, far from cementing his power, only confirmed an uneasy compromise.

Early in 1958, the balance shifted decisively away from Lamine and the advance guarantee toward Abbas. The new element in the picture was President Habib Bourguiba of Tunisia. Since Bourguiba's arms agreement with Oumrane in March 1957, the Tunisian border had played an increasingly large role in the Algerian fighting. The French had fortified their side of the frontier heavily, and proclaimed the right of hot pursuit against rebel soldiers taking refuge on the Tunisian side of the line. A series of minor incidents led up, on February 8, 1958, to a French bombing raid against the Tunisian border town of Sakiet-Sidi-Youssef. The Sakiet incident raised for Bourguiba a real threat that the war might spread to Tunisian territory. He redoubled efforts to have the rebels moderate terms for an agreement with France; the rebel leadership asked, in return, further support from Tunis, notably recognition of a rebel government if one were established. Some time in March, a deal was struck. Persuaded and cajoled by Bourguiba, Belkacem Krim—and with him the military—threw support from Lamine and Abane to the Abbas faction. Early in April, Abane was killed in mysterious circumstances (his death was not announced until the end of May when it was laid at the door of the French). At the end of April, the deal was formalized at a four-day conference in Tangier, bringing together FLN representatives with political leaders from Morocco and Tunisia. In a communiqué issued at the conclusion of the Tangier conference, the Algerians modified slightly their demand that independence be a precondition for negotiations with France. Instead they set as "the only condition" recognition of the "*right* of the Algerian people to sovereignty and independence" (my italics). The *préalable* was on its way to being buried. In return for that concession, Tunisia and Morocco sanctioned the future establishment of an Algerian government. The communiqué said:

> The conference recommends (after consultation with the Tunisian and Moroccan governments) the creation of an Algerian government.

When the new regime—the Provisional Government of the Algerian Republic, or GPRA—was finally formed on September 19, the full extent of the switch in policy became apparent. Leadership was in the hands of a coalition linking Krim and the armed forces with Abbas and his group. Abbas was at the helm as Premier. Krim was Vice Premier and Minister of Armed Forces. Ben Bella, an Abbas backer, although in prison was also a Vice Premier, while the other imprisoned leaders were Ministers of State. Two key ministerial posts went to Krim lieutenants: Lakhdar ben Tobbal, former head of Villaya II, was Minister of Interior; Abdelhafid Boussouf, former head of Villaya V, was Minister of Communications and Liaison. Sympathizers with Abbas took four posts: Mahmoud Cherif was Minister of Arms and Supply; Ahmed Francis was Minister of Finance; Abdelhamid Mehri was Minister of North African Affairs; M'hammed Yazid was Minister of Information. All that remained of the Abane group were three isolated ministers: Lamine-Debaghine as Foreign Minister; Benyussuf Benkhedda as Minister of Social Affairs; Tewfik el Madani as Minister of Cultural Affairs. The moderate wing had won a smashing victory.

With the establishment of the GPRA, a firm rebel strategy emerged for the first time. The Provisional Government was to act as trustee for the Algerian people in the struggle for independence from France. Against Paris it would wield military and diplomatic weapons. But the overriding aim was to force negotiations, and the essential character of the rebel government was that of a negotiating instrument. "The Provisional Government of the Algerian Republic," Abbas said in his first declaration as Premier, "is ready to begin negotiations. It is ready at any time to meet with the representatives of the French government." To that overriding goal the GPRA at all times adjusted military tactics, diplomatic action, and its own structure and composition.

Militarily the need was to maintain trouble to the point where neither France nor the world could forget Algeria. That required a fairly brisk pace of terrorist activity, and thus the rebels maintained an effective underground in all the main Algerian towns. Through 1958, 1959, 1960, and the early months of 1961, more or less spectacular acts of sabotage and assassination continued without cease. Because they were at once easy to reach and challenged the rebel claim to be representative, Moslems working with the French were the principal victims. At no time did the rate of killing fall below ten a day. But in such a pin-prick campaign, the main rebel force, the Army of National Liberation, was of little use. As French army action increased, and as border crossing became more and more difficult, a major change in ALN function took place. In a few remote areas—the Aurès range, the Collo Peninsula, the Kabyle ranges, the Ouarsenis—ALN units dug in, tying up large numbers of French troops. But for the most part, the rebel force was withdrawn beyond French lines on the Tunisian and Moroccan frontiers. Between these lines and the frontiers, large ALN bases were established. From these bases, rebel forces sallied out occasionally, convoying arms, or recruits for the underground, into Algeria. Generally, however, the ALN stuck to its bases—a reserve army, giving continual earnest of rebel capacity to keep up the fight indefinitely. "We're ready," Defense Minister Krim put it in 1958, "for a ten-year war."

On the diplomatic front, the GPRA pursued the same tactic of waging pin-prick war while storing up reserves of strength. The U.N. General Assembly was a principal theater of operations, for the rebels calculated—and not wrongly—that the threat of international intervention would push Paris to negotiate, or at least push Washington to push Paris. The task of rebel diplomacy was to maximize the threat, and to that end the GPRA came year after year to the General Assembly, each time backing increasingly stringent resolutions. Thus in 1958 it proposed "negotiations between the parties concerned with a view to reaching a solution" (of the Algerian war); in 1959 it asked for recognition of Algeria's right to independence; in 1960 it called for U.N. supervision of a referendum in which Algeria would choose between independence and some other status. That none of these proposals passed was of little moment to the rebels. Indeed passage of a resolution—which would have opened a dubious test between the world organization and the Paris government—was no part of their purpose; what they wanted was to keep up the threat of passage. Still, even that limited goal required a steadily expanding circle of friends in the outside world. And requirements for arms and money underscored the rebel need to cultivate good relations with as many powers as possible.

Such foreign ties as it had, the GPRA, accordingly, nursed very carefully. Tunis became the seat of government, and all ministers, notably Ferhat Abbas, worked closely with President Bourguiba. As a mark of respect for Egypt, the GPRA foreign office was kept in Cairo. Permanent offices were established in Rabat, where the King was consulted on all major actions, and in each of the Arab capitals. Regional meetings of Asians and Africans, as the capitals of all Asian, African, and Latin American states, became regular ports of call for traveling rebel leaders. With the coming to independence of the African states, the GPRA speedily established diplomatic missions in their capitals. Beginning in 1958, a series of diplomatic and miltary missions voyaged to Peiping. In October 1960, the GPRA was granted "*de facto*" recognition by the Soviet Union.

Inside the rebel organization there inevitably grew up impatience with the policy of slowly accumulating and husbanding military and diplomatic power. The soldiers, as always, wanted more arms and more action. Among the political leadership there remained sympathy for Abane's position of No Compromise with France. Some of those based in Cairo, and some in touch with Peiping, felt that concessions to the Communists would bring quick and decisive military support. The position of all these dissidents was strengthened in the fall of 1958 and 1959 when Paris offered negotiating terms clearly unsatisfactory to the rebels.

A showdown came at a critical meeting of the GPRA held in Tripoli, Libya, in December-January, 1959–60. The result was a complete victory for Ferhat Abbas and the policy of seeking negotiations with France. Mohammed Lamine-Debaghine, at once the chief holdover from the diehard Abane faction and the rebel leader most deeply rooted in Cairo, was replaced as Foreign Minister by Belkacem Krim. Tewfik el Madani, the Ulema leader, also in close touch with Cairo, was dropped from the government entirely. So was one of the three main negotiators with Communist China: former Supply Minister Mahmoud Cherif. The other two were demoted: Omar Oussedik from Minister of State to the post of representative in Guinea; Benyussuf Benkhedda from Minister of Social Affairs to traveling representative in Latin America. The soldiers were put under closer subordination to the government through establishment of a three-man general staff: Belkacem Krim, who held the Defense Ministry as well as the foreign post; Interior Minister Lakhdar ben Tobbal; and Communications Minister Abdelhafid Boussouf. Lastly, in the most important single decision, the GPRA was authorized to negotiate with France without always seeking new mandates from the field commands.

Apart from a decisive endorsement of the policy of negotiations, there also emerged from the Tripoli meeting a stable power relationship within the GPRA. Belkacem Krim was obviously the strong man. The only surviving member of the CRUA, a former head of Villaya III, active on the exterior since 1957, he had contacts with rebel troops in the field, with the leaders imprisoned in Paris, and with the chief leaders of states supporting the rebel regime. Working with him were two highly effective lieutenants, Lakhdar ben Tobbal and Abdelhafid Boussouf, both former field commanders in constant touch with rebel fighters. To be sure, Krim and Ben Tobbal, both self-educated, were rough men of few words and no great grasp of ideas; while Boussouf, though of good education and family (and dress), was a young man, prone to harsh judgments, notably of the French, and extreme suspicions, notably of the Americans. But Krim had a distinct sense of his own limitations. "I'm over my head here," he once said about the complex maneuvering in a U.N. debate. For better or worse, he had thrown his support to the political leaders favoring negotiations with France.

Of these the chief was, of course, Ferhat Abbas. The leader best known in France, and for that matter in Algeria, he was a standing symbol of rebel willingness to negotiate. To be sure, he had no power base of his own. Other ministers treated him with disdain, calling him the premier in slippers, interrupting him repeatedly, even, in public, letting strangers know that he was not very clever. Only as long as Krim backed him, his place was secure. When the prospects for negotiations took a bad turn in August 1961, Abbas was replaced with the tougher and younger Benyussuf Benkhedda. Benkhedda as much as Abbas is partisan of negotiation but differed in being more willing to back up his position by recourse to Communist diplomatic support.

For all its shortcomings, in short, the GPRA was something to reckon with. It fielded a team of ministers any new country might envy. It controlled an army of 30,000 troops. It had a clear, and feasible, policy. It had diplomatic offices across the world; and a highly organized party system, built up over many years, maintained close contact between government and people. What it mainly lacked, as Boussouf wryly observed, was an *interlocuteur valable* on the other side, a strong French government willing to negotiate. Before that could emerge, it was required that France set in order her own political house. She had above all to master a force converted by war into the first political party of the nation—the army.

# 4. THE ARMY

To ASK why the settlers want to stay on in Algeria is to speculate on the Queen's motives for eating bread and honey: everybody knows so why analyze? But to the French army, Algeria provides a case of Hecuba to him. A conscript force emanating from a people which never cared two pins for what was not France, it was led by officers raised up in a tradition of obedience to civil authority as old as the American republic. Yet it consistently affronted the political establishment of Paris, occasionally taking supreme risks, for the sake of staying on in Algeria. Why? What was Algeria to the army?

The special kind of limited war called Pacification supplies the answer. The great mass of conscripts it neutralized in a massive but innocuous show of the French presence: *quadrillage*. The regulars it plunged into passionate adventure. A struggle with some fighting, it enough resembled war to whet further an appetite for triumph born of years without victory. Aimed at containing and penetrating a whole population, it involved the assumption of governmental and political duties in an atmosphere breeding callous brutality toward individuals. Carried through in many social service missions, it fostered a conviction of spotless purpose. Connected with a struggle for men's minds, it produced a doctrine, void of ideas but rich in slogans, and a wild energy clouded in Hegelian doctrine. Coincident with the East-West rivalry, its outcome came to take on the character of historic importance.

The conversion of all these lines made Algeria a focus of dreams, and a last proving point of frustrations. A genuine obsession, it sucked the army into politics with a force that no other French party commanded.

II

THE initial response of the French army to the rebellion was a classic example of fighting the last war. "At first we thought," the commanding general Paul Chérrière wrote later, "that we faced a tribal uprising similar to those that had marked our history in North Africa. It seemed sufficient for the army to reduce some dissident local tribes . . . and for the police to maintain order elsewhere." Accordingly while the gendarmes arrested known nationalist leaders, the soldiers converged on the trouble spots in the Aurès. Wherever an incident took place, tanks surrounded the area, while spotter and fighter planes flew overhead, and heavily armed troops, transported by truck and jeep, moved from village to village, searching for weapons and suspects. Wherever they encountered rebel bands in open combat, the regular troops, better armed and better trained, came off victorious. Thus in one engagement in the Aurès, on November 29, 1954, two companies of paratroopers killed twenty-nine rebels and captured eighteen, while themselves losing only two men. But moving about the countryside in trucks and tanks was a sure way to give alarm, and usually the expeditions found nothing. Here, for example, are three entries from the diary of a paratroop captain:

At our approach there were cries and headlong flight of the whole population. After three hours of searching in the huts and the woods surrounding them, no one could be found.

We searched a village. Not a human being except a few old men.

The patrol couldn't find a single inhabitant. Everyone, women, children, and old men had time to flee.

Even when suspects were rounded up, moreover, there was rarely any means of establishing guilt. The army killed thousands of innocent individuals and destroyed hundreds of homes that never harbored a rebel. On the other hand, there were no legal means of detaining suspects. General Chérrière complained regularly of having to recapture, "arms in hand, rebels released by the courts for lack of proof."

The spread of the rebellion through 1955, and especially the Philippeville attacks of August 20, made it plain that the classic tactic for fighting tribal war was only alienating more and more Moslems. By the beginning of 1956, the army had worked out a completely new strategy. In February 1956, the main lines were approved by the government of Premier Guy Mollet. The new strategy was Pacification.

The principal visible change was a sudden increase in the number of troops available. On April 13, 1956, acting under a special powers law passed a month earlier, Defense Minister Maurice Bourgès-Maunoury decreed the dispatch of draftees to Algeria. In the next four months French forces rose from 200,000, all regulars or reservists, to over 400,000 men.

The new recruits represented a fair sampling of civilian France: fishermen from Brittany, metal workers from the Paris suburbs, dockers from Marseilles, peasants from the Jura, furniture workers from the Nord. Apart from putting on the uniform, their lives continued much as before. They were scattered across the countryside in the vast *quadrillage*—a grid operation garrisoning in strength all major cities and, in diminishing force, all the towns, villages, and farms of Algeria. They were quartered in housing projects, barracks, requisitioned hotels, and, very occasionally, tents. They ate French bread, drank French wine, read French papers, smoked French cigarettes. Many kept their civilian occupations as clerks, chauffeurs, mechanics, bakers. Mounting guard was their principal military function. Here are three different accounts of life in Algeria by draftees:

> Our regiment never went on operations, but guarded several farms warehouses and transformers.

> What I did there was to mount guard day and night, protecting the harvest.

> Our lives are not much disjointed. We do night police and escort civilian transport. Every morning we go down to the river where we wash. The colors are rich and various. I paint when I have time off, surrounded by wondrous children.

The civilian soldiers had approached the Algerian war with considerable misgiving. Throughout the early months of conscription, there were mutinous demonstrations and remarks, much exploited by the French Communists and considerably inflated by the French press. Once inside Algeria, however, they settled down, and there was a minimum of difficulty: a testament to the mildness of their service. It was not an indication, despite the suspicions of the French Left, that the recruits were taken in tow by the settlers. On the contrary, all the evidence is that the draftees, while keeping great distances from the Moslems, never felt at home with the settlers either. In *Ceux d'Algérie*, a volume of letters home, one veteran speaks of "guarding a haystack while the owners tanned themselves on the Côte d'Azur with ten American cars." A second remembers "certain *colons* who went so far as to refuse water to the wounded." A third laments having to leave his mother alone on his farm, which was "much less well equipped than those we found over here." A fourth says of the settlers; "I think it is especially the *colons*, the Spanish and Italian *colons* particularly, who are the most responsible for this rebellion. I have a very bad impression of them as they did not appreciate the efforts of the soldier, but acted as though we were there for our pleasure." Such criticism is no doubt atypical, but what does seem the major mood is a mood of indifference. "We have become," one lieutenant wrote, "part of the landscape to them [the settlers]. We are among them as strangers, like a policeman on the Avenue de l'Opéra whom you might ask for some help or information, but whom you'd never think to ask about his wife or children or housing problems."

Part of the landscape—that, indeed, was the moral status of the great bulk of the French army in Algeria. Bored, cut off from home, devoid of personal purpose, undergoing life in a form so mild it could hardly be called experience, most of the army in Algeria was a detached mass—putty in the hands of elite troops and regular officers.

### III

THESE approached Algeria in a mood of absolute alienation from the French nation. Where the bulk of the nation participated during the postwar in a steadily expanding prosperity, the military suffered a relative drop in prestige and salary only partially expressed by the five-star general who, in protest, rode to his Paris office on a bicycle. Moreover, where the country at large, except for brief lapses in 1940 and 1944, had been at peace since 1918, the professional warriors had been in the breach since 1939. Of victory and the chance for heroism that binds buckler to hearth they had no taste. Fighting seemed to be their constant diet, defeat their regular dessert.

Nineteen forty in particular had been an unforgettable shock. At last the army's hour had come round again; the test so long avoided at hand. A martial *frisson* shook the land, and the soldier was now the savior; none more so than the two Vieux Glorieux: Pétain, extolled in the press as "the noblest and most humane of our military chiefs," and Weygand, the alter ego of Foch. As late as May 1940, an old woman, recognizing Weygand, had exclaimed, "How can I be frightened, now you are here."

Three weeks later the bubble had burst. Not only was the army outmanned, outgunned, and outthought—absolutely routed—but it became the foremost symbol of capitulation. As hard as anyone Weygand pushed for surrender. Pétain led the nation defeated. Where only a handful of officers rallied to De Gaulle, thousands stood by Vichy—many of them in the colonies under no threat from the Germans; others even streaming back from Britain. As always with beaten soldiers, the politicians were the main scapegoats. "I cannot allow," Pétain said, "the army to be blamed for errors of policy. The real culprit is Daladier, for it was he who created the Popular Front." "It is out of the question," Weygand agreed, "to punish the generals and not the teachers who have refused to develop in the children the sentiment of patriotism and sacrifice." In this climate of defeat, recrimination among the soldiers flourished. At Dakar and in Syria, French officers loyal to the Marshal fired on those aligned with De Gaulle. Many who left the Marshal's side made a special point of rallying to the Allies rather than the Free French. Not even participation in the final Allied victory could wipe clean the stain of collaboration in a moral collapse. For foreigners to talk with French regulars about the war, meaning 1939–45, was to trench on forbidden ground. "They think," a British officer once said, "we're needling them." And as protection against real or fancied slights they concocted an elaborate fiction giving victory to France thanks to moral regeneration by the army. "*Combat pour l'honneur,*" one general called his account of the 1940 fighting, as if the soldiers saved the one thing it would have been fatal to lose. "In 1940," two other officers wrote recently to *Le Monde*, "the army averted for France an end like that of Greece." And the group of officers who write under the collective pen name

Milites referred to the war period as "five years in which the army stood in the breach to remake France."

Indochina hardened the 1940 complex. For eight years the regulars of the Legion and the pride of St. Cyr slogged through distant jungles and rice paddies against a people in arms. Over that period the equivalent of two thirds of each year's graduating class was killed annually, with the other third suffering wounds. But back home officers found not sympathy but contempt. Parliament after parliament stipulated against the use of conscript troops in "the dirty war." Toward the end, thanks to American loans, the country was making money out of the war—buying the gold of its allies, so it seemed in the rice paddies, with the blood of its soldiers. Just before the very end there came, at Dienbienphu, a defeat to rank with Waterloo and Sedan. And then Geneva, once more, opened the door to the excuse of political betrayal. Hundreds of junior officers, who had rallied Indochinese to the French cause by personal pledges, felt their honor compromised by Paris. "Eight years of war, to achieve this," a captain exclaimed. "And Paris doesn't give a damn. The rotten bastards play with our lives." "Geneva, not Dienbienphu," a general wrote, "marks the defeat of France. It is her politicians, not her soldiers, that owe an explanation."

The granting of independence to Morocco and to Tunisia, after brief fighting in 1955, only firmed up the army's case against the politicians. A colonel reaching Algeria in 1955 told a general, "I'm fed up with hauling down the flag. For fifteen years I've done it. If it happens in Algeria, I'll go to the other side, I'll become a Communist." By 1956, a general was saying, "They dished us in Indochina . . . They dished us in Tunisia . . . They dished us in Morocco. They'll never dish us in Algeria. I swear it, and you can tell Paris."

For 40,000 regulars, in short, Algeria was to be revenge on the years of defeat. While Pacification used the conscripts only as tools, it became for the regulars a grand design. They would crush the rebellion and vindicate their honor by fencing Algeria off from the world, taking the population in hand and binding it to the standard of France.

IV

THE fencing off of Algeria began at the frontiers. Back of both the Moroccan and Tunisian borders the French army constructed long nets of heavily fortified positions. The Morice Line, on the Tunisian border, stretched 200 miles from desert to sea, and encompassed thick strands of widely spaced barbed and electrified wire, mine fields, rocket and gun emplacements, and a complex system of automatic alarms and searchlights. While the Western Line along the Moroccan frontier was less formidable, it too presented a powerful deterrent against incursions. Moreover, inside Algeria, the army marked off huge areas heavy with rebel forces—the Collo Peninsula, parts of the Aurès and Kabylia ranges, the Ouarsenis—as zones of security. All persons living in these areas were removed and their dwellings burned. Planes, tanks, armored cars, and infantry patrols coursed over the forbidden ground, shooting anything that moved. Together with the frontier areas, the zones of security became the principal theaters of operations.

For fighting there was. Between 1954 and the end of 1960, official army figures record 13,000 deaths on the French side; and on the rebel side over 100,000 dead. And of the odds and murderous savagery of the fighting, the figures give no idea. For combat purposes the French army relied almost exclusively on paratroopers and the Foreign Legion. Well-trained, tough troops, with the most modern arms and transport, these were nonetheless limited in number. Pierre Clostermann, a Gaullist deputy who served as a pilot in Algeria, estimated that French troops on operations in Algeria numbered usually about 40,-000—"roughly equivalent to what the FLN mustered."

As in numbers so in tactics, the fighting French troops were similar to the rebel soldiers. Along the frontiers there were small arms duels almost nightly—rebel units advancing to probe for weaknesses, or to fire on French forts or trucks, while the French fired back to hold them off and inflict casualties. In the security zones, picked French troops moved about in small units, living off the land as they trailed rebel units across the rough countryside. A typical engagement I saw in the Aurès Mountains involved a company of French paratroopers and a twelve-man section of rebels. The paratroopers had been following the tracks of the rebel unit for five days through desolate mountainous terrain. On the morning of the sixth day, after a full night's marching, they caught sight of the rebels for the first time, bedded down in a remote hollow. The paras put in a radio call for spotter planes and tank support, then took up positions on three ridges around the hollow. Toward noon, two tanks rolled up to guard the base of the hollow, while almost simultaneously the spotter plane, a helicopter, appeared. The captain leading the company came down from the hills and with one tank commander set up a command post, in touch by radio with the plane, the tanks, and the troops. Then, very methodically, moving under orders from their captain, a squad at a time, the paras began to converge from the ridges toward the foot of the hollow where the tanks stood guard. They moved no more than a hundred feet at a jump, firing tommy guns as they advanced from cover to cover. The first volley drew return rifle fire from the rebels. Then the *fellagha*, as the army calls the rebels, lit a brush fire, sending up clouds of billowing smoke that hid them from view, and dispersed. For the next six hours, under a broiling sun, the operation continued—the paras advancing slowly down the hills, the rebels seeking singly or in groups of two or three to scoot through the closing cordon. Toward dusk when the paratroops finally collected at the foot of the hollow, they had killed two rebels. From the corpses, each riddled across the middle with machine-gun bullets, they stripped weapons: belt grenades and old Spanish hunting rifles.

"*Pas brilliant*," the captain muttered when shown the booty, and after a short rest the company was off again, on the track of the fleeing rebels.

Having sealed off the frontiers and security zones, the army more and more found itself drawn to managing and penetrating the rest of the country. The prime motive was protection of the inhabitants from the FLN. Unable to extend the *quadrillage* to the distant villages housing so many of the Moslems, the army, under Pacification, brought the villages to the *quadrillage*. The whole populations—men, women, children, old people—of many remote places were transported, with their goods, to specially built camps and villages adjacent to military posts. No doubt some of the people came voluntarily, seeking shelter from the rebels. But it is equally clear that many were coerced. In some cases the old villages were simply bombed out. In others, the roads of access were blocked and the villagers were starved out. In all, according to an official report, more than a million persons were moved by the army from the distant countryside to population centers near military strong points. It was one of the largest—and least reported—population movements of the postwar period. Still, it represented only a fraction of the administrative controls exercised by the army over the Moslem population.

For while the concentration of the population brought Moslems under the wing of the *quadrillage*, it also stimulated the rebels to step up underground operations. The success of these as reflected in the terrorist campaign and Algiers general strike of 1957, made the Moslem population, in the eyes of the French army, not only an object of protection but a source of information. No rebel action in the cities could be planned or carried out without the knowledge of some, if not a great, portion of the Moslem population. Advance knowledge of such actions was of inestimable use to the military: it enabled them to prevent bombings and acts of sabotage, and to save lives. Thus the search for information on the rebels became a major army operation in the settled parts of Algeria. As the military correspondent for *Le Monde* put it, "the search for information, once the concern of general staffs, has become for everybody a question of life or death."

From there it was but a step to widespread brutality and torture. The beginning seems to have been quite casual. One paratrooper recounts with no sense of wrongdoing that when he took a prisoner he would say, "We are among paratroopers. If you help us we will be especially merciful. If not we will be especially nasty." Another gives this account of the interrogation of a fifteen-year-old boy:

Q. Do you know what a *fellagha* is?
A. A what?
Q. A *fellagha*?
A. No. I never heard of it. I don't even know whether it's an animal or a tree.

That cost him a couple of smacks. He began sobbing, but did not talk . . . After two other smacks, the result of enormous lies, the kid burst into tears, and promised to tell the truth.

Before very long the phrase for a couple of smacks (*deux gifles*) came to cover a wide variety of far more ferocious and systematic treatment. In military posts and police stations all across Algeria frequent use was made of the "magneto," or hand-telephone generator, for applying electric shocks to prisoners. The ducking of bound prisoners to the point of drowning, as well as the application of burning cigarettes to tender skin, and the internal use of pressurized gases and liquids—all became standard operating procedures. Not only were these practices attested by individuals in countless statements, and by reliable organizations, including the International Red Cross, but many of those responsible on the highest level were at pains to justify them. General Jacques Massu, reportedly after consultation with a spiritual adviser, reasoned thus: "It is torture to give a couple of smacks to an innocent person. But is it torture to give a couple of smacks to a bomb thrower?

The rights of the innocent are superior to those of the guilty." A high civil official put his case to a member of the Commission on Safeguards, appointed by Paris to investigate torture charges, in these terms:

> We've just caught a terrorist, grenade in hand. We're sure that he knows the names of thirty other terrorists, each one ready to throw a bomb. What should we do? Give him a few unpleasant minutes or put three hundred innocent lives in danger? You make the decision in my place.

A similar logic served to justify a practice at least as awful as torture: reprisals. Though less notorious and less well documented, there is absolutely no doubt of their existence. A former rebel leader who deserted to the French tells in a confession circulated by the French of an Arab forest guard killed by rebel troops under his command. "French soldiers," he writes, "two days after the murder, shot in reprisal twelve inhabitants of the village." A priest from western Algeria reports that when a French truck was blown up, with loss of its cargo though not of life, the colonel in the region "killed five prisoners and had their corpses exposed for 48 hours near the explosion." The priest reports that eighty villagers were killed after the murder of a French officer in their village. When a mine was found on a road, forty-three Moslems from the adjacent village were killed. "Next day," according to the priest, "the rebels came to tell the army where additional mines had been placed. If the army hadn't killed the 43 men, this warning would not have come." In short, what had begun as a movement of protection, passed through a quest for information, and emerged as the use of terror to divorce the Moslems from the FLN. And once having achieved divorce through terror, the army quickly moved to take the whole Moslem population in hand. "The population," an article in the March 1958 issue of *Perspectives Militaires* declared, "must be cleaned up, assisted, helped, organized, administered."

The take-over of the Moslem population began in Algiers in January 1957. The French response to a protest general strike called by the rebels, it was signalized by the blanket grant of police authority to the 10th Paratroop Division under General Massu. In a statement to the *Echo d'Alger*, Massu announced his plan of operations:

> I have a plan for offensive action, very simple and ready to be put in execution next week. Take a census of the whole population of Algiers. Above all we must know all the local people, know what they do and how they make their living. Then in a second stage, raise the living standards of those who need it; give them work and quarters.
>
> The population is the target of two adversaries. Up to now there is no concealing that the FLN has made notable progress in the conquest of the Moslem population. We will have that much more trouble in winning it back.

The first step in the operation was a census of the whole population of Algiers. Every man, woman, and child in the city was registered and issued an identification card indicating name, address, occupation, and place of business. To enforce this control on the Moslems, a special headquarters was established at the main gate linking the Casbah with the rest of the city. A regiment of paratroopers was made available. Mobile units, stationed at strategic corners throughout the Casbah, were in constant radio touch with the headquarters. At any time the paras were able to stop Moslems in the streets and ask for identification. It became a common sight to see long lines of Moslems awaiting clearance at some check point. At random times through the day and night the paras conducted *rattisages*, or raking operations, in which homes were cordoned off and searched for suspicious persons, literature, and arms stores. Any show of resistance evoked bullets, and arrests were made on the slightest suspicion. Prisoners were without legal rights, and were generally taken direct to various paratroop installations near Algiers for questioning. About these centers there grew well-substantiated stories of brutal tortures, arranged "suicides," bizarre cases of prisoners shot "trying to escape." Survivors of the "questioning" were generally sent, for indefinite periods, to concentration camps scattered all across Algeria. Here, besides the poorest living conditions and brutal treatment, the prisoners were exposed to indoctrination courses stressing their duties toward France.

By September 1957, the paras had won the battle of Algiers —the major French victory of the war. Out of a total Casbah population of 75,000, there were 3,000 dead, another 5,000 in prison or concentration camps. The formidable FLN network responsible for the terror tactics of 1956–57 was completely broken up. In its place the paras established a network of their own—the "*îlot*" system. Under this system, one person in each family group was designated as responsible for the whereabouts of all other members of the family. The responsible family man on every floor in every building was in turn made responsible to a floor chief. Each floor chief was responsible to a building chief; all the building men to a block leader, and so forth until there was a chain of command stretching down from French headquarters to the bosom of every family. With this system in operation the French command could lay hands on any Moslem in the Casbah within a matter of minutes. Moreover, the chiefs at every level from the family upward constituted a potent means of influencing opinion. Many were former FLN organizers who changed sides after a spell in the prison camps. They met regularly with French officers (they were dubbed "*bleus*" by the rebels after the Moslems who used to hang around French military camps for odd jobs and were known by that name because they wore blue jeans). Through them, the army passed down orders for demonstrations, and even how to vote. There came a time, indeed, through 1958 and 1959, when the Moslem population would not make any move without a signal from the *bleus*. At that point, in the winter of 1958–59, the army had penetrated the Casbah completely. As surely as the soldier grips his rifle, it held Moslem opinion in its hand.

To be sure, the Casbah, with a heavily concentrated population cheek by jowl with the high command, was a special case. But in diluted form, the same kind of penetration tactics were pursued across Algeria. Moreover, outside the big cities, the grip of the army on the local Moslems was reinforced by control over all basic services. In the back country, the military controlled transportation and the food supply, provided work, education, and medical attention, registered births and marriages, ran the postal service, published newspapers, and, of course, managed elections.

The backbone of this system of rural administration were the Sections Administratives Specialisées, or SAS. Some six hundred SAS installations were scattered through the countryside, each one commanded by a French officer, usually with a squad of French troops under his direct command. As in Algiers, each SAS officer took a census and kept a register on the local population. Each also had his *bleus*: a troop, or *harka*, of Moslem soldiers used as auxiliaries to the French squad. But while force was present, the dominant motif was social service. "At once mayors and architects," Philippe Herreman wrote of the SAS in *Le Monde*, "the officers draw up plans for the village, build the houses, trace out the streets, open work projects, receive the complaints of the inhabitants, and arbitrate their *chicayas*" (disputes). A typical SAS installation near Blida was responsible for a group of villages housing 5,000 persons. It maintained a newly built school, a canteen for children, a program of medical and dental care serviced by visiting physicians, a work project, and a census control. The officer there, a regular just out of school, rose every morning at five, did an hour of administrative work, then took breakfast and walked through the village and the work project (a road-building job), keeping in touch with his charges. Back in his office he met with a local Moslem notable to receive names of new pupils wishing to attend school, then worked out with the notable a schedule for buses to Blida on the next market day. After lunch he met with all the men of the village and discussed for several hours improvement plans for fountains, a public bath, and extension of crop credits. Before dinner he made another visit to the work project, and afterwards he heard the *chicaya*, typical domestic disputes involving men who had left their wives, or quarrelsome neighbors. Before turning in, he looked over the weekly newspaper, a single page mimeographed on both sides which had been put out that day by the SAS secretary. It contained lists of deaths, births, and marriages, announcments of coming events, and a few political comments. "Our effort," one said, "will be pursued as long as necessary. We will undertake, without awaiting the good will of the enemy, the construction of a New Algeria."

As the emphasis on the new Algeria suggests, the army concentrated its social service efforts on young people. The detailed, deliberate care with which the soldiers sought to mold young minds is perhaps without parallel in military annals. At a paratroop vocational school near Algiers, for example, all boys lived with their soldier-teachers, who were called monitors, and the curriculum reached into the most private affairs. Apart from academic subjects (French, math, geography) and practical work with wood, metals, and in industrial design, instruction included courses on Moral Life, Initiation to Modern Life, and something called *Savoir Vivre*, or manners. Many of the lessons were simple homilies. Thus in an hour given over to The Conscience, the student learned that "to do our duty we must listen to our conscience." In a lesson on the school, the student was taught "to love my school and respect it." But he was equally taught, in a lesson on Brothers and Sisters, that "parents are only happy when they have several children," and, in a lesson on The Government, that "the law is the expression of the will of the people, and must be obeyed as the rules of a game one is playing." And frequently these subtle political themes gave way to far grosser dogma. The lesson on Work taught the student to believe that:

> Work is the sacred law of the world . . . I want to choose my work well, and do it well, whatever it may be. I will work with all my strength and all my soul to the end that France be reborn.

And this is what the student was supposed to learn about the home:

> I love my home where I have the luck to live happily amidst those who hold me dear. I want to remain close to it all my life . . . I will never forget that the grandeur of France depends on the solidarity of the hearth.

Because of its detailed application as well as its broad scope the pacification campaign had immense impact on the Moslems. Resettlement caught up more than a million persons. At least that many, and probably more, were left in rebel territory by the fencing-off policy. Several hundred thousand from the border territories crossed the frontiers as refugees in Morocco and Tunisia. At least a hundred thousand were held prisoner under suspicion of rebel activity in more than a score of prisons and concentration camps. It is literally true, in other words, that there was no Moslem family in Algeria untouched by the French effort.

The main effect was a fragmentation of opinion. By far the largest portion of the Moslem population simply followed the lines of force. Under FLN sway, they paid taxes to the rebels, gave them help and information, and otherwise did what they were told. They acted similarly with respect to the French army. Of the war, their only hope was that it would end soon. If they favored one side or another they kept it to themselves with a muteness that was striking. On one occasion an American reporter, riding with a bunch of Moslem workers in the back of a truck, struck up a friendship, and carefully steered the talk to politics. But when he put a pointed question, six men in a row refused to answer. The seventh pointed to the cab where a French sergeant was driving, and said, "Ask him what I think."

Without much doubt, a substantial fraction of the population was alienated by Pacification, and driven into the arms of the rebels. Such sentiments were especially notable among the young men: though suffering casualties of over 20,000 annually, the FLN at no time had difficulty recruiting new volunteers. Even where the social service work of the French had yielded tangible benefits, the sentiment of youth for the FLN was marked. Polls in some areas—notably around Sétif—seemed to indicate that FLN sympathies were especially strong where the French army had come in force, cleansed the area of rebels, and then moved on. In other words, the schooling and rehousing occasioned by Pacification stirred in some breasts an appetite for more. In others benefits were received only as part of the French response to the rebellion, and thus were credited to the account of the FLN. However, a very large fraction was undoubtedly won over. These included not only French stooges but many beneficiaries of the new social services, plus all those *bleus* who had elected to help France, among them 200,000 *harka*, in Pacification. Many of these rightly feared severe reprisals if the rebels came to power; and they were a constant source of pressure upon the French army to hold firm against any attempt to pursue the military struggle against the FLN to the bitter end. For the fact is that whatever its impact upon the Moslems, Pacification exerted a far greater influence in shaping the attitudes and outlook of the men who carried it out, that is upon the regular French army. For the soldiers had gained the distinct impression of doing good works. They acquired, as Maurice Duverger put it, "a taste for their jobs." They "became the priests of the African Middle Ages." As a lieutenant leaving Algeria wrote, "The future may hold great joys in store, but certainly there is no greater happiness than having won back the souls of the 25,000 persons placed in our charge for the past year . . . We have rid them of their terrors and restored them to life. We have shared their problems, their sufferings, their joys."

What spoke there was a Messianic faith. It found expression in a dogma that brought the army into the inner recesses of social and political life: the dogma of Psychological Warfare.


v


IN A typically droll conceit, the *Canard Enchâiné* once imagined itself conducting by telephone a long-distance panel show. The first guest was General Massu, and the program broke down at the outset because Massu was too busy to come to the phone. He was reading the works of Mao Tse-tung.

The concealed butt of the *Canard's* conceit was the "Seventh Arm" of the French General Staff—the Service of Psychological Action and Information. Nominally its function in Algeria was the winning of a favorable public for the army and its projects: its men conducted the indoctrination courses in the prison camps; its field units broadcast over portable loudspeakers all over the territory, and put about propaganda tracts and wall stickers, all advertising the strength and benevolence of French forces as contrasted with the weakness and malignity of the rebels. But actually the psychological warfare service owed its genesis to the frustration of the French army when it found itself, in Indochina, being beaten by an enemy short on steel, long on ideology. "It is time," one officer who had served in Indochina and who backed creation of the Seventh Arm had written, "that the army ceased being the Great Mute. The time has come for the free world, if it does not want to die a violent death, to apply certain of the methods of its enemy. One of these methods, and without doubt the most important, lies in the ideological role." In introducing their brother officers to "the ideological role," the Psychological Warriors laid great stress on a body of well-known writers in the psychological and political field. Apart from the selected works of Mao, a typical reading list included the *History of the Russian Revolution* by Walter; *Political Propaganda* by Domenach; *The Adventure of Western Man* by Denis de Rougemont; *The Revolt of Israel* by Begin; *The Star and the Cross* by Dufay; as well as selections from the works of Freud, Kierkegaard, Nietzsche, and Pavlov. A typical lecture according to Pierre Nora, included citations from Spinoza, Hegel, Alain, Bergson, and Romain Rolland. If nothing else, the soldiers were fed a fairly heady brew.

Not all of them took to it, of course. Older officers showed little taste for a course so remote from the traditional military curriculum. This was notably true of the generals, like Raoul Salan, commanding officer in Algeria from 1956 through 1958, who saw the struggle only from on high and kept their eyes fixed on the source of promotion in Paris. But among the younger officers actually effecting Pacification, Psychological Warfare found a ready reception. In time psychological warfare experts came to hold most of the major intelligence and information posts in Algiers, notably in the paratroop headquarters of General Massu. Their slogans dominated the conversation, and their teachings permeated the mental outlook, of the most active officers in Algeria. Psychological Warfare become the ruling doctrine of the little knot of colonels— Broizat, Lacheroy, Gardes, Trinquier, Godard, Argoud—who time after time were to push their superiors to make trouble for Paris.

A good deal of what they said resembled what illiterates suddenly possessed by the Higher Criticism might have produced. "Man," one officer could write, "is an individual endowed with a unique personality, but marked by a historic heritage (ethnic, religious, cultural factors, etc.) and by current events. He is a member of a collectivity, that is one of a milieu or social group, with his personality affected by its specific characteristics, namely: age group, family cell, local group or habitat (rural or urban center), professional (or ethnic) group."

But amidst the gibberish, there was a discernible doctrine—the doctrine of Revolutionary War—that appealed to the soldiers because it raised their experience to the level of historic accomplishment in the cause of Christian civilization. Despite criticism, many officers came to look on Psychological Warfare as a solid asset of indisputable virtue. "You can't be against it," one officer once said. "It's like being against artillery."

The central thesis of the Psychological Warrior was that in 1917 the Bolsheviks unleashed a new technique of aggression —Revolutionary War—which has ever since been sapping the foundations of Christian civilization all over the world. What distinguishes the new technique is its target. For it aims not at the destruction of cities, still less at the conquest of territory or the taking of cities, but at the mind of man. It is, wrote Colonel Charles Lacheroy, the first head of the Psychological Warfare Bureau at the Army General Staff in Paris and subsequently spokesman for General Salan, "war amidst the crowd, a war with the mass, in which the masses are the objective to be won over." In such struggles, another French officer wrote, "the population (mass) becomes completely engaged. Intelligence, harassment, sabotage, paralyzing the enemy are everyone's business, not the affair of a few specialists."

Though the Communists invented the technique they are not its only practitioners. "Revolutionary War," according to one writer in an issue of the *Revue Militaire d'Information* given over completely to discussion of that subject, "is the most commonplace and permanent feature of modern history." "That's all we have," Colonel Lacheroy once said, and an account of "a few revolutionary wars in the twentieth century" lists eighteen such conflicts, including: "Spain, 1931–36; Palestine, 1936–39 and 1947–48; Indonesia, 1945–46; Burma, 1946–53; and Tunisia, Morocco, and Algeria." For it is especially nationalist parties struggling for independence who, so the doctrine goes, use the tactics of Revolutionary War; and as an instrument devised by the devil does Nick's work, so Revolutionary War, having been devised by the Communists, inevitably works to Moscow's advantage. "Revolutionary War," Colonel Lacheroy asserted, "is waged directly when the local Communist party is strong, or indirectly when the Marxist-Leninist parties choose to support nationalist parties." "The road from Moscow to Paris," another officer wrote, affecting to quote Lenin, "passes by Peiping, Saigon, and Calcutta—and we may add by Cairo, Algiers, and Dakar." Still a third officer puts the case with a show of sweet reason:

> At first glance, it may seem strange to consider the troubles in dependent countries as examples of Revolutionary War. Many nonexperienced people suppose that the essential criterion of this form of war consists in the presence of the Communist party in the highest positions. But the official statements of the Soviet leaders have indicated, and experience has shown, that nationalist parties—even non-Marxist-Leninist ones—are aided directly by the local Communist parties and the Popular Democracies, etc. In fact, in its first stage, the Revolutionary War that the Communists, notably in France, taught the nationalists to prepare and guide, aims at the eviction of the protecting power. But it also has as its goal, witness Marx and Lenin, the conquest of power at a later stage by the local party of the extreme Left which takes over as soon as independence is achieved.

In the view of the Psychological Warriors, in other words, Communists and nationalists are practically identical. "The enemy," as one put it, "is always the same."

Fortunately, the doctrine continues, the enemy can be beaten at his own game. What is required is the application of psychological warfare techniques against him. That entails, first, the establishment on the disputed territory of a large, disciplined force—namely the army. "In the Western world," one officer put it, "the army is destined to play the role which, in Communist countries, has fallen to the party." "We," another officer used to say, "are the missionaries of a new gospel." As a general rule, "there must be one soldier for every ten or fifteen people, a battalion for every sixty miles." Once in place, the army must develop a series of "parallel hierarchies"—trade unions, peasant groups, sports clubs, veterans' organizations— as a means of penetrating the disputed population. "It is necessary above all and without delay to organize the whole population of the country in a system of self-defense based on army units . . ." "The inhabitants must be engaged against the rebels and organized to fight for themselves. This can be achieved only by an integrated action at every level in the fields of politics, administration, economic welfare, and culture." The army must also "eliminate suspects and regroup the inhabitants . . . Recalcitrants or known rebels are interned, not in a prison but in a camp of disindoctrination. At the end of more or less time —without using violent methods, but on the contrary persuasive and humane ones—the great majority of the internees become adapted to the 'New System'."

If that prescription sounds familiar, it should. It is an exact description of Pacification—with its 400,000 soldiers, its penetration of the local population, its concentration camps, and its *bleus* "adapted to the New System." But to that mixture the Psychological Warriors added two new ingredients, both heavily political in content. One was stress on some catch phrase or slogan that could be put across "by all the latest developments of experimental psychology" as a means of rallying mass support. In Indochina, according to Colonel Lacheroy, the Communists had had to deal with a "simple people . . . at bottom ill-disposed . . . toward communism" by reason of "genie worship, Buddhism . . . and natural reluctance to accept totalitarianism." How did the Communists overcome these obstacles? This way, according to Colonel Lacheroy:

> The enemy began, following a well-known formula, by finding in the arsenal of words, a word which closely corresponded with their war aims and which sounded good. It took the word independence—*Doclap* in Vietnamese. Suddenly everything was *Doclap*.

In Algeria, the Psychological Warriors sought a *Doclap* of their own. The word they came up with was Integration—meaning the integration of all Algerians into France as equal citizens with equal rights. Though never endorsed by the French parliament, which leaned far more toward autonomy, Integration became the slogan pushed by the army across Algeria in all its multifold propaganda activities. And if the Moslems did not necessarily believe the propaganda, the French army did. "In Algeria," one officer told Jean-Raymond Tournoux, "the magic word was Integration, as distinct from the myth of independence."

Voluntarism—that view of affairs that holds that the will *is* the way—was the second original contribution of the Psychological Warriors to the military mind in Algeria. It was a cardinal tenet of their doctrine that will could move political mountains and sweep back historical tides. "If you hold the vase tightly enough," Colonel Lacheroy put it, "you can put into it anything you want." "Political, economic, and social reasons," another officer wrote in the *Revue Militaire*, "are not the decisive cause in the revolt; what is is the action of revolutionary organizations." "After Napoleon," a highly placed officer on General Salan's staff once theorized, "nationalism swept Europe as it now sweeps Asia and Africa. But one man said No—Metternich; and for a hundred years, trouble ceased. Like Metternich, I say No."

The most concrete expression of Voluntarism in Algeria was a phrase heard from one end of the country to the other, and at all levels of the officer corps: "We will never abandon Algeria." In part, of course, the pledge was aimed at the uncommitted Moslem mass—a show of strength to convince the fearful. But harsh resolution—determination for determination's sake—had an impact also in Paris. For it was clear to the Psychological Warriors that bitter-endism was above all sapped by the principles of liberal, internationalist democracy. And the Psychological Warriors attacked these principles with a vengeance.

"Revolutionary wars cannot be won with the Napoleonic Code," was Colonel Lacheroy's answer to those who deplored brutal and extralegal practices. To those who favored political concessions to the Moslems or special consideration for international opinion, one of his fellows declared, "The more one gives reforms to a territory, the more the resistance grows . . . The more international opinion expresses interest in the cause of the revolt, the more its manifestations increase." From these generalizations to specific political attacks was only a short step, a step the Psychological Warriors did not forbear to take. Their Algerian journal, *Le Bled*, systematically derided the political leaders of Paris. In their book the liberal former Premier Pierre Mendès-France was "M. Mendès, curiously called France." Beneath a photo of Premier Felix Gaillard playing tennis, *Bled* placed the caption: "The man of the backhand."

In sum, Psychological Warfare underwrote the passions and prejudices of the army in Algeria. By the pale cast of thought, it thickened the native hue of resolution. It represented the military effort there as a vital salient in the defense of the free world against communism. It licensed the soldiers to pursue their methods with relentless determination against all opposition. It enjoined them especially to take stands on political matters. "Lyautey," as one officer put it, "wrote of the social role of the officer. We are concerned with his political role."

VI

MONTH after month through 1956, 1957, and the first part of 1958, the political role of the officer made steady inroads against the power of decision in Paris. In October 1956, while Paris sought to negotiate with the rebel leaders, the army took them prisoner. In November 1957, while Paris sought to back away from Pacification, the soldiers threatened "to find alone the road to total victory." In February 1958, while Paris hoped to deal through Tunisia and Morocco, the army staged the border raid at Sakiet. In May 1958, while Paris once more sought accommodation with the rebels, the army played the major role in killing the Fourth Republic. Briefly the soldiers held supreme power, and thereafter, for a long time, weighed heavily as a political force. But void of practical programs themselves, they placed their hopes in a man bound to bring them to heel. For want of anything better, in short, *Exercitus fecit Imperatorem.* Twice—in January 1960, and, more directly, in April 1961—the soldiers moved against their master. But these tests showed that if much of the army's strength was in itself, much also was an illusion—given special color by the peculiar weakness of the Fourth Republic.

# 5.   THE POLITICS

"You can talk sense to the American people," Adlai Stevenson once said, and on that article of faith pitched a national campaign. But it is not a phrase one would hear in France. The beginning of wisdom about French politics is that you can't talk sense to the French people.

The reasons, mutually re-enforcing and thus difficult to trace, have to do with splits so deep and diverse as to suppress consensus. Politically France is what Hazlitt called Macbeth: "a huddling together of fierce extremes." Majority public opinion, the stuff of which mandates are made, does not exist. Government, in the absence of a clear lead from below, is by mystification from above, and historically French regimes have swung between two kinds of bamboozlement. There is the mass intoxication of one-man rule, whether by Napoleon, his nephew, Pétain, or De Gaulle. There is the unfathomable complexity of government by ever-changing cabinets representing multiparty assemblies: *le système*, practiced in the Third and Fourth Republics.

Each has its characteristic strengths and weaknesses. The

Man becomes a focus of renaissance and heroic actions: *gesta Dei per Francos*; but then dreams dreams, and enters the road to disaster, moving at breakneck pace toward unreachable goals. The Machine fosters prosperity and cultural achievement; but, a mere convenience, strikes no loyalties and founders when crisis supervenes.

It was the fate of the Fourth Republic to crumble ignominiously under the weight of the Algerian crisis. Unloved, no one mourns its death. But there is a case to be made. Real gains were registered during its brief life. It fell under pressures no polity could easily withstand. And in ways it is important to comprehend, it answered the peculiar genius of a sorely divided people.

## II

Top people read the *Times* from Land's End to John O'Groats, and a traveler in Russia once complained that his sleeping car had not moved during the night, for on waking he found the same birches he had seen before retiring. But how infinitely varied is France. Marseilles is a shrine of Latinity on the sunny Mediterranean; Paris a misty city of the North. Around the capital and in the areas fringing Belgium, heavy industry and an urban proletariat are the rule. But besides Paris and Marseilles, only twenty-two other cities have populations of more than 100,000 people, and much of the rest of the country is, literally, underdeveloped. During the trial of Père Dominici—a farmer from the Southwest of France implicated in the murder of a British civil servant—it came out that Dominici had a working vocabulary of about 200 words: the figure generally given for the number of novels written by Georges Simenon. I have lived on a French farm not thirty miles from Paris where horse cart was the means of transport, and the knowledge of supply and demand so limited that the farmer's wife would complain about her hens that they seemed to slow down on the laying at exactly the time the price of eggs rose. I used there to take the London *Observer* and *Economist*, and Mme. Cherel, proprietress of the local café and village Solomon to boot, once expressed astonishment that an American was so much at home in English: "We are all French, but I do not understand the Alsatians easily, still less the Bretons, and the Basques can talk only to themselves."

With narrow provincialism goes jealous patriotism. The Germans have a phrase "to live like a king in France." Good Americans, when they die, are supposed to go to Paris. "I've always wanted to see the rue de Rivoli" is a believable line put by Nevil Shute into the mouth of one of his Australian characters. But the French grenadier retreating from Moscow had no thought of stopping in Vienna or Frankfurt. "It's a long way to Carcassonne," he said. Montesquieu, representing his Frenchmen as Persians, had one of them ask incredulously, "How could anyone not be a Persian?" Even Villon, of whom Rabelais could say that he cared only for "last year's snow," wrote a "Ballad Against Those Who Missay France."

No doubt, it is a pleasant place. But if Douce France is more than a song title—and it is—it is because the French have made it so. Baudelaire's worship of "*dandysme*" expresses nothing more sinister than a preference for the elegantly wrought-over crude nature, and Voltaire's injunction was "Cultivate your garden." Fifth Avenue bears witness that the French have taken the enjoinder to heart in all the luxurious arts—dress, cooking, love. At more reasonable prices there is conversation. In argument the Paris cabby is as sharp and nasty as his New York colleague; but the insult direct he eschews for subtler thrusts: "My regards to Mademoiselle *votre mère*," for example. And what pains are not taken for a little comfort? More care goes into the annual *Guide Michelin* than is lavished on many an encyclopedia. A peasant I know spent a full day making the sides of his wheelbarrow detachable, so that he could use it as a chaise longue. Adjoining the Esso station near my little town was a rose garden with tables and chairs; the motorist waiting for a grease job could take refreshments alfresco.

*Incivisme*—the Frenchman's refusal to render unto Caesar what everyone else agrees is his, notably taxes—is supposed to be the little man's reflex in the face of centralized bureaucracy: "*le citoyen contre les pouvoirs*," as Alain put it. But *l'avare*—the miser—also plays a part. Having worked so hard to attain his ease, the Frenchman is understandably tight-fisted. That the taxes could easily be paid counts for nothing; not long ago several million francs were raised by a check on Parisians owning foreign cars: most of them had filed no returns at all. Neither does it make any difference that the blood tax—the draft—has been paid without complaint. A Frenchman will cast his bread upon the waters; not his cake. And if the sweet morsel happens to be connected with a locale, resistance becomes bitter to the point of comedy. When the coal mines of central France began to play out, it was of no avail for the government to offer the miners transportation and new homes and jobs in the North. "I suppose," one of them said in refusing, "you'll move the graveyard too."

Local attachment tends to give the French past an intimate character, as of felt experience rather than recorded events. There are peasants in Lorraine who still think of the enemy as the Swedes who came down from the north in the first part of the seventeenth century. Few French towns are without their rue de Richelieu or Place St. Louis. Historic dates—not only Bastille Day on July 14, but September 4, August 4, the 18th Brumaire—have a living political reality. Still, the past is upon the French in another way. When the military and the settlers in Algiers moved against Paris in May 1958, they established a Committee of Public Safety—a harking back to the members of the Great Revolution. These in turn had modeled themselves on the stern republicans of Rome. To imitate imitators is to go beyond the living memory of things past. No way of life, it is a state of mind.

One definition of a Jewish joke is a story no Gentile comprehends and every Jew has heard before. The French too have their secret understanding—something they think and we do not. Hard to define, it is connected with a passion for paradox, once expressed in a startling conceit by the patriot-poet Charles Péguy: " 'It will be a nuisance,' God said, 'when there are no more Frenchmen. There are things I do no one else understands.' " A concrete example is the ubiquitous *rond-point*, the broad traffic circle at the juncture of eight or so absolutely similar avenues: "so neat," an Englishman once observed, "and so easy to get lost in." Less obvious, but more important, is the taste for orderly texts bearing no relation, as everyone knows, to the chaotic affairs they are supposed to govern. Mere words, they put a heavy premium on the work of the intellectual.

There is ludicrous exaggeration in the case of the deputy during the Third Republic who proclaimed in debate, "Gentlemen, this can't go on. We must act; we must strike a blow. I'm going to write an article in the *Revue des Deux Mondes*." But no Frenchman would endorse Stanley Baldwin's view that the intelligentsia bears to intelligence the same relation as gents to gentlemen. Over 40 per cent of the deputies elected in the 1956 election were classed as intellectuals (as against 4 per cent of the general population). That Mauriac, Malraux, Sartre, and Camus should participate prominently in political discussions is only normal. Every party has its intellectuals. Even Pierre Poujade, a leader of shopkeepers and peasants who seemed to eschew thought, acknowledged he had to have a doctrine—"*pour embêter les autres*"; to confound his rivals. As that admission suggests, the role of the intellectual is to generate heat, not light. Clouds of irrelevant rhetoric and dubious history obscure the simplest political transaction. Let a politician talk of "authority," and Bonaparte is on a thousand lips. On complex issues, armies of words take the field. "In Algeria," Raymond Aron observed, "we fight over words"; and Germaine Tillon once listed a dozen of these bones of contention: "Nationalism, Federalism, Separatism, Colonialism, Terrorism, Fatalism, Fanaticism, Communism, Elections, Integration, Negotiations, Capitulation." Words to be sure, but with the effect of music, which is to set men marching. A deputy of the Radical party, on being told that Alain had written his *Elements of a Radical Doctrine*, protested to fellow deputies, "If a Radical doctrine existed, wouldn't we be the first to know it?" But the peasants of southern France seem to vote Communist out of a historic affection for the slogans of the Left. "This region," Daniel Halévy wrote in 1920, "has always been Republican, Radical, or Socialist, depending upon the time. Comes a fourth word: Communist, or Bolshevik, or even Anarchist. It will be adopted. What does a word mean? The intellectuals invent it . . . The peasants repeat it." It was precisely the habit of coining words without value that led Julien Benda to debase the mental currency further by striking off the term: *Trahaison des Clercs*, Betrayal of the Intellectuals. And André Siegfried used to wonder if well-governed countries were not those in which people didn't think very much.

For all this, of course, has a central political impact. Geographical disunity, fierce attachment to the past and its quarrels, unwillingness to surrender the tiniest portion of one's worldly goods, a false intellectualism apt to make a martyr's cause of the meanest interest—this is the very atmosphere of political France. It at once generates and enflames the three principal issues of French politics.

## III

ONE is familiar enough. In every modern country, the industrial workers and large segments of the white-collar class seek economic security and a modicum of ease: full employment, high wages, old-age and disability pensions, plentiful housing, public recreation facilities. For nearly half a century they have been pressing these claims through the medium of the state. Since the claims involve higher taxes and an extension of government regulation, they are generally contested by elements of the business community, and a section, at least, of the farm population. The consequent struggle is a political universal: the basic dividing line between Right and Left in the twentieth century, and to this fight France has no immunity. On the contrary, the struggle is more intense. In Britain and the United States, not to mention the Scandinavian countries, the vast popular majority and all major parties are won over to the principle of the Welfare State. All the skirmishing centers on marginal advances or retreats. But in France, the principle itself is at stake. The Welfare State, in root and branch, is contested by static France, the section south of the Loire dominated by small landholders and petty tradesmen living in tiny villages. Comprising about 20 per cent of the total French population, they fall below the average in every respect: income, education, birth rate. Most of them live on farms yielding an average income of less than $750 annually. A large fraction operate shops with a total business turnover of less than $2,000 per annum. Of the thirteen departments with a per capita production of less than 70 per cent of the French average, twelve are in the region. Tax yields per person in the region run as much as 40 per cent below the national average. Well-organized static France is not, but the instinct for survival pits it remorselessly against all the creatures of northern France and its cities. Its negative power is immense. The Vichy regime, in one sense, was the revenge of backward France upon the Popular Front. Most of the social legislation now on the books (and it is sweeping) was put through in a month's period just after Liberation while static France was still discredited by association with the Germans. Since then, the French Left has never been able to enforce its demands against the combined resistance of French business and static France. Static France, indeed, can boast of one supreme, and seemingly lasting, victory. In defending its cause it has been able to confuse the issue completely by foisting upon the nation two issues appropriate not to the twentieth century but to the nineteenth and eighteenth.

The nineteenth-century issue is the state of the state: what kind of constitution? In the United States and Britain, the issue was settled so long ago that precise dates are hard to fix. But France since 1789 has known two monarchies, two empires, five republics, a French state (Vichy), and fifteen constitutions. Through all the republican decades Bonapartist sentiment persisted, "like a latent state of mind," as Siegfried put it. Faced with such opposition, republicans clung to clichés fit for a Jeffersonian democracy of small-holders—notably the works of Alain and the famous mot of Jules Ferry, "What France needs is weak government." In the context of a century's struggle between authoritarians and liberals, every change was a restoration, making an indent for the next, and producing, psychologically at least, a new crop of *émigrés*. Joined to the present discontents, the partisans of what was gone tended to make up a near majority. The Constitution of the Fourth Republic, rejected in one referendum, was finally adopted by a vote of 9 million against 8 million, with 8.5 million abstentions. Assuming the anti-republican character of the Communists and Gaullists, the partisans of the Fourth Republic never won more than half the total vote cast. What especially marked opponents of the regime, moreover, was not their number but the violence of their views. During the Third Republic, Charles Maurras, the darling of respectable right-wing Paris, was convicted of conspiracy to incite the murder of Léon Blum. In no other country have political strikes assumed so widespread and durable a character as the Communist walkouts of 1947. It is because the opposition is almost always disloyal that France has for so long been plagued by political trials—*les affaires*. The Dreyfus case was no mere outcropping of anti-Semitism, still less a matter involving theft of state secrets; it was a challenge to the regime. For that reason too the sordid affairs of Stavisky took on importance. And this was one of the exchanges in a trial held in 1955:

> DEFENSE ATTORNEY: "No need to go into that; the regime is low enough already."
> INTERIOR MINISTER: "You are seeing to that."
> DEFENSE ATTORNEY: "Enthusiastically! And I shall continue until the regime disappears."

Less choler attaches to the eighteenth-century issue which is the place of the Church in the state. But popular division on the matter splits France almost exactly in two. In the 1951 elections, 50.9 per cent of the population voted for parties favoring state aid to Catholic schools; 49.1 per cent were opposed. And the nature of the issue focuses attention on the pettiest details. In 1951, parliamentary business was held up while the Socialists argued that since Ascension Day was a legal holiday, Labor Day ought to be also. During the same parliament another Socialist deputy harangued the Assembly on the grievous wrong of paying a stipend to a priest for acting as watchman over his church, which was also a national monument: a matter of principle, to be sure, for the stipend was $40 annually. Trivial as the issues seem, events of moment hang upon them. One reason the European Defense Community project did not pass the Assembly is that the Socialists, who had voted en bloc for the Coal and Steel Community, regarded it as a Catholic project: the Vaticform. Catholic support kept a corrupt and incompetent High Commissioner in Indochina, largely because he had been attacked by anti-clericals. And at all times the parties of the Right have been able to divide the Center from the Left by raising the clerical issue.

With three issues (economic, constitutional, religious) and

the possibility of a pro or con stand on each, there was a theoretical possibility of eight different parties. During the Fourth Republic, six of the places were filled. There were the Gaullists, left on economic matters, authoritarian on the Constitution, clerical; the Independents, right on economic matters, liberal on the Constitution, clerical; the Popular Republicans (MRP), left on economic matters, liberal on the Constitution, clerical; the Socialists, left on economic matters, liberal on the Constitution, anticlerical; the Communists, left on the economy, authoritarian on the Constitution, anticlerical. Thus, on the economic issue, there was a potential majority of the Left: Gaullists, Popular Republicans, Socialists, and Communists. But the Gaullists and Communists had authoritarian leanings, as against the liberal inclinations of the Socialists and Popular Republicans; and the Socialists and Communists voted against the Gaullists and Popular Republicans on religious questions.

Moreover, atop the three basic issues were piled local and commerical interests, personal splits, and a vast corpus of tiny causes. Repeatedly candidates sought election on the ticket of National Discontent. There were independent Independents. In the 1956 elections the founder and president of the League for Illegitimate Children ran on a platform emphasizing a new deal for bastards. The one thing there was not was a majority party. For fragmentation is writ in the *moeurs* of the nation. "Our weakness is our division," Charles Maurras said for the authoritarian Right. Maurice Thorez, eschewing the Communist myth of monolithic unity, used to complain of "deviations in the proletariat brought on by the petit bourgeois." And Adolphe Thiers, second President of the Third Republic, spoke from the center perhaps the best words ever said for *le système*: "It divides us least."

IV

"ALL government," Burke wrote, "indeed every human benefit and enjoyment, every virtue and every prudent act, is founded on compromise and barter." The central political problem of France is to square the need for "compromise and barter" with the circle of a public opinion atomized into tiny fragments of irreconcilable belief. *Le système* achieved that miracle by using the very diversity of opinion as a screen behind which political bosses could strike bargains without incurring the responsibility for the deals they made. Under it, as Jacques Fauvet noted, Frenchmen were right or left, governments nearly always in the center.

This is not to call the system dishonest. On the contrary, for rigid devotion to the abstract principles of perfect democracy, few regimes could match the Fourth Republic. Elections were orderly and by universal suffrage. An exceptionally large portion of the eligible voters went to the polls: 83 per cent in the general election of January 2, 1956, as against 55 per cent in the American Presidential poll of that year; and 76.8 per cent in the British general election of 1955. In most areas, proportional representation, or some variant of it, insured that minority opinion would not be lost. The multitude of different parties gave expression to a multitude of different opinions. So little did mere organization count, that the most mercurial changes of sentiment showed up in the vote proportions. Between the elections of 1945 and 1946, the Socialists lost a quarter of their total vote; the MRP a third. General de Gaulle's RPF, the largest single party in 1951, lost 3 million votes and shrank to a mere shadow in 1956. Pierre Poujade's Union for the Defense of Tradesmen and Artisans, a blank in 1951, won 2.5 million votes, or 14 per cent of the poll, in 1956, and became a blank again in 1958.

But if the electoral machinery was a sensitive instrument for recording nuance, the Assembly was a gigantic engine for its blunting. The existence of so many parties made necessary government by coalition. Of the twenty-six governments holding office under the Fourth Republic only one—the Blum regime of 1947—was not a coalition, and it lasted only a month. But in the process of putting together coalitions—a behind-the-scenes process—the parties perforce diluted some of their principles. Moreover, whenever hard issues arose and militant extremes tended to assert themselves, there could be thrown into the breach the device of the cabinet crisis. A ritual to outsiders and to not a few Frenchmen, the aim of the cabinet crisis was to force reasonable behavior upon the intransigent. What it did was, first, to isolate the party holding out on a matter of principle; then, thrust upon it the obloquy of obstructing government; and lastly, draw the party into the ways of compromise. As an example of this process, consider the cabinet crisis of spring 1953. On May 21, the cabinet of René Mayer was voted from office, thanks in large measure to opposition from the MRP. Four successive candidates (Paul Reynaud, Pierre Mendès-France, Georges Bidault, André Marie) represented themselves as possible premiers, but failed to win sufficient support. Except for Bidault, their own man, the MRP voted in opposition each time. Against Marie their stand was unanimous. But by that time twenty-nine days had elapsed since the fall of René Mayer. With the Bermuda Big Three conference in the offing, it looked as though France might have no one to sit for her, and blame was beginning to pile upon the shoulders of the MRP. When Joseph Laniel was nominated as Premier eight days later, "the party," as Philip Williams noted, "thought it prudent to support him." The first act of the Laniel government was to pass, with MRP approval, the bill on which M. René Mayer had been defeated. That pattern, indeed, became traditional. The government of Maurice Bourgès-Maunoury passed as first measure the wages bill on which his predecessor, Guy Mollet, went down; and when

Bourgès fell, his successor, Felix Gaillard, very early won approval of the measure which had been Bourgès's undoing. "There was no case," Jacques Fauvet commented, "of a new government which was not conceded more than its predecessors." As Edgar Faure wrote, the cabinet crisis was "not a mandate for a policy," but "an excuse for a concession—a sort of method of government by shakes."

Two favorable consequences flowed from the method of government by shakes. First, extremes were either kept from power or obliged to modulate their harshest views in the interest of the emoluments of office. Through most of the life of the Fourth Republic well over 40 per cent of the electorate voted for anti-Republican parties: Communists, Gaullists, and Poujadists. The Communists, in the early days, joined the government, and paid for it by consenting to the dissolution of paramilitary formations built up during the Liberation and by accepting a hold-the-line policy on wages. Later, after being expelled from the coalition, the Communist leadership, in daily contact with the seedy politicians of the Center, seemed to undergo an embourgeoisement. "Our Communists," Fauvet wrote, "have a middle-class face; they offer reassurances." A deputy of another party once remarked on the strangely sweet tone of their conversations, "You'd think they were the only Frenchmen who never read *l'Humanité*." At all times, moreover, the presence of the large Communist bloc inside France served to make the deputies of the system keenly anti-Soviet and eager to cooperate with other Western countries. Without benefit of real popular support, the system took France into the Brussels Pact and Atlantic Alliance and the Coal and Steel Community. The old tradition of diplomatic partnership with Russia against Germany was foregone, and it was only when General de Gaulle arrived again that fears of a revived Paris-Moscow axis, unfounded as it turned out, began to mount.

As to the Gaullists, they were first kept at arm's length. One group split from the leadership in 1952 to join the Pinay government. The rump participated, without much effect, in the Mendès-France and Faure governments. By 1955 the party was in complete disarray. That its doctrine had been corrupted and its unity broken by the spoils of office was an open secret. One story had it that the General, reproaching one of the straying Gaullists, said, "But for me, you never would have been a deputy." "On the contrary," the reply went, "but for you I would have been a minister long ago." So withering, indeed, were the effects of the system on party doctrine and unity, that to be out of office was considered the cure for what ailed a party, as witness the phrase *le guérison d'opposition*—the cure of opposition. Precisely because of those withering effects, right-wing groups in France have tended to take the form of extraparliamentary leagues; while trade unionists, to keep cohesion, incline toward apolitical syndicalism. Raymond Aron, noting the cases of the Socialists and Radicals, set it down as a rule of thumb that when a party entered a government, it was over the hill.

The second consequence of the system was the power of the higher civil service. Put together out of disparate elements, coalitions rarely held together for more than a year, the average lasting about eight months under the Fourth Republic. At the Quai d'Orsay, Robert Schuman and Georges Bidault between them held the Foreign Ministry through twenty different governments stretching over ten years. But usually ministers were barely able to familiarize themselves with the complex and ever-changing problems making up the daily business of the modern state. For continuity, they relied to an increasing extent on the civil service. "France," André Siegfried wrote of the Fourth Republic, "was not governed; she was administered." Under the Fourth, though, the civil service was a superb elite corps. The financial and economic administration, in particular, was staffed by far-seeing central planners, many of them educated abroad, all of them familiar with Keynesian doctrine and far advanced in their thinking over the pedestrian views

of the average French businessman, not to say peasant. "I
feel like a foreigner whenever I talk economics with another
Frenchman," one young Inspecteur de Finances, educated at
Harvard, once confessed. But given wide autonomy as chiefs
of the nationalized industries or in government bodies like
Jean Monnet's Commissariat du Plan, and protected by the
system from extremist pressures, the Inspecteurs de Finance,
mining engineers, and managers put France through the paces
of an economic expansion almost unknown in her history. Its
effects are seen in growth in every area of economic activity.
The most telling figures of all come in what is beginning to
emerge as the prime national resource: power to consume. Between 1950 and 1957, French consumption rose by 40 per cent,
an annual growth of 5 per cent, surpassed only by West Germany (8 per cent), and well ahead of Britain (1.1 per cent),
Belgium (2.5 per cent), and the U.S. (3.8 per cent). Especially
revealing are the areas of increased consumption: household
furnishings and electrical equipment up 110 per cent; toys up
100 per cent; autos and motorcycles up 50 per cent; meat, fowl,
fish, and eggs up 41 per cent; radio and TV up 85 per cent.
What these figures spell out is a modernization, not to say
Americanization, of consuming habits. Not only was prosperity achieved, but there was laid down a base for its continuation and growth; a proclivity to consume. "You have to go back
more than a century, to the beginning of the Second Empire,"
Maurice Duverger wrote in retrospect, "to find in our country
such industrial dynamism." To its eternal glory, *le système* presided over a French miracle.

v

Who cannot recite the weaknesses of *le système?* Short gover-
ments which grew weaker as they grew older; interminable debate on mere trivialities; absence of authority at moments of
crisis; inabilty to face up to hard decisions—it was a regular

litany. But even where the criticism is just, most of the trouble
derived less from the system than from the spirit of mystification forced upon it by the French body politic. Two major
weaknesses there were, however, endemic to the system. It
made lukewarm friends, and passionate enemies.

Working the system required a rare kind of political leader.
All the tedious club-room skills—slapping backs, remembering
names, clasping hands, asking after family, making dull little
jokes—were prerequisites. *Habileté*—the adroitness implicit in
masking intentions and soothing suspicions—was another essential. So was a keen intelligence and firm sense of purpose.
Without them it was possible to tack so much as to lose
direction.

Of the men who reached the top of the greasy pole in the
Fourth Republic, perhaps only Edgar Faure filled the bill: a
hero of the system. Once the youngest member of the Paris
bar, a writer of mystery stories, trained economist and student
of Russian, Faure possessed a mind of real power, but was also
witty ("I was born old and aged rapidly") and sociable. At
home in the best Paris salons—one of them run by his wife
Lucie Faure—he could also knock back shots of red wine with
the toughest of his mining and mountaineer constituents in
the Jura. Journalists almost without exception would refer to
him as "Edgar," with a knowing wink or roguish glint in the
eye. It is a mark of his standing with the deputies, and a reason
for the knowing wink, that Edgar, though he once advocated
a measure whereby ministers in one government would be debarred from sitting in the next, participated as Finance Minister in the cabinets of almost diametrically opposite but
successive governments—those of Joseph Laniel and Pierre
Mendès-France—and then himself succeeded Mendès. Of tim-
ing he was a master: in the fall of 1955, at a meeting of the
Radical party which was absolutely dominated by followers of
Mendès, Edgar delayed his appearance to the point where the
prime matter of interest became whether he would show or

not; when he finally arrived, the whole hall rose and shouted, "He's coming, he's coming." Making use of confusion was a special forte. When Mendès, in the fall of 1955, sought to change the voting system before the general election due in the spring, Edgar allowed him to push through motion after motion in both the Assembly and Senate. To thicken the soup, he came out himself for a system of electoral reform involving a redrawing of the whole voting map of France. Then he announced he would put his own system before the Assembly on a vote of confidence. Thanks to opposition by Mendès, it was defeated. But by an overlooked constitutional clause, Edgar had the right to dissolve the Assembly after the defeat. That he promptly did, forcing immediate elections under the old system: his objective from the very first. Through all the slyness, though, there shone clear purpose. Slipping and sliding, palming off deuces here, and there slipping aces from a sleeve, he put across settlements of the Moroccan and Tunisian issues despite the sharpest opposition. As Finance Minister, he presided over the onset of the economic miracle, and, unlike some other Finance Ministers, knew exactly what he was doing. At the Radical Congress of 1955, he was able to document the boom in one of the most sensitive areas: housing. And it was a statement of real faith when Faure told the congress, "We believe in social reform."

Unfortunately not all trimmers are like Edgar Faure. Toward the end of the Fourth Republic there began to emerge a kind of false Edgar. Felix Gaillard and Maurice Bourgès-Maunoury, for instance, were, like Edgar, "young and dynamic," but did next to nothing in office. Bourgès, when a delegation of striking gendarmes sought him out, hid in the Assembly basement. Gaillard was able to accuse Mendès of "intellectual masochism" in a formal speech, and then put it about that someone else had written the speech. Lack of stature, indeed, was the rule, for the men who made good during the latter half of the Fourth Republic. According to one story, the more meaningful for perhaps being legendary, Antoine Pinay, on being introduced to a famous polar explorer, could think of only one question: "What do they say in the North Pole about France?" Guy Mollet could believe that Nasser was Hitler, and persist in the belief even after the rather telling differences between Germany and Egypt had been explained. Robert Lacoste used to refer to himself as "*un vieux con*," and when it once was suggested that he might become Premier, a friend interpolated, "What a catastrophe for the French language." André le Troquer, president of the Assembly, was shown, by the Ballet Rose scandal, to be a sexual pervert. André Morice, Defense Minister under Bourgès, denied that he had profiteered on building military installations in Algeria, but not that he had built Atlantic defenses for the Nazis in 1943, using slave labor. The list of the second rate could be multiplied *ad nauseam*.

"Geese who saved the Capitol," Clemenceau had said of the men nurtured by the system. The tragedy is that the geese drove out the eagles. Churchill could call himself a "House of Commons man," but apart from Edgar Faure, the impressive Frenchmen of the postwar era were distinguished by absence, or alienation, from the Assembly. Charles de Gaulle and Jean Monnet, in fact, retained prestige by holding themselves aloof. Neither made any secret of contempt for the deputies, and ultimately both depended for power on external supports: Monnet on Washington, Wall Street, and his allies in united Europe; De Gaulle on the Algerian crisis. The case of Pierre Mendès-France provides one measure of what happened to men of great capacity and drive who lacked pliability but tried to remain within the system.

Mendès's basic push was in the direction of the economic modernization accomplished by the system in its special, wavering fashion of doing precisely what it seemed not to do. But where the system moved under cover and by indirection, Mendès wanted to come into the open. His very first acts—the settlement in Indochina; the interdependence agreement with Tunisia; the solution, by death and resurrection, of the European Defense Community issue—were for him only a clearing of the ground. Thereafter he set to work. Open war was declared on probably the worst symbols of static France: the *bouilliers de cru,* or private distillers, most of them working for marginal vineyards and selling wine which, except for government support, sometimes to the point of diluting gasoline with it, could not have been sold at all. His milk drinking, light lunches, and swift dashes back and forth (the *Canard Enchaîné* once imagined him darting about Paris by helicopter) were equally symbolic boosts to modernity. In his ministry, the young Keynesian economists who had operated behind the scenes stepped front and center. Hand in hand with the economic program went an all-out drive for political reform. Instead of playing the coalition game inside the Assembly, Mendès sought popular mandates in weekly national radio broadcasts. In his scheme for electoral reform he advocated the single-member constituency, re-enforcing each deputy's responsibility to his voters. And he sought to make over the Radical party, traditionally a collection of notable figures able to coalesce to the right or to the left, into a monolithic disciplined party, like Labour in Britain.

The result proved, on the one hand, the impossibility of achieving reforms without the mystification of the system. In the country at large, Mendès roused the most passionate hatreds. Pierre Poujade, whose movement drew immense sustenance as an opposition to Mendès, used at dinner to nod at a water jug in the shape of a pig and say, "Please pass the Mendès." Threats of physical violence drove Mendès, a most courageous man, to use bodyguards and to enlist a squad of personal bully boys for protection at his meetings. In the Assembly he was equally disliked. A storm of shouts and whistles was deliberately whipped up to drown out the speech he tried to make after being defeated. "You have no business to make this speech," a Communist shouted. "The tribune isn't meant for personal propaganda," an MRP delegate crowed. And when Mendés asserted the debate wasn't over, an Independent, known for mild manners, interjected, "Yes it is." Mendès left the hall. Alexander Werth, a Mendèsist to the core, wrote on the occasion, "amid loud booing." For his own part, Mendès's reaction to the trials of power, and the sharp bite of defeat, was almost like that of De Gaulle and Monnet. Without pronouncing the words, he turned on *le système*. "*Le gang*," Mendès told Werth, "*le gang*—it's not just this or that lobby; it's not only the beet growers or the colonialists—it's an ensemble, the whole damned lot of them, who have become, as it were, part of our system."

Passionate devotion to democratic forms attached Mendès to the Fourth Republic to its dying day—and even beyond. What happened when devotion was less passionate is suggested by the case of Jacques Soustelle. By background and career he seemed almost a caricature of left-wing France. A Protestant and son of a worker, he made his mark as a brilliant student in the social sciences (anthropology) and first entered politics as secretary to a fellow-traveling anti-Fascist organization. During the resistance he did prodigies for the Free French in South America, ending the war as a trusted lieutenant of General de Gaulle with special responsibility in the intelligence field. Thereafter he plunged into politics as deputy from Lyons and principal organizer of the Gaullist parties. Second man to De Gaulle, and to Herriot in the Lyons constituency, he was prey to a not unfamiliar kind of ambition. But few men worked harder. I once interviewed Soustelle early in the morning in an apartment to which he had just moved. Crates of books, bits of covered furniture, unhung pictures, piles of linens were scattered all about the room. In one corner was Soustelle's desk. He was writing a pamphlet reply to Raymond Aron on Algeria. With industry went enlightened views. A strong proponent of economic modernization, Soustelle had

pushed as few men the cause of the backward peoples. In Mexico he had taken up the cudgels for the Indians, and he
favored a loose federal arrangement for the French Empire.
Then it happened to him to take power—as Mendès-France's
nominee for Governor General of Algeria.

Foes of Soustelle now cite his case as an example of Acton's
famous mot; in fact, it is the opposite: corruption by impotence. The FLN would not negotiate with him; but neither
would Arab victims of FLN terror cooperate. The settlers
hated Soustelle, put it about he was a Jew called Ben Soussan.
With the civil service, Soustelle acknowledged in a memoir of
his Algerian year, his "authority was often without effect." The
army he found geared to "large operations, useless because of
their very size, and which too often thrust the people into the
arms of the rebels." Paris, Soustelle deluged with pleas for decision: "Say Yes or No"; "I insist more than ever on the need
to take the initiative very quickly"; "the hour has come to take
a stand and stick to it." In season and out, he was fobbed off:
"One hardly heard any but negative voices"; "How many
times did I see, sadly, the poisons of campaigns led by irre-
sponsibles." In the end of his term, when the Faure government decided upon dissolution of the French Assembly and
new elections—a step which had the gravest import for security
in Algeria—Soustelle learned of the decision only by chance
from a minister he met casually at an airport. "I could hardly
believe my ears," he writes. Disillusioned beyond measure,
Soustelle returned to France in 1956, a confirmed foe of the
whole system. And he held in his hands an issue which made
him dangerous—Algeria.

VI

IN AN earlier day, the putting off of good men might have been
absorbed. Disaffection of strong leaders could even have been
cited as a sign of democratic strength, in keeping with France's

supposed need for weak governments, or even the Jeffersonian concept of the best government as being that which governs least. But those concepts derive from the infant days of democracy when it was building on the ruins of monarchical power. As self-protection there then developed a doctrinal bias against individual authority which seemed to hold the seeds of monarchial restoration. But the more democratic government has become implanted and the more industrialism has taken root, the more individual authority has revived. Very few men in the history of the world have held more power than Presidents Roosevelt, Truman, Eisenhower, and Kennedy. Macmillan, not to say Churchill, commanded authority the most ambitious Stuart would envy. As much as Stalin, if not more, Khrushchev embodies the Cult of Personality.

The explanation for this personification of power is not very difficult. On the one hand, events by their complexity have assumed a nonhuman scale; only by identifying policies with individuals can the great mass of us even begin to comprehend the alternate possibilities available in domestic or foreign politics. On the other hand, to be effective, modern government requires the cooperation and sacrifices of great masses of men. Far more than in a monarchy or dictatorship, people must believe that the government is their creature. But the evocation of such faith is the work of men, not systems. There must be an Ike to like.

The system closed off the possibility of personal devotion. While stirring individuals were exiled from office, the seats of power were screened and insulated from the great mass of Frenchmen. The President was elected not by the people but by the deputies. Thanks to the complexities of coalition making, it was almost impossible for a Frenchman to identify his vote with the choice of Premier. A Briton voting Tory knows that he is striking a blow for Mr. Macmillan. But a Frenchman who wanted to see a right-winger, say M. Pinay, as Premier, might find that he should vote Communist, on the theory that in reaction to a strong Left, the Right would hold together. Before the 1956 elections which resulted in the government of Guy Mollet, a most reliable public-opinion poll showed that only 2 per cent of the electorate favored Mollet as Premier. Not 1 per cent wanted the two men who succeeded Mollet—Bourgès-Maunoury and Felix Gaillard. The one man substantial numbers of voters wanted had no chance at all. He was Pierre Mendès-France, with 27 per cent of the poll. Most striking, 40 per cent of the polled electorate had no choice for Premier.

What that 40 per cent indicates is a break in the circuit between governors and governed. Baffled by its complexities and unable to identify with any single heroic figure, Frenchmen simply lost interest in the Fourth Republic. Crisis after crisis passed with, headlines apart, no sign of public concern. Taxi drivers, knowledgeable about the meanest back street, would stare blankly when directed to the Matignon—the Premier's official residence. A steady decline was registered in the active membership of all political parties, and in the subscription lists of opinion journals. During the summer-long strikes of 1953, Catherine Gavin noted that "the annual Tour de France bicycle race was followed with even more than the usual passionate enthusiasm. The hero of France . . . was neither soldier nor statesman: he was Louis Bobet, the first Frenchman for years to win the 3,000-mile race . . ." As Fauvet, quoting Lamartine, put it, "La France s'ennuie"—France was bored.

But while most of the country prospered and ignored politics, one section of the nation intensified a destructive interest. The static France of small shopkeepers and peasants south of the Loire, being largely self-sufficient, had enormous advantages in weathering the period of wartime shortages. It is estimated that during the liberation period some 150,000 laborers acquired small shops. For the next five or six years the number mounted by over 5,000 annually. The total was at all times too great for any but the luckiest to thrive; according to a study made in 1956, France had 942,000 retail shops, or one for every 54 persons as against a European ratio of 1:71; and 410,-000 food shops, or one for every 101 persons as against a European ratio of 1:134. With reconstruction new problems multiplied for the small shopkeeper, notably south of the Loire. Prosperity up North drew consumers away; the Departments of Lozère and Upper Loire, for instance, underwent a 9 per cent population decrease between 1946 and 1954. Retail chains began to mushroom: between 1947 and 1954, the number of chain stores almost doubled. Then in 1953, the inflation which had permitted shopkeepers to pass inefficiency along in rising costs abruptly ceased. The cost of living, mounting by 10 per cent before, stood still in 1953 and in the next four years inched upward only 6 per cent. With a stable currency went a beginning of tax reform: notably an increase in basic assessment, long overdue: a tightening of general control over tax collection; and a stiffening in the penalties for tax fraud. The result was to push the small shopkeeper to the wall. The general prosperity of France, the chief accomplishment of the system, meant for him bankruptcy and the prospect of sinking to proletarian ranks.

In Pierre Poujade these victims of progress found a remarkable champion. A shopkeeper himself, he had worked as a traveling salesman, and had a wide network of contacts throughout the South. His own town, St. Céré in the Lot Department, had witnessed a decline in population of nearly 50 per cent over the past century; but the number of shopkeepers had held constant at about 300—a fifth of the town's active population. Son of an architect, he embodied in his career the dreaded slide toward proletarian stature ("Because I want to be independent and work like a madman, do I have to lose caste?" he once asked). A veteran and not bad-looking, he had a personal flair to which was added the supreme gift of the demagogue: the knack of focusing all discontents by attacking what the mass instinctively feared and envied. He was against: the system ("the mess"); Paris ("the monster"); the Assembly ("a den of iniquity"); the deputies ("old rubbish and young traitors"); the Communists (the party of "free shaves"); the Socialists ("mechanized irresponsibility"); the Independents ("snot-nosed cockroaches"); Pinay ("the leather Premier"); Edgar Faure ("the worst bandit of the Fourth Republic"); the press ("a cheese, the more admired the smellier it is"); the unions ("bodyguards of the Republic"); big business (the "unpatriotic and inhuman financial power"); foreigners ("We want to live as we do today on the banks of the Seine and the Garonne, and if there are people who like life on the banks of the Moskva and the Mississippi, well, let them go there"); the Jews ("Frenchmen of recent date"); and the educated classes ("France suffers overproduction of people with degrees, engineers, economists, philosophers, and other dreamers who have lost touch with reality").

Against all these he posed the past and the people. Valmy and Verdun were favorite references in Poujadist literature; one of his supporters once suggested giving power to an "incontestable military authority." "We must save the French Union" was the master slogan of one of his meetings. On the economic plane he backed what Stanley Hoffman has called sclerosis: "We defend the traditional structure of the French economy; we are against conversion." Politically his pamphlets spoke of a Committee of Public Safety, and a basic goal was a convening of the Estates General, as in 1789. "We are peaceful citizens who want some order in the house" was one cry, and another was a call for a "return to the basic principles of the republic" and "to the people." The exponents of basic principle, the true people, were, of course, his own followers. They were: "our fathers who were at Verdun, and now and then take a drink"; "David against Goliath"; "the free men who say '*merde*' when they want to."

Striking success was enjoyed by the Poujadist movement from its inception in July 1953, when M. Poujade, warned by a Communist municipal official of an impending tax audit, organized a successful resistance among the shopkeepers of St. Céré. By the end of that year Poujadists held office in the Lot Department. Before another year was out they had held their first national congress—in Algiers. By January 1955, Poujadist representatives had been received by a group in the National Assembly, and held a Paris meeting drawing a crowd of 100,-000 persons. In March, they forced Edgar Faure to promise an eventual watering down of the hated tax reforms. In June, the clientele, originally shopkeepers, was widened to include peasants, workers, and white-collar workers. In July, at the second national congress, Save the French Union was made a chief slogan. In December, Poujadists swept the elections to the Paris Chamber of Commerce. For the general elections of January 2, 1956, the Poujadists, running on the theme of—"*Sortez Les Sortants*," in effect, throw the rascals out—presented candidates in eighty-two Departments, less only than the Communists and Socialists. They carried at least 5 per cent of the vote in all but three Departments. Their total was over 2.5 million voters or 9.2 per cent of the poll; fifty-two Poujadist deputies were elected.

From this death rattle of static France, there emerged no practical programs. "You don't think," M. Poujade once said, "that we're going to rack our brains for solutions so that [others] can say, 'We are the saviors.'" Void of programmatic ideas, Poujadism had to expire. But it raised to the surface of French politics two emotion-charged themes: a hatred of system and its politicians and bureaucrats; and, by contrast, a xenophobic nationalism. The two themes put static France in harmony with the Europeans of Algeria, with the army, and with disaffected leaders, like Soustelle, willing to use Algeria as a sword against the system. Together they prepared the ground for the political treatment of Algeria—the ground down which the Fourth Republic plunged headlong to ruin.

VII

IN ANY country the liquidation of empire is a political trans-action of the utmost difficulty. National pride works at all times against the cession of territory, hence the flames gener-ated by such trivial irredentist matters as Trieste or Cyprus or western New Guinea. Even where resignation rules, dema-gogues can stir interest and force the pace: once "54:40 or fight" is pronounced, no one dare accept 54:39. In the guise of pa-triotism, moreover, the most unreasonable claims can be made to seem just. Political freebooters long convinced Britain she had title to Ireland; behind the cry, heard not long ago in this country, that treason lost China, there lurked the assumption that somehow the United States had China to lose. And par-ticularly when fighting has already begun, "our boys" can be thrown into the scales to outweigh the most unreasonable concessions.

To such tactics no country was more vulnerable than post-war France. Hurt feelings of *amour-propre,* easy to play upon when not smarting by themselves, had been induced by a drop in national prestige reaching back to Napoleon's day and un-derlined in the debacle of 1940. Prosperity fostered a cocky tone in public affairs, and made it possible to support the luxury of colonial ventures. The army was only one powerful vested interest ceaselessly opposed to a yielding up of territories. A second was the group of marginal firms unloading on a pro-tected market what they could not sell elsewhere: in 1952, for instance, 25 per cent of French textile production went to the colonies. To these were added local interests. In Indochina there was the Catholic Church with a big native following as well as the planters, merchants, bankers, and profiteers in the piaster trade. Tunisia was the fief of some 10,000 French civil servants; Morocco besides mining concerns and a French ad-ministration housed some 375,000 Europeans holding French citizenship. To all these private interests, the divided character of the French Assembly lent a formidable negative power, and overriding the resistance was the more difficult for a basic flaw in the French overseas system. Nations tend to project their own images abroad, and where Britain had planted local government—a base on which independence could be reared—France transmitted direct administration. "Self-determination" was not even part of the vocabulary of the French Union. There was thus no acceptable juridical approach to independence; no schedule of easy stages for progress from dependence to sovereignty. The pass had to be forced. It is a mark of the difficulty that only the catastrophe of Dienbienphu made an Indochina settlement possible.

It is a tribute to the system that its paladins learned the Indochinese lesson and applied it in Morocco and Tunisia. Facing up at last to the task of liquidating empire, they evolved a characteristically zigzag device for giving independence without seeming to—the device of the *solution truquée,* or trick solution. Its elements included: a *choc psychologique,* or dramatic move, awakening France to the issue; an abstract and complex formula granting independence under the guise of seeming to assure continued French control; and the use of well-known French nationalists, associated with the army or the Right, as a cover for the whole operation: "*un homme du droit,*" as the saying went, "*pour une politique de la gauche.*"

In Tunisia the shock was a flight by Mendès-France to Tunis on July 31, 1954—the first of its kind by a French Premier. With him as cover, Mendès took Marshal Pierre-Alphonse Juin, the son of an Algerian policeman and a darling of the North African lobby. The formula was "internal autonomy." Gilbert Grandval, years later, accurately described it as a phrase which sounded well but rang false. But at the time, Pierre Joly could say of the agreement giving Tunisia "internal autonomy" that "Far from weakening the position of France, the conventions you are asked to ratify on the contrary confirm the essential rights held by France under former treaties, and give her every means of enforcing them. I would even say they are reinforced." And most of the Assembly agreed. Of the 625 deputies, 538 voted for the conventions. In less than a year Tunisia was independent.

In Morocco, the shock was the murder of a score of French settlers by nationalist tribesmen on August 20, 1955: the so-called massacre of Oued Zem. No doubt Premier Faure did not will the killing; neither, though warned in advance, did he do anything to forefend it. And he turned it very swiftly to account. Immediately after Oued Zem, Faure came up with the formula: return of the exiled Sultan of Morocco, Mohammed ben Youssef, from Madagascar to Paris for negotiations. As cover Faure used General Georges Catroux, who arranged the Sultan's trip to Paris, and Foreign Minister Antoine Pinay, who negotiated directly with the Sultan when the monarch reached Paris. The understanding pledged by Faure less than a week before the Sultan's arrival in France was that Mohammed ben Youssef would never go back to Morocco. The fruit of the negotiations, less than a month later, was the Sultan's return to Morocco bearing unconditional independence. So close had Faure kept his intentions that an aide, told the Sultan was coming to Paris, exclaimed to Faure, "But that means independence." To which Faure replied, "Did you ever doubt it?" And doubt or not, once the deed was done it could not be undone. On November 14, 1956, the Assembly approved Faure's Moroccan settlement by a 477–140 vote.

Six weeks later, in the general election of January 2, 1956, Algeria came center stage in French politics. The subsequent history of the Fourth Republic is the story of failure to find a *solution truquée* for Algeria. What blocked it was the interaction of two opposing groups which also came to prominence with the 1956 general elections. One was the Socialist party; the other the Algeria Firsters.

VIII

THE Socialists took on special importance because of the breakdown of the new Assembly. More than 200 of the 595 deputies
(150 Communists, 52 Poujadists) were beyond the pale of coalition making. United, any one of the other four major parties
could block a coalition. But the hundred or so Independents
could get together only in advocacy of right-wing economic
measures. The MRP with 85 deputies had suffered losses in
the poll and was bent on moving from association with the
Independents to liaison with the Socialists under cover of a
period outside office. The Radicals were divided between Men-
dèsists, linked for campaign purposes with the Socialists in the
Republican Front, and old-line placemen, ready to participate
in any combination. Only the Socialists had firm party discipline. With 95 sure votes, a standing alliance with the Men-
dèsists, and a covert tie to the MRP, they were the key to the
Assembly. Alone able to block any combination, they were
perforce the party on which all coalitions had to rest. Three
weeks after the election they took office in a minority coalition
of the Republican Front. Its chief was Guy Mollet, the first
Socialist Premier in a decade. Mendès was minister without
portfolio.

During the electoral campaign the Socialists had lined up
behind Mendès in stressing an Algerian settlement as a primary
party plank. "At any price we must find a solution to the Algerian conflict"; "We cannot maintain ourselves there if we depend upon the army, the police, and repression"; "no solution
by armed force is possible"—these were a few of Mendès's
watchwords. If anything, Guy Mollet was even more out-
spoken: "Do you want our boys to die for the millions of the
colonial exploiters?" he asked the electors of Arras. One of his
chief lieutenants, Robert Lacoste, had nailed his colors directly
to Mendès's staff: "The Socialists support Mendès-France be-

cause he liquidated the Indochina war, and . . . in working up the conventions with Tunisia opened the way to peace in North Africa." Some Socialists even came out obliquely for negotiations with the FLN. "The solution," Max Lejeune told the electors of the Somme, "can be found only in political negotiations." Christian Pineau, Foreign Minister in the Mollet government and those of Maurice Bourgès-Maunoury and Felix Gaillard as well, had as an electoral formula: "Negotiate, negotiate, negotiate."

The coming of the Socialists to office thus upset one of the primary ground rules of the *solution truquée*. Out in the open, they had no right-wing associates behind which to take cover. Having all but proclaimed the fact themselves, they were universally suspected of willingness to deal Algeria away. The policy of the Left would, this time, have to be conducted by men of the Left.

Halfhearted men of the Left to boot. Over the years the Socialist party had passed from an advanced guard of revolution to an interest group of provincial, middle-aged civil servants. Nearly 90 per cent of the Socialist votes came from cities of less than 100,000 inhabitants; over 40 per cent from hamlets of less than 2,000. Among party workers, close to 70 per cent were over forty years old; more than a third past fifty. Among party candidates in the past three elections, there were ten times as many civil servants as industrial workers. A full third of the party hierarchy were state employees by profession: the majority of them schoolteachers. If the economic interest of the party still lay to the left, the emphasis was more on comfort than on structural reform of the nation and its business. The chief economic innovation of the Mollet government was characteristic: an increase from two to three weeks in annual paid vacations. The anticolonial stance of the party was purely doctrinaire, a holdover from the days when imperialism was "the last stage of capitalism." The sharpest interest of the party clientele was in power and the patronage that went with it.

The Socialists had become the kinds of politicians who live not for, but on, politics. Toward office the Mollet government, as André Philippe, a Socialist himself, put it, acted "like a *nouveau riche* toward money." The administration was colonized on a scandalous scale, and there was vividly apparent the cronyism of men who fear to hang apart. "Not one of ours," was Guy Mollet's comment when Mendès eventually left the government. But when pressed to oust Lacoste, Mollet stuck fast: "He's a Socialist . . . a friend." In clinging to office the Socialists were above all determined not to lay themselves open to a charge and a defeat which most of them could count as their most vivid political experience. The charge of being un-French which, when leveled against Léon Blum, did so much to bring down the Popular Front. To provincial suspicion of the cosmopolitan, the Socialists joined a horror of seeming less patriotic than the ultranationalists. "We're fed up with internationals," Max Lejeune put it.

The weakness of the Socialists was the strength of the Algeria Firsters. These had commenced operations as political agents of the settlers: a mere handful of deputies and senators. But where the Socialists were defensive about patriotism, the Algeria Firsters wrapped themselves in the Tricolor, shrieked high the national grandeur, and hurled against doubters the charge of being un-French. That program held out a natural appeal for any opposition, and very quickly backers began to swarm. For Gaullists like Soustelle and Michel Debré, Algeria First was a battering ram against the Fourth Republic. The Poujadists used it to raise tax resistance to a national cause. For some of the Independents it was a weapon against Socialist economic policy. And within every party men on the make took the high ground of Algeria First as a vantage point for directing shots against men who were already made. It served to give Roger Duchet the whip hand over Antoine Pinay and Paul Reynaud among the Independents; it was Georges Bidault's spearhead against the leadership of the MRP; André

Morice and, at times, Maurice Bourgès-Maunoury and Felix
Gaillard used it against such fellow Radicals as Mendès and
Faure. Among the Socialists, when dissidence cropped up,
there were some leaders, Lacoste particularly but also Max Lejeune and occasionally Guy Mollet, ready to use Algeria First
as a disciplinary whip.

The doctrine itself bore the marks of a motley following.
The beginning point was *Algérie Française*. "They are our
brothers," Soustelle cried of the Algerians, and every Algeria
Firster echoed the nonsense (broadcast by Hervé Alphand, the
French Ambassador to Washington) that "Algeria has been
French since 1834, as Brittany since 1491, Alsace since 1648,
Corsica since 1769, Savoy since 1860." To lose Algeria was not
only to slice off a section of the national domain, but also an
immoral act. "One million two hundred thousand Frenchmen
aren't cattle to be sold," Soustelle thundered. For Algeria itself,
independence would be a disaster: "It will become Pan-Arab,
Communist, or American, perhaps all three," Soustelle predicted. The gravest consequences would follow for France. According to Soustelle's reasoning there would be in automobiles
alone a loss of sales which "support 20,000 workers earning 10
billion francs in annual salary." "The Sahara," he claimed,
"offers the only chance of meeting France's needs without depending on the Arabs or Americans." Worse still, France
would be reduced first to a small European state, another Portugal, then to nothingness. "After falling back on the [metro-
pole]," Soustelle wrote, "there will be a retreat to the immaterial. For the fight is not over Algeria, it is over decadence,"
which, Algeria lost, would be France's certain fate.

Fortunately, the argument continued, there was an easy way
to ward off these miseries. Pacification, the military repression
of the rebellion, was that way, and it was a cardinal tenet of
the Algeria Firsters that the job was virtually done anyhow.
Lacoste, in June 1956, predicted victory "in six months." In
September, the next month would see "a package of highly sig-

nificant results." In December, he uttered the lapidary phrase "last quarter of an hour." In January: "the FLN has lost." If anything was needed, it was only the crowding on of a little more sail. "The whole country," said André Morice, "must be at the side of her 450,000 sons who fight to save the future." "What we have to do," Soustelle enjoined, is "to perfect and step up day by day" the policy being followed in Algeria. "You remember when we were at Verdun," Lacoste told a meeting of his constituency, "and Clemenceau told us to hold fast. In Algeria too we have to hold fast."

But let anyone suggest some different approach and the furies gave tongue. Did the intellectuals express misgivings about brutal methods? Bidault wrote them off as "masochists," and Soustelle said, "Our intelligentsia gives the enemy arguments, slogans, propaganda themes." Was the Quai d'Orsay in favor of negotiations? "We have a diplomatic corps," Lacoste blustered, "made up of *cons*." Did the Tunisians offer to mediate? Bourguiba, according to Soustelle, was a "pocket Hitler." Did the United Nations take an interest? "It suffices to be European to be wrong in the U.N.," Soustelle argued. Did the United States lean toward a North African federation? "A Franco-African federation," André Morice shot back, "is a betrayal of France." Did this country aid the Tunisians? "How would they like it," Bidault asked, "if we began arming Cuba or Puerto Rico?" and Soustelle said, "If there are Frenchmen dying across the Mediterranean, it is thanks to Mr. Dulles." As to criticism of Pacification, it was intolerable. "We are in 1917," Roger Duchet declared. "We are ready to back any man who will finally be able to accomplish the task of tracking down traitors." "We are at war," Bourgès echoed, "and should show only the will to crush the enemy." "We have asked the Premier to act with toughness against the Fifth Column of demoralization," André Morice said. And when *l'Express* intimated that Morice had worked for the Germans in World War II, he retorted, "The enemies of France who attack me will be destroyed . . . It is a plot which goes beyond me personally. They want to rob us of our victory, to steal from the nation the fruits of the victory which the army already has within its grasp."

That such rantings had a deep or broad effect on French public opinion seems doubtful. There is only slight evidence for the theory that in the mid-fifties a chauvinist wave overwhelmed France. On the contrary, during this period the Saar passed out of French hands without stirring a murmur, and the steps taken toward European integration and the eventual independence of French holdings south of the Sahara excited only feeble protests. At all times, moreover, public-opinion polls showed a distinct disposition for peace in Algeria. But the sentiment for peace was never compressed against the pistons of political action. The Socialists, fearful of the un-French charge, gave no lead. Barely touched by the war in blood or money losses, the ordinary citizens did not force the pace. Serious partisans of negotiations thus found themselves attacked by the Algeria Firsters without winning compensating benefits from any other quarter. Not unnaturally they tended to hold their tongues. As during the Korean war in this country the China Lobby, without real popular backing, managed to drive from the field so many proponents of a sensible policy, so in France the Algeria Firsters, equally bereft of mass support, silenced men with reasonable ideas about Algeria. Mendès, after three months in the Mollet cabinet, left the government, and in the eighteen months thereafter addressed the Assembly only three times. Edgar Faure took time out for long trips to the Soviet Union and Communist China. Raymond Aron published his *Tragédie algérienne* with an anguished *cri du coeur* ("each citizen is obliged to die for his country; none is obliged to lie for it") after holding the manuscript away from the publisher for a year. When Pierre Viansson-Ponté, a leading political journalist, sought to poll eight prominent deputies on their reaction to a declaration made by Bourguiba, six refused to answer. "Dangerous," "useless," "not desirable in the current state of opinion"—these were some of the reasons offered for failure to respond. And in that climate the marvelous engine of the system, the device of the *solution truquée*, was stood upon its head. To the bitter end, the men of the Left were made to follow a policy of the Right.

IX

THE inversion made itself felt a week after the Mollet government took office. True to campaign promises M. Mollet raised Algeria to the first order of state business. "This problem," he said in his investiture speech, "dominates all those which France must solve." He promised "above all to restore peace," and in the phrase "Algerian personality" found a polite formula for saying that Algeria is not France. With his blessing, Mendès opened negotiations through the medium of Professor André Mandouze with the Algiers rebel leader, Ramdane Abane. General Georges Catroux, the World War II hero who had served Edgar Faure as cover in dealing with the Sultan of Morocco, was appointed Minister Resident in Algeria. In an interview with *Le Monde*, General Catroux spoke of free elections for an Algerian Assembly. "There will be an Algerian Assembly," he said, "which might in the future be endowed with an embryo executive power."

What that portended was fairly clear. The Mollet government was offering free elections to an Assembly which would then write the Algerian future—independence not excluded. Mendès was to win the cooperation of the rebels; General Catroux to hold the army and settlers in check. To launch the whole project Mollet himself would make a gesture reminiscent of Mendès's famous flight to Tunis. On February 6, 1956, a week after taking office, the Premier flew to Algiers.

The settlers were waiting for him. Factories, shops, restaurants, cafés, bakeries were closed; public services were down to a bare minimum. Black crepe hung from downtown windows. As Mollet drove through the suburbs, passers-by kept silence and averted their eyes. But at the Monument des Morts, where the Premier was to lay a wreath, a crowd of thousands had assembled. As he stepped from his car the *Marseillaise* struck up. It was as if lightning had unchained the elements. Thunderous boos roared from ten thousand throats. There followed a hail of rotten fruit, of lumps of grass and dried horse manure. Tear gas held the crowd at a distance. But as Mollet left the monument, pale, thin-lipped, and misty-eyed, the mob broke past the guards, seized the wreath, tore it to shreds, then trampled the sprigs in the dust. Nearly berserk, they ran through the streets chanting the slogans of "*Algérie Française*," shouting, "Catroux to the Gallows."

The effect on Guy Mollet was not so much terror as revelation. A schoolteacher trained in Socialist doctrine but with little experience of affairs, especially foreign ones, he had figured the Algerian problem as a struggle between powerful private interests and masses of the meek. "Do you want our boys to die for the millions of the colonial exploiters?" he had asked during the election campaign. But here were no colonial exploiters. The throwers of fruit, the men who had menaced his person and trampled his offering were shopkeepers, skilled workers, and civil servants. A telephone operator had interrupted one of Guy Mollet's calls to Paris to tell him that though she was a Socialist, she too wanted Algeria to stay French. And Guy Mollet remembered, and reported the incident back home. For what most struck him was that the protests came from ordinary people, the stuff of socialism, even such as had elected Guy Mollet in Arras. He was not against, but with, them, and his reaction he summed up next morning in a statement to a veterans' group. "I came," Guy Mollet said. "I saw. I understood."

That kind of understanding meant a reversal of policy. Catroux was replaced on the spot by Robert Lacoste, a rough and

But if the nationalist line solidified Mollet's majority, it cost him control over events. Three incidents, all occurring in the mid-season of Suez popularity, underlined the government's impotence in the face of the army, the settlers, and the Algeria Firsters. The first was the seizure of the top FLN leaders. M. Pineau's talk with Nasser back in April 1956 had led to a series of conversations with the rebels. Four times in April and on May 1, two Quai d'Orsay officials met with Mohammed Khider in Cairo. In July 1956, Pierre Commin and Pierre Herbaut of the Socialist party bureaucracy, acting under Guy Mollet's instructions, talked with M'hammed Yazid in Belgrade. On September 2 and 3, Commin and his party met with Yazid, Khider, and Ahmed Kiouane in Rome. On September 20, contact was renewed in Belgrade in talks between M. Herbaut and Mohammed Lamine-Debaghine. There is no reason to believe that any of these parleys had been fruitful; but they had moved from the stage of diplomacy to political soundings; and on both sides the hope for continued contact had been expressed. One likely area was Tunis in October. Alain Savary, Guy Mollet's Minister of Moroccan and Tunisian Affairs, had made known to both Mohammed V of Morocco and President Bourguiba of Tunisia the hope that they might act as bridge between the FLN and Paris. In mid-October four of the top FLN leaders (Ben Bella, Boudiaf, Khider, Hocine Ait-Ahmed) visited Morocco. At the Sultan's request and despite some misgivings, they agreed to accompany him in his official train on a state visit he was paying to Tunis. The four left Rabat for Tunis at noon on October 23, in a DC-3 aircraft manned by a French crew but owned by the Moroccan airways. The route lay entirely outside French territory, with a midway refueling stop at Palma de Mallorca.

At 5:20 in the afternoon, five minutes before landing at Palma, the pilot received a radio message from Paris ordering him to proceed from Palma to Algiers. During the stopover the pilot cabled back to Rabat for instructions. Twice Rabat cabled back to Palma, enjoining the pilot not to take off until further orders had been issued. The messages never got through; presumably they were held up by French officials running the Moroccan telegraph system. At 6:14 the DC-3 left Palma, still bound for Tunis. At 6:35 there came an order from Algiers to land at the Algiers military airport, Maison Blanche. At 6:50 the pilot wired Rabat that, having received no further instructions, he was going in to Algiers. Four and a half hours later, after sweeping in circles through the skies, in order to fill up the time required to reach Tunis, the DC-3 was circling Maison Blanche. Passengers were requested to fasten seat belts and extinguish cigarettes. "Tunis," the hostess announced, and then the lights went out. Minutes later the FLN leaders were in French hands.

Ever since the captain's message at 6:50, the Moroccans had realized something was afoot. By 7:30, Bourguiba and the Sultan had been informed in Tunis. In a stormy interview with the French Ambassador, the Sultan declared the worst consequences would follow if anything happened to the Algerian leaders whom he regarded as his guests. The Ambassador called Alain Savary at the Ministry of Moroccan and Tunisian Affairs. Thunderstruck, Savary tried to call Bourgès-Maunoury and Max Lejeune at the Defense Ministry. In vain. Toward eight o'clock he reached Guy Mollet, who for the first time learned of what was going on. "It's mad," Mollet said. "I don't believe it. Anyway, if it's true do everything to stop this abomination." All Savary could do was to call Lacoste in Algiers. "It's serious," Savary warned, "and Guy Mollet is not in agreement." But Lacoste, just back from a trip to France, knew nothing. Only two hours later, at 10:15, did Lacoste call back to affirm that the trap was indeed being sprung. Savary immediately brought the news to Mollet, who was attending a farewell dinner for the NATO commander, Alfred Gruenther. Mollet paled; then ordered Savary to go to the Elysée Palace, inform President Coty, and arrange for a cabinet meeting. In the cabinet, it transpired that the Under Secretary of Defense, Max Lejeune, had known all about the capture plot from the beginning. Rather than disavow one of his own, Mollet decided to sleep on the matter. Next morning the front pages were full of talk of the government's master stroke. The Algeria Firsters crowed that with the head cut off, the body of rebellion could not long survive. In the end it was Alain Savary, not Max Lejeune, who resigned. Guy Mollet told the Assembly, "If I do not take credit for this deed, it is only because others deserve the praise."

The second incident revolved around General Jacques Faure, a veteran career officer, second in command of the division of Algiers, and long known for his violent political views. A Pétainist (in London in June 1940, he had returned to France, in effect choosing Pétain over De Gaulle), Faure had knitted up ties with the Gaullists in opposing the European Defense Community treaty. As commander of the Reserve School at St. Maxient he had made contact with veterans' organizations inside France, and with a number of leading Poujadists, including the deputies Jean Didès and Jean Le Pen. In Algiers he had been responsible for organizing the Territorial Units, composed of European reservists, many of them ultras and activists. From these contacts it was a short step to hatching plots. One of the men General Faure asked to help him, Paul Teitgen, secretary general of the Algiers prefecture and cousin of an MRP deputy, reported Faure's overtures to Lacoste. Highly skeptical, Lacoste ordered Teitgen to meet Faure again and make a tape recording of the conversation. The trick worked, and what Faure had to say was eye opening indeed. He had been in touch with Soustelle and Debré among the Gaullists; with General René Cogny who was hoping to replace Salan as commander in chief in Algeria; with commanders of military units in metropolitan France, and with police and fire department officials there; also, with a host of Poujadists. His plan was for a military coup in Algiers. The first step was to be seizure of the Government General building. Salan, if he refused to go along, would be arrested. Lacoste was to be made prisoner. The seriousness of the plan was indicated by a police search of Faure's quarters, made on Lacoste's instructions after hearing the tape recording. The search turned up batches of orders, with forged signatures, proclaiming the military take-over of Algiers.

On December 27, 1956, General Faure was called before Defense Minister Bourgès-Maunoury in Paris. Bourgès made known the fruits of the investigation, then politely asked General Faure to keep quiet and to refrain from returning to Algiers. "Nuts to you," Faure said in effect, in fact using far stronger language, and immediately he sought to regain Algiers. Only after the police had twice prevented Faure from going back to Algiers did Bourgès take action. For what amounted to treason, not denied and virtually proved, he meted out a sentence of thirty days' confinement to quarters. So that it wouldn't look like discrimination, the same sentence was given another general, Paris de Bollardière who had criticized army methods, notably the tortures. And far from being held back, General Faure was promoted. His sentence served, he was made second in command of French troops in West Germany.

The third incident was the so-called Bazooka Affair. At 7:00 P.M. on January 17, 1957, there exploded in General Salan's Algiers office a rocket fired from a homemade bazooka. Salan, having been called by Lacoste to the Government General building, was untouched. But one of his aides, Major Rodier, was killed; a second, Colonel Basset, wounded. Investigation, pursued with special vigor on the theory that the FLN had committed the murder, led to a group of European counterterrorists under the direction of René Kovacs, a 34-year-old dentist, well known in Algeria as a former swimming champion, and for a life led in a style (American car; hillside villa; frequent trips) well beyond the ordinary income of an ordi nary dentist. Among other things, the investigation turned up Kovacs' headquarters, a villa fitted out as a military command post and equipped with all the accouterments of a torture chamber. On the first floor was a fake general staff room with maps, and a tribunal before which kidnaped Moslems were hauled as if undergoing regular trial. On the second floor were stocks, a plunging pool, an electric generator. In the cellar were loudspeakers, and a pile of pamphlets proclaiming rebellion. One said, "We took Algeria to liberate France."

The tale Kovacs told was of a piece with the villa. He admitted the plot against General Salan, "a republican, Freemason, and the seller-out of Indochina." He described the purchase of the equipment to construct the bazooka, and told of trials made on a deserted beach outside Algiers. He claimed that he had been working with General Faure and with General Cogny, who, he said, was slated to take command in Algeria once Salan was out of the way. He said that his own operation was part of a much larger scheme directed by a general staff of six leaders. Among them he named Soustelle, Debré, the Corsican deputy Pascal Arrighi, and General Cogny.

Before that line-up of Algeria Firsters, the government once again quailed. Kovacs and the men directly involved in buying and firing the bazooka were released on bail. On his own insistence, Cogny gave evidence denying Kovacs' story. Soustelle, Debré, and Arrighi were not even questioned. The dossier of the affair shuttled back and forth between Paris and Algiers. The press treated the matter, as the Bromberger brothers put it, "as an everyday affair." Not until after the end of the Fourth Republic did the case come to trial; and by that time Kovacs had skipped to Spanish territory. There remain, accordingly, many uncertainties. But one thing is certain. The Mollet government gave way before a gang of confessed murderers, simply because they claimed alliance with the Algeria Firsters. It was as though in the United States, midway during the Korean war, a group of thugs, caught in an attempt to murder

General MacArthur, won immunity from prosecution, and from unfavorable publicity, by claiming a connection with General Eisenhower and a group of Republican Congressmen. In a word, it was fantastic.

And of course it was not only in the matter of Algeria that the Mollet government lost control. The effects spread to the domain closest to the Socialist heart: social and economic policy. To be sure, pension coverage was extended and a third week of paid vacation was added to the benefits of industrial workers. But in paying for the Algerian war, a charge of about $750 million annually, the Socialist regime followed a path the greediest war profiteer might have traced out. Taxes remained as before, and purchasing power ran on unabated. The extra expenses were met in a way no Frenchman felt immediately— by drawing down foreign reserves, notably dollar balances accumulated as American aid to the effort in Indochina. From January 1956 through April 1957, French gold and dollar holdings plummeted from a high of over $2 billion to around $800 million. "We finance economic expansion," the Socialist Finance Minister Paul Ramadier said, "with the foreign deficit." And when price rises tended, through the mechanism of an escalator clause, to force up wages, the government juggled with the wage-price index—a step, as Maurice Duverger pointed out, which no right-wing government would have dared to take.

On those terms, the Independents continued to support the government, and to keep a certain distance from the Independents. But in the spring of 1957, with the price index threatening to take off and the bottom of the foreign balances in sight, the government came up with a measure to raise taxes. At once the Independents edged over toward the Algeria Firsters. Sensing trouble, Guy Mollet tried to play the super-patriot. As an evocation of his moment of glory he referred to the U.N. Security Council a complaint on Colonel Nasser's handling of traffic through the Suez Canal. Economic aid to Tunisia was suspended. The Algeria Firsters were not to be brought round.

"We've had enough of compromising," one said in the debate. "This is a government of bankruptcy. Let's throw it out." On May 21, 1957, by a vote of 250 to 213, with 52 Independents joining the opposition, the Mollet government was ousted from office.

Since a ministerial crisis had come, the idea, as René Pleven said, was "to make use of it." That meant finding a man of the Right to pursue a policy of the Left—setting the system back on its feet. As a first condition a way had to be found to undo Guy Mollet's capitulation of February 6. Lacoste had to be derricked. M. Pleven, appointed by President Coty to take soundings on the state of political opinion, found a way: change the office of Minister Resident in Algeria back to the office of Governor General, and in the process quietly drop Lacoste. Antoine Pinay, asked to undertake that mission, ducked out. Pierre Pflimlin of the MRP was willing. But Guy Mollet was not yet ready to abandon the Socialist hold on office. When he refused to countenance Lacoste's dismissal, Pflimlin withdrew as candidate for Premier. At Mollet's suggestion, President Coty nominated and the Assembly invested Mollet's Defense Minister, Maurice Bourgès-Maunoury.

Bourgès's government was in effect Guy Mollet's second team. Two liberals of the first team, Gaston Deferre as Minister for Overseas Territories and François Mitterrand at Justice, were dropped. At Defense one of the most virulent of the Algeria Firsters, André Morice, filled Bourgès's shoes. At Finance, the younger and more conservative Felix Gaillard took over from Paul Ramadier. But Lacoste remained in Algiers as Minister Resident—"a February 6 for Bourgès," as one observer put it, "even before he took office." Once again it was going to be a government based on Socialist support which would follow the line of the Right. As Lacoste said, "There will be no changes in policy."

He was more right than he knew. At the outset Bourgès pushed through the Assembly an even stiffer special powers law, many provisions for dictatorial authority being now extended to metropolitan France. Construction of the Morice Line, got under way. Then Bourgès turned to political means for settling the conflict. At once he ran athwart the Algeria Firsters, blooded on their victory over Guy Mollet. The fight lasted two short rounds.

In the first, Bourgès, seeking to re-establish contact with the rebel leadership, dispatched a young member of Foreign Minister Christian Pineau's cabinet, Yves Geou-Brissonière, to a congress of the World Federation of Free Trade Unions meeting in Tunis at the end of July. Geou-Brissonière buttonholed M'hammed Yazid and, by means of a note from the French embassy in Tunis, established his bona fides. Before going into substantive matters, Yazid wanted clearance from the four rebel leaders captured in the plane and since then held prisoner in Paris. A Tunisian lawyer, Ali Chakal, was sent to Paris to seek their approval. But the Algiers police had got wind of the matter. On landing in Paris, Chakal was searched and arrested. The Tunisian embassy protested at once, exposing the whole business. Bourgès, like Guy Mollet before him, simply went along. Asked about Geou-Brissonière, he said, "I never saw him in my whole life."

In the second round, Bourgès moved to win Moslem public opinion (and a respite at the United Nations) with a new political statute for Algeria—the so-called *loi cadre*. The project did away with the double electoral college. Otherwise, it held out no appeal to the Moslems. Its first paragraph stipulated that Algeria was an "integral part of France." It also provided that the territory be divided into twelve regions; that each region elect by universal suffrage a representative assembly; that the regional assemblies send delegates to a territory-wide assembly which would legislate for the whole of Algeria under direction of a Governor General appointed from Paris. In the territory-wide assembly, the Algeria Firsters saw, or affected to see, the means whereby the Moslem majority could vote independence to Algeria. Within the government, André Morice maneuvered against the project. Outside it, Jacques Soustelle was on the offensive. Once more the Independents went into opposition. On September 30, by a 279–253 vote, with 38 Independents in the majority, the *loi cadre* was defeated and Bourgès pushed from office.

With Bourgès gone, the way seemed open for Guy Mollet to come back. Like malicious boys pricking balloons, the Socialists rejected rival bids for power, one by one. First René Pleven was blocked; then Antoine Pinay; then Robert Schuman of the MRP. The stage was set for Mollet, only by October 1958 the Algeria Firsters had picked up enough support from the Independents not only to knock down, but to prevent, the formation of governments. To his surprise and chagrin ("The French Right is the stupidest in the world"), Guy Mollet was beaten back, 290 votes to 227 with 81 Independents voting against him. The only alternative was an all-party coalition. Formed under the leadership of the former radical Finance Minister, Felix Gaillard, it included Independents, Gaullists, Radicals, MRP, and Socialists. "At last," Felix Gaillard said, "we have a government of the majority." In fact, the old problem of winning enough votes in the Assembly had simply been translated to another plane. The fight now was to hold the cabinet together.

It lasted just one round. The first punch was thrown in February with the incident of Sakiet-Sidi-Youssef. A small town on the Algerian-Tunisian frontier, Sakiet included a couple of hundred houses, a few shops, a school, a post office, a customs house, and an abandoned mine. Moslem refugees from Algeria had crowded into the town using the mine as a shelter, and the area had long been in the thick of skirmishes between French and FLN troops. In December a French unit had crossed the frontier at Sakiet in hot pursuit of an FLN band. In January an FLN company operating around Sakiet had ambushed a French patrol, killing fifteen soldiers and taking four prisoner. In riposte, three crack paratroop regiments moved up to the frontier area and began serious clean-up operations. A Tunisian company stationed at Sakiet did what it could to keep both belligerents on the other side of the line. But no doubt sympathies leaned toward the FLN, and in practice about all the Tunisians could do was to take pot shots at French planes which strayed across the frontier. On February 7, more by luck than skill, the Tunisians happened to wing a T-6 which had edged across the border on scouting duty.

That evening in Constantine, Lacoste met with the generals of Algeria. A review was made of the border tension, and evidently it was decided to take reprisals for the next incident. In an address that evening Lacoste said, "We are experiencing a stepped-up drive of rebels coming from Tunisia. This must be stopped. I have brought here the determination to deal them a hard blow; means for this action will not be lacking. This trip had as its purpose to put an end to the operations of Bourguiba, that's all I have to say to that gentleman."

Next day, February 8, was market day in Sakiet. Farmers from the surrounding countryside trekked into town. A Red Cross mission, ministering to the Algerian refugees, was due. For that reason if no other, FLN troops were not in the vicinity. Around nine o'clock, the Tunisian battery near town fired on a Mystère jet which had strayed across the frontier. At 11:03, the reprisals began. A first wave of B-26 bombers showered 500-pound missiles on the school, the post office, the customs house. A second wave hit the abandoned mine and church. In a third wave, the planes strafed their targets. In all, 130 houses were destroyed and 85 stores wiped out. There were 63 persons killed, and 102 wounded, including twenty-five children between six and thirteen, hit as they sat over their lessons. Not a single Algerian soldier or political figure was among the casualties.

In Algiers, the army immediately took credit for the feat. General Salan's headquarters issued a statement saying only military personnel and matériel had been hit, and that Salan himself was responsible for the operation. In Paris the government followed suit. Very briefly Foreign Minister Christian Pineau did treat the matter as a deliberate case of murder on the big scale. In an interview with Joseph Alsop, he characterized the bombing as a "sad mistake" and said, "Paris knew nothing of the operation, and had never authorized it." But next day Pineau denied ever saying such a thing. Premier Gaillard, before the Assembly, uttered no word of regret, and when a proposition for an indemnity was hooted by the Algeria Firsters, he promptly withdrew the offer. In the vote, only twenty-nine non-Communist deputies chose to condemn the government for Sakiet.

Gaillard was still not home free. The Tunisians had lodged a formal complaint with the U.N. Security Council. Except for France, all Council members were sympathetic to the Tunisian cause, the U.S. and Britain the more so for fear of opening a propaganda field in which the Russians could make hay. France, of course, could veto; but the Tunisians held some important hostages: some 25,000 French citizens; a string of air bases; the big naval base at Bizerte. Under popular pressure President Bourguiba had already expelled four French consuls from the country and placed police cordons around the French bases. Much worse might easily happen. Rather than force the issue, both sides agreed to accept the services of an Anglo-French good offices team. Shuttling back and forth between Paris and Tunis, Robert Murphy of the State Department and Harold Beeley of the Foreign Office put together an agreement which appeared to save face all around. The one French concession to President Bourguiba was abandonment of four air bases in southern Tunisia, which the French, months earlier, had agreed to give up as useless anyway.

That was enough for the Algeria Firsters. Atop the abuse heaped on the British and Americans, and on Bourguiba and the Tunisians, there was now piled a case for the airdromes.

It was even alleged that they would become a base for Tunisian attacks on Algeria; the Tunisians lacked the planes for any such venture, which would have been suicidal anyway. But at one juncture, an Independent holding office as Under Secretary for Air sounded the alarm on a flight of unknown aircraft, spotted as they moved toward Algeria from Tunis. It turned out to be a swarm of locusts; but that made no difference. The alarm had been raised. In an Assembly vote on the issue of the four airfields, Gaillard was beaten on April 16, by a vote of 321 to 255. Nearly one hundred Independent delegates joined the Algeria Firsters in opposition. It was a blow from which the men of the system never recovered. For two and a half years they had been going through the motions of government, paying lip service to principles they did not hold, endorsing events they abhorred, providing cover for actions they did not take. But practice without faith begets malaise. The ranks of the system had become totally demoralized. On all hands there was present a sense of weakness, a precognition of catastrophe, an intimation of doom. Mendès had spoken of being "in 1788." Roger Duchet had told the Independents, "Unless we remodel the regime, tomorrow we will enter into adventures." To the Socialists, Alain Savary said, "We must be very prudent, for given the weaknesses of the regime, a reaction could have the gravest consequences." "The country," said François de Menthon of the MRP, "has misgivings not only about the government, but about the parliament and all the constituted powers. The malaise is universal. Partisans of a tough policy share it with partisans of surrender. It translates the common conviction of waiting for a new fact . . . something new." "Everyone," Maurice Duverger wrote, "talks of General de Gaulle's return to power. The question is not whether De Gaulle will come back. The real question is when."

What was to happen—the "when" of May 13—came as a shock. But general anticipation made it possible. As so often in the past, the surprise was universally expected.

# 6. *THE IDES OF MAY*

To THE long list of red-letter days on the calendar of French history—to the 14th July of 1789, the 18th Brumaire of 1799, the 2nd December of 1851, the 4th September of 1870, the 18th June of 1940—the Algerian conflict in 1958 added the 13th May. Like all the others it was a day marked by stormy drama. As they did, it signified an end of sorts to an *ancien régime*. Otherwise, its meaning, like theirs, was a legacy of conflicting claims.

"Revolution," the settlers called it, implying thereby a spontaneous mass act, moving with the flow of history; but while amateurs took part, their aim was to ward off a universal process, and the leads were played by well-rehearsed professionals, acting deliberately and not without histrionics. "Mutiny" became the term of opprobrium dear to the French Left, and it is true that there were plots to begin with, an astonishing absence of mass action in France throughout, and, at the close, a paroxysm of wire pulling; still, if conspiracy was afoot, it succeeded because, for one reason or another, practically everybody who was anybody in every place that was any place, was in the plot. In fact, May 13 was shot through with elements of restoration, riot, putsch, civil war, popular rising, and pronunciamento. What was unique amidst this combination of classic troubles was the special role of the fashionable world of inside dopesters. Celebrities of every walk but politics—well-known jurists, the titled and the active rich, society leaders, heroes of the battle and the playing fields—all entered the drama. "It's always the same familiar faces," the Gaullist Raymond Dronne was told by a fellow resistance figure when they met en route to Algiers. At one point events turned around a former rugby champion, Defense Minister Jacques Chaban-Delmas. At another the ex-Davis Cup player, Robert Abdessalem, bulked large. A gossip columnist might have picked the cast that managed one crucial affair: the escape of Jacques Soustelle from Paris to Algiers. Funds were made available by the flashiest of the postwar nouveaux riches, Marcel Bloch-Dassault. A fashionable publisher, Guillain de Benouville, and a society diplomat, Geoffroy de la Tour du Pin, spirited Soustelle over the border to Switzerland and flew with him across the Mediterranean. In Paris, the escape car was driven past the police guard by Monique Dufour, the Brazilian wife of a French golf champion. Before embarking she asked about the most appropriate dress: "I have a little suit by Dior, very practical . . ."

If the dramatis personnae is easily identifiable, the action is harder to follow. Turbulent events, accompanied at the time by clouds of deliberately planted, self-serving rumors, have combined with grossly slanted restrospective accounts to fuzz over the details of what happened. Even so the main outline emerges sharply. Several trains of unrelated incidents came to a junction on a fatal day: the Ides of May. Opportunity was seized by two groups long planning the death of the Fourth Republic: the crackpot bully boys of Algiers; and the Gaullist Algeria Firsters, ready to use the trouble as a detonator. The first planned and brought about the single most decisive action: seizure of the Government General building. By that stroke they forced the Army of Algeria to declare against Paris. The second filched the "revolution," and with the willing help of the society world channeled its force against the administrative underpinning of the Fourth Republic. Disaffected to begin with, then worked on by their peers, the army, police, militia, and local administrators, one by one, slipped into the Gaullist camp. Power shifted as water in a tilting glass. Then at the eleventh hour, the men of the system performed a final rite of mystification: the euthanasia of the Fourth Republic.

II

WEEK after week, from February through May, events seemed to march in giant steps toward negotiated peace in Algeria. The Sakiet incident brought the whole matter before the international bar. A full-dress United Nations debate was staved off by the Anglo-American Good Offices Commission, but that itself raised the prospect of a federal solution for all North Africa gently imposed upon France in the name of the U.N. by the Anglo-Saxon allies. "It is very difficult," Secretary Dulles told the press before the commission began its work, "to isolate the problem of Algeria from the problem of Tunisia." When the commission ended its work, the American representative, Robert Murphy, told the press that the United States was "increasingly convinced of the need for a non-military settlement of the Algerian rebellion." He did not rule out "the possibility of negotiations with the FLN."

What Mr. Murphy did not rule out, French politics seemed to rule in. On April 16, a day before his statement, the Gaillard government fell from office. Thereafter, in rapid succession, the four principal Algeria Firsters were pushed from the path to power. On the sixteenth, all the principal leaders combined to prevail upon President René Coty not even to consider Jacques Soustelle as a possible Premier. On the twenty-third, Georges

Bidault abandoned efforts to form a ministry when his own Popular Republican party refused to support him. On May 5, the Socialists, in an announcement that they would support but not enter a cabinet headed by René Pleven, spelled the end of Robert Lacoste's tenure in Algiers. On May 8, Pleven gave up cabinet building when the Radicals balked at backing a cabinet including André Morice. Within three weeks, in short, Soustelle, Bidault, Lacoste, and Morice had been put *hors de combat.*

All along, the chief Popular Republican leader, Pierre Pflimlin, had been issuing bold-faced calls for dealings with the FLN. "We refuse," he wrote on April 23, "to be locked in the dilemma of toughness or surrender. We believe that there exists a third policy: talks with the representatives of those with whom we fight." "I am one of those," he said on May 2, "who believes that there is no true solution for Algeria, except of a political kind. I think that we must take every opportunity to open talks for a cease-fire." A week later Pflimlin was designated to form a new government. His cabinet, announced on May 11, was bare of Algeria Firsters, and included some of the best-known exemplars of the system's instinct for the liquidation of empire. Besides Pflimlin, its stars were Foreign Minister René Pleven, Defense Minister at the time of Dienbienphu, and Finance Minister Edgar Faure, Premier at the time of the Moroccan settlement. The Assembly's investiture vote on the prospective government was set for the day after the political week-end, Tuesday, May 13.

In harmony with the French political and the international developments, the FLN had been orchestrating its own policy. For months it had been sharpening for France the twin alternatives of negotiation or endless bloodshed, matching concession with concession, toughness with toughness. In the wake of the Good Offices Commission and the progressive elimination of the Algeria Firsters, the FLN held out at the Tangier Conference of April 27–30 with the Tunisians and the Moroccans the prospect of a federated North Africa, independent yet bound by the closest ties to France. But on April 24, the French command in Algiers had announced the guillotining of three FLN students convicted of terrorism in Algiers. The rebels replied in kind. On May 9, the FLN bureau in Tunis announced that on April 25, in retaliation for the Algiers killings, they had executed three French soldiers, allegedly tried and convicted by military tribunal of rape and torture.

The rebel execution announcement struck Algiers as a lash across a smarting wound. Step by step from Sakiet forward, whippers of opinion had been underlining and overexaggerating the meaning of events. The *Echo d'Alger* had stigmatized the Good Offices as "a discreet operation sellout." The Tangier federation offer was "a conspiracy which would lead inevitably to the enslavement of all Africa by Pan-Arabism." Socialist action in the political crisis was "a smokescreen designed to cover . . . the goal of eliminating Robert Lacoste." M. Lacoste himself had already defended Sakiet by invoking the Communist menace. "A huge amount of arms," he said in a defiant speech in Philippeville, "were coming to Tunis this month from the Communist bloc. We could not allow such an arsenal to be piled up on our doorstep." With removal in sight, he began a campaign of open incitement. In a widely quoted interview, he predicted a "diplomatic Dienbienphu" for Algeria. Speaking on the same theme to the assembled generals of Algiers, he used what one reporter called "a language whose brutality defies ink." In Paris, asked if he would return to Algiers to soften feelings toward Pflimlin, he turned on his heel, patted his rump, and declared, "My ass."

"By the end of April," one settler wrote, "the great majority of the population of Algeria had the feeling that 'liquidation' was only a matter of time." Spontaneous and directed gestures of defiance began to mushroom. On April 26, 30,000 settlers marched through the streets of Algiers in protest against possible formation of a Pleven government. In all quarters, tracts began to appear: "The last hope of France is a Government of Public Safety"; "If Pflimlin gets in, Algeria will be lost before October . . . In August 1958, when you're all on vacation, the cease-fire conference will begin . . . When you get back in October, everything will be arranged . . . Unless you oppose by all means, there will be no more Frenchmen of Algeria . . . Pflimlin is the last hope of an exhausted system . . . The sole strength of the enemy is the division of France . . . Keep vigilant . . . At the first sign of weakening, at the first surrender we will call you to action."

In that climate, the rebel announcement of the execution of the three French soldiers offered a new source of excitement, and a marvelous pretext for mass demonstrations. Veterans' and student organizations announced memorial parades. A general sympathy strike was called, and examinations in the schools postponed. The military high command arranged a program of military honors for the dead soldiers. The day fixed for commemoration was the day scheduled for debate on Pierre Pflimlin's investiture—May 13. A time to strike was at hand.

III

OF THE two groups plotting to seize the hour, the Gaullists were the more formidable by far. They had a specific, workable, long-term objective: to put the General in the saddle. Their leadership included men of undoubted substance in France. Besides Soustelle, there was Senator Michel Debré, Defense Minister Jacques Chaban-Delmas, the jurist Maxime Bloc-Masquart, the general, René Cogny. As well-known figures in their own right, they had the usual contacts in the press, business, and administration. Through two talented rabble rousers, the Corsican deputies Jean-Baptiste Biaggi and Pascal Arrighi, they had connections with the bully boys of the right-wing veterans' organizations in Paris. As partisans of Algeria First, they enjoyed the sympathy of the large ex-settler population in southwest France. The old Gaullist party, the Social Republicans, gave them an administrative shell and more business connections. Past work in the resistance tied them close to many of the top army officers. The Chief of the General Staff, General Paul Ely, and his three principal deputies—Generals Maurice Challe, André Petit, Grout de Beaufort—had been convinced, well before the spring of 1958, that in a showdown for the regime, the army would turn to General de Gaulle.

Across the Mediterranean, to be sure, the Gaullists were not so strong. The settlers had preferred Pétain, and still did: probably less than a hundred were full-fledged members of the Social Republican party. Still Soustelle's was a name with which to conjure, and he had long since been working closely with such settler figures as Alain de Serigny. Through Chaban-Delmas at Defense, moreover, the Gaullist conspiracy had set up in Algiers a branch office, the so-called antenna. It was headed by three young Social Republican organizers from France, Leon Delbecque, Lucien Neuwirth, and Guy Ribeaud—all ostensibly employed as special assistants to the army in matters of psychological warfare. The antenna penetrated the main veterans' organization in Algiers, established a beachhead in the local civil service, and made contact with the local extremist organizations in a "Committee of Vigilance." It did not net the very biggest of the military fish—Generals Salan, Allard, and Massu of the Algiers command. But it did have some important catches, among them General Jean Gilles, commanding the Army Corps in Constantine; Colonel Marcel Bigeard of the 3rd Regiment of Colonial Paratroopers and, after April 1958, chief of the paratroop school at Philippeville; Colonel Jean Thomazo of Allard's staff; and Lieutenant Colonel Yves Godard, responsible for security in Algiers.

What the Gaullists most lacked was the sense of desperation that alone imparts reality to subversion. "*Pas de bêtises,*" no nonsense, De Gaulle who knew at least dimly of their doings used to warn them—and with reasons. For their preparations present the spectacle of children playing an imperfectly known, adult game. In their Algiers antenna, for example, Delbecque and Ribeaud fashioned an elaborate system of fantastic code names. Massu was "rabbit"; Gaillard, "tin can"; Lacoste, "string"; Debré, "archangel"; De Gaulle, "Mr. Pigeon." Not only was the whole code known to the authorities through a plant, but the plotters themselves frequently forgot it and often improvised names. After one crucial interview, Delbecque, whose regular code name was "Lefebvre," told his interlocutor to refer to him in future clandestine correspondence as "Big Leon." One of "Big Leon's" most widely advertised coups, in fact, turned out to be a dud, and almost a backfire. At his suggestion, on May 11, the 3rd Regiment of Colonial Paratroops (3rd RPC) was transferred by Chaban-Delmas's office from duty on the Tunisian frontier to the rest camp in Algiers. Evidently the reasoning was that the former commander and ardent Gaullist, Colonel Bigeard, would hold sway over his troops. In fact, the actual commander, Lieutenant Colonel Roger Trinquier, held sway. A protégé of General Massu who had private reasons for being cool to Bigeard, Colonel Trinquier was not only not a Gaullist but, if anything, was partial to the extremists of Algiers.

Not surprisingly, very few of the eminent plotters in France had any faith in the doings of the antenna in Algiers. "If you count on the Algiers antenna to change anything," Soustelle once said—and finished the sentence with a shrug. And lacking faith, the Gaullists chopped and changed their plots in season and out. One called for replacement of Salan by Cogny, a declaration by the army in Algiers against the government in Paris, and a call to General de Gaulle to arbitrate the matter. A second looked to replacement of Salan by Gilles and Bigeard, a series of riots in France, dispatch of troops from Algeria to quell the troubles, and an army appeal to De Gaulle to take power in the interests of order. As the testing time drew near, the Gaullists cast about for still other schemes. On

May 8, with Soustelle's blessing, Delbecque and De Serigny proposed to Lacoste that he issue a pronouncement stating refusal to leave Algiers until a government under De Gaulle had been seated. When Lacoste turned them down, they hatched a plan for Soustelle to come to Algiers, take over Lacoste's office, and demand a Gaullist government. Through General Petit on General Ely's staff a military plane was made available to bring the former Governor General back to Algiers on the evening of May 13. Delbecque, in Paris for the negotiations with Soustelle, was sent posthaste back to Algiers to try to coordinate the demonstrations scheduled for May 13 with Soustelle's arrival. Then Soustelle began to backtrack. He asked for, and as he no doubt foresaw, did not get, a green light from General de Gaulle. On the evening of May 12, he called off the trip. His real place, he told some of the plotters, was in the Assembly, beating back Pflimlin's bid for investiture. To another he said, "I'm waiting for the generals to declare."

## IV

THE other group of plotters, the Algiers activists, commanded none of the Gaullist assets. Their leadership was a gaggle of discredited crackpots: Martel and Crespin of the Union des Français Nord Africains (UFNA); Lagaillarde of the students; Dr. Lefèvre and the two restaurateurs, Ortiz and Goutallier of the Poujadists. Their immediate followers numbered no more than 10,000. They had military connections—with Colonel Thomazo of Allard's staff and with Colonel Trinquier of the 3rd RPC—but not with any important generals. In France, they had been put in touch through the offices of a free-lance Belgian journalist, Pierre Joly, with a certain Dr. Martin, a disciple of Maurras and one of the last survivors of the Cagoule, the clandestine Fascist league, active in political terror during the 1930's, and in collaboration through the Vichy period. Dr. Martin had put together a new counterrevolutionary organization, the Big O. In it he held the role of Big V, while two disgruntled generals, Lionel Chassin and Paul Cherrière, were the Big A and B respectively. Little a was Yves Gignac, secretary general of the Veterans of Indochina, numbering some 3,000 toughs in Paris, including 300 Hungarian refugees. It was not, all in all, a very impressive outfit.

Still the activists had a clearly defined immediate aim. Against the system, and anti-Gaullist ("Soustelle," Lefèvre once said, "is the worst product of the system"), they placed their faith in a military regime: the army in power in Algeria and in France was their goal. Moreover, what might seem like fantasy to more sophisticated men was to them intensely real. Night after night, from April 26 through May 12, the Group of Seven, as the activists called their general staff, concerted their plans. On May 11, they fixed on the demonstrations of the thirteenth as an occasion for striking. Next night, at a meeting at Dr. Lefèvre's home, they took the deliberate decision that made May 13 a historic date. They decided to seize the Government General building. Their purpose was to force the army to declare itself. "We must thrust upon the army a dilemma," Dr. Lefèvre said that night. "Either they fire upon us, or work with us." "Tomorrow," Lagaillarde pledged, "I take the GG . . . Salan will be forced to power. I swear not to stop until I'm in Lacoste's office."

## V

THE dawn of May 13 brought to Algiers a sparkling day of brilliant sunshine. Up betimes, the activists were sowing seeds of trouble. In town, teams moved from office to office, spreading word of the general strike that afternoon. Martel himself toured the surrounding countryside by car. One of his henchmen buzzed outlying towns, dropping from a rented plane freshly printed tracts calling for a levee en masse. Twice in the morning the activist leaders met to renew the oath of the night before. Around noon, they set 6:00 P.M. as the time to attack the GG. Then each moved back to his troops.

Just after noon, a strange silence fell over downtown Algiers. Shops, offices, and factories closed down for the day. Streetcars and buses ceased to run. Private cars, usually bumper to bumper through the midday hour, were few. Police were not to be seen. Colonel Godard had evidently pulled them off the streets. In case of trouble he was going to rely on three companies of CRS—the Republican Guards or militia—and the paras of the 3rd RPC.

Around 2:30, like an abandoned ant hill suddenly come to life, the city began to stir. From all quarters European workers, clerks, students, and hangers-on converged on a sloping rectangle hung between the sky and sea that is the heart of Algiers. The magnet was a huge statue, the Monument aux Morts, set in a small park about a hundred yards in width and running, in length, about a quarter mile from the Boulevard Carnot, which overlooks the docks, past the war memorial to an enormous staircase, three flights of thirty-three steps each, mounting straight to the giant parking lot, or Forum, outside the GG. By 2:45 the park itself was jammed, and knots of people were collecting on the Boulevard Carnot, a little way up the stairs, and out on the two roadways of the Boulevard Laferrière which fringes the park. By 3:00, the throng was choking the principal thoroughfares leading toward the park: the rue Albert Lelluch, the Boulevard Baudin, the rue d'Isly, the rue Michelet. For the next three hours the crowd continued to swell, reaching by six an estimated 100,000 persons. Buzzing with excitement at all times, they sang the *Marseillaise* whenever marchers appeared, and roared out the thunderous slogans of settlerdom: "*Algérie Française*; The Army to Power; Shoot Ben Bella; *Vive Massu*; Bourguiba to the Stake; *Vive Soustelle*; Down with the Americans." Not long after 3:00, the first marchers appeared, two cohorts of high-school students dressed in jeans and T-shirts. After parading past the monument, one marched up the rue Michelet, and, before Colonel Trinquier's 3rd RPC could intervene, sacked the American Cultural Center; the other marched down the rue d'Isly, and was with difficulty held from attacking the liberal organ of Mayor Jacques Chevallier, the *Journal d'Alger*.

By 3:30 groups representing outlying townships were beginning to pile in. From Ménerville and Castiglione, from St. Eugène and Guyotville, from El-Affroun, Ameur-el-Ain and Blida they came, marching with banners overhead, singing patriotic songs, then taking up position around the war memorial. At 4:30, amidst a peal of cheers, an armless war hero led a contingent of 300 veterans from Algiers to the monument. By that time, Martel and Lagaillarde had sallied forth, mounted in an open sound truck and bearing aloft a huge banner. For nearly an hour, standing as a tribune upon the war memorial, dressed in his paratroop uniform with Martel's banner overhead, Lagaillarde worked over the crowd. "All to the GG," he kept shouting. "Today is the day or never. Will you let them sell out French Algeria? Do you want traitors to govern?" And back came the chant: "No, no; *Algérie française* against all; Shoot Ben Bella; Bourguiba to the Stake." "Lagaillarde," Martel said later, "was in the best of form."

At 6:00 came the blare of trumpets, and strains of martial music. The high command of Algiers—Generals Salan, Jouhaud, Massu, Allard—had arrived. Salan mounted the pedestal of the monument, pronounced two innocuous sentences, laid down a wreath. The band played taps. Slowly the generals withdrew. As they left, the crowd began to disperse. Suddenly Lagaillarde was back at the tribune. "All to the GG," he shouted. "Against the rotten regime." And with Martel in his wake he began to make his way up the ninety-nine steps.

It could have been a perilous venture. The GG is one of the most easily defended public buildings in the world. Virtually unassailable from below, the forum at the top of the steps stretches over an open expanse of 4,000 square feet: classic terrain for the whiff of grapeshot. A paling of high iron gates separates the forum from the entrance way to the building itself. "I could have held it," Jules Moch, an expert in handling unruly mobs, said later, "with a company of Republican Guards." In fact the Republican Guard stationed outside the GG had kept the forum clear for most of the afternoon without strain. But at 5:30 they were ordered off the forum and inside the paling by Colonel Godard. At once the forum began to fill with demonstrators from below. At 5:45, on orders from Lacoste's Directeur de Cabinet, Pierre Maisoneuve, the Republican Guards sallied out from the paling. With tear gas they easily cleared the forum anew. Then, for a second time, Colonel Godard ordered them back inside the paling. In their place he brought up by trucks and half-tracks a section of Colonel Trinquier's 3rd RPC. These were in position on the forum, with their vehicles behind them, when Lagaillarde and Martel began their charge.

Far from barring the way, the paras opened ranks. Moments later Lagaillarde and Martel were over the top. There was a brief flurry of fighting as the Republican Guards threw tear gas from behind the paling and the crowd hurled back stones. Most of the demonstrators retreated. But Lagaillarde slipped into the building through a broken window and dashed to the fifth floor. Screaming and waving from a balcony high above, he rallied his followers onward. One mounted a truck and drove it, like a battering ram, through the paling. A half-track, following behind, went up the entrance steps and through the doors. In its wake poured the mob. In the front hall a statue of the republican symbol, Marianne, was broken from its pedestal. Books were torn from library shelves and ripped apart. In a first-floor office a small fire was started, then extinguished by water which flooded the area. From windows all over the building there fell a gentle paper rain: the dossiers of the GG, snatched from file cabinets and scattered to the winds.

By 7:00, the initial spasm of fury had been spent. Shep-
herded by Lagaillarde a small group of the rioters made their
way to Maisoneuve's office, a spacious second-floor suite with a
balcony fronting on the forum. There they encountered the
bulk of Lacoste's administrative staff, including Maisoneuve,
and the military aide Colonel Paul Ducournau. For fifteen
minutes while a crowd of several thousand stamped and
shouted outside, the two groups exchanged verbal blows. "We
want a Committee of Public Safety," Lagaillarde bellowed.

"You're crazy," Ducournau shot back. "You'll spoil everything."

At 7:15 Massu arrived in the second-floor office, loud with
rude words from both the rioters and the Republican Guards.
He was trying to find out what had happened when, a quarter
of an hour later, Salan appeared. The commanding general had
been authorized, in a phone call from the Gaillard government
in Paris, to assume all of Lacoste's powers. Thinking to announce the news, he stepped to the balcony. From below rose
a chorus of catcalls and boos: "Indochina! Get the hell out!
*Vive Massu!*" Shaken, Salan re-entered the office and again
called Paris. This time he was authorized to delegate full powers to Massu. The paratroop general had all the while been
going hot and heavy with the demonstrators inside the office.
"What do you want?" he asked. "Does anyone have any ideas?
Those people outside have to go back home."

"Oh, no," Lagaillarde countered, "they're not going home.
They're staying right here."

"Well, what do you want me to do?"

"A Committee of Public Safety, or the riot continues."

Massu turned to Salan. The supreme commander gave no
sign to the contrary. Massu turned back: "Who do you want
on the committee?"

On the spot, a list was drawn up from among those present.
For reasons easy to guess, settler partisans, including Alain de
Serigny and Michael Clark, have insisted that most of the

members were merely ordinary people. In fact, of the eleven names on the list, four were military men: Massu and his deputy, Colonel Ducasse, plus two colonels in touch with the activists, Trinquier and Thomazo. Three of the civilians belonged to no organization at all. A fourth was an innocent bystander who happened to be seeing Colonel Ducournau on other business when trouble broke out. But three were definitely organization men: Lagaillarde himself, and two of Martel's followers, Armand Perrou and Gilbert Montigny.

With the list completed, Massu spoke by phone to Lacoste in Paris, fired off to the capital a telegram announcing formation of the Committee of Public Safety and demanding formation of a Government of Public Safety. He ordered the paratroops, this time with results, to clear the building. A new attempt by Salan to speak from the balcony was hissed down. But then one of the civilian members of the committee took the rostrum. "The army," he said, "is with us. We have formed a Committee of Public Safety. General Salan is with us." A moment later, Massu confirmed the news: "The army is at one with you."

With that announcement, Act I of May 13 came to a close. The activists had stolen a clear march on the Gaullists. They had taken the GG. They had formed a Committee of Public Safety packed with their own men and void of Gaullists. They had, above all, thrust the army to power in Algeria. In only one way did their plans misfire. Early on the morning of May 14, the National Assembly, in a defiant mood, voted the investiture of the Pflimlin government.

VI

As THE curtain rose on Act II of the drama of May 13 the army held center stage. It had been catapulted to power in Algiers. It was at once the main hope of the activists, the main hope of the Gaullists, and the main hope of the Pflimlin government.

For themselves, the soldiers were united on one thing only. They wanted to show that they had victory in their grasp; that they were not the goon squads of colonial reaction; that they had done deeds worthy of honor; that, in a word, the Moslems were with them. Even in the turbulence of the assault on the GG, Massu insisted on that objective. On his orders, four Moslems were added to the Committee of Public Safety during the evening of May 13. Next day orders went out for public demonstrations of Moslem support. "It is not some Moslems we need," General Massu said to the security chief, Colonel Godard. "It is *the* Moslems."

On May 15, Colonel Godard and his deputy in the Casbah, Captain Sirvent, brought the *îlot* system into play. Leaders from all over the Casbah were summoned to a meeting where they elected a Casbah Committee of Public Safety. In a moving appeal, Colonel Godard called on the Moslems to demonstrate on behalf of the French army:

> For the first time [he told the Casbah leaders], Frenchmen of Algeria are making a demonstration that is not directed against you. No Arab has been harmed. This revolution is yours too. We give you equality of rights. Come to the Forum.

Banners were passed out; transportation made available; leave from work secured. Next morning Godard told a group of journalists, "You are going to see something you've never seen before."

What they saw was the so-called Miracle of Algiers. On the evening of May 16, 30,000 Moslems poured from the Casbah and made their way to the Forum. There they joined hands with waiting Europeans, paraded back and forth in long circling chains, singing the *Marseillaise*, shouting the slogans of Europeans: "*Vive Massu; Vive Soustelle; Vive Salan; Vive l'Algérie Française.*" To these well-worked themes they added one phrase that spoke exactly the army's message to the world: "The Casbah is present."

In the hysteria of that evening, the organized base of the demonstration was forgotten. An observer as well informed and skeptical as the *Time* correspondent Stanley Karnow was "stupefied." "Nothing," the Brombergers wrote, "more honors the French army." A cautious army report spoke of an "extraordinary revolution . . . in the direction of total spiritual unity of the two communities which comprises the decisive element in the situation." It may even be said that on the night of May 16, the French army came closer than at any time before or since to victory in the Algerian war. But it was still far, far away. For the Miracle of Algiers shared with all other miracles the property of not solving political problems. It did not solve the problem of the FLN. It did not solve the problem of the regime in Paris. It did not solve the problem of struggle between Gaullists and activists. And in facing these problems the military mixed the impatient frustration of miracle workers with the political emptiness common to soldiers. "Above all," one captain told a meeting in Constantine on May 14, "we want to depoliticalize the regime. The political parties are the cause of our humiliations, of defeat wherever the French army fights. We've had enough kicks in the ass. Today we command in Algeria. We will keep up the fight no matter what happens." But when General Massu was asked what would happen he replied, "I don't know nothing."

In that curious atmosphere—an atmosphere of absolute certainty as to ends and absolute uncertainty as to means—military power came naturally to rest in the hands of a man who could take on any purpose while avoiding all means. General Raoul Salan, supreme commander in Algeria, had built a reputation as "the best politician in the French army." Nature made him impassive and good to look upon, with broad forehead, silvery hair, a roman nose and tight mouth. Long and deep experience in the Far East (he was known as "the Chinese General," had a son by an Asian wife, and was reputed to take opium and carry at all times, as a good luck charm, a miniature elephant of yellow jade) had accustomed him to the ruse and bluff and fast-moving loyalties of political intrigue. He had accompanied Italian troops to Ethiopia in the guise of a newspaper reporter. He had fired on Anglo-American troops at Dakar, and then joined them in the assault on the Continent. He had negotiated with the Chinese and the Vietminh over French reoccupation of Indochina, and then come back to fight the Vietminh as De Lattre's successor in Indochina. As a military man he was known for carefully plotted defensive action. The *quadrillage* was his tactic in Algeria; and in Indochina he had held the line around Hanoi during the interim between De Lattre's operations up the Red River and the Navarre Plan. De Lattre once wrote of him, "He never leaves port without the biscuits."

In Algeria Salan was, perforce, a loner. Suspected of being a favorite of the Paris politicians, he was cut off from the army, and so unpopular with the Europeans that whenever he appeared they made a point of cheering Massu. Activists had tried to kill him in the bazooka plot. The Gaullists were widely known to have sought his replacement by General Cogny. In self-defense Salan had put together an information system of his own—leading through the Indochina Veterans to Gaullist groups in France, and through Colonel Thomazo to the activists. Informed but not committed, on the phone to Paris all the time, very mindful of self ("I'm risking my neck in this business," he said once; and on another occasion, "I'm preparing my defense before a court of treason"), capable of veering with the winds (at one point he denied privately words he had uttered only a moment earlier before thousands of people), Salan developed a cautious survival policy, wrapped in calculated ambiguity. By that means he became, on the morrow of May 13, the arbiter of the struggle among activists, Gaullists, and the Paris government.

Cautious ambiguity was the climate least healthful for the activists. Recapitulating in little the glorious night of May 13, they stirred popular demonstrations the next day against the civil power in Oran and Constantine. At their instigation the remaining vestiges of the system's rule in Algiers—notably the staff of the Governor General—were toppled. One group of activists for a while held the Algiers Radio station. And they packed the Algiers Committee of Public Safety, adding to the three original activist members three more full members (Lefèvre, Martel, and Merlo) and four alternate members (Ortiz, Crespin, Goutallier, and Roseau).

But at every turn, Salan placed the army over the activists. Members of Lacoste's staff were taken under military protection, then packed off to Paris. Generals were made prefects, taking over the deposed civil authority in Algiers, Oran, and Constantine. Within a matter of hours after seizure by the activists, the radio was in military hands. With the army in control, there was increasingly less scope for the activists. Their specialty was making trouble "mobilizing the crowd," as Dr. Lefèvre once put it. But there was no chance to mobilize the crowd against the army, nor basically any purpose. And thus inside Algeria, the activists steadily lost influence.

Outside Algeria they were ludicrous. Most of the Paris activists, long since known to the police, were arrested on the night of May 13, or driven into flight. Probably the most important, General Chassin, managed to slip away to the south. But his attempt to found an underground resistance to the regime petered out in farce. What was to have been a "march" on the town of St. Etienne dissolved when the local prefect confronted Chassin's forces one night and told them to go to bed. According to one report, Chassin thereupon went into hiding in a small village near the Swiss border, taking to himself the code name of "the Pope." Not long thereafter, in the dead of night, a messenger seeking Chassin knocked at the wrong door. "I'm a friend of the Pope," he called out when an irate householder looked out from a second-floor window.

"You're crazy," was the response.

"Of the Pope, I tell you," the messenger persisted.

"The Pope is over here," interjected a voice from Chassin's hide-out across the street.

"You're both crazy," said the householder. It was a fit end to the revolt of the activists.

As the activists faded, the Gaullists, left at the post during the taking of the GG, forged to the fore. All through the afternoon of May 13, Delbecque had been on the phone to Paris insisting that either Soustelle or Debré make for Algiers. Only at 10:30 that evening, with Ribeaud and Neuwirth in tow, did Delbecque finally reach the GG. His reception was, to put it mildly, cool. Ducournau denounced him as a "hooligan." But Delbecque announced the imminent arrival of Soustelle and declared himself to be Soustelle's representative. Massu, at least, was impressed. "So there has been a plot," he said. Delbecque was admitted on the spot to the Committee of Public Safety, and Neuwirth became its official spokesman. Later in the evening other Gaullists were admitted, including Count de Serigny who took on the post of liaison between the CSP and General Salan. With General Petit in the lead, all the Gaullists immediately started, as Delbecque put it later, "to canalize the revolution." In essence that meant facing Salan in the direction of De Gaulle.

The first effort came that very evening in the GG. The Gaullists proposed that Salan wire Paris urging a "Government of Public Safety presided over by General de Gaulle." The Mandarin balked: "I'm risking my neck in this business." But he did consent to a telegram urging "an appeal to a national arbiter." It was a first step toward De Gaulle.

Next day Salan drew back sharply. Far from arriving, Soustelle was being held under guard in Paris. De Gaulle had not spoken. There was reason to take cover, and in an order of the day Salan announced the retreat. It stipulated that he had assumed "military and civil powers for the purpose of assuring order." The Committee of Public Safety, "set up under the pressure of events," would be restricted to the role of "liaison between" the local population "and the command which would issue orders." The administration was to be set in order; the population calm and dignified. It was as though nothing had happened.

Massu fell smartly into line. He called a press conference that day at General Salan's headquarters—a sign of submission underlined by Massu's statement that he was talking to the press with the permission of General Salan. He asked for "an end to the insurrectional atmosphere" and insisted that he was "not a fractious general." The Committee of Public Safety would sit only until a Minister of Algeria could arrive from Paris. As to the night before, it was an accident, and a bad one at that. "I am in this thing," Massu explained, "only by chance."

Next day, May 15, Algiers heard General de Gaulle announce from Paris that he was ready to take power. Salan inched forward again. At the end of a short speech from the GG, he used the ritual closing: "*Vive la France, Vive l'Algérie Française.*" As he turned to go, Delbecque stepped to his side and whispered a word. Salan did an about-face and shouted to the crowd, "*Vive De Gaulle.*"

But moments later, back in his office, Salan denied ever having uttered these words, and they did not appear in the official transcript of his remarks. On the next day, moreover, the first official sanctions were taken against the Gaullists in Algiers. The victim was one of the principal Gaullist plotters—the Corsican deputy Jean-Baptiste Biaggi. "The Bat" arrived in Algiers on May 16 in a chartered plane from Madrid. He had bold plans for assuring the escape of Soustelle from Paris, and for an assault on the capital from Algiers. Instead of being helped, he found himself being taken directly to General

Massu who received him with contempt: "We don't want you in Algiers . . . my orders are to fling you back to Madrid. You are a conspirator." That night Biaggi spent under guard in the GG. Next morning he was put on a plane and dispatched— not to Madrid as promised—but 1,600 miles south, to a remote oasis in the Sahara. Salan and with him Massu had turned their backs on the Gaullists. "We're lost," Thomazo moaned at a meeting with Delbecque. "With my own eyes I have seen the preparation of the arrest orders for you, the Gaullists . . ."

A few hours changed the outlook completely. Just after noon that day, May 17, Jacques Soustelle in flight from the Paris police, arrived in Algiers by air from Switzerland. Salan hastened to the airport, intending to send him back. "*Monsieur le Ministre*," the Commanding General told Soustelle, "your presence here is not required. Algeria will stay French. Everything is being arranged . . . Rest a little while. And then fly back. Believe me, it is in the public interest."

Soustelle was on the point of believing. But one of his companions was already on the phone to Delbecque. "Tell him to stay," Delbecque shouted. "Whatever it costs. I'll get out the people." Minutes later the word was being passed through Algiers: "Soustelle is here. All to the Forum." Before the afternoon was over, Soustelle was on the balcony of the GG addressing a delirious crowd. That evening he plunged into conferences at Salan's headquarters.

The reception of Jacques Soustelle in Algiers was an event, as Jean-Raymond Tournoux points out, "more important than the taking of the GG." It was, to be precise, the Gaullist version of the assault on the GG. Not, as some have claimed, because Soustelle added the factor of a political brain. But because the reception of a fugitive deputy symbolized the end of all co-operation between General Salan and the Pflimlin government. For all his caution, duplicity, and digging in of heels, General Salan had been pushed into the Rubicon. As the activists had forced the army to take power, so the Gaullists forced the military to turn that power against Paris. Only four days after Soustelle's coming to Algiers, the new alliance was announced in an emotional speech by Salan. "You must know," he told the crowd on the Forum on the night of May 21, "that we are now all united, and that thus we shall march together up the Champs Elysées, and we shall be covered with flowers."

Behind the scenes, in fact, plans for military action to force General de Gaulle's investiture had been under way since Soustelle's arrival. Corsica was to be the stepping stone to Paris. The climate was favorable. Ever since May 13, Gaullists on the island, led by one of the General's cousins, and the numerous relatives of Algerian settlers had been agitating for a change. The means were ready to hand. On the night of May 23, the Corsican deputy, Pascal Arrighi, broadcast from Algiers to the island in his native tongue, a call to action. Early on the morning of the twenty-fourth, Arrighi with a paratroop officer and three Corsican settlers flew from Algiers to Ajaccio. By late afternoon, after a token resistance by a handful of civil officials, the whole island had fallen to the army of Algeria.

Thereafter, all efforts were bent in the direction of a strike on Paris. "Operation Resurrection" had been in the works since May 17 (the day of Soustelle's arrival in Algiers), when two junior officers on Massu's staff had been secretly ferried from Algiers to the paratroop base at Pau in southwestern France. Four different headquarters—General Salan's in Algiers, General Miquel's in southwest France; the general staff in Paris; and the second armored division under General Gribius at Rambouillet outside Paris—were in on the plan. It involved seizure of Paris by an armored column from Rambouillet working in conjunction with two groups of paratroopers who were to be brought in from Algiers and Pau. The armored column was to hold the airfields around Paris for the arrival of the paratroops. Once on the ground, the paras, sup-

ported by the Paris police, were to take the principal buildings
of the capital. In those circumstances, it was thought, the
deputies would turn to General de Gaulle. If necessary, Generals Massu and Miquel would move by helicopter to General
de Gaulle's country home and bring him back to Paris for investiture.

No doubt Operation Resurrection was militarily feasible.
But politically, as the final grace note makes plain, it was
giddy. At any stage, matters could have gone wrong, plunging
France into open civil war. The habitual prudence—not to use
a stronger word—of both Raoul Salan and Jacques Soustelle
suggests that at all times a large element of bluff entered into
Operation Resurrection. In any case the mere possibility of
such action was enough to project Algiers into the midst of
Paris. It was there that the political leaders played out the
third and final act of the drama of May 13.

VII

HAD there never been a May 13 in Algiers, there might never
have been a Pflimlin government in Paris. Doubts about support from the Independents, the Socialists, and the Communists put a majority in question until the last minute. The
senior citizens of the system at no time wanted an MRP government. But the news from Algiers solidified behind M.
Pflimlin a militant majority, which fastened upon the system
a policy it instinctively abhorred. The story of the Pflimlin
government is the story of how, after four successive defeats,
the men of the system finally disentangled themselves from the
awful embarrassment of an overwhelming majority favoring a
clear course of action.

The lines were drawn early on May 13. At the first news of
insurrection, the reigning members of the system foregathered
with M. Pflimlin and began dropping broad hints that he efface
himself. Duchet of the Independents pointed out that M.

Pflimlin's investiture would only increase tension between Algiers and Paris. Lacoste of the Socialists asserted that there was no way of forcing a retreat in Algiers. Mollet cited that one as among the advantages of withdrawal by M. Pflimlin. A member of Pflimlin's own party, Robert Lecourt, suggested that the Independents ought to vote en bloc against him, thus assuring his defeat. Antoine Pinay asked, "Is the current political situation good? I wonder. I don't know. I pose the question." Pflimlin took the hint without blinking. "I'm ready to step down," he said, "on condition that some other solution is immediately possible."

There was one, and everybody knew it: a new government headed by Guy Mollet. But—and it was the system at its most typical—what everyone knew could not be said aloud. For the whiff of insurrection in Algiers put the frustrated party militants of the Center and Left in the presence of a great cause. At long last the time had come for action, for open struggle with the Algeria Firsters, with the right-wingers, with the hated *colons*, with the army itself. Old memories of the Republic in Danger, of its great triumphs and humiliating defeats, came surging to the fore. "It's 1934 again," a veteran Socialist cried out, evoking the fight against the Rightist Leagues that prefigured the Popular Front. "This time I will be one of the eighty," a Radical deputy swore, in reference to the minority that had opposed Pétain in the Chamber. "Fascism shall not pass," an echo of Verdun, became the watchword of Communist and Socialist deputies. Even as M. Pflimlin conferred with the heads of the system, a delegation of eighty Socialists implored him to hold fast. From the center, Mendès-France, Daladier, Mitterrand joined the chorus for a fight to the finish. In the presence of such a tide, none of the more mellow men of the system were willing to counsel that M. Pflimlin yield to M. Mollet. In the absence of such counseling M. Pflimlin did his duty: he struck the pose of holding fast.

There was thus set up a contradiction which dictated the course of the crisis, an ambiguity from which the Premier never recovered. Privately he wished to compose matters, to reach agreement with the Europeans of Algeria, with the army, with the Gaullists. But publicly he was cast as the hero defying these enemies of the Republican faith. Time after time he sought to extend the carrot, only to find that he was holding a stick. At each juncture the power at his disposal ebbed away, thus causing his backers to take even stronger and stronger stands while making more and more difficult accomplishment of the unavowed design of concord and harmony. At the moment of his greatest strength in the parliament, the Premier was at his weakest outside. At the moment the deputies most wanted him to continue, he was most bent on resigning. He was in the position, as Georges Bidault pointed out, of the man who first offers to surrender standing up, then bowing low, then on bended knee, then prostrate on the ground, and then . . . But on the fifth try, the Pflimlin regime succeeded.

The first test came on the night of May 13–14. In public, before the Chamber, with Socialists, Communists, and the republican stalwarts of the Center calling for blood from Algiers, the Premier took a tough stand. "In Algiers," he told the deputies, "Frenchmen whose anguish I understand have let themselves be dragged into grave actions, and military leaders have taken an attitude which, I regret to say, is an attitude of insurrection against republican law." He easily won investiture —280–126, with the Communists in benevolent abstention. Back at the Matignon his aides drew plans for a blockade cutting communications with Algeria, and for the hunting down and guarding in France of activists and Algeria Firsters. The message seemed clear: the government was determined to stand against insurrection. But at 3:00 in the morning, in the privacy of the President's office at the Elysée Palace, M. Pflimlin took the soft line. "I think that we must have confidence in Salan," he told a meeting of the cabinet. And in a telephone

exchange with the supreme commander he confirmed, on behalf of the new government, Salan's powers over Algeria, cau-
tioning him "not to act outside the laws."

For a full day the agreement with Salan seemed to work.
It brought about the Algiers retreat of May 14. But M. Pflimlin took no step to cement the alliance or follow up his advantage. In the meantime he had thrown away one card. He
had committed his government to the military hierarchy. He
had closed off the possibility of naming a new high command,
of setting general against general in a contest to do the government's bidding.

Thus weakened, M. Pflimlin faced the second test. It was
posed by General de Gaulle's statement of May 15—an open,
and not unsophistical, challenge to the regime:

> The degradation of the state leads infallibly to the estrange-
> ment of the associated peoples, the distress of the army in ac-
> tion, national dislocation, the loss of independence. For twelve
> years, France, beset by problems too harsh for the regime of the
> parties, has been caught in a disastrous process. Not so long ago,
> the country from its depths put its trust in me to guide all of it
> to its salvation. Today, in the face of the trials that are again
> mounting, it should know that I am ready to assume the powers
> of the Republic.

Outraged determination not to yield was the public reaction
of the government. M. Pflimlin announced "a state of urgency
bill" authorizing search without warrant and control of all
public media. The Socialists lined up en bloc behind the government, permitting Guy Mollet to join as Vice Premier, and
Jules Moch and Albert Gazier to take the key Ministries of Interior and Information. In Assembly debate on the "urgency
bill," M. Pflimlin boldly rang the changes on the theme of "republican liberties and national unity." M. Mendès-France, stirring memories of Robespierre, called for the revolutionary
ardor of the *Conventionnels* of '93. A Socialist orator once
prominently linked with the Algeria Firsters, former Governor

General Naegelen, hit directly at General de Gaulle: "His declaration is the threadbare plea of all dictators in all countries . . . He asks dictatorship."

But privately the government was once more moving to compose. The daily record of M. Pflimlin's chief administrative assistant, Michel Poniatowski, included these conclusions from a conversation with the Premier on May 16: (1) "Preserve French unity with Algeria, avoid any act of rupture . . . Re-establish . . . transport as quickly as possible"; (2) "Do not attack the army"; (3) "Avoid any attitude or measure susceptible of leading to civil war." And then there followed a certain sign that the Premier was already thinking of bowing to General de Gaulle:

> Avoid any attack or criticism on General de Gaulle [the notebook said]. Do not compromise the possibility of a solution through him.

In that spirit, on the sixteenth, the Premier formally canceled the orders for blockade of Algeria. It was another card thrown away. In admitting De Gaulle's right to take up the cudgels for the army and the Algeria Firsters, he had accepted disaffection at home. Cessation of the blockade was merely the formal announcement that he would not play Frenchmen of France against Frenchmen of Algeria.

The third test was double barreled: the escape of Jacques Soustelle and his reception in Algiers on May 17; the reiteration by General de Gaulle, at a Paris press conference on May 19, of willingness to take power. Once again the government made a public show of vigorous response. A stringent press censorship was instituted. It was made illegal for any citizen to leave France without express permission. The most prominent civil servant in Algeria, Serge Baret, Prefect of Algiers, was dismissed for receiving Soustelle. And at the Ministry of Algeria, Jules Moch assembled all the prefects of France and rallied them for a coming struggle. He set as "Number One objective" the finding of "a counterweight" to the forces massing in Algiers. "We must lean on the people," he told the prefects, "on the working class."

But privately Premier Pflimlin once more drew back. He raised before M. Moch the specter of the Spanish Civil War and of the Prague coup, warning that the "Communists were as dangerous to liberty as the fascist elements." At a meeting with President Coty he expressed again willingness to resign provided "a substitute combination is ready." And by that time the Premier's closest associates were trafficking with De Gaulle. On May 20, Guy Mollet, acting without the Premier's knowledge, initiated conversations with General de Gaulle's chief administrative assistant, Olivier Guichard. Next day, Antoine Pinay sought and got the Premier's permission for a visit to Colombey. Pinay's ostensible mission was to wring from De Gaulle a repudiation of Algiers. What he got instead was a recognition of Paris. In reporting back to the Premier, Pinay spoke of De Gaulle as if he were the hero of the system. "He was very affable, very receptive," Pinay said. "He offered me a cup of tea." Still another card, in effect, had been thrown away. Having failed to use the army, the country, and people against revolt, M. Pflimlin was now acknowledging that the system itself was not going to be brought into play against its enemies.

The fourth test came two days later with the coup in Corsica. Once more the Premier found himself center stage astride the charger of resistance. "The Algerian crisis," he said in a radio address that day, "is explained to a large extent by popular emotion which insofar as it expresses a will to remain French is legitimate. But in Corsica other factors are at work. No popular emotion can explain or justify the acts committed there by a handful of rebels." Next day he put through the Chamber a measure depriving the Corsican leader and deputy, Pascal Arrighi, of his parliamentary immunity—the kind of measure traditionally resisted by all parliaments. This time, on a vote of confidence, the majority was overwhelming—393–169. But that night, in the privacy of the cabinet room, he vetoed Jules Moch's project for an expedition against Corsica from the mainland. Even in the presence of what he, and everyone else, acknowledged to be rebellion, the Premier would not assert his government. He had, without a fight, lost the power to keep the public peace.

The fifth test ensued next day, May 26, when the Premier agreed to meet with General de Gaulle. The parley, held at the house of the Curator of the Park of St. Cloud, ended in a comic stand-off. The Premier said that the way would be open to De Gaulle if only the General first repudiated the insurrectionists of Algiers. The General refused to renounce his supporters, but assured the Premier that he would take power only by legal means. After two and a half hours of fruitless haggling, the two men parted, agreeing only to announce that they had met. M. Pflimlin had in mind the blandest of communiqués. General de Gaulle, apparently convinced that the strike from Algiers was imminent, thought otherwise. On the morning of May 27, his headquarters issued a shocker:

I began last night the regular process leading up to the formation of a republican government capable of assuring the unity and independence of the country.

From the militants of the Left and Center there rose a new chorus of outraged protest. "Pflimlin surrendered last night and dare not admit it," was the cry in the corridors of the Assembly. "De Gaulle tricked him." M. Mitterrand accused the government of "disintegrating under the first puff of wind from Colombey." The old Socialist Paul Ramadier begged the Premier to rally fast: "We are ready to follow you for the safety of the Republic: we will stand by you to defend it and to make it triumph." For the Communists, Pierre Cot threatened what M. Ramadier promised: "Our duty is to close ranks around you, if need be to hang ourselves to your coat-tails, in order to prevent you from getting out." Not to be outdone, the Socialists, in caucus, voted 111–3 "never to approve the candidacy of General de Gaulle."

This time the Premier was not to be goaded. It was true that the General had usurped the Premier's right even to speak for his own government. At the first word of the General's statement he had been furious. "A cheat," he had remarked to his *chef de cabinet.* But reports and rumors of impending military action from Algiers had been pouring in. Both Mollet and Moch were convinced that De Gaulle's statement was aimed at staving off attack from Algiers. So credible and anti-Gaullist a source as the American embassy believed, and let the Premier know it believed, that an attack was in the making. On the afternoon of May 27, M. Pflimlin officially accepted that view. "De Gaulle," he told a caucus of the MRP, "must have learned that the landing was set for the near future . . . In that case the General was right."

That night the Premier found a device peculiarly fit to take him off the hook with the parliament. It was the device of constitutional reform. Throughout the whole history of the Fourth Republic, no issue had been more roundly abused. Endorsed in principle by practically all deputies, desired in fact by practically none, it had been the favorite smokescreen for the discontented of all brands. Standpatters regularly espoused the cause in order to seem progressive—while in fact doing nothing. Communists and Gaullists used it to heap discredit upon the regime. Every new government professed to abhor the rules by which it came to power, and to hunger for reform. In keeping with that tradition, M. Pflimlin had announced on taking office that he would offer a bill reforming the Constitution. He added that once the bill was passed, the government would resign.

On May 25, a reform bill of sweeping dimensions was introduced. On the night of May 27, the Premier brought it to a vote in the Chamber as a matter of confidence. On its merits hardly anybody liked the bill. But defeat would have given the government the excuse it now plainly sought—the excuse to resign. Accordingly, all the anti-Gaullist militants, whatever their feelings about M. Pflimlin or the Constitution, rallied round. "We will not," Jacques Duclos said in announcing Communist support, "give you an alibi to resign." The measure passed by a lopsided majority: 408–165.

Briefly it appeared that the majority was too stout to admit resignation. At a cabinet meeting immediately after the vote, all the Socialist ministers counseled the Premier against stepping down. As they talked, René Pleven scribbled on a sheet of foolscap. At length someone said the inevitable: that resignation would produce a power vacuum. "Power vacuum," M. Pleven took up. "Gentlemen, we have no power. We are the government, but what government? Here is the Minister of Algeria, he can't go to Algeria. Here is the Minister of the Sahara, he can't go to the Sahara. The Minister of Defense has no army. The Minister of Interior has no police . . ." There was a moment of silence. Then M. Pflimlin made known his decision. "I am going to propose the resignation of the government to President Coty."

Early on the morning of May 28, the President accepted the government's resignation, pending establishment of a new government. For the next five days all the men of the system labored to line up a majority for General de Gaulle. The sitting President, M. Coty, took soundings of all the parties and threatened his own resignation if General de Gaulle were not approved. An ancient former President, Vincent Auriol, came out of retirement to help Mollet, Moch, and Ramadier soften up the Socialists. While M. Pinay held the Independents for De Gaulle, and Edgar Faure lined up Radical votes, Pflimlin won over the MRP with only two exceptions. At length De Gaulle himself consented to meet with the deputies, and after coaching from Auriol and Coty, played his role as a veteran of the system. "After sedition, seduction," one deputy said of the performance. Even so it was no landslide. On June 1, by a vote of 329–224, the Assembly invested Charles de Gaulle as Premier. In effect, it was the end of the Fourth Republic.

Could it have been otherwise? Could the Pflimlin government, by fighting troubles, have mastered them? There is evidence—but only slight evidence—for thinking so. Where the government did dig in and fight it found little backing. Early in the crisis the Minister of Defense, M. Chevigné, placed two generals on the general staff under house arrest; the result was the resignation of the Chief of Staff, General Paul Ely. When Jules Moch sought to rally the prefects, there was obvious resistance. "Are you still the man of 1947," one of them asked the Minister, alluding to his breaking of Communist strikes in that year, "still the man of the implacable fight against communism?" M. Moch himself reported later that he could "barely trust" the police, and that the weakness of the "loyal forces" at his disposal was "humiliating." And there was certainly no sign of popular resistance to the men from Algiers —not even among the communized workers: a Communist call for a protest strike on May 19 brought out only 1,000 of the 35,000 workers at the Renault plant in Paris; only 1,000 of the 300,000 in the mines of the North.

But these are straws in the wind; not evidence. At bottom the whole question is academic. There was never a serious possibility that the system would fight. Its character was its fate, and nothing in its life became it as the leaving it. As never before, legerdemain, sleight-of-hand, and mystification were triumphant. A revolution was accomplished with less bloodshed than an ordinary election. A government without power yielded up the seals of office on the ground that its mission had been accomplished. An unshakable majority for the men of the system was translated overnight to its sworn public enemy. And as a final irony, the men of the system, constrained to act against their will, brought to power a man of huge proportions but made in their own image—the greatest mystifier of them all.

# 7. DE GAULLE

"I AM not Bonaparte, I am not Boulanger," he once protested, and no doubt rightly. But who is Charles André Joseph Marie de Gaulle?

"The man who belongs to nobody and to everyone," he once said of himself. "The man of destiny," Churchill called him, and later, "The Constable of France." "The necessary man, or rather the only possible man," was Léon Blum's verdict. "A new kind of man—the liberal hero," Malraux asserted. "The man of the day before yesterday," said Edmond Michelet, "and of the day after tomorrow." But to Stalin, he was "not complicated." Roosevelt found him "essentially an egoist." Georges Bidault saw "a man of intelligence, and a man of caprice." Vincent Auriol—and how many others—likened him to Hitler. A woman, on whom he took mean revenge, spoke of "a palpable coldness that hid him as a damp cloth hides a sculptor's clay." "To me," wrote Emmanuel d'Astier, "he remains a mystery."

It is easy to see why. A child of the urban, industrial North, born in 1890 amidst the clang of machines in Lille, raised in the bustle of Paris, devotee of a mechanized army and a modernized France, De Gaulle was equally a product of traditional France, heir to a literary tradition, schooled in the legends of a glorious history, at home in the mysteries, abstractions, and absolutes of a medieval religion. A proper bourgeois who first met his wife "by arrangement" at an art gallery, he spent his most formative period in that academy of sour revolutionaries: a prison camp. A soldier in an army contemptuous of intellectuals, and even of articulation, he scribbled as the veriest professor, producing between the ages of thirty-four and forty-four, four different books. Precise in mind and well ordered in personal habit, he addressed his writings and lectures with fatal insistence to the misty borderland of "the soldier and politics," as he called one of his essays. A general, he fought virtually without troops, taking territory in the baggage of foreign armies, and winning struggle by intrigue and maneuver. A self-proclaimed savior, he was party to squalid intrigue: Joan of Arc amid the Florentines. An ally, he specialized in unilateral action. An apostle of national unity, he stirred dissension in every quarter. A conquering hero, he cast away power at a moment of grave crisis. A political leader, he headed a party which he called a rally but which became a rout. Retired, he was as active politically as any minister. An imperialist, he came back to supreme office, destined to preside over the liquidation of empire.

What emerges from the record is more than paradox. There is a mystery, a genuine enigma, expressed in systematic incongruity between promise and performance. De Gaulle combines immense personal force with high purpose and capacity for constructive achievement: the elements of greatness. What is missing is the gift of cooperation. Working with others, De Gaulle acts like a man on the make who has a "thing" about power. With the features of the great, he blends the instinct of the petty: to the head of the hero, he adds the heart of the rebel.

II

Few men have been more richly endowed with the stuff of
greatness. From his mother (daughter of an industrialist and
parent of two engineers and a bank executive) he drew the future: an understanding that this was an age when "technology
dominated the universe." From his father (a historian among
the Jesuits) he drew the past—and a name to conjure with if
there ever was one. Great height and peculiar features set him
apart as surely as any public figure of the century. A wave of
those enormous flippers was enough to encompass a province,
or dismiss forever the fatuous. Churchill, seeing him for only
the third time, standing slightly aloof from his colleagues
in the cabinet of Paul Reynaud, was moved to whisper,
"*L'homme du destin.*" Of his first encounter with De Gaulle,
Admiral Muselier, who was no friend, wrote:

> I was immediately struck by the physique of the man: by his
> great height, with a disproportionately small head and a too low
> forehead; his eyes, small and gray . . . his chin of very unusual
> shape . . . his mouth, medium in size . . . his nose, almost
> Bourbon . . . his ears, badly shaped.

Emmanuel d'Astier, on his first meeting, noted especially the
height: "He was even taller than I had thought." In addition,
there were "his small head," his "waxy face," "a body of uncertain architecture . . . frail wrists, very white, somewhat
feminine hands." Most of all D'Astier was impressed by the
voice. Greatness, he acknowledged, lay in "that inspired voice
with its broken cadences." To have heard it once was to understand how an unknown brigadier first made himself known,
broadcasting from London on the Free French radio.

Like the body, the mind was cut in generous dimensions.
Noble in interest (De Gaulle's quotations range from Homer
through Shakespeare to Valéry and Bergson), it harbored that
special understanding of massive events fostered by a feel for

history and geography. To Duff Cooper, De Gaulle once confided that he tried "every day, for a short time, to imagine himself looking down on events without prejudice, from the point of view of the future historian." In all his works, the past lives as a real world, peopled with familiars; connecting events together is for him a matter of course; and history is his favorite mode of argument and explanation. He made his famous case against the Maginot Line by citing the record from Roman Gaul to 1870 to show that the "age-old weakness of the country" lay in vulnerability to attack at precisely those places undefended by the Line. Pleading the importance of the French army, he asks, "How can one understand Greece without Salamis, Rome without the Legions, Christianity without the sword, Islam without the scimitar, our own Revolution without Valmy?" He fell easily into the habit of defining leadership by reference to Alexander, Caesar, Joan of Arc, Napoleon. He knew his own country through the "agonized cry of our chiefs" in time gone by:

> The grim orders of the day of Joffre and Gallieni; Gambetta's abjuration: "Lift up your hearts!"; Danton's outcry: "The country is in danger"; the sad utterance of Louis XIV: "There is no happiness in our age!"; Francis I's sorrow: "All is lost save honor!"; the Maid's tears over our "piteous condition"; the despair of Philip VI in flight: "Open the door! It is the wretched king of France!"

Space was as deep to him as time. "Charles de Gaulle," David Thompson wrote, "is, in the Churchillian sense, an imperialist. Both in military and political affairs, he thinks on a world-wide scale and studies the large maps." Throughout all his work runs the assumption that "the map tells our fortune," that "the policy of a state is decided by its geography." His most important military work, *Vers l'Armée du Métier*, opens with a geographical précis of France, then expands to a strategic view of the world circa 1935:

The sea protects England, America, and Japan. The immense arc of the Alps prevents access to Italy on all sides. Distance makes Russia impregnable. The Pyrenees defend Spain. How distant and scattered are the active centers of the German Empire, the Ruhr, the Harz Mountains, Saxony, Silesia.

The memoirs sparkle with similar tours of the geographic horizon. And as a man of action, consciousness of the empire and the world outside France, as much as anything else, set De Gaulle apart from other French soldiers in 1940. Always he talked of a France 100 million strong. In the last weeks of the Third Republic, he met Weygand as the Germans were fighting their way across the Somme. This was De Gaulle's account of the conversation:

DE GAULLE: So they cross the Somme. And then after that?
WEYGAND: After that? It's the Seine and the Marne.
DE GAULLE: Yes. And after that?
WEYGAND: After that? Then it's all over.
DE GAULLE: How over? What about the world? The Empire?

The same kind of "worldliness" separated him from the politicians of the Fourth Republic. "They occupy themselves with the trivialities of county politics," he wrote in 1946, in the post-resignation speech that Blum and Auriol convinced him not to deliver, "as if the world had not become the measuring stick of all problems."

In a curious passage in one of the early books, De Gaulle defined method as "the habit of never being surprised." By which he means the habit of bringing to bear on current transactions the wide world and its past. Among modern leaders perhaps not even Churchill mastered so thoroughly the art of investing what is daily and local with what is eternal and ecumenical. There lies the intellectual *sine qua non* of greatness among men: the heroic mind, simultaneously penetrating to the heart of events and raising circumstance to drama. "There has been no illustrious captain," De Gaulle put it, "who did not possess taste and a feeling for the human mind. At the root of Alexander's victories, one will always find Aristotle."

Demosthenes too, in De Gaulle's case, for with the gift of divination goes the gift of tongues. Supreme powers of articulation account for much, if not most, of the Gaullist legend, and from perfunctory pleasantries through sharp repartee there is style in every line. "I must let you go now," the General says to visitors who have overstayed their time. "Close the parenthesis," he told a political leader who objected that the General had "opened a parenthesis" in their association by founding his own party. "If you agree there's nothing more to say," was his comment when a minister prefaced objection with the line, "I agree, but . . ." "France has lost the battle but not the war" was one of the great rallying cries of World War II, even if De Gaulle did not say it on the day he was supposed to. The *Memoirs* are a work of art, rich in gems of portraiture and descriptive prose. *"Vers l'Orient compliquée je volais avec des idées simples"* is a sentence, too perfectly balanced to be spoiled by translation, which speaks volumes about De Gaulle and the Middle East. Of Pétain he wrote, "Too proud for intrigue, too strong for mediocrity, too ambitious to be pushy, he nursed in solitude a passion to dominate, long hardened by awareness of his own worth, by difficulties mastered, and by a mistrust he felt for others." Here is the justly well-known self-portrait at the very end:

> Old man, exhausted by ordeal, detached from human deeds, feeling the approach of the eternal cold, but always watching in the shadows for the gleam of hope!

It is Proust's famous opener—*"Longtemps je me suis couché de bonne heure"*—that is the model for cadence, though not the equal for brilliance, of De Gaulle's beginning: *"Toute ma vie je me suis fait une certaine idée de la France."*

But what was that certain idea of France? De Gaulle answers over and over again. His France is the "France that cannot be France without grandeur"; the France of the "princess in the fairy tales and the Madonna on the walls"; the France of "primacy in western Europe"; the France of "independence, the sword, and the Empire"; the France of "night falling on Notre Dame, of majestic evenings at Versailles, of the Arc de Triomphe in the sun." That is, the France of Richelieu, Louis XIV, and Napoleon; the France "that is only herself at the top of the ladder."

Whatever else may be in doubt about De Gaulle, that vision of France is not. It is the subject of his days and works, the touchstone of his being, the focus of passions, hopes, illusions, and absurdities. "His only motive force," D'Astier put it, "is the greatness of France. [It is] a road that replaces all other roads, those of God, of men, or progress, and of all ideologies."

No doubt the Gaullist aspiration for a great France has immense creative vitality. It inspired the General's flight to Britain in 1940 amidst the debacle of defeat. It sustained him in the lonely years of building a Free French force and a provisional government. It contributed to the unprecedented record of reform measures he put through in 1945: adoption of cradle-to-grave social security with an emphasis on family that spurred the birth rate; nationalization of credit institutions, the railways, the coal, gas, and electrical industries; establishment of a first-rate school of public administration. From these aspirations, most of all, flowed the Gaullist legend, the mystique that made it possible, once the government decided not to fight, for everyone, in May 1958, to turn to Charles de Gaulle.

Even so De Gaulle's vision of France was a jealous passion. Remote from the empty vessel of Maurras's *France seule*, it still shared with that barren concept qualities of invidious destructiveness. Foreign states, even allies, were automatically excluded. Behind every one of De Gaulle's wartime quarrels with Roosevelt and Churchill lies that "certain idea of France." There is no shred of French sovereignty on which he is not capable of believing them to harbor designs. He suspects them of wanting Madagascar, the Chad, Syria and the Lebanon, the right to direct affairs in metropolitan France. To assert France's right to the tiny islands of St. Pierre and Miquelon—for only the briefest spell—he courted, and won, the lasting enmity of the American State Department. In the *Memoirs* he is forever complaining about having to use Allied planes and review Allied soldiers; he makes particular note of the fact if a plane happens to be French, and at one point even exults because "the cars were French." His notion of serious objectives at the first, organizational meeting of the United Nations was a list headed by recognition of French "as one of the three official languages." Despite a great show of concern for eastern Europe, all indications are that he was willing to underwrite Soviet control in return for Communist endorsement of a special French position in the Ruhr. That other countries, or their nationals, might have interests of higher priority to which France might reasonably yield, he does not imagine. Of Duff Cooper he writes, "If he was not Prime Minister in London, he was to be Ambassador to Paris." As if the two posts were roughly comparable. That France should be left out of anything he cannot abide: "Any large-scale human edifice will be arbitrary and ephemeral if the seal of France is not affixed to it." Neither could he imagine that other countries might not reasonably want to accommodate their interests to those of France: "What was to the advantage of France was to the advantage of all."

It is not only against foreigners, moreover, that the Grandeur of France is a weapon. De Gaulle uses it mercilessly on his own countrymen. Under its ban fall all but Gaullist causes, movements, parties, institutions, and leaders. In the *Memoirs*, he writes off the "causes" of the 1890's—freedom for Dreyfus, decent living conditions for the workers, separation of church and state—as examples of "our weakness and our errors." The Right he dismissed as "against the state"; the Left as "against the country." Representative bodies were "ruled by fear of action."

Political parties were agents of "ignorance . . . bad faith . . . incompetence." "Voices heard from the pulpit and in faculties and academies were . . . the clamor of partisans." As to individuals, "he referred," Herbert Leuthy wrote, "to his opponents as those who do not play the French game."

The fact is, and it goes to the heart of the Gaullist mystery, that the true vision of the Grandeur of France is vouchsafed to only one man—Charles de Gaulle. There lies the base of the transformation trick whereby first person becomes third, and third merges with historic figures from Joan of Arc through Napoleon to Clemenceau. In his own words, De Gaulle is "an almost legendary character," "a man serving as an instrument of destiny," "a man endowed with a mission of pre-eminent character," a man "inspired with a national task." The Task is nothing less than "to constitute around myself the unity of lacerated France," to be "the guide of France," "to assume French sovereignty."

How this singular notion was conceived is a matter of guesswork. But suggestive evidence abounds in the astonishing poverty of De Gaulle's human contacts. All his life, as Duff Cooper remarked, he has had "an ineptitude for happiness," and "no capacity for making friends." As a boy, his family life was cold and formal: "My father," he writes of his parents, "opened history to me. My mother bore for the country a proud love equal only to her religious piety." His professional colleagues liked him little: he was known as the Big Asparagus at St. Cyr, and later "as the most undisciplined officer in the army." Paris society was open to him, but, as one host reports, "De Gaulle was the dullest dinner companion we ever had." Women seem to have held for him no charms; apart from his mother, his wife has been the only woman in his life, and even now at Gaullist functions, as at intellectual parties in New York, an unspoken rule drives the sexes into opposite corners. Malice tinges all De Gaulle's humor, and stiffness pervades his sentiment. "Oh, it's you," was all he could think to say when Mme.

de Gaulle arrived in Britain after a perilous journey from France in 1940. To an aide, whom he saw for the first time after a long separation, his only personal comment was, "You've grown thinner." A sentry to whom, at the suggestion of an aide, he once addressed a personal comment, was convinced something had gone wrong. The sparsest taste governs his table, offices, and dwellings, and the *Memoirs* are bare of comment on surroundings—be they Chequers or the *bidonvilles* of Algiers. Colombey expresses chiefly a passion for being alone, as does De Gaulle's chief relaxation, walking. Probably his most productive period was the two years (1916–18) passed in German prison camps where he wrote most of his first two books. He speaks often of the need to confront destiny "alone"; greatness to him is "*triste*"; and in his book "the man of character . . . is a jealous lover and will not share the prizes or pains that may be his." In his proud solitude, De Gaulle took France as mistress. She became the love of his life, his revenge on people, the crown of his ambition.

For ambitious De Gaulle was from the earliest years. He is supposed to have had a sense of great things in store when he was only twelve. It is clear that he joined the army to make his way: "What fundamentally tempts [men of ability] to adopt the profession of arms," he wrote in *The Edge of the Sword*, "is the prospect of power." In World War I he repeatedly volunteered for the most dangerous missions, earning mention in dispatches and three wounds before his capture at Verdun. Fame was a spur to the books, and they won him steady promotion, at the top of his class, until he made lieutenant colonel and secretary of the Supreme War Council in 1933. In that post he lobbied among the press and politicians with the insistence of the most importunistic Pentagon colonel. After his flight to London in 1940, he wrested and held supreme power with something like fanaticism. The low point of his life, apparently, a time when he was smoking three packs of cigarettes daily, came in 1942–43, when it appeared that General Henri Giraud might win control of Free French forces. His resignation as Premier in 1946 was almost certainly submitted in the hope—a hope justified by repeated refusals of past resignations—that he would immediately be called back to office. The Gaullist party (RPF) was formed as a vehicle for bringing the General back to power at a moment when the country was threatened by Communist pressure from within and without. Even in retirement, De Gaulle was in touch with generals, ministers, ambassadors, businessmen, and not a few plotters, to whom at all times he made clear that he "would face up to his responsibilities." The guide line of his life, in short, was the prospect of power. There is not much doubt about whom he is talking in the peroration of *The Edge of the Sword*:

> What is important is that the ambitious be obsessed by the necessity of finding in life an opportunity to leave their mark upon events; that from the shore on which they live their uneventful lives they should direct their eyes with longing to the stormy seas of history.

Stormy, of course, because in De Gaulle's temper, ambition blends with hostility. He is the very reverse of the Organization Man. "His instinct," Duff Cooper wrote, "is to say no whenever ordinary people would say yes." Not by cooperating with others did he make his way, but by individual effort (the daring missions during the war, as well as the books) and by swimming against the tide. Before 1914, he joined the Pétainists in opposing the doctrine of defense in depth to the ruling precept of mass attack. Between the wars, he opposed to the ruling Pétainist dogma the idea of attack by armored forces. As a colonel heading a tank regiment in 1938, he wrote to a friend, "A unit commander is purely and simply a person who uses up his time and effort in a struggle against his superiors." In 1940, he carried the fight to Britain in the face of explicit orders to the contrary. As chief of the Free French, though only a brigadier, he at all times showed elaborate suspicion of those who outranked him—Vice Admiral Muselier, General Catroux, General Giraud—and he insisted that, as he put it, he had a "mission outside the hierarchy of rank." The theme of disobedience runs through his books, and while being condemned as untimely in the German army of 1918, it is explicity endorsed in *The Edge of the Sword* as a virtue proper to the Man of Character. The supreme aim of the Man of Character, he wrote, was "to rise above himself in order to dominate others." For De Gaulle, in other words, to lead is to dominate.

The taste for domination finds fixed expression in De Gaulle's concept of the state. For him the only state worth the name is a strong state. That comprises first a powerful army, for "the sword is the axis of the world." It includes also empire of some kind, for "if overseas territories cut themselves off from metropolitan France, or if our forces were engaged there, what consequence could we have?" Lastly, there is a nearly omnipotent executive. The role of the chief executive in the constitutional scheme blocked out by De Gaulle at Bayeux in 1946 has been likened to that of the American President. It includes, to be sure, all of the American President's powers —but also one more: the power to dissolve the parliament. It thus combines the strengths of the President and the Prime Minister, while eliminating the vulnerability these have to legislative disapproval. It is, in other words, a vehicle of executive domination unique in non-authoritarian states. Its true nature is revealed by a remark in the *Memoirs*: "Without parliament, elections, and parties no politics were played . . . My task of leadership was therefore facilitated."

Domination is an unpopular theme in a democratic age, and men primarily concerned to get better things for themselves are not easily rallied by appeals for a stronger executive, a stronger army, a stronger empire. But it is notable that from the list of things De Gaulle could best rule without, the people are missing. On the contrary, innumerable remarks, the taste for plebiscites, and in the *Memoirs* the accounts *ad nauseam* of enthusiastic reception in town after town, all testify to De Gaulle's respect for popular sovereignty. He repudiated forceful seizure of power with contempt: *"On n'insiste pas,"* he said when a project was broached to him after his resignation. But neither would he enter that vast world that lies between perfect democracy and the *coup d'état*—the world of orderly political procedure. To do that was to be on the same footing with other seekers after office. But De Gaulle was not *comme les autres*. He had a mission that placed him "outside the hierarchy of rank." Thus, there existed for him at all times the problem of how to assume power: the problem of legitimacy.

His answer to the legitimacy problem is the Gaullist method, a recipe for action that takes the form of a philosophy of history heavily dosed with hocus-pocus. A principal element is the Man of Character, playing a role blocked out by De Gaulle in *The Edge of the Sword*. He appears in public often and dramatically ("great leaders have always stage-managed their effects carefully"). He maintains prestige by keeping distance ("familiarity breeds contempt") and secrets ("give nothing away"). His policy he wraps in silence ("nothing more enhances authority") and calculated obscurantism ("there must always be a 'something' which others cannot fathom"). Withdrawal, the tactic of Achilles, is his supreme weapon. That is how "it constantly happens that men with an unbroken record of success and public approval suddenly lay the burden down."

Around the leader are a small band of trusty aides, not so much givers of advice as arrangers and intriguers, masters of the political sleight-of-hand. Their task is to help history on its way, to open the path, and their principal instrument is guile. "Surprise," the General wrote in *The Army of the Future*, "must be organized . . . If one is willing to mislead the very people one intends to employ, or by clever artifice to use all the means which are now available in order to spread misleading rumors, one can hide reality behind falsehood."

For the rest, there is the play of events. The Man of Character is at all times ready to maneuver with circumstance. He has "a keen eye for contingency." His "principles are adapted to the circumstance of the given situation." And the long-term flow of history works for him. Like Yeats, De Gaulle believes that things fall apart. When catastrophe, cataclysm, or disaster supervenes, the rules go by the board and the times are ripe for De Gaulle. "A few years from now," he wrote casually in a letter in 1929, "they will be after me to save the country." Or, as he said more formally in *The Edge of the Sword:*

> When the situation becomes serious, when the nation is in need of a leader with initiative who can be relied upon, and is willing to take risks, then a sort of ground swell brings the Man of Character to the fore. Everything he asks is granted.

In May 1958, things fell out so. At Colombey, De Gaulle had kept his distance and a grand silence. Mystery shrouded his policies: he seemed the great hope to the right-wing veterans who wanted to cling to Algeria, while to a large group of those on the Left who favored negotiations with the FLN he was the only man of the Right fit to put through a policy of the Left. His entourage—Soustelle, Debré, Chaban-Delmas, Delbecque—was neck deep in plots. At three contingencies—in the statement of readiness on May 15; in the press conference of May 19; in the claim to be forming a government on May 27—he intervened to give a twist to events. Yet in the end it seemed inevitable, the logical culmination of a historic sweep that made Charles de Gaulle the one man who could save France. It was not, as he remarked later to Delbecque, badly played. Not badly at all.

## 8.  PEACE OF THE BRAVE

ONCE back in office, the General lost no time in impressing himself upon events. Within four months he had his plebiscite—the referendum of September 28, 1958, returning a majority of 79.5 per cent for a Fifth Republic. The new Constitution put in place two components of his strong state: a President made lord and master of the Assembly by the right to dissolve; and a federalized empire called the French Community. A third element was added by sweeping economic reforms: convertibility and a 17.5 per cent devaluation of the franc; increase of commodity and personal income taxes; reduction and abolition of pensions and subsidies. By the end of 1959 the adverse balance of payments had been righted; on January 1, 1960, a new "hard" franc made its debut. As a final touch, in the military field, De Gaulle stirred to life a drowsy nuclear weapons program. On February 13, 1960, deep in the Sahara, France successfully tested a rudimentary atom bomb. "Hurrah for France," De Gaulle cried. "She is stronger and prouder."

Long before his own garden was thus in order, the General

was looking over the walls. In September 1958, he staked a claim to parity with Washington and London in the famous memorandum to Dulles and Macmillan asking an American-British-French directorate over NATO. In a series of meetings with Konrad Adenauer that fall, he moved to make good the claim through the device of a Paris-Bonn axis. One result was the European Common Market, put into effect, to the exclusion of Britain, on January 1, 1959. A second was the emergence of De Gaulle as the principal spokesman for the very stiff West German view of Western negotiations with Moscow. All through the long approach to the summit that dominated the diplomacy of 1959, De Gaulle dragged his feet. The summit meeting itself, initially scheduled for December, was postponed until May to allow De Gaulle to share with Eisenhower and Macmillan the satisfaction of private talks with Khrushchev. When the summit conference finally convened, the General emerged as arbiter among the other three. In two years, in short, he had climbed to the topmost rung of world diplomacy. By standing atop Adenauer, he had raised himself to the level of Eisenhower and Khrushchev. He had recalled the Old World to existence to redress the balance of the New.

Undoubtedly the achievement was magnificent. Whether it was politic was open to doubt. The new Constitution was cut to fit a man so special that it probably could never clothe another. The French Community sprung a leak at the start when Guinea contracted out in the referendum, and it all but sank in 1960 when all the member states became independent. The bid for a NATO triumvirate, backed by withdrawal of the French fleet from NATO and refusal to allow the use of French soil for U.S. nuclear weapons, demonstrably weakened the alliance. The French bomb, complicating greatly the task of armaments control, exerted a powerful claim to be the most untoward event of 1960. But good or bad, all events made one thing clear. The years out of office may have mellowed De Gaulle's spirit, weakened his eyes, and thickened his frame. But above all things he still wanted his country to count in the world. He was still eager to write his signature across the pages of history. He was, in short, still the same old De Gaulle. And nothing showed it so much as his Algerian policy.

II

HIS aim was simple: to maintain French presence and influence in Algeria. Over and over again, and in many different ways, he made the same point:

> Algeria must be forever body and soul with France.

> Algeria should be built on the dual basis of its personality and its close solidarity with metropolitan France.

> Algeria will be transformed, developing her personality herself, and closely associated with France.

To Guy Mollet he once confided that the word that to him symbolized the proper relationship between Algeria and France was *avec*. In his perorations, the phrase he repeatedly used was "Algeria with France."

He differed widely, of course, from those settlers who supposed the objective could be achieved by reimposing the old domination. "The Algeria of Papa," as he put it in an interview with Pierre Laffont, had to go. Neither did he accept the Soustelle-army formula of Integration. He refused, with one exception, to mouth the slogan *Algérie c'est la France*—a feat roughly akin to not saying "image," on Madison Avenue. But he did believe that by economic and political reform it would be possible to build a peaceful and prosperous Algeria linked to France by the free choice of the majority. By way of economic reform, he laid down, on October 3, 1958, the Constantine Plan. It held out the prospect of a dramatic rise in the economic status of the Moslems: more jobs, more houses, more land, more schools, more welfare benefits. Stretched out over a five-year period, it intertwined more than ever the French and

Algerian economies. By way of political reform, he accepted from the first the principle of a single electoral college in Algeria, and applied it in repeated votes: the referendum of 1958, then national legislative elections, then municipal elections, then elections to the provincial councils, then the referendum of 1960. His hope was to form a Moslem elite, a third force free from domination by either the settlers or the rebels. With this group, as he said in Algiers on June 4, 1958, he planned "to do the rest"—that is build a new Algeria aligned with France.

Inevitably the General's program came into conflict with two different groups. The rebels viewed the building of a Moslem third force as an attempt to bind Algeria over to the hands of French puppets: Bao-Daiism. Against the General, and in favor of peace negotiations that would put them in the driver's seat, they mustered whatever pressures they could: their army in the field; the threat of U.N. intervention; support from African, Asian, and Communist states. The settlers, French army, and Algeria Firsters, on the other hand, saw cession of political power to the Moslems as an opening for independence. Against the General, and on behalf of a war fought until victory, they mobilized their nearly infinite capacity for making trouble.

De Gaulle, of course, had anticipated trouble in both quarters. His strategy with the rebels was to take them in tow by an offer of physical safety while at the same time holding over their heads the threat of annihilation by the army. In a simile continually endorsed by his intimates as an accurate reflection of his views, he likened liquidation of the Algerian revolt to Napoleon's successful treatment of the revolt of the Vendée in 1801. As reported by Jean Letang in the *Bulletin de Paris*, the General remarked:

> They brought the heads of the rebellion to Paris, and told them: Now it's all over. You can have your churches and your priests. You won't get the King, but France will begin anew.

For the settlers and the army, the General prescribed discipline and the firm tones of command. "The army," he said at one cabinet meeting, "is made for obeying. Give it work and it will think less . . . The settlers are Frenchmen like the others, and must obey the government. Paris governs in Algeria—even in Algiers."

For three years events turned on the efforts of General de Gaulle to take the FLN into camp while imposing his will upon the army and the settlers. To these efforts a rhythmic pattern was imparted, for each year De Gaulle launched his initiatives just before the FLN made its annual autumn bid in the U.N. Assembly. He had, as Raymond Aron once put it, "his Septembers." Early in fall, he opened the prospect of talks with the rebels. While the General Assembly deliberated, the prospect was kept alive. Counteraction from the settlers and army closed that prospect around midwinter. Summer became the fighting season: the army venturing forth inside Algeria, the rebels gathering strength in diplomatic missions abroad. In fall, De Gaulle once more resumed the initiative.

Twice events followed the appointed round. In 1958, De Gaulle nearly cornered the rebel leadership with his offer of the Peace of the Brave. But blatant army "managing" of legislative elections at the end of the year gave the FLN a way out. In 1959, the General again seemed to trap the rebels with an offer of self-determination for Algeria. But a settler-army revolt in January 1960 unloosed the trap and pushed De Gaulle into a very unfavorable position at the abortive Melun peace talks. In 1960, De Gaulle again threatened the rebels with an offer of Algerian Algeria. But this time they broke the mold with a show of unbeatable strength in the Algiers demonstrations of December. And when the professional soldiers moved to strike De Gaulle himself in April 1961, the General crushed the putsch by turning conscripts against regulars.

In the end, character proved to be fate. De Gaulle chose to dominate the army and the settlers, and by his tested recipe—

by using the threat of disaster to acquire full power—he succeeded. But from the rebels he needed cooperation. Not all his ruses, tricks, and pressures availed to bring them into the Gaullist camp.

III

THE General opened his campaign to take the FLN into camp six weeks after returning to power. In mid-July he began casting about for a middle-of-the-road Algerian, widely known and not hostile to the FLN, who might join his cabinet. Ferhat Abbas being unavailable (De Gaulle once indicated that he would have considered Abbas ideal), he hit upon Abderrahmane Farès, a well-known Algerian politician, formerly head of the Algerian Assembly, who had previously indicated that no solution in Algeria was possible without the cooperation of the FLN. Farès visited Abbas in Montreux, Switzerland, to ask FLN backing if he joined the Gaullist government. The rebels, fearing that Farès's participation would give a spur to Integration, refused. But they expressed eagerness to negotiate with De Gaulle.

In August, Farès came back to Montreux, initiating a series of trips that embraced two proposals from De Gaulle. In one, the rebels were asked to support, or at least not to oppose, the referendum. They refused on the ground that the referendum only solidified French sovereignty in Algeria. In the other, De Gaulle suggested that the rebels send a delegation to Paris to discuss cease-fire terms. This also they refused, expressing preference for a neutral country (out of fear, no doubt, that the delegation might be held prisoner) and indicating that they could not lay down their weapons without discussing political conditions as well. When De Gaulle took no notice of their objection to the referendum, the FLN took a step designed to show that French-supervised votes in Algeria would only harden their resistance. They formed, on September 19, 1958, the Provisional Government of the Algerian Republic (GPRA). "It was our response," one member of the Provisional Government declared, "to the referendum." But even in announcing the government, Premier Abbas reiterated willingness to enter into negotiations.

On October 10, De Gaulle renewed negotiations through Jean Amrouche, a well-known poet of Kabyle stock, personally friendly with De Gaulle, who had accompanied Farès on a few of the earlier missions. Amrouche laid before the GPRA Defense Minister Belkacem Krim a memorandum suggesting talks in Paris and guaranteeing the safety of an FLN delegation. Having asked for negotiations, the rebels were in poor position to refuse. But before accepting, the GPRA decided to seek backing from their field commands. Communications Minister Abdelhafid Boussouf crossed the lines into Algeria, and in talks with the field commanders sought and won a mandate to negotiate for a cease-fire. "The time has come," Abbas said in an interview on October 19, "when I can meet any French government without preconditions, because now we have a government holding legitimate authority from the people." As he spoke GPRA ministers were converging on Cairo for a plenary meeting, called to make reply to the French offer of October 10. The meeting was set for October 24.

One day before, General de Gaulle sprung his trap. On October 23, in a carefully prepared answer to a plainly planted question at a press conference in Paris, he made his famous offer of the Peace of the Brave. It was a move toward a cease-fire. But it affected to treat differently the rebel fighters inside Algeria and the political leaders of the GPRA. To the fighters, De Gaulle said:

> Wherever they are organized for combat, their leaders need only enter into contact with the French command. The old warrior's procedure, long used when one wanted to silence the guns, was to wave the white flag of truce.

To the political leaders, De Gaulle said:

> As to the external organization . . . I strongly repeat what I have
> already made known. If delegates are designated to come and
> regulate the end of hostilities with the authority, they have only
> to address themselves to the embassy of France at Tunis or at
> Rabat. The one or the other will assure their transport to the
> Metropole. Their entire security will be assured them and I
> guarantee them their freedom of departure.

To most of the world, it looked like a fair enough offer. President Bourguiba called it "a step forward." The United States put heavy pressure on the rebels to accept. "No French government," wrote Maurice Duverger, a bitter critic of De Gaulle and firm partisan of negotiations with the rebels, "could go further than the present Premier in his offer of negotiations."

But to the rebels, the offer was a poisoned chalice. In their eyes, the reference to the white flag signified surrender. The separate message to fighter and "external organization" seemed a crude device to split their ranks. Besides, General de Gaulle had raised to the public level matters they had wanted secret, and had put forward, under conditions of maximum pressure, terms they had previously rejected. Despite the pressure, the GPRA rejected the Peace of the Brave in the strongest fashion. "We ask," Ferhat Abbas said in a statement on October 24, "a peaceful solution through negotiation. We are offered unconditional surrender."

"Troublemakers," was De Gaulle's *mot* when he heard the news, and he predicted that the force of international opinion would swing against the GPRA. Rightly. At the U.N. General Assembly, despite last-minute concessions on the text of a resolution, the rebels could not secure a mandate for any action. Thus De Gaulle not only passed through the Assembly season, he left the rebels in awkward position with most of the rest of the world. But that victory was speedily annulled by the army's role in the legislative elections in Algeria.

## IV

GENERAL de Gaulle had come to grips with the army and settlers within a week of his accession to office. On a flying visit to Algeria from June 4 to 6, 1958, he sketched out in general terms his New Deal for the Moslems. In the economic, social, and political domains they were to become first-class citizens —"*citoyens à part entière*," as he told a huge crowd in Algiers.

That sounded like Integration, and very briefly the settlers were jubilant. "This is marvelous," said a spokesman for the Algiers Committee of Public Safety. But directly the settlers tried to harden ambiguity and force the pace of events, De Gaulle stiffened. At Oran when the crowd persisted in shouting integrationist slogans, De Gaulle, in a white fury, shouted back, "That's enough . . . shut up." A speech by Leon Delbecque calling for vigilance by the Committee of Public Safety ("Do no more Bastilles remain to be taken?") was partially suppressed; and De Gaulle, in a thinly veiled allusion, told a settler crowd, "You have no more revolutions to make . . ." Positions became fully clear on June 11, when the Committee of Public Safety sent the Premier a memorandum demanding "total, unreserved integration." De Gaulle, in a public statement, called the memorandum "offensive."

To spike the settler guns in Paris the Premier took in his cabinet, in the relatively innocuous post of Minister of Information, their biggest piece—Jacques Soustelle. At the same time he called on the army to hold the settlers in check in Algeria. "Authority here," De Gaulle proclaimed, "is in the hands of General Salan. It must not be contested." Salan was continued as Delegate General with full military and civil powers. Massu was given a promotion. Lesser officers who had assumed civil powers as prefects and subprefects were maintained in their posts. On his second trip to Algeria, on July 1, De Gaulle skipped the civilian population centers to visit army installations at Batna, Fort National, and Sidi-bel-Abbès, headquarters of the Foreign Legion. "For General de Gaulle," a beaming General Salan said in the course of the trip, "we will give the magnificent performance he has asked."

For the rest of the summer the principal task confronting the army was the organization of the referendum, scheduled in Algeria for September 26, 27, and 28. The army's performance was literally magnificent. All over Algeria, from Morocco to Tunis, from the sea to the desert, protected polling places were established. Information on where and how to vote was circulated to the remotest villages. Trucks were made available to bring thousands from the towns to the voting booths. Escorts were provided people who had no road connections to the voting centers. Despite threats from the FLN, the vote itself transpired with a minimum of violence. And it was, for Algeria, a model of democratic procedure. For the first time Europeans and Moslems voted together in a single college. For the first time women went to the polls. Journalists were allowed, within the security regulations, almost free run to cover the vote. Apart from one or two rare cases, there was no interference with the secrecy of the voting. The transportation and counting of the ballots were rigorously honest. And the results, for the army at least, were especially gratifying. Of 3.4 million valid votes, 3.3 million were cast in the Yes column: a majority of 96.5 per cent. Putting together No votes (115,000), abstentions (890,000), and nonregistered voters (about a million), the FLN could claim, at the very best, only 40 per cent of the population.

Still, for General de Gaulle, the referendum carried a distinctly disquieting message. Only in the most formal sense could the vote be called honest. By posters and leaflets, in the papers, on the radio, and at meetings, the army had waged a vigorous campaign for the Yes vote. If there was one thing every Moslem in Algeria knew, it was that the army wanted him to vote, and wanted him to vote affirmatively. In this pressure there was nothing untoward. Given the counterpressure by the FLN, it was in fact normal. But the army's active role posed the question of whether it could ever be neutral; whether it could ever act with enough restraint to leave to the Moslems a genuinely free choice; whether, in other words, the army did not, by its very presence, count as a barrier against General de Gaulle's hopes for raising an independent Moslem elite.

The test came by invitation of Charles de Gaulle in the parliamentary elections of November 30, 1958. Directly after the referendum, in a letter to General Salan, the Premier issued instructions enjoining the strictest neutrality upon the army. Soldiers were to leave the Public Safety Committees forthwith. In the upcoming poll, they were to admit, "except for those taking part in terrorist activity," unfettered campaigning by all parties.

> I attach [De Gaulle wrote] the greatest importance to the fact that there should be genuine competition, i.e. complete with rival electoral lists; the worst possible mistake would be to run lists solely favored by the authorities. What we must aim at is that an Algerian political elite should freely emerge from the election. Only thus can we fill the political vacuum which has opened the void to the leaders of the Algerian rebellion.

With a few grumbles, the officers followed De Gaulle's order to quit the Public Safety Committees. But at that point obedience ran out. Just as in the referendum, the army made known—by posters, at meetings, in the press, and on the air— its preference for candidates favoring Integration. This order of the day was a typical interpretation of De Gaulle's letter to Salan:

> While remaining impartial and keeping out of struggles between persons and parties, the army shall more than ever play its national part in Algeria . . . Promoting fusion of the two communities, counseling and guiding the Moslem population . . . indicating the prospects open to the Algerians within the French frame-

work . . . the army will enable the population to vote for those lists that will best serve the cause of French Algeria.

In consequence of that attitude, the poll, though nominally free once again, was as controlled as any in the past. In three major constituencies (Tiaret, Tizi-Ouzou, and Orléansville) there was only one list on the ballot—the list patronized by the army and local Public Safety Committees. In seven others, there was more than a single list—but no competition for the official candidates. Alain Savary, a Socialist friendly to De Gaulle but also to independence, withdrew his intended candidacy "because the conditions for the functioning of a democratic system do not exist at present in Algeria." "Looking for an independent candidate," Eugene Mannoni wrote in *Le Monde*, "is like waiting for Godot." "Candidates representing the spirit of May 13," Henry Tanner reported in the New York *Times*, "have a virtual monopoly." In the end, no candidate favoring even eventual independence emerged from either the Moslem or European communities. At least 60 of the 71 Algerian seats were filled by puppets. Doubt was cast over De Gaulle's whole project of raising an Algerian third force. It was only clear that he had to bring the army out of politics and under his discipline.

It was on that indecisive note that, at the end of 1958, the first phase of the three-cornered struggle among De Gaulle, the rebels, and the army came to a close.

## v

The second phase opened in the fall of 1959 with all parties in stronger positions. General de Gaulle was President of the Fifth Republic, with the right to overwhelming emergency powers. Beneath him as Premier he had a man of the warmest personal loyalty—Michel Debré. Most of the old parties had been crushed in the elections of November 1958, while a large fraction of the new deputies had come to power on De Gaulle's coat-tails. The President had already secured the support of Dr. Adenauer and was beginning to emerge as the leading statesman of the West. In Algeria, he had replaced General Salan with two personal protégés. Salan's civil authority as Governor General he vested in the economist Paul Delouvrier; Delouvrier rapidly moved to take administrative powers in Algeria back under civilian control. Salan's military authority De Gaulle handed to General Maurice Challe, an officer very active in helping the Gaullist cause during the May days of 1958.

The army had launched a new offensive—the Challe Plan —in the spring of 1959. While it fell far short of crushing the rebels, it did have the effect of imbuing General Challe with the spirit of Pacification. "I believe in a military solution to the Algerian question," General Challe told an interviewer in June 1959. "The army will not leave for a long time. The security of the Western world demands that France stay in Algeria." Moreover, the army's political allies in Paris, including Soustelle, who remained in the Debré cabinet, and Delbecque and Thomazo, held important posts in the two parties supporting the Debré government—the Independents and the Gaullist Union for the New Republic (UNR).

As to the rebels, they had suffered losses in the Challe offensive, but mere survival constituted for them a kind of victory. Moreover, two missions to Peiping, in the spring and early summer of 1959, assured them that, in a pinch, outside support was available. And by the end of summer all indications were that the rebel plaint would fare exceedingly well at the coming General Assembly meeting.

Suddenly De Gaulle took the initiative again. On August 24, at a four-hour cabinet meeting officially dubbed "very important," the President heard nineteen ministers, one by one, present their views on Algeria. Next day he was off on a tour of the officers' messes in Algeria—his first visit since becoming President in January. Back in Paris, on September 2, he met with President Eisenhower and developed plans for a new departure in Algerian policy. A week later he outlined his views at a meeting of the heads of states of the French Community. Then on September 16, in a nationally televised address, he broached his plan.

The centerpiece was a pledge of self-determination for Algeria. Four years after a cease-fire, or after killings in Algeria fell below the level of 200 annually, the Algerians were to choose their destiny in a free vote. The choice was to lie among three alternatives.

One was integration, making "the Algerians part and parcel of the French people who would then, in effect, spread from Dunkirk to Tamanrasset." A second was association with France—"the government of Algerians by the Algerians, backed up by French help and in close relation with her [France] as regards the economy, education, defense, and foreign relations. In that case the internal regime of Algeria should be of the federal type, so that the various communities—French, Arab, Kabyle, Mozabite—who live together in the country would find guarantees for their own way of life and a framework for cooperation." Finally there was independence, or as General de Gaulle called it, "secession." On this point he said:

> France would then leave the Algerians who had expressed their wish to become separated from her. They would organize, without her, the territory in which they live, the resources they have at their disposal, the government which they desire. I am convinced personally that such an outcome would be incredible and disastrous . . .

What the build-up implied, the text had confirmed. General de Gaulle was seeking to win international favor without alienating the army, and thus to cross safely the danger zone of the General Assembly. "I must gain an international victory," he told one army officer at the time, "while simultaneously you follow through with your pacification effort. The only way to do this is to affirm that my policy is liberal." Accepting the principle of "self-determination," in effect turned the trick. The White House found the new plan "completely in accord with our hopes to see a just and liberal program for Algeria." From Moscow, Khrushchev, then angling for a summit meeting, expressed his blessing: General de Gaulle's offer "could play an important role in the settlement of the Algerian problem." President Bourguiba, speaking for much of moderate African opinion, counseled the rebels to make terms with Paris forthwith.

In fact, the De Gaulle plan was anything but hopeful from the rebel viewpoint. To be sure, it admitted the eventual possibility of independence. But it asserted that independence would go with partition, slicing the Sahara and parts of the coast from the Algerian state. It threatened the complete cessation of French economic support for an independent Algeria. It implied that the French army would conduct the vote determining Algeria's future. It opened the door to a postponement of a vote for four years after the rebels had ceased fighting. Above all, it said nothing about negotiations with the rebels. "De Gaulle," as a diplomat put it, "is moving forward as if the FLN didn't exist at all."

In these circumstances, the rebel tactic was to underline all the difficulties in the De Gaulle plan without refusing it. Their hope was to place the onus of a negative stand upon Paris. That basic decision was made on September 18 at an all-day meeting in Tunis at the home of Ferhat Abbas. Thereafter, for a full week, the rebels mustered diplomatic support. Rabat and Cairo were invoked against pressure for agreement from Tunis and Washington. A second meeting on September 23 was followed by leaks to the press that the rebel response would be "positive." Then on September 28, at a press conference in the Hotel Majestic in Tunis, Ferhat Abbas made known the GPRA position.

The response stressed all the particular points in dispute be-

tween the rebels and General de Gaulle. It denied
claim to sovereignty over the Sahara: "prospecting an
ration cannot be changed into the right of ownership." It expressed "unshakable determination to oppose partition." It
scouted the assumption that France itself could supervise a free
choice in Algeria: "The free choice of the Algerian people cannot be exercised under the pressure of an army of occupation."
Still, while pointing out all these matters to be settled by negotiation, the rebels accepted Self-Determination as a basis for
talks. And to shift the onus of reply to Paris they crowded an
urgent hope into their statement. "Peace," it said, "can be immediate."

The response of Paris was to pretend that everything was
going swimmingly, and that nothing could be easier than talks.
A day after the GPRA statement, Foreign Minister Couve de
Murville announced that France was "prepared to discuss a
cease-fire with all those who fight, and that, of course, includes
the FLN." Two weeks later Premier Debré declared that if the
rebels wanted to negotiate they had only to present themselves
at the French Embassy in Rabat or Tunis in keeping with the
Peace of the Brave offer of the year before. "This offer," he
said, "still stands." Then on November 10, in a press conference, General de Gaulle made it formal. "I say once again,"
he told the press, "that if the leaders of the insurrection wish to
discuss with the authorities the conditions of an end to the
fighting, they can do it. The conditions will be honorable, will
respect the liberty and dignity of everyone. If the representatives of the external organization decide to come to France to
discuss them, it depends only on them to do so, either secretly
or in public."

Once again the ball was back in the FLN court. The rebels
were obliged to shatter the illusion fostered by De Gaulle that
everything was coming up roses. As one of them put it: "General de Gaulle, in moving on November 10, obliged us to make
response. French opinion was beginning to think that the FLN

had really decided to negotiate, even to order a cease-fire before the conditions of achieving self-determination had been worked out . . ." The response made by the FLN was a maneuver designed to dramatize one of the main points at issue between the rebels and the French government. On November 17, the GPRA announced willingness to negotiate with France in Paris on the conditions of a cease-fire. As rebel delegates the GPRA named five ministers long since held prisoner by the French: Ben Bella; Ait-Ahmed, Bitat, Boudiaf, and Khider.

The maneuver fooled nobody. De Gaulle himself rejected it contemptuously: "Too bad for them, the war will continue." When the U.N. General Assembly opened debate on Algeria on November 30, it was plain that tempers had turned against the GPRA. In the vote on December 12, the rebels failed even to muster a two-thirds majority for a resolution backing informal talks with France and recognizing Algeria's right to self-determination. Thus, for the second straight year, General de Gaulle had traversed the danger zone. But a month later— also for the second year in a row—his victory was dissipated when the army and settlers took to the warpath.

The self-determination offer had from the beginning aroused their unmixed hostility. For while favoring association between France and Algeria, and admitting the possibility of integration, the proposal also allowed in theory for independence. However theoretical, allowing that awful possibility was to the settlers and to the army an omen of capitulation. Self-Determination became in their mouths Indetermination. "Like Mali, eh?" General Massu said, likening De Gaulle's program for Algeria to the chain of events that was bringing independence in Black Africa.

To fight the program of September 16 there was formed on September 18 in Paris the RAF, or Rassemblement de l'Algérie Française. Its membership included most of the old Algeria Firsters—minus Jacques Soustelle, but plus some forty of the new Algerian deputies. It was financed by the chief settler bagman—Alain de Serigny. It had the usual connections with bully boys in Paris and Algiers. Military sympathizers included Marshal Juin, General André Zeller, Army Chief of Staff in Paris, and Generals Faure and Mirambeau in Algeria. The strategy was to force the government to come out so strongly for integration that the whole program for self-determination would be wrecked. The tactic was familiar: pressure from the army in Algeria.

To effect that goal a complex plot was worked out and scheduled for the second week of October. In the Assembly, a hundred or so deputies, nominally supporting the government, were to declare in the most violent terms their adherence to the Integration principle. Simultaneously there was to be in Algiers and Paris a rash of spectacular assassination attempts and political incidents. The military would then petition General de Gaulle, in the interests of France, for a government that could maintain order. The calculation was that Premier Debré, with his majority threatened and public order in doubt, would step aside; that General de Gaulle would be obliged to appoint a new government headed by Georges Bidault and including most of the Algeria Firsters; that the new government would then declare itself in favor of Integration, thus effectively junking the self-determination program.

As it developed, President de Gaulle was alerted to the plot by the Defense Chief of Staff, General Paul Ely. De Gaulle summoned General Challe from Algeria and assured him that there would never be political negotiations with the rebels, and that the army would remain in Algeria. Challe passed the reassurances down the line in Algeria. On October 10, in an order of the day, Massu declared, "I will maintain order." The army had contracted out of the plot.

With the danger gone, loyal Gaullists and advocates of a liberal policy in Algeria began cultivating the fiction that a plot was still in the works. On the night of October 15–16 came the mysterious attempt by Robert Pesquet to assassinate former Interior Minister François Mitterrand—an attempt which, by pre-arrangement, failed. Hours earlier Lucien Neuwirth, a faithful Gaullist, had warned the Assembly in the most dramatic terms: "The plot may come off tomorrow. Already groups of killers have crossed the border from Spain. The men to be assassinated have already been designated." A few days later, Albert Chalandin, secretary general of the Gaullist UNR, officially warned of "a subversive plot." Under cover of this fiction, the loyal Gaullists moved against their opponents. Fifteen leading ultras, including Delbecque and Thomazo, were expelled from the UNR; and a series of raids were staged by police on bully-boy offices in Paris and Algiers. Marshal Juin was rebuked for an article criticizing the September 16 speech.

But no officers implicated in the original plot were apprehended. On the contrary, De Gaulle's reliance on Massu's support made it more apparent where real power lay. And the army's strength and sentiments emerged with utter clarity when a new test developed. The occasion was an interview given, on January 16, 1960, by General Massu to Hans Ulrich Kempski of Munich's *Suddeutsche Zeitung*. As the story appeared, on January 19, Massu said of General de Gaulle:

> We do not understand his policy. The army could never have expected him to take such a stand. That is true for more than his Algerian policy. The Constantine Plan, formerly accepted by the army, now appears without any purpose, because it is clear that the African peoples to whom he guaranteed the right of self-determination are only using it to quit the community sooner or later.
>
> Our greatest disappointment is that General de Gaulle has become a man of the Left. [On May 13] he was the only man available. But the army perhaps made a mistake.

When Kempski observed that perhaps De Gaulle was still the only man available, General Massu commented:

> The big question is to know when a successor to De Gaulle will come.

On January 20, De Gaulle ordered Massu back to Paris. On January 22, over the protests of Premier Debré, Defense Minister Guillaumat, Delegate General Delouvrier, and General Challe, the President relieved Massu of his command. Almost immediately Algiers was aflame. On January 23, violent calls to action were heard in all quarters. "De Gaulle," said a settler tract, "wants a free hand to sell out Algeria . . . The hour to rise has come." "Our silence," an editorial in the *Echo d'Alger* declared, "would be cowardice." "We'll go get Massu in Paris," an activist leader told his troops. "They've laid hands on Massu," another said at a meeting. "They don't know what heavy consequences will follow." "The die," Pierre Lagaillarde threatened, "is cast," and he promised to be on the barricades the following day.

On the morning of January 24, Lagaillarde established a small armed redoubt in the grounds of the University of Algiers. That afternoon a protest demonstration was called by the Front National Français of Joseph Ortiz in downtown Algiers. To break up the demonstration, General Challe called up two detachments of paratroops and a company of CRS guards. But the paratroopers refused to march; and when the CRS moved on the settlers, there was a short but bloody exchange, killing twenty-four and wounding 136—mainly of the CRS. The taste of blood, and confidence that the army would not fire upon them, rallied the great mass of settlers round Lagaillarde and Ortiz. By the morning of January 25, all of settler Algiers was out on a sympathy strike. Three different redoubts, well manned and well armed, had been set up in downtown Algiers. Lagaillarde and Ortiz, in friendly communication with both the army high command and all settler groups, were the men of the hour. "Tomorrow," Ortiz exulted, "I'll be in power in Paris."

For five days, the strange insurrection continued. Night after night the settlers brought arms, provisions, reinforcements, and expressions of sympathy to the men in the redoubts. Day after day, despite orders and appeals from Paris and General Challe's headquarters, the troops mingled freely and amicably with the men in the redoubts. Only after the government had taken the most serious measures—only after special trips from Paris by General Ely and Premier Debré; only after a retreat from Algiers by General Challe and M. Delouvrier; only after the replacement of the Algiers paras by fresh musters from the field; only after a personal appeal from General de Gaulle; only, in short, after the gulf of disaster opened before the Fifth Republic—did the insurrection peter out.

When it did, it appeared that General de Gaulle had won a smashing victory over the soldiers. In his broadcast appeal he had seemed to stand by Self-Determination: "It is the policy which has been defined by the President of the Republic, decided upon by the government, approved by the parliament, and adopted by the French nation." Immediately after the redoubts were emptied, leaders of the rising were rounded up for trial. A cabinet reshuffle ousted Jacques Soustelle from office.

But it soon emerged that in the negotiations preceding collapse of the insurrection, the army had won some crucial concessions. Except for one officer, Colonel Jean Gardes, a psychological warfare expert, the soldiers active in the revolt escaped without sanction. Moreover, in his public speech, General de Gaulle had expressed a kind word for Pacification. He urged the soldiers to "liquidate the rebel force which is seeking to drive France out of Algeria, and to impose upon that land its dictatorship of want and sterility." He promised that if a referendum on Self-Determination were held "it will be your responsibility to guarantee the complete freedom and sincerity of this vote."

In March, in the course of a tour of army posts in Algeria, General de Gaulle re-emphasized those themes in unmistakable language. "There will be no Dienbienphu," he said at Catinat. "This is going to end in a military success that will assure the active presence of France." "Solving the problem," he told another group of officers, "will be long. It cannot be approached until after a complete military victory." "Nothing," he said to still another group, "can be built without Pacification. There is nothing more important . . . than operations." And at Batna, he made it plain that the eventual cease-fire he had in mind was a surrender: "If the rebels lay down their arms, the army will take them up."

It was in the same spirit that General de Gaulle, fortified by his personal success at the abortive summit meeting in May, issued to the rebels his invitation to what became the abortive talks of Melun. On June 14, in a televized address, he said:

> Once again I turn in the name of France to the leaders of the insurrection. I say to them that we await them here in order to find an honorable end to the fighting which drags on, to fix the disposal of weapons and decide the fate of the fighters.

For three reasons, the offer seemed worth exploring to the GPRA. First, the term "honorable end to the fighting" seemed to rule out surrender. Second, the reference to "the fate of the fighters" might open a broad highway for negotiations on the guarantees, that is to say political conditions, that would accompany a cease-fire. Third, in secret unofficial contacts, the FLN had been told that De Gaulle preferred France to a neutral country as a locus of negotiations, because he himself wanted to participate directly. Accordingly on June 20, the GPRA accepted De Gaulle's offer. As an indication of the understanding that there would be meetings with De Gaulle himself, and that political issues would be discussed, it announced that it would send a delegation headed by Ferhat Abbas. It equally indicated that it would send in advance, to work out technical details of the trip, a preliminary mission. On June 25, the preliminary negotiators, Ahmed Boumendjel and Mohammed ben Yahia, left Tunis for Paris by a regular flight of Air Tunis. For the first time since 1954, rebel officials were meeting French officials on a formal, public basis.

Very quickly it became apparent that there was, to put it mildly, a misunderstanding. Where the GPRA looked to broad negotiations between Abbas and De Gaulle, the French seemed bent on drawing them into a narrow discussion of how to lay down arms. The two rebel negotiators were whisked by helicopter from Orly to the city hall at Melun. Except for tele-communications with Tunis, they were denied all contact with the outside world. Though Boumendjel had hoped to leave the matter ambiguous, the French negotiators from the start insisted the coming talks could deal only with military matters. For two days, in question after question, Boumendjel tried to find scope for broader talks. He was told that the Abbas mission would have no chance for outside contacts with the press. He was told that it would be denied access to the im-prisoned rebel leaders. When he asked the composition of the French delegation, the answer indicated that it would be largely military. When he asked whether Abbas would have a chance to meet with De Gaulle, the answer was: not until after the cease-fire.

While the talks advanced in that unpropitious climate, the French press, acting under official guidance, was giving the impression that all was moving smoothly. "There is no reason to believe," the official news agency, Agence France Presse, said in one dispatch, "that the talks will not reach a satisfactory conclusion." To the rebels in Tunis, it looked, once again, like a trap. As they saw it, they were being handed unacceptable terms without an opportunity to explain what was unaccept-able. The build-up of happy expectation looked to them like a new move to bundle them into surrender. On instructions from Tunis accordingly, Boumendjel posed a decisive ques-tion: Were the conditions of Abbas's visit subject to any ne-gotiations at all? The answer was that France would establish the conditions for the rebels to take or leave. At that point, Boumendjel broke off the talks. "In present circumstances," a communiqué issued by the GPRA from Tunis said, "the coming to France of a delegation from the GPRA is not appropriate." "Even in negotiations," Ferhat Abbas said in a speech, "France acts like a colonial power."

On that sour note the second phase came to a close. It had been as indecisive as the first. De Gaulle had launched the idea of self-determination. But the rebels regarded the offer as merely a blind for capitulation. The General had also begun the game of military musical chairs—a policy that in 1960 removed from Algeria every officer involved in the January insurrection. But there was no sign that the new officers sent to Algeria differed from the old. A settlement, in short, seemed as far away as ever.

## VI

WHEN phase three opened in the fall of 1960, General de Gaulle was still in the mood of Melun. At a news conference on September 5, he showed open disdain for the "so-called United Nations." "No matter what does, or does not, happen in New York," he said, "France will pursue her course." He told the rebels that the only terms on which he would talk to them were the terms they believed to verge on surrender. "Why fail to recognize," he asked without pronouncing the word surrender, "what the nature of negotiations must be?"

At that point, there supervened for the rebels their biggest diplomatic break of the war. Though they had long had ties with the Chinese Communists, it was clear that effective aid could come only from the Russians. But Khrushchev, apparently in the hope of using De Gaulle to break open NATO, had long refrained from antagonizing Paris on Algeria. The collapse of the summit must have shaken these hopes. And in September, when he found himself at the table-pounding session of the U.N. in direct conflict with the West in a bid for African and Asian support, he decided to play the Algerian card. On October 2, after a two-hour meeting with three

GPRA ministers at the Soviet mission's summer place in Glen Cove, he indicated that he considered Algeria, "apart from disarmament, the principal subject of the Assembly." Six days later he stepped up support. "Our meetings and our talks with the Algerian leaders," he said in response to a question, "constitute a *de facto* recognition of their government."

By that time General de Gaulle was already readjusting his policy to meet the new rebel success. At the end of October, in a swing through Brittany, he climbed down from the harsh stand of Melun and the September 4 address. On November 4, in a radio-television address, he broke dramatically with the policy of the past four months. In his speech he endorsed anew the principle of self-determination. He sketched in glowing colors "the Algeria of tomorrow"—an "Algerian Algeria" . . . with "her own government, her institutions, and her laws." He expressed conviction that at the time of self-determination Algeria would be "united with France for economic, technical, educational, and defense matters." By omission, at least it appeared that the Algerian Algeria would have its own foreign office and policy. As to the rebels, he invited them anew "to participate without restriction" in the construction of the new Algeria, but demanded that "beforehand we should stop killing each other." And if they did not agree, well, France would go forward anyway.

> That is why [he said] without abandoning the hope that one day common sense will finally prevail and that general negotiations will be opened after the fighting and acts of terrorism have ceased, we are going, with the Algerians of Algeria to continue along the road to an Algerian Algeria . . . What was begun by instituting the single electoral college, the election of deputies and senators, of municipal councilors and mayors, of general councilors and their chairmen . . . will be continued and developed.

What this meant, in effect, was a new constitution for Algeria, written under French auspices but guaranteeing home rule, and put into effect even before an agreement with the rebels supervened. The Elysée indicated that a referendum to approve the general policy would be held in Algeria and in France early in 1961.

To the rebels, the new plan looked like Bao-Daiism with a vengeance. Immediately after De Gaulle made the offer, they made it clear that any French move to establish, without them, a new statute for Algeria would only complicate peace negotiations. They labeled the program a new move to circumvent the General Assembly, where they were moving to seek direct U.N. intervention in Algeria. But it was equally clear that the November 5 program held out the possibility of negotiations —if only between the home-rule government established in Algeria and the GPRA. Moreover, the Algiers insurrection of January 1960 had made it plain that without De Gaulle, the army would rule in Paris. De Gaulle, as President Bourguiba pointed out at the end of November, was "the man best qualified to solve the Algerian problem." In that move, the General Assembly once more issued a reprieve. Direct U.N. intervention in Algeria was voted down overwhelmingly. For the third straight year, De Gaulle had steered by the U.N. reef.

Even before the U.N. vote came, he was in the thick of the referendum campaign. He had asked a mandate in the following terms:

> Do you approve the projected law . . . concerning self-determination for the Algerian peoples, and the organization of public powers in Algeria before self-determination?

A clever formula, it thrust into opposition only two groups: the settlers hostile to self-determination, and the rebel supporters opposed to the "organization of public power in Algeria before self-determination." Thus by securing a large mandate, De Gaulle could expect to discredit both the settlers and the GPRA.

He set to his task with a will. Speaking tours and a series of nation-wide addresses were organized. The patronage weapon was used openly. In the press there was a vigorous campaign. All over France, Gaullist organizations chalked up pleas to vote Yes. When the President himself swung into action early in December, there was no doubt he would win in the vote. For his first step in the campaign he picked the only tough area in the nation: Algeria. There he found the event that threw the negotiations out of phase, the most surprising and important development of the whole Algerian war—the Moslem May 13.

VII

DE GAULLE flew from Paris to Ain-Témouchent in western Algeria on the morning of Friday, December 9. His itinerary for the next four days included main centers of Moslem settlement removed from the coast: Tlemcen, Blida, Orléansville, Télergma, Biskra, Batna. Plainly he was bidding for Moslem support. "It is up to you," he told a Moslem crowd at Tlemcen on Friday, "to assume Algerian responsibilities." Equally plainly he expected trouble in the European centers of Oran and Algiers. Neither city was on his route. During the preceding week, large contingents of CRS and police from France were flown to the two big settler towns. As a further insurance against trouble, army units heavily staffed with draftees were moved from the countryside for guard duty in the big cities.

Friday morning trouble came as expected. A new settler activist organization—the FAF or Front pour l'Algérie Française—had decreed protest strikes in all the main coastal cities. In Algiers, early in the morning, youth gangs ran through the streets, warning workers and shopkeepers to stay home and dismantling private cars. Though public transport continued to function, and though Moslem shops remained open, the strike was 90 per cent effective by 10 o'clock that morning. Around 10:30, in downtown Algiers, groups of FAF sympathizers began demonstrating against the referendum. But wherever large crowds formed, contingents of CRS men moved in to break them up. Several times during the day the CRS loosed tear-gas bombs, or concussion grenades, and the crowd, returning a hail of stones, fell back. Much the same picture presented itself in other coastal cities, though in Oran the strife was quicker. At one point 2,000 protesting settlers crowded into the central square, blocking the approaches by setting buses with punctured tires athwart the streets. There was a hail of missiles, and some shots, when the CRS launched tear gas to break up the crowd. In all, some 45 persons were hurt—25 settlers and 20 from the CRS.

Saturday, as De Gaulle moved eastward from Tlemcen, a heavy rain drenched Algiers. The downtown area was empty, save for CRS patrols, and groups of settler youths honking horns to sound out the code for Algérie Française. Around noon, a push by the settlers toward the Summer Palace was broken up by the CRS. There was tear gas, a throwing of rocks, and the firing of some shots from balconies overlooking the street. But at two in the afternoon everything seemed calm. It was—downtown. But in Belcourt, an eastern suburb of the city heavily settled with Europeans and relatively well-off Moslems, a fatal spark had been struck.

During all of Friday and most of Saturday, Belcourt had been quiet, as the Europeans observed, and the Moslems ignored, the strike call. Saturday afternoon, two armed Europeans approached a group of Moslems in the rue de Lyon, the main street of Belcourt, and bade them cease work. The Moslems protested, and tempers were mounting when a *harka* of Moslem soldiers in the French army intervened. The sergeant commanding the unit started to disarm one of the Europeans. The other fired at the sergeant. But immediately word spread —growing in enormity as it passed from person to person—that Europeans were shooting down Moslems. For the rebel organizers planted through the Moslem community, a moment had come round at last. Banners, emblems, and stickers were broken out; parades and demonstrations organized. By late afternoon every Moslem sector of Algiers was marching for the FLN.

In Belcourt, 5,000 Moslems, women and children in the van, paraded up and down the rue de Lyon bearing FLN banners and stickers and shouting, "*Vive le FLN, Algérie Libre, Vive De Gaulle,* Down with De Gaulle, Abbas to Power, Negotiations with the FLN, Lagaillarde to the stake." A company of draftees watched impassively as the Moslems worked their way up and down the street. Settlers pelted the marchers with stones from the balconies, and there were some shots.

At the southern extremity of the city, in the Valley of the Shrieking Woman, several hundred Moslems marched through the alleys shouting FLN slogans. One group broke out arms and set up a barrier athwart a main road. At least one European who tried to penetrate was killed. A military troop saw the barrier and detoured.

At the southeast fringes of the city, in the new housing developments of Diar el Mahçoul and Diar es Saada, FLN stickers suddenly appeared at every window; Moslem singing FLN songs danced through the courtyards, then moved down on the city, driving European families from their apartments and burning two gas stations owned by settlers.

At the western edge of the city, in the heavily European quarter of Bab-el-Oued, several thousand Moslems, singing Arabic songs and bearing FLN banners, marched behind a Simca plastered with FLN stickers, straight down the main street, tangling as they moved with settlers who hurled missiles and fruit.

In the very heart of town, in the Casbah, a cortege of several hundred Moslems paraded past French soldiers from the top of the Casbah to its base at the rue de Lyre. Checked there by the CRS and a volley of shots by armed settlers, they stopped and yelled slogans: "Algeria will be Independent; Free Ben

Bella; Lagaillarde to the Stake; Ferhat Abbas to Power; Moslem Algeria." When a shot rang out near the synagogue, the demonstrators burst in, broke windows, ransacked a dozen neighboring shops, and then ran the FLN flag up atop the temple. When reporters entered the Casbah, they found, instead of a distant and suspicious population, extreme volubility. One young Moslem, a civil servant, told the correspondent from Le Monde:

We want De Gaulle to negotiate with the GPRA. That is the only possible referendum. Elections were never free in this country. We are not against De Gaulle. We are not against France. We are against colonialism. We have had enough now. We say it; we will show it; and we will never stop.

Most of Monday witnessed similar demonstrations in Oran and Bône as well as Algiers. But where on the first day troops and CRS stood by, only intervening in clashes between settlers and Moslems, on the second they moved vigorously to crush the Moslem demonstrations. Republican guards walled off the Moslem quarters in the suburbs and then went in, breaking up crowds and tearing down FLN stickers. Regular troops occupied the Casbah and Bab-el-Oued. Almost everywhere clashes marked the return to order. On Monday night the Delegate General's office announced that ninety-six persons had been killed in the demonstrations—five of them Europeans.

That same evening, General de Gaulle, cutting his trip short by a day, flew back to Paris. On arrival at the airport, he spoke as if nothing had happened: "There is only one policy. It must be followed." In the same spirit he went through the motions of the referendum. But in fact everything had changed. The settler myth of integration was shattered. Through two days of ebullient settler demonstrations against De Gaulle, no significant Moslem voice was raised in support of the Europeans of Algeria. Equally bankrupt was the army argument of voluntarism: of holding firm to keep the Moslems in line. In Algiers

—the very stronghold of Pacification—under the muzzles of French guns, the Moslem community had expressed its loyalty to the FLN and its hope for a Moslem Algeria. Similarly engulfed was the policy of Charles de Gaulle. For the demonstrators of December 12 were precisely those Moslems with whom De Gaulle had hoped to build a third force against the FLN. Economically they were those who had benefited most from French development projects: they lived in the new apartments of Diar el Mahçoul, not in the mud huts of the countryside; they worked in the factories, and shops and offices of Belcourt, not on the stony soil of the Bled. Politically they were the burghers quickened to life by De Gaulle's incessant elections. They had voted in the referendum of 1958; they had voted for deputies; they had voted for provincial officials; they had voted for municipal officials. They stood on the eve of a statute that would be without doubt the most liberal in Algerian history. And they rejected it in the only way they could. They plebiscited the FLN.

On De Gaulle the lesson was not wasted. Immediately after the referendum, he buried its principal subject: the projected statute for an Algerian Algeria. Through President Bourguiba of Tunisia, he moved for direct negotiations with the FLN on the political future of Algeria. Forgotten was the old policy of taking the rebels into camp. "Melun," De Gaulle told one of the Tunisians, "never happened." Of the December days in Algiers, he said:

The FLN created a spirit; hence a people; hence a policy; hence a state.

But what De Gaulle learned inevitably was also known to the professional diehards of the army. They remained resolutely opposed to negotiations with the FLN, and even more to Algerian independence. But where once they were content to force De Gaulle's hand, they now saw in his change of policy the need to eliminate him entirely. And where once they were content to work behind the screen of settler pressure—affecting to play the role of mediators—they now saw in De Gaulle's determination the need to take the lead. On those principles, a handful of officers, previously removed by De Gaulle from Algeria, wove together plans for a military putsch. Their leaders included a quartet of generals (Maurice Challe, Raoul Salan, Edmond Jouhaud, André Zeller) and a dozen or so colonels. Their troops amounted to a corporal's guard: some 7,500 paras and Legionnaires personally loyal to General Challe, with whom they had fought in the Challe Plan operations of 1959. Their plan was to seize Algiers, to rally the armed forces in the name of army unity and French Algeria, and then to seize Paris, driving De Gaulle from office.

Thanks largely to overconfidence in Paris ("It is unthinkable that the French army would rebel against higher authority," Defense Minister Pierre Messmer said in mid-April), the plotters enjoyed the advantage of virtually complete surprise. Between 2:00 and 6:00 on the morning of Saturday, April 22, they took over Algiers without firing a shot, or even waking many people. Before 9:00, General Challe was on the radio addressing to all soldiers a call to stand united in the cause of French Algeria. He called the Gaullist regime a "surrender government" and raised the specter that Algeria would furnish "Soviet bases tomorrow." Reinforced by flying squads of paratroopers, General Challe's call for unity won over generals commanding in Oran, Constantine, and the Sahara. But that was the high-water mark of the putsch.

With his own head at stake, De Gaulle, for the first time, struck directly at the rebellious soldiers. On Saturday, the first day of the putsch, he sent his Minister of State, Louis Joxe, hopping across Algeria by jet to rally resistance to the coup. By Sunday it was clear that the navy, while not supporting the government, was not going along with the insurgents either. Active resistance was coming from the air force in Algeria, and from draftee units south of Oran and Constantine. That evening, De Gaulle went over to the offensive. He formally invoked Article XVI of the Constitution, according the President of the Republic dictatorial powers in times of supreme emergency. He stripped the leaders of the putsch of their military titles. In a televised appeal to the armed forces and the nation, he swung against the generals one of his favorite weapons: the weapon of disobedience.

> In the name of France [he said] I order that all means, I say all means, be employed to bar the way . . . I forbid every Frenchman, and foremost every soldier, to execute any of their orders.

In response to this appeal, airmen began flying empty transports from Algiers to France. By Monday night, it was clear that Algiers lacked the means to reach France. Next morning De Gaulle ordered the fleet based at Toulon to sail for Algeria, presumably to commence operations against the army insurrection. In the apparent hope of presenting a solid front of resistance, General Challe directed his paras to take the naval base at Mers-el-Kebir. But when the sailors there showed signs of fight, the paras declined to force the issue. With the navy, air force, and conscript elements of the army taking De Gaulle's side, the battle was over. Tuesday evening, April 25, Challe in a direct call to Paris announced willingness to surrender. A brief coda followed when some of the colonels summoned the settler population to the Forum and began distributing arms. But conscript units, unmoved by a promise to reduce the length of conscription, speedily acted to hold the settlers in check. By Wednesday morning, Challe himself was in custody; his fellow plotters in flight; their shock troops back in barracks. For the ultras of the army, the end had come. "All that is left," one of the paratroop officers said, "is to go out and die."

## VIII

With the end of the generals' revolt, De Gaulle moved rapidly down the path of negotiation. On May 20, less than a month after the Challe *Putsch*, French and rebel negotiators were meeting publicly at the resort town of Évian-les-Bains. For the first time high-level representatives were involved: Minister of State Louis Joxe for France; Vice Premier and Foreign Minister Belkacem Krim for the rebels. For the first time, too, serious substantive issues were on the agenda. The talks turned on three main issues.

Of these, the most important by far was the fate of the settlers. In the long run it was clear that the European minority would either merge with the Moslem population or make its way back across the Mediterranean. Currently outnumbered ten to one by the Moslems, the settlers, because their own birthrate is static while that of the Moslems gallops, will be outnumbered by twenty to one in 1980, and by forty to one at the turn of the century. Still, for the interim period, there remains a serious question of assuring their personal safety, and at least some of their property rights, against the Moslem majority.

A second, related, issue was the question of the French army. The withdrawal of most of the 400,000-man force is a *sine qua non* of an independent Algeria. But an abrupt pullback poses immense political problems in Paris, and with the settlers and the soldiers themselves, while juridical protection for the European minority assumes a far more effective cast if it is backed by the presence of at least some French troops on Algerian soil.

The third issue was the Sahara. Since 1955, a crash program of development by (mainly) French companies has uncovered in the Sahara oil reserves estimated at about 20 billion barrels, and gas reserves of about 20 trillion cubic feet. For France, Saharan oil could supply, after 1965, all her petroleum needs (some 650,000 barrels per day), thus eliminating the heavy drain on her foreign exchange imposed by purchase of oil and coal abroad. For an independent Algeria, Saharan oil could provide petroleum for all local needs and, sold on a royalty basis to foreign producers, yield revenues of more than $200,-000,000 annually.

A wide area of conflict on all three issues was explored in the first phase of the Évian-les-Bains talks. With respect to the settlers, the rebels offered to allow them full citizenship in an Algerian republic, or an option of keeping French citizenship without prejudice to their rights. M. Joxe replied that it was not enough for the rebels to say, "Be confident." France had to have "guarantees" for the safety of the European minority. He suggested dual Algerian-French citizenship, and intimated that a federal regime in Algeria might afford the settlers a measure of autonomy within the independent state. These suggestions the rebels rejected as a breach of Algerian sovereignty. In these circumstances, General de Gaulle let loose from off stage a threat that Algeria might be partitioned into European and Moslem states. The rebels, in riposte, called for protest demonstrations by Moslems throughout Algeria on July 5. The demonstrations resulted in heavy casualties, and a revival of counter-terrorism by settlers and the military remnants of the generals' revolt. But the FLN appeal met with almost 100 per cent response on the part of the Moslems. If nothing else, it was clear that partition, far from ending the war, would only transfer hostilities to new lines.

With respect to the army, the French, simultaneous with the opening of the Évian-les-Bains talks, ordered their forces in Algeria not to fire except in self-defense. Later they pulled a reserve division back to France. At Évian-les-Bains, M. Joxe raised the possibility of a continuing French military presence in Algeria, notably at the great naval base outside Oran, Mers-el-Kebir. The rebels denounced the unilateral "cease fire" and the withdrawal of the division as a "trick." By words and a drumfire of military action, they indicated they would keep fighting until their political conditions were accepted. They equally made plain that Mers-el-Kebir, and a continuing French military presence, would have to await Algerian independence and future negotiations between two sovereign states. Still, the precedent had been set for a staged French withdrawal and the peaceful presence of French forces on Algerian soil.

As to the Sahara, the French took the position it was their territory. They stipulated they would negotiate transit rights for moving the oil with all the adjoining states, including Algeria but also Tunisia, Morocco, and Mauritania. The rebels insisted the Sahara was part of Algeria, and expressed willingness to negotiate a royalty agreement allowing continued exploitation by French companies. In side negotiations, they won support for their position from Morocco and Mauritania. When President Bourguiba refused to bring Tunisia into line, the rebels denounced his stand publicly, and stimulated expressions of disapproval both inside Tunisia, and from the other Arab states. Under pressure to demonstrate he was no colonial puppet, M. Bourguiba renewed in strong terms his long-standing complaint against continued French tenure of the Bizerte naval base. There ensued bitter fighting, U.N. debate, and a general worsening in French relations with all North Africa. It was clear that in competing for support on the Saharan issue among the neighboring states, the rebels could easily outbid the French.

Despite all the attendant strains, Évian-les-Bains pointed the way to a potential solution through a Franco-Algerian agreement stretching over a long period of time. It would provide for transition to an independent Algeria within a year or so; a staged withdrawal by the French army, spread over five years or more; exploitation of the Sahara by French interests paying royalties to an Algerian state which would provide the neighbors with a cut. Independence would satisfy the prime rebel demand. The continuing presence of French troops would supply the best available surety for the European minority. Joint exploitation of the Sahara would seal—and sweeten—the bargain for both sides.

Between a pattern so logical and the course of events, there subsisted, to be sure, an enormous gap. The vulnerability of a France dependent upon one man; the deliberate trickiness, and harsh bargaining tactics, of De Gaulle; the infinite capacity of the settlers and army for absurd adventure; and the instability of relations inside the rebel government provided unsettling materials in abundance. Still, negotiations had reached the trading stage: the stage of finding the right price. The principle of Algerian independence was implicitly conceded. It was equally acknowledged that the FLN would largely dominate the new country. Except for details, the struggle for Algeria was over.

# 9.   THE LESSON

THE lesson it teaches is the pain of living in the same world as the underdeveloped countries. For Algeria shows in acute form the process by which Asia and Africa came suddenly awake. Their vast tracts, a century ago, were peopled by primitive agricultural communities, virtually immune to change and limited in horizon to a radius of a few hundred miles. Suddenly, and in some cases brutally, there supervened contact with the advanced civilization of the West. Economic development and exploitation began: the trader's frontier. With it went doctrines of emancipation and improvement: the missionary's frontier. For administrative purposes, tiny units were absorbed in larger entities: the carving up of the continents. Willy-nilly the dormant communities stirred. In places of immediate contact, a cash economy was substituted for subsistence agriculture; there grew up small trading communities and pockets of propertyless workers. Almost everywhere sanitation and medicine introduced a population rise. There followed a decisive break: urbanization, the rise of the cities.

And what pestilential holes these are. Jerry-built piles of rotten wood and dried mud; stinking alleys strewn with bits of excrement; mattresses crawling with vermin; tiny dark rooms smelling of food and sweat; tawdry shops and stalls swarming with flies; disease-ridden and disfigured beggars; child prostitutes—these are the staple features, and each city has its specialties as well. The Algiers Casbah houses 80,000 people on seventy-five acres. Baghdad sits on a cesspool. Thirty per cent of Cairo's dwellings are uninhabitable—"houses of certain death"—and one quarter of its population is below the age of six. The blacks of Johannesburg call their section of town, proudly, "our slum." Bombay's permanent quota of jobless numbers half the working population. Forty thousand lepers walk the streets of Rangoon.

By occupation, the denizens of these sinkholes are workers, petty civil servants, clerks, and shopkeepers, with a sprinkling of intellectuals. Perversion thrives among them, as does crime. The yellowest journalism and rawest Hollywood films make up their cultural fare. Ill-educated though able to read, they are half-baked in their ideas and brutal in manner. Street brawls, like the beating of women and children, are an everyday affair. Among them, the insolence of office knows no bounds. And in politics the street mob is the characteristic mode of expression. Mobs were the makers of Cairo's Black Thursday, in June 1953; of the brutal murder of King Feisal in Iraq; of the language riots of Bombay and the school riots of Kerala; of the labor troubles in Singapore; and of the anti-American demonstrations that barred President Eisenhower from Tokyo. "Give me the street," it has been said, "and I can move the world."

For these unhappy masses are the torchbearers of their communities. In touch with modernity, they have advanced much further than their fellows down the path from traditional societies. Their needs shape political forms; their desires force the pace of development; from their ranks spring the leaders of the future. They are, in effect, the culture heroes, the creative minorities, of the underdeveloped world. And no early mellowing of temper is in the works. Chief protagonists in the drama of the underdeveloped nations, the city masses follow a road which runs athwart a mountain of economic obstacles, through a jungle of social tension, to a political desert.

On the economic plane what they seek is industrialization, higher wages, full employment, free education, better housing, plus an infinity of consumer goods. Even to approach these goals requires the covering of enormous distances. The economic misery of the underdeveloped countries—their starting point in the drive ahead—beggars description. In French West Africa 97 per cent of the population is illiterate. Two thirds of Egypt's population is infected by Bilharzia. Average income in India is about $60 annually. Over 20 per cent of Tunisia's working population is unemployed, while 40 per cent of Ceylon's workers are considered to be underemployed. Absence of trained personnel is a major drag on any advance in the underdeveloped countries. So, in many, are shortages of power, transport, industrial materials, and markets. Not being in the Temperate Zone works incalculably bad effects. And on top of all this there comes, as principal obstacle, population growth. Because of population pressures, the poor peoples of the world are getting poorer and poorer. We are witnessing the pauperization of a large fraction of mankind.

To reverse the trend, to support an increasing population at a rising standard of living while insuring future economic growth, requires that a country every year be able to put about 15 per cent of its national product into productive investment. That is roughly the rate of investment in this country and in western Europe, while in the Soviet bloc it sometimes approaches 25 per cent. But the prevailing investment rate in Asia (China and Japan excluded) is about 5 per cent; and in Africa the average is perhaps 8 per cent, with only Southern Rhodesia and the Union breaking through the 15 per cent barrier. And to raise the rate is to plunge in' ` the thickets of social maladjustment.

The obvious way is to raise production of salable commodities, plowing back the profit as investment. Countries with mineral or specialized agricultural resources can easily follow this pattern, though even they are at the mercy of wildly fluctuating international prices. But oil, tin, rubber, bauxite, and cocoa are not found everywhere. Indeed, the "wealth of Africa" and the "riches of the East" are often as mythical as the "perfumes of Araby." Underdeveloped countries may not be undevelopable, but they tend to be poor rather than rich. In most the prime resource is nonspecialized agriculture. It absorbs between 50 and 90 per cent of the population of the southern continents. In general, accordingly, the first prerequisite for economic growth is an agricultural revolution.

In outlook and structure the agrarian population of the underdeveloped countries is the polar opposite of the dynamic urban masses. An archaic peasant mass, it is organized in small village or tribal units, governed by tradition, usually religious, and almost completely illiterate. Land tenure is by custom, often with widely separated strips assigned to different families, and with some land held in common. Farming methods are primitive; and the rise in population, putting new pressure on the land, results in a breakdown of ancient methods of soil protection. Shortages of machines, fertilizer, and adequate irrigation are chronic. Yields per man per acre are incredibly depressed. Often the entire peasantry is in the hands of moneylenders; sometimes a few wealthy landlords, usually absentee, hold very large tracts of land, which may or may not be farmed by modern methods, but which in any case, is not worked to the benefit of the local population.

Land reform is the traditional answer to these problems; and at first glance, in most places, it seems politically promising. On the one hand, what the peasants want is more land. On the other, the urban masses, as a matter of instinct, seek to level inequalities and are bitterly hostile to rich landowners. The two groups thus work hand in hand to effect a redistribu-

tion of land at the expense of big owners. Virtually every new
country from Morocco to Vietnam has enacted a land reform
along those lines. But once land is distributed, the partnership
between city and country ceases abruptly. There occurs on the
broadest scale something like what happened to the pious East
European Jew of the last century, who, wanting to read on a
sabbath evening, but being debarred from striking a match,
trusted to his peasant servant. "Ivan," he called out. "Would
you like a drink? Here is the key to the closet; light the candle
and help yourself." All of this Ivan did; but after a few gulps
he was satisfied. He blew out the candle and went back to sleep.

The peasant will always take his land and go back to sleep.
Not only will the ancient customs and outworn production
methods survive, but because of the clash between small holdings and the large tracts most favorable for machine farming,
there may even be a drop in yields. Moreover, having acquired
land, the peasant will add to a fanatic clinging to the old ways
the special tenacity of a vested interest. The urban masses,
though, want the lights to go on. They seek the transformation
of the peasant into a producer of surpluses which may be taxed
to provide investment capital. To achieve that goal they must
keep up the pace of change after land distribution. Specifically,
they must prevail upon the peasantry to pool fragmented holdings so that the land can be worked by modern methods and
its produce sold in bulk. Inevitably, however, moves in that
direction call forth the fierce resistance of the peasant. Thus,
wherever land reform has gone beyond distribution, coercion
has been required. The measures taken by the Communists to
force collectivization are harsher, but not more coercive, than
the sanctions accompanying land reform in countries as re-
nowned for humane leadership as India and Tunisia.

Thus, even where land reform works, it yields a bitter conflict
between urban and rural forces, and the strife is the more ugly
for coinciding with other tensions. Old-time religions generally
hold sway among the rural masses, but not in the cities. Small

administrative units—cores, often, of language and other minorities—characterize the country, while the urban masses drive toward centralization and a sweeping away of differences. Thus the urban-rural fight may emerge nakedly, as in Ghana or in Jordan; or take a religious form, as in India and northern Iraq; or be fought along states' rights lines, as in Ceylon and Burma. One way or another, though, the basic tension permeates the underdeveloped world, sharpening into conflict and upheaval at every step toward development.

Bearing that burden would strain the most deeply rooted political systems. As it happens, the underdeveloped countries entered political life with almost no roots. Occupying powers may have left, as in the Sudan and India, an effective civil service. To this there were usually joined borrowed ideas about constitutions, representative assemblies, and chief executives. On that basis, most Asian and African countries set up shop as working democracies. With rare exceptions, they have all gone to the wall. And midst the rubble of the ruined democracies, one can discern the growth of three political forms appropriate to the new countries.

One of these is the classic expression of aggressive urban masses working through the agency of mobs: plebiscitarian dictatorship. The chief characteristic of mob action is the sweeping away of superiorities in education, wealth, and social position. That kind of leveling, as every political philosopher from Plato through Tocqueville has noted, prepares the void which is filled by the tyrant: the monolatry of the political desert. At the same time, the mob requires some rallying point, a simple figure known to all, a leader fit to be an object of religious frenzy. Thus by a double process there exists innate harmony between mob power and one-man rule. Breeders without par of urban mobs, the underdeveloped countries are a forcing ground of messianic leadership.

Equally common, though for different reasons, is the one-party state. The new nations usually threw off colonial wraps by political pressures brought to bear through underground movements. Necessarily secret and hardened in discipline by police persecution, these movements generally emerged at independence as dominant parties. The Neo-Destour in Tunisia, Congress in India, and the Convention People's party of Ghana are all examples of that kind of development. Moreover, because the two principal social segments of political life in the underdeveloped countries—the rural and urban masses—are locked in death struggle, it is generally impossible to develop "loyal opposition." The dominant party crushes its rivals and absorbs all other private groupings. As President Sekou Touré of Guinea put it:

> Thus it is the party which determines and directs the action of the nation, the action of the districts, the action of the villages, the action of every group and of the totality of groups . . . Everywhere it is the party that is pre-eminent.

Mixed with both dictatorship and one-party rule is a third form, which sometimes emerges independently: military rule. As the most obvious agent of coercion in any state, the army has at all times attracted the attention of minorities bent on forcing through rapid economic change. In both Germany and Japan, an alliance of private businessmen with the military powered the drive toward industrialization at the end of the last century. Substitute the urban masses for the progressive entrepreneurs, and advance the action by fifty years, and there are present the components of Nasserism and Peronism. Among other things, one-man rule and one-party rule are a means for mobilizing the army behind the push toward development. When either of these systems crumble, force generally shows itself naked and unashamed in a military coup.

Together with authoritarian features, all three forms of government have in common grave problems of legitimacy. Caesar has no heirs is history's epitaph on all dictatorships; and neither do one-party states or military juntas provide means for the orderly transmission of power. In the absence of an accepted basis of rule, leaders are under constant pressure to satisfy the merest whims of their followers. Reactionary or Communist governments excepted, no new regime has been able to hold back the inflationary pressures implicit in the drive of the urban masses for consumption, or for such non-revenue-producing investments as schools. Where bread lacks, there is a virtual compulsion to divert attention by circuses. And for these diversionary tactics the underdeveloped world holds out the broadest opportunities. Hardly a nation in Asia or Africa is without some traces of the hated foreigner: every Cairo has its Shepheards. Because the carving up of the continents did not coincide with ethnic groupings, border problems abound: every India has its Kashmir. For the same reason, there is a plenitude of minority problems: every Iraq has its Kurds. And when the going gets rough, when desperate economic conditions assert themselves or social tension rises, it is a rare leader indeed who will not play these cards.

For all these reasons, then, it is the normal thing for the underdeveloped countries to be seats of unrest. Controlled by aggressive minorities, faced with near insoluble economic problems, riven by social tensions, void of stable political institutions, they are anything but pacific. They want, quite literally, to do terrible things to one another and the world; they have a stake in trouble. Thus for the foreseeable future, the convulsions of Africa and Asia are a fixture which not even the Big Two can control.

On the contrary, a deep gulf stands between the Great Powers and the world of the underdeveloped countries. The United States is predominantly white, rich, and capitalistic. The Asians and Africans are poor, socialistic, and not white. Russia starts with the advantage of being not capitalistic and, within recent memory anyway, poor. To this is added the natural tendency of former colonies to flirt with the East in order to show they are not married to the West. Still, what the Rus-

sians seek is political power: they are finally satisfied only when
fellow Communists hold office. But power—their own power
—is precisely the objective of the new class of leaders rising
through the underdeveloped world. As experience in Egypt,
India, Argentina, and Ghana demonstrates, the Communists
run athwart local nationalism as soon as the issue of political
domination comes into question.

Not only do the Big Two start off at odds with the underdeveloped world, but they have only the most limited means of
influence. It had been hoped, notably by Secretary General
Dag Hammarskjöld, that the United Nations could play a decisive role in promoting stability in the new countries. But the
Suez aftermath suggests that the U.N. solves problems by post-
poning them, while the Congo underscores the pathetic weakness of the U.N. in staff and resources. Moreover, the stuffing
of the General Assembly has made it possible for virtually any
group of nations to block any but the most innocuous action.
The U.N. may continue to flourish as a forum of debate—an
important function. But all signs indicate that as an agent of
intervention its role is diminishing. It works at all only when
the Big Two agree. When they part company, they look, perforce, to unilateral means of influence.

Military force, the last resort, has obvious uses. Still, nuclear
weapons are hardly germane in the southern continents: one
does not burn down the house to fry an egg. Conventional
forces are more applicable, as the case of the Lebanon landings
of 1958 indicates. But whether they can be used far inland is
a question. Moreover, it is not always easy to keep a limited
war limited. And the case of the French army in Algeria—perhaps the most rugged conventional force in the world—suggests
that the long-term commitment of modern armies in the underdeveloped countries works disastrous effects.

Foreign aid, the *wunderkind* of the postwar decade, is an
obvious conduit between the Big Two and the southern continents. But the needs of the underdeveloped far outrun the

combined resources of the Great Powers and their allies. Leaving Japan and China aside, the rest of Asia, just to maintain its present exceedingly low living standards over the next ten years, would require an estimated $7 billion annually—twice the annual average of American aid in the postwar years. The huge Soviet outlays for the Aswan Dam will leave the Egyptian standard of living a decade hence just about where it is now. Moreover, in international politics the man who pays the piper does not call the tune. As a political weapon, foreign aid is a gamble. It worked for the United States in western Europe, but not in Laos. It works for the Soviet Union in Afghanistan, but not in Iraq.

Far larger dividends, in fact, seem to flow from a more pointedly political approach. Between nations, as between people, there are hidden currents of sympathy that work secretly but far more effectively than the logic of interest or of force. It is by these secret bonds, far more than by economic or military connections, that the revolutionary governments of the world —the regimes of Colonel Nasser and President Touré, for instance—are drawn to the Soviet Union. By the same process, more conservative regimes find protection for themselves— and the status quo—at the side of the United States. No doubt this country can accomplish something like a reversal of alliances. It requires mainly an internal transformation—what President Kennedy used to call "getting the country moving again." But even then, picking and choosing among competing political movements and leaders from the underdeveloped world is a tricky business. It is still unclear whether ties with Hussein of Jordan or the Shah of Iran are an asset or a liability.

Perhaps all that is certain is that, for good or ill, the choices must be made. Left to themselves, the Big Two might—probably would—work out stable arrangements for peaceful competition. But they are trammeled beyond release in the social maladjustments, economic problems, and crumbling politics of the underdeveloped world. Non-intervention is a myth that yields at every test to invidious fears, to the pleas of clients and protégés, or even to humanitarian instincts. The duel between Washington and Moscow cannot keep clear of the struggle between the rich of the North and the poor of the South. For the settlement of that struggle promises to be the central process of the next half-century.